BLACK SLAVERY IN THE AMERICAS

BLACK SLAVERY IN THE AMERICAS

An Interdisciplinary Bibliography, 1865–1980

VOLUME 2

Compiled by JOHN DAVID SMITH

Foreword by Stanley L. Engerman

GREENWOOD PRESS
Westport, Connecticut • London, England

Library of Congress Cataloging in Publication Data

Smith, John David, 1949-
  Black slavery in the Americas.

  Includes indexes.
    1. Slavery—America—Bibliography. 2. Slavery—
United States—Bibliography. I. Title.
Z7164.S6S63 1982   016.306'362'0973   82-11736
[HT1049]
ISBN 0-313-23118-4 (lib. bdg.) (set)
ISBN 0-313-23675-5 (lib. bdg.) (vol. 1)
ISBN 0-313-23676-3 (lib. bdg.) (vol. 2)

Copyright © 1982 by John David Smith

Library of Congress Catalog Card Number: 82-11736
ISBN: 0-313-23676-3

First published in 1982

Greenwood Press
A division of Congressional Information Service, Inc.
88 Post Road West, Westport, Connecticut 06881

Printed in the United States of America

10 9 8 7 6 5 4 3 2 1

For My Parents,
Doris Woronock Smith and Leonard Calgut Smith,
With Love

Contents

VOLUME 2

BLACK SLAVERY IN THE AMERICAS

15.
Slavery in the Lower South

GENERAL

11656   ALDEN, JOHN R.   THE SOUTH IN THE REVOLUTION, 1763-1789.
        BATON ROUGE: LOUISIANA STATE UNIVERSITY PRESS, 1957.

11657   BAREFIELD, JAMES T.   "THE PLANTATION SYSTEM IN THE
        SOUTHEASTERN COTTON STATES, 1848-1853." M.A. THESIS,
        FLORIDA STATE UNIVERSITY, 1977.

11658   BERTRAM, WINIFRED E.   "THE PLANTATION OVERSEER IN THE
        LOWER SOUTH PRIOR TO THE CIVIL WAR."   M.A. THESIS,
        UNIVERSITY OF CHICAGO, 1928.

11659   BROWN, WILLIAM G.   THE LOWER SOUTH IN AMERICAN HISTORY.
        NEW YORK: MACMILLAN COMPANY, 1902.

11660   CLARK, JOHN G.   "THE ANTEBELLUM GULF COAST: A STUDY OF
        WORLD VIEWS, TRADITIONALISM AND BACKWARDNESS."   IN
        ELLSWORTH, LUCIUS F. (ED.).   THE AMERICANIZATION OF
        THE GULF COAST, 1803-1350.   PENSACOLA: HISTORIC
        PENSACOLA PRESERVATION BOARD, 1972, PP. 1-19.

11661   CLARK, THOMAS D.   "THE SLAVE TRADE BETWEEN KENTUCKY AND
        THE COTTON KINGDOM."   MISSISSIPPI VALLEY HISTORICAL
        REVIEW, 21 (DECEMBER, 1934):   331-342.

11662   CLARK, THOMAS D.   "THE TRADE BETWEEN KENTUCKY AND THE
        COTTON KINGDOM IN LIVESTOCK, HEMP AND SLAVES FROM 1840
        TO 1860."   M.A. THESIS, UNIVERSITY OF KENTUCKY, 1929.

11663   DRAKE, RICHARD B.   "APPALACHIAN WHITES IN THE ERA OF
        SLAVERY: A CRITICAL REVIEW OF EUGENE D. GENOVESE'S
        ROLL, JORDAN, ROLL."   APPALACHIAN NOTES, 4 (1976):
        60-62.

11664   FULLER, JOHN D.P.   "SLAVERY PROPAGANDA DURING THE MEXICAN
        WAR."   SOUTHWESTERN HISTORICAL QUARTERLY, 38 (APRIL,
        1935):   235-245.

11665   FULLER, JOHN D.P.   "THE SLAVERY QUESTION AND THE MOVEMENT
        TO ACQUIRE MEXICO, 1846-1848."   MISSISSIPPI VALLEY
        HISTORICAL REVIEW, 21 (JUNE, 1934):   31-48.

11666   GREEN, FLETCHER M.   THE LIDES GO SOUTH AND WEST: THE
        RECORD OF A PLANTER MIGRATION IN 1835.   COLUMBIA:
        UNIVERSITY OF SOUTH CAROLINA PRESS, 1952.

11667   HODGSON, JOSEPH.   THE CRADLE OF THE CONFEDERACY; OR, THE
        TIMES OF TROUP, QUITMAN, AND YANCEY.   MOBILE:
        REGISTER PUBLISHING OFFICE, 1876.

11668   JACKSON, HARVEY H. "'AMERICAN SLAVERY, AMERICAN FREEDOM' AND THE REVOLUTION IN THE LOWER SOUTH: THE CASE OF LACHLAN MCINTOSH." SOUTHERN STUDIES, 19 (SPRING, 1980): 81-93.

11669   JORDAN, TERRY G. "THE IMPRINT OF THE UPPER AND LOWER SOUTH ON MID-NINETEENTH CENTURY TEXAS." ANNALS OF THE ASSOCIATION OF AMERICAN GEOGRAPHERS, 57 (DECEMBER, 1967): 667-690.

11670   LACK, PAUL D. "URBAN SLAVERY IN THE SOUTHWEST." PH.D. DISSERTATION, TEXAS TECH UNIVERSITY, 1973.

11671   MENN, JOSEPH K. "THE LARGE SLAVEHOLDERS OF THE DEEP SOUTH, 1860." PH.D. DISSERTATION, UNIVERSITY OF TEXAS, 1964.

11672   MYERS, MINNIE W. ROMANCE AND REALISM OF THE SOUTH GULF COAST. CINCINNATI: ROBERT CLARKE COMPANY, 1898.

11673   NULL, ALVIN E. "THE EXPANSION OF THE COTTON GROWING INDUSTRY INTO THE LOWER SOUTH." M.A. THESIS, UNIVERSITY OF CHICAGO, 1926.

11674   RICHARD, HENRY T. "EVIDENCE OF NEGRO MIGRATION FROM THE UPPER TO THE LOWER SOUTH, 1820-1845." M.A. THESIS, UNIVERSITY OF CHICAGO, 1931.

11675   RIGGS, ELEANOR. "THE GROWTH OF THE INSTITUTION OF SLAVERY AS AN INTEGRAL PART IN THE DEVELOPMENT OF THE LOWER MISSISSIPPI VALLEY." M.A. THESIS, TULANE UNIVERSITY, 1912.

11676   ROHRBOUGH, MALCOLM J. THE TRANS-APPALACHIAN FRONTIER: PEOPLE, SOCIETIES, AND INSTITUTIONS, 1775-1850. NEW YORK: OXFORD UNIVERSITY PRESS, 1978.

11677   SMITH, JULIA F. "RACIAL ATTITUDES IN THE OLD SOUTHWEST." IN ELLSWORTH, LUCIUS F. (ED.). THE AMERICANIZATION OF THE GULF COAST, 1803-1850. PENSACOLA: HISTORIC PENSACOLA PRESERVATION BOARD, 1972, PP. 68-77.

LOWER SOUTH COLONIES/STATES

ALABAMA

11678   ABERNETHY, THOMAS P. THE FORMATIVE PERIOD IN ALABAMA, 1815-1828. UNIVERSITY, AL: UNIVERSITY OF ALABAMA PRESS, 1965.

11679   ALEXANDER, CLAUDE H. "THE BANK OF THE STATE OF ALABAMA AND ITS BRANCHES." M.A. THESIS, UNIVERSITY OF ALABAMA, 1928.

11680   AVANT, GLADYS B. "HISTORY OF WASHINGTON COUNTY TO 1860."
         M.A. THESIS, UNIVERSITY OF ALABAMA, 1929.

11681   BAILEY, HUGH C. AND DALE, WILLIAM P. "MISSUS ALONE IN DE
         'BIG HOUSE.'" ALABAMA REVIEW, 8 (JANUARY, 1955):
         43-54.

11682   BALL, TIMOTHY H. A GLANCE INTO THE GREAT SOUTH-EAST; OR,
         CLARKE COUNTY ALABAMA, AND ITS SURROUNDINGS, FROM 1540
         TO 1877. CHICAGO: PRESS OF KNIGHT & LEONARD, 1882.

11683   BARNEY, WILLIAM L. "PATTERNS OF CRISIS: ALABAMA WHITE
         FAMILIES AND SOCIAL CHANGE, 1850-1870." SOCIOLOGY AND
         SOCIAL RESEARCH, 63 (APRIL, 1979): 524-543.

11684   BARNEY, WILLIAM L. THE SECESSIONIST IMPULSE: ALABAMA
         AND MISSISSIPPI IN 1860. PRINCETON: PRINCETON
         UNIVERSITY PRESS, 1974.

11685   BELSER, THOMAS A., JR. "ALABAMA PLANTATION TO GEORGIA
         FARM, JOHN HORRY DENT AND RECONSTRUCTION." ALABAMA
         HISTORICAL QUARTERLY, 25 (SPRING-SUMMER, 1963):
         136-148.

11686   BEVERLY, JOHN W. HISTORY OF ALABAMA, FOR USE IN SCHOOLS
         AND FOR GENERAL READING. MONTGOMERY: THE AUTHOR,
         1901.

11687   BIRNEY, WILLIAM. JAMES G. BIRNEY AND HIS TIMES. NEW
         YORK: D. APPLETON, 1889.

11688   "BLACK BELT." IN SCHAPSMEIER, EDWARD L. AND SCHAPSMEIER,
         FREDERICK H. ENCYCLOPEDIA OF AMERICAN AGRICULTURAL
         HISTORY. WESTPORT: GREENWOOD PRESS, 1975, P. 39.

11689   BOND, HORACE M. NEGRO EDUCATION IN ALABAMA: A STUDY IN
         COTTON AND STEEL. WASHINGTON: ASSOCIATED PUBLISHERS,
         1939.

11690   BOOTHE, CHARLES O. THE CYCLOPEDIA OF THE COLORED BAPTIST
         OF ALABAMA. BIRMINGHAM: BIRMINGHAM PUBLISHING
         COMPANY, 1895.

11691   BOUCHER, MORRIS R. "THE FREE NEGRO IN ALABAMA PRIOR TO
         1860." PH.D. DISSERTATION, UNIVERSITY OF IOWA, 1950.

11692   BOYD, MINNIE C. ALABAMA IN THE FIFTIES: A SOCIAL STUDY.
         NEW YORK: COLUMBIA UNIVERSITY PRESS, 1931.

11693   BOYD, MINNIE C. "ALABAMA IN THE FIFTIES: A SOCIAL
         STUDY." PH.D. DISSERTATION, COLUMBIA UNIVERSITY, 1931.

11694   BRANTLEY, WILLIAM H. THREE CAPITALS. UNIVERSITY, AL:
         UNIVERSITY OF ALABAMA PRESS, 1976.

11695   BROWN, WILLIAM G.   A HISTORY OF ALABAMA.   NEW YORK:
         UNIVERSITY PUBLISHING COMPANY, 1900.

11696   BURTON, ANNIE L.   MEMORIES OF CHILDHOOD'S SLAVERY DAYS.
         BOSTON: ROSS PUBLISHING COMPANY, 1909.

11697   CHAPPELL, GORDON T.   "JOHN COFFEE: LAND SPECULATOR AND
         PLANTER."   ALABAMA REVIEW, 22 (JANUARY, 1969):   24-43.

11698   CHRISTIAN, ELLA S.   "THE DAYS THAT ARE NO LONGER; OR
         PLANTATION LIFE AS IT WAS."   ALABAMA HISTORICAL
         QUARTERLY, 14 (MARCH-APRIL, 1952):   331-336; 15
         (JANUARY, 1953):   127-168.

11699   CHRISTIAN, ELLA S.   "PLANTATION LIFE AS IT WAS."
         UNPUBLISHED PAPER, N.D., ALABAMA DEPARTMENT OF
         ARCHIVES AND HISTORY.

11700   CLAYTON, VICTORIA H.   WHITE AND BLACK UNDER THE OLD
         REGIME.   MILWAUKEE: YOUNG CHURCHMAN COMPANY, 1899.

11701   CLEVELAND, GORDON B.   "SOCIAL CONDITIONS IN ALABAMA AS
         SEEN BY TRAVELERS, 1840-1850."   ALABAMA REVIEW, 2
         (JANUARY, 1949):   3-23.

11702   CLEVELAND, HERDMAN F.   "THE BLACK BELT OF ALABAMA."
         GEOGRAPHICAL REVIEW, 10 (DECEMBER, 1920):   375-387.

11703   CLEVELAND, LEN G.   "LETTER FROM A FORMER ALABAMA SLAVE TO
         HIS OLD MASTER."   ALABAMA REVIEW, 28 (APRIL, 1975):
         151-152.

11704   COCHRAN, JOHN P.   "JAMES ASBURY TAIT AND HIS
         PLANTATIONS."   M.A. THESIS, UNIVERSITY OF ALABAMA,
         1951.

11705   COMINGS, L.L. NEWCOMB AND ALBARS, MARTH M.   A BRIEF
         HISTORY OF BALDWIN COUNTY.   FAIRHOPE, AL: THE
         AUTHORS, 1928.

11706   DAVIS, BARBARA J.   "A COMPARATIVE ANALYSIS OF THE
         ECONOMIC STRUCTURE OF MOBILE COUNTY, ALABAMA, BEFORE
         AND AFTER THE CIVIL WAR, 1860 AND 1870."   M.A. THESIS,
         UNIVERSITY OF ALABAMA, 1963.

11707   DAVIS, CHARLES S.   THE COTTON KINGDOM IN ALABAMA.
         MONTGOMERY: ALABAMA STATE DEPARTMENT OF ARCHIVES AND
         HISTORY, 1939.

11708   DAVIS, CHARLES S.   "THE PLANTATION SYSTEM IN ALABAMA
         BEFORE 1860."   PH.D. DISSERTATION, DUKE UNIVERSITY,
         1938.

11709   DAVIS, GEORGE A. AND DONALDSON, O. FRED.   BLACKS IN THE
         UNITED STATES: A GEOGRAPHIC PERSPECTIVE.   BOSTON:

HOUGHTON MIFFLIN, 1975.

11710 DENMAN, CLARENCE P. THE SECESSION MOVEMENT IN ALABAMA.
MONTGOMERY: ALABAMA STATE DEPARTMENT OF ARCHIVES,
1933.

11711 DENSON, JOHN V. "SLAVERY LAWS IN ALABAMA." ALABAMA
POLYTECHNIC INSTITUTE HISTORICAL STUDIES, 3RD SER.,
(1908): 1-47.

11712 DUBOSE, J.W. "THE CANEBRAKE NEGRO, 1850-1865."
UNPUBLISHED MANUSCRIPT, N.D., DUBOSE PAPERS, ALABAMA
DEPARTMENT OF ARCHIVES AND HISTORY.

11713 DUBOSE, JOHN W. "RECOLLECTIONS OF THE PLANTATION."
ALABAMA HISTORICAL QUARTERLY, 1 (SPRING, SUMMER,
1930): 63-75, 107-113.

11714 EISTERHOLD, JOHN A. "MOBILE: LUMBER CENTER OF THE GULF
COAST." ALABAMA REVIEW, 26 (APRIL, 1973): 83-104.

11715 FLADELAND, BETTY. JAMES GILLESPIE BIRNEY: SLAVEHOLDER
TO ABOLITIONIST. ITHACA: CORNELL UNIVERSITY PRESS,
1955.

11716 FULLER, WILLIE J. BLACKS IN ALABAMA, 1528-1865.
MONTICELLO, IL: COUNCIL OF PLANNING LIBRARIANS, 1976.

11717 GREENBERG, STANLEY B. RACE AND STATE IN CAPITALIST
DEVELOPMENT: COMPARATIVE PERSPECTIVES. NEW HAVEN:
YALE UNIVERSITY PRESS, 1980.

11718 GRIFFIN, RICHARD W. "COTTON MANUFACTURE IN ALABAMA TO
1860." ALABAMA HISTORICAL QUARTERLY, 18 (FALL, 1956):
289-307.

11719 HAMILTON, PETER J. (ED.). COLONIAL MOBILE: AN HISTORICAL
STUDY, LARGELY FROM ORIGINAL SOURCES. BOSTON:
HOUGHTON MIFFLIN, 1897.

11720 HAMMETT, HUGH B. HILARY ABNER HERBERT: A SOUTHERNER
RETURNS TO THE UNION. PHILADELPHIA: AMERICAN
PHILOSOPHICAL SOCIETY, 1976.

11721 HARVEY, MERIWETHER. "SLAVERY IN AUBURN, ALABAMA."
ALABAMA POLYTECHNIC INSTITUTE HISTORICAL STUDIES, 3RD
SER., (1907): 1-18.

11722 HAZEL, JOSEPH A. "THE GEOGRAPHY OF NEGRO AGRICULTURAL
SLAVERY IN ALABAMA, FLORIDA, AND MISSISSIPPI, CIRCA
1860." PH.D. DISSERTATION, COLUMBIA UNIVERSITY, 1963.

11723 HERBERT, HILARY A. "ALABAMA IN FEDERAL POLITICS." IN
MEMORIAL RECORD OF ALABAMA, VOLUME 2. MADISON: BRANT
& FULLER, 1893, PP. 17-106.

11724   HERZBERG, LOUIS F. "NEGRO SLAVERY IN TUSCALOOSA COUNTY, ALABAMA, 1818-1865." M.A. THESIS, UNIVERSITY OF ALABAMA, 1955.

11725   HOLDERFIELD, HORACE M. "THE FREEDMEN'S BUREAU IN ALABAMA IN 1865 AND 1866." M.A. THESIS, AUBURN UNIVERSITY, 1970.

11726   HOLMES, JACK D.L. "THE ROLE OF BLACKS IN SPANISH ALABAMA: THE MOBILE DISTRICT, 1780-1813." ALABAMA HISTORICAL QUARTERLY, 37 (SPRING, 1975): 5-18.

11727   HOOLE, W. STANLEY. "ADVICE TO AN OVERSEER: EXTRACTS FROM THE 1840-1842 PLANTATION JOURNAL OF JOHN HORRY DENT." ALABAMA REVIEW, 1 (JANUARY, 1948): 50-63.

11728   INMAN, HENRY F. "MIGRATION IN THE COTTON SOUTH: THE GEOGRAPHIC MOBILITY OF ALABAMA FARMERS, 1850-1860." M.A. THESIS, UNIVERSITY OF ALABAMA, BIRMINGHAM, 1980.

11729   JAMISON, MONROE F. AUTOBIOGRAPHY AND WORK OF BISHOP M.E. JAMISON. NASHVILLE: THE AUTHOR, 1912.

11730   JOHNSON, KENNETH R. "SOME ASPECTS OF SLAVERY IN THE MUSCLE SHOALS AREA." JOURNAL OF MUSCLE SHOALS HISTORY, 2 (1974): 35-59.

11731   JORDAN, WEYMOUTH T. "AGRICULTURAL SOCIETIES IN ANTE-BELLUM ALABAMA." ALABAMA REVIEW, 4 (OCTOBER, 1951): 241-253.

11732   JORDAN, WEYMOUTH T. ANTE-BELLUM ALABAMA: TOWN AND COUNTRY. TALLAHASSEE: FLORIDA STATE UNIVERSITY STUDIES, 1957.

11733   JORDAN, WEYMOUTH T. "EARLY ANTE-BELLUM MARION, ALABAMA: A BLACK BELT TOWN." ALABAMA HISTORICAL QUARTERLY, 5 (SPRING, 1943): 12-31.

11734   JORDAN, WEYMOUTH T. "THE ELISHA F. KING FAMILY, PLANTERS OF THE ALABAMA BLACK BELT." AGRICULTURAL HISTORY, 19 (JULY, 1945): 152-162.

11735   JORDAN, WEYMOUTH T. HUGH DAVIS AND HIS ALABAMA PLANTATION. UNIVERSITY, AL: UNIVERSITY OF ALABAMA PRESS, 1948.

11736   JORDAN, WEYMOUTH T. "THE MANAGEMENT RULES OF AN ALABAMA BLACK BELT PLANTATION, 1848-1862." AGRICULTURAL HISTORY, 18 (JANUARY, 1944): 53-64.

11737   JORDAN, WEYMOUTH T. (ED.). "MARTIN MARSHALL'S BOOK: HERB MEDICINE." ALABAMA HISTORICAL QUARTERLY, 2 (WINTER, 1940): 443-459.

11738 JORDAN, WEYMOUTH T. (ED.). "MARTIN MARSHALL'S BOOK:
       HOMEMADE MEDICINE." ALABAMA HISTORICAL QUARTERLY, 3
       (SPRING, 1941): 117-129.

11739 JORDAN, WEYMOUTH T. "NOAH B. CLOUD'S ACTIVITIES ON
       BEHALF OF SOUTHERN AGRICULTURE." AGRICULTURAL
       HISTORY, 25 (APRIL, 1951): 53-58.

11740 JORDAN, WEYMOUTH T. (ED.). "'SYSTEM OF FARMING AT BEAVER
       BEND,' ALABAMA, 1862." JOURNAL OF SOUTHERN HISTORY, 7
       (FEBRUARY, 1941): 76-34.

11741 KELLER, MARK. "ALABAMA PLANTATION LIFE IN 1860:
       GOVERNOR BENJAMIN FITZPATRICK'S 'OAK GROVE.'" ALABAMA
       HISTORICAL QUARTERLY, 38 (FALL, 1976): 218-227.

11742 KIGER, JOSEPH C. "SOME SOCIAL AND ECONOMIC FACTORS
       RELATING TO THE ANTEBELLUM ALABAMA LARGE PLANTER."
       M.A. THESIS, UNIVERSITY OF ALABAMA, 1947.

11743 KOLCHIN, PETER. FIRST FREEDOM: THE RESPONSES OF
       ALABAMA'S BLACKS TO EMANCIPATION AND RECONSTRUCTION.
       WESTPORT: GREENWOOD PRESS, 1972.

11744 KOLCHIN, PETER R. "FIRST FREEDOM: THE RESPONSES OF
       ALABAMA'S BLACKS TO EMANCIPATION AND RECONSTRUCTION."
       PH.D. DISSERTATION, JOHNS HOPKINS UNIVERSITY, 1970.

11745 KRAMER, EDWARD M. "ALABAMA NEGROES, 1861-1865." M.A.
       THESIS, AUBURN UNIVERSITY, 1955.

11746 LITTLE, JOHN B. HISTORY OF BUTLER COUNTY, ALABAMA, FROM
       1815 TO 1885. CINCINNATI: ELM PRINTING COMPANY, 1885.

11747 MASON, SARA E. "SECTIONALISM IN ALABAMA, 1840-1860."
       M.A. THESIS, UNIVERSITY OF CHICAGO, 1938.

11748 MATHIS, RAY. JOHN HORRY DENT: SOUTH CAROLINA ARISTOCRAT
       ON THE ALABAMA FRONTIER. UNIVERSITY, AL: UNIVERSITY
       OF ALABAMA PRESS, 1979.

11749 MATHIS, RAY AND MATHIS, MARY. INTRODUCTION AND INDEX TO
       THE JOHN HORRY DENT FARM JOURNALS AND ACCOUNT BOOKS,
       1840-1892. UNIVERSITY, AL: UNIVERSITY OF ALABAMA
       PRESS, 1977.

11750 MCWHINEY, GRADY. "THE REVOLUTION IN NINETEENTH-CENTURY
       ALABAMA AGRICULTURE." ALABAMA REVIEW, 31 (JANUARY,
       1978): 3-32.

11751 MELLOWN, WILLIAM E. "SOME SOCIAL AND ECONOMIC ASPECTS OF
       MARENGO COUNTY IN 1850." M.A. THESIS, UNIVERSITY OF
       ALABAMA, 1955.

11752 MILLER, RANDALL M. THE COTTON MILL MOVEMENT IN

ANTEBELLUM ALABAMA. NEW YORK: ARNO PRESS, 1978.

11753 MILLER, RANDALL M. "DANIEL PRATT'S INDUSTRIAL URBANISM:
       THE COTTON MILL TOWN IN ANTE-BELLUM ALABAMA." ALABAMA
       HISTORICAL QUARTERLY, 34 (SPRING, 1972): 5-36.

11754 MOBLEY, JOE A. "FLUSH TIMES, WAR, AND RECONSTRUCTION IN
       A SOUTHERN TOWN, MOBILE, 1850-1867." M.A. THESIS,
       NORTH CAROLINA STATE UNIVERSITY, 1976.

11755 MONTGOMERY, MARGARET L. (ED.). "ALABAMA FREEDMEN: SOME
       RECONSTRUCTION DOCUMENTS." PHYLON, 13 (THIRD QUARTER,
       1952): 245-251.

11756 MOORE, ALBERT B. HISTORY OF ALABAMA AND HER PEOPLE.
       CHICAGO: AMERICAN HISTORICAL SOCIETY, 1927.

11757 NEIGHBORS, RUBYE G. "PLANTATION LIFE IN HALE COUNTY."
       M.A. THESIS, UNIVERSITY OF ALABAMA, 1927.

11758 NUERMBERGER, RUTH K. THE CLAYS OF ALABAMA: A
       PLANTER-POLITICIAN-LAWYER FAMILY. LEXINGTON:
       UNIVERSITY OF KENTUCKY PRESS, 1958.

11759 "OLD OAKBOWERY, CHAMBERS COUNTY, ALABAMA." BULLETIN OF
       THE CHATTAHOOCHEE VALLEY HISTORICAL SOCIETY, 5
       (NOVEMBER, 1961): 124-172, 191-198.

11760 OWSLEY, FRANK L. PLAIN FOLK OF THE OLD SOUTH. BATON
       ROUGE: LOUISIANA STATE UNIVERSITY PRESS, 1949.

11761 PETERSON, WALTER F. "RURAL LIFE IN ANTE-BELLUM ALABAMA."
       ALABAMA REVIEW, 19 (APRIL, 1966): 137-146.

11762 PETERSON, WALTER F. "SLAVERY IN THE 1850S: THE
       RECOLLECTIONS OF AN ALABAMA UNIONIST." ALABAMA
       HISTORICAL QUARTERLY, 30 (FALL/WINTER, 1968): 219-227.

11763 PICKARD, KATE E.R. "THE KIDNAPPED AND THE RANSOMED."
       AMERICAN JEWISH ARCHIVES, 9 (APRIL, 1957): 3-31.

11764 PICKETT, ALBERT J. THE HISTORY OF ALABAMA AND
       INCIDENTALLY OF GEORGIA AND MISSISSIPPI, FROM THE
       EARLIEST PERIOD. ATLANTA: T.J. DOONAN, 1900.

11765 PRAYTOR, ROBERT E. "FROM CONCERN TO NEGLECT, ALABAMA
       BAPTISTS' RELATIONSHIPS TO THE NEGRO, 1823-1870."
       M.A. THESIS, SAMFORD UNIVERSITY, 1971.

11766 PYRNELLE, LOUISA-CLARK. DIDDIE, DUMPS, AND TOT; OR,
       PLANTATION CHILD-LIFE. NEW YORK: HARPER, 1898.

11767 RACHLEFF, MARSHALL. "BIG JOE, LITTLE JOE, BILL, AND
       JACK: AN EXAMPLE OF SLAVE RESISTANCE IN ALABAMA."
       ALABAMA REVIEW, 32 (APRIL, 1979): 141-146.

11768 RACHLEFF, MARSHALL. "DAVID WALKER'S SOUTHERN AGENT."
JOURNAL OF NEGRO HISTORY, 62 (JANUARY, 1977): 100-103.

11769 RACHLEFF, MARSHALL J. "RACIAL FEAR AND POLITICAL
FACTIONALISM: A STUDY OF THE SECESSION MOVEMENT IN
ALABAMA, 1819-1861." PH.D. DISSERTATION, UNIVERSITY
OF MASSACHUSETTS, 1974.

11770 REID, ROBERT D. "THE NEGRO IN ALABAMA DURING THE CIVIL
WAR." JOURNAL OF NEGRO HISTORY, 35 (JULY, 1950):
265-288.

11771 REID, ROBERT D. "RELIGION AND RECREATION AMONG SLAVES IN
ANTE-BELLUM ALABAMA." MIDWEST JOURNAL, 2 (WINTER,
1949): 29-36.

11772 REID, ROBERT D. "SLAVERY IN ALABAMA." PH.D.
DISSERTATION, UNIVERSITY OF MINNESOTA, 1945.

11773 REYNOLDS, MARYLEE. "A SOCIAL AND ECONOMIC HISTORY OF
SUMTER COUNTY, ALABAMA, IN THE ANTEBELLUM PERIOD."
M.A. THESIS, UNIVERSITY OF ALABAMA, 1953.

11774 ROBERSON, NANCY C. "THE NEGRO AND THE BAPTISTS OF
ANTE-BELLUM ALABAMA." M.A. THESIS, UNIVERSITY OF
ALABAMA, 1954.

11775 ROBERSON, NANCY C. "SOCIAL MOBILITY IN ANTE-BELLUM
ALABAMA." ALABAMA REVIEW, 13 (JANUARY, 1960):
135-145.

11776 ROBERTS, FRANCES C. "AN EXPERIMENT IN EMANCIPATION OF
SLAVES BY AN ALABAMA PLANTER." M.A. THESIS,
UNIVERSITY OF ALABAMA, 1940.

11777 ROCHE, EMMA L. "AN ENGLISHMAN'S IMPRESSIONS OF ALABAMA
IN 1846." SOUTH ATLANTIC QUARTERLY, 7 (JULY, 1908):
223-231.

11778 ROCHE, EMMA L. HISTORIC SKETCHES OF THE SOUTH. NEW
YORK: KNICKERBOCKER PRESS, 1914.

11779 ROHRBOUGH, MALCOLM J. THE TRANS-APPALACHIAN FRONTIER:
PEOPLE, SOCIETIES, AND INSTITUTIONS, 1775-1850. NEW
YORK: OXFORD UNIVERSITY PRESS, 1978.

11780 ROSS, MELVIN L., JR. "BLACKS, MULATTOES AND CREOLES IN
MOBILE DURING THE EUROPEAN AND AMERICAN PERIODS."
M.A. THESIS, PURDUE UNIVERSITY, 1971.

11781 RUTLEDGE, WILLIAM S. "AN ECONOMIC AND SOCIAL HISTORY OF
ANTE-BELLUM JEFFERSON COUNTY, ALABAMA." M.A. THESIS,
UNIVERSITY OF ALABAMA, 1939.

11782 SELLERS, JAMES B. SLAVERY IN ALABAMA. UNIVERSITY, AL:

UNIVERSITY OF ALABAMA PRESS, 1950.

11783   SHERER, ROBERT G.   "LET US MAKE MAN: NEGRO EDUCATION IN
        NINETEENTH CENTURY ALABAMA."   PH.D. DISSERTATION,
        UNIVERSITY OF NORTH CAROLINA, 1970.

11784   SISK, GLENN N.   "AGRICULTURAL DIVERSIFICATION IN THE
        ALABAMA BLACK BELT."   AGRICULTURAL HISTORY, 26 (APRIL,
        1952):   42-45.

11785   SMITH, WARREN I.   "LAND PATTERNS IN ANTE-BELLUM
        MONTGOMERY COUNTY, ALABAMA."   ALABAMA REVIEW, 8 (JULY,
        1955):   196-208.

11786   SMITH, WARREN I.   "STRUCTURE OF LANDHOLDING AND SLAVE
        OWNERSHIP IN ANTE-BELLUM MONTGOMERY COUNTY, ALABAMA."
        PH.D. DISSERTATION, UNIVERSITY OF ALABAMA, 1952.

11787   STOCKHOLM, RICHARD J.   "ALABAMA IRON FOR THE CONFEDERACY:
        THE SELMA IRON WORKS."   ALABAMA REVIEW, 21 (JULY,
        1968):   163-172.

11788   THOMAS, COBURN.   "AN ECONOMIC AND SOCIAL HISTORY OF
        JACKSON COUNTY."   M.S. THESIS, AUBURN UNIVERSITY, 1938.

11789   THOMPSON, ALANA S.   "MOBILE, ALABAMA, 1850-1861:
        ECONOMIC, POLITICAL, PHYSICAL AND POPULATION
        CHARACTERISTICS."   PH.D. DISSERTATION, UNIVERSITY OF
        ALABAMA, 1979.

11790   THORNTON, J. MILLS.   POLITICS AND POWER IN A SLAVE
        SOCIETY: ALABAMA, 1800-1860.   BATON ROUGE: LOUISIANA
        STATE UNIVERSITY PRESS, 1978.

11791   THORNTON, JONATHAN M.   "POLITICS AND POWER IN A SLAVE
        SOCIETY: ALABAMA, 1806-1860."   PH.D. DISSERTATION,
        YALE UNIVERSITY, 1974.

11792   VANDIVER, FRANK E.   "THE SHELBY IRON COMPANY IN THE CIVIL
        WAR: A STUDY OF A CONFEDERATE INDUSTRY."   ALABAMA
        REVIEW, 1 (JANUARY, 1948):   12-26.

11793   VANDIVER, FRANK E.   "THE SHELBY IRON WORKS: A STUDY IN
        CONFEDERATE INDUSTRY."   ALABAMA REVIEW, 1 (JULY,
        1948):   203-217.

11794   WHATLEY, GEORGE C.   "THE ALABAMA PRESBYTERIAN AND HIS
        SLAVE."   ALABAMA REVIEW, 13 (JANUARY, 1960):   40-51.

11795   WIENER, JONATHAN M.   "FEMALE PLANTERS AND PLANTERS' WIVES
        IN CIVIL WAR AND RECONSTRUCTION: ALABAMA, 1850-1870."
        ALABAMA REVIEW, 30 (APRIL, 1977):   135-149.

11796   WIENER, JONATHAN M.   "PLANTATIONS, POLITICS AND INDUSTRY:
        ALABAMA, 1850-1890."   PH.D. DISSERTATION, HARVARD

UNIVERSITY, 1972.

11797   WIENER, JONATHAN M.   "PLANTER PERSISTENCE AND SOCIAL
        CHANGE: ALABAMA, 1850-1870."   JOURNAL OF
        INTERDISCIPLINARY HISTORY, 7 (AUTUMN, 1976):   235-260.

11798   WIENER, JONATHAN M.   SOCIAL ORIGINS OF THE NEW SOUTH:
        ALABAMA, 1860-1885.   BATON ROUGE: LOUISIANA STATE
        UNIVERSITY PRESS, 1978.

11799   WIGINTON, DOLLIE.   "SOME SOCIAL AND ECONOMIC FACTORS IN
        SOUTHEASTERN ALABAMA IN 1860."   M.A. THESIS,
        UNIVERSITY OF ALABAMA, 1941.

11800   WILLIAMS, CLANTON.   "EARLY ANTE-BELLUM MONTGOMERY."
        UNPUBLISHED MANUSCRIPT, ALABAMA DEPARTMENT OF ARCHIVES
        AND HISTORY, 1941.

11801   WILLIAMS, CLANTON W.   "EARLY ANTE-BELLUM MONTGOMERY: A
        BLACK-BELT CONSTITUENCY."   JOURNAL OF SOUTHERN
        HISTORY, 7 (NOVEMBER, 1941):   495-525.

11802   WOODRUFF, JAMES F.   "SOME CHARACTERISTICS OF THE ALABAMA
        SLAVE POPULATION IN 1850."   GEOGRAPHICAL REVIEW, 52
        (JULY, 1962):   379-388.

11803   WOODRUFF, JAMES F.   "A STUDY OF THE CHARACTERISTICS OF
        THE ALABAMA SLAVE POPULATION IN 1850."   ANNALS OF THE
        ASSOCIATION OF AMERICAN GEOGRAPHERS, 51 (DECEMBER,
        1961):   427.

11804   WOODWARD, JOSEPH H.   "ALABAMA IRON MANUFACTURING,
        1860-1865."   ALABAMA REVIEW, 7 (JULY, 1954):   199-207.

11805   YANKOVIC, DONALD J.   "A MICRO STUDY OF THE COTTON
        PLANTATION ECONOMY OF DALLAS COUNTY, ALABAMA, BASED ON
        THE MANUSCRIPT CENSUS RETURNS OF 1860."   PH.D.
        DISSERTATION, UNIVERSITY OF PITTSBURGH, 1972.

11806   YOUNG, HUGH P.   "A SOCIAL AND ECONOMIC HISTORY OF
        MONTGOMERY, ALABAMA, 1846-1860."   M.A. THESIS,
        UNIVERSITY OF ALABAMA, 1948.

ARKANSAS

11807   BARR, ALWYN.   "BLACK MIGRATION INTO SOUTHWESTERN CITIES,
        1865-1900."   IN GALLAGHER, GARY W. (ED.).   ESSAYS IN
        SOUTHERN HISTORY WRITTEN IN HONOR OF BARNES F.
        LATHROP.   AUSTIN: GENERAL LIBRARIES, UNIVERSITY OF
        TEXAS, 1980, PP. 15-38.

11808   BEATTY-BROWN, FLORENCE R.   "LEGAL STATUS OF ARKANSAS
        NEGROES BEFORE EMANCIPATION."   ARKANSAS HISTORICAL
        QUARTERLY, 28 (SPRING, 1969):   6-13.

11809   BELL, H.S.   "PLANTATION LIFE OF THE NEGRO IN THE LOWER
        MISSISSIPPI VALLEY."   SOUTHERN WORKMAN, 28 (AUGUST,
        1899):   313-314.

11810   BROWN, MATTIE.   "A HISTORY OF RIVER TRANSPORTATION IN
        ARKANSAS FROM 1819-1880."   M.A. THESIS, UNIVERSITY OF
        ARKANSAS, 1934.

11811   CAMP, ALONZO D.   "LITIGATION INVOLVING ARKANSAS SLAVES."
        PULASKI COUNTY HISTORICAL SOCIETY BULLETIN, 13 (MARCH,
        1962):   1-6.

11812   CARMICHAEL, MAUDE S.   "FEDERAL EXPERIMENTS WITH NEGRO
        LABOR ON ABANDONED PLANTATIONS IN ARKANSAS:
        1862-1865."   ARKANSAS HISTORICAL QUARTERLY, 1 (MARCH,
        1942):   101-116.

11813   CARMICHAEL, MAUDE S.   "THE PLANTATION SYSTEM IN ARKANSAS,
        1850-1876."   PH.D. DISSERTATION, RADCLIFFE COLLEGE,
        1935.

11814   CARMICHAEL, MAUDE S.   "SLAVERY IN ARKANSAS."   M.A.
        THESIS, COLUMBIA UNIVERSITY, 1924.

11815   CATHEY, CLYDE W.   "SLAVERY IN ARKANSAS."   ARKANSAS
        HISTORICAL QUARTERLY, 3 (SPRING, SUMMER, 1944):
        66-90, 150-163.

11816   CATHEY, CLYDE W.   "SLAVERY IN ARKANSAS."   M.A. THESIS,
        UNIVERSITY OF ARKANSAS, 1936.

11817   CHESTER, SAMUEL H.   "AFRICAN SLAVERY AS I KNEW IT IN
        SOUTHERN ARKANSAS."   TENNESSEE HISTORICAL MAGAZINE, 9
        (OCTOBER, 1925):   178-184.

11818   CHESTER, SAMUEL H.   PIONEER DAYS IN ARKANSAS.   RICHMOND:
        PRESBYTERIAN COMMITTEE OF PUBLICATION, 1927.

11819   CLAYTON, LOUISE.   "LEGAL STATUS AND SOCIAL LIFE OF THE
        SLAVES IN ARKANSAS."   M.A. THESIS, UNIVERSITY OF
        CHICAGO, 1928.

11820   DALTON, LAWRENCE.   HISTORY OF RANDOLPH COUNTY, ARKANSAS.
        LITTLE ROCK: DEMOCRAT PRINT AND LITHOGRAPHING
        COMPANY, 1946.

11821   DOUGAN, MICHAEL B.   CONFEDERATE ARKANSAS: THE PEOPLE AND
        POLICIES OF A FRONTIER STATE IN WARTIME.   UNIVERSITY,
        AL: UNIVERSITY OF ALABAMA PRESS, 1976.

11822   GUINN, NANCY C.   "RURAL ARKANSAS IN THE '20'S."   ARKANSAS
        PIONEERS, 1 (SEPTEMBER, 1912):   11-12.

11823   HARVIN, E.L.   "ARKANSAS AND THE CRISIS OF 1860-1861."
        M.A. THESIS, UNIVERSITY OF TEXAS, 1926.

11824   HEMPSTEAD, FAY. HISTORICAL REVIEW OF ARKANSAS. 3 VOLS.
         CHICAGO: LEWIS PUBLISHING COMPANY, 1911.

11825   JOHNSON, FANNY A. "THE ASHLEY MANSION AND THE ASHLEY
         BAND--THE JOHNSON RESIDENCE." ARKANSAS PIONEERS, 1
         (SEPTEMBER, 1912): 10-11.

11826   KEESEE, IRENE. "THE MUTED VOICES OF MAGUIRETOWN."
         OZARKS MOUNTAINEER, 24 (APRIL, 1976): 16.

11827   KNIGHT, HANNAH D. "HOSPITALITY OF EARLY DAYS." ARKANSAS
         PIONEERS, 1 (SEPTEMBER, 1912): 10-11.

11828   LEWIS, ELSIE M. "FROM NATIONALISM TO DISUNION: A STUDY
         IN THE SECESSION MOVEMENT IN ARKANSAS, 1850-1861."
         PH.D. DISSERTATION, UNIVERSITY OF CHICAGO, 1947.

11829   MERRILL, PIERCE K. "RACE AS A FACTOR IN ACHIEVEMENT IN
         PLANTATION AREAS IN ARKANSAS." PH.D. DISSERTATION,
         VANDERBILT UNIVERSITY, 1951.

11830   MOFFATT, WALTER. "MEDICINE AND DENTISTRY IN PIONEER
         ARKANSAS." ARKANSAS HISTORICAL QUARTERLY, 10 (SUMMER,
         1951): 89-94.

11831   MORGAN, GORDON D. AND KUNKEL, PETER. "ARKANSAS' OZARK
         MOUNTAIN BLACKS: AN INTRODUCTION." PHYLON, 34
         (SEPTEMBER, 1973): 283-288.

11832   OTTO, JOHN S. "CANNON'S POINT PLANTATION AND THE HARDY
         BANKS FARM: MATERIAL LIVING CONDITIONS OF OLD SOUTH
         SLAVES." UNPUBLISHED PAPER PRESENTED AT MEETING OF
         SOCIETY FOR HISTORICAL ARCHAEOLOGY, NASHVILLE,
         TENNESSEE, 1979.

11833   OTTO, JOHN S. "SLAVERY IN THE MOUNTAINS: YELL COUNTY,
         ARKANSAS, 1840-1860." ARKANSAS HISTORICAL QUARTERLY,
         39 (SPRING, 1980): 35-52.

11834   PEAY, SUE C. AND CREASE, SOPHIA. "GOOD CHEER OF EARLY
         DAYS." ARKANSAS PIONEERS, 1 (JANUARY, 1913): 11.

11835   PIPKIN, JOHN G. "SLAVERY IN ARKANSAS." M.A. THESIS,
         UNIVERSITY OF CHICAGO, 1923.

11836   RHODES, ROBERT C. "ATTITUDE TOWARD SLAVERY AND SECESSION
         OF THE ARKANSAS REPRESENTATIVES IN CONGRESS." M.A.
         THESIS, VANDERBILT UNIVERSITY, 1908.

11837   "SLAVEOWNERS AND SLAVES IN PULASKI COUNTY, ARKANSAS,
         1861." PULASKI COUNTY HISTORICAL SOCIETY BULLETIN, 8
         (JUNE, 1960): 22-28.

11838   "SLAVERY (IN EARL, ARKANSAS)." COMMONWEAL, 25 (DECEMBER
         11, 1936): 188.

11839 "SLAVERY IN PULASKI COUNTY IN 1861." PULASKI COUNTY
HISTORICAL SOCIETY BULLETIN, 18 (SEPTEMBER, 1970): 39.

11840 TATUM, GEORGIA L. DISLOYALTY IN THE CONFEDERACY. CHAPEL
HILL: UNIVERSITY OF NORTH CAROLINA PRESS, 1934.

11841 TAYLOR, ORVILLE W. "BAPTISTS AND SLAVERY IN ARKANSAS:
RELATIONSHIPS AND ATTITUDES." ARKANSAS HISTORICAL
QUARTERLY, 38 (AUTUMN, 1979): 199-226.

11842 TAYLOR, ORVILLE W. "'JUMPING THE BROOMSTICK': SLAVE
MARRIAGE AND MORALITY IN ARKANSAS." ARKANSAS
HISTORICAL QUARTERLY, 17 (AUTUMN, 1958): 217-231.

11843 TAYLOR, ORVILLE W. (ED.). "A LETTER FROM GOVERNOR JAMES
S. CONWAY TO HIS PLANTATION OVERSEER." ARKANSAS
HISTORICAL QUARTERLY, 18 (SUMMER, 1959): 90-92.

11844 TAYLOR, ORVILLE W. NEGRO SLAVERY IN ARKANSAS. DURHAM:
DUKE UNIVERSITY PRESS, 1958.

11845 TAYLOR, ORVILLE W. "NEGRO SLAVERY IN ARKANSAS." PH.D.
DISSERTATION, DUKE UNIVERSITY, 1956.

11846 "TERRITORIAL TAX LIST, ARKANSAS COUNTY, 1817." GRAND
PRAIRIE HISTORICAL SOCIETY BULLETIN, 4 (APRIL, 1961):
10-13.

11847 THANET, OCTAVE. "PLANTATION LIFE IN ARKANSAS." ATLANTIC
MONTHLY, 68 (JULY, 1891): 32-49.

11848 THOMAS, DAVID Y. ARKANSAS IN WAR AND RECONSTRUCTION,
1861-1874. LITTLE ROCK: UNITED DAUGHTERS OF THE
CONFEDERACY, 1926.

11849 THORPE, REED. "THE SOUTHWEST AND SLAVERY." M.S. THESIS,
UNIVERSITY OF UTAH, 1943.

11850 TRIEBER, JACOB. "LEGAL STATUS OF NEGROES IN ARKANSAS
BEFORE THE CIVIL WAR." PUBLICATIONS OF THE ARKANSAS
HISTORICAL ASSOCIATION, 3 (1911): 175-183.

11851 VAN DEBURG, WILLIAM L. "THE SLAVE DRIVERS OF ARKANSAS:
A NEW VIEW FROM THE NARRATIVES." ARKANSAS HISTORICAL
QUARTERLY, 35 (AUTUMN, 1976): 231-245.

11852 WALZ, ROBERT B. "ARKANSAS SLAVEHOLDINGS AND SLAVEHOLDERS
IN 1850." ARKANSAS HISTORICAL QUARTERLY, 12 (SPRING,
1953): 38-74.

11853 WHITE, LONNIE J. POLITICS ON THE SOUTHWESTERN FRONTIER:
ARKANSAS TERRITORY, 1819-1836. MEMPHIS: MEMPHIS
STATE UNIVERSITY PRESS, 1964.

11854 WORLEY, TED R. (ED.). "AT HOME IN CONFEDERATE ARKANSAS:

LETTERS FROM PULASKI COUNTIANS, 1861-1865." PULASKI
COUNTY HISTORICAL SOCIETY BULLETIN, 2 (DECEMBER,
1955): 36-42.

11855   WORLEY, TED R. (ED.). "STORY OF AN EARLY SETTLEMENT IN
        CENTRAL ARKANSAS." ARKANSAS HISTORICAL QUARTERLY, 10
        (SUMMER, 1951): 117-137.

FLORIDA

11856   ABBEY, KATHRYN T. "DOCUMENTS RELATING TO EL DESTINO AND
        CHEMONIE PLANTATIONS, MIDDLE FLORIDA, 1828-1868."
        FLORIDA HISTORICAL QUARTERLY, 7 (JANUARY, APRIL,
        1929): 179-213, 291-329; 8 (JULY, OCTOBER, 1929):
        3-46, 79-111.

11857   AGRESTI, BARBARA F. "THE FIRST DECADES OF FREEDOM:
        BLACK FAMILIES IN A SOUTHERN COUNTY, 1870 AND 1885."
        JOURNAL OF MARRIAGE AND THE FAMILY, 40 (NOVEMBER,
        1978): 697-706.

11858   APPLEYARD, LULA D.K. "PLANTATION LIFE IN MIDDLE FLORIDA,
        1821-1845." M.A. THESIS, FLORIDA STATE COLLEGE FOR
        WOMEN, 1940.

11859   BARR, RUTH B. AND HARGIS, MODESTE. "THE VOLUNTARY EXILE
        OF FREE NEGROES OF PENSACOLA." FLORIDA HISTORICAL
        QUARTERLY, 17 (JULY, 1938): 3-14.

11860   BATES, THELMA. "THE LEGAL STATUS OF THE NEGRO IN
        FLORIDA." FLORIDA HISTORICAL QUARTERLY, 6 (JANUARY,
        1928): 159-181.

11861   BATES, THELMA. "A PRELIMINARY STUDY OF THE LEGAL STATUS
        OF THE NEGRO IN FLORIDA." M.A. THESIS, FLORIDA STATE
        COLLEGE FOR WOMEN, 1927.

11862   BOOTH, NORMAN E. "TALLAHASSEE AND TRINITY'S ANTE-BELLUM
        TIMES, 1824-1861." M.A. THESIS, FLORIDA STATE
        UNIVERSITY, 1971.

11863   BOYD, MARK F. "HISTORIC SITES IN AND AROUND THE JIM
        WOODRUFF RESERVOIR AREA, FLORIDA-GEORGIA." IN U.S.
        BUREAU OF AMERICAN ETHNOLOGY. RIVER BASIN SURVEYS:
        INTER-AGENCY ARCHEOLOGICAL SALVAGE PROGRAM PAPERS NO.
        13. WASHINGTON: U.S. GOVERNMENT PRINTING OFFICE,
        1958, PP. 195-314.

11864   BRAGAW, DONALD H. "LOSS OF IDENTITY ON PENSACOLA'S PAST:
        A CREOLE FOOTNOTE." FLORIDA HISTORICAL QUARTERLY, 50
        (APRIL, 1972): 414-418.

11865   BRUMBAUGH, RODERICK. "BLACK MAROONS IN FLORIDA,
        1800-1830." UNPUBLISHED PAPER PRESENTED AT MEETING OF

ORGANIZATION OF AMERICAN HISTORIANS, BOSTON, 1975.

11866   BUKER, GEORGE E.   SWAMP SAILOR: RIVERINE WARFARE IN THE
        EVERGLADES, 1835-1842.   GAINESVILLE: UNIVERSITY
        PRESSES OF FLORIDA, 1975.

11867   CHATHAM, KATHERINE.   "PLANTATION SLAVERY IN MIDDLE
        FLORIDA."   M.A. THESIS, UNIVERSITY OF NORTH CAROLINA,
        1938.

11868   CHERRY, ADA L.   "THE UNITED STATES NAVY YARD AT
        PENSACOLA, FLORIDA, 1823-1862."   M.A. THESIS, FLORIDA
        STATE UNIVERSITY, 1953.

11869   COTTON, BARBARA R.   "THE EFFECTS OF ANTEBELLUM CONDITIONS
        UPON POST-WAR ECONOMIC ADJUSTMENT OF BLACKS IN
        JACKSONVILLE."   NEGRO HISTORY BULLETIN, 42 (JULY,
        AUGUST, SEPTEMBER, 1979):   68-69, 72-73.

11870   COVINGTON, JAMES W.   "AN EPISODE IN THE THIRD SEMINOLE
        WAR."   FLORIDA HISTORICAL QUARTERLY, 45 (JULY, 1966):
        45-59.

11871   DAVIS, JESS G.   HISTORY OF ALACHUA COUNTY, 1824-1969.
        GAINESVILLE: ALACHUA COUNTY HISTORICAL COMMISSION,
        1970.

11872   DAVIS, T. FREDERICK.   "UNITED STATES TROOPS IN SPANISH
        EAST FLORIDA, 1812-1813."   FLORIDA HISTORICAL
        QUARTERLY, 9 (JULY, OCTOBER, 1930, JANUARY, APRIL,
        1931):   3-23, 96-116, 135-155, 259-278; 10 (JULY,
        1931):   24-34.

11873   DIBBLE, ERNEST F.   ANTEBELLUM PENSACOLA AND THE MILITARY
        PRESENCE.   PENSACOLA: MAYES PRINTING COMPANY, 1974.

11874   DIBBLE, ERNEST F.   "SLAVE RENTALS TO THE MILITARY:
        PENSACOLA AND THE GULF COAST."   CIVIL WAR HISTORY, 23
        (JUNE, 1977):   101-113.

11875   DODD, DOROTHY.   "FLORIDA IN 1845."   FLORIDA HISTORICAL
        QUARTERLY, 24 (JULY, 1945):   3-27.

11876   DODD, DOROTHY.   "FLORIDA'S POPULATION IN 1845."   FLORIDA
        HISTORICAL QUARTERLY, 24 (JULY, 1945):   28-29.

11877   DODD, DOROTHY.   "THE SCHOONER 'EMPEROR'; AN INCIDENT OF
        THE ILLEGAL SLAVE TRADE IN FLORIDA."   FLORIDA
        HISTORICAL SOCIETY QUARTERLY, 13 (JANUARY, 1935):
        117-128.

11878   DOHERTY, HERBERT J., JR.   "FLORIDA AND THE CRISIS OF
        1850."   JOURNAL OF SOUTHERN HISTORY, 19 (FEBRUARY,
        1953):   32-47.

11879   DOHERTY, HERBERT J., JR. (ED.). "A FREE NEGRO PURCHASES
        HIS DAUGHTER." FLORIDA HISTORICAL QUARTERLY, 29
        (JULY, 1950): 38-43.

11880   DOUGLAS, MARJORY S. FLORIDA: THE LONG FRONTIER. NEW
        YORK: HARPER & ROW, 1967.

11881   DJFFNER, MICHAEL P. "THE SEMINOLE-BLACK ALLIANCE IN
        FLORIDA: AN EXAMPLE OF MINORITY COOPERATION." M.A.
        THESIS, GEORGE MASON UNIVERSITY, 1973.

11882   EISTERHOLD, JOHN A. "LUMBER AND TRADE IN PENSACOLA AND
        WEST FLORIDA: 1800-1860." FLORIDA HISTORICAL
        QUARTERLY, 51 (JANUARY, 1973): 267-280.

11883   EPPES, MRS. NICHOLAS W. THE NEGRO OF THE OLD SOUTH, A
        BIT OF PERIOD HISTORY. CHICAGO: JOSEPH G. BRANCH,
        1925.

11884   FAIRBANKS, CHARLES H. "THE KINGSLEY SLAVE CABINS IN
        DUVAL COUNTY, FLORIDA, 1968." THE CONFERENCE ON
        HISTORIC SITE ARCHAEOLOGY PAPERS, 1972, NO. 7 (1974):
        62-93.

11885   FAIRBANKS, CHARLES H. "SPANIARDS, PLANTERS, SHIPS, AND
        SLAVES: HISTORICAL ARCHAEOLOGY IN FLORIDA AND
        GEORGIA." ARCHAEOLOGY, 29 (JULY, 1976): 164-172.

11886   FOX, GRACE I. "RING GAMES AND OTHER GAMES OF THE FLORIDA
        NEGRO." PH.D. DISSERTATION, INDIANA UNIVERSITY, 1951.

11887   FRETWELL, MARK E. AND ARANA, EUGENIA B. (EDS.). "MAJOR
        PONCE AND CASTILLO DE SAN MARCOS, 1673-1675."
        ESCRIBANO, 9 (1972): 174-185.

11888   GILLIAM, FARLEY M. "THE 'BLACK CODES' OF FLORIDA."
        APALACHEE, 6 (1963-1967): 111-120.

11889   GLUNT, JAMES D. "PLANTATION AND FRONTIER RECORDS OF EAST
        AND MIDDLE FLORIDA, 1789-1868." PH.D. DISSERTATION,
        UNIVERSITY OF MICHIGAN, 1931.

11890   GOLD, ROBERT L. BORDERLAND EMPIRES IN TRANSITION: THE
        TRIPLE-NATION TRANSFER OF FLORIDA. CARBONDALE:
        SOUTHERN ILLINOIS UNIVERSITY PRESS, 1969.

11891   GRANADE, RAY. "SLAVE UNREST IN FLORIDA." FLORIDA
        HISTORICAL QUARTERLY, 55 (JULY, 1976): 18-36.

11892   GROENE, BERTRAM H. "ANTE-BELLUM TALLAHASSEE; IT WAS A
        GAY TIME THEN." PH.D. DISSERTATION, FLORIDA STATE
        UNIVERSITY, 1967.

11893   HADD, DONALD R. "THE SECESSION MOVEMENT IN FLORIDA,
        1850-1861." M.A. THESIS, FLORIDA STATE UNIVERSITY,

1960.

11894   HARPER, ROLAND M.   "ANTE-BELLUM CENSUS ENUMERATIONS IN
        FLORIDA."   ELORIDA HISTORICAL SOCIETY QUARTERLY, 6
        (JULY, 1927):   42-52.

11895   HAYNES, ROBERT V.   THE NATCHEZ DISTRICT AND THE AMERICAN
        REVOLUTION.   JACKSON: UNIVERSITY PRESS OF
        MISSISSIPPI, 1976.

11896   HAZEL, JOSEPH A.   "THE GEOGRAPHY OF NEGRO AGRICULTURAL
        SLAVERY IN ALABAMA, FLORIDA, AND MISSISSIPPI, CIRCA
        1860."   PH.D. DISSERTATION, COLUMBIA UNIVERSITY, 1963.

11897   HERING, JULIA F.   "PLANTATION ECONOMY IN LEON COUNTY,
        1830-1840."   ELORIDA HISTORICAL QUARTERLY, 33 (JULY,
        1954):   32-47.

11898   HERING, JULIA F.   "PLANTATION ECONOMY IN LEON COUNTY FROM
        1830 TO 1840."   M.S. THESIS, FLORIDA STATE UNIVERSITY,
        1954.

11899   HOLMES, JACK D.L.   "INDIGO IN COLONIAL LOUISIANA AND THE
        FLORIDAS."   LOUISIANA HISTORY, 8 (FALL, 1967):
        329-350.

11900   HOLMES, JACK D.L.   "NAVAL STORES IN COLONIAL LOUISIANA
        AND THE FLORIDAS."   LOUISIANA HISTORY, 7 (WINTER,
        1968):   295-309.

11901   HOWARD, CLINTON N.   THE BRITISH DEVELOPMENT OF WEST
        ELORIDA, 1763-1769.   BERKELEY: UNIVERSITY OF
        CALIFORNIA PRESS, 1947.

11902   HOWE, BENNIE W.   "THE FUGITIVE SLAVE PROBLEM IN SOUTH
        CAROLINA AND FLORIDA, 1670-1763:   A CONTRAST IN
        ATTITUDES."   M.A. THESIS, OHIO STATE UNIVERSITY, 1962.

11903   JACKSON, JESSE J.   "THE NEGRO AND THE LAW IN FLORIDA,
        1821-1921; LEGAL PATTERNS OF SEGREGATION AND CONTROL
        IN FLORIDA, 1821-1921."   M.A. THESIS, FLORIDA STATE
        UNIVERSITY, 1960.

11904   JOHNS, JOHN E.   ELORIDA DURING THE CIVIL WAR.
        GAINESVILLE: UNIVERSITY OF FLORIDA PRESS, 1963.

11905   JOHNSON, CECIL S.   BRITISH WEST ELORIDA, 1763-1783.   NEW
        HAVEN: YALE UNIVERSITY PRESS, 1943.

11906   KIPLE, KENNETH F.   "THE CASE AGAINST A NINETEENTH-CENTURY
        CUBA-FLORIDA SLAVE TRADE."   ELORIDA HISTORICAL
        QUARTERLY, 49 (APRIL, 1971):   346-355.

11907   KITTREDGE, FRANK E.   THE MAN WITH THE BRANDED HAND: AN
        AUTHENTIC SKETCH OF THE LIFE AND SERVICE OF CAPTAIN

JONATHAN WALKER. ROCHESTER: H.L. WILSON, 1899.

11908 KLINGMAN, PETER D. "A FLORIDA SLAVE SALE." _FLORIDA HISTORICAL QUARTERLY_, 52 (JULY, 1973): 62-66.

11909 LOCKEY, JOSEPH B. _EAST FLORIDA, 1783-1785_. BERKELEY: UNIVERSITY OF CALIFORNIA PRESS, 1949.

11910 LONG, ELLEN C. _FLORIDA BREEZES: OR, FLORIDA, NEW AND OLD_. JACKSONVILLE: ASHMEAD BROTHERS, 1882.

11911 LOTT, AUDREY P. "SLAVERY IN FLORIDA--A STUDY." M.A. THESIS, DUKE UNIVERSITY, 1937.

11912 LYON, EUGENE. _THE ENTERPRISE OF FLORIDA: PEDRO MENENDEZ DE AVILES AND THE SPANISH CONQUEST OF 1565-1568_. GAINESVILLE: UNIVERSITY PRESSES OF FLORIDA, 1976.

11913 MAHON, JOHN K. _HISTORY OF THE SECOND SEMINOLE WAR, 1835-1842_. GAINESVILLE: UNIVERSITY OF FLORIDA PRESS, 1967.

11914 MARTIN, SIDNEY W. _FLORIDA DURING THE TERRITORIAL DAYS_. ATHENS: UNIVERSITY OF GEORGIA PRESS, 1944.

11915 MCCONNELL, ROLAND C. "BLACK LIFE AND ACTIVITIES IN WEST FLORIDA AND ON THE GULF COAST, 1762-1803." IN PROCTOR, SAMUEL (ED.). _EIGHTEENTH-CENTURY FLORIDA: LIFE ON THE FRONTIER_. GAINESVILLE: UNIVERSITY PRESSES OF FLORIDA, 1976, PP. 75-90.

11916 MCRORY, MARY O. AND BARROWS, EDITH C. _HISTORY OF JEFFERSON COUNTY, FLORIDA_. MONTICELLO: JEFFERSON COUNTY KIWANIS CLUB, 1935.

11917 MILLIGAN, JOHN D. "SLAVE REBELLIOUSNESS AND THE FLORIDA MAROON." _PROLOGUE_, 6 (SPRING, 1974): 4-18.

11918 MOWAT, CHARLES. _EAST FLORIDA AS A BRITISH PROVINCE, 1763-1784_. BERKELEY: UNIVERSITY OF CALIFORNIA PRESS, 1934.

11919 MURDOCH, RICHARD K. "THE RETURN OF RUNAWAY SLAVES, 1790-1794." _FLORIDA HISTORICAL QUARTERLY_, 38 (OCTOBER, 1959): 96-113.

11920 PALMER, HENRY E. "PHYSICIANS OF EARLY TALLAHASSEE AND VICINITY." _APALACHEE, THE PUBLICATION OF THE FLORIDA HISTORICAL SOCIETY_, (1944-1956): 29-46.

11921 PALMER, HENRY E. "THE PROCTORS--A TRUE STORY OF ANTE-BELLUM DAYS AND SINCE." _TALLAHASSEE HISTORICAL SOCIETY ANNUAL_, 1 (1934): 14-16.

11922 PHILLIPS, ULRICH B. AND GLUNT, JAMES D. (EDS.). _FLORIDA_

PLANTATION RECORDS FROM THE PAPERS OF GEORGE NOBLE JONES. ST. LOUIS: MISSOURI HISTORICAL SOCIETY, 1927.

11923 PORTER, KENNETH W. "ABRAHAM." PHYLON, 2 (SECOND QUARTER, 1941): 107-116.

11924 PORTER, KENNETH W. "THE EARLY LIFE OF LUIS PACHECO, NEE FATIO." NEGRO HISTORY BULLETIN, 7 (DECEMBER, 1943): 52.

11925 PORTER, KENNETH W. "FLORIDA SLAVES AND FREE NEGROES IN THE SEMINOLE WAR, 1835-1842." JOURNAL OF NEGRO HISTORY, 28 (OCTOBER, 1943): 390-421.

11926 PORTER, KENNETH W. "JOHN CAESAR: A FORGOTTEN HERO OF THE SEMINOLE WAR." JOURNAL OF NEGRO HISTORY, 28 (JANUARY, 1943): 53-65.

11927 PORTER, KENNETH W. "JOHN CAESAR: SEMINOLE NEGRO PARTISAN." JOURNAL OF NEGRO HISTORY, 31 (APRIL, 1946): 190-207.

11928 PORTER, KENNETH W. "LOUIS PACHECO: THE MAN AND THE MYTH." JOURNAL OF NEGRO HISTORY, 28 (JANUARY, 1943): 65-72.

11929 PORTER, KENNETH W. "THE NEGRO ABRAHAM." FLORIDA HISTORICAL QUARTERLY, 25 (JULY, 1946): 1-43.

11930 PORTER, KENNETH W. "NEGRO GUIDES AND INTERPRETERS IN THE EARLY STAGES OF THE SEMINOLE WAR, DECEMBER 28, 1835-MARCH 6, 1837." JOURNAL OF NEGRO HISTORY, 35 (APRIL, 1950): 174-188.

11931 PORTER, KENNETH W. "NEGROES AND THE EAST FLORIDA ANNEXATION PLOT, 1811-1813." JOURNAL OF NEGRO HISTORY, 30 (JANUARY, 1945): 9-29.

11932 PORTER, KENNETH W. "NEGROES AND THE SEMINOLE WAR, 1817-1818." JOURNAL OF NEGRO HISTORY, 36 (JULY, 1951): 249-280.

11933 PORTER, KENNETH W. "NEGROES AND THE SEMINOLE WAR, 1835-1842." JOURNAL OF SOUTHERN HISTORY, 30 (NOVEMBER, 1964): 427-450.

11934 PORTER, KENNETH W. "NOTES ON SEMINOLE NEGROES IN THE BAHAMAS." FLORIDA HISTORICAL QUARTERLY, 24 (JULY, 1945): 56-60.

11935 PORTER, KENNETH W. "OSCEOLA AND THE NEGROES." FLORIDA HISTORICAL QUARTERLY, 33 (JANUARY/APRIL, 1955): 235-239.

11936 PORTER, KENNETH W. "SEMINOLE FLIGHT FROM FORT MARION."

FLORIDA HISTORICAL QUARTERLY, 22 (JANUARY, 1944):
112-133.

11937   RANDALL, STANLEY J.   HISTORY OF JACKSON COUNTY.
        MARIANNA, FL: JACKSON COUNTY HISTORICAL SOCIETY, 1950.

11938   REA, ROBERT R.   "PLANTERS AND PLANTATIONS IN BRITISH WEST
        FLORIDA."   ALABAMA REVIEW, 29 (JULY, 1976):   220-235.

11939   RICHARDSON, BARBARA A.   "A HISTORY OF BLACKS IN
        JACKSONVILLE, FLORIDA, 1860-1895:   A SOCIO-ECONOMIC
        AND POLITICAL STUDY."   D.A. DISSERTATION,
        CARNEGIE-MELLON UNIVERSITY, 1975.

11940   RICHARDSON, JOE M.   "CHRISTIAN ABOLITIONISM: THE
        AMERICAN MISSIONARY ASSOCIATION AND THE FLORIDA
        NEGRO."   JOURNAL OF NEGRO EDUCATION, 40 (WINTER,
        1971):   35-44.

11941   RICHARDSON, JOE M.   THE NEGRO IN THE RECONSTRUCTION OF
        FLORIDA, 1865-1877.   TALLAHASSEE: FLORIDA STATE
        UNIVERSITY PRESS, 1965.

11942   RICHARDSON, JOE M.   "THE NEGRO IN THE RECONSTRUCTION OF
        FLORIDA."   PH.D. DISSERTATION, FLORIDA STATE
        UNIVERSITY, 1963.

11943   SEFTON, JAMES E.   "BLACK SLAVES, RED MASTERS, WHITE
        MIDDLEMEN: A CONGRESSIONAL DEBATE OF 1852."   FLORIDA
        HISTORICAL QUARTERLY, 51 (OCTOBER, 1972):   113-128.

11944   SHELDON, JANE M.   "SEMINOLE ATTACKS NEAR NEW SMYRNA,
        1835-1856."   FLORIDA HISTORICAL QUARTERLY, 8 (APRIL,
        1930):   188-196.

11945   SHELLEY, DIAN L.   "THE EFFECTS OF INCREASING RACISM ON
        THE CREOLE COLORED IN THREE GULF COAST CITIES BETWEEN
        1803 AND 1860."   M.A. THESIS, UNIVERSITY OF WEST
        FLORIDA, 1971.

11946   SHOFNER, JERRELL H.   HISTORY OF JEFFERSON COUNTY.
        TALLAHASSEE: SENTRY PRESS, 1976.

11947   SHOFNER, JERRELL H. AND ROGERS, WILLIAM W.   "SEA ISLAND
        COTTON IN ANTE-BELLUM FLORIDA."   FLORIDA HISTORICAL
        QUARTERLY, 40 (APRIL, 1962):   373-380.

11948   SIEBERT, WILBUR H.   "THE EARLY SUGAR INDUSTRY IN
        FLORIDA."   FLORIDA HISTORICAL QUARTERLY, 35 (APRIL,
        1957):   312-319.

11949   SIEBERT, WILBUR H.   "HISTORY OF SLAVERY IN EAST FLORIDA,
        1776-1785."   FLORIDA HISTORICAL SOCIETY QUARTERLY, 10
        (JANUARY, 1932):   139-161.

11950   SIEBERT, WILBUR H.   "SLAVERY AND WHITE SERVITUDE IN EAST
         FLORIDA, 1726-1776." FLORIDA HISTORICAL SOCIETY
         QUARTERLY, 10 (JULY, 1931): 3-23.

11951   SMITH, JULIA F.   "COTTON AND THE FACTORAGE SYSTEM IN
         ANTEBELLUM FLORIDA." FLORIDA HISTORICAL QUARTERLY, 49
         (JULY, 1970): 36-48.

11952   SMITH, JULIA F.   "THE PLANTATION BELT IN MIDDLE FLORIDA,
         1850-1860." PH.D. DISSERTATION, FLORIDA STATE
         UNIVERSITY, 1964.

11953   SMITH, JULIA F.   "PLANTATION ECONOMY IN LEON COUNTY FROM
         1830-1840." M.S. THESIS, FLORIDA STATE UNIVERSITY,
         1954.

11954   SMITH, JULIA F.   SLAVERY AND PLANTATION GROWTH IN
         ANTEBELLUM FLORIDA, 1821-1860. GAINESVILLE:
         UNIVERSITY OF FLORIDA PRESS, 1973.

11955   SMITH, JULIA F.   "SLAVETRADING IN ANTEBELLUM FLORIDA."
         FLORIDA HISTORICAL QUARTERLY, 50 (JANUARY, 1972):
         252-261.

11956   SMITH, RHEA.   "RACIAL STRAINS IN FLORIDA." FLORIDA
         HISTORICAL SOCIETY QUARTERLY, 11 (JULY, 1932): 17-32.

11957   SOUTHALL, EUGENE P.   "NEGROES IN FLORIDA PRIOR TO THE
         CIVIL WAR." JOURNAL OF NEGRO HISTORY, 19 (JANUARY,
         1934): 77-86.

11958   STAKELY, CHARLES A.   "INTRODUCTION OF THE NEGRO INTO THE
         UNITED STATES--FLORIDA, NOT VIRGINIA, THE FIRST STATE
         TO RECEIVE HIM." MAGAZINE OF AMERICAN HISTORY, 26
         (NOVEMBER, 1891): 349-363.

11959   STARR, J. BARTON.   TORIES, DONS, AND REBELS: THE
         AMERICAN REVOLUTION IN BRITISH WEST FLORIDA.
         GAINESVILLE: UNIVERSITY PRESSES OF FLORIDA, 1976.

11960   STEPHENS, JEAN B.   "ZEPHANIA KINGSLEY AND THE RECAPTURED
         AFRICANS." ESCRIBANO, 15 (1978): 71-78.

11961   TANNER, EARL C. (ED.).   "THE EARLY CAREER OF EDWIN T.
         JENCKES: A FLORIDA PIONEER OF THE 1830'S." FLORIDA
         HISTORICAL QUARTERLY, 30 (JANUARY, 1952): 270-275.

11962   TENNEY, JOHN F.   SLAVERY, SECESSION AND SUCCESS: THE
         MEMOIRS OF A FLORIDA PIONEER. SAN ANTONIO: SOUTHERN
         LITERARY INSTITUTE, 1934.

11963   TEPASKE, JOHN J.   "THE FUGITIVE SLAVE: INTERCOLONIAL
         RIVALRY AND SPANISH SLAVE POLICY, 1687-1764." IN
         PROCTOR, SAMUEL (ED.). EIGHTEENTH-CENTURY FLORIDA AND
         ITS BORDERLANDS. GAINESVILLE: UNIVERSITY PRESSES OF

FLORIDA, 1975, PP. 1-12.

11964   WEINBERG, SYDNEY J. "SLAVERY AND SECESSION IN FLORIDA,
        1845-1861." M.A. THESIS, UNIVERSITY OF FLORIDA, 1940.

11965   WEST, FRANCIS D. (ED.). "JOHN BARTRAM AND SLAVERY."
        SOUTH CAROLINA HISTORICAL MAGAZINE, 56 (APRIL, 1955):
        115-119.

11966   WIGHT, WILLARD E. "BISHOP VEROT AND THE CIVIL WAR."
        CATHOLIC HISTORICAL REVIEW, 47 (JULY, 1961): 153-163.

11967   WILLIAMS, EDWIN L., JR. "FLORIDA IN THE UNION,
        1845-1861." PH.D. DISSERTATION, UNIVERSITY OF NORTH
        CAROLINA, 1951.

11968   WILLIAMS, EDWIN L., JR. "NEGRO SLAVERY IN FLORIDA."
        FLORIDA HISTORICAL QUARTERLY, 28 (OCTOBER, 1949,
        JANUARY, 1950): 182-204.

11969   WRIGHT, ALBERT H. OUR GEORGIA-FLORIDA FRONTIER: THE
        OKEFENOKEE SWAMP, ITS HISTORY AND CARTOGRAPHY.
        ITHACA: A.H. WRIGHT, 1945.

11970   WRIGHT, J. LEITCH. "BRITISH EAST FLORIDA: LOYALIST
        BASTION." IN PROCTOR, SAMUEL (ED.).
        EIGHTEENTH-CENTURY FLORIDA: THE IMPACT OF THE
        AMERICAN REVOLUTION. GAINESVILLE: UNIVERSITY PRESSES
        OF FLORIDA, 1978, PP. 1-13.

11971   WRIGHT, J. LEITCH JR. "BLACKS IN BRITISH EAST FLORIDA."
        FLORIDA HISTORICAL QUARTERLY, 54 (APRIL, 1976):
        425-442.

11972   WRIGHT, J. LEITCH JR. FLORIDA IN THE AMERICAN
        REVOLUTION. GAINESVILLE: UNIVERSITY PRESSES OF
        FLORIDA, 1975.

11973   WRIGHT, J. LEITCH JR. "A NOTE ON THE FIRST SEMINOLE WAR
        AS SEEN BY THE INDIANS, NEGROES, AND THEIR BRITISH
        ADVISERS." JOURNAL OF SOUTHERN HISTORY, 34 (NOVEMBER,
        1968): 565-575.

11974   ZACHARIAS, DIANNA. "AN INTERPRETATION OF THE FLORIDA
        EX-SLAVES' MEMORIES OF SLAVERY AND THE CIVIL WAR."
        M.A. THESIS, WESTERN KENTUCKY UNIVERSITY, 1976.

GEORGIA

11975   ALBANESE, ANTHONY G. "THE PLANTATION AS A SCHOOL: THE
        SEA-ISLANDS OF GEORGIA AND SOUTH CAROLINA, A TEST
        CASE, 1800-1860." ED.D. DISSERTATION, RUTGERS
        UNIVERSITY, 1970.

11976 ALBERT, OCTAVIA V.R. THE HOUSE OF BONDAGE: OR,
       CHARLOTTE BROOKS AND OTHER SLAVES. NEW YORK: HUNT
       AND EATON, 1890.

11977 "AMELIA M. MURRAY ON SLAVERY--AN UNPUBLISHED LETTER."
       GEORGIA HISTORICAL QUARTERLY, 33 (DECEMBER, 1949):
       314-317.

11978 ANDREWS, GARNETT. REMINISCENCES OF AN OLD GEORGIA
       LAWYER. ATLANTA: FRANKLIN STEAM PRINTING HOUSE, 1870.

11979 ANGEL, ROBERT. "THE ARGUMENT OVER THE INTRODUCTION OF
       SLAVERY INTO GEORGIA IN THE COLONIAL PERIOD." M.A.
       THESIS, CATHOLIC UNIVERSITY OF AMERICA, 1964.

11980 ARMSTRONG, THOMAS F. "FROM TASK LABOR TO FREE LABOR:
       THE TRANSITION ALONG GEORGIA'S RICE COAST, 1820-1880."
       GEORGIA HISTORICAL QUARTERLY, 64 (WINTER, 1980):
       432-447.

11981 ASCHER, ROBERT AND FAIRBANKS, CHARLES H. "EXCAVATION OF
       A SLAVE CABIN: GEORGIA, USA." HISTORICAL
       ARCHAEOLOGY, 5 (1971): 3-17.

11982 AVERY, ISAAC W. HISTORY OF THE STATE OF GEORGIA,
       1850-1881. NEW YORK: BROWN, 1881.

11983 BAILEY, HUGH C. "SLAVE OWNERS WITHIN THE FIRST
       ASSESSMENT DISTRICT OF BURKE COUNTY, GEORGIA, IN
       1798--A TAX LIST." NATIONAL GENEALOGICAL SOCIETY
       QUARTERLY, 50 (1962): 69-72.

11984 BANKS, ENOCH M. "ECONOMICS OF LAND TENURE IN GEORGIA."
       PH.D. DISSERTATION, COLUMBIA UNIVERSITY, 1905.

11985 BARNWELL, STEPHEN B. "THE CONFEDERATE EPISCOPACY,
       SLAVERY, AND STEPHEN ELLIOT." MICHIGAN ACADEMICIAN, 1
       (SPRING, 1969): 57-67.

11986 BARROW, DAVID C. "A GEORGIA PLANTATION." SCRIBNER'S
       MONTHLY, 21 (APRIL, 1881): 830-836.

11987 BASCOM, WILLIAM R. "ACCULTURATION AMONG THE GULLAH
       NEGROES." AMERICAN ANTHROPOLOGIST, 43 (JANUARY-MARCH,
       1941): 43-50.

11988 BELLEGARDE, IDA R. "A HISTORICAL ANALYSIS OF
       TENSION-MAKING FACTORS IN GEORGIA." PH.D.
       DISSERTATION, LAVAL UNIVERSITY, 1943.

11989 BLASSINGAME, JOHN W. "BEFORE THE GHETTO: THE MAKING OF
       THE BLACK COMMUNITY IN SAVANNAH, GEORGIA, 1865-1880."
       JOURNAL OF SOCIAL HISTORY, 6 (SUMMER, 1973): 463-488.

11990 BONEY, F.N. "DOCTOR THOMAS HAMILTON: TWO VIEWS OF A

GENTLEMAN OF THE OLD SOUTH." PHYLON, 28 (FALL, 1967): 288-292.

11991 BONEY, F.N. "THOMAS STEVENS, ANTEBELLUM GEORGIAN." SOUTH ATLANTIC QUARTERLY, 72 (SPRING, 1973): 226-242.

11992 BONNER, JAMES C. "AGRICULTURAL REFORM IN THE GEORGIA PIEDMONT, 1820-1860." PH.D. DISSERTATION, UNIVERSITY OF NORTH CAROLINA, 1943.

11993 BONNER, JAMES C. A HISTORY OF GEORGIA AGRICULTURE, 1732-1860. ATHENS: UNIVERSITY OF GEORGIA PRESS, 1964

11994 BONNER, JAMES C. "PROFILE OF A LATE ANTE-BELLUM COMMUNITY." AMERICAN HISTORICAL REVIEW, 49 (JULY, 1944): 663-680.

11995 BREEDEN, JAMES O. JOSEPH JONES, M.D.: SCIENTIST OF THE OLD SOUTH. LEXINGTON: UNIVERSITY PRESS OF KENTUCKY, 1975.

11996 BROOKS, ROBERT P. "ECONOMIC AND SOCIAL ASPECTS OF SLAVERY." IN SEBBA, GREGOR (ED.). GEORGIA STUDIES: SELECTED WRITINGS OF ROBERT PRESTON BROOKS. ATHENS: UNIVERSITY OF GEORGIA PRESS, 1952, PP. 205-215.

11997 BROOKS, ROBERT P. "A LOCAL STUDY OF THE RACE PROBLEM." POLITICAL SCIENCE QUARTERLY, 26 (JUNE, 1911): 193-221

11998 BROOKS, ROBERT P. "ORIGIN OF THE BLACK BELT IN GEORGIA." HISTORY OF GEORGIA. BOSTON: ATKINSON, MENTZER & COMPANY, 1913, PP. 208-220.

11999 BROOKS, ROBERT P. "SLAVERY: ECONOMIC AND SOCIAL ASPECTS." HISTORY OF GEORGIA. BOSTON: ATKINSON, MENTZER & COMPANY, 1913, PP. 232-236.

12000 BROUCEK, JACK W. "EIGHTEENTH CENTURY MUSIC IN SAVANNAH, GEORGIA." ED.D. DISSERTATION, FLORIDA STATE UNIVERSITY, 1963.

12001 BROWN, THOMAS I. (ED.). ECONOMIC CO-OPERATION AMONG THE NEGROES OF GEORGIA. ATLANTA: ATLANTA UNIVERSITY, 1917.

12002 BROZEAL, ERNESTINE E. "LABOR PROBLEMS IN COLONIAL GEORGIA." M.A. THESIS, UNIVERSITY OF CHICAGO, 1937.

12003 BRYAN, THOMAS C. CONFEDERATE GEORGIA. ATHENS: UNIVERSITY OF GEORGIA PRESS, 1953.

12004 BYRNE, WILLIAM A. "SLAVERY IN SAVANNAH, GEORGIA, DURING THE CIVIL WAR." M.A. THESIS, FLORIDA STATE UNIVERSITY, 1970.

12005   BYRNE, WILLIAM A., JR.   "THE BURDEN AND HEAT OF THE DAY:
        SLAVERY AND SERVITUDE IN SAVANNAH: 1733-1865."   PH.D.
        DISSERTATION, FLORIDA STATE UNIVERSITY, 1979.

12006   CALLAWAY, JAMES E.   THE EARLY SETTLEMENT OF GEORGIA.
        ATHENS: UNIVERSITY OF GEORGIA PRESS, 1948.

12007   CANDLER, MARK A.   "THE BEGINNINGS OF SLAVERY IN GEORGIA."
        MAGAZINE OF HISTORY, 13 (JULY, 1911):   342-351.

12008   CANDLER, MYRTIE L.   "REMINISCENCES OF LIFE IN GEORGIA
        DURING THE 1850S AND 1860S."   GEORGIA HISTORICAL
        QUARTERLY, 33 (MARCH, JUNE, SEPTEMBER, DECEMBER,
        1949):   36-48, 110-123, 213-227, 303-313; 34 (MARCH,
        1950):   10-18.

12009   CATE, MARGARET D.   EARLY DAYS OF COASTAL GEORGIA.   ST.
        SIMONS ISLAND, GA: FORT FREDERICA ASSOCIATION, 1955.

12010   CATE, MARGARET D.   OUR TODAYS AND YESTERDAYS: A STORY OF
        BRUNSWICK AND THE COASTAL ISLANDS.   BRUNSWICK, GA:
        GLOVER BROTHERS, 1930.

12011   CATES, GERALD L.   "'THE SEASONING':   DISEASE AND DEATH
        AMONG THE FIRST COLONISTS OF GEORGIA."   GEORGIA
        HISTORICAL QUARTERLY, 64 (SUMMER, 1980):   146-158.

12012   CLARK, HORACE S.   "THE ADMINISTRATION OF LEGAL JUSTICE AS
        APPLIED TO BLACKS IN THOMAS COUNTY, GEORGIA,
        1826-1885."   M.A. THESIS, FLORIDA STATE UNIVERSITY,
        1977.

12013   CLIFTON, JAMES M.   "A HALF-CENTURY OF A GEORGIA RICE
        PLANTATION."   NORTH CAROLINA HISTORICAL REVIEW, 47
        (AUTUMN, 1970):   388-415.

12014   CLIFTON, JAMES M. (ED.).   LIFE AND LABOR ON ARGYLE
        ISLAND: LETTERS AND DOCUMENTS OF A SAVANNAH RIVER
        RICE PLANTATION, 1833-1867.   SAVANNAH: BEEHIVE PRESS,
        1978.

12015   COBB, HERSCHEL P.   "OLD SLAVE LAWS OF GEORGIA."   CASE AND
        COMMENT, 23 (JUNE, 1916):   7-10.

12016   COBB, NORMAN J. AND MCWALTERS, DON.   "HISTORICAL REPORT
        ON EVELYN PLANTATION."   GEORGIA HISTORICAL QUARTERLY,
        55 (FALL, 1971):   417-436.

12017   COLE, ARTHUR J.   "CHANGES IN SENTIMENT IN GEORGIA TOWARD
        SECESSION, 1850-1861."   M.A. THESIS, UNIVERSITY OF
        ILLINOIS, 1938.

12018   COLEMAN, KENNETH.   THE AMERICAN REVOLUTION IN GEORGIA,
        1763-1789.   ATHENS: UNIVERSITY OF GEORGIA PRESS, 1958.

12019   CONRAD, GEORGIA B. "REMINISCENCES OF A SOUTHERN WOMAN."
        SOUTHERN WORKMAN, 30 (FEBRUARY, MARCH, MAY, JUNE,
        JULY, 1901): 77-80, 167-171, 252-257, 357-359,
        409-411.

12020   COPENHAUSER, J.E. "CULTURE OF INDIGO IN THE PROVINCES OF
        SOUTH CAROLINA AND GEORGIA." INDUSTRIAL AND
        ENGINEERING CHEMISTRY, 22 (AUGUST, 1930): 894-896.

12021   CORRY, JOHN P. "RACIAL ELEMENTS IN COLONIAL GEORGIA."
        GEORGIA HISTORICAL QUARTERLY, 20 (MARCH, 1936): 30-40.

12022   COULTER, E. MERTON. AURARIA: THE STORY OF A GEORGIA
        GOLD MINING TOWN. ATHENS: UNIVERSITY OF GEORGIA
        PRESS, 1965.

12023   COULTER, E. MERTON. "A CENTURY OF A GEORGIA PLANTATION."
        AGRICULTURAL HISTORY, 3 (OCTOBER, 1929): 147-159.

12024   COULTER, E. MERTON. "A CENTURY OF A GEORGIA PLANTATION."
        MISSISSIPPI VALLEY HISTORICAL REVIEW, 16 (DECEMBER,
        1929): 334-346.

12025   COULTER, E. MERTON. DANIEL LEE, AGRICULTURIST: HIS LIFE
        NORTH AND SOUTH. ATHENS: UNIVERSITY OF GEORGIA
        PRESS, 1972.

12026   COULTER, E. MERTON. "FOUR SLAVE TRIALS IN ELBERT COUNTY,
        GEORGIA." GEORGIA HISTORICAL QUARTERLY, 41
        (SEPTEMBER, 1957): 237-246.

12027   COULTER, E. MERTON. JAMES MONROE SMITH, GEORGIA PLANTER:
        BEFORE DEATH AND AFTER. ATHENS: UNIVERSITY OF
        GEORGIA PRESS, 1961.

12028   COULTER, E. MERTON. A SHORT HISTORY OF GEORGIA. CHAPEL
        HILL: UNIVERSITY OF NORTH CAROLINA PRESS, 1933.

12029   COULTER, E. MERTON. "SLAVERY AND FREEDOM IN ATHENS,
        GEORGIA, 1860-1866." GEORGIA HISTORICAL QUARTERLY, 49
        (SEPTEMBER, 1965): 264-293.

12030   COULTER, E. MERTON. THOMAS SPALDING OF SAPELO.
        UNIVERSITY, LA: LOUISIANA STATE UNIVERSITY PRESS,
        1940.

12031   COURLANDER, HAROLD. THE AFRICAN. NEW YORK: CROWN, 1967.

12032   CRAWFORD, JEWELL R. "THE LEGISLATION OF GEORGIA IN
        REFERENCE TO SLAVERY PRIOR TO 1860." M.A. THESIS,
        HOWARD UNIVERSITY, 1937.

12033   CUNNINGHAM, EILEEN S. AND SCHNEIDER, MABEL A. "A SLAVE'S
        AUTOBIOGRAPHY RETOLD." WESTERN ILLINOIS REGIONAL
        STUDIES, 2 (1979): 109-126.

12034   CUNNINGHAM, RUTH R.   "THE CIVIL STATUS OF THE NEGRO IN
        GEORGIA PRIOR TO THE CIVIL WAR."   M.A. THESIS, ATLANTA
        UNIVERSITY, 1936.

12035   DAVIS, HAROLD E.   "A SOCIAL HISTORY OF GEORGIA:
        1733-1776."   PH.D. DISSERTATION, EMORY UNIVERSITY,
        1972.

12036   DAVIS, JOHN W.   "GEORGE LIELE AND ANDREW BRYAN, PIONEER
        NEGRO BAPTIST PREACHERS."   JOURNAL OF NEGRO HISTORY, 3
        (APRIL, 1918): 119-127.

12037   DILL, FLOYD R.   "THE INSTITUTIONAL POSSIBILITIES AND
        LIMITATIONS OF ECONOMIC PROGRESS IN ANTEBELLUM
        GEORGIA: A SOCIAL SYSTEMS APPROACH."   PH.D.
        DISSERTATION, CORNELL UNIVERSITY, 1973.

12038   DONNELLY, RALPH W.   "THE BARTOW COUNTY CONFEDERATE
        SALTPETRE WORKS."   GEORGIA HISTORICAL QUARTERLY, 54
        (FALL, 1970): 305-319.

12039   DORSEY, JAMES E.   FOOTPRINTS ALONG THE HOOPEE: A HISTORY
        OF EMANUEL COUNTY, 1812-1900. SPARTANBURG, SC:
        REPRINT COMPANY, 1978.

12040   DRAGO, EDMUND L.   "BLACK GEORGIA DURING RECONSTRUCTION."
        PH.D. DISSERTATION, UNIVERSITY OF CALIFORNIA, 1975.

12041   DRAGO, EDMUND L.   "HOW SHERMAN'S MARCH THROUGH GEORGIA
        AFFECTED THE SLAVES."   GEORGIA HISTORICAL QUARTERLY,
        57 (FALL, 1973): 361-375.

12042   DUBOIS, W.E.B.   "GEORGIA NEGROES."   COLORED AMERICAN
        MAGAZINE, 16 (MAY, 1909): 264-273.

12043   EDWARDS, JOHN C.   "SLAVE JUSTICE IN FOUR MIDDLE GEORGIA
        COUNTIES."   GEORGIA HISTORICAL QUARTERLY, 57 (SUMMER,
        1973): 265-273.

12044   EISTERHOLD, JOHN A.   "SAVANNAH: LUMBER CENTER OF THE
        SOUTH ATLANTIC."   GEORGIA HISTORICAL QUARTERLY, 57
        (WINTER, 1973): 526-543.

12045   FAIRBANKS, CHARLES H.   "SPANIARDS, PLANTERS, SHIPS, AND
        SLAVES: HISTORICAL ARCHAEOLOGY IN FLORIDA AND
        GEORGIA."   ARCHAEOLOGY, 29 (JULY, 1976): 164-172.

12046   FLANDERS, RALPH B.   PLANTATION SLAVERY IN GEORGIA.
        CHAPEL HILL: UNIVERSITY OF NORTH CAROLINA PRESS, 1933.

12047   FLANDERS, RALPH B.   "PLANTATION SLAVERY IN THE STATE OF
        GEORGIA."   PH.D. DISSERTATION, DUKE UNIVERSITY, 1929.

12048   FLANDERS, RALPH B.   "PLANTERS' PROBLEMS IN ANTE-BELLUM
        GEORGIA."   GEORGIA HISTORICAL QUARTERLY, 14 (MARCH,

1930): 17-40.

12049 FLANDERS, RALPH B. "TWO PLANTATIONS AND A COUNTY OF
       ANTE-BELLUM GEORGIA." GEORGIA HISTORICAL QUARTERLY,
       12 (MARCH, 1928): 1-37.

12050 FRANCIS, JAMES P. "MOTHER LAVENDER AND HER HOLIDAY
       DINNERS." NEW YORK FOLKLORE QUARTERLY, 8 (WINTER,
       1952): 283-290.

12051 FURLOW, HENRY J. "THE LEGAL CONTROL OF THE NEGRO IN
       GEORGIA DURING THE CIVIL WAR." M.A. THESIS, ATLANTA
       UNIVERSITY, 1952.

12052 GENOVESE, EUGENE D. "A GEORGIA SLAVEHOLDER LOOKS AT
       AFRICA." GEORGIA HISTORICAL QUARTERLY, 51 (JUNE,
       1967): 186-193.

12053 "GEORGIA THE ONLY FREE COLONY: HOW THE NEGRO CAME."
       MAGAZINE OF AMERICAN HISTORY, 22 (OCTOBER, 1889):
       280-306.

12054 GEORGIA WRITERS' PROJECT. "COLERAIN PLANTATION."
       GEORGIA HISTORICAL QUARTERLY, 24 (DECEMBER, 1940):
       342-373; 25 (MARCH, JUNE, SEPTEMBER, 1941): 39-66,
       120-140, 225-243.

12055 GEORGIA WRITERS' PROJECT. "DRAKIES PLANTATION." GEORGIA
       HISTORICAL QUARTERLY, 24 (SEPTEMBER, 1940): 207-235.

12056 GEORGIA WRITERS' PROJECT. DRUMS AND SHADOWS: SURVIVAL
       STUDIES AMONG THE GEORGIA COASTAL NEGROES. ATHENS:
       UNIVERSITY OF GEORGIA PRESS, 1940.

12057 GEORGIA WRITERS' PROJECT. "PLANTATION DEVELOPMENT IN
       CHATHAM COUNTY." GEORGIA HISTORICAL QUARTERLY, 22
       (DECEMBER, 1938): 305-330.

12058 GEORGIA WRITERS' PROJECT. "RICHMOND OAKGROVE
       PLANTATION." GEORGIA HISTORICAL QUARTERLY, 24 (MARCH,
       JUNE, 1940): 1-21, 124-144.

12059 GEORGIA WRITERS' PROJECT. "WHITEHALL PLANTATION, PART
       I." GEORGIA HISTORICAL QUARTERLY, 25 (DECEMBER,
       1941): 340-363.

12060 GIFFORD, JAMES M. "BLACK HOPE AND DESPAIR IN ANTEBELLUM
       GEORGIA: THE WILLIAM MOSS CORRESPONDENCE." PROLOGUE,
       8 (FALL, 1976): 153-162.

12061 GIFFORD, JAMES M. "THE CONSCIENCE OF A SLAVEHOLDER."
       RESEARCH STUDIES, 42 (SEPTEMBER, 1974): 185-187.

12062 GIFFORD, JAMES M. "EMILY TUBMAN AND THE AFRICAN
       COLONIZATION MOVEMENT IN GEORGIA." GEORGIA HISTORICAL

QUARTERLY, 59 (SPRING, 1975): 10-24.

12063 GORDON, ASA H. THE GEORGIA NEGRO: A HISTORY. ANN
ARBOR: EDWARDS BROTHERS, 1937.

12064 GRAY, RALPH AND WOOD, BETTY. "THE TRANSITION FROM
INDENTURED TO INVOLUNTARY SERVITUDE IN COLONIAL
GEORGIA." EXPLORATIONS IN ECONOMIC HISTORY, 13
(OCTOBER, 1976): 353-370.

12065 GREEN, FLETCHER M. "GEORGIA'S FORGOTTEN INDUSTRY: GOLD
MINING." GEORGIA HISTORICAL QUARTERLY, 19 (JUNE,
SEPTEMBER, 1935): 93-111, 210-228.

12066 GREEN, THOMAS M. "SMALL SLAVEHOLDERS IN CRAWFORD COUNTY,
GEORGIA, 1822-1861." B.A. THESIS, HARVARD UNIVERSITY,
1978.

12067 GROGAN, ELMIRA F. "ROSE HILL; A PLANTATION SKETCH."
YALE REVIEW, N.S., 17 (OCTOBER, 1927): 153-164.

12068 GUNN, VICTORIA R. HOFWYL PLANTATION. ATLANTA: GEORGIA
DEPARTMENT OF NATURAL RESOURCES, 1976.

12069 GUNN, VICTORIA R. JARRELL PLANTATION: A HISTORY.
ATLANTA: GEORGIA DEPARTMENT OF NATURAL RESOURCES,
1974.

12070 HARN, JULIA. "OLD CANOOCHEE--OGEECHEE CHRONICLES."
GEORGIA HISTORICAL QUARTERLY, 16 (DECEMBER, 1932):
298-312.

12071 HARPER, ROLAND M. "DEVELOPMENT OF AGRICULTURE IN LOWER
GEORGIA FROM 1850 TO 1880." GEORGIA HISTORICAL
QUARTERLY, 6 (MARCH, 1922): 3-27.

12072 HARVEY, DIANE. "THE TERRI, AUGUSTA'S BLACK ENCLAVE."
RICHMOND COUNTY HISTORY, 5 (SUMMER, 1973): 60-75.

12073 HAUNTON, RICHARD H. "LAW AND ORDER IN SAVANNAH,
1850-1860." GEORGIA HISTORICAL QUARTERLY, 56 (SPRING,
1972): 1-24.

12074 HAVARD, WILLIAM C. "PRIDE AND FALL: A NEW SOURCE FOR
INTERPRETING SOUTHERN EXPERIENCE." SOUTHERN REVIEW,
10 (OCTOBER, 1974): 823-839.

12075 HEARD, GEORGE A. "ST. SIMON'S ISLAND DURING THE WAR
BETWEEN THE STATES." GEORGIA HISTORICAL QUARTERLY, 22
(SEPTEMBER, 1938): 249-272.

12076 HEMPHILL, SUSAN L. "FROM EMANCIPATION TO EVANGELIZATION:
THE ATTITUDE AND ACTION OF THE METHODIST EPISCOPAL
CHURCH IN GEORGIA TOWARDS NEGRO SLAVES, 1784-1844."
B.A. THESIS, EMORY UNIVERSITY, 1966.

12077 HERTZBERG, STEVEN. STRANGERS WITHIN THE GATE CITY: THE JEWS OF ATLANTA, 1845-1915. PHILADELPHIA: JEWISH PUBLICATION SOCIETY OF AMERICA, 1978.

12078 HERTZLER, JAMES R. "SLAVERY IN THE YEARLY SERMONS BEFORE THE GEORGIA TRUSTEES." GEORGIA HISTORICAL QUARTERLY, 59 (SUPPLEMENT, 1975): 118-126.

12079 HILLIARD, SAM B. "ANTEBELLUM TIDEWATER RICE CULTURE IN SOUTH CAROLINA AND GEORGIA." IN GIBSON, JAMES R. (ED.). EUROPEAN SETTLEMENT AND DEVELOPMENT IN NORTH AMERICA: ESSAYS ON GEOGRAPHICAL CHANGE IN HONOUR AND MEMORY OF ANDREW HILL CLARK. BUFFALO: UNIVERSITY OF TORONTO PRESS, 1978, PP. 91-115.

12080 HILLIARD, SAM B. "BIRDSONG: SEQUENT OCCUPANCE ON A SOUTHWESTERN GEORGIA PLANTATION." M.A. THESIS, UNIVERSITY OF GEORGIA, 1961.

12081 HOFFMAN, EDWIN D. "FROM SLAVERY TO SELF-RELIANCE." JOURNAL OF NEGRO HISTORY, 41 (JANUARY, 1956): 8-42.

12082 HOUSE, A.V. PLANTER MANAGEMENT AND CAPITALISM IN ANTEBELLUM GEORGIA: THE JOURNAL OF HUGH FRASER GRANT, RICE GROWER. NEW YORK: COLUMBIA UNIVERSITY PRESS, 1954.

12083 HOUSE, ALBERT V. "LABOR MANAGEMENT PROBLEMS ON GEORGIA RICE PLANTATIONS, 1840-1860." AGRICULTURAL HISTORY, 28 (OCTOBER, 1954): 149-154.

12084 HOUSE, ALBERT V., JR. (ED.). "DETERIORATION OF A GEORGIA RICE PLANTATION DURING FOUR YEARS OF CIVIL WAR." JOURNAL OF SOUTHERN HISTORY, 9 (FEBRUARY, 1943): 98-113.

12085 HOUSE, ALBERT V., JR. "THE MANAGEMENT OF A RICE PLANTATION IN GEORGIA, 1834-1861, AS REVEALED IN THE JOURNAL OF HUGH FRASER GRANT." AGRICULTURAL HISTORY, 13 (OCTOBER, 1939): 208-217.

12086 HULSEY, HAL. "A HISTORY OF THE INTRODUCTION OF SLAVERY INTO THE COLONY OF GEORGIA, 1732-1750." M.A. THESIS, UNIVERSITY OF GEORGIA, 1917.

12087 HUNNICUTT, GEORGE F. DAVID DICKSON'S AND JAMES M. SMITH'S FARMING. ATLANTA: CULTIVATOR PUBLISHING COMPANY, 1910.

12088 HURST, D.; SOUTH, S.; AND LARSON, C.S. "RICH MAN, POOR MAN: OBSERVATIONS ON THREE ANTEBELLUM BURIALS FROM THE GEORGIA COAST." ANTHROPOLOGICAL PAPERS OF THE AMERICAN MUSEUM OF NATURAL HISTORY, 54 (1977): 397-420.

12089 HYNDS, ERNEST C. ANTEBELLUM ATHENS AND CLARK COUNTY
       GEORGIA. ATHENS: UNIVERSITY OF GEORGIA PRESS, 1974.

12090 "ITINERANT OBSERVATIONS IN AMERICA." COLLECTIONS OF THE
       GEORGIA HISTORICAL SOCIETY, 4. SAVANNAH: J.H.
       ESTILL, 1878.

12091 IVERS, LARRY E. BRITISH DRUMS ON THE SOUTHERN FRONTIER:
       THE MILITARY COLONIZATION OF GEORGIA, 1733-1749.
       CHAPEL HILL: UNIVERSITY OF NORTH CAROLINA PRESS, 1974.

12092 JACKSON, SUSAN. "CURRENT RESEARCH: SOUTHEAST." SOCIETY
       FOR HISTORICAL ARCHAEOLOGY NEWSLETTER, 9 (1976):
       15-19.

12093 JAMISON, MONROE F. AUTOBIOGRAPHY AND WORK OF BISHOP M.E.
       JAMISON. NASHVILLE: THE AUTHOR, 1912.

12094 JENKINS, WILLIAM T. "ANTE BELLUM MACON AND BIBB COUNTY,
       GEORGIA." PH.D. DISSERTATION, UNIVERSITY OF GEORGIA,
       1966.

12095 JOHNSON, AMANDA. GEORGIA AS A COLONY AND STATE.
       ATLANTA: WALTER W. BROWN, 1938.

12096 JOHNSON, J.G. "NOTES ON MANUFACTURING IN ANTE-BELLUM
       GEORGIA." GEORGIA HISTORICAL QUARTERLY, 16
       (SEPTEMBER, 1932): 214-231.

12097 JOHNSON, MICHAEL P. "SECESSION AND CONSERVATISM IN THE
       LOWER SOUTH: THE SOCIAL AND IDEOLOGICAL BASES OF
       SECESSION IN GEORGIA, 1860-1861." PH.D. DISSERTATION,
       STANFORD UNIVERSITY, 1973.

12098 JOHNSON, MICHAEL P. TOWARD A PATRIARCHAL REPUBLIC: THE
       SECESSION OF GEORGIA. BATON ROUGE: LOUISIANA STATE
       UNIVERSITY PRESS, 1977.

12099 JOHNSON, R.M. "NEGROES IN GEORGIA, BEFORE, DURING AND
       SINCE THE WAR." AMERICAN CATHOLIC QUARTERLY REVIEW, 6
       (APRIL, 1881): 353.

12100 JONES, CHARLES C., JR. THE HISTORY OF GEORGIA.
       CLEVELAND: BURROWS BROTHERS, 1883.

12101 JONES, J. RALPH AND LANDESS, TOM (EDS.). "PORTRAITS OF
       GEORGIA SLAVES." GEORGIA REVIEW, 21 (SPRING-WINTER,
       1967): 126-132, 268-273, 407-411, 521-525; 22
       (SPRING-SUMMER, 1968): 125-127, 254-257.

12102 JONES, RUBYE M. "THE NEGRO IN COLONIAL GEORGIA,
       1735-1805." M.A. THESIS, ATLANTA UNIVERSITY, 1938.

12103 KILLION, R.G. "REMINISCENCES OF THE 'PECULIAR
       INSTITUTION.'" SANDLAPPER, 5 (OCTOBER, 1972): 49-54,

68.

12104　KILLION, RONALD G. AND WALLER, CHARLES (EDS.). SLAVERY TIME WHEN I WAS CHILLUN DOWN ON MARSTER'S PLANTATION: INTERVIEWS WITH GEORGIA SLAVES. SAVANNAH: BEEHIVE PRESS, 1973.

12105　KNIGHT, LUCIAN L. A STANDARD HISTORY OF GEORGIA AND GEORGIANS. 6 VOLS. ATLANTA: DEPARTMENT OF ARCHIVES AND HISTORY, 1917.

12106　LAWRENCE, JAMES B. "RELIGIOUS EDUCATION OF THE NEGRO IN THE COLONY OF GEORGIA." GEORGIA HISTORICAL QUARTERLY, 14 (MARCH, 1930): 41-57.

12107　LEE, ANNE S. AND LEE, EVERETT S. "THE HEALTH OF SLAVES AND THE HEALTH OF FREEDMEN: A SAVANNAH STUDY." PHYLON, 38 (SUMMER, 1977): 170-180.

12108　LEIGH, FRANCES B. TEN YEARS ON A GEORGIA PLANTATION SINCE THE WAR. LONDON: R. BENTLEY AND SON, 1883.

12109　"LETTERS OF JAMES HAMILTON COUPER TO HIS WIFE, 1833-1836." GEORGIA HISTORICAL QUARTERLY, 14 (JUNE, 1930): 150-173.

12110　LEWIS, GEORGE. "THE NEGRO IN ANTE-BELLUM THOMAS COUNTY, GEORGIA, 1825-1860." M.A. THESIS, ATLANTA UNIVERSITY, 1963.

12111　LOEWALD, KLAUS G.; STARIDA, BEVERLY; AND TAYLOR, PAUL S. (EDS.). "JOHANN MARTIN BOLZIUS ANSWERS A QUESTIONNAIRE ON CAROLINA AND GEORGIA." WILLIAM AND MARY QUARTERLY, 3RD SER., 14 (APRIL, 1957): 218-261; 15 (APRIL, 1958): 228-252.

12112　LUDLOW, HELEN W. "GEORGIA'S INVESTMENT." SOUTHERN WORKMAN, 36 (1907): 219-235.

12113　LUMPKIN, KATHARINE D. THE MAKING OF A SOUTHERNER. NEW YORK: ALFRED A. KNOPF, 1947.

12114　MAGOFFIN, DOROTHY S. "A GEORGIA PLANTER AND HIS PLANTATIONS, 1837-1861." NORTH CAROLINA HISTORICAL REVIEW, 15 (OCTOBER, 1938): 354-377.

12115　MALLARD, ROBERT Q. PLANTATION LIFE BEFORE EMANCIPATION. RICHMOND: WHITTET AND SHEPPERSON, 1892.

12116　MALONE, HENRY T. "CHEROKEE CIVILIZATION IN THE LOWER APPALACHIANS, ESPECIALLY IN NORTH GEORGIA, BEFORE 1830." M.A. THESIS, EMORY UNIVERSITY, 1949.

12117　MALONE, HENRY T. CHEROKEES OF THE OLD SOUTH: A PEOPLE IN TRANSITION. ATHENS: UNIVERSITY OF GEORGIA PRESS,

898

1956.

12118 MARION, ERNESTINE A. "THE UNINDEXED OFFICIAL RECORD OF
       THE NEGRO IN GEORGIA, 1733-1766." M.A. THESIS,
       ATLANTA UNIVERSITY, 1937.

12119 MARTIN, SIDNEY W. "A NEW ENGLANDER'S IMPRESSIONS OF
       GEORGIA IN 1817-1818: EXTRACTS FROM THE DIARY OF
       EBENEZER KELLOGG." JOURNAL OF SOUTHERN HISTORY, 12
       (MAY, 1946): 247-262.

12120 MCCAIN, JAMES R. "EARLY HISTORY OF SLAVERY IN GEORGIA."
       M.A. THESIS, UNIVERSITY OF CHICAGO, 1911.

12121 MCCRARY, ROYCE C. "THE GOLDEN AGE AND DISSATISFACTION:
       A STUDY OF THE AGRICULTURAL REFORM MOVEMENT IN GEORGIA
       DURING THE EIGHTEEN-FIFTIES." M.A. THESIS, UNIVERSITY
       OF GEORGIA, 1968.

12122 MCFARLANE, SUZANNE S. "THE ETHNOHISTORY OF A SLAVE
       COMMUNITY: THE COUPER PLANTATION SITE." M.A. THESIS,
       UNIVERSITY OF FLORIDA, 1975.

12123 MCMICHAEL, LOIS. HISTORY OF BUTTS COUNTY, GEORGIA,
       1825-1976. ATLANTA: CHEROKEE PUBLISHING COMPANY,
       1978.

12124 MCPHERSON, ROBERT G. (ED.). "GEORGIA SLAVE TRIALS,
       1837-1849." AMERICAN JOURNAL OF LEGAL HISTORY, 4
       (JULY, OCTOBER, 1960): 257-284, 364-377.

12125 MILLER, MARY E.W. SLAVERY DAYS IN GEORGIA. RICHLAND,
       GA: N.P., N.D.

12126 MILLER, RANDALL M. "A BACKCOUNTRY LOYALIST PLAN TO
       RETAKE GEORGIA AND THE CAROLINAS, 1778." SOUTH
       CAROLINA HISTORICAL MAGAZINE, 75 (OCTOBER, 1974):
       207-214.

12127 MILLER, RANDALL M. "THE FAILURE OF THE COLONY OF GEORGIA
       UNDER THE TRUSTEES." GEORGIA HISTORICAL QUARTERLY, 53
       (MARCH, 1969): 1-17.

12128 MOHR, CLARENCE L. "BEFORE SHERMAN: GEORGIA BLACKS AND
       THE UNION WAR EFFORT, 1861-1864." JOURNAL OF SOUTHERN
       HISTORY, 45 (AUGUST, 1979): 331-352.

12129 MOHR, CLARENCE L. "GEORGIA BLACKS DURING SECESSION AND
       CIVIL WAR, 1859-1865." PH.D. DISSERTATION, UNIVERSITY
       OF GEORGIA, 1975.

12130 MOHR, CLARENCE L. "SLAVERY IN OGLETHORPE COUNTY,
       GEORGIA, 1773-1865." PHYLON, 33 (SPRING, 1972): 4-21.

12131 MULLING, VICTOR H. "A BRIEF ACCOUNT OF SLAVERY IN

COLONIAL GEORGIA WITH SPECIAL EMPHASIS ON ITS LEGAL
ASPECTS." M.A. THESIS, UNIVERSITY OF GEORGIA, 1939.

12132 MURRAY, PAUL. "AGRICULTURE IN THE INTERIOR OF GEORGIA,
1830-1860." GEORGIA HISTORICAL QUARTERLY, 19
(DECEMBER, 1935): 291-312.

12133 MYERS, ROBERT (ED.). THE CHILDREN OF PRIDE: A TRUE
STORY OF GEORGIA AND THE CIVIL WAR. NEW HAVEN: YALE
UNIVERSITY PRESS, 1971.

12134 NOBLE, WILLIAM A. "SEQUENT OCCUPANCE OF HOPETON-ALTAMA,
1816-1956." M.A. THESIS, UNIVERSITY OF GEORGIA, 1957.

12135 O'GRADY, PATRICIA D. "THE OCCUPATION OF SAPELO SINCE
1733." WEST GEORGIA COLLEGE STUDIES IN THE SOCIAL
SCIENCES, 19 (JUNE, 1980): 1-8.

12136 OTTO, JOHN S. "ARTIFACTS AND STATUS DIFFERENCES--A
COMPARISON OF CERAMICS FROM PLANTER, OVERSEER, AND
SLAVE SITES ON AN ANTEBELLUM PLANTATION." IN SOUTH,
STANLEY (ED.). RESEARCH STRATEGIES IN HISTORICAL
ARCHEOLOGY. NEW YORK: ACADEMIC PRESS, 1977, PP.
91-118.

12137 OTTO, JOHN S. "CANNON'S POINT PLANTATION AND THE HARDY
BANKS FARM: MATERIAL LIVING CONDITIONS OF OLD SOUTH
SLAVES." UNPUBLISHED PAPER PRESENTED AT MEETING OF
SOCIETY FOR HISTORICAL ARCHAEOLOGY, NASHVILLE,
TENNESSEE, 1979.

12138 OTTO, JOHN S. "A NEW LOOK AT SLAVE LIFE." NATURAL
HISTORY, 88 (JANUARY, 1979): 8, 16, 20, 22, 24, 30.

12139 OTTO, JOHN S. "SLAVERY IN A COASTAL COMMUNITY--GLYNN
COUNTY (1790-1860)." GEORGIA HISTORICAL QUARTERLY, 64
(WINTER, 1979): 461-468.

12140 OTTO, JOHN S. "STATUS DIFFERENCES AND THE ARCHEOLOGICAL
RECORD--A COMPARISON OF PLANTER, OVERSEER, AND SLAVE
SITES FROM CANNON'S POINT PLANTATION (1794-1861), ST.
SIMON'S ISLAND, GEORGIA." PH.D. DISSERTATION,
UNIVERSITY OF FLORIDA, 1975.

12141 OWENS, JAMES L. "THE NEGRO IN GEORGIA DURING
RECONSTRUCTION, 1864-1872: A SOCIAL HISTORY." PH.D.
DISSERTATION, UNIVERSITY OF GEORGIA, 1975.

12142 OWSLEY, FRANK L. PLAIN FOLK OF THE OLD SOUTH. BATON
ROUGE: LOUISIANA STATE UNIVERSITY PRESS, 1949.

12143 PARKER, D.M. "SOME EARLY LAWS OF GEORGIA." CASE AND
COMMENT, 24 (OCTOBER, 1917): 389-392.

12144 PARRISH, LYDIA A. SLAVE SONGS OF THE GEORGIA SEA

ISLANDS. NEW YORK: CREATIVE AGE PRESS, 1942.

12145 PENNYPACKER, FRANCES W. "A LETTER FROM AUGUSTA, 1821."
RICHMOND COUNTY HISTORY, 4 (1972): 17-24.

12146 "PEONAGE IN GEORGIA." CRISIS, 20 (JULY, 1920): 139.

12147 PERDUE, ROBERT E. "THE NEGRO IN SAVANNAH, 1865-1900."
PH.D. DISSERTATION, UNIVERSITY OF GEORGIA, 1971.

12148 PHILLIPS, ULRICH B. GEORGIA AND STATE RIGHTS.
WASHINGTON: GOVERNMENT PRINTING OFFICE, 1902.

12149 PHILLIPS, ULRICH B. "GEORGIA LOCAL ARCHIVES." ANNUAL
REPORT OF THE AMERICAN HISTORICAL ASSOCIATION FOR THE
YEAR 1904. WASHINGTON: GOVERNMENT PRINTING OFFICE,
1905, PP. 555-596.

12150 PHILLIPS, ULRICH B. "HISTORICAL NOTES OF MILLEDGEVILLE,
GA." GULF STATES HISTORICAL MAGAZINE, 2 (NOVEMBER,
1903): 161-171.

12151 PHILLIPS, ULRICH B. "THE ORIGIN AND GROWTH OF THE
SOUTHERN BLACK BELTS." AMERICAN HISTORICAL REVIEW, 11
(JULY, 1906): 798-816.

12152 PHILLIPS, ULRICH B. "THE PUBLIC ARCHIVES OF GEORGIA."
ANNUAL REPORT OF THE AMERICAN HISTORICAL ASSOCIATION
FOR THE YEAR 1903. 2 VOLS. WASHINGTON: GOVERNMENT
PRINTING OFFICE, 1904, VOL. 1, PP. 439-474.

12153 PICKETT, ALBERT J. THE HISTORY OF ALABAMA AND
INCIDENTALLY OF GEORGIA AND MISSISSIPPI, FROM THE
EARLIEST PERIOD. ATLANTA: T.J. DOONAN, 1900.

12154 POE, WILLIAM A. "GEORGIA INFLUENCE IN THE DEVELOPMENT OF
LIBERIA." GEORGIA HISTORICAL QUARTERLY, 57 (MARCH,
1973): 9-13.

12155 POTTER, DAVID M., JR. "THE RISE OF THE PLANTATION SYSTEM
IN GEORGIA." GEORGIA HISTORICAL QUARTERLY, 16 (JUNE,
1932): 114-135.

12156 "THE PRESBYTERIAN CHURCH IN GEORGIA ON SECESSION AND
SLAVERY." GEORGIA HISTORICAL QUARTERLY, 1 (SEPTEMBER,
1917): 263-265.

12157 PROCTOR, WILLIAM G. "THE AMBIGUOUS AUCTION BLOCK."
GEORGIA REVIEW, 23 (SPRING, 1969): 63-71.

12158 PROCTOR, WILLIAM G. "THE AMBIGUOUS AUCTION BLOCK; A
STUDY OF THE SIGNIFICANCE OF THE ATTITUDES OF THE
SLAVEHOLDERS OF SOUTHWEST GEORGIA TOWARD THEIR NEGRO
SLAVES, 1820-1865." B.A. THESIS, HARVARD UNIVERSITY,
1963.

12159 PROCTOR, WILLIAM G. "SLAVERY IN SOUTHWEST GEORGIA."
        GEORGIA HISTORICAL QUARTERLY, 49 (MARCH, 1965): 1-22.

12160 RAMAGE, BURR J. "GEORGIA AND THE CHEROKEES." AMERICAN
        HISTORICAL MAGAZINE AND TENNESSEE HISTORICAL SOCIETY
        QUARTERLY, 7 (1902): 199-203.

12161 RANGE, WILLARD. A CENTURY OF GEORGIA AGRICULTURE,
        1850-1950. ATHENS: UNIVERSITY OF GEORGIA PRESS, 1954.

12162 READY, M.L. "AN ECONOMIC HISTORY OF COLONIAL GEORGIA,
        1732-1754." PH.D. DISSERTATION, UNIVERSITY OF
        GEORGIA, 1970.

12163 RODGERS, AVA D. THE HOUSING OF OGLETHORPE COUNTY,
        GEORGIA: 1790-1860. TALLAHASSEE: FLORIDA STATE
        UNIVERSITY PRESS, 1971.

12164 ROGERS, WILLIAM W. ANTE-BELLUM THOMAS COUNTY, 1825-1861.
        TALLAHASSEE: FLORIDA STATE UNIVERSITY STUDIES, NO.
        39, 1963.

12165 SCARBOROUGH, RUTH. THE OPPOSITION TO SLAVERY IN GEORGIA
        PRIOR TO 1860. NASHVILLE: GEORGE PEABODY COLLEGE FOR
        TEACHERS, 1933.

12166 SCARBOROUGH, RUTH. "THE OPPOSITION TO SLAVERY IN GEORGIA
        PRIOR TO 1860." PH.D. DISSERTATION, GEORGE PEABODY
        COLLEGE FOR TEACHERS, 1933.

12167 SCOMP, H.A. "GEORGIA THE ONLY FREE COLONY. HOW THE
        NEGRO CAME." MAGAZINE OF AMERICAN HISTORY, 22
        (OCTOBER, 1889): 280-306.

12168 "THE SEA ISLANDS." HARPER'S NEW MONTHLY MAGAZINE, 57
        (NOVEMBER, 1878): 839-861.

12169 SEAY, DOROTHY. "A GEORGIA PLANTER AND HIS PLANTATIONS,
        1837-1861." M.A. THESIS, UNIVERSITY OF NORTH
        CAROLINA, 1937.

12170 SEBBA, GREGOR (ED.). GEORGIA STUDIES: SELECTED WRITINGS
        OF ROBERT PRESTON BROOKS. ATHENS: UNIVERSITY OF
        GEORGIA PRESS, 1952.

12171 SECRIST, PHILIP. "MILITARY DEFENSE AND LAW ENFORCEMENT
        IN THE COLONY OF GEORGIA, 1754-1776." ATLANTA
        HISTORICAL BULLETIN, 18 (FALL-WINTER, 1973): 7-18.

12172 SHELTON, JANE T. PINES AND PIONEERS: A HISTORY OF
        LOWNDES COUNTY, GEORGIA, 1825-1900. ATLANTA:
        CHEROKEE PUBLISHING COMPANY, 1976.

12173 SHINGLETON, ROYCE G. "THE TRIAL AND PUNISHMENT OF SLAVES
        IN BALDWIN COUNTY, GEORGIA, 1812-1826." SOUTHERN

HUMANITIES REVIEW, 8 (WINTER, 1974): 67-73.

12174   SHRYOCK, RICHARD H. GEORGIA AND THE UNION IN 1850.
        DURHAM: DUKE UNIVERSITY PRESS, 1926.

12175   SINGLETON, THERESA A. "THE ARCHAEOLOGY OF AFRO-AMERICAN
        SLAVERY IN COASTAL GEORGIA: A REGIONAL PERCEPTION OF
        SLAVE HOUSEHOLD AND COMMUNITY PATTERNS." PH.D.
        DISSERTATION, UNIVERSITY OF FLORIDA, 1980.

12176   SINGLETON, THERESA A. "SLAVES AND EX-SLAVE SITES IN
        COASTAL GEORGIA." UNPUBLISHED PAPER PRESENTED AT
        MEETING OF SOCIETY FOR HISTORICAL ARCHAEOLOGY,
        NASHVILLE, TENNESSEE, 1979.

12177   SINGLETON, WILLIAM H. RECOLLECTIONS OF MY SLAVERY DAYS
        BY WILLIAM HENRY SINGLETON. PEEKSKILL, NY: HIGHLAND
        DEMOCRAT COMPANY, 1922.

12178   SISK, GLENN. "CONTEMPORARY SITUATION OF: 'THE NEGRO IN
        ATLANTA.'" NEGRO HISTORY BULLETIN, 27 (APRIL, 1964):
        174-176.

12179   SPALDING, PHINIZY. OGLETHORPE IN AMERICA. CHICAGO:
        UNIVERSITY OF CHICAGO PRESS, 1977.

12180   "STATE OF GEORGIA PASSED RESOLUTION TO BUY SLAVE WHO
        SAVED W. & A. TRESTLE." ATLANTA CONSTITUTION,
        NOVEMBER 5, 1916.

12181   STEPHENS, LESTER D. "A FORMER SLAVE AND THE GEORGIA
        CONVICT LEASE SYSTEM." NEGRO HISTORY BULLETIN, 39
        (JANUARY, 1976): 505-507.

12182   STEPHENSON, MASON W. AND STEPHENSON, D. GRIER. "'TO
        PROTECT AND DEFEND': JOSEPH HENRY LUMPKIN, THE
        SUPREME COURT OF GEORGIA, AND SLAVERY." EMORY LAW
        JOURNAL, 25 (SUMMER, 1976): 579-608.

12183   STEWART, MARJORIE A. "A COMPARATIVE ANALYTICAL STUDY OF
        THE BLACK CODE AND SLAVE CODE OF GEORGIA." M.A.
        THESIS, ATLANTA UNIVERSITY, 1934.

12184   STODDARD, ALBERT H. "ORIGIN, DIALECT, BELIEFS, AND
        CHARACTERISTICS OF THE NEGROES OF SOUTH CAROLINA AND
        GEORGIA COASTS." GEORGIA HISTORICAL QUARTERLY, 28
        (SEPTEMBER, 1944): 186-195.

12185   STONE, JAMES H. "BLACK LEADERSHIP IN THE OLD SOUTH: THE
        SLAVE DRIVERS OF THE RICE KINGDOM." PH.D.
        DISSERTATION, FLORIDA STATE UNIVERSITY, 1976.

12186   STUART, GEORGE R. "NUMBER AND DISTRIBUTION OF
        PLANTATIONS IN GEORGIA (1800-1860)." M.A. THESIS,
        EMORY UNIVERSITY, 1925.

12187   TALMADGE, JOHN E. "BEN: PERLEY POORE'S STAY IN ATHENS."
         GEORGIA HISTORICAL QUARTERLY, 41 (SEPTEMBER, 1957):
         247-254.

12188   TAYLOR, SUSIE K. REMINISCENCES OF MY LIFE IN CAMP WITH
         THE 33RD UNITED STATES COLORED TROOPS LATE 1ST S.C.
         VOLUNTEERS. BOSTON: THE AUTHOR, 1902.

12189   TERRELL, LLOYD P. BLACKS IN AUGUSTA: A CHRONOLOGY,
         1741-1977. AUGUSTA, GA: PRESTON PUBLICATIONS, 1977.

12190   THOMAS, DAVID H.; SOUTH, STANLEY; AND LARSEN, CLARK S.
         "RICH MAN, POOR MEN: OBSERVATIONS ON THREE ANTEBELLUM
         BURIALS FROM THE GEORGIA COAST." ANTHROPOLOGICAL
         PAPERS OF THE AMERICAN MUSEUM OF NATURAL HISTORY, 54
         (1977): 397-420.

12191   THOMPSON, C. MILDRED. "THE FREEDMEN'S BUREAU IN GEORGIA
         IN 1865-1866." GEORGIA HISTORICAL QUARTERLY, 5
         (MARCH, 1921): 40-49.

12192   TRESP, LOTHAR L. "EARLY NEGRO BAPTISMS IN COLONIAL
         GEORGIA BY THE SALZBURGERS AT EBENEZER."
         AMERICANA-AUSTRIACA, 2 (1970): 159-170.

12193   TURNER, LORENZO D. AFRICANISMS IN THE GULLAH DIALECT.
         CHICAGO: UNIVERSITY OF CHICAGO PRESS, 1949.

12194   TWINING, MARY A. "AN EXAMINATION OF AFRICAN RETENTIONS
         IN THE FOLK CULTURE OF THE SOUTH CAROLINA AND GEORGIA
         SEA ISLANDS." PH.D. DISSERTATION, INDIANA UNIVERSITY,
         1977.

12195   TWINING, MARY A. "SOURCES IN THE FOLKLORE AND FOLKLIFE
         OF THE SEA ISLANDS." SOUTHERN FOLKLORE QUARTERLY, 39
         (JUNE, 1975): 135-150.

12196   VARN, SALLIE R. "THE INTRODUCTION OF SLAVERY INTO
         GEORGIA." M.A. THESIS, UNIVERSITY OF SOUTH CAROLINA,
         1922.

12197   VER STEEG, CLARENCE L. "REASSESSING THE FOUNDING OF
         GEORGIA: ENRICHING OF THE SOCIAL MOSAIC." ORIGINS OF
         A SOUTHERN MOSAIC: STUDIES OF EARLY CAROLINA AND
         GEORGIA. ATHENS: UNIVERSITY OF GEORGIA PRESS, 1975,
         PP. 69-102.

12198   WAGNER, CLARENCE M. PROFILES OF BLACK GEORGIA BAPTISTS:
         TWO HUNDRED AND SIX YEARS OF BLACK GEORGIA BAPTIST
         HISTORY, ONE HUNDRED YEARS OF NATIONAL BAPTIST
         HISTORY. GAINESVILLE, GA: WAGNER, 1980.

12199   WASHINGTON, AUSTIN D. "THE DOLLYS: AN ANTEBELLUM BLACK
         FAMILY OF SAVANNAH, GEORGIA." SAVANNAH STATE COLLEGE
         BULLETIN, 26 (DECEMBER, 1972): 101-103.

12200　WASHINGTON, AUSTIN D. "SOME ASPECTS OF EMANCIPATION IN
　　　　　EIGHTEENTH CENTURY SAVANNAH, GEORGIA." SAVANNAH STATE
　　　　　COLLEGE BULLETIN, 26 (DECEMBER, 1972): 104-106.

12201　WAX, DAROLD D. "GEORGIA AND THE NEGRO BEFORE THE
　　　　　AMERICAN REVOLUTION." GEORGIA HISTORICAL QUARTERLY,
　　　　　51 (MARCH, 1967): 63-77.

12202　WERNICK, ROBERT. "GLAMOROUS ACTRESS FOUND NO GLAMOR IN
　　　　　GEORGIA SLAVERY: FANNY KEMBLE'S LIFE ON AN ANTEBELLUM
　　　　　PLANTATION." SMITHSONIAN, 5 (NOVEMBER, 1974): 74-81.

12203　WHITMAN, LOWELL A. "ECONOMIC AND SOCIAL ASPECTS OF THE
　　　　　HISTORY OF COLONIAL GEORGIA." M.A. THESIS, UNIVERSITY
　　　　　OF CHICAGO, 1933.

12204　WILLIAMS, WALTER L. "THE 'SAMBO' DECEPTION: THE
　　　　　EXPERIENCE OF JOHN MCELROY IN ANDERSONVILLE PRISON."
　　　　　PHYLON, 39 (FALL, 1978): 261-263.

12205　WILMS, DOUGLAS C. "THE DEVELOPMENT OF RICE CULTURE IN
　　　　　EIGHTEENTH CENTURY GEORGIA." SOUTHEASTERN GEOGRAPHER,
　　　　　12 (MAY, 1972): 45-57.

12206　WILSON, ADELAIDE. HISTORIC AND PICTURESQUE SAVANNAH.
　　　　　BOSTON: BOSTON PHOTOGRAVURE COMPANY, 1889.

12207　WOOD, BETTY. "THOMAS STEPHENS AND THE INTRODUCTION OF
　　　　　BLACK SLAVERY IN GEORGIA." GEORGIA HISTORICAL
　　　　　QUARTERLY, 58 (SPRING, 1974): 24-40.

12208　WOOD, BETTY C. "A NOTE ON THE GEORGIA MALCONTENTS."
　　　　　GEORGIA HISTORICAL QUARTERLY, 63 (SUMMER, 1979):
　　　　　264-278.

12209　WOOD, BETTY C. "THE ONE THING NEEDFUL: THE SLAVERY
　　　　　DEBATE IN GEORGIA, 1732-1750." PH.D. DISSERTATION,
　　　　　UNIVERSITY OF PENNSYLVANIA, 1975.

12210　WRITERS' PROGRAM, GEORGIA. THE STORY OF
　　　　　WASHINGTON-WILKES. ATHENS: UNIVERSITY OF GEORGIA
　　　　　PRESS, 1941.

12211　WRITERS PROJECT, GEORGIA. DRUMS AND SHADOWS: SURVIVAL
　　　　　STUDIES AMONG THE GEORGIA COASTAL NEGROES. ATHENS:
　　　　　UNIVERSITY OF GEORGIA PRESS, 1940.

12212　WYLLY, CHARLES S. THE SEED THAT WAS SOWN IN THE COLONY
　　　　　OF GEORGIA: THE HARVEST AND AFTERMATH, 1740-1870.
　　　　　NEW YORK: NEALE PUBLISHING COMPANY, 1910.

LOUISIANA

12213　AERTKER, ROBERT J. "A SOCIAL HISTORY OF BATON ROUGE

DURING THE CIVIL WAR AND EARLY RECONSTRUCTION." M.A.
THESIS, LOUISIANA STATE UNIVERSITY, 1937.

12214   AIME, VALCOUR. PLANTATION DIARY OF THE LATE MR. VALCOUR
        AIME. NEW ORLEANS: CLARK & HOFELINE, 1878.

12215   ALLAIN, MATHE. "LIST OF INHABITANTS WHO PRESENTED THE
        COUNCIL WITH A REQUEST FOR NEGROES, AND THE NUMBER
        THEY REQUEST, PAYABLE AND SET BY THE COMPANY."
        ATTAKAPAS GAZETTE, 10 (FALL, 1975): 155-162.

12216   ALLAIN, MATHE. "SLAVE POLICIES IN FRENCH LOUISIANA."
        LOUISIANA HISTORY, 21 (SPRING, 1980): 127-138.

12217   ALLAIN, MATHE AND CASSIDY, VINCENT H. "BLAMPAIN, TRADER
        AMONG THE ATTAKAPAS." ATTAKAPAS GAZETTE, 3 (DECEMBER,
        1968): 32-38.

12218   ALLAN, WILLIAM. LIFE AND WORK OF JOHN MCDONOGH.
        BALTIMORE: ISAAC FRIEDENWALD, 1886.

12219   ANDERSON, JOHN Q. "DR. JAMES GREEN CARSON, ANTE-BELLUM
        PLANTER OF MISSISSIPPI AND LOUISIANA." JOURNAL OF
        MISSISSIPPI HISTORY, 18 (OCTOBER, 1956): 243-301.

12220   ARGUEDES, JEANNE. "VARIOUS SUPERSTITIONS KNOWN IN NEW
        ORLEANS AND BELIEVED BY THE OLD COLORED PEOPLE
        DESCENDANTS OF SLAVES, EMPLOYED IN THE OLD CREOLE
        FAMILIES." UNPUBLISHED MANUSCRIPT, N.D., TULANE
        UNIVERSITY LIBRARY.

12221   BAADE, ANNE A. "SLAVE INDEMNITIES: A GERMAN COAST
        RESPONSE, 1795." LOUISIANA HISTORY, 20 (WINTER,
        1979): 102-109.

12222   BACON, DORIS Y. "THE HEALTH OF SLAVES ON LOUISIANA
        PLANTATIONS, 1840-1860." M.A. THESIS, LOUISIANA STATE
        UNIVERSITY, 1958.

12223   BAKER, VAUGHAN. "THE ACADIANS IN ANTEBELLUM LOUISIANA:
        A STUDY OF ACCULTURATION." IN CONRAD, GLENN R. (ED.).
        THE CAJUNS: ESSAYS ON THEIR HISTORY AND CULTURE.
        LAFAYETTE, LA: CENTER FOR LOUISIANA STUDIES,
        UNIVERSITY OF SOUTHWESTERN LOUISIANA, 1978, PP.
        115-128.

12224   BAKER, VAUGHAN (ED.). "GLIMPSES OF IBERIA IN THE CIVIL
        WAR." ATTAKAPAS GAZETTE, 6 (SEPTEMBER, 1971): 73-94.

12225   BAKER, VAUGHAN. "PATTERNS OF ACADIAN SLAVE OWNERSHIP IN
        LAFAYETTE PARISH, 1850." ATTAKAPAS GAZETTE, 10
        (SEPTEMBER, 1974): 144-148.

12226   BARKER, DOROTHY M. "AN ECONOMIC SURVEY OF NEW ORLEANS
        DURING THE CIVIL WAR AND RECONSTRUCTION." M.A.

THESIS, TULANE UNIVERSITY, 1942.

12227   BATES, RUTH. "CONDITIONS OF SLAVE LIFE." M.A. THESIS,
        LOUISIANA STATE UNIVERSITY, 1913.

12228   BINNING, F. WAYNE. "COOPERATION AND OBSTRUCTION IN THE
        LOUISIANA SECESSION CRISIS." M.A. THESIS, LOUISIANA
        STATE UNIVERSITY, 1965.

12229   BLACK BICENTENNIAL COMMITTEE. CONTRIBUTIONS OF OUACHITA
        PARISH: A HISTORY OF BLACKS TO COMMEMORATE THE
        BICENTENNIAL OF THE UNITED STATES OF AMERICA. MONROE,
        LA: BLACK BICENTENNIAL COMMITTEE OF OUACHITA PARISH,
        1976.

12230   BLASSINGAME, JOHN W. BLACK NEW ORLEANS, 1860-1880.
        CHICAGO: UNIVERSITY OF CHICAGO PRESS, 1973.

12231   BORELLO, FRANK C. "FREE BLACKS IN LAFAYETTE PARISH TO
        1860." ATTAKAPAS GAZETTE, 10 (SUMMER, 1975): 103-104.

12232   BOSTICK, CLYDE M. "SELECTED ASPECTS OF SLAVE HEALTH IN
        LOUISIANA, 1804-1861." M.A. THESIS, LOUISIANA STATE
        UNIVERSITY, 1960.

12233   BRASSEAUX, CARL A. "THE ADMINISTRATION OF SLAVE
        REGULATIONS IN FRENCH LOUISIANA, 1724-1766."
        LOUISIANA HISTORY, 21 (SPRING, 1980): 139-158.

12234   BRASSEAUX, CARL A. "THE BRAZIL EXILES: A FORGOTTEN
        CHAPTER IN THE HISTORY OF ST. LANDRY PARISH."
        ATTAKAPAS GAZETTE, 13 (SUMMER, 1978): 78-84.

12235   BRASSEAUX, CARL A. (ED.). A COMPARATIVE VIEW OF FRENCH
        LOUISIANA, 1699 AND 1762: THE JOURNALS OF PIERRE
        LEMOYNE D'IBERVILLE AND JEAN-JACQUES-BLAISE D'ABBADIE.
        LAFAYETTE, LA: UNIVERSITY OF SOUTHWESTERN LOUISIANA
        HISTORY SERIES, 1979.

12236   BRASSEAUX, CARL A. (ED.). "THE GLORY DAYS: E.T. KING
        RECALLS THE CIVIL WAR YEARS." ATTAKAPAS GAZETTE, 11
        (SPRING, 1976): 3-33.

12237   BRINGER, GLADYS S. "TRANSITION FROM SLAVE TO FREE LABOR
        IN LOUISIANA AFTER THE CIVIL WAR." M.A. THESIS,
        TULANE UNIVERSITY, 1927.

12238   BROWN, EVERETT S. THE CONSTITUTIONAL HISTORY OF THE
        LOUISIANA PURCHASE, 1803-1812. BERKELEY: UNIVERSITY
        OF CALIFORNIA PRESS, 1920.

12239   BURNS, FRANCIS P. "THE BLACK CODE." LOYOLA LAW JOURNAL,
        5 (DECEMBER, 1923): 15-25.

12240   BUTLER, PIERCE. "SLAVERY." IN CHANDLER, JULIAN A.C.

(ED.). THE SOUTH IN THE BUILDING OF THE NATION. 12
VOLS. RICHMOND: SOUTHERN HISTORICAL PUBLICATION
SOCIETY, 1909, VOL. 3, PP. 121-126.

12241 CABLE, GEORGE W. "CREOLE SLAVE DANCES: THE DANCE IN
PLACE CONGO." CENTURY MAGAZINE, 31 (FEBRUARY, 1886):
517-532.

12242 CABLE, GEORGE W. "CREOLE SLAVE SONGS." CENTURY
MAGAZINE, 31 (APRIL, 1886): 807-828.

12243 CABLE, GEORGE W. THE CREOLES OF LOUISIANA. NEW YORK:
CHARLES SCRIBNER'S SONS, 1884.

12244 CAPERS, GERALD M. OCCUPIED CITY: NEW ORLEANS UNDER THE
FEDERALS, 1862-1865. LEXINGTON: UNIVERSITY OF
KENTUCKY PRESS, 1965.

12245 CARAVAGLIOS, MARIA G. "A ROMAN CRITIQUE OF THE
PRO-SLAVERY VIEWS OF BISHOP MARTIN OF NATCHITOCHES,
LOUISIANA." RECORDS OF THE AMERICAN CATHOLIC
HISTORICAL SOCIETY OF PHILADELPHIA, 83 (JUNE, 1972):
67-81.

12246 CARTER, DORIS D. "REFUSING TO RELINQUISH THE STRUGGLES:
THE SOCIAL ROLE OF THE BLACK WOMAN IN LOUISIANA
HISTORY." IN MACDONALD, ROBERT R.; KEMP, JOHN R.; AND
HAAS, EDWARD F. (EDS.). LOUISIANA'S BLACK HERITAGE.
NEW ORLEANS: LOUISIANA STATE MUSEUM, 1979, PP.
163-189.

12247 CASTELLANOS, HENRY C. NEW ORLEANS AS IT WAS, EPISODES OF
LOUISIANA LIFE. NEW ORLEANS: L. GRAHAM & SON, 1895.

12248 CHILDS, WILLIAM T. JOHN MCDONOGH, HIS LIFE AND WORK.
BALTIMORE: MEYER & THALHEIMER, 1939.

12249 CHRISTIAN, MARCUS B. NEGRO IRONWORKERS OF LOUISIANA,
1718-1900. GRETNA, LA: PELICAN PUBLISHING COMPANY,
1972.

12250 CLARK, JOHN G. NEW ORLEANS, 1718-1812: AN ECONOMIC
HISTORY. BATON ROUGE: LOUISIANA STATE UNIVERSITY
PRESS, 1970.

12251 CLAYTON, RONNIE W. "THE FEDERAL WRITERS' PROJECT FOR
BLACKS IN LOUISIANA." LOUISIANA HISTORY, 19 (SUMMER,
1978): 327-335.

12252 COLES, HARRY L., JR. "SOME NOTES ON SLAVEOWNERSHIP AND
LANDOWNERSHIP IN LOUISIANA, 1850-1860." JOURNAL OF
SOUTHERN HISTORY, 9 (AUGUST, 1943): 381-394.

12253 CONRAD, GLENN R. (ED.). NEW IBERIA: ESSAYS ON THE TOWN
AND ITS PEOPLE. LAFAYETTE, LA: UNIVERSITY OF

SOUTHWESTERN LOUISIANA HISTORY SERIES, 1979.

12254 CONRAD, GLENN R. "SHOULD WE TAKE ANOTHER LOOK AT
       ANTE-BELLUM LOUISIANA?" LOUISIANA REVUE, 8 (SUMMER,
       1978): 35-48.

12255 CONRAD, GLENN R. (ED.). ST. CHARLES: ABSTRACTS OF THE
       CIVIL RECORDS OF ST. CHARLES PARISH, 1770-1803.
       LAFAYETTE, LA: UNIVERSITY OF SOUTHWESTERN LOUISIANA
       HISTORY SERIES, 1974.

12256 CONRAD, GLENN R. (ED.). ST.-JEAN-BAPTISTE DES ALLEMANDS:
       ABSTRACTS OF THE CIVIL RECORDS OF ST. JOHN-THE-BAPTIST
       PARISH WITH GENEALOGY AND INDEX, 1753-1803.
       LAFAYETTE, LA: UNIVERSITY OF SOUTHWESTERN LOUISIANA
       HISTORY SERIES, 1972.

12257 COOK, CHARLES O. AND POTEET, JAMES M. (EDS.). "'DEM WAS
       BLACK TIMES, SURE 'NOUGH': THE SLAVE NARRATIVES OF
       LYDIA JEFFERSON AND STEPHEN WILLIAMS." LOUISIANA
       HISTORY, 20 (SUMMER, 1979): 281-292.

12258 COOK, PHILLIP C. "ANTE-BELLUM BIENVILLE PARISH." M.A.
       THESIS, LOUISIANA TECH UNIVERSITY, 1965.

12259 CORLEY, DANIEL B. A VISIT TO UNCLE TOM'S CABIN.
       CHICAGO: LAIRD & LEE, 1892.

12260 COTTON, ROLAND M. "SLAVERY IN CATAHOULA PARISH,
       LOUISIANA." M.A. THESIS, LOUISIANA STATE UNIVERSITY,
       1968.

12261 COULON, EARL C. "ATTITUDE OF NEW ORLEANS NEWSPAPERS
       TOWARDS SLAVERY AND SECESSION." M.A. THESIS, TULANE
       UNIVERSITY, 1939.

12262 CRAVEN, AVERY O. RACHEL OF OLD LOUISIANA. BATON ROUGE:
       LOUISIANA STATE UNIVERSITY PRESS, 1975.

12263 CRAVENS, JOHN N. "FELIX 'ZERO' ERVIN: LOUISIANA NEGRO
       SLAVE AND EAST TEXAS FREEMAN." EAST TEXAS HISTORICAL
       JOURNAL, 10 (FALL, 1972): 125-130.

12264 CRUZAT, HELOISE H. "TRIAL AND SENTENCE OF BIRON, RUNAWAY
       NEGRO SLAVE, BEFORE THE SUPERIOR COUNCIL OF LOUISIANA,
       1728." LOUISIANA HISTORICAL QUARTERLY, 8 (JANUARY,
       1925): 23-27.

12265 DALRYMPLE, MARGARET F. (ED.). THE MERCHANT OF MANCHAC:
       THE LETTERBOOKS OF JOHN FITZPATRICK, 1768-1790. BATON
       ROUGE: LOUISIANA STATE UNIVERSITY PRESS, 1978.

12266 DART, HENRY P. (ED.). "CABILDO ARCHIVES--FRENCH PERIOD."
       LOUISIANA HISTORICAL QUARTERLY, 4 (JULY, 1921):
       361-368.

12267   DART, HENRY P. (ED.). "EMANCIPATION OF MARIE ARAM, A
        SLAVE, REDEEMED BY HER HUSBAND'S LABOR DURING SEVEN
        YEARS." LOUISIANA HISTORICAL QUARTERLY, 3 (OCTOBER,
        1920): 551-553.

12268   DART, HENRY P. (ED.). "THE FIRST CARGO OF AFRICAN SLAVES
        FOR LOUISIANA, 1718." LOUISIANA HISTORICAL QUARTERLY,
        14 (APRIL, 1931): 163-177.

12269   DART, HENRY P. "A LOUISIANA INDIGO PLANTATION ON BAYOU
        TECHE, 1773." LOUISIANA HISTORICAL QUARTERLY, 9
        (OCTOBER, 1926): 565-589.

12270   DART, HENRY P. "A MURDER CASE TRIED IN NEW ORLEANS IN
        1773." LOUISIANA HISTORICAL QUARTERLY, 22 (JULY,
        1939): 623-641.

12271   DART, HENRY P. (ED.). "SUIT FOR DAMAGES FOR PERSONAL
        INJURIES TO A SLAVE; DAGOBERT, SUPERIOR OF THE
        CAPUCHINS VS. SIEUR LOQUET, BEFORE THE SUPERIOR
        COUNCIL OF LOUISIANA, 1764." LOUISIANA HISTORICAL
        QUARTERLY, 5 (JANUARY, 1922): 58-62.

12272   DAVIS, E.A. "BENNET H. BARROW, ANTE-BELLUM PLANTER OF
        THE FELICIANAS." JOURNAL OF SOUTHERN HISTORY, 5
        (NOVEMBER, 1939): 431-446.

12273   DAVIS, EDWIN A. LOUISIANA, THE PELICAN STATE. BATON
        ROUGE: LOUISIANA STATE UNIVERSITY PRESS, 1959.

12274   DAVIS, EDWIN A. PLANTATION LIFE IN THE FLORIDA PARISHES
        OF LOUISIANA, 1836-1846, AS REFLECTED IN THE DIARY OF
        BENNET H. BARROW. NEW YORK: COLUMBIA UNIVERSITY
        PRESS, 1943.

12275   DAVIS, EDWIN A. "SOCIAL AND ECONOMIC LIFE IN WEST
        FELICIANA PARISH, LOUISIANA, 1830-1850, AS REFLECTED
        IN THE PLANTATION DIARY OF BENNET H. BARROW." PH.D.
        DISSERTATION, LOUISIANA STATE UNIVERSITY, 1936.

12276   DAWES, EMMA L.M. "JUDGE THOMAS BUTLER, OF LOUISIANA, A
        BIOGRAPHICAL STUDY OF AN ANTE-BELLUM JURIST AND
        PLANTER." M.A. THESIS, LOUISIANA STATE UNIVERSITY,
        1953.

12277   DEGRUMMOND, JEWEL L. "A SOCIAL HISTORY OF ST. MARY
        PARISH, 1845-1860." LOUISIANA HISTORICAL QUARTERLY,
        32 (JANUARY, 1949): 17-102.

12278   "DESTEHAN'S SLAVE ROLL." LOUISIANA HISTORICAL QUARTERLY,
        7 (APRIL, 1924): 302-303.

12279   DIN, GILBERT C. "CIMARRONES AND THE SAN MALO BAND IN
        SPANISH LOUISIANA." LOUISIANA HISTORY, 21 (SUMMER,
        1980): 237-262.

12280   DORMON, JAMES H. "ASPECTS OF ACADIANA PLANTATION LIFE IN
         THE MID-NINETEENTH CENTURY: A MICROCOSMIC VIEW."
         LOUISIANA HISTORY, 16 (FALL, 1975): 361-370.

12281   DORMON, JAMES H. "ASPECTS OF SLAVE MANAGEMENT AND
         MAINTENANCE ON A LOUISIANA SUGAR PLANTATION: PETITE
         ANSE, 1840-1860." ATTAKAPAS GAZETTE, 7 (MARCH, 1972):
         23-30.

12282   DORMON, JAMES H. "THE PERSISTENT SPECTER: SLAVE
         REBELLION IN TERRITORIAL LOUISIANA." LOUISIANA
         HISTORY, 18 (FALL, 1977): 389-404.

12283   DOUGLAS, MURIEL L. "SOME ASPECTS OF THE SOCIAL HISTORY
         OF BATON ROUGE FROM 1830 TO 1850." M.A. THESIS,
         LOUISIANA STATE UNIVERSITY, 1955.

12284   DUBROCA, ISABELLE C. "A STUDY OF NEGRO EMANCIPATION IN
         LOUISIANA, 1803-1865." M.A. THESIS, TULANE
         UNIVERSITY, 1924.

12285   DUFFY, JOHN. THE RUDOLPH MATAS HISTORY OF MEDICINE IN
         LOUISIANA. 2 VOLS. BATON ROUGE: LOUISIANA STATE
         UNIVERSITY PRESS, 1958-1962.

12286   DUFFY, JOHN. "SLAVERY AND SLAVE HEALTH IN LOUISIANA,
         1766-1825." BULLETIN OF THE TULANE UNIVERSITY MEDICAL
         FACULTY, 26 (FEBRUARY, 1967): 1-6.

12287   DUFOUR, CHARLES L. "THE PEOPLE OF NEW ORLEANS." IN
         CARTER, HODDING (ED.). THE PAST AS PRELUDE: NEW
         ORLEANS, 1718-1968. NEW ORLEANS: TULANE UNIVERSITY,
         1968, PP. 20-41.

12288   DUNBAR-NELSON, ALICE. "PEOPLE OF COLOR IN LOUISIANA."
         JOURNAL OF NEGRO HISTORY, 1 (OCTOBER, 1916): 359-374;
         2 (JANUARY, 1917): 51-78.

12289   "EDUCATION OF THE COLORED POPULATION OF LOUISIANA."
         HARPER'S NEW MONTHLY MAGAZINE, 33 (JULY, 1866):
         244-250.

12290   ELLIS, ISABELLA D.C. "THE TRANSITION FROM SLAVE LABOR TO
         FREE LABOR WITH SPECIAL REFERENCE TO LOUISIANA." M.A.
         THESIS, LOUISIANA STATE UNIVERSITY, 1932.

12291   ENGELSMAN, JOHN C. "THE FREEDMEN'S BUREAU IN LOUISIANA."
         LOUISIANA HISTORICAL QUARTERLY, 32 (JANUARY, 1949):
         145-224.

12292   EVANS, OLIVER. "MELTING POT IN THE BAYOUS." AMERICAN
         HERITAGE, 15 (DECEMBER, 1963): 30-51, 106-107.

12293   FARNOWSKI, MARY S. "NATCHITOCHES DURING THE CIVIL WAR
         AND RECONSTRUCTION PERIOD." M.A. THESIS, CATHOLIC

UNIVERSITY OF AMERICA, 1951.

12294   FEDERAL WRITERS' PROGRAM, LOUISIANA. GUMBO YA=YA.
        BOSTON: HOUGHTON MIFFLIN COMPANY, 1945.

12295   FIEHRER, THOMAS M. "THE AFRICAN PRESENCE IN COLONIAL
        LOUISIANA: AN ESSAY ON THE CONTINUITY OF CARIBBEAN
        CULTURE." IN MACDONALD, ROBERT R.; KEMP, JOHN R.; AND
        HAAS, EDWARD F. (EDS.). LOUISIANA'S BLACK HERITAGE.
        NEW ORLEANS: LOUISIANA STATE MUSEUM, 1979, PP. 3=31.

12296   FISCHER, ROGER A. "RACIAL SEGREGATION IN ANTE BELLUM NEW
        ORLEANS." AMERICAN HISTORICAL REVIEW, 74 (FEBRUARY,
        1969): 926=957.

12297   FISCHER, ROGER A. "THE SEGREGATION STRUGGLE IN
        LOUISIANA, 1850=1890." PH.D. DISSERTATION, TULANE
        UNIVERSITY, 1967.

12298   FISCHER, ROGER A. THE SEGREGATION STRUGGLE IN LOUISIANA,
        1862=1877. URBANA: UNIVERSITY OF ILLINOIS PRESS,
        1974.

12299   FONER, LAURA. "THE FREE PEOPLE OF COLOR IN LOUISIANA AND
        ST. DOMINGUE: A COMPARATIVE PORTRAIT OF TWO
        THREE=CASTE SOCIETIES." JOURNAL OF SOCIAL HISTORY, 3
        (SUMMER, 1970): 406=430.

12300   FORTIER, ALCEE. "CUSTOMS AND SUPERSTITIONS IN
        LOUISIANA." JOURNAL OF AMERICAN FOLKLORE, 1
        (JULY=SEPTEMBER, 1888): 136=140.

12301   FORTIER, ALCEE. LOUISIANA FOLK=TALES. BOSTON:
        HOUGHTON, MIFFLIN AND COMPANY, 1895.

12302   FOSSIER, ALBERT E. NEW ORLEANS: THE GLAMOUR PERIOD,
        1800=1840. NEW ORLEANS: PELICAN PRESS, 1957.

12303   GATELL, FRANK O. "DOCTOR PALFREY FREES HIS SLAVES." NEW
        ENGLAND QUARTERLY, 34 (MARCH, 1961): 74=86.

12304   GAYARRE, CHARLES. HISTORY OF LOUISIANA. 4 VOLS. NEW
        YORK: REDFIELD, 1854=1866.

12305   GAYARRE, CHARLES. "A LOUISIANA SUGAR PLANTATION OF THE
        OLD REGIME." HARPER'S NEW MONTHLY MAGAZINE, 74
        (MARCH, 1887): 606=621.

12306   GREEN, GEORGE D. FINANCE AND ECONOMIC DEVELOPMENT IN THE
        OLD SOUTH: LOUISIANA BANKING, 1804=1861. STANFORD:
        STANFORD UNIVERSITY PRESS, 1972.

12307   GREENWALD, BRUCE C.N. ADVERSE SELECTION IN THE LABOR
        MARKET. NEW YORK: GARLAND PUBLISHERS, 1979.

12308   GREENWALD, BRUCE C.N.   "ADVERSE SELECTION IN THE LABOR
         MARKET."   PH.D. DISSERTATION, MASSACHUSETTS INSTITUTE
         OF TECHNOLOGY, 1978.

12309   GREER, JAMES K.   "LOUISIANA AND THE SOUTH, 1848-1860."
         M.A. THESIS, UNIVERSITY OF TEXAS, 1922.

12310   GREGORY, HIRAM.   "AFRICA IN THE DELTA."   LOUISIANA
         STUDIES, 1 (SPRING, 1962):   16-23.

12311   GRIGSBY, ROBERT W.   "THE MANUMISSION OF SLAVES IN
         LOUISIANA."   M.A. THESIS, LOUISIANA STATE UNIVERSITY,
         1938.

12312   HACKETT, D.L.A.   "SLAVERY, ETHNICITY, AND SUGAR: AN
         ANALYSIS OF VOTING BEHAVIOUR IN LOUISIANA, 1828-1844."
         LOUISIANA STUDIES, 13 (SUMMER, 1974):   73-118.

12313   HAGGARD, JUAN V.   "THE NEUTRAL GROUND BETWEEN LOUISIANA
         AND TEXAS, 1806-1821."   PH.D. DISSERTATION, UNIVERSITY
         OF TEXAS, 1942.

12314   HAMLETT, JAMES A.   "THE FOLKLORE OF THE FRENCH-SPEAKING
         NEGRO OF EVANGELINE PARISH."   M.A. THESIS, LOUISIANA
         STATE UNIVERSITY, 1954.

12315   HARKINS, JOHN E.   "THE REGULATORY FUNCTIONS OF THE NEW
         ORLEANS CABILDO, 1769-1803."   M.A. THESIS, LOUISIANA
         STATE UNIVERSITY, 1971.

12316   HASKINS, JAMES.   THE CREOLES OF COLOR OF NEW ORLEANS.
         NEW YORK: CROWELL, 1975.

12317   HATCH, JAMES R.   "LIFE AND LABOR IN ANTE BELLUM CLAIBORNE
         PARISH."   M.A. THESIS, LOUISIANA TECH UNIVERSITY, 1968.

12318   HAYWOOD, JACQUELYN S.   "THE AMERICAN MISSIONARY
         ASSOCIATION IN LOUISIANA DURING RECONSTRUCTION."
         PH.D. DISSERTATION, UNIVERSITY OF CALIFORNIA, LOS
         ANGELES, 1974.

12319   HELPLER, MORRIS K.   "NEGROES AND CRIME IN NEW ORLEANS,
         1850-1861."   M.A. THESIS, TULANE UNIVERSITY, 1960.

12320   HENDERSON, DWIGHT F.   "FEDERAL JUSTICE IN LOUISIANA: THE
         FIRST QUARTER CENTURY."   IN GALLAGHER, GARY W. (ED.).
         ESSAYS IN SOUTHERN HISTORY WRITTEN IN HONOR OF BARNES
         E. LATHROP.   AUSTIN: GENERAL LIBRARIES, UNIVERSITY OF
         TEXAS, 1980, PP. 39-58.

12321   HENDRIX, JAMES P.   "THE EFFORTS TO REOPEN THE AFRICAN
         SLAVE TRADE IN LOUISIANA."   LOUISIANA HISTORY, 10
         (SPRING, 1969):   97-124.

12322   HENDRIX, JAMES P.   "THE EFFORTS TO REOPEN THE AFRICAN

SLAVE TRADE IN LOUISIANA." M.A. THESIS, LOUISIANA
STATE UNIVERSITY, 1968.

12323   HEPBURN, DAVID. "THE NEGRO CATHOLIC IN NEW ORLEANS."
        OUR WORLD, 5 (APRIL, 1950): 16-32.

12324   HICKS, WILLIAM. HISTORY OF LOUISIANA NEGRO BAPTISTS,
        1804 TO 1914. NASHVILLE: NATIONAL BAPTIST PUBLISHING
        BOARD, 1915.

12325   HIGHSMITH, WILLIAM E. "SOCIAL AND ECONOMIC CONDITIONS IN
        RAPIDES PARISH DURING RECONSTRUCTION." M.A. THESIS,
        LOUISIANA STATE UNIVERSITY, 1947.

12326   HIGHSMITH, WILLIAM E. "SOME ASPECTS OF RECONSTRUCTION IN
        THE HEART OF LOUISIANA." JOURNAL OF SOUTHERN HISTORY,
        13 (NOVEMBER, 1947): 460-491.

12327   HOLMES, JACK. GAYOSO: THE LIFE OF A SPANISH GOVERNOR IN
        THE MISSISSIPPI VALLEY, 1789-1799. BATON ROUGE:
        LOUISIANA STATE UNIVERSITY PRESS, 1965.

12328   HOLMES, JACK D.L. "THE ABORTIVE SLAVE REVOLT AT POINTE
        COUPEE, LOUISIANA, 1795." LOUISIANA HISTORY, 11
        (FALL, 1970): 341-362.

12329   HOLMES, JACK D.L. "INDIGO IN COLONIAL LOUISIANA AND THE
        FLORIDAS." LOUISIANA HISTORY, 8 (FALL, 1967):
        329-350.

12330   HOLMES, JACK D.L. "NAVAL STORES IN COLONIAL LOUISIANA
        AND THE FLORIDAS." LOUISIANA HISTORY, 7 (WINTER,
        1968): 295-309.

12331   HOSMER, JAMES K. THE HISTORY OF THE LOUISIANA PURCHASE.
        NEW YORK: D. APPLETON & COMPANY, 1902.

12332   HULEN, RICHARD. "FIDDLING AMONG THE SLAVES IN
        LOUISIANA." DEVIL'S BOX, 9 (JULY 4, 1969): 14.

12333   HUNTER, BEN. "THE IMAGE OF THE NEGRO IN LOUISIANA
        HISTORY: THE PERIOD OF SLAVERY, 1803-1860." M.A.
        THESIS, PRAIRIE VIEW AGRICULTURAL AND MECHANICAL
        UNIVERSITY, 1970.

12334   JACKSON, HARVEY H. "THE CALM BEFORE THE STORM: A
        LOUISIANA OVERSEER'S WORLD ON THE EVE OF THE CIVIL
        WAR." SOUTHERN STUDIES, 13 (SUMMER, 1979): 241-246.

12335   JARREAU, LAFAYETTE. "CREOLE FOLKLORE OF POINT COUPEE
        PARISH." M.A. THESIS, LOUISIANA STATE UNIVERSITY,
        1931.

12336   JOHNSON, CLIFTON H. "SOME MANUSCRIPT SOURCES IN
        LOUISIANA ARCHIVAL REPOSITORIES FOR STUDY OF THE

HISTORY OF LOUISIANA BLACKS." IN MACDONALD, ROBERT
R.; KEMP, JOHN R.; AND HAAS, EDWARD F. (EDS.).
LOUISIANA'S BLACK HERITAGE. NEW ORLEANS: LOUISIANA
STATE MUSEUM, 1979, PP. 209-230.

12337 KENDALL, JOHN S. "NEW ORLEANS' 'PECULIAR INSTITUTION.'"
LOUISIANA HISTORICAL QUARTERLY, 23 (JULY, 1940):
864-886.

12338 KENDALL, JOHN S. (ED.). NEW ORLEANS' "PECULIAR
INSTITUTION." NEW ORLEANS: LOUISIANA HISTORICAL
SOCIETY, 1940.

12339 KENDALL, JOHN S. "SHADOW OVER THE CITY." LOUISIANA
HISTORICAL QUARTERLY, 22 (JANUARY, 1939): 142-165.

12340 KENDALL, LANE C. "JOHN MCDONOGH--SLAVE-OWNER."
LOUISIANA HISTORICAL QUARTERLY, 15 (OCTOBER, 1932):
646-654; 16 (JANUARY, 1933): 125-134.

12341 KENNEDY, ROBERT E. MELLOWS, A CHRONICLE OF UNKNOWN
SINGERS. NEW YORK: A. AND C. BONI, 1925.

12342 KILMAN, GRADY W. "SLAVERY AND AGRICULTURE IN LOUISIANA:
1699-1731." ATTAKAPAS GAZETTE, 6 (JUNE, 1971): 39-50.

12343 KILMAN, GRADY W. "SLAVERY AND FORCED LABOR IN COLONIAL
LOUISIANA, 1699-1803." M.A. THESIS, UNIVERSITY OF
SOUTHWESTERN LOUISIANA, 1972.

12344 KING, AMEDA R. "SOCIAL AND ECONOMIC LIFE IN SPANISH
LOUISIANA, 1763-1783." PH.D. DISSERTATION, UNIVERSITY
OF ILLINOIS, 1931.

12345 KING, RUTH A. "SOCIAL AND ECONOMIC LIFE IN SPANISH
LOUISIANA, 1763-1783." PH.D. DISSERTATION, UNIVERSITY
OF ILLINOIS, 1931.

12346 KLEIN, SELMA L. "SOCIAL INTERACTIONS OF THE CREOLES AND
ANGLO-AMERICANS IN NEW ORLEANS, 1803-1860." M.A.
THESIS, TULANE UNIVERSITY, 1940.

12347 KMEN, HENRY A. "SINGING AND DANCING IN NEW ORLEANS--A
SOCIAL HISTORY OF THE BIRTH AND GROWTH OF BALLS AND
OPERA, 1791-1841." PH.D. DISSERTATION, TULANE
UNIVERSITY, 1961.

12348 KOTLIKOFF, LAURENCE J. "THE STRUCTURE OF SLAVE PRICES IN
NEW ORLEANS, 1804 TO 1862." ECONOMIC INQUIRY, 17
(OCTOBER, 1979): 496-518.

12349 KOTLIKOFF, LAURENCE J. "TOWARDS A QUANTITATIVE
DESCRIPTION OF THE NEW ORLEANS SLAVE MARKET."
UNPUBLISHED PAPER PRESENTED TO UNIVERSITY OF CHICAGO
WORKSHOP ON ECONOMIC HISTORY, 1975.

12350 KOTLIKOFF, LAURENCE J. AND RUPERT, ANTON J. "THE
MANUMISSION OF SLAVES IN NEW ORLEANS, 1827-1846."
SOUTHERN STUDIES, 19 (SUMMER, 1980): 172-181.

12351 KRAMER, ELIZABETH K. "SLAVERY LEGISLATION IN ANTE-BELLUM
LOUISIANA, 1803-1860." M.A. THESIS, LOUISIANA STATE
UNIVERSITY, 1944.

12352 KUNKEL, PAUL A. "MODIFICATIONS IN LOUISIANA LEGAL STATUS
UNDER LOUISIANA CONSTITUTIONS, 1812-1957." JOURNAL OF
NEGRO HISTORY, 44 (JANUARY, 1959): 1-25.

12353 LABBE, DOLORES E. "WOMEN IN EARLY NINETEENTH-CENTURY
LOUISIANA." PH.D. DISSERTATION, UNIVERSITY OF
DELAWARE, 1975.

12354 LACHANCE, PAUL F. "THE POLITICS OF FEAR: FRENCH
LOUISIANIANS AND THE SLAVE TRADE, 1786-1809."
PLANTATION SOCIETY IN THE AMERICAS, 1 (JUNE, 1979):
162-197.

12355 LATHROP, BARNES F. "THE PUGH PLANTATIONS, 1860-1865: A
STUDY OF LIFE IN LOWER LOUISIANA." PH.D.
DISSERTATION, UNIVERSITY OF TEXAS, 1945.

12356 LAWRENCE, GRACE M. "SLAVERY IN LOUISIANA." M.A. THESIS,
LOUISIANA STATE UNIVERSITY, 1922.

12357 LAWS, J. BRADFORD. "THE NEGROES OF CINCLARE CENTRAL
FACTORY AND CALUMET PLANTATION, LOUISIANA." BULLETIN
OF THE DEPARTMENT OF LABOR, 7 (JANUARY, 1902): 95-120.

12358 LEBRETON, MARIETTA M. "A HISTORY OF THE TERRITORY OF
ORLEANS, 1803-1812." PH.D. DISSERTATION, LOUISIANA
STATE UNIVERSITY, 1969.

12359 LEE, CHAN. "A CULTURE HISTORY OF RICE WITH SPECIAL
REFERENCE TO LOUISIANA." PH.D. DISSERTATION,
LOUISIANA STATE UNIVERSITY, 1960.

12360 LEWIS, NEIL M. "SLAVERY IN LOUISIANA DURING THE FRENCH
AND SPANISH REGIMES." M.A. THESIS, LOUISIANA STATE
UNIVERSITY, 1913.

12361 LOGSDON, JOSEPH. "DIARY OF A SLAVE: RECOLLECTION AND
PROPHECY." IN SHADE, WILLIAM G. AND HERRENKOHL, ROY
C. (EDS.). SEVEN ON BLACK: REFLECTIONS ON THE NEGRO
EXPERIENCE IN AMERICA. PHILADELPHIA: J.B.
LIPPINCOTT, 1969, PP. 24-48.

12362 LUKE, JOSEPHINE. "FROM SLAVERY TO FREEDOM IN LOUISIANA,
1862-1865." M.A. THESIS, TULANE UNIVERSITY, 1939.

12363 MALLORY, WILLIAM. OLD PLANTATION DAYS. N.P., 1902.

12364 MARTIN, JERRYE L.B. "NEW ORLEANS SLAVERY, 1840-1860: TESTING THE WADE THEORY." M.A. THESIS, TULANE UNIVERSITY, 1972.

12365 MCCANTS, DOROTHEA O. (ED.). THEY CAME TO LOUISIANA: LETTERS OF A CATHOLIC MISSION, 1854-1882. BATON ROUGE: LOUISIANA STATE UNIVERSITY PRESS, 1970.

12366 MCCONNELL, ROLAND C. "BLACK LIFE AND ACTIVITIES IN WEST FLORIDA AND ON THE GULF COAST, 1762-1803." IN PROCTOR, SAMUEL (ED.). EIGHTEENTH-CENTURY FLORIDA: LIFE ON THE FRONTIER. GAINESVILLE: UNIVERSITY PRESSES OF FLORIDA, 1976, PP. 75-90.

12367 MCCONNELL, ROLAND C. "LOUISIANA'S BLACK MILITARY HISTORY, 1729-1865." IN MACDONALD, ROBERT R.; KEMP, JOHN R.; AND HAAS, EDWARD F. (EDS.). LOUISIANA'S BLACK HERITAGE. NEW ORLEANS: LOUISIANA STATE MUSEUM, 1979, PP. 32-62.

12368 MCCONNELL, ROLAND C. NEGRO TROOPS OF ANTEBELLUM LOUISIANA. BATON ROUGE: LOUISIANA STATE UNIVERSITY PRESS, 1968.

12369 MCCRARY, PEYTON. ABRAHAM LINCOLN AND RECONSTRUCTION: THE LOUISIANA EXPERIMENT. PRINCETON: PRINCETON UNIVERSITY PRESS, 1978.

12370 MCDONALD, RODERICK. "'GOODS AND CHATTELS': THE ECONOMY OF SLAVES ON SUGAR PLANTATIONS IN JAMAICA AND LOUISIANA." PH.D. DISSERTATION, UNIVERSITY OF KANSAS, 1980.

12371 MCGIMSEY, RICHARD. "POLICE AND SLAVE PATROL REGULATIONS, 1823-1857." ATTAKAPAS GAZETTE, 10 (FALL, 1975): 147-152.

12372 MCGOWAN, JAMES T. "CREATION OF A SLAVE SOCIETY: LOUISIANA PLANTATIONS IN THE EIGHTEENTH CENTURY." PH.D. DISSERTATION, UNIVERSITY OF ROCHESTER, 1976.

12373 MCGOWAN, JAMES T. "PLANTERS WITHOUT SLAVES: ORIGINS OF A NEW WORLD LABOR SYSTEM." SOUTHERN STUDIES, 16 (SPRING, 1977): 5-26.

12374 MCGRATH, ROSEMARIE C. "THE ISSUE OF THE FOREIGN SLAVE TRADE IN THE LOUISIANA TERRITORY, 1803-1810." M.A. THESIS, UNIVERSITY OF VIRGINIA, 1967.

12375 MCILHENNY, EDWARD A. BEFO' DE WAR SPIRITUALS: WORDS AND MELODIES COLLECTED BY E.A. MCILHENNY. BOSTON: CHRISTOPHER PUBLISHING HOUSE, 1933.

12376 MCTIGUE, GERALDINE. "PATTERNS OF RESIDENCE: HOUSING DISTRIBUTION BY COLOR IN TWO LOUISIANA TOWNS,

1860-1880." LOUISIANA STUDIES, 15 (WINTER, 1976):
345-388.

12377　MCTIGUE, GERALDINE M. "FORMS OF RACIAL INTERACTION IN
LOUISIANA, 1860-1880." PH.D. DISSERTATION, YALE
UNIVERSITY, 1975.

12378　MENEZES, MARY N. "A COMPARATIVE STUDY OF THE FRENCH AND
SPANISH NEGRO SLAVE POLICY IN COLONIAL LOUISIANA,
1700-1803." M.A. THESIS, GEORGETOWN UNIVERSITY, 1965.

12379　MENN, JOSEPH K. "THE LARGE SLAVEHOLDERS OF LOUISIANA,
1860." M.A. THESIS, UNIVERSITY OF TEXAS, 1961.

12380　MENN, JOSEPH K. THE LARGE SLAVEHOLDERS OF
LOUISIANA--1860. NEW ORLEANS: PELICAN PUBLISHING
COMPANY, 1964.

12381　MENN, JOSEPH K. "THE LARGE SLAVEHOLDERS OF THE DEEP
SOUTH, 1860." PH.D. DISSERTATION, UNIVERSITY OF
TEXAS, 1964.

12382　MESSNER, WILLIAM F. "BLACK EDUCATION IN LOUISIANA,
1863-1865." CIVIL WAR HISTORY, 22 (MARCH, 1976):
41-59.

12383　MESSNER, WILLIAM F. "BLACK VIOLENCE AND WHITE RESPONSE:
LOUISIANA, 1862." JOURNAL OF SOUTHERN HISTORY, 41
(FEBRUARY, 1975): 19-38.

12384　MESSNER, WILLIAM F. FREEDMEN AND THE IDEOLOGY OF FREE
LABOR: LOUISIANA, 1862-1865. LAFAYETTE, LA:
UNIVERSITY OF SOUTHWESTERN LOUISIANA HISTORY SERIES,
1978.

12385　MEYERS, ROSE. A HISTORY OF BATON ROUGE, 1699-1812.
BATON ROUGE: LOUISIANA STATE UNIVERSITY PRESS, 1976.

12386　MICELI, MARY V. "THE INFLUENCE OF THE ROMAN CATHOLIC
CHURCH ON SLAVERY IN COLONIAL LOUISIANA UNDER FRENCH
DOMINATION, 1718-1763." PH.D. DISSERTATION, TULANE
UNIVERSITY, 1979.

12387　MILLS, GARY. MELROSE. NATCHITOCHES, LA: PRESERVATION
OF HISTORIC NATCHITOCHES, 1973.

12388　MILLS, GARY B. "CANE RIVER COUNTRY, 1860-1866."
PROCEEDINGS OF THE SEVENTEENTH ANNUAL GENEALOGICAL
INSTITUTE. BATON ROUGE: LOUISIANA GENEALOGICAL AND
HISTORICAL SOCIETY, 1974, PP. 1-12.

12389　MILLS, GARY B. THE FORGOTTEN PEOPLE: CANE RIVER'S
CREOLES OF COLOR. BATON ROUGE: LOUISIANA STATE
UNIVERSITY PRESS, 1977.

12390   MILLS, GARY B. "THE FORGOTTEN PEOPLE: CANE RIVER'S
        CREOLES OF COLOR." PH.D. DISSERTATION, MISSISSIPPI
        STATE UNIVERSITY, 1974.

12391   MILLS, GARY B. "A PORTRAIT OF ACHIEVEMENT: AUGUSTIN
        METOYER. . . ." RED RIVER VALLEY HISTORICAL REVIEW, 2
        (FALL, 1975): 333-348.

12392   MOODY, V. ALTON. "SLAVERY ON LOUISIANA SUGAR
        PLANTATIONS." LOUISIANA HISTORICAL QUARTERLY, 7
        (APRIL, 1924): 187-301.

12393   MOODY, VERNIE A. SLAVERY ON LOUISIANA SUGAR PLANTATIONS.
        NEW ORLEANS: N.P., 1924.

12394   MOODY, VERNIE A. "SLAVERY ON LOUISIANA SUGAR
        PLANTATIONS." PH.D. DISSERTATION, UNIVERSITY OF
        MICHIGAN, 1923.

12395   MORAN, ROBERT E. "THE NEGRO DEPENDENT CHILD IN
        LOUISIANA, 1800-1935." SOCIAL SERVICE REVIEW, 45
        (MARCH, 1971): 53-61.

12396   MORAN, ROBERT E. ONE HUNDRED YEARS OF CHILD WELFARE IN
        LOUISIANA, 1860-1960. LAFAYETTE, LA: UNIVERSITY OF
        SOUTHWESTERN LOUISIANA HISTORY SERIES, 1980.

12397   MORAZAN, RONALD R. "'QUADROON' BALLS IN THE SPANISH
        PERIOD." LOUISIANA HISTORY, 14 (SUMMER, 1973):
        310-315.

12398   MUSTACCHI, PIERO. "CESARE BRESSA (1785-1836) ON DIRT
        EATING IN LOUISIANA: A CRITICAL ANALYSIS OF HIS
        UNPUBLISHED MANUSCRIPT DE LA DISSOLUTION SCORBUTIQUE."
        JOURNAL OF THE AMERICAN MEDICAL ASSOCIATION, 218
        (OCTOBER 11, 1971): 229-232.

12399   NAU, JOHN F. THE GERMAN PEOPLE OF NEW ORLEANS,
        1850-1900. LEIDEN: E.J. BRILL, 1958.

12400   NELSON, ALICE D. "PEOPLE OF COLOR IN LOUISIANA."
        JOURNAL OF NEGRO HISTORY, 1 (OCTOBER, 1916): 361-376;
        2 (JANUARY, 1917): 51-78.

12401   NICKERSON, CAMILLE L. "AFRICO-CREOLE MUSIC IN LOUISIANA:
        A THESIS ON THE PLANTATION SONGS CREATED BY THE CREOLE
        NEGROES OF LOUISIANA." M.M. THESIS, OBERLIN COLLEGE,
        1932.

12402   NIEHAUS, EARL F. THE IRISH IN NEW ORLEANS, 1800-1860.
        BATON ROUGE: LOUISIANA STATE UNIVERSITY PRESS, 1965.

12403   NORDMANN, C.A. "SOME ASPECTS OF THE REGULATION AND
        CONTROL OF SLAVES AND FREE PERSONS OF COLOR IN ST.
        LANDRY PARISH." M.A. THESIS, UNIVERSITY OF

12404 NUHRAH, ARTHUR G. "JOHN MCDONOGH: LIBERAL SLAVEHOLDER."
       M.A. THESIS, TULANE UNIVERSITY, 1947.

12405 "OBSERVATIONS ON THE NEGROES OF LOUISIANA." JOURNAL OF
       NEGRO HISTORY, 2 (APRIL, 1917): 164-185.

12406 OPPENHEIM, LEONARD. "THE LAW OF SLAVES--A COMPARATIVE
       STUDY OF THE ROMAN AND LOUISIANA SYSTEMS." TULANE LAW
       REVIEW, 14 (APRIL, 1940): 384-406.

12407 OWSLEY, FRANK L. PLAIN FOLK OF THE OLD SOUTH. BATON
       ROUGE: LOUISIANA STATE UNIVERSITY PRESS, 1949.

12408 PADGETT, JAMES A. "A YANKEE SCHOOL TEACHER IN LOUISIANA,
       1835-1837: THE DIARY OF CAROLINE B. POOLE."
       LOUISIANA HISTORICAL QUARTERLY, 20 (JULY, 1937):
       651-679.

12409 PAQUETTE, ROBERT L. "SLAVERY IN LOUISIANA AND CUBA: A
       DEMOGRAPHIC APPROACH." M.A. THESIS, BOWLING GREEN
       STATE UNIVERSITY, 1976.

12410 PECOT, SHIRLEY C. "THE BLACK CODE OF LOUISIANA." A.B.
       THESIS, LOYOLA UNIVERSITY, NEW ORLEANS, 1938.

12411 PELLEGRIN, ROLAND J. AND PARENTON, VERNON J. "THE IMPACT
       OF SOCIO-ECONOMIC CHANGE ON RACIAL GROUPS IN A RURAL
       SETTING." PHYLON, 23 (SPRING, 1962): 55-60.

12412 PORTEOUS, LAURA L. "INDEX TO THE SPANISH JUDICIAL
       RECORDS OF LOUISIANA." LOUISIANA HISTORICAL
       QUARTERLY, 6 (JANUARY, 1926): 145-163.

12413 PORTER, ALICE T. "AN ECONOMIC VIEW OF ANTE-BELLUM NEW
       ORLEANS, 1845-1860." M.A. THESIS, TULANE UNIVERSITY,
       1942.

12414 PORTER, BETTY. "THE HISTORY OF NEGRO EDUCATION IN
       LOUISIANA." M.A. THESIS, LOUISIANA STATE UNIVERSITY,
       1938.

12415 POSTELL, PAUL E. "JOHN HAMPDEN RANDOLPH, A LOUISIANA
       PLANTER." LOUISIANA HISTORICAL QUARTERLY, 25
       (JANUARY, 1942): 149-223.

12416 POSTELL, PAUL E. "JOHN HAMPDEN RANDOLPH, A SOUTHERN
       PLANTER." M.A. THESIS, LOUISIANA STATE UNIVERSITY,
       1936.

12417 PREJEAN, HAROLD (ED.). "ESTIMATE OF LANDS AND SLAVES:
       RETURN OF THE LANDS AND SLAVES OF THE COUNTY
       OPELOUSAS." ATTAKAPAS GAZETTE, 9 (MARCH, 1974):
       19-32.

12418   PRICE, JOHN M. "SLAVERY IN WINN PARISH." LOUISIANA
        HISTORY, 8 (SPRING, 1967): 137-148.

12419   PRICHARD, WALTER. "THE EFFECTS OF THE CIVIL WAR ON THE
        LOUISIANA SUGAR INDUSTRY." JOURNAL OF SOUTHERN
        HISTORY, 5 (AUGUST, 1939): 315-332.

12420   PRICHARD, WALTER (ED.). "LEASE OF A LOUISIANA PLANTATION
        AND SLAVES." LOUISIANA HISTORICAL QUARTERLY, 21
        (OCTOBER, 1938): 995-997.

12421   PRICHARD, WALTER. "ROUTINE ON A LOUISIANA SUGAR
        PLANTATION UNDER THE SLAVERY REGIME." MISSISSIPPI
        VALLEY HISTORICAL REVIEW, 14 (SEPTEMBER, 1927):
        168-178.

12422   PJLWERS, JACOB E. "HENRY MARSTON, ANTE-BELLUM PLANTER
        AND BUSINESSMAN OF EAST FELICIANA." M.A. THESIS,
        LOUISIANA STATE UNIVERSITY, 1955.

12423   RANKIN, DAVID C. "THE POLITICS OF CASTE: FREE COLORED
        LEADERSHIP IN NEW ORLEANS DURING THE CIVIL WAR." IN
        MACDONALD, ROBERT R.; KEMP, JOHN R.; AND HAAS, EDWARD
        F. (EDS.). LOUISIANA'S BLACK HERITAGE. NEW ORLEANS:
        LOUISIANA STATE MUSEUM, 1979, PP. 107-146.

12424   RANKIN, DAVID C. "THE TANNENBAUM THESIS RECONSIDERED:
        SLAVERY AND RACE RELATIONS IN ANTEBELLUM LOUISIANA."
        SOUTHERN STUDIES, 18 (SPRING, 1979): 5-32.

12425   REDDICK, LAWRENCE D. "THE NEGRO IN THE NEW ORLEANS
        PRESS, 1850-60: A STUDY IN ATTITUDES AND PROPAGANDA."
        PH.D. DISSERTATION, UNIVERSITY OF CHICAGO, 1939.

12426   REED, GERMAINE A. "RACE LEGISLATION IN LOUISIANA,
        1864-1920." LOUISIANA HISTORY, 6 (FALL, 1965):
        379-392.

12427   REHDER, JOHN B. "DIAGNOSTIC LANDSCAPE TRAITS OF SUGAR
        PLANTATIONS IN SOUTHERN LOUISIANA." GEOSCIENCE AND
        MAN, 19 (JUNE 30, 1978): 135-150.

12428   REILLY, TIMOTHY. "GENTEEL REFORM VERSUS SOUTHERN
        ALLEGIANCE: EPISCOPALIAN DILEMMA IN OLD NEW ORLEANS."
        HISTORICAL MAGAZINE OF THE PROTESTANT EPISCOPAL
        CHURCH, 44 (DECEMBER, 1975): 437-450.

12429   REILLY, TIMOTHY F. "RELIGIOUS LEADERS AND SOCIAL
        CRITICISM IN NEW ORLEANS, 1800-1861." PH.D.
        DISSERTATION, UNIVERSITY OF MISSOURI, 1972.

12430   REILLY, TIMOTHY F. "SLAVERY AND THE SOUTHWESTERN
        EVANGELIST IN NEW ORLEANS, (1800-1861)." JOURNAL OF
        MISSISSIPPI HISTORY, 41 (NOVEMBER, 1979): 301-318.

12431   REINDERS, ROBERT C.   "THE CHURCHES AND THE NEGRO IN NEW
          ORLEANS, 1850-1860."   PHYLON, 22 (FALL, 1961):
          241-248.

12432   REINDERS, ROBERT C.   "DR. JAMES G. CARSON'S CANEBRAKE: A
          VIEW OF AN ANTE-BELLUM LOUISIANA PLANTATION."
          LOUISIANA HISTORICAL QUARTERLY, 33 (OCTOBER, 1950):
          353-363.

12433   REINDERS, ROBERT C.   END OF AN ERA: NEW ORLEANS,
          1850-1860.   NEW ORLEANS: PELICAN PUBLISHING COMPANY,
          1964.

12434   REINDERS, ROBERT C.   "SLAVERY IN NEW ORLEANS IN THE
          DECADE BEFORE THE CIVIL WAR."   MID-AMERICA, 44
          (OCTOBER, 1962):   211-221.

12435   REINDERS, ROBERT C.   "A SOCIAL HISTORY OF NEW ORLEANS,
          1850-1860."   PH.D. DISSERTATION, UNIVERSITY OF TEXAS,
          1957.

12436   RICHARDSON, FRANCIS D.   "THE TECHE COUNTRY FIFTY YEARS
          AGO."   ATTAKAPAS GAZETTE, 6 (DECEMBER, 1971):   119-129.

12437   RICHTER, WILLIAM L.   "SLAVERY IN BATON ROUGE, 1820-1860."
          LOUISIANA HISTORY, 10 (SPRING, 1969):   125-146.

12438   RIPLEY, C. PETER.   "THE BLACK FAMILY IN TRANSITION:
          LOUISIANA, 1860-1865."   JOURNAL OF SOUTHERN HISTORY,
          41 (AUGUST, 1975):   369-380.

12439   RIPLEY, C. PETER.   SLAVES AND FREEDMEN IN CIVIL WAR
          LOUISIANA.   BATON ROUGE: LOUISIANA STATE UNIVERSITY
          PRESS, 1976.

12440   RIPLEY, CHARLES P.   "BLACK, BLUE AND GRAY: SLAVES AND
          FREEDMEN IN CIVIL WAR LOUISIANA."   PH.D. DISSERTATION,
          FLORIDA STATE UNIVERSITY, 1973.

12441   RIPLEY, ELIZA M.C.H.   SOCIAL LIFE IN OLD NEW ORLEANS.
          NEW YORK: D. APPLETON AND COMPANY, 1912.

12442   ROBERTSON, JAMES A.   LOUISIANA UNDER THE RULE OF SPAIN,
          FRANCE, AND THE UNITED STATES.   2 VOLS.   CLEVELAND:
          ARTHUR H. CLARK COMPANY, 1911.

12443   ROGERS, TOMMY W.   "ORIGIN AND CULTURAL ASSIMILATION OF
          THE POPULATION OF LOUISIANA."   MISSISSIPPI QUARTERLY,
          25 (WINTER, 1971-1972):   45-68.

12444   ROHRBOUGH, MALCOLM J.   THE TRANS-APPALACHIAN FRONTIER:
          PEOPLE, SOCIETIES, AND INSTITUTIONS, 1775-1850.   NEW
          YORK: OXFORD UNIVERSITY PRESS, 1978.

12445   ROLAND, CHARLES P.   "DIFFICULTIES OF CIVIL WAR SUGAR

PLANTING IN LOUISIANA." LOUISIANA HISTORICAL
QUARTERLY, 38 (OCTOBER, 1955): 40-62.

12446 ROLAND, CHARLES P. LOUISIANA SUGAR PLANTATIONS DURING
       THE AMERICAN CIVIL WAR. LEIDEN: E.J. BRILL, 1957.

12447 ROLAND, CHARLES P. "LOUISIANA SUGAR PLANTATIONS DURING
       THE CIVIL WAR." PH.D. DISSERTATION, LOUISIANA STATE
       UNIVERSITY, 1951.

12448 ROUSSEVE, CHARLES B. THE NEGRO IN LOUISIANA: ASPECTS OF
       HIS HISTORY AND HIS LITERATURE. NEW ORLEANS: XAVIER
       UNIVERSITY PRESS, 1937.

12449 "SALVAGING THE LOAD OF A SUNKEN KEELBOAT." PIONEER
       AMERICA, 10 (DECEMBER 1, 1978): 28-31.

12450 SANDERS, MARY E. "LIST OF LANDOWNERS AND SLAVEOWNERS OF
       THE ATTAKAPAS." ATTAKAPAS GAZETTE, 11 (SUMMER, 1976):
       84-90.

12451 SAXON, LYLE. OLD LOUISIANA. NEW YORK: CENTURY, 1929.

12452 SAXON, LYLE; DREYER, EDWARD; AND TALLANT, ROBERT. GUMBO
       YA-YA: A COLLECTION OF LOUISIANA FOLK TALES. BOSTON:
       HOUGHTON MIFFLIN, 1945.

12453 SCHAFER, JUDITH K. "THE IMMEDIATE IMPACT OF NAT TURNER'S
       INSURRECTION ON NEW ORLEANS." LOUISIANA HISTORY, 21
       (FALL, 1980): 361-376.

12454 SCHMITZ, MARK D. "ECONOMIC ANALYSIS OF ANTEBELLUM SUGAR
       PLANTATIONS IN LOUISIANA." PH.D. DISSERTATION,
       UNIVERSITY OF NORTH CAROLINA, 1974.

12455 SCHWENINGER, LOREN. "A NEGRO SOJOURNER IN ANTEBELLUM NEW
       ORLEANS." LOUISIANA HISTORY, 20 (SUMMER, 1979):
       305-314.

12456 SCOTT, STERLING C. "ASPECTS OF THE LIBERIAN COLONIZATION
       MOVEMENT IN LOUISIANA." M.A. THESIS, TULANE
       UNIVERSITY, 1952.

12457 SEIP, TERRY L. "SLAVES AND FREE NEGROES IN ALEXANDRIA,
       1850-1860." LOUISIANA HISTORY, 10 (SPRING, 1969):
       147-165.

12458 SHENKEL, J. RICHARD AND HUDSON, JACK. "HISTORIC
       ARCHAEOLOGY IN NEW ORLEANS." THE CONFERENCE ON
       HISTORIC SITE ARCHAEOLOGY PAPERS, 6 (1971): 40-44.

12459 SHUGG, ROGER W. ORIGINS OF CLASS STRUGGLE IN LOUISIANA:
       A SOCIAL HISTORY OF WHITE FARMERS AND LABORERS DURING
       SLAVERY AND AFTER, 1840-1875. UNIVERSITY, LA:
       LOUISIANA STATE UNIVERSITY PRESS, 1939.

12460   SIMMS, MARION. "BLACK MAGIC IN NEW ORLEANS." _TRAVEL_, 81
        (JULY, 1943): 18-19, 32.

12461   SITTERSON, J.C. "THE SUGAR INDUSTRY IN THE OLD SOUTH."
        M.A. THESIS, UNIVERSITY OF NORTH CAROLINA, 1932.

12462   SITTERSON, J. CARLYLE. "EXPANSION, REVERSION, AND
        REVOLUTION IN THE SOUTHERN SUGAR INDUSTRY:
        1850-1910." _BULLETIN OF THE BUSINESS HISTORICAL
        SOCIETY_, 27 (SEPTEMBER, 1953): 129-140.

12463   SITTERSON, J. CARLYLE. "HIRED LABOR ON SUGAR PLANTATIONS
        OF THE ANTE-BELLUM SOUTH." _JOURNAL OF SOUTHERN
        HISTORY_, 14 (MAY, 1948): 192-205.

12464   SITTERSON, J. CARLYLE. "LEWIS THOMPSON, A CAROLINIAN AND
        HIS LOUISIANA PLANTATION, 1848-1888, A STUDY IN
        ABSENTEE OWNERSHIP." IN GREEN, FLETCHER (ED.).
        _ESSAYS IN SOUTHERN HISTORY PRESENTED TO JOSEPH
        GREGOIRE DE ROULHAC HAMILTON, BY HIS FORMER STUDENTS
        AT THE UNIVERSITY OF NORTH CAROLINA_. CHAPEL HILL:
        UNIVERSITY OF NORTH CAROLINA PRESS, 1949, PP. 16-27.

12465   SITTERSON, J. CARLYLE. "MAGNOLIA PLANTATION, 1853-1862:
        A DECADE OF A LOUISIANA SUGAR ESTATE." _MISSISSIPPI
        VALLEY HISTORICAL REVIEW_, 25 (SEPTEMBER, 1938):
        197-210.

12466   SITTERSON, J. CARLYLE. "THE MCCOLLAMS: A PLANTER FAMILY
        OF THE OLD AND NEW SOUTH." _JOURNAL OF SOUTHERN
        HISTORY_, 6 (AUGUST, 1940): 347-367.

12467   SITTERSON, J. CARLYLE. "THE TRANSITION FROM SLAVE TO
        FREE ECONOMY ON THE WILLIAM J. MINOR PLANTATIONS."
        AGRICULTURAL HISTORY, 17 (OCTOBER, 1943): 216-224.

12468   SITTERSON, J. CARLYLE. "THE WILLIAM J. MINOR
        PLANTATIONS: A STUDY IN ANTE-BELLUM ABSENTEE
        OWNERSHIP." _JOURNAL OF SOUTHERN HISTORY_, 9 (FEBRUARY,
        1943): 59-74.

12469   SITTERSON, JOSEPH C. _SUGAR COUNTRY: THE CANE SUGAR
        INDUSTRY IN THE SOUTH, 1753-1950_. LEXINGTON:
        UNIVERSITY OF KENTUCKY PRESS, 1953.

12470   "SLAVERY DAY CEREMONY." _CURRENT LITERATURE_, 23 (APRIL,
        1898): 329.

12471   SMALLEY, EUGENE V. "SUGAR MAKING IN LOUISIANA." _CENTURY
        MAGAZINE_, 35 (NOVEMBER, 1887): 100-120.

12472   SMITH, WALTER R. _BRIEF HISTORY OF THE LOUISIANA
        TERRITORY_. ST. LOUIS: ST. LOUIS NEWS COMPANY, 1904.

12473   SNYDER, PERRY A. "SHREVEPORT, LOUISIANA, DURING THE

CIVIL WAR AND RECONSTRUCTION." PH.D. DISSERTATION, FLORIDA STATE UNIVERSITY, 1979.

12474 SPAIN, DAPHNE. "RACE RELATIONS AND RESIDENTIAL SEGREGATION IN NEW ORLEANS: TWO CENTURIES OF PARADOX." ANNALS OF THE AMERICAN ACADEMY OF POLITICAL AND SOCIAL SCIENCE, 441 (JANUARY, 1979): 82-96.

12475 STEPHENSON, WENDELL H. ALEXANDER PORTER, WHIG PLANTER OF OLD LOUISIANA. BATON ROUGE: LOUISIANA STATE UNIVERSITY PRESS, 1934.

12476 STEPHENSON, WENDELL H. "ANTE-BELLUM NEW ORLEANS AS AN AGRICULTURAL FOCUS." AGRICULTURAL HISTORY, 15 (OCTOBER, 1941): 161-174.

12477 STEVENSON, ROBERT. "AFRO-AMERICAN MUSIC--THE COLONIAL PERIOD." IN SADIE, STANLEY (ED.). THE NEW GROVE DICTIONARY OF MUSIC AND MUSICIANS. 20 VOLS. LONDON: MACMILLAN, 1980, VOL. 10, PP. 522-525.

12478 STOKES, BEATRICE M. "JOHN BISLAND, MISSISSIPPI PLANTER, 1776-1821." M.A. THESIS, LOUISIANA STATE UNIVERSITY, 1941.

12479 SUAREZ, RALEIGH A., JR. "RURAL LIFE IN LOUISIANA, 1850-1860." PH.D. DISSERTATION, LOUISIANA STATE UNIVERSITY, 1954.

12480 "SUMMARY OF TRIAL PROCEEDINGS OF THOSE ACCUSED OF PARTICIPATING IN THE SLAVE UPRISING OF JANUARY 9, 1811." LOUISIANA HISTORY, 18 (FALL, 1977): 472-473.

12481 SURREY, NANCY M. THE COMMERCE OF LOUISIANA DURING THE FRENCH REGIME, 1679-1763. NEW YORK: COLUMBIA UNIVERSITY PRESS, 1916.

12482 TAYLOR, JOE G. "THE FOREIGN SLAVE TRADE IN LOUISIANA AFTER 1808." LOUISIANA HISTORY, 1 (WINTER, 1960): 36-43.

12483 TAYLOR, JOE G. "INTRODUCTION." LOUISIANA HISTORY, 10 (SPRING, 1969): 93-96.

12484 TAYLOR, JOE G. NEGRO SLAVERY IN LOUISIANA. BATON ROUGE: LOUISIANA HISTORICAL ASSOCIATION, 1963.

12485 TAYLOR, JOE G. "NEGRO SLAVERY IN LOUISIANA." PH.D. DISSERTATION, LOUISIANA STATE UNIVERSITY, 1952.

12486 TAYLOR, JOE G. "A NEW LOOK AT SLAVERY IN LOUISIANA." IN MACDONALD, ROBERT R.; KEMP, JOHN R.; AND HAAS, EDWARD F. (EDS.). LOUISIANA'S BLACK HERITAGE. NEW ORLEANS: LOUISIANA STATE MUSEUM, 1979, PP. 190-208.

12487   TAYLOR, JOE G.   "SLAVERY IN FOUR NORTHEASTERN PARISHES IN
        LOUISIANA."   M.A. THESIS, LOUISIANA STATE UNIVERSITY,
        1948.

12488   TAYLOR, JOE G.   "SLAVERY IN LOUISIANA DURING THE CIVIL
        WAR."   LOUISIANA HISTORY, 8 (WINTER, 1967):   27-34.

12489   TIEDEMAN, ARTHUR E.   "SLAVERY IN LOUISIANA."   M.A.
        THESIS, COLUMBIA UNIVERSITY, 1949.

12490   TOLLE, CHARLES O.   "SLAVE SALE TO ST. MARC DARBY--1828."
        ATTAKAPAS GAZETTE, 8 (JUNE, 1975):   89.

12491   TREGLE, JOSEPH G., JR.   "EARLY NEW ORLEANS SOCIETY: A
        REAPPRAISAL."   JOURNAL OF SOUTHERN HISTORY, 18
        (FEBRUARY, 1952):   20-36.

12492   TUNNELL, TED.   "ANVIL OF THE REVOLUTION: THE MAKING OF
        RADICAL LOUISIANA, 1862-1877."   PH.D. DISSERTATION,
        UNIVERSITY OF CALIFORNIA, 1978.

12493   TURNER, SUZANNE L.   "PLANTATION PAPERS AS A SOURCE FOR
        LANDSCAPE DOCUMENTATION AND INTERPRETATION: THE
        THOMAS BUTLER PAPERS."   APT BULLETIN, 12 (1980):
        28-45.

12494   U.S. ARMY, BUREAU OF FREE LABOR.   THE FREEDMEN OF
        LOUISIANA.   NEW ORLEANS: NEW ORLEANS TIMES BOOK AND
        JOB OFFICE, 1865.

12495   USNER, DANIEL H., JR.   "FROM AFRICAN CAPTIVITY TO
        AMERICAN SLAVERY: THE INTRODUCTION OF BLACK LABORERS
        TO COLONIAL LOUISIANA."   LOUISIANA HISTORY, 20
        (WINTER, 1979):   25-48.

12496   VINCENT, CHARLES.   "BLACK LOUISIANIANS DURING THE CIVIL
        WAR AND RECONSTRUCTION: ASPECTS OF THEIR STRUGGLES
        AND ACHIEVEMENTS."   IN MACDONALD, ROBERT R.; KEMP,
        JOHN R.; AND HAAS, EDWARD F. (EDS.).   LOUISIANA'S
        BLACK HERITAGE.   NEW ORLEANS: LOUISIANA STATE MUSEUM,
        1979, PP. 85-106.

12497   VOSS, LOUIS.   "SALLY MUELLER, THE GERMAN SLAVE."
        LOUISIANA HISTORICAL QUARTERLY, 12 (JULY, 1929):
        447-460.

12498   WEGENER, WERNER A.   "NEGRO SLAVERY IN NEW ORLEANS."   M.A.
        THESIS, TULANE UNIVERSITY, 1935.

12499   WELLS, TOM H.   "MOVING A PLANTATION TO LOUISIANA."
        LOUISIANA STUDIES, 6 (FALL, 1967):   280-289.

12500   WHITE, ALICE P.   "THE PLANTATION EXPERIENCE OF JOSEPH AND
        LAVINIA ERWIN, 1807-1836."   LOUISIANA HISTORICAL
        QUARTERLY, 27 (APRIL, 1944):   343-478.

12501 WHITTEN, DAVID O. "ANTEBELLUM SUGAR AND RICE
        PLANTATIONS, LOUISIANA AND SOUTH CAROLINA: A
        PROFITABILITY STUDY." PH.D. DISSERTATION, TULANE
        UNIVERSITY, 1970.

12502 WHITTEN, DAVID O. "A BLACK ENTREPRENEUR IN ANTEBELLUM
        LOUISIANA." BUSINESS HISTORY REVIEW, 45 (SUMMER,
        1971): 201-219.

12503 WHITTEN, DAVID O. "MEDICAL CARE OF SLAVES: LOUISIANA
        SUGAR REGION AND SOUTH CAROLINA RICE DISTRICT."
        SOUTHERN STUDIES, 16 (SUMMER, 1977):   153-180.

12504 WHITTEN, DAVID O. "SLAVE BUYING IN 1835 VIRGINIA AS
        REVEALED BY LETTERS OF A BLACK LOUISIANA SUGAR
        PLANTER." LOUISIANA HISTORY, 11 (SUMMER, 1970):
        231-244.

12505 WHITTEN, DAVID O. "SUGAR SLAVERY: A PROFITABILITY MODEL
        FOR SLAVE INVESTMENTS IN THE ANTEBELLUM LOUISIANA
        SUGAR INDUSTRY." LOUISIANA STUDIES, 12 (SUMMER,
        1973):   423-442.

12506 WHITTEN, DAVID O. "TARIFF AND PROFIT IN THE ANTEBELLUM
        LOUISIANA SUGAR INDUSTRY." BUSINESS HISTORY REVIEW,
        44 (SUMMER, 1970):   226-233.

12507 WHITTINGTON, G.P. (ED.). "CONCERNING THE LOYALTY OF
        SLAVES IN NORTH LOUISIANA IN 1862." LOUISIANA
        HISTORICAL QUARTERLY, 14 (OCTOBER, 1931):   487-502.

12508 WILLEY, NATHAN. "EDUCATION OF THE COLORED POPULATION OF
        LOUISIANA." HARPER'S NEW MONTHLY MAGAZINE, 33 (JULY,
        1866):   244-250.

12509 WILLIAMS, E. RUSS JR. (ED.). "SLAVE PATROL ORDINANCES OF
        ST. TAMMANY PARISH, LOUISIANA, 1835-1838." LOUISIANA
        HISTORY, 13 (FALL, 1972):   399-412.

12510 WILLIAMS, ORA G. (ED.). PLANTATION MEMO: PLANTATION
        LIFE IN LOUISIANA, 1750-1790 AND OTHER MATTERS.   BATON
        ROUGE: CLAITOR'S PUBLISHING DIVISION, 1972.

12511 WILSON, SAMUEL JR. (ED.). IMPRESSIONS RESPECTING NEW
        ORLEANS: DIARY AND SKETCHES, 1818-1820.   NEW YORK:
        COLUMBIA UNIVERSITY PRESS, 1951.

12512 WINSTON, JAMES E. "THE FREE NEGRO IN NEW ORLEANS,
        1803-1860." LOUISIANA HISTORICAL QUARTERLY, 21
        (OCTOBER, 1938):   1075-1085.

12513 WOESSNER, HERMAN C. "NEW ORLEANS, 1840-1860:   A STUDY IN
        URBAN SLAVERY." M.A. THESIS, LOUISIANA STATE
        UNIVERSITY, 1967.

12514   WOOD, MINTER. "LIFE IN NEW ORLEANS IN THE SPANISH
        PERIOD." LOUISIANA HISTORICAL QUARTERLY, 22 (JULY,
        1939): 642-709.

12515   WOOD, MINTER. "LIFE IN NEW ORLEANS IN THE SPANISH
        PERIOD." M.A. THESIS, TULANE UNIVERSITY, 1938.

12516   WOODS, FRANCES J. MARGINALITY AND IDENTITY: A COLORED
        CREOLE FAMILY THROUGH TEN GENERATIONS. BATON ROUGE:
        LOUISIANA STATE UNIVERSITY PRESS, 1972.

12517   YOUNG, TOMMY R. "THE UNITED STATES ARMY AND THE
        INSTITUTION OF SLAVERY IN LOUISIANA: 1803-1815."
        LOUISIANA STUDIES, 13 (FALL, 1974): 201-222.

MISSISSIPPI

12518   ALFORD, TERRY. PRINCE AMONG SLAVES. NEW YORK: HARCOURT
        BRACE JOVANOVICH, 1977.

12519   ALFORD, TERRY L. "LETTER FROM LIBERIA, 1848."
        MISSISSIPPI QUARTERLY, 22 (SPRING, 1969): 150-151.

12520   ALFORD, TERRY L. "SOME MANUMISSIONS RECORDED IN THE
        ADAMS COUNTY DEED BOOKS IN CHANCERY CLERK'S OFFICE,
        NATCHEZ, MISSISSIPPI, 1795-1835." JOURNAL OF
        MISSISSIPPI HISTORY, 33 (FEBRUARY, 1971): 39-50.

12521   ANDERSON, JOHN Q. "DR. JAMES GREEN CARSON, ANTE-BELLUM
        PLANTER OF MISSISSIPPI AND LOUISIANA." JOURNAL OF
        MISSISSIPPI HISTORY, 18 (OCTOBER, 1956): 243-301.

12522   ANDERSON, SOLENA. "BACK IN 'DEM DAYS: A BLACK FAMILY
        REMINISCES." JOURNAL OF MISSISSIPPI HISTORY, 36 (MAY,
        1974): 179-186.

12523   APPLEWHITE, RIVERS. "THE CONSTITUTIONAL ASPECT OF
        SLAVERY AS A CAUSE OF SECESSION IN 1861." M.A.
        THESIS, UNIVERSITY OF MISSISSIPPI, 1925.

12524   BARADELL, WILLIAM L. "RUNAWAY SLAVES IN MISSISSIPPI."
        M.A. THESIS, UNIVERSITY OF SOUTHERN MISSISSIPPI, 1974.

12525   BARNEY, WILLIAM L. THE SECESSIONIST IMPULSE: ALABAMA
        AND MISSISSIPPI IN 1860. PRINCETON: PRINCETON
        UNIVERSITY PRESS, 1974.

12526   BEASLEY, JONATHAN. "BLACKS--SLAVE AND FREE--VICKSBURG,
        1850-1860." JOURNAL OF MISSISSIPPI HISTORY, 38
        (FEBRUARY, 1976): 1-32.

12527   BELL, H.S. "PLANTATION LIFE OF THE NEGRO IN THE LOWER
        MISSISSIPPI VALLEY." SOUTHERN WORKMAN, 28 (AUGUST,
        1899): 313-314.

12528   BIGELOW, MARTHA M. "VICKSBURG: EXPERIMENT IN FREEDOM."
        JOURNAL OF MISSISSIPPI HISTORY, 26 (FEBRUARY, 1964):
        28-44.

12529   "BLACK BELT." IN SCHAPSMEIER, EDWARD L. AND SCHAPSMEIER,
        FREDERICK H. ENCYCLOPEDIA OF AMERICAN AGRICULTURAL
        HISTORY. WESTPORT: GREENWOOD PRESS, 1975, P. 39.

12530   BOMAN, MARTHA. "A CITY OF THE OLD SOUTH: JACKSON,
        MISSISSIPPI, 1850-1860." JOURNAL OF MISSISSIPPI
        HISTORY, 15 (JANUARY, 1953): 1-32.

12531   BOX, MRS. EUGENE. "ANTE-BELLUM TRAVELERS IN
        MISSISSIPPI." JOURNAL OF MISSISSIPPI HISTORY, 17
        (APRIL, 1955): 110-126.

12532   BOYD, JESSE L. A POPULAR HISTORY OF THE BAPTISTS IN
        MISSISSIPPI. JACKSON: BAPTIST PRESS, 1930.

12533   BOZEMAN, WILLIAM F. "MARTIN WILSON PHILIPS, MISSISSIPPI
        PLANTER." M.A. THESIS, LOUISIANA STATE UNIVERSITY,
        1937.

12534   BROUGH, CHARLES H. "HISTORY OF TAXATION IN MISSISSIPPI."
        PUBLICATIONS OF THE MISSISSIPPI HISTORICAL SOCIETY, 2
        (1899): 113-124.

12535   BROWN, MAUD M. "THE WAR COMES TO COLLEGE HILL." JOURNAL
        OF MISSISSIPPI HISTORY, 16 (JANUARY, 1954): 22-30.

12536   CALDWELL, JOAN P. "CHRISTMAS IN OLD NATCHEZ." JOURNAL
        OF MISSISSIPPI HISTORY, 21 (OCTOBER, 1959): 257-269.

12537   CROCKER, LES. "AN EARLY IRON FOUNDRY IN NORTHERN
        MISSISSIPPI." JOURNAL OF MISSISSIPPI HISTORY, 35
        (MAY, 1973): 113-126.

12538   CURRIE, JAMES T. ENCLAVE: VICKSBURG AND HER
        PLANTATIONS, 1863-1870. JACKSON: UNIVERSITY PRESS OF
        MISSISSIPPI, 1980.

12539   CURRIE, JAMES T. "FROM SLAVERY TO FREEDOM IN
        MISSISSIPPI'S LEGAL SYSTEM." JOURNAL OF NEGRO
        HISTORY, 65 (SPRING, 1980): 112-125.

12540   DANIELS, JONATHAN. THE DEVIL'S BACKBONE: THE STORY OF
        THE NATCHEZ TRACE. NEW YORK: MCGRAW-HILL, 1962.

12541   DAVENPORT, F. GARVIN (ED.). "JUDGE SHARKEY PAPERS."
        MISSISSIPPI VALLEY HISTORICAL REVIEW, 20 (JUNE, 1933):
        76-90.

12542   DAVIS, EDWIN A. AND HOGAN, WILLIAM R. (EDS.). THE BARBER
        OF NATCHEZ. BATON ROUGE: LOUISIANA STATE UNIVERSITY
        PRESS, 1954.

12543 DORSON, RICHARD M. "RHYMING TALES FROM BOLIVAR COUNTY,
       MISSISSIPPI." SOUTHERN FOLKLORE QUARTERLY, 19 (1955):
       104-116.

12544 DUBAY, ROBERT W. "JOHN JONES PETTUS: A STUDY IN
       SECESSION." M.A. THESIS, UNIVERSITY OF SOUTHERN
       MISSISSIPPI, 1966.

12545 DUBAY, ROBERT W. JOHN JONES PETTUS: MISSISSIPPI
       FIRE-EATER: HIS LIFE AND TIMES, 1813-1867. JACKSON:
       UNIVERSITY PRESS OF MISSISSIPPI, 1975.

12546 DYER, STANFORD P. "A BLACK VIEW OF MISSISSIPPI
       RECONSTRUCTION." M.A. THESIS, LOUISIANA TECH
       UNIVERSITY, 1974.

12547 EATON, CLEMENT. JEFFERSON DAVIS. NEW YORK: MACMILLAN
       COMPANY, 1977.

12548 EUDY, JOHN C. "A MISSISSIPPI LOG WAGON." JOURNAL OF
       MISSISSIPPI HISTORY, 30 (MAY, 1968): 143-150.

12549 EVERETT, FRANK E. BRIERFIELD, PLANTATION HOME OF
       JEFFERSON DAVIS. HATTIESBURG: UNIVERSITY AND COLLEGE
       PRESS OF MISSISSIPPI, 1971.

12550 FLEMING, WALTER L. JEFFERSON DAVIS, THE NEGROES AND THE
       NEGRO PROBLEM. BATON ROUGE: LOUISIANA STATE
       UNIVERSITY BULLETIN, 6TH SER., 1908.

12551 FLEMING, WALTER L. "JEFFERSON DAVIS, THE NEGROES AND THE
       NEGRO PROBLEM." SEWANEE REVIEW, 16 (OCTOBER, 1908):
       407-427.

12552 FLEMING, WALTER L. "PLANTATION LIFE IN THE OLD SOUTH AND
       THE PLANTATION NEGROES." JOURNAL OF AMERICAN HISTORY,
       3 (APRIL-JULY, 1909): 233-246.

12553 FULKERSON, HORACE S. "TREATMENT OF SLAVES AT THIS
       PERIOD, ETC." RANDOM RECOLLECTIONS OF EARLY DAYS IN
       MISSISSIPPI. VICKSBURG: VICKSBURG PRINTING AND
       PUBLISHING COMPANY, 1885, PP. 128-140.

12554 GIBSON, GEORGE H. (ED.). "THE MISSISSIPPI MARKET FOR
       WOOLEN GOODS: AN 1822 ANALYSIS." JOURNAL OF SOUTHERN
       HISTORY, 31 (FEBRUARY, 1965): 80-90.

12555 GLADNEY, LOUISE. "HISTORY OF PLEASANT HILL PLANTATION,
       1811-1867." M.A. THESIS, LOUISIANA STATE UNIVERSITY,
       1932.

12556 GRIFFITH, LUCILLE. "THE PLANTATION RECORD BOOK OF
       BROOKDALE FARM, 1856-1857." JOURNAL OF MISSISSIPPI
       HISTORY, 7 (JANUARY, 1945): 23-31.

12557   HADSKEY, JOHN W.   "A HISTORY OF FRANKLIN COUNTY,
        MISSISSIPPI, TO 1865."   M.A. THESIS, MISSISSIPPI STATE
        COLLEGE, 1954.

12558   HAMILTON, HOLMAN.   ZACHARY TAYLOR: SOLDIER IN THE WHITE
        HOUSE.   INDIANAPOLIS: BOBBS-MERRILL COMPANY, 1951.

12559   HAMILTON, W.B.   "MISSISSIPPI 1817: A SOCIOLOGICAL AND
        ECONOMIC ANALYSIS."   JOURNAL OF MISSISSIPPI HISTORY,
        29 (NOVEMBER, 1967):   270-292.

12560   HAMILTON, WILLIAM B. AND MCCAIN, WILLIAM D. (EDS.).
        "WEALTH IN THE NATCHEZ REGION: INVENTORIES OF THE
        ESTATE OF CHARLES PERCY, 1794 AND 1804."   JOURNAL OF
        MISSISSIPPI HISTORY, 10 (OCTOBER, 1948):   290-316.

12561   HAWES, RUTH B.   "SLAVERY IN MISSISSIPPI."   SEWANEE
        REVIEW, 21 (APRIL, 1913):   223-234.

12562   HAZEL, JOSEPH A.   "THE GEOGRAPHY OF NEGRO AGRICULTURAL
        SLAVERY IN ALABAMA, FLORIDA, AND MISSISSIPPI, CIRCA
        1860."   PH.D. DISSERTATION, COLUMBIA UNIVERSITY, 1963.

12563   HEARN, WALTER C.   "TOWNS IN ANTEBELLUM MISSISSIPPI."
        PH.D. DISSERTATION, UNIVERSITY OF MISSISSIPPI, 1969.

12564   HEARON, CLEO C.   "SECESSION OF MISSISSIPPI, 1849-1861;
        ECONOMIC, SOCIAL AND POLITICAL FORCES."   PH.D.
        DISSERTATION, UNIVERSITY OF CHICAGO, 1913.

12565   HEIDELBERG, NELL A.   "THE FRONTIER IN MISSISSIPPI."   M.A.
        THESIS, LOUISIANA STATE UNIVERSITY, 1940.

12566   HERMANN, JANET S.   "THE BLACK COMMUNITY AT DAVIS BEND:
        THE PURSUIT OF A DREAM."   PH.D. DISSERTATION,
        UNIVERSITY OF CALIFORNIA, 1979.

12567   HOGAN, WILLIAM R. AND DAVIS, EDWIN A. (EDS.).   WILLIAM
        JOHNSON'S NATCHEZ: THE ANTE-BELLUM DIARY OF A FREE
        NEGRO.   BATON ROUGE: LOUISIANA STATE UNIVERSITY
        PRESS, 1951.

12568   HOLDER, RAY.   WILLIAM WINANS: METHODIST LEADER IN
        ANTEBELLUM MISSISSIPPI.   JACKSON: UNIVERSITY PRESS OF
        MISSISSIPPI, 1977.

12569   HOOD, A.P.   THE NEGRO AT MOUND BAYOU.   NASHVILLE:
        AFRICAN METHODIST EPISCOPAL SUNDAY SCHOOL UNION, 1910.

12570   JACKSON, MAURICE J.   "MOUND BAYOU--A STUDY IN SOCIAL
        DEVELOPMENT."   M.A. THESIS, UNIVERSITY OF ALABAMA,
        1937.

12571   JAMES, D. CLAYTON.   ANTEBELLUM NATCHEZ.   BATON ROUGE:
        LOUISIANA STATE UNIVERSITY PRESS, 1968.

12572   JAMES, D. CLAYTON.   "MISSISSIPPI AGRICULTURE, 1861-1865."
        JOURNAL OF MISSISSIPPI HISTORY, 24 (MAY, 1962):
        129-141.

12573   JAMES, DORIS C.   "ANTE-BELLUM NATCHEZ."   PH.D.
        DISSERTATION, UNIVERSITY OF TEXAS, 1964.

12574   "JEFFERSON DAVIS' SLAVE."   NEW YORK SUN, SEPTEMBER 11,
        1900.

12575   KELL, PATRICIA A.   "THE ARISTOCRACY IN LATE ANTEBELLUM
        MISSISSIPPI."   M.A. THESIS, LAMAR UNIVERSITY, 1977.

12576   KELLEY, DONALD B.   "HARPER'S FERRY: PRELUDE TO CRISIS IN
        MISSISSIPPI."   JOURNAL OF MISSISSIPPI HISTORY, 27
        (NOVEMBER, 1965):   351-372.

12577   KNOX, THOMAS W.   CAMP FIRE AND COTTON FIELD: SOUTHERN
        ADVENTURE IN TIME OF WAR.   LIFE WITH THE UNION ARMIES
        AND A RESIDENCE ON A LOUISIANA PLANTATION.   NEW YORK:
        BLELOCK, 1865.

12578   LANG, MEREDITH.   DEFENDER OF THE FAITH: THE HIGH COURT
        OF MISSISSIPPI, 1817-1875.   JACKSON: UNIVERSITY PRESS
        OF MISSISSIPPI, 1977.

12579   MAGRUDER, W.W.   "THE LEGAL STATUS OF SLAVES IN
        MISSISSIPPI BEFORE THE WAR."   PUBLICATIONS OF THE
        MISSISSIPPI HISTORICAL SOCIETY, 4 (1901):   133-142.

12580   MARSHALL, THEODORA B. AND EVANS, GLADYS C.   "PLANTATION
        REPORTS FROM THE PAPERS OF LEVIN R. MARSHALL OF
        'RICHMOND,' NATCHEZ, MISSISSIPPI (1836)."   JOURNAL OF
        MISSISSIPPI HISTORY, 3 (JANUARY, 1941):   45-55.

12581   MAY, ROBERT E.   "JOHN A. QUITMAN AND HIS SLAVES:
        RECONCILING SLAVE RESISTANCE WITH THE PROSLAVERY
        DEFENSE."   JOURNAL OF SOUTHERN HISTORY, 46 (NOVEMBER,
        1980):   551-570.

12582   MCCAIN, WILLIAM D.   "THE EMANCIPATION OF INDIANA
        OSBORNE."   JOURNAL OF MISSISSIPPI HISTORY, 8 (APRIL,
        1946):   97-98.

12583   MCINTIRE, CARL.   "SLAVE MADE MARKERS."   JACKSON (MS)
        CLARION LEDGER AND JACKSON DAILY NEWS, MAY 4, 1969.

12584   MCKIBBEN, DAVIDSON B.   "NEGRO SLAVE INSURRECTIONS IN
        MISSISSIPPI, 1800-1865."   JOURNAL OF NEGRO HISTORY, 34
        (JANUARY, 1949):   73-90.

12585   MCMILLAN, LUCY M.   "NATCHEZ, 1763-1779."   M.A. THESIS,
        UNIVERSITY OF VIRGINIA, 1938.

12586   MESSNER, WILLIAM F.   "THE MISSISSIPPI BLACK CODE OF

1865." M.A. THESIS, UNIVERSITY OF WISCONSIN, 1965.

12587 MICKLES, ALEXANDER. LIFE OF ALEXANDER MICKLES, ONE
HUNDRED YEARS OLD: FIFTY-FOUR YEARS A SLAVE; FORTY-SIX
YEARS A FREE MAN: THE OLDEST DARKEY IN MISSISSIPPI.
JACKSON, MS: TUCKER PRINTING HOUSE, 1911.

12588 MILES, EDWIN A. JACKSONIAN DEMOCRACY IN MISSISSIPPI.
CHAPEL HILL: UNIVERSITY OF NORTH CAROLINA PRESS, 1960.

12589 MILES, EDWIN A. "THE MISSISSIPPI SLAVE INSURRECTION
SCARE OF 1835." JOURNAL OF NEGRO HISTORY, 42
(JANUARY, 1957): 48-60.

12590 MOORE, JOHN HEBRON. AGRICULTURE IN ANTE-BELLUM
MISSISSIPPI. NEW YORK: BOOKMAN ASSOCIATES, 1958.

12591 MOORE, JOHN HEBRON. "A LETTER FROM A FUGITIVE SLAVE."
JOURNAL OF MISSISSIPPI HISTORY, 24 (APRIL, 1962):
99-101.

12592 MOORE, JOHN HEBRON. (ED.). "TWO DOCUMENTS RELATING TO
PLANTATION OVERSEERS OF THE VICKSBURG REGION,
1831-1832." JOURNAL OF MISSISSIPPI HISTORY, 16
(JANUARY, 1954): 31-36.

12593 MOSLEY, MRS. CHARLES C. THE NEGRO IN MISSISSIPPI
HISTORY. JACKSON, MS: HEDERMAN BROTHERS, 1950.

12594 MURPHEE, DENNIS. "HURRICANE AND BRIERFIELD: THE DAVIS
PLANTATIONS." JOURNAL OF MISSISSIPPI HISTORY, 9
(APRIL, 1947): 98-107.

12595 NELSON, MARY L. "BENEVOLENT ASPECTS OF THE 'PECULIAR
INSTITUTION' IN MISSISSIPPI." M.A. THESIS,
MISSISSIPPI STATE UNIVERSITY, 1965.

12596 OLSON, CARL I. "THE NEGRO AND CONFEDERATE MORALE." M.A.
THESIS, UNIVERSITY OF MISSISSIPPI, 1951.

12597 OSBORN, GEORGE C. "PLANTATION LIFE IN CENTRAL
MISSISSIPPI AS REVEALED IN THE CLAY SHARKEY PAPERS."
JOURNAL OF MISSISSIPPI HISTORY, 3 (OCTOBER, 1941):
277-288.

12598 OWSLEY, FRANK L. PLAIN FOLK OF THE OLD SOUTH. BATON
ROUGE: LOUISIANA STATE UNIVERSITY PRESS, 1949.

12599 PHILLIPS, ULRICH B. "THE ORIGIN AND GROWTH OF THE
SOUTHERN BLACK BELTS." AMERICAN HISTORICAL REVIEW, 11
(JULY, 1906): 798-816.

12600 PICKETT, ALBERT J. THE HISTORY OF ALABAMA AND
INCIDENTALLY OF GEORGIA AND MISSISSIPPI, FROM THE
EARLIEST PERIOD. ATLANTA: T.J. DOONAN, 1900.

12601 PILLAR, JAMES J. THE CATHOLIC CHURCH IN MISSISSIPPI, 1837-1865. NEW ORLEANS: HAUSER, 1964.

12602 POWDERMAKER, HORTENSE. AFTER FREEDOM: A CULTURAL STUDY IN THE DEEP SOUTH. NEW YORK: VIKING PRESS, 1939.

12603 PYRNELLE, LOUISA-CLARK. DIDDIE, DUMPS, AND TOT; OR, PLANTATION CHILD-LIFE. NEW YORK: HARPER, 1898.

12604 RILEY, FRANKLIN L. (ED.). "DIARY OF A MISSISSIPPI PLANTER, JANUARY 1, 1840, TO APRIL, 1863." PUBLICATIONS OF THE MISSISSIPPI HISTORICAL SOCIETY, 10 (1909): 305-481.

12605 RODABOUGH, JOHN E. "A HISTORY OF NEGROES OF ABERDEEN AND MONROE COUNTY, MISSISSIPPI, 1790-1816." M.A. THESIS, MISSISSIPPI STATE UNIVERSITY, 1964.

12606 ROHRBOUGH, MALCOLM J. THE TRANS-APPALACHIAN FRONTIER: PEOPLE, SOCIETIES, AND INSTITUTIONS, 1775-1850. NEW YORK: OXFORD UNIVERSITY PRESS, 1978.

12607 ROSS, STEVEN J. "FREED SOIL, FREED LABOR, FREED MEN: JOHN EATON AND THE DAVIS BEND EXPERIMENT." JOURNAL OF SOUTHERN HISTORY, 44 (MAY, 1978): 213-232.

12608 ROTHSTEIN, MORTON. "THE CHANGING SOCIAL NETWORKS AND INVESTMENT BEHAVIOR OF A SLAVEHOLDING ELITE IN THE ANTE BELLUM SOUTH: SOME NATCHEZ 'NABOBS,' 1800-1860." IN GREENFIELD, SIDNEY M.; STRICKON, ARNOLD; AND AUBEY, ROBERT T. (EDS.). ENTREPRENEURS IN CULTURAL CONTEXT. ALBUQUERQUE: UNIVERSITY OF NEW MEXICO PRESS, 1979, PP. 65-88.

12609 ROTHSTEIN, MORTON. "THE NATCHEZ NABOBS: KINSHIP AND FRIENDSHIP IN AN ECONOMIC ELITE." IN TREFOUSSE, HANS L. (ED.). TOWARD A NEW VIEW OF AMERICA: ESSAYS IN HONOR OF ARTHUR C. COLE. NEW YORK: BURT FRANKLIN AND COMPANY, 1977, PP. 97-112.

12610 ROWLAND, DUNBAR. HISTORY OF MISSISSIPPI, THE HEART OF THE SOUTH. 2 VOLS. CHICAGO: S.J. CLARKE, 1925.

12611 ROWLAND, DUNBAR. "PLANTATION LIFE IN MISSISSIPPI BEFORE THE WAR." PUBLICATIONS OF THE MISSISSIPPI HISTORICAL SOCIETY, 3 (1900): 85-95.

12612 ROWLAND, THOMAS B. "LEGAL STATUS OF THE NEGRO IN MISSISSIPPI FROM 1832 TO 1860." M.A. THESIS, UNIVERSITY OF WISCONSIN, 1933.

12613 SCARBOROUGH, WILLIAM K. "HEARTLAND OF THE COTTON KINGDOM." IN MCLEMORE, RICHARD A. (ED.). A HISTORY OF MISSISSIPPI. 2 VOLS. HATTIESBURG: UNIVERSITY AND COLLEGE PRESS OF MISSISSIPPI, 1973, VOL. 1, PP.

310-351.

12614 SEAL, A.G. "JOHN CARMICHAEL JENKINS: SCIENTIFIC PLANTER OF THE NATCHEZ DISTRICT." JOURNAL OF MISSISSIPPI HISTORY, 1 (JANUARY, 1939): 14-28.

12615 SEAL, ALBERT G. "JOHN CARMICHAEL JENKINS, SCIENTIFIC PLANTER OF THE NATCHEZ DISTRICT." M.A. THESIS, LOUISIANA STATE UNIVERSITY, 1937.

12616 SEAL, ALBERT G. (ED.). "LETTERS FROM THE SOUTH: A MISSISSIPPIAN'S DEFENSE OF SLAVERY." JOURNAL OF MISSISSIPPI HISTORY, 2 (OCTOBER, 1940): 212-231.

12617 SEWELL, GEORGE A. MISSISSIPPI BLACK HISTORY MAKERS. JACKSON: UNIVERSITY PRESS OF MISSISSIPPI, 1977.

12618 SHEPPERD, GLADYS B. "THE MONTGOMERY SAGA: FROM SLAVERY TO BLACK POWER." UNPUBLISHED MANUSCRIPT, N.D., BENJAMIN MONTGOMERY FAMILY PAPERS, MANUSCRIPT DIVISION, LIBRARY OF CONGRESS.

12619 SMEDES, SUSAN D. MEMORIALS OF A SOUTHERN PLANTER. BALTIMORE: CUSHINGS AND BAILEY, 1887.

12620 SPELL, SUZANNE. "A HISTORY OF JONES COUNTY, MISSISSIPPI." M.A. THESIS, MISSISSIPPI COLLEGE, 1961.

12621 STEPHENSON, WENDELL H. "A QUARTER-CENTURY OF A MISSISSIPPI PLANTATION: ELI J. CAPELL OF 'PLEASANT HILL.'" MISSISSIPPI VALLEY HISTORICAL REVIEW, 23 (DECEMBER, 1936): 355-374

12622 STONE, ALFRED H. "THE EARLY SLAVE LAWS OF MISSISSIPPI." PUBLICATIONS OF THE MISSISSIPPI HISTORICAL SOCIETY, 2 (1899): 133-145.

12623 SWEARINGEN, MACK. "THIRTY YEARS OF A MISSISSIPPI PLANTATION: CHARLES WHITMORE OF 'MONTPELIER.'" JOURNAL OF SOUTHERN HISTORY, 1 (MAY, 1935): 198-211.

12624 SYDNOR, CHARLES S. "THE BIOGRAPHY OF A SLAVE." SOUTH ATLANTIC QUARTERLY, 36 (JANUARY, 1937): 59-73.

12625 SYDNOR, CHARLES S. A GENTLEMAN OF THE OLD NATCHEZ REGION: BENJAMIN L.C. WAILES. DURHAM: DUKE UNIVERSITY PRESS, 1938.

12626 SYDNOR, CHARLES S. "LIFE SPAN OF MISSISSIPPI SLAVES." AMERICAN HISTORICAL REVIEW, 35 (APRIL, 1930): 566-574.

12627 SYDNOR, CHARLES S. SLAVERY IN MISSISSIPPI. NEW YORK: D. APPLETON-CENTURY COMPANY, 1933.

12628 THIGPEN, SAMUEL G. A BOY IN RURAL MISSISSIPPI AND OTHER

STORIES. PICAYUNE, MS: THE AUTHOR, 1966.

12629 THOMPSON, PATRICK H. THE HISTORY OF NEGRO BAPTISTS IN MISSISSIPPI. JACKSON: R.W. BAILEY, 1898.

12630 WARREN, HARRIS G. "AGRICULTURAL STATISTICS OF CLAIBORNE COUNTY, 1850 AND 1860." JOURNAL OF MISSISSIPPI HISTORY, 15 (OCTOBER, 1953): 230-241.

12631 WARREN, HARRIS G. "PEOPLE AND OCCUPATIONS IN PORT GIBSON, 1860." JOURNAL OF MISSISSIPPI HISTORY, 10 (APRIL, 1948): 104-115.

12632 WARREN, HARRIS G. "POPULATION ELEMENTS OF CLAIBORNE COUNTY, 1820-1860." JOURNAL OF MISSISSIPPI HISTORY, 9 (APRIL, 1947): 75-87.

12633 WAYNE, MICHAEL S. "ANTE-BELLUM PLANTERS IN THE POST-BELLUM SOUTH: THE NATCHEZ DISTRICT, 1860-1880." PH.D. DISSERTATION, YALE UNIVERSITY, 1979.

12634 WEAVER, HERBERT. MISSISSIPPI FARMERS, 1850-1860. NASHVILLE: VANDERBILT UNIVERSITY PRESS, 1945.

12635 WHARTON, VERNON L. "THE NEGRO IN MISSISSIPPI, 1865-1890." PH.D. DISSERTATION, UNIVERSITY OF NORTH CAROLINA, 1940.

12636 WHARTON, VERNON L. "SLAVERY AND THE NEGRO IN 1865." THE NEGRO IN MISSISSIPPI, 1865-1890. CHAPEL HILL: UNIVERSITY OF NORTH CAROLINA PRESS, 1947, PP. 9-22.

12637 WHITING, BARTLETT J. "WILLIAM JOHNSON OF NATCHEZ: FREE NEGRO." SOUTHERN FOLKLORE QUARTERLY, 16 (JUNE, 1952): 145-153.

12638 WINGFIELD, C.L. "THE SUGAR PLANTATIONS OF WILLIAM J. MINOR, 1830-1860." M.A. THESIS, LOUISIANA STATE UNIVERSITY, 1950.

12639 WOODS, WILLIAM L. "THE TRAVAIL OF FREEDOM: MISSISSIPPI BLACKS, 1862-1870." PH.D. DISSERTATION, PRINCETON UNIVERSITY, 1979.

12640 WRIGHT, G. FREDERICK. "AN OLD TIME MISSISSIPPI PLANTATION." NATION, 79 (NOVEMBER 3, 1904): 351-352.

NORTH CAROLINA

12641 AFRICA, PHILIP. "SLAVEHOLDING IN THE SALEM COMMUNITY, 1771-1851." NORTH CAROLINA HISTORICAL REVIEW, 54 (SUMMER, 1977): 271-307.

12642 ANDERSON, JEAN. "PAUL CARRINGTON CAMERON AS PLANTER."

CAROLINA COMMENTS, 27 (SEPTEMBER, 1979): 114-120.

12643 ARNETT, ETHEL S. GREENSBORO, NORTH CAROLINA, THE COUNTY SEAT OF GUILFORD. CHAPEL HILL: UNIVERSITY OF NORTH CAROLINA PRESS, 1955.

12644 "AUTOBIOGRAPHY OF OMAR IBN SAID, SLAVE IN NORTH CAROLINA, 1831." AMERICAN HISTORICAL REVIEW, 30 (JULY, 1925): 787-795.

12645 BARFIELD, RODNEY. "NORTH CAROLINA BLACK MATERIAL CULTURE: A RESEARCH OPPORTUNITY." NORTH CAROLINA FOLKLORE JOURNAL, 27 (NOVEMBER, 1979): 61-66.

12646 BARRINGER, PAUL B. THE NATURAL BENT: THE MEMOIRS OF DR. PAUL B. BARRINGER. CHAPEL HILL: UNIVERSITY OF NORTH CAROLINA PRESS, 1949.

12647 BASSETT, JOHN S. ANTI-SLAVERY LEADERS OF NORTH CAROLINA. BALTIMORE: JOHNS HOPKINS PRESS, 1898.

12648 BASSETT, JOHN S. "THE CASE OF THE STATE VS. WILL." HISTORICAL PAPERS PUBLISHED BY THE TRINITY COLLEGE HISTORICAL SOCIETY, 2ND SER., (1898): 12-20.

12649 BASSETT, JOHN S. "NORTH CAROLINA METHODISM AND SLAVERY." HISTORICAL PAPERS PUBLISHED BY THE TRINITY COLLEGE HISTORICAL SOCIETY, 4TH SER., (1900): 1-11.

12650 BASSETT, JOHN S. SLAVERY AND SERVITUDE IN THE COLONY OF NORTH CAROLINA. BALTIMORE: JOHNS HOPKINS PRESS, 1896.

12651 BASSETT, JOHN S. SLAVERY IN THE STATE OF NORTH CAROLINA. BALTIMORE: JOHNS HOPKINS PRESS, 1899.

12652 BASSETT, JOHN S. "SOME PHASES OF EARLY PLANTATION LIFE IN NORTH CAROLINA." TRINITY ARCHIVE, 6 (DECEMBER, 1892): 98-103.

12653 BASTIN, BRUCE. "BLACK MUSIC IN NORTH CAROLINA." IN CROW, JEFFREY J. AND WINTERS, ROBERT E., JR. (EDS.). THE BLACK PRESENCE IN NORTH CAROLINA. RALEIGH: NORTH CAROLINA MUSEUM OF HISTORY, 1978, PP. 41-52.

12654 BASTIN, BRUCE. "BLACK MUSIC IN NORTH CAROLINA." NORTH CAROLINA FOLKLORE JOURNAL, 27 (MAY, 1979): 3-19.

12655 BATTLE, GEORGE G. "THE STATE OF NORTH CAROLINA V. NEGRO WILL, A SLAVE OF JAMES S. BATTLE; A CAUSE-CELEBRE OF ANTE-BELLUM TIMES." VIRGINIA LAW REVIEW, 6 (APRIL, 1920): 515-530.

12656 BATTLE, KEMP P. MEMORIES OF AN OLD-TIME TAR HEEL. CHAPEL HILL: UNIVERSITY OF NORTH CAROLINA PRESS, 1945.

12657   BATTLE, KEMP P.   SKETCH OF THE LIFE AND CHARACTER OF
         WILSON CALDWELL. CHAPEL HILL: UNIVERSITY PRESS
         COMPANY PRINT, 1895.

12658   BELLAMY, DONNIE D.   "SLAVERY IN MICROCOSM: ONSLOW
         COUNTY, NORTH CAROLINA." JOURNAL OF NEGRO HISTORY, 62
         (OCTOBER, 1977): 339-350.

12659   BIVINS, JOHN JR.   THE MORAVIAN POTTERS IN NORTH CAROLINA.
         CHAPEL HILL: UNIVERSITY OF NORTH CAROLINA PRESS, 1972.

12660   BLAND, LINDA A.   "GUILFORD COUNTY QUAKERS AND SLAVERY IN
         NORTH CAROLINA." M.A. THESIS, WAKE FOREST UNIVERSITY,
         1968.

12661   BONNER, JAMES C. (ED.).   "PLANTATION EXPERIENCES OF A NEW
         YORK WOMAN." NORTH CAROLINA HISTORICAL REVIEW, 33
         (JULY, 1956): 384-412.

12662   BOWEN, MICHAEL L.   "SLAVERY AMONG THE BRETHREN."   M.A.
         THESIS, WESTERN CAROLINA UNIVERSITY, 1975.

12663   BOYD, WILLIAM K.   "AD VALOREM SLAVE TAXATION, 1858-1860."
         HISTORICAL PAPERS PUBLISHED BY THE TRINITY COLLEGE
         HISTORICAL SOCIETY, 5TH SER., (1905): 31-38.

12664   BOYD, WILLIAM K.   HISTORY OF NORTH CAROLINA. NEW YORK:
         LEWIS PUBLISHING COMPANY, 1919.

12665   BOYKIN, JAMES H.   THE NEGRO IN NORTH CAROLINA PRIOR TO
         1861: AN HISTORICAL MONOGRAPH. NEW YORK: PAGEANT
         PRESS, 1958.

12666   BOYKIN, JAMES H.   NORTH CAROLINA IN 1861. NEW YORK:
         BOOKMAN ASSOCIATES, 1961.

12667   BRADY, P.S.   "SLAVERY, RACE, AND THE CRIMINAL LAW IN
         ANTEBELLUM NORTH CAROLINA: A RECONSIDERATION OF THE
         THOMAS RUFFIN COURT." NORTH CAROLINA CENTRAL LAW
         JOURNAL, 10 (SPRING, 1979): 248-260.

12668   BRAWLEY, JAMES S.   ROWAN COUNTY: A BRIEF HISTORY.
         RALEIGH: NORTH CAROLINA DEPARTMENT OF CULTURAL
         RESOURCES, 1974.

12669   BREWER, JAMES H.   "AN ACCOUNT OF NEGRO SLAVERY IN THE
         CAPE FEAR REGION PRIOR TO 1860." PH.D. DISSERTATION,
         UNIVERSITY OF PITTSBURGH, 1949.

12670   BREWER, JAMES H.   "LEGISLATION DESIGNED TO CONTROL
         SLAVERY IN WILMINGTON AND FAYETTEVILLE." NORTH
         CAROLINA HISTORICAL REVIEW, 30 (APRIL, 1953): 155-165.

12671   BRINN, SUSAN H.   "BLACKS IN COLONIAL NORTH CAROLINA,
         1660-1723." M.A. THESIS, UNIVERSITY OF NORTH

CAROLINA, 1978.

12672 BROWNING, JAMES B. "THE NORTH CAROLINA BLACK CODE."
       JOURNAL OF NEGRO HISTORY, 15 (OCTOBER, 1930): 461-473.

12673 BUTTS, DONALD C. "A CHALLENGE TO PLANTER RULE: THE
       CONTROVERSY OVER THE AD VALOREM TAXATION OF SLAVES IN
       NORTH CAROLINA: 1858-1862." PH.D. DISSERTATION, DUKE
       UNIVERSITY, 1978.

12674 CALLAHAN, BENJAMIN F. "THE NORTH CAROLINA SLAVE PATROL."
       M.A. THESIS, UNIVERSITY OF NORTH CAROLINA, 1973.

12675 CAPEHART, L.C. REMINISCENCES OF ISAAC AND SUKEY, SLAVES
       OF B.F. MOORE, OF RALEIGH, N.C. RALEIGH: EDWARDS AND
       BROUGHTON PRINTING COMPANY, 1907.

12676 CAPPON, LESTER J. "IRON-MAKING--A FORGOTTEN INDUSTRY OF
       NORTH CAROLINA." NORTH CAROLINA HISTORICAL REVIEW, 9
       (OCTOBER, 1932): 331-348.

12677 CARROLL, WILLIAM. "NAKED GENIUS: THE POETRY OF GEORGE
       MOSES HORTON, SLAVE BARD OF NORTH CAROLINA,
       1797(?)-1883." PH.D. DISSERTATION, UNIVERSITY OF
       NORTH CAROLINA, 1978.

12678 CATHEY, BOYD D. "RACE, REPRESENTATION, AND RELIGION; THE
       NORTH CAROLINA CONSTITUTIONAL CONVENTION OF 1835."
       M.A. THESIS, UNIVERSITY OF VIRGINIA, 1971.

12679 CATHEY, CORNELIUS O. AGRICULTURAL DEVELOPMENTS IN NORTH
       CAROLINA, 1783-1860. CHAPEL HILL: UNIVERSITY OF
       NORTH CAROLINA PRESS, 1956.

12680 CATHEY, CORNELIUS O. "AGRICULTURAL IMPLEMENTS IN NORTH
       CAROLINA, 1783-1865." AGRICULTURAL HISTORY, 25 (JULY,
       1951): 128-135.

12681 CATHEY, CORNELIUS O. "SYDNEY WELLER: ANTE-BELLUM
       PROMOTER OF REFORM." NORTH CAROLINA HISTORICAL
       REVIEW, 31 (JANUARY, 1954): 1-17.

12682 CENSER, JANE T. "PARENTS AND CHILDREN: NORTH CAROLINA
       PLANTER FAMILIES, 1800-1860." PH.D. DISSERTATION,
       JOHNS HOPKINS UNIVERSITY, 1980.

12683 CHESNUTT, CHARLES W. "THE FREE COLORED PEOPLE OF NORTH
       CAROLINA." SOUTHERN WORKMAN, 31 (MARCH, 1902):
       136-141.

12684 CLARK, ERNEST J. "ASPECTS OF THE NORTH CAROLINA SLAVE
       CODE, 1715-1860." NORTH CAROLINA HISTORICAL REVIEW,
       39 (SPRING, 1962): 148-164.

12685 CLARK, ERNEST J., JR. "SLAVE CASES BEFORE THE NORTH

CAROLINA SUPREME COURT, 1818-1858." M.A. THESIS,
UNIVERSITY OF NORTH CAROLINA, 1959.

12686 CLARK, JAMES W., JR. "BURLEY TOBACCO CULTURE: A
NORTHAMPTON SLAVE'S ACCOUNT." NORTH CAROLINA
FOLKLORE, 16 (MAY, 1968): 15-19.

12687 CLIFTON, JAMES M. "GOLDEN GRAINS OF WHITE: RICE
PLANTING ON THE LOWER CAPE FEAR." NORTH CAROLINA
HISTORICAL REVIEW, 50 (OCTOBER, 1973): 365-393.

12688 CLONTS, F.W. "TRAVEL AND TRANSPORTATION IN COLONIAL
NORTH CAROLINA." NORTH CAROLINA HISTORICAL REVIEW, 3
(JANUARY, 1926): 16-35.

12689 CONYNGHAM, DAVID P. SHERMAN'S MARCH THROUGH THE SOUTH.
NEW YORK: SHELDON AND COMPANY, 1865.

12690 CRABTREE, BETH G. AND PATTON, JAMES W. (EDS.). "JOURNAL
OF A SECESH LADY": THE DIARY OF CATHERINE DEVEREUX
EDMONDSTON, 1860-1866. RALEIGH: NORTH CAROLINA
DIVISION OF ARCHIVES AND HISTORY, 1979.

12691 CRAIG, JAMES H. THE ARTS AND CRAFTS IN NORTH CAROLINA,
1699-1840. WINSTON-SALEM: MUSEUM OF EARLY SOUTHERN
DECORATIVE ARTS, 1965.

12692 CROW, JEFFREY J. THE BLACK EXPERIENCE IN REVOLUTIONARY
NORTH CAROLINA. RALEIGH: NORTH CAROLINA DEPARTMENT
OF CULTURAL RESOURCES, 1977.

12693 CROW, JEFFREY J. "SLAVE REBELLIOUSNESS AND SOCIAL
CONFLICT IN NORTH CAROLINA, 1775 TO 1802." WILLIAM
AND MARY QUARTERLY, 3RD SER., 37 (JANUARY, 1980):
79-102.

12694 CROW, JEFFREY J. AND WINTERS, ROBERT E. (EDS.). THE
BLACK PRESENCE IN NORTH CAROLINA. RALEIGH: NORTH
CAROLINA MUSEUM OF HISTORY, 1978.

12695 DABNEY, VIRGINIUS. LIBERALISM IN THE SOUTH. CHAPEL
HILL: UNIVERSITY OF NORTH CAROLINA PRESS, 1932.

12696 DAVIS, ARCHIBALD K. "THE LADY FROM BOSTON."
MASSACHUSETTS HISTORICAL SOCIETY PROCEEDINGS, 91
(1979): 67-85.

12697 DAVIS, J.R. "RECONSTRUCTION IN CLEVELAND COUNTY."
HISTORICAL PAPERS PUBLISHED BY THE TRINITY COLLEGE
HISTORICAL SOCIETY, 10 (1914): 1-170.

12698 DESCHAMPS, MARGARET B. "JOHN CHAVIS AS A PREACHER TO
WHITES." NORTH CAROLINA HISTORICAL REVIEW, 32 (APRIL,
1955): 165-172.

12699 DOWD, JEROME. "REVEREND MOSES HESTER: SKETCH OF A
       QUAINT NEGRO PREACHER IN NORTH CAROLINA." _TRINITY
       ARCHIVE_, 9 (FEBRUARY, 1896): 283-296.

12700 ENNIS, BARBARA S. "THE NEGRO FARM LABORER IN NORTH
       CAROLINA, 1865-1867: FROM SLAVE TO SERVANT OF
       SOCIETY." M.A. THESIS, WAKE FOREST UNIVERSITY, 1966.

12701 ERVIN, EDDIE M. "RUNAWAY SLAVES IN ANTE-BELLUM NORTH
       CAROLINA." M.A. THESIS, NORTH CAROLINA CENTRAL
       UNIVERSITY, 1946.

12702 ERVIN, SAMUEL J. _A COLONIAL HISTORY OF ROWAN COUNTY
       NORTH CAROLINA_. CHAPEL HILL: UNIVERSITY OF NORTH
       CAROLINA PRESS, 1917.

12703 EVANS, W. MCKEE. _BALLOTS AND FENCE RAILS:
       RECONSTRUCTION ON THE LOWER CAPE FEAR_. CHAPEL HILL:
       UNIVERSITY OF NORTH CAROLINA PRESS, 1966.

12704 FARLOW, GALE J. "BLACK CRAFTSMEN IN NORTH CAROLINA
       BEFORE 1850." M.A. THESIS, UNIVERSITY OF NORTH
       CAROLINA, GREENSBORO, 1979.

12705 FARRISON, W. EDWARD. "GEORGE MOSES HORTON: POET FOR
       FREEDOM." _CLA JOURNAL_, 14 (MARCH, 1971): 227-241.

12706 FARRISON, WILLIAM E. "THE NEGRO POPULATION OF GUILFORD
       COUNTY, NORTH CAROLINA, BEFORE THE CIVIL WAR." _NORTH
       CAROLINA HISTORICAL REVIEW_, 21 (OCTOBER, 1944):
       319-329.

12707 FELTS, JOE M. "THE INTERPRETATION OF THE SLAVE CODE BY
       THE NORTH CAROLINA SUPREME COURT." M.A. THESIS,
       WESTERN CAROLINA UNIVERSITY, 1974.

12708 FEREBEE, LONDON R. _BRIEF HISTORY OF THE SLAVE LIFE OF
       REV. L.R. FEREBEE_. RALEIGH: EDWARDS & BROUGHTON,
       1882.

12709 FLEMING, JOHN E. "OUT OF BONDAGE: THE ADJUSTMENT OF
       BURKE COUNTY NEGROES AFTER THE CIVIL WAR, 1865-1890."
       PH.D. DISSERTATION, HOWARD UNIVERSITY, 1974.

12710 FRANKLIN, JOHN H. "THE ENSLAVEMENT OF FREE NEGROES IN
       NORTH CAROLINA." _JOURNAL OF NEGRO HISTORY_, 29
       (OCTOBER, 1944): 401-428.

12711 FRANKLIN, JOHN H. "NEGRO EPISCOPALIANS IN ANTE-BELLUM
       NORTH CAROLINA." _HISTORICAL MAGAZINE OF THE
       PROTESTANT EPISCOPAL CHURCH_, 13 (SEPTEMBER, 1944):
       216-234.

12712 FRANKLIN, JOHN H. "SLAVES VIRTUALLY FREE IN ANTE-BELLUM
       NORTH CAROLINA." _JOURNAL OF NEGRO HISTORY_, 28 (JULY,

1943):   284-310.

12713   FRANKLIN, W. NEIL.   "AGRICULTURE IN COLONIAL NORTH
        CAROLINA."   NORTH CAROLINA HISTORICAL REVIEW, 3
        (OCTOBER, 1926):   539-574.

12714   FRIES, ADELAIDE (ED.).   FORSYTH: THE HISTORY OF A COUNTY
        ON THE MARCH.   CHAPEL HILL: UNIVERSITY OF NORTH
        CAROLINA PRESS, 1976.

12715   GAVINS, RAYMOND.   "BLACK LEADERSHIP IN NORTH CAROLINA TO
        1900."   IN CROW, JEFFREY J. AND WINTERS, ROBERT E.,
        JR. (EDS.).   THE BLACK PRESENCE IN NORTH CAROLINA.
        RALEIGH: NORTH CAROLINA MUSEUM OF HISTORY, 1978, PP.
        1-8.

12716   GEHRKE, WILLIAM H.   "NEGRO SLAVERY AMONG THE GERMANS IN
        NORTH CAROLINA."   NORTH CAROLINA HISTORICAL REVIEW, 14
        (OCTOBER, 1937):   307-324.

12717   GILLESPIE, J. DAVID AND GILLESPIE, JUDI F.   "STRUGGLE FOR
        IDENTITY: THE LIFE OF JORDAN CHAMBERS."   PHYLON, 40
        (SUMMER, 1979):   107-113.

12718   GREEN, FLETCHER M.   "GOLD MINING: A FORGOTTEN INDUSTRY
        OF ANTEBELLUM NORTH CAROLINA."   NORTH CAROLINA
        HISTORICAL REVIEW, 14 (JANUARY, OCTOBER, 1937):   1-19,
        357-366.

12719   GREEN, FLETCHER M.   "SLAVERY IN ORANGE COUNTY."   IN
        LEFLER, HUGH T. AND WAGER, PAUL W. (EDS.).   ORANGE
        COUNTY--1752-1952.   CHAPEL HILL: THE ORANGE
        PRINTSHOP, 1953, PP. 95-106.

12720   GRIFFITH, CYNTHIA A.   "THE ECONOMIC EFFECTS OF THE CIVIL
        WAR AND RECONSTRUCTION ON THIRTY-THREE PLANTERS OF
        CHOWAN COUNTY, NORTH CAROLINA."   M.A. THESIS, WAKE
        FOREST UNIVERSITY, 1972.

12721   HARRELL, ISAAC S.   "GATES COUNTY TO 1860."   HISTORICAL
        PAPERS PUBLISHED BY THE TRINITY COLLEGE HISTORICAL
        SOCIETY, 12 (1916):   56-106.

12722   HIGGINBOTHAM, DON AND PRICE, WILLIAM S., JR.   "WAS IT
        MURDER FOR A WHITE MAN TO KILL A SLAVE? CHIEF JUSTICE
        MARTIN HOWARD CONDEMNS THE PECULIAR INSTITUTION IN
        NORTH CAROLINA."   WILLIAM AND MARY QUARTERLY, 3RD
        SER., 36 (OCTOBER, 1979):   593-601.

12723   HILTY, HIRAM H.   "NORTH CAROLINA QUAKERS AND SLAVERY."
        PH.D. DISSERTATION, DUKE UNIVERSITY, 1969.

12724   HIRSCH, CHARLES B.   "THE EXPERIENCES OF THE S.P.G. IN
        EIGHTEENTH CENTURY NORTH CAROLINA."   PH.D.
        DISSERTATION, INDIANA UNIVERSITY, 1954.

12725 HOLT, BRYCE R. "THE SUPREME COURT OF NORTH CAROLINA AND
       SLAVERY." HISTORICAL PAPERS PUBLISHED BY THE TRINITY
       COLLEGE HISTORICAL SOCIETY, 17TH SER., (1927): 71-99.

12726 HORTON, FRAZIER R. "NEGRO LIFE IN WATAUGA COUNTY." B.A.
       THESIS, AGRICULTURAL AND TECHNICAL COLLEGE OF NORTH
       CAROLINA, 1942.

12727 HURLEY, CHARLES F. "SLAVERY IN ANTE-BELLUM NORTH
       CAROLINA, 1783-1861: A STUDY BASED ON TRAVELERS'
       WRITINGS." M.A. THESIS, NORTH CAROLINA STATE
       UNIVERSITY, 1973.

12728 JACKSON, BLYDEN. "BLACK LITERATURE IN NORTH CAROLINA."
       IN CROW, JEFFREY J. AND WINTERS, ROBERT E. (EDS.).
       THE BLACK PRESENCE IN NORTH CAROLINA. RALEIGH: NORTH
       CAROLINA MUSEUM OF HISTORY, 1978, PP. 25-40.

12729 JACKSON, BLYDEN. "GEORGE MOSES HORTON, NORTH
       CAROLINIAN." NORTH CAROLINA HISTORICAL REVIEW, 53
       (SPRING, 1976): 140-147.

12730 JACKSON, SUSAN. "CURRENT RESEARCH: SOUTHEAST." SOCIETY
       FOR HISTORICAL ARCHAEOLOGY NEWSLETTER, 10 (1977):
       21-24.

12731 JOHNSON, G.G. "SOCIAL CONDITIONS IN NORTH CAROLINA,
       1800-1860." PH.D. DISSERTATION, UNIVERSITY OF NORTH
       CAROLINA, 1927.

12732 JOHNSON, GUION G. ANTE-BELLUM NORTH CAROLINA: A SOCIAL
       HISTORY. CHAPEL HILL: UNIVERSITY OF NORTH CAROLINA
       PRESS, 1937.

12733 KAY, MARVIN L.M. AND CARY, LORIN L. "CLASS, MOBILITY,
       AND CONFLICT IN CAROLINA ON THE EVE OF THE
       REVOLUTION." IN CROW, JEFFREY J. AND TISE, LARRY E.
       (EDS.). THE SOUTHERN EXPERIENCE IN THE AMERICAN
       REVOLUTION. CHAPEL HILL: UNIVERSITY OF NORTH
       CAROLINA PRESS, 1978, PP. 109-151.

12734 KAY, MARVIN L.M. AND CARY, LORIN L. "'THE PLANTERS
       SUFFER LITTLE OR NOTHING': NORTH CAROLINA
       COMPENSATIONS FOR EXECUTED SLAVES, 1748-1772."
       SCIENCE AND SOCIETY, 40 (FALL, 1976): 288-306.

12735 KEYS, LINDA D. "SOME ASPECTS OF SLAVERY IN NORTH
       CAROLINA." M.A. THESIS, NORTH CAROLINA CENTRAL
       UNIVERSITY, 1975.

12736 LATTA, MORGAN L. THE HISTORY OF MY LIFE AND WORK.
       RALEIGH: M.L. LATTA, 1903.

12737 LEAMING, HUGO P. "HIDDEN AMERICANS: MAROONS OF VIRGINIA
       AND THE CAROLINAS." PH.D. DISSERTATION, UNIVERSITY OF

ILLINOIS, CHICAGO CIRCLE, 1979.

12738 LEE, LAWRENCE. THE LOWER CAPE FEAR IN COLONIAL DAYS.
       CHAPEL HILL: UNIVERSITY OF NORTH CAROLINA PRESS, 1965.

12739 LEFLER, HUGH T. AND WAGER, PAUL W. (EDS.). ORANGE
       COUNTY--1752-1952. CHAPEL HILL: THE ORANGE
       PRINTSHOP, 1953.

12740 LINCOLN, C. ERIC. "BLACK RELIGION IN NORTH CAROLINA:
       FROM COLONIAL TIMES TO 1900." IN CROW, JEFFREY J. AND
       WINTERS, ROBERT E., JR. (EDS.). THE BLACK PRESENCE IN
       NORTH CAROLINA. RALEIGH: NORTH CAROLINA MUSEUM OF
       HISTORY, 1978, PP. 9-24.

12741 LITTLE, JOYCE B. "THE CONTROL OF BLACKS IN NORTH
       CAROLINA FROM 1829 TO 1840." M.A. THESIS, NORTH
       CAROLINA CENTRAL UNIVERSITY, 1977.

12742 MALLORY, WILLIAM. OLD PLANTATION DAYS. N.P., 1902.

12743 MATTHEWS, ESSIE C. AUNT PHOEBE, UNCLE TOM AND OTHERS:
       CHARACTER STUDIES AMONG THE OLD SLAVES OF THE SOUTH
       FIFTY YEARS AFTER. COLUMBUS: CHAMPLIN PRESS, 1915.

12744 MCGEACHY, KAHERINE A. "THE NORTH CAROLINA SLAVE CODE."
       M.A. THESIS, UNIVERSITY OF NORTH CAROLINA, 1948.

12745 MCKIEVER, CHARLES F. "SLAVERY AND THE EMIGRATION OF
       NORTH CAROLINA FRIENDS." M.A. THESIS, EAST CAROLINA
       UNIVERSITY, 1962.

12746 MCKIEVER, CHARLES F. SLAVERY AND THE EMIGRATION OF NORTH
       CAROLINA FRIENDS. MURFREESBORO, NC: JOHNSON
       PUBLISHING COMPANY, 1970.

12747 MERRENS, HARRY R. COLONIAL NORTH CAROLINA IN THE
       EIGHTEENTH CENTURY: A STUDY IN HISTORICAL GEOGRAPHY.
       CHAPEL HILL: UNIVERSITY OF NORTH CAROLINA PRESS, 1964

12748 MILLER, RANDALL M. "'IT IS GOOD TO BE RELIGIOUS': A
       LOYAL SLAVE ON GOD, MASTERS, AND THE CIVIL WAR."
       NORTH CAROLINA HISTORICAL REVIEW, 54 (WINTER, 1977):
       66-71.

12749 MODEY, YAO F. "BLACK JUSTICE UNDER WHITE LAW: CRIMINAL
       PROSECUTIONS OF BLACKS IN ANTEBELLUM NORTH CAROLINA."
       M.A. THESIS, WAKE FOREST UNIVERSITY, 1978.

12750 MONTGOMERY, WALTER A. THE DAYS OF OLD AND THE YEARS THAT
       ARE PAST. CHARLOTTESVILLE: PRIVATELY PRINTED, 1939.

12751 MORDECAI, ELLEN. GLEANINGS FROM LONG AGO. SAVANNAH:
       BRAID & HUTTON, 1933.

12752   MORRIS, CHARLES E. "PANIC AND REPRISAL: REACTION IN
         NORTH CAROLINA TO THE NAT TURNER INSURRECTION." M.A.
         THESIS, NORTH CAROLINA STATE UNIVERSITY, 1979.

12753   MORRIS, FRANCIS G. AND MORRIS, PHYLLIS M. "ECONOMIC
         CONDITIONS IN NORTH CAROLINA ABOUT 1780, PART
         II--OWNERSHIP OF TOWN LOTS, SLAVES, AND CATTLE."
         NORTH CAROLINA HISTORICAL REVIEW, 16 (JULY, 1939):
         296-327.

12754   MORROW, DECATUR F. THEN AND NOW: REMINISCENCES AND
         HISTORICAL ROMANCE, 1856-1865. MACON, GA: J.W.
         BURKE, 1926.

12755   MORTON, RICHARD L. (ED.). "A 'YANKEE TEACHER' IN NORTH
         CAROLINA, BY MARGARET NEWBOLD THORPE." NORTH CAROLINA
         HISTORICAL REVIEW, 30 (OCTOBER, 1953): 564-582.

12756   MUTUNHU, TENDAI. "THE NORTH CAROLINA QUAKERS AND
         SLAVERY: THE EMIGRATION AND SETTLEMENT OF THEIR
         FORMER SLAVES IN HAITI." JOURNAL OF
         AFRICAN-AFRO-AMERICAN AFFAIRS, 4 (SPRING, 1980):
         54-67.

12757   NELSON, B.H. "SOME ASPECTS OF NEGRO LIFE IN NORTH
         CAROLINA DURING THE CIVIL WAR." NORTH CAROLINA
         HISTORICAL REVIEW, 25 (APRIL, 1948): 143-166.

12758   NUERMBERGER, RUTH K. THE FREE PRODUCE MOVEMENT: A QUAKER
         PROTEST AGAINST SLAVERY. DURHAM: DUKE UNIVERSITY
         PRESS, 1942.

12759   OPPER, PETER K. "NORTH CAROLINA QUAKERS: RELUCTANT
         SLAVEHOLDERS." NORTH CAROLINA HISTORICAL REVIEW, 52
         (JANUARY, 1975): 37-58.

12760   OPPER, PETER K. "'OLD JANE SEEMS TO BE A COMING TOO'; A
         HISTORY OF THE MIGRATION, EMIGRATION, AND COLONIZATION
         OF THE NORTH CAROLINA NEGRO, 1816-1836." M.A. THESIS,
         UNIVERSITY OF NORTH CAROLINA, 1969.

12761   PADGETT, JAMES A. "FROM SLAVERY TO PROMINENCE IN NORTH
         CAROLINA." JOURNAL OF NEGRO HISTORY, 22 (OCTOBER,
         1937): 433-487.

12762   PADGETT, JAMES A. "THE STATUS OF SLAVES IN COLONIAL
         NORTH CAROLINA." JOURNAL OF NEGRO HISTORY, 14 (JULY,
         1929): 300-327.

12763   PARKER, ALLEN. RECOLLECTIONS OF SLAVERY TIMES.
         WORCESTER, MA: CHARLES W. BURBANK & COMPANY, 1895.

12764   PARKER, FREDDIE L. "SLAVE PROTEST IN NORTH CAROLINA,
         1775-1835." M.A. THESIS, NORTH CAROLINA CENTRAL
         UNIVERSITY, 1976.

12765   PARRAMORE, THOMAS C. "THE 'COUNTY DISTEMPER' IN COLONIAL
        NORTH CAROLINA." NORTH CAROLINA HISTORICAL REVIEW, 48
        (JANUARY, 1971): 44-52.

12766   PHIFER, EDWARD W. "SLAVERY IN MICROCOSM: BURKE COUNTY,
        NORTH CAROLINA." JOURNAL OF SOUTHERN HISTORY, 28
        (MAY, 1962): 137-165.

12767   POE, CLARENCE H. "INDIANS, SLAVES AND TORIES: OUR 18TH
        CENTURY LEGISLATION REGARDING THEM." NORTH CAROLINA
        BOOKLET, 9 (JULY, 1909): 3-15.

12768   POWELL, WILLIAM S. WHEN THE PAST REFUSED TO DIE: A
        HISTORY OF CASWELL COUNTY, NORTH CAROLINA, 1777-1977.
        DURHAM: MOORE PUBLISHING COMPANY, 1977.

12769   PRICE, WILLIAM S., JR. (ED.). NORTH CAROLINA
        HIGHER-COURT MINUTES, 1709-1723. RALEIGH: DEPARTMENT
        OF CULTURAL RESOURCES, DIVISION OF ARCHIVES AND
        HISTORY, 1974.

12770   RAPER, DENNIS L. "THE EFFECTS OF DAVID WALKER'S APPEAL
        AND NAT TURNER'S INSURRECTION ON NORTH CAROLINA."
        M.A. THESIS, UNIVERSITY OF NORTH CAROLINA, 1969.

12771   RIGHTS, DOUGLAS L. THE AMERICAN INDIAN IN NORTH
        CAROLINA. WINSTON-SALEM: J.F. BLAIR, 1957.

12772   RIVERS, ROBERT H. "THE RELATIONSHIP BETWEEN WHITE AND
        NEGRO BAPTISTS IN THE CHURCHES OF NORTH CAROLINA FROM
        1830 TO 1870." M.A. THESIS, DUKE UNIVERSITY, 1971.

12773   ROBERT, JOSEPH C. "THE TOBACCO INDUSTRY IN ANTE-BELLUM
        NORTH CAROLINA." NORTH CAROLINA HISTORICAL REVIEW, 15
        (APRIL, 1938): 119-130.

12774   ROBERT, JOSEPH C. THE TOBACCO KINGDOM: PLANTATION,
        MARKET, AND FACTORY IN VIRGINIA AND NORTH CAROLINA,
        1800-1860. DURHAM: DUKE UNIVERSITY PRESS, 1938.

12775   SADLER, LYNN B. "DR. STEPHEN GRAHAM'S NARRATION OF THE
        'DUPLIN INSURRECTION': ADDITIONAL EVIDENCE OF THE
        IMPACT OF NAT TURNER." JOURNAL OF AMERICAN STUDIES,
        12 (DECEMBER, 1978): 359-367.

12776   SANDERS, CHARLES R. THE CAMERON PLANTATION IN CENTRAL
        NORTH CAROLINA (1776-1973) AND ITS FOUNDER RICHARD
        BENNEHAN. DURHAM: THE AUTHOR, 1974.

12777   SANDROCK, MARGUERITA J. "SLAVEHOLDERS BEFORE AND AFTER
        THE CIVIL WAR: DAVIDSON COUNTY, NORTH CAROLINA,
        1820-1880." M.A. THESIS, UNIVERSITY OF NORTH
        CAROLINA, GREENSBORO, 1979.

12778   SAVAGE, W. SHERMAN. "THE INFLUENCE OF JOHN CHAVIS AND

LUNSFORD LANE ON THE HISTORY OF NORTH CAROLINA."
JOURNAL OF NEGRO HISTORY, 25 (JANUARY, 1940): 14-24.

12779 SAVITT, TODD L. "SLAVE LIFE INSURANCE IN VIRGINIA AND
NORTH CAROLINA." JOURNAL OF SOUTHERN HISTORY, 43
(NOVEMBER, 1977): 583-600.

12780 SCHNEIDER, TRACY W. "THE INSTITUTION OF SLAVERY IN NORTH
CAROLINA, 1860-1865." PH.D. DISSERTATION, DUKE
UNIVERSITY, 1979.

12781 SCHWENINGER, LOREN. "A SLAVE FAMILY IN THE ANTEBELLUM
SOUTH." JOURNAL OF NEGRO HISTORY, 60 (JANUARY, 1975):
29-44.

12782 SHERRILL, P.M. "THE QUAKERS AND THE NORTH CAROLINA
MANUMISSION SOCIETY." HISTORICAL PAPERS PUBLISHED BY
THE TRINITY COLLEGE HISTORICAL SOCIETY, (1914): 32-51.

12783 SHINODA, YASUKO I. "LANDS AND SLAVES IN NORTH CAROLINA
IN 1860." PH.D. DISSERTATION, UNIVERSITY OF NORTH
CAROLINA, 1971.

12784 "SIGNIFICANT WILLS—NORTHAMPTON COUNTY, NORTH CAROLINA."
JOURNAL OF NEGRO HISTORY, 16 (JULY, 1931): 328-337.

12785 SIMPKINS, PATRICK L. "NORTH CAROLINA QUAKERS AND BLACKS:
EDUCATION AND MEMBERSHIP." NEGRO HISTORY BULLETIN, 35
(NOVEMBER, 1972): 160-162.

12786 SINGLETON, WILLIAM H. RECOLLECTIONS OF MY SLAVERY DAYS
BY WILLIAM HENRY SINGLETON. PEEKSKILL, NY: HIGHLAND
DEMOCRAT COMPANY, 1922.

12787 SITTERSON, JOSEPH C. "ECONOMIC SECTIONALISM IN
ANTE-BELLUM NORTH CAROLINA." NORTH CAROLINA
HISTORICAL REVIEW, 16 (APRIL, 1939): 134-146.

12788 "SLAVERY IN THE CAROLINAS (1663-1770)." IN RYWELL,
MARTIN (ED.). AFRO-AMERICAN ENCYCLOPEDIA. 10 VOLS.
NORTH MIAMI: EDUCATIONAL BOOK PUBLISHERS, 1974, VOL.
8, PP. 2445-2447.

12789 SLAVERY IN THE STATES: SELECTED ESSAYS. NEW YORK:
NEGRO UNIVERSITIES PRESS, 1969.

12790 SMITH, ELIZABETH S. "VESUVIUS FURNACE PLANTATION."
HISTORIC PRESERVATION, 28 (APRIL-JUNE, 1976): 24-27.

12791 SONDLEY, FOSTER A. A HISTORY OF BUNCOMBE COUNTY, NORTH
CAROLINA. 2 VOLS. ASHEVILLE: ADVOCATE PRINTING
COMPANY, 1930.

12792 SOWLE, PATRICK. "THE NORTH CAROLINA MANUMISSION SOCIETY,
1816-1834." NORTH CAROLINA HISTORICAL REVIEW, 42

(SPRING, 1965): 47-69.

12793   STANDARD, DIFFEE W. AND GRIFFIN, RICHARD. "THE COTTON
         TEXTILE INDUSTRY IN ANTE-BELLUM NORTH CAROLINA: AN
         ERA OF BOOM AND CONSOLIDATION, 1830-1860." NORTH
         CAROLINA HISTORICAL REVIEW, 34 (APRIL, 1957): 131-164.

12794   STANDARD, DIFFEE W. AND GRIFFIN, RICHARD. "THE COTTON
         TEXTILE INDUSTRY IN ANTE-BELLUM NORTH CAROLINA:
         ORIGIN AND GROWTH TO 1830." NORTH CAROLINA HISTORICAL
         REVIEW, 34 (JANUARY, 1957): 15-35.

12795   SYDNOR, CHARLES S. "A SLAVE OWNER AND HIS OVERSEERS."
         NORTH CAROLINA HISTORICAL REVIEW, 14 (JANUARY, 1937):
         31-38.

12796   TAYLOR, ROSSER H. "HUMANIZING THE SLAVE CODE OF NORTH
         CAROLINA." NORTH CAROLINA HISTORICAL REVIEW, 2 (JULY,
         1925): 323-331.

12797   TAYLOR, ROSSER H. "SLAVE CONSPIRACIES IN NORTH
         CAROLINA." NORTH CAROLINA HISTORICAL REVIEW, 5
         (JANUARY, 1928): 20-34.

12798   TAYLOR, ROSSER H. SLAVEHOLDING IN NORTH CAROLINA: AN
         ECONOMIC VIEW. CHAPEL HILL: UNIVERSITY OF NORTH
         CAROLINA PRESS, 1926.

12799   THORNBURG, OPAL (ED.). "FROM INDIANA TO NORTH CAROLINA:
         THE DIARY OF WILLIAM REES." QUAKER HISTORY, 59
         (AUTUMN, 1970): 67-80.

12800   TODD, WILLIE G. "NORTH CAROLINA BAPTISTS AND SLAVERY."
         NORTH CAROLINA HISTORICAL REVIEW, 24 (APRIL, 1947):
         135-159.

12801   TOMPKINS, D.A. HISTORY OF MECKLENBURG COUNTY AND THE
         CITY OF CHARLOTTE FROM 1740 TO 1903. CHARLOTTE:
         OBSERVER PRINTING HOUSE, 1903.

12802   TURNER, J. KELLY AND BRIDGES, JONATHAN L., JR. HISTORY
         OF EDGECOMBE COUNTY NORTH CAROLINA. RALEIGH: EDWARDS
         AND BROUGHTON PRINTING COMPANY, 1920.

12803   TURNER, JAMES K. "SLAVERY IN EDGECOMBE COUNTY."
         HISTORICAL PAPERS PUBLISHED BY THE TRINITY COLLEGE
         HISTORICAL SOCIETY, 12TH SER., (1916): 5-36.

12804   UZZELL, W.E. "HISTORY OF TOBACCO IN NORTH CAROLINA
         BEFORE THE CIVIL WAR." M.A. THESIS, UNIVERSITY OF
         NORTH CAROLINA, 1929.

12805   VLOCK, LAUREL F. AND LEVITCH, JOEL A. CONTRABAND OF WAR:
         THE STORY OF WILLIAM HENRY SINGLETON: SLAVE AND
         SOLDIER IN THE CIVIL WAR. NEW YORK: FUNK AND

948

WAGNALLS, 1970.

12806 WALKER, JACQUELINE B. "BLACKS IN NORTH CAROLINA DURING
       RECONSTRUCTION." PH.D. DISSERTATION, DUKE UNIVERSITY,
       1979.

12807 WALL, BENNETT H. "EBENEZER PETTIGREW, AN ECONOMIC STUDY
       OF AN ANTE-BELLUM PLANTER." PH.D. DISSERTATION,
       UNIVERSITY OF NORTH CAROLINA, 1947.

12808 WALL, BENNETT H. "THE FOUNDING OF THE PETTIGREW
       PLANTATIONS." NORTH CAROLINA HISTORICAL REVIEW, 27
       (OCTOBER, 1950): 395-418.

12809 WALL, BENNETT H. "MEDICAL CARE OF EBENEZER PETTIGREW'S
       SLAVES." MISSISSIPPI VALLEY HISTORICAL REVIEW, 37
       (DECEMBER, 1950): 451-470.

12810 WALL, JAMES W. DAVIE COUNTY: A BRIEF HISTORY. RALEIGH:
       NORTH CAROLINA DEPARTMENT OF CULTURAL RESOURCES, 1976.

12811 "WAS A SLAVE IN NORTH CAROLINA." BALTIMORE LEDGER, APRIL
       30, 1898.

12812 WATSON, ALAN D. "HOUSEHOLD SIZE AND COMPOSITION IN
       PRE-REVOLUTIONARY NORTH CAROLINA." MISSISSIPPI
       QUARTERLY, 31 (FALL, 1978): 551-569.

12813 WATSON, ALAN D. "IMPULSE TOWARD INDEPENDENCE:
       RESISTANCE AND REBELLION AMONG NORTH CAROLINA SLAVES,
       1750-1755." JOURNAL OF NEGRO HISTORY, 63 (FALL,
       1978): 317-328.

12814 WATSON, ALAN D. "SOCIETY AND ECONOMY IN COLONIAL
       EDGECOMBE COUNTY." NORTH CAROLINA HISTORICAL REVIEW,
       50 (JULY, 1973): 231-255.

12815 WATSON, ALAN D. SOCIETY IN COLONIAL NORTH CAROLINA.
       RALEIGH: NORTH CAROLINA DEPARTMENT OF CULTURAL
       RESOURCES, 1975.

12816 WATTERS, FANNY C. PLANTATION MEMORIES OF THE CAPE FEAR
       RIVER COUNTRY. ASHEVILLE: STEPHENS PRESS, 1944.

12817 WEARN, CORNELLA. "SOCIAL CONDITIONS IN NORTH CAROLINA IN
       THE EIGHTEENTH CENTURY." M.A. THESIS, UNIVERSITY OF
       NORTH CAROLINA, 1926.

12818 WELLMAN, MANLY W. THE COUNTY OF WARREN, NORTH CAROLINA.
       CHAPEL HILL: UNIVERSITY OF NORTH CAROLINA PRESS, 1959.

12819 WILLIAMS, ELIZABETH J. "THE GRAMMAR OF PLANTATION
       OVERSEER'S LETTERS, ROCKINGHAM COUNTY, 1829-1860."
       M.A. THESIS, UNIVERSITY OF NORTH CAROLINA, 1953.

12820   WILLIAMS, ROBERT. CLEAR VIEWS IN 1782, CONCERNING THE
         EFFECTS OF SLAVERY, EXPRESSED BY ROBERT WILLIAMS, OF
         CARTERET COUNTY, NORTH CAROLINA. CINCINNATI:
         WRIGHTSON AND COMPANY, 1867.

12821   WOODSON, CARTER G. FREEDOM AND SLAVERY IN APPALACHIAN
         AMERICA. HUNTINGTON: APPALACHIAN MOVEMENT PRESS,
         1973.

12822   WOODSON, CARTER G. "FREEDOM AND SLAVERY IN APPALACHIAN
         AMERICA." JOURNAL OF NEGRO HISTORY, 1 (APRIL, 1916):
         132-150.

12823   YANUCK, JULIUS. "THOMAS RUFFIN AND NORTH CAROLINA SLAVE
         LAW." JOURNAL OF SOUTHERN HISTORY, 21 (NOVEMBER,
         1955): 456-475.

12824   YONKER, THOMAS W. "THE NEGRO CHURCH IN NORTH CAROLINA,
         1700-1900." M.A. THESIS, DUKE UNIVERSITY, 1955.

SOUTH CAROLINA

12825   ABBOTT, ALBERT. "STONO SLAVE CONSPIRACY." IN ROLLER,
         DAVID C. AND TWYMAN, ROBERT W. (EDS.). THE
         ENCYCLOPEDIA OF SOUTHERN HISTORY. BATON ROUGE:
         LOUISIANA STATE UNIVERSITY PRESS, 1979, P. 1164.

12826   ABBOTT, MARTIN. THE FREEDMEN'S BUREAU IN SOUTH CAROLINA:
         1865-1877. CHAPEL HILL: UNIVERSITY CF NORTH CAROLINA
         PRESS, 1967.

12827   ABBOTT, MARTIN L. "THE FREEDMEN'S BUREAU IN SOUTH
         CAROLINA, 1865-1872." PH.D. DISSERTATION, EMORY
         UNIVERSITY, 1954.

12828   ACKERMAN, ROBERT K. "COLONIAL LAND POLICIES AND THE
         SLAVE PROBLEM." PROCEEDINGS OF THE SOUTH CAROLINA
         HISTORICAL ASSOCIATION, (1965): 28-35.

12829   ACKERMAN, ROBERT K. SOUTH CAROLINA COLONIAL LAND
         POLICIES. COLUMBIA: UNIVERSITY OF SOUTH CAROLINA
         PRESS, 1977.

12830   ADAMS, EDWARD C.L. CONGAREE SKETCHES. SCENES FROM NEGRO
         LIFE IN THE SWAMPS OF THE CONGAREE AND TALES BY TAD
         AND SCIP OF HEAVEN AND HELL WITH OTHER MISCELLANY.
         CHAPEL HILL: UNIVERSITY OF NORTH CAROLINA PRESS, 1927.

12831   ADGER, JOHN B. MY LIFE AND TIMES, 1810-1899. RICHMOND:
         PRESBYTERIAN COMMITTEE OF PUBLICATION, 1899.

12832   ALBANESE, ANTHONY G. "THE PLANTATION AS A SCHOOL: THE
         SEA-ISLANDS OF GEORGIA AND SOUTH CAROLINA, A TEST
         CASE, 1800-1860." ED.D. DISSERTATION, RUTGERS

UNIVERSITY, 1970.

12833 ALBANESE, ANTHONY G. THE PLANTATION SCHOOL. NEW YORK:
       VANTAGE PRESS, 1976.

12834 ALECKSON, SAM. BEFORE THE WAR, AND AFTER THE UNION: AN
       AUTOBIOGRAPHY. BOSTON: GOLD MIND PUBLISHING COMPANY,
       1929.

12835 AMES, MARY. FROM A NEW ENGLAND WOMAN'S DIARY IN DIXIE IN
       1865. NORWOOD, MA: PLIMPTON PRESS, 1906.

12836 APPLEWHITE, JOSEPH D. "SOME ASPECTS OF SOCIETY IN RURAL
       SOUTH CAROLINA IN 1850." NORTH CAROLINA HISTORICAL
       REVIEW, 29 (JANUARY, 1952): 39-63.

12837 APPLEWHITE, JOSEPH D. "SOME ASPECTS OF SOCIETY IN RURAL
       SOUTH CAROLINA, 1850." PH.D. DISSERTATION, VANDERBILT
       UNIVERSITY, 1949.

12838 BALDWIN, CLINTON T. "THE RICE INDUSTRY OF SOUTH
       CAROLINA, PRIMARILY COLONIAL." M.A. THESIS, DUKE
       UNIVERSITY, 1935.

12839 BARNWELL, JOSEPH W. (ED.). "DIARY OF TIMOTHY FORD,
       1785-1786." SOUTH CAROLINA HISTORICAL AND
       GENEALOGICAL MAGAZINE, 13 (APRIL, 1912): 132-147.

12840 BASCOM, WILLIAM R. "ACCULTURATION AMONG THE GULLAH
       NEGROES." AMERICAN ANTHROPOLOGIST, 43 (JANUARY-MARCH,
       1941): 43-50.

12841 BATTALIO, RAYMOND C. AND KAGEL, JOHN. "THE STRUCTURE OF
       ANTEBELLUM SOUTHERN AGRICULTURE: SOUTH CAROLINA, A
       CASE STUDY." AGRICULTURAL HISTORY, 44 (JANUARY,
       1970): 25-38.

12842 BELIN, H.E. "SIDE LIGHTS ON CAROLINA HISTORY." MAGAZINE
       OF AMERICAN HISTORY, (FEBRUARY, MARCH, 1905): 91-96,
       142-149.

12843 BENTLEY, WILLIAM G. "WEALTH DISTRIBUTION IN COLONIAL
       SOUTH CAROLINA." PH.D. DISSERTATION, GEORGIA STATE
       UNIVERSITY, 1977.

12844 BIRNIE, C.W. "THE EDUCATION OF THE NEGRO IN CHARLESTON,
       SOUTH CAROLINA, BEFORE THE CIVIL WAR." JOURNAL OF
       NEGRO HISTORY, 12 (JANUARY, 1927): 13-21.

12845 BLAKE, RUSSELL. "SLAVE RUNAWAYS IN COLONIAL SOUTH
       CAROLINA." UNPUBLISHED PAPER, UNIVERSITY OF MICHIGAN,
       1972.

12846 BLASSINGAME, JOHN W. "BLACK MAJORITY: AN ESSAY-REVIEW."
       GEORGIA HISTORICAL QUARTERLY, 59 (SPRING, 1975):

67-71.

12847   BOLTON, H. CARRINGTON. "DECORATION OF NEGRO GRAVES IN
        SOUTH CAROLINA." JOURNAL OF AMERICAN FOLKLORE, 4
        (JULY-SEPTEMBER, 1891): 214.

12848   BOLTON, S.C. "SOUTH CAROLINA AND THE REVEREND DOCTOR
        FRANCIS LE JAU: SOUTHERN SOCIETY AND THE CONSCIENCE
        OF AN ANGLICAN MISSIONARY." HISTORICAL MAGAZINE OF
        THE PROTESTANT EPISCOPAL CHURCH, 40 (MARCH, 1971):
        63-79.

12849   BOTUME, ELIZABETH H. FIRST DAYS AMONGST THE CONTRABANDS.
        BOSTON: LEE AND SHEPHERD, 1893.

12850   BRADLEY, JOHN L. "SLAVE MANUMISSION IN SOUTH CAROLINA,
        1820-1860." M.A. THESIS, UNIVERSITY OF SOUTH
        CAROLINA, 1964.

12851   BRADY, PATRICK S. "THE SLAVE TRADE AND SECTIONALISM IN
        SOUTH CAROLINA, 1787-1808." JOURNAL OF SOUTHERN
        HISTORY, 38 (NOVEMBER, 1972): 601-620.

12852   BREWER, J. MASON. "HUMOROUS FOLKTALES OF THE SOUTH
        CAROLINA NEGRO." PUBLICATIONS OF THE SOUTH CAROLINA
        FOLKLORE GUILD, NO. 1 (1945): 1-64.

12853   BROWN, PHILIP M. "EARLY INDIAN TRADE IN THE DEVELOPMENT
        OF SOUTH CAROLINA: POLITICS, ECONOMICS, AND SOCIAL
        MOBILITY DURING THE PROPRIETORY PERIOD, 1670-1719."
        SOUTH CAROLINA HISTORICAL MAGAZINE, 76 (JULY, 1975):
        118-128.

12854   BRYAN, LEON S. "SLAVERY ON A PEEDEE RIVER RICE
        PLANTATION, 1825-1865." M.A. THESIS, JOHNS HOPKINS
        UNIVERSITY, 1963.

12855   BULL, ELIAS B. "STORM TOWERS OF THE SANTEE DELTA."
        SOUTH CAROLINA HISTORICAL MAGAZINE, 81 (APRIL, 1980):
        95-101.

12856   BURTON, ORVILLE V. "UNGRATEFUL SERVANTS? EDGEFIELD'S
        BLACK RECONSTRUCTION: PART 1 OF THE TOTAL HISTORY OF
        EDGEFIELD COUNTY, SOUTH CAROLINA." PH.D.
        DISSERTATION, PRINCETON UNIVERSITY, 1976.

12857   CANN, MARVIN L. "WAR IN THE BACKCOUNTRY: THE SIEGE OF
        NINETY SIX, MAY 22-JUNE 19, 1781." SOUTH CAROLINA
        HISTORICAL MAGAZINE, 72 (JANUARY, 1971): 1-14.

12858   CARAWAN, GUY AND CARAWAN, CANDIE. AIN' I YOU GOT A RIGHT
        TO THE TREE OF LIFE? THE PEOPLE OF JOHNS ISLAND,
        SOUTH CAROLINA--THEIR FACES, THEIR WORDS AND THEIR
        SONGS. NEW YORK: SIMON & SCHUSTER, 1966.

12859   CHANNING, STEVEN A. _CRISIS OF FEAR: SECESSION IN SOUTH
        CAROLINA._ NEW YORK: SIMON AND SCHUSTER, 1970.

12860   CHANNING, STEVEN A. "CRISIS OF FEAR; SECESSION IN SOUTH
        CAROLINA, 1859-1860." PH.D. DISSERTATION, UNIVERSITY
        OF NORTH CAROLINA, 1963.

12861   CHAPMAN, ANNE W. "INADEQUACIES OF THE 1848 CHARLESTON
        CENSUS." _SOUTH CAROLINA HISTORICAL MAGAZINE,_ 81
        (JANUARY, 1980): 24-34.

12862   CHARTOCK, LEWIS C. "A HISTORY AND ANALYSIS OF LABOR
        CONTRACTS ADMINISTERED BY THE BUREAU OF REFUGEES,
        FREEDMEN, AND ABANDONED LANDS IN EDGEFIELD, ABBEVILLE
        AND ANDERSON COUNTIES IN SOUTH CAROLINA, 1865-1868."
        PH.D. DISSERTATION, BRYN MAWR COLLEGE, 1974.

12863   CHESTER, ARNOT. "A SOUTH CAROLINA RICE PLANTATION OF 'YE
        OLDEN TIME.'" _SOUTHERN STATES,_ 3 (MAY, 1895):
        106-108.

12864   CHILDS, ARNEY R. _PLANTERS AND BUSINESSMEN: THE GUIGNARD
        FAMILY OF SOUTH CAROLINA._ COLUMBIA: UNIVERSITY OF
        SOUTH CAROLINA PRESS, 1957.

12865   CHILDS, ARNEY R. (ED.). _THE PRIVATE JOURNAL OF HENRY
        WILLIAM RAVENEL, 1859-1887._ COLUMBIA: UNIVERSITY OF
        SOUTH CAROLINA PRESS, 1947.

12866   CHILDS, ARNEY R. (ED.). _RICE PLANTER AND SPORTSMAN: THE
        RECOLLECTIONS OF J. MOTTE ALSTON, 1821-1909._
        COLUMBIA: UNIVERSITY OF SOUTH CAROLINA PRESS, 1953.

12867   CHILDS, ST. JULIEN RAVENEL. "KITCHEN PHYSICK; MEDICAL
        AND SURGICAL CARE OF SLAVES ON AN EIGHTEENTH CENTURY
        RICE PLANTATION." _MISSISSIPPI VALLEY HISTORICAL
        REVIEW,_ 20 (MARCH, 1934): 549-554.

12868   CHILDS, ST. JULIEN RAVENEL. _MALARIA AND COLONIZATION IN
        THE CAROLINA LOW COUNTRY, 1526-1696._ BALTIMORE:
        JOHNS HOPKINS UNIVERSITY, 1940.

12869   CLARKE, ERSKINE. "AN EXPERIMENT IN PATERNALISM:
        PRESBYTERIANS AND SLAVES IN CHARLESTON, SOUTH
        CAROLINA." _JOURNAL OF PRESBYTERIAN HISTORY,_ 53 (FALL,
        1975): 223-238.

12870   CLARKE, ERSKINE. _WRESTLIN' JACOB: A PORTRAIT OF
        RELIGION IN THE OLD SOUTH._ ATLANTA: JOHN KNOX PRESS,
        1979.

12871   CLAY-CLOPTON, VIRGINIA. _A BELLE OF THE FIFTIES._ NEW
        YORK: DOUBLEDAY, PAGE & COMPANY, 1905.

12872   CLIFTON, JAMES M. "THE ANTE-BELLUM RICE PLANTER AS

REVEALED IN THE LETTERBOOK OF CHARLES MANIGAULT, 1846-1848." _SOUTH CAROLINA HISTORICAL MAGAZINE_, 74 (JULY, OCTOBER, 1973): 119-127, 300-310.

12873 CLINKSCALES, JOHN G. _ON THE OLD PLANTATION: REMINISCENCES OF HIS CHILDHOOD_. SPARTANBURG, SC: BAND AND WHITE, 1916.

12874 CLOWSE, CONVERSE D. _ECONOMIC BEGINNINGS IN COLONIAL SOUTH CAROLINA, 1670-1730_. COLUMBIA: UNIVERSITY OF SOUTH CAROLINA PRESS, 1971.

12875 COBB, JIMMY G. "A STUDY OF WHITE PROTESTANTS' ATTITUDES TOWARD NEGROES IN CHARLESTON, SOUTH CAROLINA, 1790-1845." PH.D. DISSERTATION, BAYLOR UNIVERSITY, 1977.

12876 CODY, CHERYLL A. "A NOTE ON CHANGING PATTERNS OF SLAVE FERTILITY IN THE SOUTH CAROLINA RICE DISTRICT, 1735-1865." _SOUTHERN STUDIES_, 16 (WINTER, 1977): 457-462.

12877 COHEN, HENNIG. "LITERARY REFLECTIONS OF SLAVERY FROM THE _SOUTH CAROLINA GAZETTE_." _JOURNAL OF NEGRO HISTORY_, 37 (APRIL, 1952): 188-193.

12878 COIT, MARGARET. _JOHN C. CALHOUN: AMERICAN PORTRAIT_. BOSTON: HOUGHTON MIFFLIN COMPANY, 1950.

12879 COLE, DAVID W. "THE ORGANIZATION AND ADMINISTRATION OF THE SOUTH CAROLINA MILITIA SYSTEM, 1670-1783." PH.D. DISSERTATION, UNIVERSITY OF SOUTH CAROLINA, 1953.

12880 COLEMAN, ANNIE C. "THE NEGRO IN VIRGINIA AND SOUTH CAROLINA, 1861-1877, AS SEEN BY CONTEMPORARY OBSERVERS AND NEWSPAPERS AND BY HISTORIANS." M.A. THESIS, VIRGINIA STATE COLLEGE, 1967.

12881 COLEMAN, MAYBELLE. "POVERTY AND POOR RELIEF IN THE PLANTATION SOCIETY OF SOUTH CAROLINA: A STUDY IN THE SOCIOLOGY OF A SOCIAL PROBLEM." PH.D. DISSERTATION, DUKE UNIVERSITY, 1943.

12882 COMBES, JOHN D. "ETHNOGRAPHY, ARCHAEOLOGY AND BURIAL PRACTICES AMONG COASTAL SOUTH CAROLINA BLACKS." _CONFERENCE ON HISTORIC SITE ARCHAEOLOGY PAPERS_, NO. 7 (1972): 52-61.

12883 COON, DAVID L. "ELIZA LUCAS PINCKNEY AND THE REINTRODUCTION OF INDIGO CULTURE IN SOUTH CAROLINA." _JOURNAL OF SOUTHERN HISTORY_, 42 (FEBRUARY, 1976): 61-76.

12884 COPENHAUSER, J.E. "CULTURE OF INDIGO IN THE PROVINCES OF SOUTH CAROLINA AND GEORGIA." _INDUSTRIAL AND_

ENGINEERING CHEMISTRY, 22 (AUGUST, 1930):   894-896.

12885 CREEL, MARGARET W. "ANTEBELLUM RELIGION AMONG THE
       GULLAHS: A STUDY OF SLAVE CONVERSION AND RELIGIOUS
       CULTURE IN THE SOUTH CAROLINA SEA ISLANDS." PH.D.
       DISSERTATION, UNIVERSITY OF CALIFORNIA, DAVIS, 1980.

12886 CRUM, MASON. GULLAH: NEGRO LIFE IN THE CAROLINA SEA
       ISLANDS. DURHAM: DUKE UNIVERSITY PRESS, 1940.

12887 DAVIDSON, CHALMERS. THE LAST FORAY: THE SOUTH CAROLINA
       PLANTERS OF 1860: A SOCIOLOGICAL STUDY. COLUMBIA:
       UNIVERSITY OF SOUTH CAROLINA PRESS, 1971.

12888 DAVIES, JULIA E. COLONIAL SOUTH CAROLINA. CINCINNATI:
       EBBERT & RICHARDSON COMPANY, 1925.

12889 DAVIS, GERALD L. "AFRO-AMERICAN COIL BASKETRY IN
       CHARLESTON COUNTY, SOUTH CAROLINA: AFFECTIVE
       CHARACTERISTICS OF A ARTISTIC CRAFT IN SOCIAL
       CONTEXT." IN YODER, DON (ED.). AMERICAN FOLKLIFE.
       AUSTIN: UNIVERSITY OF TEXAS PRESS, 1976, PP. 151-184.

12890 DAVIS, HENRY C. "NEGRO FOLK-LORE IN SOUTH CAROLINA."
       JOURNAL OF AMERICAN FOLKLORE, 27 (JULY-SEPTEMBER,
       1914):   241-254.

12891 DAVIS, MARIANNA (ED.). SOUTH CAROLINA'S BLACKS AND
       NATIVE AMERICANS, 1776-1976. COLUMBIA: STATE HUMAN
       AFFAIRS COMMISSION, 1976.

12892 DAVIS, RICHARD B. "THE BALL PAPERS: A PATTERN OF LIFE
       IN THE LOW COUNTRY, 1800-1825." SOUTH CAROLINA
       HISTORICAL MAGAZINE, 65 (JANUARY, 1964): 1-15.

12893 DICKERMAN, G.S. "A GLIMPSE OF CHARLESTON HISTORY."
       SOUTHERN WORKMAN, 36 (JANUARY, 1907): 15-22.

12894 DISMUKES, CAMILLUS J. "INVENTORY OF A PLANTER'S ESTATE."
       SOUTH CAROLINA HISTORICAL MAGAZINE, 73 (JANUARY,
       1972): 37-38.

12895 DOAR, DAVID. RICE AND RICE PLANTING IN THE SOUTH
       CAROLINA LOW COUNTRY. CHARLESTON: CHARLESTON MUSEUM,
       1936.

12896 DOAR, DAVID. A SKETCH OF THE AGRICULTURAL SOCIETY OF ST.
       JAMES, SANTEE, SOUTH CAROLINA; AND AN ADDRESS ON THE
       TRADITIONS AND REMINISCENCES OF THE PARISH, DELIVERED
       BEFORE THE SOCIETY ON THE 4TH OF JULY, 1907.
       CHARLESTON: CALDER-FLADGER COMPANY, 1908.

12897 DODGE, N.S. "A CHARLESTON VENDUE IN 1842." GALAXY, 7
       (JANUARY, 1869): 119-123.

12898   DONNAN, ELIZABETH.   "THE SLAVE TRADE INTO SOUTH CAROLINA
        BEFORE THE REVOLUTION." AMERICAN HISTORICAL REVIEW,
        33 (JULY, 1928): 804-828.

12899   DRUCKER, LESLEY M.   "SPIERS LANDING: A SOCIOECONOMIC
        STUDY OF AN UNDOCUMENTED LATE EIGHTEENTH CENTURY SITE
        IN BERKELEY COUNTY, SOUTH CAROLINA." UNPUBLISHED
        PAPER DELIVERED AT MEETING OF SOCIETY FOR HISTORICAL
        ARCHAEOLOGY, NASHVILLE, TENNESSEE, 1979.

12900   DRUCKER, LESLEY M. AND ANTHONY, RONALD W. THE SPIERS
        LANDING SITE: ARCHAEOLOGICAL INVESTIGATIONS IN
        BERKELEY COUNTY, SOUTH CAROLINA. COLUMBIA: CAROLINA
        ARCHAEOLOGICAL SERVICES, 1979.

12901   DUFFY, JOHN. "EIGHTEENTH-CENTURY CAROLINA HEALTH
        CONDITIONS." JOURNAL OF SOUTHERN HISTORY, 18 (AUGUST,
        1952): 289-302.

12902   DUNCAN, JOHN D. "SERVITUDE AND SLAVERY IN COLONIAL SOUTH
        CAROLINA, 1670-1776." PH.D. DISSERTATION, EMORY
        UNIVERSITY, 1971.

12903   DUNCAN, JOHN D. "SLAVE EMANCIPATION IN COLONIAL SOUTH
        CAROLINA." AMERICAN CHRONICLE, A MAGAZINE OF HISTORY,
        1 (JANUARY, 1972): 64-66.

12904   DUNN, RICHARD S. "THE ENGLISH SUGAR ISLANDS AND THE
        FOUNDING OF SOUTH CAROLINA." SOUTH CAROLINA
        HISTORICAL MAGAZINE, 72 (APRIL, 1971): 81-93.

12905   DURDEN, ROBERT F. "THE ESTABLISHMENT OF CALVARY
        PROTESTANT EPISCOPAL CHURCH FOR NEGROES IN
        CHARLESTON." SOUTH CAROLINA HISTORICAL MAGAZINE, 65
        (JANUARY, 1964): 63-84.

12906   EASTERBY, JAMES H. "THE SOUTH CAROLINA RICE FACTOR AS
        REVEALED IN THE PAPERS OF ROBERT F.W. ALLSTON."
        JOURNAL OF SOUTHERN HISTORY, 7 (MAY, 1941): 160-172.

12907   EASTERBY, JAMES H. THE SOUTH CAROLINA RICE PLANTATION AS
        REVEALED IN THE PAPERS OF ROBERT F.W. ALLSTON.
        CHICAGO: UNIVERSITY OF CHICAGO PRESS, 1945.

12908   EASTERBY, JAMES H. "THE SOUTH CAROLINA RICE PLANTATION
        AS REVEALED IN THE PAPERS OF ROBERT F.W. ALLSTON."
        PH.D. DISSERTATION, UNIVERSITY OF CHICAGO, 1946.

12909   EASTERBY, JAMES H. "SOUTH CAROLINA THROUGH NEW ENGLAND
        EYES." SOUTH CAROLINA HISTORICAL AND GENEALOGICAL
        MAGAZINE, 45 (JULY, 1944): 127-136.

12910   EDGAR, WALTER B. (ED.). THE LETTERBOOK OF ROBERT
        PRINGLE. 2 VOLS. COLUMBIA: UNIVERSITY OF SOUTH
        CAROLINA PRESS, 1972.

12911   EISTERHOLD, JOHN A. "CHARLESTON: LUMBER AND TRADE IN A
         DECLINING SOUTHERN PORT." SOUTH CAROLINA HISTORICAL
         MAGAZINE, 74 (APRIL, 1973): 61-72.

12912   FARLEY, M. FOSTER. "THE FEAR OF NEGRO SLAVE REVOLTS IN
         SOUTH CAROLINA, 1690-1865." AFRO-AMERICAN STUDIES, 3
         (DECEMBER, 1972): 199-207.

12913   FARLEY, M. FOSTER. "A HISTORY OF NEGRO SLAVE REVOLTS IN
         SOUTH CAROLINA." AFRO-AMERICAN STUDIES, 3 (SEPTEMBER,
         1972): 97-102.

12914   FARLEY, M. FOSTER. "THE SOUTH CAROLINA NEGRO DURING THE
         AMERICAN REVOLUTION." AFRO-AMERICAN STUDIES, 3
         (DECEMBER, 1972): 209-215.

12915   FARLEY, M. FOSTER. "THE SOUTH CAROLINA NEGRO IN THE
         AMERICAN REVOLUTION, 1775-1783." SOUTH CAROLINA
         HISTORICAL MAGAZINE, 79 (APRIL, 1978): 75-86.

12916   FAUST, DREW G. "CULTURE, CONFLICT AND COMMUNITY: THE
         MEANING OF POWER ON AN ANTE-BELLUM PLANTATION."
         JOURNAL OF SOCIAL HISTORY, 14 (FALL, 1980): 83-98.

12917   FAUST, DREW G. "THE RHETORIC AND RITUAL OF AGRICULTURE
         IN ANTEBELLUM SOUTH CAROLINA." JOURNAL OF SOUTHERN
         HISTORY, 45 (NOVEMBER, 1979): 541-568.

12918   FERGUSON, LELAND G. "AFRO-AMERICAN SLAVERY AND THE
         'INVISIBLE' ARCHAEOLOGICAL RECORD OF SOUTH CAROLINA."
         UNPUBLISHED PAPER PRESENTED AT THE CONFERENCE ON
         HISTORIC SITE ARCHAEOLOGY, ST. AUGUSTINE, FLORIDA,
         1979.

12919   FICKLING, SUSAN M. "CHRISTIANIZATION OF THE NEGRO IN
         SOUTH CAROLINA, 1830-1860." M.A. THESIS, UNIVERSITY
         OF SOUTH CAROLINA, 1923.

12920   FICKLING, SUSAN M. "SLAVE-CONVERSION IN SOUTH CAROLINA,
         1830-1860." BULLETIN OF THE UNIVERSITY OF SOUTH
         CAROLINA, NO. 146 (SEPTEMBER 1, 1924): 1-59.

12921   FISHBURNE, ANN S. BELVIDERE: A PLANTATION MEMORY.
         COLUMBIA: UNIVERSITY OF SOUTH CAROLINA PRESS, 1949.

12922   FLEMING, JOHN E. "THE STONO RIVER REBELLION AND ITS
         IMPACT ON THE SOUTH CAROLINA SLAVE CODE." NEGRO
         HISTORY BULLETIN, 42 (JULY-AUGUST-SEPTEMBER, 1979):
         66-68.

12923   FREDRICKSON, GEORGE M. "MASTERS AND MUDSILLS: THE ROLE
         OF RACE IN THE PLANTER IDEOLOGY OF SOUTH CAROLINA."
         IN CENSER, JACK R.; STEINERT, N. STEVEN; MCCANDLESS,
         AMY M. (EDS.). SOUTH ATLANTIC URBAN STUDIES, VOLUME
         2. COLUMBIA: UNIVERSITY OF SOUTH CAROLINA PRESS,

1978, PP. 34-48.

12924　FREEHLING, WILLIAM W.　PRELUDE TO CIVIL WAR:　THE
NULLIFICATION CONTROVERSY IN SOUTH CAROLINA,
1816-1836.　NEW YORK:　HARPER & ROW, 1966.

12925　GONZALES, WILLIAM E.　"THE NEGRO SLAVES."　IN CHANDLER,
JULIAN A.C. (ED.).　THE SOUTH IN THE BUILDING OF THE
NATION.　12 VOLS.　RICHMOND:　SOUTHERN HISTORICAL
PUBLICATION SOCIETY, 1909, VOL. 2, PP. 90-91.

12926　GORDON, ASA H.　SKETCHES OF NEGRO LIFE AND HISTORY IN
SOUTH CAROLINA.　HAMMOND, IN:　W.B. CONKEY, 1929.

12927　GORDON, ASA H.　"THE SLAVES' STRUGGLE FOR FREEDOM IN
SOUTH CAROLINA."　M.A. THESIS, COLUMBIA UNIVERSITY,
1932.

12928　GORDON, ROBERT W.　"THE NEGRO SPIRITUAL."　IN SMYTHE,
AUGUSTINE T.　THE CAROLINA LOW-COUNTRY.　NEW YORK:
MACMILLAN, 1931, PP. 191-221.

12929　GREENBERG, KENNETH S.　"REVOLUTIONARY IDEOLOGY AND THE
PROSLAVERY ARGUMENT:　THE ABOLITION OF SLAVERY IN
ANTEBELLUM SOUTH CAROLINA."　JOURNAL OF SOUTHERN
HISTORY, 42 (AUGUST, 1976):　365-384.

12930　GREENE, JACK P.　"'SLAVERY OR INDEPENDENCE':　SOME
REFLECTIONS ON THE RELATIONSHIP AMONG LIBERTY, BLACK
BONDAGE, AND EQUALITY IN REVOLUTIONARY SOUTH
CAROLINA."　SOUTH CAROLINA HISTORICAL MAGAZINE, 80
(JULY, 1979):　193-214.

12931　GRIGGS, GEORGIA.　"THE SOUTH CAROLINA SLAVEHOLDER'S
DEFENSE OF SLAVERY AND OF CERTAIN INSTITUTIONS WITHIN
HIS STATE."　M.A. THESIS, DUKE UNIVERSITY, 1938.

12932　GUTHRIE, PATRICIA.　"CATCHING SENSE:　THE MEANING OF
PLANTATION MEMBERSHIP AMONG BLACKS ON ST. HELENA
ISLAND, SOUTH CAROLINA."　PH.D. DISSERTATION,
UNIVERSITY OF ROCHESTER, 1977.

12933　GUTMAN, HERBERT G.　"FAMILY AND KINSHIP GROUPINGS AMONG
THE ENSLAVED AFRO-AMERICANS ON THE SOUTH CAROLINA GOOD
HOPE PLANTATION:　1760-1860."　IN RUBIN, VERA AND
TUDEN, ARTHUR (EDS.).　COMPARATIVE PERSPECTIVES ON
SLAVERY IN NEW WORLD PLANTATION SOCIETIES.　NEW YORK:
NEW YORK ACADEMY OF SCIENCES, 1977, PP. 242-258.

12934　GWINN, JANE W.　"THE GEORGETOWN SLAVE INSURRECTION OF
1829."　IN JOYNER, CHARLES W. (ED.).　BLACK
CAROLINIANS:　STUDIES IN THE HISTORY OF SOUTH CAROLINA
NEGROES IN THE NINETEENTH CENTURY.　LAURINBURG, NC:
ST. ANDREWS PRESBYTERIAN COLLEGE, 1969, PP. 72-76.

12935   HALL, HENRY L.   "THE CHARLESTON FIRE SCARE OF 1826."   IN
        JOYNER, CHARLES W. (ED.).   BLACK CAROLINIANS: STUDIES
        IN THE HISTORY OF SOUTH CAROLINA NEGROES IN THE
        NINETEENTH CENTURY.   LAURINBURG, NC: ST. ANDREWS
        PRESBYTERIAN COLLEGE, 1969, PP. 88-93.

12936   HAMER, MARGUERITE B.   "A CENTURY BEFORE
        MANUMISSION--SIDELIGHTS ON SLAVERY IN MID-EIGHTEENTH
        CENTURY SOUTH CAROLINA."   NORTH CAROLINA HISTORICAL
        REVIEW, 17 (JULY, 1940):   232-236.

12937   HAMER, PHILIP M.   "BRITISH CONSULS AND THE NEGRO SEAMEN
        ACTS, 1850-1860."   JOURNAL OF SOUTHERN HISTORY, 1
        (MAY, 1935):   138-168.

12938   HAMER, PHILIP M.   "GREAT BRITAIN, THE UNITED STATES, AND
        THE NEGRO SEAMEN ACTS, 1822-1848."   JOURNAL OF
        SOUTHERN HISTORY, 1 (FEBRUARY, 1935):   3-28.

12939   HATCH, TERRY B.   "MEDICAL CARE OF SLAVES."   IN JOYNER,
        CHARLES W. (ED.).   BLACK CAROLINIANS: STUDIES IN THE
        HISTORY OF SOUTH CAROLINA NEGROES IN THE NINETEENTH
        CENTURY.   LAURINBURG, NC: ST. ANDREWS PRESBYTERIAN
        COLLEGE, 1969, PP. 21-23.

12940   HAWKINS, FRANK R.   "LEGISLATION GOVERNING THE INSTITUTION
        OF SLAVERY IN COLONIAL SOUTH CAROLINA."   M.A. THESIS,
        UNIVERSITY OF WISCONSIN, 1968.

12941   HAYDEN, J. CARLETON.   "CONVERSION AND CONTROL: DILEMMA
        OF EPISCOPALIANS IN PROVIDING FOR THE RELIGIOUS
        INSTRUCTION OF SLAVES, CHARLESTON, SOUTH CAROLINA,
        1845-1860."   HISTORICAL MAGAZINE OF THE PROTESTANT
        EPISCOPAL CHURCH, 40 (JUNE, 1971):   143-171.

12942   HEAD, JOSEPH L.   "ATTITUDES TOWARD THE NEGRO IN SOUTH
        CAROLINA, 1670 TO 1822."   M.A. THESIS, UNIVERSITY OF
        GEORGIA, 1970.

12943   HELWIG, ADELAIDE B.   "THE EARLY HISTORY OF BARBADOS AND
        HER INFLUENCE UPON THE EARLY DEVELOPMENT OF SOUTH
        CAROLINA."   PH.D. DISSERTATION, UNIVERSITY OF
        CALIFORNIA, 1931.

12944   HELWIG, ADELAIDE B.   "THE POLITICAL DEVELOPMENT OF THE
        CAROLINA COLONY, 1663-1720."   M.A. THESIS, UNIVERSITY
        OF CALIFORNIA, 1924.

12945   HENDERSON, DALE E.   "METHODIST MISSIONS TO THE PLANTATION
        SLAVES OF THE SOUTH CAROLINA CONFERENCE."   M.A.
        THESIS, OLD DOMINION UNIVERSITY, 1971.

12946   HENDERSON, WILLIAM C.   "THE SLAVE COURT SYSTEM IN
        SPARTANBURG COUNTY."   PROCEEDINGS OF THE SOUTH
        CAROLINA HISTORICAL ASSOCIATION, (1976):   24-38.

12947   HENDERSON, WILLIAM C.   "SPARTAN SLAVES: A DOCUMENTARY
        ACCOUNT OF BLACKS ON TRIAL IN SPARTANBURG, SOUTH
        CAROLINA, 1830 TO 1865." PH.D. DISSERTATION,
        NORTHWESTERN UNIVERSITY, 1978.

12948   HENRY, HOWELL M. THE POLICE CONTROL OF THE SLAVE IN
        SOUTH CAROLINA. EMORY, VA: THE AUTHOR, 1914.

12949   HENRY, HOWELL M. "THE POLICE CONTROL OF THE SLAVE IN
        SOUTH CAROLINA." PH.D. DISSERTATION, VANDERBILT
        UNIVERSITY, 1913.

12950   HEYWARD, DUBOSE. "THE NEGRO IN THE LOW-COUNTRY."   IN
        SMYTHE, AUGUSTINE T. THE CAROLINA LOW-COUNTRY. NEW
        YORK: MACMILLAN, 1931, PP. 171-187.

12951   HEYWARD, DUNCAN C. SEED FROM MADAGASCAR. CHAPEL HILL:
        UNIVERSITY OF NORTH CAROLINA PRESS, 1937.

12952   HIGGINS, W. ROBERT. "CHARLES TOWN MERCHANTS AND FACTORS
        DEALING IN THE EXTERNAL NEGRO TRADE, 1735-1775."
        SOUTH CAROLINA HISTORICAL MAGAZINE, 65 (OCTOBER,
        1964): 205-217.

12953   HIGGINS, W. ROBERT. "CHARLESTON: TERMINUS AND ENTREPOT
        OF THE COLONIAL SLAVE TRADE." IN KILSON, MARTIN L.
        AND ROTBERG, ROBERT I. (EDS.). THE AFRICAN DIASPORA:
        INTERPRETIVE ESSAYS. CAMBRIDGE: HARVARD UNIVERSITY
        PRESS, 1976, PP. 114-131.

12954   HIGGINS, W. ROBERT. "THE GEOGRAPHICAL ORIGINS OF NEGRO
        SLAVES IN COLONIAL SOUTH CAROLINA." SOUTH ATLANTIC
        QUARTERLY, 70 (WINTER, 1971): 34-47.

12955   HIGGINS, W. ROBERT. "THE SOUTH CAROLINA NEGRO DUTY LAW,
        1703-1775." M.A. THESIS, UNIVERSITY OF SOUTH
        CAROLINA, 1967.

12956   HILLIARD, SAM B. "ANTEBELLUM TIDEWATER RICE CULTURE IN
        SOUTH CAROLINA AND GEORGIA." IN GIBSON, JAMES R.
        (ED.). EUROPEAN SETTLEMENT AND DEVELOPMENT IN NORTH
        AMERICA: ESSAYS ON GEOGRAPHICAL CHANGE IN HONOUR AND
        MEMORY OF ANDREW HILL CLARK. BUFFALO: UNIVERSITY OF
        TORONTO PRESS, 1978, PP. 91-115.

12957   HINDUS, MICHAEL S. "BLACK JUSTICE UNDER WHITE LAW:
        CRIMINAL PROSECUTIONS OF BLACKS IN ANTEBELLUM SOUTH
        CAROLINA." JOURNAL OF AMERICAN HISTORY, 63 (DECEMBER,
        1976): 575-599.

12958   HINDUS, MICHAEL S. PRISON AND PLANTATION: CRIME,
        JUSTICE, AND AUTHORITY IN MASSACHUSETTS AND SOUTH
        CAROLINA, 1767-1878. CHAPEL HILL: UNIVERSITY OF
        NORTH CAROLINA PRESS, 1980.

12959   HINDUS, MICHAEL S.   "PRISON AND PLANTATION: CRIMINAL
        JUSTICE IN NINETEENTH-CENTURY MASSACHUSETTS AND SOUTH
        CAROLINA."   PH.D. DISSERTATION, UNIVERSITY OF
        CALIFORNIA, 1975.

12960   HINDUS, MICHAEL S.   "THE SOCIOLOGY OF CRIME AND JUSTICE
        IN SOUTH CAROLINA."   IN JOHNSON, HERBERT A. (ED.).
        SOUTH CAROLINA LEGAL HISTORY.   COLUMBIA: SOUTHERN
        STUDIES PROGRAM, UNIVERSITY OF SOUTH CAROLINA, 1980,
        PP. 155-177.

12961   HOFFMAN, EDWIN D.   "FROM SLAVERY TO SELF-RELIANCE."
        JOURNAL OF NEGRO HISTORY, 41 (JANUARY, 1956):   8-42.

12962   HOLLAND, RUPERT S. (ED.).   LETTERS AND DIARY OF LAURA M.
        TOWNE: WRITTEN FROM THE SEA ISLANDS OF SOUTH CAROLINA,
        1862-1884.   CAMBRIDGE: RIVERSIDE PRESS, 1912.

12963   HOWE, BENNIE W.   "THE FUGITIVE SLAVE PROBLEM IN SOUTH
        CAROLINA AND FLORIDA, 1670-1763:   A CONTRAST IN
        ATTITUDES."   M.A. THESIS, OHIO STATE UNIVERSITY, 1962.

12964   HUFF, ARCHIE V., JR.   LANGDON CHEVES OF SOUTH CAROLINA.
        COLUMBIA: UNIVERSITY OF SOUTH CAROLINA PRESS, 1977.

12965   HUGER, ALFRED.   "THE STORY OF THE LOW-COUNTRY."   IN
        SMYTHE, AUGUSTINE T.   THE CAROLINA LOW-COUNTRY.   NEW
        YORK: MACMILLAN, 1931, PP. 33-122.

12966   HUGHSON, SHIRLEY C.   "CAROLINA SLAVE LAWS."   NEW YORK
        EVENING POST, MARCH 18, 25, APRIL 8, 1893.

12967   HUNEYCUTT, DWIGHT J.   "THE ECONOMICS OF THE INDIGO
        INDUSTRY IN SOUTH CAROLINA."   M.S. THESIS, UNIVERSITY
        OF SOUTH CAROLINA, 1949.

12968   INABINET, L. GLEN.   "'THE JULY FOURTH INCIDENT' OF 1816:
        AN INSURRECTION PLOTTED BY SLAVES IN CAMDEN, SOUTH
        CAROLINA."   IN JOHNSON, HERBERT A. (ED.).   SOUTH
        CAROLINA LEGAL HISTORY.   COLUMBIA: SOUTHERN STUDIES
        PROGRAM, UNIVERSITY OF SOUTH CAROLINA, 1980, PP.
        209-221.

12969   JACKSON, JUANITA; SLAUGHTER, SABRA; AND BLAKE, J. HERMAN.
        "THE SEA ISLANDS AS A CULTURAL RESOURCE."   BLACK
        SCHOLAR, 5 (MARCH, 1974):   32-39.

12970   JACKSON, LUTHER P.   "RELIGIOUS INSTRUCTION OF NEGROES,
        1830 TO 1860, WITH SPECIFIC REFERENCES TO SOUTH
        CAROLINA."   JOURNAL OF NEGRO HISTORY, 15 (JANUARY,
        1930):   72-114.

12971   JACKSON, SUSAN.   "CURRENT RESEARCH: SOUTHEAST."   SOCIETY
        FOR HISTORICAL ARCHAEOLOGY NEWSLETTER, 10 (1977):
        42-45.

12972   JANUARY, ALAN F. "THE FIRST NULLIFICATION: THE NEGRO
         SEAMEN ACTS CONTROVERSY IN SOUTH CAROLINA, 1822-1860."
         PH.D. DISSERTATION, UNIVERSITY OF IOWA, 1976.

12973   JANUARY, ALAN F. "THE SOUTH CAROLINA ASSOCIATION: AN
         AGENCY FOR RACE CONTROL IN ANTEBELLUM CHARLESTON."
         SOUTH CAROLINA HISTORICAL MAGAZINE, 78 (OCTOBER,
         1977): 191-201.

12974   JERVEY, SUSAN R. AND RAVENEL, CHARLOTTE ST. J. TWO
         DIARIES FROM MIDDLE ST. JOHN'S BERKELEY, SOUTH
         CAROLINA, FEBRUARY-MAY, 1865. PINOPOLIS, SC: ST.
         JOHN'S HUNTING CLUB, 1921.

12975   JERVEY, THEODORE D. ROBERT Y. HAYNE AND HIS TIMES. NEW
         YORK: MACMILLAN, 1909.

12976   JOHNSON, C.A. "NEGROES." IN HENNIG, HELEN K. (ED.).
         COLUMBIA: CAPITAL CITY OF SOUTH CAROLINA, 1786-1936.
         COLUMBIA: R.L. BRYAN COMPANY, 1936, 303-314.

12977   JOHNSON, GUION G. A SOCIAL HISTORY OF THE SEA ISLANDS
         WITH SPECIAL REFERENCE TO ST. HELENA ISLAND, SOUTH
         CAROLINA. CHAPEL HILL: UNIVERSITY OF NORTH CAROLINA
         PRESS, 1930.

12978   JOHNSON, GUY B. FOLK CULTURE ON ST. HELENA ISLAND, SOUTH
         CAROLINA. CHAPEL HILL: UNIVERSITY OF NORTH CAROLINA
         PRESS, 1930.

12979   JOHNSON, MICHAEL P. "PLANTERS AND PATRIARCHY:
         CHARLESTON, 1800-1860." JOURNAL OF SOUTHERN HISTORY,
         46 (FEBRUARY, 1980): 45-72.

12980   JORDAN, LAYLON W. "POLICE POWER AND PUBLIC SAFETY IN
         ANTEBELLUM CHARLESTON: THE EMERGENCE OF A NEW POLICE,
         1800-1860." IN CENSER, JACK R.; STEINERT, N. STEVEN;
         AND MCCANDLESS, AMY M. (EDS.). SOUTH ATLANTIC URBAN
         STUDIES, VOLUME 3. COLUMBIA: UNIVERSITY OF SOUTH
         CAROLINA PRESS, 1979, PP. 122-140.

12981   JOYNER, CHARLES W. (ED.). BLACK CAROLINIANS: STUDIES IN
         THE HISTORY OF SOUTH CAROLINA NEGROES. LAURINBURG,
         NC: ST. ANDREWS PRESBYTERIAN COLLEGE, 1969.

12982   JOYNER, CHARLES W. "THE CREOLIZATION OF SLAVE FOLKLIFE:
         ALL-SAINTS PARISH, SOUTH CAROLINA, AS A TEST CASE."
         HISTORICAL REFLECTIONS, 6 (WINTER, 1979): 435-453.

12983   JOYNER, CHARLES W. "SLAVE FOLKLIFE ON THE WACCAMAW NECK:
         ANTEBELLUM BLACK CULTURE IN THE SOUTH CAROLINA
         LOWCOUNTRY." PH.D. DISSERTATION, UNIVERSITY OF
         PENNSYLVANIA, 1977.

12984   KEECH, MICHAEL R. "THE BLACK SEAMEN'S CONTROVERSY,

1822-1823." IN JOYNER, CHARLES W. (ED.). BLACK
CAROLINIANS: STUDIES IN THE HISTORY OF SOUTH CAROLINA
NEGROES IN THE NINETEENTH CENTURY. LAURINBURG, NC:
ST. ANDREWS PRESBYTERIAN COLLEGE, 1969, PP. 94-100.

12985 KILLION, R.G. "REMINISCENCES OF THE 'PECULIAR
INSTITUTION.'" SANDLAPPER, 5 (OCTOBER, 1972): 49-54,
68.

12986 KIMMEL, ROBERT E. "JAMES HENRY HAMMOND: SOUTHERN
PLANTER." M.A. THESIS, MIAMI UNIVERSITY, 1976.

12987 KING, CAROLINE O. (ED.). "JOURNAL OF A VISIT TO
GREENVILLE FROM CHARLESTON IN THE SUMMER OF 1825."
SOUTH CAROLINA HISTORICAL MAGAZINE, 72 (JULY, 1971):
164-173.

12988 KING, JOE M. A HISTORY OF SOUTH CAROLINA BAPTISTS.
COLUMBIA: GENERAL BOARD OF THE SOUTH CAROLINA BAPTIST
CONVENTION, 1964.

12989 KIRKLAND, THOMAS J. AND KENNEDY, ROBERT M. HISTORIC
CAMDEN. 2 VOLS. COLUMBIA, SC: THE STATE COMPANY,
1905-1926.

12990 KLEIN, RACHEL. "THE RISE OF THE PLANTERS IN THE SOUTH
CAROLINA BACKCOUNTRY, 1767-1808." PH.D. DISSERTATION,
YALE UNIVERSITY, 1979.

12991 KLINGBERG, FRANK J. AN APPRAISAL OF THE NEGRO IN
COLONIAL SOUTH CAROLINA: A STUDY IN AMERICANIZATION.
WASHINGTON: ASSOCIATED PUBLISHERS, 1941.

12992 KLINGBERG, FRANK J. CAROLINA CHRONICLE: THE PAPERS OF
COMMISSARY GIDEON JOHNSON, 1707-1716. BERKELEY:
UNIVERSITY OF CALIFORNIA PRESS, 1946.

12993 LACHIOTTE, ALBERTA M. GEORGETOWN RICE PLANTATIONS.
COLUMBIA, SC: THE STATE COMPANY, 1955.

12994 LANDER, ERNEST M. "SLAVE LABOR IN SOUTH CAROLINA COTTON
MILLS." JOURNAL OF NEGRO HISTORY, 38 (APRIL, 1953):
162-173.

12995 LANDER, ERNEST M., JR. "THE DEVELOPMENT OF TEXTILES IN
THE SOUTH CAROLINA PIEDMONT BEFORE 1860." COTTON
HISTORY REVIEW, 1 (1960): 88-100.

12996 LANDER, ERNEST M., JR. "THE IRON INDUSTRY IN ANTE-BELLUM
SOUTH CAROLINA." JOURNAL OF SOUTHERN HISTORY, 20
(AUGUST, 1954): 337-355.

12997 LAWSON, DENNIS T. NO HEIR TO TAKE ITS PLACE: THE STORY
OF RICE IN GEORGETOWN COUNTY, SOUTH CAROLINA.
GEORGETOWN: RICE MUSEUM, 1972.

12998   LEAMING, HUGO P.   "HIDDEN AMERICANS: MAROONS OF VIRGINIA
        AND THE CAROLINAS."   PH.D. DISSERTATION, UNIVERSITY OF
        ILLINOIS, CHICAGO CIRCLE, 1979.

12999   LEE, RUTH A.   "GULLAH ROOTS IN THE SEA ISLANDS."   ENCORE,
        7 (OCTOBER 16, 1978):   38-39.

13000   LIFE OF MAUMER JUNO, OF CHARLESTON, S.C..   ATLANTA:
        FOOTE & DAVIES PRINTERS, 1892.

13001   LITTLEFIELD, DANIEL C.   "PLANTER PREFERENCES: A STUDY OF
        SLAVERY AND THE SLAVE TRADE IN COLONIAL SOUTH
        CAROLINA."   PH.D. DISSERTATION, JOHNS HOPKINS
        UNIVERSITY, 1977.

13002   LJEWALD, KLAUS G.; STARIDA, BEVERLY; AND TAYLOR, PAUL S.
        (EDS.).   "JOHANN MARTIN BOLZIUS ANSWERS A
        QUESTIONNAIRE ON CAROLINA AND GEORGIA."   WILLIAM AND
        MARY QUARTERLY, 3RD SER., 14 (APRIL, 1957):   218-261;
        15 (APRIL, 1958):   228-252.

13003   LOFTON, JOHN.   INSURRECTION IN SOUTH CAROLINA: THE
        TURBULENT WORLD OF DENMARK VESEY.   YELLOW SPRINGS, OH:
        ANTIOCH PRESS, 1964.

13004   LOFTON, JOHN.   "NEGRO INSURRECTIONIST."   ANTIOCH REVIEW,
        18 (SUMMER, 1958):   133-196.

13005   LOFTON, JOHN M.   "SLAVERY IN THE TIME AND LANDS OF
        DENMARK VESEY'S CAPTIVITY."   M.A. THESIS, UNIVERSITY
        OF PITTSBURGH, 1956.

13006   LOFTON, JOHN M., JR.   "DENMARK VESEY'S CALL TO ARMS."
        JOURNAL OF NEGRO HISTORY, 33 (OCTOBER, 1948):   395-417.

13007   LOWERY, IRVING E.   LIFE ON THE OLD PLANTATION IN
        ANTE-BELLUM DAYS; OR, A STORY BASED ON FACTS.
        COLUMBIA, SC: THE STATE COMPANY, 1911.

13008   MACARTHUR, WILLIAM J.   "ANTEBELLUM POLITICS IN AN UP
        COUNTRY COUNTY: NATIONAL, STATE AND LOCAL ISSUES IN
        SPARTANBURG COUNTY, SOUTH CAROLINA, 1850-1860."   M.A.
        THESIS, UNIVERSITY OF SOUTH CAROLINA, 1966.

13009   MALLARD, ANNIE H.   "RELIGIOUS WORK OF SOUTH CAROLINA
        BAPTISTS AMONG THE SLAVES FROM 1781 TO 1830."   M.A.
        THESIS, UNIVERSITY OF SOUTH CAROLINA, 1946.

13010   MARSZALEK, JOHN F., JR.   COURT-MARTIAL: A BLACK MAN IN
        AMERICA.   NEW YORK: CHARLES SCRIBNER'S SONS, 1972.

13011   MARTIN, JOSEPHINE W.   "THE EDUCATIONAL EFFORTS OF THE
        MAJOR FREEDMEN'S AID SOCIETIES AND THE FREEDMEN'S
        BUREAU IN SOUTH CAROLINA: 1862-1870."   PH.D.
        DISSERTATION, UNIVERSITY OF SOUTH CAROLINA, 1971.

13012 MARTIN, THOMAS P. (ED.). "THE ADVENT OF WILLIAM GREGG
       AND THE GRANITEVILLE COMPANY." JOURNAL OF SOUTHERN
       HISTORY, 11 (AUGUST, 1945): 389-423.

13013 MASLOWSKI, PETER. "NATIONAL POLICY TOWARD THE USE OF
       BLACK TROOPS IN THE REVOLUTION." SOUTH CAROLINA
       HISTORICAL MAGAZINE, 73 (JANUARY, 1972): 1-17.

13014 MCCANTS, E.C. "THE BEGINNING OF SLAVERY." SOUTHERN
       MAGAZINE, 2 (1936): 7, 42.

13015 MCCOWEN, GEORGE S., JR. THE BRITISH OCCUPATION OF
       CHARLESTON, 1780-1782. COLUMBIA: UNIVERSITY OF SOUTH
       CAROLINA PRESS, 1972.

13016 MCCRADY, EDWARD. THE HISTORY OF SOUTH CAROLINA UNDER
       PROPRIETARY GOVERNMENT. NEW YORK: MACMILLAN, 1897.

13017 MCCRADY, EDWARD. THE HISTORY OF SOUTH CAROLINA UNDER
       ROYAL GOVERNMENT, 1719-1776. NEW YORK: MACMILLAN,
       1899.

13018 MCCRADY, EDWARD. "SLAVERY IN THE PROVINCE OF SOUTH
       CAROLINA, 1670-1770." ANNUAL REPORT OF THE AMERICAN
       HISTORICAL ASSOCIATION FOR THE YEAR 1895. WASHINGTON:
       GOVERNMENT PRINTING OFFICE, 1896, PP. 631-673.

13019 MCINTOSH, JAMES. "THE FUTURE OF THE NEGRO RACE."
       TRANSACTIONS OF THE SOUTH CAROLINA MEDICAL
       ASSOCIATION, (1891): 133-188.

13020 MCLOUGHLIN, WILLIAM G. AND JORDAN, WINTHROP D. (EDS.).
       "BAPTISTS FACE THE BARBARITIES OF SLAVERY IN 1710."
       JOURNAL OF SOUTHERN HISTORY, 29 (NOVEMBER, 1963):
       495-501.

13021 MELNICK, RALPH. "BILLY SIMONS: THE BLACK JEW OF
       CHARLESTON." AMERICAN JEWISH ARCHIVES, 32 (APRIL,
       1980): 3-8.

13022 MENDENHALL, M.S. "A HISTORY OF AGRICULTURE IN SOUTH
       CAROLINA, 1790 TO 1860: AN ECONOMIC AND SOCIAL
       STUDY." PH.D. DISSERTATION, UNIVERSITY OF NORTH
       CAROLINA, 1940.

13023 MENDENHALL, MARJORIE S. AND RAVENEL, HENRY W. (EDS.).
       "RECOLLECTIONS OF SOUTHERN PLANTATION LIFE." YALE
       REVIEW, N.S., 25 (JUNE, 1936): 748-777.

13024 MERCER, P.M. "TAPPING THE SLAVE NARRATIVE COLLECTION FOR
       THE RESPONSE OF BLACK SOUTH CAROLINIANS TO
       EMANCIPATION AND RECONSTRUCTION." AUSTRALIAN JOURNAL
       OF POLITICS AND HISTORY, 25 (AUGUST, 1979): 358-374.

13025 MERIWETHER, ROBERT L. THE EXPANSION OF SOUTH CAROLINA,

          1729-1765. KINGSPORT, TN: SOUTHERN PUBLISHERS, 1940.

13026 MERRENS, H. ROY. "A VIEW OF COASTAL SOUTH CAROLINA IN
          1778: THE JOURNAL OF EBENEZER HAZARD." SOUTH
          CAROLINA HISTORICAL MAGAZINE, 73 (OCTOBER, 1972):
          177-193.

13027 MIKELL, I. JENKINS. RUMBLING OF THE CHARIOT WHEELS.
          COLUMBIA, SC: THE STATE COMPANY, 1923.

13028 MILLER, RANDALL M. "A BACKCOUNTRY LOYALIST PLAN TO
          RETAKE GEORGIA AND THE CAROLINAS, 1778." SOUTH
          CAROLINA HISTORICAL MAGAZINE, 75 (OCTOBER, 1974):
          207-214.

13029 MOERMAN, DANIEL E. "EXTENDED FAMILY AND POPULAR MEDICINE
          ON ST. HELENA ISLAND, S.C.: ADAPTATIONS TO
          MARGINALITY." PH.D. DISSERTATION, UNIVERSITY OF
          MICHIGAN, 1974.

13030 MOFFATT, FRED T., JR. "JAMES HENRY HAMMOND'S VIEWS ON
          SLAVERY AND SECESSION." M.A. THESIS, UNIVERSITY OF
          KENTUCKY, 1958.

13031 MOFFATT, JOSIAH. "A MERCHANT-PLANTER OF THE OLD SOUTH."
          SOUTH ATLANTIC QUARTERLY, 34 (JANUARY, 1935): 91-104.

13032 MOORE, JANIE G. "AFRICANISMS AMONG BLACKS OF THE SEA
          ISLANDS." JOURNAL OF BLACK STUDIES, 10 (JUNE, 1980):
          467-480.

13033 MOORE, JOHN HAMMOND. "A HYMN OF FREEDOM; SOUTH CAROLINA,
          1813." JOURNAL OF NEGRO HISTORY, 50 (JANUARY, 1965):
          50-53.

13034 MOORE, JOHN HAMMOND. "JARED SPARKS VISITS SOUTH
          CAROLINA." SOUTH CAROLINA HISTORICAL MAGAZINE, 72
          (JULY, 1971): 150-160.

13035 MORGAN, P.D. "AFRO-AMERICAN CULTURAL CHANGE; THE CASE OF
          COLONIAL SOUTH CAROLINA SLAVES." UNPUBLISHED PAPER,
          1979.

13036 MORRISON, CHARLES E. "SLAVERY AND NULLIFICATION IN SOUTH
          CAROLINA." M.A. THESIS, COLUMBIA UNIVERSITY, 1901.

13037 MOSES, JANET S. "THE NEGRO FAMILY IN SLAVERY AND
          FREEDOM." IN JOYNER, CHARLES W. (ED.). BLACK
          CAROLINIANS: STUDIES IN THE HISTORY OF SOUTH CAROLINA
          NEGROES IN THE NINETEENTH CENTURY. LAURINBURG, NC:
          ST. ANDREWS PRESBYTERIAN COLLEGE, 1969, PP. 134-143.

13038 MULLIN, MICHAEL. "BRITISH CARIBBEAN AND NORTH AMERICAN
          SLAVES IN AN ERA OF WAR AND REVOLUTION, 1775-1807."
          IN CROW, JEFFREY J. AND TISE, LARRY E. (EDS.). THE

SOUTHERN EXPERIENCE IN THE AMERICAN REVOLUTION.
CHAPEL HILL: UNIVERSITY OF NORTH CAROLINA PRESS,
1978, PP. 235-267.

13039 NADELHAFT, JEROME J. "SOUTH CAROLINA AND THE SLAVE
       TRADE, 1783-1787." M.A. THESIS, UNIVERSITY OF
       WISCONSIN, 1961.

13040 NASH, A.E. KEIR. "NEGRO RIGHTS, UNIONISM, AND GREATNESS
       ON THE SOUTH CAROLINA COURT OF APPEALS: THE
       EXTRAORDINARY CHIEF JUSTICE JOHN BELTON O'NEALL."
       SOUTH CAROLINA LAW REVIEW, 21 (SPRING, 1969): 141-190.

13041 "NEGROES EXECUTED BY BURNING." SOUTH CAROLINA HISTORICAL
       AND GENEALOGICAL MAGAZINE, 2 (OCTOBER, 1901): 299.

13042 OHLINE, HOWARD A. "GEORGETOWN, SOUTH CAROLINA: RACIAL
       ANXIETIES AND MILITANT BEHAVIOR, 1802." SOUTH
       CAROLINA HISTORICAL MAGAZINE, 73 (JULY, 1972):
       130-140.

13043 OLSBERG, ROBERT N. "A GOVERNMENT OF CLASS AND RACE:
       WILLIAM HENRY TRESCOT AND THE SOUTH CAROLINA CHIVALRY,
       1860-1865." PH.D. DISSERTATION, UNIVERSITY OF SOUTH
       CAROLINA, 1972.

13044 PAYNE, DANIEL A. RECOLLECTIONS OF SEVENTY YEARS.
       NASHVILLE: PUBLISHING HOUSE OF THE A.M.E. SUNDAY
       SCHOOL UNION, 1888.

13045 PEARSON, ELIZABETH W. (ED.). LETTERS FROM PORT ROYAL
       WRITTEN AT THE TIME OF THE CIVIL WAR. BOSTON: W.B.
       CLARKE COMPANY, 1906.

13046 PHILLIPS, ULRICH B. "THE ORIGIN AND GROWTH OF THE
       SOUTHERN BLACK BELTS." AMERICAN HISTORICAL REVIEW, 11
       (JULY, 1906): 798-816.

13047 PHILLIPS, ULRICH B. "THE SLAVE LABOR PROBLEM IN THE
       CHARLESTON DISTRICT." POLITICAL SCIENCE QUARTERLY, 22
       (SEPTEMBER, 1907): 416-439.

13048 PINCKNEY, C.C. FIRE FROM MAGNOLIA. RALEIGH: GRAPHIC
       PRESS, 1952.

13049 PINCKNEY, ELISE (ED.). THE LETTERBOOK OF ELIZA LUCAS
       PINCKNEY, 1739-1762. CHAPEL HILL: UNIVERSITY OF
       NORTH CAROLINA PRESS, 1972.

13050 POPE, THOMAS H. THE HISTORY OF NEWBERRY COUNTY, SOUTH
       CAROLINA: VOLUME ONE, 1749-1860. COLUMBIA:
       UNIVERSITY OF SOUTH CAROLINA PRESS, 1973.

13051 POWELL, VIRGIL S. FROM THE SLAVE CABIN OF YANI.
       HICKSVILLE, NY: EXPOSITION PRESS, 1977.

13052   PRATT-THOMAS, H. RAWLINGS.   "PLANTATION MEDICINE."
        JOURNAL OF THE SOUTH CAROLINA MEDICAL ASSOCIATION, 66
        (MAY, 1970):   152-159.

13053   PRINGLE, ELIZABETH W.   CHRONICLES OF CHICORA WOOD.   NEW
        YORK: CHARLES SCRIBNER'S SONS, 1922.

13054   RADFORD, JOHN P.   "THE CHARLESTON PLANTERS IN 1860."
        SOUTH CAROLINA HISTORICAL MAGAZINE, 77 (OCTOBER,
        1976):   227-235.

13055   RADFORD, JOHN P.   "CULTURE, ECONOMY AND RESIDENTIAL
        STRUCTURE IN CHARLESTON, SOUTH CAROLINA, 1860-1880."
        PH.D. DISSERTATION, CLARK UNIVERSITY, 1974.

13056   RADFORD, JOHN P.   "DELICATE SPACE: RACE AND RESIDENCE IN
        CHARLESTON, SOUTH CAROLINA, 1860-1880."   WEST GEORGIA
        COLLEGE STUDIES IN THE SOCIAL SCIENCES, 16 (JUNE,
        1977):   17-37.

13057   RADFORD, JOHN P.   "RACE, RESIDENCE AND IDEOLOGY:
        CHARLESTON, SOUTH CAROLINA IN THE MID-NINETEENTH
        CENTURY."   JOURNAL OF HISTORICAL GEOGRAPHY, 2
        (OCTOBER, 1976):   329-346.

13058   RAVENEL, HENRY W.   "RECOLLECTIONS OF SOUTHERN PLANTATION
        LIFE."   YALE REVIEW, 25 (JUNE, 1936):   748-777.

13059   RAVENEL, ROSE P.   PIAZZA TALES: A CHARLESTON MEMORY.
        CHARLESTON: SHAFTESBURY, 1952.

13060   RAVITZ, ABE C.   "JOHN PIERPONT AND THE SLAVES'
        CHRISTMAS."   PHYLON, 21 (WINTER, 1960):   383-386.

13061   REED, HARRY A.   "SLAVERY IN ASHANTI AND COLONIAL SOUTH
        CAROLINA."   BLACK WORLD, 20 (FEBRUARY, 1971):   37-40,
        70-74.

13062   REICHLIN, ELINOR.   "FACES OF SLAVERY: A HISTORICAL
        FIND."   AMERICAN HERITAGE, 28 (JUNE, 1977):   4-11.

13063   RHETT, ROBERT G.   CHARLESTON: AN EPIC OF CAROLINA.
        RICHMOND: GARRETT AND MASSIE, 1940.

13064   RICARDS, SHERMAN L. AND BLACKBURN, GEORGE M.   "A
        DEMOGRAPHIC HISTORY OF SLAVERY: GEORGETOWN COUNTY,
        SOUTH CAROLINA, 1850."   SOUTH CAROLINA HISTORICAL
        MAGAZINE, 76 (OCTOBER, 1975):   215-224.

13065   ROBBINS, GERALD.   "THE RECRUITING AND ARMING OF NEGROES
        IN THE SOUTH CAROLINA SEA ISLANDS--1862-1865."   NEGRO
        HISTORY BULLETIN, 28 (APRIL, 1965):   150-151.

13066   ROBBINS, GERALD.   "WILLIAM F. ALLEN: CLASSICAL SCHOLAR
        AMONG THE SLAVES."   HISTORY OF EDUCATION QUARTERLY, 5

(DECEMBER, 1965): 211-223.

13067   ROGERS, GEORGE C. (ED.). THE PAPERS OF HENRY LAURENS. 9
        VOLS. COLUMBIA: UNIVERSITY OF SOUTH CAROLINA PRESS,
        1968-1980.

13068   ROGERS, GEORGE C., JR. CHARLESTON IN THE AGE OF THE
        PINCKNEYS. NORMAN: UNIVERSITY OF OKLAHOMA PRESS,
        1969.

13069   ROGERS, GEORGE C., JR. EVOLUTION OF A FEDERALIST:
        WILLIAM LOUGHTON SMITH OF CHARLESTON (1758-1812).
        COLUMBIA: UNIVERSITY OF SOUTH CAROLINA PRESS, 1962.

13070   ROGERS, GEORGE C., JR. "THE GEORGETOWN RICE PLANTERS ON
        THE EVE OF THE CIVIL WAR." SOUTH CAROLINA HISTORY
        ILLUSTRATED, 1 (1970): 24-33.

13071   ROGERS, GEORGE C., JR. THE HISTORY OF GEORGETOWN COUNTY,
        SOUTH CAROLINA. COLUMBIA: UNIVERSITY OF SOUTH
        CAROLINA PRESS, 1970.

13072   ROGERS, GEORGE C., JR. "SOUTH CAROLINA FEDERALISTS AND
        THE ORIGINS OF THE NULLIFICATION MOVEMENT." SOUTH
        CAROLINA HISTORICAL MAGAZINE, 71 (JANUARY, 1970):
        17-32.

13073   ROLAND, HAROLD. TRICENTENNIAL: ORANGEBURG COUNTY'S
        BLACK HERITAGE. ORANGEBURG, SC: N.P., 1970.

13074   ROPER, JOHN A. "WHITE ON BLACK: WHITE RACISM IN
        NINETEENTH CENTURY SOUTH CAROLINA." IN JOYNER,
        CHARLES W. (ED.). BLACK CAROLINIANS: STUDIES IN THE
        HISTORY OF SOUTH CAROLINA NEGROES. LAURINBURG, NC:
        ST. ANDREWS PRESBYTERIAN COLLEGE, 1969, PP. 125-133.

13075   ROSE, LISLE A. "A COMMUNICATION." WILLIAM AND MARY
        QUARTERLY, 3RD SER., 26 (JANUARY, 1969): 162-164.

13076   ROSE, WILLIE LEE. REHEARSAL FOR RECONSTRUCTION: THE
        PORT ROYAL EXPERIMENT. INDIANAPOLIS: BOBBS-MERRILL,
        1964.

13077   RYAN, FRANK. "TRAVELLERS IN SOUTH CAROLINA IN THE
        EIGHTEENTH CENTURY." M.A. THESIS, UNIVERSITY OF NORTH
        CAROLINA, 1949.

13078   SALLEY, ALEXANDER S. (ED.). THE INTRODUCTION OF RICE
        CULTURE INTO SOUTH CAROLINA. COLUMBIA: HISTORICAL
        COMMISSION OF SOUTH CAROLINA, 1919.

13079   SALLEY, ALEXANDER S. (ED.). NARRATIVES OF EARLY
        CAROLINA, 1650-1708. NEW YORK: C. SCRIBNERS, 1911.

13080   SCHAPER, WILLIAM A. "SECTIONALISM AND REPRESENTATION IN

SOUTH CAROLINA." ANNUAL REPORT OF THE AMERICAN
HISTORICAL ASSOCIATION FOR THE YEAR 1900. 2 VOLS.
WASHINGTON: GOVERNMENT PRINTING OFFICE, 1901, VOL. 1,
PP. 237-463.

13081   SCHREYER, GEORGE M. "METHODIST WORK AMONG THE PLANTATION
        NEGROES IN THE SOUTH CAROLINA CONFERENCE FROM 1829 TO
        1865." B.D. THESIS, DUKE UNIVERSITY, 1939.

13082   SCOTT, EDWIN J. RANDOM RECOLLECTIONS OF A LONG LIFE,
        1806 TO 1876. COLUMBIA, SC: C.A. CALVO, JR.,
        PRINTER, 1884.

13083   "THE SEA ISLANDS." HARPER'S NEW MONTHLY MAGAZINE, 57
        (NOVEMBER, 1878): 839-861.

13084   SELLERS, LEILA. CHARLESTON BUSINESS ON THE EVE OF THE
        AMERICAN REVOLUTION. CHAPEL HILL: UNIVERSITY OF
        NORTH CAROLINA PRESS, 1934.

13085   SENESE, DONALD J. "LEGAL THOUGHT IN SOUTH CAROLINA,
        1800-1860." PH.D. DISSERTATION, UNIVERSITY OF SOUTH
        CAROLINA, 1970.

13086   SHARRER, G. TERRY. "THE INDIGO BONANZA IN SOUTH
        CAROLINA, 1740-1790." TECHNOLOGY AND CULTURE, 12
        (JULY, 1971): 447-455.

13087   SHERWOOD, HENRY N. (ED.). "THE JOURNAL OF MISS SUSAN
        WALKER, MARCH 3RD TO JUNE 6TH, 1862." QUARTERLY
        PUBLICATION OF THE HISTORICAL AND PHILOSOPHICAL
        SOCIETY OF OHIO, 7 (1912): 3-48.

13088   SIRMANS, M. EUGENE. COLONIAL SOUTH CAROLINA: A
        POLITICAL HISTORY, 1663-1763. CHAPEL HILL:
        UNIVERSITY OF NORTH CAROLINA PRESS, 1966.

13089   SIRMANS, M. EUGENE. "THE LEGAL STATUS OF THE SLAVE IN
        SOUTH CAROLINA, 1670-1740." JOURNAL OF SOUTHERN
        HISTORY, 28 (NOVEMBER, 1962): 462-473.

13090   "SLAVERY IN THE CAROLINAS (1663-1770)." IN RYWELL,
        MARTIN (ED.). AFRO-AMERICAN ENCYCLOPEDIA. 10 VOLS.
        NORTH MIAMI: EDUCATIONAL BOOK PUBLISHERS, 1974, VOL.
        8, PP. 2445-2447.

13091   SMITH, ALFRED G. ECONOMIC READJUSTMENT OF AN OLD COTTON
        STATE: SOUTH CAROLINA, 1820-1860. COLUMBIA:
        UNIVERSITY OF SOUTH CAROLINA PRESS, 1958.

13092   SMITH, ALFRED G., JR. "ECONOMIC READJUSTMENT OF AN OLD
        COTTON STATE: SOUTH CAROLINA, 1820-1860." PH.D.
        DISSERTATION, COLUMBIA UNIVERSITY, 1954.

13093   SMITH, ALICE R.H. A CAROLINA RICE PLANTATION OF THE

FIFTIES. NEW YORK: WILLIAM MORROW, 1936.

13094 SMITH, DANIEL E.H.; SMITH, ALICE R.H.; AND CHILDS, ARNEY
       R. (EDS.). MASON SMITH FAMILY LETTERS, 1860-1868.
       COLUMBIA: UNIVERSITY OF SOUTH CAROLINA PRESS, 1950.

13095 SMITH, DORIS W. "TROUBLESOME PROPERTY: FUGITIVES,
       SABOTEURS, AND MALINGERERS." IN JOYNER, CHARLES W.
       (ED.). BLACK CAROLINIANS: STUDIES IN THE HISTORY OF
       SOUTH CAROLINA NEGROES. LAURINBURG, NC: ST. ANDREWS
       PRESBYTERIAN COLLEGE, 1969, PP. 43-49.

13096 SMITH, JOHN DAVID. "MORE THAN SLAVES, LESS THAN
       FREEDMEN: THE 'SHARE WAGES' LABOR SYSTEM DURING
       RECONSTRUCTION." CIVIL WAR HISTORY, 26 (SEPTEMBER,
       1980): 256-266.

13097 SMITH, JOHN DAVID. "NEGLECTED BUT NOT FORGOTTEN: HOWELL
       M. HENRY AND THE 'POLICE CONTROL' OF SLAVES IN SOUTH
       CAROLINA." PROCEEDINGS OF THE SOUTH CAROLINA
       HISTORICAL ASSOCIATION, (1980): 94-110.

13098 SMITH, WARREN B. WHITE SERVITUDE IN COLONIAL SOUTH
       CAROLINA. COLUMBIA: UNIVERSITY OF SOUTH CAROLINA
       PRESS, 1961.

13099 SMITH, WILLIAM R. SOUTH CAROLINA AS A ROYAL PROVINCE,
       1719-1776. NEW YORK: MACMILLAN, 1903.

13100 SNELL, WILLIAM R. "INDIAN SLAVERY IN COLONIAL SOUTH
       CAROLINA, 1671-1795." PH.D. DISSERTATION, UNIVERSITY
       OF ALABAMA, 1972.

13101 STARNES, HUGH N. "THE RICE FIELDS OF SOUTH CAROLINA."
       SOUTHERN BIVOUAC, 2 (1886): 329-342.

13102 STAROBIN, ROBERT S. (ED.). DENMARK VESEY: THE SLAVE
       CONSPIRACY OF 1822. ENGLEWOOD CLIFFS: PRENTICE-HALL,
       1970.

13103 STAROBIN, ROBERT S. "DENMARK VESEY'S SLAVE CONSPIRACY OF
       1822: A STUDY IN REBELLION AND REPRESSION." IN
       BRACEY, JOHN H., JR.; MEIER, AUGUST; AND RUDWICK,
       ELLIOTT (EDS.). AMERICAN SLAVERY: THE QUESTION OF
       RESISTANCE. BELMONT, CA: WADSWORTH PUBLISHING
       COMPANY, 1971, PP. 142-157.

13104 STAVISKY, LEONARD P. "INDUSTRIALISM IN ANTE BELLUM
       CHARLESTON." JOURNAL OF NEGRO HISTORY, 36 (JULY,
       1951): 302-322.

13105 STAVISKY, LEONARD P. "THE NEGRO ARTISAN IN THE SOUTH
       ATLANTIC STATES, 1800-1860: A STUDY OF STATUS AND
       ECONOMIC OPPORTUNITY WITH SPECIAL REFERENCE TO
       CHARLESTON." PH.D. DISSERTATION, COLUMBIA UNIVERSITY,

1958.

13106   STERLING, DOROTHY.   CAPTAIN OF THE PLANTER: THE STORY OF
        ROBERT SMALLS.   GARDEN CITY: DOUBLEDAY AND COMPANY,
        1958.

13107   STEVENSON, MARY (ED.).   THE DIARY OF CLARISSA ADGER
        BOWEN, ASHTABULA PLANTATION, 1865.   PENDLETON, SC:
        FOUNDATION FOR HISTORIC RESTORATION IN PENDLETON AREA,
        1973.

13108   STODDARD, ALBERT H.   "ORIGIN, DIALECT, BELIEFS, AND
        CHARACTERISTICS OF THE NEGROES OF SOUTH CAROLINA AND
        GEORGIA COASTS."   GEORGIA HISTORICAL QUARTERLY, 28
        (SEPTEMBER, 1944):   186-195.

13109   STONE, JAMES H.   "BLACK LEADERSHIP IN THE OLD SOUTH: THE
        SLAVE DRIVERS OF THE RICE KINGDOM."   PH.D.
        DISSERTATION, FLORIDA STATE UNIVERSITY, 1976.

13110   STONEY, SAMUEL G.   PLANTATIONS OF THE CAROLINA LOW
        COUNTRY.   CHARLESTON: CAROLINA ART ASSOCIATION, 1955.

13111   STROUP, RODGER E.   "BEFORE AND AFTER: THREE LETTERS FROM
        E.B. HEYWARD."   SOUTH CAROLINA HISTORICAL MAGAZINE, 74
        (APRIL, 1973):   98-102.

13112   STROYER, JACOB.   SKETCHES OF MY LIFE IN THE SOUTH.
        SALEM, MA: SALEM PRESS, 1379.

13113   "SWAMP RICE NEGROES."   IN ROLLER, DAVID C. AND TWYMAN,
        ROBERT W. (EDS.).   THE ENCYCLOPEDIA OF SOUTHERN
        HISTORY.   BATON ROUGE: LOUISIANA STATE UNIVERSITY
        PRESS, 1979, P. 1171.

13114   TAKAKI, RONALD.   "THE MOVEMENT TO REOPEN THE SLAVE TRADE
        IN SOUTH CAROLINA."   SOUTH CAROLINA HISTORICAL
        MAGAZINE, 66 (JANUARY, 1965):   38-54.

13115   TAYLOR, ALRUTHEUS A.   THE NEGRO IN SOUTH CAROLINA DURING
        THE RECONSTRUCTION.   WASHINGTON: ASSOCIATION FOR THE
        STUDY OF NEGRO LIFE AND HISTORY, 1924.

13116   TAYLOR, ROSSER H.   ANTE-BELLUM SOUTH CAROLINA: A SOCIAL
        AND CULTURAL HISTORY.   CHAPEL HILL: UNIVERSITY OF
        NORTH CAROLINA PRESS, 1342.

13117   "TELLS OF LOW COUNTRY NEGROES."   COLUMBIA (SC) STATE,
        JANUARY 25, 1920.

13118   TERRY, GEORGE D.   "CHAMPAIGN COUNTRY: A SOCIAL HISTORY
        OF AN EIGHTEENTH CENTURY LOWCOUNTRY PARISH--ST.
        JOHN'S, BERKELEY COUNTY, SOUTH CAROLINA."   PH.D.
        DISSERTATION, UNIVERSITY OF SOUTH CAROLINA, 1980.

13119 TERRY, GEORGE D. "SOUTH CAROLINA'S FIRST NEGRO SEAMEN
       ACTS, 1793-1803." PROCEEDINGS OF THE SOUTH CAROLINA
       HISTORICAL ASSOCIATION, (1980): 78-93.

13120 TERRY, GEORGE D. "A STUDY OF THE IMPACT OF THE FRENCH
       REVOLUTION AND THE INSURRECTIONS IN SAINT-DOMINGUE
       UPON SOUTH CAROLINA: 1790-1805." M.A. THESIS,
       UNIVERSITY OF SOUTH CAROLINA, 1975.

13121 TINDALL, GEORGE B. SOUTH CAROLINA NEGROES, 1877-1900.
       COLUMBIA: UNIVERSITY OF SOUTH CAROLINA PRESS, 1952.

13122 TOWNE, LAURA M. LETTERS AND DIARY OF LAURA M. TOWNE
       WRITTEN FROM THE SEA ISLANDS OF SOUTH CAROLINA,
       1862-1884. CAMBRIDGE: PRIVATELY PRINTED, 1912.

13123 TRAYNOR, MARTIN J. "RUNAWAY SLAVES IN COLONIAL AMERICA,
       SOUTH CAROLINA, 1750-1776." M.A. THESIS, ROOSEVELT
       UNIVERSITY, 1970.

13124 TUCKER, ROBERT C. "JAMES H. HAMMOND AS AN
       AGRICULTURIST." FURMAN STUDIES, 34 (WINTER, 1951):
       32-45.

13125 TURNER, LORENZO D. AFRICANISMS IN THE GULLAH DIALECT.
       CHICAGO: UNIVERSITY OF CHICAGO PRESS, 1949.

13126 TURNER, LORENZO D. "PROBLEMS CONFRONTING THE
       INVESTIGATOR OF GULLAH." PUBLICATION OF THE AMERICAN
       DIALECT SOCIETY, NO. 9 (APRIL, 1948): 74-84.

13127 TWINING, MARY A. BIBLIOGRAPHY OF THE SEA ISLANDS.
       ATLANTA: ATLANTA UNIVERSITY CENTER FOR AFRICAN AND
       AFRICAN-AMERICAN STUDIES, 1971.

13128 TWINING, MARY A. "AN EXAMINATION OF AFRICAN RETENTIONS
       IN THE FOLK CULTURE OF THE SOUTH CAROLINA AND GEORGIA
       SEA ISLANDS." PH.D. DISSERTATION, INDIANA UNIVERSITY,
       1977.

13129 TWINING, MARY A. "SOURCES IN THE FOLKLORE AND FOLKLIFE
       OF THE SEA ISLANDS." SOUTHERN FOLKLORE QUARTERLY, 39
       (JUNE, 1975): 135-150.

13130 TYLER, LYON G. "PRISONERS ALL--THE SLAVE AND JAMES LOUIS
       PETIGRU." PROCEEDINGS OF THE SOUTH CAROLINA
       HISTORICAL ASSOCIATION, (1980): 55-72.

13131 "UP THE EDISTO." ATLANTIC MONTHLY, 20 (AUGUST, 1867):
       157-165.

13132 UYA, OKON E. "FROM SERVITUDE TO SERVICE: ROBERT SMALLS,
       1839-1915." PH.D. DISSERTATION, UNIVERSITY OF
       WISCONSIN, 1969.

13133 UYA, OKON E. FROM SLAVERY TO PUBLIC SERVICE: ROBERT
       SMALLS, 1839-1915. NEW YORK: OXFORD UNIVERSITY
       PRESS, 1971.

13134 VAN PELT, W. WELLS. "THE 'HIRING OUT' OF SLAVES IN
       CHARLESTON." IN JOYNER, CHARLES W. (ED.). BLACK
       CAROLINIANS: STUDIES IN THE HISTORY OF SOUTH CAROLINA
       NEGROES. LAURINBURG, NC: ST. ANDREWS PRESBYTERIAN
       COLLEGE, 1969, PP. 29-42.

13135 VER STEEG, CLARENCE L. "SLAVES, SLAVERY, AND THE GENESIS
       OF THE PLANTATION SYSTEM IN SOUTH CAROLINA: AN
       EVOLVING SOCIAL-ECONOMIC MOSAIC." ORIGINS OF A
       SOUTHERN MOSAIC: STUDIES OF EARLY CAROLINA AND
       GEORGIA. ATHENS: UNIVERSITY OF GEORGIA PRESS, 1975,
       PP. 103-132.

13136 VLACH, JOHN M. "PHILLIP SIMMONS: AFRO-AMERICAN
       BLACKSMITH." IN SHAPIRO, LINN (ED.). BLACK PEOPLE
       AND THEIR CULTURE: SELECTED WRITINGS FROM THE AFRICAN
       DIASPORA. WASHINGTON: SMITHSONIAN INSTITUTION, 1976,
       PP. 35-57.

13137 VLACH, JOHN M. "SLAVE POTTERS." CERAMICS MONTHLY, 26
       (SEPTEMBER, 1978): 66-69.

13138 WADE, RICHARD C. "THE VESEY PLOT: A RECONSIDERATION."
       JOURNAL OF SOUTHERN HISTORY, 30 (MAY, 1964): 143-161.

13139 WALKER, JULIET E.K. "'FREE' FRANK AND NEW PHILADELPHIA:
       SLAVE AND FREEDMAN, FRONTIERSMAN AND TOWN FOUNDER."
       PH.D. DISSERTATION, UNIVERSITY OF CHICAGO, 1976.

13140 WALLACE, DAVID D. "SLAVERY, 1790 TO 1860." IN CHANDLER,
       JULIAN A.C. (ED.). THE SOUTH IN THE BUILDING OF THE
       NATION. 12 VOLS. RICHMOND: SOUTHERN HISTORICAL
       PUBLICATION SOCIETY, 1909, VOL. 2, PP. 45-49.

13141 WALLACE, DAVID D. SOUTH CAROLINA: A SHORT HISTORY,
       1520-1948. CHAPEL HILL: UNIVERSITY OF NORTH CAROLINA
       PRESS, 1951.

13142 WALSH, RICHARD. "THE CHARLESTON MECHANICS: A BRIEF
       STUDY, 1760-1776." SOUTH CAROLINA HISTORICAL
       MAGAZINE, 60 (JULY, 1959): 123-144.

13143 WARING, JOSEPH I. (ED.). "CORRESPONDENCE BETWEEN
       ALEXANDER GARDEN, M.D., AND THE ROYAL SOCIETY OF
       ARTS." SOUTH CAROLINA HISTORICAL MAGAZINE, 64
       (JANUARY, APRIL, 1963): 86-94.

13144 WATSON, LARRY D. "THE QUEST FOR ORDER: ENFORCING SLAVE
       CODES IN REVOLUTIONARY SOUTH CAROLINA, 1760-1800."
       PH.D. DISSERTATION, UNIVERSITY OF SOUTH CAROLINA, 1980.

13145   WHITE, HENRY A. "LABOR CONDITIONS IN THE COLONY:
        SLAVERY." IN CHANDLER, JULIAN A.C. (ED.). THE SOUTH
        IN THE BUILDING OF THE NATION. 12 VOLS. RICHMOND:
        SOUTHERN HISTORICAL PUBLICATION SOCIETY, 1909, VOL. 2,
        PP. 23-24.

13146   WHITNEY, EDSON L. "CONSTITUTIONAL, ECONOMIC, AND SOCIAL
        HISTORY OF THE COLONY OF SOUTH CAROLINA." PH.D.
        DISSERTATION, HARVARD UNIVERSITY, 1890.

13147   WHITNEY, EDSON L. GOVERNMENT OF THE COLONY OF SOUTH
        CAROLINA. BALTIMORE: JOHNS HOPKINS UNIVERSITY PRESS,
        1895.

13148   WHITTEN, DAVID O. "ANTEBELLUM SUGAR AND RICE
        PLANTATIONS, LOUISIANA AND SOUTH CAROLINA: A
        PROFITABILITY STUDY." PH.D. DISSERTATION, TULANE
        UNIVERSITY, 1970.

13149   WHITTEN, DAVID O. "MEDICAL CARE OF SLAVES: LOUISIANA
        SUGAR REGION AND SOUTH CAROLINA RICE DISTRICT."
        SOUTHERN STUDIES, 16 (SUMMER, 1977): 153-180.

13150   WHITTEN, DAVID O. "THE MEDICAL CARE OF SLAVES ON SOUTH
        CAROLINA RICE PLANTATIONS." M.A. THESIS, UNIVERSITY
        OF SOUTH CAROLINA, 1963.

13151   "WHO BROUGHT NEGROES TO CHARLESTON AND SOLD THEM AS
        SLAVES?" HISTORICAL MAGAZINE, 2ND SER., 5 (MARCH,
        1869): 209.

13152   WILKS, OSCAR C. "THE SOUTH CAROLINA ATTITUDE TOWARD
        SLAVERY AS REFLECTED IN THE CHARLESTON PRESS
        1820-1845." M.A. THESIS, UNIVERSITY OF TEXAS, 1929.

13153   WILLET, N.L. BEAUFORT COUNTY, SOUTH CAROLINA, THE
        SHRINES, EARLY HISTORY AND TOPOGRAPHY. N.P.:
        CHARLESTON AND WESTERN CAROLINA RAILWAY COMPANY, 1929.

13154   WILLIAMS, EDWARD W. A HISTORY OF THE COLORED PEOPLE OF
        SOUTH CAROLINA WITH AN ACCOUNT OF THE ORIGIN AND
        PROGRESS OF THE COLORED RACE, AND HUMAN SLAVERY.
        PHILADELPHIA: HARPER AND BROTHER, 1882.

13155   WILLIAMS, JACK K. "CRIME AND PUNISHMENT IN SOUTH
        CAROLINA, 1790-1860." PH.D. DISSERTATION, EMORY
        UNIVERSITY, 1953.

3156   WILLIAMS, JACK K. VOGUES IN VILLAINY: CRIME AND
        RETRIBUTION IN ANTEBELLUM SOUTH CAROLINA. COLUMBIA:
        UNIVERSITY OF SOUTH CAROLINA PRESS, 1959.

3157   WILLIAMS, JOHN G. "DE OLE PLANTATION." CHARLESTON:
        WALKER, EVANS, AND COGSWELL COMPANY, 1895.

975

13158   WILLIAMSON, JOEL. AFTER SLAVERY: THE NEGRO IN SOUTH
         CAROLINA DURING RECONSTRUCTION, 1861-1877. CHAPEL
         HILL: UNIVERSITY OF NORTH CAROLINA PRESS, 1965.

13159   WILLIAMSON, JOEL R. "THE NEGRO IN SOUTH CAROLINA DURING
         RECONSTRUCTION, 1861-1877." PH.D. DISSERTATION,
         UNIVERSITY OF CALIFORNIA, 1964.

13160   WILLIS, WILLIAM S. "DIVIDE AND RULE: RED, WHITE, AND
         BLACK IN THE SOUTHEAST." JOURNAL OF NEGRO HISTORY, 48
         (JULY, 1963): 157-176.

13161   WILSON, MIRIAM B. SLAVE DAYS, CONDENSED FROM FACTUAL
         INFORMATION GATHERED BY MIRIAM BELLANGEE WILSON.
         CHARLESTON: OLD SLAVE MART FOUNDATION, 1946.

13162   WILSON, ROBERT. "AT THE OLD PLANTATION." LIPPINCOTT'S
         MAGAZINE, 17 (JANUARY, 1876): 113-124.

13163   WINDLEY, LATHAN A. "A PROFILE OF RUNAWAY SLAVES IN
         VIRGINIA AND SOUTH CAROLINA FROM 1730 THROUGH 1787."
         PH.D. DISSERTATION, UNIVERSITY OF IOWA, 1974.

13164   WINSLOW, DAVID J. "A NEGRO CORN-SHUCKING." JOURNAL OF
         AMERICAN FOLKLORE, 86 (JANUARY-MARCH, 1973): 61-62.

13165   WOOD, PETER H. BLACK MAJORITY: NEGROES IN COLONIAL
         SOUTH CAROLINA, 1670 TO THE STONO REBELLION. NEW
         YORK: ALFRED A. KNOPF, 1974.

13166   WOOD, PETER H. "BLACK MAJORITY: NEGROES IN COLONIAL
         SOUTH CAROLINA FROM 1670 THROUGH THE STONO REBELLION."
         PH.D. DISSERTATION, HARVARD UNIVERSITY, 1972.

13167   WOOD, PETER H. "'IT WAS A NEGRO TAUGHT THEM', A NEW LOOK
         AT AFRICAN LABOR IN EARLY SOUTH CAROLINA." JOURNAL OF
         ASIAN AND AFRICAN STUDIES, 9 (JULY/OCTOBER, 1974):
         160-179.

13168   WOOD, PETER H. "'MORE LIKE A NEGRO COUNTRY':
         DEMOGRAPHIC PATTERNS IN COLONIAL SOUTH CAROLINA,
         1700-1740." IN ENGERMAN, STANLEY L. AND GENOVESE,
         EUGENE D. (EDS.). RACE AND SLAVERY IN THE WESTERN
         HEMISPHERE: QUANTITATIVE STUDIES. PRINCETON:
         PRINCETON UNIVERSITY PRESS, 1975, PP. 131-172.

13169   WOOD, PETER H. "'TAKING CARE OF BUSINESS' IN
         REVOLUTIONARY SOUTH CAROLINA: REPUBLICANISM AND THE
         SLAVE SOCIETY." IN CENSER, JACK R.; STEINERT, N.
         STEVEN; AND MCCANDLESS, AMY M. (EDS.). SOUTH ATLANTIC
         URBAN STUDIES, VOLUME 2. COLUMBIA: UNIVERSITY OF
         SOUTH CAROLINA PRESS, 1978, PP. 49-72.

13170   WOOD, PETER H. "'TAKING CARE OF BUSINESS' IN
         REVOLUTIONARY SOUTH CAROLINA: REPUBLICANISM AND THE

SLAVE SOCIETY." IN CROW, JEFFREY J. AND TISE, LARRY
E. (EDS.). *THE SOUTHERN EXPERIENCE IN THE AMERICAN
REVOLUTION.* CHAPEL HILL: UNIVERSITY OF NORTH
CAROLINA PRESS, 1978, PP. 268-294.

13171 WOOFTER, JAMES J., JR. *BLACK YEOMANRY: LIFE ON ST.
HELENA ISLAND.* NEW YORK: HENRY HOLT AND COMPANY,
1930.

13172 ZORNOW, DAVID M. "A TROUBLESOME COMMUNITY: BLACKS IN
REVOLUTIONARY CHARLES TOWN, 1765-1775." B.A. THESIS,
HARVARD UNIVERSITY, 1976.

TENNESSEE

13173 ABERNETHY, THOMAS P. *FROM FRONTIER TO PLANTATION IN
TENNESSEE: A STUDY IN FRONTIER DEMOCRACY.* CHAPEL
HILL: UNIVERSITY OF NORTH CAROLINA PRESS, 1932.

13174 ADAIR, THOMAS J. "BISHOP ISAAC LANE: A PORTRAIT,
1834-1914." M.S. THESIS, TENNESSEE A&I STATE
UNIVERSITY, 1956.

13175 ALDERSON, WILLIAM T. (ED.). "THE CIVIL WAR REMINISCENCES
OF JOHN JOHNSON, 1861-1866." *TENNESSEE HISTORICAL
QUARTERLY,* 13 (MARCH, JUNE, SEPTEMBER, DECEMBER,
1954): 65-82, 156-178, 244-276, 329-355; 14 (MARCH,
JUNE, 1955): 43-81, 142-176.

13176 ALLISON, JOHN. *DROPPED STITCHES IN TENNESSEE HISTORY.*
NASHVILLE: MARSHALL & BRUCE, 1899.

13177 ARMYTAGE, W.H.G. "NASHOBAN NARRATIVE." *DALHOUSIE
REVIEW,* 33 (SUMMER, 1953): 110-116.

13178 BAILEY, E. BRASHER. "THE NEGRO IN EAST TENNESSEE." M.A.
THESIS, NEW YORK UNIVERSITY, 1947.

13179 BECKER, CARL M. "A BUCKEYE IN TENNESSEE: SOJOURN OF
ALIENATION." *TENNESSEE HISTORICAL QUARTERLY,* 22
(DECEMBER, 1963): 335-346.

13180 BERKELEY, KATHLEEN C. "'LIKE A PLAGUE OF LOCUST':
IMMIGRATION AND SOCIAL CHANGE IN MEMPHIS, TENNESSEE,
1850-1880." PH.D. DISSERTATION, UNIVERSITY OF
CALIFORNIA, LOS ANGELES, 1980.

13181 BOWEN, DAVID W. "ANDREW JOHNSON AND THE NEGRO." PH.D.
DISSERTATION, UNIVERSITY OF TENNESSEE, 1976.

13182 BRYAN, LOUISE M. "SOME ASPECTS OF SLAVERY IN TENNESSEE."
M.A. THESIS, GEORGE PEABODY COLLEGE FOR TEACHERS, 1924.

13183 BURKETT, E. VANN. "AN INVESTIGATION OF UNION AND

CONFEDERATE ARMY DOCUMENTS ADVOCATING THE USE OF THE
NEGRO IN OCCUPATIONAL PURSUITS, 1861-1865." M.A.
THESIS, TENNESSEE STATE UNIVERSITY, 1968.

13184 CANSLER, CHARLES W. THREE GENERATIONS: THE STORY OF A
COLORED FAMILY OF EASTERN TENNESSEE. KINGSPORT, TN:
KINGSPORT PRESS, 1939.

13185 CARROLL, ROSEMARY F. "MARGARET CLARK GRIFFIS, PLANTATION
TEACHER." TENNESSEE HISTORICAL QUARTERLY, 26 (FALL,
1967): 295-303.

13186 CHAPPELL, GORDON T. "LAND SPECULATION AND TAXATION IN
TENNESSEE, 1790-1834." M.A. THESIS, VANDERBILT
UNIVERSITY, 1936.

13187 CHURCH, ANNETTE E. AND CHURCH, ROBERTA. THE ROBERT R.
CHURCHES OF MEMPHIS: A FATHER AND SON WHO ACHIEVED IN
SPITE OF RACE. MEMPHIS: A.E. CHURCH, 1974.

13188 CIMPRICH, JOHN. "THE BEGINNING OF THE BLACK SUFFRAGE
MOVEMENT IN TENNESSEE, 1863-1865." JOURNAL OF NEGRO
HISTORY, 65 (SUMMER, 1980): 185-195.

13189 CIMPRICH, JOHN. "MILITARY GOVERNOR JOHNSON AND TENNESSEE
BLACKS, 1862-1865." TENNESSEE HISTORICAL QUARTERLY,
39 (WINTER, 1980): 459-470.

13190 CIMPRICH, JOHN V., JR. "SLAVERY AMIDST THE CIVIL WAR IN
TENNESSEE: THE DEATH OF AN INSTITUTION." PH.D.
DISSERTATION, OHIO STATE UNIVERSITY, 1977.

13191 CLARK, BLANCHE H. THE TENNESSEE YEOMEN, 1840-1860.
NASHVILLE: VANDERBILT UNIVERSITY PRESS, 1942.

13192 CLAYTON, W.W. HISTORY OF DAVIDSON COUNTY, TENNESSEE.
PHILADELPHIA: J.W. LEWIS AND COMPANY, 1880.

13193 CORLEW, ROBERT E. "SOME ASPECTS OF SLAVERY IN DICKSON
COUNTY." TENNESSEE HISTORICAL QUARTERLY, 10
(SEPTEMBER, DECEMBER, 1951): 224-248, 344-365.

13194 CORLEW, ROBERT E. "SOME ASPECTS OF SLAVERY IN DICKSON
COUNTY, TENNESSEE." BULLETIN OF VANDERBILT
UNIVERSITY, 49 (AUGUST, 1949): 71.

13195 CORLEW, ROBERT E. "SOME ASPECTS OF SLAVERY IN DICKSON
COUNTY, TENNESSEE." M.A. THESIS, VANDERBILT
UNIVERSITY, 1949.

13196 COULTER, E. MERTON. WILLIAM G. BROWNLOW: FIGHTING
PARSON OF THE SOUTHERN HIGHLANDS. CHAPEL HILL:
UNIVERSITY OF NORTH CAROLINA PRESS, 1937.

13197 COULTER, ROY D. "THE NEGROES OF CHATTANOOGA, TENNESSEE."

B.D. THESIS, VANDERBILT UNIVERSITY, 1934.

13198   CURTIS, JAMES C.   ANDREW JACKSON AND THE SEARCH FOR
        VINDICATION.   BOSTON: LITTLE, BROWN AND COMPANY, 1976.

13199   DAVIS, J. TREADWELL.   "NASHOBA: FRANCES WRIGHT'S
        EXPERIMENT IN SELF-EMANCIPATION."   SOUTHERN QUARTERLY,
        11 (OCTOBER, 1972):   63-90.

13200   DEBERRY, JOHN H.   "ANTI-SLAVERY IN TENNESSEE."   TENNESSEE
        VALLEY HISTORICAL REVIEW, 2 (WINTER, 1973):   19-25, 64.

13201   DESCHAMPS, MARGARET B.   "EARLY DAYS IN THE CUMBERLAND
        COUNTRY."   TENNESSEE HISTORICAL QUARTERLY, 6
        (SEPTEMBER, 1947):   195-229.

13202   EGERTON, JOHN.   VISIONS OF UTOPIA: NASHOBA, RUGBY,
        RUSKIN, AND THE "NEW COMMUNITIES" IN TENNESSEE'S PAST.
        KNOXVILLE: UNIVERSITY OF TENNESSEE PRESS, 1977.

13203   EGYPT, OPHELIA S.; MASUOKA, J.; AND JOHNSON, CHARLES S.
        UNWRITTEN HISTORY OF SLAVERY: AUTOBIOGRAPHICAL
        ACCOUNTS OF NEGRO EX-SLAVES.   NASHVILLE: SOCIAL
        SCIENCE INSTITUTE, FISK UNIVERSITY, 1945.

13204   ELLIOTT, HELEN.   "FRANCES WRIGHT'S EXPERIMENT WITH NEGRO
        EMANCIPATION."   INDIANA MAGAZINE OF HISTORY, 35
        (MARCH, 1939):   141-157.

13205   EMERSON, O.B.   "FRANCIS WRIGHT AND THE NASHOBA
        EXPERIMENT."   TENNESSEE HISTORICAL QUARTERLY, 6
        (DECEMBER, 1947):   291-314.

13206   FERTIG, JAMES W.   THE SECESSION AND RECONSTRUCTION OF
        TENNESSEE.   CHICAGO: UNIVERSITY OF CHICAGO PRESS,
        1898.

13207   FULLER, THOMAS O.   HISTORY OF THE NEGRO BAPTISTS OF
        TENNESSEE.   MEMPHIS: HASKINS PRINT, 1936.

13208   GATEWOOD, WILLARD B., JR. (ED.).   SLAVE AND FREEMAN: THE
        AUTOBIOGRAPHY OF GEORGE L. KNOX.   LEXINGTON:
        UNIVERSITY OF KENTUCKY PRESS, 1979.

13209   GOLDEN, DEAN C.   "THE OPERATION OF THE FREEDMEN'S BUREAU
        IN TENNESSEE, 1865-1870."   M.A. THESIS, MEMPHIS STATE
        UNIVERSITY, 1963.

13210   GOODSTEIN, ANITA S.   "BLACK HISTORY ON THE NASHVILLE
        FRONTIER, 1780-1810."   TENNESSEE HISTORICAL QUARTERLY,
        38 (WINTER, 1979):   401-420.

13211   GOWER, HERSCHEL.   "BELLE MEADE: QUEEN OF TENNESSEE
        PLANTATIONS."   TENNESSEE HISTORICAL QUARTERLY, 22
        (SEPTEMBER, 1963):   203-222.

13212   GRACY, DAVID B. AND ABRAHAMS, ROGER D. "SOME PLANTATION
        REMEDIES AND RECIPES." TENNESSEE FOLKLORE SOCIETY
        BULLETIN, 29 (JUNE, 1963): 29-34.

13213   GUNTER, CHARLES JR. "BEDFORD COUNTY DURING THE CIVIL
        WAR." M.A. THESIS, UNIVERSITY OF TENNESSEE, 1963.

13214   HALE, WILLIAM T. HISTORY OF DEKALB COUNTY, TENNESSEE.
        NASHVILLE: PAUL HUNTER, 1915.

13215   HARRISON, LOWELL H. "RECOLLECTIONS OF SOME TENNESSEE
        SLAVES." TENNESSEE HISTORICAL QUARTERLY, 33 (SUMMER,
        1974): 175-190.

13216   HAY, ROBERT P. "AND TEN DOLLARS EXTRA, FOR EVERY HUNDRED
        LASHES ANY PERSON WILL GIVE HIM, TO THE AMOUNT OF
        THREE HUNDRED: A NOTE ON ANDREW JACKSON'S RUNAWAY
        SLAVE AD OF 1804 AND ON THE HISTORIAN'S USE OF
        EVIDENCE." TENNESSEE HISTORICAL QUARTERLY, 36
        (WINTER, 1977): 468-478.

13217   HEDRICK, CHARLES E. "SOCIAL AND ECONOMIC ASPECTS OF
        SLAVERY IN THE TRANSMONTANE PRIOR TO 1850." PH.D.
        DISSERTATION, GEORGE PEABODY COLLEGE FOR TEACHERS,
        1927.

13218   HEISKELL, C.W. "REMARKABLE SLAVE HISTORY IN TENNESSEE."
        CONFEDERATE VETERAN, 16 (MARCH, 1908): 124.

13219   HENRY, HOWELL M. "THE SLAVE LAWS OF TENNESSEE."
        TENNESSEE HISTORICAL MAGAZINE, 2 (SEPTEMBER, 1916):
        175-203.

13220   HIGHSAW, MARY W. "A HISTORY OF ZION COMMUNITY IN MAURY
        COUNTY, 1806-1860." TENNESSEE HISTORICAL QUARTERLY, 5
        (MARCH, JUNE, SEPTEMBER, 1946): 3-34, 111-140,
        222-233.

13221   HOOPER, ERNEST W. "MEMPHIS, TENNESSEE: FEDERAL
        OCCUPATION AND RECONSTRUCTION, 1862-1870." PH.D.
        DISSERTATION, UNIVERSITY OF NORTH CAROLINA, 1957.

13222   HOWINGTON, ARTHUR. "'ACCORDING TO LAW': THE TRIAL AND
        PUNISHMENT OF BLACK DEFENDANTS IN ANTEBELLUM
        TENNESSEE." PAPER PRESENTED AT MEETING OF
        ORGANIZATION OF AMERICAN HISTORIANS, NEW YORK, APRIL
        13, 1978.

13223   HOWINGTON, ARTHUR F. "'NOT IN THE CONDITION OF A HORSE
        OR AN OX': FORD V. FORD, THE LAW OF TESTAMENTARY
        MANUMISSION, AND THE TENNESSEE COURT'S RECOGNITION OF
        SLAVE HUMANITY." TENNESSEE HISTORICAL QUARTERLY, 34
        (FALL, 1975): 249-263.

13224   HUBBARD, G.W. (ED.). A HISTORY OF THE COLORED SCHOOLS OF

NASHVILLE, TENNESSEE. NASHVILLE: WHEELER, MARSHALL & BRUCE, 1874.

13225 IMES, WILLIAM L. "THE LEGAL STATUS OF FREE NEGROES AND SLAVES IN TENNESSEE." JOURNAL OF NEGRO HISTORY, 4 (JULY, 1919): 254-272.

13226 IMES, WILLIAM L. "THE NEGRO IN TENNESSEE BEFORE THE CIVIL WAR, A SOCIOLOGICAL STUDY." M.A. THESIS, FISK UNIVERSITY, 1912.

13227 INGRAHAM, J.H. NOT 'A FOOL'S ERRAND': LIFE AND EXPERIENCE OF A NORTHERN GOVERNESS IN THE SUNNY SOUTH. NEW YORK: G.W. CARLETON, 1880.

13228 JENNINGS, THELMA. "TENNESSEE AND THE NASHVILLE CONVENTIONS OF 1850." TENNESSEE HISTORICAL QUARTERLY, 30 (SPRING, 1971): 70-82.

13229 KINARD, MARGARET. "FRONTIER DEVELOPMENT OF WILLIAMSON COUNTY." TENNESSEE HISTORICAL QUARTERLY, 8 (MARCH, 1949): 3-33.

13230 LACY, VIRGINIA J. AND HARRELL, DAVID E., JR. "PLANTATION HOME REMEDIES: MEDICINAL RECIPES FROM THE DIARIES OF JOHN POPE." TENNESSEE HISTORICAL QUARTERLY, 22 (SEPTEMBER, 1963): 259-265.

13231 LANE, ISAAC. AUTOBIOGRAPHY OF BISHOP ISAAC LANE, LL.D.: WITH A SHORT HISTORY OF THE C.M.E. CHURCH IN AMERICA AND OF METHODISM. NASHVILLE: M.E. CHURCH, SOUTH, 1916.

13232 LOVETT, BOBBY L. "THE NEGRO IN TENNESSEE, 1861-1866: A SOCIO-MILITARY HISTORY OF THE CIVIL WAR ERA." PH.D. DISSERTATION, UNIVERSITY OF ARKANSAS, 1978.

13233 LOVETT, BOBBY L. "THE NEGRO'S CIVIL WAR IN TENNESSEE, 1861-1865." JOURNAL OF NEGRO HISTORY, 61 (JANUARY, 1976): 36-50.

13234 "MANAGEMENT OF SOUTHERN ESTATES." TENNESSEE HISTORICAL MAGAZINE, 5 (JULY, 1919): 97-103.

13235 MASLOWSKI, PETER. TREASON MUST BE MADE ODIOUS: MILITARY OCCUPATION AND WARTIME RECONSTRUCTION IN NASHVILLE, TENNESSEE, 1862-1865. MILLWOOD, NY: KRAUS-THOMSON ORGANIZATION, 1978.

13236 MASLOWSKI, PETER. "'TREASON MUST BE MADE ODIOUS': MILITARY OCCUPATION AND WARTIME RECONSTRUCTION IN NASHVILLE, TENNESSEE, 1862-1865." PH.D. DISSERTATION, OHIO STATE UNIVERSITY, 1972.

13237 MATTHEWS, PAUL A. "FRANCES WRIGHT AND THE NASHOBA

EXPERIMENT: A TRANSITIONAL PERIOD IN ANTISLAVERY ATTITUDES." EAST TENNESSEE HISTORICAL SOCIETY PUBLICATIONS, 46 (1974): 37-52.

13238 MCCORMACK, EDWARD M. SLAVERY ON THE TENNESSEE FRONTIER. NASHVILLE: TENNESSEE AMERICAN REVOLUTION BICENTENNIAL COMMISSION, 1977.

13239 MCNEILLY, JAMES H. RELIGION AND SLAVERY: A VINDICATION OF THE SOUTHERN CHURCHES. NASHVILLE: PUBLISHING HOUSE OF THE M.E. CHURCH, SOUTH, 1911.

13240 MERIWETHER, ELIZABETH A. RECOLLECTIONS OF 92 YEARS, 1824-1916. NASHVILLE: TENNESSEE HISTORICAL COMMISSION, 1958.

13241 MILLER, RANDALL M. "'DEAR MASTER': LETTERS FROM NASHVILLE, 1862." TENNESSEE HISTORICAL QUARTERLY, 33 (SPRING, 1974): 85-92.

13242 MOODY, DAVID W. "LEGAL PHASES OF EMANCIPATION IN TENNESSEE." M.A. THESIS, GEORGE PEABODY COLLEGE FOR TEACHERS, 1934.

13243 MOONEY, CHASE C. "THE QUESTION OF SLAVERY AND THE FREE NEGRO IN THE TENNESSEE CONSTITUTIONAL CONVENTION OF 1834." JOURNAL OF SOUTHERN HISTORY, 12 (NOVEMBER, 1946): 487-509.

13244 MOONEY, CHASE C. "SLAVERY IN DAVIDSON COUNTY, TENNESSEE." M.A. THESIS, VANDERBILT UNIVERSITY, 1936.

13245 MOONEY, CHASE C. SLAVERY IN TENNESSEE. BLOOMINGTON: INDIANA UNIVERSITY PRESS, 1957.

13246 MOONEY, CHASE C. "SLAVERY IN TENNESSEE." PH.D. DISSERTATION, VANDERBILT UNIVERSITY, 1939.

13247 MOONEY, CHASE C. "SOME INSTITUTIONAL AND STATISTICAL ASPECTS OF SLAVERY IN TENNESSEE." TENNESSEE HISTORICAL QUARTERLY, 1 (SEPTEMBER, 1942): 195-228.

13248 ORR, HORACE E. "THE TENNESSEE CHURCHES AND SLAVERY; WITH SPECIAL REFERENCE TO EAST TENNESSEE." M.A. THESIS, UNIVERSITY OF TENNESSEE, 1924.

13249 OWSLEY, FRANK L. PLAIN FOLK OF THE OLD SOUTH. BATON ROUGE: LOUISIANA STATE UNIVERSITY PRESS, 1949.

13250 OWSLEY, FRANK L. AND OWSLEY, HARRIET C. "THE ECONOMIC STRUCTURE OF RURAL TENNESSEE, 1850-1860." JOURNAL OF SOUTHERN HISTORY, 8 (MAY, 1942): 161-182.

13251 PARKS, EDD W. "DREAMER'S VISION: FRANCES WRIGHT AT NASHOBA, 1825-1830." TENNESSEE HISTORICAL MAGAZINE,

2ND SER., 2 (JANUARY, 1932): 75-86.

13252 PATTERSON, CALEB P. THE NEGRO IN TENNESSEE, 1790-1865: A STUDY IN SOUTHERN POLITICS. AUSTIN: UNIVERSITY OF TEXAS BULLETIN NO. 2205; FEBRUARY 1, 1922.

13253 PATTERSON, CALEB P. "THE NEGRO IN TENNESSEE, 1790-1865: A STUDY IN SOUTHERN POLITICS." PH.D. DISSERTATION, COLUMBIA UNIVERSITY, 1923.

13254 PATTON, JAMES W. "THE PROGRESS OF EMANCIPATION IN TENNESSEE, 1796-1860." JOURNAL OF NEGRO HISTORY, 17 (JANUARY, 1932): 67-102.

13255 PAYNE-GAPOSCHKIN, CECILIA H. "THE NASHOBA PLAN FOR REMOVING THE EVIL OF SLAVERY: LETTERS OF FRANCES AND CAMILLA WRIGHT, 1820-1829." HARVARD LIBRARY BULLETIN, 23 (JULY, OCTOBER, 1975): 221-251, 429-461.

13256 PEASE, WILLIAM H. AND PEASE, JANE H. "A NEW VIEW OF NASHOBA." TENNESSEE HISTORICAL QUARTERLY, 19 (JUNE, 1960): 99-109.

13257 RATCLIFFE, ROBERTA M. "THE CHURCH FAMILY OF MEMPHIS." M.A. THESIS, TENNESSEE STATE UNIVERSITY, 1972.

13258 RAULSTON, J. LEONARD AND LIVINGOOD, JAMES W. SEQUATCHIE: A STORY OF THE SOUTHERN CUMBERLANDS. KNOXVILLE: UNIVERSITY OF TENNESSEE PRESS, 1974.

13259 ROBBINS, PEGGY. "EXPERIMENT AT NASHOBA PLANTATION." AMERICAN HISTORY ILLUSTRATED, 15 (APRIL, 1980): 12-19.

13260 ROBINSON, ARMSTEAD L. "IN THE AFTERMATH OF SLAVERY: BLACKS AND RECONSTRUCTION IN MEMPHIS, 1865-1870." B.A. THESIS, YALE UNIVERSITY, 1969.

13261 ROBINSON, JAMES H. "A SOCIAL HISTORY OF THE NEGRO IN MEMPHIS AND IN SHELBY COUNTY." PH.D. DISSERTATION, YALE UNIVERSITY, 1934.

13262 SCHAEFER, DONALD F. "PRODUCTIVITY IN THE ANTEBELLUM SOUTH: THE WESTERN TOBACCO REGION." RESEARCH IN ECONOMIC HISTORY, 3 (1978): 305-346.

13263 SCHWENINGER, LOREN. "JAMES RAPIER AND RECONSTRUCTION." PH.D. DISSERTATION, UNIVERSITY OF CHICAGO, 1972.

13264 SCHWENINGER, LOREN. JAMES T. RAPIER AND RECONSTRUCTION. CHICAGO: UNIVERSITY OF CHICAGO PRESS, 1978.

13265 SCHWENINGER, LOREN. "JOHN H. RAPIER, SR.: A SLAVE AND FREEDMAN IN THE ANTE-BELLUM SOUTH." CIVIL WAR HISTORY, 20 (MARCH, 1974): 23-34.

13266   SHELDEN, RANDALL G. "FROM SLAVE TO CASTE SOCIETY: PENAL
        CHANGES IN TENNESSEE, 1830-1915." TENNESSEE
        HISTORICAL QUARTERLY, 38 (WINTER, 1979): 462-478.

13267   "SLAVERY IN TENNESSEE (1790-1860)." IN RYWELL, MARTIN
        (ED.). AFRO-AMERICAN ENCYCLOPEDIA. 10 VOLS. NORTH
        MIAMI: EDUCATIONAL BOOK PUBLISHERS, 1974, VOL. 8, PP.
        2452-2454.

13268   SMITH, C.O. "THE EVANGELICAL LUTHERAN TENNESSEE SYNOD'S
        ATTITUDE TOWARD THE NEGRO BOTH AS A SLAVE AND AS
        FREEDMAN." CONCORDIA HISTORICAL INSTITUTE QUARTERLY,
        21 (JANUARY, 1949): 145-149.

13269   SMITH, SAM B. (ED.). TENNESSEE HISTORY: A BIBLIOGRAPHY.
        KNOXVILLE: UNIVERSITY OF TENNESSEE PRESS, 1974.

13270   SMITH, SAMUEL D. "AN ARCHAEOLOGICAL AND HISTORICAL
        ASSESSMENT OF THE FIRST HERMITAGE." TENNESSEE
        DIVISION OF ARCHAEOLOGY RESEARCH SERIES 2. NASHVILLE:
        TENNESSEE DEPARTMENT OF CONSERVATION, 1976.

13271   SMITH, SAMUEL D. ARCHAEOLOGICAL EXPLORATIONS AT THE
        CASTALIAN SPRINGS, TENNESSEE, HISTORIC SITE.
        NASHVILLE: TENNESSEE HISTORICAL COMMISSION, 1975.

13272   SMITH, SAMUEL D. "PLANTATION ARCHAEOLOGY AT THE
        HERMITAGE: SOME SUGGESTED PATTERNS." TENNESSEE
        ANTHROPOLOGIST, 2 (1977): 152-163.

13273   TAYLOR, ALRUTHEUS A. THE NEGRO IN TENNESSEE, 1865-1880.
        WASHINGTON: ASSOCIATED PUBLISHERS, 1941.

13274   TILLY, BETTE B. "ASPECTS OF SOCIAL AND ECONOMIC LIFE IN
        WEST TENNESSEE BEFORE THE CIVIL WAR." PH.D.
        DISSERTATION, MEMPHIS STATE UNIVERSITY, 1974.

13275   TILLY, BETTE B. "THE SPIRIT OF IMPROVEMENT: REFORMISM
        AND SLAVERY IN WEST TENNESSEE." WEST TENNESSEE
        HISTORICAL SOCIETY PAPERS, 28 (1974): 25-42.

13276   TRABUE, CHARLES C. "THE VOLUNTARY EMANCIPATION OF SLAVES
        IN TENNESSEE AS REFLECTED IN THE STATE'S LEGISLATION
        AND JUDICIAL DECISIONS." TENNESSEE HISTORICAL
        MAGAZINE, 4 (MARCH, 1913): 50-68.

13277   TRIMBLE, SARAH R. (ED.). "BEHIND THE LINES IN MIDDLE
        TENNESSEE, 1863-1865: THE JOURNAL OF BETTIE RIDLEY
        BLACKMORE." TENNESSEE HISTORICAL QUARTERLY, 12
        (MARCH, 1953): 48-80.

13278   WALKER, ARDA. "ANDREW JACKSON: PLANTER." EAST
        TENNESSEE HISTORICAL SOCIETY PUBLICATIONS, 15 (1943):
        19-34.

13279   WALKER, JOSEPH E.   "THE NEGRO IN TENNESSEE DURING THE
        RECONSTRUCTION PERIOD."   M.A. THESIS, UNIVERSITY OF
        TENNESSEE, 1933.

13280   WILEY, BELL I.   "COTTON AND SLAVERY IN THE HISTORY OF
        WESTERN TENNESSEE."   M.A. THESIS, UNIVERSITY OF
        KENTUCKY, 1929.

13281   WILLIAMS, EMMA I.   "JACKSON AND MADISON COUNTY; AN INLAND
        COTTON CENTER OF THE GROWING WEST, 1821-1850."
        TENNESSEE HISTORICAL QUARTERLY, 3 (MARCH, 1944):
        24-45.

13282   WILLIAMS, JOSEPH S.   OLD TIMES IN WEST TENNESSEE.
        MEMPHIS: W.G. CHEENEY, 1873.

13283   WILLS, RIDLEY.   "LETTERS FROM NASHVILLE, 1862, I: A
        PORTRAIT OF BELLE MEADE."   TENNESSEE HISTORICAL
        QUARTERLY, 33 (SPRING, 1974):   70-84.

13284   WINGFIELD, MARSHALL (ED.).   "THE DIARY OF WILLIAMSON
        YOUNGER (1817-1876)."   WEST TENNESSEE HISTORICAL
        SOCIETY PAPERS, 13 (1959):   55-77.

TEXAS

13285   ABEL, ANNIE H.   "MEXICO AS A FIELD FOR SYSTEMATIC BRITISH
        COLONIZATION."   SOUTHWESTERN HISTORICAL QUARTERLY, 30
        (JULY, 1926):   63-67.

13286   ADDINGTON, WENDELL G.   "SLAVE INSURRECTIONS IN TEXAS."
        JOURNAL OF NEGRO HISTORY, 35 (OCTOBER, 1950):   408-434.

13287   ASHBURN, KARL E.   "THE DEVELOPMENT OF COTTON PRODUCTION
        IN TEXAS."   PH.D. DISSERTATION, DUKE UNIVERSITY, 1934.

13288   ASHBURN, KARL E.   "SLAVERY AND COTTON PRODUCTION IN
        TEXAS."   SOUTHWESTERN SOCIAL SCIENCE QUARTERLY, 14
        (DECEMBER, 1933):   257-271.

13289   ATKINSON, BERTHA.   "THE HISTORY OF BELL COUNTY, TEXAS."
        M.A. THESIS, UNIVERSITY OF TEXAS, 1929.

13290   ATKINSON, LILLIE E.   "SLAVERY IN THE ECONOMY OF COLORADO
        COUNTY, 1822-1863."   M.A. THESIS, PRAIRIE VIEW
        AGRICULTURAL AND MECHANICAL COLLEGE, 1963.

13291   AURENTZ, JANET.   "THE INTERNATIONAL SLAVE TRADE IN TEXAS:
        A HALF-CENTURY OF CONFLICT."   ESSAYS IN HISTORY: THE
        E.C. BARKSDALE STUDENT LECTURES, 3 (1974):   18-28.

13292   BACHMANN, FREDERICK W. (ED.).   "CORRESPONDENCE BETWEEN
        JEAN AND PIERRE LAFITTE AND JOSEPH ROBIDOUX CONCERNING
        SALE OF SLAVES AT GALVESTON AND ST. LOUIS, 1818."   NEW

MEXICO HISTORICAL REVIEW, 27 (APRIL, 1952):   168-170.

13293   BARKER, EUGENE C.   "THE AFRICAN SLAVE TRADE IN TEXAS."
        QUARTERLY OF THE TEXAS STATE HISTORICAL ASSOCIATION, 6
        (JULY, 1902):   145-158.

13294   BARKER, EUGENE C.   "THE INFLUENCE OF SLAVERY IN THE
        COLONIZATION OF TEXAS."   SOUTHWESTERN HISTORICAL
        QUARTERLY, 28 (JULY, 1924):   1-33.

13295   BARKER, EUGENE C.   "THE INFLUENCE OF SLAVERY ON THE
        COLONIZATION OF TEXAS."   MISSISSIPPI VALLEY HISTORICAL
        REVIEW, 11 (JUNE, 1924):   3-36.

13296   BARKER, EUGENE C.   MEXICO AND TEXAS, 1821-1835.   DALLAS:
        P.L. TURNER, 1928.

13297   BARKER, EUGENE C.   "NOTES ON THE COLONIZATION OF TEXAS."
        SOUTHWESTERN HISTORICAL QUARTERLY, 27 (OCTOBER, 1923):
        108-119.

13298   BARR, ALWYN.   BLACK TEXANS: A HISTORY OF NEGROES IN
        TEXAS, 1528-1971.   AUSTIN: JENKINS PUBLISHING
        COMPANY, 1973.

13299   BARRIFFE, EUGENE.   "SOME ASPECTS OF SLAVERY AND
        ANTI-SLAVERY MOVEMENTS IN TEXAS, 1830-1860."   M.A.
        THESIS, UNIVERSITY OF SOUTHWESTERN LOUISIANA, 1968.

13300   BELL, MATTIE.   "THE GROWTH AND DISTRIBUTION OF THE TEXAS
        POPULATION."   M.A. THESIS, BAYLOR UNIVERSITY, 1935.

13301   BENJAMIN, GILBERT G.   "THE GERMANS IN TEXAS, A STUDY IN
        IMMIGRATION."   PH.D. DISSERTATION, YALE UNIVERSITY,
        1909.

13302   BERTLETH, ROSA G.   "JARED ELLISON GRACE."   SOUTHWESTERN
        HISTORICAL QUARTERLY, 20 (APRIL, 1917):   358-368.

13303   BLOCK, W.T.   "THE ROMANCE OF SABINE LAKE, 1777-1846:
        SCENE OF SLAVING, SMUGGLING, STEAMBOATING, BORDER
        CONFLICT, AND COTTON COMMERCE UNDER THE TEXAS
        REPUBLIC."   TEXAS GULF HISTORICAL AND BIOGRAPHICAL
        RECORD, 9 (NOVEMBER, 1973):   9-43.

13304   BOYKIN, MARY A.   "SLAVERY IN THE DIPLOMATIC RELATIONS
        BETWEEN GREAT BRITAIN AND THE TEXAS REPUBLIC,
        1836-1842."   M.A. THESIS, CATHOLIC UNIVERSITY OF
        AMERICA, 1947.

13305   BREWER, JOHN M. (ED.).   AN HISTORICAL OUTLINE OF THE
        NEGRO IN TRAVIS COUNTY, BY THE NEGRO HISTORY CLASS OF
        SAMUEL HUSTON COLLEGE, SUMMER, 1940.   AUSTIN: SAMUEL
        HUSTON COLLEGE, 1940.

13306   BREWER, JOHN M.   "NEGRO PREACHER TALES FROM THE TEXAS
        'BRAZOS BOTTOMS.'" M.A. THESIS, INDIANA UNIVERSITY,
        1949.

13307   BREWER, JOHN MASON.   "SLAVERY AND ITS LEGACY." DOG
        GHOSTS AND OTHER TEXAS NEGRO FOLK TALES. AUSTIN:
        UNIVERSITY OF TEXAS PRESS, 1958, PP. 7-24.

13308   BRIDGES, CLARENCE A.   "TEXAS AND THE CRISIS OF 1850."
        M.A. THESIS, UNIVERSITY OF TEXAS, 1925.

13309   BRIGHT, MARGARET D.   "THE SOCIAL DEVELOPMENT OF HOUSTON,
        TEXAS, 1836-1860." M.A. THESIS, UNIVERSITY OF TEXAS,
        1940.

13310   BROWNE, PHILIP D.   "THE EARLY HISTORY OF FREESTONE COUNTY
        TO 1865." M.A. THESIS, UNIVERSITY OF TEXAS, 1925.

13311   BUGBEE, LESTER G.   "SLAVERY IN EARLY TEXAS." POLITICAL
        SCIENCE QUARTERLY, 13 (SEPTEMBER, DECEMBER, 1898):
        389-412, 648-668.

13312   BURNS, ALVIN E.   "SLAVE LIFE ON THE RICHARD ELLIS
        PLANTATION." JUNIOR HISTORIAN OF THE TEXAS STATE
        HISTORICAL ASSOCIATION, 10 (NOVEMBER, 1949): 27-29.

13313   CAIN, JERRY B.   "THE THOUGHT AND ACTION OF SOME EARLY
        TEXAS BAPTISTS CONCERNING THE NEGRO." EAST TEXAS
        HISTORICAL JOURNAL, 13 (SPRING, 1975): 3-12.

13314   CAMPBELL, RANDOLPH B.   "HUMAN PROPERTY: THE NEGRO SLAVE
        IN HARRISON COUNTY, 1850-1860." SOUTHWESTERN
        HISTORICAL QUARTERLY, 76 (APRIL, 1973): 384-396.

13315   CAMPBELL, RANDOLPH B.   "LOCAL ARCHIVES AS A SOURCE OF
        SLAVE PRICES: HARRISON COUNTY, TEXAS AS A TEST CASE."
        HISTORIAN, 36 (AUGUST, 1974): 660-669.

13316   CAMPBELL, RANDOLPH B.   "PLANTERS AND PLAIN FOLK:
        HARRISON COUNTY, TEXAS, AS A TEST CASE, 1850-1860."
        JOURNAL OF SOUTHERN HISTORY, 40 (AUGUST, 1974):
        369-398.

13317   CAMPBELL, RANDOLPH B.   "THE PRODUCTIVITY OF SLAVE LABOR
        IN EAST TEXAS: A RESEARCH NOTE." LOUISIANA STUDIES,
        13 (SUMMER, 1974): 154-172.

13318   CAMPBELL, RANDOLPH B.   "SLAVEHOLDING IN HARRISON COUNTY,
        1850-1860: A STATISTICAL PROFILE." EAST TEXAS
        HISTORICAL JOURNAL, 11 (SPRING, 1973): 18-27.

13319   CAMPBELL, RANDOLPH B. AND LOWE, RICHARD G.   "SOME
        ECONOMIC ASPECTS OF ANTEBELLUM TEXAS AGRICULTURE."
        SOUTHWESTERN HISTORICAL QUARTERLY, 82 (APRIL, 1979):
        351-378.

13320 CAMPBELL, RANDOLPH B. AND LOWE, RICHARD G. WEALTH AND
       POWER IN ANTEBELLUM TEXAS. COLLEGE STATION: TEXAS A
       & M UNIVERSITY PRESS, 1977.

13321 CAMPBELL, RANDOLPH B. AND PICKENS, DONALD K. "'MY DEAR
       HUSBAND': A TEXAS SLAVE'S LOVE LETTER, 1862."
       JOURNAL OF NEGRO HISTORY, 65 (FALL, 1980): 361-364.

13322 CARNATHAN, W.J. "THE ATTEMPT TO REOPEN THE AFRICAN SLAVE
       TRADE IN TEXAS, 1857-1858." IN PROCEEDINGS OF THE
       SIXTH ANNUAL CONVENTION OF THE SOUTHWESTERN POLITICAL
       AND SOCIAL SCIENCE ASSOCIATION, (1925): 134-144.

13323 COOPER, MADIE. "TEXAS COLONIZATION UNDER MEXICAN
       RESTRICTIONS, 1821-1835." M.A. THESIS, SAM HOUSTON
       STATE TEACHERS COLLEGE, 1940.

13324 COTTON, WALTER. HISTORY OF THE NEGROES OF LIMESTONE
       COUNTY. MEXIA, TX: NEWS PRINT COMPANY, 1939.

13325 COTTRELL, DANNELL G. "THE AMERICANIZATION OF TEXAS."
       M.A. THESIS, UNIVERSITY OF UTAH, 1941.

13326 CROOK, CARLAND E. "SAN ANTONIO, TEXAS, 1846-1861." M.A.
       THESIS, RICE UNIVERSITY, 1964.

13327 CROUCH, BARRY A. "HIDDEN SOURCES OF BLACK HISTORY: THE
       TEXAS FREEDMEN'S BUREAU RECORDS AS A CASE STUDY."
       SOUTHWESTERN HISTORICAL QUARTERLY, 83 (JANUARY, 1980):
       211-226.

13328 CURLEE, ABIGAIL. "THE HISTORY OF A TEXAS SLAVE
       PLANTATION, 1831-1863." M.A. THESIS, UNIVERSITY OF
       TEXAS, 1922.

13329 CURLEE, ABIGAIL. "THE HISTORY OF A TEXAS SLAVE
       PLANTATION, 1831-1863." SOUTHWESTERN HISTORICAL
       QUARTERLY, 26 (OCTOBER, 1922): 79-127.

13330 CURLEE, ABIGAIL. "A STUDY OF TEXAS SLAVE PLANTATIONS,
       1822 TO 1865." PH.D. DISSERTATION, UNIVERSITY OF
       TEXAS, 1932.

13331 DOBIE, BERTHA M. "THE DEATH BELL OF THE BRAZOS."
       PUBLICATIONS OF THE TEXAS FOLKLORE SOCIETY, 3 (1924):
       141-142.

13332 EDWARDS, MARY JO. "TEXAS AGRICULTURE AS REFLECTED IN
       LETTERS TO THE SOUTHERN CULTIVATOR PRIOR TO 1861."
       M.A. THESIS, EAST TEXAS STATE TEACHERS COLLEGE, 1948.

13333 ELLIS, MARY H. "SOCIAL CONDITIONS IN TEXAS ABOUT 1850."
       M.A. THESIS, UNIVERSITY OF TEXAS, 1927.

13334 ELLSWORTH, LOIS C. "SAN ANTONIO DURING THE CIVIL WAR."

M.A. THESIS, UNIVERSITY OF TEXAS, 1938.

13335 ENGELKING, JOHANNA R. "SLAVERY IN TEXAS." M.A. THESIS,
       BAYLOR UNIVERSITY, 1933.

13336 EVERETT, MARY. "TEXAN PLANTATION: THEN AND NOW."
       SEWANEE REVIEW, 44 (OCTOBER, 1936): 386-404.

13337 FALER, KAREN B. "THE SLAVE QUESTION IN ANGLO-TEXAN
       RELATIONS, 1836-1845; AN ANALYSIS OF BRITISH POLICY."
       M.A. THESIS, UNIVERSITY OF WISCONSIN, 1966.

13338 FAULK, ODIE B. THE LAST YEARS OF SPANISH TEXAS,
       1778-1821. THE HAGUE: MOUTON & COMPANY, 1964.

13339 FAULK, ODIE B. A SUCCESSFUL FAILURE. AUSTIN:
       STECK-VAUGHN COMPANY, 1965.

13340 FEHRENBACH, T.R. LONE STAR: A HISTORY OF TEXAS AND THE
       TEXANS. NEW YORK: MACMILLAN COMPANY, 1968.

13341 FORNELL, EARL W. "THE ABDUCTION OF FREE NEGROES AND
       SLAVES IN TEXAS." SOUTHWESTERN HISTORICAL QUARTERLY,
       60 (JANUARY, 1957): 369-380.

13342 FORNELL, EARL W. "AGITATION IN TEXAS FOR REOPENING THE
       SLAVE TRADE." SOUTHWESTERN HISTORICAL QUARTERLY, 60
       (OCTOBER, 1956): 244-259.

13343 FORNELL, EARL W. THE GALVESTON ERA: THE TEXAS CRESCENT
       ON THE EVE OF SECESSION. AUSTIN: UNIVERSITY OF TEXAS
       PRESS, 1961.

13344 FREEMAN, MARCUS A. "TAXES AND SLAVERY IN TEXAS,
       1845-1860." M.A. THESIS, PRAIRIE VIEW AGRICULTURAL
       AND MECHANICAL COLLEGE, 1956.

13345 GLASRUD, BRUCE A. "JIM CROW'S EMERGENCE IN TEXAS."
       AMERICAN STUDIES, 15 (SPRING, 1974): 47-60.

13346 GOLDMANN, PAULINE S. "LETTERS FROM THREE MEMBERS OF
       TERRY'S TEXAS RANGERS, 1861-1865." M.A. THESIS,
       UNIVERSITY OF TEXAS, 1930.

13347 GORDON, RAMSEY J. "THE NEGRO IN MCLENNAN COUNTY, TEXAS."
       M.A. THESIS, BAYLOR UNIVERSITY, 1932.

13348 GRAHAM, PHILIP (ED.). "TEXAS MEMOIRS OF AMELIA E. BARR."
       SOUTHWESTERN HISTORICAL QUARTERLY, 69 (APRIL, 1966):
       473-498.

13349 GRIFFIN, SAMUEL F. SLAVEHOLDERS OF TEXAS. OAKHURST, CA:
       GOLD SIDE BOOK, 1972.

13350 HAGGARD, J. VILLSANA. "A BRIEF STUDY OF THE IMPRESSMENT

OF SLAVE LABOR IN TEXAS, 1861-1865." M.A. THESIS, UNIVERSITY OF TEXAS, 1938.

13351 HAGGARD, JUAN V. "THE NEUTRAL GROUND BETWEEN LOUISIANA AND TEXAS, 1806-1821." PH.D. DISSERTATION, UNIVERSITY OF TEXAS, 1942.

13352 HAGOOD, LOUISE W. "NEGROES IN NORTHEAST TEXAS, 1859-1875." M.A. THESIS, EAST TEXAS STATE UNIVERSITY, 1965.

13353 HALE, LAURA E. "THE GROCES AND THE WHARTONS IN THE EARLY HISTORY OF TEXAS." M.A. THESIS, UNIVERSITY OF TEXAS, 1942.

13354 HALEY, J. EVETTS. GEORGE W. LITTLEFIELD, TEXAN. NORMAN: UNIVERSITY OF OKLAHOMA PRESS, 1943.

13355 HAWKINS, MARJORIE B. "RUNAWAY SLAVES IN TEXAS, 1830-1860." M.A. THESIS, PRAIRIE VIEW AGRICULTURAL AND MECHANICAL COLLEGE, 1952.

13356 HAYMAN, BETTIE. "A SHORT HISTORY OF THE NEGRO OF WALKER COUNTY, 1860-1942." M.A. THESIS, SAM HOUSTON STATE TEACHERS COLLEGE, 1942.

13357 HAYNES, ROSE MARY F. "SOME FEATURES OF NEGRO PARTICIPATION IN TEXAS HISTORY THROUGH 1879." M.A. THESIS, TEXAS COLLEGE OF ARTS AND INDUSTRIES, KINGSVILLE, 1948.

13358 HENRY, WILLIE R. "SLAVERY IN THE ECONOMY OF BRAZOS COUNTY, 1821-1860." M.A. THESIS, PRAIRIE VIEW AGRICULTURAL AND MECHANICAL COLLEGE, 1954.

13359 HENSON, MARGARET S. "DEVELOPMENT OF SLAVE CODES IN TEXAS, 1821-1845." M.A. THESIS, UNIVERSITY OF HOUSTON, 1969.

13360 HOGAN, WILLIAM R. THE TEXAS REPUBLIC: A SOCIAL AND ECONOMIC HISTORY. AUSTIN: UNIVERSITY OF TEXAS PRESS, 1946.

13361 HOLBROOK, ABIGAIL C. "COTTON MARKETING IN ANTEBELLUM TEXAS." SOUTHWESTERN HISTORICAL QUARTERLY, 73 (APRIL, 1970): 431-455.

13362 HOLBROOK, ABIGAIL C. "A GLIMPSE OF LIFE ON ANTEBELLUM SLAVE PLANTATIONS IN TEXAS." SOUTHWESTERN HISTORICAL QUARTERLY, 76 (APRIL, 1973): 361-383.

13363 HOLLON, W. EUGENE. FRONTIER VIOLENCE: ANOTHER LOOK. NEW YORK: OXFORD UNIVERSITY PRESS, 1974.

13364 HOLLON, W. EUGENE (ED.). WILLIAM BOLLAERT'S TEXAS.

NORMAN: UNIVERSITY OF OKLAHOMA PRESS, 1956.

13365   HUNTER, IRENE P.   "SLAVERY IN THE ECONOMY OF CHEROKEE
        COUNTY, TEXAS, 1846-1860."   M.A. THESIS, PRAIRIE VIEW
        AGRICULTURAL AND MECHANICAL COLLEGE, 1956.

13366   HUTSON, CHARLES W.   "THE SLAVE TRADE IN TEXAS."   IN
        CHANDLER, JULIAN A.C. (ED.).   THE SOUTH IN THE
        BUILDING OF THE NATION.   12 VOLS.   RICHMOND: SOUTHERN
        HISTORICAL PUBLICATION SOCIETY, 1909, VOL. 3, PP.
        351-352.

13367   INSTITUTE OF TEXAN CULTURES.   THE AFRO-AMERICAN TEXANS.
        SAN ANTONIO: THE INSTITUTE, 1975.

13368   JACKSON, SUSAN.   "SLAVERY IN HOUSTON: THE 1850S."
        HOUSTON REVIEW, 2 (SUMMER, 1980):   66-82.

13369   JENKINS, JOHN H. (ED.).   "LETTERS AND DOCUMENTS."
        TEXANA, 3 (FALL, 1965):   275-281.

13370   JOHNSON, WILLIAM R.   A SHORT HISTORY OF THE SUGAR
        INDUSTRY IN TEXAS.   HOUSTON: TEXAS GULF COAST
        ASSOCIATION PUBLICATIONS, 1961.

13371   JONES, CLYDE V.   "FAYETTE COUNTY, TEXAS, DURING CIVIL WAR
        AND RECONSTRUCTION."   M.A. THESIS, ST. MARY'S
        UNIVERSITY, SAN ANTONIO, 1948.

13372   JORDAN, TERRY G.   "THE IMPRINT OF THE UPPER AND LOWER
        SOUTH ON MID-NINETEENTH CENTURY TEXAS."   ANNALS OF THE
        ASSOCIATION OF AMERICAN GEOGRAPHERS, 57 (DECEMBER,
        1967):   667-690.

13373   JUNKINS, ENDA.   "SLAVE PLOTS, INSURRECTIONS, AND ACTS OF
        VIOLENCE IN THE STATE OF TEXAS, 1828-1865."   M.A.
        THESIS, BAYLOR UNIVERSITY, 1969.

13374   KAHN, JOAN M.   "SLAVE LABOR ON AN ANTE-BELLUM TEXAS
        PLANTATION AS REVEALED IN THE ASHBEL SMITH PAPERS."
        M.A. THESIS, COLUMBIA UNIVERSITY, 1951.

13375   LACK, PAUL.   "SLAVERY ON THE SOUTHWESTERN URBAN FRONTIER:
        AUSTIN, TEXAS, 1845-1860."   UNPUBLISHED PAPER, TEXAS
        TECH UNIVERSITY, 1970.

13376   LAKE, MARY D.   "PIONEER CHRISTMAS CUSTOMS OF TARRANT
        COUNTY."   PUBLICATIONS OF THE TEXAS FOLKLORE SOCIETY,
        NO. 5 (1926):   107-111.

13377   LALE, MAX S. AND CAMPBELL, RANDOLPH B. (EDS.).   "THE
        PLANTATION JOURNAL OF JOHN B. WEBSTER, FEBRUARY 17,
        1858-NOVEMBER 5, 1859."   SOUTHWESTERN HISTORICAL
        QUARTERLY, 84 (JULY, 1980):   49-80.

13378 LATHROP, BARNES F. MIGRATION INTO EAST TEXAS, 1835-1860:
       A STUDY FROM THE UNITED STATES CENSUS. AUSTIN: TEXAS
       STATE HISTORICAL ASSOCIATION, 1949.

13379 LEDBETTER, BARBARA A. "BLACK AND MEXICAN SLAVES IN YOUNG
       COUNTY, TEXAS, 1856-1865." WEST TEXAS HISTORICAL
       ASSOCIATION YEAR BOOK, 56 (1980): 100-102.

13380 LEDBETTER, BILLY D. "SLAVE UNREST AND WHITE PANIC: THE
       IMPACT OF BLACK REPUBLICANISM IN ANTE-BELLUM TEXAS."
       IEXANA, 10 (1972): 335-350.

13381 LEDBETTER, BILLY D. "SLAVERY, FEAR, AND DISUNION IN THE
       LONE STAR STATE: TEXANS' ATTITUDES TOWARD SECESSION
       AND THE UNION, 1846-1861." PH.D. DISSERTATION, NORTH
       TEXAS STATE UNIVERSITY, 1972.

13382 LEDBETTER, BILLY D. "WHITE OVER BLACK IN TEXAS: RACIAL
       ATTITUDES IN THE ANTE-BELLUM PERIOD." PHYLON, 34
       (DECEMBER, 1973): 406-418.

13383 LOCKHART, W.E. "THE SLAVE CODE OF TEXAS." M.A. THESIS,
       BAYLOR UNIVERSITY, 1929.

13384 LOWE, RICHARD AND CAMPBELL, RANDOLPH. "SLAVE PROPERTY
       AND THE DISTRIBUTION OF WEALTH IN TEXAS, 1860."
       JOURNAL OF AMERICAN HISTORY, 63 (SEPTEMBER, 1976):
       316-324.

13385 LUMPKINS, JOSEPHINE. "ANTISLAVERY OPPOSITION TO THE
       ANNEXATION OF TEXAS, WITH SPECIAL REFERENCE TO JOHN
       QUINCY ADAMS." PH.D. DISSERTATION, CORNELL
       UNIVERSITY, 1941.

13386 LYON, ANNIE L.K. "SLAVERY AS AN ECONOMIC AND POLITICAL
       FACTOR IN THE TEXAS GUBERNATORIAL ELECTIONS OF 1857
       AND 1859." M.A. THESIS, UNIVERSITY OF HOUSTON, 1964.

13387 MADDOX, JOLENE. "SLAVERY IN TEXAS, 1836-1860." M.A.
       THESIS, SOUTHWEST TEXAS STATE UNIVERSITY, 1969.

13388 MARR, JOHN C. "THE HISTORY OF MATAGORDA COUNTY, TEXAS."
       M.A. THESIS, UNIVERSITY OF TEXAS, 1928.

13389 MARSHALL, ELMER G. "THE HISTORY OF BRAZOS COUNTY,
       TEXAS." M.A. THESIS, UNIVERSITY OF TEXAS, 1937.

13390 MCCOMB, DAVID G. HOUSTON: THE BAYOU CITY. AUSTIN:
       UNIVERSITY OF TEXAS PRESS, 1969.

13391 MCDONALD, LAWRENCE H. "BRITAIN AND SLAVERY IN THE
       REPUBLIC OF TEXAS." M.A. THESIS, GEORGETOWN
       UNIVERSITY, 1968.

13392 MCPHERSON, HALLIE M. "SLAVERY IN TEXAS." M.A. THESIS,

UNIVERSITY OF CHICAGO, 1924.

13393   MEINIG, D.W.   IMPERIAL TEXAS: AN INTERPRETIVE ESSAY IN
        CULTURAL GEOGRAPHY.   AUSTIN: UNIVERSITY OF TEXAS
        PRESS, 1969.

13394   MERK, FREDERICK.   THE MONROE DOCTRINE AND AMERICAN
        EXPANSIONISM, 1843-1849.   NEW YORK: ALFRED A. KNOPF,
        1966.

13395   MERK, FREDERICK.   SLAVERY AND THE ANNEXATION OF TEXAS.
        NEW YORK: ALFRED A. KNOPF, 1972.

13396   MOORE, CHARLES L.   "TEXAS AND THE KANSAS-NEBRASKA ACT OF
        1854."   M.A. THESIS, NORTH TEXAS STATE UNIVERSITY,
        1974.

13397   MOORE, COUNCIL S.   "SLAVERY IN THE ECONOMY OF FALLS
        COUNTY."   M.A. THESIS, PRAIRIE VIEW AGRICULTURAL AND
        MECHANICAL COLLEGE, 1954.

13398   MUIR, ANDREW F.   "THE FREE NEGRO IN GALVESTON COUNTY,
        TEXAS."   NEGRO HISTORY BULLETIN, 22 (DECEMBER, 1958):
        68-70.

13399   "MY MASTER," THE INSIDE STORY OF SAM HOUSTON AND HIS
        TIMES, BY HIS FORMER SLAVE, JEFF HAMILTON, AS TOLD TO
        LENOIR HUNT.   DALLAS: MANFRED, VAN NORT, AND COMPANY,
        1940.

13400   NASH, A.E.K.   "THE TEXAS SUPREME COURT AND THE TRIAL
        RIGHTS OF BLACKS, 1845-1860."   JOURNAL OF AMERICAN
        HISTORY, 58 (DECEMBER, 1971):   622-642.

13401   NASH, A.E. KEIR.   "TEXAS JUSTICE IN THE AGE OF SLAVERY:
        APPEALS CONCERNING BLACKS AND THE ANTEBELLUM STATE
        SUPREME COURT."   HOUSTON LAW REVIEW, 8 (JANUARY,
        1971):   438-456.

13402   NELSON, ROBERT E.   "BRITAIN AND THE ANNEXATION OF TEXAS,
        WITH PARTICULAR REFERENCE TO THE SLAVERY QUESTION
        (1836-1845)."   M.A. THESIS, MONTANA STATE UNIVERSITY,
        1964.

13403   NEWTON, LEWIS W. AND GAMBRELL, HERPERT P.   A SOCIAL AND
        POLITICAL HISTORY OF TEXAS.   DALLAS: SOUTHWEST PRESS,
        1932.

13404   NORTON, WESLEY.   "THE METHODIST EPISCOPAL CHURCH AND THE
        CIVIL DISTURBANCES IN NORTH TEXAS IN 1859 AND 1860."
        SOUTHWESTERN HISTORICAL QUARTERLY, 68 (JANUARY, 1965):
        317-341.

13405   O'BANION, MAURINE M.   "THE HISTORY OF CALDWELL COUNTY."
        M.A. THESIS, UNIVERSITY OF TEXAS, 1931.

13406   ODELL, ABRABELLA G.   "REOPENING THE AFRICAN SLAVE TRADE
        IN TEXAS."   M.A. THESIS, UNIVERSITY OF TEXAS, 1946.

13407   ORREN, G.G.   "THE HISTORY OF HOPKINS COUNTY."   M.A.
        THESIS, EAST TEXAS STATE TEACHERS COLLEGE, 1938.

13408   OSBORNE, FRED Y.   "STUDY OF SOCIAL AND RELIGIOUS
        ACTIVITIES IN DALLAS COUNTY, 1841-1861."   M.A. THESIS,
        SOUTHERN METHODIST UNIVERSITY, 1947.

13409   OWENS, WILLIAM A.   "RETURN TO PIN HOOK."   IN ABERNETHY,
        FRANCIS E. (ED.).   OBSERVATIONS & REFLECTIONS ON TEXAS
        FOLKLORE.   AUSTIN: ENCINO PRESS, 1972, PP. 31-34.

13410   PALM, REBA W.   "PROTESTANT CHURCHES AND SLAVERY IN
        MATAGORDA COUNTY."   EAST TEXAS HISTORICAL JOURNAL, 14
        (SPRING, 1976):   3-8.

13411   PIERCE, BURNETT C.   "TITUS COUNTY, TEXAS: ITS BACKGROUND
        AND HISTORY IN ANTEBELLUM DAYS."   M.A. THESIS,
        UNIVERSITY OF COLORADO, 1932.

13412   PLATTER, ALLEN A.   "EDUCATIONAL, SOCIAL, AND ECONOMIC
        CHARACTERISTICS OF THE PLANTATION CULTURE OF BRAZORIA
        COUNTY, TEXAS."   PH.D. DISSERTATION, UNIVERSITY OF
        HOUSTON, 1961.

13413   POOL, WILLIAM C., JR.   "THE HISTORY OF BOSQUE COUNTY."
        M.A. THESIS, UNIVERSITY OF TEXAS, 1946.

13414   PORTER, KENNETH W.   "NEGROES AND INDIANS ON THE TEXAS
        FRONTIER, 1831-1876."   JOURNAL OF NEGRO HISTORY, 41
        (JULY, OCTOBER, 1956):   185-214, 285-310.

13415   PORTER, KENNETH W.   "NEGROES AND INDIANS ON THE TEXAS
        FRONTIER, 1834-1874."   SOUTHWESTERN HISTORICAL
        QUARTERLY, 53 (OCTOBER, 1949):   151-163.

13416   PRINCE, DIANE E.   "WILLIAM GOYENS, FREE NEGRO ON THE
        TEXAS FRONTIER."   M.A. THESIS, STEPHEN F. AUSTIN STATE
        UNIVERSITY, 1961.

13417   REDWINE, W.A.   BRIEF HISTORY OF THE NEGRO IN FIVE
        COUNTIES.   TYLER, TX: N.P., 1901.

13418   REDWINE, W.A.   "HISTORY OF FIVE COUNTIES."   CHRONICLES OF
        SMITH COUNTY, 11 (FALL, 1972):   13-68.

13419   REFSELL, OLIVER M.   "THE MASSIES OF VIRGINIA: A
        DOCUMENTARY HISTORY OF A PLANTER FAMILY."   PH.D.
        DISSERTATION, UNIVERSITY OF TEXAS, 1959.

13420   "REMINISCENCES OF MRS. DILUE HARRIS."   QUARTERLY OF THE
        TEXAS STATE HISTORICAL ASSOCIATION, 4 (OCTOBER, 1900):
        85-128, (JANUARY, 1901):   155-189.

13421   REYNOLDS, DONALD E.   "SMITH COUNTY AND ITS NEIGHBORS
        DURING THE SLAVE INSURRECTION PANIC OF 1860."
        CHRONICLES OF SMITH COUNTY, TEXAS, 10 (FALL, 1971):
        1-8.

13422   ROBBINS, FRED.   "THE ORIGIN AND DEVELOPMENT OF THE
        AFRICAN SLAVE TRADE IN GALVESTON, TEXAS, AND
        SURROUNDING AREAS FROM 1816 TO 1836."   EAST TEXAS
        HISTORICAL JOURNAL, 9 (OCTOBER, 1971):   153-161.

13423   ROBBINS, FRED.   "THE ORIGINS AND DEVELOPMENT OF THE
        AFRICAN SLAVE TRADE INTO TEXAS, 1816-1860."   M.A.
        THESIS, UNIVERSITY OF HOUSTON, 1972.

13424   ROBBINS, HAL.   "SLAVERY IN THE ECONOMY OF MATAGORDA
        COUNTY, TEXAS, 1839-1860."   M.A. THESIS, PRAIRIE VIEW
        AGRICULTURAL AND MECHANICAL COLLEGE, 1952.

13425   ROBINSON, RICHARDSON R.   "RACISM AS AN ASPECT OF THE
        VIOLENT HISTORY OF THE STATE OF TEXAS IN THE 1830'S
        AND 1840'S."   M.A. THESIS, KEAN COLLEGE OF NEW JERSEY,
        1979.

13426   SHAW, ELTON R.   THE CONQUEST OF THE SOUTHWEST: A
        DISCUSSION OF THE CHARGES THAT THE COLONIZATION OF
        TEXAS AND THE REVOLUTION AGAINST MEXICO WERE THE
        RESULTS OF A MOVEMENT OF THE 'SLAVOCRACY' TO INCREASE
        SLAVE TERRITORY, OR OF THE ACTIVITY OF ANDREW JACKSON,
        THROUGH SAMUEL HOUSTON, TO ACCOMPLISH THE SAME RESULT.
        BERWYN, IL: SHAW PUBLISHING COMPANY, 1924.

13427   SHIMKIN, DEMITRI B.   "TEXAS INDEED IS DIFFERENT: SOME
        HISTORICAL AND DEMOGRAPHIC OBSERVATIONS."   IN SHIMKIN,
        DEMITRI B.; SHIMKIN, EDITH M.; AND FRATE, DENNIS A.
        (EDS.).   THE EXTENDED FAMILY IN BLACK SOCIETIES.   THE
        HAGUE: MOUTON PUBLISHERS, 1978, PP. 363-378.

13428   SIBLEY, MARILYN M.   TRAVELERS IN TEXAS, 1761-1860.
        AUSTIN: UNIVERSITY OF TEXAS PRESS, 1967.

13429   "SLAVE INSURRECTIONS."   IN WEBB, WALTER P. (ED.).   THE
        HANDBOOK OF TEXAS.   2 VOLS.   AUSTIN: TEXAS STATE
        HISTORICAL ASSOCIATION, 1952, VOL. 2, PP. 618-619.

13430   "SLAVERY IN TEXAS (1821-1861)."   IN RYWELL, MARTIN (ED.).
        AFRO-AMERICAN ENCYCLOPEDIA.   10 VOLS.   NORTH MIAMI:
        EDUCATIONAL BOOK PUBLISHERS, 1974, VOL. 8, P. 2454.

13431   SMALLWOOD, JAMES.   "BLACKS IN ANTEBELLUM TEXAS: A
        REAPPRAISAL."   RED RIVER VALLEY HISTORICAL REVIEW, 2
        (WINTER, 1975):   443-466.

13432   SMALLWOOD, JAMES M.   "BLACK TEXANS DURING RECONSTRUCTION,
        1865-1874."   PH.D. DISSERTATION, TEXAS TECH
        UNIVERSITY, 1974.

13433   SMITH, PATRICIA A.   "NEGRO COWBOYS."   NEGRO HISTORY
        BULLETIN, 29 (FEBRUARY, 1966):   107-108.

13434   SMITH, RALPH A.   "THE MAMELUKES OF WEST TEXAS AND
        MEXICO."   WEST TEXAS HISTORY YEARBOOK, 4 (1963):   5-22.

13435   SMITH, RALPH A.   "MEXICAN AND ANGLO-SAXON TRAFFIC IN
        SCALPS, SLAVES, AND LIVESTOCK, 1835-1841."   WEST TEXAS
        HISTORICAL ASSOCIATION YEARBOOK, 36 (OCTOBER, 1960):
        98-115.

13436   SMITHER, HARRIET.   "ENGLISH ABOLITIONISM AND THE
        ANNEXATION OF TEXAS."   SOUTHWESTERN HISTORICAL
        QUARTERLY, 32 (JANUARY, 1929):   193-205.

13437   SMYRL, FRANK H.   "UNIONISM, ABOLITIONISM, AND VIGILANTISM
        IN TEXAS, 1856-1865."   M.A. THESIS, UNIVERSITY OF
        TEXAS, 1961.

13438   ST. CLAIR, LAWRENCE W.   "HISTORY OF ROBERTSON COUNTY."
        M.A. THESIS, UNIVERSITY OF TEXAS, 1931.

13439   STARK, ANNE.   "A HISTORY OF DALLAS COUNTY."   M.A. THESIS,
        UNIVERSITY OF TEXAS, 1935.

13440   STENBERG, RICHARD R.   "THOMAS HART BENTON AND TEXAS,
        1818-1845."   M.A. THESIS, UNIVERSITY OF TEXAS, 1929.

13441   STROBEL, ABNER J.   THE OLD PLANTATIONS AND THEIR OWNERS
        OF BRAZORIA COUNTY, TEXAS.   HOUSTON: N.P., 1926.

13442   TARLTON, DEWITT T.   "THE HISTORY OF THE COTTON INDUSTRY
        IN TEXAS, 1820-1850."   M.A. THESIS, UNIVERSITY OF
        TEXAS, 1923.

13443   TELFORD, MARGARET J.A.   "SLAVE RESISTANCE IN TEXAS."
        M.A. THESIS, SOUTHERN METHODIST UNIVERSITY, 1975.

13444   THORPE, REED.   "THE SOUTHWEST AND SLAVERY."   M.S. THESIS,
        UNIVERSITY OF UTAH, 1943.

13445   TYLER, RONNIE C.   "SLAVE OWNERS AND RUNAWAY SLAVES IN
        TEXAS."   M.A. THESIS, TEXAS CHRISTIAN UNIVERSITY, 1965.

13446   TYLER, RONNIE C. AND MURPHY, LAWRENCE R. (EDS.).   THE
        SLAVE NARRATIVES OF TEXAS.   AUSTIN: ENCINO PRESS,
        1974.

13447   WALLACE, JAMES O.   "SAN ANTONIO DURING THE CIVIL WAR."
        M.A. THESIS, ST. MARY'S UNIVERSITY, SAN ANTONIO, 1940.

13448   WATSON, TOM V.   "A STUDY IN AGRICULTURE IN COLONIAL
        TEXAS, 1821-1836."   M.A. THESIS, TEXAS TECHNOLOGICAL
        COLLEGE, 1935.

13449   WHEELER, KENNETH W.   TO WEAR A CITY'S CROWN: THE
        BEGINNINGS OF URBAN GROWTH IN TEXAS, 1836-1865.
        CAMBRIDGE: HARVARD UNIVERSITY PRESS, 1968.

13450   WHITE, FRANK B.   "A HISTORY OF THE TERRITORY THAT NOW
        CONSTITUTES WALLER COUNTY, TEXAS, FROM 1821 TO 1884."
        M.A. THESIS, UNIVERSITY OF TEXAS, 1936.

13451   WHITE, RAYMOND E.   "COTTON GINNING IN TEXAS TO 1861."
        SOUTHWESTERN HISTORICAL QUARTERLY, 61 (OCTOBER, 1957):
        257-269.

13452   WHITE, WILLIAM W.   "MIGRATION INTO WEST TEXAS,
        1845-1860." M.A. THESIS, UNIVERSITY OF TEXAS, 1948.

13453   WHITE, WILLIAM W.   "THE TEXAS SLAVE INSURRECTION OF
        1860." SOUTHWESTERN HISTORICAL QUARTERLY, 52
        (JANUARY, 1949): 259-285.

13454   WILDY, CLARISSA H.   "FRANCIS MARION RAY: HIS LIFE AS
        SLAVE AND FREEDMAN IN TEXAS AND CALIFORNIA." M.A.
        THESIS, UNIVERSITY OF HAWAII, 1976.

13455   WINFREY, DORMAN H.   "JULIEN SIDNEY DEVEREUX AND HIS MONTE
        VERDI, TEXAS, PLANTATION." PH.D. DISSERTATION,
        UNIVERSITY OF TEXAS, 1962.

13456   WINNINGHAM, MRS. DAVID W.   "SAM HOUSTON AND SLAVERY."
        TEXANA, 3 (SUMMER, 1965): 93-104.

13457   WOOD, WILLIAM.   "GROWTH OF ANTI-SLAVERY SENTIMENT." GULF
        STATES HISTORICAL MAGAZINE, 2 (SEPTEMBER, 1903): 99.

13458   WOOLFOLK, GEORGE R.   "COTTON CAPITALISM AND SLAVE LABOR
        IN TEXAS." SOUTHWESTERN SOCIAL SCIENCE QUARTERLY, 37
        (JUNE, 1956): 43-52.

13459   WOOLFOLK, GEORGE R.   "SOURCES OF THE HISTORY OF THE NEGRO
        IN TEXAS WITH SPECIAL REFERENCE TO THEIR IMPLICATIONS
        FOR RESEARCH IN SLAVERY." JOURNAL OF NEGRO HISTORY,
        42 (JANUARY, 1957): 38-47.

13460   WOOLFOLK, GEORGE R.   "SOURCES OF THE HISTORY OF THE NEGRO
        IN TEXAS, WITH SPECIAL REFERENCE TO THEIR IMPLICATIONS
        FOR RESEARCH IN SLAVERY." NEGRO HISTORY BULLETIN, 20
        (FEBRUARY, 1957): 105-107, 112.

13461   WOOLFOLK, GEORGE R.   "TURNER'S SAFETY-VALVE AND FREE
        NEGRO WESTWARD MIGRATION." PACIFIC NORTHWEST
        QUARTERLY, 56 (JULY, 1965): 125-130.

13462   WOOSTER, RALPH A.   "NOTES ON TEXAS' LARGEST SLAVEHOLDERS,
        1860." SOUTHWESTERN HISTORICAL QUARTERLY, 65 (JULY,
        1961): 72-79.

13463 WOOSTER, RALPH A. "WEALTHY TEXANS, 1860." SOUTHWESTERN
       HISTORICAL QUARTERLY, 71 (OCTOBER, 1967): 163-180.

13464 WORTHAM, SUE C. "THE ROLE OF THE NEGRO ON THE TEXAS
       FRONTIER, 1821-1836." M.A. THESIS, SOUTHWEST TEXAS
       STATE UNIVERSITY, 1970.

VIRGINIA

13465 ALBERT, PETER J. "THE PROTEAN INSTITUTION: THE
       GEOGRAPHY, ECONOMY, AND IDEOLOGY OF SLAVERY IN
       POST-REVOLUTIONARY VIRGINIA." PH.D. DISSERTATION,
       UNIVERSITY OF MARYLAND, 1976.

13466 AMBLER, CHARLES H. "THE CLEAVAGE BETWEEN EASTERN AND
       WESTERN VIRGINIA." AMERICAN HISTORICAL REVIEW, 15
       (JULY, 1910): 762-780.

13467 AMBLER, CHARLES H. SECTIONALISM IN VIRGINIA FROM 1776 TO
       1861. CHICAGO: UNIVERSITY OF CHICAGO PRESS, 1910.

13468 AMES, SUSIE M. READING, WRITING AND ARITHMETIC IN
       VIRGINIA, 1607-1699. WILLIAMSBURG: HISTORICAL
       BOOKLET NUMBER 15, 1957.

13469 AMES, SUSIE M. STUDIES OF THE VIRGINIA EASTERN SHORE IN
       THE SEVENTEENTH CENTURY. RICHMOND: DIETZ PRESS, 1940.

13470 ARMSTRONG, THOMAS F. "URBAN VISION IN VIRGINIA: A
       COMPARATIVE STUDY OF ANTE-BELLUM FREDERICKSBURG,
       LYNCHBURG, AND STAUNTON." PH.D. DISSERTATION,
       UNIVERSITY OF VIRGINIA, 1974.

13471 ARNOLD, B.W., JR. "CONCERNING THE NEGROES OF THE CITY OF
       LYNCHBURG, VIRGINIA." PUBLICATIONS OF THE SOUTHERN
       HISTORY ASSOCIATION, 10 (JANUARY, 1906): 19-30.

13472 ARTHUR, T.S. AND CARPENTER, W.H. THE HISTORY OF VIRGINIA
       FROM ITS EARLIEST SETTLEMENT TO THE PRESENT TIME.
       PHILADELPHIA: J.B. LIPPINCOTT, 1865.

13473 AYRES, S. EDWARD. "ALBEMARLE COUNTY, 1744-1770: AN
       ECONOMIC, POLITICAL, AND SOCIAL ANALYSIS." MAGAZINE
       OF ALBEMARLE COUNTY HISTORY, 25 (1966-1967): 37-72.

13474 BABCOCK, THEODORE S. "MANUMISSION IN VIRGINIA,
       1782-1806." M.A. THESIS, UNIVERSITY OF VIRGINIA, 1974.

13475 BAILEY, CLAY. "JOSEPH R. ANDERSON OF TREDEGAR."
       COMMONWEALTH, 12 (NOVEMBER, 1959): 2, 36, 38.

13476 BAILEY, RAYMOND C. "RACIAL DISCRIMINATION AGAINST FREE
       BLACKS IN ANTEBELLUM VIRGINIA: THE CASE OF HARRY
       JACKSON." WEST VIRGINIA HISTORY, 39 (JANUARY-APRIL,

1978): 181-186.

13477   BAILOR, KENNETH M. "JOHN TAYLOR OF CAROLINE:
        CONTINUITY, CHANGE AND DISCONTINUITY IN VIRGINIA'S
        SENTIMENTS TOWARD SLAVERY." VIRGINIA MAGAZINE OF
        HISTORY AND BIOGRAPHY, 75 (JULY, 1967): 290-304.

13478   BAILYN, BERNARD. "POLITICS AND SOCIAL STRUCTURE IN
        VIRGINIA." IN SMITH, JAMES M. (ED.).
        SEVENTEENTH-CENTURY AMERICA: ESSAYS IN COLONIAL
        HISTORY. CHAPEL HILL: UNIVERSITY OF NORTH CAROLINA
        PRESS, 1959, PP. 90-115.

13479   BALLAGH, JAMES C. "THE ANTI-SLAVERY SENTIMENT IN
        VIRGINIA." SOUTH ATLANTIC QUARTERLY, 1 (APRIL, 1902):
        107-117.

13480   BALLAGH, JAMES C. A HISTORY OF SLAVERY IN VIRGINIA.
        BALTIMORE: JOHNS HOPKINS PRESS, 1902.

13481   BALLAGH, JAMES C. WHITE SERVITUDE IN THE COLONY OF
        VIRGINIA. BALTIMORE: JOHNS HOPKINS PRESS, 1895.

13482   BARBER, JAMES G. "ALEXANDRIA IN THE CIVIL WAR,
        1861-1865." M.A. THESIS, VIRGINIA POLYTECHNIC
        INSTITUTE AND STATE UNIVERSITY, 1977.

13483   BARRINGER, PAUL B. THE NATURAL BENT: THE MEMOIRS OF DR.
        PAUL B. BARRINGER. CHAPEL HILL: UNIVERSITY OF NORTH
        CAROLINA PRESS, 1949.

13484   BARROW, ROBERT M. "WILLIAMSBURG AND NORFOLK: MUNICIPAL
        GOVERNMENT AND JUSTICE IN COLONIAL VIRGINIA." M.A.
        THESIS, COLLEGE OF WILLIAM AND MARY, 1960.

13485   BARRY, WAYNE E. "SLAVES AGAINST THEIR MASTERS' WILL: A
        JUDICIAL HISTORY OF VIRGINIA'S MANUMISSION LAW,
        1800-1860." M.A. THESIS, UNIVERSITY OF MINNESOTA,
        1979.

13486   BASKIN, ANDREW L. "PEOPLE OF COLOR IN BEDFORD COUNTY AND
        FRANKLIN COUNTY, 1850-1865." IN TALBERT, ROY JR.
        (ED.). STUDIES IN THE LOCAL HISTORY OF SLAVERY:
        ESSAYS PREPARED FOR THE BOOKER T. WASHINGTON NATIONAL
        MONUMENT. FERRUM, VA: UNITED STATES NATIONAL PARK
        SERVICE, 1978, PP. 88-127.

13487   BASSETT, JOHN S. (ED.). THE WESTOVER JOURNAL OF JOHN A.
        SELDEN, ESQUIRE, 1858-1862. NORTHAMPTON, MA: SMITH
        COLLEGE STUDIES IN HISTORY, 1921.

13488   BEAR, JAMES A., JR. (ED.). JEFFERSON AT MONTICELLO:
        MEMOIRS OF A MONTICELLO SLAVE AS DICTATED TO CHARLES
        CAMPBELL BY ISAAC. CHARLOTTESVILLE: UNIVERSITY PRESS
        OF VIRGINIA, 1967.

13489   BEARSS, EDWIN C. THE BURROUGHS PLANTATION AS A LIVING
        HISTORICAL FARM. WASHINGTON: UNITED STATES NATIONAL
        PARK SERVICE, 1969.

13490   BEATTY, JAMES P. "THOMAS JEFFERSON AND SLAVERY." M.A.
        THESIS, NORTH TEXAS STATE UNIVERSITY, 1973.

13491   BEAUCHAMP, HELEN C. "SLAVERY AS AN ISSUE IN VIRGINIA
        POLITICS, 1828-1836." M.A. THESIS, UNIVERSITY OF
        CHICAGO, 1930.

13492   BEEMAN, RICHARD R. "LABOR FORCES AND RACE RELATIONS: A
        COMPARATIVE VIEW OF THE COLONIZATION OF BRAZIL AND
        VIRGINIA." POLITICAL SCIENCE QUARTERLY, 86 (DECEMBER,
        1971): 609-636.

13493   BEEMAN, RICHARD R. THE OLD DOMINION AND THE NEW NATION,
        1788-1801. LEXINGTON: UNIVERSITY PRESS OF KENTUCKY,
        1972.

13494   BEEMAN, RICHARD R. "THE OLD DOMINION AND THE NEW NATION,
        1788-1801." PH.D. DISSERTATION, UNIVERSITY OF
        CHICAGO, 1968.

13495   BEEMAN, RICHARD R. "SOCIAL CHANGE AND CULTURAL CONFLICT
        IN VIRGINIA: LUNENBURG COUNTY, 1746 TO 1774."
        WILLIAM AND MARY QUARTERLY, 3RD SER., 35 (JULY, 1978):
        455-476.

13496   BERKELEY, FRANCIS L., JR. DUNMORE'S PROCLAMATION OF
        EMANCIPATION. CHARLOTTESVILLE: TRACEY W. MCGREGOR
        LIBRARY, UNIVERSITY OF VIRGINIA, 1941.

13497   BETTS, EDWIN M. AND BEAR, JAMES A., JR. (EDS.). THE
        FAMILY LETTERS OF THOMAS JEFFERSON. COLUMBIA:
        UNIVERSITY OF MISSOURI PRESS, 1966.

13498   BILLINGS, WARREN M. "THE CASES OF FERNANDO AND ELIZABETH
        KEY: A NOTE ON THE STATUS OF BLACKS IN
        SEVENTEENTH-CENTURY VIRGINIA." WILLIAM AND MARY
        QUARTERLY, 3RD SER., 30 (JULY, 1973): 467-474.

13499   BLACKFORD, L. MINOR. MINE EYES HAVE SEEN THE GLORY: THE
        STORY OF A VIRGINIA LADY. CAMBRIDGE: HARVARD
        UNIVERSITY PRESS, 1954.

13500   BOGGER, TOMMY L. "THE SLAVE AND FREE BLACK COMMUNITY IN
        NORFOLK, 1775-1865." PH.D. DISSERTATION, UNIVERSITY
        OF VIRGINIA, 1976.

13501   BONEKEMPER, EDWARD H. "NEGROES' FREEDOM OF CONTACT IN
        ANTE-BELLUM VIRGINIA, 1620-1860." M.A. THESIS, OLD
        DOMINION UNIVERSITY, 1971.

13502   BONEY, F.N. "THE BLUE LIZARD: ANOTHER VIEW OF NAT

TURNER'S COUNTRY ON THE EVE OF REBELLION." PHYLON, 31
(WINTER, 1970): 351-358.

13503   BONEY, F.N. "NATHANIEL FRANCIS, REPRESENTATIVE
ANTEBELLUM SOUTHERNER." PROCEEDINGS OF THE AMERICAN
PHILOSOPHICAL SOCIETY, 118 (OCTOBER, 1974): 449-458.

13504   BOOKER, H. MARSHALL. "THOMAS RODERICK DEW: FORGOTTEN
VIRGINIAN." VIRGINIA CAVALCADE, 19 (AUTUMN, 1969):
20-29.

13505   BOSKIN, JOSEPH. INTO SLAVERY: RACIAL DECISIONS IN THE
VIRGINIA COLONY. PHILADELPHIA: J.B. LIPPINCOTT
COMPANY, 1976.

13506   BOWERS, JAMES C., JR. "SLAVERY AND SECESSION SENTIMENT
IN VIRGINIA, 1860-1861." M.A. THESIS, UNIVERSITY OF
VIRGINIA, 1928.

13507   BOWMAN, LARRY G. "VIRGINIA'S USE OF BLACKS IN THE FRENCH
AND INDIAN WAR." WESTERN PENNSYLVANIA HISTORICAL
MAGAZINE, 53 (JANUARY, 1970): 57-63.

13508   BRACEY, SUSAN L. LIFE BY THE ROARING ROANOKE: A HISTORY
OF MECKLENBURG COUNTY, VIRGINIA. MECKLENBURG COUNTY,
VA: MECKLENBURG COUNTY BICENTENNIAL COMMISSION, 1977.

13509   BRADFORD, S. SYDNEY. "THE NEGRO IRONWORKER IN
ANTE-BELLUM VIRGINIA." JOURNAL OF SOUTHERN HISTORY,
25 (MAY, 1959): 194-206.

13510   BRADFORD, SAMUEL S. "THE ANTE-BELLUM CHARCOAL IRON
INDUSTRY OF VIRGINIA." PH.D. DISSERTATION, COLUMBIA
UNIVERSITY, 1958.

13511   BRANSCOME, JAMES L. "IMPRESSMENT IN THE STATE OF
VIRGINIA DURING THE CIVIL WAR." M.A. THESIS, WAKE
FOREST UNIVERSITY, 1976.

13512   BRATTON, MARY J. (ED.). "FIELDS'S OBSERVATIONS: THE
SLAVE NARRATIVE OF A NINETEENTH-CENTURY VIRGINIAN."
VIRGINIA MAGAZINE OF HISTORY AND BIOGRAPHY, 88
(JANUARY, 1980): 75-93.

13513   BRATTON, MARY J. "JOHN JASPER OF RICHMOND: FROM SLAVE
PREACHER TO COMMUNITY LEADER." VIRGINIA CAVALCADE, 29
(SUMMER, 1979): 32-39.

13514   BREEN, T.H. "A CHANGING LABOR FORCE AND RACE RELATIONS
IN VIRGINIA, 1660-1710." JOURNAL OF SOCIAL HISTORY, 6
(FALL, 1973): 3-25.

13515   BREEN, T.H. PURITANS AND ADVENTURERS: CHANGE AND
PERSISTENCE IN EARLY AMERICA. NEW YORK: OXFORD
UNIVERSITY PRESS, 1980.

13516   BREEN, T.H. AND INNES, STEPHEN. "MYNE OWNE GROUND":
        RACE AND FREEDOM ON VIRGINIA'S EASTERN SHORE,
        1640-1676. NEW YORK: OXFORD UNIVERSITY PRESS, 1980.

13517   BREWER, JAMES H. THE CONFEDERATE NEGRO: VIRGINIA'S
        CRAFTSMEN AND MILITARY LABORERS, 1861-1865. DURHAM:
        DUKE UNIVERSITY PRESS, 1969.

13518   BREWER, JAMES H. "NEGRO PROPERTY OWNERS IN
        SEVENTEENTH-CENTURY VIRGINIA." WILLIAM AND MARY
        QUARTERLY, 3RD SER., 12 (OCTOBER, 1955): 575-580.

13519   BRIDENBAUGH, CARL. JAMESTOWN, 1544-1699. NEW YORK:
        OXFORD UNIVERSITY PRESS, 1980.

13520   BROCK, ROBERT A. "THE FOURTH CHARTER OF THE ROYAL
        AFRICAN COMPANY OF ENGLAND, SEPTEMBER 27, 1672, WITH
        PREFATORY NOTE, EXHIBITING THE PAST RELATION OF
        VIRGINIA TO AFRICAN SLAVERY." COLLECTIONS OF THE
        VIRGINIA HISTORICAL SOCIETY, N.S., 6 (1887): 1-60.

13521   BROCK, ROBERT A. "PREFATORY NOTE, EXHIBITING THE PAST
        RELATION OF VIRGINIA TO AFRICAN SLAVERY." COLLECTIONS
        OF THE VIRGINIA HISTORICAL SOCIETY, N.S., 6 (1887):
        1-36.

13522   BRODIE, FAWN M. "THE GREAT JEFFERSON TABOO." AMERICAN
        HERITAGE, 23 (JUNE, 1972): 49-57, 97-100.

13523   BRODIE, FAWN M. THOMAS JEFFERSON: AN INTIMATE HISTORY.
        NEW YORK: W.W. NORTON, 1974.

13524   BRODIE, FAWN M. "THOMAS JEFFERSON'S UNKNOWN
        GRANDCHILDREN: A STUDY IN HISTORICAL SILENCE."
        AMERICAN HERITAGE, 27 (OCTOBER, 1976): 28-33, 94-99.

13525   BROMBERG, ALAN B. "SLAVERY IN THE VIRGINIA TOBACCO
        FACTORIES, 1800-1860." M.A. THESIS, UNIVERSITY OF
        VIRGINIA, 1968.

13526   BROOKS, ALBERT N.O. "EDUCATION OF THE NEGRO IN VIRGINIA
        PRIOR TO 1861." M.A. THESIS, HOWARD UNIVERSITY, 1938.

13527   BROWN, ELISABETH D. "SOME ECONOMIC ASPECTS OF SLAVERY IN
        VIRGINIA DURING THE COLONIAL AND NATIONAL PERIODS."
        M.A. THESIS, UNIVERSITY OF CHICAGO, 1933.

13528   BROWN, LETITIA W. FREE NEGROES IN THE DISTRICT OF
        COLUMBIA, 1790-1846. NEW YORK: OXFORD UNIVERSITY
        PRESS, 1972.

13529   BROWN, MARY V. "A HISTORY OF NEGROES IN MONONGALIA
        COUNTY." M.A. THESIS, WEST VIRGINIA UNIVERSITY, 1930.

13530   BROWN, MRS. DOUGLAS. "CEDAR CREEK MONTHLY MEETING AND

ITS MEETING HOUSE." _WILLIAM AND MARY QUARTERLY_, 2ND
SER., 19 (JULY, 1939): 293-298.

13531 BROWN, ROBERT E. AND BROWN, B. KATHERINE. _VIRGINIA,_
1705-1786: DEMOCRACY OR ARISTOCRACY? EAST LANSING:
MICHIGAN STATE UNIVERSITY PRESS, 1964.

13532 BROWN, W.H. _THE EDUCATION AND ECONOMIC DEVELOPMENT OF_
THE NEGRO IN VIRGINIA. CHARLOTTESVILLE:
SURBER-ARUNDALE COUNTY, 1923.

13533 BRUCE, KATHLEEN. "SLAVE LABOR IN THE VIRGINIA IRON
INDUSTRY." _WILLIAM AND MARY COLLEGE QUARTERLY_
HISTORICAL MAGAZINE, 2ND SER., 6 (OCTOBER, 1926):
289-303; 7 (JANUARY, 1927): 21-31.

13534 BRUCE, KATHLEEN. _VIRGINIA IRON MANUFACTURE IN THE SLAVE_
ERA. NEW YORK: CENTURY COMPANY, 1930.

13535 BRUCE, KATHLEEN. "VIRGINIA IRON MANUFACTURE IN THE SLAVE
ERA." PH.D. DISSERTATION, RADCLIFFE COLLEGE, 1924.

13536 BRUCE, KATHLEEN. "VIRGINIAN AGRICULTURAL DECLINE TO
1860: A FALLACY." _AGRICULTURAL HISTORY_, 6 (JANUARY,
1932): 3-13.

13537 BRUCE, PHILIP A. _ECONOMIC HISTORY OF VIRGINIA IN THE_
SEVENTEENTH CENTURY. 2 VOLS. NEW YORK: MACMILLAN,
1896.

13538 BRUCE, PHILIP A. _INSTITUTIONAL HISTORY OF VIRGINIA IN_
THE SEVENTEENTH CENTURY. 2 VOLS. NEW YORK: G.P.
PUTNAM'S SONS, 1910.

13539 BRUCE, PHILIP A. "THE SUPERIORITY OF SLAVE LABOR." IN
CHANDLER, JULIAN A.C. (ED.). _THE SOUTH IN THE_
BUILDING OF THE NATION. 12 VOLS. RICHMOND: SOUTHERN
HISTORICAL PUBLICATION SOCIETY, 1909, VOL. 1, PP.
55-58.

13540 BRUCE, PHILIP A. _THE VIRGINIA PLUTARCH._ 2 VOLS. CHAPEL
HILL: UNIVERSITY OF NORTH CAROLINA PRESS, 1929.

13541 BRUCE, WILLIAM C. "A PLANTATION RETROSPECT." _VIRGINIA_
QUARTERLY REVIEW, 7 (OCTOBER, 1931): 547-561.

13542 BRYAN, C. BRAXTON. "THE NEGRO IN VIRGINIA." _SOUTHERN_
WORKMAN, 34 (JANUARY, FEBRUARY, MARCH, 1905): 51-53,
100-107, 170-178.

13543 BRYAN, CORBIN B. _THE NEGRO IN VIRGINIA._ HAMPTON:
HAMPTON INSTITUTE PRESS, 1905.

13544 BRYDON, G. MACLAREN. "THE BRISTOL IRON WORKS IN KING
GEORGE COUNTY." _VIRGINIA MAGAZINE OF HISTORY AND_

BIOGRAPHY, 42 (APRIL, 1934): 97-102.

13545 BRYDON, GEORGE M. "THE WEALTH OF THE CLERGY OF VIRGINIA
       IN 1791." HISTORICAL MAGAZINE OF THE PROTESTANT
       EPISCOPAL CHURCH, 22 (MARCH, 1953): 91-98.

13546 BUEHLER, RICHARD D. "VIRGINIA'S ATTITUDE TOWARD SLAVERY,
       1776-1800." M.A. THESIS, COLUMBIA UNIVERSITY, 1964.

13547 BURWELL, LETITIA M. A GIRL'S LIFE IN VIRGINIA BEFORE THE
       WAR. NEW YORK: F.A. STOKES, 1895.

13548 BURWELL, LETITIA M. PLANTATION REMINISCENCES.
       OWENSBORO, KY: N.P., 1878.

13549 BUZZELL, L.H. "SLAVERY IN RANDOLPH COUNTY." RANDOLPH
       COUNTY HISTORICAL SOCIETY MAGAZINE OF HISTORY AND
       BIOGRAPHY, NO. 9 (1937): 58-62.

13550 CALLAHAN, JAMES M. SEMI-CENTENNIAL HISTORY OF WEST
       VIRGINIA. CHARLESTON: SEMI-CENTENNIAL COMMISSION OF
       WEST VIRGINIA, 1913.

13551 CAMPBELL, T.E. COLONIAL CAROLINE: A HISTORY OF CAROLINE
       COUNTY, VIRGINIA. RICHMOND: DIETZ PRESS, 1954.

13552 CARDWELL, GARY L. "SLAVERY AND SOCIETY IN THE TOBACCO
       KINGDOM: FRANKLIN AND BEDFORD COUNTIES, VIRGINIA,
       1850-1865." IN TALBERT, ROY JR. (ED.). STUDIES IN
       THE LOCAL HISTORY OF SLAVERY: ESSAYS PREPARED FOR THE
       BOOKER T. WASHINGTON NATIONAL MONUMENT. FERRUM, VA:
       UNITED STATES NATIONAL PARK SERVICE, 1978, PP. 1-8.

13553 CAREY, PAUL M. "JEFFERSON AND SLAVERY." M.A. THESIS,
       UNIVERSITY OF VIRGINIA, 1952.

13554 CASSELL, FRANK A. "SLAVES OF THE CHESAPEAKE BAY AREA AND
       THE WAR OF 1812." JOURNAL OF NEGRO HISTORY, 57
       (APRIL, 1972): 144-155.

13555 CHAMBERLAYNE, C.G. (ED.). THE VESTRY BOOK AND REGISTER
       OF ST. PETER'S PARISH, NEW KENT AND JAMES CITY
       COUNTIES, VIRGINIA, 1684-1786. RICHMOND: VIRGINIA
       STATE LIBRARY, 1937.

13556 "CHARLES CITY COUNTY PETITIONS." TYLER'S QUARTERLY
       HISTORICAL AND GENEALOGICAL MAGAZINE, 2 (JANUARY,
       1921): 160-176.

13557 CLAIBORNE, WILLIAM B. "RUNAWAY SLAVES IN VIRGINIA."
       M.A. THESIS, VIRGINIA STATE UNIVERSITY, 1978.

13558 CLARK, CHARLES B. THE EASTERN SHORE OF MARYLAND AND
       VIRGINIA. 3 VOLS. NEW YORK: LEWIS HISTORICAL
       PUBLISHING COMPANY, 1950.

13559   CLAY, EARL C. "THE NEGRO IN GREENBRIER COUNTY." M.A.
       THESIS, VIRGINIA STATE COLLEGE, 1946.

13560   CLEMENT, SAMUEL S. MEMOIRS OF SAMUEL SPOTTFORD CLEMENT:
       RELATING INTERESTING EXPERIENCES IN DAYS OF SLAVERY
       AND FREEDOM. STEUBENVILLE, OH: HERALD PRINTING
       COMPANY, 1908.

13561   CLICK, PATRICIA C. "SLAVERY AND SOCIETY IN THE
       SHENANDOAH VALLEY OF VIRGINIA, 1790-1830." M.A.
       THESIS, UNIVERSITY OF VIRGINIA, 1974.

13562   COHEN, WILLIAM. "THOMAS JEFFERSON AND THE PROBLEM OF
       SLAVERY." JOURNAL OF AMERICAN HISTORY, 56 (DECEMBER,
       1969): 503-526.

13563   COLEMAN, ANNIE C. "THE NEGRO IN VIRGINIA AND SOUTH
       CAROLINA, 1861-1877, AS SEEN BY CONTEMPORARY OBSERVERS
       AND NEWSPAPERS AND BY HISTORIANS." M.A. THESIS,
       VIRGINIA STATE COLLEGE, 1967.

13564   COLEMAN, ELIZABETH D. "SOME BELOVED VIRGINIA MAMMIES."
       VIRGINIA CAVALCADE, 4 (SUMMER, 1954): 28-33.

13565   COLEMAN, MRS. GEORGE P. (ED.). VIRGINIA SILHOUETTES:
       CONTEMPORARY LETTERS CONCERNING NEGRO SLAVERY IN THE
       STATE OF VIRGINIA. RICHMOND: DIETZ PRINTING COMPANY,
       1934.

13566   COMETTI, ELIZABETH. "DEPREDATIONS IN VIRGINIA DURING THE
       REVOLUTION." IN RUTMAN, DARRETT B. (ED.). THE OLD
       DOMINION: ESSAYS FOR THOMAS PERKINS ABERNETHY.
       CHARLOTTESVILLE: UNIVERSITY PRESS OF VIRGINIA, 1964,
       PP. 135-151.

13567   CONDIT, WILLIAM W. "VIRGINIA'S EARLY IRON AGE." IRON
       WORKER, 23 (SUMMER, 1959): 1-7.

13568   CONLEY, PHIL. HISTORY OF THE WEST VIRGINIA COAL
       INDUSTRY. CHARLESTON, WV: EDUCATIONAL FOUNDATIONS,
       1960.

13569   COPE, ROBERT S. CARRY ME BACK: SLAVERY AND SERVITUDE IN
       SEVENTEENTH-CENTURY VIRGINIA. PIKEVILLE, KY:
       PIKEVILLE COLLEGE PRESS, 1973.

13570   COPE, ROBERT S. "SLAVERY AND SERVITUDE IN THE COLONY OF
       VIRGINIA IN THE SEVENTEENTH CENTURY." PH.D.
       DISSERTATION, OHIO STATE UNIVERSITY, 1951.

13571   CORBIN, FRANCIS. "SLAVERY IN VIRGINIA, 1819."
       MASSACHUSETTS HISTORICAL SOCIETY PROCEEDINGS, 43
       (1910): 261-265.

13572   COTTER, JOHN L. "CURRENT RESEARCH: NORTHEAST." SOCIETY

FOR HISTORICAL ARCHAEOLOGY NEWSLETTER, 10 (1977): 12-21.

13573 COX, HAROLD E. "FEDERALISM AND ANTI-FEDERALISM IN VIRGINIA--1787: A STUDY OF POLITICAL ECONOMIC MOTIVATIONS." PH.D. DISSERTATION, UNIVERSITY OF VIRGINIA, 1958.

13574 COYLE, BETTY W. "THE TREATMENT OF SERVANTS AND SLAVES IN COLONIAL VIRGINIA." M.A. THESIS, COLLEGE OF WILLIAM AND MARY, 1974.

13575 COYNER, MARTIN B., JR. "JOHN HARTWELL COCKE OF BREMO: AGRICULTURE AND SLAVERY IN THE ANTE-BELLUM SOUTH." PH.D. DISSERTATION, UNIVERSITY OF VIRGINIA, 1961.

13576 CRAPSEY, ALGERNON S. THE LAST OF THE HERETICS. NEW YORK: ALFRED A. KNOPF, 1924.

13577 CRAVEN, AVERY O. EDMUND RUFFIN SOUTHERNER: A STUDY IN SECESSION. NEW YORK: D. APPLETON AND COMPANY, 1932.

13578 CRAVEN, AVERY O. SOIL EXHAUSTION AS A FACTOR IN THE AGRICULTURAL HISTORY OF VIRGINIA AND MARYLAND, 1606-1860. URBANA: UNIVERSITY OF ILLINOIS STUDIES IN THE SOCIAL SCIENCES, 1925.

13579 CRAVEN, WESLEY F. "TWENTY NEGROES TO JAMESTOWN IN 1619?" VIRGINIA QUARTERLY REVIEW, 47 (SUMMER, 1971): 416-420.

13580 CRAVEN, WESLEY F. WHITE, RED, AND BLACK: THE SEVENTEENTH-CENTURY VIRGINIAN. CHARLOTTESVILLE: UNIVERSITY PRESS OF VIRGINIA, 1971.

13581 CRESSEY, PAMELA J. "AN ENDURING AFRO-AMERICAN NEIGHBORHOOD: AN ARCHAEOLOGICAL PERSPECTIVE FROM ALEXANDRIA, VIRGINIA." BLACK HERITAGE, 20 (SEPTEMBER-OCTOBER, 1980): 1-10.

13582 CULMER, FREDERIC A. "FLEMING TERRELL OF VIRGINIA AND MISSOURI AND THE CURIOUS CASE OF HIS SLAVES." VIRGINIA MAGAZINE OF HISTORY AND BIOGRAPHY, 58 (APRIL, 1950): 194-208.

13583 DABNEY, ROBERT L. A DEFENCE OF VIRGINIA (AND THROUGH HER, OF THE SOUTH) IN RECENT AND PENDING CONTESTS AGAINST THE SECTIONAL PARTY. NEW YORK: E.J. HALE AND SON, 1867.

13584 DAIN, NORMAN. DISORDERED MINDS: THE FIRST CENTURY OF EASTERN STATE HOSPITAL IN WILLIAMSBURG, VIRGINIA, 1766-1866. CHARLOTTESVILLE: UNIVERSITY PRESS OF VIRGINIA, 1971.

13585 DANIEL, W. HARRISON. "VIRGINIA BAPTISTS AND THE NEGRO IN

THE ANTEBELLUM ERA." JOURNAL OF NEGRO HISTORY, 56
(JANUARY, 1971): 1-16.

13586   DANIEL, W. HARRISON. "VIRGINIA BAPTISTS AND THE NEGRO IN
THE EARLY REPUBLIC." VIRGINIA MAGAZINE OF HISTORY AND
BIOGRAPHY, 80 (JANUARY, 1972): 60-69.

13587   DAVIS, J.E. "THE LOWER VIRGINIA PENINSULA--LIFE IN THE
SEVENTEENTH CENTURY." SOUTHERN WORKMAN, 29 (AUGUST,
1900): 478-483.

13588   DAVIS, J.E. "THE LOWER VIRGINIA PENINSULA--THE COMING OF
THE ENGLISH TO KECOUGHTAN." SOUTHERN WORKMAN, 29
(MAY, 1900): 283-287.

13589   DAVIS, J.E. "THE LOWER VIRGINIA PENINSULA--THE EARLY
YEARS OF THE EIGHTEENTH CENTURY." SOUTHERN WORKMAN,
31 (JANUARY, 1902): 21-26.

13590   DAVIS, RICHARD B. INTELLECTUAL LIFE IN JEFFERSON'S
VIRGINIA, 1790-1830. CHAPEL HILL: UNIVERSITY OF
NORTH CAROLINA PRESS, 1964.

13591   DAVIS, RICHARD B. (ED.). WILLIAM FITZHUGH AND HIS
CHESAPEAKE WORLD, 1676-1701. CHAPEL HILL: UNIVERSITY
OF NORTH CAROLINA PRESS, 1963.

13592   DAY, RICHARD E. RHAPSODY IN BLACK: THE LIFE STORY OF
JOHN JASPER. PHILADELPHIA: JUDSON PRESS, 1953.

13593   DECORSE, HELEN C. CHARLOTTESVILLE--A STUDY OF NEGRO LIFE
AND PERSONALITY. CHARLOTTESVILLE: UNIVERSITY OF
VIRGINIA PRESS, 1933.

13594   DEW, CHARLES B. IRONMAKER TO THE CONFEDERACY: JOSEPH R.
ANDERSON AND THE TREDEGAR IRON WORKS. NEW HAVEN:
YALE UNIVERSITY PRESS, 1966.

13595   DEW, CHARLES B. "SOUTHERN INDUSTRY IN THE CIVIL WAR ERA:
JOSEPH REID ANDERSON AND THE TREDEGAR IRON WORKS,
1859-1867." PH.D. DISSERTATION, JOHNS HOPKINS
UNIVERSITY, 1964.

13596   DREWRY, WILLIAM S. "SLAVE INSURRECTIONS IN VIRGINIA
(1830-1865)." PH.D. DISSERTATION, JOHNS HOPKINS
UNIVERSITY, 1900.

13597   DREWRY, WILLIAM S. THE SOUTHAMPTON INSURRECTION.
WASHINGTON: NEALE COMPANY, 1900.

13598   DUNN, RICHARD S. "A TALE OF TWO PLANTATIONS: SLAVE LIFE
AT MESOPOTAMIA IN JAMAICA AND MOUNT AIRY IN VIRGINIA,
1799 TO 1828." WILLIAM AND MARY QUARTERLY, 3RD SER.,
34 (JANUARY, 1977): 32-65.

13599   EARNEST, JOSEPH B.   THE RELIGIOUS DEVELOPMENT OF THE
        NEGRO IN VIRGINIA. CHARLOTTESVILLE: MICHIE COMPANY,
        1914.

13600   EARNEST, JOSEPH B.   "THE RELIGIOUS DEVELOPMENT OF THE
        NEGRO IN VIRGINIA." PH.D. DISSERTATION, UNIVERSITY OF
        VIRGINIA, 1914.

13601   EASTON, CHARLES E.   "NEGRO CONTRIBUTIONS TO THE POLITICAL
        AND LEGAL HISTORY OF THE SOUTHERN COUNTIES OF WEST
        VIRGINIA." M.A. THESIS, MARSHALL UNIVERSITY, 1964.

13602   EAVES, CHARLES D.   THE VIRGINIA TOBACCO INDUSTRY,
        1780-1860. LUBBOCK, TX: TEXAS TECHNOLOGICAL COLLEGE,
        1945.

13603   ECKENRODE, H.J.   "NEGROES IN RICHMOND IN 1864." VIRGINIA
        MAGAZINE OF HISTORY AND BIOGRAPHY, 46 (JULY, 1938):
        193-200.

13604   EGGLESTON, GEORGE C.   "THE OLD REGIME IN THE OLD
        DOMINION." ATLANTIC MONTHLY, 36 (NOVEMBER, 1875):
        603-616.

13605   EGGLESTON, JOSEPH D.   THE ATTITUDE OF VIRGINIA LEADERS
        TOWARD SLAVERY AND SECESSION. HARRISONBURG, VA:
        N.P., 1932.

13606   EMMERTH, BARBARA L.   "SLAVERY IN PRESENT WEST VIRGINIA IN
        1860." WEST VIRGINIA HISTORY, 21 (JULY, 1960):
        275-277.

13607   ENGS, ROBERT F.   FREEDOM'S FIRST GENERATION: BLACK
        HAMPTON, VIRGINIA, 1861-1890. PHILADELPHIA:
        UNIVERSITY OF PENNSYLVANIA PRESS, 1979.

13608   ERNST, WILLIAM J.   "CHANGES IN THE SLAVE POPULATION OF
        THE VIRGINIA TIDEWATER AND PIEDMONT, 1830-1860:   A
        STABLE POPULATION ANALYSIS." ESSAYS IN HISTORY, 19
        (1975):   75-88.

13609   ESSIG, JAMES D.   "A VERY WINTRY SEASON: VIRGINIA
        BAPTISTS AND SLAVERY, 1785-1797." VIRGINIA MAGAZINE
        OF HISTORY AND BIOGRAPHY, 88 (APRIL, 1980):   170-185.

13610   ETHERIDGE, HARRISON M.   "THE JORDAN HATCHER AFFAIR OF
        1852:   COLD JUSTICE AND WARM COMPASSION." VIRGINIA
        MAGAZINE OF HISTORY AND BIOGRAPHY, 84 (OCTOBER, 1976):
        446-463.

13611   EVANS, EMORY G. (ED.).   "A QUESTION OF COMPLEXION:
        DOCUMENTS CONCERNING THE NEGRO AND THE FRANCHISE IN
        EIGHTEENTH-CENTURY VIRGINIA." VIRGINIA MAGAZINE OF
        HISTORY AND BIOGRAPHY, 71 (OCTOBER, 1963):   411-415.

13612   EVANS, ROBLEY D.   A SAILOR'S LOG: RECOLLECTIONS OF FORTY
        YEARS OF NAVAL LIFE. NEW YORK: D. APPLETON, 1901.

13613   FARISH, HUNTER D. (ED.).   JOURNAL & LETTERS OF PHILIP
        VICKERS FITHIAN, 1773-1774: A PLANTATION TUTOR OF THE
        OLD DOMINION. WILLIAMSBURG: COLONIAL WILLIAMSBURG,
        INC., 1943.

13614   FARMER, H.H.   VIRGINIA BEFORE AND DURING THE WAR.
        HENDERSON, KY: THE AUTHOR, 1892.

13615   FIELDS, EMMETT B.   "THE AGRICULTURAL POPULATION OF
        VIRGINIA, 1850-1860." PH.D. DISSERTATION, VANDERBILT
        UNIVERSITY, 1953.

13616   FLEETWOOD, GEORGE B.   "SOUTHSIDE VIRGINIA IN THE MIDDLE
        PERIOD, WITH SPECIFIC REFERENCE TO THE RELATIONS
        BETWEEN LOCAL GOVERNMENT AND SLAVERY." M.A. THESIS,
        WAKE FOREST UNIVERSITY, 1940.

13617   FRANK, WILLARD.   "COLONIAL DISEQUILIBRIUM AND THE
        AMERICAN REVOLUTION: A REVIEW OF SOME RECENT WRITING
        OF HISTORY." IN RUTYNA, RICHARD A. AND STEWART, PETER
        C. (EDS.).   VIRGINIA IN THE AMERICAN REVOLUTION: A
        COLLECTION OF ESSAYS. NORFOLK: OLD DOMINION
        UNIVERSITY, 1977, PP. 1-37.

13618   "FREE AND SLAVE, NORFOLK COUNTY, 1782."   LOWER NORFOLK
        COUNTY VIRGINIA ANTIQUARY, 4 (1903):   163-166.

13619   FREEHLING, ALISON H.G.   "DRIFT TOWARD DISSOLUTION: THE
        VIRGINIA SLAVERY DEBATE OF 1831-1832." PH.D.
        DISSERTATION, UNIVERSITY OF MICHIGAN, 1974.

13620   FREEMAN, DOUGLAS S.   "THE ATTITUDE OF POLITICAL PARTIES
        IN VIRGINIA TO SLAVERY AND TO SECESSION (1846-1861)."
        PH.D. DISSERTATION, JOHNS HOPKINS UNIVERSITY, 1908.

13621   FUNKE, CAROL N.   "THE EMERGENCE OF AN AFRO-AMERICAN
        SOCIETY IN COLONIAL AMELIA COUNTY, VIRGINIA." M.A.
        THESIS, UTAH STATE UNIVERSITY, 1980.

13622   GAMBLE, ROBERT S.   SULLY: THE BIOGRAPHY OF A HOUSE.
        CHANTILLY, VA: SULLY FOUNDATION, 1973.

13623   GARA, LARRY (ED.).   "A NEW ENGLANDER'S VIEW OF PLANTATION
        LIFE: LETTERS OF EDWIN HALL TO CYRUS WOODMAN, 1837."
        JOURNAL OF SOUTHERN HISTORY, 18 (AUGUST, 1952):
        343-354.

13624   GEWEHR, WESLEY.   THE GREAT AWAKENING IN VIRGINIA,
        1740-1790. DURHAM: DUKE UNIVERSITY PRESS, 1930.

13625   GOLDFIELD, DAVID R.   "FRIENDS AND NEIGHBORS: URBAN-RURAL
        RELATIONS IN ANTEBELLUM VIRGINIA."   VIRGINIA

CAVALCADE, 25 (SUMMER, 1975): 14-27.

13626 GOLDFIELD, DAVID R. URBAN GROWTH IN THE AGE OF
       SECTIONALISM, VIRGINIA, 1847-1861. BATON ROUGE:
       LOUISIANA STATE UNIVERSITY PRESS, 1977.

13627 GOLDFIELD, DAVID R. "URBAN-RURAL RELATIONS IN THE OLD
       SOUTH: THE EXAMPLE OF VIRGINIA." JOURNAL OF URBAN
       HISTORY, 2 (FEBRUARY, 1976): 146-168.

13628 GOODWIN, MARY F. (ED.). "A LIBERIAN PACKET." VIRGINIA
       MAGAZINE OF HISTORY AND BIOGRAPHY, 59 (JANUARY, 1951):
       72-88.

13629 GORDON, ARMISTEAD C. "THE OLD REGIME IN VIRGINIA." IN
       MITCHELL, SAMUEL C. (ED.). THE SOUTH IN THE BUILDING
       OF THE NATION. 12 VOLS. RICHMOND: SOUTHERN
       HISTORICAL PUBLICATION SOCIETY, 1909, VOL. 10, PP.
       77-96.

13630 GRAGG, LARRY D. MIGRATION IN EARLY AMERICA: THE
       VIRGINIA QUAKER EXPERIENCE. ANN ARBOR: UMI RESEARCH
       PRESS, 1980.

13631 GREEN, RODNEY D. "URBAN INDUSTRY, BLACK RESISTANCE AND
       RACIAL RECONSTRUCTION IN THE ANTEBELLUM SOUTH: A
       GENERAL MODEL AND CASE STUDY IN URBAN VIRGINIA."
       PH.D. DISSERTATION, AMERICAN UNIVERSITY, 1980.

13632 GREENBERG, MICHAEL. "WILLIAM BYRD II AND THE WORLD OF
       THE MARKET." SOUTHERN STUDIES, 16 (WINTER, 1977):
       429-456.

13633 GREENBERG, MICHAEL S. "GENTLEMEN SLAVEHOLDERS: THE
       SOCIAL OUTLOOK OF THE VIRGINIA PLANTER CLASS." PH.D.
       DISSERTATION, RUTGERS UNIVERSITY, 1972

13634 GREENE, JACK P. (ED.). THE DIARY OF COLONEL LANDON
       CARTER OF SABINE HALL, 1752-1778. 2 VOLS.
       CHARLOTTESVILLE: UNIVERSITY PRESS OF VIRGINIA, 1965.

13635 GRINNAN, A.G. "THE BURNING OF EVE IN VIRGINIA."
       VIRGINIA MAGAZINE OF HISTORY AND BIOGRAPHY, 3
       (JANUARY, 1896): 307-310.

13636 GUILD, JUNE P. BLACK LAWS OF VIRGINIA: A SUMMARY OF THE
       LEGISLATIVE ACTS OF VIRGINIA CONCERNING NEGROES FROM
       EARLIEST TIMES TO THE PRESENT. RICHMOND: WHITTER &
       SHEPPERTON, 1936.

13637 HANDLIN, OSCAR AND HANDLIN, MARY F. "ORIGINS OF THE
       SOUTHERN LABOR SYSTEM." WILLIAM AND MARY QUARTERLY,
       3RD SER., 7 (APRIL, 1950): 199-222.

13638 HARLAN, LOUIS R. BOOKER T. WASHINGTON: THE MAKING OF A

BLACK LEADER, 1856-1901. NEW YORK: OXFORD UNIVERSITY
         PRESS, 1972.

13639 HARLAN, LOUIS R. "BOOKER T. WASHINGTON'S WEST VIRGINIA
         BOYHOOD." WEST VIRGINIA HISTORY, 32 (JANUARY, 1971):
         63-85.

13640 HARRISON, LOWELL H. "THOMAS RODERICK DEW: PHILOSOPHER
         OF THE OLD SOUTH." VIRGINIA MAGAZINE OF HISTORY AND
         BIOGRAPHY, 57 (OCTOBER, 1949): 390-404.

13641 HART, FREEMAN H. THE VALLEY OF VIRGINIA IN THE AMERICAN
         REVOLUTION, 1763-1789. CHAPEL HILL: UNIVERSITY OF
         NORTH CAROLINA PRESS, 1942.

13642 HAST, ADELE. "THE LEGAL STATUS OF THE NEGRO IN VIRGINIA,
         1705-1765." JOURNAL OF NEGRO HISTORY, 54 (JULY,
         1969): 217-239.

13643 HAUGHT, JAMES A. "INSTITUTE: IT SPRINGS FROM EPIC LOVE
         STORY." WEST VIRGINIA HISTORY, 32 (JANUARY, 1971):
         101-107.

13644 HAYMOND, HENRY. HISTORY OF HARRISON COUNTY, WEST
         VIRGINIA. MORGANTOWN, WV: ACME, 1910.

13645 HEDRICK, CHARLES E. "SOCIAL AND ECONOMIC ASPECTS OF
         SLAVERY IN THE TRANSMONTANE PRIOR TO 1850." PH.D.
         DISSERTATION, GEORGE PEABODY COLLEGE FOR TEACHERS,
         1927.

13646 HEMPHILL, JOHN. "VIRGINIA AND THE ENGLISH CONTINENTAL
         SYSTEM, 1689-1733: STUDIES IN THE DEVELOPMENT AND
         FLUCTUATIONS OF A COLONIAL ECONOMY UNDER IMPERIAL
         CONTROL." PH.D DISSERTATION, PRINCETON UNIVERSITY,
         1964.

13647 HENRY, GEORGE. LIFE OF GEORGE HENRY: TOGETHER WITH A
         BRIEF HISTORY OF THE COLORED PEOPLE OF AMERICA. N.P.:
         THE AUTHOR, 1894.

13648 HERNDON, G. MELVIN. "FROM ORPHANS TO MERCHANTS TO
         PLANTERS: THE GALT BROTHERS, WILLIAM AND JAMES."
         VIRGINIA CAVALCADE, 29 (SUMMER, 1979): 22-31.

13649 HERNDON, G. MELVIN. "SLAVERY IN ANTEBELLUM VIRGINIA:
         WILLIAM GALT, JR., 1839-1851, A CASE STUDY." SOUTHERN
         STUDIES, 16 (FALL, 1977): 309-320.

13650 HERNDON, G. MELVIN. "A WAR-INSPIRED INDUSTRY: THE
         MANUFACTURE OF HEMP IN VIRGINIA DURING THE
         REVOLUTION." VIRGINIA MAGAZINE OF HISTORY AND
         BIOGRAPHY, 74 (JULY, 1966): 301-311.

13651 HERNDON, GEORGE M. "THE STORY OF HEMP IN COLONIAL

VIRGINIA." PH.D. DISSERTATION, UNIVERSITY OF
VIRGINIA, 1959.

13652   HICKEY, DONALD R. (ED.). "SLAVERY AND THE REPUBLICAN
        EXPERIMENT: A VIEW FROM WESTERN VIRGINIA IN 1806."
        WEST VIRGINIA HISTORY, 39 (JANUARY-APRIL, 1978):
        236-240.

13653   HICKIN, P.E.P. "'SITUATION ETHICS' AND ANTISLAVERY
        ATTITUDES IN THE VIRGINIA CHURCHES." IN BOLES, JOHN
        B. (ED.). AMERICA: THE MIDDLE PERIOD: ESSAYS IN
        HONOR OF BERNARD MAYO. CHARLOTTESVILLE: UNIVERSITY
        PRESS OF VIRGINIA, 1973, PP. 138-215.

13654   HICKIN, PATRICIA. "GENTLE AGITATOR: SAMUEL M. JANNEY
        AND THE ANTISLAVERY MOVEMENT IN VIRGINIA, 1842-1851."
        JOURNAL OF SOUTHERN HISTORY, 37 (MAY, 1971): 159-190.

13655   HOLLAND, C.G. "THE SLAVE POPULATION ON THE PLANTATION OF
        JOHN C. COHOON, JR., NANSEMOND COUNTY, VIRGINIA,
        1811-1863: SELECTED DEMOGRAPHIC CHARACTERISTICS."
        VIRGINIA MAGAZINE OF HISTORY AND BIOGRAPHY, 80
        (JANUARY, 1972): 333-340.

13656   HOLLAND, FRANCIS R., JR. "THREE VIRGINIA IRON COMPANIES,
        1825-1865." M.A. THESIS, UNIVERSITY CF TEXAS, 1958.

13657   HOOK, FRANCIS M. "THE NEGRO IN COLONIAL VIRGINIA,
        1619-1765." M.A. THESIS, COLLEGE OF WILLIAM AND MARY,
        1952.

13658   HUGGINS, NATHAN I. SLAVE AND CITIZEN: THE LIFE OF
        FREDERICK DOUGLASS. BOSTON: LITTLE, BROWN AND
        COMPANY, 1980.

13659   HUGHES, SARAH S. "ELIZABETH CITY COUNTY, VIRGINIA,
        1782-1810: THE ECONOMIC AND SOCIAL STRUCTURE OF A
        TIDEWATER COUNTY IN THE EARLY NATIONAL YEARS." PH.D.
        DISSERTATION, COLLEGE OF WILLIAM AND MARY, 1975.

13660   HUGHES, SARAH S. "SLAVES FOR HIRE: THE ALLOCATION OF
        BLACK LABOR IN ELIZABETH CITY COUNTY VIRGINIA, 1792 TO
        1810." WILLIAM AND MARY QUARTERLY, 3RD SER., 35
        (APRIL, 1978): 260-286.

13661   JACKSON, LUTHER P. "THE EARLY STRIVINGS OF THE NEGRO IN
        VIRGINIA." JOURNAL OF NEGRO HISTORY, 25 (JANUARY,
        1940): 25-34.

13662   JACKSON, LUTHER P. "MANUMISSION IN CERTAIN VIRGINIA
        CITIES." JOURNAL OF NEGRO HISTORY, 15 (JULY, 1930):
        278-314.

13663   JACKSON, LUTHER P. "NEGRO ENTERPRISE IN NORFOLK DURING
        THE DAYS OF SLAVERY." QUARTERLY JOURNAL OF THE

FLORIDA AGRICULTURAL AND MECHANICAL COLLEGE, 8 (APRIL, 1939): 5-12.

13664 JACKSON, LUTHER P. "RELIGIOUS DEVELOPMENT OF THE NEGRO IN VIRGINIA FROM 1760 TO 1860." JOURNAL OF NEGRO HISTORY, 16 (APRIL, 1931): 168-239.

13665 JACKSON, LUTHER P. "VIRGINIA NEGRO SOLDIERS AND SEAMEN IN THE AMERICAN REVOLUTION." JOURNAL OF NEGRO HISTORY, 27 (JULY, 1942): 247-287.

13666 JACKSON, LUTHER P. VIRGINIA NEGRO SOLDIERS AND SEAMEN IN THE REVOLUTIONARY WAR. NORFOLK: GUIDE QUALITY PRESS, 1944.

13667 JAMES, EDWARD W. "FREE AND SLAVE, GLOUCESTER COUNTY." VIRGINIA MAGAZINE OF HISTORY AND BIOGRAPHY, 12 (JULY, OCTOBER, 1904, JANUARY, APRIL, 1905): 14-16, 185-187, 269-271, 414-416.

13668 JAMES, EDWARD W. "SLAVE OWNERS, ABINGDON PARISH, GLOUCESTER COUNTY, VIRGINIA, APRIL, 1786." VIRGINIA MAGAZINE OF HISTORY AND BIOGRAPHY, 3 (JANUARY, 1896): 324-326.

13669 JAMES, EDWARD W. "SLAVE OWNERS 'SPOTSYLVANIA' COUNTY, 1783." VIRGINIA MAGAZINE OF HISTORY AND BIOGRAPHY, 4 (JULY, 1896, JANUARY, 1897): 104-106, 292-299.

13670 JAMES, EDWARD W. "SLAVE OWNERS, WESTMORELAND COUNTY, VIRGINIA, 1782." VIRGINIA MAGAZINE OF HISTORY AND BIOGRAPHY, 10 (JANUARY, 1903): 229-235.

13671 JAMES, JACQUELINE. "UNCLE TOM? NOT BOOKER T." AMERICAN HERITAGE, 19 (AUGUST, 1968): 50-63, 95-100.

13672 JANSEN, MARY L. "AGRICULTURE IN VIRGINIA IN THE POST-COLONIAL PERIOD." M.A. THESIS, COLUMBIA UNIVERSITY, 1935.

13673 JESTER, ANNIE L. DOMESTIC LIFE IN VIRGINIA IN THE SEVENTEENTH CENTURY. WILLIAMSBURG: VIRGINIA 350TH ANNIVERSARY CELEBRATION CORPORATION, 1957.

13674 JETER, HENRY N. JETER'S TWENTY-FIVE YEARS' EXPERIENCE WITH THE SHILOH BAPTIST CHURCH AND HER HISTORY. PROVIDENCE: REMINGTON PRINTING COMPANY, 1901.

13675 JOHNSON, THOMAS L. TWENTY-EIGHT YEARS A SLAVE; OR, THE STORY OF MY LIFE IN THREE CONTINENTS. BOURNEMOUTH, ENGLAND: W. MATE & SONS, 1909.

13676 JOHNSTON, JAMES H. "THE PARTICIPATION OF WHITE MEN IN VIRGINIA NEGRO INSURRECTIONS." JOURNAL OF NEGRO HISTORY, 16 (APRIL, 1931): 158-167.

13677   JOHNSTON, JAMES H.   RACE RELATIONS IN VIRGINIA AND
         MISCEGENATION IN THE SOUTH, 1776-1860. AMHERST:
         UNIVERSITY OF MASSACHUSETTS PRESS, 1970.

13678   JOHNSTON, JAMES H.   "RACE RELATIONS IN VIRGINIA AND
         MISCEGENATION IN THE SOUTH, 1776-1860." PH.D.
         DISSERTATION, UNIVERSITY OF CHICAGO, 1937.

13679   JONES, GEORGE F.   MYSELF AND OTHERS; OR REMINISCENCES,
         RECOLLECTIONS AND EXPERIENCES IN A LIFE OF SEVENTY-SIX
         YEARS, 1811-1887. PHILADELPHIA: GLOBE PRINTING
         HOUSE, 1887.

13680   JORDAN, ERVIN L.   "A PAINFUL CASE: THE WRIGHT-SANBORN
         INCIDENT IN NORFOLK, VIRGINIA, JULY-OCTOBER, 1863."
         M.A. THESIS, OLD DOMINION UNIVERSITY, 1979.

13681   KELLY, KEVIN P.   "ECONOMIC AND SOCIAL DEVELOPMENT OF
         SEVENTEENTH-CENTURY SURRY COUNTY, VIRGINIA." PH.D.
         DISSERTATION, UNIVERSITY OF WASHINGTON, 1972.

13682   KELLY, KEVIN P.   "'IN DISPERS'D COUNTRY PLANTATIONS':
         SETTLEMENT PATTERNS IN SEVENTEENTH-CENTURY SURRY
         COUNTY, VIRGINIA." IN TATE, THAD W. AND AMMERMAN,
         DAVID L. (EDS.). THE CHESAPEAKE IN THE SEVENTEENTH
         CENTURY: ESSAYS ON ANGLO-AMERICAN SOCIETY. NEW YORK:
         W.W. NORTON, 1979, PP. 183-205.

13683   KELSO, WILLIAM M.   "THE COLONIAL SILENT MAJORITY:
         TENANT, SERVANT AND SLAVE SETTLEMENT SITES AT
         KINGSMILL, VIRGINIA." UNPUBLISHED PAPER PRESENTED AT
         MEETING OF AMERICAN ANTHROPOLOGICAL ASSOCIATION,
         WASHINGTON, 1976.

13684   KETCHAM, RALPH L. (ED.).   "THE DICTATES OF CONSCIENCE:
         EDWARD COLES AND SLAVERY." VIRGINIA QUARTERLY REVIEW,
         36 (WINTER, 1960): 46-62.

13685   KILLINGER, CHARLES L.   "THE ROYAL COMPANY SLAVE TRADE TO
         VIRGINIA, 1689-1713." M.A. THESIS, COLLEGE OF WILLIAM
         AND MARY, 1969.

13686   KIMBALL, WILLIAM J.   "THE GABRIEL INSURRECTION OF 1800."
         NEGRO HISTORY BULLETIN, 34 (NOVEMBER, 1971): 153-156.

13687   KLEIN, HERBERT S.   "SLAVERY IN CUBA AND VIRGINIA; A
         COMPARATIVE HISTORY OF THE FIRST HUNDRED YEARS." M.A.
         THESIS, UNIVERSITY OF CHICAGO, 1959.

13688   KLEIN, HERBERT S.   SLAVERY IN THE AMERICAS: A
         COMPARATIVE STUDY OF VIRGINIA AND CUBA. CHICAGO:
         UNIVERSITY OF CHICAGO PRESS, 1967.

13689   KLEIN, HERBERT S.   "SLAVES AND SHIPPING IN
         EIGHTEENTH-CENTURY VIRGINIA." JOURNAL OF

INTERDISCIPLINARY HISTORY, 5 (WINTER, 1975): 383-412.

13690 KLINGAMAN, DAVID. "THE SIGNIFICANCE OF GRAIN IN THE
       DEVELOPMENT OF THE TOBACCO COLONIES." JOURNAL OF
       ECONOMIC HISTORY, 29 (JUNE, 1969): 268-278.

13691 KULIKOFF, ALLAN. "THE COLONIAL CHESAPEAKE: SEEDBED OF
       ANTEBELLUM SOUTHERN CULTURE?" JOURNAL OF SOUTHERN
       HISTORY, 45 (NOVEMBER, 1979): 513-540.

13692 KULIKOFF, ALLAN. "THE ORIGINS OF AFRO-AMERICAN SOCIETY
       IN TIDEWATER MARYLAND AND VIRGINIA, 1700 TO 1790."
       WILLIAM AND MARY QUARTERLY, 3RD SER., 35 (APRIL,
       1978): 226-259.

13693 KULIKOFF, ALLAN. "A 'PROLIFICK' PEOPLE: BLACK
       POPULATION GROWTH IN THE CHESAPEAKE COLONIES."
       SOUTHERN STUDIES, 16 (WINTER, 1977): 391-428.

13694 LAING, JAMES T. "THE EARLY DEVELOPMENT OF THE COAL
       INDUSTRY IN THE WESTERN COUNTIES OF VIRGINIA,
       1800-1865." WEST VIRGINIA HISTORY, 27 (JANUARY,
       1966): 144-155.

13695 "LAND AND SLAVE OWNERS IN PRINCESS ANNE COUNTY, 1778."
       LOWER NORFOLK COUNTY VIRGINIA ANTIQUARY, 4 (1902):
       1-7.

13696 LANGHORNE, ORRA. "CHANGES OF A HALF CENTURY IN
       VIRGINIA." AMERICAN JOURNAL OF SOCIAL SCIENCE, 38
       (DECEMBER, 1900): 168.

13697 LANGHORNE, ORRA. "FREE NEGROES IN VIRGINIA BEFORE THE
       WAR." SOUTHERN WORKMAN, 23 (JANUARY, 1899): 678-682.

13698 LATANE, JOHN H. "SLAVERY." IN CHANDLER, JULIAN A.C.
       (ED.). THE SOUTH IN THE BUILDING OF THE NATION. 12
       VOLS. RICHMOND: SOUTHERN HISTORICAL PUBLICATION
       SOCIETY, 1909, VOL. 1, PP. 110-111.

13699 LAWSON, HAROLD L. "THE NEGRO IN PAGE COUNTY, VIRGINIA--A
       SOCIAL, ECONOMIC AND EDUCATIONAL STUDY." M.S. THESIS,
       VIRGINIA STATE COLLEGE, 1951.

13700 LAWSON, HERBERT H. "THE GENESIS AND GROWTH OF STATEHOOD
       IN WEST VIRGINIA, 1776-1863." M.A. THESIS, MIAMI
       UNIVERSITY, 1959.

13701 LEAMING, HUGO P. "HIDDEN AMERICANS: MAROONS OF VIRGINIA
       AND THE CAROLINAS." PH.D. DISSERTATION, UNIVERSITY OF
       ILLINOIS, CHICAGO CIRCLE, 1979.

13702 LEE, FLORENCE W. "CHRISTMAS IN VIRGINIA BEFORE THE WAR."
       SOUTHERN WORKMAN, 37 (DECEMBER, 1908): 686-689.

13703   LEE, FLORENCE W.   "HARVEST TIME IN OLD VIRGINIA."
        SOUTHERN WORKMAN, 37 (OCTOBER, 1908):   566-567.

13704   LEWIS, RONALD L.   "BLACK LABOR IN THE EASTERN VIRGINIA
        COAL FIELD, 1765-1865."   IN NEWTON, JAMES E. AND LEWIS
        (EDS.).   THE OTHER SLAVES: MECHANICS, ARTISANS AND
        CRAFTSMEN.   BOSTON: G.K. HALL, 1978, PP. 87-108.

13705   LEWIS, RONALD L.   COAL, IRON, AND SLAVES: INDUSTRIAL
        SLAVERY IN MARYLAND AND VIRGINIA, 1715-1865.
        WESTPORT: GREENWOOD PRESS, 1979.

13706   LEWIS, RONALD L.   "'THE DARKEST ABODE OF MAN'--BLACK
        MINERS IN THE FIRST SOUTHERN COAL FIELD, 1780-1865."
        VIRGINIA MAGAZINE OF HISTORY AND BIOGRAPHY, 87 (APRIL,
        1979):   190-202.

13707   LEWIS, RONALD L.   "SLAVE FAMILIES AT EARLY CHESAPEAKE
        IRONWORKS."   VIRGINIA MAGAZINE OF HISTORY AND
        BIOGRAPHY, 86 (APRIL, 1978):   169-179.

13708   LEWIS, RONALD L.   "SLAVERY IN THE CHESAPEAKE IRON
        INDUSTRY, 1716-1865."   PH.D. DISSERTATION, UNIVERSITY
        OF AKRON, 1974.

13709   LEWIS, RONALD L.   "THE USE AND EXTENT OF SLAVE LABOR IN
        THE CHESAPEAKE IRON INDUSTRY: THE COLONIAL ERA."
        LABOR HISTORY, 17 (SUMMER, 1976):   388-405.

13710   LEWIS, RONALD L.   "THE USE AND EXTENT OF SLAVE LABOR IN
        THE VIRGINIA IRON INDUSTRY: THE ANTE-BELLUM ERA."
        WEST VIRGINIA HISTORY, 38 (JANUARY, 1977):   141-156.

13711   LOGAN, RAYFORD W. (ED.).   MEMOIRS OF A MONTICELLO SLAVE,
        AS DICTATED TO CHARLES CAMPBELL IN THE 1840'S BY
        ISAAC, ONE OF THOMAS JEFFERSON'S SLAVES.
        CHARLOTTESVILE: UNIVERSITY OF VIRGINIA PRESS, 1951.

13712   LOGAN, RAYFORD W. (ED.).   "MEMOIRS OF A MONTICELLO SLAVE,
        AS DICTATED TO CHARLES CAMPBELL IN THE 1840'S BY
        ISAAC, ONE OF THOMAS JEFFERSON'S SLAVES."   WILLIAM AND
        MARY QUARTERLY, 3RD SER., 8 (OCTOBER, 1951):   561-582.

13713   LOKEN, GREGORY A.   "THE SONS OF THEIR FATHERS; THE 1832
        SLAVERY DEBATE IN VIRGINIA."   B.A. THESIS, HARVARD
        UNIVERSITY, 1974.

13714   LOWERY, CHARLES D.   "JAMES BARBOUR, A PROGRESSIVE FARMER
        OF ANTEBELLUM VIRGINIA."   IN BOLES, JOHN B. (ED.).
        AMERICA: THE MIDDLE PERIOD--ESSAYS IN HONOR OF
        BERNARD MAYO.   CHARLOTTESVILLE: UNIVERSITY PRESS OF
        VIRGINIA, 1973, PP. 168-187.

13715   LOWMAN, DAVID ST. CLAIR.   "UNWANTED RESIDENTS: THE
        PLIGHT OF THE EMANCIPATED SLAVE IN VIRGINIA,

1806-1835." M.A. THESIS, COLLEGE OF WILLIAM AND MARY, 1977.

13716 MACKINTOSH, BARRY. GENERAL BACKGROUND STUDIES: THE BURROUGHS PLANTATION, 1856-1865. WASHINGTON: NATIONAL PARK SERVICE, U.S. DEPARTMENT OF THE INTERIOR, 1968.

13717 MACMASTER, RICHARD K. "ARTHUR LEE'S 'ADDRESS ON SLAVERY': AN ASPECT OF VIRGINIA'S STRUGGLE TO END THE SLAVE TRADE, 1765-1774." VIRGINIA MAGAZINE OF HISTORY AND BIOGRAPHY, 80 (APRIL, 1972): 141-157.

13718 MADDEX, JACK P., JR. THE VIRGINIA CONSERVATIVES, 1867-1879: A STUDY IN RECONSTRUCTION POLITICS. CHAPEL HILL: UNIVERSITY OF NORTH CAROLINA PRESS, 1970.

13719 MAIN, JACKSON T. "THE DISTRIBUTION OF PROPERTY IN POST-REVOLUTIONARY VIRGINIA." MISSISSIPPI VALLEY HISTORICAL REVIEW, 41 (SEPTEMBER, 1954): 241-258.

13720 MAIN, JACKSON T. "THE ONE HUNDRED." WILLIAM AND MARY QUARTERLY, 3RD SER., 11 (JULY, 1954): 354-384.

13721 MALONE, DUMAS. JEFFERSON THE VIRGINIAN. BOSTON: LITTLE, BROWN AND COMPANY, 1948.

13722 "MANUMISSION PETITIONS PRESENTED TO THE VIRGINIA LEGISLATURE." JOURNAL OF NEGRO HISTORY, 13 (JANUARY, 1928): 87-101.

13723 MARAMBAUD, PIERRE. WILLIAM BYRD OF WESTOVER, 1674-1744. CHARLOTTESVILLE: UNIVERSITY PRESS OF VIRGINIA, 1971.

13724 MARSZALEK, JOHN F. "BATTLE FOR FREEDOM--GABRIEL'S INSURRECTION." NEGRO HISTORY BULLETIN, 39 (MARCH, 1976): 540-543.

13725 MARSZALEK, JOHN F. "GABRIEL'S INSURRECTION." IN ROLLER, DAVID C. AND TWYMAN, ROBERT W. (EDS.). THE ENCYCLOPEDIA OF SOUTHERN HISTORY. BATON ROUGE: LOUISIANA STATE UNIVERSITY PRESS, 1979, P. 502.

13726 MATTHEWS, ALBERT. NOTES ON THE PROPOSED ABOLITION OF SLAVERY IN VIRGINIA IN 1785. CAMBRIDGE: COLONIAL SOCIETY OF MASSACHUSETTS, 1903.

13727 MATTHEWS, ALBERT. "NOTES ON THE PROPOSED ABOLITION OF SLAVERY IN VIRGINIA IN 1785." PUBLICATIONS OF THE COLONIAL SOCIETY OF MASSACHUSETTS, 6 (1899-1900): 370-380.

13728 MAZYCK, WALTER H. GEORGE WASHINGTON AND THE NEGRO. WASHINGTON: ASSOCIATED PUBLISHERS, 1932.

13729   MCCOLLEY, ROBERT. SLAVERY AND JEFFERSONIAN VIRGINIA.
        URBANA: UNIVERSITY OF ILLINOIS PRESS, 1964.

13730   MCCOLLEY, ROBERT. "SLAVERY IN JEFFERSON'S VIRGINIA."
        JOURNAL OF THE CENTRAL MISSISSIPPI VALLEY AMERICAN
        STUDIES ASSOCIATION, 1 (SPRING, 1960): 23-31.

13731   MCCOLLEY, ROBERT M. "GENTLEMEN AND SLAVERY IN
        JEFFERSON'S VIRGINIA." PH.D. DISSERTATION, UNIVERSITY
        OF CALIFORNIA, 1961.

13732   MCDONALD, JAMES J. LIFE IN OLD VIRGINIA. NORFOLK: OLD
        VIRGINIA PUBLISHING COMPANY, 1907.

13733   MENARD, RUSSELL R. "FROM SERVANTS TO SLAVES: THE
        TRANSFORMATION OF THE CHESAPEAKE LABOR SYSTEM."
        SOUTHERN STUDIES, 16 (WINTER, 1977): 355-390.

13734   MENARD, RUSSELL R. "THE TOBACCO INDUSTRY IN THE
        CHESAPEAKE COLONIES, 1617-1730: AN INTERPRETATION."
        RESEARCH IN ECONOMIC HISTORY, 5 (1980): 109-178.

13735   MEYERS, MARVIN (ED.). THE MIND OF THE FOUNDER.
        INDIANAPOLIS: BOBBS-MERRILL, 1973.

13736   MILLER, JOHN C. THE WOLF BY THE EARS--THOMAS JEFFERSON
        AND SLAVERY. NEW YORK: FREE PRESS, 1977.

13737   MILLER, RANDALL M. (ED.). "DEAR MASTER": LETTERS OF A
        SLAVE FAMILY. ITHACA: CORNELL UNIVERSITY PRESS, 1978.

13738   MITCHELL, ROBERT D. COMMERCIALISM AND FRONTIER:
        PERSPECTIVES ON THE EARLY SHENANDOAH VALLEY.
        CHARLOTTESVILLE: UNIVERSITY PRESS OF VIRGINIA, 1977.

13739   MITCHELL, ROBERT D. "CONTENT AND CONTEXT: TIDEWATER
        CHARACTERISTICS IN THE EARLY SHENANDOAH VALLEY."
        MARYLAND HISTORIAN, 5 (FALL, 1974): 79-92.

13740   MONICO, FRANCIS W. "THE NEGRO AND THE MARTINSBURG
        GAZETTE, 1799-1833." M.A. THESIS, WEST VIRGINIA
        UNIVERSITY, 1959.

13741   MOORE, GEORGE E. "SLAVERY AS A FACTOR IN THE FORMATION
        OF WEST VIRGINIA." M.A. THESIS, WEST VIRGINIA
        UNIVERSITY, 1947.

13742   MOORE, GEORGE E. "SLAVERY AS A FACTOR IN THE FORMATION
        OF WEST VIRGINIA." WEST VIRGINIA HISTORY, 18
        (OCTOBER, 1956): 5-89.

13743   MORGAN, EDMUND S. AMERICAN SLAVERY, AMERICAN FREEDOM:
        THE ORDEAL OF COLONIAL VIRGINIA. NEW YORK: W.W.
        NORTON, 1975.

13744   MORGAN, EDMUND S.   THE CHALLENGE OF THE AMERICAN
         REVOLUTION.   NEW YORK: W.W. NORTON, 1976.

13745   MORGAN, EDMUND S.   "THE LABOR PROBLEM AT JAMESTOWN,
         1607-1618."   AMERICAN HISTORICAL REVIEW, 76 (JUNE,
         1971):   595-611.

13746   MORGAN, EDMUND S.   "SLAVERY AND FREEDOM: THE AMERICAN
         PARADOX."   JOURNAL OF AMERICAN HISTORY, 59 (JUNE,
         1972):   5-29.

13747   MORGAN, EDMUND S.   VIRGINIANS AT HOME: FAMILY LIFE IN
         THE EIGHTEENTH CENTURY.   WILLIAMSBURG: COLONIAL
         WILLIAMSBURG, 1952.

13748   MORGAN, TIMOTHY E.   "TURMOIL IN AN ORDERLY SOCIETY:
         COLONIAL VIRGINIA, 1607-1754."   PH.D. DISSERTATION,
         COLLEGE OF WILLIAM AND MARY, 1977.

13749   MORRIS, GEORGE G.   "CONFEDERATE LYNCHBURG, 1861-1865."
         M.A. THESIS, VIRGINIA POLYTECHNIC INSTITUTE AND STATE
         UNIVERSITY, 1977.

13750   MORTON, LOUIS.   ROBERT CARTER OF NOMINI HALL: A VIRGINIA
         TOBACCO PLANTER OF THE EIGHTEENTH CENTURY.
         CHARLOTTESVILLE: UNIVERSITY PRESS OF VIRGINIA, 1941.

13751   MORTON, LOUIS.   "ROBERT WORMELEY CARTER OF SABINE HALL:
         NOTES ON THE LIFE OF A VIRGINIA PLANTER."   JOURNAL OF
         SOUTHERN HISTORY, 12 (AUGUST, 1946):   345-365.

13752   MORTON, RICHARD L.   COLONIAL VIRGINIA.   2 VOLS.   CHAPEL
         HILL: UNIVERSITY OF NORTH CAROLINA PRESS, 1960.

13753   MORTON, RICHARD L. (ED.).   "'CONTRABANDS' AND QUAKERS IN
         THE VIRGINIA PENINSULA, 1862-1869."   VIRGINIA MAGAZINE
         OF HISTORY AND BIOGRAPHY, 61 (OCTOBER, 1953):   419-429.

13754   MOSS, CHARLES G.G.   "THE VIRGINIA PLANTATION SYSTEM,
         1700-1750."   PH.D. DISSERTATION, YALE UNIVERSITY, 1932.

13755   MULLIN, GERALD W.   FLIGHT AND REBELLION: SLAVE
         RESISTANCE IN EIGHTEENTH CENTURY VIRGINIA.   NEW YORK:
         OXFORD UNIVERSITY PRESS, 1972.

13756   MULLIN, GERALD W.   "GABRIEL'S INSURRECTION."   IN ROSE,
         PETER I. (ED.).   AMERICANS FROM AFRICA.   2 VOLS.   NEW
         YORK: ATHERTON PRESS, 1970, VOL. 2, PP. 53-73.

13757   MULLIN, GERALD W., JR.   "PATTERNS OF SLAVE BEHAVIOR IN
         EIGHTEENTH-CENTURY VIRGINIA."   PH.D. DISSERTATION,
         UNIVERSITY OF CALIFORNIA, 1968.

13758   MULLIN, MICHAEL.   "BRITISH CARIBBEAN AND NORTH AMERICAN
         SLAVES IN AN ERA OF WAR AND REVOLUTION, 1775-1807."

IN CROW, JEFFREY J. AND TISE, LARRY E. (EDS.). THE
SOUTHERN EXPERIENCE IN THE AMERICAN REVOLUTION.
CHAPEL HILL: UNIVERSITY OF NORTH CAROLINA PRESS,
1978, PP. 235-267.

13759 MUNFORD, BEVERLY B. VIRGINIA'S ATTITUDE TOWARD SLAVERY
       AND SECESSION. NEW YORK: LONGMANS, GREEN AND
       COMPANY, 1909.

13760 MUSSER, CARL W. "ECONOMIC AND SOCIAL ASPECTS OF NEGRO
       SLAVERY IN WYTHE COUNTY, VIRGINIA, 1790-1860." M.A.
       THESIS, GEORGE WASHINGTON UNIVERSITY, 1958.

13761 NAY, ROBERT F. "THE CRIMINAL PROCEEDINGS OF THE COURT OF
       AUGUSTA COUNTY, VIRGINIA, 1746-1769." M.A. THESIS,
       GEORGE MASON UNIVERSITY, 1977.

13762 "THE NEGRO AS SUPPLIANT AND CONTRABAND." TYLER'S
       QUARTERLY HISTORICAL AND GENEALOGICAL MAGAZINE, 2
       (OCTOBER, 1920): 78-79.

13763 "NEGRO EDUCATION IN VIRGINIA IN THE EIGHTEENTH CENTURY."
       VIRGINIA MAGAZINE OF HISTORY AND BIOGRAPHY, 2 (APRIL,
       1895): 429.

13764 NEILL, EDWARD D. "VIRGINIA SLAVEHOLDERS, FEBRUARY,
       1625." NEW-ENGLAND HISTORICAL AND GENEALOGICAL
       REGISTER, 31 (JANUARY, 1877): 22.

13765 NETHERTON, NAN; SWEIG, DONALD; ARTEMEL, JANICE; HICKIN,
       PATRICIA; AND REED, PATRICK. FAIRFAX COUNTY,
       VIRGINIA: A HISTORY. FAIRFAX, VA: FAIRFAX COUNTY
       BOARD OF SUPERVISORS, 1978.

13766 NEURATH, PETER F. "THE ROLE OF SLAVERY IN THE FORMATION
       OF WEST VIRGINIA." M.A. THESIS, UNIVERSITY OF
       WASHINGTON, 1966.

13767 NICHOLLS, MICHAEL L. "ORIGINS OF THE VIRGINIA SOUTHSIDE,
       1703-1753: A SOCIAL AND ECONOMIC STUDY." PH.D.
       DISSERTATION, COLLEGE OF WILLIAM AND MARY, 1972.

13768 OATES, STEPHEN B. "TURNER'S REBELLION." IN ROLLER,
       DAVID C. AND TWYMAN, ROBERT W. (EDS.). THE
       ENCYCLOPEDIA OF SOUTHERN HISTORY. BATON ROUGE:
       LOUISIANA STATE UNIVERSITY PRESS, 1975, P. 1255.

13769 OBERSEIDER, NANCY L. "A SOCIO-DEMOGRAPHIC STUDY OF THE
       FAMILY AS A SOCIAL UNIT IN TIDEWATER VIRGINIA,
       1660-1776." PH.D. DISSERTATION, UNIVERSITY OF
       MARYLAND, 1975.

13770 O'BRIEN, JOHN T. "FACTORY, CHURCH, AND COMMUNITY:
       BLACKS IN ANTEBELLUM RICHMOND." JOURNAL OF SOUTHERN
       HISTORY, 44 (NOVEMBER, 1978): 509-536.

13771　O'BRIEN, JOHN T.　"FROM BONDAGE TO CITIZENSHIP:　THE
　　　　RICHMOND BLACK COMMUNITY, 1865-1867."　PH.D.
　　　　DISSERTATION, UNIVERSITY OF ROCHESTER, 1974.

13772　OSBORNE, JOSEPH A.　"SLAVERY AND SERVANTS."　WILLIAMSBURG
　　　　IN COLONIAL TIMES.　RICHMOND:　DIETZ PRESS, 1935, PP.
　　　　79-100.

13773　OWEN, H.T.　"SLAVERY AND ABOLITION IN VIRGINIA."
　　　　CONFEDERATE VETERAN, 25 (OCTOBER, 1917):　458.

13774　PAGE, THOMAS N.　SOCIAL LIFE IN OLD VIRGINIA BEFORE THE
　　　　WAR.　NEW YORK:　CHARLES SCRIBNER'S SONS, 1897.

13775　PALMER, PAUL C.　"SERVANT INTO SLAVE:　THE EVOLUTION OF
　　　　THE LEGAL STATUS OF THE NEGRO LABORER IN COLONIAL
　　　　VIRGINIA."　SOUTH ATLANTIC QUARTERLY, 65 (SUMMER,
　　　　1966):　355-370.

13776　PARKER, WILLIAM H.　"THE NAT TURNER INSURRECTION."　OLD
　　　　VIRGINIA YARNS, 1 (JANUARY, 1893):　14-29.

13777　PARRAMORE, THOMAS C.　SOUTHAMPTON COUNTY, VIRGINIA.
　　　　CHARLOTTESVILLE:　UNIVERSITY PRESS OF VIRGINIA, 1978.

13778　PERDUE, CHARLES L., JR.　"SLAVE LIFE STYLES IN EARLY
　　　　VIRGINIA."　PROCEEDINGS OF THE PIONEER AMERICA
　　　　SOCIETY, 2 (1973):　54-58.

13779　PERDUE, CHARLES L., JR.; BARDEN, THOMAS E.; AND PHILLIPS,
　　　　ROBERT K. (EDS.).　WEEVILS IN THE WHEAT:　INTERVIEWS
　　　　WITH VIRGINIA EX-SLAVES.　CHARLOTTESVILLE:　UNIVERSITY
　　　　PRESS OF VIRGINIA, 1976.

13780　PETERSON, MERRILL D.　THE JEFFERSON IMAGE IN THE AMERICAN
　　　　MIND.　NEW YORK:　OXFORD UNIVERSITY PRESS, 1960.

13781　PFISTER, FREDERICK W.　"THE NEGRO SLAVE EXPERIENCE IN
　　　　COLONIAL VIRGINIA."　M.A. THESIS, BOWLING GREEN STATE
　　　　UNIVERSITY, 1972.

13782　PHILLIPS, ULRICH B.　LIFE AND LABOR IN THE OLD SOUTH.
　　　　BOSTON:　LITTLE, BROWN AND COMPANY, 1929.

13783　PHILLIPS, ULRICH B.　"THE PLANTATION AS A CIVILIZING
　　　　FACTOR."　SEWANEE REVIEW, 12 (JULY, 1904):　257-267.

13784　PHILLIPS, ULRICH B.　"SLAVE CRIME IN VIRGINIA."　AMERICAN
　　　　HISTORICAL REVIEW, 20 (JANUARY, 1915):　336-340.

13785　PILCHER, GEORGE W.　"SAMUEL DAVIES AND THE INSTRUCTION OF
　　　　NEGROES IN VIRGINIA."　VIRGINIA MAGAZINE OF HISTORY
　　　　AND BIOGRAPHY, 74 (JULY, 1966):　293-300.

13786　PILCHER, GEORGE W.　SAMUEL DAVIES:　APOSTLE OF DISSENT IN

COLONIAL VIRGINIA. KNOXVILLE: UNIVERSITY OF
TENNESSEE PRESS, 1971.

13787 PINCHBECK, RAYMOND B. THE VIRGINIA NEGRO ARTISAN AND
TRADESMAN. RICHMOND: WILLIAM BYRD PRESS, 1926.

13788 PLEASANTS, SALLY. OLD VIRGINIA DAYS AND WAYS. MENASHA,
WI: GEORGE BANTA PUBLISHING COMPANY, 1916.

13789 POLK, LEE R. "AN ANALYSIS OF ARGUMENTATION IN THE
VIRGINIA SLAVERY DEBATE OF 1832." PH.D. DISSERTATION,
PURDUE UNIVERSITY, 1967.

13790 POSEY, THOMAS E. THE NEGRO CITIZEN OF WEST VIRGINIA.
INSTITUTE, WV: PRESS OF WEST VIRGINIA STATE COLLEGE,
1934.

13791 PREISSER, THOMAS M. "EIGHTEENTH-CENTURY ALEXANDRIA,
VIRGINIA, BEFORE THE REVOLUTION, 1749-1776." PH.D.
DISSERTATION, COLLEGE OF WILLIAM AND MARY, 1977.

13792 PREISSER, THOMAS M. "THE VIRGINIA DECISION TO USE NEGRO
SOLDIERS IN THE CIVIL WAR, 1864-1865." VIRGINIA
MAGAZINE OF HISTORY AND BIOGRAPHY, 83 (JANUARY, 1975):
98-113.

13793 PRICE, JACOB M. "THE BEGINNINGS OF TOBACCO MANUFACTURE
IN VIRGINIA." VIRGINIA MAGAZINE OF HISTORY AND
BIOGRAPHY, 64 (JANUARY, 1956): 3-29.

13794 PUGH, EVELYN L. "WOMEN AND SLAVERY: JULIA GARDINER
TYLER AND THE DUCHESS OF SUTHERLAND." VIRGINIA
MAGAZINE OF HISTORY AND BIOGRAPHY, 88 (APRIL, 1980):
186-202.

13795 PULLEY, RICHARD D. "THE ROLE OF THE VIRGINIA SLAVE IN
IRON AND TOBACCO MANUFACTURING." M.A. THESIS,
UNIVERSITY OF RICHMOND, 1962.

13796 QUARLES, BENJAMIN. "LORD DUNMORE AS LIBERATOR." WILLIAM
AND MARY QUARTERLY, 3RD SER., 15 (OCTOBER, 1958):
494-507.

13797 RABE, HARRY G. "THE REVEREND DEVEREAUX JARRATT AND THE
VIRGINIA SOCIAL ORDER." HISTORICAL MAGAZINE OF THE
PROTESTANT EPISCOPAL CHURCH, 33 (DECEMBER, 1964):
299-336.

13798 RAINBOLT, JOHN C. "THE ALTERATION IN THE RELATIONSHIP
BETWEEN LEADERSHIP AND CONSTITUENTS IN VIRGINIA, 1660
TO 1720." WILLIAM AND MARY QUARTERLY, 3RD SER., 27
(JULY, 1970): 411-434.

13799 RANDOLPH, PETER. FROM SLAVE CABIN TO THE PULPIT: THE
AUTOBIOGRAPHY OF REV. PETER RANDOLPH: THE SOUTHERN

QUESTION ILLUSTRATED, AND SKETCHES OF SLAVE LIFE.
BOSTON: J.H. EARLE, 1893.

13800   RANSON, A.R.H.   "PLANTATION LIFE IN VIRGINIA BEFORE THE
        WAR."   SEWANEE REVIEW, 21 (OCTOBER, 1913):   428-447.

13801   REID, GURNEY H.   "THE NEGRO IN RICHMOND ON THE EVE OF AND
        DURING THE CIVIL WAR."   M.A. THESIS, COLLEGE OF
        WILLIAM AND MARY, 1936.

13802   RICE, OTIS K.   "COAL MINING IN THE KANAWHA VALLEY TO
        1861:   A VIEW OF INDUSTRIALISM IN THE OLD SOUTH."
        JOURNAL OF SOUTHERN HISTORY, 31 (NOVEMBER, 1965):
        393-416.

13803   "RICHARD STANUP WHO HAD CHARGE OF GEORGE WASHINGTON'S
        SLAVES."   NEGRO HISTORY BULLETIN, 32 (FEBRUARY, 1969):
        12-13.

13804   RICHARDSON, EUDORA R.   "TRAGIC ACCIDENT."   SOUTH ATLANTIC
        QUARTERLY, 51 (JULY, 1952):   413-418.

13805   RICHES, WILLIAM T.M.   "RACE, SLAVERY, AND SERVITUDE:
        VIRGINIA, 1607-1705."   M.A. THESIS, UNIVERSITY OF
        TENNESSEE, 1969.

13806   RIDGEWAY, MICHAEL A.   "A PECULIAR BUSINESS: SLAVE
        TRADING IN ALEXANDRIA, VIRGINIA, 1825-1861."   M.A.
        THESIS, GEORGETOWN UNIVERSITY, 1976.

13807   RIPLEY, WILLIAM Z.   "THE TAX UPON SLAVES IMPORTED."   THE
        FINANCIAL HISTORY OF VIRGINIA, 1609-1776.   NEW YORK:
        COLUMBIA UNIVERSITY PRESS, 1893, PP. 73-78.

13808   ROBERT, JOSEPH C.   "EXCOMMUNICATION, VIRGINIA STYLE:
        CHURCH DISCIPLINE AS APPLIED TO NEGRO MEMBERS IN THE
        DAYS OF SLAVERY."   SOUTH ATLANTIC QUARTERLY, 40 (JULY,
        1941):   243-258.

13809   ROBERT, JOSEPH C.   "LEE THE FARMER."   JOURNAL OF SOUTHERN
        HISTORY, 3 (AUGUST, 1937):   422-440.

13810   ROBERT, JOSEPH C.   THE ROAD FROM MONTICELLO: A STUDY OF
        THE VIRGINIA SLAVERY DEBATE OF 1832.   DURHAM: DUKE
        UNIVERSITY PRESS, 1941.

13811   ROBERT, JOSEPH C.   THE TOBACCO KINGDOM: PLANTATION,
        MARKET, AND FACTORY IN VIRGINIA AND NORTH CAROLINA,
        1800-1860.   DURHAM: DUKE UNIVERSITY PRESS, 1938.

13812   ROBERTSON, MARY D. (ED.).   "THE DUSKY WINGS OF WAR: THE
        JOURNAL OF LUCY G. BRECKINRIDGE, 1862-1864."   CIVIL
        WAR HISTORY, 23 (MARCH, 1977):   26-51.

13813   ROCKWELL, TIM O.   BELLE GROVE EXCAVATIONS, MIDDLETOWN,

VIRGINIA, 1972-1973. WASHINGTON: NATIONAL TRUST FOR
HISTORIC PRESERVATION, N.D.

13814 ROUSE, PARKE JR. PLANTERS AND PIONEERS: LIFE IN
COLONIAL VIRGINIA. NEW YORK: HASTINGS HOUSE, 1968.

13815 RUSSELL, JOHN H. "COLORED FREEMEN AS SLAVEOWNERS IN
VIRGINIA." JOURNAL OF NEGRO HISTORY, 1 (JULY, 1916):
233-242.

13816 RUSSELL, JOHN H. THE FREE NEGRO IN VIRGINIA, 1619-1865.
BALTIMORE: JOHNS HOPKINS PRESS, 1913.

13817 RUTMAN, DARRETT B.; WETHERELL, CHARLES; AND RUTMAN, ANITA
H. "RHYTHMS OF LIFE: BLACK AND WHITE SEASONALITY IN
THE EARLY CHESAPEAKE." JOURNAL OF INTERDISCIPLINARY
HISTORY, 11 (SUMMER, 1930): 29-54.

13818 RYLAND, ROBERT. "ORIGINS AND HISTORY OF THE FIRST
AFRICAN BAPTIST CHURCH." IN TUPPER, HENRY A. (ED.).
THE FIRST CENTURY OF THE FIRST BAPTIST CHURCH IN
RICHMOND, VIRGINIA. RICHMOND: CARLTON MCCARTHY,
1880, PP. 245-272.

13819 SAMS, CONWAY W. THE CONQUEST OF VIRGINIA: THE THIRD
ATTEMPT, 1610-1624. NEW YORK: G.P. PUTNAM'S SONS,
1939.

13820 SAUNDERS, ROBERT M. "CRIME AND PUNISHMENT IN EARLY
NATIONAL AMERICA: RICHMOND, VIRGINIA, 1784-1820."
VIRGINIA MAGAZINE OF HISTORY AND BIOGRAPHY, 86
(JANUARY, 1978): 33-44.

13821 SAVITT, TODD L. MEDICINE AND SLAVERY: THE DISEASES AND
HEALTH CARE OF BLACKS IN ANTEBELLUM VIRGINIA. URBANA:
UNIVERSITY OF ILLINOIS PRESS, 1978.

13822 SAVITT, TODD L. "SLAVE LIFE INSURANCE IN VIRGINIA AND
NORTH CAROLINA." JOURNAL OF SOUTHERN HISTORY, 43
(NOVEMBER, 1977): 583-600.

13823 SAVITT, TODD L. "SOUND MINDS AND SOUND BODIES: THE
DISEASES AND HEALTH CARE OF BLACKS IN ANTEBELLUM
VIRGINIA." PH.D. DISSERTATION, UNIVERSITY OF
VIRGINIA, 1975.

13824 SCHLOTTERBECK, JOHN. "PLANTATION AND FARM: SOCIAL AND
ECONOMIC CHANGE IN ORANGE AND GREEN COUNTIES,
VIRGINIA, 1716-1860." PH.D. DISSERTATION, JOHNS
HOPKINS UNIVERSITY, 1979.

13825 SCHWARTZ, L.P. "SLAVE DISCIPLINE IN VIRGINIA." M.A.
THESIS, COLUMBIA UNIVERSITY, 1947.

13826 SCOTT, ARTHUR P. CRIMINAL LAW IN COLONIAL VIRGINIA.

CHICAGO: UNIVERSITY OF CHICAGO PRESS, 1930.

13827   SCRIBNER, ROBERT L.   "'IN MEMORY OF FRANK PADGET.'"
        VIRGINIA CAVALCADE, 3 (WINTER, 1953):   7-11.

13828   SCRIBNER, ROBERT L.   "SLAVE GANGS ON THE MARCH: BEFORE
        1861 TRAVELERS IN VIRGINIA WITNESSED THE SOUTHWARD
        TREK OF THE SURPLUS SLAVE POPULATION, GUIDED BY SIMON
        LEGREES OF THE HIGHROAD."   VIRGINIA CAVALCADE, 3
        (AUTUMN, 1953):   10-13.

13829   SHAW, ERNEST.   "FROM WILLIAMSBURG TO NEW HAVEN: A STUDY
        OF RURAL PEOPLE IN AN URBAN ENVIRONMENT."   M.A.
        THESIS, UNIVERSITY OF CONNECTICUT, 1975.

13830   SHEELER, J. REUBEN.   "THE NEGRO ON THE VIRGINIA
        FRONTIER."   JOURNAL OF NEGRO HISTORY, 43 (OCTOBER,
        1958):   279-297.

13831   SHEELER, J. REUBEN.   "SERVITUDE AND SLAVERY OF VIRGINIA
        IN SEVENTEENTH CENTURY."   NEGRO HISTORY BULLETIN, 10
        (APRIL, 1947):   161-164.

13832   SHEELER, JOHN R.   "THE NEGRO IN WEST VIRGINIA BEFORE
        1900."   PH.D. DISSERTATION, WEST VIRGINIA UNIVERSITY,
        1954.

13833   SHEELER, JOHN R.   "THE SPIRIT OF FREEDOM IN WESTERN
        VIRGINIA AFTER 1800."   WEST VIRGINIA HISTORY, 17
        (JULY, 1956):   285-303.

13834   SHELDON, MARIANNE B.   "BLACK-WHITE RELATIONS IN RICHMOND,
        VIRGINIA, 1782-1820."   JOURNAL OF SOUTHERN HISTORY, 45
        (FEBRUARY, 1979):   27-44.

13835   SHIMKIN, DEMITRI B.; LOUIE, GLORIA J.; AND FRATE, DENNIS
        A.   "THE BLACK EXTENDED FAMILY: A BASIC RURAL
        INSTITUTION AND A MECHANISM OF URBAN ADAPTATION."   IN
        SHIMKIN, DEMITRI B.; SHIMKIN, EDITH M.; AND FRATE,
        DENNIS A. (EDS.).   THE EXTENDED FAMILY IN BLACK
        SOCIETIES.   THE HAGUE: MOUTON PUBLISHERS, 1978, PP.
        25-148.

13836   SIEGEL, FRED.   "THE PATERNALIST THESIS: VIRGINIA AS A
        TEST CASE."   CIVIL WAR HISTORY, 25 (SEPTEMBER, 1979):
        246-261.

13837   "SLAVE OWNERS, PRINCESS ANNE COUNTY."   LOWER NORFOLK
        COUNTY VIRGINIA ANTIQUARY, 4 (1902):   24-26, 34-35,
        64-69, 76-77.

13838   "SLAVE OWNERS, PRINCESS ANNE COUNTY, 1840."   LOWER
        NORFOLK COUNTY VIRGINIA ANTIQUARY, 4 (1903):   174-182.

13839   "SLAVERY IN VIRGINIA."   VIRGINIA MAGAZINE OF HISTORY AND

BIOGRAPHY, 36 (JULY, 1928): 275-281.

13840   "SLAVERY IN VIRGINIA (1691-1798)." IN RYWELL, MARTIN
         (ED.). AFRO-AMERICAN ENCYCLOPEDIA. 10 VOLS. NORTH
         MIAMI: EDUCATIONAL BOOK PUBLISHERS, 1974, VOL. 8, PP.
         2447-2449.

13841   "SLAVES AS PERSONAL PROPERTY." VIRGINIA MAGAZINE OF
         HISTORY AND BIOGRAPHY, 11 (APRIL, 1904): 351-354.

13842   "SLAVES ON A FEDERAL PROJECT." BULLETIN OF THE BUSINESS
         HISTORICAL SOCIETY, 8 (MARCH, 1934): 32-33.

13843   SMITH, DOUGLAS C. "RACE RELATIONS AND INSTITUTIONAL
         RESPONSES IN WEST VIRGINIA--A HISTORY; WEST VIRGINIA
         AND THE BLACK EXPERIENCE: AN HISTORICAL OVERVIEW,
         PART I." WEST VIRGINIA HISTORY, 39 (FALL, 1977):
         30-48.

13844   SMITH, JAMES L. AUTOBIOGRAPHY OF JAMES L. SMITH,
         INCLUDING ALSO, REMINISCENCES OF SLAVE LIFE,
         RECOLLECTIONS OF THE WAR, EDUCATION OF THE FREEDMEN,
         CAUSES OF THE EXODUS, ETC. NORWICH: PRESS OF THE
         BULLETIN COMPANY, 1881.

13845   SMITH, PAGE. JEFFERSON, A REVEALING BIOGRAPHY. NEW
         YORK: AMERICAN HERITAGE PUBLISHING COMPANY, 1976.

13846   SPENCER, SAMUEL R., JR. BOOKER T. WASHINGTON AND THE
         NEGRO'S PLACE IN AMERICAN LIFE. BOSTON: LITTLE,
         BROWN AND COMPANY, 1955.

13847   STARKE, BARBARA M. "A MINI VIEW OF THE MICROENVIRONMENT
         OF SLAVES AND FREED BLACKS LIVING IN VIRGINIA AND
         MARYLAND AREAS FROM THE SEVENTEENTH THROUGH THE
         NINETEENTH CENTURIES." NEGRO HISTORY BULLETIN, 41
         (SEPTEMBER/OCTOBER, 1978): 877-880.

13848   STARKEY, MARION L. THE FIRST PLANTATION: A HISTORY OF
         HAMPTON AND ELIZABETH CITY COUNTY, VIRGINIA,
         1607-1887. HAMPTON: HOUSTON PRINTING AND PUBLISHING
         HOUSE, 1936.

13849   STEALEY, JOHN E. "THE RESPONSIBILITIES AND LIABILITIES
         OF THE BAILEE OF SLAVE LABOR IN VIRGINIA." AMERICAN
         JOURNAL OF LEGAL HISTORY, 12 (OCTOBER, 1968): 336-353.

13850   STEALEY, JOHN E. "THE SALT INDUSTRY OF THE GREAT KANAWAH
         VALLEY OF VIRGINIA: A STUDY OF ANTE-BELLUM INTERNAL
         COMMERCE." PH.D. DISSERTATION, WEST VIRGINIA
         UNIVERSITY, 1970.

13851   STEALEY, JOHN E. "SLAVERY AND THE WESTERN VIRGINIA SALT
         INDUSTRY." JOURNAL OF NEGRO HISTORY, 59 (APRIL,
         1974): 105-131.

13852   STEEL, EDWARD M., JR. "BLACK MONONGALIANS: A JUDICIAL
         VIEW OF SLAVERY AND THE NEGRO IN MONONGALIA COUNTY,
         1776-1865." WEST VIRGINIA HISTORY, 34 (JULY, 1973):
         331-359.

13853   STEEL, EDWARD M., JR. "BYPATH TO FREEDOM." WEST
         VIRGINIA HISTORY, 31 (OCTOBER, 1969): 33-39.

13854   STEINER, BRUCE E. "A PLANTER'S TROUBLED CONSCIENCE."
         JOURNAL OF SOUTHERN HISTORY, 28 (AUGUST, 1962):
         343-347.

13855   STEPHENSON, MARY A. "NOTES ON THE NEGRO SCHOOL IN
         WILLIAMSBURG, 1760-1774." UNPUBLISHED PAPER, N.D.,
         COLONIAL WILLIAMSBURG, INC.

13856   STIVERSON, GREGORY A. AND BUTLER, PATRICK H. (EDS.).
         "VIRGINIA IN 1732: THE TRAVEL JOURNAL OF WILLIAM HUGH
         GROVE." VIRGINIA MAGAZINE OF HISTORY AND BIOGRAPHY,
         85 (JANUARY, 1977): 18-44.

13857   SUTTELL, ELIZABETH L. "THE BRITISH SLAVE TRADE TO
         VIRGINIA, 1698-1728." M.A. THESIS, COLLEGE OF WILLIAM
         AND MARY, 1965.

13858   SYDNOR, CHARLES S. AMERICAN REVOLUTIONARIES IN THE
         MAKING. CHAPEL HILL: UNIVERSITY OF NORTH CAROLINA
         PRESS, 1952.

13859   TALBERT, ROY JR. (ED.). STUDIES IN THE LOCAL HISTORY OF
         SLAVERY: ESSAYS PREPARED FOR THE BOOKER T. WASHINGTON
         NATIONAL MONUMENT. FERRUM, VA: UNITED STATES
         NATIONAL PARK SERVICE, 1978.

13860   TALPALAR, MORRIS. THE SOCIOLOGY OF COLONIAL VIRGINIA.
         NEW YORK: PHILOSOPHICAL LIBRARY, 1968.

13861   TATE, THAD W. THE NEGRO IN EIGHTEENTH-CENTURY
         WILLIAMSBURG. CHARLOTTESVILLE: UNIVERSITY OF
         VIRGINIA PRESS, 1965.

13862   TAYLOR, A.A. "MAKING WEST VIRGINIA A FREE STATE."
         JOURNAL OF NEGRO HISTORY, 6 (APRIL, 1921): 131-173.

13863   TAYLOR, ALRUTHEUS A. THE NEGRO IN THE RECONSTRUCTION OF
         VIRGINIA. WASHINGTON: ASSOCIATION FOR THE STUDY OF
         NEGRO LIFE AND HISTORY, 1926.

13864   THOMAS, EMORY M. THE CONFEDERATE STATE OF RICHMOND: A
         BIOGRAPHY OF THE CAPITAL. AUSTIN: UNIVERSITY OF
         TEXAS PRESS, 1971.

13865   THOMAS, PERCIAL M. "PLANTATIONS IN TRANSITION: A STUDY
         OF FOUR VIRGINIA PLANTATIONS, 1860-1870." PH.D.
         DISSERTATION, UNIVERSITY OF VIRGINIA, 1979.

13866   TINLING, MARION. "CAWSONS, VIRGINIA, IN 1795-1796."
         WILLIAM AND MARY QUARTERLY, 3RD SER., 3 (APRIL, 1946):
         281-291.

13867   TOWNES, A. JANE. "THE EFFECT OF EMANCIPATION ON LARGE
         LANDHOLDINGS, NELSON AND GOOCHLAND COUNTIES,
         VIRGINIA." JOURNAL OF SOUTHERN HISTORY, 45 (AUGUST,
         1979): 403-412.

13868   TRAGLE, HENRY I. NAT TURNER'S SLAVE REVOLT--1831. NEW
         YORK: GROSSMAN, 1972.

13869   TRAGLE, HENRY I. "THE SOUTHAMPTON SLAVE REVOLT." PH.D.
         DISSERTATION, UNIVERSITY OF MASSACHUSETTS, 1971.

13870   TRAUBERT, ANNA E. "ABOLITION OF NEGRO SLAVERY IN WEST
         VIRGINIA." M.A. THESIS, COLUMBIA UNIVERSITY, 1933.

13871   TSCHAN, FRANCIS J. "THE VIRGINIA PLANTER, 1700-1775."
         PH.D. DISSERTATION, UNIVERSITY OF CHICAGO, 1916.

13872   TUCKER, ST. GEORGE. "LETTERS TO DR. BELKNAP ON SLAVES IN
         VIRGINIA." MASSACHUSETTS HISTORICAL SOCIETY
         COLLECTIONS, 5TH SER., 3 (1877): 401-412, 416-431.

13873   TURNER, CHARLES W. "VIRGINIA RAILROAD HISTORY,
         1827-1860." M.A. THESIS, UNIVERSITY OF MINNESOTA,
         1946.

13874   VAUGHAN, ALDEN T. "BLACKS IN VIRGINIA: A NOTE ON THE
         FIRST DECADE." WILLIAM AND MARY QUARTERLY, 3RD SER.,
         29 (JULY, 1972): 469-478.

13875   VINIKAS, VINCE. "A SURVEY AT THE SURFACE OF SLAVERY:
         VIEWS ON TWO COLONIAL VIRGINIA COUNTIES." M.A.
         THESIS, COLUMBIA UNIVERSITY, 1974.

13876   "THE VIRGINIA CENSUS, 1624-1625." VIRGINIA MAGAZINE OF
         HISTORY AND BIOGRAPHY, 7 (APRIL, 1900): 364-365.

13877   WARD, HARRY M. AND GREER, HAROLD E., JR. RICHMOND DURING
         THE REVOLUTION, 1775-1783. CHARLOTTESVILLE:
         UNIVERSITY PRESS OF VIRGINIA, 1977.

13878   WASHINGTON, BOOKER T. "CHRISTMAS DAYS IN OLD VIRGINIA."
         SUBURBAN LIFE, 5 (DECEMBER, 1907): 336-337.

13879   WASHINGTON, BOOKER T. "CHRISTMAS DAYS IN OLD VIRGINIA."
         TUSKEGEE STUDENT, 19 (DECEMBER 21, 1907): 1.

13880   WAX, DAROLD D. "NEGRO IMPORT DUTIES IN COLONIAL
         VIRGINIA: A STUDY IN BRITISH COMMERCIAL POLICY AND
         LOCAL PUBLIC POLICY." VIRGINIA MAGAZINE OF HISTORY
         AND BIOGRAPHY, 79 (JANUARY, 1971): 29-44.

13881   WAYLAND, JOHN W.   A HISTORY OF ROCKINGHAM COUNTY,
        VIRGINIA.   DAYTON, VA: RUEBUSH-ELKINS COMPANY, 1912.

13882   WERTENBAKER, THOMAS J.   PATRICIAN AND PLEBIAN IN
        VIRGINIA.   CHARLOTTESVILLE: MICHIE COMPANY, 1910.

13883   WERTENBAKER, THOMAS J.   VIRGINIA UNDER THE STUARTS.
        PRINCETON: UNIVERSITY PRESS, 1912.

13884   WEST, GERALD M.   "THE STATUS OF THE NEGRO IN VIRGINIA
        DURING THE COLONIAL PERIOD."   PH.D. DISSERTATION,
        COLUMBIA UNIVERSITY, 1890.

13885   WEST, LANDON.   LIFE OF ELDER SAMUEL WEIR.   TUSKEGEE:
        NORMAL SCHOOL STEAM PRESS, 1896.

13886   WHITFIELD, THEODORE M.   SLAVERY AGITATION IN VIRGINIA,
        1829-1832.   BALTIMORE: JOHNS HOPKINS UNIVERSITY
        PRESS, 1930.

13887   WHITFIELD, THEODORE M.   "SLAVERY AGITATION IN VIRGINIA,
        1829-1832."   PH.D. DISSERTATION, JOHNS HOPKINS
        UNIVERSITY, 1929.

13888   WILLIAMS, EDNA G.   "THOMAS JEFFERSON, SLAVERY AND THE
        NEGRO."   M.A. THESIS, HOWARD UNIVERSITY, 1938.

13889   WILSTACH, PAUL.   JEFFERSON AND MONTICELLO.   NEW YORK:
        DOUBLEDAY, PAGE AND COMPANY, 1925.

13890   WINDLEY, LATHAN A.   "A PROFILE OF RUNAWAY SLAVES IN
        VIRGINIA AND SOUTH CAROLINA FROM 1730 THROUGH 1787."
        PH.D. DISSERTATION, UNIVERSITY OF IOWA, 1974.

13891   WOOD, WALTER K.   "HENRY EDMUNDSON, THE ALLEGHANY
        TURNPIKE, AND 'FOTHERINGAY' PLANTATION, 1805-1847:
        PLANTING AND TRADING IN MONTGOMERY COUNTY, VIRGINIA."
        VIRGINIA MAGAZINE OF HISTORY AND BIOGRAPHY, 83 (JULY,
        1975):   304-320.

13892   WOODSON, C.G.   "EARLY NEGRO EDUCATION IN WEST VIRGINIA."
        JOURNAL OF NEGRO HISTORY, 7 (JANUARY, 1922):   23-63.

13893   WOODSON, CARTER G.   FREEDOM AND SLAVERY IN APPALACHIAN
        AMERICA.   HUNTINGTON: APPALACHIAN MOVEMENT PRESS,
        1973.

13894   WOODSON, CARTER G.   "FREEDOM AND SLAVERY IN APPALACHIAN
        AMERICA."   JOURNAL OF NEGRO HISTORY, 1 (APRIL, 1916):
        132-150.

13895   WOODSON, CARTER G.   "THE NEGRO IN EARLY VIRGINIA."   NEGRO
        HISTORY BULLETIN, 12 (MAY, 1949):   173-180, 191.

13896   WRIGHT, LOUIS B.   "ANTIDOTE TO ROMANTIC CONCEPTS OF

COLONIAL VIRGINIA." <u>VIRGINIA QUARTERLY REVIEW</u>, 42
(WINTER, 1966): 137-141.

13897 WRIGHT, LOUIS B. <u>THE FIRST GENTLEMEN OF VIRGINIA</u>. SAN
MARINO: HUNTINGTON LIBRARY, 1940.

13898 WRIGHT, LOUIS B. (ED.). <u>LETTERS OF ROBERT CARTER,
1720-1727: THE COMMERCIAL INTERESTS OF A VIRGINIA
GENTLEMAN</u>. SAN MARINO: HUNTINGTON LIBRARY, 1940.

13899 WRITERS' PROGRAM, VIRGINIA. <u>THE NEGRO IN VIRGINIA</u>. NEW
YORK: HASTINGS HOUSE, 1940.

13900 WUST, KLAUS. <u>THE VIRGINIA GERMANS</u>. CHARLOTTESVILLE:
UNIVERSITY PRESS OF VIRGINIA, 1969.

13901 ZUCKERMAN, MICHAEL. "WILLIAM BYRD'S FAMILY."
<u>PERSPECTIVES IN AMERICAN HISTORY</u>, 12 (1979): 253-312.

13902   ABEL, ANNIE H.   THE AMERICAN INDIAN AS SLAVEHOLDER AND
        SECESSIONIST: AN OMITTED CHAPTER IN THE DIPLOMATIC
        HISTORY OF THE SOUTHERN CONFEDERACY.   CLEVELAND:
        ARTHUR H. CLARK COMPANY, 1915.

13903   ALDEN, JOHN R.   JOHN STUART AND THE SOUTHERN COLONIAL
        FRONTIER, 1754-1775:   A STUDY OF INDIAN RELATIONS,
        WAR, TRADE, AND LAND PROBLEMS IN THE SOUTHERN
        WILDERNESS, 1774-1775.   ANN ARBOR: UNIVERSITY OF
        MICHIGAN PRESS, 1944.

13904   ALDRICH, GENE.   BLACK HERITAGE OF OKLAHOMA.   EDMOND, OK:
        THOMPSON BOOK AND SUPPLY COMPANY, 1973.

13905   ANDERSON, ROBERT L.   "THE END OF AN IDYLL."   FLORIDA
        HISTORICAL QUARTERLY, 42 (JULY, 1963):   35-47.

13906   ANDREWS, THOMAS F.   "FREEDMEN IN INDIAN TERRITORY: A
        POST-CIVIL WAR DILEMMA."   JOURNAL OF THE WEST, 4
        (JULY, 1965):   367-376.

13907   ASH, HARRY C.   "ETHNOLOGY OF THE INDIAN TRIBES FORMERLY
        OCCUPYING THE TERRITORY OF GEORGIA."   M.A. THESIS,
        EMORY UNIVERSITY, 1932.

13908   AXTELL, JAMES.   "THROUGH A GLASS DARKLY, COLONIAL
        ATTITUDES TOWARD THE NATIVE AMERICANS."   AMERICAN
        INDIAN CULTURE AND RESEARCH JOURNAL, 1 (1974):   17-28.

13909   BAILEY, LYNN R.   INDIAN SLAVE TRADE IN THE SOUTHWEST: A
        STUDY OF SLAVE-TAKING AND THE TRAFFIC OF INDIAN
        CAPTIVES.   LOS ANGELES: WESTERNLORE PRESS, 1966.

13910   BAILEY, MINNIE T.   RECONSTRUCTION IN INDIAN TERRITORY: A
        STORY OF AVARICE, DISCRIMINATION AND OPPORTUNISM.
        PORT WASHINGTON, NY: KENNIKAT PRESS, 1972.

13911   BAIRD, W. DAVID.   "SPENCER ACADEMY, CHOCTAW NATION,
        1842-1890."   CHRONICLES OF OKLAHOMA, 45 (SPRING,
        1967):   25-43.

13912   BEARSS, EDWIN C.   "THE CIVIL WAR COMES TO INDIAN
        TERRITORY, 1861:   THE FLIGHT OF OPOTHLEYOHOLO."
        JOURNAL OF THE WEST, 11 (JANUARY, 1972):   9-42.

13913   BELTON, BILL.   "THE INDIAN HERITAGE OF CRISPUS ATTUCKS."
        NEGRO HISTORY BULLETIN, 35 (NOVEMBER, 1972):   149-152.

13914   BENNETT, LERONE JR.   "RED AND BLACK: THE INDIANS AND THE
        AFRICANS."   EBONY, 26 (DECEMBER, 1970):   70-80.

13915   BENNETT, LERONE JR. "THE ROAD NOT TAKEN: COLONIES TURN
        FATEFUL FORK BY SYSTEMATICALLY DIVIDING THE RACES."
        EBONY, 25 (AUGUST, 1970): 71-77.

13916   BERKHOFER, ROBERT F., JR. "PROTESTANTS, PAGANS, AND
        SEQUENCES AMONG THE NORTH AMERICAN INDIANS,
        1760-1860." ETHNOHISTORY, 10 (1963): 201-233.

13917   BERKHOFER, ROBERT F., JR. SALVATION AND THE SAVAGE: AN
        ANALYSIS OF PROTESTANT MISSIONS AND AMERICAN INDIAN
        RESPONSE. LEXINGTON: UNIVERSITY OF KENTUCKY PRESS,
        1965.

13918   BITTLE, WILLIAM E. AND GEIS, GILBERT. THE LONGEST WAY
        HOME. DETROIT: WAYNE STATE UNIVERSITY PRESS, 1964.

13919   BLOOM, LEONARD. "THE ACCULTURATION OF THE EASTERN
        CHEROKEES." NORTH CAROLINA HISTORICAL REVIEW, 19
        (OCTOBER, 1942): 323-358.

13920   BLOOM, LEONARD. "ROLE OF THE INDIAN IN THE RACE
        RELATIONS COMPLEX OF THE SOUTH." SOCIAL FORCES, 19
        (DECEMBER, 1940): 268-273.

13921   BOLT, CHRISTINE. "RED, BLACK AND WHITE IN
        NINETEENTH-CENTURY AMERICA." IN HEPBURN, A.C. (ED.).
        MINORITIES IN HISTORY. LONDON: EDWARD ARNOLD, 1978,
        PP. 116-134.

13922   BONNIFIELD, PAUL. "CHOCTAW NATION ON THE EVE OF THE
        CIVIL WAR." JOURNAL OF THE WEST, 12 (JULY, 1973):
        386-402.

13923   BRINTON, DANIEL G. "ON CERTAIN SUPPOSED NANTICOKE WORDS,
        SHOWN TO BE AFRICAN." AMERICAN ANTIQUARIAN AND
        ORIENTAL JOURNAL, 9 (NOVEMBER, 1887): 350-354.

13924   BROWN, JOHN P. OLD FRONTIERS: THE STORY OF THE CHEROKEE
        INDIANS FROM THE EARLIEST TIMES TO THE DATE OF THEIR
        REMOVAL TO THE WEST, 1838. KINGSPORT, TN: SOUTHERN
        PUBLISHERS, 1938.

13925   BROWN, RICHARD M. THE SOUTH CAROLINA REGULATORS.
        CAMBRIDGE: HARVARD UNIVERSITY PRESS, 1963.

13926   BUKER, GEORGE E. "RIVERINE WARFARE: NAVAL COMBAT IN THE
        SECOND SEMINOLE WAR, 1835-1842." PH.D. DISSERTATION,
        UNIVERSITY OF FLORIDA, 1969.

13927   CHAMBERLAIN, ALEXANDER F. "AFRICAN AND AMERICAN: THE
        CONTACT OF NEGRO AND INDIAN." SCIENCE, 17 (FEBRUARY
        13, 1891): 85-90.

13928   CHAMBERLAIN, ALEXANDER F. "NEGRO AND INDIAN." IN HODGE,
        FREDERICK W. (ED.). HANDBOOK OF AMERICAN INDIANS

NORTH OF MEXICO. 2 VOLS. WASHINGTON: GOVERNMENT
PRINTING OFFICE, 1912, VOL. 2, PP. 51-53.

13929   CORKRAN, DAVID H. THE CHEROKEE FRONTIER: CONFLICT AND
        SURVIVAL, 1740-1762. NORMAN: UNIVERSITY OF OKLAHOMA
        PRESS, 1962.

13930   CORKRAN, DAVID H. THE CREEK FRONTIER, 1540-1783.
        NORMAN: UNIVERSITY OF OKLAHOMA PRESS, 1967.

13931   CORRY, JOHN P. "INDIAN AFFAIRS IN GEORGIA, 1732-1756."
        PH.D. DISSERTATION, UNIVERSITY OF PENNSYLVANIA, 1935.

13932   CORRY, JOHN P. INDIAN AFFAIRS IN GEORGIA, 1732-1756.
        PHILADELPHIA: N.P., 1936.

13933   COTTERILL, ROBERT S. THE SOUTHERN INDIANS: THE STORY OF
        THE CIVILIZED TRIBES BEFORE REMOVAL. NORMAN:
        UNIVERSITY OF OKLAHOMA PRESS, 1954.

13934   CROCKETT, NORMAN L. THE BLACK TOWNS. LAWRENCE: REGENTS
        PRESS OF KANSAS, 1979.

13935   CROWE, CHARLES. "INDIANS AND BLACKS IN WHITE AMERICA."
        IN HUDSON, CHARLES M. (ED.). FOUR CENTURIES OF
        SOUTHERN INDIANS. ATHENS: UNIVERSITY OF GEORGIA
        PRESS, 1975, PP. 148-169.

13936   DALE, EDWARD E. "THE CHEROKEES IN THE CONFEDERACY."
        JOURNAL OF SOUTHERN HISTORY, 13 (MAY, 1947): 159-185.

13937   DAVIS, J.B. "SLAVERY IN THE CHEROKEE NATION."
        CHRONICLES OF OKLAHOMA, 11 (DECEMBER, 1933):
        1056-1072.

13938   DEBO, ANGIE. THE ROAD TO DISAPPEARANCE. NORMAN:
        UNIVERSITY OF OKLAHOMA PRESS, 1941.

13939   DEROSIER, ARTHUR H. THE REMOVAL OF THE CHOCTAW INDIANS.
        KNOXVILLE: UNIVERSITY OF TENNESSEE PRESS, 1970.

13940   DEROSIER, ARTHUR H., JR. "PIONEERS WITH CONFLICTING
        IDEALS: CHRISTIANITY AND SLAVERY IN THE CHOCTAW
        NATION." JOURNAL OF MISSISSIPPI HISTORY, 21 (MAY,
        1959): 174-189.

13941   DOBYNS, HENRY F.; EZELL, PAUL H.; EZELL, GRETA S. "DEATH
        OF A SOCIETY: THE HALCHIDHOMAS." ETHNOHISTORY, 10
        (1963): 105-161.

13942   DORAN, MICHAEL F. "NEGRO SLAVES OF THE FIVE CIVILIZED
        TRIBES." ANNALS OF THE ASSOCIATION OF AMERICAN
        GEOGRAPHERS, 68 (SEPTEMBER, 1978): 335-350.

13943   DORAN, MICHAEL F. "POPULATION STATISTICS OF NINETEENTH

CENTURY INDIAN TERRITORY." CHRONICLES OF OKLAHOMA, 53
(WINTER, 1975-1976): 492-515.

13944   DUFFNER, MICHAEL P. "THE SEMINOLE-BLACK ALLIANCE IN
        FLORIDA: AN EXAMPLE OF MINORITY COOPERATION." M.A.
        THESIS, GEORGE MASON UNIVERSITY, 1973.

13945   DUNCAN, JAMES W. "INTERESTING ANTE-BELLUM LAWS OF THE
        CHEROKEES, NOW OKLAHOMA HISTORY." CHRONICLES OF
        OKLAHOMA, 6 (JUNE, 1928): 178-180.

13946   DUNCAN, OTIS D. "THE FUSION OF WHITE, NEGRO AND INDIAN
        CULTURES AT THE CONVERGING OF THE NEW SOUTH AND THE
        WEST." SOUTHWESTERN SOCIAL SCIENCE QUARTERLY, 14
        (MARCH, 1934): 357-369.

13947   DUNDES, ALAN. "AFRICAN TALES AMONG THE NORTH AMERICAN
        INDIANS." SOUTHERN FOLKLORE QUARTERLY, 29 (SEPTEMBER,
        1965): 207-219.

13948   FISCHER, LEROY H. "THE CIVIL WAR ERA IN INDIAN
        TERRITORY." JOURNAL OF THE WEST, 12 (JULY, 1973):
        345-355.

13949   FLEMING, WALTER L. "SLAVE-HOLDING INDIANS IN THE CIVIL
        WAR." DIAL, 59 (SEPTEMBER 16, 1915): 216-218.

13950   FORBES, G. "PART PLAYED BY INDIAN SLAVERY IN REMOVAL OF
        TRIBES TO OKLAHOMA." CHRONICLES OF OKLAHOMA, 16
        (JUNE, 1938): 163-170.

13951   FOREMAN, GRANT. ADVANCING THE FRONTIER, 1830-1860.
        NORMAN: UNIVERSITY OF OKLAHOMA PRESS, 1933.

13952   FOREMAN, GRANT. THE FIVE CIVILIZED TRIBES. NORMAN:
        UNIVERSITY OF OKLAHOMA PRESS, 1937.

13953   FOREMAN, GRANT. INDIAN REMOVAL: THE EMIGRATION OF THE
        FIVE CIVILIZED TRIBES OF INDIANS. NORMAN: UNIVERSITY
        OF OKLAHOMA PRESS, 1932.

13954   FOSTER, GEORGE E. "THE ABOLITION OF SLAVERY BY THE
        CHEROKEES." CENTURY MAGAZINE, 36 (AUGUST, 1888): 638.

13955   FOSTER, LAURENCE. "NEGRO-INDIAN RELATIONSHIPS IN THE
        SOUTHEAST." PH.D. DISSERTATION, UNIVERSITY OF
        PENNSYLVANIA, 1935.

13956   FOSTER, LAURENCE. NEGRO-INDIAN RELATIONSHIPS IN THE
        SOUTHEAST. PHILADELPHIA: UNIVERSITY OF PENNSYLVANIA
        PRESS, 1935.

13957   FOSTER, LAURENCE AND MCREYNOLDS, EDWIN C. THE SEMINOLES.
        NORMAN: UNIVERSITY OF OKLAHOMA PRESS, 1954.

13958   FRANKLIN, JIMMIE L. THE BLACKS IN OKLAHOMA. NORMAN:
        UNIVERSITY OF OKLAHOMA PRESS, 1980.

13959   GAMMON, TIM. "BLACK FREEDMEN AND THE CHEROKEE NATION."
        JOURNAL OF AMERICAN STUDIES, 11 (DECEMBER, 1977):
        357-364.

13960   GEIST, CHRISTOPHER D. "SLAVERY AMONG THE INDIANS: AN
        OVERVIEW." NEGRO HISTORY BULLETIN, 38
        (OCTOBER/NOVEMBER, 1975): 465-467.

13961   GILBERT, WILLIAM H., JR. THE EASTERN CHEROKEES.
        WASHINGTON: U.S. GOVERNMENT PRINTING OFFICE, 1943.

13962   GRAEBNER, NORMAN A. "PIONEER INDIAN AGRICULTURE IN
        OKLAHOMA." CHRONICLES OF OKLAHOMA, 23 (AUTUMN, 1945):
        232-248.

13963   GRIFFIN, LARRY D. "(A-NI-JA-LA-GA JU-NI-NA-TLA
        A-NI-GV-NE-GE) BLACK SLAVES IN THE CHEROKEE NATION."
        ESSAYS IN HISTORY: THE E.G. BARKSDALE STUDENT
        LECTURES, 2 (1973): 111-134.

13964   HALLIBURTON, JANET. "BLACK SLAVERY IN THE CREEK NATION."
        CHRONICLES OF OKLAHOMA, 56 (FALL, 1978): 298-314.

13965   HALLIBURTON, R., JR. "BLACK SLAVE CONTROL IN THE
        CHEROKEE NATION." JOURNAL OF ETHNIC STUDIES, 3
        (SUMMER, 1975): 23-36.

13966   HALLIBURTON, R., JR. "BLACK SLAVERY AMONG THE
        CHEROKEES." AMERICAN HISTORY ILLUSTRATED, 11
        (OCTOBER, 1976): 12-19.

13967   HALLIBURTON, R., JR. "ORIGINS OF BLACK SLAVERY AMONG THE
        CHEROKEES." CHRONICLES OF OKLAHOMA, 52 (WINTER,
        1974-1975): 483-496.

13968   HALLIBURTON, R., JR. RED OVER BLACK: BLACK SLAVERY
        AMONG THE CHEROKEE INDIANS. WESTPORT: GREENWOOD
        PRESS, 1977.

13969   HALLOWELL, A. IRVING. "AMERICAN INDIANS, WHITE AND
        BLACK: THE PHENOMENON OF TRANSCULTURALIZATION."
        CURRENT ANTHROPOLOGY, 4 (1963): 519-531.

13970   HENSHAW, HENRY W. "SLAVERY." IN HODGE, FREDERICK W.
        (ED.). HANDBOOK OF AMERICAN INDIANS NORTH OF MEXICO.
        2 VOLS. WASHINGTON: GOVERNMENT PRINTING OFFICE,
        1907-1910, VOL. 2, PP. 597-600.

13971   HERZOG, GEORGE. "AFRICAN INFLUENCES IN NORTH AMERICAN
        INDIAN MUSIC." PAPERS READ AT THE INTERNATIONAL
        CONGRESS OF MUSICOLOGY HELD AT NEW YORK, SEPTEMBER
        11TH TO 16TH, 1939. NEW YORK: MUSIC EDUCATORS

NATIONAL CONFERENCE FOR THE AMERICAN MUSICOLOGICAL SOCIETY, 1944, PP. 130-143.

13972 HOLLAND, REID A. "LIFE IN THE CHEROKEE NATION, 1855-1860." CHRONICLES OF OKLAHOMA, 49 (AUTUMN, 1971): 284-301.

13973 HOOVER, DWIGHT W. THE RED AND THE BLACK. CHICAGO: RAND MCNALLY, 1976.

13974 HUDSON, CHARLES M. (ED.). FOUR CENTURIES OF SOUTHERN INDIANS. ATHENS: UNIVERSITY OF GEORGIA PRESS, 1975.

13975 HUDSON, CHARLES M. (ED.). RED, WHITE, AND BLACK: SYMPOSIUM ON INDIANS IN THE OLD SOUTH. ATHENS: SOUTHERN ANTHROPOLOGICAL SOCIETY, 1971.

13976 HUDSON, CHARLES M. THE SOUTHEASTERN INDIANS. KNOXVILLE: UNIVERSITY OF TENNESSEE PRESS, 1976.

13977 HUNT, H.F. "SLAVERY AMONG THE INDIANS OF NORTHWEST AMERICA." WASHINGTON HISTORICAL QUARTERLY, 9 (OCTOBER, 1918): 277-283.

13978 JAMES, JAMES A. ENGLISH INSTITUTIONS AND THE AMERICAN INDIAN. BALTIMORE: JOHNS HOPKINS PRESS, 1894.

13979 JELTZ, WYATT F. "THE RELATIONS OF NEGROES AND CHOCTAW AND CHICKASAW INDIANS." JOURNAL OF NEGRO HISTORY, 33 (JANUARY, 1948): 24-37.

13980 JOSEPHY, ALVIN M. THE INDIAN HERITAGE OF AMERICA. NEW YORK: ALFRED A. KNOPF, 1968.

13981 KATZ, WILLIAM L. "BLACK AND INDIAN COOPERATION AND RESISTANCE TO SLAVERY." FREEDOMWAYS, 17 (THIRD QUARTER, 1977): 164-174.

13982 KERSEY, HARRY A., JR. "THE CHEROKEE, CREEK, AND SEMINOLE RESPONSES TO REMOVAL: A COMPARISON." IN MAHON, JOHN K. (ED.). INDIANS OF THE LOWER SOUTH: PAST AND PRESENT. PENSACOLA: GULF COAST HISTORY AND HUMANITIES CONFERENCE, 1975, PP. 112-117.

13983 LAUBER, ALMON W. INDIAN SLAVERY IN COLONIAL TIMES WITHIN THE PRESENT LIMITS OF THE UNITED STATES. NEW YORK: LONGMANS, GREEN AND COMPANY, 1913.

13984 LAUBER, ALMON W. "INDIAN SLAVERY IN COLONIAL TIMES WITHIN THE PRESENT LIMITS OF THE UNITED STATES." PH.D. DISSERTATION, COLUMBIA UNIVERSITY, 1913.

13985 LITTLEFIELD, DANIEL F., JR. AFRICANS AND CREEKS: FROM THE COLONIAL PERIOD TO THE CIVIL WAR. WESTPORT: GREENWOOD PRESS, 1979.

13986   LITTLEFIELD, DANIEL F., JR. AFRICANS AND SEMINOLES:
        FROM REMOVAL TO EMANCIPATION. WESTPORT: GREENWOOD
        PRESS, 1977.

13987   LITTLEFIELD, DANIEL F., JR. THE CHEROKEE FREEDMEN: FROM
        EMANCIPATION TO AMERICAN CITIZENSHIP. WESTPORT:
        GREENWOOD PRESS, 1978.

13988   LITTLEFIELD, DANIEL F., JR. THE CHICKASAW FREEDMEN: A
        PEOPLE WITHOUT A COUNTRY. WESTPORT: GREENWOOD PRESS,
        1980.

13989   LITTLEFIELD, DANIEL F., JR. AND UNDERHILL, LONNIE E.
        "SLAVE 'REVOLT' IN THE CHEROKEE NATION, 1842."
        AMERICAN INDIAN QUARTERLY, 3 (SUMMER, 1977): 121-133.

13990   LOFTON, JOHN M., JR. "WHITE, INDIAN, AND NEGRO CONTACTS
        IN COLONIAL SOUTH CAROLINA." SOUTHERN INDIAN STUDIES,
        1 (1949): 3-12.

13991   LOVE, EDGAR F. "LEGAL RESTRICTIONS ON AFRO-INDIAN
        RELATIONS IN COLONIAL MEXICO." JOURNAL OF NEGRO
        HISTORY, 55 (APRIL, 1970): 131-139.

13992   MACLEOD, WILLIAM C. "DEBTOR AND CHATTEL SLAVERY IN
        ABORIGINAL NORTH AMERICA." AMERICAN ANTHROPOLOGIST,
        27 (JULY, 1925): 370-380.

13993   MACLEOD, WILLIAM C. "ECONOMIC ASPECTS OF INDIGENOUS
        AMERICAN SLAVERY." AMERICAN ANTHROPOLOGIST, 30
        (OCTOBER, 1928): 632-650.

13994   MACLEOD, WILLIAM C. "SOME ASPECTS OF CHATTEL SLAVERY."
        JOURNAL OF SOCIAL FORCES, 4 (SEPTEMBER, 1925):
        137-141.

13995   MAGNAGHI, RUSSELL M. "THE ROLE OF INDIAN SLAVERY IN
        COLONIAL ST. LOUIS." BULLETIN OF THE MISSOURI
        HISTORICAL SOCIETY, 31 (JULY, 1975): 264-272.

13996   MAHON, JOHN K. HISTORY OF THE SECOND SEMINOLE WAR,
        1835-1842. GAINESVILLE: UNIVERSITY OF FLORIDA PRESS,
        1967.

13997   MALONE, HENRY T. "CHEROKEE CIVILIZATION IN THE LOWER
        APPALACHIANS, ESPECIALLY IN NORTH GEORGIA, BEFORE
        1830." M.A. THESIS, EMORY UNIVERSITY, 1949.

13998   MALONE, HENRY T. CHEROKEES OF THE OLD SOUTH: A PEOPLE
        IN TRANSITION. ATHENS: UNIVERSITY OF GEORGIA PRESS,
        1956.

13999   MCKEE, JESSE O. AND SCHLENKER, JON A. THE CHOCTAWS:
        CULTURAL EVOLUTION OF A NATIVE AMERICAN TRIBE.
        JACKSON: UNIVERSITY PRESS OF MISSISSIPPI, 1980.

14000   MCLOUGHLIN, WILLIAM G.   "CHEROKEE ANOMIE, 1794-1809:   NEW
        ROLES FOR RED MEN, RED WOMEN, AND BLACK SLAVES."   IN
        BUSHMAN, RICHARD L.; HARRIS, NEIL; ROTHMAN, DAVID;
        SOLOMON, BARBARA M.; AND THERNSTROM, STEPHAN (EDS.).
        UPROOTED AMERICANS: ESSAYS TO HONOR OSCAR HANDLIN.
        BOSTON: LITTLE, BROWN AND COMPANY, 1979, PP. 125-160.

14001   MCLOUGHLIN, WILLIAM G.   "THE CHOCTAW SLAVE BURNING: A
        CRISIS IN MISSION WORK AMONG THE INDIANS."   JOURNAL OF
        THE WEST, 13 (JANUARY, 1974):   113-127.

14002   MCLOUGHLIN, WILLIAM G.   "INDIAN SLAVEHOLDERS AND
        PRESBYTERIAN MISSIONARIES, 1837-1861."   CHURCH
        HISTORY, 42 (DECEMBER, 1973):   535-551.

14003   MCLOUGHLIN, WILLIAM G.   "RED INDIANS, BLACK SLAVERY AND
        WHITE RACISM: AMERICA'S SLAVEHOLDING INDIANS."
        AMERICAN QUARTERLY, 26 (OCTOBER, 1974):   367-385.

14004   MCLOUGHLIN, WILLIAM G.   "RED, WHITE, AND BLACK IN THE
        ANTEBELLUM SOUTH."   BAPTIST HISTORY AND HERITAGE, 7
        (JANUARY, 1972):   69-75.

14005   MERRELL, JAMES H.   "THE PROBLEM OF SLAVERY IN CHEROKEE
        CULTURE."   REVIEWS IN AMERICAN HISTORY, 7 (DECEMBER,
        1979):   509-514.

14006   MILLING, CHAPMAN J.   RED CAROLINIANS.   CHAPEL HILL:
        UNIVERSITY OF NORTH CAROLINA PRESS, 1940.

14007   MOONEY, JAMES.   MYTHS OF THE CHEROKEES.   CAMBRIDGE:
        RIVERSIDE PRESS, 1888.

14008   NASH, GARY B.   "AFRICAN-INDIAN CONTACT."   RED, WHITE AND
        BLACK: THE PEOPLES OF EARLY AMERICA.   ENGLEWOOD
        CLIFFS: PRENTICE-HALL, 1974, PP. 290-297.

14009   NASH, GARY B.   "RED, WHITE AND BLACK: THE ORIGINS OF
        RACISM IN COLONIAL AMERICA."   IN NASH AND WEISS,
        RICHARD (EDS.).   THE GREAT FEAR: RACE IN THE MIND OF
        AMERICA.   NEW YORK: HOLT, RINEHART AND WINSTON, 1970,
        PP. 1-26.

14010   NEELY, SHARLOTTE.   "ACCULTURATION AND PERSISTENCE AMONG
        NORTH CAROLINA'S EASTERN BAND OF CHEROKEE INDIANS."
        IN WILLIAMS, WALTER L. (ED.).   SOUTHEASTERN INDIANS
        SINCE THE REMOVAL ERA.   ATHENS: UNIVERSITY OF GEORGIA
        PRESS, 1979, PP. 154-173.

14011   O'DONNELL, JAMES H.   SOUTHERN INDIANS IN THE AMERICAN
        REVOLUTION.   KNOXVILLE: UNIVERSITY OF TENNESSEE
        PRESS, 1973.

14012   PASCHAL, ANDREW G.   "HISTORY SHOWS INDIANS AND BLACKS
        NATURAL ALLIES IN BATTLE AGAINST AMERICAN TREACHERY."

MUHAMMAD SPEAKS, 8 (NOVEMBER 22, 1968):   27, 30, 32.

14013   PERDUE, THEDA.   "CHEROKEE PLANTERS: THE DEVELOPMENT OF
        PLANTATION SLAVERY BEFORE REMOVAL."   IN KING, DUANE H.
        (ED.).   THE CHEROKEE INDIAN NATION: A TROUBLED
        HISTORY.   KNOXVILLE: UNIVERSITY OF TENNESSEE PRESS,
        1979, PP. 110-128.

14014   PERDUE, THEDA.   NATIONS REMEMBERED: AN ORAL HISTORY OF
        THE FIVE CIVILIZED TRIBES, 1865-1907.   WESTPORT:
        GREENWOOD PRESS, 1980.

14015   PERDUE, THEDA.   "PEOPLE WITHOUT A PLACE: ABORIGINAL
        CHEROKEE BONDAGE."   INDIAN HISTORIAN, 9 (SUMMER,
        1976):   31-37.

14016   PERDUE, THEDA.   SLAVERY AND THE EVOLUTION OF CHEROKEE
        SOCIETY, 1540-1866.   KNOXVILLE: UNIVERSITY OF
        TENNESSEE PRESS, 1979.

14017   PERDUE, THEDA.   "SLAVERY AND THE EVOLUTION OF CHEROKEE
        SOCIETY, 1540-1838."   M.A. THESIS, UNIVERSITY OF
        GEORGIA, 1974.

14018   PERDUE, THEDA.   "SLAVERY AND THE EVOLUTION OF CHEROKEE
        SOCIETY, 1540-1866."   PH.D. DISSERTATION, UNIVERSITY
        OF GEORGIA, 1976.

14019   PETERS, VIRGINIA B.   THE FLORIDA WARS.   HAMDEN, CT: SHOE
        STRING PRESS, 1979.

14020   PETERSON, JOHN H., JR.   "THE INDIANS IN THE OLD SOUTH."
        IN HUDSON, CHARLES M. (ED.).   RED, WHITE, AND BLACK:
        SYMPOSIUM ON INDIANS IN THE OLD SOUTH.   ATHENS:
        SOUTHERN ANTHROPOLOGICAL SOCIETY, 1971, PP. 116-133.

14021   PORTER, KENNETH W.   "FAREWELL TO JOHN HORSE: AN EPISODE
        OF SEMINOLE NEGRO FOLK HISTORY."   PHYLON, 8 (THIRD
        QUARTER, 1947):   265-273.

14022   PORTER, KENNETH W.   "NEGROES AND THE SEMINOLE WAR,
        1835-1842."   JOURNAL OF SOUTHERN HISTORY, 30
        (NOVEMBER, 1964):   427-450.

14023   PORTER, KENNETH W.   "NEGROES ON THE SOUTHERN FRONTIER,
        1670-1763."   JOURNAL OF NEGRO HISTORY, 33 (JANUARY,
        1948):   53-78.

14024   PORTER, KENNETH W.   "NOTES SUPPLEMENTARY TO RELATIONS
        BETWEEN NEGROES AND INDIANS."   JOURNAL OF NEGRO
        HISTORY, 18 (JULY, 1933):   282-321.

14025   PORTER, KENNETH W.   "RELATIONS BETWEEN NEGROES AND
        INDIANS WITHIN THE PRESENT LIMITS OF THE UNITED
        STATES."   JOURNAL OF NEGRO HISTORY, 17 (JULY, 1932):

287-367.

14026 PRICE, EDWARD T. "A GEOGRAPHIC ANALYSIS OF
       WHITE-NEGRO-INDIAN RACIAL MIXTURES IN THE EASTERN
       UNITED STATES." ANNALS OF THE ASSOCIATION OF AMERICAN
       GEOGRAPHERS, 43 (JUNE, 1953): 138-156.

14027 PRUCHA, FRANCIS P. A BIBLIOGRAPHICAL GUIDE TO THE
       HISTORY OF INDIAN-WHITE RELATIONS IN THE UNITED
       STATES. CHICAGO: UNIVERSITY OF CHICAGO PRESS, 1977.

14028 RAMAGE, BURR J. "GEORGIA AND THE CHEROKEES." AMERICAN
       HISTORICAL MAGAZINE AND TENNESSEE HISTORICAL SOCIETY
       QUARTERLY, 7 (1902): 199-208.

14029 REID, JOHN P. A BETTER KIND OF HATCHET: LAW, TRADE, AND
       DIPLOMACY IN THE CHEROKEE NATION DURING THE EARLY
       YEARS OF EUROPEAN CONTACT. UNIVERSITY PARK:
       PENNSYLVANIA STATE UNIVERSITY PRESS, 1976.

14030 RIGHTS, DOUGLAS L. THE AMERICAN INDIAN IN NORTH
       CAROLINA. WINSTON-SALEM: J.F. BLAIR, 1957.

14031 ROETHLER, MICHAEL D. "NEGRO SLAVERY AMONG THE CHEROKEE
       INDIANS, 1540-1866." PH.D. DISSERTATION, FORDHAM
       UNIVERSITY, 1964.

14032 ROYCE, CHARLES C. THE CHEROKEE NATION OF INDIANS: A
       NARRATIVE OF THEIR OFFICIAL RELATIONS WITH THE
       COLONIAL AND FEDERAL GOVERNMENTS. WASHINGTON:
       GOVERNMENT PRINTING OFFICE, 1887.

14033 RUCKER, ALVIN. "THE STORY OF SLAVE UPRISING IN
       OKLAHOMA." OKLAHOMA CITY DAILY OKLAHOMAN, OCTOBER 30,
       1932.

14034 SAMETH, SIGMUND. "CREEK NEGROES: A STUDY OF RACE
       RELATIONS." M.A. THESIS, UNIVERSITY OF OKLAHOMA, 1940.

14035 SATZ, RONALD N. TENNESSEE'S INDIAN PEOPLES. KNOXVILLE:
       UNIVERSITY OF TENNESSEE PRESS, 1979.

14036 SEFTON, JAMES E. "BLACK SLAVES, RED MASTERS, WHITE
       MIDDLEMEN: A CONGRESSIONAL DEBATE OF 1852." FLORIDA
       HISTORICAL QUARTERLY, 51 (OCTOBER, 1972): 113-128.

14037 SHAW, HELLEN L. BRITISH ADMINISTRATION OF THE SOUTHERN
       INDIANS, 1756-1783. LANCASTER, PA: LANCASTER PRESS,
       1931.

14038 SIEGEL, BERNARD J. "SOME METHODOLOGICAL CONSIDERATIONS
       FOR A COMPARATIVE STUDY OF SLAVERY." AMERICAN
       ANTHROPOLOGIST, N.S., 47 (JULY/SEPTEMBER, 1945):
       357-392.

14039   SMITH, C. CALVIN. "THE OPPRESSED OPPRESSORS: NEGRO
        SLAVERY AMONG THE CHOCTAW INDIANS OF OKLAHOMA." RED
        RIVER VALLEY HISTORICAL REVIEW, 2 (SUMMER, 1975):
        240-254.

14040   SPECK, F.G. "THE NEGROES AND THE CREEK NATION."
        SOUTHERN WORKMAN, 37 (FEBRUARY, 1908): 106-110.

14041   SPECK, FRANK G. "A COMPARATIVE STUDY OF THE NATIVE
        MYTHOLOGY OF THE SOUTH-EASTERN UNITED STATES." M.A.
        THESIS, COLUMBIA UNIVERSITY, 1905.

14042   STARKEY, MARION L. THE CHEROKEE NATION. NEW YORK:
        ALFRED A. KNOPF, 1946.

14043   STARR, EMMET. CHEROKEES "WEST", 1794-1839. CLAREMORE,
        OK: THE AUTHOR, 1910.

14044   STEWART, LEROY E. "A HISTORY OF THE CHICKASAWS,
        1830-1855." M.A. THESIS, UNIVERSITY OF OKLAHOMA, 1938.

14045   SWANTON, JOHN R. THE INDIANS OF THE SOUTHEASTERN UNITED
        STATES. WASHINGTON: U.S. GOVERNMENT PRINTING OFFICE,
        1946.

14046   THOBURN, JOSEPH B. AND WRIGHT, MURIEL H. OKLAHOMA--A
        HISTORY OF THE STATE AND ITS PEOPLE. 4 VOLS. NEW
        YORK: LEWIS HISTORICAL PUBLISHING COMPANY, 1929.

14047   TROPER, HAROLD M. "THE CREEK-NEGROES OF OKLAHOMA AND
        CANADIAN IMMIGRATION, 1909-1911." CANADIAN HISTORICAL
        REVIEW, 53 (SEPTEMBER, 1972): 272-288.

14048   WALTON, GEORGE. FEARLESS AND FREE: THE SEMINOLE INDIAN
        WAR, 1835-1842. INDIANAPOLIS: BOBBS-MERRILL, 1977.

14049   WARDELL, MORRIS L. A POLITICAL HISTORY OF THE CHEROKEE
        NATION, 1838-1907. NORMAN: UNIVERSITY OF OKLAHOMA
        PRESS, 1938.

14050   WHIPPLE, CHARLES K. THE RELATION OF THE A.B.C.F.M. TO
        SLAVERY. BOSTON: R.F. WALLCUT, 1871.

14051   WILLIAMS, SAMUEL C. EARLY TRAVELS IN THE TENNESSEE
        COUNTRY, 1540-1800. JOHNSON CITY, TN: WATAUGA PRESS,
        1928.

14052   WILLIAMS, WALTER L. "SOUTHEASTERN INDIANS BEFORE
        REMOVAL: PREHISTORY, CONTACT, DECLINE." IN WILLIAMS
        (ED.). SOUTHEASTERN INDIANS SINCE THE REMOVAL ERA.
        ATHENS: UNIVERSITY OF GEORGIA PRESS, 1979, PP. 3-26.

14053   WILLIS, WILLIAM S. "DIVIDE AND RULE: RED, WHITE, AND
        BLACK IN THE SOUTHEAST." JOURNAL OF NEGRO HISTORY, 48
        (JULY, 1963): 157-176.

14054　WILLIS, WILLIAM S., JR. "DIVIDE AND RULE: RED, WHITE, AND BLACK IN THE SOUTHEAST." IN HUDSON, CHARLES M. (ED.). RED, WHITE, AND BLACK: SYMPOSIUM ON INDIANS IN THE OLD SOUTH. ATHENS: SOUTHERN ANTHROPOLOGICAL SOCIETY, 1971, PP. 99-115.

14055　WILMS, DOUGLAS C. "CHEROKEE SLAVE OWNERSHIP PRIOR TO THE REMOVAL." PAPER PRESENTED AT SYMPOSIUM ON NEW DIRECTIONS IN CHEROKEE STUDIES, MEETING OF THE SOUTHERN ANTHROPOLOGICAL SOCIETY, BLACKSBURG, VIRGINIA, 1974.

14056　WILSON, L.W. "REMINISCENCES OF JIM TOMM." CHRONICLES OF OKLAHOMA, 44 (AUTUMN, 1966): 290-306.

14057　WILSON, RALEIGH A. "NEGRO AND INDIAN RELATIONS IN THE FIVE CIVILIZED TRIBES FROM 1865 TO 1907." PH.D. DISSERTATION, UNIVERSITY OF IOWA, 1949.

14058　WOODWARD, GRACE S. THE CHEROKEES. NORMAN: UNIVERSITY OF OKLAHOMA PRESS, 1963.

14059　WRIGHT, J. LEITCH JR. THE ONLY LAND THEY KNEW: THE TRAGIC STORY OF THE AMERICAN INDIANS IN THE OLD SOUTH. NEW YORK: FREE PRESS, 1980.

14060　WRIGHT, MURIEL H. "ORGANIZATION OF COUNTIES IN THE CHOCTAW AND CHICKASAW NATIONS." CHRONICLES OF OKLAHOMA, 8 (SEPTEMBER, 1930): 315-334.

14061　YOUNG, MARY E. REDSKINS, RUFFLESHIRTS AND REDNECKS: INDIAN ALLOTMENTS IN ALABAMA AND MISSISSIPPI. NORMAN: UNIVERSITY OF OKLAHOMA PRESS, 1961.

Economics of Slavery

GENERAL

14062 AIKEN, CHARLES S. "COTTON GINNING." IN ROLLER, DAVID C. AND TWYMAN, ROBERT W. (EDS.). THE ENCYCLOPEDIA OF SOUTHERN HISTORY. BATON ROUGE: LOUISIANA STATE UNIVERSITY PRESS, 1979, PP. 302-303.

14063 ALDRIDGE, HAROLD R. "SLAVE TRADE ECONOMICS; ACCOUNT-BOOK KEPT BY THE CAPTAIN OF A LIVERPOOL SCHOONER, 1785-1787." BRITISH MUSEUM QUARTERLY, 9 (MAY, 1935): 119-121.

14064 ALEXANDER, THOMAS B.; ENGERMAN, STANLEY L.; MCDONALD, FORREST; MCWHINEY, GRADY; AND PESSEN, EDWARD. "ANTEBELLUM NORTH AND SOUTH IN COMPARATIVE PERSPECTIVE: A DISCUSSION." AMERICAN HISTORICAL REVIEW, 85 (DECEMBER, 1980): 1150-1170.

14065 ALLEN, JAMES S. THE NEGRO QUESTION IN THE UNITED STATES. NEW YORK: INTERNATIONAL PUBLISHERS, 1936.

14066 AMERICA, RICHARD. "A NEW RATIONALE FOR INCOME REDISTRIBUTION." REVIEW OF BLACK POLITICAL ECONOMY, 2 (WINTER, 1972): 3-21.

14067 AMUNDSON, RICHARD J. "SUGAR INDUSTRY." IN ROLLER, DAVID C. AND TWYMAN, ROBERT W. (EDS.). THE ENCYCLOPEDIA OF SOUTHERN HISTORY. BATON ROUGE: LOUISIANA STATE UNIVERSITY PRESS, 1979, PP. 1169-1170.

14068 ANDERSON, RALPH V. "LABOR UTILIZATION AND PRODUCTIVITY, DIVERSIFICATION AND SELF SUFFICIENCY, SOUTHERN PLANTATIONS, 1800-1840." PH.D. DISSERTATION, UNIVERSITY OF NORTH CAROLINA, 1974.

14069 ANDERSON, RALPH V. AND GALLMAN, ROBERT E. "SLAVES AS FIXED CAPITAL: SLAVE LABOR AND SOUTHERN ECONOMIC DEVELOPMENT." JOURNAL OF AMERICAN HISTORY, 64 (JUNE, 1977): 24-46.

14070 ANDREANO, RALPH L. "SOME ISSUES IN ANTE-BELLUM U.S. ECONOMIC GROWTH AND WELFARE." CAHIERS INTERNATIONAL HISTOIRE ECONOMIQUE SOCIETE, 5 (1975): 357-379.

14071 APTHEKER, HERBERT. THE LABOR MOVEMENT IN THE SOUTH DURING SLAVERY. NEW YORK: INTERNATIONAL PUBLISHERS, 1954.

14072 ARMSTRONG, THOMAS F. "FROM TASK LABOR TO FREE LABOR: THE TRANSITION ALONG GEORGIA'S RICE COAST, 1820-1880."

GEORGIA HISTORICAL QUARTERLY, 64 (WINTER, 1980):
432-447.

14073   ASHBURN, KARL E. "THE DEVELOPMENT OF COTTON PRODUCTION
        IN TEXAS." PH.D. DISSERTATION, DUKE UNIVERSITY, 1934.

14074   ASHBURN, KARL E. "SLAVERY AND COTTON PRODUCTION IN
        TEXAS." SOUTHWESTERN SOCIAL SCIENCE QUARTERLY, 14
        (DECEMBER, 1933): 257-271.

14075   ASHTON, THOMAS S. THE INDUSTRIAL REVOLUTION, 1760-1830.
        NEW YORK: OXFORD UNIVERSITY PRESS, 1948.

14076   AUFHAUSER, R. KEITH. "SLAVERY AND SCIENTIFIC
        MANAGEMENT." JOURNAL OF ECONOMIC HISTORY, 33
        (DECEMBER, 1973): 811-824.

14077   AUFHAUSER, R. KEITH. "SLAVERY AND TECHNOLOGICAL CHANGE."
        JOURNAL OF ECONOMIC HISTORY, 34 (MARCH, 1974):   36-50.

14078   AUFHAUSER, ROBERT K. "WORK AND SLAVERY." PH.D.
        DISSERTATION, HARVARD UNIVERSITY, 1972.

14079   BAGLEY, WILLIAM C., JR. SOIL EXHAUSTION AND THE CIVIL
        WAR. WASHINGTON: AMERICAN COUNCIL ON PUBLIC AFFAIRS,
        1942.

14080   BAILEY, DAVID C. "THE MARITIME SLAVE TRADE TO BRITISH
        AMERICA CONSIDERED AS A PROBLEM IN THE HISTORY OF
        BUSINESS ADMINISTRATION." M.A. THESIS, UNIVERSITY OF
        NOTRE DAME, 1959.

14081   BALLAGH, JAMES C. "CHARACTERISTIC METHODS OF SOUTHERN
        AGRICULTURAL PRODUCTION." IN BALLAGH (ED.). THE
        SOUTH IN THE BUILDING OF THE NATION. 12 VOLS.
        RICHMOND: SOUTHERN HISTORICAL PUBLICATION SOCIETY,
        1909, VOL. 5, PP. 152-158.

14082   BALLAGH, JAMES C. "INTRODUCTION TO SOUTHERN ECONOMIC
        HISTORY--THE LAND SYSTEM." ANNUAL REPORT OF THE
        AMERICAN HISTORICAL ASSOCIATION FOR THE YEAR 1897.
        WASHINGTON: GOVERNMENT PRINTING OFFICE, 1898, PP.
        99-130.

14083   BALLAGH, JAMES C. "LABOR--THE DEVELOPMENT OF LABOR
        SYSTEMS IN THE COLONIAL SOUTH." IN BALLAGH (ED.).
        THE SOUTH IN THE BUILDING OF THE NATION. 12 VOLS.
        RICHMOND: SOUTHERN HISTORICAL PUBLICATION SOCIETY,
        1909, VOL. 5, PP. 86-104.

14084   BALLAGH, JAMES C. "SOUTHERN ECONOMIC HISTORY: TARIFF
        AND PUBLIC LANDS." ANNUAL REPORT OF THE AMERICAN
        HISTORICAL ASSOCIATION FOR THE YEAR 1898. WASHINGTON:
        GOVERNMENT PRINTING OFFICE, 1899, PP. 221-264.

14085   BANKS, ENOCH M. "ECONOMICS OF LAND TENURE IN GEORGIA."
         PH.D. DISSERTATION, COLUMBIA UNIVERSITY, 1905.

14086   BAREFIELD, JAMES T. "THE PLANTATION SYSTEM IN THE
         SOUTHEASTERN COTTON STATES, 1848-1853." M.A. THESIS,
         FLORIDA STATE UNIVERSITY, 1977.

14087   BARNEY, WILLIAM L. IHE ROAD TO SECESSION: A NEW
         PERSPECTIVE ON THE OLD SOUTH. NEW YORK: PRAEGER,
         1972.

14088   BARON, HAROLD M. "THE DEMAND FOR BLACK LABOR:
         HISTORICAL NOTES ON THE POLITICAL ECONOMY OF RACISM."
         RADICAL AMERICA, 5 (1971): 1-46.

14089   BARON, HAROLD M. IHE DEMAND FOR BLACK LABOR: HISTORICAL
         NOTES ON THE ECONOMY OF RACISM. SOMERVILLE, MA: NEW
         ENGLAND FREE PRESS, 1971.

14090   BARRINGER, R. "WHY THE SOUTH DOES NOT RAISE ITS
         PROVISIONS." CHARLOTTE MECKLENBURG TIMES, FEBRUARY
         19, 1892.

14091   BARZEL, YORAM. "ECONOMIC ANALYSIS OF SLAVERY." JOURNAL
         OF LAW AND ECONOMICS, 20 (APRIL, 1977): 87-110.

14092   BATIE, ROBERT C. "A COMPARATIVE ECONOMIC HISTORY OF THE
         SPANISH, FRENCH, AND ENGLISH IN THE CARIBBEAN ISLANDS
         DURING THE SEVENTEENTH CENTURY." PH.D. DISSERTATION,
         UNIVERSITY OF WASHINGTON, 1972.

14093   BATIE, ROBERT C. "WHY SUGAR? ECONOMIC CYCLES AND THE
         CHANGING OF STAPLES ON THE ENGLISH AND FRENCH
         ANTILLES, 1624-1654." JOURNAL OF CARIBBEAN HISTORY, 8
         (NOVEMBER, 1976): 1-41.

14094   BATTALIO, RAYMOND C. AND KAGEL, JOHN. "THE STRUCTURE OF
         ANTEBELLUM SOUTHERN AGRICULTURE: SOUTH CAROLINA, A
         CASE STUDY." AGRICULTURAL HISTORY, 44 (JANUARY,
         1970): 25-38.

14095   BAUGHMAN, JAMES P. "NEW DIRECTIONS IN AMERICAN ECONOMIC
         AND BUSINESS HISTORY." IN BILLIAS, GEORGE A. AND
         GROB, GERALD N. (EDS.). AMERICAN HISTORY: RETROSPECT
         AND PROSPECT. NEW YORK: FREE PRESS, 1971, PP.
         271-314.

14096   BEAN, RICHARD N. AND THOMAS, ROBERT P. "THE ADOPTION OF
         SLAVE LABOR IN BRITISH AMERICA." IN GEMERY, HENRY AND
         HOGENDORN, JAN S. (EDS.). IHE UNCOMMON MARKET:
         ESSAYS IN THE ECONOMIC HISTORY OF THE ATLANTIC SLAVE
         TRADE. NEW YORK: ACADEMIC PRESS, 1979, PP. 377-398.

14097   BEAN, RICHARD N. AND THOMAS, ROBERT P. "THE FISHERS OF
         MEN: THE PROFITS OF THE SLAVE TRADE." UNPUBLISHED

PAPER, 1973.

14098   BEARSS, EDWIN C. THE BURROUGHS PLANTATION AS A LIVING
         HISTORICAL FARM. WASHINGTON: UNITED STATES NATIONAL
         PARK SERVICE, 1969.

14099   BECKER, GARY. "INVESTMENTS IN HUMAN CAPITAL: A
         THEORETICAL ANALYSIS." JOURNAL OF POLITICAL ECONOMY,
         SUPPLEMENT 70 (OCTOBER, 1962): 9-49.

14100   BELISLE, JOHN. BLACK SLAVERY AND CAPITALISM. NEW YORK:
         NATIONAL EDUCATION DEPARTMENT, SOCIALIST WORKERS
         PARTY, 1969.

14101   BENNETT, J. HARRY. "THE PROBLEM OF SLAVE LABOR SUPPLY AT
         THE CODRINGTON PLANTATIONS." JOURNAL OF NEGRO
         HISTORY, 36 (APRIL, 1952): 115-141.

14102   BERGSTROM, T. "ON THE EXISTENCE AND OPTIMALITY OF
         COMPETITIVE EQUILIBRIUM FOR A SLAVE ECONOMY." REVIEW
         OF ECONOMIC STUDIES, 38 (JANUARY, 1971): 23-36.

14103   BERLIN, IRA. SLAVES WITHOUT MASTERS: THE FREE NEGRO IN
         THE ANTEBELLUM SOUTH. NEW YORK: PANTHEON, 1974.

14104   BOGART, ERNEST L. ECONOMIC HISTORY OF AMERICAN
         AGRICULTURE. NEW YORK: LONGMANS, GREEN, 1923.

14105   BONAICH, EDNA. "ABOLITION, THE EXTENSION OF SLAVERY AND
         THE POSITION OF FREE BLACKS: A STUDY OF SPLIT LABOR
         MARKETS IN THE UNITED STATES, 1830-1863." AMERICAN
         JOURNAL OF SOCIOLOGY, 81 (NOVEMBER, 1975): 601-628.

14106   BONAICH, EDNA. "ADVANCED CAPITALISM AND BLACK-WHITE
         RELATIONS IN THE UNITED STATES: A SPLIT LABOR MARKET
         INTERPRETATION." AMERICAN SOCIOLOGICAL REVIEW, 41
         (FEBRUARY, 1976): 34-51.

14107   BONAICH, EDNA. "A THEORY OF ETHNIC ANTAGONISM: THE
         SPLIT LABOR MARKET." AMERICAN SOCIOLOGICAL REVIEW, 37
         (OCTOBER, 1972): 547-559.

14108   BONAICH, EDNA. "A THEORY OF MIDDLEMEN MINORITIES."
         AMERICAN SOCIOLOGICAL REVIEW, 39 (OCTOBER, 1973):
         583-594.

14109   BONNER, JAMES C. "ADVANCING TRENDS IN SOUTHERN
         AGRICULTURE, 1840-1860." AGRICULTURAL HISTORY, 22
         (OCTOBER, 1948): 248-259.

14110   BONNER, JAMES C. "THE GENESIS OF AGRICULTURAL REFORM IN
         THE COTTON BELT." JOURNAL OF SOUTHERN HISTORY, 9
         (NOVEMBER, 1943): 475-500.

14111   BONNER, JAMES C. A HISTORY OF GEORGIA AGRICULTURE,

1732-1860. ATHENS: UNIVERSITY OF GEORGIA PRESS, 1964.

14112 BOUCHER, CHAUNCEY S. "THE ANTE-BELLUM ATTITUDE OF SOUTH
        CAROLINA TOWARDS MANUFACTURING AND AGRICULTURE."
        WASHINGTON UNIVERSITY STUDIES, 3 (APRIL, 1916):
        243-270.

14113 BOYD, WILLIAM K. "AD VALOREM SLAVE TAXATION, 1858-1860."
        HISTORICAL PAPERS PUBLISHED BY THE TRINITY COLLEGE
        HISTORICAL SOCIETY, 5TH SER., (1905): 31-38.

14114 BOYKIN, EUGENE M. "ENTERPRISE AND ACCUMULATION OF
        NEGROES PRIOR TO 1860." M.A. THESIS, COLUMBIA
        UNIVERSITY, 1933.

14115 BRANNEN, CLAUDE O. RELATION OF LAND TENURE TO PLANTATION
        ORGANIZATION. WASHINGTON: GOVERNMENT PRINTING
        OFFICE, 1924.

14116 BRATHWAITE, EDWARD K. "QUANTITATIVE AND ECONOMIC
        ANALYSIS OF WEST INDIAN SLAVE SOCIETIES: RESEARCH
        PROBLEMS: A COMMENTARY." IN RUBIN, VERA AND TUDEN,
        ARTHUR (EDS.). COMPARATIVE PERSPECTIVES ON SLAVERY IN
        NEW WORLD PLANTATION SOCIETIES. NEW YORK: NEW YORK
        ACADEMY OF SCIENCES, 1977, PP. 610-612.

14117 BREWER, WILLIAM M. "SOME EFFECTS OF THE PLANTATION
        SYSTEM UPON THE ANTE-BELLUM SOUTH." GEORGIA
        HISTORICAL QUARTERLY, 11 (SEPTEMBER, 1927): 250-273.

14118 BRINSMADE, R.B. "SLAVERY AND LAND VALUES." PUBLIC, 13
        (JULY 22, 1910): 690.

14119 BROOKS, ROBERT P. "ECONOMIC AND SOCIAL ASPECTS OF
        SLAVERY." IN SEBBA, GREGOR (ED.). GEORGIA STUDIES:
        SELECTED WRITINGS OF ROBERT PRESTON BROOKS. ATHENS:
        UNIVERSITY OF GEORGIA PRESS, 1952, PP. 205-215.

14120 BROOKS, ROBERT P. "SLAVERY: ECONOMIC AND SOCIAL
        ASPECTS." HISTORY OF GEORGIA. BOSTON: ATKINSON,
        MENTZER & COMPANY, 1913, PP. 232-236.

14121 BROUGH, CHARLES H. "HISTORY OF TAXATION IN MISSISSIPPI."
        PUBLICATIONS OF THE MISSISSIPPI HISTORICAL SOCIETY, 2
        (1899): 113-124.

14122 BROWN, ELISABETH D. "SOME ECONOMIC ASPECTS OF SLAVERY IN
        VIRGINIA DURING THE COLONIAL AND NATIONAL PERIODS."
        M.A. THESIS, UNIVERSITY OF CHICAGO, 1933.

14123 BROWN, KENNETH S. "NEGRO SLAVERY: THE FORMATION OF THE
        SOUTH'S PECULIAR LABOR SYSTEM." M.A. THESIS,
        UNIVERSITY OF PENNSYLVANIA, 1978.

14124 BROWNE, ROBERT S. "THE ECONOMIC CASE FOR REPARATIONS TO

BLACK AMERICA." AMERICAN ECONOMIC REVIEW, 62 (MAY, 1972): 39-46.

14125 BROWNLEE, W. ELLIOT. "THE ECONOMICS OF URBAN SLAVERY." REVIEWS IN AMERICAN HISTORY, 5 (JUNE, 1977): 230-235.

14126 BRUCE, KATHLEEN. "VIRGINIAN AGRICULTURAL DECLINE TO 1860: A FALLACY." AGRICULTURAL HISTORY, 6 (JANUARY, 1932): 3-13.

14127 BRUCE, PHILIP A. "THE SUPERIORITY OF SLAVE LABOR." IN CHANDLER, JULIAN A.C. (ED.). THE SOUTH IN THE BUILDING OF THE NATION. 12 VOLS. RICHMOND: SOUTHERN HISTORICAL PUBLICATION SOCIETY, 1909, VOL. 1, PP. 55-58.

14128 BRUCHEY, STUART (ED.). COTTON AND THE GROWTH OF THE AMERICAN ECONOMY, 1790-1860: SOURCES AND READINGS. BALTIMORE: JOHNS HOPKINS UNIVERSITY PRESS, 1967.

14129 BURGESS, AMY P. "SLAVE PRICES, 1830 TO 1860." M.A. THESIS, EMORY UNIVERSITY, 1933.

14130 BURRELL, W.P. "THE NEGRO IN INSURANCE." PROCEEDINGS OF THE HAMPTON NEGRO CONFERENCE, 8 (1904): 14-15.

14131 BUTLIN, NOEL G. ANTE-BELLUM SLAVERY--A CRITIQUE OF A DEBATE. CANBERRA, AUSTRALIA: DEPARTMENT OF ECONOMIC HISTORY, RESEARCH SCHOOL OF SOCIAL SCIENCES, AUSTRALIAN NATIONAL UNIVERSITY, 1971.

14132 BUTTS, DONALD C. "A CHALLENGE TO PLANTER RULE: THE CONTROVERSY OVER THE AD VALOREM TAXATION OF SLAVES IN NORTH CAROLINA: 1858-1862." PH.D. DISSERTATION, DUKE UNIVERSITY, 1978.

14133 CALLENDER, GUY S. (ED.). SELECTIONS FROM THE ECONOMIC HISTORY OF THE UNITED STATES, 1765-1860. BOSTON: GINN AND COMPANY, 1909.

14134 CAMPBELL, RANDOLPH B. AND LOWE, RICHARD G. "SOME ECONOMIC ASPECTS OF ANTEBELLUM TEXAS AGRICULTURE." SOUTHWESTERN HISTORICAL QUARTERLY, 82 (APRIL, 1979): 351-378.

14135 CARLISLE, WILLIAM T. "THE ECONOMICS OF SLAVERY: A REEXAMINATION." INTELLECT, 106 (FEBRUARY, 1978): 335-337.

14136 CARRIER, LYMAN. THE BEGINNINGS OF AGRICULTURE IN AMERICA. NEW YORK: MCGRAW-HILL, 1923.

14137 CLOWSE, CONVERSE D. ECONOMIC BEGINNINGS IN COLONIAL SOUTH CAROLINA, 1670-1720. COLUMBIA: UNIVERSITY OF SOUTH CAROLINA PRESS, 1971.

14138   COHN, DAVID L. THE LIFE AND TIMES OF KING COTTON. NEW
         YORK: OXFORD UNIVERSITY PRESS, 1956.

14139   COLE, ARTHUR H. "THE TEMPO OF MERCANTILE LIFE IN
         COLONIAL AMERICA." BUSINESS HISTORY REVIEW, 33 (FALL,
         1959): 277-299.

14140   COLE, FRED C. "THE TEXAS CAREER OF THOMAS AFFLECK."
         PH.D. DISSERTATION, LOUISIANA STATE UNIVERSITY, 1942.

14141   CONDE, ROBERTO C. AND STEIN, STANLEY J. (EDS.). LATIN
         AMERICA: A GUIDE TO ECONOMIC HISTORY, 1830-1930.
         BERKELEY: UNIVERSITY OF CALIFORNIA PRESS, 1977.

14142   CONRAD, ALFRED H.; FOGEL, ROBERT W.; BRUCHEY, STUART; AND
         CHANDLER, ALFRED. "ECONOMETRICS AND SOUTHERN
         HISTORY." EXPLORATIONS IN ENTREPRENEURIAL HISTORY,
         2ND SER., 6 (FALL, 1968): 34-74.

14143   CONRAD, ALFRED H.; MEYER, JOHN R.; DOWD, DOUGLAS F.;
         ENGERMAN, STANLEY L.; GINSBURG, E.; KELSO, C.;
         SCHEIBER, H.N.; AND SUTCH, RICHARD. "SLAVERY AS AN
         OBSTACLE TO ECONOMIC GROWTH IN THE UNITED STATES."
         JOURNAL OF ECONOMIC HISTORY, 27 (DECEMBER, 1967):
         518-560.

14144   COOPER, WILLIAM J., JR. "THE COTTON CRISIS IN THE
         ANTEBELLUM SOUTH: ANOTHER LOOK." AGRICULTURAL
         HISTORY, 49 (APRIL, 1975): 381-391.

14145   COPENHAUSER, J.E. "CULTURE OF INDIGO IN THE PROVINCES OF
         SOUTH CAROLINA AND GEORGIA." INDUSTRIAL AND
         ENGINEERING CHEMISTRY, 22 (AUGUST, 1930): 894-896.

14146   COX, LAWANDA F. "AGRICULTURAL LABOR IN THE UNITED
         STATES, 1865-1900, WITH SPECIAL REFERENCE TO THE
         SOUTH." PH.D. DISSERTATION, UNIVERSITY OF CALIFORNIA,
         1941.

14147   CRAVEN, AVERY O. EDMUND RUFFIN SOUTHERNER: A STUDY IN
         SECESSION. NEW YORK: D. APPLETON AND COMPANY, 1932.

14148   DABNEY, CHARLES W. "THE NEW FARMER IN THE NEW SOUTH."
         SOUTHERN STATES, 5 (MARCH, 1897): 6-14.

14149   DAVID, PAUL A.; GUTMAN, HERBERT G.; SUTCH, RICHARD;
         TEMIN, PETER; AND WRIGHT, GAVIN. "TIME ON THE CROSS
         AND THE BURDEN OF QUANTITATIVE HISTORY." RECKONING
         WITH SLAVERY: A CRITICAL STUDY IN THE QUANTITATIVE
         HISTORY OF AMERICAN NEGRO SLAVERY. NEW YORK: OXFORD
         UNIVERSITY PRESS, 1976, PP. 339-357.

14150   DAVID, PAUL A. AND TEMIN, PETER. "SLAVERY: THE
         PROGRESSIVE INSTITUTION?" IN DAVID; TEMIN; GUTMAN,
         HERBERT G.; SUTCH, RICHARD; AND WRIGHT, GAVIN.

RECKONING WITH SLAVERY: A CRITICAL STUDY IN THE
QUANTITATIVE HISTORY OF AMERICAN NEGRO SLAVERY. NEW
YORK: OXFORD UNIVERSITY PRESS, 1976, PP. 165-230.

14151   DAVID, PAUL A. AND TEMIN, PETER. "SLAVERY: THE
        PROGRESSIVE INSTITUTION?" JOURNAL OF ECONOMIC
        HISTORY, 34 (SEPTEMBER, 1974): 739-783.

14152   DAVIS, BARBARA J. "A COMPARATIVE ANALYSIS OF THE
        ECONOMIC STRUCTURE OF MOBILE COUNTY, ALABAMA, BEFORE
        AND AFTER THE CIVIL WAR, 1860 AND 1870." M.A. THESIS,
        UNIVERSITY OF ALABAMA, 1963.

14153   DAVIS, RONALD. "'GOOD AND FAITHFUL LABOR': A STUDY OF
        THE DEVELOPMENT AND ECONOMICS OF SOUTHERN
        SHARECROPPING, 1860-1880." PH.D. DISSERTATION,
        UNIVERSITY OF MISSOURI, 1974.

14154   DECANIO, STEPHEN J. AGRICULTURE IN THE POSTBELLUM SOUTH:
        THE ECONOMICS OF PRODUCTION AND SUPPLY. CAMBRIDGE:
        MASSACHUSETTS INSTITUTE OF TECHNOLOGY PRESS, 1974.

14155   DECANIO, STEPHEN J. "A NEW ECONOMIC HISTORY OF SLAVERY
        IN THE UNITED STATES." REVIEWS IN AMERICAN HISTORY, 2
        (DECEMBER, 1974): 474-487.

14156   DEERR, NOEL. THE HISTORY OF SUGAR. 2 VOLS. LONDON:
        CHAPMAN & HALL, 1949-1950.

14157   DEGLER, CARL N. "STARR ON SLAVERY." JOURNAL OF ECONOMIC
        HISTORY, 19 (JUNE, 1959): 271-277.

14158   DESAI, M. "CONSOLATION OF SLAVERY." ECONOMIC HISTORY
        REVIEW, 29 (AUGUST, 1976): 491-503.

14159   DESTLER, CHESTER M. "DAVID DICKSON'S 'SYSTEM OF FARMING'
        AND THE AGRICULTURAL REVOLUTION IN THE DEEP SOUTH,
        1850-1885." AGRICULTURAL HISTORY, 31 (JULY, 1957):
        30-39.

14160   DEW, CHARLES B. "TWO APPROACHES TO SOUTHERN HISTORY:
        PSYCHOLOGY AND QUANTIFICATION." SOUTH ATLANTIC
        QUARTERLY, 66 (SUMMER, 1967): 307-325.

14161   DICKERMAN, G.S. "SOME LABOR TENDENCIES IN THE SOUTH."
        SOUTHERN WORKMAN, 36 (OCTOBER, 1907): 522-526.

14162   DICKEY, G. EDWARD AND WILSON, WARREN W. "ECONOMICS OF
        SCALE IN COTTON AGRICULTURE, 1850-1860." UNPUBLISHED
        PAPER, 1972.

14163   DILL, FLOYD R. "THE INSTITUTIONAL POSSIBILITIES AND
        LIMITATIONS OF ECONOMIC PROGRESS IN ANTEBELLUM
        GEORGIA: A SOCIAL SYSTEMS APPROACH." PH.D.
        DISSERTATION, CORNELL UNIVERSITY, 1973.

14164   DILLINGHAM, WILLIAM P.   "THE ECONOMICS OF SEGREGATION."
        IN THE NEGRO IN AMERICAN SOCIETY. TALLAHASSEE:
        FLORIDA STATE UNIVERSITY, 1958, PP. 29-39.

14165   DIRKS, ROBERT.   "RESOURCE FLUCTUATIONS AND COMPETITIVE
        TRANSFORMATIONS IN WEST INDIAN SLAVE SOCIETIES." IN
        LAUGHLIN, CHARLES D., JR. AND BRADY, IVAN A. (EDS.).
        EXTINCTION AND SURVIVAL IN HUMAN POPULATIONS. NEW
        YORK: COLUMBIA UNIVERSITY PRESS, 1978, PP. 122-180.

14166   DISMUKES, CAMILLUS J.   "INVENTORY OF A PLANTER'S ESTATE."
        SOUTH CAROLINA HISTORICAL MAGAZINE, 73 (JANUARY,
        1972): 37-38.

14167   DONNELL, EZEKIEL J.   CHRONOLOGICAL AND STATISTICAL
        HISTORY OF COTTON. NEW YORK: J. SUTTON, 1872.

14168   DORMON, JAMES H.   "ASPECTS OF SLAVE MANAGEMENT AND
        MAINTENANCE ON A LOUISIANA SUGAR PLANTATION: PETITE
        ANSE, 1840-1860." ATTAKAPAS GAZETTE, 7 (MARCH, 1972):
        23-30.

14169   DORRIS, JONATHAN T.   "MAJOR SQUIRE TURNER: LAWYER,
        STATESMAN, AND ECONOMIST." FILSON CLUB HISTORY
        QUARTERLY, 25 (JANUARY, 1951): 33-50.

14170   DOUGLAS, PAUL H.   AMERICAN APPRENTICESHIP AND INDUSTRIAL
        EDUCATION. NEW YORK: COLUMBIA UNIVERSITY PRESS, 1921.

14171   DOWD, DOUGLAS F.   "A COMPARATIVE ANALYSIS OF ECONOMIC
        DEVELOPMENT IN THE AMERICAN WEST AND SOUTH." JOURNAL
        OF ECONOMIC HISTORY, 16 (DECEMBER, 1956): 558-574.

14172   DRIMMER, MELVIN.   "WAS SLAVERY DYING BEFORE THE COTTON
        GIN?" IN DRIMMER (ED.). BLACK HISTORY: A
        REAPPRAISAL. GARDEN CITY: DOUBLEDAY & COMPANY, 1968,
        PP. 96-115.

14173   DUBOIS, W.E.B.   "THE ECONOMIC FUTURE OF THE NEGRO."
        PUBLICATIONS OF THE AMERICAN ECONOMIC ASSOCIATION, 3RD
        SER., (1906): 219-242.

14174   DUBOIS, W.E.B.   "THE ECONOMIC REVOLUTION IN THE SOUTH."
        IN WASHINGTON, BOOKER T. AND DUBOIS. THE NEGRO IN THE
        SOUTH. PHILADELPHIA: GEORGE W. JACOBS AND COMPANY,
        1907, PP. 77-122.

14175   DUNBAR, CHARLES F.   "ECONOMIC SCIENCE IN AMERICA,
        1776-1876." NORTH AMERICAN REVIEW, 122 (JANUARY,
        1876): 124-154.

14176   EARLE, CARVILLE AND HOFFMAN, RONALD.   "THE FOUNDATION OF
        THE MODERN ECONOMY: AGRICULTURE AND THE COSTS OF
        LABOR IN THE UNITED STATES AND ENGLAND, 1800-1860."
        AMERICAN HISTORICAL REVIEW, 85 (DECEMBER, 1980):

1055-1094.

14177   EARLE, CARVILLE V. "STAPLE INTERPRETATION OF SLAVERY AND FREE LABOR." GEOGRAPHICAL REVIEW, 68 (JANUARY, 1978): 51-65.

14178   EASTERLIN, RICHARD A. "REGIONAL INCOME TRENDS, 1840-1950." IN HARRIS, SEYMOUR E. (ED.). AMERICAN ECONOMIC HISTORY. NEW YORK: MCGRAW-HILL, 1961, PP. 525-547.

14179   EDEL, MATTHEW. "THE BRAZILIAN SUGAR CYCLE OF THE SEVENTEENTH CENTURY AND THE RISE OF WEST INDIAN COMPETITION." CARIBBEAN STUDIES, 9 (APRIL, 1969): 24-44.

14180   EISTERHOLD, JOHN A. "CHARLESTON: LUMBER AND TRADE IN A DECLINING SOUTHERN PORT." SOUTH CAROLINA HISTORICAL MAGAZINE, 74 (APRIL, 1973): 61-72.

14181   EISTERHOLD, JOHN A. "LUMBER AND TRADE IN PENSACOLA AND WEST FLORIDA: 1800-1860." FLORIDA HISTORICAL QUARTERLY, 51 (JANUARY, 1973): 267-280.

14182   EISTERHOLD, JOHN A. "LUMBER AND TRADE IN THE SEABOARD CITIES OF THE OLD SOUTH, 1607-1860." PH.D. DISSERTATION, UNIVERSITY OF MISSISSIPPI, 1970.

14183   EISTERHOLD, JOHN A. "MOBILE: LUMBER CENTER OF THE GULF COAST." ALABAMA REVIEW, 26 (APRIL, 1973): 83-104.

14184   EISTERHOLD, JOHN A. "SAVANNAH: LUMBER CENTER OF THE SOUTH ATLANTIC." GEORGIA HISTORICAL QUARTERLY, 57 (WINTER, 1973): 526-543.

14185   ELKINS, STANLEY AND MCKITRICK, ERIC. "INSTITUTIONS AND THE LAW OF SLAVERY: THE DYNAMICS OF UNOPPOSED CAPITALISM." AMERICAN QUARTERLY, 9 (SPRING, 1957): 3-21.

14186   EMERSON, F.V. "GEOGRAPHIC INFLUENCES IN AMERICAN SLAVERY." BULLETIN OF THE AMERICAN GEOGRAPHICAL SOCIETY, 43 (JANUARY, FEBRUARY, MARCH, 1911): 13-26, 106-118, 170-181.

14187   ENGERMAN, STANLEY L. "THE ECONOMIC IMPACT OF THE CIVIL WAR." EXPLORATIONS IN ENTREPRENEURIAL HISTORY, 2ND SER., 3 (SPRING-SUMMER, 1966): 176-199.

14188   ENGERMAN, STANLEY L. "THE EFFECTS OF SLAVERY UPON THE SOUTHERN ECONOMY: A REVIEW OF THE RECENT DEBATE." EXPLORATIONS IN ENTREPRENEURIAL HISTORY, 4 (WINTER, 1967): 71-97.

14189   ENGERMAN, STANLEY L. "THE LEGACY OF SLAVERY."

UNPUBLISHED PAPER PRESENTED AT DUKE UNIVERSITY
SYMPOSIUM ON ONE KIND OF FREEDOM, DURHAM, FEBRUARY 11,
1978.

14190   ENGERMAN, STANLEY L.   "NOTES ON THE PATTERNS OF ECONOMIC
        GROWTH IN THE BRITISH NORTH AMERICAN COLONIES IN THE
        SEVENTEENTH, EIGHTEENTH, AND NINETEENTH CENTURIES."
        IN FLINN, MICHAEL (ED.).   PROCEEDINGS OF THE SEVENTH
        INTERNATIONAL ECONOMIC HISTORY CONGRESS.   EDINBURGH:
        EDINBURGH UNIVERSITY PRESS, 1978, PP. 187-198.

14191   ENGERMAN, STANLEY L.   "QUANTITATIVE AND ECONOMIC ANALYSIS
        OF WEST INDIAN SLAVE SOCIETIES: RESEARCH PROBLEMS."
        IN RUBIN, VERA AND TUDEN, ARTHUR (EDS.).   COMPARATIVE
        PERSPECTIVES ON SLAVERY IN NEW WORLD PLANTATION
        SOCIETIES.   NEW YORK: NEW YORK ACADEMY OF SCIENCES,
        1977, PP. 597-609.

14192   ENGERMAN, STANLEY L.   "A RECONSIDERATION OF SOUTHERN
        ECONOMIC GROWTH, 1770-1860."   AGRICULTURAL HISTORY, 49
        (APRIL, 1975):   343-361.

14193   ENGERMAN, STANLEY L.   "SOME CONSIDERATIONS RELATING TO
        PROPERTY RIGHTS IN MAN."   JOURNAL OF ECONOMIC HISTORY,
        33 (MARCH, 1973):   43-65.

14194   ENGERMAN, STANLEY L.   "SOME ECONOMIC AND DEMOGRAPHIC
        COMPARISONS OF SLAVERY IN THE UNITED STATES AND THE
        BRITISH WEST INDIES."   ECONOMIC HISTORY REVIEW, 29
        (MAY, 1976):   258-275.

14195   ENGERMAN, STANLEY L.   "SOME ECONOMIC FACTORS IN SOUTHERN
        BACKWARDNESS IN THE NINETEENTH CENTURY."   IN KAIN,
        JOHN F. AND MEYER, JOHN R. (EDS.).   ESSAYS IN REGIONAL
        ECONOMICS.   CAMBRIDGE: HARVARD UNIVERSITY PRESS,
        1971, PP. 279-306.

14196   ENGERMAN, STANLEY L.   "THE SOUTHERN SLAVE ECONOMY."   IN
        OWENS, HARRY P. (ED.).   PERSPECTIVES AND IRONY IN
        AMERICAN SLAVERY.   JACKSON: UNIVERSITY PRESS OF
        MISSISSIPPI, 1976, PP. 71-102.

14197   ENGERMAN, STANLEY L. AND ELTIS, DAVID.   "ECONOMIC ASPECTS
        OF THE ABOLITION DEBATE."   IN BOLT, CHRISTINE AND
        DRESCHER, SEYMOUR (EDS.).   ANTI-SLAVERY, RELIGION, AND
        REFORM: ESSAYS IN MEMORY OF ROGER ANSTEY.   HAMDEN,
        CT: ARCHON BOOKS, 1980, PP. 272-293.

14198   ENGERMAN, STANLEY L. AND GENOVESE, EUGENE D. (EDS.).
        RACE AND SLAVERY IN THE WESTERN HEMISPHERE:
        QUANTITATIVE STUDIES.   PRINCETON: PRINCETON
        UNIVERSITY PRESS, 1975.

14199   "ESTIMATES OF THE VALUE OF SLAVES, 1815."   AMERICAN
        HISTORICAL REVIEW, 19 (JULY, 1914):   813-838.

14200   EVANS, ROBERT JR. "THE ECONOMICS OF AMERICAN NEGRO
        SLAVERY, 1830-1860." IN UNIVERSITIES--NATIONAL BUREAU
        COMMITTEE FOR ECONOMIC RESEARCH. ASPECTS OF LABOR
        ECONOMICS. PRINCETON: PRINCETON UNIVERSITY PRESS,
        1962, PP. 185-243.

14201   EVANS, ROBERT JR. "THE ECONOMICS OF AMERICAN NEGRO
        SLAVERY, 1830-1860." PH.D. DISSERTATION, UNIVERSITY
        OF CHICAGO, 1959.

14202   EVANS, ROBERT JR. "THE MILITARY DRAFT AS A SLAVE SYSTEM:
        AN ECONOMIC VIEW." SOCIAL SCIENCE QUARTERLY, 50
        (1969): 535-543.

14203   EVANS, ROBERT JR. "SOME ECONOMIC ASPECTS OF THE DOMESTIC
        SLAVE TRADE, 1830-1860." SOUTHERN ECONOMIC JOURNAL,
        27 (APRIL, 1961): 329-337.

14204   EVANS, ROBERT JR. "SOME NOTES ON COERCED LABOR."
        JOURNAL OF ECONOMIC HISTORY, 30 (DECEMBER, 1970):
        861-866.

14205   FIELDING, RONALD H. "AMERICAN SLAVE EMANCIPATION: THE
        COSTS IN THE SOUTH, THE DISTRICT OF COLUMBIA, AND THE
        NORTH." UNPUBLISHED PAPER, 1973.

14206   FIELDS, EMMETT B. "THE AGRICULTURAL POPULATION OF
        VIRGINIA, 1850-1860." PH.D. DISSERTATION, VANDERBILT
        UNIVERSITY, 1953.

14207   FISCHBAUM, MARVIN AND RUBIN, JULIUS. "SLAVERY AND THE
        ECONOMIC DEVELOPMENT OF THE AMERICAN SOUTH."
        EXPLORATIONS IN ENTREPRENEURIAL HISTORY, 6 (FALL,
        1968): 116-127.

14208   FITZHUGH, GEORGE. "THE FREEDMAN AND HIS FUTURE."
        LIPPINCOTT'S MAGAZINE, 4 (OCTOBER, 1869): 436-439.

14209   FLANDERS, RALPH B. "PLANTATION SYSTEM OF THE SOUTH." IN
        ADAMS, JAMES T. (ED.). DICTIONARY OF AMERICAN
        HISTORY. 5 VOLS. NEW YORK: CHARLES SCRIBNER'S SONS,
        1940, VOL. 4, PP. 283-284.

14210   FLEISIG, HAYWOOD. "SLAVERY, THE SUPPLY OF AGRICULTURAL
        LABOR, AND THE INDUSTRIALIZATION OF THE SOUTH."
        JOURNAL OF ECONOMIC HISTORY, 36 (SEPTEMBER, 1976):
        572-597.

14211   FLEMING, WALTER L. "THE SLAVE-LABOR IN THE ANTE-BELLUM
        SOUTH." IN BALLAGH, JAMES C. (ED.). THE SOUTH IN THE
        BUILDING OF THE NATION. 12 VOLS. RICHMOND: SOUTHERN
        HISTORICAL PUBLICATION SOCIETY, 1909, VOL. 5, PP.
        104-120.

14212   FOGEL, ROBERT W. AND ENGERMAN, STANLEY L. "A COMPARISON

OF THE RELATIVE EFFICIENCY OF SLAVE AND FREE
AGRICULTURE IN THE UNITED STATES DURING 1860." PAPERS
AND PROCEEDINGS OF THE FIFTH INTERNATIONAL CONFERENCE
OF ECONOMIC HISTORY. 8 VOLS. PARIS: MOUTON
PUBLISHERS, 1970, VOL. 7, PP. 141-146.

14213 FOGEL, ROBERT W. AND ENGERMAN, STANLEY L. "THE ECONOMICS
OF SLAVERY." IN FOGEL AND ENGERMAN (EDS.). THE
REINTERPRETATION OF AMERICAN ECONOMIC HISTORY. NEW
YORK: HARPER & ROW, 1971, PP. 311-341.

14214 FOGEL, ROBERT W. AND ENGERMAN, STANLEY L. "EXPLAINING
THE RELATIVE EFFICIENCY OF SLAVE AGRICULTURE IN THE
ANTEBELLUM SOUTH." AMERICAN ECONOMIC REVIEW, 67
(JUNE, 1977): 275-296.

14215 FOGEL, ROBERT W. AND ENGERMAN, STANLEY L. "EXPLAINING
THE RELATIVE EFFICIENCY OF SLAVE AGRICULTURE IN THE
ANTEBELLUM SOUTH: A REPLY TO CRITICS." UNPUBLISHED
PAPER, DEPARTMENT OF ECONOMICS, HARVARD UNIVERSITY,
1976.

14216 FOGEL, ROBERT W. AND ENGERMAN, STANLEY L. "EXPLAINING
THE RELATIVE EFFICIENCY OF SLAVE AGRICULTURE IN THE
ANTEBELLUM SOUTH: REPLY." AMERICAN ECONOMIC REVIEW,
70 (SEPTEMBER, 1980): 672-690.

14217 FOGEL, ROBERT W. AND ENGERMAN, STANLEY L. "THE MARKET
EVALUATION OF HUMAN CAPITAL: THE CASE OF SLAVERY."
UNPUBLISHED PAPER PRESENTED TO CLIOMETRICS CONFERENCE,
MADISON, WISCONSIN, APRIL, 1972.

14218 FOGEL, ROBERT W. AND ENGERMAN, STANLEY L. "PHILANTHROPY
AT BARGAIN PRICES: NOTES ON THE ECONOMICS OF GRADUAL
EMANCIPATION." JOURNAL OF LEGAL STUDIES, 3 (JUNE,
1974): 377-401.

14219 FOGEL, ROBERT W. AND ENGERMAN, STANLEY L. "THE RELATIVE
EFFICIENCY OF SLAVERY: A COMPARISON OF NORTHERN AND
SOUTHERN AGRICULTURE IN 1860." EXPLORATIONS IN
ECONOMIC HISTORY, 8 (SPRING, 1971): 353-367.

14220 FOGEL, ROBERT W. AND ENGERMAN, STANLEY L. TIME ON THE
CROSS: THE ECONOMICS OF AMERICAN NEGRO SLAVERY. 2
VOLS. BOSTON: LITTLE, BROWN AND COMPANY, 1974.

14221 FORNELL, EARL W. "TEXANS AND FILIBUSTERS IN THE 1850S."
SOUTHWESTERN HISTORICAL QUARTERLY, 59 (APRIL, 1956):
411-428.

14222 FOUST, JAMES D. THE YEOMAN FARMER AND WESTWARD EXPANSION
OF U.S. COTTON PRODUCTION. NEW YORK: ARNO PRESS,
1975.

14223 FOUST, JAMES D. "THE YEOMAN FARMER AND WESTWARD

EXPANSION OF U.S. COTTON PRODUCTION." PH.D.
DISSERTATION, UNIVERSITY OF NORTH CAROLINA, 1968.

14224 FREEMAN, MARCUS A. "TAXES AND SLAVERY IN TEXAS,
1845-1860." M.A. THESIS, PRAIRIE VIEW AGRICULTURAL
AND MECHANICAL COLLEGE, 1956.

14225 GALENSON, DAVID W. AND MENARD, RUSSELL R. "APPROACHES TO
THE ANALYSIS OF ECONOMIC GROWTH IN COLONIAL BRITISH
AMERICA." HISTORICAL METHODS, 13 (WINTER, 1980):
3-18.

14226 GALLMAN, ROBERT E. "HUMAN CAPITAL IN THE 80 YEARS OF THE
REPUBLIC: HOW MUCH DID AMERICA OWE THE REST OF THE
WORLD?" AMERICAN ECONOMIC REVIEW, 67 (FEBRUARY,
1977): 27-31.

14227 GALLMAN, ROBERT E. "SELF-SUFFICIENCY IN THE COTTON
ECONOMY OF THE ANTEBELLUM SOUTH." AGRICULTURAL
HISTORY, 44 (JANUARY, 1970): 5-23.

14228 GALLMAN, ROBERT E. "SLAVERY AND SOUTHERN ECONOMIC
GROWTH." SOUTHERN ECONOMIC JOURNAL, 45 (APRIL, 1979):
1007-1022.

14229 GALLMAN, ROBERT E. "SOUTHERN ANTE-BELLUM INCOME
RECONSIDERED." EXPLORATIONS IN ECONOMIC HISTORY, 12
(JANUARY, 1975): 89-99.

14230 GALLMAN, ROBERT E. "TRENDS IN SIZE DISTRIBUTION OF
WEALTH IN THE NINETEENTH CENTURY: SOME SPECULATIONS."
IN SOLTOW, LEE (ED.). SIX PAPERS ON THE SIZE
DISTRIBUTION OF WEALTH AND INCOME. NEW YORK:
NATIONAL BUREAU OF ECONOMIC RESEARCH, 1969, PP. 1-24.

14231 GALLMAN, ROBERT E. AND ANDERSON, RALPH V. "SLAVES AS
FIXED CAPITAL: SLAVE LABOR AND SOUTHERN ECONOMIC
DEVELOPMENT." JOURNAL OF AMERICAN HISTORY, 64 (JUNE,
1977): 24-46.

14232 GARRETT, RICHARD D. "PRIMITIVE ACCUMULATION IN THE
ANTEBELLUM COTTON SOUTH." PH.D. DISSERTATION, NEW
SCHOOL FOR SOCIAL RESEARCH, 1978.

14233 GASSETT, MATTYELU. "SOME ECONOMIC ASPECTS OF ANTE-BELLUM
SLAVERY." M.A. THESIS, UNIVERSITY OF GEORGIA, 1938.

14234 GATES, PAUL W. THE FARMER'S AGE: AGRICULTURE,
1815-1860. NEW YORK: HOLT, RINEHART & WINSTON, 1960.

14235 GEGGUS, DAVID P. "THE SLAVES OF BRITISH-OCCUPIED SAINT
DOMINGUE: AN ANALYSIS OF THE WORKFORCES OF 197
ABSENTEE PLANTATIONS, 1796-1797." CARIBBEAN STUDIES,
18 (APRIL-JULY, 1978): 5-42.

14236   GEMERY, H.A. AND HOGENDORN, J.S. "ELASTICITY OF SLAVE
        LABOR SUPPLY AND THE DEVELOPMENT OF SLAVE ECONOMIES IN
        THE BRITISH CARIBBEAN: THE SEVENTEENTH CENTURY
        EXPERIENCE." IN RUBIN, VERA AND TUDEN, ARTHUR (EDS.).
        COMPARATIVE PERSPECTIVES ON SLAVERY IN NEW WORLD
        PLANTATION SOCIETIES. NEW YORK: NEW YORK ACADEMY OF
        SCIENCES, 1977, PP. 72-83.

14237   GEMERY, HENRY A. AND HOGENDORN, JAN S. "TECHNOLOGICAL
        CHANGE, SLAVERY, AND THE SLAVE TRADE." IN DEWEY,
        CLIVE J. AND HOPKINS, A.G. (EDS.). THE IMPERIAL
        IMPACT: STUDIES IN THE ECONOMIC HISTORY OF AFRICA AND
        INDIA. LONDON: ATHLONE PRESS FOR THE INSTITUTE OF
        COMMONWEALTH STUDIES, UNIVERSITY OF LONDON, 1978, PP.
        243-258.

14238   GENOVESE, EUGENE D. "COTTON, SLAVERY AND SOIL EXHAUSTION
        IN THE OLD SOUTH." COTTON HISTORY REVIEW, 2 (JANUARY,
        1961):   3-17.

14239   GENOVESE, EUGENE D. IN RED AND BLACK: MARXIAN
        EXPLORATIONS IN SOUTHERN AND AFRO-AMERICAN HISTORY.
        NEW YORK: PANTHEON, 1968.

14240   GENOVESE, EUGENE D. "THE LIMITS OF AGRARIAN REFORM IN
        THE SLAVE SOUTH." PH.D. DISSERTATION, COLUMBIA
        UNIVERSITY, 1959.

14241   GENOVESE, EUGENE D. "LIVESTOCK IN THE SLAVE ECONOMY OF
        THE OLD SOUTH--A REVISED VIEW." AGRICULTURAL HISTORY,
        36 (JULY, 1962):   143-149.

14242   GENOVESE, EUGENE D. "THE MEDICAL AND INSURANCE COSTS OF
        SLAVEHOLDING IN THE COTTON BELT." JOURNAL OF NEGRO
        HISTORY, 45 (JULY, 1960):   141-155.

14243   GENOVESE, EUGENE D. THE POLITICAL ECONOMY OF SLAVERY:
        STUDIES IN THE ECONOMY AND SOCIETY OF THE SLAVE SOUTH.
        NEW YORK: VINTAGE, 1961.

14244   GENOVESE, EUGENE D. "THE SIGNIFICANCE OF THE SLAVE
        PLANTATION FOR SOUTHERN ECONOMIC DEVELOPMENT."
        JOURNAL OF SOUTHERN HISTORY, 28 (NOVEMBER, 1962):
        422-437.

14245   GENOVESE, EUGENE D. (ED.). THE SLAVE ECONOMIES. 2 VOLS.
        NEW YORK: JOHN WILEY AND SONS, 1973.

14246   GENOVESE, EUGENE D. "THE SLAVE SOUTH: AN
        INTERPRETATION." SCIENCE AND SOCIETY, 25 (DECEMBER,
        1961):   320-337.

14247   GENOVESE, EUGENE D. THE WORLD THE SLAVEHOLDERS MADE:
        TWO ESSAYS IN INTERPRETATION. NEW YORK: VINTAGE,
        1969.

14248   GENOVESE, EUGENE D. "YEOMEN FARMERS IN A SLAVEHOLDERS'
        DEMOCRACY." AGRICULTURAL HISTORY, 49 (APRIL, 1975):
        331-342.

14249   GENOVESE, EUGENE D. AND FOX-GENOVESE, ELIZABETH. "THE
        SLAVE ECONOMIES IN POLITICAL PERSPECTIVE." JOURNAL OF
        AMERICAN HISTORY, 66 (JUNE, 1979): 7-23.

14250   GERSHMAN, SALLY. "ALEXIS DE TOCQUEVILLE AND SLAVERY."
        FRENCH HISTORICAL STUDIES, 9 (SPRING, 1976): 467-483.

14251   GIBSON, GEORGE H. (ED.). "THE MISSISSIPPI MARKET FOR
        WOOLEN GOODS: AN 1822 ANALYSIS." JOURNAL OF SOUTHERN
        HISTORY, 31 (FEBRUARY, 1965): 80-90.

14252   GOLDBERG, BARRY H. "BEYOND FREE LABOR: LABOR, SOCIALISM
        AND THE IDEA OF WAGE SLAVERY, 1890-1920." PH.D.
        DISSERTATION, COLUMBIA UNIVERSITY, 1979.

14253   GOLDIN, CLAUDIA. "AMERICAN SLAVERY: DE JURE AND DE
        FACTO." JOURNAL OF INTERDISCIPLINARY HISTORY, 10
        (SUMMER, 1979): 129-135.

14254   GOLDIN, CLAUDIA D. "THE ECONOMICS OF EMANCIPATION."
        JOURNAL OF ECONOMIC HISTORY, 33 (MARCH, 1973): 66-85.

14255   GOLDIN, CLAUDIA D. "THE ECONOMICS OF URBAN SLAVERY:
        1820 TO 1860." PH.D. DISSERTATION, UNIVERSITY OF
        CHICAGO, 1972.

14256   GOLDIN, CLAUDIA D. "A MODEL TO EXPLAIN THE RELATIVE
        DECLINE OF URBAN SLAVERY: EMPIRICAL RESULTS." IN
        ENGERMAN, STANLEY L. AND GENOVESE, EUGENE D. (EDS.).
        RACE AND SLAVERY IN THE WESTERN HEMISPHERE:
        QUANTITATIVE STUDIES. PRINCETON: PRINCETON
        UNIVERSITY PRESS, 1975, PP. 427-454.

14257   GOLDIN, CLAUDIA D. URBAN SLAVERY IN THE AMERICAN SOUTH,
        1820-1860: A QUANTITATIVE HISTORY. CHICAGO:
        UNIVERSITY OF CHICAGO PRESS, 1976.

14258   GORDON, ARMISTEAD C. "VALUE AND EXCHANGE--REAL AND
        PERSONAL PROPERTY VALUES IN THE ANTE-BELLUM SOUTH."
        IN BALLAGH, JAMES C. (ED.). THE SOUTH IN THE BUILDING
        OF THE NATION. 12 VOLS. RICHMOND: SOUTHERN
        HISTORICAL PUBLICATION SOCIETY, 1909, VOL. 5, PP.
        418-422.

14259   GORDON, ASA H. SKETCHES OF NEGRO LIFE AND HISTORY IN
        SOUTH CAROLINA. HAMMOND, IN: W.B. CONKEY, 1929.

14260   GOVAN, THOMAS P. "AMERICANS BELOW THE POTOMAC." IN
        SELLERS, CHARLES G. (ED.). THE SOUTHERNER AS
        AMERICAN. CHAPEL HILL: UNIVERSITY OF NORTH CAROLINA
        PRESS, 1960, PP. 19-39.

14261   GOVAN, THOMAS P. "WAS THE OLD SOUTH DIFFERENT?" JOURNAL
         OF SOUTHERN HISTORY, 21 (NOVEMBER, 1955): 447-455.

14262   GRAY, LEWIS C. HISTORY OF AGRICULTURE IN THE SOUTHERN
         UNITED STATES TO 1860. 2 VOLS. WASHINGTON: CARNEGIE
         INSTITUTION OF WASHINGTON, 1932.

14263   GRAY, LEWIS C. "SOUTHERN AGRICULTURE, PLANTATION SYSTEM,
         AND THE NEGRO PROBLEM." ANNALS OF THE AMERICAN
         ACADEMY OF POLITICAL AND SOCIAL SCIENCE, 40 (MARCH,
         1912): 90-99.

14264   GREEN, WILLIAM A. "THE PLANTER CLASS AND BRITISH WEST
         INDIAN SUGAR PRODUCTION, BEFORE AND AFTER
         EMANCIPATION." ECONOMIC HISTORY REVIEW, 26 (AUGUST,
         1973): 448-463.

14265   GREENBERG, MICHAEL. "THE NEW ECONOMIC HISTORY AND THE
         UNDERSTANDING OF SLAVERY: A METHODOLOGICAL CRITIQUE."
         DIALECTICAL ANTHROPOLOGY, 2 (MAY, 1977): 131-141.

14266   GREENE, LARRY A. "BLACKS." IN PORTER, GLENN (ED.).
         ENCYCLOPEDIA OF AMERICAN ECONOMIC HISTORY: STUDIES OF
         THE PRINCIPAL MOVEMENTS AND IDEAS. 3 VOLS. NEW YORK:
         SCRIBNERS, 1980, VOL. 3, PP. 1001-1011.

14267   GUJER, BRUNO. "FREE TRADE AND SLAVERY: CALHOUN'S
         DEFENSE OF SOUTHERN INTERESTS AGAINST BRITISH
         INTERFERENCE, 1811-1848." PH.D. DISSERTATION,
         UNIVERSITAT ZURICH, 1971.

14268   GUNDER FRANK, ANDRE. "ON WORLD CAPITAL ACCUMULATION,
         INTERNATIONAL EXCHANGE, AND THE DIVERSITY OF MODES OF
         PRODUCTION IN THE NEW WORLD." ACTES DU XLII CONGRES
         INTERNATIONAL DES AMERICANISTES, VOLUME I. PARIS:
         SOCIETE DES AMERICANISTES, 1977, PP. 187-208.

14269   GUNDERSON, GERALD. "SLAVERY." IN PORTER, GLENN (ED.).
         ENCYCLOPEDIA OF AMERICAN ECONOMIC HISTORY: STUDIES OF
         THE PRINCIPAL MOVEMENTS AND IDEAS. 3 VOLS. NEW YORK:
         SCRIBNERS, 1980, VOL. 2, PP. 552-561.

14270   GUNDERSON, GERALD. "SOUTHERN ANTE-BELLUM INCOME
         RECONSIDERED." EXPLORATIONS IN ECONOMIC HISTORY, 10
         (WINTER, 1973): 151-176.

14271   GUNDERSON, GERALD. "SOUTHERN INCOME RECONSIDERED: A
         REPLY." EXPLORATIONS IN ECONOMIC HISTORY, 12
         (JANUARY, 1975): 101-102.

14272   GUTMAN, HERBERT AND SUTCH, RICHARD. "SAMBO MAKES GOOD,
         OR WERE SLAVES IMBUED WITH THE PROTESTANT WORK ETHIC?"
         IN DAVID, PAUL A.; GUTMAN; SUTCH; TEMIN, PETER; AND
         WRIGHT, GAVIN (EDS.). RECKONING WITH SLAVERY: A
         CRITICAL STUDY IN THE QUANTITATIVE HISTORY OF AMERICAN

NEGRO SLAVERY. NEW YORK: OXFORD UNIVERSITY PRESS,
1976, PP. 55-93.

14273 HALL, ARTHUR R.   "SOIL EROSION AND AGRICULTURE IN THE
       SOUTHERN PIEDMONT: A HISTORY." PH.D. DISSERTATION,
       DUKE UNIVERSITY, 1948.

14274 HALL, DOUGLAS. "THE SOCIAL AND ECONOMIC BACKGROUND TO
       SUGAR IN SLAVE DAYS (WITH SPECIAL REFERENCE TO
       JAMAICA)." CARIBBEAN HISTORICAL REVIEW, 3-4
       (DECEMBER, 1954): 149-169.

14275 HAMMOND, M.B.   "THE SOUTHERN FARMER AND THE COTTON
       QUESTION." POLITICAL SCIENCE QUARTERLY, 12
       (SEPTEMBER, 1897): 450-475.

14276 HAMMOND, MATTHEW B.   THE COTTON INDUSTRY: AN ESSAY IN
       AMERICAN ECONOMIC HISTORY. NEW YORK: MACMILLAN
       COMPANY, 1897.

14277 HAMMOND, MATTHEW B.   "THE HISTORY OF COTTON PLANTING IN
       THE SOUTH." IN BALLAGH, JAMES C. (ED.). THE SOUTH IN
       THE BUILDING OF THE NATION. 12 VOLS. RICHMOND:
       SOUTHERN HISTORICAL PUBLICATION SOCIETY, 1909, VOL. 5,
       PP. 197-212.

14278 HANDLER, JEROME S.   "SMALL-SCALE SUGAR CANE FARMING IN
       BARBADOS." ETHNOLOGY, 5 (1966): 264-283.

14279 HART, ALBERT B.   SLAVERY AND ABOLITION, 1831-1841. NEW
       YORK: HARPER AND BROTHERS, 1906.

14280 HARTWELL, E.C.   "THE ECONOMICS OF SLAVERY." HISTORY
       TEACHER'S MAGAZINE, 4 (FEBRUARY, 1913): 50.

14281 HARTWELL, RONALD M.   "SLAVE LABOUR AND FACTORY LABOUR; A
       COMPARISON OF THE HISTORICAL DEBATES ON AMERICAN
       SLAVERY AND ON LIVING STANDARDS DURING THE ENGLISH
       INDUSTRIAL REVOLUTION." UNPUBLISHED PAPER PRESENTED
       AT MSSB--UNIVERSITY OF ROCHESTER CONFERENCE: "TIME ON
       THE CROSS: A FIRST APPRAISAL," OCTOBER 24-26, 1974.

14282 HASKINS, RALPH W.   "THE COTTON FACTOR, 1800-1860: A
       STUDY IN SOUTHERN ECONOMIC AND SOCIAL HISTORY." PH.D.
       DISSERTATION, UNIVERSITY OF CALIFORNIA, 1950.

14283 HASKINS, RALPH W.   "PLANTER AND COTTON FACTOR IN THE OLD
       SOUTH: SOME AREAS OF FRICTION." AGRICULTURAL
       HISTORY, 29 (JANUARY, 1955): 1-14.

14284 HAWK, EMORY Q.   ECONOMIC HISTORY OF THE SOUTH. NEW YORK:
       PRENTICE-HALL, 1934.

14285 HAYWOOD, C. ROBERT.   "MERCANTILISM AND COLONIAL SLAVE
       LABOR, 1700-1763." JOURNAL OF SOUTHERN HISTORY, 23

(NOVEMBER, 1957):   454-464.

14286   HEDRICK, CHARLES E. "SOCIAL AND ECONOMIC ASPECTS OF
        SLAVERY IN THE TRANSMONTANE PRIOR TO 1850." PH.D.
        DISSERTATION, GEORGE PEABODY COLLEGE FOR TEACHERS,
        1927.

14287   HEYWARD, DUNCAN C. SEED FROM MADAGASCAR. CHAPEL HILL:
        UNIVERSITY OF NORTH CAROLINA PRESS, 1937.

14288   HIGGS, ROBERT. COMPETITION AND COERCION: BLACKS IN THE
        AMERICAN ECONOMY, 1865-1914. NEW YORK: CAMBRIDGE
        UNIVERSITY PRESS, 1977.

14289   HIGMAN, BARRY W. SLAVE POPULATION AND ECONOMY IN
        JAMAICA, 1807-1834. CAMBRIDGE: CAMBRIDGE UNIVERSITY
        PRESS, 1976.

14290   HILL, JAMES D. "SOME ECONOMIC ASPECTS OF SLAVERY,
        1850-1860." SOUTH ATLANTIC QUARTERLY, 26 (APRIL,
        1927): 161-177.

14291   HILL, WILLIAM. FIRST STAGES OF THE TARIFF POLICY OF THE
        UNITED STATES. BALTIMORE: AMERICAN ECONOMIC
        ASSOCIATION, 1893.

14292   HILLIARD, SAM B. "ANTEBELLUM TIDEWATER RICE CULTURE IN
        SOUTH CAROLINA AND GEORGIA." IN GIBSON, JAMES R.
        (ED.). EUROPEAN SETTLEMENT AND DEVELOPMENT IN NORTH
        AMERICA: ESSAYS ON GEOGRAPHICAL CHANGE IN HONOUR AND
        MEMORY OF ANDREW HILL CLARK. BUFFALO: UNIVERSITY OF
        TORONTO PRESS, 1978, PP. 91-115.

14293   HINE, DARLENE C. "FEMALE SLAVE RESISTANCE: THE
        ECONOMICS OF SEX." WESTERN JOURNAL OF BLACK STUDIES,
        3 (SUMMER, 1979): 123-127.

14294   HINE, WILLIAM C. "AMERICAN SLAVERY AND RUSSIAN SERFDOM:
        A PRELIMINARY COMPARISON." PHYLON, 36 (WINTER, 1975):
        378-384.

14295   HOBSBAWM, E.J. "THE SEVENTEENTH CENTURY IN THE
        DEVELOPMENT OF CAPITALISM." SCIENCE AND SOCIETY, 24
        (SPRING, 1960): 97-112.

14296   HOPKINS, JAMES F. "HEMP." IN ROLLER, DAVID C. AND
        TWYMAN, ROBERT W. (EDS.). THE ENCYCLOPEDIA OF
        SOUTHERN HISTORY. BATON ROUGE: LOUISIANA STATE
        UNIVERSITY PRESS, 1979, P. 588.

14297   HUGHES, SARAH S. "SLAVES FOR HIRE: THE ALLOCATION OF
        BLACK LABOR IN ELIZABETH CITY COUNTY VIRGINIA, 1782 TO
        1810." WILLIAM AND MARY QUARTERLY, 3RD SER., 35
        (APRIL, 1978): 260-286.

14298 HUNEYCUTT, DWIGHT J. "THE ECONOMICS OF THE INDIGO
       INDUSTRY IN SOUTH CAROLINA." M.S. THESIS, UNIVERSITY
       OF SOUTH CAROLINA, 1949.

14299 HUNT, WILLIAM A. "THE ECONOMIC HAZARDS OF SLAVERY."
       M.A. THESIS, SOUTHERN METHODIST UNIVERSITY, 1933.

14300 HYPPS, IRENE C. "CHANGES IN BUSINESS ATTITUDES AND
       ACTIVITIES OF THE NEGRO IN THE UNITED STATES SINCE
       1619." PH.D. DISSERTATION, NEW YORK UNIVERSITY, 1943.

14301 "INDIGO." IN SCHAPSMEIER, EDWARD L. AND SCHAPSMEIER,
       FREDERICK H. ENCYCLOPEDIA OF AMERICAN AGRICULTURAL
       HISTORY. WESTPORT: GREENWOOD PRESS, 1975, P. 176.

14302 INIKORI, JOSEPH E. "THE SLAVE TRADE AND THE ATLANTIC
       ECONOMIES, 1451-1870." IN THE AFRICAN SLAVE TRADE
       FROM THE FIFTEENTH TO THE NINETEENTH CENTURY. PARIS:
       UNITED NATIONS EDUCATIONAL, SCIENTIFIC AND CULTURAL
       ORGANIZATION, 1979, PP. 56-85.

14303 JACOBSTEIN, MEYER. "TOBACCO CULTURE IN THE SOUTH." IN
       BALLAGH, JAMES C. (ED.). THE SOUTH IN THE BUILDING OF
       THE NATION. 12 VOLS. RICHMOND: SOUTHERN HISTORICAL
       PUBLICATION SOCIETY, 1909, VOL. 5, PP. 158-169.

14304 JACOBSTEIN, MEYER. THE TOBACCO INDUSTRY IN THE UNITED
       STATES. NEW YORK: COLUMBIA UNIVERSITY PRESS, 1907.

14305 JERNEGAN, MARCUS W. LABORING AND DEPENDENT CLASSES IN
       COLONIAL AMERICA, 1607-1783: STUDIES OF THE ECONOMIC,
       EDUCATIONAL, AND SOCIAL SIGNIFICANCE OF SLAVES,
       SERVANTS, APPRENTICES, AND POOR FOLK. CHICAGO:
       UNIVERSITY OF CHICAGO PRESS, 1931.

14306 JERNEGAN, MARCUS W. "SLAVERY AND THE BEGINNINGS OF
       INDUSTRIALISM IN THE AMERICAN COLONIES." AMERICAN
       HISTORICAL REVIEW, 25 (JANUARY, 1920): 220-240.

14307 JERVEY, THEODORE D. THE RAILROAD, THE CONQUEROR.
       COLUMBIA, SC: STATE COMPANY, 1913.

14308 JOHNSON, C. "COTTON PICKERS." OUTING MAGAZINE, 45
       (OCTOBER, 1904): 80-97.

14309 JOHNSON, HARRY G. "THE ANTE-BELLUM SOUTH: NEGRO
       SLAVERY." ENCOUNTER, 44 (JANUARY, 1975): 56-59.

14310 JOHNSON, THAVOLIA G. "WAGES, SHARE WAGES, SHARECROPPING:
       THE TRANSITION FROM SLAVERY TO FREEDOM IN THE RURAL
       SOUTH, 1860-1880." UNPUBLISHED PAPER PRESENTED AT
       MEETING OF THE ASSOCIATION FOR THE STUDY OF
       AFRO-AMERICAN LIFE AND HISTORY, 1976.

14311 JOHNSON, WHITTINGTON B. "NEGRO LABORING CLASSES IN EARLY

AMERICA, 1750-1820." PH.D. DISSERTATION, UNIVERSITY
OF GEORGIA, 1970.

14312   JONES, ARCHER AND CARLSSON, ROBERT J. "SLAVERY AND
        SAVING." AMERICAN JOURNAL OF ECONOMICS AND SOCIOLOGY,
        30 (APRIL, 1971): 171-177.

14313   JONES, ARCHER AND HOEPNER, PAUL H. "THE SOUTH'S ECONOMIC
        INVESTMENT IN SLAVERY." AMERICAN JOURNAL OF ECONOMICS
        AND SOCIOLOGY, 26 (JULY, 1967): 297-299.

14314   KEMMERER, DONALD L. "THE CHANGING PATTERN OF AMERICAN
        ECONOMIC DEVELOPMENT." JOURNAL OF ECONOMIC HISTORY,
        16 (DECEMBER, 1956): 575-589.

14315   KEMMERER, DONALD L. "THE PRE-CIVIL WAR SOUTH'S LEADING
        CROP: CORN." AGRICULTURAL HISTORY, 23 (OCTOBER,
        1949): 236-239.

14316   KILLEBREW, J.B. "THE OLD PLANTATION VERSUS INTENSIVE
        FARMING." SOUTHERN STATES FARM MAGAZINE, 5 (NOVEMBER,
        1897): 397-401.

14317   KLEIN, HERBERT S. SLAVERY IN THE AMERICAS: A
        COMPARATIVE STUDY OF VIRGINIA AND CUBA. CHICAGO:
        UNIVERSITY OF CHICAGO PRESS, 1967.

14318   KLINGAMAN, DAVID. "THE SIGNIFICANCE OF GRAIN IN THE
        DEVELOPMENT OF THE TOBACCO COLONIES." JOURNAL OF
        ECONOMIC HISTORY, 29 (JUNE, 1969): 268-278.

14319   KOVAL, B.I. "COLONIAL PLANTATION SLAVERY AND PRIMARY
        CAPITAL ACCUMULATION IN WESTERN EUROPE (BASED ON
        SOURCES FROM THE HISTORY OF BRAZIL)." IN BARTLEY,
        RUSSELL H. (ED.). SOVIET HISTORIANS ON LATIN AMERICA:
        RECENT SCHOLARLY CONTRIBUTIONS. MADISON: UNIVERSITY
        OF WISCONSIN PRESS, 1978, PP. 89-108.

14320   KULIKOFF, ALLAN. "BLACK SOCIETY AND THE ECONOMICS OF
        SLAVERY." MARYLAND HISTORICAL MAGAZINE, 70 (SUMMER,
        1975): 203-210.

14321   KUZNESOF, ELIZABETH A. "HOUSEHOLD COMPOSITION AND THE
        ECONOMY IN AN URBANIZING COMMUNITY: SAO PAULO,
        1765-1836." PH.D. DISSERTATION, UNIVERSITY OF
        CALIFORNIA, 1976.

14322   LACK, PAUL D. "THE ANTE-BELLUM SOUTHERN WORKER: AN
        ECONOMIC AND SOCIAL HISTORY." M.A. THESIS, TEXAS TECH
        UNIVERSITY, 1969.

14323   LAMB, ROBERT B. THE MULE IN SOUTHERN AGRICULTURE.
        BERKELEY: UNIVERSITY OF CALIFORNIA PUBLICATIONS IN
        GEOGRAPHY NO. 15, 1963.

14324   LAND, AUBREY C. (ED.).   BASES OF THE PLANTATION SOCIETY.
        NEW YORK: HARPER & ROW, 1969.

14325   LAND, AUBREY C.   "THE TOBACCO STAPLE AND THE PLANTER'S
        PROBLEMS: TECHNOLOGY, LABOR, AND CROPS."
        AGRICULTURAL HISTORY, 43 (JANUARY, 1969):   69-82.

14326   "LAND TENURE IN THE SOUTH." NEW YORK TIMES, SEPTEMBER
        30, 1881.

14327   LANDON, FRED.   "AGRICULTURE AMONG THE NEGRO REFUGEES IN
        UPPER CANADA." JOURNAL OF NEGRO HISTORY, 21 (JULY,
        1936):   304-312.

14328   "LARGE VS. SMALL COTTON PLANTATIONS."   AMERICAN
        AGRICULTURIST, 26 (JULY, 1867):   249-250.

14329   LEE, SUSAN P.   "THE WESTWARD MOVEMENT OF THE COTTON
        ECONOMY, 1840-1860:   PERCEIVED INTERESTS AND ECONOMIC
        REALITIES." PH.D. DISSERTATION, COLUMBIA UNIVERSITY,
        1975.

14330   LEFF, NATHANIEL H.   "LONG-TERM VIABILITY OF SLAVERY IN A
        BACKWARD CLOSED ECONOMY." JOURNAL OF
        INTERDISCIPLINARY HISTORY, 5 (SUMMER, 1974):   103-108.

14331   LERNER, EUGENE.   "SOUTHERN OUTPUT AND AGRICULTURAL
        INCOME, 1860-1880." AGRICULTURAL HISTORY, 33 (JULY,
        1959):   117-125.

14332   LINDEN, FABIAN.   "NOTES ON SOME PREVAILING FALLACIES IN
        SOUTHERN ANTE-BELLUM HISTORY." GEORGIA HISTORICAL
        QUARTERLY, 25 (JUNE, 1941):   141-150.

14333   LINDSTROM, DIANE L.   "SOUTHERN DEPENDENCE UPON
        INTERREGIONAL GRAIN SUPPLIES: A REVIEW OF THE TRADE
        FLOWS, 1840-1860." AGRICULTURAL HISTORY, 44 (JANUARY,
        1970):   101-114.

14334   LORIA, A.   "THE HISTORICAL ORIGIN OF SLAVERY: A FRAGMENT
        OF THE 'ANALYSIS OF THE THEORY OF CAPITAL.'" SEWANEE
        REVIEW, 8 (OCTOBER, 1900):   466-477.

14335   LOWE, RICHARD G. AND CAMPBELL, RANDOLPH B.   "THE
        SLAVE-BREEDING HYPOTHESIS: A DEMOGRAPHIC COMMENT ON
        THE 'BUYING' AND 'SELLING' STATES." JOURNAL OF
        SOUTHERN HISTORY, 42 (AUGUST, 1976):   401-412.

14336   LURAGHI, RAIMONDO.   "THE CIVIL WAR AND THE MODERNIZATION
        OF AMERICAN SOCIETY: SOCIAL STRUCTURE AND INDUSTRIAL
        REVOLUTION IN THE OLD SOUTH BEFORE AND DURING THE
        WAR." CIVIL WAR HISTORY, 18 (SEPTEMBER, 1972):
        230-250.

14337   LURAGHI, RAIMONDO.   "WAGE LABOR IN THE 'RICE BELT' OF

NORTHERN ITALY AND SLAVE LABOR IN THE AMERICAN
SOUTH--A FIRST APPROACH." SOUTHERN STUDIES, 16
(SUMMER, 1977):   109-123.

14338 LURAGHI, RAIMONDO. "WAGE LABOR IN THE 'RICE BELT' OF
NORTHERN ITALY AND SLAVE LABOR IN THE AMERICAN
SOUTH--A FIRST APPROACH." UNPUBLISHED PAPER PRESENTED
AT MSSB--UNIVERSITY OF ROCHESTER CONFERENCE: "TIME ON
THE CROSS: A FIRST APPRAISAL," OCTOBER 24-26, 1974.

14339 LYON, ANNIE L.K. "SLAVERY AS AN ECONOMIC AND POLITICAL
FACTOR IN THE TEXAS GUBERNATORIAL ELECTIONS OF 1857
AND 1859." M.A. THESIS, UNIVERSITY OF HOUSTON, 1964.

14340 MACLEOD, DUNCAN. "THE POLITICAL ECONOMY OF JOHN TAYLOR
OF CAROLINE." JOURNAL OF AMERICAN STUDIES, 14
(DECEMBER, 1980):   387-406.

14341 MAIN, B.J. "TOWARD THE MEASUREMENT OF HISTORIC DEBTS."
REVIEW OF BLACK POLITICAL ECONOMY, 2 (WINTER, 1972):
22-42.

14342 MAIN, JACKSON T. THE SOCIAL STRUCTURE OF REVOLUTIONARY
AMERICA. PRINCETON: PRINCETON UNIVERSITY PRESS, 1965.

14343 MANDEL, BERNARD. "SLAVERY AND THE SOUTHERN WORKERS."
NEGRO HISTORY BULLETIN, 17 (DECEMBER, 1953):   57-62.

14344 MANDLE, JAY R. "THE PLANTATION ECONOMY: AN ESSAY IN
DEFINITION." SCIENCE AND SOCIETY, 36 (SPRING, 1972):
49-62.

14345 MANDLE, JAY R. THE ROOTS OF BLACK POVERTY: THE SOUTHERN
PLANTATION ECONOMY AFTER THE CIVIL WAR. DURHAM: DUKE
UNIVERSITY PRESS, 1978.

14346 MARCILIO, MARIA L. "THE PRICE OF SLAVES IN XIXTH CENTURY
BRAZIL: A QUANTITATIVE ANALYSIS OF THE REGISTRATION
OF SLAVE SALES IN BAHIA." IN STUDI IN MEMORIA DE
FEDERIGO MELIS. NAPOLI: GIANNINI EDITORE, 1978, PP.
83-97.

14347 MARKS, BAYLY E. "ECONOMICS AND SOCIETY IN A STAPLE
PLANTATION SYSTEM: ST. MARY'S COUNTY, MARYLAND,
1790-1840." PH.D. DISSERTATION, UNIVERSITY OF
MARYLAND, 1979.

14348 MATHEWS, THOMAS. "CARIBBEAN ECONOMIC HISTORY."
CARIBBEAN REVIEW, 3 (SPRING, 1971):   4-6.

14349 MCCARTHY, TERENCE. "400 YEARS LATER." CANADIAN
DIMENSION, 11 (1976):   5-11.

14350 MCCOY, A.D. THOUGHTS ON LABOR IN THE SOUTH, PAST,
PRESENT AND FUTURE. NEW ORLEANS: BLELOCK & COMPANY,

1865.

14351   MCCRARY, ROYCE C. "THE GOLDEN AGE AND DISSATISFACTION:
        A STUDY OF THE AGRICULTURAL REFORM MOVEMENT IN GEORGIA
        DURING THE EIGHTEEN-FIFTIES." M.A. THESIS, UNIVERSITY
        OF GEORGIA, 1968.

14352   MCCUSKER, JOHN J. "THE RUM TRADE AND THE BALANCE OF
        PAYMENTS OF THE THIRTEEN CONTINENTAL COLONIES,
        1650-1770." PH.D. DISSERTATION, UNIVERSITY OF
        PITTSBURGH, 1970.

14353   MCDONALD, RODERICK. "'GOODS AND CHATTELS': THE ECONOMY
        OF SLAVES ON SUGAR PLANTATIONS IN JAMAICA AND
        LOUISIANA." PH.D. DISSERTATION, UNIVERSITY OF KANSAS,
        1980.

14354   MCKENZIE, EDNA C. "SELF-HIRE AMONG SLAVES, 1820-1860:
        INSTITUTIONAL VARIATION OR ABERRATION?" PH.D.
        DISSERTATION, UNIVERSITY OF PITTSBURGH, 1973.

14355   MCKENZIE, ROBERT H. "THE ECONOMIC IMPACT OF FEDERAL
        OPERATIONS IN ALABAMA DURING THE CIVIL WAR." ALABAMA
        HISTORICAL QUARTERLY, 38 (SPRING, 1976): 51-68.

14356   MELL, PATRICK H. "RICE PLANTING IN THE AGRICULTURAL
        DEVELOPMENT OF THE SOUTH." IN BALLAGH, JAMES C.
        (ED.). THE SOUTH IN THE BUILDING OF THE NATION. 12
        VOLS. RICHMOND: SOUTHERN HISTORICAL PUBLICATION
        SOCIETY, 1909, VOL. 5, PP. 169-177.

14357   MELLO, PEDRO C. DE. "THE ECONOMICS OF LABOR IN BRAZILIAN
        COFFEE PLANTATIONS, 1850-1888." PAPER PRESENTED AT
        WORKSHOP IN ECONOMIC HISTORY, UNIVERSITY OF CHICAGO,
        1974.

14358   MELLO, PEDRO CARVAHLO DE. "THE ECONOMICS OF LABOR IN
        BRAZILIAN COFFEE PLANTATIONS, 1850-1888." PH.D.
        DISSERTATION, UNIVERSITY OF CHICAGO, 1977.

14359   MELOM, HALVOR G. "THE ECONOMIC DEVELOPMENT OF ST. LOUIS,
        1803-1846." PH.D. DISSERTATION, UNIVERSITY OF
        MISSOURI, 1948.

14360   MENDENHALL, M.S. "A HISTORY OF AGRICULTURE IN SOUTH
        CAROLINA, 1790 TO 1860: AN ECONOMIC AND SOCIAL
        STUDY." PH.D. DISSERTATION, UNIVERSITY OF NORTH
        CAROLINA, 1940.

14361   MERRITT, J.E. "THE LIVERPOOL SLAVE TRADE, 1789-1792: AN
        ANALYTICAL STUDY OF THE RETURNS TO THE COMMITTEE OF
        ENQUIRY INTO THE SLAVE TRADE, 1788, 1790, 1791, WITH
        SPECIAL REFERENCE TO THE PROFITABILITY OF THE SLAVE
        TRADE AND THE NATURE OF THE TRIANGULAR TRADE." M.A.
        THESIS, UNIVERSITY OF NOTTINGHAM, 1959.

14362   METZER, JACOB. "INSTITUTIONAL CHANGE AND ECONOMIC
        ANALYSIS: SOME ISSUES RELATED TO AMERICAN SLAVERY."
        LOUISIANA STUDIES, 15 (WINTER, 1976): 321-344.

14363   METZER, JACOB. "RATIONAL MANAGEMENT, MODERN BUSINESS
        PRACTICES, AND ECONOMIES OF SCALE IN THE ANTE-BELLUM
        SOUTHERN PLANTATION." EXPLORATIONS IN ECONOMIC
        HISTORY, 12 (APRIL, 1975): 123-150.

14364   MILLER, KELLY. "THE NEGRO AS A WORKINGMAN." AMERICAN
        MERCURY, 6 (NOVEMBER, 1925): 310-313.

14365   MILLER, KENNETH J. "SOME ECONOMIC ASPECTS OF AMERICAN
        NEGRO SLAVERY." M.A. THESIS, STANFORD UNIVERSITY,
        1950.

14366   MILLER, MARION M. AMERICAN DEBATE: A HISTORY OF
        POLITICAL AND ECONOMIC CONTROVERSY IN THE UNITED
        STATES. 2 VOLS. NEW YORK: PUTNAM, 1916.

14367   MILLER, WILLIAM L. "J.E. CAIRNES ON THE ECONOMICS OF
        AMERICAN NEGRO SLAVERY." SOUTHERN ECONOMIC JOURNAL,
        30 (APRIL, 1964): 333-341.

14368   MILLER, WILLIAM L. "A NOTE ON THE IMPORTANCE OF THE
        INTER-STATE SLAVE TRADE OF THE ANTE BELLUM SOUTH."
        JOURNAL OF POLITICAL ECONOMY, 73 (APRIL, 1965):
        181-187.

14369   MILLER, WILLIAM L. "SLAVERY AND THE POPULATION OF THE
        SOUTH." SOUTHERN ECONOMIC JOURNAL, 28 (JULY, 1961):
        46-54.

14370   MINTZ, SIDNEY. WAS THE PLANTATION SLAVE A PROLETERIAN?
        BINGHAMTON, NY: FERNAND BRAUDEL CENTER, STATE
        UNIVERSITY OF NEW YORK, SEMINAR I WORKING PAPERS, 1977.

14371   MINTZ, SIDNEY W. "THE DIGNITY OF HONEST TOIL: A REVIEW
        ARTICLE." COMPARATIVE STUDIES IN SOCIETY AND HISTORY,
        21 (OCTOBER, 1979): 558-566.

14372   MINTZ, SIDNEY W. "WAS THE PLANTATION SLAVE A
        PROLETARIAN?" REVIEW, 2 (SUMMER, 1978): 81-98.

14373   MIRSKY, JEANETTE AND NEVINS, ALLAN. THE WORLD OF ELI
        WHITNEY. NEW YORK: MACMILLAN COMPANY, 1952.

14374   MITCHELL, BROADUS. "ECONOMIC EFFECTS OF SLAVERY."
        FREDERICK LAW OLMSTED: A CRITIC OF THE OLD SOUTH.
        BALTIMORE: JOHNS HOPKINS PRESS, 1924, PP. 114-156.

14375   MITCHELL, BROADUS. THE RISE OF COTTON MILLS IN THE
        SOUTH. BALTIMORE: JOHNS HOPKINS PRESS, 1921.

14376   MITCHELL, BROADUS. WILLIAM GREGG, FACTORY MASTER OF THE

OLD SOUTH. CHAPEL HILL: UNIVERSITY OF NORTH CAROLINA
PRESS, 1928.

14377 MOES, JOHN E. "THE ABSORPTION OF CAPITAL IN SLAVE LABOR
IN THE ANTE-BELLUM SOUTH AND ECONOMIC GROWTH."
AMERICAN JOURNAL OF ECONOMICS AND SOCIOLOGY, 20
(OCTOBER, 1961): 535-541.

14378 MOES, JOHN E. "THE ECONOMICS OF SLAVERY IN THE
ANTE-BELLUM SOUTH: ANOTHER COMMENT." JOURNAL OF
POLITICAL ECONOMY, 68 (APRIL, 1960): 183-187.

14379 MOORE, JOHN HEBRON. "COTTON BREEDING IN THE OLD SOUTH."
AGRICULTURAL HISTORY, 30 (JULY, 1956): 95-103.

14380 MOORE, JOHN HEBRON. "THE TEXTILE INDUSTRY OF THE OLD
SOUTH." JOURNAL OF ECONOMIC HISTORY, 16 (JUNE, 1956):
200-205.

14381 MORGAN, EDWIN V. "PRICE OF SLAVES IN NEW YORK
(1659-1818)." MAGAZINE OF AMERICAN HISTORY, 29
(MAY-JUNE, 1893): 523-524.

14382 MORRILL, RICHARD L. AND DONALDSON, O. FRED.
"GEOGRAPHICAL PERSPECTIVES ON THE HISTORY OF BLACK
AMERICA." ECONOMIC GEOGRAPHY, 48 (JANUARY, 1972):
1-23.

14383 MUSSER, CARL W. "ECONOMIC AND SOCIAL ASPECTS OF NEGRO
SLAVERY IN WYTHE COUNTY, VIRGINIA, 1790-1860." M.A.
THESIS, GEORGE WASHINGTON UNIVERSITY, 1958.

14384 NETTELS, CURTIS P. "THE MONEY SUPPLY OF THE AMERICAN
COLONIES BEFORE 1720." UNIVERSITY OF WISCONSIN
STUDIES IN THE SOCIAL SCIENCES AND HISTORY, NO. 20
(1934): 1-300.

14385 NEVINS, ALLAN. "THE CASH ACCOUNT OF SLAVERY." ORDEAL OF
THE UNION. 2 VOLS. NEW YORK: CHARLES SCRIBNER'S
SONS, 1947, VOL. 1, PP. 462-497.

14386 NICHOLLS, W.H. "SOME FOUNDATIONS OF ECONOMIC DEVELOPMENT
IN THE UPPER EAST TENNESSEE VALLEY, 1850-1900:
SLAVERY AND SOCIOPOLITICAL STRUCTURE." JOURNAL OF
POLITICAL ECONOMY, 64 (OCTOBER, 1956): 403-405.

14387 NIEMI, ALBERT W., JR. "INEQUALITY IN THE DISTRIBUTION OF
SLAVE WEALTH: THE COTTON SOUTH AND OTHER SOUTHERN
AGRICULTURAL REGIONS." JOURNAL OF ECONOMIC HISTORY,
37 (SEPTEMBER, 1977): 747-754.

14388 NORTH, DOUGLASS C. THE ECONOMIC GROWTH OF THE UNITED
STATES, 1790-1860. ENGLEWOOD CLIFFS: PRENTICE-HALL,
1961.

14389   NOVACK, GEORGE.   THE RISE AND FALL OF THE COTTON KINGDOM:
        THE ULTIMATE STAGE OF CHATTEL SLAVERY IN THE SOUTH.
        NEW YORK: SOCIALIST WORKERS PARTY, 1968.

14390   NOVACK, GEORGE E.   "NEGRO SLAVERY IN NORTH AMERICA."   IN
        HIMMEL, ROBERT (ED.).   MARXIST ESSAYS IN AMERICAN
        HISTORY.   NEW YORK: MERIT PUBLISHERS, 1969, PP. 33-36.

14391   NOYES, JAMES O.   "SOUTHERN TROUBLES AND THEIR REMEDY."
        GALAXY, 5 (MARCH, 1863):   355-374.

14392   OLSEN, OTTO H.   "HISTORIANS AND THE EXTENT OF SLAVE
        OWNERSHIP IN THE SOUTHERN UNITED STATES."   CIVIL WAR
        HISTORY, 18 (JUNE, 1972):   101-116.

14393   OWSLEY, FRANK L. AND OWSLEY, HARRIET C.   "THE ECONOMIC
        BASIS OF SOCIETY IN THE LATE ANTE-BELLUM SOUTH."
        JOURNAL OF SOUTHERN HISTORY, 6 (FEBRUARY, 1940):
        24-45.

14394   PAPENFUSE, EDWARD C., JR.   "PLANTER BEHAVIOR AND ECONOMIC
        OPPORTUNITY IN A STAPLE ECONOMY."   AGRICULTURAL
        HISTORY, 46 (APRIL, 1972):   297-311.

14395   PARKER, WILLIAM N.   "THE SLAVE PLANTATION IN AMERICAN
        AGRICULTURE."   IN FIRST INTERNATIONAL CONFERENCE OF
        ECONOMIC HISTORY.   PARIS: MOUTON & COMPANY, 1960, PP.
        321-331.

14396   PARKER, WILLIAM N.   "SLAVERY AND SOUTHERN ECONOMIC
        DEVELOPMENT: AN HYPOTHESIS AND SOME EVIDENCE."
        AGRICULTURAL HISTORY, 44 (JANUARY, 1970):   115-126.

14397   PARKER, WILLIAM N. (ED.).   THE STRUCTURE OF THE COTTON
        ECONOMY OF THE ANTEBELLUM SOUTH.   WASHINGTON:
        AGRICULTURAL HISTORY SOCIETY, 1970.

14398   PARKINS, A.E.   "THE ANTEBELLUM SOUTH: A GEOGRAPHER'S
        INTERPRETATION."   ANNALS OF THE ASSOCIATION OF
        AMERICAN GEOGRAPHERS, 21 (MARCH, 1931):   1-33.

14399   PARKINS, ALMON E.   THE SOUTH: ITS ECONOMIC-GEOGRAPHIC
        DEVELOPMENT.   NEW YORK: JOHN WILEY AND SONS, 1938.

14400   PASSELL, PETER.   "ESSAYS IN THE ECONOMICS OF UNITED
        STATES ANTEBELLUM LAND POLICY."   PH.D. DISSERTATION,
        YALE UNIVERSITY, 1970.

14401   PASSELL, PETER.   "THE IMPACT OF COTTON LAND DISTRIBUTION
        ON THE ANTEBELLUM ECONOMY."   JOURNAL OF ECONOMIC
        HISTORY, 31 (DECEMBER, 1971):   917-937.

14402   PASSELL, PETER AND WRIGHT, GAVIN.   "THE EFFECTS OF
        PRE-CIVIL WAR TERRITORIAL EXPANSION ON THE PRICE OF
        SLAVES."   JOURNAL OF POLITICAL ECONOMY, 80

(NOVEMBER/DECEMBER, 1972): 1183-1202.

14403 PATTERSON, ORLANDO. "THE STRUCTURAL ORIGINS OF SLAVERY:
A CRITIQUE OF THE NIEBOER-DOMAR HYPOTHESIS FROM A
COMPARATIVE PERSPECTIVE." IN RUBIN, VERA AND TUDEN,
ARTHUR (EDS.). COMPARATIVE PERSPECTIVES ON SLAVERY IN
NEW WORLD PLANTATION SOCIETIES. NEW YORK: NEW YORK
ACADEMY OF SCIENCES, 1977, PP. 12-34.

14404 PEASE, JANE H. "A NOTE ON PATTERNS OF CONSPICUOUS
CONSUMPTION AMONG SEABOARD PLANTERS, 1820-1860."
JOURNAL OF SOUTHERN HISTORY, 35 (AUGUST, 1969):
381-393.

14405 PERRY, PERCIVAL. "NAVAL STORES." IN ROLLER, DAVID C.
AND TWYMAN, ROBERT W. (EDS.). THE ENCYCLOPEDIA OF
SOUTHERN HISTORY. BATON ROUGE: LOUISIANA STATE
UNIVERSITY PRESS, 1979, P. 884.

14406 PHILLIPS, ULRICH B. AMERICAN NEGRO SLAVERY: A SURVEY OF
THE SUPPLY, EMPLOYMENT AND CONTROL OF NEGRO LABOR AS
DETERMINED BY THE PLANTATION REGIME. NEW YORK: D.
APPLETON, 1918.

14407 PHILLIPS, ULRICH B. "AN AMERICAN STATE-OWNED RAILROAD."
YALE REVIEW, 15 (NOVEMBER, 1906): 259-282.

14408 PHILLIPS, ULRICH B. "BLACK-BELT LABOR, SLAVE AND FREE."
IN UNIVERSITY OF VIRGINIA, PHELPS-STOKES FELLOWSHIP
PAPERS. LECTURES AND ADDRESSES ON THE NEGRO IN THE
SOUTH. CHARLOTTESVILLE: MICHIE COMPANY, 1915, PP.
29-36.

14409 PHILLIPS, ULRICH B. "CONSERVATISM AND PROGRESS IN THE
COTTON BELT." SOUTH ATLANTIC QUARTERLY, 3 (JANUARY,
1904): 1-10.

14410 PHILLIPS, ULRICH B. "THE DECADENCE OF THE PLANTATION
SYSTEM." ANNALS OF THE AMERICAN ACADEMY OF POLITICAL
AND SOCIAL SCIENCE, 35 (JANUARY, 1910): 37-41.

14411 PHILLIPS, ULRICH B. "THE ECONOMIC COST OF SLAVEHOLDING
IN THE COTTON BELT." POLITICAL SCIENCE QUARTERLY, 20
(JUNE, 1905): 257-275.

14412 PHILLIPS, ULRICH B. "THE ECONOMICS OF SLAVE LABOR IN THE
SOUTH." IN BALLAGH, JAMES C. (ED.). THE SOUTH IN THE
BUILDING OF THE NATION. 12 VOLS. RICHMOND: SOUTHERN
HISTORICAL PUBLICATION SOCIETY, 1909, VOL. 5, PP.
121-124.

14413 PHILLIPS, ULRICH B. "THE ECONOMICS OF THE PLANTATION."
SOUTH ATLANTIC QUARTERLY, 2 (JULY, 1903): 231-236.

14414 PHILLIPS, ULRICH B. "THE ECONOMICS OF THE SLAVE TRADE,

FOREIGN AND DOMESTIC." IN BALLAGH, JAMES C. (ED.).
THE SOUTH IN THE BUILDING OF THE NATION. 12 VOLS.
RICHMOND: SOUTHERN HISTORICAL PUBLICATION SOCIETY,
1909, VOL. 5, PP. 124-129.

14415 PHILLIPS, ULRICH B. "FINANCIAL CRISES IN THE ANTE-BELLUM
       SOUTH." IN BALLAGH, JAMES C. (ED.). THE SOUTH IN THE
       BUILDING OF THE NATION. 12 VOLS. RICHMOND: SOUTHERN
       HISTORICAL PUBLICATION SOCIETY, 1909, VOL. 5, PP.
       435-441.

14416 PHILLIPS, ULRICH B. A HISTORY OF TRANSPORTATION IN THE
       EASTERN COTTON BELT TO 1860. NEW YORK: COLUMBIA
       UNIVERSITY PRESS, 1908.

14417 PHILLIPS, ULRICH B. "A JAMAICA SLAVE PLANTATION."
       AMERICAN HISTORICAL REVIEW, 19 (APRIL, 1914): 543-558.

14418 PHILLIPS, ULRICH B. LIFE AND LABOR IN THE OLD SOUTH.
       BOSTON: LITTLE, BROWN AND COMPANY, 1929.

14419 PHILLIPS, ULRICH B. "MAKING COTTON PAY." WORLD'S WORK,
       8 (MAY, 1904): 4782-4792.

14420 PHILLIPS, ULRICH B. "ON THE ECONOMICS OF SLAVERY,
       1815-1860." ANNUAL REPORT OF THE AMERICAN HISTORICAL
       ASSOCIATION FOR THE YEAR 1912. WASHINGTON:
       GOVERNMENT PRINTING OFFICE, 1914, PP. 150-151.

14421 PHILLIPS, ULRICH B. "THE ORIGIN AND GROWTH OF THE
       SOUTHERN BLACK BELTS." AMERICAN HISTORICAL REVIEW, 11
       (JULY, 1906): 798-816.

14422 PHILLIPS, ULRICH B. "THE OVERPRODUCTION OF COTTON AND A
       POSSIBLE REMEDY." SOUTH ATLANTIC QUARTERLY, 4 (APRIL,
       1905): 148-158.

14423 PHILLIPS, ULRICH B. (ED.). PLANTATION AND FRONTIER
       DOCUMENTS: 1649-1863, ILLUSTRATIVE OF INDUSTRIAL
       HISTORY IN THE COLONIAL AND ANTE-BELLUM SOUTH. 2
       VOLS. CLEVELAND: A.H. CLARK, 1909.

14424 PHILLIPS, ULRICH B. "PLANTATIONS EAST AND WEST OF SUEZ."
       AGRICULTURAL HISTORY, 5 (JULY, 1931): 93-109.

14425 PHILLIPS, ULRICH B. "PLANTATIONS WITH SLAVE LABOR AND
       FREE." AMERICAN HISTORICAL REVIEW, 30 (JULY, 1925):
       738-753.

14426 PHILLIPS, ULRICH B. "THE SLAVE LABOR PROBLEM IN THE
       CHARLESTON DISTRICT." POLITICAL SCIENCE QUARTERLY, 22
       (SEPTEMBER, 1907): 416-439.

14427 PHILLIPS, ULRICH B. "TRANSPORTATION IN THE ANTE-BELLUM
       SOUTH: AN ECONOMIC ANALYSIS." QUARTERLY JOURNAL OF

ECONOMICS, 19 (MAY, 1905): 434-451.

14428 "PLANTATION." IN SCHAPSMEIER, EDWARD L. AND SCHAPSMEIER,
FREDERICK H. ENCYCLOPEDIA OF AMERICAN AGRICULTURAL
HISTORY. WESTPORT: GREENWOOD PRESS, 1975, P. 271.

14429 PREYER, NORRIS W. "THE HISTORIAN, THE SLAVE, AND THE
ANTE-BELLUM TEXTILE INDUSTRY." JOURNAL OF NEGRO
HISTORY, 46 (APRIL, 1961): 67-82.

14430 PRICE, JACOB M. "THE BEGINNINGS OF TOBACCO MANUFACTURE
IN VIRGINIA." VIRGINIA MAGAZINE OF HISTORY AND
BIOGRAPHY, 64 (JANUARY, 1956): 3-29.

14431 "THE PRICE OF SLAVES." BULLETIN OF THE BUSINESS
HISTORICAL SOCIETY, 1 (DECEMBER, 1926): 3-4.

14432 PRUNTY, MERLE JR. "THE RENAISSANCE OF THE SOUTHERN
PLANTATION." GEOGRAPHICAL REVIEW, 45 (OCTOBER, 1955):
459-491.

14433 QUINLAN, JOHN. "NEGRO SLAVERY AND INDUSTRIAL SLAVERY."
CATHOLIC WORLD, 140 (JANUARY, 1935): 482-484.

14434 RAGATZ, LOWELL J. THE FALL OF THE PLANTER CLASS IN THE
BRITISH CARIBBEAN, 1763-1833; A STUDY IN SOCIAL AND
ECONOMIC HISTORY. NEW YORK: CENTURY COMPANY, 1928.

14435 RANSOM, ROGER AND SUTCH, RICHARD. "THE IMPACT OF THE
CIVIL WAR AND OF EMANCIPATION ON SOUTHERN
AGRICULTURE." EXPLORATIONS IN ECONOMIC HISTORY, 12
(JANUARY, 1975): 1-28.

14436 RANSOM, ROGER L. AND SUTCH, RICHARD. "THE EX-SLAVE IN
THE POST-BELLUM SOUTH: A STUDY OF THE ECONOMIC IMPACT
OF RACISM IN A MARKET ENVIRONMENT." JOURNAL OF
ECONOMIC HISTORY, 33 (MARCH, 1973): 131-148.

14437 RANSOM, ROGER L. AND SUTCH, RICHARD. ONE KIND OF
FREEDOM: THE ECONOMIC CONSEQUENCES OF EMANCIPATION.
CAMBRIDGE: CAMBRIDGE UNIVERSITY PRESS, 1977.

14438 REID, JOSEPH D. "SHARECROPPING AS AN UNDERSTANDABLE
MARKET RESPONSE: THE POSTBELLUM SOUTH." JOURNAL OF
ECONOMIC HISTORY, 33 (MARCH, 1973): 106-130.

14439 REIS, JAIME. "ABOLITION AND THE ECONOMICS OF
SLAVEHOLDING IN NORTH EAST BRAZIL." BOLETIN DE
ESTUDIOS LATINOAMERICANOS Y DEL CARIBE, 17 (DECEMBER,
1974): 3-20.

14440 REIS, JAIME. ABOLITION AND THE ECONOMICS OF SLAVEHOLDING
IN NORTH EAST BRAZIL. GLASGOW: INSTITUTE OF LATIN
AMERICAN STUDIES, UNIVERSITY OF GLASGOW, 1974.

14441   "RICE." IN SCHAPSMEIER, EDWARD L. AND SCHAPSMEIER,
         FREDERICK H. ENCYCLOPEDIA OF AMERICAN AGRICULTURAL
         HISTORY. WESTPORT: GREENWOOD PRESS, 1975, P. 295.

14442   RICHARDSON, CORA L. "THE ECONOMIC EFFICIENCY OF SLAVERY
         IN THE SOUTHERN UNITED STATES." M.A. THESIS,
         UNIVERSITY OF GEORGIA, 1939.

14443   ROBBINS, HAL. "SLAVERY IN THE ECONOMY OF MATAGORDA
         COUNTY, TEXAS, 1839-1360." M.A. THESIS, PRAIRIE VIEW
         AGRICULTURAL AND MECHANICAL COLLEGE, 1952.

14444   ROBBINS, I.M. "THE ECONOMIC ASPECTS OF THE NEGRO
         PROBLEM." INTERNATIONAL SOCIALIST REVIEW, 8
         (FEBRUARY-JUNE, 1908): 480-488, 543-554, 614-619,
         691-700, 765-777; 9 (JULY, SEPTEMBER, OCTOBER, 1908):
         51-61, 161-171, 282-292.

14445   ROGERS, GEORGE C., JR. EVOLUTION OF A FEDERALIST:
         WILLIAM LOUGHTON SMITH OF CHARLESTON (1758-1812).
         COLUMBIA: UNIVERSITY OF SOUTH CAROLINA PRESS, 1962.

14446   ROSE, LOUIS A. "CAPITAL LOSSES OF SOUTHERN SLAVEHOLDERS
         DUE TO EMANCIPATION." WESTERN ECONOMIC JOURNAL, 3
         (FALL, 1964): 39-51.

14447   ROTHSTEIN, MORTON. "THE ANTE-BELLUM PLANTATION AS A
         BUSINESS ENTERPRISE: A REVIEW OF SCARBOROUGH'S THE
         OVERSEER." EXPLORATIONS IN ENTREPRENEURIAL HISTORY, 6
         (FALL, 1968): 128-133.

14448   ROTHSTEIN, MORTON. "THE ANTEBELLUM SOUTH AS A DUAL
         ECONOMY: A TENTATIVE HYPOTHESIS." AGRICULTURAL
         HISTORY, 41 (OCTOBER, 1967): 373-382.

14449   ROTHSTEIN, MORTON. "THE CHANGING SOCIAL NETWORKS AND
         INVESTMENT BEHAVIOR OF A SLAVEHOLDING ELITE IN THE
         ANTE BELLUM SOUTH: SOME NATCHEZ 'NABOBS,' 1800-1860."
         IN GREENFIELD, SIDNEY M.; STRICKON, ARNOLD; AND AUBEY,
         ROBERT T. (EDS.). ENTREPRENEURS IN CULTURAL CONTEXT.
         ALBUQUERQUE: UNIVERSITY OF NEW MEXICO PRESS, 1979,
         PP. 65-88.

14450   ROTHSTEIN, MORTON. "MEASUREMENT, CALCULUS, AND
         DIRECTION: PROMETHUS IN THE ANTEBELLUM SOUTHLAND."
         UNPUBLISHED PAPER PRESENTED AT MSSB--UNIVERSITY OF
         ROCHESTER CONFERENCE: "TIME ON THE CROSS: A FIRST
         APPRAISAL," OCTOBER 24-26, 1974.

14451   RUBIN, JULIUS. "THE LIMITS OF AGRICULTURAL PROGRESS IN
         THE NINETEENTH-CENTURY SOUTH." AGRICULTURAL HISTORY,
         49 (APRIL, 1975): 362-373.

14452   RUSSEL, ROBERT R. CRITICAL STUDIES IN ANTEBELLUM
         SECTIONALISM: ESSAYS IN AMERICAN POLITICAL AND

ECONOMIC HISTORY. WESTPORT: GREENWOOD PUBLISHING
COMPANY, 1972.

14453 RUSSEL, ROBERT R. ECONOMIC ASPECTS OF SOUTHERN
SECTIONALISM, 1840-1861. URBANA: UNIVERSITY OF
ILLINOIS PRESS, 1924.

14454 RUSSEL, ROBERT R. "THE ECONOMIC HISTORY OF NEGRO SLAVERY
IN THE UNITED STATES." AGRICULTURAL HISTORY, 11
(OCTOBER, 1937): 308-321.

14455 RUSSEL, ROBERT R. "THE EFFECTS OF SLAVERY UPON
NONSLAVEHOLDERS IN THE ANTE BELLUM SOUTH."
AGRICULTURAL HISTORY, 15 (APRIL, 1941): 112-126.

14456 RUSSEL, ROBERT R. "THE GENERAL EFFECTS OF SLAVERY UPON
SOUTHERN ECONOMIC PROGRESS." JOURNAL OF SOUTHERN
HISTORY, 4 (FEBRUARY, 1938): 39-54.

14457 RYAN, TERRENCE C.I. "THE ECONOMICS OF TRADING IN
SLAVES." PH.D. DISSERTATION, MASSACHUSETTS INSTITUTE
OF TECHNOLOGY, 1975.

14458 SARAYDAR, EDWARD. "A NOTE ON THE PROFITABILITY OF ANTE
BELLUM SLAVERY." SOUTHERN ECONOMIC JOURNAL, 30
(APRIL, 1964): 325-332.

14459 SAUNDERS, EMANUEL. "THE CRISIS OF THE PLANTATION:
CAPITAL OR LABOR, 1834-1917." M.A. THESIS, HOWARD
UNIVERSITY, 1969.

14460 SAYLOR, W. CROMWELL. "EFFECT OF THE COTTON GIN UPON THE
POLITICS OF THE UNITED STATES FROM 1787 TO 1857."
MECHANICAL ENGINEERING, 48 (DECEMBER, 1926):
1397-1401.

14461 SCARBOROUGH, WILLIAM K. (ED.). THE DIARY OF EDMUND
RUFFIN. 2 VOLS. BATON ROUGE: LOUISIANA STATE
UNIVERSITY PRESS, 1972-1976.

14462 SCHMITZ, MARK D. "ECONOMIC ANALYSIS OF ANTEBELLUM SUGAR
PLANTATIONS IN LOUISIANA." PH.D. DISSERTATION,
UNIVERSITY OF NORTH CAROLINA, 1974.

14463 SCHMITZ, MARK D. "ECONOMIES OF SCALE AND FARM SIZE IN
THE ANTEBELLUM SUGAR SECTOR." JOURNAL OF ECONOMIC
HISTORY, 37 (DECEMBER, 1977): 959-980.

14464 SCHMITZ, MARK D. AND SCHAEFER, DONALD F. "SLAVERY,
FREEDOM, AND THE ELASTICITY OF SUBSTITUTION."
EXPLORATIONS IN ECONOMIC HISTORY, 15 (JULY, 1978):
327-337.

14465 SCHULTZ, THEODORE W. "INVESTMENT IN HUMAN CAPITAL."
AMERICAN ECONOMIC REVIEW, 51 (MARCH, 1961): 1-17.

14466   SEAGRAVE, CHARLES E.   "THE SOUTHERN NEGRO AGRICULTURAL
         WORKER, 1850-1870."   JOURNAL OF ECONOMIC HISTORY, 31
         (MARCH, 1971):   279-280.

14467   SHARP, WILLIAM F.   "FORSAKEN BUT FOR GOLD: AN ECONOMIC
         STUDY OF SLAVERY AND MINING IN THE COLOMBIAN CHOCO,
         1680-1810."   PH.D. DISSERTATION, UNIVERSITY OF NORTH
         CAROLINA, 1970.

14468   SHERIDAN, RICHARD B.   "THE PLANTATION REVOLUTION AND THE
         INDUSTRIAL REVOLUTION, 1625-1775."   CARIBBEAN STUDIES,
         9 (OCTOBER, 1969):   5-25.

14469   SHERIDAN, RICHARD B.   SUGAR AND SLAVERY: AN ECONOMIC
         HISTORY OF THE BRITISH WEST INDIES, 1623-1775.
         BARBADOS: CARIBBEAN UNIVERSITIES PRESS, 1974.

14470   SHUGG, ROGER W.   ORIGINS OF CLASS STRUGGLE IN LOUISIANA:
         A SOCIAL HISTORY OF WHITE FARMERS AND LABORERS DURING
         SLAVERY AND AFTER, 1840-1875.   UNIVERSITY, LA:
         LOUISIANA STATE UNIVERSITY PRESS, 1939.

14471   SIMON, JULIAN L.   "THE WORTH TODAY OF UNITED STATES
         SLAVES' IMPUTED WAGES."   JOURNAL OF ECONOMIC ISSUES, 5
         (SEPTEMBER, 1971):   110-113.

14472   SIMONS, A.M.   "ECONOMIC ASPECTS OF CHATTEL SLAVERY IN
         AMERICA."   INTERNATIONAL SOCIALIST REVIEW, 4 (JULY,
         AUGUST, SEPTEMBER, 1903):   25-33, 95-105, 164-173.

14473   SINZHEIMER, G.P.G.   "THE ECONOMICS OF RUSSIAN SERFDOM AND
         THE ECONOMICS OF AMERICAN SLAVERY--A HISTORICAL
         COMPARISON."   JAHRBUCHER FUR GESCHICHTE OSTEUROPAS, 14
         (1966):   513-528.

14474   SITTERSON, J.C.   "THE SUGAR INDUSTRY IN THE OLD SOUTH."
         M.A. THESIS, UNIVERSITY OF NORTH CAROLINA, 1932.

14475   SITTERSON, J. CARLYLE.   "ANTE-BELLUM SUGAR CULTURE IN THE
         SOUTH ATLANTIC STATES."   JOURNAL OF SOUTHERN HISTORY,
         3 (MAY, 1937):   175-187.

14476   SITTERSON, J. CARLYLE.   "FINANCING AND MARKETING THE
         SUGAR CROP OF THE OLD SOUTH."   JOURNAL OF SOUTHERN
         HISTORY, 10 (MAY, 1944):   188-199.

14477   SITTERSON, J. CARLYLE.   "THE TRANSITION FROM SLAVE TO
         FREE ECONOMY ON THE WILLIAM J. MINOR PLANTATIONS."
         AGRICULTURAL HISTORY, 17 (OCTOBER, 1943):   216-224.

14478   SITTERSON, JOSEPH C.   SUGAR COUNTRY: THE CANE SUGAR
         INDUSTRY IN THE SOUTH, 1753-1950.   LEXINGTON:
         UNIVERSITY OF KENTUCKY PRESS, 1953.

14479   "SLAVE GANG."   IN NUNEZ, BENJAMIN.   DICTIONARY OF

AFRO-LATIN AMERICAN CIVILIZATION. WESTPORT:
GREENWOOD PRESS, 1980, P. 435.

14480 "SLAVE LABOR: EFFECTS ON AMERICAN ECONOMY (1630-1750)."
       IN RYWELL, MARTIN (ED.). AFRO-AMERICAN ENCYCLOPEDIA.
       10 VOLS. NORTH MIAMI: EDUCATIONAL BOOK PUBLISHERS,
       1974, VOL. 8, PP. 2430-2431.

14481 "SLAVE PRICE." IN NUNEZ, BENJAMIN. DICTIONARY OF
       AFRO-LATIN AMERICAN CIVILIZATION. WESTPORT:
       GREENWOOD PRESS, 1980, P. 437.

14482 "SLAVE WORKDAY." IN NUNEZ, BENJAMIN. DICTIONARY OF
       AFRO-LATIN AMERICAN CIVILIZATION. WESTPORT:
       GREENWOOD PRESS, 1980, P. 438.

14483 "SLAVES: HIERARCHY OF OCCUPATIONS." IN RYWELL, MARTIN
       (ED.). AFRO-AMERICAN ENCYCLOPEDIA. 10 VOLS. NORTH
       MIAMI: EDUCATIONAL BOOK PUBLISHERS, 1974, VOL. 8, PP.
       2487-2489.

14484 "SLAVES ON A FEDERAL PROJECT." BULLETIN OF THE BUSINESS
       HISTORICAL SOCIETY, 8 (MARCH, 1934): 32-33.

14485 "SLAVOCRACIA." IN NUNEZ, BENJAMIN. DICTIONARY OF
       AFRO-LATIN AMERICAN CIVILIZATION. WESTPORT:
       GREENWOOD PRESS, 1980, P. 439.

14486 SLENES, ROBERT W. "THE DEMOGRAPHY AND ECONOMICS OF
       BRAZILIAN SLAVERY: 1850-1888." PH.D. DISSERTATION,
       STANFORD UNIVERSITY, 1976.

14487 SMITH, ALFRED G., JR. "ECONOMIC READJUSTMENT OF AN OLD
       COTTON STATE: SOUTH CAROLINA, 1820-1860." PH.D.
       DISSERTATION, COLUMBIA UNIVERSITY, 1954.

14488 SMITH, ROBERT W. "WAS SLAVERY UNPROFITABLE IN THE
       ANTE-BELLUM SOUTH?" AGRICULTURAL HISTORY, 20
       (JANUARY, 1946): 62-64.

14489 SOLTOW, LEE. "ECONOMIC INEQUALITY IN THE UNITED STATES
       IN THE PERIOD FROM 1790 TO 1860." JOURNAL OF ECONOMIC
       HISTORY, 31 (DECEMBER, 1971): 822-839.

14490 SPENGLER, J.J. "MALTHUSIANISM AND THE DEBATE ON
       SLAVERY." SOUTH ATLANTIC QUARTERLY, 34 (APRIL, 1935):
       170-189.

14491 STAROBIN, ROBERT S. "THE ECONOMICS OF INDUSTRIAL SLAVERY
       IN THE OLD SOUTH." BUSINESS HISTORY REVIEW, 44
       (SUMMER, 1970): 131-174.

14492 STAROBIN, ROBERT S. INDUSTRIAL SLAVERY IN THE OLD SOUTH.
       NEW YORK: OXFORD UNIVERSITY PRESS, 1970.

14493   STARR, CHESTER G. "AN OVERDOSE OF SLAVERY." JOURNAL OF
         ECONOMIC HISTORY, 18 (MARCH, 1958):   17-32.

14494   STECKEL, RICHARD. "THE ECONOMICS OF U.S. SLAVE AND
         SOUTHERN FREE-WHITE FERTILITY." UNPUBLISHED PAPER,
         UNIVERSITY OF CHICAGO, 1973.

14495   STECKEL, RICHARD H. "THE ECONOMICS OF THE UNITED STATES
         SLAVE AND SOUTHERN WHITE FERTILITY." PH.D.
         DISSERTATION, JNIVERSITY OF CHICAGO, 1977.

14496   STETSON, KENNETH W. "A QUANTITATIVE APPROACH TO
         BRITAIN'S AMERICAN SLAVE TRADE, 1770-1773." M.S.
         THESIS, UNIVERSITY OF WISCONSIN, 1967.

14497   STIVERSON, GREGORY A. "EARLY AMERICAN FARMING: A
         COMMENT." AGRICULTURAL HISTORY, 50 (JANUARY, 1976):
         37-44.

14498   STONE, ALFRED H. "THE COTTON FACTORAGE SYSTEM OF THE
         SOUTHERN STATES." AMERICAN HISTORICAL REVIEW, 25
         (APRIL, 1915):   557-565.

14499   STONE, ALFRED H. "SOME PROBLEMS OF SOUTHERN ECONOMIC
         HISTORY." AMERICAN HISTORICAL REVIEW, 13 (JULY,
         1908):   779-797.

14500   STUBBS, W.C. CULTIVATION OF SUGAR CANE, IN TWO
         PARTS--PART I, SUGAR CANE: A TREATISE ON ITS HISTORY,
         BOTANY AND AGRICULTURE. PART II, SUGAR CANE: ITS
         HISTORY IN GEORGIA AND SOUTH CAROLINA, 1767-1900, WITH
         RECOLLECTIONS OF HOPETON PLANTATION, BY O.G. PURSE.
         SAVANNAH: MORNING NEWS PRINT, 1900.

14501   STUBBS, WILLIAM C. "SUGAR PRODUCTS IN THE SOUTH." IN
         BALLAGH, JAMES C. (ED.). THE SOUTH IN THE BUILDING OF
         THE NATION. 12 VOLS. RICHMOND: SOUTHERN HISTORICAL
         PUBLICATION SOCIETY, 1909, VOL. 5, PP. 184-197.

14502   "SUGAR CANE." IN SCHAPSMEIER, EDWARD L. AND SCHAPSMEIER,
         FREDERICK. ENCYCLOPEDIA OF AMERICAN AGRICULTURAL
         HISTORY. WESTPORT: GREENWOOD PRESS, 1975, P. 335.

14503   SUTCH, RICHARD. THE BREEDING OF SLAVES FOR SALE AND THE
         WESTERN EXPANSION OF SLAVERY, 1850-1860. SOUTHERN
         ECONOMIC HISTORY PROJECT WORKING PAPER SERIES NO. 10.
         BERKELEY: UNIVERSITY OF CALIFORNIA, INSTITUTE OF
         BUSINESS AND ECONOMIC RESEARCH, 1972.

14504   SUTCH, RICHARD. "THE BREEDING OF SLAVES FOR SALE AND THE
         WESTWARD EXPANSION OF SLAVERY, 1850-1860." IN
         ENGERMAN, STANLEY L. AND GENOVESE, EUGENE D. (EDS.).
         RACE AND SLAVERY IN THE WESTERN HEMISPHERE:
         QUANTITATIVE STUDIES. PRINCETON: PRINCETON
         UNIVERSITY PRESS, 1975, PP. 173-210.

14505   SUTCH, RICHARD AND RANSOM, ROGER. "SHARECROPPING:
        MARKET RESPONSE OR MECHANISM OF RACE CONTROL?" IN
        SANSING, DAVID G. (ED.). WHAT WAS FREEDOM'S PRICE?
        JACKSON: UNIVERSITY PRESS OF MISSISSIPPI, 1978, PP.
        51-70.

14506   SWAN, DALE E. THE STRUCTURE AND PROFITABILITY OF THE
        ANTEBELLUM RICE INDUSTRY, 1859. NEW YORK: ARNO
        PRESS, 1975.

14507   SWAN, DALE E. "THE STRUCTURE AND PROFITABILITY OF THE
        ANTEBELLUM RICE INDUSTRY: 1859." PH.D. DISSERTATION,
        UNIVERSITY OF NORTH CAROLINA, 1972.

14508   TANG, ANTHONY M. ECONOMIC DEVELOPMENT IN THE SOUTHERN
        PIEDMONT, 1860-1950: ITS IMPACT ON AGRICULTURE.
        CHAPEL HILL: UNIVERSITY OF NORTH CAROLINA PRESS, 1958.

14509   TARLTON, DEWITT T. "THE HISTORY OF THE COTTON INDUSTRY
        IN TEXAS, 1920-1850." M.A. THESIS, UNIVERSITY OF
        TEXAS, 1923.

14510   TAYLOR, GEORGE R. THE TRANSPORTATION REVOLUTION,
        1815-1860. NEW YORK: HOLT, RINEHART AND WINSTON,
        1951.

14511   TAYLOR, KIT S. "THE ECONOMICS OF SUGAR AND SLAVERY IN
        NORTHEAST BRAZIL." AGRICULTURAL HISTORY, 44 (JULY,
        1970): 267-280.

14512   TAYLOR, PAUL S. "PLANTATION AGRICULTURE IN THE UNITED
        STATES: SEVENTEENTH TO TWENTIETH CENTURIES." LAND
        ECONOMICS, 30 (MAY, 1954): 141-152.

14513   TAYLOR, PAUL S. "PLANTATION LABORER BEFORE THE CIVIL
        WAR." AGRICULTURAL HISTORY, 28 (JANUARY, 1954): 1-20.

14514   TAYLOR, PAUL S. SLAVE TO FREEDMAN. BERKELEY: INSTITUTE
        OF BUSINESS AND ECONOMIC RESEARCH, UNIVERSITY OF
        CALIFORNIA, 1970.

14515   TAYLOR, ROSSER H. SLAVEHOLDING IN NORTH CAROLINA: AN
        ECONOMIC VIEW. CHAPEL HILL: UNIVERSITY OF NORTH
        CAROLINA PRESS, 1926.

14516   TEMIN, PETER. "THE CAUSES OF COTTON PRICE FLUCTUATIONS
        IN THE 1830'S." REVIEW OF ECONOMICS AND STATISTICS,
        49 (NOVEMBER, 1967): 463-470.

14517   THOMPSON, EDGAR. "THE PLANTATION." PH.D. DISSERTATION,
        UNIVERSITY OF CHICAGO, 1932.

14518   THOMPSON, EDGAR T. "THE CLIMATIC THEORY OF THE
        PLANTATION." AGRICULTURAL HISTORY, 15 (JANUARY,
        1941): 49-60.

14519   THOMPSON, EDGAR T.   "THE NATURAL HISTORY OF AGRICULTURAL
        LABOR IN THE SOUTH."   IN JACKSON, DAVID K. (ED.).
        AMERICAN STUDIES IN HONOR OF WILLIAM KENNETH BOYD.
        DURHAM: DUKE UNIVERSITY PRESS, 1940, PP. 110-174.

14520   THOMPSON, EDGAR T.   "THE PLANTATION AS A SOCIAL SYSTEM."
        PLANTATION SYSTEMS OF THE NEW WORLD.   WASHINGTON: PAN
        AMERICAN UNION, 1959, PP. 26-36.

14521   "THOSE BIG SLAVE OWNERS."   SOUTHERN FARM MAGAZINE, 10
        (JUNE, 1902):   16-17.

14522   "TOBACCO."   IN SCHAPSMEIER, EDWARD L. AND SCHAPSMEIER,
        FREDERICK.   ENCYCLOPEDIA OF AMERICAN AGRICULTURAL
        HISTORY.   WESTPORT: GREENWOOD PRESS, 1975, P. 347.

14523   TREXLER, HARRISON A.   SLAVERY IN MISSOURI, 1804-1865.
        BALTIMORE: JOHNS HOPKINS PRESS, 1914.

14524   TREXLER, HARRISON A.   "SLAVERY IN MISSOURI, 1804-1865."
        PH.D. DISSERTATION, JOHNS HOPKINS UNIVERSITY, 1914.

14525   TREXLER, HARRISON A.   "THE VALUE AND THE SALE OF THE
        MISSOURI SLAVE."   MISSOURI HISTORICAL REVIEW, 8
        (JANUARY, 1914):   69-85.

14526   TROUTMAN, RICHARD L.   "THE SOCIAL AND ECONOMIC STRUCTURE
        OF KENTUCKY AGRICULTURE, 1850-1860."   PH.D.
        DISSERTATION, UNIVERSITY OF KENTUCKY, 1958.

14527   TURNER, FREDERICK J.   "THE SOUTH, 1820-1830."   AMERICAN
        HISTORICAL REVIEW, 11 (APRIL, 1906):   559-573.

14528   VAN DEUSEN, JOHN G.   ECONOMIC BASES OF DISUNION IN SOUTH
        CAROLINA.   NEW YORK: COLUMBIA UNIVERSITY PRESS, 1928.

14529   VANCE, RUPERT B.   HUMAN FACTORS IN COTTON CULTURE: A
        STUDY IN THE SOCIAL GEOGRAPHY OF THE AMERICAN SOUTH.
        CHAPEL HILL: UNIVERSITY OF NORTH CAROLINA PRESS,
        1929.

14530   VANRIEL, WESLEY B.   "THE POLITICAL ECONOMY OF NEW WORLD
        SLAVERY."   M.S. THESIS, UNIVERSITY OF THE WEST INDIES,
        1979.

14531   VEDDER, RICHARD K.   "THE SLAVE EXPLOITATION
        (EXPROPRIATION) RATE."   EXPLORATIONS IN ECONOMIC
        HISTORY, 12 (OCTOBER, 1975):   453-457.

14532   VEDDER, RICHARD K.; KLINGAMAN, DAVID C.; AND GALLAWAY,
        LOWELL E.   "THE PROFITABILITY OF ANTE-BELLUM
        AGRICULTURE IN THE COTTON BELT: SOME NEW EVIDENCE."
        ATLANTIC ECONOMIC JOURNAL, 2 (NOVEMBER, 1974):   30-47.

14533   VERLINDEN, CHARLES.   "MEDIEVAL 'SLAVERS.'"   EXPLORATIONS

IN ECONOMIC HISTORY, 7 (FALL-WINTER, 1969): 1-14.

14534   WALL, BENNETT H. "EBENEZER PETTIGREW, AN ECONOMIC STUDY
        OF AN ANTE-BELLUM PLANTER." PH.D. DISSERTATION,
        UNIVERSITY OF NORTH CAROLINA, 1947.

14535   WALL, BENNETT H. "EBENEZER PETTIGREW'S EFFORTS TO
        CONTROL THE MARKETING OF HIS CROPS." AGRICULTURAL
        HISTORY, 27 (OCTOBER, 1953): 123-132.

14536   WALLACE, DAVID D. "SOUTHERN AGRICULTURE: ITS CONDITION
        AND NEEDS." POPULAR SCIENCE MONTHLY, 64 (JANUARY,
        1904): 245-261.

14537   WALLENSTEIN, PETER. "FROM SLAVE SOUTH TO NEW SOUTH:
        TAXES AND SPENDING IN GEORGIA FROM 1850 THROUGH
        RECONSTRUCTION." JOURNAL OF ECONOMIC HISTORY, 36
        (MARCH, 1976): 287-290.

14538   WALLENSTEIN, PETER R. "FROM SLAVE SOUTH TO NEW SOUTH:
        TAXES AND SPENDING IN GEORGIA FROM 1850 THROUGH
        RECONSTRUCTION." PH.D. DISSERTATION, JOHNS HOPKINS
        UNIVERSITY, 1973.

14539   WALLERSTEIN, IMMANUEL. "THE THREE STAGES OF AFRICAN
        INVOLVEMENT IN THE WORLD-ECONOMY." IN GUTKIND, PETER
        C.W. AND WALLERSTEIN (EDS.). THE POLITICAL ECONOMY OF
        CONTEMPORARY AFRICA. BEVERLY HILLS: SAGE
        PUBLICATIONS, 1976, PP. 30-57.

14540   WASHINGTON, BOOKER T. "THE AMERICAN NEGRO AND HIS
        ECONOMIC VALUE." INTERNATIONAL MONTHLY, 2 (DECEMBER,
        1900): 672-686.

14541   WASHINGTON, BOOKER T. "THE ECONOMIC DEVELOPMENT OF THE
        NEGRO RACE IN SLAVERY." IN WASHINGTON AND DUBOIS,
        W.E.B. THE NEGRO IN THE SOUTH. PHILADELPHIA: GEORGE
        W. JACOBS AND COMPANY, 1907, PP. 7-42.

14542   WASHINGTON, BOOKER T. "THE ECONOMIC DEVELOPMENT OF THE
        NEGRO RACE SINCE ITS EMANCIPATION." IN WASHINGTON AND
        DUBOIS, W.E.B. THE NEGRO IN THE SOUTH. PHILADELPHIA:
        GEORGE W. JACOBS AND COMPANY, 1907, PP. 43-75.

14543   WHARTENBY, FRANKLEE. "LAND AND LABOR PRODUCTIVITY IN
        U.S. COTTON PRODUCTION, 1800-1840." PH.D.
        DISSERTATION, UNIVERSITY OF NORTH CAROLINA, 1963.

14544   WHITE, HENRY C. "THE PLANTATION AND FARM SYSTEMS IN
        SOUTHERN AGRICULTURE." IN BALLAGH, JAMES C. (ED.).
        THE SOUTH IN THE BUILDING OF THE NATION. 12 VOLS.
        RICHMOND: SOUTHERN HISTORICAL PUBLICATION SOCIETY,
        1909, VOL. 5, PP. 73-85.

14545   WILEY, BELL I. "SALIENT CHANGES IN SOUTHERN AGRICULTURE

SINCE THE CIVIL WAR." AGRICULTURAL HISTORY, 13
(APRIL, 1939): 65-76.

14546 WILEY, BELL I. "VICISSITUDES OF EARLY RECONSTRUCTION
FARMING IN THE LOWER MISSISSIPPI VALLEY." JOURNAL OF
SOUTHERN HISTORY, 3 (NOVEMBER, 1937): 441-452.

14547 WILLIAMS, E.E. "THE ECONOMIC ASPECT OF THE ABOLITION OF
THE WEST INDIAN SLAVE TRADE AND SLAVERY." PH.D.
DISSERTATION, UNIVERSITY OF OXFORD, 1938.

14548 WILLIAMS, ERIC. CAPITALISM AND SLAVERY. CHAPEL HILL:
UNIVERSITY OF NORTH CAROLINA PRESS, 1944.

14549 WILLIAMS, ERIC. "LAISSEZ FAIRE, SUGAR AND SLAVERY."
POLITICAL SCIENCE QUARTERLY, 58 (MARCH, 1943): 67-85.

14550 WOODMAN, HAROLD D. "ITINERANT COTTON MERCHANTS OF THE
ANTEBELLUM SOUTH." AGRICULTURAL HISTORY, 40 (APRIL,
1966): 79-90.

14551 WOODMAN, HAROLD D. "KING COTTON AND HIS RETAINERS: A
STUDY OF COTTON MARKETING IN THE SOUTH." PH.D.
DISSERTATION, UNIVERSITY OF CHICAGO, 1964.

14552 WOODMAN, HAROLD D. KING COTTON AND HIS RETAINERS:
FINANCING AND MARKETING THE COTTON CROPS OF THE SOUTH,
1800-1925. LEXINGTON: UNIVERSITY OF KENTUCKY PRESS,
1968.

14553 WOODMAN, HAROLD D. "NEW PERSPECTIVES ON SOUTHERN
ECONOMIC DEVELOPMENT: A COMMENT." AGRICULTURAL
HISTORY, 49 (APRIL, 1975): 374-380.

14554 WOODWARD, C. VANN. "SOUTHERN SLAVES IN THE WORLD OF
THOMAS MALTHUS." AMERICAN COUNTERPOINT: SLAVERY AND
RACISM IN THE NORTH-SOUTH DIALOGUE. BOSTON: LITTLE,
BROWN AND COMPANY, 1964, PP. 78-106.

14555 WOOLFOLK, GEORGE R. "PLANTER CAPITALISM AND SLAVERY:
THE LABOR THESIS." JOURNAL OF NEGRO HISTORY, 41
(APRIL, 1956): 103-116.

14556 WOOLFOLK, GEORGE R. "TAXES AND SLAVERY IN THE ANTE
BELLUM SOUTH." JOURNAL OF SOUTHERN HISTORY, 26 (MAY,
1960): 180-200.

14557 WOOSTER, RALPH A. "WEALTHY SOUTHERNERS ON THE EVE OF THE
CIVIL WAR." IN GALLAGHER, GARY W. (ED.). ESSAYS ON
SOUTHERN HISTORY WRITTEN IN HONOR OF BARNES F.
LATHROP. AUSTIN: GENERAL LIBRARIES, UNIVERSITY OF
TEXAS, 1980, PP. 131-160.

14558 WRIGHT, GAVIN. "AN ECONOMETRIC STUDY OF COTTON
PRODUCTION AND TRADE, 1830-1860." REVIEW OF ECONOMICS

AND STATISTICS, 53 (MAY, 1971): 111-120.

14559   WRIGHT, GAVIN. "'ECONOMIC DEMOCRACY' AND THE
        CONCENTRATION OF AGRICULTURAL WEALTH IN THE COTTON
        SOUTH, 1850-1860." AGRICULTURAL HISTORY, 44 (JANUARY,
        1970): 63-94.

14560   WRIGHT, GAVIN. "THE ECONOMICS OF COTTON IN THE
        ANTEBELLUM SOUTH." PH.D. DISSERTATION, YALE
        UNIVERSITY, 1969.

14561   WRIGHT, GAVIN. "THE EFFICIENCY OF SLAVERY: ANOTHER
        INTERPRETATION." AMERICAN ECONOMIC REVIEW, 69 (MARCH,
        1979): 219-226.

14562   WRIGHT, GAVIN. "NEW AND OLD VIEWS ON THE ECONOMICS OF
        SLAVERY." JOURNAL OF ECONOMIC HISTORY, 33 (JUNE,
        1973): 452-466.

14563   WRIGHT, GAVIN. THE POLITICAL ECONOMY OF THE COTTON
        SOUTH: HOUSEHOLDS, MARKETS, AND WEALTH IN THE
        NINETEENTH CENTURY. NEW YORK: W.W. NORTON, 1978.

14564   WRIGHT, GAVIN. "SLAVERY AND THE COTTON BOOM."
        EXPLORATIONS IN ECONOMIC HISTORY, 12 (OCTOBER, 1975):
        439-451.

14565   WRIGHT, GAVIN AND KUNREUTHER, HOWARD. "COTTON, CORN AND
        RISK IN THE NINETEENTH CENTURY." JOURNAL OF ECONOMIC
        HISTORY, 25 (SEPTEMBER, 1975): 526-551.

14566   YARBROUGH, WILLIAM H. ECONOMIC ASPECTS OF SLAVERY IN
        RELATION TO SOUTHERN AND SOUTHWESTERN MIGRATION.
        NASHVILLE: GEORGE PEABODY COLLEGE FOR TEACHERS, 1932.

14567   YARBROUGH, WILLIAM H. "ECONOMIC ASPECTS OF SLAVERY IN
        RELATION TO SOUTHERN AND SOUTHWESTERN MIGRATION."
        PH.D. DISSERTATION, GEORGE PEABODY COLLEGE FOR
        TEACHERS, 1932.

14568   YASUBA, YASUKICHI. "THE PROFITABILITY AND VIABILITY OF
        PLANTATION SLAVERY IN THE UNITED STATES." ECONOMIC
        STUDIES QUARTERLY, 12 (SEPTEMBER, 1961): 60-67.

14569   YEO, C.A. "THE ECONOMICS OF ROMAN AND AMERICAN SLAVERY."
        FINANZARCHIV, 13 (1952): 445-485.

14570   ZEPP, THOMAS M. "ON RETURNS TO SCALE AND INPUT
        SUBSTITUTABILITY IN SLAVE AGRICULTURE." EXPLORATIONS
        IN ECONOMIC HISTORY, 13 (APRIL, 1976): 165-178.

PROFITABILITY OF SLAVERY

14571 AITKEN, HUGH G.J. (ED.). DID SLAVERY PAY? READINGS IN THE ECONOMICS OF BLACK SLAVERY IN THE UNITED STATES. BOSTON: HOUGHTON MIFFLIN COMPANY, 1971.

14572 AUFHAUSER, R. KEITH. "PROFITABILITY OF SLAVERY IN THE BRITISH CARIBBEAN." JOURNAL OF INTERDISCIPLINARY HISTORY, 5 (SUMMER, 1974): 45-68.

14573 BARRINGER, PAUL B. "MEMORANDA FOR ADDRESS BEFORE RADFORD CHAPTER OF THE U.D.C.: THE OLD SOUTH AND HOW IT MET THE BLOCKADE IN '65. THE PLANTATION. THE SOCIAL AND ECONOMIC UNIT OF THE SOUTH." UNPUBLISHED MANUSCRIPT, N.D., BARRINGER FAMILY PAPERS, UNIVERSITY OF VIRGINIA.

14574 BELL, RUDOLPH M. "SLAVERY AS AN INVESTMENT: DOLLARS AND HUMANS." HISTORICAL METHODS NEWSLETTER, 10 (DECEMBER, 1976): 1-9.

14575 BUTLIN, NOEL G. ANTE-BELLUM SLAVERY--A CRITIQUE OF A DEBATE. CANBERRA, AUSTRALIA: DEPARTMENT OF ECONOMIC HISTORY, RESEARCH SCHOOL OF SOCIAL SCIENCES, AUSTRALIAN NATIONAL UNIVERSITY, 1971.

14576 CAMPBELL, RANDOLPH B. "LOCAL ARCHIVES AS A SOURCE OF SLAVE PRICES: HARRISON COUNTY, TEXAS AS A TEST CASE." HISTORIAN, 36 (AUGUST, 1974): 660-669.

14577 CAMPBELL, RANDOLPH B. "THE PRODUCTIVITY OF SLAVE LABOR IN EAST TEXAS: A RESEARCH NOTE." LOUISIANA STUDIES, 13 (SUMMER, 1974): 154-172.

14578 CANARELLA, GIORGIO AND TOMASKE, JOHN A. "THE OPTIMAL UTILIZATION OF SLAVES." JOURNAL OF ECONOMIC HISTORY, 35 (SEPTEMBER, 1975): 621-629.

14579 "CONDITIONS BEFORE THE CIVIL WAR." SOUTHWESTERN CHRISTIAN ADVOCATE, 34 (FEBRUARY 16, 1899): 14.

14580 CONRAD, ALFRED H. AND MEYER, JOHN R. "THE ECONOMICS OF SLAVERY IN THE ANTE BELLUM SOUTH." JOURNAL OF POLITICAL ECONOMY, 66 (APRIL, 1958): 95-130.

14581 CONRAD, ALFRED H. AND MEYER, JOHN R. "THE ECONOMICS OF SLAVERY IN THE ANTEBELLUM SOUTH." THE ECONOMICS OF SLAVERY AND OTHER ESSAYS IN ECONOMETRIC HISTORY. CHICAGO: ALDINE PUBLISHING COMPANY, 1964, PP. 43-92.

14582 CONRAD, ALFRED H. AND MEYER, JOHN R. "A POLEMICAL POSTSCRIPT ON ECONOMIC GROWTH." THE ECONOMICS OF SLAVERY AND OTHER STUDIES IN ECONOMETRIC HISTORY. CHICAGO: ALDINE PUBLISHING COMPANY, 1964, PP. 223-236.

14583 CONRAD, ALFRED H. AND MEYER, JOHN R. "REPLY." JOURNAL

OF POLITICAL ECONOMY, 66 (OCTOBER, 1958):   442-443.

14584   CONRAD, ALFRED H. AND MEYER, JOHN R.   "REPLY."   JOURNAL
        OF POLITICAL ECONOMY, 68 (APRIL, 1960):   187-189.

14585   DAVID, PAUL A. AND TEMIN, PETER.   "EXPLAINING THE
        RELATIVE EFFICIENCY OF SLAVE AGRICULTURE IN THE
        ANTEBELLUM SOUTH: COMMENT."   AMERICAN ECONOMIC
        REVIEW, 69 (MARCH, 1979):   213-218.

14586   DOWD, DOUGLAS F.   "THE ECONOMICS OF SLAVERY IN THE
        ANTE-BELLUM SOUTH: A COMMENT."   JOURNAL OF POLITICAL
        ECONOMY, 66 (OCTOBER, 1958):   440-442.

14587   DYER, G.W.   DEMOCRACY IN THE SOUTH BEFORE THE CIVIL WAR.
        NASHVILLE: M.E. SOUTH PUBLISHING COMPANY, 1905.

14588   EATON, CLEMENT.   "SLAVE-HIRING IN THE UPPER SOUTH: A
        STEP TOWARD FREEDOM."   MISSISSIPPI VALLEY HISTORICAL
        REVIEW, 46 (MARCH, 1960):   663-678.

14589   FOGEL, ROBERT W.   "THE LIMITS OF QUANTITATIVE METHODS IN
        HISTORY."   AMERICAN HISTORICAL REVIEW, 80 (APRIL,
        1975):   329-350.

14590   FOGEL, ROBERT W. AND ENGERMAN, STANLEY L.   "A COMPARISON
        OF THE RELATIVE EFFICIENCY OF SLAVE AND FREE
        AGRICULTURE IN THE UNITED STATES DURING 1860."   PAPERS
        AND PROCEEDINGS OF THE FIFTH INTERNATIONAL CONFERENCE
        OF ECONOMIC HISTORY.   8 VOLS.   PARIS: MOUTON
        PUBLISHERS, 1970, VOL. 7, PP. 141-146.

14591   FOGEL, ROBERT W. AND ENGERMAN, STANLEY L.   "THE ECONOMICS
        OF SLAVERY."   IN FOGEL AND ENGERMAN (EDS.).   THE
        REINTERPRETATION OF AMERICAN ECONOMIC HISTORY.   NEW
        YORK: HARPER & ROW, 1971, PP. 311-341.

14592   FOGEL, ROBERT W. AND ENGERMAN, STANLEY L.   "EXPLAINING
        THE RELATIVE EFFICIENCY OF SLAVE AGRICULTURE IN THE
        ANTEBELLUM SOUTH."   AMERICAN ECONOMIC REVIEW, 67
        (JUNE, 1977):   275-296.

14593   FOGEL, ROBERT W. AND ENGERMAN, STANLEY L.   "EXPLAINING
        THE RELATIVE EFFICIENCY OF SLAVE AGRICULTURE IN THE
        ANTEBELLUM SOUTH: REPLY."   AMERICAN ECONOMIC REVIEW,
        70 (SEPTEMBER, 1980):   672-690.

14594   FOGEL, ROBERT W. AND ENGERMAN, STANLEY L.   TIME ON THE
        CROSS: THE ECONOMICS OF AMERICAN NEGRO SLAVERY.   2
        VOLS.   BOSTON: LITTLE, BROWN AND COMPANY, 1974.

14595   FOUST, JAMES D. AND SWAN, DALE E.   "PRODUCTIVITY AND
        PROFITABILITY OF ANTEBELLUM SLAVE LABOR: A
        MICRO-APPROACH."   AGRICULTURAL HISTORY, 44 (JANUARY,
        1970):   39-62.

14596   GENOVESE, EUGENE D. "THE LOW PRODUCTIVITY OF SOUTHERN SLAVE LABOR: CAUSES AND EFFECTS." CIVIL WAR HISTORY, 9 (DECEMBER, 1963): 365-382.

14597   GENOVESE, EUGENE D. "THE MEDICAL AND INSURANCE COSTS OF SLAVEHOLDING IN THE COTTON BELT." JOURNAL OF NEGRO HISTORY, 45 (JULY, 1960): 141-155.

14598   GENOVESE, EUGENE D. "PLANTATION SLAVERY: ITS UNPROFITABILITY AND ITS RELATIONSHIP TO CAPITALISM." M.A. THESIS, COLUMBIA UNIVERSITY, 1955.

14599   GENOVESE, EUGENE D. THE POLITICAL ECONOMY OF SLAVERY: STUDIES IN THE ECONOMY AND SOCIETY OF THE SLAVE SOUTH. NEW YORK: VINTAGE, 1961.

14600   GOVAN, THOMAS P. "WAS PLANTATION SLAVERY PROFITABLE?" JOURNAL OF SOUTHERN HISTORY, 8 (NOVEMBER, 1942): 513-535.

14601   GRAY, LEWIS C. "ECONOMIC EFFICIENCY AND COMPETITIVE ADVANTAGES OF SLAVERY UNDER THE PLANTATION SYSTEM." AGRICULTURAL HISTORY, 4 (MARCH, 1930): 31-47.

14602   GRAY, LEWIS C. "THE GENESIS AND EXPANSION OF THE PLANTATION SYSTEM IN THE SOUTHERN STATES OF NORTH AMERICA DURING THE COLONIAL PERIOD." PH.D. DISSERTATION, UNIVERSITY OF WISCONSIN, 1911.

14603   GRAY, LEWIS C. HISTORY OF AGRICULTURE IN THE SOUTHERN UNITED STATES TO 1860. 2 VOLS. WASHINGTON: CARNEGIE INSTITUTION OF WASHINGTON, 1932.

14604   GRAY, RALPH AND WOOD, BETTY. "THE TRANSITION FROM INDENTURED TO INVOLUNTARY SERVITUDE IN COLONIAL GEORGIA." EXPLORATIONS IN ECONOMIC HISTORY, 13 (OCTOBER, 1976): 353-370.

14605   GREENBERG, MICHAEL. "THE NEW ECONOMIC HISTORY AND THE UNDERSTANDING OF SLAVERY: A METHODOLOGICAL CRITIQUE." DIALECTICAL ANTHROPOLOGY, 2 (MAY, 1977): 131-141.

14606   GREEN-PEDERSEN, SVEND E. "THE HISTORY OF THE DANISH NEGRO SLAVE TRADE, 1733-1807. AN INTERIM SURVEY RELATING IN PARTICULAR TO ITS VOLUME, STRUCTURE, PROFITABILITY AND ABOLITION." REVUE FRANCAISE D'HISTOIRE D'OUTRE-MER, 62 (1975): 196-220.

14607   HASKELL, THOMAS L. "EXPLAINING THE RELATIVE EFFICIENCY OF SLAVE AGRICULTURE IN THE ANTEBELLUM SOUTH: A REPLY TO FOGEL-ENGERMAN." AMERICAN ECONOMIC REVIEW, 69 (MARCH, 1979): 206-207.

14608   HASKELL, THOMAS L. "WERE SLAVES MORE EFFICIENT? SOME DOUBTS ABOUT 'TIME ON THE CROSS.'" NEW YORK REVIEW OF

BOOKS, 21 (SEPTEMBER 19, 1974): 38-42.

14609 HIGMAN, BARRY W. SLAVE POPULATION AND ECONOMY IN JAMAICA, 1807-1834. CAMBRIDGE: CAMBRIDGE UNIVERSITY PRESS, 1976.

14610 HUERTAS, THOMAS. "DAMNIFYING GROWTH IN THE SOUTH, 1820-1860." JOURNAL OF ECONOMIC HISTORY, 39 (MARCH, 1979): 87-100.

14611 JONES, ARCHER AND HOEPNER, PAUL H. "THE SOUTH'S ECONOMIC INVESTMENT IN SLAVERY." AMERICAN JOURNAL OF ECONOMICS AND SOCIOLOGY, 26 (JULY, 1967): 297-299.

14612 KOTLIKOFF, LAURENCE J. "THE STRUCTURE OF SLAVE PRICES IN NEW ORLEANS, 1804 TO 1862." ECONOMIC INQUIRY, 17 (OCTOBER, 1979): 496-518.

14613 KOTLIKOFF, LAURENCE J. "TOWARDS A QUANTITATIVE DESCRIPTION OF THE NEW ORLEANS SLAVE MARKET." UNPUBLISHED PAPER PRESENTED TO UNIVERSITY OF CHICAGO WORKSHOP ON ECONOMIC HISTORY, 1975.

14614 KOTLIKOFF, LAURENCE J. AND PINERA, SEBASTIAN E. "THE OLD SOUTH'S STAKE IN THE INTER-REGIONAL MOVEMENT OF SLAVES, 1850-1860." JOURNAL OF ECONOMIC HISTORY, 37 (JUNE, 1977): 434-450.

14615 LEIMAN, M.M. "SLAVE PROFITABILITY AND ECONOMIC GROWTH; AN EXAMINATION OF THE CONRAD-MEYER THESIS." SOCIAL AND ECONOMIC STUDIES, 16 (JUNE, 1967): 211-215.

14616 MERRITT, J.E. "THE LIVERPOOL SLAVE TRADE, 1789-1792: AN ANALYTICAL STUDY OF THE RETURNS TO THE COMMITTEE OF ENQUIRY INTO THE SLAVE TRADE, 1788, 1790, 1791, WITH SPECIAL REFERENCE TO THE PROFITABILITY OF THE SLAVE TRADE AND THE NATURE OF THE TRIANGULAR TRADE." M.A. THESIS, UNIVERSITY OF NOTTINGHAM, 1959.

14617 MOES, JOHN E. "THE ABSORPTION OF CAPITAL IN SLAVE LABOR IN THE ANTE-BELLUM SOUTH AND ECONOMIC GROWTH." AMERICAN JOURNAL OF ECONOMICS AND SOCIOLOGY, 20 (OCTOBER, 1961): 535-541.

14618 NEVINS, ALLAN. "THE CASH ACCOUNT OF SLAVERY." ORDEAL OF THE UNION. 2 VOLS. NEW YORK: CHARLES SCRIBNER'S SONS, 1947, VOL. 1, PP. 462-497.

14619 NEWDING, STANLEY. "PROFITABILITY OF SLAVERY: A STUDY IN THE METHODOLOGY OF HISTORICAL INFERENCE." M.A. THESIS, TEXAS TECH UNIVERSITY, 1968.

14620 PARKINS, A.E. "THE ANTEBELLUM SOUTH: A GEOGRAPHER'S INTERPRETATION." ANNALS OF THE ASSOCIATION OF AMERICAN GEOGRAPHERS, 21 (MARCH, 1931): 1-33.

14621 PASSELL, PETER AND WRIGHT, GAVIN. "THE EFFECTS OF
       PRE-CIVIL WAR TERRITORIAL EXPANSION ON THE PRICE OF
       SLAVES." JOURNAL OF POLITICAL ECONOMY, 80
       (NOVEMBER/DECEMBER, 1972): 1188-1202.

14622 PHILLIPS, ULRICH B. AMERICAN NEGRO SLAVERY: A SURVEY OF
       THE SUPPLY, EMPLOYMENT, AND CONTROL OF NEGRO LABOR AS
       DETERMINED BY THE PLANTATION REGIME. NEW YORK: D.
       APPLETON, 1918.

14623 PHILLIPS, ULRICH B. "BLACK-BELT LABOR, SLAVE AND FREE."
       IN UNIVERSITY OF VIRGINIA, PHELPS-STOKES FELLOWSHIP
       PAPERS. LECTURES AND ADDRESSES ON THE NEGRO IN THE
       SOUTH. CHARLOTTESVILLE: MICHIE COMPANY, 1915, PP.
       29-36.

14624 PHILLIPS, ULRICH B. "THE DECADENCE OF THE PLANTATION
       SYSTEM." ANNALS OF THE AMERICAN ACADEMY OF POLITICAL
       AND SOCIAL SCIENCE, 35 (JANUARY, 1910): 37-41.

14625 PHILLIPS, ULRICH B. "THE ECONOMIC COST OF SLAVEHOLDING
       IN THE COTTON BELT." POLITICAL SCIENCE QUARTERLY, 20
       (JUNE, 1905): 257-275.

14626 PHILLIPS, ULRICH B. "A JAMAICA SLAVE PLANTATION."
       AMERICAN HISTORICAL REVIEW, 19 (APRIL, 1914): 543-558.

14627 PHILLIPS, ULRICH B. LIFE AND LABOR IN THE OLD SOUTH.
       BOSTON: LITTLE, BROWN AND COMPANY, 1929.

14628 PHILLIPS, ULRICH B. "ON THE ECONOMICS OF SLAVERY,
       1815-1860." ANNUAL REPORT OF THE AMERICAN HISTORICAL
       ASSOCIATION FOR THE YEAR 1912. WASHINGTON:
       GOVERNMENT PRINTING OFFICE, 1914, PP. 150-151.

14629 PHILLIPS, ULRICH B. "THE SLAVE LABOR PROBLEM IN THE
       CHARLESTON DISTRICT." POLITICAL SCIENCE QUARTERLY, 22
       (SEPTEMBER, 1907): 416-439.

14630 RANSOM, ROGER L. AND SUTCH, RICHARD. ONE KIND OF
       FREEDOM: THE ECONOMIC CONSEQUENCES OF EMANCIPATION.
       CAMBRIDGE: CAMBRIDGE UNIVERSITY PRESS, 1977.

14631 RICHARDSON, CORA L. "THE ECONOMIC EFFICIENCY OF SLAVERY
       IN THE SOUTHERN UNITED STATES." M.A. THESIS,
       UNIVERSITY OF GEORGIA, 1939.

14632 ROARK, JAMES L. MASTERS WITHOUT SLAVES: SOUTHERN
       PLANTERS IN THE CIVIL WAR AND RECONSTRUCTION. NEW
       YORK: W.W. NORTON, 1977.

14633 ROSE, LOUIS A. "CAPITAL LOSSES OF SOUTHERN SLAVEHOLDERS
       DUE TO EMANCIPATION." WESTERN ECONOMIC JOURNAL, 3
       (FALL, 1964): 39-51.

14634   RUSSEL, ROBERT R.   "THE ECONOMIC HISTORY OF NEGRO SLAVERY
        IN THE UNITED STATES."   AGRICULTURAL HISTORY, 11
        (OCTOBER, 1937):   308-321.

14635   RUSSEL, ROBERT R.   "THE GENERAL EFFECTS OF SLAVERY UPON
        SOUTHERN ECONOMIC PROGRESS."   JOURNAL OF SOUTHERN
        HISTORY, 4 (FEBRUARY, 1938):   39-54.

14636   SARAYDAR, EDWARD.   "A NOTE ON THE PROFITABILITY OF ANTE
        BELLUM SLAVERY."   SOUTHERN ECONOMIC JOURNAL, 30
        (APRIL, 1964):   325-332.

14637   SARAYDAR, EDWARD.   "THE PROFITABILITY OF ANTE BELLUM
        SLAVERY--A REPLY."   SOUTHERN ECONOMIC JOURNAL, 31
        (APRIL, 1965):   377-397.

14638   SCHAEFER, DONALD F.   "PRODUCTIVITY IN THE ANTEBELLUM
        SOUTH: THE WESTERN TOBACCO REGION."   RESEARCH IN
        ECONOMIC HISTORY, 3 (1978):   305-340.

14639   SCHAEFER, DONALD AND SCHMITZ, M.D.   "THE RELATIVE
        EFFICIENCY OF SLAVE AGRICULTURE: A COMMENT."
        AMERICAN ECONOMIC REVIEW, 69 (MARCH, 1979):   208-212.

14640   SHARP, WILLIAM F.   "THE PROFITABILITY OF SLAVERY IN THE
        COLOMBIAN CHOCO, 1680-1810."   HISPANIC AMERICAN
        HISTORICAL REVIEW, 55 (AUGUST, 1975):   468-495.

14641   SHERWOOD, MORGAN B.   "AN HISTORICAL NOTE ON 'A
        RECONSIDERATION OF THE LANCASHIRE COTTON FAMINE.'"
        AGRICULTURAL HISTORY, 37 (JULY, 1963):   163-165.

14642   SMITH, ROBERT W.   "WAS SLAVERY UNPROFITABLE IN THE
        ANTE-BELLUM SOUTH?"   AGRICULTURAL HISTORY, 20
        (JANUARY, 1946):   62-64.

14643   STAMPP, KENNETH M.   THE PECULIAR INSTITUTION: SLAVERY IN
        THE ANTE-BELLUM SOUTH.   NEW YORK: ALFRED A. KNOPF,
        1956.

14644   STEIN, ROBERT.   "THE PROFITABILITY OF THE NANTES SLAVE
        TRADE, 1783-1792."   JOURNAL OF ECONOMIC HISTORY, 35
        (DECEMBER, 1975):   779-793.

14645   SUTCH, RICHARD.   "THE PROFITABILITY OF ANTE BELLUM
        SLAVERY--REVISITED."   SOUTHERN ECONOMIC JOURNAL, 31
        (APRIL, 1965):   365-377.

14646   THOMAS, WILLIAM H.   "TOIL AND TRUST."   A.M.E. CHURCH
        REVIEW, 4 (APRIL, 1888):   369-376.

14647   VEDDER, RICHARD K. AND STOCKDALE, DAVID C.   "THE
        PROFITABILITY OF SLAVERY REVISITED: A DIFFERENT
        APPROACH."   AGRICULTURAL HISTORY, 49 (APRIL, 1975):
        392-404.

14648   WHITTEN, DAVID O.   "ANTEBELLUM SUGAR AND RICE
        PLANTATIONS, LOUISIANA AND SOUTH CAROLINA: A
        PROFITABILITY STUDY." PH.D. DISSERTATION, TULANE
        UNIVERSITY, 1970.

14649   WHITTEN, DAVID O.   "SUGAR SLAVERY: A PROFITABILITY MODEL
        FOR SLAVE INVESTMENTS IN THE ANTEBELLUM LOUISIANA
        SUGAR INDUSTRY." LOUISIANA STUDIES, 12 (SUMMER,
        1973): 423-442.

14650   WHITTEN, DAVID O.   "TARIFF AND PROFIT IN THE ANTEBELLUM
        LOUISIANA SUGAR INDUSTRY." BUSINESS HISTORY REVIEW,
        44 (SUMMER, 1970): 226-233.

14651   WOODMAN, HAROLD D.   "THE PROFITABILITY OF SLAVERY: A
        HISTORICAL PERENNIAL." JOURNAL OF SOUTHERN HISTORY,
        29 (AUGUST, 1963): 303-325.

14652   WRIGHT, GAVIN. THE POLITICAL ECONOMY OF THE COTTON
        SOUTH: HOUSEHOLDS, MARKETS, AND WEALTH IN THE
        NINETEENTH CENTURY. NEW YORK: W.W. NORTON, 1978.

14653   YASUBA, YASUKICHI. "THE PROFITABILITY AND VIABILITY OF
        PLANTATION SLAVERY IN THE UNITED STATES." ECONOMIC
        STUDIES QUARTERLY, 12 (SEPTEMBER, 1961): 60-67.

14654   ZILVERSMIT, ARTHUR. THE FIRST EMANCIPATION: THE
        ABOLITION OF SLAVERY IN THE NORTH. CHICAGO:
        UNIVERSITY OF CHICAGO PRESS, 1967.

INDUSTRIAL SLAVERY

14655   BAILEY, CLAY. "JOSEPH R. ANDERSON OF TREDEGAR."
        COMMONWEALTH, 12 (NOVEMBER, 1959):   2, 36, 38.

14656   BAKER, HENRY E. THE COLORED INVENTOR. NEW YORK: CRISIS
        PUBLISHING COMPANY, 1913.

14657   BAKER, HENRY E. "THE NEGRO IN THE FIELD OF INVENTION."
        JOURNAL OF NEGRO HISTORY, 2 (JANUARY, 1917): 21-36.

14658   BATEMAN, FRED; FOUST, JAMES; AND WEISS, THOMAS. "THE
        PARTICIPATION OF PLANTERS IN MANUFACTURING IN THE
        ANTE-BELLUM SOUTH." AGRICULTURAL HISTORY, 48 (APRIL,
        1974): 277-297.

14659   BATEMAN, FRED; FOUST, JAMES D.; AND WEISS, THOMAS J.
        "LARGE-SCALE MANUFACTURING IN THE SOUTH AND WEST,
        1850-1860." BUSINESS HISTORY REVIEW, 45 (SPRING,
        1971): 1-17.

14660   BATEMAN, FRED AND WEISS, THOMAS J. "MANUFACTURING IN THE
        ANTEBELLUM SOUTH." RESEARCH IN ECONOMIC HISTORY, 1
        (1976): 1-44.

14661 BAZANT, JAN. "EVOLUTION OF THE TEXTILE INDUSTRY OF
       PUEBLA, 1544-1845." COMPARATIVE STUDIES IN SOCIETY
       AND HISTORY, 7 (OCTOBER, 1964): 56-69.

14662 BERRY, THOMAS S. "THE RISE OF FLOUR MILLING IN
       RICHMOND." VIRGINIA MAGAZINE OF HISTORY AND
       BIOGRAPHY, 78 (OCTOBER, 1970): 387-408.

14663 BLACK, ROBERT C. THE RAILROADS OF THE CONFEDERACY.
       CHAPEL HILL: UNIVERSITY OF NORTH CAROLINA PRESS, 1952.

14664 BOYD-BOWMAN, PETER. "SPANISH AND EUROPEAN TEXTILES IN
       SIXTEENTH CENTURY MEXICO." AMERICAS, 29 (JANUARY,
       1973): 334-358.

14665 BRADFORD, S. SYDNEY. "THE NEGRO IRONWORKER IN
       ANTE-BELLUM VIRGINIA." JOURNAL OF SOUTHERN HISTORY,
       25 (MAY, 1959): 194-206.

14666 BRADFORD, SAMUEL S. "THE ANTE-BELLUM CHARCOAL IRON
       INDUSTRY OF VIRGINIA." PH.D. DISSERTATION, COLUMBIA
       UNIVERSITY, 1958.

14667 BRAINERD, ALFRED F. "COLORED MINING LABOR."
       TRANSACTIONS OF THE AMERICAN INSTITUTE OF MINING
       ENGINEERS, 14 (JUNE, 1835-MAY, 1886): 78-80.

14668 BREWER, JAMES H. THE CONFEDERATE NEGRO: VIRGINIA'S
       CRAFTSMEN AND MILITARY LABORERS, 1861-1865. DURHAM:
       DUKE UNIVERSITY PRESS, 1969.

14669 BRIDENBAUGH, CARL. THE COLONIAL CRAFTSMAN. CHICAGO:
       UNIVERSITY OF CHICAGO PRESS, 1974.

14670 BROMBERG, ALAN B. "SLAVERY IN THE VIRGINIA TOBACCO
       FACTORIES, 1800-1860." M.A. THESIS, UNIVERSITY OF
       VIRGINIA, 1968.

14671 "BROWN SKIN AND BRIGHT LEAF: THE STORY OF THE NEGRO'S
       ROLE IN THE TOBACCO INDUSTRY." NEGRO HISTORY
       BULLETIN, 19 (OCTOBER, NOVEMBER, 1955): 3-10, 27-33.

14672 BRUCE, KATHLEEN. "SLAVE LABOR IN THE VIRGINIA IRON
       INDUSTRY." WILLIAM AND MARY COLLEGE QUARTERLY
       HISTORICAL MAGAZINE, 2ND SER., 6 (OCTOBER, 1926):
       289-303; 7 (JANUARY, 1927): 21-31.

14673 BRUCE, KATHLEEN. VIRGINIA IRON MANUFACTURE IN THE SLAVE
       ERA. NEW YORK: CENTURY COMPANY, 1930.

14674 BRUCE, KATHLEEN. "VIRGINIA IRON MANUFACTURE IN THE SLAVE
       ERA." PH.D. DISSERTATION, RADCLIFFE COLLEGE, 1924.

14675 BRYDON, G. MACLAREN. "THE BRISTOL IRON WORKS IN KING
       GEORGE COUNTY." VIRGINIA MAGAZINE OF HISTORY AND

BIOGRAPHY, 42 (APRIL, 1934): 97-102.

14676 CALLOWAY, THOMAS J. "THE AMERICAN NEGRO ARTISAN."
       CASSIER'S MAGAZINE, 25 (MARCH, 1904): 435-445.

14677 CAPPON, LESTER J. "HISTORY OF THE SOUTHERN IRON INDUSTRY
       TO THE CLOSE OF THE CIVIL WAR." PH.D. DISSERTATION,
       HARVARD UNIVERSITY, 1928.

14678 CAPPON, LESTER J. "IRON-MAKING--A FORGOTTEN INDUSTRY OF
       NORTH CAROLINA." NORTH CAROLINA HISTORICAL REVIEW, 9
       (OCTOBER, 1932): 331-348.

14679 CAPPON, LESTER J. (ED.). IRON WORKS AT TUBALL: TERMS
       AND CONDITIONS FOR THEIR LEASE AS STATED BY ALEXANDER
       SPOTSWOOD ON THE TWENTIETH DAY OF JULY 1739.
       CHARLOTTESVILLE: MCGREGOR LIBRARY, UNIVERSITY OF
       VIRGINIA, 1945.

14680 CAPPON, LESTER J. "TREND OF THE SOUTHERN IRON INDUSTRY
       UNDER THE PLANTATION SYSTEM." JOURNAL OF ECONOMIC AND
       BUSINESS HISTORY, 2 (FEBRUARY, 1930): 353-381.

14681 CHRISTIAN, MARCUS B. NEGRO IRONWORKERS OF LOUISIANA,
       1713-1900. GRETNA, LA: PELICAN PUBLISHING COMPANY,
       1972.

14682 COLEMAN, J. WINSTON JR. "OLD KENTUCKY IRON FURNACES."
       FILSON CLUB HISTORY QUARTERLY, 31 (JULY, 1957):
       227-242.

14683 COLLINS, HERBERT. "THE SOUTHERN INDUSTRIAL GOSPEL BEFORE
       1860." JOURNAL OF SOUTHERN HISTORY, 12 (AUGUST,
       1946): 386-402.

14684 CONDIT, WILLIAM W. "VIRGINIA'S EARLY IRON AGE." IRON
       WORKER, 23 (SUMMER, 1959): 1-7.

14685 CONLEY, PHIL. HISTORY OF THE WEST VIRGINIA COAL
       INDUSTRY. CHARLESTON, WV: EDUCATIONAL FOUNDATIONS,
       1960.

14686 CORLEW, ROBERT E. "SOME ASPECTS OF SLAVERY IN DICKSON
       COUNTY." TENNESSEE HISTORICAL QUARTERLY, 10
       (SEPTEMBER, DECEMBER, 1951): 224-248, 344-365.

14687 CORLEW, ROBERT E. "SOME ASPECTS OF SLAVERY IN DICKSON
       COUNTY, TENNESSEE." BULLETIN OF VANDERBILT
       UNIVERSITY, 49 (AUGUST, 1949): 71.

14688 CORLEW, ROBERT E. "SOME ASPECTS OF SLAVERY IN DICKSON
       COUNTY, TENNESSEE." M.A. THESIS, VANDERBILT
       UNIVERSITY, 1949.

14689 COTTER, JOHN L. "CURRENT RESEARCH: NORTHEAST." SOCIETY

FOR HISTORICAL ARCHAEOLOGY NEWSLETTER, 10 (1977):
12-21.

14690   COULTER, E. MERTON.   AURARIA: THE STORY OF A GEORGIA
        GOLD MINING TOWN.   ATHENS: UNIVERSITY OF GEORGIA
        PRESS, 1965.

14691   COZZENS, ARTHUR B.   "THE IRON INDUSTRY OF MISSOURI."
        MISSOURI HISTORICAL REVIEW, 35 (JULY, 1941):   509-538;
        36 (OCTOBER, 1941):   48-59.

14692   CROCKER, LES.   "AN EARLY IRON FOUNDRY IN NORTHERN
        MISSISSIPPI."   JOURNAL OF MISSISSIPPI HISTORY, 35
        (MAY, 1973):   113-126.

14693   DAVIDSON, PHILIP G.   "INDUSTRIALISM IN THE ANTE-BELLUM
        SOUTH."   SOUTH ATLANTIC QUARTERLY, 27 (OCTOBER, 1928):
        405-425.

14694   DEW, CHARLES B.   "BLACK IRONWORKERS AND THE SLAVE
        INSURRECTION PANIC OF 1856."   JOURNAL OF SOUTHERN
        HISTORY, 16 (AUGUST, 1975):   321-338.

14695   DEW, CHARLES B.   "DAVID ROSS AND THE OXFORD IRON WORKS:
        A STUDY OF INDUSTRIAL SLAVERY IN THE EARLY
        NINETEENTH-CENTURY SOUTH."   WILLIAM AND MARY
        QUARTERLY, 3RD SER., 31 (APRIL, 1974):   189-224.

14696   DEW, CHARLES B.   "DISCIPLINING SLAVE IRONWORKERS IN THE
        ANTEBELLUM SOUTH: COERCION, CONCILIATION, AND
        ACCOMMODATION."   AMERICAN HISTORICAL REVIEW, 79
        (APRIL, 1974):   393-418.

14697   DEW, CHARLES B.   IRONMAKER TO THE CONFEDERACY: JOSEPH R.
        ANDERSON AND THE TREDEGAR IRON WORKS.   NEW HAVEN:
        YALE UNIVERSITY PRESS, 1966.

14698   DEW, CHARLES B.   "SOUTHERN INDUSTRY IN THE CIVIL WAR ERA:
        JOSEPH REID ANDERSON AND THE TREDEGAR IRON WORKS,
        1859-1867."   PH.D. DISSERTATION, JOHNS HOPKINS
        UNIVERSITY, 1964.

14699   DONNELLY, RALPH W.   "THE BARTOW COUNTY CONFEDERATE
        SALTPETRE WORKS."   GEORGIA HISTORICAL QUARTERLY, 54
        (FALL, 1970):   305-319.

14700   DOWD, JEROME.   "COLORED MEN AS COTTON MANUFACTURERS."
        GUNTON'S MAGAZINE, 23 (SEPTEMBER, 1902):   254-256.

14701   DOZIER, RICHARD K.   "A HISTORICAL SURVEY: BLACK
        ARCHITECTS AND CRAFTSMEN."   BLACK WORLD, 23 (MAY,
        1974):   4-15.

14702   DUBOIS, W.E.B. (ED.).   THE NEGRO ARTISAN.   ATLANTA:
        ATLANTA UNIVERSITY PRESS, 1902.

14703   DUBOIS, W.E.B. AND DILL, AUGUSTJS G. (EDS.). THE NEGRO
        AMERICAN ARTISAN. ATLANTA: ATLANTA UNIVERSITY
        PUBLICATIONS, 1912.

14704   DURHAM, JOHN S. "THE LABOR UNIONS AND THE NEGRO."
        ATLANTIC MONTHLY, 81 (FEBRUARY, 1898): 222-231.

14705   EATON, CLEMENT. "SLAVE-HIRING IN THE UPPER SOUTH: A
        STEP TOWARD FREEDOM." MISSISSIPPI VALLEY HISTORICAL
        REVIEW, 46 (MARCH, 1960): 663-678.

14706   EISTERHOLD, JOHN A. "COLONIAL BEGINNINGS IN THE SOUTH'S
        LUMBER INDUSTRY: 1607-1800." SOUTHERN LUMBERMAN, 223
        (DECEMBER 15, 1971): 150-153.

14707   EISTERHOLD, JOHN A. "LUMBER AND TRADE IN THE LOWER
        MISSISSIPPI VALLEY AND NEW ORLEANS, 1800-1860."
        LOUISIANA HISTORY, 13 (WINTER, 1972): 71-92.

14708   FARLOW, GALE J. "BLACK CRAFTSMEN IN NORTH CAROLINA
        BEFORE 1850." M.A. THESIS, UNIVERSITY OF NORTH
        CAROLINA, GREENSBORO, 1979.

14709   FISHWICK, MARSHALL W. "JOHN JORDAN, MAN OF IRON." IRON
        WORKER, 21 (AUTUMN, 1957): 1-8.

14710   FLISCH, JULIA A. "THE COMMON PEOPLE OF THE OLD SOUTH."
        ANNUAL REPORT OF THE AMERICAN HISTORICAL ASSOCIATION
        FOR THE YEAR 1908. 2 VOLS. WASHINGTON: GOVERNMENT
        PRINTING OFFICE, 1909, VOL. 1, PP. 133-143.

14711   FOGEL, ROBERT W. AND ENGERMAN, STANLEY L. TIME ON THE
        CROSS: THE ECONOMICS OF AMERICAN NEGRO SLAVERY. 2
        VOLS. BOSTON: LITTLE, BROWN AND COMPANY, 1974.

14712   GEGGUS, DAVID P. "THE SLAVES OF BRITISH-OCCUPIED SAINT
        DOMINGUE: AN ANALYSIS OF THE WORKFORCES OF 197
        ABSENTEE PLANTATIONS, 1796-1797." CARIBBEAN STUDIES,
        18 (APRIL-JULY, 1978): 5-42.

14713   GENOVESE, EUGENE D. THE POLITICAL ECONOMY OF SLAVERY:
        STUDIES IN THE ECONOMY AND SOCIETY OF THE SLAVE SOUTH.
        NEW YORK: VINTAGE, 1961.

14714   GREEN, BARBARA L. "SLAVE LABOR AT THE MARAMEC IRON
        WORKS, 1828-1850." MISSOURI HISTORICAL REVIEW, 73
        (JANUARY, 1979): 150-164.

14715   GREEN, FLETCHER M. "GEORGIA'S FORGOTTEN INDUSTRY: GOLD
        MINING." GEORGIA HISTORICAL QUARTERLY, 19 (JUNE,
        SEPTEMBER, 1935): 93-111, 210-228.

14716   GREEN, FLETCHER M. "GOLD MINING: A FORGOTTEN INDUSTRY
        OF ANTEBELLUM NORTH CAROLINA." NORTH CAROLINA
        HISTORICAL REVIEW, 14 (JANUARY, OCTOBER, 1937): 1-19,

357-366.

14717   GREEN, RODNEY D. "URBAN INDUSTRY, BLACK RESISTANCE AND
        RACIAL RECONSTRUCTION IN THE ANTEBELLUM SOUTH: A
        GENERAL MODEL AND CASE STUDY IN URBAN VIRGINIA."
        PH.D. DISSERTATION, AMERICAN UNIVERSITY, 1980.

14718   GREENLEAF, RICHARD E. "THE OBRAJE IN THE LATE MEXICAN
        COLONY." AMERICAS, 23 (JANUARY, 1967): 239-250.

14719   GREENLEAF, RICHARD E. "VICEREGAL POWER AND THE OBRAJES
        OF THE CORTES ESTATE, 1595-1708." HISPANIC AMERICAN
        HISTORICAL REVIEW, 48 (AUGUST, 1968): 365-379.

14720   GRIFFIN, RICHARD W. "ANTE BELLUM INDUSTRIAL FOUNDATIONS
        OF THE (ALLEGED) 'NEW SOUTH.'" TEXTILE HISTORY
        REVIEW, 5 (APRIL, 1964): 33-43.

14721   GRIFFIN, RICHARD W. "COTTON MANUFACTURE IN ALABAMA TO
        1860." ALABAMA HISTORICAL QUARTERLY, 18 (FALL, 1956):
        289-307.

14722   GRIFFIN, RICHARD W. "MANUFACTURING INTERESTS OF
        MISSISSIPPI PLANTERS, 1810-1832." JOURNAL OF
        MISSISSIPPI HISTORY, 22 (APRIL, 1960): 110-122.

14723   GRIFFIN, RICHARD W. "NORTH CAROLINA, THE ORIGIN AND RISE
        OF THE COTTON TEXTILE INDUSTRY, 1830-1880." PH.D.
        DISSERTATION, OHIO STATE UNIVERSITY, 1954.

14724   GRIFFIN, RICHARD W. "AN ORIGIN OF THE INDUSTRIAL
        REVOLUTION IN MARYLAND: THE TEXTILE INDUSTRY,
        1789-1836." MARYLAND HISTORICAL MAGAZINE, 61 (MARCH,
        1966): 24-36.

14725   GRIFFIN, RICHARD W. "AN ORIGIN OF THE NEW SOUTH: THE
        SOUTH CAROLINA HOMESPUN COMPANY, 1808-1815." BUSINESS
        HISTORY REVIEW, 35 (AUTUMN, 1961): 402-414.

14726   GRIFFIN, RICHARD W. "ORIGINS OF SOUTHERN COTTON
        MANUFACTURE, 1807-1816." COTTON HISTORY REVIEW, 1
        (1960): 5-12.

14727   GRIFFIN, RICHARD W. "THE ORIGINS OF THE INDUSTRIAL
        REVOLUTION IN GEORGIA: COTTON TEXTILES, 1810-1865."
        GEORGIA HISTORICAL QUARTERLY, 42 (DECEMBER, 1958):
        355-375.

14728   GRIFFIN, RICHARD W. AND WILSON, HAROLD S. "THE
        ANTE-BELLUM TEXTILE INDUSTRY OF GEORGIA." UNPUBLISHED
        MANUSCRIPT, N.D.

14729   GRIMKE, ARCHIBALD H. "MODERN INDUSTRIALISM AND THE
        NEGROES OF THE UNITED STATES." AMERICAN NEGRO ACADEMY
        OCCASIONAL PAPERS, NO. 12. WASHINGTON: AMERICAN

NEGRO ACADEMY, 1908.

14730 HART, ALBERT B. SLAVERY AND ABOLITION, 1831-1841. NEW
YORK: HARPER AND BROTHERS, 1906.

14731 HERRING, JAMES V. "THE AMERICAN NEGRO AS CRAFTSMAN AND
ARTIST." CRISIS, 49 (APRIL, 1942): 116-118.

14732 HOLLAND, FRANCIS R., JR. "THREE VIRGINIA IRON COMPANIES,
1825-1865." M.A. THESIS, UNIVERSITY OF TEXAS, 1958.

14733 HOWARD, JOHN C. THE NEGRO IN THE LUMBER INDUSTRY.
PHILADELPHIA: UNIVERSITY OF PENNSYLVANIA PRESS, 1970.

14734 HUDSON, J. PAUL. "IRON MANUFACTURING DURING THE
EIGHTEENTH CENTURY." IRON WORKER, 21 (AUTUMN, 1957):
9-13.

14735 JERNEGAN, MARCUS W. "SLAVERY AND THE BEGINNINGS OF
INDUSTRIALISM IN THE AMERICAN COLONIES." AMERICAN
HISTORICAL REVIEW, 25 (JANUARY, 1920): 220-240.

14736 JOHNSON, CHARLES S. "THE CONFLICT OF CASTE AND CLASS IN
AN AMERICAN INDUSTRY." AMERICAN JOURNAL OF SOCIOLOGY,
42 (JULY, 1936): 55-65.

14737 JOHNSON, J.G. "NOTES ON MANUFACTURING IN ANTE-BELLUM
GEORGIA." GEORGIA HISTORICAL QUARTERLY, 16
(SEPTEMBER, 1932): 214-231.

14738 JOHNSON, KEACH D. "ESTABLISHMENT OF THE BALTIMORE IRON
COMPANY: A CASE STUDY OF THE AMERICAN IRON INDUSTRY
IN THE EIGHTEENTH CENTURY." PH.D. DISSERTATION,
UNIVERSITY OF IOWA, 1949.

14739 JOHNSON, WILLIAM R. A SHORT HISTORY OF THE SUGAR
INDUSTRY IN TEXAS. HOUSTON: TEXAS GULF COAST
ASSOCIATION PUBLICATIONS, 1961.

14740 LAING, JAMES T. "THE EARLY DEVELOPMENT OF THE COAL
INDUSTRY IN THE WESTERN COUNTIES OF VIRGINIA,
1800-1865." WEST VIRGINIA HISTORY, 27 (JANUARY,
1966): 144-155.

14741 LANDER, ERNEST M. "SLAVE LABOR IN SOUTH CAROLINA COTTON
MILLS." JOURNAL OF NEGRO HISTORY, 38 (APRIL, 1953):
162-173.

14742 LANDER, ERNEST M., JR. "THE DEVELOPMENT OF TEXTILES IN
THE SOUTH CAROLINA PIEDMONT BEFORE 1860." COTTON
HISTORY REVIEW, 1 (1960): 88-100.

14743 LANDER, ERNEST M., JR. "THE IRON INDUSTRY IN ANTE-BELLUM
SOUTH CAROLINA." JOURNAL OF SOUTHERN HISTORY, 20
(AUGUST, 1954): 337-355.

14744 LANGLEY, HAROLD D. "THE NEGRO IN THE NAVY AND MERCHANT
       SERVICE." JOURNAL OF NEGRO HISTORY, 52 (OCTOBER,
       1967): 273-286.

14745 LEWIS, RONALD L. "BLACK LABOR IN THE EASTERN VIRGINIA
       COAL FIELD, 1765-1865." IN NEWTON, JAMES E. AND LEWIS
       (EDS.). THE OTHER SLAVES: MECHANICS, ARTISANS AND
       CRAFTSMEN. BOSTON: G.K. HALL, 1978, PP. 87-108.

14746 LEWIS, RONALD L. COAL, IRON, AND SLAVES: INDUSTRIAL
       SLAVERY IN MARYLAND AND VIRGINIA, 1715-1865.
       WESTPORT: GREENWOOD PRESS, 1979.

14747 LEWIS, RONALD L. "'THE DARKEST ABODE OF MAN'--BLACK
       MINERS IN THE FIRST SOUTHERN COAL FIELD, 1780-1865."
       VIRGINIA MAGAZINE OF HISTORY AND BIOGRAPHY, 87 (APRIL,
       1979): 190-202.

14748 LEWIS, RONALD L. "SLAVE FAMILIES AT EARLY CHESAPEAKE
       IRONWORKS." VIRGINIA MAGAZINE OF HISTORY AND
       BIOGRAPHY, 86 (APRIL, 1978): 169-179.

14749 LEWIS, RONALD L. "SLAVERY IN THE CHESAPEAKE IRON
       INDUSTRY, 1716-1865." PH.D. DISSERTATION, UNIVERSITY
       OF AKRON, 1974.

14750 LEWIS, RONALD L. "SLAVERY ON CHESAPEAKE IRON PLANTATIONS
       BEFORE THE AMERICAN REVOLUTION." JOURNAL OF NEGRO
       HISTORY, 59 (JULY, 1974): 242-254.

14751 LEWIS, RONALD L. "THE USE AND EXTENT OF SLAVE LABOR IN
       THE CHESAPEAKE IRON INDUSTRY: THE COLONIAL ERA."
       LABOR HISTORY, 17 (SUMMER, 1976): 388-405.

14752 LEWIS, RONALD L. "THE USE AND EXTENT OF SLAVE LABOR IN
       THE VIRGINIA IRON INDUSTRY: THE ANTE-BELLUM ERA."
       WEST VIRGINIA HISTORY, 38 (JANUARY, 1977): 141-156.

14753 LOWRY, ROBERT. "THE NEGRO AS A MECHANIC." NORTH
       AMERICAN REVIEW, 156 (APRIL, 1893): 472-477.

14754 MARTIN, THOMAS P. (ED.). "THE ADVENT OF WILLIAM GREGG
       AND THE GRANITEVILLE COMPANY." JOURNAL OF SOUTHERN
       HISTORY, 11 (AUGUST, 1945): 389-423.

14755 MARTINS, ROBERTO B. "GROWING IN SILENCE: THE SLAVE
       ECONOMY OF NINETEENTH-CENTURY MINAS GERAIS, BRAZIL."
       PH.D. DISSERTATION, VANDERBILT UNIVERSITY, 1980.

14756 MAY, EARL C. PRINCIPIO TO WHEELING, 1715-1945: A
       PAGEANT OF IRON AND STEEL. NEW YORK: HARPER &
       BROTHERS, 1945.

14757 MENARD, W.T. "THE LABOR PROBLEM." INDIANAPOLIS FREEMAN,
       DECEMBER 29, 1900.

14758   MILLER, MARY E.W.   SLAVERY DAYS IN GEORGIA.   RICHLAND,
        GA: N.P., N.D.

14759   MILLER, RANDALL M.   THE COTTON MILL MOVEMENT IN
        ANTEBELLUM ALABAMA.   NEW YORK: ARNO PRESS, 1978.

14760   MILLER, RANDALL M.   "THE COTTON MILL MOVEMENT IN
        ANTEBELLUM ALABAMA."   PH.D. DISSERTATION, OHIO STATE
        UNIVERSITY, 1971.

14761   MILLER, RANDALL M.   "DANIEL PRATT'S INDUSTRIAL URBANISM:
        THE COTTON MILL TOWN IN ANTE-BELLUM ALABAMA."   ALABAMA
        HISTORICAL QUARTERLY, 34 (SPRING, 1972):   5-36.

14762   MILLER, RANDALL M.   "THE FABRIC OF CONTROL: BLACK SLAVES
        IN ANTEBELLUM SOUTHERN TEXTILE MILLS."   UNPUBLISHED
        PAPER, 1980.

14763   MITCHELL, BROADUS.   THE RISE OF COTTON MILLS IN THE
        SOUTH.   BALTIMORE: JOHNS HOPKINS PRESS, 1921.

14764   MITCHELL, BROADUS.   WILLIAM GREGG, FACTORY MASTER OF THE
        OLD SOUTH.   CHAPEL HILL: UNIVERSITY OF NORTH CAROLINA
        PRESS, 1928.

14765   MOORE, BRENT.   A STUDY OF THE PAST, THE PRESENT AND THE
        POSSIBILITIES OF THE HEMP INDUSTRY IN KENTUCKY.
        LEXINGTON: PRESS OF J.E. HUGHES, 1905.

14766   MOORE, JOHN HEBRON.   ANDREW BROWN AND CYPRESS LUMBERING
        IN THE OLD SOUTHWEST.   BATON ROUGE: LOUISIANA STATE
        UNIVERSITY PRESS, 1967.

14767   MOORE, JOHN HEBRON.   "MISSISSIPPI'S ANTE-BELLUM TEXTILE
        INDUSTRY."   JOURNAL OF MISSISSIPPI HISTORY, 16 (APRIL,
        1954):   81-98.

14768   MOORE, JOHN HEBRON.   "SIMON GRAY, RIVERMAN: A SLAVE WHO
        WAS ALMOST FREE."   MISSISSIPPI VALLEY HISTORICAL
        REVIEW, 49 (DECEMBER, 1962):   472-484.

14769   MORRIS, RICHARD B.   "LABOR MILITANCY IN THE OLD SOUTH."
        LABOR AND NATION, 4 (MAY/JUNE, 1948):   32-36.

14770   NELSON, LEE H.   "BRICKMAKING IN BALTIMORE, 1798."
        JOURNAL OF THE SOCIETY OF ARCHITECTURAL HISTORIANS, 18
        (MARCH, 1959):   33-34.

14771   NEWTON, JAMES E. AND LEWIS, RONALD L. (EDS.).   THE OTHER
        SLAVES: MECHANICS, ARTISANS AND CRAFTSMEN.   BOSTON:
        G.K. HALL, 1978.

14772   NORTHRUP, HERBERT R.   THE NEGRO IN THE TOBACCO INDUSTRY.
        PHILADELPHIA: UNIVERSITY OF PENNSYLVANIA PRESS, 1970.

14773   O'BRIEN, JOHN T. "FACTORY, CHURCH, AND COMMUNITY:
         BLACKS IN ANTEBELLUM RICHMOND." JOURNAL OF SOUTHERN
         HISTORY, 44 (NOVEMBER, 1978): 509-536.

14774   PENISTON, GREGORY S. "THE SLAVE BUILDER-ARTISAN."
         WESTERN JOURNAL OF BLACK STUDIES, 2 (WINTER, 1978):
         284-295.

14775   PERRY, PERCIVAL. "THE NAVAL STORES INDUSTRY IN THE
         ANTE-BELLUM SOUTH, 1789-1861." PH.D. DISSERTATION,
         DUKE UNIVERSITY, 1947.

14776   PERRY, PERCIVAL. "THE NAVAL-STORES INDUSTRY IN THE OLD
         SOUTH, 1790-1860." JOURNAL OF SOUTHERN HISTORY, 34
         (NOVEMBER, 1968): 509-526.

14777   PINCHBECK, RAYMOND B. "THE VIRGINIA NEGRO ARTISAN AND
         TRADESMAN." PH.D. DISSERTATION, UNIVERSITY OF
         VIRGINIA, 1925.

14778   PINCHBECK, RAYMOND B. THE VIRGINIA NEGRO ARTISAN AND
         TRADESMAN. RICHMOND: WILLIAM BYRD PRESS, 1926.

14779   PRATT, FRANCIS E. "THE OBRAJE IN NEW SPAIN: A CASE
         STUDY IN THE FAILURE OF ROYAL AUTHORITY TO IMPOSE ITS
         WILL." M.A. THESIS, UNIVERSITY OF THE AMERICAS,
         MEXICO CITY, 1965.

14780   PREYER, NORRIS W. "THE HISTORIAN, THE SLAVE, AND THE
         ANTE-BELLUM TEXTILE INDUSTRY." JOURNAL OF NEGRO
         HISTORY, 46 (APRIL, 1961): 67-82.

14781   PREYER, NORRIS W. "WHY DID INDUSTRIALIZATION LAG IN THE
         OLD SOUTH?" GEORGIA HISTORICAL QUARTERLY, 55 (FALL,
         1971): 378-396.

14782   PRICE, JACOB M. "THE BEGINNINGS OF TOBACCO MANUFACTURE
         IN VIRGINIA." VIRGINIA MAGAZINE OF HISTORY AND
         BIOGRAPHY, 64 (JANUARY, 1956): 3-29.

14783   PULLEY, RICHARD D. "THE ROLE OF THE VIRGINIA SLAVE IN
         IRON AND TOBACCO MANUFACTURING." M.A. THESIS,
         UNIVERSITY OF RICHMOND, 1962.

14784   ROBBINS, MICHAEL W. "THE PRINCIPIO COMPANY: IRON-MAKING
         IN COLONIAL MARYLAND, 1720-1781." PH.D. DISSERTATION,
         GEORGE WASHINGTON UNIVERSITY, 1972.

14785   ROBERT, JOSEPH C. THE STORY OF TOBACCO IN AMERICA. NEW
         YORK: A.A. KNOPF, 1949.

14786   ROBERT, JOSEPH C. "THE TOBACCO INDUSTRY IN ANTE-BELLUM
         NORTH CAROLINA." NORTH CAROLINA HISTORICAL REVIEW, 15
         (APRIL, 1938): 119-130.

14787   ROBERT, JOSEPH C.   THE TOBACCO KINGDOM: PLANTATION,
        MARKET, AND FACTORY IN VIRGINIA AND NORTH CAROLINA,
        1800-1860. DURHAM: DUKE UNIVERSITY PRESS, 1938.

14788   ROWAN, RICHARD L.   THE NEGRO IN THE TEXTILE INDUSTRY.
        PHILADELPHIA: UNIVERSITY OF PENNSYLVANIA PRESS, 1970.

14789   SCARBOROUGH, W.S.   "THE NEGRO AND THE TRADES."   SOUTHERN
        WORKMAN, 26 (FEBRUARY, 1897):   26-27.

14790   SHELDON, MARIANNE B.   "BLACK-WHITE RELATIONS IN RICHMOND,
        VIRGINIA, 1782-1820."   JOURNAL OF SOUTHERN HISTORY, 45
        (FEBRUARY, 1979):   27-44.

14791   SHOFNER, JERRELL H.   "NEGRO LABORERS AND THE FOREST
        INDUSTRIES IN RECONSTRUCTION FLORIDA."   JOURNAL OF
        FOREST HISTORY, 18 (OCTOBER, 1975):   180-191.

14792   SITTERSON, J. CARLYLE.   "HIRED LABOR ON SUGAR PLANTATIONS
        OF THE ANTE-BELLUM SOUTH."   JOURNAL OF SOUTHERN
        HISTORY, 14 (MAY, 1948):   192-205.

14793   SITTERSON, JOSEPH C.   SUGAR COUNTRY: THE CANE SUGAR
        INDUSTRY IN THE SOUTH, 1753-1950. LEXINGTON:
        UNIVERSITY OF KENTUCKY PRESS, 1953.

14794   "SLAVERY: SKILLED AND UNSKILLED LABOR IN COLONIAL PERIOD
        (1630-1770)."   IN RYWELL, MARTIN (ED.).   AFRO-AMERICAN
        ENCYCLOPEDIA.   10 VOLS.   NORTH MIAMI: EDUCATIONAL
        BOOK PUBLISHERS, 1974, VOL. 8, P. 2431.

14795   SMITH, ELIZABETH S.   "VESUVIUS FURNACE PLANTATION."
        HISTORIC PRESERVATION, 28 (APRIL-JUNE, 1976):   24-27.

14796   SPERO, STERLING D. AND HARRIS, ABRAM L.   THE BLACK
        WORKER: THE NEGRO AND THE LABOR MOVEMENT.   NEW YORK:
        COLUMBIA UNIVERSITY PRESS, 1931.

14797   STANDARD, DIFFEE W. AND GRIFFIN, RICHARD.   "THE COTTON
        TEXTILE INDUSTRY IN ANTE-BELLUM NORTH CAROLINA: AN
        ERA OF BOOM AND CONSOLIDATION, 1830-1860."   NORTH
        CAROLINA HISTORICAL REVIEW, 34 (APRIL, 1957):   131-164.

14798   STANDARD, DIFFEE W. AND GRIFFIN, RICHARD.   "THE COTTON
        TEXTILE INDUSTRY IN ANTE-BELLUM NORTH CAROLINA:
        ORIGIN AND GROWTH TO 1830."   NORTH CAROLINA HISTORICAL
        REVIEW, 34 (JANUARY, 1957):   15-35.

14799   STAROBIN, ROBERT.   "RACE RELATIONS IN OLD SOUTH
        INDUSTRIES."   IN WEINSTEIN, ALLEN AND GATELL, FRANK O.
        (EDS.).   AMERICAN NEGRO SLAVERY: A MODERN READER.
        NEW YORK: OXFORD UNIVERSITY PRESS, 1968, PP. 299-309.

14800   STAROBIN, ROBERT S.   "DISCIPLINING INDUSTRIAL SLAVES IN
        THE OLD SOUTH."   JOURNAL OF NEGRO HISTORY, 53 (APRIL,

1968):   111-128.

14801   STAROBIN, ROBERT S.   "THE ECONOMICS OF INDUSTRIAL SLAVERY
        IN THE OLD SOUTH."   BUSINESS HISTORY REVIEW, 44
        (SUMMER, 1970):   131-174.

14802   STAROBIN, ROBERT S.   INDUSTRIAL SLAVERY IN THE OLD SOUTH.
        NEW YORK: OXFORD UNIVERSITY PRESS, 1970.

14803   STAROBIN, ROBERT S.   "INDUSTRIAL SLAVERY IN THE OLD
        SOUTH, 1790-1861:   A STUDY IN POLITICAL ECONOMY."
        PH.D. DISSERTATION, UNIVERSITY OF CALIFORNIA, 1968.

14804   STAVISKY, LEONARD.   "THE ORIGINS OF NEGRO CRAFTSMANSHIP
        IN COLONIAL AMERICA."   JOURNAL OF NEGRO HISTORY, 32
        (JULY, 1947):   417-429.

14805   STAVISKY, LEONARD P.   "INDUSTRIALISM IN ANTE BELLUM
        CHARLESTON."   JOURNAL OF NEGRO HISTORY, 36 (JULY,
        1951):   302-322.

14806   STAVISKY, LEONARD P.   "THE NEGRO ARTISAN IN THE SOUTH
        ATLANTIC STATES, 1800-1860:   A STUDY OF STATUS AND
        ECONOMIC OPPORTUNITY WITH SPECIAL REFERENCE TO
        CHARLESTON."   PH.D. DISSERTATION, COLUMBIA UNIVERSITY,
        1958.

14807   STAVISKY, LEONARD P.   "NEGRO CRAFTSMANSHIP IN EARLY
        AMERICA."   AMERICAN HISTORICAL REVIEW, 54 (JANUARY,
        1949):   315-325.

14808   STEALEY, JOHN E.   "THE SALT INDUSTRY OF THE GREAT KANAWAH
        VALLEY OF VIRGINIA: A STUDY OF ANTE-BELLUM INTERNAL
        COMMERCE."   PH.D. DISSERTATION, WEST VIRGINIA
        ·UNIVERSITY, 1970.

14809   STEALEY, JOHN E.   "SLAVERY AND THE WESTERN VIRGINIA SALT
        INDUSTRY."   JOURNAL OF NEGRO HISTORY, 59 (APRIL,
        1974):   105-131.

14810   STEFFEN, CHARLES G.   "CHANGES IN THE ORGANIZATION OF
        ARTISAN PRODUCTION IN BALTIMORE, 1790 TO 1820."
        WILLIAM AND MARY QUARTERLY, 3RD SER., 36 (JANUARY,
        1979):   101-117.

14811   STEFFEN, CHARLES G.   "THE PRE-INDUSTRIAL IRON WORKER:
        NORTHAMPTON IRON WORKS, 1780-1820."   LABOR HISTORY, 20
        (WINTER, 1979):   89-110.

14812   STOCKHOLM, RICHARD J.   "ALABAMA IRON FOR THE CONFEDERACY:
        THE SELMA IRON WORKS."   ALABAMA REVIEW, 21 (JULY,
        1968):   163-172.

14813   STOKES, ALLEN H.   "BLACK AND WHITE LABOR AND THE
        DEVELOPMENT OF THE SOUTHERN TEXTILE INDUSTRY,

          1800-1920." PH.D. DISSERTATION, UNIVERSITY OF SOUTH
          CAROLINA, 1977.

14814   SUPER, JOHN C. "QUERETARO OBRAJES: INDUSTRY AND SOCIETY
        IN PROVINCIAL MEXICO, 1600-1810." HISPANIC AMERICAN
        HISTORICAL REVIEW, 56 (MAY, 1976): 197-216.

14815   TERRILL, TOM E. "EAGER HANDS: LABOR FOR SOUTHERN
        TEXTILES, 1850-1860." JOURNAL OF ECONOMIC HISTORY, 36
        (MARCH, 1976): 84-99.

14816   TUCKER, HELEN A. "NEGRO CRAFTSMEN IN AFRICA AND THE
        SOUTH." SOUTHERN WORKMEN, 36 (NOVEMBER, 1907):
        613-615.

14817   VANDIVER, FRANK E. "THE SHELBY IRON COMPANY IN THE CIVIL
        WAR: A STUDY OF A CONFEDERATE INDUSTRY." ALABAMA
        REVIEW, 1 (JANUARY, 1948): 12-26.

14818   VANDIVER, FRANK E. "THE SHELBY IRON WORKS: A STUDY IN
        CONFEDERATE INDUSTRY." ALABAMA REVIEW, 1 (JULY,
        1948): 203-217.

14819   VEDDER, RICHARD K.; GALLAWAY, LOWELL E.; AND KLINGAMAN,
        DAVID C. "DISCRIMINATION AND EXPLOITATION IN
        ANTEBELLUM AMERICAN COTTON TEXTILE MANUFACTURING."
        RESEARCH IN ECONOMIC HISTORY, 3 (1978): 217-262.

14820   WADE, RICHARD C. SLAVERY IN THE CITIES: THE SOUTH,
        1820-1860. NEW YORK: OXFORD UNIVERSITY PRESS, 1964.

14821   WADE, RICHARD C. THE URBAN FRONTIER: THE RISE OF
        WESTERN CITIES, 1790-1830. CAMBRIDGE: HARVARD
        UNIVERSITY PRESS, 1959.

14822   WALKER, JOSEPH E. HOPEWELL VILLAGE: A SOCIAL AND
        ECONOMIC HISTORY OF AN IRON COMMUNITY. PHILADELPHIA:
        UNIVERSITY OF PENNSYLVANIA PRESS, 1966.

14823   WALKER, JOSEPH E. "NEGRO LABOR IN THE CHARCOAL IRON
        INDUSTRY OF SOUTHEASTERN PENNSYLVANIA." PENNSYLVANIA
        MAGAZINE OF HISTORY AND BIOGRAPHY, 93 (OCTOBER, 1969):
        466-486.

14824   WALSH, RICHARD. "THE CHARLESTON MECHANICS: A BRIEF
        STUDY, 1760-1776." SOUTH CAROLINA HISTORICAL
        MAGAZINE, 60 (JULY, 1959): 123-144.

14825   WHITELY, WILLIAM G. "THE PRINCIPIO COMPANY: A
        HISTORICAL SKETCH OF THE FIRST IRON-WORKS IN
        MARYLAND." PENNSYLVANIA MAGAZINE OF HISTORY AND
        BIOGRAPHY, 11 (1887): 63-68, 190-198, 288-295.

14826   WOOD, PETER H. "WHETTING, SETTING AND LAYING
        TIMBERS--BLACK BUILDERS IN THE EARLY SOUTH." SOUTHERN

EXPOSURE, 8 (SPRING, 1930): 3-8.

14827   WOODWARD, JOSEPH H.   "ALABAMA IRON MANUFACTURING,
        1860-1865."   ALABAMA REVIEW, 7 (JULY, 1954):   199-207.

14828   WOODWORTH, J.B.   "THE HISTORY OF CONDITIONS OF MINING IN
        THE RICHMOND COAL-BASIN, VIRGINIA."   TRANSACTIONS OF
        THE AMERICAN INSTITUTE OF MINING ENGINEERS, 31 (1902):
        477-484.

14829   WRIGHT, GAVIN.   "CHEAP LABOR AND SOUTHERN TEXTILES BEFORE
        1880."   JOURNAL OF ECONOMIC HISTORY, 39 (SEPTEMBER,
        1979):   655-680.

SLAVE DRIVERS

14830   BRAZIL, BLAS.   "A HISTORY OF THE OBRAJES IN NEW SPAIN,
        1535-1630."   M.A. THESIS, UNIVERSITY OF NEW MEXICO,
        1962.

14831   COULTER, E. MERTON.   THOMAS SPALDING OF SAPELO.
        UNIVERSITY, LA: LOUISIANA STATE UNIVERSITY PRESS,
        1940.

14832   EATON, CLEMENT.   "THE MIND OF THE SOUTHERN NEGRO: THE
        REMARKABLE INDIVIDUALS."   THE MIND OF THE OLD SOUTH.
        BATON ROUGE: LOUISIANA STATE UNIVERSITY PRESS, 1967,
        PP. 170-199.

14833   EATON, CLEMENT.   THE WANING OF THE OLD SOUTH
        CIVILIZATION.   ATHENS: UNIVERSITY OF GEORGIA PRESS,
        1968.

14834   FOGEL, ROBERT W. AND ENGERMAN, STANLEY L.   TIME ON THE
        CROSS: THE ECONOMICS OF AMERICAN NEGRO SLAVERY.   2
        VOLS.   BOSTON: LITTLE, BROWN AND COMPANY, 1974.

14835   GEGGUS, DAVID P.   "THE SLAVES OF BRITISH-OCCUPIED SAINT
        DOMINGUE: AN ANALYSIS OF THE WORKFORCES OF 197
        ABSENTEE PLANTATIONS, 1796-1797."   CARIBBEAN STUDIES,
        18 (APRIL-JULY, 1978):   5-42.

14836   GENOVESE, EUGENE D.   ROLL, JORDAN, ROLL: THE WORLD THE
        SLAVES MADE.   NEW YORK: PANTHEON, 1974.

14837   GRAY, LEWIS C.   HISTORY OF AGRICULTURE IN THE SOUTHERN
        UNITED STATES TO 1860.   2 VOLS.   WASHINGTON: CARNEGIE
        INSTITUTION OF WASHINGTON, 1932.

14838   HART, ALBERT B.   SLAVERY AND ABOLITION, 1831-1841.   NEW
        YORK: HARPER AND BROTHERS, 1906.

14839   HASKELL, JOSEPH A.   "SACRIFICIAL OFFERINGS AMONG NORTH
        CAROLINA NEGROES."   JOURNAL OF AMERICAN FOLKLORE, 4

(JULY—SEPTEMBER, 1891):   267-269.

14840   JACKSON, SHIRLEY M. "BLACK SLAVE DRIVERS IN THE
        ANTEBELLUM SOUTH." M.A. THESIS, PURDUE UNIVERSITY,
        1973.

14841   JACKSON, SHIRLEY M. "BLACK SLAVE DRIVERS IN THE SOUTHERN
        UNITED STATES." PH.D. DISSERTATION, BOWLING GREEN
        STATE UNIVERSITY, 1977.

14842   LITWACK, LEON F. BEEN_IN_THE_STORM_SO_LONG:__THE
        AFTERMATH_OF_SLAVERY. NEW YORK: ALFRED A. KNOPF,
        1979.

14843   MILLER, RANDALL M. "THE MAN IN THE MIDDLE: THE BLACK
        SLAVE DRIVER." AMERICAN_HERITAGE, 30
        (OCTOBER—NOVEMBER, 1979): 40-49.

14844   OWENS, LESLIE H. THIS_SPECIES_OF_PROPERTY:__SLAVE_LIFE
        AND_CULTURE_IN_THE_OLD_SOUTH. NEW YORK: OXFORD
        UNIVERSITY PRESS, 1976.

14845   PERDUE, CHARLES L., JR.; BARDEN, THOMAS E.; AND PHILLIPS,
        ROBERT K. (EDS.). WEEVILS_IN_THE_WHEAT:__INTERVIEWS
        WITH_VIRGINIA_EX-SLAVES. CHARLOTTESVILLE: UNIVERSITY
        PRESS OF VIRGINIA, 1976.

14846   SCARBOROUGH, WILLIAM K. THE_OVERSEER:__PLANTATION
        MANAGEMENT_IN_THE_OLD_SOUTH. BATON ROUGE: LOUISIANA
        STATE UNIVERSITY PRESS, 1966.

14847   "SLAVE DRIVER." IN SCHAPSMEIER, EDWARD L. AND
        SCHAPSMEIER, FREDERICK H. ENCYCLOPEDIA_OF_AMERICAN
        AGRICULTURAL_HISTORY. WESTPORT: GREENWOOD PRESS,
        1975, P. 320.

14848   SNEED, LEONORA. "TYPES OF RICE PLANTATION NEGROES."
        SOUTHERN_WORKMAN, 32 (FEBRUARY, 1903): 107-114.

14849   STAROBIN, ROBERT. BLACKS_IN_BONDAGE:__LETTERS_OF
        AMERICAN_SLAVES. NEW YORK: NEW VIEWPOINTS, 1974.

14850   STAROBIN, ROBERT S. "PRIVILEGED BONDSMEN AND THE PROCESS
        OF ACCOMMODATION: THE ROLE OF HOUSESERVANTS AND
        DRIVERS AS SEEN IN THEIR OWN LETTERS." JOURNAL_OF
        SOCIAL_HISTORY, 5 (FALL, 1971): 46-70.

14851   STONE, JAMES H. "BLACK LEADERSHIP IN THE OLD SOUTH: THE
        SLAVE DRIVERS OF THE RICE KINGDOM." PH.D.
        DISSERTATION, FLORIDA STATE UNIVERSITY, 1976.

14852   VAN DEBURG, WILLIAM L. "ELITE SLAVE BEHAVIOR DURING THE
        CIVIL WAR: BLACK DRIVERS AND FOREMEN IN
        HISTORIOGRAPHICAL PERSPECTIVE." SOUTHERN_STUDIES, 16
        (FALL, 1977): 253-269.

14853   VAN DEBURG, WILLIAM L.   "SLAVE DRIVERS AND SLAVE
        NARRATIVES: A NEW LOOK AT THE 'DEHUMANIZED ELITE.'"
        HISTORIAN, 39 (AUGUST, 1977): 717-732.

14854   VAN DEBURG, WILLIAM L.   THE SLAVE DRIVERS: BLACK
        AGRICULTURAL LABOR SUPERVISORS IN THE ANTEBELLUM
        SOUTH. WESTPORT: GREENWOOD PRESS, 1979.

14855   VAN DEBURG, WILLIAM L.   "THE SLAVE DRIVERS OF ARKANSAS:
        A NEW VIEW FROM THE NARRATIVES." ARKANSAS HISTORICAL
        QUARTERLY, 35 (AUTUMN, 1976): 231-245.

14856   VAN DEBURG, WILLIAM L.   "WHO WERE THE SLAVE DRIVERS?"
        NEGRO HISTORY BULLETIN, 41 (MARCH, 1978): 808-810.

14857   WILEY, BELL I.   SOUTHERN NEGROES, 1861-1865. NEW HAVEN:
        YALE UNIVERSITY PRESS, 1938.

OVERSEERS

14858   BASSETT, JOHN S.   THE SOUTHERN PLANTATION OVERSEER AS
        REVEALED IN HIS LETTERS. NORTHAMPTON, MA: SMITH
        COLLEGE FIFTIETH ANNIVERSARY PUBLICATIONS, 1925.

14859   BERTRAM, WINIFRED E.   "THE PLANTATION OVERSEER IN THE
        LOWER SOUTH PRIOR TO THE CIVIL WAR." M.A. THESIS,
        UNIVERSITY OF CHICAGO, 1928.

14860   BONNER, JAMES C.   "THE PLANTATION OVERSEER AND SOUTHERN
        NATIONALISM AS REVEALED IN THE CAREER OF GARLAND D.
        HARMON." AGRICULTURAL HISTORY, 19 (JANUARY, 1945):
        1-10.

14861   BREEDEN, JAMES O. (ED.).   ADVICE AMONG MASTERS: THE
        IDEAL IN SLAVE MANAGEMENT IN THE OLD SOUTH. WESTPORT:
        GREENWOOD PRESS, 1980.

14862   BRYANT, CHARLES A.   "OVERSEERS OF THE SOUTHERN SLAVE
        PLANTATION." M.A. THESIS, SOUTHERN METHODIST
        UNIVERSITY, 1931.

14863   COULTER, E. MERTON.   THOMAS SPALDING OF SAPELO.
        UNIVERSITY, LA: LOUISIANA STATE UNIVERSITY PRESS,
        1940.

14864   DAVENPORT, F. GARVIN (ED.).   "JUDGE SHARKEY PAPERS."
        MISSISSIPPI VALLEY HISTORICAL REVIEW, 20 (JUNE, 1933):
        76-90.

14865   EATON, CLEMENT.   "THE MIND OF THE SOUTHERN NEGRO: THE
        REMARKABLE INDIVIDUALS." THE MIND OF THE OLD SOUTH.
        BATON ROUGE: LOUISIANA STATE UNIVERSITY PRESS, 1967,
        PP. 170-199.

14866   FOGEL, ROBERT W. AND ENGERMAN, STANLEY L. _TIME ON THE CROSS: THE ECONOMICS OF AMERICAN NEGRO SLAVERY_. 2 VOLS. BOSTON: LITTLE, BROWN AND COMPANY, 1974.

14867   GENOVESE, EUGENE D. _ROLL, JORDAN, ROLL: THE WORLD THE SLAVES MADE_. NEW YORK: PANTHEON, 1974.

14868   GRAY, LEWIS C. _HISTORY OF AGRICULTURE IN THE SOUTHERN UNITED STATES TO 1860_. 2 VOLS. WASHINGTON: CARNEGIE INSTITUTION OF WASHINGTON, 1932.

14869   HART, ALBERT B. _SLAVERY AND ABOLITION, 1831-1841_. NEW YORK: HARPER AND BROTHERS, 1906.

14870   HASKELL, JOSEPH A. "SACRIFICIAL OFFERINGS AMONG NORTH CAROLINA NEGROES." _JOURNAL OF AMERICAN FOLKLORE_, 4 (JULY-SEPTEMBER, 1891): 267-269.

14871   HOOLE, W. STANLEY. "ADVICE TO AN OVERSEER: EXTRACTS FROM THE 1840-1842 PLANTATION JOURNAL OF JOHN HORRY DENT." _ALABAMA REVIEW_, 1 (JANUARY, 1948): 50-63.

14872   JACKSON, HARVEY H. "THE CALM BEFORE THE STORM: A LOUISIANA OVERSEER'S WORLD ON THE EVE OF THE CIVIL WAR." _SOUTHERN STUDIES_, 13 (SUMMER, 1979): 241-246.

14873   LITWACK, LEON F. _BEEN IN THE STORM SO LONG: THE AFTERMATH OF SLAVERY_. NEW YORK: ALFRED A. KNOPF, 1979.

14874   MOORE, JOHN HEBRON. (ED.). "TWO DOCUMENTS RELATING TO PLANTATION OVERSEERS OF THE VICKSBURG REGION, 1831-1832." _JOURNAL OF MISSISSIPPI HISTORY_, 16 (JANUARY, 1954): 31-36.

14875   MORTON, LOUIS. "ROBERT WORMELEY CARTER OF SABINE HALL: NOTES ON THE LIFE OF A VIRGINIA PLANTER." _JOURNAL OF SOUTHERN HISTORY_, 12 (AUGUST, 1946): 345-365.

14876   NEVINS, ALLAN. "THE LOT OF THE BONDSMAN." _ORDEAL OF THE UNION_. 2 VOLS. NEW YORK: CHARLES SCRIBNER'S SONS, 1947, VOL. 1, PP. 412-461.

14877   OTTO, JOHN S. "ARTIFACTS AND STATUS DIFFERENCES--A COMPARISON OF CERAMICS FROM PLANTER, OVERSEER, AND SLAVE SITES ON AN ANTEBELLUM PLANTATION." IN SOUTH, STANLEY (ED.). _RESEARCH STRATEGIES IN HISTORICAL ARCHEOLOGY_. NEW YORK: ACADEMIC PRESS, 1977, PP. 91-118.

14878   OTTO, JOHN S. "STATUS DIFFERENCES AND THE ARCHEOLOGICAL RECORD--A COMPARISON OF PLANTER, OVERSEER, AND SLAVE SITES FROM CANNON'S POINT PLANTATION (1794-1861), ST. SIMON'S ISLAND, GEORGIA." PH.D. DISSERTATION, UNIVERSITY OF FLORIDA, 1975.

14879   "OVERSEER." IN SCHAPSMEIER, EDWARD L. AND SCHAPSMEIER,
        FREDERICK H. ENCYCLOPEDIA OF AMERICAN AGRICULTURAL
        HISTORY. WESTPORT: GREENWOOD PRESS, 1975, P. 258.

14880   PERDUE, CHARLES L., JR.; BARDEN, THOMAS E.; AND PHILLIPS,
        ROBERT K. (EDS.). WEEVILS IN THE WHEAT: INTERVIEWS
        WITH VIRGINIA EX-SLAVES. CHARLOTTESVILLE: UNIVERSITY
        PRESS OF VIRGINIA, 1976.

14881   PHILLIPS, ULRICH B. AMERICAN NEGRO SLAVERY: A SURVEY OF
        THE SUPPLY, EMPLOYMENT AND CONTROL OF NEGRO LABOR AS
        DETERMINED BY THE PLANTATION REGIME. NEW YORK: D.
        APPLETON, 1918.

14882   PHILLIPS, ULRICH B. LIFE AND LABOR IN THE OLD SOUTH.
        BOSTON: LITTLE, BROWN AND COMPANY, 1929.

14883   "RICHARD STANUP WHO HAD CHARGE OF GEORGE WASHINGTON'S
        SLAVES." NEGRO HISTORY BULLETIN, 32 (FEBRUARY, 1969):
        12-13.

14884   ROTHSTEIN, MORTON. "THE ANTE-BELLUM PLANTATION AS A
        BUSINESS ENTERPRISE: A REVIEW OF SCARBOROUGH'S THE
        OVERSEER." EXPLORATIONS IN ENTREPRENEURIAL HISTORY, 6
        (FALL, 1968):   128-133.

14885   SCARBOROUGH, WILLIAM K. THE OVERSEER: PLANTATION
        MANAGEMENT IN THE OLD SOUTH. BATON ROUGE: LOUISIANA
        STATE UNIVERSITY PRESS, 1966.

14886   SCARBOROUGH, WILLIAM K. "PLANTATION MANAGEMENT IN THE
        ANTE-BELLUM SOUTH: THE OVERSEER." PH.D.
        DISSERTATION, UNIVERSITY OF NORTH CAROLINA, 1962.

14887   SCARBOROUGH, WILLIAM K. "THE PLANTATION OVERSEER: A
        RE-EVALUATION." AGRICULTURAL HISTORY, 38 (JANUARY,
        1964):   13-20.

14888   SITTERSON, J. CARLYLE. "HIRED LABOR ON SUGAR PLANTATIONS
        OF THE ANTE-BELLUM SOUTH." JOURNAL OF SOUTHERN
        HISTORY, 14 (MAY, 1948):   192-205.

14889   SITTERSON, J. CARLYLE. "MAGNOLIA PLANTATION, 1853-1862:
        A DECADE OF A LOUISIANA SUGAR ESTATE." MISSISSIPPI
        VALLEY HISTORICAL REVIEW, 25 (SEPTEMBER, 1938):
        197-210.

14890   SOLTOW, LEE. "ECONOMIC INEQUALITY IN THE UNITED STATES
        IN THE PERIOD FROM 1790 TO 1860." JOURNAL OF ECONOMIC
        HISTORY, 31 (DECEMBER, 1971):   822-839.

14891   STAMPP, KENNETH M. THE PECULIAR INSTITUTION: SLAVERY IN
        THE ANTE-BELLUM SOUTH. NEW YORK: ALFRED A. KNOPF,
        1956.

14892　STAROBIN, ROBERT.　BLACKS IN BONDAGE:　LETTERS OF
　　　　AMERICAN SLAVES.　NEW YORK:　NEW VIEWPOINTS, 1974.

14893　SYDNOR, CHARLES S.　"A SLAVE OWNER AND HIS OVERSEERS."
　　　　NORTH CAROLINA HISTORICAL REVIEW, 14 (JANUARY, 1937):
　　　　31-38.

14894　SYDNOR, CHARLES S.　SLAVERY IN MISSISSIPPI.　NEW YORK:
　　　　D. APPLETON-CENTURY COMPANY, 1933.

14895　TAYLOR, ORVILLE W. (ED.).　"A LETTER FROM GOVERNOR JAMES
　　　　S. CONWAY TO HIS PLANTATION OVERSEER."　ARKANSAS
　　　　HISTORICAL QUARTERLY, 18 (SUMMER, 1959):　90-92.

14896　VAN DEBURG, WILLIAM L.　THE SLAVE DRIVERS:　BLACK
　　　　AGRICULTURAL LABOR SUPERVISORS IN THE ANTEBELLUM
　　　　SOUTH.　WESTPORT:　GREENWOOD PRESS, 1979.

14897　WILEY, BELL I.　SOUTHERN NEGROES, 1861-1865.　NEW HAVEN:
　　　　YALE UNIVERSITY PRESS, 1938.

14898　WILLIAMS, ELIZABETH J.　"THE GRAMMAR OF PLANTATION
　　　　OVERSEER'S LETTERS, ROCKINGHAM COUNTY, 1829-1860."
　　　　M.A. THESIS, UNIVERSITY OF NORTH CAROLINA, 1953.

SLAVE DEMOGRAPHY

14899　ADELAIDE, JACQUES.　"DEMOGRAPHY AND NAMES OF SLAVES OF LE
　　　　MAULE 1845 TO MAY 1848."　IN MARSHALL, WOODVILLE K.
　　　　(ED.).　PAPERS PRESENTED AT THE THIRD CONFERENCE OF
　　　　CARIBBEAN HISTORIANS.　N.P., 1971, PP. 86-90.

14900　ANDREWS, GEORGE R.　THE AFRO-ARGENTINES OF BUENOS AIRES,
　　　　1800-1900.　MADISON:　UNIVERSITY OF WISCONSIN PRESS,
　　　　1980.

14901　ATKINSON, THOMAS P.　"REPORT ON THE ANATOMICAL,
　　　　PHYSIOLOGICAL AND PATHOLOGICAL DIFFERENCES BETWEEN THE
　　　　WHITE AND THE BLACK RACES, AND ON THE MODIFICATIONS OF
　　　　THE TREATMENT OF THE DISEASES OF THE LATTER RENDERED
　　　　NECESSARY THEREBY."　TRANSACTIONS OF THE MEDICAL
　　　　SOCIETY OF VIRGINIA, 4 (1872-1875):　65-71, 105-114.

14902　BELL, MATTIE.　"THE GROWTH AND DISTRIBUTION OF THE TEXAS
　　　　POPULATION."　M.A. THESIS, BAYLOR UNIVERSITY, 1935.

14903　"BLACK AND WHITE RATIOS FOR ELEVEN DECADES."　NATION, 73
　　　　(NOVEMBER 21, 1901):　391-392.

14904　BONSAL, LEIGH.　"POST-REVOLUTIONARY MOVEMENT OF SLAVES
　　　　SOUTHWARD."　NATION, 46 (FEBRUARY 16, 1888):　135-136.

14905　BOSSY, JOHN.　"DEMOGRAPHY AND DEMAGOGY; ON THE HISTORY OF
　　　　RURAL PEOPLE."　ENCOUNTER, 46 (JANUARY, 1976):　62-66.

14906   BRINKLEY, FRANCES K. "AN ANALYSIS OF THE 1750 CARRIACOU
        CENSUS." CARIBBEAN QUARTERLY, 24 (MARCH-JUNE, 1978):
        44-60.

14907   BROWNING, DAVID G. AND ROBINSON, DAVID J. "THE ORIGIN
        AND COMPARABILITY OF PERUVIAN POPULATION DATA:
        1776-1815." JAHRBUCH FUR GESCHICHTE VON STAAT,
        WIRTSCHAFT UND GESELLSCHAFT, 14 (1977): 199-223.

14908   CAMPBELL, RANDOLPH B. "SLAVEHOLDING IN HARRISON COUNTY,
        1850-1860: A STATISTICAL PROFILE." EAST TEXAS
        HISTORICAL JOURNAL, 11 (SPRING, 1973): 18-27.

14909   CARMAGNANI, MARCELLO. "COLONIAL LATIN AMERICAN
        DEMOGRAPHY: GROWTH OF CHILEAN POPULATION, 1700-1830."
        JOURNAL OF SOCIAL HISTORY, 1 (WINTER, 1967): 179-191.

14910   CARROLL, PATRICK J. "BLACK LABORERS AND THEIR EXPERIENCE
        IN COLONIAL JALAPA." IN REUNION DE HISTORIADORES
        MEXICANOS Y NORTEAMERICANOS Y LOS TRABAJADORES EN LA
        HISTORIA DE MEXICO. MEXICO: COLEGIO DE MEXICO, 1979,
        PP. 119-132.

14911   CASSEDY, JAMES H. DEMOGRAPHY IN EARLY AMERICA:
        BEGINNINGS OF THE STATISTICAL MIND, 1600-1800.
        CAMBRIDGE: HARVARD UNIVERSITY PRESS, 1969.

14912   CHAPMAN, ANNE W. "INADEQUACIES OF THE 1848 CHARLESTON
        CENSUS." SOUTH CAROLINA HISTORICAL MAGAZINE, 81
        (JANUARY, 1980): 24-34.

14913   CLARKE, ROBERT L. "SOME SOURCES IN THE NATIONAL ARCHIVES
        FOR STUDIES OF AFRO-AMERICAN POPULATION: GROWTH AND
        MOVEMENT." IN EHRENBERG, RALPH E. (ED.). PATTERN AND
        PROCESS: RESEARCH IN HISTORICAL GEOGRAPHY.
        WASHINGTON: HOWARD UNIVERSITY PRESS, 1975, PP. 73-80.

14914   "COLORED STATISTICS." NATION, 77 (NOVEMBER 19, 1903):
        400-401.

14915   COOK, SHERBURNE F. AND BORAH, WOODROW. ESSAYS IN
        POPULATION HISTORY: MEXICO AND THE CARIBBEAN.
        BERKELEY: UNIVERSITY OF CALIFORNIA PRESS, 1971.

14916   COOK, SHERBURNE F. AND SIMPSON, LESLEY B. THE POPULATION
        OF CENTRAL MEXICO IN THE SIXTEENTH CENTURY. BERKELEY:
        UNIVERSITY OF CALIFORNIA PRESS, 1948.

14917   CRATON, MICHAEL J. "JAMAICAN SLAVE MORTALITY: FRESH
        LIGHT FROM WORTHY PARK, LONGVILLE AND THE THARP
        ESTATES." JOURNAL OF CARIBBEAN HISTORY, 3 (NOVEMBER,
        1971): 1-27.

14918   CURTIN, PHILIP D. "THE AFRICAN DIASPORA." HISTORICAL
        REFLECTIONS, 6 (SUMMER, 1979): 1-17.

14919   CURTIN, PHILIP D. THE ATLANTIC SLAVE TRADE: A CENSUS.
         MADISON: UNIVERSITY OF WISCONSIN PRESS, 1969.

14920   CURTIN, PHILIP D. "MEASURING THE ATLANTIC SLAVE TRADE."
         IN ENGERMAN, STANLEY L. AND GENOVESE, EUGENE D.
         (EDS.). RACE AND SLAVERY IN THE WESTERN HEMISPHERE:
         QUANTITATIVE STUDIES. PRINCETON: PRINCETON
         UNIVERSITY PRESS, 1975, PP. 107-128.

14921   CURTIN, PHILIP D. "MEASURING THE ATLANTIC SLAVE TRADE
         ONCE AGAIN: A COMMENT." JOURNAL OF AFRICAN HISTORY,
         17 (1976): 595-605.

14922   CUSHNER, NICHOLAS P. "SLAVE MORTALITY AND REPRODUCTION
         ON HACIENDAS IN COLONIAL PERU." HISPANIC AMERICAN
         HISTORICAL REVIEW, 55 (MAY, 1975): 177-199.

14923   DAVIS, GEORGE A. AND DONALDSON, O. FRED. BLACKS IN THE
         UNITED STATES: A GEOGRAPHIC PERSPECTIVE. BOSTON:
         HOUGHTON MIFFLIN, 1975.

14924   DAVIS, JAMES E. FRONTIER AMERICA, 1800-1840: A
         COMPARATIVE DEMOGRAPHIC ANALYSIS OF THE SETTLEMENT
         PROCESS. GLENDALE, CA: ARTHUR H. CLARK COMPANY, 1977.

14925   DAVIS, THOMAS J. "POPULATION AND SLAVERY IN NEW YORK."
         M.A. THESIS, COLUMBIA UNIVERSITY, 1968.

14926   DEAN, JOHN G. "THE FREE NEGRO IN DELAWARE: A
         DEMOGRAPHIC AND ECONOMIC STUDY, 1790-1860." M.A.
         THESIS, UNIVERSITY OF DELAWARE, 1970.

14927   DORAN, MICHAEL F. "POPULATION STATISTICS OF NINETEENTH
         CENTURY INDIAN TERRITORY." CHRONICLES OF OKLAHOMA, 53
         (WINTER, 1975-1976): 492-515.

14928   DUBLIN, LOUIS I. "LIFE, DEATH AND THE NEGRO." AMERICAN
         MERCURY, 12 (SEPTEMBER, 1927): 37-45.

14929   DUNN, RICHARD S. "THE BARBADOS CENSUS OF 1680: PROFILE
         OF THE RICHEST COLONY IN ENGLISH AMERICA." JOURNAL OF
         THE BARBADOS MUSEUM AND HISTORICAL SOCIETY, 33
         (NOVEMBER, 1969): 57-75.

14930   DUNN, RICHARD S. "THE BARBADOS CENSUS OF 1680: PROFILE
         OF THE RICHEST COLONY IN ENGLISH AMERICA." WILLIAM
         AND MARY QUARTERLY, 3RD SER., 26 (JANUARY, 1969):
         3-30.

14931   EBLEN, JACK. "NEW ESTIMATES OF THE VITAL RATES OF THE
         UNITED STATES BLACK POPULATION DURING THE NINETEENTH
         CENTURY." IN VINOVSKIS, MARIS A. (ED.). STUDIES IN
         AMERICAN HISTORICAL DEMOGRAPHY. NEW YORK: ACADEMIC
         PRESS, 1979, PP. 339-357.

14932   EBLEN, JACK E.   "GROWTH OF THE BLACK POPULATION IN ANTE
         BELLUM AMERICA, 1820-1860."   POPULATION STUDIES, 26
         (JULY, 1972):   273-289.

14933   EBLEN, JACK E.   "NEW ESTIMATES OF THE VITAL RATES OF THE
         UNITED STATES BLACK POPULATION DURING THE NINETEENTH
         CENTURY."   DEMOGRAPHY, 11 (MAY, 1974):   301-319.

14934   EBLEN, JACK E.   "ON THE NATURAL INCREASE OF SLAVE
         POPULATIONS: THE EXAMPLE OF THE CUBAN BLACK
         POPULATION, 1775-1900."   IN ENGERMAN, STANLEY L. AND
         GENOVESE, EUGENE D. (EDS.).   RACE AND SLAVERY IN THE
         WESTERN HEMISPHERE: QUANTITATIVE STUDIES.   PRINCETON:
         PRINCETON UNIVERSITY PRESS, 1975, PP. 211-247.

14935   ELLSWORTH, ROBERT A.   "REGIONAL DEMOGRAPHIC TRENDS IN
         ANTEBELLUM AMERICA."   PH.D. DISSERTATION, UNIVERSITY
         OF UTAH, 1974.

14936   ENGERMAN, STANLEY L.   "BLACK FERTILITY AND FAMILY
         STRUCTURE IN THE UNITED STATES, 1880-1940."   JOURNAL
         OF FAMILY HISTORY, 2 (SUMMER, 1977):   117-138.

14937   ENGERMAN, STANLEY L.   "COMMENTARY."   HISTORICAL
         REFLECTIONS, 6 (SUMMER, 1979):   204-211.

14938   ENGERMAN, STANLEY L.   "THE HEIGHT OF SLAVES IN THE UNITED
         STATES."   LOCAL POPULATION STUDIES, 16 (SPRING, 1976):
         45-50.

14939   ENGERMAN, STANLEY L.   "SOME ECONOMIC AND DEMOGRAPHIC
         COMPARISONS OF SLAVERY IN THE UNITED STATES AND THE
         BRITISH WEST INDIES."   ECONOMIC HISTORY REVIEW, 29
         (MAY, 1976):   258-275.

14940   ERNST, WILLIAM J.   "CHANGES IN THE SLAVE POPULATION OF
         THE VIRGINIA TIDEWATER AND PIEDMONT, 1830-1860:   A
         STABLE POPULATION ANALYSIS."   ESSAYS IN HISTORY, 19
         (1975):   75-88.

14941   FAGE, J.D.   "THE EFFECT OF THE EXPORT SLAVE TRADE ON
         AFRICAN POPULATIONS."   IN RATHBONE, R.J.A.R. AND MOSS,
         R.P. (EDS.).   THE POPULATION FACTOR IN AFRICAN
         STUDIES.   LONDON: UNIVERSITY OF LONDON PRESS, 1975,
         PP. 15-23.

14942   FARLEY, REYNOLDS.   "THE DEMOGRAPHIC RATES AND SOCIAL
         INSTITUTIONS OF THE NINETEENTH CENTURY NEGRO
         POPULATION: A STABLE POPULATION ANALYSIS."
         DEMOGRAPHY, 2 (1965):   386-398.

14943   FARLEY, REYNOLDS.   GROWTH OF THE BLACK POPULATION: A
         STUDY OF DEMOGRAPHIC TRENDS.   CHICAGO: MARKHAM
         PUBLISHING COMPANY, 1970.

14944   FOGEL, ROBERT W.   "RECENT DEVELOPMENTS IN THE DEMOGRAPHY
        OF SLAVERY." UNPUBLISHED PAPER, 1977.

14945   FOGEL, ROBERT W. AND ENGERMAN, STANLEY L.   "RECENT
        FINDINGS IN THE STUDY OF SLAVE DEMOGRAPHY AND FAMILY
        STRUCTURE." SOCIOLOGY AND SOCIAL RESEARCH, 63 (APRIL,
        1979):   566-589.

14946   FOGEL, ROBERT W. AND ENGERMAN, STANLEY L.   TIME ON THE
        CROSS: THE ECONOMICS OF AMERICAN NEGRO SLAVERY.   2
        VOLS.   BOSTON: LITTLE, BROWN AND COMPANY, 1974.

14947   FOGEL, ROBERT W. AND ENGERMAN, STANLEY L.   "WHY THE U.S.
        SLAVE POPULATION GREW SO RAPIDLY: FERTILITY,
        MORTALITY, AND HOUSEHOLD STRUCTURE." UNPUBLISHED
        PAPER, 1975.

14948   FOGEL, ROBERT W.; ENGERMAN, STANLEY L.; TRUSSELL, JAMES;
        FLOUD, RODERICK; POPE, CLAYNE L.; AND WIMMER, LARRY T.
        "THE ECONOMICS OF MORTALITY IN NORTH AMERICA,
        1650-1910:   A DESCRIPTION OF A RESEARCH PROJECT."
        HISTORICAL METHODS, 11 (SPRING, 1978):   75-108.

14949   FORTUNE, T. THOMAS. "MOVEMENT OF THE AFRO-AMERICAN
        POPULATION FROM THE SOUTHERN STATES." A.M.E. CHURCH
        REVIEW, 33 (JANUARY, 1917):   127-129.

14950   FRAGINALS, MANUEL M. "AFRICA IN CUBA: A QUANTITATIVE
        ANALYSIS OF THE AFRICAN POPULATION IN THE ISLAND OF
        CUBA."   IN RUBIN, VERA AND TUDEN, ARTHUR (EDS.).
        COMPARATIVE PERSPECTIVES ON SLAVERY IN NEW WORLD
        PLANTATION SOCIETIES.   NEW YORK: NEW YORK ACADEMY OF
        SCIENCES, 1977, PP. 187-201.

14951   GEGGUS, DAVID P.   "THE SLAVES OF BRITISH-OCCUPIED SAINT
        DOMINGUE: AN ANALYSIS OF THE WORKFORCES OF 197
        ABSENTEE PLANTATIONS, 1796-1797."   CARIBBEAN STUDIES,
        18 (APRIL-JULY, 1978):   5-42.

14952   GREENE, EVARTS B. AND HARRINGTON, VIRGINIA D.   AMERICAN
        POPULATION BEFORE THE FEDERAL CENSUS OF 1790.   NEW
        YORK: COLUMBIA UNIVERSITY PRESS, 1932.

14953   HARDING, LEONARD L.   "THE NEGRO IN CINCINNATI, 1860-1870;
        A DEMOGRAPHIC STUDY OF A TRANSITIONAL DECADE."   M.A.
        THESIS, UNIVERSITY OF CINCINNATI, 1967.

14954   HARRIS, JOSEPH E.   "A COMMENTARY ON THE SLAVE TRADE."   IN
        THE AFRICAN SLAVE TRADE FROM THE FIFTEENTH TO THE
        NINETEENTH CENTURY.   PARIS: UNITED NATIONS
        EDUCATIONAL, SCIENTIFIC AND CULTURAL ORGANIZATION,
        1979, PP. 289-295.

14955   HARRIS, MARVIN.   PATTERNS OF RACE IN THE AMERICAS.   NEW
        YORK: WALKER AND COMPANY, 1964.

14956   HENRETTA, JAMES A.   THE EVOLUTION OF AMERICAN SOCIETY,
        1700-1815:   AN INTERDISCIPLINARY ANALYSIS.   LEXINGTON,
        MA: D.C. HEATH AND COMPANY, 1973.

14957   HIGMAN, B.W.   "THE DEMOGRAPHY OF SLAVERY IN JAMAICA,
        1817-1834."   IN PAPERS PRESENTED AT THE THIRD ANNUAL
        CONFERENCE OF CARIBBEAN HISTORIANS, APRIL 15-17, 1971.
        GEORGETOWN: UNIVERSITY OF GUYANA, 1971, PP. 32-40.

14958   HIGMAN, B.W.C.   "THE POPULATION GEOGRAPHY OF SLAVERY IN
        THE BRITISH CARIBBEAN, 1807-1834."   PH.D.
        DISSERTATION, UNIVERSITY OF LIVERPOOL, 1976.

14959   HIGMAN, BARRY W.   "GROWTH IN AFRO-CARIBBEAN SLAVE
        POPULATIONS."   AMERICAN JOURNAL OF PHYSICAL
        ANTHROPOLOGY, 50 (MARCH, 1979):   373-386.

14960   HIGMAN, BARRY W.   "HOUSEHOLD STRUCTURE AND FERTILITY ON
        JAMAICAN SLAVE PLANTATIONS: A NINETEENTH-CENTURY
        EXAMPLE."   POPULATION STUDIES: A JOURNAL OF
        DEMOGRAPHY, 27 (NOVEMBER, 1973):   527-550.

14961   HIGMAN, BARRY W.   SLAVE POPULATION AND ECONOMY IN
        JAMAICA, 1807-1834.   CAMBRIDGE: CAMBRIDGE UNIVERSITY
        PRESS, 1976.

14962   HIGMAN, BARRY W.   "SLAVE POPULATION AND ECONOMY IN
        JAMAICA AT THE TIME OF EMANCIPATION (WITH A
        STATISTICAL COMPARISON)."   PH.D. DISSERTATION,
        UNIVERSITY OF THE WEST INDIES, 1971.

14963   HOEPPLI, R.   PARASITIC DISEASES IN AFRICA AND THE WESTERN
        HEMISPHERE: EARLY DOCUMENTATION AND TRANSMISSION BY
        THE SLAVE TRADE.   ACTA TROPICA, SUPPLEMENTUM 10.
        BASEL: VERLAG FUR RECHT UND GESELLSCHAFT AG., BASEL,
        1969, PP. V-XII, 3-240.

14964   HOFFMAN, FREDERICK L.   "RACE TRAITS AND TENDENCIES OF THE
        AMERICAN NEGRO."   PUBLICATIONS OF THE AMERICAN
        ECONOMIC ASSOCIATION, 11 (AUGUST, 1896):   1-329.

14965   HOLLAND, C.G.   "THE SLAVE POPULATION ON THE PLANTATION OF
        JOHN C. COHOON, JR., NANSEMOND COUNTY, VIRGINIA,
        1811-1863:   SELECTED DEMOGRAPHIC CHARACTERISTICS."
        VIRGINIA MAGAZINE OF HISTORY AND BIOGRAPHY, 80
        (JANUARY, 1972):   333-340.

14966   JOHNSON, LYMAN L. AND SOCOLOW, SUSAN M.   "POPULATION AND
        SPACE IN EIGHTEENTH-CENTURY BUENOS AIRES."   IN
        ROBINSON, DAVID J. (ED.).   SOCIAL FABRIC AND SPATIAL
        STRUCTURE IN COLONIAL LATIN AMERICA.   ANN ARBOR:
        UNIVERSITY MICROFILMS INTERNATIONAL, 1979, PP. 339-368.

14967   JOHNSON, RICHARD H.   THE PHYSICAL DEGENERACY OF THE
        MODERN NEGRO: WITH STATISTICS FROM THE PRINCIPAL

CITIES, SHOWING HIS MORTALITY FROM A.D. 1700 TO 1897.
BRUNSWICK, GA: N.P., 1897.

14968   KAKE, I.B. "THE SLAVE TRADE AND THE POPULATION DRAIN
        FROM BLACK AFRICA TO NORTH AFRICA AND THE MIDDLE
        EAST." IN THE AFRICAN SLAVE TRADE FROM THE FIFTEENTH
        TO THE NINETEENTH CENTURY. PARIS: UNITED NATIONS
        EDUCATIONAL, SCIENTIFIC AND CULTURAL ORGANIZATION,
        1979, PP. 164-174.

14969   KARINEN, ARTHUR E. "MARYLAND POPULATION: 1631-1730:
        NUMERICAL AND DISTRIBUTIONAL ASPECTS." MARYLAND
        HISTORICAL MAGAZINE, 54 (DECEMBER, 1959): 365-407.

14970   KAY, MARVIN L.M. AND CARY, LORIN L. "CLASS, MOBILITY,
        AND CONFLICT IN CAROLINA ON THE EVE OF THE
        REVOLUTION." IN CROW, JEFFREY J. AND TISE, LARRY E.
        (EDS.). THE SOUTHERN EXPERIENCE IN THE AMERICAN
        REVOLUTION. CHAPEL HILL: UNIVERSITY OF NORTH
        CAROLINA PRESS, 1978, PP. 109-151.

14971   KILSON, MARION D. DE B. "AFRO-AMERICAN SOCIAL STRUCTURE,
        1790-1970." IN KILSON, MARTIN L. AND ROTBERG, ROBERT
        I. (EDS.). THE AFRICAN DIASPORA: INTERPRETIVE
        ESSAYS. CAMBRIDGE: HARVARD UNIVERSITY PRESS, 1976,
        PP. 414-458.

14972   KIPLE, KENNETH F. BLACKS IN COLONIAL CUBA, 1774-1899.
        GAINESVILLE: UNIVERSITY PRESSES OF FLORIDA, 1976.

14973   KIPLE, KENNETH F. "THE CUBAN SLAVE TRADE, 1820-1862:
        THE DEMOGRAPHIC IMPLICATIONS FOR COMPARATIVE STUDIES."
        PH.D. DISSERTATION, UNIVERSITY OF FLORIDA, 1970.

14974   KIPLE, KENNETH F. AND KIPLE, VIRGINIA H. "DEFICIENCY
        DISEASES IN THE CARIBBEAN." JOURNAL OF
        INTERDISCIPLINARY HISTORY, 11 (AUTUMN, 1980): 197-215.

14975   KIPLE, KENNETH F. AND KIPLE, VIRGINIA H. "SLAVE CHILD
        MORTALITY: SOME NUTRITIONAL ANSWERS TO A PERENNIAL
        PUZZLE." IN BRANCA, PATRICIA (ED.). MEDICINE SHOW:
        PATIENTS, PHYSICIANS, AND THE PERPLEXITIES OF THE
        HEALTH REVOLUTION IN MODERN SOCIETY. NEW YORK:
        SCIENCE HISTORY PUBLISHERS, 1977, PP. 21-46.

14976   KIPLE, KENNETH F. AND KIPLE, VIRGINIA H. "SLAVE CHILD
        MORTALITY: SOME NUTRITIONAL ANSWERS TO A PERENNIAL
        PUZZLE." JOURNAL OF SOCIAL HISTORY, 10 (MARCH, 1977):
        284-309.

14977   KLEIN, HERBERT S. THE MIDDLE PASSAGE: COMPARATIVE
        STUDIES IN THE ATLANTIC SLAVE TRADE. PRINCETON:
        PRINCETON UNIVERSITY PRESS, 1978.

14978   KLEIN, HERBERT S. "PATTERNS OF SETTLEMENT OF THE

AFRO-AMERICAN POPULATION IN THE NEW WORLD." IN
HUGGINS, NATHAN I.; KILSON, MARTIN; AND FOX, DANIEL M.
(EDS.). KEY ISSUES IN THE AFRO-AMERICAN EXPERIENCE.
2 VOLS. NEW YORK: HARCOURT, BRACE, JOVANOVICH, 1971,
VOL. 1, PP. 99-115.

14979 KLEIN, HERBERT S. "THE TRADE IN AFRICAN SLAVES TO RIO DE
       JANEIRO, 1795-1811: ESTIMATES OF MORTALITY AND
       PATTERNS OF VOYAGES." JOURNAL OF AFRICAN HISTORY, 10
       (1969): 533-549.

14980 KLEIN, HERBERT S. AND ENGERMAN, STANLEY L. "THE
       DEMOGRAPHIC STUDY OF THE AMERICAN SLAVE POPULATIONS."
       PAPER PRESENTED AT THIRD INTERNATIONAL COLLOQUIUM ON
       DEMOGRAPHIC HISTORY, MONTREAL, 1975.

14981 KLEIN, HERBERT S. AND ENGERMAN, STANLEY L. "A NOTE ON
       MORTALITY IN THE FRENCH SLAVE TRADE IN THE EIGHTEENTH
       CENTURY." IN GEMERY, HENRY A. AND HOGENDORN, JAN S.
       (EDS.). THE UNCOMMON MARKET: ESSAYS IN THE ECONOMIC
       HISTORY OF THE ATLANTIC SLAVE TRADE. NEW YORK:
       ACADEMIC PRESS, 1979, PP. 261-272.

14982 KLEIN, HERBERT S. AND ENGERMAN, STANLEY L. "SHIPPING
       PATTERNS AND MORTALITY IN THE AFRICAN SLAVE TRADE TO
       RIO DE JANEIRO, 1825-1830." CAHIERS D'ETUDES
       AFRICAINES, 15 (1975): 381-398.

14983 KLEIN, HERBERT S. AND ENGERMAN, STANLEY L. "SLAVE
       MORTALITY ON BRITISH SHIPS, 1791-1797." IN ANSTEY,
       ROGER AND HAIR, P.E.H. (EDS.). LIVERPOOL, THE AFRICAN
       SLAVE TRADE, AND ABOLITION. BRISTOL: HISTORIC
       SOCIETY OF LANCASHIRE AND CHESHIRE OCCASIONAL SERIES
       VOL. 2, 1976, PP. 113-125.

14984 KNIGHT, FRANKLIN W. "SEXUAL COMPOSITION AND THE AFRICAN
       SLAVE TRADE TO THE CARIBBEAN." PAPER PRESENTED AT
       VIRGINIA STATE UNIVERSITY SLAVE TRADE SYMPOSIUM,
       PETERSBURG, VA, OCTOBER 4-5, 1979.

14985 KULIKOFF, ALLAN. "A 'PROLIFICK' PEOPLE: BLACK
       POPULATION GROWTH IN THE CHESAPEAKE COLONIES."
       SOUTHERN STUDIES, 16 (WINTER, 1977): 391-428.

14986 LAMUR, HUMPHREY E. "DEMOGRAPHY OF SURINAM PLANTATION
       SLAVES IN THE LAST DECADE BEFORE EMANCIPATION: THE
       CASE OF CATHARINA SOPHIA." IN RUBIN, VERA AND TUDEN,
       ARTHUR (EDS.). COMPARATIVE PERSPECTIVES ON SLAVERY IN
       NEW WORLD PLANTATION SOCIETIES. NEW YORK: NEW YORK
       ACADEMY OF SCIENCES, 1977, PP. 161-173.

14987 LANTZ, HERMAN AND HENDRIX, LEWELLYN. "BLACK FERTILITY
       AND THE BLACK FAMILY IN THE NINETEENTH CENTURY: A
       RE-EXAMINATION OF THE PAST." JOURNAL OF FAMILY
       HISTORY, 3 (FALL, 1978): 251-261.

14988   LATHROP, BARNES F.   MIGRATION INTO EAST TEXAS, 1835-1860:
         A STUDY FROM THE UNITED STATES CENSUS. AUSTIN: TEXAS
         STATE HISTORICAL ASSOCIATION, 1949.

14989   LOMBARDI, JOHN V.   PEOPLES AND PLACES IN COLONIAL
         VENEZUELA. BLOOMINGTON: INDIANA UNIVERSITY PRESS,
         1976.

14990   LOWE, RICHARD G. AND CAMPBELL, RANDOLPH B.   "THE
         SLAVE-BREEDING HYPOTHESIS: A DEMOGRAPHIC COMMENT ON
         THE 'BUYING' AND 'SELLING' STATES." JOURNAL OF
         SOUTHERN HISTORY, 42 (AUGUST, 1976): 401-412.

14991   LOWENTHAL, DAVID. "POPULATION CONTRASTS IN THE GUIANAS."
         GEOGRAPHICAL REVIEW, 50 (JANUARY, 1960): 41-58.

14992   LUTZ, CHRISTOPHER H. "SANTIAGO DE GUATEMALA, 1541-1773:
         THE SOCIO-DEMOGRAPHIC HISTORY OF A SPANISH AMERICAN
         COLONIAL CITY." PH.D. DISSERTATION, UNIVERSITY OF
         WISCONSIN, 1976.

14993   MAIN, GLORIA L. "PERSONAL WEALTH IN COLONIAL AMERICA:
         EXPLORATIONS IN THE USE OF PROBATE RECORDS FROM
         MARYLAND AND MASSACHUSETTS, 1650-1720." PH.D.
         DISSERTATION, COLUMBIA UNIVERSITY, 1972.

14994   MEEKER, EDWARD. "MORTALITY TRENDS OF SOUTHERN BLACKS,
         1850-1910: SOME PRELIMINARY FINDINGS." EXPLORATIONS
         IN ECONOMIC HISTORY, 13 (JANUARY, 1976): 13-42.

14995   MENARD, RUSSELL R. "IMMIGRANTS AND THEIR INCREASE: THE
         PROCESS OF POPULATION GROWTH IN EARLY COLONIAL
         MARYLAND." IN LAND, AUBREY C.; CARR, LOIS G.; AND
         PAPENFUSE, EDWARD C. (EDS.). LAW, SOCIETY, AND
         POLITICS IN EARLY MARYLAND. BALTIMORE: JOHNS HOPKINS
         UNIVERSITY PRESS, 1977, PP. 88-110.

14996   MENARD, RUSSELL R. "THE MARYLAND SLAVE POPULATION, 1658
         TO 1730: A DEMOGRAPHIC PROFILE OF BLACKS IN FOUR
         COUNTIES." WILLIAM AND MARY QUARTERLY, 3RD SER., 32
         (JANUARY, 1975): 29-54.

14997   MILLER, WILLIAM L. "SLAVERY AND THE POPULATION OF THE
         SOUTH." SOUTHERN ECONOMIC JOURNAL, 28 (JULY, 1961):
         46-54.

14998   MODELL, JOHN. "HERBERT GUTMAN'S THE BLACK FAMILY IN
         SLAVERY AND FREEDOM, 1750-1925: DEMOGRAPHIC
         PERSPECTIVES." SOCIAL SCIENCE HISTORY, 3 (OCTOBER,
         1979): 45-55.

14999   MOLEN, PATRICIA A. "POPULATION AND SOCIAL PATTERNS IN
         BARBADOS IN THE EARLY EIGHTEENTH CENTURY." WILLIAM
         AND MARY QUARTERLY, 3RD SER., 28 (APRIL, 1971):
         287-300.

15000   MORRILL, RICHARD L. AND DONALDSON, O. FRED.
         "GEOGRAPHICAL PERSPECTIVES ON THE HISTORY OF BLACK
         AMERICA." ECONOMIC GEOGRAPHY, 48 (JANUARY, 1972):
         1-23.

15001   MURRAY, D.R. "STATISTICS OF THE SLAVE TRADE TO CUBA,
         1790-1867." JOURNAL OF LATIN AMERICAN STUDIES, 3
         (NOVEMBER, 1971): 131-149.

15002   "THE NEGRO RACE IN THE SOUTH." AFRICAN REPOSITORY, 50
         (APRIL, 1874): 128.

15003   NORTHRUP, DAVID. "AFRICAN MORTALITY IN THE SUPPRESSION
         OF THE SLAVE TRADE: THE CASE OF THE BIGHT OF BIAFRA."
         JOURNAL OF INTERDISCIPLINARY HISTORY, 9 (SUMMER,
         1978): 47-64.

15004   OBERSEIDER, NANCY L. "A SOCIO-DEMOGRAPHIC STUDY OF THE
         FAMILY AS A SOCIAL UNIT IN TIDEWATER VIRGINIA,
         1660-1776." PH.D. DISSERTATION, UNIVERSITY OF
         MARYLAND, 1975.

15005   OGOT, BETHWELL A. "POPULATION MOVEMENTS BETWEEN EAST
         AFRICA, THE HORN OF AFRICA AND THE NEIGHBOURING
         COUNTRIES." IN THE AFRICAN SLAVE TRADE FROM THE
         FIFTEENTH TO THE NINETEENTH CENTURY. PARIS: UNITED
         NATIONS EDUCATIONAL, SCIENTIFIC AND CULTURAL
         ORGANIZATION, 1979, PP. 175-182.

15006   OWSLEY, FRANK L. PLAIN FOLK OF THE OLD SOUTH. BATON
         ROUGE: LOUISIANA STATE UNIVERSITY PRESS, 1949.

15007   PAPENFUSE, EDWARD C., JR. "PLANTER BEHAVIOR AND ECONOMIC
         OPPORTUNITY IN A STAPLE ECONOMY." AGRICULTURAL
         HISTORY, 46 (APRIL, 1972): 297-311.

15008   PAQUETTE, ROBERT L. "SLAVERY IN LOUISIANA AND CUBA: A
         DEMOGRAPHIC APPROACH." M.A. THESIS, BOWLING GREEN
         STATE UNIVERSITY, 1976.

15009   PATTERSON, J. STAHL. "INCREASE AND MOVEMENT OF THE
         COLORED POPULATION." POPULAR SCIENCE MONTHLY, 19
         (SEPTEMBER, OCTOBER, 1881): 665-675, 784-790.

15010   PHILLIPS, ULRICH B. "A JAMAICA SLAVE PLANTATION."
         AMERICAN HISTORICAL REVIEW, 19 (APRIL, 1914): 543-558.

15011   PHILLIPS, ULRICH B. "THE ORIGIN AND GROWTH OF THE
         SOUTHERN BLACK BELTS." AMERICAN HISTORICAL REVIEW, 11
         (JULY, 1906): 798-816.

15012   PHILLIPS, ULRICH B. "THE SLAVE LABOR PROBLEM IN THE
         CHARLESTON DISTRICT." POLITICAL SCIENCE QUARTERLY, 22
         (SEPTEMBER, 1907): 416-439.

15013   POLLARD, LESLIE J.   "AGE AND PATERNALISM IN A SLAVE
        SOCIETY."   PERSPECTIVE ON AGING, 7 (NOVEMBER-DECEMBER,
        1978):   4-8.

15014   "POPULATION OF BARBADOS."   JOURNAL OF THE BARBADOS MUSEUM
        AND HISTORICAL SOCIETY, 8 (NOVEMBER, 1945-FEBRUARY,
        1946):   3-20.

15015   POSTELL, WILLIAM D.   "BIRTH AND MORTALITY RATES AMONG
        SLAVE INFANTS ON SOUTHERN PLANTATIONS."   PEDIATRICS,
        10 (NOVEMBER, 1952):   538-541.

15016   POSTELL, WILLIAM D.   "SLAVES AND THEIR LIFE EXPECTANCY."
        BULLETIN OF THE TULANE UNIVERSITY MEDICAL FACULTY, 26
        (FEBRUARY, 1967):   7-11.

15017   POSTMA, JOHANNES.   "MORTALITY IN THE DUTCH SLAVE TRADE,
        1675-1795."   IN GEMERY, HENRY A. AND HOGENDORN, JAN S.
        (EDS.).   THE UNCOMMON MARKET: ESSAYS IN THE ECONOMIC
        HISTORY OF THE ATLANTIC SLAVE TRADE.   NEW YORK:
        ACADEMIC PRESS, 1979, PP. 239-260.

15018   POTTER, J.   "THE GROWTH OF POPULATION IN AMERICA,
        1700-1860."   IN GLASS, D.V. AND EVERSLEY, D.E.C.
        (EDS.).   POPULATION IN HISTORY.   CHICAGO: ALDINE
        PUBLISHING COMPANY, 1965, PP. 631-688.

15019   RICARDS, SHERMAN L. AND BLACKBURN, GEORGE M.   "A
        DEMOGRAPHIC HISTORY OF SLAVERY: GEORGETOWN COUNTY,
        SOUTH CAROLINA, 1850."   SOUTH CAROLINA HISTORICAL
        MAGAZINE, 76 (OCTOBER, 1975):   215-224.

15020   ROBERTS, G.W.   "IMMIGRATION OF AFRICANS INTO THE BRITISH
        CARIBBEAN."   POPULATION STUDIES, 7 (1953-1954):
        235-263.

15021   ROBERTS, G.W.   "MOVEMENTS IN SLAVE POPULATION OF THE
        CARIBBEAN DURING THE PERIOD OF SLAVE REGISTRATION."
        IN RUBIN, VERA AND TUDEN, ARTHUR (EDS.).   COMPARATIVE
        PERSPECTIVES ON SLAVERY IN NEW WORLD PLANTATION
        SOCIETIES.   NEW YORK: NEW YORK ACADEMY OF SCIENCES,
        1977, PP. 145-160.

15022   ROBERTS, GEORGE W.   "A LIFE TABLE FOR A WEST INDIAN SLAVE
        POPULATION."   POPULATION STUDIES, 5 (MARCH, 1952):
        238-243.

15023   RUTMAN, DARRETT B.; WETHERELL, CHARLES; AND RUTMAN, ANITA
        H.   "RHYTHMS OF LIFE: BLACK AND WHITE SEASONALITY IN
        THE EARLY CHESAPEAKE."   JOURNAL OF INTERDISCIPLINARY
        HISTORY, 11 (SUMMER, 1980):   29-54.

15024   RYAN, TERRENCE C.I.   "THE ECONOMICS OF TRADING IN
        SLAVES."   PH.D. DISSERTATION, MASSACHUSETTS INSTITUTE
        OF TECHNOLOGY, 1975.

15025   SCOTT, ROLAND B. AND WINSTON, MICHAEL R. "THE HEALTH AND
        WELFARE OF THE BLACK FAMILY IN THE UNITED STATES: A
        HISTORICAL AND INSTITUTIONAL ANALYSIS." AMERICAN
        JOURNAL OF DISEASES OF CHILDREN, 130 (JULY, 1976):
        704-707.

15026   SHIMKIN, DEMITRI B. "TEXAS INDEED IS DIFFERENT: SOME
        HISTORICAL AND DEMOGRAPHIC OBSERVATIONS." IN SHIMKIN,
        DEMITRI B.; SHIMKIN, EDITH M.; AND FRATE, DENNIS A.
        (EDS.). THE EXTENDED FAMILY IN BLACK SOCIETIES. THE
        HAGUE: MOUTON PUBLISHERS, 1978, PP. 363-378.

15027   SLENES, ROBERT W. "THE DEMOGRAPHY AND ECONOMICS OF
        BRAZILIAN SLAVERY: 1850-1888." PH.D. DISSERTATION,
        STANFORD UNIVERSITY, 1976.

15028   THE SOCIAL AND ECONOMIC STATUS OF THE BLACK POPULATION IN
        THE UNITED STATES: AN HISTORICAL VIEW, 1790-1978.
        WASHINGTON: GOVERNMENT PRINTING OFFICE, 1979.

15029   SPENGLER, JOSEPH J. "POPULATION THEORY IN THE
        ANTE-BELLUM SOUTH." JOURNAL OF SOUTHERN HISTORY, 2
        (NOVEMBER, 1936): 360-389.

15030   STECKEL, RICHARD. "THE ECONOMICS OF U.S. SLAVE AND
        SOUTHERN FREE-WHITE FERTILITY." UNPUBLISHED PAPER,
        UNIVERSITY OF CHICAGO, 1973.

15031   STECKEL, RICHARD. "NEGRO SLAVERY IN THE WESTERN
        HEMISPHERE." UNPUBLISHED PAPER, UNIVERSITY OF
        CHICAGO, 1971.

15032   STECKEL, RICHARD H. "ANTEBELLUM SOUTHERN WHITE
        FERTILITY: A DEMOGRAPHIC AND ECONOMIC ANALYSIS."
        JOURNAL OF ECONOMIC HISTORY, 40 (JUNE, 1980): 331-350.

15033   STECKEL, RICHARD H. "THE ECONOMICS OF THE UNITED STATES
        SLAVE AND SOUTHERN WHITE FERTILITY." PH.D.
        DISSERTATION, UNIVERSITY OF CHICAGO, 1977.

15034   STECKEL, RICHARD H. "MISCEGENATION AND THE AMERICAN
        SLAVE SCHEDULES." JOURNAL OF INTERDISCIPLINARY
        HISTORY, 11 (AUTUMN, 1980): 251-263.

15035   STECKEL, RICHARD H. "SLAVE HEIGHT PROFILES FROM
        COASTWISE MANIFESTS." EXPLORATIONS IN ECONOMIC
        HISTORY, 16 (OCTOBER, 1979): 363-380.

15036   STECKEL, RICHARD H. "SLAVE MORTALITY: ANALYSIS OF
        EVIDENCE FROM PLANTATION RECORDS." SOCIAL SCIENCE
        HISTORY, 3 (OCTOBER, 1979): 86-114.

15037   SUTCH, RICHARD. THE BREEDING OF SLAVES FOR SALE AND THE
        WESTERN EXPANSION OF SLAVERY, 1850-1860. SOUTHERN
        ECONOMIC HISTORY PROJECT WORKING PAPER SERIES NO. 10.

BERKELEY: UNIVERSITY OF CALIFORNIA, INSTITUTE OF BUSINESS AND ECONOMIC RESEARCH, 1972.

15038 SUTCH, RICHARD. "THE BREEDING OF SLAVES FOR SALE AND THE WESTWARD EXPANSION OF SLAVERY, 1850-1860." IN ENGERMAN, STANLEY L. AND GENOVESE, EUGENE D. (EDS.). RACE AND SLAVERY IN THE WESTERN HEMISPHERE: QUANTITATIVE STUDIES. PRINCETON: PRINCETON UNIVERSITY PRESS, 1975, PP. 173-210.

15039 SYDNOR, CHARLES S. "LIFE SPAN OF MISSISSIPPI SLAVES." AMERICAN HISTORICAL REVIEW, 35 (APRIL, 1930): 566-574.

15040 TAYLOR, ALRUTHEUS A. "THE MOVEMENT OF THE NEGROES FROM THE EAST TO THE GULF STATES FROM 1830 TO 1850." JOURNAL OF NEGRO HISTORY, 8 (OCTOBER, 1923): 367-383.

15041 THOMAS, HERBERT A., JR. "VICTIMS OF CIRCUMSTANCE: NEGROES IN A SOUTHERN TOWN, 1865-1880." REGISTER OF THE KENTUCKY HISTORICAL SOCIETY, 71 (JULY, 1973): 253-271.

15042 THOMPSON, ALANA S. "MOBILE, ALABAMA, 1850-1861: ECONOMIC, POLITICAL, PHYSICAL AND POPULATION CHARACTERISTICS." PH.D. DISSERTATION, UNIVERSITY OF ALABAMA, 1979.

15043 THORNTON, JOHN. "THE SLAVE TRADE IN EIGHTEENTH CENTURY ANGOLA: EFFECTS ON DEMOGRAPHIC STRUCTURES." CANADIAN JOURNAL OF AFRICAN STUDIES, 14 (1980): 417-428.

15044 TRUSSELL, JAMES AND STECKEL, RICHARD. "THE AGE OF SLAVES AT MENARCHE AND THEIR FIRST BIRTH." JOURNAL OF INTERDISCIPLINARY HISTORY, 8 (WINTER, 1978): 477-505.

15045 TULLY, ALAN. "PATTERNS OF SLAVEHOLDING IN COLONIAL PENNSYLVANIA: CHESTER AND LANCASTER COUNTIES, 1729-1758." JOURNAL OF SOCIAL HISTORY, 6 (SPRING, 1973): 284-305.

15046 U.S. DEPARTMENT OF COMMERCE, CENSUS BUREAU. NEGRO POPULATION GROWTH, 1790-1909. WASHINGTON: GOVERNMENT PRINTING OFFICE, 1909.

15047 U.S. DEPARTMENT OF COMMERCE, CENSUS BUREAU. NEGRO POPULATION IN THE UNITED STATES, 1790-1915. WASHINGTON: GOVERNMENT PRINTING OFFICE, 1918.

15048 UNITED STATES, BUREAU OF THE CENSUS. THE SOCIAL AND ECONOMIC STATUS OF THE BLACK POPULATION IN THE UNITED STATES, 1790-1978: AN HISTORICAL VIEW. WASHINGTON: U.S. GOVERNMENT PRINTING OFFICE, 1979.

15049 VINOVSKIS, MARIS A. "THE DEMOGRAPHY OF THE SLAVE POPULATION IN ANTEBELLUM AMERICA." JOURNAL OF

INTERDISCIPLINARY HISTORY, 5 (WINTER, 1975): 459-467.

15050 "THE VIRGINIA CENSUS, 1624-1625." VIRGINIA MAGAZINE OF
HISTORY AND BIOGRAPHY, 7 (APRIL, 1900): 364-365.

15051 WALKER, FRANCIS A. "STATISTICS OF THE COLORED RACE IN
THE UNITED STATES." PUBLICATIONS OF THE AMERICAN
STATISTICAL ASSOCIATION, N.S., 2 (SEPTEMBER, DECEMBER,
1890): 91-106.

15052 WATSON, ALAN D. "HOUSEHOLD SIZE AND COMPOSITION IN
PRE-REVOLUTIONARY NORTH CAROLINA." MISSISSIPPI
QUARTERLY, 31 (FALL, 1978): 551-569.

15053 WELLS, ROBERT V. THE POPULATION OF THE BRITISH COLONIES
IN AMERICA BEFORE 1776: A SURVEY OF CENSUS DATA.
PRINCETON: PRINCETON UNIVERSITY PRESS, 1975.

15054 WESSMAN, JAMES W. "THE DEMOGRAPHIC STRUCTURE OF SLAVERY
IN PUERTO RICO: SOME ASPECTS OF AGRARIAN CAPITALISM
IN THE LATE NINETEENTH CENTURY." JOURNAL OF LATIN
AMERICAN STUDIES, 12 (NOVEMBER, 1980): 271-289.

15055 WEYL, NATHANIEL. "SOME GENETIC ASPECTS OF PLANTATION
SLAVERY." PERSPECTIVES IN BIOLOGY AND MEDICINE, 13
(SUMMER, 1970): 618-625.

15056 WHITE, WILLIAM W. "MIGRATION INTO WEST TEXAS,
1845-1860." M.A. THESIS, UNIVERSITY OF TEXAS, 1948.

15057 WILLIAMS, MELVIN R. "A STATISTICAL STUDY OF BLACKS IN
WASHINGTON, D.C., IN 1860." RECORDS OF THE COLUMBIA
HISTORICAL SOCIETY OF WASHINGTON, D.C., 50 (1980):
172-179.

15058 WILLIAMSON, JOEL. NEW PEOPLE: MISCEGENATION AND
MULATTOES IN THE UNITED STATES. NEW YORK: MACMILLAN
COMPANY, 1980.

15059 WOOD, PETER H. BLACK MAJORITY: NEGROES IN COLONIAL
SOUTH CAROLINA, 1670 TO THE STONO REBELLION. NEW
YORK: ALFRED A. KNOPF, 1974.

15060 WOOD, PETER H. "'MORE LIKE A NEGRO COUNTRY':
DEMOGRAPHIC PATTERNS IN COLONIAL SOUTH CAROLINA,
1700-1740." IN ENGERMAN, STANLEY L. AND GENOVESE,
EUGENE D. (EDS.). RACE AND SLAVERY IN THE WESTERN
HEMISPHERE: QUANTITATIVE STUDIES. PRINCETON:
PRINCETON UNIVERSITY PRESS, 1975, PP. 131-172.

15061 WOODRUFF, JAMES F. "SOME CHARACTERISTICS OF THE ALABAMA
SLAVE POPULATION IN 1850." GEOGRAPHICAL REVIEW, 52
(JULY, 1962): 379-388.

15062 WOODRUFF, JAMES F. "A STUDY OF THE CHARACTERISTICS OF

THE ALABAMA SLAVE POPULATION IN 1850." ANNALS OF THE
ASSOCIATION OF AMERICAN GEOGRAPHERS, 51 (DECEMBER,
1961): 427.

15063 WOODSON, CARTER G. FREE NEGRO HEADS OF FAMILIES IN THE
UNITED STATES IN 1830: TOGETHER WITH A BRIEF
TREATMENT OF THE FREE NEGRO. WASHINGTON: ASSOCIATION
FOR THE STUDY OF NEGRO LIFE AND HISTORY, 1925.

15064 WOOSTER, RALPH A. THE PEOPLE IN POWER: COURTHOUSE AND
STATEHOUSE IN THE LOWER SOUTH, 1850-1860. KNOXVILLE:
UNIVERSITY OF TENNESSEE PRESS, 1969.

15065 WOOSTER, RALPH A. POLITICIANS, PLANTERS, AND PLAIN FOLK:
COURTHOUSE AND STATEHOUSE IN THE UPPER SOUTH,
1850-1860. KNOXVILLE: UNIVERSITY OF TENNESSEE PRESS,
1975.

15066 ZELINSKY, WILBUR. "THE HISTORICAL GEOGRAPHY OF THE NEGRO
POPULATION OF LATIN AMERICA." JOURNAL OF NEGRO
HISTORY, 34 (APRIL, 1949): 153-221.

15067 ZELINSKY, WILBUR. "THE POPULATION GEOGRAPHY OF THE FREE
NEGRO IN ANTE-BELLUM AMERICA." POPULATION STUDIES, 3
(MARCH, 1950): 386-401.

15068 ZELNIK, MELVIN. "FERTILITY OF THE AMERICAN NEGRO IN 1830
AND 1850." POPULATION STUDIES, 20 (JULY, 1966):
77-83.

18.
Domestic Slave Trade

15069   "ANTE-BELLUM ECHOES." INDIANAPOLIS FREEMAN, FEBRUARY 11, 1893.

15070   ARMSTRONG, WILLIAM N. "VIGNETTES OF SLAVERY DAYS." SOUTHERN WORKMAN, 31 (NOVEMBER, 1902): 604-611.

15071   ATKINSON, EDWARD. "'THE NEGRO A BEAST.'" NORTH AMERICAN REVIEW, 181 (AUGUST, 1905): 202-215.

15072   BACHMANN, FREDERICK W. (ED.). "CORRESPONDENCE BETWEEN JEAN AND PIERRE LAFITTE AND JOSEPH ROBIDOUX CONCERNING SALE OF SLAVES AT GALVESTON AND ST. LOUIS, 1818." NEW MEXICO HISTORICAL REVIEW, 27 (APRIL, 1952): 168-170.

15073   BANCROFT, FREDERIC. SLAVE TRADING IN THE OLD SOUTH. BALTIMORE: J.H. FURST COMPANY, 1931.

15074   BANKS, MELVIN J. "THE COASTWIDE SLAVE TRADE." M.A. THESIS, HOWARD UNIVERSITY, 1925.

15075   BERNS, WALTER. "THE CONSTITUTION AND THE MIGRATION OF SLAVES." YALE LAW JOURNAL, 78 (DECEMBER, 1968): 198-228.

15076   "BILL OF SALE FOR SEVEN SLAVES." HOBBIES, 45 (MARCH, 1940): 117.

15077   BLOCK, W.T. "THE ROMANCE OF SABINE LAKE, 1777-1846: SCENE OF SLAVING, SMUGGLING, STEAMBOATING, BORDER CONFLICT, AND COTTON COMMERCE UNDER THE TEXAS REPUBLIC." TEXAS GULF HISTORICAL AND BIOGRAPHICAL RECORD, 9 (NOVEMBER, 1973): 9-43.

15078   BOMAN, MARTHA. "A CITY OF THE OLD SOUTH: JACKSON, MISSISSIPPI, 1850-1860." JOURNAL OF MISSISSIPPI HISTORY, 15 (JANUARY, 1953): 1-32.

15079   BONSAL, LEIGH. "POST-REVOLUTIONARY MOVEMENT OF SLAVES SOUTHWARD." NATION, 45 (FEBRUARY 16, 1888): 135-136.

15080   BRATTON, MARY J. "CREOLE SLAVE CASE (1841)." IN ROLLER, DAVID C. AND TWYMAN, ROBERT W. (EDS.). THE ENCYCLOPEDIA OF SOUTHERN HISTORY. BATON ROUGE: LOUISIANA STATE UNIVERSITY PRESS, 1979, PP. 310-311.

15081   BROWER, ELIZABETH E. "THE AMERICAN SLAVE TRADE: (COLONIAL PERIOD)." M.A. THESIS, COLUMBIA UNIVERSITY, 1925.

15082   CALDERHEAD, WILLIAM L. "DOMESTIC SLAVE TRADE." IN

ROLLER, DAVID C. AND TWYMAN, ROBERT W. (EDS.). THE
ENCYCLOPEDIA OF SOUTHERN HISTORY. BATON ROUGE:
LOUISIANA STATE UNIVERSITY PRESS, 1979, PP. 1117-1118.

15083   CALDERHEAD, WILLIAM L. "FRANKLIN & ARMFIELD COMPANY."
IN ROLLER, DAVID C. AND TWYMAN, ROBERT W. (EDS.). THE
ENCYCLOPEDIA OF SOUTHERN HISTORY. BATON ROUGE:
LOUISIANA STATE UNIVERSITY PRESS, 1979, P. 486.

15084   CALDERHEAD, WILLIAM L. "HOW EXTENSIVE WAS THE BORDER
STATE SLAVE TRADE? A NEW LOOK." CIVIL WAR HISTORY,
18 (MARCH, 1972): 42-55.

15085   CALDERHEAD, WILLIAM L. "THE PROFESSIONAL SLAVE TRADER IN
A SLAVE ECONOMY: AUSTIN WOOLFOLK, A CASE STUDY."
CIVIL WAR HISTORY, 23 (SEPTEMBER, 1977): 195-211.

15086   CARSTENSEN, F.V. AND GOODMAN, S.E. "TROUBLE ON THE
AUCTION BLOCK: INTERREGIONAL SLAVE SALES AND THE
RELIABILITY OF A LINEAR EQUATION." JOURNAL OF
INTERDISCIPLINARY HISTORY, 8 (AUTUMN, 1977): 315-318.

15087   CHANDLER, JULIAN A.C. "SLAVE TRADE." IN RILEY, FRANKLIN
L. (ED.). THE SOUTH IN THE BUILDING OF THE NATION. 12
VOLS. RICHMOND: SOUTHERN HISTORICAL PUBLICATION
SOCIETY, 1909, VOL. 4, PP. 293-294.

15088   CLARK, THOMAS D. "INTERNAL SLAVE TRADE." SOCIAL
STUDIES, 35 (FEBRUARY, 1944): 64-65.

15089   CLARK, THOMAS D. "THE SLAVE TRADE BETWEEN KENTUCKY AND
THE COTTON KINGDOM." MISSISSIPPI VALLEY HISTORICAL
REVIEW, 21 (DECEMBER, 1934): 331-342.

15090   CLARK, THOMAS D. "THE TRADE BETWEEN KENTUCKY AND THE
COTTON KINGDOM IN LIVESTOCK, HEMP AND SLAVES FROM 1840
TO 1860." M.A. THESIS, UNIVERSITY OF KENTUCKY, 1929.

15091   COLEMAN, J. WINSTON JR. "LEXINGTON'S SLAVE DEALERS AND
THEIR SOUTHERN TRADE." FILSON CLUB HISTORY QUARTERLY,
12 (JANUARY, 1938): 1-23.

15092   COLLINS, WINFIELD H. THE DOMESTIC SLAVE TRADE OF THE
SOUTHERN STATES. NEW YORK: BROADWAY PUBLISHING
COMPANY, 1904.

15093   COLVIN, AUDREY T. "THE SLAVE TRADE IN THE DISTRICT OF
COLUMBIA, 1825-1850." M.A. THESIS, HOWARD UNIVERSITY,
1955.

15094   CONNER, ELOISE. "THE SLAVE MARKET IN LEXINGTON,
KENTUCKY, 1850-1860." M.A. THESIS, UNIVERSITY OF
KENTUCKY, 1931.

15095   CUNNINGHAM, EILEEN S. AND SCHNEIDER, MABEL A. "A SLAVE'S

AUTOBIOGRAPHY RETOLD." _WESTERN ILLINOIS REGIONAL STUDIES_, 2 (1979): 109-126.

15096 DANIELS, JONATHAN. _THE DEVIL'S BACKBONE: THE STORY OF THE NATCHEZ TRACE_. NEW YORK: MCGRAW-HILL, 1962.

15097 DART, HENRY P. "THE SLAVE DEPOT OF THE COMPANY OF THE INDIES AT NEW ORLEANS." _LOUISIANA HISTORICAL QUARTERLY_, 9 (APRIL, 1926): 286-287.

15098 DODGE, N.S. "A CHARLESTON VENDUE IN 1842." _GALAXY_, 7 (JANUARY, 1869): 119-123.

15099 EASTERBY, JAMES H. "THE SOUTH CAROLINA RICE FACTOR AS REVEALED IN THE PAPERS OF ROBERT F.W. ALLSTON." _JOURNAL OF SOUTHERN HISTORY_, 7 (MAY, 1941): 160-172.

15100 EVANS, ROBERT JR. "SOME ECONOMIC ASPECTS OF THE DOMESTIC SLAVE TRADE, 1830-1860." _SOUTHERN ECONOMIC JOURNAL_, 27 (APRIL, 1961): 329-337.

15101 FINLEY, MRS. H.R. "THE AMERICAN SLAVE TRADE." _AMERICANA_, 18 (JULY, 1924): 252-257.

15102 FISHER, JOHN E. "SLAVERY AND THE SLAVE TRADE IN THE LOUISIANA PURCHASE." _ESSAYS IN HISTORY_, 13 (1967-1968): 42-58.

15103 FORBES, GEORGE W. "COLORED SLAVE OWNERS AND TRADERS IN THE OLD DAYS." _A.M.E. CHURCH REVIEW_, 29 (JANUARY, 1913): 300-303.

15104 FURNAS, J.C. _GOODBYE TO UNCLE TOM_. NEW YORK: WILLIAM SLOANE ASSOCIATES, 1956.

15105 GOLDFIELD, DAVID R. "FRIENDS AND NEIGHBORS: URBAN-RURAL RELATIONS IN ANTEBELLUM VIRGINIA." _VIRGINIA CAVALCADE_, 25 (SUMMER, 1975): 14-27.

15106 GRAY, LEWIS C. _HISTORY OF AGRICULTURE IN THE SOUTHERN UNITED STATES TO 1860_. 2 VOLS. WASHINGTON: CARNEGIE INSTITUTION OF WASHINGTON, 1932.

15107 GREEN, BARBARA L. "SLAVES, SHIPS, AND CITIZENSHIP: CONGRESSIONAL RESPONSE TO THE COASTWIDE SLAVE TRADE AND STATUS OF SLAVES ON THE HIGH SEAS, 1830-1842." M.A. THESIS, NORTH TEXAS STATE UNIVERSITY, 1975.

15108 GREEN, FLETCHER M. "SLAVE TRADE, AMERICAN." IN ADAMS, JAMES T. (ED.). _CONCISE DICTIONARY OF AMERICAN HISTORY_. NEW YORK: CHARLES SCRIBNER'S SONS, 1962, PP. 876-878.

15109 GREEN, FLETCHER M. "SLAVE TRADE, THE AMERICAN." IN ADAMS, JAMES T. (ED.). _DICTIONARY OF AMERICAN_

HISTORY. 5 VOLS. NEW YORK: CHARLES SCRIBNER'S SONS, 1940, VOL. 5, PP. 91-93.

15110   GREENWALD, BRUCE C.N. ADVERSE SELECTION IN THE LABOR MARKET. NEW YORK: GARLAND PUBLISHERS, 1979.

15111   GREENWALD, BRUCE C.N. "ADVERSE SELECTION IN THE LABOR MARKET." PH.D. DISSERTATION, MASSACHUSETTS INSTITUTE OF TECHNOLOGY, 1978.

15112   GUTMAN, HERBERT AND SUTCH, RICHARD. "THE SLAVE FAMILY: PROTECTED AGENT OF CAPITALIST MASTERS OR VICTIM OF THE SLAVE TRADE?" IN DAVID, PAUL A.; GUTMAN; SUTCH; TEMIN, PETER; AND WRIGHT, GAVIN (EDS.). RECKONING WITH SLAVERY: A CRITICAL STUDY IN THE QUANTITATIVE HISTORY OF AMERICAN NEGRO SLAVERY. NEW YORK: OXFORD UNIVERSITY PRESS, 1976, PP. 94-133.

15113   HENRY, ROBERT S. "FIRST WITH THE MOST" FORREST. INDIANAPOLIS: BOBBS-MERRILL COMPANY, 1944.

15114   HERMANN, JANET S. "THE MCINTOSH AFFAIR." BULLETIN OF THE MISSOURI HISTORICAL SOCIETY, 26 (JANUARY, 1970): 123-143.

15115   HOWE, M.A. DEWOLFE. BRISTOL, RHODE ISLAND, A TOWN BIOGRAPHY. CAMBRIDGE: HARVARD UNIVERSITY PRESS, 1930.

15116   HOWELL, ISABEL. "JOHN ARMFIELD, SLAVE-TRADER." TENNESSEE HISTORICAL QUARTERLY, 2 (MARCH, 1943): 2-39.

15117   HUTSON, CHARLES W. "THE SLAVE TRADE IN TEXAS." IN CHANDLER, JULIAN A.C. (ED.). THE SOUTH IN THE BUILDING OF THE NATION. 12 VOLS. RICHMOND: SOUTHERN HISTORICAL PUBLICATION SOCIETY, 1909, VOL. 3, PP. 351-352.

15118   "IMMIGRATION TO TEXAS AND THE DOMESTIC SLAVE TRADE." QUARTERLY OF THE TEXAS STATE HISTORICAL ASSOCIATION, 9 (APRIL, 1906): 285-286.

15119   JAMES, JACQUELINE. "UNCLE TOM? NOT BOOKER T." AMERICAN HERITAGE, 19 (AUGUST, 1968): 50-63, 95-100.

15120   JERVEY, EDWARD D. AND HUBER, C. HAROLD. "THE CREOLE AFFAIR." JOURNAL OF NEGRO HISTORY, 65 (SUMMER, 1980): 196-211.

15121   JOHNSON, CLIFTON H. "THE CREOLE AFFAIR." CRISIS, 78 (OCTOBER, 1971): 248-250.

15122   JOHNSTON, JAMES H. "A NEW INTERPRETATION OF THE DOMESTIC SLAVE SYSTEM." JOURNAL OF NEGRO HISTORY, 18 (JANUARY, 1933): 39-45.

15123   JONES, ELSIE C. "WATERWAYS OF THE DOMESTIC SLAVE TRADE
        AS SHOWN BY SHIP MANIFESTS, 1808-1860." M.A. THESIS,
        HOWARD UNIVERSITY, 1935.

15124   KELLAR, HERBERT A. (ED.). "A JOURNEY THROUGH THE SOUTH
        IN 1836: DIARY OF JAMES D. DAVIDSON." JOURNAL OF
        SOUTHERN HISTORY, 1 (AUGUST, 1935): 345-377.

15125   KLINGMAN, PETER D. "A FLORIDA SLAVE SALE." FLORIDA
        HISTORICAL QUARTERLY, 52 (JULY, 1973): 62-66.

15126   KOCH, FELIX J. "KENTUCKY ASSOCIATIONS WITH 'UNCLE TOM'S
        CABIN.'" SOUTHERN WORKMAN, 36 (MAY, 1907): 279-284.

15127   KOTLIKOFF, LAURENCE J. "TOWARDS A QUANTITATIVE
        DESCRIPTION OF THE NEW ORLEANS SLAVE MARKET."
        UNPUBLISHED PAPER PRESENTED TO UNIVERSITY OF CHICAGO
        WORKSHOP ON ECONOMIC HISTORY, 1975.

15128   KOTLIKOFF, LAURENCE J. AND PINERA, SEBASTIAN E. "THE OLD
        SOUTH'S STAKE IN THE INTER-REGIONAL MOVEMENT OF
        SLAVES, 1850-1860." JOURNAL OF ECONOMIC HISTORY, 37
        (JUNE, 1977): 434-450.

15129   LAPRADE, WILLIAM T. "THE DOMESTIC SLAVE TRADE IN THE
        DISTRICT OF COLUMBIA." JOURNAL OF NEGRO HISTORY, 11
        (JANUARY, 1926): 17-34.

15130   LORD, DONALD C. "SLAVE ADS AS HISTORICAL EVIDENCE."
        HISTORY TEACHER, 5 (MAY, 1972): 10-16.

15131   LOWE, RICHARD G. AND CAMPBELL, RANDOLPH B. "THE
        SLAVE-BREEDING HYPOTHESIS: A DEMOGRAPHIC COMMENT ON
        THE 'BUYING' AND 'SELLING' STATES." JOURNAL OF
        SOUTHERN HISTORY, 42 (AUGUST, 1976): 401-412.

15132   MARSH, J.O. "DOMESTIC SLAVE TRADE IN THE U.S." M.A.
        THESIS, OHIO STATE UNIVERSITY, 1930.

15133   MAY, PHILIP S. "ZEPHANIA KINGSLEY--NONCONFORMIST."
        FLORIDA HISTORICAL QUARTERLY, 23 (JANUARY, 1945):
        145-159.

15134   MCGETTIGAN, JAMES W. "SLAVE SALES, ESTATE DIVISIONS, AND
        THE SLAVE FAMILY IN BOONE COUNTY, MISSOURI,
        1820-1865." M.A. THESIS, UNIVERSITY OF MISSOURI, 1976.

15135   MCGETTIGAN, JAMES W., JR. "BOONE COUNTY SLAVES: SALES,
        ESTATE DIVISIONS, AND FAMILIES, 1820-1865." MISSOURI
        HISTORICAL REVIEW, 72 (JANUARY, APRIL, 1978):
        176-197, 271-295.

15136   MIDDLETON, ARTHUR P. TOBACCO COAST: A MARITIME HISTORY
        OF CHESAPEAKE BAY IN THE COLONIAL ERA. NEWPORT NEWS:
        MARINER'S MUSEUM, 1953.

15137   MILLER, M. SAMMY. "LEGEND OF A KIDNAPPER." CRISIS, 82
         (APRIL, 1975): 118-120.

15138   MILLER, M. SAMMY. "PATTY CANNON: MURDERER AND KIDNAPPER
         OF FREE BLACKS: A REVIEW OF THE EVIDENCE." MARYLAND
         HISTORICAL MAGAZINE, 72 (FALL, 1977): 419-423.

15139   MILLER, WILLIAM L. "A NOTE ON THE IMPORTANCE OF THE
         INTER-STATE SLAVE TRADE OF THE ANTE BELLUM SOUTH."
         JOURNAL OF POLITICAL ECONOMY, 73 (APRIL, 1965):
         181-187.

15140   "MISSOURI FORMER SLAVES." PHILADELPHIA SUNDAY ITEM, JULY
         24, 1892.

15141   MOOREN, ROBERT L. "THE SLAVE TRADE AND FUGITIVE SLAVES
         DURING THE CIVIL WAR." M.A. THESIS, UNIVERSITY OF
         WISCONSIN, 1949.

15142   NEVINS, ALLAN. "THE LOT OF THE BONDSMAN." ORDEAL OF THE
         UNION. 2 VOLS. NEW YORK: CHARLES SCRIBNER'S SONS,
         1947, VOL. 1, PP. 412-461.

15143   OWENS, LESLIE H. THIS SPECIES OF PROPERTY: SLAVE LIFE
         AND CULTURE IN THE OLD SOUTH. NEW YORK: OXFORD
         UNIVERSITY PRESS, 1976.

15144   PERDUE, CHARLES L., JR.; BARDEN, THOMAS E.; AND PHILLIPS,
         ROBERT K. (EDS.). WEEVILS IN THE WHEAT: INTERVIEWS
         WITH VIRGINIA EX-SLAVES. CHARLOTTESVILLE: UNIVERSITY
         PRESS OF VIRGINIA, 1976.

15145   PHILLIPS, ULRICH B. AMERICAN NEGRO SLAVERY: A SURVEY OF
         THE SUPPLY, EMPLOYMENT AND CONTROL OF NEGRO LABOR AS
         DETERMINED BY THE PLANTATION REGIME. NEW YORK: D.
         APPLETON, 1918.

15146   PHILLIPS, ULRICH B. "THE ECONOMICS OF THE SLAVE TRADE,
         FOREIGN AND DOMESTIC." IN BALLAGH, JAMES C. (ED.).
         THE SOUTH IN THE BUILDING OF THE NATION. 12 VOLS.
         RICHMOND: SOUTHERN HISTORICAL PUBLICATION SOCIETY,
         1909, VOL. 5, PP. 124-129.

15147   PHILLIPS, ULRICH B. LIFE AND LABOR IN THE OLD SOUTH.
         BOSTON: LITTLE, BROWN AND COMPANY, 1929.

15148   PHILLIPS, ULRICH B. "RACIAL PROBLEMS, ADJUSTMENTS AND
         DISTURBANCES." IN RILEY, FRANKLIN L. (ED.). THE
         SOUTH IN THE BUILDING OF THE NATION. 12 VOLS.
         RICHMOND: SOUTHERN HISTORICAL PUBLICATION SOCIETY,
         1909, VOL. 4, PP. 194-241.

15149   PRESTON, DICKSON J. "FREDERICK DOUGLASS WAS RIGHT ABOUT
         HIMSELF." BALTIMORE SUN MAGAZINE, APRIL 17, 1977.

15150   "REVIEWS AND PREVIEWS--CHARLES WHITE." ART_NEWS, 69
           (APRIL, 1970): 76.

15151   RICE, ARNOLD S. "SOLD DOWN THE RIVER." IN ROLLER, DAVID
           C. AND TWYMAN, ROBERT W. (EDS.). THE_ENCYCLOPEDIA_OF
           SOUTHERN_HISTORY. BATON ROUGE: LOUISIANA STATE
           UNIVERSITY PRESS, 1979, P. 1124.

15152   RIDGEWAY, MICHAEL A. "A PECULIAR BUSINESS: SLAVE
           TRADING IN ALEXANDRIA, VIRGINIA, 1825-1861." M.A.
           THESIS, GEORGETOWN UNIVERSITY, 1976.

15153   ROPPOLO, JOSEPH P. "HARRIET BEECHER STOWE AND NEW
           ORLEANS: A STUDY IN HATE." NEW_ENGLAND_QUARTERLY, 30
           (SEPTEMBER, 1957): 346-362.

15154   SCRIBNER, ROBERT L. "SLAVE GANGS ON THE MARCH: BEFORE
           1861 TRAVELERS IN VIRGINIA WITNESSED THE SOUTHWARD
           TREK OF THE SURPLUS SLAVE POPULATION, GUIDED BY SIMON
           LEGREES OF THE HIGHROAD." VIRGINIA_CAVALCADE, 3
           (AUTUMN, 1953): 10-13.

15155   SHELTON, HORACE H. TEXAS_HEROES. AUSTIN: TEXAS
           HERITAGE FOUNDATION, 1951.

15156   SHEPHERD, JAMES F. AND WILLIAMSON, SAMUEL H. "THE
           COASTAL TRADE OF THE NORTH AMERICAN COLONIES,
           1768-1772." JOURNAL_OF_ECONOMIC_HISTORY, 32
           (DECEMBER, 1972): 783-810.

15157   SHERWIN, OSCAR. "SLAVE AUCTIONS AND JAILS." NEGRO
           HISTORY_BULLETIN, 8 (FEBRUARY, 1945): 101-104, 106,
           119.

15158   SHERWIN, OSCAR. "TRADING IN NEGROES." NEGRO_HISTORY
           BULLETIN, 8 (APRIL, 1945): 160-164, 166.

15159   "SLAVE AUCTION (1827)." IN RYWELL, MARTIN (ED.).
           AFRO-AMERICAN_ENCYCLOPEDIA. 10 VOLS. NORTH MIAMI:
           EDUCATIONAL BOOK PUBLISHERS, 1974, VOL. 8, PP.
           2391-2393.

15160   "SLAVE AUCTION (1829)." IN RYWELL, MARTIN (ED.).
           AFRO-AMERICAN_ENCYCLOPEDIA. 10 VOLS. NORTH MIAMI:
           EDUCATIONAL BOOK PUBLISHERS, 1974, VOL. 8, PP.
           2381-2391.

15161   "SLAVE AUCTION (1841)." IN RYWELL, MARTIN (ED.).
           AFRO-AMERICAN_ENCYCLOPEDIA. 10 VOLS. NORTH MIAMI:
           EDUCATIONAL BOOK PUBLISHERS, 1974, VOL. 8, P. 2393.

15162   "SLAVE BREEDING." IN NUNEZ, BENJAMIN. DICTIONARY_OF
           AFRO-LATIN_AMERICAN_CIVILIZATION. WESTPORT:
           GREENWOOD PRESS, 1980, P. 433.

15163   "SLAVE-TRADERS IN MISSOURI." MISSOURI HISTORICAL REVIEW,
         26 (JANUARY, 1932): 184-135.

15164   "SLAVERY AND THE SLAVE TRADE IN THE DISTRICT OF
         COLUMBIA." NEGRO HISTORY BULLETIN, 14 (OCTOBER,
         1950): 7-8, 18.

15165   "SLAVES, BUYING AND SELLING OF." IN RYWELL, MARTIN
         (ED.). AFRO-AMERICAN ENCYCLOPEDIA. 10 VOLS. NORTH
         MIAMI: EDUCATIONAL BOOK PUBLISHERS, 1974, VOL 8, PP.
         2378-2381.

15166   SMILEY, DAVID L. LION OF WHITE HALL: THE LIFE OF
         CASSIUS M. CLAY. MADISON: UNIVERSITY OF WISCONSIN
         PRESS, 1962.

15167   SMITH, ALFRED G. ECONOMIC READJUSTMENT OF AN OLD COTTON
         STATE: SOUTH CAROLINA, 1820-1860. COLUMBIA:
         UNIVERSITY OF SOUTH CAROLINA PRESS, 1958.

15168   SMITH, JULIA F. "SLAVETRADING IN ANTEBELLUM FLORIDA."
         FLORIDA HISTORICAL QUARTERLY, 50 (JANUARY, 1972):
         252-261.

15169   STAMPP, KENNETH M. THE PECULIAR INSTITUTION: SLAVERY IN
         THE ANTE-BELLUM SOUTH. NEW YORK: ALFRED A. KNOPF,
         1956.

15170   STEPHENSON, WENDELL H. ISAAC FRANKLIN, SLAVE TRADER AND
         PLANTER OF THE OLD SOUTH. BATON ROUGE: LOUISIANA
         STATE UNIVERSITY PRESS, 1938.

15171   STOCKBRIDGE, HENRY. "BALTIMORE IN 1346." MARYLAND
         HISTORICAL MAGAZINE, 6 (MARCH, 1911): 20-34.

15172   SUTCH, RICHARD. THE BREEDING OF SLAVES FOR SALE AND THE
         WESTERN EXPANSION OF SLAVERY, 1850-1860. SOUTHERN
         ECONOMIC HISTORY PROJECT WORKING PAPER SERIES NO. 10.
         BERKELEY: UNIVERSITY OF CALIFORNIA, INSTITUTE OF
         BUSINESS AND ECONOMIC RESEARCH, 1972.

15173   SUTCH, RICHARD. "THE BREEDING OF SLAVES FOR SALE AND THE
         WESTWARD EXPANSION OF SLAVERY, 1850-1860." IN
         ENGERMAN, STANLEY L. AND GENOVESE, EUGENE D. (EDS.).
         RACE AND SLAVERY IN THE WESTERN HEMISPHERE:
         QUANTITATIVE STUDIES. PRINCETON: PRINCETON
         UNIVERSITY PRESS, 1975, PP. 173-210.

15174   SWEIG, DONALD M. "REASSESSING THE HUMAN DIMENSION OF THE
         INTERSTATE SLAVE TRADE." PROLOGUE, 12 (SPRING, 1980):
         5-22.

15175   SYDNOR, CHARLES S. SLAVERY IN MISSISSIPPI. NEW YORK:
         D. APPLETON-CENTURY COMPANY, 1933.

15176 TADMAN, MICHAEL. "SLAVE TRADING IN THE ANTE-BELLUM
       SOUTH: AN ESTIMATE OF THE EXTENT OF THE
       INTER-REGIONAL SLAVE TRADE." JOURNAL OF AMERICAN
       STUDIES, 13 (AUGUST, 1979): 195-220.

15177 TADMAN, MICHAEL. "SPECULATORS AND SLAVES IN THE OLD
       SOUTH: A STUDY OF THE AMERICAN DOMESTIC SLAVE TRADE,
       1820-1860." PH.D. DISSERTATION, UNIVERSITY OF HULL,
       1978.

15178 TAYLOR, ALRUTHEUS A. "THE MOVEMENT OF THE NEGROES FROM
       THE EAST TO THE GULF STATES FROM 1830 TO 1850."
       JOURNAL OF NEGRO HISTORY, 3 (OCTOBER, 1923): 367-383.

15179 THOMAS, MRS. Z.V. HISTORY OF JEFFERSON COUNTY. MACON:
       J.W. BURKE, 1927.

15180 TIERMAN, STANTON. "BALTIMORE'S OLD SLAVE MARKET."
       BALTIMORE SUN, SEPTEMBER 13, 1936.

15181 TREXLER, HARRISON A. "THE VALUE AND THE SALE OF THE
       MISSOURI SLAVE." MISSOURI HISTORICAL REVIEW, 8
       (JANUARY, 1914): 69-85.

15182 TRYON, WARREN S. (ED.). THE COTTON KINGDOM. CHICAGO:
       UNIVERSITY OF CHICAGO PRESS, 1952.

15183 "VIGINTAL CROP." IN SCHAPSMEIER, EDWARD L. AND
       SCHAPSMEIER, FREDERICK. ENCYCLOPEDIA OF AMERICAN
       AGRICULTURAL HISTORY. WESTPORT: GREENWOOD PRESS,
       1975, P. 362.

15184 WADE, RICHARD C. SLAVERY IN THE CITIES: THE SOUTH,
       1820-1860. NEW YORK: OXFORD UNIVERSITY PRESS, 1964.

15185 WADE, RICHARD C. THE URBAN FRONTIER: THE RISE OF
       WESTERN CITIES, 1790-1330. CAMBRIDGE: HARVARD
       UNIVERSITY PRESS, 1959.

15186 WAX, DAROLD D. "THE NEGRO SLAVE TRADE IN COLONIAL
       PENNSYLVANIA." M.A. THESIS, UNIVERSITY OF WASHINGTON,
       1958.

15187 WAX, DAROLD D. "THE NEGRO SLAVE TRADE IN COLONIAL
       PENNSYLVANIA." PH.D. DISSERTATION, UNIVERSITY OF
       WASHINGTON, 1962.

15188 WAX, DAROLD D. "QUAKER MERCHANTS AND THE SLAVE TRADE IN
       COLONIAL PENNSYLVANIA." PENNSYLVANIA MAGAZINE OF
       HISTORY AND BIOGRAPHY, 36 (APRIL, 1962): 143-159.

15189 WEEDEN, WILLIAM B. "THE EARLY AFRICAN SLAVE-TRADE IN NEW
       ENGLAND." PROCEEDINGS OF THE AMERICAN ANTIQUARIAN
       SOCIETY, N.S., 5 (OCTOBER, 1889): 107-128.

15190   WESLEY, CHARLES H.   "MANIFESTS OF SLAVE SHIPMENTS ALONG
         THE WATERWAYS, 1808-1864."   JOURNAL_OF_NEGRO_HISTORY,
         27 (APRIL, 1942):   155-174.

15191   WHITTEN, DAVID O.   "SLAVE BUYING IN 1835 VIRGINIA AS
         REVEALED BY LETTERS OF A BLACK LOUISIANA SUGAR
         PLANTER."   LOUISIANA_HISTORY, 11 (SUMMER, 1970):
         231-244.

15192   WILEY, BELL I.   SOUTHERN_NEGROES,_1861-1865.   NEW HAVEN:
         YALE UNIVERSITY PRESS, 1938.

15193   WILLIAMSON, JOEL.   NEW_PEOPLE:__MISCEGENATION_AND
         MULATTOES_IN_THE_UNITED_STATES.   NEW YORK: MACMILLAN
         COMPANY, 1980.

GENERAL

15194   ANDREWS, EVANGELINE W. (ED.).   JOURNAL OF A LADY OF
        QUALITY: BEING THE NARRATIVE OF A JOURNEY FROM
        SCOTLAND TO THE WEST INDIES, NORTH CAROLINA, AND
        PORTUGAL IN THE YEARS 1774 TO 1776.   NEW HAVEN: YALE
        UNIVERSITY PRESS, 1922.

15195   BAKER, S.C.   "THE SOUTHERN NEGRO--HIS RECENT EROTIC
        TENDENCIES--THE CAUSES--SUGGESTIONS AS TO PREVENTION."
        CAROLINA MEDICAL JOURNAL, 45 (MARCH, 1900):   89-94.

15196   BAKER, THOMAS N.   THE NEGRO WOMAN.   PHILADELPHIA: A.M.E.
        BOOK CONCERN, N.D.

15197   BALLAGH, JAMES C.   "THE SOCIAL CONDITION OF THE
        ANTEBELLUM NEGRO."   CONSERVATIVE REVIEW, 3 (MARCH,
        1900):   211-223.

15198   BARKSDALE, RICHARD K.   "WHITE TRIANGLES, BLACK CIRCLES."
        CLA JOURNAL, 18 (JUNE, 1975):   465-476.

15199   BARRINGER, PAUL B.   THE AMERICAN NEGRO, HIS PAST AND
        FUTURE.   RALEIGH: EDWARDS & BROUGHTON, 1900.

15200   BARRINGER, PAUL B.   "THE SACRIFICE OF A RACE."   RALEIGH:
        EDWARDS & BROUGHTON, 1900.

15201   BATES, RUTH.   "CONDITIONS OF SLAVE LIFE."   M.A. THESIS,
        LOUISIANA STATE UNIVERSITY, 1913.

15202   BENNETT, LERONE JR.   "THE BREAKING OF THE BOND."   NEGRO
        DIGEST, 15 (FEBRUARY, 1966):   68-87.

15203   BENNETT, LERONE JR.   "THE WORLD OF THE SLAVE."   EBONY, 26
        (FEBRUARY, 1971):   44-56.

15204   BLASSINGAME, JOHN W.   "THE AMERICANIZATION OF THE SLAVE
        AND THE AFRICANIZATION OF THE SOUTH."   THE SLAVE
        COMMUNITY: PLANTATION LIFE IN THE ANTEBELLUM SOUTH.
        NEW YORK: OXFORD UNIVERSITY PRESS, 1979, PP. 49-104.

15205   BLASSINGAME, JOHN W.   "STATUS AND SOCIAL STRUCTURE IN THE
        SLAVE COMMUNITY: EVIDENCE FROM NEW SOURCES."   IN
        OWENS, HARRY P. (ED.).   PERSPECTIVES AND IRONY IN
        AMERICAN SLAVERY.   JACKSON: UNIVERSITY PRESS OF
        MISSISSIPPI, 1976, PP. 137-152.

15206   BLOCH, H.   "MEDICAL-SOCIAL CONDITIONS OF SLAVES IN THE
        SOUTH."   JOURNAL OF THE NATIONAL MEDICAL ASSOCIATION,

61 (SEPTEMBER, 1969): 442-444.

15207   BONEKEMPER, EDWARD H. "NEGROES' FREEDOM OF CONTACT IN
        ANTE-BELLUM VIRGINIA, 1620-1860." M.A. THESIS, OLD
        DOMINION UNIVERSITY, 1971.

15208   BREWER, JAMES H. "LEGISLATION DESIGNED TO CONTROL
        SLAVERY IN WILMINGTON AND FAYETTEVILLE." NORTH
        CAROLINA HISTORICAL REVIEW, 30 (APRIL, 1953): 155-166.

15209   BRYCE-LAPORTE, ROY S. "THE CONCEPTUALIZATION OF THE
        AMERICAN SLAVE PLANTATION AS A TOTAL INSTITUTION."
        PH.D. DISSERTATION, UNIVERSITY OF CALIFORNIA, LOS
        ANGELES, 1968.

15210   BRYCE-LAPORTE, ROY S. "THE SLAVE PLANTATION: BACKGROUND
        TO PRESENT CONDITIONS OF URBAN BLACKS." IN ORLEANS,
        PETER A. AND ELLIS, WILLIAM R. (EDS.). RACE, CHANGE,
        AND URBAN SOCIETY. BEVERLY HILLS: SAGE PUBLICATIONS,
        1971, PP. 257-284.

15211   BURGESS, JOHN W. REMINISCENCES OF AN AMERICAN SCHOLAR.
        NEW YORK: COLUMBIA UNIVERSITY PRESS, 1934.

15212   CLAIBORNE, JOHN H. "THE NEGRO--HIS ENVIRONMENTS AS A
        SLAVE--HIS ENVIRONMENTS AS A FREEDMAN." TRANSACTIONS
        OF THE SECOND ANNUAL SESSION OF THE TRI-STATE MEDICAL
        ASSOCIATION OF THE CAROLINAS AND VIRGINIA, FEBRUARY
        20-22, 1900. RICHMOND: WILLIAM PRINTING COMPANY,
        1900, PP. 91-97.

15213   CLARKE, ERSKINE. WRESTLIN' JACOB: A PORTRAIT OF
        RELIGION IN THE OLD SOUTH. ATLANTA: JOHN KNOX PRESS,
        1979.

15214   CONRAD, GEORGIA B. "REMINISCENCES OF A SOUTHERN WOMAN."
        SOUTHERN WORKMAN, 30 (FEBRUARY, MARCH, MAY, JUNE,
        JULY, 1901): 77-80, 167-171, 252-257, 357-359,
        409-411.

15215   CUNNINGHAM, EILEEN S. AND SCHNEIDER, MABEL A. "A SLAVE'S
        AUTOBIOGRAPHY RETOLD." WESTERN ILLINOIS REGIONAL
        STUDIES, 2 (1979): 109-126.

15216   DABNEY, ROBERT L. "WHAT THE NEGRO DID FOR THE OLD
        SOUTH." SOUTHERN STATES FARM MAGAZINE, 5 (JANUARY,
        1898): 477-482.

15217   DORMON, JAMES H. AND JONES, ROBERT R. THE AFRO-AMERICAN
        EXPERIENCE: A CULTURAL HISTORY THROUGH EMANCIPATION.
        NEW YORK: JOHN WILEY & SONS, 1974.

15218   DOUGLASS, FREDERICK. "THE CONDITION OF THE FREEDMEN."
        HARPER'S WEEKLY, 27 (DECEMBER 8, 1883): 782-783.

15219   DUBOIS, W.E.B.   EFFORTS FOR SOCIAL BETTERMENT AMONG NEGRO
        AMERICANS.   ATLANTA: ATLANTA UNIVERSITY PUBLICATIONS,
        1909.

15220   FAIRBANKS, CHARLES H. AND MULLINS-MOORE, SUE A.   "HOW DID
        SLAVES LIVE?"   EARLY MAN, 2 (SUMMER, 1980):   2-6.

15221   FEDERAL WRITERS' PROJECT.   AMERICAN STUFF: AN ANTHOLOGY
        OF PROSE & VERSE.   NEW YORK: VIKING PRESS, 1937.

15222   FLOYD, SILAS X.   LIFE OF CHARLES T. WALKER, D.D.
        NASHVILLE: NATIONAL BAPTIST PUBLISHING BOARD, 1902.

15223   "FREDERICK DOUGLASS AS A SLAVE BOY."   AMERICAN
        MISSIONARY, 63 (MAY, 1909):   247-248.

15224   FURNAS, J.C.   GOODBYE TO UNCLE TOM.   NEW YORK: WILLIAM
        SLOANE ASSOCIATES, 1956.

15225   GAINES, W.J.   "THE EVILS OF AFRICAN SLAVERY."   THE NEGRO
        AND THE WHITE MAN.   PHILADELPHIA: A.M.E. PUBLISHING
        HOUSE, 1897, PP. 22-31.

15226   GATES, PAUL W.   AGRICULTURE AND THE CIVIL WAR.   NEW YORK:
        ALFRED A. KNOPF, 1965.

15227   GUTMAN, HERBERT G.   THE BLACK FAMILY IN SLAVERY AND
        FREEDOM, 1750-1925.   NEW YORK: PANTHEON BOOKS, 1976.

15228   HARPER, C.W.   "HOUSE SERVANTS AND FIELD HANDS:
        FRAGMENTATION IN THE ANTEBELLUM SLAVE COMMUNITY."
        NORTH CAROLINA HISTORICAL REVIEW, 58 (JANUARY, 1978):
        42-59.

15229   HARRIS, JOEL C.   "THE WOMEN OF THE SOUTH."   SOUTHERN
        HISTORICAL SOCIETY PAPERS, 18 (JANUARY-DECEMBER,
        1890):   277-281.

15230   HARRIS, MARK.   "HOW SLAVES BOUGHT THEIR OWN FREEDOM."
        NEGRO DIGEST, 7 (NOVEMBER, 1948):   40-43.

15231   HAVARD, WILLIAM C., JR.   "THE SELF-INTERPRETATION OF THE
        SOUTH THROUGH REFORM, REBELLION AND RECONSTRUCTION."
        IN SPIRIT OF A FREE SOCIETY: ESSAYS IN HONOR OF
        SENATOR JAMES WILLIAM FULBRIGHT ON THE OCCASION OF THE
        TENTH ANNIVERSARY OF THE GERMAN FULBRIGHT PROGRAM.
        HEIDELBERG: QUELLE & MEYER, 1962, PP. 74-103.

15232   HEAP, JOHN P.   "FUTURE OF THE NEGRO IN AMERICA: WILL THE
        RACE BECOME EXTINCT?"   NATIONAL MAGAZINE, 23 (OCTOBER,
        1905):   105-108.

15233   HODGES, J. ALLISON.   "THE EFFECT OF FREEDOM UPON THE
        PHYSICAL AND PSYCHOLOGICAL DEVELOPMENT OF THE NEGRO."
        PROCEEDINGS OF THE AMERICAN MEDICO-PSYCHOLOGICAL

ASSOCIATION, 7 (1900): 88-98.

15234 HUNTER, FRANCES L. "SLAVE SOCIETY ON THE SOUTHERN
       PLANTATION." JOURNAL OF NEGRO HISTORY, 7 (JANUARY,
       1922): 1-10.

15235 JACKSON, MARGARET Y. "AN INVESTIGATION OF BIOGRAPHIES
       AND AUTOBIOGRAPHIES OF AMERICAN SLAVES PUBLISHED
       BETWEEN 1840 AND 1860: BASED UPON THE CORNELL SPECIAL
       SLAVERY COLLECTION." PH.D. DISSERTATION, CORNELL
       UNIVERSITY, 1954.

15236 JACKSON, MARGARET Y. THE STRUGGLE FOR FREEDOM, PHASE I:
       AS REVEALED IN SLAVE NARRATIVES OF THE PRE-CIVIL WAR
       PERIOD, 1840-1860. CHICAGO: ADAMS PRESS, 1976.

15237 JESSE, C. "DU TERTRE AND LABAT ON SEVENTEENTH CENTURY
       SLAVE LIFE IN THE FRENCH ANTILLES." CARIBBEAN
       QUARTERLY, 7 (DECEMBER, 1961): 137-157.

15238 JOHNSON, CHARLES S. SHADOW OF THE PLANTATION. CHICAGO:
       UNIVERSITY OF CHICAGO PRESS, 1934.

15239 KNIGHT, FRANKLIN W. "THE EXPERIENCE OF SLAVERY." THE
       AFRICAN DIMENSION IN LATIN AMERICAN SOCIETY. NEW
       YORK: MACMILLAN, 1974, PP. 5-50.

15240 LALE, MAX S. AND CAMPBELL, RANDOLPH B. (EDS.). "THE
       PLANTATION JOURNAL OF JOHN B. WEBSTER, FEBRUARY 17,
       1853-NOVEMBER 5, 1859." SOUTHWESTERN HISTORICAL
       QUARTERLY, 84 (JULY, 1980): 49-80.

15241 LEWIS, MARY. FUNNY STORIES OF OLD TIME NEGROES.
       BUFFALO: M.S. LEWIS, 1913.

15242 MAGDOL, EDWARD. "THE LEGACY OF THE SLAVE COMMUNITY." A
       RIGHT TO THE LAND: ESSAYS ON THE FREEDMEN'S
       COMMUNITY. WESTPORT: GREENWOOD PRESS, 1977, PP.
       16-34.

15243 MALLARD, ROBERT Q. PLANTATION LIFE BEFORE EMANCIPATION.
       RICHMOND: WHITTET AND SHEPPERSON, 1892.

15244 MATTHEWS, ESSIE C. AUNT PHOEBE, UNCLE TOM AND OTHERS:
       CHARACTER STUDIES AMONG THE OLD SLAVES OF THE SOUTH
       FIFTY YEARS AFTER. COLUMBUS: CHAMPLIN PRESS, 1915.

15245 MCWHINEY, GRADY. "BLACK HISTORY OR PROPAGANDA?"
       SOUTHERNERS AND OTHER AMERICANS. NEW YORK: BASIC
       BOOKS, 1973, PP. 182-198.

15246 MEADE, ANNA H. WHEN I WAS A LITTLE GIRL: THE YEAR'S
       ROUND ON THE PLANTATION. LOS ANGELES: FRED S. LANG,
       1916.

15247   METCALFE, JAMES S.   "THE AMERICAN SLAVE--THE LIFE OF THE
         SLAVE."   PEARSON'S MAGAZINE, 4 (NOVEMBER, 1900):
         473-482.

15248   MOORE, JOHN HAMMOND (ED.).   BEFORE AND AFTER OR THE
         RELATIONS OF THE RACES AT THE SOUTH BY ISAAC DUBOSE
         SEABROOK.   BATON ROUGE: LOUISIANA STATE UNIVERSITY
         PRESS, 1967.

15249   MORGAN, CLAIRE S.   "THE CONDITIONS OF SLAVE LIFE."   IN
         JOYNER, CHARLES W. (ED.).   BLACK CAROLINIANS: STUDIES
         IN THE HISTORY OF SOUTH CAROLINA NEGROES IN THE
         NINETEENTH CENTURY.   LAURINBURG, NC: ST. ANDREWS
         PRESBYTERIAN COLLEGE, 1969, PP. 1-9.

15250   MORGAN, EDMUND S.   VIRGINIANS AT HOME: FAMILY LIFE IN
         THE EIGHTEENTH CENTURY.   WILLIAMSBURG: COLONIAL
         WILLIAMSBURG, 1952.

15251   MORSE, RICHARD M.   "THE NEGRO IN SAO PAULO, BRAZIL."
         JOURNAL OF NEGRO HISTORY, 38 (JULY, 1953):   290-306.

15252   NEEDHAM, J.B.   "THE PROGRESS OF THE NEGRO IN CITIES."
         TRINITY ARCHIVE, 11 (APRIL, 1898):   373-376.

15253   NEVINS, ALLAN.   "THE LOT OF THE BONDSMAN."   ORDEAL OF THE
         UNION.   2 VOLS.   NEW YORK: CHARLES SCRIBNER'S SONS,
         1947, VOL. 1, PP. 412-461.

15254   NORTHRUP, DAVID.   "AFRICAN MORTALITY IN THE SUPPRESSION
         OF THE SLAVE TRADE: THE CASE OF THE BIGHT OF BIAFRA."
         JOURNAL OF INTERDISCIPLINARY HISTORY, 9 (SUMMER,
         1978):   47-64.

15255   OWENS, LESLIE H.   "'THIS SPECIES OF PROPERTY':   SLAVE
         PERSONALITY AND BEHAVIOR IN THE OLD SOUTH, 1776-1861."
         PH.D. DISSERTATION, UNIVERSITY OF CALIFORNIA,
         RIVERSIDE, 1973.

15256   PERDUE, CHARLES L., JR.   "SLAVE LIFE STYLES IN EARLY
         VIRGINIA."   PROCEEDINGS OF THE PIONEER AMERICA
         SOCIETY, 2 (1973):   54-58.

15257   PLEASANTS, MARY M.   WHICH ONE? AND OTHER ANTE BELLUM
         DAYS.   BOSTON: JAMES H. EARLE COMPANY, 1910.

15258   PRICHARD, WALTER.   "ROUTINE ON A LOUISIANA SUGAR
         PLANTATION UNDER THE SLAVERY REGIME."   MISSISSIPPI
         VALLEY HISTORICAL REVIEW, 14 (SEPTEMBER, 1927):
         168-178.

15259   RANDOLPH, PETER.   FROM SLAVE CABIN TO THE PULPIT: THE
         AUTOBIOGRAPHY OF REV. PETER RANDOLPH: THE SOUTHERN
         QUESTION ILLUSTRATED, AND SKETCHES OF SLAVE LIFE.
         BOSTON: J.H. EARLE, 1893.

15260   RANSON, A.R.H.   "PLANTATION LIFE IN VIRGINIA BEFORE THE
        WAR."   SEWANEE REVIEW, 21 (OCTOBER, 1913):   428-447.

15261   RIDDELL, WILLIAM R.   "LE CODE NOIR."   JOURNAL OF NEGRO
        HISTORY, 10 (JULY, 1925):   321-329.

15262   RISINGER, ROBERT G.   "ROUTINE SLAVE LIFE IN THE
        ANTE-BELLUM SOUTH, 1830-1860."   M.A. THESIS,
        UNIVERSITY OF CHICAGO, 1947.

15263   ROBINSON, AVIS P.   "SOCIAL CONDITIONS OF SLAVERY AS TAKEN
        FROM SLAVE NARRATIVES."   M.A. THESIS, HOWARD
        UNIVERSITY, 1938.

15264   ROSENGARTEN, THEODORE.   ALL GOD'S DANGERS: THE LIFE OF
        NATE SHAW. NEW YORK: ALFRED A. KNOPF, 1974.

15265   RUTHERFORD, MILDRED L.   FOUR ADDRESSES. BIRMINGHAM: THE
        MILDRED RUTHERFORD HISTORICAL CIRCLE, 1912-1916.

15266   SCARBOROUGH, WILLIAM K.   "HEARTLAND OF THE COTTON
        KINGDOM."   IN MCLEMORE, RICHARD A. (ED.).   A HISTORY
        OF MISSISSIPPI. 2 VOLS. HATTIESBURG: UNIVERSITY AND
        COLLEGE PRESS OF MISSISSIPPI, 1973, VOL. 1, PP.
        310-351.

15267   "SEASONING OF SLAVES." IN NUNEZ, BENJAMIN. DICTIONARY
        OF AFRO-LATIN AMERICAN CIVILIZATION. WESTPORT:
        GREENWOOD PRESS, 1980, P. 422.

15268   SINGLETON, THERESA A.   "THE ARCHAEOLOGY OF AFRO-AMERICAN
        SLAVERY IN COASTAL GEORGIA: A REGIONAL PERCEPTION OF
        SLAVE HOUSEHOLD AND COMMUNITY PATTERNS." PH.D.
        DISSERTATION, UNIVERSITY OF FLORIDA, 1980.

15269   SINGLETON, THERESA A.   "SLAVES AND EX-SLAVE SITES IN
        COASTAL GEORGIA." UNPUBLISHED PAPER PRESENTED AT
        MEETING OF SOCIETY FOR HISTORICAL ARCHAEOLOGY,
        NASHVILLE, TENNESSEE, 1979.

15270   "SLAVE LIFE IN THE SOUTH." CONFEDERATE VETERAN, 40
        (MARCH, 1932):   103, 118.

15271   SMITH, G.W.   "SLAVERY, CONTENTMENT, AND SOCIAL FREEDOM."
        PHILOSOPHICAL QUARTERLY, 27 (JULY, 1977):   236-248.

15272   "SOMETHING OF SLAVERY AS IT EXISTED." CONFEDERATE
        VETERAN, 1 (JUNE, 1893):   171.

15273   STAMPP, KENNETH M.   "THE DAILY LIFE OF THE SOUTHERN
        SLAVE."   IN HUGGINS, NATHAN I.; KILSON, MARTIN; AND
        FOX, DANIEL M. (EDS.).   KEY ISSUES IN THE
        AFRO-AMERICAN EXPERIENCE. 2 VOLS. NEW YORK:
        HARCOURT BRACE JOVANOVICH, 1971, VOL. 1, PP. 116-137.

15274 STAROBIN, ROBERT S. "PRIVILEGED BONDSMEN AND THE PROCESS
       OF ACCOMMODATION: THE ROLE OF HOUSE SERVANTS AND
       DRIVERS AS SEEN IN THEIR OWN LETTERS." JOURNAL OF
       SOCIAL HISTORY, 5 (FALL, 1971): 46-70.

15275 STEARNS, CHARLES. THE BLACK MAN OF THE SOUTH, AND THE
       REBELS; OR, THE CHARACTERISTICS OF THE FORMER, AND THE
       RECENT OUTRAGES OF THE LATTER. BOSTON: AMERICAN NEWS
       COMPANY, 1872.

15276 TARVER, HAROLD M. THE NEGRO IN THE HISTORY OF THE UNITED
       STATES. AUSTIN: STATE PRINTING COMPANY, 1905.

15277 TAYLOR, CLARE. "ASPECTS OF PLANTER SOCIETY IN THE
       BRITISH WEST INDIES BEFORE EMANCIPATION." CYLCHGRAWN
       LLYFRGELL GENEDLAETHOL CYMRU, 20 (1978): 361-372.

15278 THOMAS, EMORY M. THE CONFEDERATE STATE OF RICHMOND: A
       BIOGRAPHY OF THE CAPITAL. AUSTIN: UNIVERSITY OF
       TEXAS PRESS, 1971.

15279 TOMICH, DALE. "HOUSEHOLD SLAVES AND BLACK
       ACCOMMODATIONISM IN THE AMERICAN SOUTH." UNPUBLISHED
       HONORS ESSAY, DEPARTMENT OF HISTORY, UNIVERSITY OF
       WISCONSIN, 1968.

15280 TREXLER, HARRISON A. SLAVERY IN MISSOURI, 1804-1865.
       BALTIMORE: JOHNS HOPKINS PRESS, 1914.

15281 TREXLER, HARRISON A. "SLAVERY IN MISSOURI, 1804-1865."
       PH.D. DISSERTATION, JOHNS HOPKINS UNIVERSITY, 1914.

15282 UYA, OKON E. "EVERYDAY LIFE IN SLAVERY." UNPUBLISHED
       MANUSCRIPT, N.D.

15283 VAN NESS, JAMES S. "ECONOMIC DEVELOPMENT, SOCIAL AND
       CULTURAL CHANGES: 1800-1850." IN WALSH, RICHARD AND
       FOX, WILLIAM L. (EDS.). MARYLAND: A HISTORY,
       1632-1974. BALTIMORE: MARYLAND HISTORICAL SOCIETY,
       1974, PP. 151-238.

15284 WEBBER, THOMAS L. DEEP LIKE THE RIVERS: EDUCATION IN
       THE SLAVE QUARTER COMMUNITY, 1831-1865. NEW YORK:
       W.W. NORTON, 1978.

15285 WHEELWRIGHT, DALE G. "AMERICAN SLAVERY AS SEEN BY
       EUROPEAN TRAVELERS, 1815-1860." M.A. THESIS,
       PENNSYLVANIA STATE UNIVERSITY, 1959.

15286 WILLIAMS, E.K. "SIDELIGHTS ON SOME OF THE SOCIAL ASPECTS
       OF SLAVERY IN DELAWARE, 1638-1865." NEGRO EDUCATIONAL
       REVIEW, 5 (JANUARY, 1954): 14-21.

SLAVE TREATMENT

15287   ABRAMS, JOSEPHINE S.   "THE TREATMENT OF NEGRO WOMEN
        DURING SLAVERY." M.A. THESIS, Y.M.C.A. GRADUATE
        SCHOOL, NASHVILLE, 1936.

15288   ANDREWS, GEORGE R.   THE AFRO-ARGENTINES OF BUENOS AIRES,
        1800-1900. MADISON: UNIVERSITY OF WISCONSIN PRESS,
        1980.

15289   BARRINGER, PAUL B.   "MEMORANDA FOR ADDRESS BEFORE RADFORD
        CHAPTER OF THE U.D.C.: THE OLD SOUTH AND HOW IT MET
        THE BLOCKADE IN '65. THE PLANTATION. THE SOCIAL AND
        ECONOMIC UNIT OF THE SOUTH." UNPUBLISHED MANUSCRIPT,
        N.D., BARRINGER FAMILY PAPERS, UNIVERSITY OF VIRGINIA.

15290   BLASSINGAME, JOHN W.   THE SLAVE COMMUNITY: PLANTATION
        LIFE IN THE ANTEBELLUM SOUTH.   NEW YORK: OXFORD
        UNIVERSITY PRESS, 1972.

15291   BONNER, JAMES C. (ED.).   "PLANTATION EXPERIENCES OF A NEW
        YORK WOMAN." NORTH CAROLINA HISTORICAL REVIEW, 33
        (JULY, 1956):   384-412.

15292   BROOKS, ROBERT P.   "SLAVERY: ECONOMIC AND SOCIAL
        ASPECTS." HISTORY OF GEORGIA. BOSTON: ATKINSON,
        MENTZER & COMPANY, 1913, PP. 232-236.

15293   CALDWELL, ROBERT G.   RED HANNAH, DELAWARE'S WHIPPING
        POST. PHILADELPHIA: UNIVERSITY OF PENNSYLVANIA
        PRESS, 1947.

15294   CLARKE, FORSTER.   "PLAN OF TREATMENT OF THE NEGROES ON
        THE ESTATES IN BARBADOS, 1823." JOURNAL OF THE
        BARBADOS MUSEUM AND HISTORICAL SOCIETY, 2 (1934):
        29-31.

15295   CLAYTON, RONNIE W.   "THE FEDERAL WRITERS' PROJECT FOR
        BLACKS IN LOUISIANA." LOUISIANA HISTORY, 19 (SUMMER,
        1978):   327-335.

15296   CLIFTON, JAMES M.   "A HALF-CENTURY OF A GEORGIA RICE
        PLANTATION." NORTH CAROLINA HISTORICAL REVIEW, 47
        (AUTUMN, 1970):   388-415.

15297   COLTHARP, ROBERT W.   "THE CARE OF SLAVES." M.A. THESIS,
        INDIANA UNIVERSITY, 1937.

15298   CRATON, MICHAEL J.   "HOBBESIAN OR PANGLOSSIAN? THE TWO
        EXTREMES OF SLAVE CONDITIONS IN THE BRITISH CARIBBEAN,
        1783-1834." WILLIAM AND MARY QUARTERLY, 3RD SER., 35
        (APRIL, 1978):   324-356.

15299   CRAWFORD, STEPHEN C.   "QUANTIFIED MEMORY: A STUDY OF THE
        WPA AND FISK UNIVERSITY SLAVE NARRATIVE COLLECTIONS."

PH.D. DISSERTATION, UNIVERSITY OF CHICAGO, 1980.

15300 DABNEY, SUSAN. "A SOUTHERN PLANTER." ACADEMY, 37 (MARCH 15, 1890): 180.

15301 DEBOW, J.D.B. "MANAGEMENT OF NEGROES UPON SOUTHERN ESTATES--AN ECHO OF SLAVE DAYS IN THE SOUTHLAND." TENNESSEE HISTORICAL MAGAZINE, 5 (JULY, 1919): 95-104.

15302 DENNEY, JOSEPH E. "THE LASH AND THE LAW: THE MECHANICS OF SLAVE CONTROL." IN JOYNER, CHARLES W. (ED.). BLACK CAROLINIANS: STUDIES IN THE HISTORY OF SOUTH CAROLINA NEGROES IN THE NINETEENTH CENTURY. LAURINBURG, NC: ST. ANDREWS PRESBYTERIAN COLLEGE, 1969, PP. 10-20.

15303 DEW, CHARLES B. "DISCIPLINING SLAVE IRONWORKERS IN THE ANTEBELLUM SOUTH: COERCION, CONCILIATION, AND ACCOMMODATION." AMERICAN HISTORICAL REVIEW, 79 (APRIL, 1974): 393-418.

15304 DOOKHAN, ISAAC. "SLAVERY AND EMANCIPATION." A HISTORY OF THE BRITISH VIRGIN ISLANDS, 1672 TO 1970. EPPING, ESSEX, ENGLAND: CARIBBEAN UNIVERSITIES PRESS, 1975, PP. 71-96.

15305 DORMON, JAMES H. "ASPECTS OF SLAVE MANAGEMENT AND MAINTENANCE ON A LOUISIANA SUGAR PLANTATION: PETITE ANSE, 1840-1860." ATTAKAPAS GAZETTE, 7 (MARCH, 1972): 23-30.

15306 DUBOIS, W.E.B. BLACK RECONSTRUCTION. NEW YORK: HARCOURT, BRACE AND COMPANY, 1935.

15307 DUBOIS, W.E.B. EFFORTS FOR SOCIAL BETTERMENT AMONG NEGRO AMERICANS. ATLANTA: ATLANTA UNIVERSITY PUBLICATIONS, 1909.

15308 EATON, CLEMENT. THE MIND OF THE OLD SOUTH. BATON ROUGE: LOUISIANA STATE UNIVERSITY PRESS, 1964.

15309 EATON, CLEMENT. THE WANING OF THE OLD SOUTH CIVILIZATION. ATHENS: UNIVERSITY OF GEORGIA PRESS, 1968.

15310 ELKINS, STANLEY M. SLAVERY: A PROBLEM IN AMERICAN INSTITUTIONAL AND INTELLECTUAL LIFE. CHICAGO: UNIVERSITY OF CHICAGO PRESS, 1959.

15311 ELKINS, STANLEY M. "SLAVERY: A PROBLEM IN AMERICAN INSTITUTIONAL AND INTELLECTUAL LIFE." PH.D. DISSERTATION, COLUMBIA UNIVERSITY, 1959.

15312 FOGEL, ROBERT W. AND ENGERMAN, STANLEY L. TIME ON THE CROSS: THE ECONOMICS OF AMERICAN NEGRO SLAVERY. 2

VOLS. BOSTON: LITTLE, BROWN AND COMPANY, 1974.

15313   FRANKLIN, JIMMIE L. THE BLACKS IN OKLAHOMA. NORMAN:
        UNIVERSITY OF OKLAHOMA PRESS, 1980.

15314   FRANKLIN, JOHN H. "SLAVES VIRTUALLY FREE IN ANTE-BELLUM
        NORTH CAROLINA." JOURNAL OF NEGRO HISTORY, 28 (JULY,
        1943): 284-310.

15315   FREDRICKSON, GEORGE M. AND LASCH, CHRISTOPHER.
        "RESISTANCE TO SLAVERY." CIVIL WAR HISTORY, 13
        (DECEMBER, 1967): 315-329.

15316   FULKERSON, HORACE S. "TREATMENT OF SLAVES AT THIS
        PERIOD, ETC." RANDOM RECOLLECTIONS OF EARLY DAYS IN
        MISSISSIPPI. VICKSBURG: VICKSBURG PRINTING AND
        PUBLISHING COMPANY, 1885, PP. 128-140.

15317   GAINES, W.J. "THE EVILS OF AFRICAN SLAVERY." THE NEGRO
        AND THE WHITE MAN. PHILADELPHIA: A.M.E. PUBLISHING
        HOUSE, 1897, PP. 22-31.

15318   GANNETT, HENRY. "ARE WE TO BECOME AFRICANIZED?" POPULAR
        SCIENCE MONTHLY, 27 (JUNE, 1885): 146-150.

15319   GENOVESE, EUGENE D. THE POLITICAL ECONOMY OF SLAVERY:
        STUDIES IN THE ECONOMY AND SOCIETY OF THE SLAVE SOUTH.
        NEW YORK: VINTAGE, 1961.

15320   GENOVESE, EUGENE D. ROLL, JORDAN, ROLL: THE WORLD THE
        SLAVES MADE. NEW YORK: PANTHEON, 1974.

15321   GENOVESE, EUGENE D. "THE TREATMENT OF SLAVES IN
        DIFFERENT COUNTRIES: PROBLEMS IN THE APPLICATIONS OF
        THE COMPARATIVE METHOD." IN FONER, LAURA AND GENOVESE
        (EDS.). SLAVERY IN THE NEW WORLD: A READER IN
        COMPARATIVE HISTORY. ENGLEWOOD CLIFFS:
        PRENTICE-HALL, 1969, PP. 202-210.

15322   GIRARDIN, J.A. "SLAVERY IN DETROIT." MICHIGAN PIONEER
        AND HISTORICAL SOCIETY COLLECTIONS, 1 (1877): 415-417.

15323   GRAY, LEWIS C. HISTORY OF AGRICULTURE IN THE SOUTHERN
        UNITED STATES TO 1860. 2 VOLS. WASHINGTON: CARNEGIE
        INSTITUTION OF WASHINGTON, 1932.

15324   GREENE, JACK P. LANDON CARTER: AN INQUIRY INTO THE
        PERSONAL VALUES AND SOCIAL IMPERATIVES OF THE
        EIGHTEENTH-CENTURY VIRGINIA GENTRY. CHARLOTTESVILLE:
        UNIVERSITY PRESS OF VIRGINIA, 1965.

15325   GRIFFITH, LUCILLE. "THE PLANTATION RECORD BOOK OF
        BROOKDALE FARM, 1856-1357." JOURNAL OF MISSISSIPPI
        HISTORY, 7 (JANUARY, 1945): 23-31.

15326   GUTMAN, HERBERT G.   THE BLACK FAMILY IN SLAVERY AND
        FREEDOM, 1750-1925.   NEW YORK: PANTHEON BOOKS, 1976.

15327   HALSTED, SARA D.   "PLANTATION LORE."   OVERLAND MONTHLY, 1
        (JUNE, 1883):   659.

15328   HAMMETT, HUGH B.   HILARY ABNER HERBERT: A SOUTHERNER
        RETURNS TO THE UNION.   PHILADELPHIA: AMERICAN
        PHILOSOPHICAL SOCIETY, 1976.

15329   HARPER, C.W.   "HOUSE SERVANTS AND FIELD HANDS:
        FRAGMENTATION IN THE ANTEBELLUM SLAVE COMMUNITY."
        NORTH CAROLINA HISTORICAL REVIEW, 58 (JANUARY, 1978):
        42-59.

15330   HART, ALBERT B.   SLAVERY AND ABOLITION, 1831-1841.   NEW
        YORK: HARPER AND BROTHERS, 1906.

15331   HAYGOOD, ATTICUS G.   "THE BLACK SHADOW IN THE SOUTH."
        FORUM, 16 (OCTOBER, 1893):   167-175.

15332   HENDRICK, ROBERT M.   "THE STATUS AND TREATMENT OF
        CHILDREN DURING SLAVERY, 1830-1860."   M.A. THESIS,
        HOWARD UNIVERSITY, 1940.

15333   HINTON, E.H.   "THE NEGRO AND THE SOUTH."   CONFEDERATE
        VETERAN, 15 (AUGUST, 1907):   367-369.

15334   HUGHES, LOUIS.   THIRTY YEARS A SLAVE.   FROM BONDAGE TO
        FREEDOM.   THE INSTITUTION OF SLAVERY AS SEEN ON THE
        PLANTATION AND IN THE HOME OF THE PLANTER.   MILWAUKEE:
        SOUTH SIDE PRINTING COMPANY, 1897.

15335   KLEBANER, BENJAMIN J.   "AMERICAN MANUMISSION LAWS AND THE
        RESPONSIBILITY FOR SUPPORTING SLAVES."   VIRGINIA
        MAGAZINE OF HISTORY AND BIOGRAPHY, 63 (OCTOBER, 1955):
        443-453.

15336   LA ROCHE, J.H.   "MASTERS AND SLAVES IN THE OLD SOUTH."
        NORTH AMERICAN REVIEW, 166 (MARCH, 1898):   383-384.

15337   LINAKER, R. HYDE.   "A SILVER SLAVE BRAND."   CONNOISSEUR,
        69 (JULY, 1924):   163-164.

15338   LITWACK, LEON F.   BEEN IN THE STORM SO LONG: THE
        AFTERMATH OF SLAVERY.   NEW YORK: ALFRED A. KNOPF,
        1979.

15339   "MANAGEMENT OF NEGROES UPON SOUTHERN ESTATES--AN ECHO OF
        SLAVE DAYS IN THE SOUTHLAND."   TENNESSEE HISTORICAL
        MAGAZINE, 5 (JULY, 1919):   97-103.

15340   MATHIS, RAY.   JOHN HORRY DENT: SOUTH CAROLINA ARISTOCRAT
        ON THE ALABAMA FRONTIER.   UNIVERSITY, AL: UNIVERSITY
        OF ALABAMA PRESS, 1979.

15341   MCINTOSH, JAMES. "THE FUTURE OF THE NEGRO RACE."
         TRANSACTIONS OF THE SOUTH CAROLINA MEDICAL
         ASSOCIATION, (1891): 133-188.

15342   MCLAURIN, MELTON. "IMAGES OF NEGROES IN DEEP SOUTH
         PUBLIC SCHOOL STATE HISTORY TEXTS." PHYLON, 32 (FALL,
         1971): 237-246.

15343   MCMASTER, JOHN B. A HISTORY OF THE PEOPLE OF THE UNITED
         STATES, FROM THE REVOLUTION TO THE CIVIL WAR. 8 VOLS.
         NEW YORK: D. APPLETON AND COMPANY, 1883-1913.

15344   MCNEILLY, JAMES H. "TREATMENT OF SLAVES IN THE SOUTH."
         CONFEDERATE VETERAN, 29 (FEBRUARY, 1921): 48-49.

15345   MERRILL, BOYNTON JR. JEFFERSON'S NEPHEWS: A FRONTIER
         TRAGEDY. PRINCETON: PRINCETON UNIVERSITY PRESS, 1976.

15346   MEULEN, VANDER. "THE NEGRO IN THE UNITED STATES."
         CONFEDERATE VETERAN, 26 (AUGUST, 1918): 342-343.

15347   NELSON, MARY L. "BENEVOLENT ASPECTS OF THE 'PECULIAR
         INSTITUTION' IN MISSISSIPPI." M.A. THESIS,
         MISSISSIPPI STATE UNIVERSITY, 1965.

15348   NEVINS, ALLAN. "THE LOT OF THE BONDSMAN." ORDEAL OF THE
         UNION. 2 VOLS. NEW YORK: CHARLES SCRIBNER'S SONS,
         1947, VOL. 1, PP. 412-461.

15349   PETERSON, WALTER F. "SLAVERY IN THE 1850S: THE
         RECOLLECTIONS OF AN ALABAMA UNIONIST." ALABAMA
         HISTORICAL QUARTERLY, 30 (FALL/WINTER, 1968): 219-227.

15350   PHILLIPS, ULRICH B. AMERICAN NEGRO SLAVERY: A SURVEY OF
         THE SUPPLY, EMPLOYMENT AND CONTROL OF NEGRO LABOR AS
         DETERMINED BY THE PLANTATION REGIME. NEW YORK: D.
         APPLETON, 1918.

15351   PHILLIPS, ULRICH B. "A JAMAICA SLAVE PLANTATION."
         AMERICAN HISTORICAL REVIEW, 19 (APRIL, 1914): 543-558.

15352   PHILLIPS, ULRICH B. LIFE AND LABOR IN THE OLD SOUTH.
         BOSTON: LITTLE, BROWN AND COMPANY, 1929.

15353   PHILLIPS, ULRICH B. "THE PLANTATION PRODUCT OF MEN."
         PROCEEDINGS OF THE SECOND ANNUAL SESSION OF THE
         GEORGIA HISTORICAL ASSOCIATION. ATLANTA: GEORGIA
         HISTORICAL ASSOCIATION, 1918, PP. 12-15.

15354   PHILLIPS, ULRICH B. "RACIAL PROBLEMS, ADJUSTMENTS AND
         DISTURBANCES." IN RILEY, FRANKLIN L. (ED.). THE
         SOUTH IN THE BUILDING OF THE NATION. 12 VOLS.
         RICHMOND: SOUTHERN HISTORICAL PUBLICATION SOCIETY,
         1909, VOL. 4, PP. 194-241.

15355   PICKENS, WILLIAM. THE HEIRS OF SLAVES: AN AUTOBIOGRAPHY.
        NEW YORK: PILGRIM PRESS, 1911.

15356   PORTER, KENNETH W. "NEGROES ON THE FRONTIER." IN LAMAR,
        HOWARD R. (ED.). THE READER'S ENCYCLOPEDIA OF THE
        AMERICAN WEST. NEW YORK: THOMAS Y. CROWELL, 1977,
        PP. 814-821.

15357   RAWICK, GEORGE P. FROM SUNDOWN TO SUNUP: THE MAKING OF
        THE BLACK COMMUNITY. WESTPORT: GREENWOOD PRESS, 1972.

15358   RHODES, JAMES F. HISTORY OF THE UNITED STATES FROM THE
        COMPROMISE OF 1850 TO THE FINAL RESTORATION OF HOME
        RULE IN THE SOUTH IN 1877. 7 VOLS. NEW YORK:
        MACMILLAN COMPANY, 1893-1917.

15359   ROSS, FITZGERALD. A VISIT TO THE CITIES AND CAMPS OF THE
        CONFEDERATE STATES. EDINBURGH: W. BLACKWOOD AND
        SONS, 1865.

15360   ROUT, LESLIE B. THE AFRICAN EXPERIENCE IN SPANISH
        AMERICA, 1502 TO THE PRESENT DAY. CAMBRIDGE:
        CAMBRIDGE UNIVERSITY PRESS, 1976.

15361   SAVITT, TODD L. MEDICINE AND SLAVERY: THE DISEASES AND
        HEALTH CARE OF BLACKS IN ANTEBELLUM VIRGINIA. URBANA:
        UNIVERSITY OF ILLINOIS PRESS, 1978.

15362   SAVITT, TODD L. "SOUND MINDS AND SOUND BODIES: THE
        DISEASES AND HEALTH CARE OF BLACKS IN ANTEBELLUM
        VIRGINIA." PH.D. DISSERTATION, UNIVERSITY OF
        VIRGINIA, 1975.

15363   SCARBOROUGH, WILLIAM K. THE OVERSEER: PLANTATION
        MANAGEMENT IN THE OLD SOUTH. BATON ROUGE: LOUISIANA
        STATE UNIVERSITY PRESS, 1966.

15364   SCARBOROUGH, WILLIAM K. "SLAVERY--THE WHITE MAN'S
        BURDEN." IN OWENS, HARRY P. (ED.). PERSPECTIVES AND
        IRONY IN AMERICAN SLAVERY. JACKSON: UNIVERSITY PRESS
        OF MISSISSIPPI, 1976, PP. 103-136.

15365   SHARPLEY, ROBERT H. "A PSYCHOHISTORICAL PERSPECTIVE OF
        THE NEGRO." AMERICAN JOURNAL OF PSYCHIATRY, 126
        (NOVEMBER, 1969): 645-650.

15366   SHARPLEY, ROBERT H. "A PSYCHOHISTORICAL PERSPECTIVE OF
        THE NEGRO." IN REINHARDT, ADINA M. AND QUINN, MILDRED
        D. (EDS.). FAMILY-CENTERED COMMUNITY NURSING: A
        SOCIOLOGICAL FRAMEWORK. SAINT LOUIS: C.V. MOSBY
        COMPANY, 1973, PP. 78-84.

15367   "SLAVE DEHUMANIZATION." IN NUNEZ, BENJAMIN. DICTIONARY
        OF AFRO-LATIN AMERICAN CIVILIZATION. WESTPORT:
        GREENWOOD PRESS, 1980, P. 434.

15368   "SLAVE JETTISONING." IN NUNEZ, BENJAMIN. DICTIONARY OF
         AFRO-LATIN AMERICAN CIVILIZATION. WESTPORT:
         GREENWOOD PRESS, 1980, P. 435.

15369   "SLAVES: TREATMENT IN THE MIDDLE COLONIES." IN RYWELL,
         MARTIN (ED.). AFRO-AMERICAN ENCYCLOPEDIA. 10 VOLS.
         NORTH MIAMI: EDUCATIONAL BOOK PUBLISHERS, 1974, VOL.
         8, PP. 2441-2442.

15370   SMITH, JULIA F. "CAT HAULING." IN ROLLER, DAVID C. AND
         TWYMAN, ROBERT W. (EDS.). THE ENCYCLOPEDIA OF
         SOUTHERN HISTORY. BATON ROUGE: LOUISIANA STATE
         UNIVERSITY PRESS, 1979, P. 189.

15371   SMITH, JULIA F. "RACIAL ATTITUDES IN THE OLD SOUTHWEST."
         IN ELLSWORTH, LUCIUS F. (ED.). THE AMERICANIZATION OF
         THE GULF COAST, 1803-1850. PENSACOLA: HISTORIC
         PENSACOLA PRESERVATION BOARD, 1972, PP. 68-77.

15372   SUTCH, RICHARD. "THE CARE AND FEEDING OF SLAVES." IN
         DAVID, PAUL A.; GUTMAN, HERBERT G.; SUTCH; TEMIN,
         PETER; AND WRIGHT, GAVIN. RECKONING WITH SLAVERY: A
         CRITICAL STUDY IN THE QUANTITATIVE HISTORY OF AMERICAN
         NEGRO SLAVERY. NEW YORK: OXFORD UNIVERSITY PRESS,
         1976, PP. 231-301.

15373   SUTCH, RICHARD. THE TREATMENT RECEIVED BY AMERICAN
         SLAVES: A CRITICAL REVIEW OF THE EVIDENCE PRESENTED
         IN TIME ON THE CROSS. BERKELEY: INSTITUTE OF
         BUSINESS AND ECONOMIC RESEARCH, UNIVERSITY OF
         CALIFORNIA, 1975.

15374   SUTCH, RICHARD. "THE TREATMENT RECEIVED BY AMERICAN
         SLAVES: A CRITICAL REVIEW OF THE EVIDENCE PRESENTED
         IN TIME ON THE CROSS." EXPLORATIONS IN ECONOMIC
         HISTORY, 12 (OCTOBER, 1975): 335-438.

15375   SUTCH, RICHARD. "THE TREATMENT RECEIVED BY AMERICAN
         SLAVES: A CRITICAL REVIEW OF THE EVIDENCE PRESENTED
         IN TIME ON THE CROSS." UNPUBLISHED PAPER PRESENTED AT
         MSSB--UNIVERSITY OF ROCHESTER CONFERENCE: "TIME ON
         THE CROSS: A FIRST APPRAISAL," OCTOBER 24-26, 1974.

15376   SYDNOR, CHARLES S. SLAVERY IN MISSISSIPPI. NEW YORK:
         D. APPLETON-CENTURY COMPANY, 1933.

15377   TAYLOR, WILLIAM B. (ED.). "THE FOUNDATION OF NUESTRA
         SENORA DE GUADALUPE DE LOS MORENOS DE AMAPA."
         AMERICAS, 26 (APRIL, 1970): 439-446.

15378   TEESDALE, WILLIAM H. "PLANTATION DISCIPLINE." M.A.
         THESIS, UNIVERSITY OF CHICAGO, 1928.

15379   TIMMONS, ROBERT. "AGED EX-SLAVES GATHER AT HOME OF OLD
         MASTER." IN PARKS, WILLIS B. THE POSSIBILITIES OF

THE NEGRO IN SYMPOSIUM. ATLANTA: FRANKLIN PUBLISHING COMPANY, 1904, PP. 69-73.

15380 "THE TREATMENT OF NEGROES IN BARBADOS IN 1786 AND IN 1823." JOURNAL OF THE BARBADOS MUSEUM AND HISTORICAL SOCIETY, 2 (NOVEMBER, 1934): 23-31.

15381 TURNER, LORENZO D. AFRICANISMS IN THE GULLAH DIALECT. CHICAGO: UNIVERSITY OF CHICAGO PRESS, 1949.

15382 VAN NESS, JAMES S. "ECONOMIC DEVELOPMENT, SOCIAL AND CULTURAL CHANGES: 1800-1850." IN WALSH, RICHARD AND FOX, WILLIAM L. (EDS.). MARYLAND: A HISTORY, 1632-1974. BALTIMORE: MARYLAND HISTORICAL SOCIETY, 1974, PP. 151-238.

15383 WASHINGTON, BOOKER T. UP FROM SLAVERY. BOSTON: HOUGHTON MIFFLIN, 1901.

15384 WHIPPLE, CHARLES K. THE RELATION OF THE A.B.C.F.M. TO SLAVERY. BOSTON: R.F. WALLCUT, 1871.

15385 WILEY, BELL I. "THE MOVEMENT TO HUMANIZE THE INSTITUTION OF SLAVERY DURING THE CONFEDERACY." EMORY UNIVERSITY QUARTERLY, 5 (DECEMBER, 1949): 207-220.

15386 WILLIAMS, MARY W. "THE TREATMENT OF NEGRO SLAVES IN THE BRAZILIAN EMPIRE: A COMPARISON WITH THE UNITED STATES OF AMERICA." CONGRESSO INTERNATIONAL DE HISTORIA DA AMERICA, 1 (1922): 271-292.

15387 WILLIAMS, MARY W. "THE TREATMENT OF NEGRO SLAVES IN THE BRAZILIAN EMPIRE: A COMPARISON WITH THE UNITED STATES OF AMERICA." JOURNAL OF NEGRO HISTORY, 15 (JULY, 1930): 315-336.

15388 WILSON, WOODROW. DIVISION AND REUNION. NEW YORK: LONGMANS, GREEN, AND COMPANY, 1893.

15389 ZILVERSMIT, ARTHUR. THE FIRST EMANCIPATION: THE ABOLITION OF SLAVERY IN THE NORTH. CHICAGO: UNIVERSITY OF CHICAGO PRESS, 1967.

SLAVE DIET

15390 BALL, TIMOTHY H. A GLANCE INTO THE GREAT SOUTH-EAST: OR, CLARKE COUNTY ALABAMA, AND ITS SURROUNDINGS, FROM 1540 TO 1877. CHICAGO: PRESS OF KNIGHT & LEONARD, 1882.

15391 BEAN, RICHARD N. "FOOD IMPORTS INTO THE BRITISH WEST INDIES: 1680-1845." IN RUBIN, VERA AND TUDEN, ARTHUR (EDS.). COMPARATIVE PERSPECTIVES ON SLAVERY IN NEW WORLD PLANTATION SOCIETIES. NEW YORK: NEW YORK ACADEMY OF SCIENCES, 1977, PP. 581-590.

15392 CARDELL, NICHOLAS AND HOPKINS, MARK M. "THE EFFECT OF
       MILK INTOLERANCE ON THE CONSUMPTION OF MILK BY SLAVES
       IN 1860." JOURNAL OF INTERDISCIPLINARY HISTORY, 8
       (WINTER, 1978): 507-514.

15393 CARGILL, KATHLEEN; GIBBS, TYSON; AND LIEBERMAN, LESLIE.
       "SLAVE DIET AND EVIDENCE OF SUPPLEMENT TO THE STANDARD
       ALLOTMENT." FLORIDA SCIENTIST, 43 (SUMMER, 1980):
       160-164.

15394 COTTON, WALTER. HISTORY OF THE NEGROES OF LIMESTONE
       COUNTY. MEXIA, TX: NEWS PRINT COMPANY, 1939.

15395 DAVIS, E.A. "BENNET H. BARROW, ANTE-BELLUM PLANTER OF
       THE FELICIANAS." JOURNAL OF SOUTHERN HISTORY, 5
       (NOVEMBER, 1939): 431-446.

15396 DOOKHAN, ISAAC. "SLAVERY AND EMANCIPATION." A HISTORY
       OF THE BRITISH VIRGIN ISLANDS, 1672 TO 1970. EPPING,
       ESSEX, ENGLAND: CARIBBEAN UNIVERSITIES PRESS, 1975,
       PP. 71-96.

15397 DRUCKER, LESLEY M. "SPIERS LANDING: A SOCIOECONOMIC
       STUDY OF AN UNDOCUMENTED LATE EIGHTEENTH CENTURY SITE
       IN BERKELEY COUNTY, SOUTH CAROLINA." UNPUBLISHED
       PAPER DELIVERED AT MEETING OF SOCIETY FOR HISTORICAL
       ARCHAEOLOGY, NASHVILLE, TENNESSEE, 1979.

15398 DRUCKER, LESLEY M. AND ANTHONY, RONALD W. THE SPIERS
       LANDING SITE: ARCHAEOLOGICAL INVESTIGATIONS IN
       BERKELEY COUNTY, SOUTH CAROLINA. COLUMBIA: CAROLINA
       ARCHAEOLOGICAL SERVICES, 1979.

15399 FAIRBANKS, CHARLES H. "THE KINGSLEY SLAVE CABINS IN
       DUVAL COUNTY, FLORIDA, 1963." THE CONFERENCE ON
       HISTORIC SITE ARCHAEOLOGY PAPERS, 1972, NO. 7 (1974):
       62-93.

15400 FOGEL, ROBERT W. "FURTHER EVIDENCE ON THE NUTRITIONAL
       ADEQUACY OF THE SLAVE DIET." UNPUBLISHED PAPER
       PRESENTED AT MSSB--UNIVERSITY OF ROCHESTER CONFERENCE:
       "TIME ON THE CROSS: A FIRST APPRAISAL," OCTOBER
       24-26, 1974.

15401 FOGEL, ROBERT W. AND ENGERMAN, STANLEY L. TIME ON THE
       CROSS: THE ECONOMICS OF AMERICAN NEGRO SLAVERY. 2
       VOLS. BOSTON: LITTLE, BROWN AND COMPANY, 1974.

15402 "FOLK-LORE AND ETHNOLOGY." SOUTHERN WORKMAN, 26 (1897):
       163.

15403 FURNAS, J.C. GOODBYE TO UNCLE TOM. NEW YORK: WILLIAM
       SLOANE ASSOCIATES, 1956.

15404 GENOVESE, EUGENE D. ROLL, JORDAN, ROLL: THE WORLD THE

SLAVES MADE. NEW YORK: PANTHEON, 1974.

15405 GIBBS, TYSON; CARGILL, KATHLEEN; LIEBERMAN, LESLIE S.;
AND REITZ, ELIZABETH. "NUTRITION IN A SLAVE
POPULATION: AN ANTHROPOLOGICAL EXAMINATION." MEDICAL
ANTHROPOLOGY, 4 (SPRING, 1980): 175-262.

15406 GRAY, LEWIS C. HISTORY OF AGRICULTURE IN THE SOUTHERN
UNITED STATES TO 1860. 2 VOLS. WASHINGTON: CARNEGIE
INSTITUTION OF WASHINGTON, 1932.

15407 GYRISCO, GEOFFREY M. AND SALWEN, BERT. "ARCHAEOLOGY OF
BLACK AMERICAN CULTURE: AN ANNOTATED BIBLIOGRAPHY."
IN SCHUYLER, ROBERT L. (ED.). ARCHAEOLOGICAL
PERSPECTIVES ON ETHNICITY IN AMERICA: AFRO-AMERICAN
AND ASIAN CULTURE HISTORY. FARMINGDALE, NY: BAYWOOD
PUBLISHING COMPANY, 1980, PP. 75-35.

15408 HART, ALBERT B. SLAVERY AND ABOLITION, 1831-1841. NEW
YORK: HARPER AND BROTHERS, 1906.

15409 HAWKES, ALTA M. "FOOD, CLOTHING AND SHELTER OF THE
AMERICAN SLAVE." M.A. THESIS, SOUTHERN METHODIST
UNIVERSITY, 1936.

15410 HIGMAN, BARRY W. "HOUSEHOLD STRUCTURE AND FERTILITY ON
JAMAICAN SLAVE PLANTATIONS: A NINETEENTH-CENTURY
EXAMPLE." POPULATION STUDIES: A JOURNAL OF
DEMOGRAPHY, 27 (NOVEMBER, 1973): 527-550.

15411 HILLIARD, SAM B. "HOG MEAT AND CORNPONE: FOOD HABITS IN
THE ANTE-BELLUM SOUTH." PROCEEDINGS OF THE AMERICAN
PHILOSOPHICAL SOCIETY, 113 (FEBRUARY, 1969): 1-13.

15412 HILLIARD, SAM B. "HOG MEAT AND HOECAKE: A GEOGRAPHICAL
VIEW OF FOOD SUPPLY IN THE HEART OF THE OLD SOUTH,
1840-1860." PH.D. DISSERTATION, UNIVERSITY OF
WISCONSIN, 1966.

15413 HILLIARD, SAM B. HOGMEAT AND HOECAKE: FOOD SUPPLY IN
THE OLD SOUTH, 1840-1860. CARBONDALE: SOUTHERN
ILLINOIS UNIVERSITY PRESS, 1972.

15414 HILLIARD, SAM B. "PORK IN THE ANTE-BELLUM SOUTH: THE
GEOGRAPHY OF SELF-SUFFICIENCY." ANNALS OF THE
ASSOCIATION OF AMERICAN GEOGRAPHERS, 59 (SEPTEMBER,
1969): 461-480.

15415 HILLIARD, SAM B. "'THE REPUBLIC OF PORKDOM': A REPLY TO
ARTICLE BY ROYCE SHINGLETON." PROCEEDINGS OF THE
AMERICAN PHILOSOPHICAL SOCIETY, 114 (OCTOBER, 1970):
409-410.

15416 "HOG AND HOMINY." IN SCHAPSMEIER, EDWARD L. AND
SCHAPSMEIER, FREDERICK H. ENCYCLOPEDIA OF AMERICAN

AGRICULTURAL HISTORY. WESTPORT: GREENWOOD PRESS, 1975, P. 163.

15417 "HOW THE SLAVES COOKED AND ATE." SOUTHERN WORKMAN, 26 (AUGUST, 1897): 163.

15418 HUNTER, JOHN M. "GEOPHAGY IN AFRICA AND IN THE UNITED STATES: A CULTURE-NUTRITION HYPOTHESIS." GEOGRAPHICAL REVIEW, 63 (APRIL, 1973): 170-195.

15419 HUTCHINSON, WILLIAM K. AND WILLIAMSON, SAMUEL H. "THE SELF-SUFFICIENCY OF THE ANTEBELLUM SOUTH: ESTIMATES OF THE FOOD SUPPLY." JOURNAL OF ECONOMIC HISTORY, 31 (SEPTEMBER, 1971): 591-612.

15420 JOYNER, CHARLES W. "SOUL FOOD AND THE SAMBO STEREOTYPE: FOODLORE IN THE SLAVE NARRATIVE COLLECTION." KEYSTONE FOLKLORE QUARTERLY, 16 (1971): 171-178.

15421 KELLAR, HERBERT A. SOLON ROBINSON: PIONEER AND AGRICULTURIST. 2 VOLS. INDIANAPOLIS: INDIANA HISTORICAL BUREAU, 1936.

15422 KIPLE, KENNETH F. AND KIPLE, VIRGINIA. "THE AFRICAN CONNECTION: SLAVERY, DISEASE AND RACISM." PHYLON, 41 (FALL, 1980): 211-222.

15423 KIPLE, KENNETH F. AND KIPLE, VIRGINIA H. "DEFICIENCY DISEASES IN THE CARIBBEAN." JOURNAL OF INTERDISCIPLINARY HISTORY, 11 (AUTUMN, 1980): 197-215.

15424 KIPLE, KENNETH F. AND KIPLE, VIRGINIA H. "SLAVE CHILD MORTALITY: SOME NUTRITIONAL ANSWERS TO A PERENNIAL PUZZLE." IN BRANCA, PATRICIA (ED.). MEDICINE SHOW: PATIENTS, PHYSICIANS, AND THE PERPLEXITIES OF THE HEALTH REVOLUTION IN MODERN SOCIETY. NEW YORK: SCIENCE HISTORY PUBLISHERS, 1977, PP. 21-46.

15425 KIPLE, KENNETH F. AND KIPLE, VIRGINIA H. "SLAVE CHILD MORTALITY: SOME NUTRITIONAL ANSWERS TO A PERENNIAL PUZZLE." JOURNAL OF SOCIAL HISTORY, 10 (MARCH, 1977): 284-309.

15426 KLEIN, HERBERT S. AND ENGERMAN, STANLEY. "FERTILITY DIFFERENTIALS BETWEEN SLAVES IN THE UNITED STATES AND THE BRITISH WEST INDIES: A NOTE ON LACTATION PRACTICES AND THEIR POSSIBLE IMPLICATIONS." WILLIAM AND MARY QUARTERLY, 3RD SER., 35 (APRIL, 1978): 357-374.

15427 KOPYTOFF, BARBARA K. "MAROON JERK PORK AND OTHER JAMAICAN COOKING." IN KUPER, JESSICA (ED.). THE ANTHROPOLOGISTS' COOKBOOK. LONDON: ROUTLEDGE AND KEGAN PAUL, 1977, PP. 141-146.

15428 "MANAGEMENT OF NEGROES UPON SOUTHERN ESTATES--AN ECHO OF
       SLAVE DAYS IN THE SOUTHLAND." *TENNESSEE HISTORICAL
       MAGAZINE*, 5 (JULY, 1919):   97-103.

15429 MAYER, JEAN.   "THE NUTRITIONAL STATUS OF AMERICAN
       NEGROES." *NUTRITION REVIEWS*, 23 (JUNE, 1965):
       161-164.

15430 MCWHINEY, GRADY. "THE REVOLUTION IN NINETEENTH-CENTURY
       ALABAMA AGRICULTURE." *ALABAMA REVIEW*, 31 (JANUARY,
       1978):   3-32.

15431 MUSTACCHI, PIERO.   "CESARE BRESSA (1785-1836) ON DIRT
       EATING IN LOUISIANA: A CRITICAL ANALYSIS OF HIS
       UNPUBLISHED MANUSCRIPT *DE LA DISSOLUTION SCORBUTIQUE*."
       JOURNAL OF THE AMERICAN MEDICAL ASSOCIATION, 218
       (OCTOBER 11, 1971):   229-232.

15432 NEVINS, ALLAN.   "THE LOT OF THE BONDSMAN." *ORDEAL OF THE
       UNION*. 2 VOLS. NEW YORK: CHARLES SCRIBNER'S SONS,
       1947, VOL. 1, PP. 412-461.

15433 O'BRIEN, MARY L.   "SLAVERY IN LOUISVILLE DURING THE
       ANTEBELLUM PERIOD: 1820-1860. A STUDY OF THE EFFECTS
       OF URBANIZATION ON THE INSTITUTION OF SLAVERY AS IT
       EXISTED IN LOUISVILLE, KENTUCKY." M.A. THESIS,
       UNIVERSITY OF LOUISVILLE, 1979.

15434 OTT, ELEANORE. *PLANTATION COOKERY OF OLD LOUISIANA*. NEW
       ORLEANS: HARMANSON, 1938.

15435 OTTO, JOHN S.   "CANNON'S POINT PLANTATION AND THE HARDY
       BANKS FARM: MATERIAL LIVING CONDITIONS OF OLD SOUTH
       SLAVES." UNPUBLISHED PAPER PRESENTED AT MEETING OF
       SOCIETY FOR HISTORICAL ARCHAEOLOGY, NASHVILLE,
       TENNESSEE, 1979.

15436 OTTO, JOHN S. "A NEW LOOK AT SLAVE LIFE." *NATURAL
       HISTORY*, 88 (JANUARY, 1979):   8, 16, 20, 22, 24, 30.

15437 OTTO, JOHN S. "STATUS DIFFERENCES AND THE ARCHEOLOGICAL
       RECORD--A COMPARISON OF PLANTER, OVERSEER, AND SLAVE
       SITES FROM CANNON'S POINT PLANTATION (1794-1861), ST.
       SIMON'S ISLAND, GEORGIA." PH.D. DISSERTATION,
       UNIVERSITY OF FLORIDA, 1975.

15438 OWENS, LESLIE H. *THIS SPECIES OF PROPERTY: SLAVE LIFE
       AND CULTURE IN THE OLD SOUTH*. NEW YORK: OXFORD
       UNIVERSITY PRESS, 1976.

15439 PARRY, JOHN H. "PLANTATION AND PROVISION GROUND--AN
       HISTORICAL SKETCH OF THE INTRODUCTION OF FOOD CROPS
       INTO JAMAICA." *REVISTA DE HISTORIA DE AMERICA*, 39
       (JUNE, 1955):   1-20.

15440   PERDUE, CHARLES L., JR.; BARDEN, THOMAS E.; AND PHILLIPS,
        ROBERT K. (EDS.). WEEVILS_IN_THE_WHEAT:__INTERVIEWS
        WITH_VIRGINIA_EX-SLAVES. CHARLOTTESVILLE: UNIVERSITY
        PRESS OF VIRGINIA, 1976.

15441   PHILLIPS, ULRICH B. AMERICAN_NEGRO_SLAVERY:_A_SURVEY_OF
        THE_SUPPLY,_EMPLOYMENT_AND_CONTROL_OF_NEGRO_LABOR_AS
        DETERMINED_BY_THE_PLANTATION_REGIME. NEW YORK: D.
        APPLETON, 1918.

15442   PHILLIPS, ULRICH B. LIFE_AND_LABOR_IN_THE_OLD_SOUTH.
        BOSTON: LITTLE, BROWN AND COMPANY, 1929.

15443   PIERSON, HAMILTON W. IN_THE_BRUSH,_OR,_OLD-TIME_SOCIAL,
        POLITICAL_AND_RELIGIOUS_LIFE_IN_THE_SOUTHWEST. NEW
        YORK: D. APPLETON, 1881.

15444   RANSOM, ROGER L. AND SUTCH, RICHARD. ONE_KIND_OF
        FREEDOM:__THE_ECONOMIC_CONSEQUENCES_OF_EMANCIPATION.
        CAMBRIDGE: CAMBRIDGE UNIVERSITY PRESS, 1977.

15445   RAWICK, GEORGE P. FROM_SUNDOWN_TO_SUNUP:__THE_MAKING_OF
        THE_BLACK_COMMUNITY. WESTPORT: GREENWOOD PRESS, 1972.

15446   ROBERTS, JOHN W. "SLAVE PROVERBS: A PERSPECTIVE."
        CALLALOO, 1 (OCTOBER, 1978): 129-140.

15447   SALWEN, BERT AND GYRISCO, GEOFFREY M. "AN ANNOTATED
        BIBLIOGRAPHY: ARCHEOLOGY OF BLACK AMERICAN CULTURE."
        11593, VOL. 3, SUPPLEMENT (FEBRUARY-MARCH, 1978): 1-4.

15448   SAVITT, TODD L. MEDICINE_AND_SLAVERY:__THE_DISEASES_AND
        HEALTH_CARE_OF_BLACKS_IN_ANTEBELLUM_VIRGINIA. URBANA:
        UNIVERSITY OF ILLINOIS PRESS, 1978.

15449   SHERIDAN, RICHARD B. "THE CRISIS OF SLAVE SUBSISTENCE IN
        THE BRITISH WEST INDIES DURING AND AFTER THE AMERICAN
        REVOLUTION." WILLIAM_AND_MARY_QUARTERLY, 3RD SER., 33
        (OCTOBER, 1976): 615-641.

15450   SHERWOOD, HENRY N. (ED.). "THE JOURNAL OF MISS SUSAN
        WALKER, MARCH 3RD TO JUNE 6TH, 1862." QUARTERLY
        PUBLICATION_OF_THE_HISTORICAL_AND_PHILOSOPHICAL
        SOCIETY_OF_OHIO, 7 (1912): 3-48.

15451   SHINGLETON, ROYCE G. "THE UTILITY OF LEISURE: GAME AS A
        SOURCE OF FOOD IN THE OLD SOUTH." MISSISSIPPI
        QUARTERLY, 25 (FALL, 1972): 429-445.

15452   SHORTER, EDWARD. "PROTEIN, PUBERTY AND PREMARITAL
        SEXUALITY: AMERICAN BLACKS V. FRENCH PEASANTS."
        UNPUBLISHED PAPER PRESENTED AT MSSB--UNIVERSITY OF
        ROCHESTER CONFERENCE: "TIME_ON_THE_CROSS: A FIRST
        APPRAISAL," OCTOBER 24-26, 1974.

15453   SIMPSON, MARTHA L. "LIQUOR SALES TO SLAVES." IN JOYNER,
        CHARLES W. (ED.). BLACK CAROLINIANS: STUDIES IN THE
        HISTORY OF SOUTH CAROLINA NEGROES. LAURINBURG, NC:
        ST. ANDREWS PRESBYTERIAN COLLEGE, 1969, PP. 109-115.

15454   "SLAVE FOOD ALLOWANCE." IN NUNEZ, BENJAMIN. DICTIONARY
        OF AFRO-LATIN AMERICAN CIVILIZATION. WESTPORT:
        GREENWOOD PRESS, 1980, P. 434.

15455   "SLAVES, FEEDING OF (1837)." IN RYWELL, MARTIN (ED.).
        AFRO-AMERICAN ENCYCLOPEDIA. 10 VOLS. NORTH MIAMI:
        EDUCATIONAL BOOK PUBLISHERS, 1974, VOL. 8, PP.
        2482-2483.

15456   "SLAVES: FOOD, MEDICINE AND MORALITY." IN RYWELL,
        MARTIN (ED.). AFRO-AMERICAN ENCYCLOPEDIA. 10 VOLS.
        NORTH MIAMI: EDUCATIONAL BOOK PUBLISHERS, 1974, VOL.
        8, PP. 2482-2486.

15457   SPEARS, JAMES E. "FAVORITE SOUTHERN NEGRO FOLK RECIPES."
        KENTUCKY FOLKLORE RECORD, 16 (JANUARY/MARCH, 1970):
        1-5.

15458   STAMPP, KENNETH M. THE PECULIAR INSTITUTION: SLAVERY IN
        THE ANTE-BELLUM SOUTH. NEW YORK: ALFRED A. KNOPF,
        1956.

15459   SUTCH, RICHARD. "THE CARE AND FEEDING OF SLAVES." IN
        DAVID, PAUL A.; GUTMAN, HERBERT G.; SUTCH; TEMIN,
        PETER; AND WRIGHT, GAVIN. RECKONING WITH SLAVERY: A
        CRITICAL STUDY IN THE QUANTITATIVE HISTORY OF AMERICAN
        NEGRO SLAVERY. NEW YORK: OXFORD UNIVERSITY PRESS,
        1976, PP. 231-301.

15460   SYDNOR, CHARLES S. SLAVERY IN MISSISSIPPI. NEW YORK:
        D. APPLETON-CENTURY COMPANY, 1933.

15461   TAYLOR, ROSSER H. "FEEDING SLAVES." JOURNAL OF NEGRO
        HISTORY, 9 (APRIL, 1924): 139-143.

15462   WADE, RICHARD C. SLAVERY IN THE CITIES: THE SOUTH,
        1820-1860. NEW YORK: OXFORD UNIVERSITY PRESS, 1964.

15463   WADE, RICHARD C. THE URBAN FRONTIER: THE RISE OF
        WESTERN CITIES, 1790-1830. CAMBRIDGE: HARVARD
        UNIVERSITY PRESS, 1959.

15464   WEBBER, THOMAS L. DEEP LIKE THE RIVERS: EDUCATION IN
        THE SLAVE QUARTER COMMUNITY, 1831-1865. NEW YORK:
        W.W. NORTON, 1978.

15465   WILSON, MARY T. "PEACEFUL INTEGRATION: THE OWNER'S
        ADOPTION OF HIS SLAVE'S FOOD." JOURNAL OF NEGRO
        HISTORY, 49 (APRIL, 1964): 116-127.

SLAVE HOUSING

15466 ABBITT OUTLAW, MERRY; BOGLEY, BEVERLY A.; AND OUTLAW,
       ALAIN C. "RICH MAN, POOR MAN: STATUS DEFINITION IN
       TWO SEVENTEENTH-CENTURY CERAMIC ASSEMBLAGES FROM
       KINGSMILL." UNPUBLISHED PAPER PRESENTED AT MEETING OF
       SOCIETY FOR HISTORICAL ARCHAEOLOGY, OTTAWA, ONTARIO,
       1977.

15467 ANTHONY, CARL. "THE BIG HOUSE AND THE SLAVE QUARTERS."
       LANDSCAPE, 20 (SPRING, 1976): 8-19; 21 (AUTUMN,
       1976): 9-15.

15468 ARMSTRONG, JIM (ED.). "THE OLD SLAVE HOUSE, HICKORY
       HILL." ELECTRIC ENERGY INK, (SEPTEMBER, 1961): 6-11.

15469 ASCHER, ROBERT AND FAIRBANKS, CHARLES H. "EXCAVATION OF
       A SLAVE CABIN: GEORGIA, USA." HISTORICAL
       ARCHAEOLOGY, 5 (1971): 3-17.

15470 BLACK, PATTI C. AND FERRIS, WILLIAM. "THE SHOTGUN, THE
       DOGTROT, AND THE ROW HOUSE . . . ." SOUTHERN VOICES,
       1 (1973): 28-32.

15471 BONNER, JAMES C. "PLANTATION ARCHITECTURE OF THE LOWER
       SOUTH ON THE EVE OF THE CIVIL WAR." JOURNAL OF
       SOUTHERN HISTORY, 11 (AUGUST, 1945): 370-454.

15472 BROWN, LETITIA W. "RESIDENCE PATTERNS OF NEGROES IN THE
       DISTRICT OF COLUMBIA, 1800-1860." RECORDS OF THE
       COLUMBIA HISTORICAL SOCIETY, 69-70 (1969-1970): 66-79.

15473 COHEN, YEHUDI A. "A STUDY OF INTERPERSONAL RELATIONS IN
       A JAMAICAN COMMUNITY." PH.D. DISSERTATION, YALE
       UNIVERSITY, 1952.

15474 COHN, MICHAEL. "COLLECTORS' NOTES: NO DOVECOT."
       ANTIQUES, 98 (FEBRUARY, 1970): 270.

15475 CONNALLY, ERNEST A. "ARCHITECTURE AT THE END OF THE
       SOUTH: CENTRAL TEXAS." JOURNAL OF THE SOCIETY OF
       ARCHITECTURAL HISTORIANS, 11 (DECEMBER, 1952): 8-12.

15476 COOLEY, ROSSA B. HOMES OF THE FREED. NEW YORK: NEW
       REPUBLIC, 1926.

15477 CRESSEY, PAMELA J. "AN ENDURING AFRO-AMERICAN
       NEIGHBORHOOD: AN ARCHAEOLOGICAL PERSPECTIVE FROM
       ALEXANDRIA, VIRGINIA." BLACK HERITAGE, 20
       (SEPTEMBER-OCTOBER, 1980): 1-10.

15478 DOOKHAN, ISAAC. "SLAVERY AND EMANCIPATION." A HISTORY
       OF THE BRITISH VIRGIN ISLANDS, 1672 TO 1970. EPPING,
       ESSEX, ENGLAND: CARIBBEAN UNIVERSITIES PRESS, 1975,
       PP. 71-96.

15479 DOUGLAS, WILLIAM L. "THE LANDSCAPE OBSERVED: OLMSTED'S
       VIEW OF THE ANTEBELLUM SOUTH." IN WHITE, DANA F. AND
       KRAMER, VICTOR A. (EDS.). OLMSTED SOUTH: OLD SOUTH
       CRITIC/NEW SOUTH PLANNER. WESTPORT: GREENWOOD PRESS,
       1979, PP. 81-90.

15480 DUBOIS, W.E.B. "THE PROBLEM OF HOUSING THE NEGRO--THE
       HOME OF THE SLAVE." SOUTHERN WORKMAN, 30 (SEPTEMBER,
       1901): 486-493.

15481 EVANS, ELLIOT A.P. "THE EAST TEXAS HOUSE." JOURNAL OF
       THE SOCIETY OF ARCHITECTURAL HISTORIANS, 11 (DECEMBER,
       1952): 1-7.

15482 FAIRBANKS, CHARLES H. "THE KINGSLEY SLAVE CABINS IN
       DUVAL COUNTY, FLORIDA, 1968." THE CONFERENCE ON
       HISTORIC SITE ARCHAEOLOGY PAPERS, 1972, NO. 7 (1974):
       62-93.

15483 FAIRBANKS, CHARLES H. AND MULLINS-MOORE, SUE A. "HOW DID
       SLAVES LIVE?" EARLY MAN, 2 (SUMMER, 1980): 2-6.

15484 FITCH, JAMES M. "CREOLE ARCHITECTURE, 1718-1860: THE
       RISE AND FALL OF A GREAT TRADITION." IN CARTER,
       HODDING (ED.). THE PAST AS PRELUDE: NEW ORLEANS,
       1718-1968. NEW ORLEANS: PELICAN PUBLISHING COMPANY,
       1968, PP. 71-87.

15485 FLOYD, M. "REVIVAL OF TABBY BUILDING IN THE NINETEENTH
       CENTURY." IN COULTER, E.M. (ED.). GEORGIA'S DISPUTED
       RUINS. CHAPEL HILL: UNIVERSITY OF NORTH CAROLINA
       PRESS, 1937, PP. 73-87.

15486 FOGEL, ROBERT W. AND ENGERMAN, STANLEY L. TIME ON THE
       CROSS: THE ECONOMICS OF AMERICAN NEGRO SLAVERY. 2
       VOLS. BOSTON: LITTLE, BROWN AND COMPANY, 1974.

15487 FORMAN, HENRY C. THE ARCHITECTURE OF THE OLD SOUTH: THE
       MEDIEVAL STYLE, 1585-1850. CAMBRIDGE: HARVARD
       UNIVERSITY PRESS, 1948.

15488 FORMAN, HENRY C. TIDEWATER MARYLAND ARCHITECTURE AND
       GARDENS. NEW YORK: ARCHITECTURAL BOOK PUBLISHING
       CORPORATION, 1957.

15489 FURNAS, J.C. GOODBYE TO UNCLE TOM. NEW YORK: WILLIAM
       SLOANE ASSOCIATES, 1956.

15490 GENOVESE, EUGENE D. ROLL, JORDAN, ROLL: THE WORLD THE
       SLAVES MADE. NEW YORK: PANTHEON, 1974.

15491 GLASSIE, HENRY. FOLK HOUSING IN MIDDLE VIRGINIA: A
       STRUCTURAL ANALYSIS OF HISTORIC ARTIFACTS. KNOXVILLE:
       UNIVERSITY OF TENNESSEE PRESS, 1975.

15492 GRAY, LEWIS C. HISTORY OF AGRICULTURE IN THE SOUTHERN
       UNITED STATES TO 1860. 2 VOLS. WASHINGTON: CARNEGIE
       INSTITUTION OF WASHINGTON, 1932.

15493 GRIDER, SYLVIA. "THE SHOTGUN HOUSE." PIONEER AMERICA, 7
       (JULY, 1975): 47-55.

15494 GRIDER, SYLVIA A. "THE SHOTGUN SHACK AS OIL BOOMTOWN
       HOUSING." FOLKLORE PREPRINT SERIES, VOL. 3, NO. 2.
       BLOOMINGTON: FOLKLORE PUBLICATIONS GROUP, 1975.

15495 GYRISCO, GEOFFREY M. AND SALWEN, BERT. "ARCHAEOLOGY OF
       BLACK AMERICAN CULTURE: AN ANNOTATED BIBLIOGRAPHY."
       IN SCHUYLER, ROBERT L. (ED.). ARCHAEOLOGICAL
       PERSPECTIVES ON ETHNICITY IN AMERICA: AFRO-AMERICAN
       AND ASIAN CULTURE HISTORY. FARMINGDALE, NY: BAYWOOD
       PUBLISHING COMPANY, 1980, PP. 76-85.

15496 HAWKES, ALTA M. "FOOD, CLOTHING AND SHELTER OF THE
       AMERICAN SLAVE." M.A. THESIS, SOUTHERN METHODIST
       UNIVERSITY, 1936.

15497 HENDERSON, GEORGE W. "LIFE IN THE LOUISIANA SUGAR BELT."
       SOUTHERN WORKMAN, 35 (1906): 207-215.

15498 HULAN, RICHARD. "MIDDLE TENNESSEE AND THE DOGTROT
       HOUSE." PIONEER AMERICA, 7 (JULY, 1975): 37-46.

15499 JACKSON, SUSAN. "CURRENT RESEARCH: SOUTHEAST." SOCIETY
       FOR HISTORICAL ARCHAEOLOGY NEWSLETTER, 9 (1976):
       15-19.

15500 JACKSON, SUSAN. "CURRENT RESEARCH: SOUTHEAST." SOCIETY
       FOR HISTORICAL ARCHAEOLOGY NEWSLETTER, 10 (1977):
       21-24.

15501 JACKSON, SUSAN. "CURRENT RESEARCH: SOUTHEAST." SOCIETY
       FOR HISTORICAL ARCHAEOLOGY NEWSLETTER, 10 (1977):
       42-45.

15502 JORDAN, TERRY G. TEXAS LOG BUILDINGS: A FOLK
       ARCHITECTURE. AUSTIN: UNIVERSITY OF TEXAS PRESS,
       1978.

15503 KELSO, WILLIAM M. "CAPTAIN JONES' WORMSLOW: A
       HISTORICAL, ARCHAEOLOGICAL, AND ARCHITECTURAL STUDY OF
       AN EIGHTEENTH-CENTURY PLANTATION SITE NEAR SAVANNAH,
       GEORGIA." PH.D. DISSERTATION, EMORY UNIVERSITY, 1971.

15504 KELSO, WILLIAM M. CAPTAIN JONES'S WORMSLOW: A
       HISTORICAL, ARCHAEOLOGICAL, AND ARCHITECTURAL STUDY OF
       AN EIGHTEENTH-CENTURY PLANTATION SITE NEAR SAVANNAH,
       GEORGIA. ATHENS: UNIVERSITY OF GEORGIA PRESS, 1979.

15505 KNIFFEN, FRED B. "THE PHYSIOGNOMY OF RURAL LOUISIANA."

LOUISIANA HISTORY, 4 (FALL, 1963): 291-299.

15506   LEWIS, KENNETH E. "EXCAVATING A COLONIAL RICE
        PLANTATION." EARLY MAN, (AUTUMN, 1979): 13-17.

15507   "MANAGEMENT OF NEGROES UPON SOUTHERN ESTATES--AN ECHO OF
        SLAVE DAYS IN THE SOUTHLAND." TENNESSEE HISTORICAL
        MAGAZINE, 5 (JULY, 1919): 97-103.

15508   MAUNCY, ALBERT C. "AMERICAN NOTES." JOURNAL OF THE
        SOCIETY OF ARCHITECTURAL HISTORIANS, 11 (DECEMBER,
        1952): 32-33.

15509   MCDANIEL, GEORGE W. "PRESERVING THE PEOPLE'S HISTORY:
        TRADITIONAL BLACK MATERIAL CULTURE IN NINETEENTH AND
        TWENTIETH CENTURY SOUTHERN MARYLAND." PH.D.
        DISSERTATION, DUKE UNIVERSITY, 1979.

15510   MCFARLANE, SUZANNE S. "THE ETHNOHISTORY OF A SLAVE
        COMMUNITY: THE COUPER PLANTATION SITE." M.A. THESIS,
        UNIVERSITY OF FLORIDA, 1975.

15511   MCTIGUE, GERALDINE. "PATTERNS OF RESIDENCE: HOUSING
        DISTRIBUTION BY COLOR IN TWO LOUISIANA TOWNS,
        1860-1880." LOUISIANA STUDIES, 15 (WINTER, 1976):
        345-388.

15512   MULLINS-MOORE, SUE. "THE ANTEBELLUM PLANTATION: IN
        SEARCH OF AN ARCHAEOLOGICAL PATTERN." PH.D.
        DISSERTATION, UNIVERSITY OF FLORIDA, 1980.

15513   O'BRIEN, MARY L. "SLAVERY IN LOUISVILLE DURING THE
        ANTEBELLUM PERIOD: 1820-1860. A STUDY OF THE EFFECTS
        OF URBANIZATION ON THE INSTITUTION OF SLAVERY AS IT
        EXISTED IN LOUISVILLE, KENTUCKY." M.A. THESIS,
        UNIVERSITY OF LOUISVILLE, 1979.

15514   OTTO, JOHN S. "CANNON'S POINT PLANTATION AND THE HARDY
        BANKS FARM: MATERIAL LIVING CONDITIONS OF OLD SOUTH
        SLAVES." UNPUBLISHED PAPER PRESENTED AT MEETING OF
        SOCIETY FOR HISTORICAL ARCHAEOLOGY, NASHVILLE,
        TENNESSEE, 1979.

15515   OTTO, JOHN S. "A NEW LOOK AT SLAVE LIFE." NATURAL
        HISTORY, 88 (JANUARY, 1979): 8, 16, 20, 22, 24, 30.

15516   OTTO, JOHN S. "STATUS DIFFERENCES AND THE ARCHEOLOGICAL
        RECORD--A COMPARISON OF PLANTER, OVERSEER, AND SLAVE
        SITES FROM CANNON'S POINT PLANTATION (1794-1861), ST.
        SIMON'S ISLAND, GEORGIA." PH.D. DISSERTATION,
        UNIVERSITY OF FLORIDA, 1975.

15517   OWENS, LESLIE H. THIS SPECIES OF PROPERTY: SLAVE LIFE
        AND CULTURE IN THE OLD SOUTH. NEW YORK: OXFORD
        UNIVERSITY PRESS, 1976.

15518   PERDUE, CHARLES L., JR.   "SLAVE LIFE STYLES IN EARLY
        VIRGINIA." PROCEEDINGS OF THE PIONEER AMERICA
        SOCIETY, 2 (1973):   54-58.

15519   PHILLIPS, ULRICH B.   AMERICAN NEGRO SLAVERY: A SURVEY OF
        THE SUPPLY, EMPLOYMENT AND CONTROL OF NEGRO LABOR AS
        DETERMINED BY THE PLANTATION REGIME. NEW YORK: D.
        APPLETON, 1918.

15520   PHILLIPS, ULRICH B.   LIFE AND LABOR IN THE OLD SOUTH.
        BOSTON: LITTLE, BROWN AND COMPANY, 1929.

15521   RADFORD, JOHN P.   "CULTURE, ECONOMY AND RESIDENTIAL
        STRUCTURE IN CHARLESTON, SOUTH CAROLINA, 1860-1880."
        PH.D. DISSERTATION, CLARK UNIVERSITY, 1974.

15522   RADFORD, JOHN P.   "DELICATE SPACE: RACE AND RESIDENCE IN
        CHARLESTON, SOUTH CAROLINA, 1860-1880." WEST GEORGIA
        COLLEGE STUDIES IN THE SOCIAL SCIENCES, 16 (JUNE,
        1977):   17-37.

15523   RADFORD, JOHN P.   "RACE, RESIDENCE AND IDEOLOGY:
        CHARLESTON, SOUTH CAROLINA IN THE MID-NINETEENTH
        CENTURY." JOURNAL OF HISTORICAL GEOGRAPHY, 2
        (OCTOBER, 1976):   329-346.

15524   RAWICK, GEORGE P.   FROM SUNDOWN TO SUNUP: THE MAKING OF
        THE BLACK COMMUNITY. WESTPORT: GREENWOOD PRESS, 1972.

15525   REHDER, JOHN B.   "DIAGNOSTIC LANDSCAPE TRAITS OF SUGAR
        PLANTATIONS IN SOUTHERN LOUISIANA." GEOSCIENCE AND
        MAN, 19 (JUNE 30, 1978):   135-150.

15526   ROLLINS, ALICE W.   "THE NEW UNCLE TOM'S CABIN." FORUM, 4
        (OCTOBER, 1887):   221-227.

15527   SALWEN, BERT AND GYRISCO, GEOFFREY M.   "AN ANNOTATED
        BIBLIOGRAPHY: ARCHEOLOGY OF BLACK AMERICAN CULTURE."
        11593, VOL. 3, SUPPLEMENT (FEBRUARY-MARCH, 1978):   1-4.

15528   SAVITT, TODD L.   MEDICINE AND SLAVERY: THE DISEASES AND
        HEALTH CARE OF BLACKS IN ANTEBELLUM VIRGINIA. URBANA:
        UNIVERSITY OF ILLINOIS PRESS, 1978.

15529   "THE SEA ISLANDS." HARPER'S NEW MONTHLY MAGAZINE, 57
        (NOVEMBER, 1878):   839-861.

15530   SHENKEL, J. RICHARD AND HUDSON, JACK.   "HISTORIC
        ARCHAEOLOGY IN NEW ORLEANS." THE CONFERENCE ON
        HISTORIC SITE ARCHAEOLOGY PAPERS, 6 (1971):   40-44.

15531   SHERWOOD, HENRY N. (ED.).   "THE JOURNAL OF MISS SUSAN
        WALKER, MARCH 3RD TO JUNE 6TH, 1862." QUARTERLY
        PUBLICATION OF THE HISTORICAL AND PHILOSOPHICAL
        SOCIETY OF OHIO, 7 (1912):   3-48.

15532   "SLAVE COTTAGES." IN NUNEZ, BENJAMIN. DICTIONARY OF
        AFRO-LATIN AMERICAN CIVILIZATION. WESTPORT:
        GREENWOOD PRESS, 1980, P. 433.

15533   SMELSER, MARSHALL. "HOUSING IN CREOLE ST. LOUIS,
        1764-1821: AN EXAMPLE OF CULTURAL CHANGE." LOUISIANA
        HISTORICAL QUARTERLY, 21 (APRIL, 1938): 337-348.

15534   SMITH, JOSEPH F. WHITE PILLARS: EARLY LIFE AND
        ARCHITECTURE OF THE LOWER MISSISSIPPI VALLEY COUNTRY.
        NEW YORK: W. HELBURN, 1941.

15535   SMITH, SAMUEL D. "AN ARCHAEOLOGICAL AND HISTORICAL
        ASSESSMENT OF THE FIRST HERMITAGE." TENNESSEE
        DIVISION OF ARCHAEOLOGY RESEARCH SERIES 2. NASHVILLE:
        TENNESSEE DEPARTMENT OF CONSERVATION, 1976.

15536   SMITH, SAMUEL D. ARCHAEOLOGICAL EXPLORATIONS AT THE
        CASTALIAN SPRINGS, TENNESSEE, HISTORIC SITE.
        NASHVILLE: TENNESSEE HISTORICAL COMMISSION, 1975.

15537   SMITH, SAMUEL D. "PLANTATION ARCHAEOLOGY AT THE
        HERMITAGE: SOME SUGGESTED PATTERNS." TENNESSEE
        ANTHROPOLOGIST, 2 (1977): 152-163.

15538   SPAIN, DAPHNE. "RACE RELATIONS AND RESIDENTIAL
        SEGREGATION IN NEW ORLEANS: TWO CENTURIES OF
        PARADOX." ANNALS OF THE AMERICAN ACADEMY OF POLITICAL
        AND SOCIAL SCIENCE, 441 (JANUARY, 1979): 82-96.

15539   STAMPP, KENNETH M. THE PECULIAR INSTITUTION: SLAVERY IN
        THE ANTE-BELLUM SOUTH. NEW YORK: ALFRED A. KNOPF,
        1956.

15540   SYDNOR, CHARLES S. SLAVERY IN MISSISSIPPI. NEW YORK:
        D. APPLETON-CENTURY COMPANY, 1933.

15541   VLACH, JOHN M. THE AFRO-AMERICAN TRADITION IN DECORATIVE
        ARTS. CLEVELAND: CLEVELAND MUSEUM OF ART, 1978.

15542   VLACH, JOHN M. "THE SHOTGUN HOUSE: AN AFRICAN
        ARCHITECTURAL LEGACY." PIONEER AMERICA, 8 (JANUARY,
        JULY, 1976): 47-56, 57-70.

15543   VLACH, JOHN M. "SHOTGUN HOUSES." NATURAL HISTORY, 86
        (FEBRUARY, 1977): 50-57.

15544   VLACH, JOHN M. "SOURCES OF THE SHOTGUN HOUSE: AFRICAN
        AND CARIBBEAN ANTECEDENTS FOR AFRO-AMERICAN
        ARCHITECTURE." PH.D. DISSERTATION, INDIANA
        UNIVERSITY, 1975.

15545   WADE, RICHARD C. SLAVERY IN THE CITIES: THE SOUTH,
        1820-1860. NEW YORK: OXFORD UNIVERSITY PRESS, 1964.

15546   WADE, RICHARD C.   THE URBAN FRONTIER: THE RISE OF
         WESTERN CITIES, 1790-1830.   CAMBRIDGE: HARVARD
         UNIVERSITY PRESS, 1959.

15547   WEATHERFORD, WILLIS D.   "THE HEARTH AND HOUSING OF THE
         NEGRO."   NEGRO LIFE IN THE SOUTH: PRESENT CONDITIONS
         AND NEEDS.   NEW YORK: ASSOCIATION PRESS, 1911, PP.
         61-83.

15548   WEBBER, THOMAS L.   DEEP LIKE THE RIVERS: EDUCATION IN
         THE SLAVE QUARTER COMMUNITY, 1831-1865.   NEW YORK:
         W.W. NORTON, 1978.

15549   WESLAGER, C.A.   "THE EXCAVATION OF A COLONIAL LOG CABIN
         NEAR WILMINGTON, DELAWARE."   BULLETIN OF THE
         ARCHAEOLOGICAL SOCIETY OF DELAWARE, 6 (APRIL, 1954):
         1-12.

15550   WILSON, EUGENE.   "THE SINGLE PEN LOG HOUSE IN THE SOUTH."
         PIONEER AMERICA, 2 (JANUARY, 1970):   21-28.

15551   WILSON, EUGENE M.   ALABAMA FOLK HOUSES.   MONTGOMERY:
         ALABAMA HISTORICAL COMMISSION, 1975.

15552   ZELINSKY, WILBUR.   "THE LOG HOUSE IN GEORGIA."
         GEOGRAPHICAL REVIEW, 43 (APRIL, 1953):   173-193.

SLAVE CLOTHING

15553   DAVID, ROBERT R., JR.   "CLOTHING."   IN ROLLER, DAVID C.
         AND TWYMAN, ROBERT W. (EDS.).   THE ENCYCLOPEDIA OF
         SOUTHERN HISTORY.   BATON ROUGE: LOUISIANA STATE
         UNIVERSITY PRESS, 1979, PP. 243-244.

15554   DOOKHAN, ISAAC.   "SLAVERY AND EMANCIPATION."   A HISTORY
         OF THE BRITISH VIRGIN ISLANDS, 1672 TO 1970.   EPPING,
         ESSEX, ENGLAND: CARIBBEAN UNIVERSITIES PRESS, 1975,
         PP. 71-96.

15555   DURAND, SALLY G.   "THE DRESS OF THE ANTEBELLUM FIELD
         SLAVE IN LOUISIANA AND MISSISSIPPI FROM 1830 TO 1860."
         M.A. THESIS, LOUISIANA STATE UNIVERSITY, 1977.

15556   FOGEL, ROBERT W. AND ENGERMAN, STANLEY L.   TIME ON THE
         CROSS: THE ECONOMICS OF AMERICAN NEGRO SLAVERY.   2
         VOLS.   BOSTON: LITTLE, BROWN AND COMPANY, 1974.

15557   "FOLK-LORE AND ETHNOLOGY."   SOUTHERN WORKMAN, 26 (1897):
         163.

15558   FURNAS, J.C.   GOODBYE TO UNCLE TOM.   NEW YORK: WILLIAM
         SLOANE ASSOCIATES, 1956.

15559   GENOVESE, EUGENE D.   ROLL, JORDAN, ROLL: THE WORLD THE

SLAVES MADE. NEW YORK: PANTHEON, 1974.

15560   GIBSON, GEORGE H. (ED.). "THE MISSISSIPPI MARKET FOR
        WOOLEN GOODS: AN 1822 ANALYSIS." JOURNAL OF SOUTHERN
        HISTORY, 31 (FEBRUARY, 1965): 80-90.

15561   GRAY, LEWIS C. HISTORY OF AGRICULTURE IN THE SOUTHERN
        UNITED STATES TO 1860. 2 VOLS. WASHINGTON: CARNEGIE
        INSTITUTION OF WASHINGTON, 1932.

15562   HARRIS, JOEL C. "THE WOMEN OF THE SOUTH." SOUTHERN
        HISTORICAL SOCIETY PAPERS, 18 (JANUARY-DECEMBER,
        1890): 277-281.

15563   HAWKES, ALTA M. "FOOD, CLOTHING AND SHELTER OF THE
        AMERICAN SLAVE." M.A. THESIS, SOUTHERN METHODIST
        UNIVERSITY, 1936.

15564   "HOW THEY WERE DRESSED." SOUTHERN WORKMAN, 26 (AUGUST,
        1897): 163.

15565   KEARNEY, BELLE. A SLAVEHOLDER'S DAUGHTER. NEW YORK:
        ABBEY PRESS, 1900.

15566   NELSON, WILLIAM. "THE AMERICAN NEWSPAPER OF THE
        EIGHTEENTH CENTURY AS SOURCES OF HISTORY." ANNUAL
        REPORT OF THE AMERICAN HISTORICAL ASSOCIATION FOR THE
        YEAR 1908. 2 VOLS. WASHINGTON: GOVERNMENT PRINTING
        OFFICE, 1909, VOL. 1, PP. 211-222.

15567   O'BRIEN, MARY L. "SLAVERY IN LOUISVILLE DURING THE
        ANTEBELLUM PERIOD: 1820-1860. A STUDY OF THE EFFECTS
        OF URBANIZATION ON THE INSTITUTION OF SLAVERY AS IT
        EXISTED IN LOUISVILLE, KENTUCKY." M.A. THESIS,
        UNIVERSITY OF LOUISVILLE, 1979.

15568   PERDUE, CHARLES L., JR. "SLAVE LIFE STYLES IN EARLY
        VIRGINIA." PROCEEDINGS OF THE PIONEER AMERICA
        SOCIETY, 2 (1973): 54-58.

15569   PERDUE, CHARLES L., JR.; BARDEN, THOMAS E.; AND PHILLIPS,
        ROBERT K. (EDS.). WEEVILS IN THE WHEAT: INTERVIEWS
        WITH VIRGINIA EX-SLAVES. CHARLOTTESVILLE: UNIVERSITY
        PRESS OF VIRGINIA, 1976.

15570   PHILLIPS, ULRICH B. AMERICAN NEGRO SLAVERY: A SURVEY OF
        THE SUPPLY, EMPLOYMENT AND CONTROL OF NEGRO LABOR AS
        DETERMINED BY THE PLANTATION REGIME. NEW YORK: D.
        APPLETON, 1918.

15571   PHILLIPS, ULRICH B. LIFE AND LABOR IN THE OLD SOUTH.
        BOSTON: LITTLE, BROWN AND COMPANY, 1929.

15572   RAWICK, GEORGE P. FROM SUNDOWN TO SUNUP: THE MAKING OF
        THE BLACK COMMUNITY. WESTPORT: GREENWOOD PRESS, 1972.

15573   SCHWARTZ, JACK. "MEN'S CLOTHING AND THE NEGRO." PHYLON,
         24 (FALL, 1963): 224-231.

15574   SHERWOOD, HENRY N. (ED.). "THE JOURNAL OF MISS SUSAN
         WALKER, MARCH 3RD TO JUNE 6TH, 1862." QUARTERLY
         PUBLICATION OF THE HISTORICAL AND PHILOSOPHICAL
         SOCIETY OF OHIO, 7 (1912): 3-48.

15575   "SLAVE CLOTHING." IN NUNEZ, BENJAMIN. DICTIONARY OF
         AFRO-LATIN AMERICAN CIVILIZATION. WESTPORT:
         GREENWOOD PRESS, 1980, P. 433.

15576   "SLAVES, CLOTHING OF." IN RYWELL, MARTIN (ED.).
         AFRO-AMERICAN ENCYCLOPEDIA. 10 VOLS. NORTH MIAMI:
         EDUCATIONAL BOOK PUBLISHERS, 1974, VOL. 8, PP.
         2486-2487.

15577   STAMPP, KENNETH M. THE PECULIAR INSTITUTION: SLAVERY IN
         THE ANTE-BELLUM SOUTH. NEW YORK: ALFRED A. KNOPF,
         1956.

15578   STAROBIN, ROBERT S. INDUSTRIAL SLAVERY IN THE OLD SOUTH.
         NEW YORK: OXFORD UNIVERSITY PRESS, 1970.

15579   SYDNOR, CHARLES S. SLAVERY IN MISSISSIPPI. NEW YORK:
         D. APPLETON-CENTURY COMPANY, 1933.

15580   WADE, RICHARD C. SLAVERY IN THE CITIES: THE SOUTH,
         1820-1860. NEW YORK: OXFORD UNIVERSITY PRESS, 1964.

15581   WADE, RICHARD C. THE URBAN FRONTIER: THE RISE OF
         WESTERN CITIES, 1790-1830. CAMBRIDGE: HARVARD
         UNIVERSITY PRESS, 1959.

15582   WEBBER, THOMAS L. DEEP LIKE THE RIVERS: EDUCATION IN
         THE SLAVE QUARTER COMMUNITY, 1831-1865. NEW YORK:
         W.W. NORTON, 1978.

SLAVE MEDICINE

15583   ALCOCK, NATHANIEL. "WHY TROPICAL MAN IS BLACK." NATURE,
         30 (AUGUST 21, 1884): 401-403.

15584   ALLEN, VIRGINIA R. "HEALTH OF SLAVES ON SOUTHERN
         PLANTATIONS." JOURNAL OF THE OKLAHOMA STATE MEDICAL
         ASSOCIATION, 64 (1971): 425-430.

15585   ANDERSON, JOHN Q.A "FOLKLORE IN THE WRITINGS OF THE
         LOUISIANA SWAMP DOCTOR." SOUTHERN FOLKLORE QUARTERLY,
         19 (DECEMBER, 1955): 243-251.

15586   ANGERMULLER, LINNEA A. "BUSH TEAS AND FOLK REMEDIES USED
         BY THE WEST INDIAN POPULATION OF COLOR, REPUBLIC OF
         PANAMA." FLORIDA STATE UNIVERSITY NOTES IN

ANTHROPOLOGY, 13 (1968): 31-50.

15587 ASHBURN, PERCY M. THE RANKS OF DEATH: A MEDICAL HISTORY OF THE CONQUEST OF AMERICA. NEW YORK: COWARD-MCCANN, 1947.

15588 ATKINSON, THOMAS P. "REPORT ON THE ANATOMICAL, PHYSIOLOGICAL AND PATHOLOGICAL DIFFERENCES BETWEEN THE WHITE AND THE BLACK RACES, AND ON THE MODIFICATIONS OF THE TREATMENT OF THE DISEASES OF THE LATTER RENDERED NECESSARY THEREBY." TRANSACTIONS OF THE MEDICAL SOCIETY OF VIRGINIA, 4 (1872-1875): 65-71, 105-114.

15589 BACON, ALICE M. "CONJURING AND CONJURE-DOCTORS." SOUTHERN WORKMAN, 24 (NOVEMBER, DECEMBER, 1895): 193-194, 209-211.

15590 BACON, DORIS Y. "THE HEALTH OF SLAVES ON LOUISIANA PLANTATIONS, 1840-1860." M.A. THESIS, LOUISIANA STATE UNIVERSITY, 1958.

15591 BARRON, ELWYN A. "SHADOWY MEMORIES OF NEGRO-LORE." FOLKLORIST, 1 (1892): 46-53.

15592 BASSETT, VICTOR H. "PLANTATION MEDICINE." JOURNAL OF THE MEDICAL ASSOCIATION OF GEORGIA, 29 (1940): 112-122.

15593 BEAN, WILLIAM B. "JOSIAH CLARK NOTT, A SOUTHERN PHYSICIAN." BULLETIN OF THE NEW YORK ACADEMY OF MEDICINE, 50 (APRIL, 1974): 529-535.

15594 BLANTON, WYNDHAM B. "EPIDEMICS, REAL AND IMAGINARY, AND OTHER FACTORS INFLUENCING SEVENTEENTH-CENTURY VIRGINIA'S POPULATION." BULLETIN OF THE HISTORY OF MEDICINE, 31 (SEPTEMBER-OCTOBER, 1957): 454-462.

15595 BLANTON, WYNDHAM B. MEDICINE IN VIRGINIA IN THE SEVENTEENTH CENTURY. RICHMOND: WILLIAM BYRD PRESS, 1930.

15596 BLANTON, WYNDHAM B. "PLANTATION MEDICINE." MEDICINE IN VIRGINIA IN THE EIGHTEENTH CENTURY. RICHMOND: GARRETT AND MASSIE, 1931, PP. 153-177.

15597 BLOCH, H. "MEDICAL-SOCIAL CONDITIONS OF SLAVES IN THE SOUTH." JOURNAL OF THE NATIONAL MEDICAL ASSOCIATION, 61 (SEPTEMBER, 1969): 442-444.

15598 BONEY, F.N. "DOCTOR THOMAS HAMILTON: TWO VIEWS OF A GENTLEMAN OF THE OLD SOUTH." PHYLON, 28 (FALL, 1967): 288-292.

15599 BOOG WATSON, W.N. "THE GUINEA TRADE AND SOME OF ITS SURGEONS." JOURNAL OF THE ROYAL COLLEGE OF SURGEONS

OF EDINBURGH, 14 (JULY, 1969): 203-214.

15600   BOSTICK, CLYDE M. "SELECTED ASPECTS OF SLAVE HEALTH IN
         LOUISIANA, 1804-1861." M.A. THESIS, LOUISIANA STATE
         UNIVERSITY, 1960.

15601   BOUSFIELD, M.O. "AN ACCOUNT OF PHYSICIANS OF COLOR IN
         THE UNITED STATES." BULLETIN OF THE HISTORY OF
         MEDICINE, 17 (JANUARY, 1945): 61-84.

15602   BOYD, MARK F. "AN HISTORICAL SKETCH OF THE PREVALENCE OF
         MALARIA IN NORTH AMERICA." AMERICAN JOURNAL OF
         TROPICAL MEDICINE, 21 (1941): 223-244.

15603   BREEDEN, JAMES O. "BODY SNATCHERS AND ANATOMY
         PROFESSORS: MEDICAL EDUCATION IN NINETEENTH CENTURY
         VIRGINIA." VIRGINIA MAGAZINE OF HISTORY AND
         BIOGRAPHY, 83 (JULY, 1975): 321-345.

15604   BREEDEN, JAMES O. JOSEPH JONES, M.D.: SCIENTIST OF THE
         OLD SOUTH. LEXINGTON: UNIVERSITY PRESS OF KENTUCKY,
         1975.

15605   BREEDEN, JAMES O. "STATES-RIGHTS MEDICINE IN THE OLD
         SOUTH." BULLETIN OF THE NEW YORK ACADEMY OF MEDICINE,
         52 (MARCH-APRIL, 1976): 373-418.

15606   BRUESCH, S.R. "THE DISASTERS AND EPIDEMICS OF A RIVER
         TOWN: MEMPHIS, TENNESSEE, 1819-1879." BULLETIN OF
         THE MEDICAL LIBRARY ASSOCIATION, 40 (JULY, 1952):
         288-305.

15607   BYERS, JAMES F. "VOODOO: TROPICAL PHARMACOLOGY OR
         PSYCHOSOMATIC PSYCHOLOGY?" NEW YORK FOLKLORE
         QUARTERLY, 26 (DECEMBER, 1970): 305-312.

15608   CADWALLADER, D.E. AND WILSON, F.J. "FOLKLORE MEDICINE
         AMONG GEORGIA'S PIEDMONT NEGROES, AFTER THE CIVIL
         WAR." GEORGIA HISTORICAL QUARTERLY, 49 (JUNE, 1965):
         217-226.

15609   CAMERON, VIVIAN. "FOLK BELIEFS PERTAINING TO HEALTH OF
         THE SOUTHERN NEGRO." M.A. THESIS, NORTHWESTERN
         UNIVERSITY, 1930.

15610   CARDELL, NICHOLAS AND HOPKINS, MARK M. "THE EFFECT OF
         MILK INTOLERANCE ON THE CONSUMPTION OF MILK BY SLAVES
         IN 1860." JOURNAL OF INTERDISCIPLINARY HISTORY, 8
         (WINTER, 1978): 507-514.

15611   CARGILL, KATHLEEN; GIBBS, TYSON; AND LIEBERMAN, LESLIE.
         "SLAVE DIET AND EVIDENCE OF SUPPLEMENT TO THE STANDARD
         ALLOTMENT." FLORIDA SCIENTIST, 43 (SUMMER, 1980):
         160-164.

15612   CARRIGAN, JO ANN. "EARLY NINETEENTH CENTURY FOLK
        REMEDIES." LOUISIANA FOLKLORE MISCELLANY, 1 (1960):
        43-61.

15613   CARRIGAN, JO ANN. "PRIVILEGE, PREJUDICE, AND THE
        STRANGERS' DISEASE IN NINETEENTH-CENTURY NEW ORLEANS."
        JOURNAL OF SOUTHERN HISTORY, 36 (NOVEMBER, 1970):
        568-578.

15614   CARRIGAN, JO ANN. "THE SAFFRON SCOURGE: A HISTORY OF
        YELLOW FEVER IN LOUISIANA, 1796-1905." PH.D.
        DISSERTATION, LOUISIANA STATE UNIVERSITY, 1961.

15615   CATES, GERALD L. "'THE SEASONING': DISEASE AND DEATH
        AMONG THE FIRST COLONISTS OF GEORGIA." GEORGIA
        HISTORICAL QUARTERLY, 64 (SUMMER, 1980): 146-158.

15616   CHANDLER, DAVID L. "HEALTH AND SLAVERY: A STUDY OF
        HEALTH CONDITIONS AMONG NEGRO SLAVES IN THE
        VICEROYALTY OF NEW GRANADA AND ITS ASSOCIATED SLAVE
        TRADE, 1600-1810." PH.D. DISSERTATION, TULANE
        UNIVERSITY, 1972.

15617   CHANDLER, DAVID L. "HEALTH CONDITIONS IN THE SLAVE TRADE
        OF COLONIAL NEW GRANADA." IN TOPLIN, ROBERT B. (ED.).
        SLAVERY AND RACE RELATIONS IN LATIN AMERICA.
        WESTPORT: GREENWOOD PRESS, 1974, PP. 51-88.

15618   CHILDS, ST. JULIEN RAVENEL. "KITCHEN PHYSICK; MEDICAL
        AND SURGICAL CARE OF SLAVES ON AN EIGHTEENTH CENTURY
        RICE PLANTATION." MISSISSIPPI VALLEY HISTORICAL
        REVIEW, 20 (MARCH, 1934): 549-554.

15619   CHILDS, ST. JULIEN RAVENEL. MALARIA AND COLONIZATION IN
        THE CAROLINA LOW COUNTRY, 1526-1696. BALTIMORE:
        JOHNS HOPKINS UNIVERSITY, 1940.

15620   CLAIBORNE, JOHN H. "THE NEGRO: HIS ENVIRONMENTS AS A
        SLAVE; HIS ENVIRONMENTS AS A FREEDMAN." VIRGINIA
        MEDICAL SEMI-MONTHLY, 5 (APRIL 13, 1900): 3-6.

15621   CLIFTON, JAMES M. "A HALF-CENTURY OF A GEORGIA RICE
        PLANTATION." NORTH CAROLINA HISTORICAL REVIEW, 47
        (AUTUMN, 1970): 388-415.

15622   CODY, CHERYLL A. "A NOTE ON CHANGING PATTERNS OF SLAVE
        FERTILITY IN THE SOUTH CAROLINA RICE DISTRICT,
        1735-1865." SOUTHERN STUDIES, 16 (WINTER, 1977):
        457-462.

15623   CORSON, EUGENE R. "THE FUTURE OF THE COLORED RACE IN THE
        UNITED STATES FROM AN ETHNIC AND MEDICAL STANDPOINT."
        NEW YORK MEDICAL TIMES, 15 (OCTOBER, 1887): 193-201.

15624   CRATON, MICHAEL J. "DEATH, DISEASE AND MEDICINE ON

JAMAICAN SLAVE PLANTATIONS; THE EXAMPLE OF WORTHY
PARK, 1792-1838." HISTOIRE SOCIALE, 9 (NOVEMBER,
1976): 237-255.

15625   CRATON, MICHAEL J.   "JAMAICAN SLAVE MORTALITY: FRESH
LIGHT FROM WORTHY PARK, LONGVILLE AND THE THARP
ESTATES."   JOURNAL OF CARIBBEAN HISTORY, 3 (NOVEMBER,
1971):   1-27.

15626   CROSBY, ALFRED W.   THE COLUMBIAN EXCHANGE: BIOLOGICAL
AND CULTURAL CONSEQUENCES OF 1492.   WESTPORT:
GREENWOOD PRESS, 1972.

15627   CROSBY, ALFRED W.   "CONQUISTADOR Y PESTILENCIA: THE
FIRST NEW WORLD PANDEMIC AND THE FALL OF THE INDIAN
EMPIRES."   HISPANIC AMERICAN HISTORICAL REVIEW, 47
(AUGUST, 1967):   321-337.

15628   CROWDER, RALPH L.   "BLACK PHYSICIANS AND THE AFRICAN
CONTRIBUTION TO MEDICINE."   WESTERN JOURNAL OF BLACK
STUDIES, 4 (SPRING, 1980):   2-20.

15629   CURTIN, PHILIP D.   "EPIDEMIOLOGY AND THE SLAVE TRADE."
IN CONGRES INTERNATIONAL DES AFRICANISTES.   PARIS:
PRESENCE AFRICAINE, 1972, PP. 87-114.

15630   CURTIN, PHILIP D.   "EPIDEMIOLOGY AND THE SLAVE TRADE."
POLITICAL SCIENCE QUARTERLY, 83 (JUNE, 1968):   190-216.

15631   CURTIN, PHILIP D.   "'THE WHITE MAN'S GRAVE':   IMAGE AND
REALITY, 1780-1850."   JOURNAL OF BRITISH STUDIES, 1
(NOVEMBER, 1961):   94-110.

15632   CUSHNER, NICHOLAS P.   "SLAVE MORTALITY AND REPRODUCTION
ON HACIENDAS IN COLONIAL PERU."   HISPANIC AMERICAN
HISTORICAL REVIEW, 55 (MAY, 1975):   177-199.

15633   DAIN, NORMAN.   DISORDERED MINDS: THE FIRST CENTURY OF
EASTERN STATE HOSPITAL IN WILLIAMSBURG, VIRGINIA,
1766-1866.   CHARLOTTESVILLE: UNIVERSITY PRESS OF
VIRGINIA, 1971.

15634   DAVIES, K.G.   "THE LIVING AND THE DEAD: WHITE MORTALITY
IN WEST AFRICA, 1684-1732."   IN ENGERMAN, STANLEY L.
AND GENOVESE, EUGENE D. (EDS.).   RACE AND SLAVERY IN
THE WESTERN HEMISPHERE: QUANTITATIVE STUDIES.
PRINCETON: PRINCETON UNIVERSITY PRESS, 1975, PP.
83-98.

15635   DICKSON, HARRIS.   "EXIT THE BLACK MAN?"   HAMPTON'S
MAGAZINE, 23 (OCTOBER, 1909):   497-505.

15636   DIDDLE, A.W.   "MEDICAL EVENTS IN HISTORY OF KEY WEST;
AFRICAN DEPOT."   JOURNAL OF THE FLORIDA MEDICAL
ASSOCIATION, 31 (NOVEMBER, 1944):   207-209.

15637   DOBYNS, H.F.   "AN OUTLINE OF ANDEAN EPIDEMIC HISTORY TO
         1720."   BULLETIN OF THE HISTORY OF MEDICINE, 37
         (NOVEMBER-DECEMBER, 1963):   493-515.

15638   DUBOIS, W.E.B.   THE HEALTH AND PHYSIQUE OF THE NEGRO
         AMERICAN.   ATLANTA: ATLANTA UNIVERSITY PRESS, 1906.

15639   DUFFY, JOHN.   "EIGHTEENTH-CENTURY CAROLINA HEALTH
         CONDITIONS."   JOURNAL OF SOUTHERN HISTORY, 18 (AUGUST,
         1952):   289-302.

15640   DUFFY, JOHN.   EPIDEMICS IN COLONIAL AMERICA.   BATON
         ROUGE: LOUISIANA STATE UNIVERSITY PRESS, 1953.

15641   DUFFY, JOHN.   THE HEALERS: THE RISE OF THE MEDICAL
         ESTABLISHMENT.   NEW YORK: MCGRAW-HILL, 1976.

15642   DUFFY, JOHN.   "MEDICAL PRACTICE IN THE ANTE BELLUM
         SOUTH."   JOURNAL OF SOUTHERN HISTORY, 25 (FEBRUARY,
         1959):   53-72.

15643   DUFFY, JOHN.   "A NOTE ON ANTE-BELLUM SOUTHERN NATIONALISM
         AND MEDICAL PRACTICE."   JOURNAL OF SOUTHERN HISTORY,
         34 (MAY, 1968):   266-276.

15644   DUFFY, JOHN.   THE RUDOLPH MATAS HISTORY OF MEDICINE IN
         LOUISIANA.   2 VOLS.   BATON ROUGE: LOUISIANA STATE
         UNIVERSITY PRESS, 1953-1962.

15645   DUFFY, JOHN.   "SLAVERY AND SLAVE HEALTH IN LOUISIANA,
         1766-1825."   BULLETIN OF THE TULANE UNIVERSITY MEDICAL
         FACULTY, 26 (FEBRUARY, 1967):   1-6.

15646   DUFFY, JOHN.   SWORD OF PESTILENCE: THE NEW ORLEANS YELLOW
         FEVER EPIDEMIC OF 1853.   BATON ROUGE: LOUISIANA STATE
         UNIVERSITY PRESS, 1966.

15647   DUGAS, L.A.   "REMARKS UPON SOME OF THE PATHOLOGICAL
         PECULIARITIES OF THE NEGRO RACE."   TRANSACTIONS OF THE
         MEDICAL ASSOCIATION OF GEORGIA, 27 (1876):   73-81.

15648   DUMMETT, CLIFTON O.   "DENTISTRY'S BEGINNINGS AMONG BLACKS
         IN THE UNITED STATES."   JOURNAL OF THE NATIONAL
         MEDICAL ASSOCIATION, 66 (JULY, 1974):   321-327.

15649   DUMMETT, CLIFTON O.   "HISTORICAL ASPECTS OF BLACKS IN
         DENTISTRY."   BULLETIN OF THE HISTORY OF DENTISTRY, 21
         (JUNE, 1973):   1-10.

15650   EASLEY, E.T.   "THE SANITARY CONDITION OF THE NEGRO."
         AMERICAN MEDICAL WEEKLY, 3 (JULY 31, 1875):   49-51.

15651   EBLEN, JACK E.   "ON THE NATURAL INCREASE OF SLAVE
         POPULATIONS: THE EXAMPLE OF THE CUBAN BLACK
         POPULATION, 1775-1900."   IN ENGERMAN, STANLEY L. AND

GENOVESE, EUGENE D. (EDS.). RACE AND SLAVERY IN THE
WESTERN HEMISPHERE: QUANTITATIVE STUDIES. PRINCETON:
PRINCETON UNIVERSITY PRESS, 1975, PP. 211-247.

15652 ELLIS, JOHN H. "BUSINESS AND PUBLIC HEALTH IN THE URBAN
       SOUTH DURING THE NINETEENTH CENTURY: NEW ORLEANS,
       MEMPHIS, AND ATLANTA." BULLETIN OF THE HISTORY OF
       MEDICINE, 44 (MAY-JUNE, JULY-AUGUST, 1970): 197-212,
       346-371.

15653 EVANS, W.A. "DOCTORS AND DISEASES IN MONROE COUNTY,
       1820-1935." JOURNAL OF MISSISSIPPI HISTORY, 5 (JULY,
       1943): 125-136.

15654 EVERETT, DONALD E. "THE NEW ORLEANS YELLOW FEVER
       EPIDEMIC OF 1853." LOUISIANA HISTORICAL QUARTERLY, 33
       (OCTOBER, 1950): 380-405.

15655 FISHER, WALTER. "PHYSICIANS AND SLAVERY IN THE
       ANTEBELLUM SOUTHERN MEDICAL JOURNAL." JOURNAL OF THE
       HISTORY OF MEDICINE AND ALLIED SCIENCES, 23 (JANUARY,
       1968): 36-49.

15656 FOGEL, ROBERT W. AND ENGERMAN, STANLEY L. TIME ON THE
       CROSS: THE ECONOMICS OF AMERICAN NEGRO SLAVERY. 2
       VOLS. BOSTON: LITTLE, BROWN AND COMPANY, 1974.

15657 FURNAS, J.C. GOODBYE TO UNCLE TOM. NEW YORK: WILLIAM
       SLOANE ASSOCIATES, 1956.

15658 GEGGUS, DAVID P. "THE SLAVES OF BRITISH-OCCUPIED SAINT
       DOMINGUE: AN ANALYSIS OF THE WORKFORCES OF 197
       ABSENTEE PLANTATIONS, 1796-1797." CARIBBEAN STUDIES,
       18 (APRIL-JULY, 1978): 5-42.

15659 GENOVESE, EUGENE D. "THE MEDICAL AND INSURANCE COSTS OF
       SLAVEHOLDING IN THE COTTON BELT." JOURNAL OF NEGRO
       HISTORY, 45 (JULY, 1960): 141-155.

15660 GENOVESE, EUGENE D. ROLL, JORDAN, ROLL: THE WORLD THE
       SLAVES MADE. NEW YORK: PANTHEON, 1974.

15661 GIBBS, TYSON; CARGILL, KATHLEEN; LIEBERMAN, LESLIE S.;
       AND REITZ, ELIZABETH. "NUTRITION IN A SLAVE
       POPULATION: AN ANTHROPOLOGICAL EXAMINATION." MEDICAL
       ANTHROPOLOGY, 4 (SPRING, 1980): 175-262.

15662 GLOSTER, JESSE E. "THE PROBLEM OF INSURANCE AMONG
       NEGROES PRIOR TO THE CIVIL WAR." NEGRO HISTORY
       BULLETIN, 27 (NOVEMBER, 1963): 42-43.

15663 GOERKE, HEINZ. "THE LIFE AND SCIENTIFIC WORKS OF DR.
       JOHN QUIER, PRACTITIONER OF PHYSIC AND SURGERY,
       JAMAICA, 1738-1822." WEST INDIAN MEDICAL JOURNAL, 5
       (1956): 23-27.

15664 GOLDFIELD, DAVID R. "THE BUSINESS OF HEALTH PLANNING:
       DISEASE PREVENTION IN THE OLD SOUTH." JOURNAL OF
       SOUTHERN HISTORY, 42 (NOVEMBER, 1976): 557-570.

15665 GRACY, DAVID B. AND ABRAHAMS, ROGER D. "SOME PLANTATION
       REMEDIES AND RECIPES." TENNESSEE FOLKLORE SOCIETY
       BULLETIN, 29 (JUNE, 1963): 29-34.

15666 GROB, GERALD N. "CLASS, ETHNICITY, AND RACE IN AMERICAN
       MENTAL HOSPITALS, 1830-1875." JOURNAL OF THE HISTORY
       OF MEDICINE AND ALLIED SCIENCES, 28 (JULY, 1973):
       207-229.

15667 GUERRA, FRANCISCO. "THE INFLUENCE OF DISEASE ON RACE,
       LOGISTICS AND COLONIZATION IN THE ANTILLES." JOURNAL
       OF TROPICAL MEDICINE AND HYGIENE, 69 (FEBRUARY, 1966):
       23-35.

15668 GUTHRIE, DOUGLAS. A HISTORY OF MEDICINE. LONDON:
       NELSON, 1958.

15669 HALLER, JOHN S., JR. "THE NEGRO AND THE SOUTHERN
       PHYSICIAN: A STUDY OF MEDICAL AND RACIAL ATTITUDES,
       1800-1860." MEDICAL HISTORY, 16 (APRIL, 1972):
       238-253.

15670 HANDLER, JEROME S. AND CORRUCCINI, R. "TEMPOROMANDIBULAR
       JOINT SIZE DECREASE IN AMERICAN BLACKS: EVIDENCE FROM
       BARBADOS." JOURNAL OF DENTAL RESEARCH, 59 (1980):
       1528.

15671 HARRIS, SEALE. "THE FUTURE OF THE NEGRO FROM THE
       STANDPOINT OF THE SOUTHERN PHYSICIAN." ALABAMA
       MEDICAL JOURNAL, 14 (JANUARY, 1902): 57-68.

15672 HARRISON, IRA E. "HEALTH STATUS AND HEALING PRACTICES:
       CONTINUATIONS FROM AN AFRICAN PAST." JOURNAL OF
       AFRICAN STUDIES, 2 (WINTER, 1975-1976): 547-560.

15673 HARRISON, IRA E. AND HARRISON, DIANA S. "THE BLACK
       FAMILY EXPERIENCE AND HEALTH BEHAVIOR." IN CRAWFORD,
       CHARLES O. (ED.). HEALTH AND THE FAMILY: A
       MEDICAL-SOCIOLOGICAL ANALYSIS. NEW YORK: MACMILLAN
       COMPANY, 1971, PP. 175-199.

15674 HART, ALBERT B. SLAVERY AND ABOLITION, 1831-1841. NEW
       YORK: HARPER AND BROTHERS, 1906.

15675 HARTWIG, GERALD W. AND PATTERSON, K. DAVID (EDS.).
       DISEASE IN AFRICAN HISTORY: AN INTRODUCTORY SURVEY
       AND CASE STUDIES. DURHAM: DUKE UNIVERSITY PRESS,
       1978.

15676 HATCH, TERRY B. "MEDICAL CARE OF SLAVES." IN JOYNER,
       CHARLES W. (ED.). BLACK CAROLINIANS: STUDIES IN THE

HISTORY OF SOUTH CAROLINA NEGROES IN THE NINETEENTH
CENTURY. LAURINBURG, NC: ST. ANDREWS PRESBYTERIAN
COLLEGE, 1969, PP. 21-23.

15677 HERRON, LEONORA. "CONJURING AND CONJURE-DOCTORS."
SOUTHERN WORKMAN, 24 (JULY, 1895): 117-118.

15678 HIGMAN, BARRY W. "GROWTH IN AFRO-CARIBBEAN SLAVE
POPULATIONS." AMERICAN JOURNAL OF PHYSICAL
ANTHROPOLOGY, 50 (MARCH, 1979): 373-386.

15679 HIGMAN, BARRY W. "HOUSEHOLD STRUCTURE AND FERTILITY ON
JAMAICAN SLAVE PLANTATIONS: A NINETEENTH-CENTURY
EXAMPLE." POPULATION STUDIES: A JOURNAL OF
DEMOGRAPHY, 27 (NOVEMBER, 1973): 527-550.

15680 HILL, CAROLE E. "BLACK HEALING PRACTICES IN THE RURAL
SOUTH." JOURNAL OF POPULAR CULTURE, 4 (SPRING, 1973):
849-853.

15681 HODGES, J. ALLISON. "THE EFFECT OF FREEDOM UPON THE
PHYSICAL AND PSYCHOLOGICAL DEVELOPMENT OF THE NEGRO."
PROCEEDINGS OF THE AMERICAN MEDICO-PSYCHOLOGICAL
ASSOCIATION, 7 (1900): 88-98.

15682 HODGES, J. ALLISON. "THE EFFECT OF FREEDOM UPON THE
PHYSICAL AND PSYCHOLOGICAL DEVELOPMENT OF THE NEGRO."
RICHMOND JOURNAL OF PRACTICE, 14 (1900): 161-171.

15683 HODGES, J. ALLISON. "THE EFFECT OF FREEDOM UPON THE
PHYSICAL AND PSYCHOLOGICAL DEVELOPMENT OF THE NEGRO."
VIRGINIA MEDICAL SEMI-MONTHLY, 5 (MAY 25, 1900):
106-110.

15684 HOEPPLI, R. PARASITIC DISEASES IN AFRICA AND THE WESTERN
HEMISPHERE: EARLY DOCUMENTATION AND TRANSMISSION BY
THE SLAVE TRADE. ACTA TROPICA, SUPPLEMENTUM 10.
BASEL: VERLAG FUR RECHT UND GESELLACHAFT AG., BASEL,
1969, PP. V-XII, 3-240.

15685 "HOT HOUSE PIECE." IN NUNEZ, BENJAMIN. DICTIONARY OF
AFRO-LATIN AMERICAN CIVILIZATION. WESTPORT:
GREENWOOD PRESS, 1980, P. 233.

15686 HUDSON, ELLIS H. "TREPONEMATOSIS AND AFRICAN SLAVERY."
BRITISH JOURNAL OF VENEREAL DISEASES, 40 (MARCH,
1964): 43-52.

15687 HUGHES, CHARLES AND HUNTER, JOHN M. "DISEASE AND
'DEVELOPMENT' IN AFRICA." SOCIAL SCIENCE AND
MEDICINE, 3 (APRIL, 1970): 443-493.

15688 HUNT, SANFORD B. "THE NEGRO AS A SOLDIER." QUARTERLY
JOURNAL OF PSYCHOLOGICAL MEDICINE AND MEDICAL
JURISPRUDENCE, 1 (OCTOBER, 1867): 161-186.

15689 HUNTER, JOHN M. "GEOPHAGY IN AFRICA AND IN THE UNITED STATES: A CULTURE-NUTRITION HYPOTHESIS." GEOGRAPHICAL REVIEW, 63 (APRIL, 1973): 170-195.

15690 HUNTER, JOHN M. "RIVER BLINDNESS IN NANGODI, NORTHERN GHANA: A HYPOTHESIS OF CYCLICAL ADVANCE AND RETREAT." GEOGRAPHICAL REVIEW, 56 (JULY, 1966): 398-416.

15691 "INDIGO NEGROES." IN ROLLER, DAVID C. AND TWYMAN, ROBERT W. (EDS.). THE ENCYCLOPEDIA OF SOUTHERN HISTORY. BATON ROUGE: LOUISIANA STATE UNIVERSITY PRESS, 1979, P. 625.

15692 JOHNSON, LEONARD W. "HISTORY OF THE EDUCATION OF NEGRO PHYSICIANS." JOURNAL OF MEDICAL EDUCATION, 42 (MAY, 1967): 439-446.

15693 JOHNSON, RICHARD H. THE PHYSICAL DEGENERACY OF THE MODERN NEGRO: WITH STATISTICS FROM THE PRINCIPAL CITIES, SHOWING HIS MORTALITY FROM A.D. 1700 TO 1897. BRUNSWICK, GA: N.P., 1897.

15694 JONES, JOSEPH. "RESEARCHES ON THE RELATIONS OF THE AFRICAN SLAVE-TRADE IN THE WEST INDIES AND TROPICAL AMERICAN TO YELLOW FEVER." VIRGINIA MEDICAL MONTHLY, 2 (1875): 11-26.

15695 JONES, S.B. "FIFTY YEARS OF NEGRO PUBLIC HEALTH." ANNALS OF THE AMERICAN ACADEMY OF POLITICAL AND SOCIAL SCIENCES, 49 (SEPTEMBER, 1913): 138-146.

15696 JORDAN, WEYMOUTH T. (ED.). "MARTIN MARSHALL'S BOOK: HERB MEDICINE." ALABAMA HISTORICAL QUARTERLY, 2 (WINTER, 1940): 443-459.

15697 JORDAN, WEYMOUTH T. (ED.). "MARTIN MARSHALL'S BOOK: HOMEMADE MEDICINE." ALABAMA HISTORICAL QUARTERLY, 3 (SPRING, 1941): 117-129.

15698 JORDAN, WEYMOUTH T. "PLANTATION MEDICINE IN THE OLD SOUTH." ALABAMA REVIEW, 3 (APRIL, 1950): 83-107.

15699 KAUFMAN, MARTIN. "MEDICINE AND SLAVERY: AN ESSAY REVIEW." GEORGIA HISTORICAL QUARTERLY, 63 (FALL, 1979): 380-390.

15700 KENNY, JOHN A. THE NEGRO IN MEDICINE. TUSKEGEE: N.P., 1912.

15701 KILGOUR, FREDERICK G. "THE RISE OF SCIENTIFIC ACTIVITY IN COLONIAL NEW ENGLAND." YALE JOURNAL OF BIOLOGY AND MEDICINE, 22 (DECEMBER, 1949): 123-138.

15702 KILPATRICK, A.R. "AN ACCOUNT OF THE COLORED POPULATION OF GRIMES COUNTY, TEXAS, A COMPARISON BETWEEN THEIR

PRESENT AND FORMER CONDITION." RICHMOND AND
LOUISVILLE MEDICAL JOURNAL, 14 (NOVEMBER, 1872):
606-623.

15703   KIPLE, KENNETH F. AND KIPLE, VIRGINIA. "THE AFRICAN
        CONNECTION: SLAVERY, DISEASE AND RACISM." PHYLON, 41
        (FALL, 1980): 211-222.

15704   KIPLE, KENNETH F. AND KIPLE, VIRGINIA H. "BLACK TONGUE
        AND BLACK MEN: PELLAGRA AND SLAVERY IN THE ANTEBELLUM
        SOUTH." JOURNAL OF SOUTHERN HISTORY, 43 (AUGUST,
        1977): 411-428.

15705   KIPLE, KENNETH F. AND KIPLE, VIRGINIA H. "BLACK YELLOW
        FEVER IMMUNITIES, INNATE AND ACQUIRED, AS REVEALED IN
        THE AMERICAN SOUTH." SOCIAL SCIENCE HISTORY, 1
        (SUMMER, 1977): 419-436.

15706   KIPLE, KENNETH F. AND KIPLE, VIRGINIA H. "DEFICIENCY
        DISEASES IN THE CARIBBEAN." JOURNAL OF
        INTERDISCIPLINARY HISTORY, 11 (AUTUMN, 1980): 197-215.

15707   KIPLE, KENNETH F. AND KIPLE, VIRGINIA H. "SLAVE CHILD
        MORTALITY: SOME NUTRITIONAL ANSWERS TO A PERENNIAL
        PUZZLE." IN BRANCA, PATRICIA (ED.). MEDICINE SHOW:
        PATIENTS, PHYSICIANS, AND THE PERPLEXITIES OF THE
        HEALTH REVOLUTION IN MODERN SOCIETY. NEW YORK:
        SCIENCE HISTORY PUBLISHERS, 1977, PP. 21-46.

15708   KIPLE, KENNETH F. AND KIPLE, VIRGINIA H. "SLAVE CHILD
        MORTALITY: SOME NUTRITIONAL ANSWERS TO A PERENNIAL
        PUZZLE." JOURNAL OF SOCIAL HISTORY, 10 (MARCH, 1977):
        284-309.

15709   KLEIN, HERBERT S. AND ENGERMAN, STANLEY. "FERTILITY
        DIFFERENTIALS BETWEEN SLAVES IN THE UNITED STATES AND
        THE BRITISH WEST INDIES: A NOTE ON LACTATION
        PRACTICES AND THEIR POSSIBLE IMPLICTIONS." WILLIAM
        AND MARY QUARTERLY, 3RD SER., 35 (APRIL, 1978):
        357-374.

15710   KLEIN, HERBERT S. AND ENGERMAN, STANLEY L. "SLAVE
        MORTALITY ON BRITISH SHIPS, 1791-1797." IN ANSTEY,
        ROGER AND HAIR, P.E.H. (EDS.). LIVERPOOL, THE AFRICAN
        SLAVE TRADE, AND ABOLITION. BRISTOL: HISTORIC
        SOCIETY OF LANCASHIRE AND CHESHIRE OCCASIONAL SERIES
        VOL. 2, 1976, PP. 113-125.

15711   KUNA, RALPH R. "HOODOO: THE INDIGENOUS MEDICINE AND
        PSYCHIATRY OF THE BLACK AMERICAN." ETHNOMEDIZIN, 3
        (1974-1975): 273-294.

15712   KUNA, RALPH R. "HOODOO: THE INDIGENOUS MEDICINE AND
        PSYCHIATRY OF THE BLACK AMERICAN." MANKIND QUARTERLY,
        18 (1977): 137-151.

15713   LACY, VIRGINIA J. AND HARRELL, DAVID E., JR.   "PLANTATION
        HOME REMEDIES: MEDICINAL RECIPES FROM THE DIARIES OF
        JOHN POPE."   TENNESSEE HISTORICAL QUARTERLY, 22
        (SEPTEMBER, 1963):   259-265.

15714   LAIRD, MARSHALL.   "OSIRIS, ASKLEPIOS, AND THE HARPIES:
        THE DEVELOPMENT OF AN AFRICAN RIVER BASIN."   IN A TIME
        TO HEAR AND ANSWER: ESSAYS FOR THE BICENTENNIAL
        SEASON.   UNIVERSITY, AL: UNIVERSITY OF ALABAMA PRESS,
        1977, PP. 108-140.

15715   LANGRIDGE, LELAND.   "ASIATIC CHOLERA IN LOUISIANA,
        1832-1873."   M.A. THESIS, LOUISIANA STATE UNIVERSITY,
        1955.

15716   LANNING, JOHN T.   "LEGITIMACY AND LIMPIEZA DE SANGRE IN
        THE PRACTICE OF MEDICINE IN THE SPANISH EMPIRE."
        JAHRBUCH FUR GESCHICHTE VON STAAT, WIRTSCHAFT UND
        GESELLSCHAFT LATEINAMERIKAS, 4 (1967):   37-60.

15717   LANTZ, HERMAN AND HENDRIX, LEWELLYN.   "BLACK FERTILITY
        AND THE BLACK FAMILY IN THE NINETEENTH CENTURY: A
        RE-EXAMINATION OF THE PAST."   JOURNAL OF FAMILY
        HISTORY, 3 (FALL, 1978):   251-261.

15718   LEE, ANNE S. AND LEE, EVERETT S.   "THE HEALTH OF SLAVES
        AND THE HEALTH OF FREEDMEN: A SAVANNAH STUDY."
        PHYLON, 38 (SUMMER, 1977):   170-180.

15719   LEGAN, MARSHALL S.   "DISEASE AND THE FREEDMEN IN
        MISSISSIPPI DURING RECONSTRUCTION."   JOURNAL OF THE
        HISTORY OF MEDICINE AND ALLIED SCIENCES, 28 (JULY,
        1973):   257-267.

15720   LETCHER, J.H.   "THE TREATMENT OF SOME DISEASES BY THE
        'OLD TIME' NEGRO."   RAILWAY SURGICAL JOURNAL, 17
        (1910-1911):   170-175.

15721   "LETTERS OF JAMES HAMILTON COUPER TO HIS WIFE,
        1833-1836."   GEORGIA HISTORICAL QUARTERLY, 14 (JUNE,
        1930):   150-173.

15722   LEVINE, LAWRENCE W.   BLACK CULTURE AND BLACK
        CONSCIOUSNESS: AFRO-AMERICAN FOLK THOUGHT FROM
        SLAVERY TO FREEDOM.   NEW YORK: OXFORD UNIVERSITY
        PRESS, 1977.

15723   LEWIS, J.H.   BIOLOGY OF THE NEGRO.   CHICAGO: UNIVERSITY
        OF CHICAGO PRESS, 1942.

15724   LEWIS, W.A.   "THE HISTORY OF MEDICINE IN THE SOUTH."
        VIRGINIA MEDICAL MONTHLY, 48 (1922):   655-660.

15725   "MANAGEMENT OF NEGROES UPON SOUTHERN ESTATES--AN ECHO OF
        SLAVE DAYS IN THE SOUTHLAND."   TENNESSEE HISTORICAL

MAGAZINE, 5 (JULY, 1919): 97-103.

15726   MARSHALL, MARY L. "PLANTATION MEDICINE." BULLETIN OF
        THE TULANE UNIVERSITY MEDICAL FACULTY, 1 (1942):
        45-58.

15727   MARSHALL, MARY L. "PLANTATION MEDICINE." BULLETIN OF
        THE MEDICAL LIBRARY ASSOCIATION, 26 (JANUARY, 1938):
        115-128.

15728   MARSHALL, MARY L. "SAMUEL A. CARTWRIGHT AND STATES'
        RIGHTS MEDICINE." NEW ORLEANS MEDICAL AND SURGICAL
        JOURNAL, 93 (AUGUST, 1940): 74-78.

15729   MARSHALL, THEODORA B. AND EVANS, GLADYS C. "PLANTATION
        REPORTS FROM THE PAPERS OF LEVIN R. MARSHALL OF
        'RICHMOND,' NATCHEZ, MISSISSIPPI (1836)." JOURNAL OF
        MISSISSIPPI HISTORY, 3 (JANUARY, 1941): 45-55.

15730   MATAS, RUDOLPH. "THE SURGICAL PECULIARITIES OF THE
        NEGRO." TRANSACTIONS OF THE AMERICAN SURGICAL
        ASSOCIATION, 14 (1896): 483-610.

15731   MAY, JUDE T. "THE MEDICAL CARE OF BLACKS IN LOUISIANA
        DURING OCCUPATION AND RECONSTRUCTION, 1862-1868: ITS
        SOCIAL AND POLITICAL BACKGROUND." PH.D. DISSERTATION,
        TULANE UNIVERSITY, 1971.

15732   MAYS, J.T. "INCREASE OF INSANITY AND CONSUMPTION AMONG
        THE NEGRO POPULATION OF THE SOUTH SINCE THE WAR."
        BOSTON MEDICAL AND SURGICAL JOURNAL, 135 (1897):
        537-540.

15733   MCCOY, AMBROSE. "VOODOOISM IN THE SOUTH." LOUISVILLE
        MEDICAL NEWS, 18 (1884): 380.

15734   MCDOWELL, A.W. "HOSPITAL OBSERVATIONS UPON NEGRO
        SOLDIERS." AMERICAN PRACTITIONER, 10 (1874): 155-158.

15735   MCINTOSH, JAMES. "THE FUTURE OF THE NEGRO RACE."
        TRANSACTIONS OF THE SOUTH CAROLINA MEDICAL
        ASSOCIATION, (1891): 183-188.

15736   MCKIE, THOMAS J. "A BRIEF HISTORY OF INSANITY AND
        TUBERCULOSIS IN THE SOUTHERN NEGRO." JOURNAL OF THE
        AMERICAN MEDICAL ASSOCIATION, 28 (1897): 537-538.

15737   MCLEAN, PATRICIA S. "CONJURE DOCTORS IN EASTERN NORTH
        CAROLINA." NORTH CAROLINA FOLKLORE, 20 (FEBRUARY,
        1972): 21-29.

15738   MCNEILL, WILLIAM H. PLAGUES AND PEOPLES. GARDEN CITY:
        ANCHOR PRESS, 1976.

15739   MEADE, MELINDA S. "THE RISE AND DEMISE OF MALARIA: SOME

REFLECTIONS ON SOUTHERN SETTLEMENT AND LANDSCAPE." SOUTHEASTERN GEOGRAPHER, 20 (NOVEMBER, 1980): 77-99.

15740   MILLER, J.F. "BRAIN AND LUNG DEGENERATION IN THE NEGRO." TRANSACTIONS OF THE SECOND ANNUAL SESSION OF THE TRI-STATE MEDICAL ASSOCIATION OF THE CAROLINAS AND VIRGINIA, FEBRUARY 20-22, 1900. RICHMOND: WILLIAMS PRINTING COMPANY, 1900, PP. 70-81.

15741   MILLER, J.F. "THE EFFECTS OF EMANCIPATION UPON THE MENTAL AND PHYSICAL HEALTH OF THE NEGRO OF THE SOUTH." NORTH CAROLINA MEDICAL JOURNAL, 38 (NOVEMBER 20, 1896): 285-294.

15742   MILLER, KELLY. "THE HISTORIC BACKGROUND OF THE NEGRO PHYSICIAN." JOURNAL OF NEGRO HISTORY, 1 (APRIL, 1916): 99-109.

15743   MITCHELL, MARTHA C. "HEALTH AND THE MEDICAL PROFESSION IN THE LOWER SOUTH, 1845-1860." JOURNAL OF SOUTHERN HISTORY, 10 (NOVEMBER, 1944): 424-446.

15744   MOFFATT, WALTER. "MEDICINE AND DENTISTRY IN PIONEER ARKANSAS." ARKANSAS HISTORICAL QUARTERLY, 10 (SUMMER, 1951): 89-94.

15745   MORAIS, HERBERT M. THE HISTORY OF THE NEGRO IN MEDICINE. NEW YORK: PUBLISHERS COMPANY, 1967.

15746   MORRILL, RICHARD L. AND DONALDSON, O. FRED. "GEOGRAPHICAL PERSPECTIVES ON THE HISTORY OF BLACK AMERICA." IN ERNST, ROBERT T. AND HUGG, LAWRENCE (EDS.). BLACK AMERICA: GEOGRAPHIC PERSPECTIVES. GARDEN CITY: ANCHOR PRESS/DOUBLEDAY, 1976, PP. 9-33.

15747   MOTON, ROBERT R. "SICKNESS IN SLAVERY DAYS." SOUTHERN WORKMAN, 28 (FEBRUARY, 1899): 74-75.

15748   MUSTACCHI, PIERO. "CESARE BRESSA (1785-1836) ON DIRT EATING IN LOUISIANA: A CRITICAL ANALYSIS OF HIS UNPUBLISHED MANUSCRIPT DE LA DISSOLUTION SCORBUTIQUE." JOURNAL OF THE AMERICAN MEDICAL ASSOCIATION, 218 (OCTOBER 11, 1971): 229-232.

15749   NASH, A.E. KEIR. "DRAPETOMANIA." IN ROLLER, DAVID C. AND TWYMAN, ROBERT W. (EDS.). THE ENCYCLOPEDIA OF SOUTHERN HISTORY. BATON ROUGE: LOUISIANA STATE UNIVERSITY PRESS, 1979, P. 369.

15750   NIXON, J.A. "HEALTH AND SICKNESS IN THE SLAVE TRADE." IN PARKINSON, C. NORTHCOTE (ED.). THE TRADE WINDS: A STUDY OF BRITISH OVERSEAS TRADE DURING THE FRENCH WARS, 1793-1815. LONDON: GEORGE ALLEN AND UNWIN, LIMITED, 1948, PP. 273-277.

15751   OWENS, LESLIE H.   THIS SPECIES OF PROPERTY: SLAVE LIFE
        AND CULTURE IN THE OLD SOUTH.   NEW YORK: OXFORD
        UNIVERSITY PRESS, 1976.

15752   PALMER, HENRY E.   "PHYSICIANS OF EARLY TALLAHASSEE AND
        VICINITY."   APALACHEE, THE PUBLICATION OF THE FLORIDA
        HISTORICAL SOCIETY, (1944-1955):   29-46.

15753   PARRAMORE, THOMAS C.   "THE 'COUNTY DISTEMPER' IN COLONIAL
        NORTH CAROLINA."   NORTH CAROLINA HISTORICAL REVIEW, 48
        (JANUARY, 1971):   44-52.

15754   PARRAMORE, THOMAS C.   "NON-VENEREAL TREPONEMATOSIS IN
        COLONIAL NORTH AMERICA."   BULLETIN OF THE HISTORY OF
        MEDICINE, 44 (NOVEMBER/DECEMBER, 1970):   571-581.

15755   PATTERSON, K. DAVID.   "DISEASE AND MEDICINE IN AFRICAN
        HISTORY: A BIBLIOGRAPHICAL ESSAY."   HISTORY OF
        AFRICA, 1 (1974):   141-148.

15756   PERDUE, CHARLES L., JR.; BARDEN, THOMAS E.; AND PHILLIPS,
        ROBERT K. (EDS.).   WEEVILS IN THE WHEAT: INTERVIEWS
        WITH VIRGINIA EX-SLAVES.   CHARLOTTESVILLE: UNIVERSITY
        PRESS OF VIRGINIA, 1976.

15757   PHILLIPS, ULRICH B.   AMERICAN NEGRO SLAVERY: A SURVEY OF
        THE SUPPLY, EMPLOYMENT AND CONTROL OF NEGRO LABOR AS
        DETERMINED BY THE PLANTATION REGIME.   NEW YORK: D.
        APPLETON, 1918.

15758   PHILLIPS, ULRICH B.   "A JAMAICA SLAVE PLANTATION."
        AMERICAN HISTORICAL REVIEW, 19 (APRIL, 1914):   543-558.

15759   PHILLIPS, ULRICH B.   LIFE AND LABOR IN THE OLD SOUTH.
        BOSTON: LITTLE, BROWN AND COMPANY, 1929.

15760   PIERSEN, WILLIAM D.   "WHITE CANNIBALS, BLACK MARTYRS:
        FEAR, DEPRESSION, AND RELIGIOUS FAITH AS CAUSES OF
        SUICIDE AMONG NEW SLAVES."   JOURNAL OF NEGRO HISTORY,
        62 (APRIL, 1977):   147-159.

15761   PINDERHUGHES, CHARLES A.   "PATHOGENIC SOCIAL STRUCTURE:
        A PRIME TARGET FOR PREVENTIVE PSYCHIATRIC
        INTERVENTION."   JOURNAL OF THE NATIONAL MEDICAL
        ASSOCIATION, 58 (NOVEMBER, 1966):   424-435.

15762   PINDERHUGHES, CHARLES A.   "RACISM AND PSYCHOTHERAPY."   IN
        WILLIE, CHARLES V.; KRAMER, BERNARD M.; AND BROWN,
        BERTRAM S. (EDS.).   RACISM AND MENTAL HEALTH: ESSAYS.
        PITTSBURGH: UNIVERSITY OF PITTSBURGH PRESS, 1973, PP.
        61-122.

15763   PLUMMER, BETTY L.   "BENJAMIN RUSH AND THE NEGRO."
        AMERICAN JOURNAL OF PSYCHIATRY, 127 (DECEMBER, 1970):
        793-798.

15764   PLUMMER, BETTY L. "BENJAMIN RUSH AND THE NEGRO." M.A.
        THESIS, HOWARD UNIVERSITY, 1969.

15765   POLLARD, LESLIE J. "AGE AND PATERNALISM IN A SLAVE
        SOCIETY." PERSPECTIVE ON AGING, 7 (NOVEMBER-DECEMBER,
        1978): 4-8.

15766   POSTELL, W.D. "SURVEY ON CHRONIC ILLNESSES AND PHYSICAL
        IMPAIRMENTS AMONG THE SLAVE POPULATION IN THE
        ANTEBELLUM SOUTH." BULLETIN OF THE MEDICAL LIBRARY
        ASSOCIATION, 42 (APRIL, 1954): 158-162.

15767   POSTELL, WILLIAM D. "BIRTH AND MORTALITY RATES AMONG
        SLAVE INFANTS ON SOUTHERN PLANTATIONS." PEDIATRICS,
        10 (NOVEMBER, 1952): 538-541.

15768   POSTELL, WILLIAM D. THE HEALTH OF SLAVES ON SOUTHERN
        PLANTATIONS. BATON ROUGE: LOUISIANA STATE UNIVERSITY
        PRESS, 1951.

15769   POSTELL, WILLIAM D. "MENTAL HEALTH AMONG THE SLAVE
        POPULATION ON SOUTHERN PLANTATIONS." AMERICAN JOURNAL
        OF PSYCHIATRY, 110 (JULY, 1953): 52-54.

15770   POSTELL, WILLIAM D. "REVIEW OF SLAVE CARE ON SOUTHERN
        PLANTATIONS." VIRGINIA MEDICAL MONTHLY, 79 (FEBRUARY,
        1952): 101-105.

15771   POSTELL, WILLIAM D. "SLAVES AND THEIR LIFE EXPECTANCY."
        BULLETIN OF THE TULANE UNIVERSITY MEDICAL FACULTY, 26
        (FEBRUARY, 1967): 7-11.

15772   POWELL, THEOPHILUS O. "THE INCREASE OF INSANITY AND
        TUBERCULOSIS IN THE SOUTHERN NEGRO SINCE 1860, AND ITS
        ALLIANCE AND SOME OF THE SUPPOSED CAUSES." JOURNAL OF
        THE AMERICAN MEDICAL ASSOCIATION, 27 (DECEMBER 5,
        1896): 1185-1188.

15773   POWELL, THEOPHILUS O. "A SKETCH OF PSYCHIATRY IN THE
        SOUTHERN STATES." AMERICAN JOURNAL OF INSANITY, 54
        (JULY, 1897): 21-36.

15774   PRATT-THOMAS, H. RAWLINGS. "PLANTATION MEDICINE."
        JOURNAL OF THE SOUTH CAROLINA MEDICAL ASSOCIATION, 66
        (MAY, 1970): 152-159.

15775   PRUDHOMME, CHARLES AND MUSTO, DAVID F. "HISTORICAL
        PERSPECTIVES ON MENTAL HEALTH AND RACISM IN THE UNITED
        STATES." IN WILLIE, CHARLES V.; KRAMER, BERNARD M.;
        AND BROWN, BERTRAM S. (EDS.). RACISM AND MENTAL
        HEALTH: ESSAYS. PITTSBURGH: UNIVERSITY OF
        PITTSBURGH PRESS, 1973, PP. 25-60.

15776   PUCKREIN, GARY. "CLIMATE, HEALTH AND BLACK LABOR IN THE
        ENGLISH AMERICAS." JOURNAL OF AMERICAN STUDIES, 13

(AUGUST, 1979):   179-193.

15777   "QUAKER RECORDS AT A MEETING OF THE MIDWIVES IN
        BARBADOS." JOURNAL OF THE BARBADOS MUSEUM AND
        HISTORICAL SOCIETY, 24 (1956-1957):   133-134.

15778   RAPHAEL, ALAN. "HEALTH AND SOCIAL WELFARE OF KENTUCKY
        BLACK PEOPLE, 1865-1870." SOCIETAS, 2 (SPRING, 1972):
        143-158.

15779   REYBURN, ROBERT. "REMARKS CONCERNING SOME OF THE
        DISEASES PREVAILING AMONG THE FREED PEOPLE IN THE
        DISTRICT OF COLUMBIA." AMERICAN JOURNAL OF THE
        MEDICAL SCIENCES, 51 (1866):   364-369.

15780   REYBURN, ROBERT. "TYPE OF DISEASE AMONG THE FREED PEOPLE
        (MIXED NEGRO RACES) OF THE UNITED STATES." MEDICAL
        NEWS, 63 (DECEMBER 2, 1893):   623-627.

15781   REYBURN, ROBERT. TYPE OF DISEASE AMONG THE FREED PEOPLE
        OF THE UNITED STATES. WASHINGTON: GIBSON BROTHERS,
        1891.

15782   ROBINSON, JEAN W. "BLACK HEALERS DURING THE COLONIAL
        PERIOD AND EARLY NINETEENTH CENTURY AMERICA." PH.D.
        DISSERTATION, SOUTHERN ILLINOIS UNIVERSITY, 1979.

15783   ROGERS, J.G. "THE EFFECT OF FREEDOM UPON THE PHYSICAL
        AND PSYCHOLOGICAL DEVELOPMENT OF THE NEGRO."
        PROCEEDINGS OF THE AMERICAN MEDICO-PSYCHOLOGICAL
        ASSOCIATION, 7 (1900):   88-98.

15784   ROSE, WILLIE LEE. REHEARSAL FOR RECONSTRUCTION: THE
        PORT ROYAL EXPERIMENT. INDIANAPOLIS: BOBBS-MERRILL,
        1964.

15785   ROUT, LESLIE B. THE AFRICAN EXPERIENCE IN SPANISH
        AMERICA, 1502 TO THE PRESENT DAY. CAMBRIDGE:
        CAMBRIDGE UNIVERSITY PRESS, 1976.

15786   RUTMAN, DARRETT B. AND RUTMAN, ANITA H. "OF AGUES AND
        FEVERS: MALARIA IN THE EARLY CHESAPEAKE." WILLIAM
        AND MARY QUARTERLY, 3RD SER., 33 (JANUARY, 1976):
        31-60.

15787   SAVITT, TODD L. "FILARIASIS IN THE UNITED STATES."
        JOURNAL OF THE HISTORY OF MEDICINE, 32 (APRIL, 1977):
        140-150.

15788   SAVITT, TODD L. MEDICINE AND SLAVERY: THE DISEASES AND
        HEALTH CARE OF BLACKS IN ANTEBELLUM VIRGINIA. URBANA:
        UNIVERSITY OF ILLINOIS PRESS, 1978.

15789   SAVITT, TODD L. "SMOTHERING AND OVERLAYING OF VIRGINIA
        SLAVE CHILDREN: A SUGGESTED EXPLANATION." BULLETIN

OF THE HISTORY OF MEDICINE, 49 (FALL, 1975): 400-404.

15790   SAVITT, TODD L. "SOUND MINDS AND SOUND BODIES: THE
        DISEASES AND HEALTH CARE OF BLACKS IN ANTEBELLUM
        VIRGINIA." PH.D. DISSERTATION, UNIVERSITY OF
        VIRGINIA, 1975.

15791   SCARBOROUGH, WILLIAM K. THE OVERSEER: PLANTATION
        MANAGEMENT IN THE OLD SOUTH. BATON ROUGE: LOUISIANA
        STATE UNIVERSITY PRESS, 1966.

15792   SCHOUTE, D. "SHIP DOCTOR'S JOURNAL OF SLAVE SHIP OF
        MIDDELBURG COMMERCE COMPANY (1761-1763)."
        NEDERLANDSCH TIJDSCHRIFT VOOR GENEESKUNDE, 92
        (NOVEMBER 6, 1948): 3645-3662.

15793   SCOTT, H. HAROLD. "THE INFLUENCE OF THE SLAVE-TRADE IN
        THE SPREAD OF TROPICAL DISEASE." TRANSACTIONS OF THE
        ROYAL SOCIETY OF TROPICAL MEDICINE AND HYGIENE, 37
        (DECEMBER, 1943): 169-188.

15794   SCOTT, HENRY H. A HISTORY OF TROPICAL MEDICINE. 2 VOLS.
        LONDON: EDWARD ARNOLD AND COMPANY, 1939.

15795   SEARCY, J.T. "THE PHYSIOLOGY OF THE RACE QUESTION."
        BELFORD'S MAGAZINE, 5 (SEPTEMBER, 1890): 495-508.

15796   SERENO, RENZO. "OBEAH: MAGIC AND SOCIAL STRUCTURE IN
        THE LESSER ANTILLES." PSYCHIATRY, 11 (FEBRUARY,
        1948): 15-31.

15797   SHALER, N.S. "THE AFRICAN ELEMENT IN AMERICA." ARENA, 2
        (NOVEMBER, 1890): 660-673.

15798   SHARPLEY, ROBERT H. "A PSYCHOHISTORICAL PERSPECTIVE OF
        THE NEGRO." AMERICAN JOURNAL OF PSYCHIATRY, 126
        (NOVEMBER, 1969): 645-650.

15799   SHARPLEY, ROBERT H. "A PSYCHOHISTORICAL PERSPECTIVE OF
        THE NEGRO." IN REINHARDT, ADINA M. AND QUINN, MILDRED
        D. (EDS.). FAMILY-CENTERED COMMUNITY NURSING: A
        SOCIOLOGICAL FRAMEWORK. SAINT LOUIS: C.V. MOSBY
        COMPANY, 1973, PP. 78-84.

15800   SHERIDAN, RICHARD B. "MORTALITY AND THE MEDICAL
        TREATMENT OF SLAVES IN THE BRITISH WEST INDIES." IN
        ENGERMAN, STANLEY L. AND GENOVESE, EUGENE D. (EDS.).
        RACE AND SLAVERY IN THE WESTERN HEMISPHERE:
        QUANTITATIVE STUDIES. PRINCETON: PRINCETON
        UNIVERSITY PRESS, 1975, PP. 285-310.

15801   SHRYOCK, RICHARD H. (ED.). "LETTERS OF RICHARD D.
        ARNOLD, M.D., 1808-1876." TRINITY COLLEGE HISTORICAL
        SOCIETY PAPERS, SER. 18-19 (1929): 1-178.

15802   SHRYOCK, RICHARD H.   "MEDICAL PRACTICE IN THE OLD SOUTH."
         SOUTH ATLANTIC QUARTERLY, 29 (APRIL, 1930):   160-178.

15803   SHRYOCK, RICHARD H.   "MEDICAL SOURCES AND THE SOCIAL
         HISTORIAN." AMERICAN HISTORICAL REVIEW, 41 (APRIL,
         1936):   458-473.

15804   SIKES, LEWRIGHT. "MEDICAL CARE FOR SLAVES: A PREVIEW OF
         THE WELFARE STATE." GEORGIA HISTORICAL QUARTERLY, 52
         (DECEMBER, 1968):   405-413.

15805   "SLAVES: FOOD, MEDICINE AND MORALITY." IN RYWELL,
         MARTIN (ED.). AFRO-AMERICAN ENCYCLOPEDIA. 10 VOLS.
         NORTH MIAMI: EDUCATIONAL BOOK PUBLISHERS, 1974, VOL.
         8, PP. 2482-2486.

15806   SMITH, SAMUEL D. "PLANTATION ARCHAEOLOGY AT THE
         HERMITAGE: SOME SUGGESTED PATTERNS." TENNESSEE
         ANTHROPOLOGIST, 2 (1977):   152-163.

15807   STAMPP, KENNETH M. THE PECULIAR INSTITUTION: SLAVERY IN
         THE ANTE-BELLUM SOUTH. NEW YORK: ALFRED A. KNOPF,
         1956.

15808   STAROBIN, ROBERT S. INDUSTRIAL SLAVERY IN THE OLD SOUTH.
         NEW YORK: OXFORD UNIVERSITY PRESS, 1970.

15809   STEWART, T.D. AND GROOME, JOHN R. "THE AFRICAN CUSTOM OF
         TOOTH MUTILATION IN AMERICA." AMERICAN JOURNAL OF
         PHYSICAL ANTHROPOLOGY, 28 (JANUARY, 1968):   31-42.

15810   STEWART, T.D. AND SPOEHR, ALEXANDER. "EVIDENCE OF THE
         PALEOPATHOLOGY OF YAWS." BULLETIN OF THE HISTORY OF
         MEDICINE, 26 (NOVEMBER/DECEMBER, 1952):   538-553.

15811   STITT, E.R. "OUR DISEASE INHERITANCE FROM SLAVERY."
         UNITED STATES NAVAL MEDICAL BULLETIN, 26 (OCTOBER,
         1928):   801-817.

15812   STRONG, KATE W. "DOCTORS LEARNED FROM SLAVES." LONG
         ISLAND FORUM, 40 (APRIL, 1977):   74-75.

15813   SWADOS, FELICE. "NEGRO HEALTH ON THE ANTE-BELLUM
         PLANTATIONS." BULLETIN OF THE HISTORY OF MEDICINE, 10
         (OCTOBER, 1941):   460-472.

15814   SYDNOR, CHARLES S. SLAVERY IN MISSISSIPPI. NEW YORK:
         D. APPLETON-CENTURY COMPANY, 1933.

15815   SZASZ, THOMAS S. "THE NEGRO IN PSYCHIATRY: AN
         HISTORICAL NOTE ON PSYCHIATRIC RHETORIC." AMERICAN
         JOURNAL OF PSYCHOTHERAPY, 25 (JULY, 1971):   469-471.

15816   SZASZ, THOMAS S. "THE SANE SLAVE: AN HISTORICAL NOTE ON
         THE USE OF MEDICAL DIAGNOSIS AS JUSTIFICATORY

RHETORIC." AMERICAN JOURNAL OF PSYCHOTHERAPY, 25
(APRIL, 1971): 228-239.

15817 SZASZ, THOMAS S. "THE SANE SLAVE, SOCIAL CONTROL AND
       LEGAL PSYCHIATRY." AMERICAN CRIMINAL LAW REVIEW, 10
       (SPRING, 1972): 337-356.

15818 TIPTON, F. "THE NEGRO PROBLEM FROM A MEDICAL
       STANDPOINT." NEW YORK MEDICAL JOURNAL, 43 (MAY 22,
       1886): 567-572.

15819 TODD, T. WINGATE. "ANTHROPOLOGY AND NEGRO SLAVERY."
       MEDICAL LIFE, 36 (MARCH, 1929): 157-167.

15820 TORCHIA, MARION M. "TUBERCULOSIS AMONG AMERICAN NEGROES:
       MEDICAL RESEARCH ON A RACIAL DISEASE, 1830-1850."
       JOURNAL OF THE HISTORY OF MEDICINE AND ALLIED
       SCIENCES, 32 (JULY, 1977): 252-279.

15821 TRUSSELL, JAMES AND STECKEL, RICHARD. "THE AGE OF SLAVES
       AT MENARCHE AND THEIR FIRST BIRTH." JOURNAL OF
       INTERDISCIPLINARY HISTORY, 8 (WINTER, 1978): 477-505.

15822 TWYMAN, ROBERT W. "THE CLAY EATER: A NEW LOOK AT AN OLD
       SOUTHERN ENIGMA." JOURNAL OF SOUTHERN HISTORY, 37
       (AUGUST, 1971): 439-448.

15823 VAN ANDEL, M.A. "HYGIENE ON SLAVE SHIPS." BIJDRAGEN TOT
       DE GESCHIEDENIS DER GENEESKUNDE, 11 (1931): 21-44.

15824 VAN ANDEL, M.A. "MEDICINE AND HYGIENE ON SLAVE SHIPS
       DURING THE SLAVE TRADE." NEDERLANDSCH TIJDSCHRIFT
       VOOR GENEESKUNDE, 75 (FEBRUARY 7, 1931): 614-637.

15825 VAN BLARCOM, CAROLYN C. "RAT PIE AMONG THE BLACK
       MIDWIVES OF THE SOUTH." HARPER'S MAGAZINE, 160
       (FEBRUARY, 1930): 322-332.

15826 WALL, BENNETT H. "MEDICAL CARE OF EBENEZER PETTIGREW'S
       SLAVES." MISSISSIPPI VALLEY HISTORICAL REVIEW, 37
       (DECEMBER, 1950): 451-470.

15827 WALTON, J.T. "THE COMPARATIVE MORTALITY OF THE WHITE AND
       COLORED RACES IN THE SOUTH." CHARLOTTE MEDICAL
       JOURNAL, 10 (1897): 291-294.

15828 WARE, E. RICHMOND. "HEALTH HAZARDS OF THE WEST AFRICAN
       TRADER, 1840-1870." AMERICAN NEPTUNE, 27 (APRIL,
       1967): 81-97.

15829 WARING, JOSEPH I. "CHARLESTON MEDICINE, 1800-1860."
       JOURNAL OF THE HISTORY OF MEDICINE AND ALLIED
       SCIENCES, 31 (JULY, 1976): 320-342.

15830 WARING, JOSEPH I. A HISTORY OF MEDICINE IN SOUTH

CAROLINA, 1670-1825. CHARLESTON: SOUTH CAROLINA
MEDICAL ASSOCIATION, 1964.

15831   WEBB, JULIE Y. "SUPERSTITIOUS INFLUENCE--VOODOO IN
        PARTICULAR--AFFECTING HEALTH PRACTICES IN A SELECTED
        POPULATION IN SOUTHERN LOUISIANA." PH.D.
        DISSERTATION, TULANE UNIVERSITY, 1974.

15832   WEYL, NATHANIEL. "SOME GENETIC ASPECTS OF PLANTATION
        SLAVERY." PERSPECTIVES IN BIOLOGY AND MEDICINE, 13
        (SUMMER, 1970): 618-625.

15833   WHITTEN, DAVID O. "MEDICAL CARE OF SLAVES: LOUISIANA
        SUGAR REGION AND SOUTH CAROLINA RICE DISTRICT."
        SOUTHERN STUDIES, 16 (SUMMER, 1977): 153-180.

15834   WHITTEN, DAVID O. "THE MEDICAL CARE OF SLAVES ON SOUTH
        CAROLINA RICE PLANTATIONS." M.A. THESIS, UNIVERSITY
        OF SOUTH CAROLINA, 1963.

15835   WIESENFELD, STEPHEN L. "SICKLE-CELL TRAIT IN HUMAN
        BIOLOGICAL AND CULTURAL EVOLUTION." SCIENCE, 157
        (SEPTEMBER, 1967): 1134-1140.

15836   WILEY, BELL I. THE LIFE OF BILLY YANK: THE COMMON
        SOLDIER OF THE UNION. INDIANAPOLIS: BOBBS-MERRILL,
        1952.

15837   WILKINS, MARY V. "MEDICAL CARE FOR SOUTHERN NEGROES,
        1861-1900." M.S. THESIS, UNIVERSITY OF WISCONSIN,
        1964.

15838   WISNER, ELIZABETH. SOCIAL WELFARE IN THE SOUTH: FROM
        COLONIAL TIMES TO WORLD WAR I. BATON ROUGE:
        LOUISIANA STATE UNIVERSITY PRESS, 1970.

15839   WOOD, PETER H. BLACK MAJORITY: NEGROES IN COLONIAL
        SOUTH CAROLINA, 1670 TO THE STONO REBELLION. NEW
        YORK: ALFRED A. KNOPF, 1974.

15840   WOOD, PETER H. "PEOPLE'S MEDICINE IN THE EARLY SOUTH."
        SOUTHERN EXPOSURE, 6 (SUMMER, 1978): 50-53.

15841   YATES, E.A. "'EFFECT OF EMANCIPATION UPON THE MENTAL AND
        PHYSICAL HEALTH OF THE NEGRO.'" NORTH CAROLINA
        CHRISTIAN ADVOCATE, 42 (JANUARY 6, 1897): 2.

SLAVE RECREATION

15842   ANDREWS, GARNETT. REMINISCENCES OF AN OLD GEORGIA
        LAWYER. ATLANTA: FRANKLIN STEAM PRINTING HOUSE, 1870.

15843   BENDER, FLORENCE R. "NEGRO AMUSEMENTS IN THE OLD SOUTH."
        M.A. THESIS, SOUTHERN METHODIST UNIVERSITY, 1941.

15844   BLACK, ELIZABETH. "A SHOW AT THE QUARTER." THEATER ARTS
        MONTHLY, 16 (JUNE, 1932): 493-500.

15845   BRUCE, DICKSON D., JR. "PLAY, WORK, AND ETHICS IN THE
        OLD SOUTH." SOUTHERN FOLKLORE QUARTERLY, 41 (1977):
        33-51.

15846   CAMERON, REBECCA. "CHRISTMAS AT BUCHOI, A NORTH CAROLINA
        RICE PLANTATION." NORTH CAROLINA BOOKLET, 13 (JULY,
        1913): 3-10.

15847   CLAYTON, LOUISE. "LEGAL STATUS AND SOCIAL LIFE OF THE
        SLAVES IN ARKANSAS." M.A. THESIS, UNIVERSITY OF
        CHICAGO, 1928.

15848   COHEN, HENNIG. "A NEGRO 'FOLK GAME' IN COLONIAL SOUTH
        CAROLINA." SOUTHERN FOLKLORE QUARTERLY, 16
        (SEPTEMBER, 1952): 183-185.

15849   DAVIS, DANIEL W. "ECHOES FROM A PLANTATION PARTY."
        SOUTHERN WORKMAN, 28 (FEBRUARY, 1899): 54-59.

15850   DIMOCK, ANNE. "CAPOEIRA ANGOLA." IN SHAPIRO, LINN
        (ED.). BLACK PEOPLE AND THEIR CULTURE: SELECTED
        WRITINGS FROM THE AFRICAN DIASPORA. WASHINGTON:
        SMITHSONIAN INSTITUTION, 1976, PP. 123-126.

15851   DIRKS, ROBERT. "SLAVES' HOLIDAY." NATURAL HISTORY, 84
        (DECEMBER, 1975): 82-84, 87-88, 90.

15852   EATON, CLEMENT. "THE MIND OF THE SOUTHERN NEGRO: THE
        REMARKABLE INDIVIDUALS." THE MIND OF THE OLD SOUTH.
        BATON ROUGE: LOUISIANA STATE UNIVERSITY PRESS, 1967,
        PP. 170-199.

15853   EMERY, LYNNE F. "BLACK DANCE OF THE CARIBBEAN,
        1518-1900." BLACK DANCE IN THE UNITED STATES FROM
        1619 TO 1970. PALO ALTO: NATIONAL PRESS BOOKS, 1972,
        PP. 15-79.

15854   EMERY, LYNNE F. "DANCE IN THE NORTH, ON THE LEVEE, AND
        IN NEW ORLEANS." BLACK DANCE IN THE UNITED STATES
        FROM 1619 TO 1970. PALO ALTO: NATIONAL PRESS BOOKS,
        1972, PP. 139-178.

15855   EMERY, LYNNE F. "DANCE ON THE PLANTATIONS." BLACK DANCE
        IN THE UNITED STATES FROM 1619 TO 1970. PALO ALTO:
        NATIONAL PRESS BOOKS, 1972, PP. 80-138.

15856   FOX, GRACE I. "RING GAMES AND OTHER GAMES OF THE FLORIDA
        NEGRO." PH.D. DISSERTATION, INDIANA UNIVERSITY, 1951.

15857   HART, ALBERT B. SLAVERY AND ABOLITION, 1831-1841. NEW
        YORK: HARPER AND BROTHERS, 1906.

15858   JOHNSTON, ELIZABETH B.   CHRISTMAS IN KENTUCKY, 1862.
        WASHINGTON: GIBSON BROTHERS, 1892.

15859   JONES, BESSIE AND HAWES, BESS L.   STEP IT DOWN: GAMES,
        PLAYS, SONGS, AND STORIES FROM THE AFRO-AMERICAN
        HERITAGE. NEW YORK: HARPER & ROW, 1972.

15860   LAKE, MARY D. "PIONEER CHRISTMAS CUSTOMS OF TARRANT
        COUNTY." PUBLICATIONS OF THE TEXAS FOLKLORE SOCIETY,
        NO. 5 (1926): 107-111.

15861   LEE, FLORENCE W. "CHRISTMAS IN VIRGINIA BEFORE THE WAR."
        SOUTHERN WORKMAN, 37 (DECEMBER, 1908): 686-689.

15862   LEE, FLORENCE W. "HARVEST TIME IN OLD VIRGINIA."
        SOUTHERN WORKMAN, 37 (OCTOBER, 1908): 566-567.

15863   MORAZAN, RONALD R. "'QUADROON' BALLS IN THE SPANISH
        PERIOD." LOUISIANA HISTORY, 14 (SUMMER, 1973):
        310-315.

15864   O'DEA, MICHAEL. "THE NEGRO GOVERNORS." AMERICAN HISTORY
        ILLUSTRATED, 15 (JULY, 1980): 22-25, 48.

15865   PETERSON, WALTER F. "SLAVERY IN THE 1850S: THE
        RECOLLECTIONS OF AN ALABAMA UNIONIST." ALABAMA
        HISTORICAL QUARTERLY, 30 (FALL/WINTER, 1968): 219-227.

15866   PLATT, ORVILLE H. "NEGRO GOVERNORS IN CONNECTICUT."
        PAPERS OF THE NEW HAVEN COLONY HISTORICAL SOCIETY, 6
        (1900): 315-335.

15867   RAWICK, GEORGE P.   FROM SUNDOWN TO SUNUP: THE MAKING OF
        THE BLACK COMMUNITY. WESTPORT: GREENWOOD PRESS, 1972.

15868   REID, ROBERT D. "RELIGION AND RECREATION AMONG SLAVES IN
        ANTE-BELLUM ALABAMA." MIDWEST JOURNAL, 2 (WINTER,
        1949): 29-36.

15869   REIDY, JOSEPH P. "'NEGRO ELECTION DAY' & BLACK COMMUNITY
        LIFE IN NEW ENGLAND, 1750-1860." MARXIST
        PERSPECTIVES, 1 (FALL, 1978): 102-117.

15870   SCHWENINGER, LOREN. "A NEGRO SOJOURNER IN ANTEBELLUM NEW
        ORLEANS." LOUISIANA HISTORY, 20 (SUMMER, 1979):
        305-314.

15871   SHELTON, JANE DE FOREST. "THE NEW ENGLAND NEGRO: A
        REMNANT." HARPER'S MONTHLY MAGAZINE, 88 (MARCH,
        1894): 533-538.

15872   "SLAVES, LEISURE HOURS OF." IN RYWELL, MARTIN (ED.).
        AFRO-AMERICAN ENCYCLOPEDIA. 10 VOLS. NORTH MIAMI:
        EDUCATIONAL BOOK PUBLISHERS, 1974, VOL. 8, PP.
        2489-2490.

15873   WADE, RICHARD C.   SLAVERY IN THE CITIES: THE SOUTH,
        1820-1860.   NEW YORK: OXFORD UNIVERSITY PRESS, 1964.

15874   WIGGINS, DAVID K.   "GOOD TIME ON THE OLD PLANTATION:
        POPULAR RECREATIONS OF THE BLACK SLAVE IN THE ANTE
        BELLUM SOUTH, 1810-1860."   JOURNAL OF SPORT HISTORY, 4
        (FALL, 1977):   260-284.

15875   WIGGINS, DAVID K.   "LEISURE TIME ON THE SOUTHERN
        PLANTATION: THE SLAVES' RESPITE FROM CONSTANT TOIL,
        1810-1860."   PROCEEDINGS OF THE NORTH AMERICAN SOCIETY
        FOR SPORT HISTORY, 8 (1980):   22-23.

15876   WIGGINS, DAVID K.   "THE PLAY OF SLAVE CHILDREN IN THE
        PLANTATION COMMUNITIES OF THE OLD SOUTH, 1820-1860."
        JOURNAL OF SPORT HISTORY, 7 (SUMMER, 1980):   21-39.

15877   WIGGINS, DAVID K.   "SPORT AND POPULAR PASTIMES IN THE
        PLANTATION COMMUNITY: THE SLAVE EXPERIENCE."   PH.D.
        DISSERTATION, UNIVERSITY OF MARYLAND, 1979.

15878   WIGGINS, DAVID K.   "SPORT AND POPULAR PASTIMES: SHADOW
        OF THE SLAVEQUARTER."   CANADIAN JOURNAL OF THE HISTORY
        OF SPORT AND PHYSICAL EDUCATION, 11 (1980):   61-88.

15879   WINFIELD, ARTHUR A., JR.   "SLAVE HOLIDAYS AND FESTIVITIES
        IN THE U.S."   M.A. THESIS, ATLANTA UNIVERSITY, 1941.

15880   WINSLOW, DAVID J.   "A NEGRO CORN-SHUCKING."   JOURNAL OF
        AMERICAN FOLKLORE, 86 (JANUARY-MARCH, 1973):   61-62.

URBAN SLAVERY

15881   ARMSTRONG, THOMAS F.   "URBAN VISION IN VIRGINIA: A
        COMPARATIVE STUDY OF ANTE-BELLUM FREDERICKSBURG,
        LYNCHBURG, AND STAUNTON."   PH.D. DISSERTATION,
        UNIVERSITY OF VIRGINIA, 1974.

15882   BARKER, DOROTHY M.   "AN ECONOMIC SURVEY OF NEW ORLEANS
        DURING THE CIVIL WAR AND RECONSTRUCTION."   M.A.
        THESIS, TULANE UNIVERSITY, 1942.

15883   BERKELEY, KATHLEEN C.   "'LIKE A PLAGUE OF LOCUST':
        IMMIGRATION AND SOCIAL CHANGE IN MEMPHIS, TENNESSEE,
        1850-1880."   PH.D. DISSERTATION, UNIVERSITY OF
        CALIFORNIA, LOS ANGELES, 1980.

15884   BERLIN, IRA AND GUTMAN, HERBERT G.   "SLAVES, FREEWORKERS,
        AND THE SOCIAL ORDER OF THE URBAN SOUTH."   UNPUBLISHED
        PAPER, DAVIS CENTER, PRINCETON UNIVERSITY, 1976.

15885   BLASSINGAME, JOHN W.   BLACK NEW ORLEANS, 1860-1880.
        CHICAGO: UNIVERSITY OF CHICAGO PRESS, 1973.

15886   BLASSINGAME, JOHN W.   "A SOCIAL AND ECONOMIC STUDY OF THE
         NEGRO IN NEW ORLEANS, 1360-1880." PH.D. DISSERTATION,
         YALE UNIVERSITY, 1971.

15887   BOGGER, TOMMY L.   "THE SLAVE AND FREE BLACK COMMUNITY IN
         NORFOLK, 1775-1865." PH.D. DISSERTATION, UNIVERSITY
         OF VIRGINIA, 1976.

15888   BRIDENBAUGH, CARL.   CITIES IN THE WILDERNESS: THE FIRST
         CENTURY OF URBAN LIFE IN AMERICA, 1625-1742. NEW
         YORK: RONALD PRESS COMPANY, 1938.

15889   BROWNE, GARY L.   BALTIMORE IN THE NATION, 1789-1861.
         CHAPEL HILL: UNIVERSITY OF NORTH CAROLINA PRESS, 1980.

15890   BROWNLEE, W. ELLIOT.   "THE ECONOMICS OF URBAN SLAVERY."
         REVIEWS IN AMERICAN HISTORY, 5 (JUNE, 1977):   230-235.

15891   BYRNE, WILLIAM A.   "SLAVERY IN SAVANNAH, GEORGIA, DURING
         THE CIVIL WAR." M.A. THESIS, FLORIDA STATE
         UNIVERSITY, 1970.

15892   BYRNE, WILLIAM A., JR.   "THE BURDEN AND HEAT OF THE DAY:
         SLAVERY AND SERVITUDE IN SAVANNAH: 1733-1865." PH.D.
         DISSERTATION, FLORIDA STATE UNIVERSITY, 1979.

15893   CAMPBELL, JANET.   "SLAVERY IN COLONIAL BOSTON." B.A.
         THESIS, HARVARD UNIVERSITY, 1977.

15894   CAPERS, GERALD M.   OCCUPIED CITY: NEW ORLEANS UNDER THE
         FEDERALS, 1862-1865. LEXINGTON: UNIVERSITY OF
         KENTUCKY PRESS, 1965.

15895   CASTELLANOS, HENRY C.   NEW ORLEANS AS IT WAS, EPISODES OF
         LOUISIANA LIFE. NEW ORLEANS: L. GRAHAM & SON, 1895.

15896   CLARK, JOHN G.   NEW ORLEANS, 1718-1812:   AN ECONOMIC
         HISTORY. BATON ROUGE: LOUISIANA STATE UNIVERSITY
         PRESS, 1970.

15897   CLARKE, T. WOOD.   "THE NEGRO PLOT OF 1741." NEW YORK
         HISTORY, 25 (APRIL, 1944):   167-181.

15898   COTTON, BARBARA R.   "TEACHING NINETEENTH CENTURY
         AFRO-AMERICAN HISTORY: THE CASE STUDY APPROACH."
         WESTERN JOURNAL OF BLACK STUDIES, 3 (SPRING, 1979):
         72-76.

15899   COTTROL, ROBERT J.   "COMPARATIVE SLAVE STUDIES: URBAN
         SLAVERY AS A MODEL, TRAVELERS' ACCOUNTS AS A
         SOURCE--BIBLIOGRAPHIC ESSAY." JOURNAL OF BLACK
         STUDIES, 8 (SEPTEMBER, 1977):   3-12.

15900   DABNEY, VIRGINIUS.   RICHMOND: THE STORY OF A CITY.
         GARDEN CITY: DOUBLEDAY AND COMPANY, 1976.

15901   DAVIS, THOMAS J. "SLAVERY IN COLONIAL NEW YORK CITY."
        PH.D. DISSERTATION, COLUMBIA UNIVERSITY, 1974.

15902   DAY, JUDY AND KEDRO, M. JAMES. "FREE BLACKS IN ST.
        LOUIS: ANTEBELLUM CONDITIONS, EMANCIPATION, AND THE
        POSTWAR ERA." BULLETIN OF THE MISSOURI HISTORICAL
        SOCIETY, 30 (JANUARY, 1974): 117-135.

15903   DELLA, M. RAY JR. "AN ANALYSIS OF BALTIMORE'S POPULATION
        IN THE 1850'S." MARYLAND HISTORICAL MAGAZINE, 68
        (SPRING, 1973): 20-35.

15904   DICKERMAN, G.S. "A GLIMPSE OF CHARLESTON HISTORY."
        SOUTHERN WORKMAN, 36 (JANUARY, 1907): 15-22.

15905   DOWTY, ALAN. "URBAN SLAVERY IN PRO-SOUTHERN FICTION OF
        THE 1850'S." JOURNAL OF SOUTHERN HISTORY, 32
        (FEBRUARY, 1966): 25-41.

15906   DUFOUR, CHARLES L. "THE PEOPLE OF NEW ORLEANS." IN
        CARTER, HODDING (ED.). THE PAST AS PRELUDE: NEW
        ORLEANS, 1718-1968. NEW ORLEANS: TULANE UNIVERSITY,
        1968, PP. 20-41.

15907   ECKENRODE, H.J. "NEGROES IN RICHMOND IN 1864." VIRGINIA
        MAGAZINE OF HISTORY AND BIOGRAPHY, 46 (JULY, 1938):
        193-200.

15908   ELLIS, JOHN H. "BUSINESS AND PUBLIC HEALTH IN THE URBAN
        SOUTH DURING THE NINETEENTH CENTURY: NEW ORLEANS,
        MEMPHIS, AND ATLANTA." BULLETIN OF THE HISTORY OF
        MEDICINE, 44 (MAY-JUNE, JULY-AUGUST, 1970): 197-212,
        346-371.

15909   EVANS, OLIVER. "MELTING POT IN THE BAYOUS." AMERICAN
        HERITAGE, 15 (DECEMBER, 1963): 30-51, 106-107.

15910   FARLEY, REYNOLDS. "THE URBANIZATION OF NEGROES IN THE
        UNITED STATES." JOURNAL OF SOCIAL HISTORY, 1 (SPRING,
        1968): 241-258.

15911   FISCHER, ROGER A. "RACIAL SEGREGATION IN ANTE BELLUM NEW
        ORLEANS." AMERICAN HISTORICAL REVIEW, 74 (FEBRUARY,
        1969): 926-957.

15912   GARONZIK, JOSEPH. "THE RACIAL AND ETHNIC MAKE-UP OF
        BALTIMORE NEIGHBORHOODS, 1850-1870." MARYLAND
        HISTORICAL MAGAZINE, 71 (FALL, 1976): 392-402.

15913   GENOVESE, EUGENE D. "ONE-TENTH IN URBAN BONDAGE."
        NATION, 200 (JANUARY 11, 1965): 38-39.

15914   GLASRUD, BRUCE A. "JIM CROW'S EMERGENCE IN TEXAS."
        AMERICAN STUDIES, 15 (SPRING, 1974): 47-60.

15915   GOLDFIELD, DAVID R. "FRIENDS AND NEIGHBORS: URBAN-RURAL
         RELATIONS IN ANTEBELLUM VIRGINIA." VIRGINIA
         CAVALCADE, 25 (SUMMER, 1975): 14-27.

15916   GOLDFIELD, DAVID R. "PURSUING THE AMERICAN DREAM:
         CITIES IN THE OLD SOUTH." IN BROWNELL, BLAINE A. AND
         GOLDFIELD (EDS.). THE CITY IN SOUTHERN HISTORY: THE
         GROWTH OF URBAN CIVILIZATION IN THE SOUTH. PORT
         WASHINGTON, NY: KENNIKAT PRESS, 1977, PP. 52-91.

15917   GOLDFIELD, DAVID R. URBAN GROWTH IN THE AGE OF
         SECTIONALISM, VIRGINIA, 1847-1861. BATON ROUGE:
         LOUISIANA STATE UNIVERSITY PRESS, 1977.

15918   GOLDIN, CLAUDIA D. "THE ECONOMICS OF URBAN SLAVERY:
         1820 TO 1860." PH.D. DISSERTATION, UNIVERSITY OF
         CHICAGO, 1972.

15919   GOLDIN, CLAUDIA D. "A MODEL TO EXPLAIN THE RELATIVE
         DECLINE OF URBAN SLAVERY: EMPIRICAL RESULTS." IN
         ENGERMAN, STANLEY L. AND GENOVESE, EUGENE D. (EDS.).
         RACE AND SLAVERY IN THE WESTERN HEMISPHERE:
         QUANTITATIVE STUDIES. PRINCETON: PRINCETON
         UNIVERSITY PRESS, 1975, PP. 427-454.

15920   GOLDIN, CLAUDIA D. URBAN SLAVERY IN THE AMERICAN SOUTH,
         1820-1860: A QUANTITATIVE HISTORY. CHICAGO:
         UNIVERSITY OF CHICAGO PRESS, 1976.

15921   GOLDIN, CLAUDIA D. "URBANIZATION AND SLAVERY: THE ISSUE
         OF COMPATIBILITY." IN SCHNORE, LEO F. (ED.). THE NEW
         URBAN HISTORY: QUANTITATIVE EXPLORATIONS BY AMERICAN
         HISTORIANS. PRINCETON: PRINCETON UNIVERSITY PRESS,
         1975, PP. 231-246.

15922   GREEN, RODNEY D. "URBAN INDUSTRY, BLACK RESISTANCE AND
         RACIAL RECONSTRUCTION IN THE ANTEBELLUM SOUTH: A
         GENERAL MODEL AND CASE STUDY IN URBAN VIRGINIA."
         PH.D. DISSERTATION, AMERICAN UNIVERSITY, 1930.

15923   HAUNTON, RICHARD H. "LAW AND ORDER IN SAVANNAH,
         1850-1860." GEORGIA HISTORICAL QUARTERLY, 56 (SPRING,
         1972): 1-24.

15924   HEARN, WALTER C. "TOWNS IN ANTEBELLUM MISSISSIPPI."
         PH.D. DISSERTATION, UNIVERSITY OF MISSISSIPPI, 1969.

15925   HELPLER, MORRIS K. "NEGROES AND CRIME IN NEW ORLEANS,
         1850-1861." M.A. THESIS, TULANE UNIVERSITY, 1960.

15926   HOGAN, DANIEL M. "THE CATHOLIC CHURCH AND THE NEGROES OF
         ST. LOUIS." M.A. THESIS, ST. LOUIS UNIVERSITY, 1955.

15927   HUNTER, LLOYD A. "SLAVERY IN ST. LOUIS, 1804-1860."
         BULLETIN OF THE MISSOURI HISTORICAL SOCIETY, 30 (JULY,

1974):   233-265.

15928   JAMES, D. CLAYTON. ANTEBELLUM NATCHEZ. BATON ROUGE:
        LOUISIANA STATE UNIVERSITY PRESS, 1968.

15929   JAMES, DORIS C. "ANTE-BELLUM NATCHEZ." PH.D.
        DISSERTATION, UNIVERSITY OF TEXAS, 1964.

15930   JORDAN, LAYLON W. "POLICE POWER AND PUBLIC SAFETY IN
        ANTEBELLUM CHARLESTON: THE EMERGENCE OF A NEW POLICE,
        1800-1860." IN CENSER, JACK R.; STEINERT, N. STEVEN;
        AND MCCANDLESS, AMY M. (EDS.). SOUTH ATLANTIC URBAN
        STUDIES, VOLUME 3. COLUMBIA: UNIVERSITY OF SOUTH
        CAROLINA PRESS, 1979, PP. 122-140.

15931   KENDALL, JOHN S. "NEW ORLEANS' 'PECULIAR INSTITUTION.'"
        LOUISIANA HISTORICAL QUARTERLY, 23 (JULY, 1940):
        864-886.

15932   KENDALL, JOHN S. (ED.). NEW ORLEANS' "PECULIAR
        INSTITUTION." NEW ORLEANS: LOUISIANA HISTORICAL
        SOCIETY, 1940.

15933   KENDALL, JOHN S. "SHADOW OVER THE CITY." LOUISIANA
        HISTORICAL QUARTERLY, 22 (JANUARY, 1939): 142-165.

15934   KENDALL, LANE C. "JOHN MCDONOGH--SLAVE-OWNER."
        LOUISIANA HISTORICAL QUARTERLY, 15 (OCTOBER, 1932):
        646-654; 16 (JANUARY, 1933): 125-134.

15935   KILSON, MARION D. DE B. "AFRO-AMERICAN SOCIAL STRUCTURE,
        1790-1970." IN KILSON, MARTIN L. AND ROTBERG, ROBERT
        I. (EDS.). THE AFRICAN DIASPORA: INTERPRETIVE
        ESSAYS. CAMBRIDGE: HARVARD UNIVERSITY PRESS, 1976,
        PP. 414-458.

15936   KING, DAVID R. "MISSIONARY VESTRYMAN." HISTORICAL
        MAGAZINE OF THE PROTESTANT EPISCOPAL CHURCH, 34
        (DECEMBER, 1965): 361-368.

15937   LACK, PAUL. "SLAVERY ON THE SOUTHWESTERN URBAN FRONTIER:
        AUSTIN, TEXAS, 1845-1860." UNPUBLISHED PAPER, TEXAS
        TECH UNIVERSITY, 1970.

15938   LACK, PAUL D. "URBAN SLAVERY IN THE SOUTHWEST." PH.D.
        DISSERTATION, TEXAS TECH UNIVERSITY, 1973.

15939   LATROBE, BENJAMIN H. IMPRESSIONS RESPECTING NEW ORLEANS.
        NEW YORK: COLUMBIA UNIVERSITY PRESS, 1951.

15940   MARTIN, JERRYE L.B. "NEW ORLEANS SLAVERY, 1840-1860:
        TESTING THE WADE THEORY." M.A. THESIS, TULANE
        UNIVERSITY, 1972.

15941   MCCOWEN, GEORGE S., JR. THE BRITISH OCCUPATION OF

CHARLESTON, 1780-1782. COLUMBIA: UNIVERSITY OF SOUTH
CAROLINA PRESS, 1972.

15942   MELOM, HALVOR G.   "THE ECONOMIC DEVELOPMENT OF ST. LOUIS,
        1803-1846." PH.D. DISSERTATION, UNIVERSITY OF
        MISSOURI, 1948.

15943   MILLER, ELINOR AND GENOVESE, EUGENE D. (EDS.).
        PLANTATION, TOWN AND COUNTY: ESSAYS ON THE LOCAL
        HISTORY OF AMERICAN SLAVE SOCIETY. URBANA:
        UNIVERSITY OF ILLINOIS PRESS, 1974.

15944   MILLER, M. SAMMY.   "SLAVERY IN AN URBAN AREA--DISTRICT OF
        COLUMBIA." NEGRO HISTORY BULLETIN, 37
        (AUGUST-SEPTEMBER, 1974): 293-295.

15945   MILLER, ZANE L.   "URBAN BLACKS IN THE SOUTH, 1865-1920:
        THE RICHMOND, SAVANNAH, NEW ORLEANS, LOUISVILLE, AND
        BIRMINGHAM EXPERIENCE." IN SCHNORE, LEO F. (ED.).
        THE NEW URBAN HISTORY. PRINCETON: PRINCETON
        UNIVERSITY PRESS, 1975, PP. 184-204.

15946   MOBLEY, JOE A.   "FLUSH TIMES, WAR, AND RECONSTRUCTION IN
        A SOUTHERN TOWN, MOBILE, 1850-1867." M.A. THESIS,
        NORTH CAROLINA STATE UNIVERSITY, 1976.

15947   MORGAN, E.V.   "SLAVERY IN NEW YORK, WITH SPECIAL
        REFERENCE TO NEW YORK CITY." HISTORIC NEW YORK, 2ND
        SER., NO. 1 (1899): 1-28.

15948   MORGAN, EDWIN V. SLAVERY IN NEW YORK, WITH SPECIAL
        REFERENCE TO NEW YORK CITY. NEW YORK: G.P. PUTNAM'S
        SONS, 1899.

15949   O'BRIEN, JOHN T.   "FACTORY, CHURCH, AND COMMUNITY:
        BLACKS IN ANTEBELLUM RICHMOND." JOURNAL OF SOUTHERN
        HISTORY, 44 (NOVEMBER, 1978): 509-536.

15950   O'BRIEN, JOHN T.   "FROM BONDAGE TO CITIZENSHIP: THE
        RICHMOND BLACK COMMUNITY, 1865-1867." PH.D.
        DISSERTATION, UNIVERSITY OF ROCHESTER, 1974.

15951   O'BRIEN, MARY L.   "SLAVERY IN LOUISVILLE DURING THE
        ANTEBELLUM PERIOD: 1820-1860. A STUDY OF THE EFFECTS
        OF URBANIZATION ON THE INSTITUTION OF SLAVERY AS IT
        EXISTED IN LOUISVILLE, KENTUCKY." M.A. THESIS,
        UNIVERSITY OF LOUISVILLE, 1979.

15952   PAUL, WILLIAM G.   "THE SHADOW OF EQUALITY: THE NEGRO IN
        BALTIMORE, 1864-1911." PH.D. DISSERTATION, UNIVERSITY
        OF WISCONSIN, 1972.

15953   PHILLIPS, ULRICH B. AMERICAN NEGRO SLAVERY: A SURVEY OF
        THE SUPPLY, EMPLOYMENT AND CONTROL OF NEGRO LABOR AS
        DETERMINED BY THE PLANTATION REGIME. NEW YORK: D.

APPLETON, 1918.

15954   PHILLIPS, ULRICH B.   "THE SLAVE LABOR PROBLEM IN THE
        CHARLESTON DISTRICT."   POLITICAL SCIENCE QUARTERLY, 22
        (SEPTEMBER, 1907):   416-439.

15955   PORTER, ALICE T.   "AN ECONOMIC VIEW OF ANTE-BELLUM NEW
        ORLEANS, 1845-1860."   M.A. THESIS, TULANE UNIVERSITY,
        1942.

15956   RADFORD, JOHN P.   "THE CHARLESTON PLANTERS IN 1860."
        SOUTH CAROLINA HISTORICAL MAGAZINE, 77 (OCTOBER,
        1976):   227-235.

15957   RADFORD, JOHN P.   "CULTURE, ECONOMY AND RESIDENTIAL
        STRUCTURE IN CHARLESTON, SOUTH CAROLINA, 1860-1880."
        PH.D. DISSERTATION, CLARK UNIVERSITY, 1974.

15958   RADFORD, JOHN P.   "DELICATE SPACE: RACE AND RESIDENCE IN
        CHARLESTON, SOUTH CAROLINA, 1860-1880."   WEST GEORGIA
        COLLEGE STUDIES IN THE SOCIAL SCIENCES, 16 (JUNE,
        1977):   17-37.

15959   RADFORD, JOHN P.   "RACE, RESIDENCE AND IDEOLOGY:
        CHARLESTON, SOUTH CAROLINA IN THE MID-NINETEENTH
        CENTURY."   JOURNAL OF HISTORICAL GEOGRAPHY, 2
        (OCTOBER, 1976):   329-346.

15960   REID, GURNEY H.   "THE NEGRO IN RICHMOND ON THE EVE OF AND
        DURING THE CIVIL WAR."   M.A. THESIS, COLLEGE OF
        WILLIAM AND MARY, 1936.

15961   REINDERS, ROBERT C.   "THE CHURCHES AND THE NEGRO IN NEW
        ORLEANS, 1850-1860."   PHYLON, 22 (FALL, 1961):
        241-248.

15962   REINDERS, ROBERT C.   "SLAVERY IN NEW ORLEANS IN THE
        DECADE BEFORE THE CIVIL WAR."   MID-AMERICA, 44
        (OCTOBER, 1962):   211-221.

15963   REINDERS, ROBERT C.   "A SOCIAL HISTORY OF NEW ORLEANS,
        1850-1860."   PH.D. DISSERTATION, UNIVERSITY OF TEXAS,
        1957.

15964   RICHARDSON, BENJAMIN H.   "THE URBAN SLAVE AS SEEN BY
        TRAVELLERS, 1820-1860."   M.A. THESIS, UNIVERSITY OF
        ROCHESTER, 1957.

15965   ROSS, MELVIN L., JR.   "BLACKS, MULATTOES AND CREOLES IN
        MOBILE DURING THE EUROPEAN AND AMERICAN PERIODS."
        M.A. THESIS, PURDUE UNIVERSITY, 1971.

15966   RYLAND, ROBERT.   "ORIGINS AND HISTORY OF THE FIRST
        AFRICAN BAPTIST CHURCH."   IN TUPPER, HENRY A. (ED.).
        THE FIRST CENTURY OF THE FIRST BAPTIST CHURCH IN

RICHMOND, VIRGINIA. RICHMOND: CARLTON MCCARTHY, 1880, PP. 245-272.

15967 SCHWENINGER, LOREN. "A NEGRO SOJOURNER IN ANTEBELLUM NEW ORLEANS." LOUISIANA HISTORY, 20 (SUMMER, 1979): 305-314.

15968 SHELDON, MARIANNE B. "BLACK-WHITE RELATIONS IN RICHMOND, VIRGINIA, 1782-1820." JOURNAL OF SOUTHERN HISTORY, 45 (FEBRUARY, 1979): 27-44.

15969 SHIMKIN, DEMITRI B.; LOUIE, GLORIA J.; AND FRATE, DENNIS A. "THE BLACK EXTENDED FAMILY: A BASIC RURAL INSTITUTION AND A MECHANISM OF URBAN ADAPTATION." IN SHIMKIN, DEMITRI B.; SHIMKIN, EDITH M.; AND FRATE, DENNIS A. (EDS.). THE EXTENDED FAMILY IN BLACK SOCIETIES. THE HAGUE: MOUTON PUBLISHERS, 1978, PP. 25-148.

15970 SIMMS, MARION. "BLACK MAGIC IN NEW ORLEANS." TRAVEL, 81 (JULY, 1943): 18-19, 32.

15971 SISK, GLENN. "CONTEMPORARY SITUATION OF: 'THE NEGRO IN ATLANTA.'" NEGRO HISTORY BULLETIN, 27 (APRIL, 1964): 174-176.

15972 SPAIN, DAPHNE. "RACE RELATIONS AND RESIDENTIAL SEGREGATION IN NEW ORLEANS: TWO CENTURIES OF PARADOX." ANNALS OF THE AMERICAN ACADEMY OF POLITICAL AND SOCIAL SCIENCE, 441 (JANUARY, 1979): 82-96.

15973 STAROBIN, ROBERT S. INDUSTRIAL SLAVERY IN THE OLD SOUTH. NEW YORK: OXFORD UNIVERSITY PRESS, 1970.

15974 STAVISKY, LEONARD P. "INDUSTRIALISM IN ANTE BELLUM CHARLESTON." JOURNAL OF NEGRO HISTORY, 36 (JULY, 1951): 302-322.

15975 THOMAS, EMORY M. THE CONFEDERATE STATE OF RICHMOND: A BIOGRAPHY OF THE CAPITAL. AUSTIN: UNIVERSITY OF TEXAS PRESS, 1971.

15976 THOMAS, HERBERT A., JR. "VICTIMS OF CIRCUMSTANCE: NEGROES IN A SOUTHERN TOWN, 1865-1880." REGISTER OF THE KENTUCKY HISTORICAL SOCIETY, 71 (JULY, 1973): 253-271.

15977 TREGLE, JOSEPH G., JR. "EARLY NEW ORLEANS SOCIETY: A REAPPRAISAL." JOURNAL OF SOUTHERN HISTORY, 18 (FEBRUARY, 1952): 20-36.

15978 VAN PELT, W. WELLS. "THE 'HIRING OUT' OF SLAVES IN CHARLESTON." IN JOYNER, CHARLES W. (ED.). BLACK CAROLINIANS: STUDIES IN THE HISTORY OF SOUTH CAROLINA NEGROES. LAURINBURG, NC: ST. ANDREWS PRESBYTERIAN

COLLEGE, 1969, PP. 29-42.

15979   WADE, RICHARD C.   "HISTORICAL ANALOGIES AND PUBLIC
        POLICY: THE BLACK AND IMMIGRANT EXPERIENCE IN URBAN
        AMERICA."   IN MORRIS, MARGARET F. AND WEST, ELLIOT
        (EDS.).   ESSAYS ON URBAN AMERICA.   AUSTIN: UNIVERSITY
        OF TEXAS PRESS, 1975, PP. 127-147.

15980   WADE, RICHARD C.   SLAVERY IN THE CITIES: THE SOUTH,
        1820-1860.   NEW YORK: OXFORD UNIVERSITY PRESS, 1964.

15981   WADE, RICHARD C.   THE URBAN FRONTIER: THE RISE OF
        WESTERN CITIES, 1790-1830.   CAMBRIDGE: HARVARD
        UNIVERSITY PRESS, 1959.

15982   WEGENER, WERNER A.   "NEGRO SLAVERY IN NEW ORLEANS."   M.A.
        THESIS, TULANE UNIVERSITY, 1935.

15983   WILKIE, JANE R.   "THE BLACK URBAN POPULATION OF THE
        PRE-CIVIL WAR SOUTH."   PHYLON, 37 (FALL, 1976):
        250-262.

15984   WOESSNER, HERMAN C.   "NEW ORLEANS, 1840-1860:   A STUDY IN
        URBAN SLAVERY."   M.A. THESIS, LOUISIANA STATE
        UNIVERSITY, 1967.

15985   WOOD, MINTER.   "LIFE IN NEW ORLEANS IN THE SPANISH
        PERIOD."   LOUISIANA HISTORICAL QUARTERLY, 22 (JULY,
        1939):   642-709.

15986   ZORNOW, DAVID M.   "A TROUBLESOME COMMUNITY: BLACKS IN
        REVOLUTIONARY CHARLES TOWN, 1765-1775."   B.A. THESIS,
        HARVARD UNIVERSITY, 1976.

MASTER/SLAVE RELATIONSHIPS

15987   "ABSENTEE OWNERSHIP OF SLAVES IN THE UNITED STATES IN
        1830."   JOURNAL OF NEGRO HISTORY, 9 (APRIL, 1924):
        196-231.

15988   ADLER, JOYCE.   "MELVILLE'S BENITO CERENO: SLAVERY AND
        VIOLENCE IN THE AMERICAS."   SCIENCE AND SOCIETY, 38
        (SPRING, 1974):   19-48.

15989   "THE ANGLO-SAXON AND THE AFRICAN."   SOUTHERN WORKMAN, 32
        (JANUARY, 1903):   9.

15990   APTHEKER, HERBERT.   "SLAVOCRACY'S SYSTEM OF CONTROL."
        NEGRO QUARTERLY, 1 (SPRING, 1942):   45-71.

15991   BAILEY, HUGH C. AND DALE, WILLIAM P.   "MISSUS ALONE IN DE
        'BIG HOUSE.'"   ALABAMA REVIEW, 8 (JANUARY, 1955):
        43-54.

15992 BALL, WILLIAM W. THE STATE THAT FORGOT: SOUTH
       CAROLINA'S SURRENDER TO DEMOCRACY. INDIANAPOLIS:
       BOBBS-MERRILL COMPANY, 1932.

15993 BLAKE, RUSSELL C. "TIES OF INTIMACY: SOCIAL VALUES AND
       PERSONAL RELATIONSHIPS OF ANTEBELLUM SLAVEHOLDERS."
       PH.D. DISSERTATION, UNIVERSITY OF MICHIGAN, 1978.

15994 BLASSINGAME, JOHN W. THE SLAVE COMMUNITY: PLANTATION
       LIFE IN THE ANTEBELLUM SOUTH. NEW YORK: OXFORD
       UNIVERSITY PRESS, 1972.

15995 BLASSINGAME, JOHN W. "STATUS AND SOCIAL STRUCTURE IN THE
       SLAVE COMMUNITY: EVIDENCE FROM NEW SOURCES." IN
       OWENS, HARRY P. (ED.). PERSPECTIVES AND IRONY IN
       AMERICAN SLAVERY. JACKSON: UNIVERSITY PRESS OF
       MISSISSIPPI, 1976, PP. 137-152.

15996 BREEDEN, JAMES O. (ED.). ADVICE AMONG MASTERS: THE
       IDEAL IN SLAVE MANAGEMENT IN THE OLD SOUTH. WESTPORT:
       GREENWOOD PRESS, 1980.

15997 BREWER, J. MASON. "SLAVE TALES AS A TYPE." PUBLICATIONS
       OF THE TEXAS FOLK-LORE SOCIETY, 10 (1932): 9-11.

15998 BRUCE, DICKSON D., JR. "SLAVERY AND VIOLENCE: THE
       MASTERS' VIEW." VIOLENCE AND CULTURE IN THE
       ANTEBELLUM SOUTH. AUSTIN: UNIVERSITY OF TEXAS PRESS,
       1979, PP. 114-136.

15999 BRUCE, PHILIP A. "THE AMERICAN NEGRO OF TODAY."
       CONTEMPORARY REVIEW, 77 (FEBRUARY, 1900): 284-297.

16000 BRUCE, PHILIP A. "THE NEGRO SERVANT OF THE PAST."
       CLIPPING, N.D., BRUCE SCRAPBOOK, PHILIP A. BRUCE
       PAPERS, UNIVERSITY OF VIRGINIA.

16001 BRYCE-LAPORTE, ROY S. "THE CONCEPTUALIZATION OF THE
       AMERICAN SLAVE PLANTATION AS A TOTAL INSTITUTION."
       PH.D. DISSERTATION, UNIVERSITY OF CALIFORNIA, LOS
       ANGELES, 1968.

16002 CLARK, JOHN G. "THE ANTEBELLUM GULF COAST: A STUDY OF
       WORLD VIEWS, TRADITIONALISM AND BACKWARDNESS." IN
       ELLSWORTH, LUCIUS F. (ED.). THE AMERICANIZATION OF
       THE GULF COAST, 1803-1850. PENSACOLA: HISTORIC
       PENSACOLA PRESERVATION BOARD, 1972, PP. 1-19.

16003 DEJARNETTE, E.M. "CREAM WHITE AND CROW BLACK." ATLANTIC
       MONTHLY, 52 (OCTOBER, 1883): 470.

16004 DENNEY, JOSEPH E. "THE LASH AND THE LAW: THE MECHANICS
       OF SLAVE CONTROL." IN JOYNER, CHARLES W. (ED.).
       BLACK CAROLINIANS: STUDIES IN THE HISTORY OF SOUTH
       CAROLINA NEGROES IN THE NINETEENTH CENTURY.

LAURINBURG, NC: ST. ANDREWS PRESBYTERIAN COLLEGE, 1969, PP. 10-20.

16005 DEW, CHARLES B. "DISCIPLINING SLAVE IRONWORKERS IN THE ANTEBELLUM SOUTH: COERCION, CONCILIATION, AND ACCOMMODATION." AMERICAN HISTORICAL REVIEW, 79 (APRIL, 1974): 393-418.

16006 EATON, CLEMENT. "SLAVE-HIRING IN THE UPPER SOUTH: A STEP TOWARD FREEDOM." MISSISSIPPI VALLEY HISTORICAL REVIEW, 46 (MARCH, 1960): 663-678.

16007 EATON, CLEMENT. THE WANING OF THE OLD SOUTH CIVILIZATION. ATHENS: UNIVERSITY OF GEORGIA PRESS, 1968.

16008 ELKINS, STANLEY M. SLAVERY: A PROBLEM IN AMERICAN INSTITUTIONAL AND INTELLECTUAL LIFE. CHICAGO: UNIVERSITY OF CHICAGO PRESS, 1959.

16009 ELKINS, STANLEY M. "SLAVERY: A PROBLEM IN AMERICAN INSTITUTIONAL AND INTELLECTUAL LIFE." PH.D. DISSERTATION, COLUMBIA UNIVERSITY, 1959.

16010 ESCOTT, PAUL D. SLAVERY REMEMBERED: A RECORD OF TWENTIETH-CENTURY SLAVE NARRATIVES. CHAPEL HILL: UNIVERSITY OF NORTH CAROLINA PRESS, 1979.

16011 FOGEL, ROBERT W. AND ENGERMAN, STANLEY L. TIME ON THE CROSS: THE ECONOMICS OF AMERICAN NEGRO SLAVERY. 2 VOLS. BOSTON: LITTLE, BROWN AND COMPANY, 1974.

16012 FORNESS, NORMAN O. "THE MASTER, THE SLAVE, AND THE PATENT LAWS: A VIGNETTE OF THE 1850S." PROLOGUE, 12 (SPRING, 1980): 23-28.

16013 FRANKLIN, JOHN H. "SLAVES VIRTUALLY FREE IN ANTE-BELLUM NORTH CAROLINA." JOURNAL OF NEGRO HISTORY, 28 (JULY, 1943): 284-310.

16014 FRY, GLADYS-MARIE. "'THE NIGHT RIDERS': A STUDY IN THE SOCIAL CONTROL OF THE NEGRO." PH.D. DISSERTATION, INDIANA UNIVERSITY, 1967.

16015 FRY, GLADYS-MARIE. NIGHT RIDERS IN BLACK FOLK HISTORY. KNOXVILLE: UNIVERSITY OF TENNESSEE PRESS, 1975.

16016 FURNAS, J.C. GOODBYE TO UNCLE TOM. NEW YORK: WILLIAM SLOANE ASSOCIATES, 1956.

16017 GENOVESE, EUGENE D. ROLL, JORDAN, ROLL: THE WORLD THE SLAVES MADE. NEW YORK: PANTHEON, 1974.

16018 GUILD, WALTER. "A PLEA FROM THE SOUTH." ARENA, 24 (NOVEMBER, 1900): 483-488.

16019   HARPER, C.W.   "HOUSE SERVANTS AND FIELD HANDS:
        FRAGMENTATION IN THE ANTEBELLUM SLAVE COMMUNITY."
        NORTH CAROLINA HISTORICAL REVIEW, 53 (JANUARY, 1978):
        42-59.

16020   HARRIS, JOEL C.   "THE NEGRO AS THE SOUTH SEES HIM I: THE
        OLD-TIME DARKY."   SATURDAY EVENING POST, 176 (JANUARY
        2, 1904):   1-2, 23.

16021   HINTON, E.H.   "THE NEGRO AND THE SOUTH."   CONFEDERATE
        VETERAN, 15 (AUGUST, 1907):   367-369.

16022   HOETINK, H.   CARIBBEAN RACE RELATIONS: A STUDY OF TWO
        VARIANTS.   NEW YORK: OXFORD UNIVERSITY PRESS, 1967.

16023   HOETINK, H.   SLAVERY AND RACE RELATIONS IN THE AMERICAS:
        COMPARATIVE NOTES ON THEIR NATURE AND NEXUS.   NEW
        YORK: HARPER AND ROW, 1973.

16024   HOETINK, HARRY.   THE TWO VARIANTS IN CARIBBEAN RACE
        RELATIONS: A CONTRIBUTION TO THE SOCIOLOGY OF
        SEGMENTED SOCIETIES.   NEW YORK: OXFORD UNIVERSITY
        PRESS, 1967.

16025   "HOW SLAVES EARNED OWNERS' CONFIDENCE."   COLUMBIA (SC)
        STATE, APRIL 4, 1915.

16026   JOHNSON, JAMES R.   "THE USEFULNESS OF RELIGIOUS TRAINING
        ON THE SOUTHERN PLANTATION AS A MEANS OF INCULCATING
        SERVILITY AND A DEEP SENSE OF INFERIORITY IN BLACK
        FOLKS DURING THE THIRTY YEARS PRECEDING THE AMERICAN
        CIVIL WAR."   UNPUBLISHED PAPER, TEACHERS COLLEGE,
        COLUMBIA UNIVERSITY, 1970.

16027   JOHNSON, MICHAEL P.   "PLANTERS AND PATRIARCHY:
        CHARLESTON, 1800-1860."   JOURNAL OF SOUTHERN HISTORY,
        46 (FEBRUARY, 1980):   45-72.

16028   JUDGE, M.T.   "ON THE DEVOTION OF SLAVES TO MASTERS."
        UNPUBLISHED MANUSCRIPT, MARCH 30, 1913, TENNESSEE
        STATE LIBRARY AND ARCHIVES, NASHVILLE.

16029   KEESEE, IRENE.   "THE MUTED VOICES OF MAGUIRETOWN."
        OZARKS MOUNTAINEER, 24 (APRIL, 1976):   16.

16030   KITCHEL, KELSEY P.   "SLAVE'S SONG."   CRISIS, 12 (MAY,
        1916):   36.

16031   LITWACK, LEON F.   BEEN IN THE STORM SO LONG: THE
        AFTERMATH OF SLAVERY.   NEW YORK: ALFRED A. KNOPF,
        1979.

16032   LIVERMORE, MARY A.   MY STORY OF THE WAR: A WOMAN'S
        NARRATIVE OF FOUR YEARS PERSONAL EXPERIENCE AS NURSE
        IN THE UNION ARMY.   HARTFORD: A.D. WORTHINGTON, 1887.

16033 "MASTER AND SLAVE." BALTIMORE LEDGER, APRIL 16, 1898.

16034 MITCHELL, JOHN JR. "THE OLD MASTER AND THE SLAVE."
RICHMOND PLANET, DECEMBER 17, 1898.

16035 ONWOOD, MAURICE. "IMPULSE AND HONOR: THE PLACE OF SLAVE
AND MASTER IN THE IDEOLOGY OF PLANTERDOM." PLANTATION
SOCIETY IN THE AMERICAS, 1 (FEBRUARY, 1979): 31-56.

16036 PAGE, THOMAS N. THE NEGRO: THE SOUTHERNER'S PROBLEM.
NEW YORK: CHARLES SCRIBNER'S SONS, 1904.

16037 PAGE, THOMAS N. "THE OLD-TIME NEGRO." SCRIBNERS
MAGAZINE, 36 (NOVEMBER, 1904): 522-532.

16038 PAGE, THOMAS N. "SLAVERY AND THE OLD RELATION BETWEEN
THE SOUTHERN WHITES AND BLACKS." MCCLURE'S MAGAZINE,
22 (MARCH, 1904): 548-554.

16039 PERKINS, A.L. "DISCOVERY." CRISIS, 41 (SEPTEMBER,
1934): 273.

16040 PHILLIPS, ULRICH B. AMERICAN NEGRO SLAVERY: A SURVEY OF
THE SUPPLY, EMPLOYMENT AND CONTROL OF NEGRO LABOR AS
DETERMINED BY THE PLANTATION REGIME. NEW YORK: D.
APPLETON, 1918.

16041 PHILLIPS, ULRICH B. "BLACK-BELT LABOR, SLAVE AND FREE."
IN UNIVERSITY OF VIRGINIA, PHELPS-STOKES FELLOWSHIP
PAPERS. LECTURES AND ADDRESSES ON THE NEGRO IN THE
SOUTH. CHARLOTTESVILLE: MICHIE COMPANY, 1915, PP.
29-36.

16042 PHILLIPS, ULRICH B. LIFE AND LABOR IN THE OLD SOUTH.
BOSTON: LITTLE, BROWN AND COMPANY, 1929.

16043 PHILLIPS, ULRICH B. "THE PLANTATION AS A CIVILIZING
FACTOR." SEWANEE REVIEW, 12 (JULY, 1904): 257-267.

16044 PHILLIPS, ULRICH B. "THE PLANTATION PRODUCT OF MEN."
PROCEEDINGS OF THE SECOND ANNUAL SESSION OF THE
GEORGIA HISTORICAL ASSOCIATION. ATLANTA: GEORGIA
HISTORICAL ASSOCIATION, 1918, PP. 12-15.

16045 PHILLIPS, ULRICH B. "RACIAL PROBLEMS, ADJUSTMENTS AND
DISTURBANCES." IN RILEY, FRANKLIN L. (ED.). THE
SOUTH IN THE BUILDING OF THE NATION. 12 VOLS.
RICHMOND: SOUTHERN HISTORICAL PUBLICATION SOCIETY,
1909, VOL. 4, PP. 194-241.

16046 RAWICK, GEORGE P. FROM SUNDOWN TO SUNUP: THE MAKING OF
THE BLACK COMMUNITY. WESTPORT: GREENWOOD PRESS, 1972.

16047 "RELATION OF SOUTHERN MASTERS TO SLAVES." CONFEDERATE
VETERAN, 5 (JANUARY, 1897): 21-22.

16048   RUTHERFORD, MILDRED L. FOUR ADDRESSES. BIRMINGHAM: THE
        MILDRED RUTHERFORD HISTORICAL CIRCLE, 1912-1916.

16049   SCARBOROUGH, WILLIAM K. "SLAVERY--THE WHITE MAN'S
        BURDEN." IN OWENS, HARRY P. (ED.). PERSPECTIVES AND
        IRONY IN AMERICAN SLAVERY. JACKSON: UNIVERSITY PRESS
        OF MISSISSIPPI, 1976, PP. 103-136.

16050   SELLERS, CHARLES G., JR. "THE TRAVAIL OF SLAVERY." IN
        SELLERS (ED.). THE SOUTHERNER AS AMERICAN. CHAPEL
        HILL: UNIVERSITY OF NORTH CAROLINA PRESS, 1960, PP.
        40-71.

16051   SHELTON, JANE DE FOREST. "THE NEW ENGLAND NEGRO: A
        REMNANT." HARPER'S MONTHLY MAGAZINE, 88 (MARCH,
        1894): 533-538.

16052   SHINN, CHARLES H. "WAS NOT THIS A MAN?" PUBLIC, 17
        (JUNE 19, 1914): 593-594.

16053   SIDES, SUDIE D. "SOUTHERN WOMEN AND SLAVERY." HISTORY
        TODAY, 20 (JANUARY, FEBRUARY, 1970): 54-60, 124-130.

16054   SIDES, SUDIE D. "WOMEN AND SLAVES: AN INTERPRETATION
        BASED ON THE WRITINGS OF SOUTHERN WOMEN." PH.D.
        DISSERTATION, UNIVERSITY OF NORTH CAROLINA, 1969.

16055   "SLAVERY IN MASSACHUSETTS." CONFEDERATE VETERAN, 5
        (JANUARY, 1897): 21-22.

16056   "SOMETHING OF SLAVERY AS IT EXISTED." CONFEDERATE
        VETERAN, 1 (JUNE, 1893): 171.

16057   SPRUILL, JULIA C. "SOUTHERN HOUSEWIVES BEFORE THE
        REVOLUTION." NORTH CAROLINA HISTORICAL REVIEW, 13
        (JANUARY, 1936): 25-46.

16058   SPRUILL, JULIA C. WOMEN'S LIFE AND WORK IN THE SOUTHERN
        COLONIES. CHAPEL HILL: UNIVERSITY OF NORTH CAROLINA
        PRESS, 1938.

16059   STAMPP, KENNETH M. THE PECULIAR INSTITUTION: SLAVERY IN
        THE ANTE-BELLUM SOUTH. NEW YORK: ALFRED A. KNOPF,
        1956.

16060   STERNE, RICHARD S. AND ROTHSEIDEN, JEANE L.
        "MASTER-SLAVE CLASHES AS FORERUNNERS OF PATTERNS IN
        MODERN AMERICAN URBAN ERUPTIONS." PHYLON, 30 (FALL,
        1969): 251-260.

16061   STOWE, STEVEN M. "THE 'TOUCHINESS' OF THE GENTLEMAN
        PLANTER: THE SENSE OF ESTEEM AND CONTINUITY IN THE
        ANTE-BELLUM SOUTH." PSYCHOHISTORY REVIEW, 8 (WINTER,
        1979): 6-15.

16062 TEBEAU, C.W. "SOME ASPECTS OF PLANTER-FREEDMAN
RELATIONS, 1865-1880." JOURNAL OF NEGRO HISTORY, 21
(APRIL, 1936): 130-150.

16063 THOMAS, EMORY M. THE CONFEDERACY AS A REVOLUTIONARY
EXPERIENCE. ENGLEWOOD CLIFFS: PRENTICE-HALL, 1971.

16064 THOMAS, EMORY M. THE CONFEDERATE NATION, 1861-1865. NEW
YORK: HARPER & ROW, 1979.

16065 TOMICH, DALE. "HOUSEHOLD SLAVES AND BLACK
ACCOMMODATIONISM IN THE AMERICAN SOUTH." UNPUBLISHED
HONORS ESSAY, DEPARTMENT OF HISTORY, UNIVERSITY OF
WISCONSIN, 1968.

16066 TYLER, LYON G. "PRISONERS ALL--THE SLAVE AND JAMES LOUIS
PETIGRU." PROCEEDINGS OF THE SOUTH CAROLINA
HISTORICAL ASSOCIATION, (1980): 55-72.

16067 VAN DEN BERGHE, PIERRE L. "DISTANCE MECHANISMS OF
STRATIFICATION." SOCIOLOGY AND SOCIAL RESEARCH, 44
(JANUARY-FEBRUARY, 1960): 155-164.

16068 WAGSTAFF, THOMAS. "CALL YOUR OLD MASTER--'MASTER':
SOUTHERN POLITICAL LEADERS AND NEGRO LABOR DURING
PRESIDENTIAL RECONSTRUCTION." LABOR HISTORY, 10
(SUMMER, 1969): 323-345.

16069 WALKER, CLARENCE E. "MASSA'S NEW CLOTHES: A CRITIQUE OF
EUGENE D. GENOVESE ON SOUTHERN SOCIETY, MASTER-SLAVE
RELATIONS, AND SLAVE BEHAVIOR." UMOJA: A SCHOLARLY
JOURNAL OF BLACK STUDIES, 4 (SUMMER, 1980): 114-130.

16070 WALTERS, RONALD G. "THE EROTIC SOUTH: CIVILIZATION AND
SEXUALITY IN AMERICAN ABOLITIONISM." AMERICAN
QUARTERLY, 25 (MAY, 1973): 177-201.

16071 WEBBER, THOMAS L. DEEP LIKE THE RIVERS: EDUCATION IN
THE SLAVE QUARTER COMMUNITY, 1831-1865. NEW YORK:
W.W. NORTON, 1978.

16072 "WHAT RIGHT HAD A FUGITIVE SLAVE OF SELF-DEFENSE AGAINST
HIS MASTER?" PENNSYLVANIA MAGAZINE OF HISTORY AND
BIOGRAPHY, 13 (1889): 106-109.

16073 WILLIAMS, HESSIE S. "A COMPARATIVE ANALYSIS OF EX-SLAVE
THOUGHTS CONCERNING THEIR MASTERS, THE UNITED STATES
ARMY, AND FREEDOM." M.A. THESIS, UNIVERSITY OF NORTH
CAROLINA, 1969.

16074 WILSON, WILLIAM J. THE DECLINING SIGNIFICANCE OF RACE,
BLACKS AND CHANGING AMERICAN INSTITUTIONS. CHICAGO:
UNIVERSITY OF CHICAGO PRESS, 1978.

16075 WOOD, GEORGE L. "REFLECTIONS ON THE INSTITUTION OF

SLAVERY." *THE SEVENTH REGIMENT*. NEW YORK: JAMES
MILLER, 1865, PP. 77-38.

20.
Slave Family

16076 ABZUG, ROBERT. "THE BLACK FAMILY DURING RECONSTRUCTION."
IN HUGGINS, NATHAN I.; KILSON, MARTIN; AND FOX, DANIEL
M. (EDS.). KEY ISSUES IN THE AFRO-AMERICAN
EXPERIENCE. 2 VOLS. NEW YORK: HARCOURT BRACE
JOVANOVICH, 1971, VOL 2, PP. 26-41.

16077 AGRESTI, BARBARA F. "THE FIRST DECADES OF FREEDOM:
BLACK FAMILIES IN A SOUTHERN COUNTY, 1870 AND 1885."
JOURNAL OF MARRIAGE AND THE FAMILY, 40 (NOVEMBER,
1978): 697-706.

16078 ALLEN, WALTER R. "BLACK FAMILY RESEARCH IN THE UNITED
STATES: A REVIEW, ASSESSMENT AND EXTENSION." JOURNAL
OF COMPARATIVE FAMILY STUDIES, 9 (SUMMER, 1978):
167-190.

16079 ALLEN, WALTER R. "THE SEARCH FOR APPLICABLE THEORIES OF
BLACK FAMILY LIFE." JOURNAL OF MARRIAGE AND THE
FAMILY, 40 (FEBRUARY, 1978): 117-129.

16080 ANDERSON, JAMES D. "BLACK CONJUGATIONS." AMERICAN
SCHOLAR, 46 (SUMMER, 1977) 384-386, 388, 390, 392-393.

16081 ANDERSON, SOLENA. "BACK IN 'DEM DAYS: A BLACK FAMILY
REMINISCES." JOURNAL OF MISSISSIPPI HISTORY, 36 (MAY,
1974): 179-186.

16082 ANTWI, SHIRLEY. "A METHOD OF TRACING THE LINEAGE OF AN
AFRICAN-AMERICAN: A STUDY OF THE VERTICAL LINEAGE OF
A U.S. BLACK." M.A. THESIS, NORTHEASTERN ILLINOIS
UNIVERSITY, 1976.

16083 ASCHENBRENNER, JOYCE. "HUMANISM IN BLACK CULTURE." IN
HENRY, FRANCES (ED.). ETHNICITY IN THE AMERICAS. THE
HAGUE: MOUTON PUBLISHERS, 1976, PP. 333-346.

16084 ASHMORE, HARRY S. THE OTHER SIDE OF JORDAN. NEW YORK:
W.W. NORTON, 1960.

16085 ATKINSON, EDWARD. "'THE NEGRO A BEAST.'" NORTH AMERICAN
REVIEW, 181 (AUGUST, 1905): 202-215.

16086 BABCHUK, NICHOLAS AND BALLWEG, JOHN A. "BLACK FAMILY
STRUCTURE AND PRIMARY RELATIONS." PHYLON, 33 (WINTER,
1972): 334-347.

16087 BANKS, FRANK D. "PLANTATION COURTSHIP." JOURNAL OF
AMERICAN FOLK-LORE, 7 (APRIL-JUNE, 1894): 147-149.

16088 BARNETT, EVELYN B. "THE CHANGING FAMILY PORTRAIT."
       RADICAL HISTORY REVIEW, 4 (SPRING-SUMMER, 1977):
       76-108.

16089 BARR, ALWYN. "BLACK MIGRATION INTO SOUTHWESTERN CITIES,
       1865-1900." IN GALLAGHER, GARY W. (ED.). ESSAYS ON
       SOUTHERN HISTORY WRITTEN IN HONOR OF BARNES F.
       LATHROP. AUSTIN: GENERAL LIBRARIES, UNIVERSITY OF
       TEXAS, 1980, PP. 15-38.

16090 BARRINGER, PAUL B. "THE INFLUENCE OF PECULIAR CONDITIONS
       IN THE EARLY HISTORY OF NORTH CAROLINA." IN
       PROCEEDINGS OF THE EIGHTEENTH ANNUAL SESSION OF THE
       STATE LITERARY AND HISTORICAL ASSOCIATION OF NORTH
       CAROLINA, RALEIGH, NOVEMBER 20-21, 1917. RALEIGH:
       EDWARDS & BROUGHTON COMPANY, 1918.

16091 BEERS, H. DWIGHT. "AFRICAN NAMES AND NAMING PRACTICES:
       A SELECTED LIST OF REFERENCES IN ENGLISH." LIBRARY OF
       CONGRESS INFORMATION BULLETIN, 36 (MARCH 25, 1977):
       206-207.

16092 BENNETT, CLIFFORD T. "BLACK ROOTS: USING GENEALOGY IN
       THE CLASSROOM." SOCIAL STUDIES, 71 (MARCH-APRIL,
       1980): 68-69.

16093 BERLIN, IRA. "HISTORIANS AND BLACK FAMILIES." NATION,
       226 (MARCH 18, 1978): 311-313.

16094 BERNARD, JESSIE. MARRIAGE AND FAMILY AMONG NEGROES.
       ENGLEWOOD CLIFFS: PRENTICE-HALL, 1966.

16095 BILLINGSLEY, ANDREW. BLACK FAMILIES IN WHITE AMERICA.
       ENGLEWOOD CLIFFS: PRENTICE-HALL, 1968.

16096 BILLINGSLEY, ANDREW. "NONE SHALL PART US FROM EACH
       OTHER: REFLECTION ON BLACK FAMILY LIFE DURING SLAVERY
       AND BEYOND." PROCEEDINGS OF THE FIFTH ANNUAL
       CONFERENCE OF THE NATIONAL ASSOCIATION OF BLACK SOCIAL
       WORKERS, HELD APRIL 18-21, 1973, NEW YORK CITY.
       DETROIT: MULT-TECH, 1974, PP. 78-88.

16097 BILLINGSLEY, ANDREW AND BILLINGSLEY, AMY T. "NEGRO
       FAMILY LIFE IN AMERICA." SOCIAL SERVICE REVIEW, 39
       (SEPTEMBER, 1965): 310-319.

16098 BILLINGSLEY, ANDREW AND GREENE, MARTHA C. "FAMILY LIFE
       AMONG THE FREE BLACK POPULATION IN THE EIGHTEENTH
       CENTURY." JOURNAL OF SOCIAL AND BEHAVIORAL SCIENCES,
       20 (SPRING, 1974): 1-18.

16099 BIMS, HAMILTON. "THE BLACK FAMILY: A PROUD
       REAPPRAISAL." EBONY, 29 (MARCH, 1974): 118-127.

16100 "BLACK FAMILIES: SURVIVING SLAVERY." TIME, 108

(NOVEMBER 22, 1976): 48.

16101 BLACK, FREDERICK R. "BIBLIOGRAPHICAL ESSAY: BENJAMIN
       DREW'S REFUGEE AND THE BLACK FAMILY." JOURNAL OF
       NEGRO HISTORY, 57 (JULY, 1972): 284-289.

16102 BLACKBURN, REGINA L. "CONSCIOUS AGENTS OF TIME AND SELF:
       THE LIVES AND STYLES OF AFRICAN-AMERICAN WOMEN AS SEEN
       THROUGH THEIR AUTOBIOGRAPHICAL WRITINGS." PH.D.
       DISSERTATION, UNIVERSITY OF NEW MEXICO, 1978.

16103 BLACKWELL, JAMES E. THE BLACK COMMUNITY: DIVERSITY AND
       UNITY. NEW YORK: DODD, MEAD AND COMPANY, 1975.

16104 BLASSINGAME, JOHN W. BLACK NEW ORLEANS, 1860-1880.
       CHICAGO: UNIVERSITY OF CHICAGO PRESS, 1973.

16105 BLASSINGAME, JOHN W. THE SLAVE COMMUNITY: PLANTATION
       LIFE IN THE ANTEBELLUM SOUTH. NEW YORK: OXFORD
       UNIVERSITY PRESS, 1972.

16106 BLASSINGAME, JOHN W. "THE SLAVE FAMILY IN AMERICA."
       AMERICAN HISTORY ILLUSTRATED, 7 (OCTOBER, 1972):
       11-17.

16107 BLASSINGAME, JOHN W. "SOUTHERN WHITE CHURCHES AND THE
       EVOLUTION OF THE SLAVE FAMILY." PAPER PRESENTED AT
       UNIVERSITY OF MISSOURI-ST. LOUIS CONFERENCE ON THE
       FIRST AND SECOND RECONSTRUCTIONS, FEBRUARY 15-17, 1978.

16108 BLASSINGAME, JOHN W. "STATUS AND SOCIAL STRUCTURE IN THE
       SLAVE COMMUNITY: EVIDENCE FROM NEW SOURCES." IN
       OWENS, HARRY P. (ED.). PERSPECTIVES AND IRONY IN
       AMERICAN SLAVERY. JACKSON: UNIVERSITY PRESS OF
       MISSISSIPPI, 1976, PP. 137-152.

16109 BROUWER, MERLE G. "MARRIAGE AND FAMILY LIFE AMONG BLACKS
       IN COLONIAL PENNSYLVANIA." PENNSYLVANIA MAGAZINE OF
       HISTORY AND BIOGRAPHY, 99 (JULY, 1975): 368-372.

16110 BROWN, BARBARA W. BLACK ROOTS IN SOUTHEASTERN
       CONNECTICUT, 1650-1900. DETROIT: GALE RESEARCH, 1980.

16111 BROWN, JAMES A. "SLAVE KINSHIP STRUCTURE." M.A. THESIS,
       UNIVERSITY OF CHICAGO, 1958.

16112 BRYCE-LAPORTE, ROY S. "THE AMERICAN SLAVE PLANTATION AND
       OUR HERITAGE OF COMMUNAL DEPRIVATION." AMERICAN
       BEHAVIORAL SCIENTIST, 12 (MARCH-APRIL, 1969): 2-8.

16113 BURGESS, ERNEST W. AND LOCKE, HARVEY J. THE FAMILY:
       FROM INSTITUTION TO COMPANIONSHIP. NEW YORK:
       AMERICAN BOOK COMPANY, 1950.

16114 BURNHAM, DOROTHY. "CHILDREN OF THE SLAVE COMMUNITY IN

THE UNITED STATES." FREEDOMWAYS, 19 (1979): 75-81.

16115 CALHOUN, ARTHUR W. A SOCIAL HISTORY OF THE AMERICAN
FAMILY FROM COLONIAL TIMES TO THE PRESENT. 3 VOLS.
CLEVELAND: A.H. CLARK, 1917-1919.

16116 CAMPBELL, DOROTHY W. "BLACK GENEALOGY AND THE PUBLIC
LIBRARY: A BIBLIOGRAPHY." PUBLIC LIBRARIES, 19
(SPRING, 1980): 22-24.

16117 CANSLER, CHARLES W. THREE GENERATIONS: THE STORY OF A
COLORED FAMILY OF EASTERN TENNESSEE. KINGSPORT, TN:
KINGSPORT PRESS, 1939.

16118 CARTER, DORIS D. "REFUSING TO RELINQUISH THE STRUGGLES:
THE SOCIAL ROLE OF THE BLACK WOMAN IN LOUISIANA
HISTORY." IN MACDONALD, ROBERT R.; KEMP, JOHN R.; AND
HAAS, EDWARD F. (EDS.). LOUISIANA'S BLACK HERITAGE.
NEW ORLEANS: LOUISIANA STATE MUSEUM, 1979, PP.
163-189.

16119 CASSITY, MICHAEL J. "SLAVES, FAMILIES, AND 'LIVING
SPACE': A NOTE ON EVIDENCE AND HISTORICAL CONTEXT."
SOUTHERN STUDIES, 17 (SUMMER, 1978): 209-215.

16120 CLARKE, EDITH. MY MOTHER WHO FATHERED ME: A STUDY OF
THE FAMILY IN THREE SELECTED COMMUNITIES IN JAMAICA.
LONDON: GEORGE ALLEN AND UNWIN, 1957.

16121 CLARKE, JOHN H. "THE BLACK FAMILY IN HISTORICAL
PERSPECTIVE." JOURNAL OF AFRO-AMERICAN ISSUES, 3
(SUMMER/FALL, 1975): 336-342.

16122 COBBS, H.A. GRIER AND PRICE, M. BLACK RAGE. NEW YORK:
BASIC BOOKS, 1968.

16123 COUSINS, WINIFRED M. "SLAVE FAMILY LIFE IN THE BRITISH
COLONIES, 1800-1834." SOCIOLOGICAL REVIEW, 27
(JANUARY, 1935): 35-55.

16124 CRATON, MICHAEL J. "CHANGING PATTERNS OF SLAVE FAMILIES
IN THE BRITISH WEST INDIES." JOURNAL OF
INTERDISCIPLINARY HISTORY, 10 (SUMMER, 1979): 1-35.

16125 CROSS, WILLIAM E., JR. "BLACK FAMILY AND BLACK IDENTITY:
A LITERATURE REVIEW." WESTERN JOURNAL OF BLACK
STUDIES, 2 (SUMMER, 1978): 111-124.

16126 DAVIS, ALLISON. CHILDREN OF BONDAGE: THE PERSONALITY
DEVELOPMENT OF NEGRO YOUTH IN THE URBAN SOUTH.
WASHINGTON: AMERICAN COUNCIL ON EDUCATION, 1940.

16127 DAVIS, LENWOOD G. THE BLACK AGED IN THE UNITED STATES:
AN ANNOTATED BIBILIOGRAPHY. WESTPORT: GREENWOOD
PRESS, 1980.

16128   DAVIS, LENWOOD G.   THE BLACK FAMILY IN THE UNITED STATES:
        A SELECTED BIBLIOGRAPHY OF ANNOTATED BOOKS, ARTICLES,
        AND DISSERTATIONS ON BLACK FAMILIES IN AMERICA.
        WESTPORT: GREENWOOD PRESS, 1978.

16129   DAVIS, OLIVIA N.   "SLAVE CHILDREN ON THE SOUTHERN
        PLANTATION." M.A. THESIS, SOUTHERN METHODIST
        UNIVERSITY, 1934.

16130   DRAKE, W.M. (ED.).   "THE ROAD TO FREEDOM." JOURNAL OF
        MISSISSIPPI HISTORY, 3 (JANUARY, 1941):   44-45.

16131   DRONAMRAJU, KRISHNA R.; SHOWELL, FRANKLIN C.; AND
        HATHAWAY, PHYLLIS S.   "GENEALOGICA MARYLANDIA:
        GENEALOGICAL STUDIES OF BLACK FAMILIES." MARYLAND
        HISTORICAL MAGAZINE, 71 (SPRING, 1976):   103-104.

16132   DUBOIS, W.E.B.   ECONOMIC CO-OPERATION AMONG NEGRO
        AMERICANS.   ATLANTA: ATLANTA UNIVERSITY PRESS, 1907.

16133   DUBOIS, W.E.B.   "MARRYING OF BLACK FOLK." INDEPENDENT,
        69 (OCTOBER 13, 1910):   812-813.

16134   DUBOIS, W.E.B. (ED.).   THE NEGRO AMERICAN FAMILY.
        ATLANTA: ATLANTA UNIVERSITY PUBLICATIONS, 1908.

16135   DUBOIS, W.E.B.   "THE NEGROES OF FARMVILLE, VIRGINIA: A
        SOCIAL STUDY." BULLETIN OF THE DEPARTMENT OF LABOR, 3
        (JANUARY, 1898):   1-38.

16136   DUBOIS, W.E.B.   THE PHILADELPHIA NEGRO: A SOCIAL STUDY.
        PHILADELPHIA: UNIVERSITY OF PENNSYLVANIA PRESS, 1899.

16137   DUBOIS, W.E.B.   "THE SOCIAL EVOLUTION OF THE BLACK
        SOUTH." AMERICAN NEGRO MONOGRAPHS, 1 (MARCH, 1911):
        1-9.

16138   DUBOIS, W.E.B.   "THE TRAINING OF NEGROES FOR SOCIAL
        POWER." OUTLOOK, 75 (OCTOBER 17, 1903):   409-414.

16139   DUBOIS, W.E.B. AND DILL, AUGUSTUS G. (EDS.).   MORALS AND
        MANNERS AMONG NEGRO AMERICANS.   ATLANTA: ATLANTA
        UNIVERSITY PUBLICATIONS, 1914.

16140   DUKE, CATHY.   "THE FAMILY IN EIGHTEENTH-CENTURY
        PLANTATION SOCIETY IN MEXICO." IN RUBIN, VERA AND
        TUDEN, ARTHUR (EDS.).   COMPARATIVE PERSPECTIVES ON
        SLAVERY IN NEW WORLD PLANTATION SOCIETIES.   NEW YORK:
        NEW YORK ACADEMY OF SCIENCES, 1977, PP. 226-241.

16141   EBLEN, JACK E.   "GROWTH OF THE BLACK POPULATION IN ANTE
        BELLUM AMERICA, 1820-1860." POPULATION STUDIES, 26
        (JULY, 1972):   273-289.

16142   ENGERMAN, STANLEY L.   "BLACK FERTILITY AND FAMILY

STRUCTURE IN THE UNITED STATES, 1880-1940." JOURNAL
OF FAMILY HISTORY, 2 (SUMMER, 1977): 117-138.

16143   ENGERMAN, STANLEY L. "COMMENTARY." HISTORICAL
REFLECTIONS, 6 (SUMMER, 1979): 204-211.

16144   ENGERMAN, STANLEY L. "STUDYING THE BLACK FAMILY: A
REVIEW OF THE BLACK FAMILY IN SLAVERY AND FREEDOM,
1750-1925." JOURNAL OF FAMILY HISTORY, 3 (SPRING,
1978): 78-101.

16145   EPPES, MRS. NICHOLAS W. THE NEGRO OF THE OLD SOUTH, A
BIT OF PERIOD HISTORY. CHICAGO: JOSEPH G. BRANCH,
1925.

16146   ESHLERMAN, J. ROSS. THE FAMILY: AN INTRODUCTION.
BOSTON: ALLYN AND BACON, 1974.

16147   FAUST, DREW G. "CULTURE, CONFLICT AND COMMUNITY: THE
MEANING OF POWER ON AN ANTE-BELLUM PLANTATION."
JOURNAL OF SOCIAL HISTORY, 14 (FALL, 1980): 83-98.

16148   FINK, LEON. "SYMPOSIUM ON HERBERT GUTMAN'S 'THE BLACK
FAMILY IN SLAVERY AND FREEDOM.'" RADICAL HISTORY
REVIEW, 4 (SPRING-SUMMER, 1977): 76-78.

16149   FLORY, MARLEEN B. "FAMILY AND 'FAMILIA': A STUDY OF
SOCIAL RELATIONS IN SLAVERY." PH.D. DISSERTATION,
YALE UNIVERSITY, 1975.

16150   FOGEL, ROBERT W. AND ENGERMAN, STANLEY L. "RECENT
FINDINGS IN THE STUDY OF SLAVE DEMOGRAPHY AND FAMILY
STRUCTURE." SOCIOLOGY AND SOCIAL RESEARCH, 63 (APRIL,
1979): 566-589.

16151   FORTUNE, T. THOMAS. "MOVEMENT OF THE AFRO-AMERICAN
POPULATION FROM THE SOUTHERN STATES." A.M.E. CHURCH
REVIEW, 33 (JANUARY, 1917): 127-129.

16152   FRAZIER, E. FRANKLIN. "THE CHANGING STATUS OF THE NEGRO
FAMILY." SOCIAL FORCES, 9 (MARCH, 1931): 386-393.

16153   FRAZIER, E. FRANKLIN. THE FREE NEGRO FAMILY: A STUDY OF
FAMILY ORIGINS BEFORE THE CIVIL WAR. NASHVILLE: FISK
UNIVERSITY PRESS, 1932.

16154   FRAZIER, E. FRANKLIN. "THE NEGRO FAMILY IN AMERICA." IN
ANSHEN, RUTH N. (ED.). THE FAMILY: ITS FUNCTION AND
DESTINY. NEW YORK: HARPER & BROTHERS, 1948, PP.
142-158.

16155   FRAZIER, E. FRANKLIN. THE NEGRO FAMILY IN THE UNITED
STATES. CHICAGO: UNIVERSITY OF CHICAGO PRESS, 1939.

16156   FRAZIER, E. FRANKLIN. "NEGRO FAMILY LIFE IN BAHIA,

BRAZIL: INFLUENCE OF AFRICAN CULTURE PATTERNS."
AMERICAN SOCIOLOGICAL REVIEW, 7 (AUGUST, 1942):
465-478.

16157   FRAZIER, E. FRANKLIN. "THE NEGRO SLAVE FAMILY." JOURNAL
        OF NEGRO HISTORY, 15 (APRIL, 1930): 198-259.

16158   FRAZIER, E. FRANKLIN. "TRADITIONS AND PATTERNS IN NEGRO
        FAMILY LIFE IN THE UNITED STATES." IN REUTER, EDWARD
        B. (ED.). RACE AND CULTURE CONTACTS. NEW YORK:
        MCGRAW-HILL, 1934, PP. 191-207.

16159   FREDRICKSON, GEORGE M. "THE GUTMAN REPORT." NEW YORK
        REVIEW OF BOOKS, 23 (SEPTEMBER 30, 1976): 18-23.

16160   FREILICH, MORRIS. "SERIAL POLYGYNY, NEGRO PEASANTS, AND
        MODERN ANALYSIS." AMERICAN ANTHROPOLOGIST, 63
        (OCTOBER, 1961): 955-975.

16161   GANS, HERBERT J. "THE NEGRO FAMILY: REFLECTIONS ON THE
        MOYNIHAN REPORT." COMMONWEAL, 33 (OCTOBER 15, 1965):
        47-51.

16162   GARRETT, SUE G. "NEGRO MATING AND FAMILY PATTERNS FROM
        WEST AFRICA TO THE NEW WORLD." M.A. THESIS,
        UNIVERSITY OF NORTH CAROLINA, 1965.

16163   GENOVESE, EUGENE D. "THE SLAVE FAMILY, WOMEN--A
        REASSESSMENT OF MATRIARCHY, EMASCULATION, WEAKNESS."
        SOUTHERN VOICES, 1 (AUGUST-SEPTEMBER, 1974): 9-16.

16164   GIBSON, WILLIAM. FAMILY LIFE AND MORALITY: STUDIES IN
        BLACK AND WHITE. WASHINGTON: UNIVERSITY PRESS OF
        AMERICA, 1980.

16165   GLAZER, NATHAN. "THE NEGRO FAMILY IN THE UNITED STATES."
        MIDWAY, NO. 26 (SPRING, 1966): 56-73.

16166   GONZALEZ, NANCIE L. BLACK CARIB HOUSEHOLD STRUCTURE.
        SEATTLE: UNIVERSITY OF WASHINGTON PRESS, 1969.

16167   GORDON, MICHAEL (ED.). THE AMERICAN FAMILY IN
        SOCIAL-HISTORICAL PERSPECTIVE. NEW YORK: ST.
        MARTIN'S PRESS, 1973.

16168   GRAHAM, RICHARD D. "SLAVE FAMILIES ON A RURAL ESTATE IN
        COLONIAL BRAZIL." JOURNAL OF SOCIAL HISTORY, 9
        (SPRING, 1976): 382-402.

16169   GREEN, MITCHELL A. "IMPACT OF SLAVERY ON THE BLACK
        FAMILY: SOCIAL, POLITICAL, AND ECONOMIC." JOURNAL OF
        AFRO-AMERICAN ISSUES, 3 (SUMMER, FALL, 1975): 343-356.

16170   GREGORY, CHESTER W. "BLACK WOMEN IN PRE-FEDERAL
        AMERICA." IN DEUTRICH, MABEL E. AND PURDY, VIRGINIA

C. (EDS.). CLIO WAS A WOMAN: STUDIES IN THE HISTORY OF AMERICAN WOMEN. WASHINGTON: HOWARD UNIVERSITY PRESS, 1980, PP. 53-72.

16171   GRENZ, SUZANNA M. "THE BLACK COMMUNITY IN BOONE COUNTY, MISSOURI, 1850-1900." PH.D. DISSERTATION, UNIVERSITY OF MISSOURI, 1979.

16172   GUTMAN, HERBERT. "THE INVISIBLE FACT: NEGRO FAMILY STRUCTURE BEFORE AND AFTER THE CIVIL WAR." PAPER PRESENTED AT MEETING OF ASSOCIATION FOR THE STUDY OF NEGRO LIFE AND HISTORY, BIRMINGHAM, OCTOBER, 1969.

16173   GUTMAN, HERBERT G. THE BLACK FAMILY IN SLAVERY AND FREEDOM, 1750-1925. NEW YORK: PANTHEON BOOKS, 1976.

16174   GUTMAN, HERBERT G. "THE BLACK FAMILY RECONSIDERED." CURRENT, 188 (DECEMBER, 1976): 3-9.

16175   GUTMAN, HERBERT G. "FAMILY AND KINSHIP GROUPINGS AMONG THE ENSLAVED AFRO-AMERICANS ON THE SOUTH CAROLINA GOOD HOPE PLANTATION: 1760-1860." IN RUBIN, VERA AND TUDEN, ARTHUR (EDS.). COMPARATIVE PERSPECTIVES ON SLAVERY IN NEW WORLD PLANTATION SOCIETIES. NEW YORK: NEW YORK ACADEMY OF SCIENCES, 1977, PP. 242-258.

16176   GUTMAN, HERBERT G. "THE MOYNIHAN REPORT: BLACK HISTORY SEDUCED AND ABANDONED." NATION, 229 (SEPTEMBER 22, 1979): 232-236.

16177   GUTMAN, HERBERT G. "PERSISTENT MYTHS ABOUT THE AFRO-AMERICAN FAMILY." IN GORDON, MICHAEL (ED.). THE AFRO-AMERICAN FAMILY IN SOCIAL-HISTORICAL PERSPECTIVE. NEW YORK: ST. MARTIN'S PRESS, 1978, PP. 467-489.

16178   GUTMAN, HERBERT G. "PERSISTENT MYTHS ABOUT THE AFRO-AMERICAN FAMILY." JOURNAL OF INTERDISCIPLINARY HISTORY, 6 (AUTUMN, 1975): 181-210.

16179   GUTMAN, HERBERT G. "SLAVE CULTURE AND SLAVE FAMILY AND KIN NETWORK: THE IMPORTANCE OF TIME." IN CENSER, JACK R.; STEINERT, N. STEVEN; MCCANDLESS, AMY M. (EDS.). SOUTH ATLANTIC URBAN STUDIES, VOLUME 2. COLUMBIA: UNIVERSITY OF SOUTH CAROLINA PRESS, 1978, PP. 73-88.

16180   GUTMAN, HERBERT G. "SLAVE FAMILY AND ITS LEGACIES." HISTORICAL REFLECTIONS, 6 (SUMMER, 1979): 183-199.

16181   GUTMAN, HERBERT AND SUTCH, RICHARD. "THE SLAVE FAMILY: PROTECTED AGENT OF CAPITALIST MASTERS OR VICTIM OF THE SLAVE TRADE?" IN DAVID, PAUL A.; GUTMAN; SUTCH; TEMIN, PETER; AND WRIGHT, GAVIN (EDS.). RECKONING WITH SLAVERY: A CRITICAL STUDY IN THE QUANTITATIVE HISTORY OF AMERICAN NEGRO SLAVERY. NEW YORK: OXFORD

UNIVERSITY PRESS, 1976, PP. 94-133.

16182   GUTMAN, HERBERT AND SUTCH, RICHARD. "VICTORIANS ALL?
        THE SEXUAL MORES AND CONDUCT OF SLAVES AND THEIR
        MASTERS." IN DAVID, PAUL A.; GUTMAN; SUTCH; TEMIN,
        PETER; AND WRIGHT, GAVIN (EDS.). RECKONING WITH
        SLAVERY: A CRITICAL STUDY IN THE QUANTITATIVE HISTORY
        OF AMERICAN NEGRO SLAVERY. NEW YORK: OXFORD
        UNIVERSITY PRESS, 1976, PP. 135-164.

16183   HALEY, ALEX. "SEARCH FOR AN ANCESTOR." LISTENER, 91
        (JANUARY 10, 1974): 43-46.

16184   HALEY, ALEX. "SEARCH FOR AN ANCESTOR." NEW COMMUNITY, 3
        (AUTUMN, 1974): 321-326.

16185   HALEY, ALEX. "SEARCH FOR AN ANCESTOR." SCOTTISH
        GENEALOGIST, 22 (JUNE, SEPTEMBER, 1975): 55-56, 57-62.

16186   HARRIS, WILLIAM G. "RESEARCH ON THE BLACK FAMILY:
        MAINSTREAM AND DISSENTING PERSPECTIVES." JOURNAL OF
        ETHNIC STUDIES, 6 (WINTER, 1979): 45-64.

16187   HARRISON, IRA E. AND HARRISON, DIANA S. "THE BLACK
        FAMILY EXPERIENCE AND HEALTH BEHAVIOR." IN CRAWFORD,
        CHARLES O. (ED.). HEALTH AND THE FAMILY: A
        MEDICAL-SOCIOLOGICAL ANALYSIS. NEW YORK: MACMILLAN
        COMPANY, 1971, PP. 175-199.

16188   HENDRICK, ROBERT M. "THE STATUS AND TREATMENT OF
        CHILDREN DURING SLAVERY, 1830-1860." M.A. THESIS,
        HOWARD UNIVERSITY, 1940.

16189   HENRIQUES, FERNANDO. CHILDREN OF CONFLICT: A STUDY OF
        INTERRACIAL SEX AND MARRIAGE. NEW YORK: DUTTON, 1975.

16190   HENRIQUES, FERNANDO. FAMILY AND COLOUR IN JAMAICA.
        LONDON: EYRE & SPOTTISWOODE, 1953.

16191   HENRIQUES, FERNANDO. "WEST INDIAN FAMILY ORGANIZATION."
        AMERICAN JOURNAL OF SOCIOLOGY, 55 (JULY, 1949): 30-37.

16192   HERSHBERG, THEODORE. "TIME ON THE CROSS AND BLACK FAMILY
        HISTORY." UNPUBLISHED PAPER PRESENTED AT
        MSSB--UNIVERSITY OF ROCHESTER CONFERENCE: "TIME ON
        THE CROSS: A FIRST APPRAISAL," OCTOBER 24-26, 1974.

16193   HERSKOVITS, MELVILLE J. AND HERSKOVITS, FRANCES S.
        TRINIDAD VILLAGE. NEW YORK: ALFRED A. KNOPF, 1947.

16194   HEWETSON, W.T. "THE SOCIAL LIFE OF THE SOUTHERN NEGRO."
        CHAUTAUQUAN, 26 (DECEMBER, 1897): 295-304.

16195   HIGMAN, B.W. "AFRICAN AND CREOLE SLAVE FAMILY PATTERNS
        IN TRINIDAD." JOURNAL OF FAMILY HISTORY, 3 (SUMMER,

1978):   163-180.

16196   HIGMAN, B.W.   "METHODOLOGICAL PROBLEMS IN THE STUDY OF
        THE SLAVE FAMILY."   IN RUBIN, VERA AND TUDEN, ARTHUR
        (EDS.).   COMPARATIVE PERSPECTIVES ON SLAVERY IN NEW
        WORLD PLANTATION SOCIETIES.   NEW YORK: NEW YORK
        ACADEMY OF SCIENCES, 1977, PP. 591-596.

16197   HIGMAN, BARRY W.   "AFRICAN AND CREOLE SLAVE FAMILY
        PATTERNS IN TRINIDAD."   IN CRAHAN, MARGARET AND
        KNIGHT, FRANKLIN W. (EDS.).   AFRICA AND THE CARIBBEAN:
        THE LEGACIES OF A LINK.   BALTIMORE: JOHNS HOPKINS
        UNIVERSITY PRESS, 1979, PP. 41-64.

16198   HIGMAN, BARRY W.   "HOUSEHOLD STRUCTURE AND FERTILITY ON
        JAMAICAN SLAVE PLANTATIONS: A NINETEENTH-CENTURY
        EXAMPLE."   POPULATION STUDIES: A JOURNAL OF
        DEMOGRAPHY, 27 (NOVEMBER, 1973):   527-550.

16199   HIGMAN, BARRY W.   "THE SLAVE FAMILY AND HOUSEHOLD IN THE
        BRITISH WEST INDIES, 1800-1834."   JOURNAL OF
        INTERDISCIPLINARY HISTORY, 6 (AUTUMN, 1975):   261-287.

16200   JACKSON, JACQUELYNE J.   "BLACK WOMEN IN A RACIST
        SOCIETY."   IN WILLIE, CHARLES V.; KRAMER, BERNARD M.;
        AND BROWN, BERTRAM S. (EDS.).   RACISM AND MENTAL
        HEALTH: ESSAYS.   PITTSBURGH: UNIVERSITY OF
        PITTSBURGH PRESS, 1973, PP. 185-268.

16201   JACOBS, HARRIET.   "THE GOOD GRANDMOTHER."   IN CHILD, L.
        MARIA (ED.).   THE FREEDMEN'S BOOK.   BOSTON: TICKNOR
        AND FIELDS, 1865, PP. 206-218.

16202   JOHNSON, KENNETH R.   "A SLAVE FAMILY'S STRUGGLE FOR
        FREEDOM."   JOURNAL OF MUSCLE SHOALS HISTORY, 6 (1978):
        10-17.

16203   JONES, BOBBY F.   "A CULTURAL MIDDLE PASSAGE: SLAVE
        MARRIAGE AND FAMILY IN THE ANTE-BELLUM SOUTH."   PH.D.
        DISSERTATION, UNIVERSITY OF NORTH CAROLINA, 1965.

16204   JONES, FAUSTINE C.   "THE LOFTY ROLE OF THE BLACK
        GRANDMOTHER."   CRISIS, 80 (JANUARY, 1973):   19-21.

16205   KETT, JOSEPH F.   "THE BLACK FAMILY UNDER SLAVERY."
        HISTORY OF EDUCATION QUARTERLY, 17 (WINTER, 1977):
        455-460.

16206   KING, JAMES R.   "AFRICAN SURVIVALS IN THE BLACK AMERICAN
        FAMILY: KEY FACTORS IN STABILITY."   JOURNAL OF
        AFRO-AMERICAN ISSUES, 4 (SPRING, 1976):   153-167.

16207   KIRK, JAMES.   "WHEN LOVE CONQUERED SLAVERY."   NEGRO
        DIGEST, 6 (JULY, 1948):   34-35.

16208   KULIKOFF, ALLAN. "THE BEGINNINGS OF THE AFRO-AMERICAN
        FAMILY IN MARYLAND." IN GORDON, MICHAEL (ED.). THE
        AMERICAN FAMILY IN SOCIAL-HISTORICAL PERSPECTIVE. NEW
        YORK: ST. MARTIN'S PRESS, 1978, PP. 444-466.

16209   KULIKOFF, ALLAN. "THE BEGINNINGS OF THE AFRO-AMERICAN
        FAMILY IN MARYLAND." IN LAND, AUBREY C.; CARR, LOIS
        G.; AND PAPENFUSE, EDWARD C. (EDS.). LAW, SOCIETY,
        AND POLITICS IN EARLY MARYLAND. BALTIMORE: JOHNS
        HOPKINS UNIVERSITY PRESS, 1977, PP. 171-196.

16210   KUYK, BETTY M. "SEEKING FAMILY RELATIONSHIPS." NEGRO
        HISTORY BULLETIN, 42 (JULY, 1979): 60.

16211   LABINJOH, JUSTIN. "THE SEXUAL LIFE OF THE OPPRESSED: AN
        EXAMINATION OF THE FAMILY LIFE OF ANTE-BELLUM SLAVES."
        PHYLON, 35 (WINTER, 1974): 375-397.

16212   LAMMERMEIER, PAUL J. "THE URBAN BLACK FAMILY OF THE
        NINETEENTH CENTURY: A STUDY OF BLACK FAMILY STRUCTURE
        IN THE OHIO VALLEY, 1850-1880." JOURNAL OF MARRIAGE
        AND THE FAMILY, 35 (AUGUST, 1973): 440-456.

16213   LANDES, RUTH. "NEGRO SLAVERY AND FEMALE STATUS."
        AFRICAN AFFAIRS, 52 (JANUARY, 1953): 54-57.

16214   LANDES, RUTH. "NEGRO SLAVERY AND FEMALE STATUS." IN LES
        AFRO-AMERICAINS. DAKAR: INSTITUT FRANCAIS D'AFRIQUE
        NOIR, 1953, PP. 265-268.

16215   LANTZ, HERMAN AND HENDRIX, LEWELLYN. "BLACK FERTILITY
        AND THE BLACK FAMILY IN THE NINETEENTH CENTURY: A
        RE-EXAMINATION OF THE PAST." JOURNAL OF FAMILY
        HISTORY, 3 (FALL, 1978): 251-261.

16216   LANTZ, HERMAN R. "FAMILY AND KIN AS REVEALED IN THE
        NARRATIVES OF EX-SLAVES." SOCIAL SCIENCE QUARTERLY,
        60 (MARCH, 1980): 667-675.

16217   LASLETT, PETER. "FOGEL AND ENGERMAN ON FAMILY AND
        HOUSEHOLD IN THE SLAVE PLANTATIONS OF THE U.S.A."
        UNPUBLISHED PAPER PRESENTED AT MSSB--UNIVERSITY OF
        ROCHESTER CONFERENCE: "TIME ON THE CROSS: A FIRST
        APPRAISAL," OCTOBER 24-26, 1974.

16218   LASLETT, PETER. "HOUSEHOLD AND FAMILY ON THE SLAVE
        PLANTATIONS OF THE U.S.A." FAMILY LIFE AND ILLICIT
        LOVE IN EARLIER GENERATIONS: ESSAYS IN HISTORICAL
        SOCIOLOGY. CAMBRIDGE: CAMBRIDGE UNIVERSITY PRESS,
        1977, PP. 233-260.

16219   LEWIS, RONALD L. "SLAVE FAMILIES AT EARLY CHESAPEAKE
        IRONWORKS." VIRGINIA MAGAZINE OF HISTORY AND
        BIOGRAPHY, 86 (APRIL, 1978): 169-179.

16220   LEWIS, ROSCOE. "THE LIFE OF PRISCILLA JOYNER." _PHYLON_,
        20 (SPRING, 1959): 71-31.

16221   "LINEAGE OF GEORGE WASHINGTON'S SLAVES TRACED, THANKS TO
        ROOTS." _JET_, 51 (MARCH 17, 1977): 32-33.

16222   MACDONALD, JOHN S. AND MACDONALD, LEATRICE D.
        "TRANSFORMATION OF AFRICAN AND INDIAN FAMILY
        TRADITIONS IN THE SOUTHERN CARIBBEAN." _COMPARATIVE
        STUDIES IN SOCIETY AND HISTORY_, 15 (MARCH, 1973):
        171-198.

16223   MACK, DELORES. "WHERE THE BLACK MATRIARCHY THEORISTS
        WENT WRONG." _PSYCHOLOGY TODAY_, 4 (JANUARY, 1971):   24.

16224   MALINO, SARAH. "CHILD REARING IN SLAVERY." M.A. THESIS,
        COLUMBIA UNIVERSITY, 1974.

16225   "MANAGEMENT OF NEGROES UPON SOUTHERN ESTATES--AN ECHO OF
        SLAVE DAYS IN THE SOUTHLAND." _TENNESSEE HISTORICAL
        MAGAZINE_, 5 (JULY, 1919): 97-103.

16226   MARTIN, ELMER P. AND MARTIN, JOANNEY M. _THE BLACK
        EXTENDED FAMILY_. CHICAGO: UNIVERSITY OF CHICAGO
        PRESS, 1978.

16227   MARTIN, JOHN E. "APPROACHES TO THE REALITY OF THE SLAVE
        FAMILY IN _UNCLE TOM'S CABIN_ AND THE WORK OF EUGENE
        GENOVESE." _ANGLO-AMERICAN FORUM_, 12 (1980): 191-208.

16228   MARTINSON, FLOYD M. _FAMILY IN SOCIETY_. NEW YORK: DODD,
        MEAD AND COMPANY, 1920.

16229   MATHIAS, ARTHUR. "CONTRASTING APPROACHES TO THE STUDY OF
        BLACK FAMILIES." _JOURNAL OF MARRIAGE AND THE FAMILY_,
        40 (NOVEMBER, 1978): 667-676.

16230   MATTHEWS, BASIL. "THE NEGRO FAMILY IN TRINIDAD." PH.D.
        DISSERTATION, FORDHAM UNIVERSITY, 1947.

16231   MCGETTIGAN, JAMES W. "SLAVE SALES, ESTATE DIVISIONS, AND
        THE SLAVE FAMILY IN BOONE COUNTY, MISSOURI,
        1820-1865." M.A. THESIS, UNIVERSITY OF MISSOURI, 1976.

16232   MCGETTIGAN, JAMES W., JR. "BOONE COUNTY SLAVES: SALES,
        ESTATE DIVISIONS, AND FAMILIES, 1820-1865." _MISSOURI
        HISTORICAL REVIEW_, 72 (JANUARY, APRIL, 1978):
        176-197, 271-295.

16233   MCKEAN, KEITH F. "SOUTHERN PATRIARCH: A PORTRAIT."
        VIRGINIA QUARTERLY REVIEW, 36 (SUMMER, 1960): 376-389.

16234   MEBANE, MARY E. "THE FAMILY IN THE WORKS OF CHARLES W.
        CHESNUTT AND SELECTED WORKS OF RICHARD WRIGHT." PH.D.
        DISSERTATION, UNIVERSITY OF NORTH CAROLINA, 1973.

16235   MERRITT, CAROLE. "SLAVE FAMILY HISTORY RECORDS: AN
        ABUNDANCE OF MATERIALS." GEORGIA ARCHIVE, 6 (SPRING,
        1978):   16-21.

16236   MILLER, RANDALL M. (ED.). "DEAR MASTER": LETTERS OF A
        SLAVE FAMILY. ITHACA: CORNELL UNIVERSITY PRESS, 1978.

16237   MINTZ, SIDNEY W. "A FINAL NOTE." SOCIAL AND ECONOMIC
        STUDIES, 10 (DECEMBER, 1961):   528-535.

16238   MODELL, JOHN. "HERBERT GUTMAN'S THE BLACK FAMILY IN
        SLAVERY AND FREEDOM, 1750-1925: DEMOGRAPHIC
        PERSPECTIVES." SOCIAL SCIENCE HISTORY, 3 (OCTOBER,
        1979):   45-55.

16239   MOLLER, HERBERT. "SEX COMPOSITION AND CORRELATED CULTURE
        PATTERNS OF COLONIAL AMERICA." WILLIAM AND MARY
        QUARTERLY, 3RD SER., 2 (APRIL, 1945):   113-153.

16240   MORGAN, KATHRYN. CHILDREN OF STRANGERS: THE STORIES OF
        A BLACK FAMILY. PHILADELPHIA: TEMPLE UNIVERSITY
        PRESS, 1980.

16241   MOSES, JANET S. "THE NEGRO FAMILY IN SLAVERY AND
        FREEDOM." IN JOYNER, CHARLES W. (ED.). BLACK
        CAROLINIANS: STUDIES IN THE HISTORY OF SOUTH CAROLINA
        NEGROES IN THE NINETEENTH CENTURY. LAURINBURG, NC:
        ST. ANDREWS PRESBYTERIAN COLLEGE, 1969, PP. 134-143.

16242   MURRAY, PAULI. PROUD SHOES: THE STORY OF AN AMERICAN
        FAMILY. NEW YORK: HARPER & BROTHERS, 1956.

16243   NASH, GARY B. "THE AFRICAN RESPONSE TO SLAVERY." RED,
        WHITE AND BLACK: THE PEOPLES OF EARLY AMERICA.
        ENGLEWOOD CLIFFS: PRENTICE-HALL, 1974, PP. 183-212.

16244   NEVINS, ALLAN. "THE LOT OF THE BONDSMAN." ORDEAL OF THE
        UNION. 2 VOLS. NEW YORK: CHARLES SCRIBNER'S SONS,
        1947, VOL. 1, PP. 412-461.

16245   NEWELL, W.W. "PLANTATION COURTSHIP." JOURNAL OF
        AMERICAN FOLKLORE, 8 (APRIL-JUNE, 1895):   106.

16246   NEWMAN, DEBORAH L. LIST OF FREE BLACK HEADS OF FAMILIES
        IN THE FIRST CENSUS OF THE UNITED STATES, 1790.
        WASHINGTON: NATIONAL ARCHIVES AND RECORDS SERVICE,
        1973.

16247   NOBLES, WADE W. "AFRICAN ROOT AND AMERICAN FRUIT: THE
        BLACK FAMILY." JOURNAL OF SOCIAL AND BEHAVIORAL
        SCIENCES, 20 (SPRING, 1974):   52-64.

16248   NOBLES, WADE W. "AFRICANITY: ITS ROLE IN BLACK
        FAMILIES." BLACK SCHOLAR, 5 (JUNE, 1974):   10-17.

16249   NOBLES, WADE W. "TOWARD AN EMPIRICAL AND THEORETICAL
        FRAMEWORK FOR DEFINING BLACK FAMILIES." JOURNAL OF
        MARRIAGE AND THE FAMILY, 40 (NOVEMBER, 1978): 679-690.

16250   OBERSEIDER, NANCY L. "A SOCIO-DEMOGRAPHIC STUDY OF THE
        FAMILY AS A SOCIAL UNIT IN TIDEWATER VIRGINIA,
        1660-1776." PH.D. DISSERTATION, UNIVERSITY OF
        MARYLAND, 1975.

16251   OTTERBEIN, KEITH F. "CARIBBEAN FAMILY ORGANIZATION: A
        COMPARATIVE ANALYSIS." AMERICAN ANTHROPOLOGIST, 67
        (FEBRUARY, 1965): 66-79.

16252   OWENS, LESLIE H. THIS SPECIES OF PROPERTY: SLAVE LIFE
        AND CULTURE IN THE OLD SOUTH. NEW YORK: OXFORD
        UNIVERSITY PRESS, 1976.

16253   PATTERSON, ORLANDO. "FROM ENDO-DEME TO MATRI-DEME: AN
        INTERPRETATION OF THE DEVELOPMENT OF KINSHIP AND
        SOCIAL ORGANIZATION AMONG THE SLAVES OF JAMAICA,
        1655-1830." IN PROCTOR, SAMUEL (ED.).
        EIGHTEENTH-CENTURY FLORIDA AND THE CARIBBEAN.
        GAINESVILLE: UNIVERSITY PRESSES OF FLORIDA, 1976, PP.
        50-59.

16254   PEEBLES, MINNIE K. "BLACK GENEALOGY." NORTH CAROLINA
        HISTORICAL REVIEW, 55 (SPRING, 1978): 164-173.

16255   PETERS, MARIE F. "THE BLACK FAMILY: PERPETUATING THE
        MYTHS: AN ANALYSIS OF FAMILY SOCIOLOGY TEXTBOOK
        TREATMENT OF BLACK FAMILIES." FAMILY COORDINATOR, 23
        (OCTOBER, 1974): 349-357.

16256   PHILLIPS, ARTHUR (ED.). SURVEY OF AFRICAN MARRIAGE AND
        FAMILY LIFE. NEW YORK: OXFORD UNIVERSITY PRESS, 1953.

16257   PICKENS, WILLIAM. THE HEIR OF SLAVES: AN AUTOBIOGRAPHY.
        NEW YORK: PILGRIM PRESS, 1911.

16258   PICOT, J. RUPERT. "TRACING YOUR ROOTS." NEGRO HISTORY
        BULLETIN, 41 (JANUARY/FEBRUARY, 1978): 780-781.

16259   PIERCE, B.E. "KINSHIP AND RESIDENCE AMONG THE URBAN
        NENGRE OF SURINAM: A RE-EVALUATION OF CONCEPTS AND
        THEORIES OF THE AFRO-AMERICAN FAMILY." PH.D.
        DISSERTATION, TULANE UNIVERSITY, 1971.

16260   PIERCE, B. EDWARD. "THE HISTORICAL CONTEXT OF NENGRE
        KINSHIP AND RESIDENCE: ETHNOHISTORY OF THE FAMILY
        ORGANIZATION OF LOWER STATUS CREOLES IN PARAMARIBO."
        IN PESCATELLO, ANN M. (ED.). OLD ROOTS IN NEW LANDS:
        HISTORICAL AND ANTHROPOLOGICAL PERSPECTIVES ON BLACK
        EXPERIENCES IN THE AMERICAS. WESTPORT: GREENWOOD
        PRESS, 1977, PP. 107-131.

16261   PINKNEY, ALPHONSO.   BLACK AMERICANS.   ENGLEWOOD CLIFFS:
        PRENTICE-HALL, 1975.

16262   POLLARD, LESLIE J.   "AGE AND PATERNALISM IN A SLAVE
        SOCIETY."   PERSPECTIVE ON AGING, 7 (NOVEMBER-DECEMBER,
        1973):   4-8.

16263   PORTER, DOROTHY B.   "FAMILY RECORDS, A MAJOR RESOURCE FOR
        DOCUMENTING THE BLACK EXPERIENCE IN NEW ENGLAND."   OLD
        TIME NEW ENGLAND, 63 (JANUARY-MARCH, 1973):   69-72.

16264   POWDERMAKER, HORTENSE.   AFTER FREEDOM: A CULTURAL STUDY
        IN THE DEEP SOUTH.   NEW YORK: VIKING PRESS, 1939.

16265   POWELL, FRANCES L.J.   "A STUDY OF THE STRUCTURE OF THE
        FREED BLACK FAMILY IN WASHINGTON, D.C., 1850-1880."
        D.A. DISSERTATION, CATHOLIC UNIVERSITY OF AMERICA,
        1980.

16266   RADCLIFFE-BROWN, ALFRED R. AND FORDE, DARYLL (EDS.).
        AFRICAN SYSTEMS OF KINSHIP AND MARRIAGE.   LONDON:
        OXFORD UNIVERSITY PRESS, 1950.

16267   RAINWATER, LEE AND YANCEY, WILLIAM L.   THE MOYNIHAN
        REPORT AND THE POLITICS OF CONTROVERSY.   CAMBRIDGE:
        MASSACHUSETTS INSTITUTE OF TECHNOLOGY PRESS, 1967.

16268   RANSOM, ROGER L. AND SUTCH, RICHARD.   ONE KIND OF
        FREEDOM: THE ECONOMIC CONSEQUENCES OF EMANCIPATION.
        CAMBRIDGE: CAMBRIDGE UNIVERSITY PRESS, 1977.

16269   RAWICK, GEORGE.   "SELF-ORGANIZATION UNDER SLAVERY."
        RADICAL HISTORY REVIEW, 4 (SPRING-SUMMER, 1977):
        79-91.

16270   REUTER, EDWARD B.   THE AMERICAN RACE PROBLEM: A STUDY OF
        THE NEGRO.   NEW YORK: THOMAS Y. CROWELL PUBLISHERS,
        1927.

16271   RICE, C. DUNCAN.   "THE INDESTRUCTIBLE INSTITUTION."
        JOURNAL OF INTERDISCIPLINARY HISTORY, 8 (AUTUMN,
        1977):   343-352.

16272   RIPLEY, C. PETER.   "THE BLACK FAMILY IN TRANSITION:
        LOUISIANA, 1860-1865."   JOURNAL OF SOUTHERN HISTORY,
        41 (AUGUST, 1975):   369-380.

16273   ROMAN, C.V.   "AN IMPENDING CRISIS."   A.M.E. CHURCH
        REVIEW, 26 (JANUARY, 1910):   226-233.

16274   ROSE, JAMES AND EICHHOLZ, ALICE.   "SLAVERY."   BLACK
        GENESIS.   DETROIT: GALE RESEARCH COMPANY, 1978, PP.
        37-48.

16275   ROSE, WILLIE LEE.   REHEARSAL FOR RECONSTRUCTION: THE

PORT_ROYAL_EXPERIMENT. INDIANAPOLIS: BOBBS-MERRILL,
1964.

16276   RUBIN, ROGER H. "MATRIARCHAL THEMES IN BLACK FAMILY
        LITERATURE: IMPLICATIONS FOR FAMILY LIFE EDUCATION."
        FAMILY_COORDINATOR, 27 (JANUARY, 1978): 33-41.

16277   RUSSELL-WOOD, A.J.R. "THE BLACK FAMILY IN THE AMERICAS."
        JAHRBUCH_FUR_GESCHICHTE_VON_STAAT,_WIRTSCHAFT_UND
        GESELLSCHAFT_LATEINAMERIKAS, 16 (1979): 267-309.

16278   RUSSELL-WOOD, A.J.R. "THE BLACK FAMILY IN THE AMERICAS."
        SOCIETAS, 8 (WINTER, 1978): 1-38.

16279   SANDERSON, WARREN C. "HERBERT GUTMAN'S THE BLACK FAMILY
        IN SLAVERY AND FREEDOM, 1750-1925: A CLIOMETRIC
        RECONSIDERATION." SOCIAL_SCIENCE_HISTORY, 3 (OCTOBER,
        1979): 66-85.

16280   SCANZONI, JOHN H. THE_BLACK_FAMILY_IN_MODERN_SOCIETY.
        BOSTON: ALLYN AND BACON, 1971.

16281   SCARBOROUGH, DOROTHY. ON_THE_TRAIL_OF_NEGRO_FOLK_SONGS.
        CAMBRIDGE: HARVARD UNIVERSITY PRESS, 1925.

16282   SCARUPA, HARRIET J. "BLACK GENEALOGY." ESSENCE, 7
        (JULY, 1976): 56-57, 84-87.

16283   SCHWENINGER, LOREN. "A SLAVE FAMILY IN THE ANTEBELLUM
        SOUTH." JOURNAL_OF_NEGRO_HISTORY, 60 (JANUARY, 1975):
        29-44.

16284   SCOTT, ROLAND B. AND WINSTON, MICHAEL R. "THE HEALTH AND
        WELFARE OF THE BLACK FAMILY IN THE UNITED STATES: A
        HISTORICAL AND INSTITUTIONAL ANALYSIS." AMERICAN
        JOURNAL_OF_DISEASES_OF_CHILDREN, 130 (JULY, 1976):
        704-707.

16285   SEWARD, RUDY R. "THE COLONIAL FAMILY IN AMERICA: TOWARD
        A SOCIO-HISTORICAL RESTORATION OF ITS STRUCTURE."
        JOURNAL_OF_MARRIAGE_AND_THE_FAMILY, 35 (FEBRUARY,
        1973): 58-70.

16286   SHIMKIN, DEMITRI B.; LOUIE, GLORIA J.; AND FRATE, DENNIS
        A. "THE BLACK EXTENDED FAMILY: A BASIC RURAL
        INSTITUTION AND A MECHANISM OF URBAN ADAPTATION." IN
        SHIMKIN, DEMITRI B.; SHIMKIN, EDITH M.; AND FRATE,
        DENNIS A. (EDS.). THE_EXTENDED_FAMILY_IN_BLACK
        SOCIETIES. THE HAGUE: MOUTON PUBLISHERS, 1978, PP.
        25-148.

16287   SHORTER, EDWARD. "PROTEIN, PUBERTY AND PREMARITAL
        SEXUALITY: AMERICAN BLACKS V. FRENCH PEASANTS."
        UNPUBLISHED PAPER PRESENTED AT MSSB--UNIVERSITY OF
        ROCHESTER CONFERENCE: "TIME_ON_THE_CROSS: A FIRST

APPRAISAL," OCTOBER 24-26, 1974.

16288   "SIGNIFICANT WILLS--NORTHAMPTON COUNTY, NORTH CAROLINA."
         JOURNAL OF NEGRO HISTORY, 16 (JULY, 1931): 328-337.

16289   SLATER, MARIAM K. THE CARIBBEAN FAMILY: LEGITIMACY IN
         MARTINIQUE. NEW YORK: ST. MARTIN'S PRESS, 1977.

16290   "SLAVE FAMILY STRUCTURE." IN NUNEZ, BENJAMIN.
         DICTIONARY OF AFRO-LATIN AMERICAN CIVILIZATION.
         WESTPORT: GREENWOOD PRESS, 1980, P. 434.

16291   "SLAVE MOTHERHOOD." IN NUNEZ, BENJAMIN. DICTIONARY OF
         AFRO-LATIN AMERICAN CIVILIZATION. WESTPORT:
         GREENWOOD PRESS, 1980, P. 436.

16292   "SLAVE POLYGAMOUS MATING." IN NUNEZ, BENJAMIN.
         DICTIONARY OF AFRO-LATIN AMERICAN CIVILIZATION.
         WESTPORT: GREENWOOD PRESS, 1980, P. 436.

16293   SMALLWOOD, JAMES. "EMANCIPATION AND THE BLACK FAMILY: A
         CASE STUDY." SOCIAL SCIENCE QUARTERLY, 57 (MARCH,
         1977): 847-849.

16294   SMITH, JULIA F. "RACIAL ATTITUDES IN THE OLD SOUTHWEST."
         IN ELLSWORTH, LUCIUS F. (ED.). THE AMERICANIZATION OF
         THE GULF COAST, 1803-1850. PENSACOLA: HISTORIC
         PENSACOLA PRESERVATION BOARD, 1972, PP. 68-77.

16295   SMITH, MICHAEL G. WEST INDIAN FAMILY STRUCTURE.
         SEATTLE: UNIVERSITY OF WASHINGTON PRESS, 1962.

16296   SMITH, RAYMOND T. "THE FAMILY IN THE CARIBBEAN." IN
         CARIBBEAN STUDIES: A SYMPOSIUM. SEATTLE: UNIVERSITY
         OF WASHINGTON PRESS, 1960, PP. 67-75.

16297   SMITH, RAYMOND T. THE NEGRO FAMILY IN BRITISH GUIANA.
         LONDON: ROUTLEDGE AND KEGAN PAUL, 1956.

16298   SMITH, RAYMOND T. "THE NUCLEAR FAMILY IN AFRO-AMERICAN
         KINSHIP." JOURNAL OF COMPARATIVE FAMILY STUDIES, 1
         (AUTUMN, 1970): 55-70.

16299   SPRADLING, MARY M. (ED.). IN BLACK AND WHITE:
         AFRO-AMERICANS IN PRINT. KALAMAZOO: KALAMAZOO PUBLIC
         LIBRARY, 1976.

16300   STAMPP, KENNETH M. "THE DAILY LIFE OF THE SOUTHERN
         SLAVE." IN HUGGINS, NATHAN I.; KILSON, MARTIN; AND
         FOX, DANIEL M. (EDS.). KEY ISSUES IN THE
         AFRO-AMERICAN EXPERIENCE. 2 VOLS. NEW YORK:
         HARCOURT BRACE JOVANOVICH, 1971, VOL. 1, PP. 116-137.

16301   STAMPP, KENNETH M. THE PECULIAR INSTITUTION: SLAVERY IN
         THE ANTE-BELLUM SOUTH. NEW YORK: ALFRED A. KNOPF,

1956.

16302 STAPLES, ROBERT. "THE BLACK AMERICAN FAMILY." IN
       MINDEL, CHARLES H. AND HABENSTEIN, ROBERT W. (EDS.).
       ETHNIC FAMILIES IN AMERICA. NEW YORK: ELSEVIER,
       1976, PP. 221-247.

16303 STAPLES, ROBERT. "THE MATRICENTRIC FAMILY: A
       CROSS-CULTURAL EXAMINATION." JOURNAL OF MARRIAGE AND
       THE FAMILY, 34 (FEBRUARY, 1972): 156-165.

16304 STAPLES, ROBERT. "THE MYTH OF THE BLACK MATRIARCHY." IN
       STAPLES (ED.). THE BLACK FAMILY. BELMONT, CA:
       WADSWORTH PUBLISHING COMPANY, 1971, PP. 149-159.

16305 STAPLES, ROBERT. "SOME MYTHS AND STEREOTYPES ABOUT THE
       BLACK FAMILY." IN GORDON, VIVIAN V. (ED.). LECTURES:
       BLACK SCHOLARS ON BLACK ISSUES. WASHINGTON:
       UNIVERSITY PRESS OF AMERICA, 1979, PP. 125-134.

16306 STECKEL, RICHARD H. "SLAVE MARRIAGE AND THE FAMILY."
       JOURNAL OF FAMILY HISTORY, 5 (WINTER, 1980): 406-421.

16307 STROMAN, CAROLYN A. "TOWARD A SOCIOLOGY OF THE BLACK
       FAMILY: A BIBLIOGRAPHIC ESSAY." M.A. THESIS, ATLANTA
       UNIVERSITY, 1973.

16308 SUDARKASA, NIARA. "AFRICAN AND AFRO-AMERICAN FAMILY
       STRUCTURE: A COMPARISON." BLACK SCHOLAR, 11
       (NOVEMBER/DECEMBER, 1980): 37-60.

16309 TANNENBAUM, FRANK. SLAVE AND CITIZEN: THE NEGRO IN THE
       AMERICAS. NEW YORK: ALFRED A. KNOPF, 1946.

16310 TENHOUTEN, WARREN D. "THE BLACK FAMILY: MYTH AND
       REALITY." PSYCHIATRY, 33 (FEBRUARY, 1970): 145-173.

16311 THOMAS, KENNETH H., JR. "A NOTE ON THE PITFALLS OF BLACK
       GENEALOGY: THE ORIGINS OF BLACK SURNAMES." GEORGIA
       ARCHIVE, 6 (SPRING, 1973): 23-30.

16312 THOMPSON, ERA B. "VAUGHN FAMILY: A TALE OF TWO
       CONTINENTS." EBONY, 30 (FEBRUARY, 1975): 53-58.

16313 "UP FROM SLAVERY." CRISIS, 44 (AUGUST, 1937): 239-240.

16314 VACHEENOS, JEAN AND VOLK, BETTY. "BORN IN BONDAGE:
       HISTORY OF A SLAVE FAMILY." NEGRO HISTORY BULLETIN,
       36 (MAY, 1973): 101-106.

16315 VAN DEBURG, WILLIAM L. THE SLAVE DRIVERS: BLACK
       AGRICULTURAL LABOR SUPERVISORS IN THE ANTEBELLUM
       SOUTH. WESTPORT: GREENWOOD PRESS, 1979.

16316 WADE, RICHARD C. THE URBAN FRONTIER: THE RISE OF

WESTERN CITIES, 1790-1830. CAMBRIDGE: HARVARD
UNIVERSITY PRESS, 1959.

16317 WASHINGTON, AUSTIN D. "THE DOLLYS: AN ANTEBELLUM BLACK
       FAMILY OF SAVANNAH, GEORGIA." SAVANNAH STATE COLLEGE
       BULLETIN, 26 (DECEMBER, 1972): 101-103.

16318 WATSON, ALAN D. "THE COLONIAL TAX LIST." NORTH CAROLINA
       GENEALOGICAL SOCIETY JOURNAL, 15 (NOVEMBER, 1979):
       218-245.

16319 WEBBER, THOMAS L. DEEP LIKE THE RIVERS: EDUCATION IN
       THE SLAVE QUARTER COMMUNITY, 1831-1865. NEW YORK:
       W.W. NORTON, 1978.

16320 WHEELER, WILLIAM H. "THE BLACK FAMILY IN PERSPECTIVE."
       PH.D. DISSERTATION, ARIZONA STATE UNIVERSITY, 1973.

16321 WHITE, JOHN. "WHATEVER HAPPENED TO THE SLAVE FAMILY IN
       THE OLD SOUTH?" JOURNAL OF AMERICAN STUDIES, 8
       (DECEMBER, 1974): 383-390.

16322 WHITTINGTON, JAMES A., JR. "KINSHIP, MATING AND FAMILY
       IN THE CHOCO OF COLOMBIA: AN AFRO-AMERICAN
       ADAPTATION." PH.D. DISSERTATION, TULANE UNIVERSITY,
       1971.

16323 WILKINSON, DORIS Y. "THE BLACK FAMILY: PAST AND
       PRESENT: A REVIEW ESSAY." JOURNAL OF MARRIAGE AND
       THE FAMILY, 40 (NOVEMBER, 1978): 829-835.

16324 WILKINSON, DORIS Y. "TOWARD A POSITIVE FRAME OF
       REFERENCE FOR ANALYSIS OF BLACK FAMILIES: A SELECTED
       BIBLIOGRAPHY." JOURNAL OF MARRIAGE AND THE FAMILY, 40
       (NOVEMBER, 1978): 707-708.

16325 WILLEMS, EMILIO. "THE STRUCTURE OF THE BRAZILIAN
       FAMILY." SOCIAL FORCES, 31 (MAY, 1953): 339-345.

16326 WILLIAMSON, ROBERT C. MARRIAGE AND FAMILY RELATIONS.
       NEW YORK: JOHN WILEY AND SONS, INC., 1972.

16327 WOOD, PETER H. BLACK MAJORITY: NEGROES IN COLONIAL
       SOUTH CAROLINA, 1670 TO THE STONO REBELLION. NEW
       YORK: ALFRED A. KNOPF, 1974.

16328 WOODSON, CARTER G. "THE NEGRO WASHERWOMAN, A VANISHING
       FIGURE." JOURNAL OF NEGRO HISTORY, 15 (JULY, 1930):
       269-277.

16329 WOODWARD, KENNETH L. AND MALSCH, S. "BLACK TIES THAT
       BIND; FAMILY AND SLAVERY; VIEWS OF HERBERT GUTMAN."
       NEWSWEEK, 88 (OCTOBER 11, 1976): 59.

16330 WYATT-BROWN, BERTRAM. "THE NEW CONSENSUS." COMMENTARY,

63 (JANUARY, 1977): 76-78.

16331   WYLIE, FLOYD M. "ATTITUDES TOWARD AGING AMONG BLACK
        AMERICANS: SOME HISTORICAL PERSPECTIVES." AGING AND
        HUMAN DEVELOPMENT, 2 (FEBRUARY, 1971): 66-70.

16332   ZILVERSMIT, ARTHUR. THE FIRST EMANCIPATION: THE
        ABOLITION OF SLAVERY IN THE NORTH. CHICAGO:
        UNIVERSITY OF CHICAGO PRESS, 1967.

SLAVE WOMEN

16333   ABRAHAMS, ROGER D. "NEGOTIATING RESPECT: PATTERNS OF
        PRESENTATION AMONG BLACK WOMEN." IN FARRAR, CLAIRE R.
        (ED.). WOMEN AND FOLKLORE. AUSTIN: UNIVERSITY OF
        TEXAS PRESS, 1975, PP. 58-80.

16334   ABRAMS, JOSEPHINE S. "THE TREATMENT OF NEGRO WOMEN
        DURING SLAVERY." M.A. THESIS, Y.M.C.A. GRADUATE
        SCHOOL, NASHVILLE, 1936.

16335   "AFRO-AMERICAN WOMANHOOD." NEW YORK AGE, FEBRUARY 22,
        1906.

16336   APTHEKER, HERBERT. "THE NEGRO WOMAN." MASSES AND
        MAINSTREAM, 2 (FEBRUARY, 1949): 10-17.

16337   ASTRACHAN, ANTHONY. "BLACK WOMAN AS SLAVE." ENCORE, 4
        (JUNE 23, 1975): 34-35.

16338   "THE AUCTION BLOCK ENDS A DREAM." ENCORE, 4 (JUNE
        23/JULY 4, 1975): 28-29.

16339   BAKER, THOMAS N. "THE NEGRO WOMAN." ALEXANDER'S
        MAGAZINE, 3 (DECEMBER 15, 1906): 71-85.

16340   BAKER, THOMAS N. THE NEGRO WOMAN. PHILADELPHIA: A.M.E.
        BOOK CONCERN, N.D.

16341   BARDWELL, J.P. "WOMAN IN SLAVERY." AMERICAN MISSIONARY,
        13 (MARCH 12, 1869): 15.

16342   BARTLETT, IRVING H. AND CAMBOR, C. GLENN. "THE HISTORY
        AND PSYCHODYNAMICS OF SOUTHERN WOMANHOOD." WOMEN'S
        STUDIES, 2 (1974): 9-24.

16343   BASTIDE, ROGER. "DUSKY VENUS, BLACK APOLLO." RACE, 3
        (NOVEMBER, 1961): 10-18.

16344   BEAL, FRANCES M. "SLAVE OF A SLAVE NO MORE: BLACK WOMEN
        IN STRUGGLE." BLACK SCHOLAR, 6 (MARCH, 1975): 2-10.

16345   BENNETT, LERONE. "THE NEGRO WOMAN." EBONY, 15 (AUGUST,
        1963): 38-46.

16346 BENNETT, LERONE. "NO CRYSTAL STAIR: THE BLACK WOMAN IN HISTORY." EBONY, 32 (AUGUST, 1977): 164-165, 167-168, 170.

16347 BENNETT, LERONE JR. "THE MYSTERY OF MARY ELLEN PLEASANT." EBONY, 34 (APRIL, 1979): 90-96.

16348 THE BLACK FAMILY AND THE BLACK WOMAN, A BIBLIOGRAPHY. BLOOMINGTON: INDIANA UNIVERSITY, 1972.

16349 "THE BLACK MAMMY OF THE SOUTH." LITERARY DIGEST, 76 (MARCH 31, 1923): 56.

16350 "BLACK WOMEN IN HISTORY; PAST AND PRESENT: A LEGACY OF COURAGE." SCHOMBURG CENTER FOR RESEARCH IN BLACK CULTURE JOURNAL, 1 (SPRING, 1977): 6-7.

16351 BLACKBURN, REGINA L. "CONSCIOUS AGENTS OF TIME AND SELF: THE LIVES AND STYLES OF AFRICAN-AMERICAN WOMEN AS SEEN THROUGH THEIR AUTOBIOGRAPHICAL WRITINGS." PH.D. DISSERTATION, UNIVERSITY OF NEW MEXICO, 1978.

16352 BOYD, GEORGIA. FUGITIVE GIRL. REXDALE, ONTARIO: IDENTITY, 1977.

16353 BRAWLEY, BENJAMIN. WOMEN OF ACHIEVEMENT. CHICAGO: WOMAN'S AMERICAN BAPTIST HOME MISSION SOCIETY, 1919.

16354 BRIDENBAUGH, CARL. "THE EARLIEST PUBLISHED POEM OF PHILLIS WHEATLEY." NEW ENGLAND QUARTERLY, 42 (DECEMBER, 1969): 583-584.

16355 BROWN, CLARENCE. "REFLECTIONS ON 119 YEARS OF LIVING." JET, 46 (JULY 4, 1974): 22-25.

16356 BROWN, MINNIE M. "BLACK WOMEN IN AMERICAN AGRICULTURE." AGRICULTURAL HISTORY, 50 (JANUARY, 1976): 202-212.

16357 BROWNE, JUANITA M. THE BLACK WOMAN. N.P., 1974.

16358 BROWNLEE, W. ELLIOT AND BROWNLEE, MARY M. "SLAVE WOMEN." WOMEN IN THE AMERICAN ECONOMY: A DOCUMENTARY HISTORY, 1675-1929. NEW HAVEN: YALE UNIVERSITY PRESS, 1976, PP. 92-98.

16359 BROWNMILLER, SUSAN. AGAINST OUR WILL: MEN, WOMEN, AND RAPE. NEW YORK: SIMON AND SCHUSTER, 1975.

16360 BURKETT, ELINOR C. "IN DUBIOUS SISTERHOOD: CLASS AND SEX IN SPANISH COLONIAL SOUTH AMERICA." LATIN AMERICAN PERSPECTIVES, 4 (WINTER, SPRING, 1977): 18-26.

16361 BURNHAM, DOROTHY. "THE LIFE OF THE AFRO-AMERICAN WOMAN IN SLAVERY." INTERNATIONAL JOURNAL OF WOMEN'S

STUDIES, 1 (JULY-AUGUST, 1978): 363-377.

16362   BURROWS, VINIE. "PHILLIS WHEATLEY--GENTLE CHILD OF
        AFRICA." JACKSON STATE REVIEW, 6 (SUMMER, 1974):
        36-38.

16363   BUSH, BARBARA M. "THE ROLE OF SLAVE WOMEN IN BRITISH
        WEST INDIAN SLAVE SOCIETY, 1650-1832." M.PHIL.
        THESIS, UNIVERSITY OF SHEFFIELD, 1979.

16364   CARRINGTON, EVELYN M. (ED.). WOMEN IN EARLY TEXAS.
        AUSTIN: JENKINS PUBLISHING COMPANY, 1975.

16365   CARROLL, MICHAEL P. "ENGELS ON THE SUBJUGATION OF WOMEN:
        SOME CROSS-CULTURAL TESTS." PACIFIC SOCIOLOGICAL
        REVIEW, 18 (APRIL, 1975): 223-241.

16366   CARTER, DORIS D. "REFUSING TO RELINQUISH THE STRUGGLES:
        THE SOCIAL ROLE OF THE BLACK WOMAN IN LOUISIANA
        HISTORY." IN MACDONALD, ROBERT R.; KEMP, JOHN R.; AND
        HAAS, EDWARD F. (EDS.). LOUISIANA'S BLACK HERITAGE.
        NEW ORLEANS: LOUISIANA STATE MUSEUM, 1979, PP.
        163-189.

16367   CLARK, ETHEL R. "AMERICAN BLACK WOMANHOOD." CRISIS, 47
        (OCTOBER, 1940): 320.

16368   CLARK, TERRI. "BLACK WOMEN: AN HISTORICAL PERSPECTIVE."
        OFF OUR BACKS, 10 (JANUARY, 1980): 16-17.

16369   CODY, CHERYLL A. "A NOTE ON CHANGING PATTERNS OF SLAVE
        FERTILITY IN THE SOUTH CAROLINA RICE DISTRICT,
        1735-1865." SOUTHERN STUDIES, 16 (WINTER, 1977):
        457-462.

16370   COHEN, DE SILVER. "IN HER OWN IMAGE: THE THEMES OF
        SELF-DEFINITION IN LITERATURE BY OR ABOUT BLACK
        WOMEN." D.A. DISSERTATION, CARNEGIE-MELLON
        UNIVERSITY, 1978.

16371   COLE, JOHNETTA. "MILITANT BLACK WOMEN IN EARLY U.S.
        HISTORY." BLACK SCHOLAR, 9 (APRIL, 1978): 38-44.

16372   CONRAD, EARL. HARRIET TUBMAN: NEGRO SOLDIER AND
        ABOLITIONIST. NEW YORK: INTERNATIONAL PRESS, 1942.

16373   COTT, NANCY F. (ED.). "NARRATIVES FROM ESCAPED SLAVES."
        ROOTS OF BITTERNESS: DOCUMENTS OF THE SOCIAL HISTORY
        OF AMERICAN WOMEN. NEW YORK: DUTTON, 1972, PP.
        186-193.

16374   CRAWFORD, MARGO. "DIAMOND IN DIRT THEORY OF SLAVERY,
        SEASONING THE FEMALE SLAVE." IN JOHNSON, WILLA D. AND
        GREEN, THOMAS L. (EDS.). PERSPECTIVES ON
        AFRO-AMERICAN WOMEN. WASHINGTON:

EDUCATIONAL-COMMUNITY COUNSELORS ASSOCIATES, 1975, PP.
22-33.

16375   DAVIS, ANGELA. "REFLECTIONS ON THE BLACK WOMAN'S ROLE IN
        THE COMMUNITY OF SLAVES." BLACK SCHOLAR, 3 (DECEMBER,
        1971): 2-16.

16376   DAVIS, ANGELA Y. "REFLECTIONS ON THE BLACK WOMAN'S ROLE
        IN THE COMMUNITY OF SLAVES." MASSACHUSETTS REVIEW, 13
        (WINTER-SPRING, 1972): 81-103.

16377   DAVIS, LENWOOD G. "THE BLACK WOMAN IN AMERICA:
        AUTOBIOGRAPHICAL AND BIOGRAPHICAL MATERIALS."
        NORTHWEST JOURNAL OF AFRICAN AND BLACK AMERICAN
        STUDIES, 2 (WINTER, 1974): 27-29.

16378   DAVIS, LENWOOD G. THE BLACK WOMAN IN AMERICAN SOCIETY:
        A SELECTED ANNOTATED BIBLIOGRAPHY. BOSTON: G.K. HALL
        AND COMPANY, 1975.

16379   DEAN, DEOLA E. "THE ANTE-BELLUM SLAVE WOMAN, 1830-1865:
        A GENERAL SURVEY." M.A. THESIS, ATLANTA UNIVERSITY,
        1975.

16380   DEGRAAF, LAWRENCE B. "RACE, SEX, AND REGION: BLACK
        WOMEN IN THE AMERICAN WEST, 1850-1920." PACIFIC
        HISTORICAL REVIEW, 49 (MAY, 1980): 285-314.

16381   DELANEY, DEBRA. "MYTHS AND IMAGES SURROUNDING THE BLACK
        WOMAN." BROWN SISTER, NO. 4 (1977): 5-14.

16382   DELANEY, LUCY A. FROM THE DARKNESS COMETH THE LIGHT OR,
        STRUGGLE FOR FREEDOM. SAINT LOUIS: J.T. SMITH, 1891.

16383   DEPAUW, LINDA G. "BLACK WOMEN." FOUNDING MOTHERS:
        WOMEN OF AMERICA IN THE REVOLUTIONARY ERA. BOSTON:
        HOUGHTON MIFFLIN COMPANY, 1975, PP. 70-98.

16384   DIETRICH, KATHERYN T. "A RE-EXAMINATION OF THE MYTH OF
        BLACK MATRIARCHY." JOURNAL OF MARRIAGE AND THE
        FAMILY, 37 (MAY, 1975): 367-374.

16385   DILL, BONNIE T. "THE DIALECTICS OF BLACK WOMANHOOD."
        SIGNS, 4 (SPRING, 1979): 543-555.

16386   DILL, BONNIE T. "THE DIALECTICS OF BLACK WOMANHOOD:
        TOWARDS A NEW MODEL OF AMERICAN FEMININITY." PAPER
        PRESENTED AT MEETING OF AMERICAN SOCIOLOGICAL
        ASSOCIATION, 1975.

16387   DUBOIS, W.E.B. "THE DAMNATION OF WOMEN." DARKWATER:
        VOICES FROM WITHIN THE VEIL. NEW YORK: HARCOURT,
        BRACE AND HOWE, 1920, PP. 163-186.

16388   DUFFY, JOHN. THE HEALERS: THE RISE OF THE MEDICAL

ESTABLISHMENT. NEW YORK: MCGRAW-HILL, 1976.

16389   DUNAYEVSKAYA, RAYA. "TWO WORLDS: THE BLACK DIMENSION IN
         WOMEN'S LIBERATION." NEWS AND LETTERS, NO. 21 (APRIL,
         1976): 5.

16390   ELIZABETH, A COLORED MINISTER OF THE GOSPEL, BORN IN
         SLAVERY. PHILADELPHIA: TRACT ASSOCIATION OF FRIENDS,
         1889.

16391   EPSTEIN, SAM AND EPSTEIN, BERYL. HARRIET TUBMAN: GUIDE
         TO FREEDOM. CHAMPAIGN: GARRARD, 1968.

16392   FARRISON, W. EDWARD. "CLOTEL, THOMAS JEFFERSON, AND
         SALLY HEMINGS." CLA JOURNAL, 17 (DECEMBER, 1973):
         147-174.

16393   FAUSET, JESSIE. "ORIFLAMME." CRISIS, 19 (JANUARY,
         1920): 128.

16394   FINCH, LUCINE. "SLAVES WHO STAYED; MAMMY." AMERICAN
         MERCURY, 65 (SEPTEMBER, 1937): 132-135.

16395   FLEMING, JOHN E. "SLAVERY, CIVIL WAR AND RECONSTRUCTION:
         A STUDY OF BLACK WOMEN IN MICROCOSM." NEGRO HISTORY
         BULLETIN, 38 (AUGUST-SEPTEMBER, 1975): 431-434.

16396   FOGEL, ROBERT W. AND ENGERMAN, STANLEY L. TIME ON THE
         CROSS: THE ECONOMICS OF AMERICAN NEGRO SLAVERY. 2
         VOLS. BOSTON: LITTLE, BROWN AND COMPANY, 1974.

16397   FOSTER, FRANCES S. "ULTIMATE VICTIMS: BLACK WOMEN IN
         SLAVE NARRATIVES." JOURNAL OF AMERICAN CULTURE, 1
         (WINTER, 1978): 845-854.

16398   FOX, GEOFFREY E. "HONOR, SHAME, AND WOMEN'S LIBERATION
         IN CUBA: VIEWS OF WORKING-CLASS EMIGRE MEN." IN
         PESCATELLO, ANN (ED.) FEMALE AND MALE IN LATIN
         AMERICA: ESSAYS. PITTSBURGH: UNIVERSITY OF
         PITTSBURGH PRESS, 1973, PP. 273-290.

16399   FRAZIER, E. FRANKLIN. THE NEGRO FAMILY IN THE UNITED
         STATES. CHICAGO: UNIVERSITY OF CHICAGO PRESS, 1939.

16400   FRY, GLADYS-MARIE. "HARRIET POWERS: PORTRAIT OF A BLACK
         QUILTER." IN WADSWORTH, ANNA (ED.). MISSING PIECES:
         GEORGIA FOLK ART, 1770-1976. ATLANTA: GEORGIA
         COUNCIL FOR THE ARTS AND HUMANITIES, 1976, PP. 16-23.

16401   FURSTENBERG, FRANK F. "THE ORIGINS OF THE FEMALE-HEADED
         BLACK FAMILY: THE DESTRUCTIVE IMPACT OF THE URBAN
         EXPERIENCE." UNPUBLISHED PAPER PRESENTED AT
         MSSB--UNIVERSITY OF ROCHESTER CONFERENCE: "TIME ON
         THE CROSS: A FIRST APPRAISAL," OCTOBER 24-26, 1974.

16402   FURSTENBERG, FRANK F.; HERSHBERG, THEODORE; AND MODELL,
        JOHN. "THE ORIGINS OF THE FEMALE-HEADED BLACK FAMILY:
        THE IMPACT OF THE URBAN EXPERIENCE." JOURNAL OF
        INTERDISCIPLINARY HISTORY, 6 (AUTUMN, 1975): 211-233.

16403   GARDNER, MARY E. "THE ROLE OF WOMEN IN AMERICAN HISTORY,
        1789-1860." M.A. THESIS, HOWARD UNIVERSITY, 1942.

16404   GEIST, CHRISTOPHER D. "VIOLENCE, PASSION, AND SEXUAL
        RACISM: THE PLANTATION NOVEL IN THE 1970S." SOUTHERN
        QUARTERLY, 18 (WINTER, 1980): 60-72.

16405   GENOVESE, EUGENE D. ROLL, JORDAN, ROLL: THE WORLD THE
        SLAVES MADE. NEW YORK: PANTHEON, 1974.

16406   GENOVESE, EUGENE D. "THE SLAVE FAMILY, WOMEN--A
        REASSESSMENT OF MATRIARCHY, EMASCULATION, WEAKNESS."
        SOUTHERN VOICES, 1 (AUGUST-SEPTEMBER, 1974): 9-16.

16407   GOODMAN, INEZ A. "THE PASSING OF THE MAMMY."
        SOUTHWESTERN CHRISTIAN ADVOCATE, JANUARY 29, 1920.

16408   GOLDIN, CLAUDIA. "FEMALE LABOR FORCE PARTICIPATION: THE
        ORIGIN OF BLACK AND WHITE DIFFERENCES, 1870 AND 1880."
        JOURNAL OF ECONOMIC HISTORY, 37 (MARCH, 1977): 87-112.

16409   GOODSON, MARTIA G. "THE SLAVE NARRATIVE COLLECTION: A
        TOOL FOR RECONSTRUCTING AFRO-AMERICAN WOMEN'S
        HISTORY." WESTERN JOURNAL OF BLACK STUDIES, 3
        (SUMMER, 1979): 116-122.

16410   GRAHAM, SHIRLEY. THE STORY OF PHILLIS WHEATLEY. NEW
        YORK: MESSNER, 1949.

16411   GREEN, THOMAS L. "THE VOYAGE OF THE SABLE VENUS--BLACK
        WOMEN IN SLAVE NARRATIVES." IN JOHNSON, WILLA D. AND
        GREEN (EDS.). PERSPECTIVES ON AFRO-AMERICAN WOMEN.
        WASHINGTON: EDUCATIONAL COMMUNITY COUNSELORS
        ASSOCIATES, INC., 1975, PP. 11-21.

16412   GREGORY, CHESTER W. "BLACK WOMEN IN PRE-FEDERAL
        AMERICA." IN DEUTRICH, MABEL E. AND PURDY, VIRGINIA
        C. (EDS.). CLIO WAS A WOMAN: STUDIES IN THE HISTORY
        OF AMERICAN WOMEN. WASHINGTON: HOWARD UNIVERSITY
        PRESS, 1980, PP. 53-72.

16413   GUTMAN, HERBERT G. THE BLACK FAMILY IN SLAVERY AND
        FREEDOM, 1750-1925. NEW YORK: PANTHEON BOOKS, 1976.

16414   GUTMAN, HERBERT G. "MARITAL AND SEXUAL NORMS AMONG SLAVE
        WOMEN." IN COTT, NANCY F. AND PLECK, ELIZABETH H.
        (EDS.). A HERITAGE OF HER OWN: TOWARD A NEW SOCIAL
        HISTORY OF AMERICAN WOMEN. NEW YORK: SIMON &
        SCHUSTER, 1979, PP. 298-310.

16415 HAHNER, JUNE E. "WOMEN AND WORK IN BRAZIL, 1850-1920: A
       PRELIMINARY INVESTIGATION." IN ALDEN, DAURIL AND
       DEAN, WARREN (EDS.). ESSAYS CONCERNING THE
       SOCIOECONOMIC HISTORY OF BRAZIL AND PORTUGUESE INDIA.
       GAINESVILLE: UNIVERSITY PRESSES OF FLORIDA, 1977, PP.
       87-117.

16416 HARLEY, SHARON AND TERBORG-PENN, ROSALYN (EDS.). THE
       AFRO-AMERICAN WOMAN: STRUGGLES AND IMAGES. PORT
       WASHINGTON, NY: KENNIKAT PRESS, 1978.

16417 HARRIS, JOEL C. "THE NEGRO AS THE SOUTH SEES HIM I: THE
       OLD-TIME DARKY." SATURDAY EVENING POST, 176 (JANUARY
       2, 1904): 1-2, 23.

16418 HEWETSON, W.T. "THE SOCIAL LIFE OF THE SOUTHERN NEGRO."
       CHAUTAUQUAN, 26 (DECEMBER, 1897): 295-304.

16419 HICKS, NORA L. SLAVE GIRL REBA AND HER DESCENDANTS IN
       AMERICA: MEMOIRS. JERICHO, NY: EXPOSITION PRESS,
       1974.

16420 HINE, DARLENE C. "FEMALE SLAVE RESISTANCE: THE
       ECONOMICS OF SEX." WESTERN JOURNAL OF BLACK STUDIES,
       3 (SUMMER, 1979): 123-127.

16421 HOLDREDGE, HELEN. MAMMY PLEASANT'S PARTNER. NEW YORK:
       PUTNAM, 1944.

16422 HUBER, JO ANNE S. "SOUTHERN WOMEN AND THE INSTITUTION OF
       SLAVERY." M.A. THESIS, LAMAR UNIVERSITY, 1980.

16423 HUNTON, ADDIE. "NEGRO WOMANHOOD DEFENDED." VOICE OF THE
       NEGRO, 1 (JULY, 1904): 280-282.

16424 HYMOWITZ, CAROL AND WEISSMAN, MICHAELE. "BLACK
       BONDAGE--WHITE PEDESTAL." A HISTORY OF WOMEN IN
       AMERICA. NEW YORK: BANTAM BOOKS, 1978, PP. 40-63.

16425 IRVIN, HELEN D. WOMEN IN KENTUCKY. LEXINGTON:
       UNIVERSITY PRESS OF KENTUCKY, 1979.

16426 ISANI, MUKHTAR ALI. "'GAMBIA ON MY SOUL': AFRICA AND
       THE AFRICANS IN THE WRITINGS OF PHILLIS WHEATLEY."
       MELUS, 6 (1979): 64-72.

16427 JACKSON, GEORGE F. "BLACK HEROINE FREEDOM FIGHTERS IN
       THE CIVIL WAR." BLACK WOMEN, MAKERS OF HISTORY: A
       PORTRAIT. SACRAMENTO: FONG & FONG, 1977, PP. 65-76.

16428 JACKSON, GEORGE F. "BLACK WOMEN PIONEERS IN CALIFORNIA
       AND NEBRASKA." BLACK WOMEN, MAKERS OF HISTORY: A
       PORTRAIT. SACRAMENTO: FONG & FONG, 1977, PP. 77-104.

16429 JACKSON, GEORGE F. "THE PECULIAR INSTITUTION." BLACK

WOMEN, MAKERS OF HISTORY: A PORTRAIT. SACRAMENTO: FONG & FONG, 1977, PP. 1-6.

16430 JACKSON, IRENE V. "BLACK WOMEN AND AFRO-AMERICAN SONG TRADITION." SING OUT, 25 (1976): 10-13.

16431 JACKSON, IRENE V. "BLACK WOMEN AND MUSIC: A SURVEY FROM AFRICA TO THE NEW WORLD." MINORITY VOICES, 2 (FALL, 1978): 15-29.

16432 JACKSON, JACQUELYNE J. "BLACK WOMEN IN A RACIST SOCIETY." IN WILLIE, CHARLES V.; KRAMER, BERNARD M.; AND BROWN, BERTRAM S. (EDS.). RACISM AND MENTAL HEALTH: ESSAYS. PITTSBURGH: UNIVERSITY OF PITTSBURGH PRESS, 1973, PP. 185-268.

16433 JONES, PAULA. "SLAVE WOMEN IN THE OLD SOUTH." M.A. THESIS, SOUTHERN METHODIST UNIVERSITY, 1934.

16434 JORDAN, WINTHROP D. THE WHITE MAN'S BURDEN: HISTORICAL ORIGINS OF RACISM IN THE UNITED STATES. NEW YORK: OXFORD UNIVERSITY PRESS, 1974.

16435 JORDAN, WINTHROP D. WHITE OVER BLACK: AMERICAN ATTITUDES TOWARD THE NEGRO, 1550-1812. CHAPEL HILL: UNIVERSITY OF NORTH CAROLINA PRESS, 1968.

16436 KING, MAE C. "THE POLITICS OF SEXUAL STEREOTYPES." BLACK SCHOLAR, 4 (MARCH-APRIL, 1973): 12-23.

16437 KLEIN, MARTIN. "WOMEN IN SLAVERY IN THE WESTERN SUDAN." UNPUBLISHED PAPER PRESENTED AT AFRICAN STUDIES ASSOCIATION ANNUAL CONVENTION, BALTIMORE, 1978.

16438 LADNER, JOYCE. TOMORROW'S TOMORROW: THE BLACK WOMAN. NEW YORK: DOUBLEDAY, 1971.

16439 LADNER, JOYCE A. "RACISM AND TRADITION: BLACK WOMANHOOD IN HISTORICAL PERSPECTIVE." IN CARROLL, BERENICE A. (ED.). LIBERATING WOMEN'S HISTORY: THEORETICAL AND CRITICAL ESSAYS. URBANA: UNIVERSITY OF ILLINOIS PRESS, 1976, PP. 179-193.

16440 LADNER, JOYCE A. "THE WOMEN: CONDITIONS OF SLAVERY LAID THE FOUNDATION FOR THEIR LIBERATION." EBONY, 30 (AUGUST, 1975): 76-78, 80-81.

16441 LANDES, RUTH. "NEGRO SLAVERY AND FEMALE STATUS." AFRICAN AFFAIRS, 52 (JANUARY, 1953): 54-57.

16442 LANDES, RUTH. "NEGRO SLAVERY AND FEMALE STATUS." IN LES AFRO-AMERICAINS. DAKAR: INSTITUT FRANCAIS D'AFRIQUE NOIR, 1953, PP. 265-268.

16443 LARISON, CORNELIUS W. SILVIA DUBOIS, (NOW 116 YEARS

OLD): A BIOGRAPHY OF THE SLAVE WHO WHIPPED HER
MISTRESS AND GAINED HER FREEDOM. RINGOES, NJ: C.W.
LARISON, 1883.

16444 LATTIMER, CATHERINE. "CATHERINE FERGUSON." NEGRO
HISTORY BULLETIN, 5 (NOVEMBER, 1951): 38-39.

16445 LAWRENCE, JACOB. HARRIET AND THE PROMISED LAND. NEW
YORK: WINDMILL BOOKS, 1968.

16446 LERNER, GERDA (ED.). BLACK WOMEN IN WHITE AMERICA: A
DOCUMENTARY HISTORY. NEW YORK: PANTHEON, 1972.

16447 "LETTERS FROM NEGRO WOMEN, 1827-1950." MASSES AND
MAINSTREAM, 4 (FEBRUARY, 1951): 24-33.

16448 LITWACK, LEON F. BEEN IN THE STORM SO LONG: THE
AFTERMATH OF SLAVERY. NEW YORK: ALFRED A. KNOPF,
1979.

16449 LOEWENBERG, BERT J. AND BOGIN, RUTH (EDS.). BLACK WOMEN
IN NINETEENTH CENTURY AMERICAN LIFE: THEIR WORDS,
THEIR THOUGHTS, THEIR FEELINGS. UNIVERSITY PARK:
PENNSYLVANIA STATE UNIVERSITY PRESS, 1976.

16450 MACK, DELORES. "WHERE THE BLACK MATRIARCHY THEORISTS
WENT WRONG." PSYCHOLOGY TODAY, 4 (JANUARY, 1971): 24.

16451 MAIR, LUCILLE M. "A HISTORICAL STUDY OF WOMEN IN JAMAICA
FROM 1655-1844." PH.D. DISSERTATION, UNIVERSITY OF
THE WEST INDIES, 1975.

16452 MAIR, LUCILLE M. THE REBEL WOMAN IN THE BRITISH WEST
INDIES DURING SLAVERY. KINGSTON: INSTITUTE OF
JAMAICA, 1975.

16453 MARTINEZ-ALIER, VERENA. MARRIAGE, CLASS AND COLOUR IN
NINETEENTH CENTURY CUBA: A STUDY OF RACIAL ATTITUDES
AND SEXUAL VALUES IN A SLAVE SOCIETY. LONDON:
CAMBRIDGE UNIVERSITY PRESS, 1974.

16454 MATHURIN, LUCILLE. "THE ARRIVALS OF BLACK WOMEN."
JAMAICA JOURNAL, 9 (1975): 2-7.

16455 MATHURIN, LUCILLE. "A HISTORICAL STUDY OF WOMEN IN
JAMAICA FROM 1655 TO 1844." PH.D. DISSERTATION,
UNIVERSITY OF THE WEST INDIES, 1974.

16456 MATHURIN, LUCILLE. THE REBEL WOMAN IN THE BRITISH WEST
INDIES DURING SLAVERY. KINGSTON: INSTITUTE OF
JAMAICA FOR THE AFRICAN-CARIBBEAN INSTITUTE OF
JAMAICA, 1975.

16457 MATHURIN, LUCILLE. "RELUCTANT MATRIARCHS." SAVACOU, 13
(1977): 1-6.

16458 MATSON, R. LYNN. "PHILLIS WHEATLEY--SOUL SISTER?" PHYLON, 33 (FALL, 1972): 222-230.

16459 MCCORMICK, V. "NEGRO SKETCHES." CATHOLIC WORLD, 122 (DECEMBER, 1925): 365-373.

16460 MCGEE, HENRY W. "THY NEIGHBOR'S SERVANTS, THY NEIGHBOR'S WIFE; WOMAN'S LIBERATION AND BLACK CIVIL RIGHTS, 1831-1919." B.A. THESIS, HARVARD UNIVERSITY, 1974.

16461 MCGOVERN, ANN. RUNAWAY SLAVE: THE STORY OF HARRIET TUBMAN. NEW YORK: FOUR WINDS PRESS, 1965.

16462 MCHENRY, SUSAN. "'SALLY HEMINGS': A KEY TO OUR NATIONAL IDENTITY: BARBARA CHASE-RIBOUD TELLS WHY SHE OUTRAGED THE JEFFERSON SCHOLARS." MS, 9 (OCTOBER, 1980): 35-40.

16463 MICHIGAN WOMEN: BIOGRAPHIES, AUTOBIOGRAPHIES, AND REMINISCENCES. LANSING: MICHIGAN DEPARTMENT OF EDUCATION, STATE LIBRARY SERVICES, 1975.

16464 MILLS, GARY B. "COINCOIN: AN EIGHTEENTH-CENTURY 'LIBERATED' WOMAN." JOURNAL OF SOUTHERN HISTORY, 42 (MAY, 1976): 205-222.

16465 MOORE, M.H. "MAMMY: A MEMORY OF THE OLD PLANTATION." NORTH CAROLINA CHRISTIAN ADVOCATE, 50 (DECEMBER 7, 1905): 2-3.

16466 MOSES, WILSON J. "DOMESTIC FEMINISM: CONSERVATISM, SEX ROLES, AND BLACK WOMEN'S CLUBS." JOURNAL OF SOCIAL AND BEHAVIORAL SCIENCES, 24 (FALL, 1978): 166-177.

16467 MUNGEN, DONNA. LIFE AND TIMES OF BIDDY MASON: FROM SLAVERY TO WEALTHY CALIFORNIA LAUNDRESS. N.P., 1976.

16468 MUSCATINE, LISSA. "'WAITING FOR GOD TO CALL': SLAVE WOMEN IN AMERICA." B.A. THESIS, HARVARD UNIVERSITY, 1976.

16469 MUSSON, NELLIE E. MIND THE ONION SEED: BLACK 'ROOTS' BERMUDA: PRESENTED DURING BERMUDA'S FIRST HERITAGE WEEK, MAY, 1979. HAMILTON, BERMUDA: MUSSON'S, 1979.

16470 MYERS, LENA W. BLACK WOMEN: DO THEY COPE BETTER? ENGLEWOOD CLIFFS: PRENTICE-HALL, 1980.

16471 NEWMAN, DEBRA. "BLACK WOMEN IN THE ERA OF THE AMERICAN REVOLUTION IN PENNSYLVANIA." JOURNAL OF NEGRO HISTORY, 61 (JULY, 1976): 276-289.

16472 NOBLE, JEANNE. "FREE AT LAST." BEAUTIFUL, ALSO, ARE THE SOULS OF MY BLACK SISTERS: A HISTORY OF THE BLACK WOMAN IN AMERICA. ENGLEWOOD CLIFFS: PRENTICE-HALL,

1978, PP. 50-71.

16473   NOBLE, JEANNE. "TO BE A SLAVE." BEAUTIFUL, ALSO, ARE
        THE SOULS OF MY BLACK SISTERS: A HISTORY OF THE BLACK
        WOMAN IN AMERICA. ENGLEWOOD CLIFFS: PRENTICE-HALL,
        1978, PP. 31-49.

16474   "THE OLD BLACK MAMMY." MONTGOMERY ADVERTISER, DECEMBER
        30, 1917.

16475   "OLD WILL SHOWS FREE NEGRO LEFT WHITE MAN WIFE."
        MONTGOMERY (AL) ADVERTISER, SEPTEMBER 25, 1916.

16476   OWENS, LESLIE H. THIS SPECIES OF PROPERTY: SLAVE LIFE
        AND CULTURE IN THE OLD SOUTH. NEW YORK: OXFORD
        UNIVERSITY PRESS, 1976.

16477   OWENS, M. LILLIANA. "JULIA GREELEY, COLORED ANGEL OF
        CHARITY." COLORADO MAGAZINE, 20 (SEPTEMBER, 1943):
        176-178.

16478   PAINTER, DIANN H. "THE BLACK WOMAN IN AMERICAN SOCIETY."
        CURRENT HISTORY, 70 (MAY, 1976): 224-227, 234.

16479   PARK, ANDREW. "OLD COLORED MAMMY'S RELIGION."
        CALIFORNIA INDEPENDENT, FEBRUARY 13, 1919.

16480   PARKHURST, JESSIE W. "THE ROLE OF THE BLACK MAMMY IN THE
        PLANTATION HOUSEHOLD." JOURNAL OF NEGRO HISTORY, 23
        (JULY, 1938): 349-369.

16481   PATTON, JUNE O. "DOCUMENT: MOONLIGHT AND MAGNOLIAS IN
        SOUTHERN EDUCATION, THE BLACK MAMMY MEMORIAL
        INSTITUTE." JOURNAL OF NEGRO HISTORY, 65 (SPRING,
        1980): 149-155.

16482   PESCATELLO, ANN. "LADIES AND WHORES IN COLONIAL BRAZIL."
        CARIBBEAN REVIEW, 5 (APRIL-JUNE, 1973): 26-30.

16483   PESCATELLO, ANN. POWER AND PAWN: THE FEMALE IN IBERIAN
        FAMILIES, SOCIETIES, AND CULTURES. WESTPORT:
        GREENWOOD PRESS, 1976.

16484   RAWICK, GEORGE P. FROM SUNDOWN TO SUNUP: THE MAKING OF
        THE BLACK COMMUNITY. WESTPORT: GREENWOOD PRESS, 1972.

16485   RENDER, SYLVIA L. "AFRO-AMERICAN WOMEN: THE OUTSTANDING
        AND THE OBSCURE." QUARTERLY JOURNAL OF THE LIBRARY OF
        CONGRESS, 32 (OCTOBER, 1975): 306-323.

16486   RICHARDSON, MARILYN. BLACK WOMEN AND RELIGION: A
        BIBLIOGRAPHY. BOSTON: G.K. HALL, 1980.

16487   RIES, ADELINE F. "MAMMY." CRISIS, 13 (JANUARY, 1917):
        117-118.

16488   ROUT, LESLIE B.   THE AFRICAN EXPERIENCE IN SPANISH
        AMERICA, 1502 TO THE PRESENT DAY.   CAMBRIDGE:
        CAMBRIDGE UNIVERSITY PRESS, 1976.

16489   RUSHING, ANDREA B.   "AN ANNOTATED BIBLIOGRAPHY OF IMAGES
        OF BLACK WOMEN IN BLACK LITERATURE."   CLA JOURNAL, 21
        (MARCH, 1978):   435-442.

16490   RUSSELL-WOOD, A.J.R.   "FEMALE AND FAMILY IN THE ECONOMY
        AND SOCIETY OF COLONIAL BRAZIL."   IN LAVRIN, ASUNCION
        (ED.).   LATIN AMERICAN WOMEN: HISTORICAL
        PERSPECTIVES.   WESTPORT: GREENWOOD PRESS, 1978, PP.
        60-100.

16491   RUSSELL-WOOD, A.J.R.   "WOMAN AND SOCIETY IN COLONIAL
        BRAZIL."   JOURNAL OF LATIN AMERICAN STUDIES, 9 (MAY,
        1977):   1-34.

16492   RYAN, MARY P.   WOMANHOOD IN AMERICA: FROM COLONIAL TIMES
        TO THE PRESENT.   NEW YORK: NEW VIEWPOINTS, 1975.

16493   SCHWENINGER, LOREN.   "A SLAVE FAMILY IN THE ANTEBELLUM
        SOUTH."   JOURNAL OF NEGRO HISTORY, 60 (JANUARY, 1975):
        29-44.

16494   SCOTT, ANNE F.   "WOMEN IN A PLANTATION CULTURE: OR WHAT
        I WISH I KNEW ABOUT SOUTHERN WOMEN."   IN CENSER, JACK
        R.; STEINERT, N. STEVEN; AND MCCANDLESS, AMY M.
        (EDS.).   SOUTH ATLANTIC URBAN STUDIES, VOLUME 2.
        COLUMBIA: UNIVERSITY OF SOUTH CAROLINA PRESS, 1978,
        PP. 24-33.

16495   SCOTT, ANNE F.   "WOMEN'S PERSPECTIVES ON THE PATRIARCHY
        IN THE 1850'S."   JOURNAL OF AMERICAN HISTORY, 61
        (JUNE, 1964):   52-64.

16496   "SHE WHO WOULD BE FREE.   RESISTANCE (THE NEGRO WOMAN IN
        SLAVERY, IN THE CIVIL WAR AND RECONSTRUCTION)."
        FREEDOMWAYS, 2 (WINTER, 1962):   60-70.

16497   SHERRARD, VIRGINIA B.   "RECOLLECTIONS OF MY MAMMY."
        SOUTHERN WORKMAN, 30 (FEBRUARY, 1901):   86-87.

16498   SHORTER, EDWARD.   "PROTEIN, PUBERTY AND PREMARITAL
        SEXUALITY: AMERICAN BLACKS V. FRENCH PEASANTS."
        UNPUBLISHED PAPER PRESENTED AT ISSB--UNIVERSITY OF
        ROCHESTER CONFERENCE: "TIME ON THE CROSS: A FIRST
        APPRAISAL,"   OCTOBER 24-26, 1974.

16499   "SILVIA DUBOIS, SLAVE OF THE SOURLANDS, RELATED LIFE
        STORY TO LARISON."   PRINCETON RECOLLECTOR, 5 (WINTER,
        1980):   1, 8-9.

16500   SIMS, JANET.   BLACK WOMEN--A SELECTED BIBLIOGRAPHY.
        WASHINGTON: MOORLAND-SPINGARN RESEARCH CENTER, HOWARD

UNIVERSITY, N.D.

16501   SIMS, JANET L. THE PROGRESS OF AFRO-AMERICAN WOMEN: A
         SELECTED BIBLIOGRAPHY AND RESOURCE GUIDE. WESTPORT:
         GREENWOOD PRESS, 1980.

16502   SLATTERY, JOHN R. "PHILLIS WHEATLEY, THE NEGRO POETESS."
         CATHOLIC WORLD, 39 (APRIL, 1884): 484-498.

16503   "SLAVE MOTHERHOOD." IN NUNEZ, BENJAMIN. DICTIONARY OF
         AFRO-LATIN AMERICAN CIVILIZATION. WESTPORT:
         GREENWOOD PRESS, 1980, P. 436.

16504   SMITH, AMANDA B. AN AUTOBIOGRAPHY: THE STORY OF THE
         LORD'S DEALINGS WITH MRS. AMANDA SMITH THE COLORED
         EVANGELIST, CONTAINING AN ACCOUNT OF HER LIFE WORK OF
         FAITH, HER TRAVELS IN AMERICA, ENGLAND, SCOTLAND,
         INDIA, AND AFRICA AS AN INDEPENDENT MISSIONARY.
         CHICAGO: MEYER AND BROTHER, 1893.

16505   SMITH, BARBARA. "DOING RESEARCH ON BLACK AMERICAN WOMEN
         OR ALL THE WOMEN ARE WHITE, ALL THE BLACKS ARE MEN,
         BUT SOME OF US ARE BRAVE." RADICAL TEACHER, NO. 3
         (1976): 25-27.

16506   SMITH, ELEANOR. "HISTORICAL RELATIONSHIPS BETWEEN BLACK
         AND WHITE WOMEN." WESTERN JOURNAL OF BLACK STUDIES, 4
         (WINTER, 1980): 251-255.

16507   SMITH, ELEANOR. "PHILLIS WHEATLEY: A BLACK
         PERSPECTIVE." JOURNAL OF NEGRO EDUCATION, 43 (SUMMER,
         1974): 401-407.

16508   STAPLES, ROBERT. THE BLACK WOMAN IN AMERICA: SEX,
         MARRIAGE, AND THE FAMILY. CHICAGO: NELSON HALL
         PUBLISHERS, 1973.

16509   STAPLES, ROBERT. "THE MYTH OF THE BLACK MATRIARCHY." IN
         STAPLES (ED.). THE BLACK FAMILY. BELMONT, CA:
         WADSWORTH PUBLISHING COMPANY, 1971, PP. 149-159.

16510   STERLING, DOROTHY. BLACK FOREMOTHERS: THREE LIVES. OLD
         WESTBURY, NY: FEMINIST PRESS, 1979.

16511   STOCKARD, JANICE L. "THE ROLE OF THE AMERICAN BLACK
         WOMAN IN FOLKTALES: AN INTERDISCIPLINARY STUDY OF
         IDENTIFICATION AND INTERPRETATION." PH.D.
         DISSERTATION, TULANE UNIVERSITY, 1980.

16512   STONE, PAULINE T. AND BROWN, CHERYL L. THE BLACK
         AMERICAN WOMAN IN THE SOCIAL SCIENCE LITERATURE. ANN
         ARBOR: MICHIGAN OCCASIONAL PAPERS IN WOMEN'S STUDIES,
         N.D.

16513   TAYLOR, MARSHALL W. AMANDA SMITH, OR THE LIFE AND

MISSION OF A SLAVE GIRL. CINCINNATI: CRANSTON AND STOWE, 1886.

16514 TELLER, WALTER. "INTRODUCTION." IN CHILD, L. MARIA (ED.). INCIDENTS IN THE LIFE OF A SLAVE GIRL. NEW YORK: HARCOURT BRACE JOVANOVICH, 1973, PP. IX-X.

16515 TERBORG-PENN, ROSALYN. "TEACHING THE HISTORY OF BLACK WOMEN: A BIBLIOGRAPHICAL ESSAY." HISTORY TEACHER, 13 (FEBRUARY, 1980): 245-250.

16516 TILLMAN, KATHERINE D. "AFRO-AMERICAN WOMEN AND THEIR WORK." A.M.E. CHURCH REVIEW, 11 (APRIL, 1895): 477-484.

16517 "TO ERECT MONUMENT FOR NEGRO 'MAMMIES.'" AFRO-AMERICAN LEDGER, JUNE 5, 1915.

16518 TRECKER, JANICE L. "TEXTBOOKS AND THE INVISIBLE WOMAN." INTERRACIAL BOOKS FOR CHILDREN, 5 (1974): 1-2.

16519 TUELON, ALAN. "NANNY--MAROON CHIEFTAINESS." CARIBBEAN QUARTERLY, 19 (DECEMBER, 1973): 20-27.

16520 TUTWILER, JULIA R. "MAMMY." ATLANTIC MONTHLY, 91 (JANUARY, 1903): 60-70.

16521 VENEY, BETHANY. THE NARRATIVE OF BETHANY VENEY, A SLAVE WOMAN. WORCESTER, MA: GEORGE H. ELLIS, 1889.

16522 WALKER, ALICE. "IN SEARCH OF OUR MOTHER'S GARDENS--HONORING THE CREATIVITY OF THE BLACK WOMAN." JACKSON STATE REVIEW, 6 (SUMMER, 1974): 44-53.

16523 WARD, HAZEL M. "THE BLACK WOMAN AS CHARACTER: IMAGES IN THE AMERICAN NOVEL, 1852-1953." PH.D. DISSERTATION, UNIVERSITY OF TEXAS, 1977.

16524 WASHINGTON, SARAH M. "AN ANNOTATED BIBLIOGRAPHY OF BLACK WOMEN BIOGRAPHIES AND AUTOBIOGRAPHIES FOR SECONDARY SCHOOL STUDENTS." PH.D. DISSERTATION, UNIVERSITY OF ILLINOIS, 1980.

16525 WATKINS, MEL AND DAVID, JAY (EDS.). TO BE A BLACK WOMAN: PORTRAITS IN FACT AND FICTION. NEW YORK: WILLIAM MORROW AND COMPANY, 1970.

16526 WATTS, A. FAULKNER. BLACK SLAVE WOMAN: PROTAGONIST FOR FREEDOM. NEW YORK: EDWARD W. BLYDEN PRESS, 1979.

16527 WEBBER, KIKANZA N. "REFLECTIONS ON BLACK AMERICAN WOMEN: THE IMAGE OF THE EIGHTIES." WESTERN JOURNAL OF BLACK STUDIES, 4 (WINTER, 1980): 242-250.

16528 WEBBER, THOMAS L. DEEP LIKE THE RIVERS: EDUCATION IN

THE_SLAVE_QUARTER_COMMUNITY,_1831-1865. NEW YORK:
W.W. NORTON, 1978.

16529 WEGELIN, OSCAR. "WAS PHILLIS WHEATLEY AMERICA'S FIRST
NEGRO POET?" LITERARY_COLLECTION, (AUGUST, 1904):
117-118.

16530 WERTHEIMER, BARBARA M. "BLACK WOMEN IN COLONIAL
AMERICA." WE_WERE_THERE:_THE_STORY_OF_WORKING_WOMEN
IN_AMERICA. NEW YORK: PANTHEON, 1977, PP. 26-37.

16531 WHITE, DEBORAH G. "AIN'T I A WOMAN? FEMALE SLAVES IN
THE ANTEBELLUM SOUTH." PH.D. DISSERTATION, UNIVERSITY
OF ILLINOIS, 1979.

16532 WHITE, JOHN. "WHATEVER HAPPENED TO THE SLAVE FAMILY IN
THE OLD SOUTH?" JOURNAL_OF_AMERICAN_STUDIES, 8
(DECEMBER, 1974): 383-390.

16533 WILEY, BELL I. CONFEDERATE_WOMEN. WESTPORT: GREENWOOD
PRESS, 1975.

16534 WILLINGHAM, N. LOUISE. "THE BLACK WOMAN: AN ANNOTATED
BIBLIOGRAPHY." UNABASHED_LIBRARIAN, 14 (WINTER,
1975): 16-17.

SLAVE_MARRIAGES

16535 AGONITO, JOSEPH. "ST. INIGOES MANOR: A NINETEENTH
CENTURY JESUIT PLANTATION." MARYLAND_HISTORICAL
MAGAZINE, 72 (SPRING, 1977): 83-98.

16536 ALEXANDER, JOHN B. REMINISCENCES_OF_THE_PAST_60_YEARS.
CHARLOTTE: RAY PRINTING COMPANY, 1908.

16537 BANKS, FRANK D. AND SMILEY, PORTIA. "OLD-TIME COURTSHIP
CONVERSATION." SOUTHERN_WORKMAN, 24 (1895): 14-15,
78.

16538 BRADWELL, JAMES B. VALIDITY_OF_SLAVE_MARRIAGES.
CHICAGO: E.B. MYERS & CHANDLER, 1866.

16539 CARTER, DORIS D. "REFUSING TO RELINQUISH THE STRUGGLES:
THE SOCIAL ROLE OF THE BLACK WOMAN IN LOUISIANA
HISTORY." IN MACDONALD, ROBERT R.; KEMP, JOHN R.; AND
HAAS, EDWARD F. (EDS.). LOUISIANA'S_BLACK_HERITAGE.
NEW ORLEANS: LOUISIANA STATE MUSEUM, 1979, PP.
163-189.

16540 CROWDER, RALPH L. "GUSSA GODFREY: BLACK-INDIAN LEADER."
MINNEAPOLIS SPOKESMAN_AND_RECORDER, FEBRUARY 4, 1976.

16541 DIETRICH, KATHERYN T. "A RE-EXAMINATION OF THE MYTH OF
BLACK MATRIARCHY." JOURNAL_OF_MARRIAGE_AND_THE

FAMILY, 37 (MAY, 1975): 367-374.

16542 "A DIFFICULT COURTSHIP." SOUTHERN WORKMAN, 25 (1896): 226.

16543 DUBOIS, W.E.B. (ED.). THE NEGRO AMERICAN FAMILY. ATLANTA: ATLANTA UNIVERSITY PUBLICATIONS, 1908.

16544 EVERLY, ELAINE C. "MARRIAGE REGISTERS OF FREEDMEN." PROLOGUE, 5 (FALL, 1973): 150-154.

16545 FOGEL, ROBERT W. AND ENGERMAN, STANLEY L. TIME ON THE CROSS: THE ECONOMICS OF AMERICAN NEGRO SLAVERY. 2 VOLS. BOSTON: LITTLE, BROWN AND COMPANY, 1974.

16546 "FOLK-LORE AND ETHNOLOGY." SOUTHERN WORKMAN, 26 (1897): 163.

16547 GARRETT, SUE G. "NEGRO MATING AND FAMILY PATTERNS FROM WEST AFRICA TO THE NEW WORLD." M.A. THESIS, UNIVERSITY OF NORTH CAROLINA, 1965.

16548 GENOVESE, EUGENE D. ROLL, JORDAN, ROLL: THE WORLD THE SLAVES MADE. NEW YORK: PANTHEON, 1974.

16549 GUTMAN, HERBERT G. THE BLACK FAMILY IN SLAVERY AND FREEDOM, 1750-1925. NEW YORK: PANTHEON BOOKS, 1976.

16550 GUTMAN, HERBERT G. "MARITAL AND SEXUAL NORMS AMONG SLAVE WOMEN." IN COTT, NANCY F. AND PLECK, ELIZABETH H. (EDS.). A HERITAGE OF HER OWN: TOWARD A NEW SOCIAL HISTORY OF AMERICAN WOMEN. NEW YORK: SIMON & SCHUSTER, 1979, PP. 298-310.

16551 JONES, BOBBY F. "A CULTURAL MIDDLE PASSAGE: SLAVE MARRIAGE AND FAMILY IN THE ANTE-BELLUM SOUTH." PH.D. DISSERTATION, UNIVERSITY OF NORTH CAROLINA, 1965.

16552 LABINJOH, JUSTIN. "THE SEXUAL LIFE OF THE OPPRESSED: AN EXAMINATION OF THE FAMILY LIFE OF ANTE-BELLUM SLAVES." PHYLON, 35 (WINTER, 1974): 375-397.

16553 LANDES, RUTH. "NEGRO SLAVERY AND FEMALE STATUS." AFRICAN AFFAIRS, 52 (JANUARY, 1953): 54-57.

16554 LANDES, RUTH. "NEGRO SLAVERY AND FEMALE STATUS." IN LES AFRO-AMERICAINS. DAKAR: INSTITUT FRANCAIS D'AFRIQUE NOIR, 1953, PP. 265-268.

16555 LASLETT, PETER. "HOUSEHOLD AND FAMILY ON THE SLAVE PLANTATIONS OF THE U.S.A." FAMILY LIFE AND ILLICIT LOVE IN EARLIER GENERATIONS: ESSAYS IN HISTORICAL SOCIOLOGY. CAMBRIDGE: CAMBRIDGE UNIVERSITY PRESS, 1977, PP. 233-260.

16556   LEVINE, ROBERT M. "SLAVE MARRIAGE." RACE AND ETHNIC
        RELATIONS IN LATIN AMERICA AND THE CARIBBEAN.
        METUCHEN, NJ: SCARECROW PRESS, 1980, P. 127.

16557   LOMBARDI, JOHN V. PEOPLES AND PLACES IN COLONIAL
        VENEZUELA. BLOOMINGTON: INDIANA UNIVERSITY PRESS,
        1976.

16558   LOVE, EDGAR F. "MARRIAGE PATTERNS OF PERSONS OF AFRICAN
        DESCENT IN A COLONIAL MEXICO CITY PARISH." HISPANIC
        AMERICAN HISTORICAL REVIEW, 51 (FEBRUARY, 1971):
        79-91.

16559   LUTZ, CHRISTOPHER H. "SANTIAGO DE GUATEMALA, 1541-1773:
        THE SOCIO-DEMOGRAPHIC HISTORY OF A SPANISH AMERICAN
        COLONIAL CITY." PH.D. DISSERTATION, UNIVERSITY OF
        WISCONSIN, 1976.

16560   "MARRIAGE AND DIVORCE--SLAVE MARRIAGE--EFFECT OF
        EMANCIPATION." YALE LAW REVIEW, 28 (MARCH, 1919):
        516-517.

16561   MARTINEZ-ALIER, VERENA. MARRIAGE, CLASS AND COLOUR IN
        NINETEENTH CENTURY CUBA: A STUDY OF RACIAL ATTITUDES
        AND SEXUAL VALUES IN A SLAVE SOCIETY. LONDON:
        CAMBRIDGE UNIVERSITY PRESS, 1974.

16562   MATHIAS, ARTHUR. "CONTRASTING APPROACHES TO THE STUDY OF
        BLACK FAMILIES." JOURNAL OF MARRIAGE AND THE FAMILY,
        40 (NOVEMBER, 1978): 667-676.

16563   MOORE, GEORGE H. "SLAVE MARRIAGES IN MASSACHUSETTS."
        HISTORICAL MAGAZINE, 2ND SER., 5 (FEBRUARY, 1869):
        135-137.

16564   OWENS, LESLIE H. THIS SPECIES OF PROPERTY: SLAVE LIFE
        AND CULTURE IN THE OLD SOUTH. NEW YORK: OXFORD
        UNIVERSITY PRESS, 1976.

16565   PERDUE, CHARLES L., JR.; BARDEN, THOMAS E.; AND PHILLIPS,
        ROBERT K. (EDS.). WEEVILS IN THE WHEAT: INTERVIEWS
        WITH VIRGINIA EX-SLAVES. CHARLOTTESVILLE: UNIVERSITY
        PRESS OF VIRGINIA, 1976.

16566   RABOTEAU, ALBERT J. SLAVE RELIGION: THE "INVISIBLE
        INSTITUTION" IN THE AMERICAN SOUTH. NEW YORK: OXFORD
        UNIVERSITY PRESS, 1978.

16567   RUBENSTEIN, HYMIE. "DIACHRONIC INFERENCE AND THE PATTERN
        OF LOWER-CLASS AFRO-CARIBBEAN MARRIAGE." SOCIAL AND
        ECONOMIC STUDIES, 26 (JUNE, 1977): 202-216.

16568   SIDES, SUDIE D. "SLAVE WEDDINGS AND RELIGION:
        PLANTATION LIFE IN THE SOUTHERN STATES BEFORE THE
        AMERICAN CIVIL WAR." HISTORY TODAY, 24 (FEBRUARY,

1974): 77-87.

16569   SLATER, MARIAM K. THE CARIBBEAN FAMILY: LEGITIMACY IN
        MARTINIQUE. NEW YORK: ST. MARTIN'S PRESS, 1977.

16570   "SLAVE MARRIAGE." IN NUNEZ, BENJAMIN. DICTIONARY OF
        AFRO-LATIN AMERICAN CIVILIZATION. WESTPORT:
        GREENWOOD PRESS, 1980, P. 436.

16571   "SLAVE MARRIAGES." SOUTHERN WORKMAN, 26 (AUGUST, 1897):
        163.

16572   "SLAVE-MARRIAGES." VIRGINIA LAW JOURNAL, 1 (NOVEMBER,
        1877): 641-652.

16573   "SLAVE MARRIAGES IN MASSACHUSETTS." HISTORICAL MAGAZINE,
        2ND SER., 5 (FEBRUARY, 1869): 135-137.

16574   "SLAVE POLYGAMOUS MATING." IN NUNEZ, BENJAMIN.
        DICTIONARY OF AFRO-LATIN AMERICAN CIVILIZATION.
        WESTPORT: GREENWOOD PRESS, 1980, P. 436.

16575   "SLAVE WOMAN MATING." IN NUNEZ, BENJAMIN. DICTIONARY OF
        AFRO-LATIN AMERICAN CIVILIZATION. WESTPORT:
        GREENWOOD PRESS, 1980, P. 438.

16576   "SLAVES' MARRIAGE BY COMMON LAW UPHELD BY COURT."
        ATLANTA CONSTITUTION, DECEMBER 11, 1920.

16577   "SLAVES, MARRIAGE OF." IN RYWELL, MARTIN (ED.).
        AFRO-AMERICAN ENCYCLOPEDIA. 10 VOLS. NORTH MIAMI:
        EDUCATIONAL BOOK PUBLISHERS, 1974, VOL. 8, P. 2491.

16578   STECKEL, RICHARD H. "SLAVE MARRIAGE AND THE FAMILY."
        JOURNAL OF FAMILY HISTORY, 5 (WINTER, 1980): 406-421.

16579   STERLING, DOROTHY. BLACK FOREMOTHERS: THREE LIVES. OLD
        WESTBURY, NY: FEMINIST PRESS, 1979.

16580   TAYLOR, ORVILLE W. "'JUMPING THE BROOMSTICK': SLAVE
        MARRIAGE AND MORALITY IN ARKANSAS." ARKANSAS
        HISTORICAL QUARTERLY, 17 (AUTUMN, 1958): 217-231.

16581   WILEY, BELL I. SOUTHERN NEGROES, 1861-1865. NEW HAVEN:
        YALE UNIVERSITY PRESS, 1938.

21.
Slave Religion

16582   ABBEY, RICHARD. PETER, NOT AN APOSTLE, BUT A CHATTEL
        WITH A STRANGE HISTORY. NASHVILLE: SOUTHERN
        METHODIST PUBLISHING HOUSE, 1885.

16583   ABBOT, ERNEST H. "RELIGIOUS TENDENCIES OF THE NEGRO."
        OUTLOOK, 69 (DECEMBER 28, 1901): 1070-1076.

16584   ADAMS, ALICE D. THE NEGLECTED PERIOD OF ANTI-SLAVERY IN
        AMERICA (1808-1831). BOSTON: GINN AND COMPANY, 1908.

16585   ADDO, LINDA D. TO BE FAITHFUL TO OUR HERITAGE: A
        HISTORY OF BLACK UNITED METHODISM IN NORTH CAROLINA.
        CHARLOTTE: WESTERN NORTH CAROLINA ANNUAL CONFERENCE,
        UNITED METHODIST CHURCH, 1980.

16586   ADEFILA, JOHNSON A. "SLAVE RELIGION IN THE ANTEBELLUM
        SOUTH: A STUDY OF THE ROLE OF AFRICANISMS IN THE
        BLACK RESPONSE TO CHRISTIANITY." PH.D. DISSERTATION,
        BRANDEIS UNIVERSITY, 1975.

16587   ADGER, JOHN B. MY LIFE AND TIMES, 1810-1899. RICHMOND:
        PRESBYTERIAN COMMITTEE OF PUBLICATION, 1899.

16588   AGONITO, JOSEPH. "ST. INIGOES MANOR: A NINETEENTH
        CENTURY JESUIT PLANTATION." MARYLAND HISTORICAL
        MAGAZINE, 72 (SPRING, 1977): 33-98.

16589   AKERS, J.N. "SLAVERY AND SECTIONALISM: SOME ASPECTS OF
        CHURCH AND SOCIETY AMONG PRESBYTERIANS IN THE AMERICAN
        SOUTH, 1789-1861." PH.D. DISSERTATION, UNIVERSITY OF
        EDINBURGH, 1973.

16590   ALHO, OLLI. THE RELIGION OF THE SLAVES: A STUDY OF THE
        RELIGIOUS TRADITION AND BEHAVIOUR OF PLANTATION SLAVES
        IN THE UNITED STATES, 1830-1865. HELSINKI, FINLAND:
        SUOMALAINEN TIEDEAKATEMIA, ACAD. SCIENTIARUM FENNICA,
        1976.

16591   ALLEN, CUTHBERT E. "THE SLAVERY QUESTION AS SEEN IN THE
        FREEMAN'S JOURNAL AND THE BALTIMORE CATHOLIC MIRROR
        (1850-1865)." M.A. THESIS, CATHOLIC UNIVERSITY OF
        AMERICA, 1935.

16592   ALLEN, CUTHBERT E. "THE SLAVERY QUESTION IN CATHOLIC
        NEWSPAPERS, 1850-1865." UNITED STATES CATHOLIC
        HISTORICAL SOCIETY RECORDS AND STUDIES, 26 (1936):
        99-179.

16593   ALLEN, HEMAN H. THE GENERAL ASSEMBLY AND ITS ACCUSERS:
        BEING A COMPILATION FROM OFFICIAL RECORDS OF THE

DELIVERANCES OF THE CHURCH (PRESBYTERIAN) ON CIVIL
AFFAIRS AND SLAVERY. LOUISVILLE: HILL & BROTHERS,
1867.

16594   ANDERSON, CHARLES A. (ED.). "PRESBYTERIANS MEET THE
        SLAVERY PROBLEM." JOURNAL OF THE PRESBYTERIAN
        HISTORICAL SOCIETY, 29 (MARCH, 1951): 9-39.

16595   ANDERSON, JOHNNY R. "THE PREACHER: A SYMBOL OF BLACK
        COMMUNITY LEADERSHIP." JOURNAL OF THE AMERICAN
        STUDIES ASSOCIATION OF TEXAS, 7 (1976): 5-13.

16596   ANDERSON, MATTHEW. PRESBYTERIANISM: ITS RELATION TO THE
        NEGRO. PHILADELPHIA: J.M. WHITE, 1897.

16597   ANSTEY, ROGER T. "SLAVERY AND THE PROTESTANT ETHIC."
        HISTORICAL REFLECTIONS, 6 (SUMMER, 1979): 157-172.

16598   APTHEKER, HERBERT. "THE QUAKERS AND NEGRO SLAVERY."
        JOURNAL OF NEGRO HISTORY, 25 (JULY, 1940): 331-362.

16599   "THE BACKGROUND OF THE NEGRO CHURCH." NEGRO HISTORY
        BULLETIN, 3 (OCTOBER, 1939): 3-4.

16600   BACON, ALICE M. "CONJURING AND CONJURE-DOCTORS."
        SOUTHERN WORKMAN, 24 (NOVEMBER, DECEMBER, 1895):
        193-194, 209-211.

16601   BAHAM, VENITA M. "MYSTICISM AND THE AFRO-AMERICAN
        RELIGIOUS EXPERIENCE." JOURNAL OF RELIGIOUS THOUGHT,
        35 (SPRING-SUMMER, 1978): 68-77.

16602   BAILEY, DAVID T. "SLAVERY AND THE CHURCHES: THE OLD
        SOUTHWEST." PH.D. DISSERTATION, UNIVERSITY OF
        CALIFORNIA, 1979.

16603   BAILEY, KENNETH K. "PROTESTANTISM AND AFRO-AMERICANS IN
        THE OLD SOUTH: ANOTHER LOOK." JOURNAL OF SOUTHERN
        HISTORY, 41 (NOVEMBER, 1975): 451-472.

16604   BAKER, ROBERT A. "THE AMERICAN BAPTIST HOME MISSION
        SOCIETY AND THE SOUTH, 1832-1894." PH.D.
        DISSERTATION, YALE UNIVERSITY, 1980.

16605   BARRETT, LEONARD E. "AFRICAN RELIGION IN THE AMERICAS:
        THE ISLANDS IN BETWEEN." IN BOOTH, NEWELL S., JR.
        (ED.). AFRICAN RELIGIONS: A SYMPOSIUM. NEW YORK:
        NOK PUBLISHERS, 1977, PP. 183-216.

16606   BARRETT, LEONARD E. "AFRICAN ROOTS IN JAMAICAN
        INDIGENOUS RELIGION." JOURNAL OF RELIGIOUS THOUGHT,
        35 (SPRING-SUMMER, 1978): 7-26.

16607   BARRETT, LEONARD E. SOUL FORCE: AFRICAN HERITAGE IN
        AFRO-AMERICAN RELIGION. NEW YORK: DOUBLEDAY, 1974.

16608   BASCOM, WILLIAM R.   "TWO FORMS OF AFRO-CUBAN DIVINATION."
        IN TAX, SOL (ED.).   ACCULTURATION IN THE AMERICAS:
        PROCEEDINGS AND SELECTED PAPERS OF THE XXIXTH
        INTERNATIONAL CONGRESS OF AMERICANISTS.   NEW YORK:
        COOPER SQUARE PUBLISHERS, 1952, PP. 169-179.

16609   BASS, BERNIE S.   "SLAVERY AND THE PRESBYTERIAN CHURCH
        BEFORE THE CIVIL WAR."   M.A. THESIS, OLD DOMINION
        UNIVERSITY, 1966.

16610   BASSETT, JOHN S.   "NORTH CAROLINA METHODISM AND SLAVERY."
        HISTORICAL PAPERS PUBLISHED BY THE TRINITY COLLEGE
        HISTORICAL SOCIETY, 4TH SER., (1900): 1-11.

16611   BASTIDE, ROGER.   THE AFRICAN RELIGIONS OF BRAZIL.
        BALTIMORE: JOHNS HOPKINS UNIVERSITY PRESS, 1978.

16612   BASTIEN, REMY.   RELIGION AND POLITICS IN HAITI.
        WASHINGTON: INSTITUTE FOR CROSS-CULTURAL RESEARCH,
        1966.

16613   BASTIN, BRUCE.   "BLACK MUSIC IN NORTH CAROLINA."   NORTH
        CAROLINA FOLKLORE JOURNAL, 27 (MAY, 1979): 3-19.

16614   BATHERSFIELD, JOAN P.   "THE TREATMENT OF BLACK RELIGION
        IN THE CARIBBEAN NOVEL."   PH.D. DISSERTATION, HOWARD
        UNIVERSITY, 1977.

16615   BEHAGUE, GERARD H.   "SOME LITURGICAL FUNCTIONS OF
        AFRO-BRAZILIAN RELIGIOUS MUSIC IN SALVADOR, BAHIA."
        WORLD OF MUSIC, 19 (1977): 4-23.

16616   BELL, HESKETH J.   OBEAH: WITCHCRAFT IN THE WEST INDIES.
        LONDON: SAMPSON, LOW, MARSTON & COMPANY, 1893.

16617   BELLOT, LELAND J.   "EVANGELICALS AND THE DEFENSE OF
        SLAVERY IN BRITAIN'S OLD COLONIAL EMPIRE."   JOURNAL OF
        SOUTHERN HISTORY, 37 (FEBRUARY, 1971): 19-40.

16618   BENNETT, ROBERT A.   "BLACK EPISCOPALIANS: A HISTORY FROM
        THE COLONIAL PERIOD TO THE PRESENT."   HISTORICAL
        MAGAZINE OF THE PROTESTANT EPISCOPAL CHURCH, 43
        (SEPTEMBER, 1974): 231-245.

16619   BETHEA, JOSEPH B.   "BLACK METHODISTS IN NORTH CAROLINA."
        IN INGRAM, O. KELLY (ED.).   METHODISM ALIVE IN NORTH
        CAROLINA.   DURHAM: DIVINITY SCHOOL, DUKE UNIVERSITY,
        1976, PP. 87-98.

16620   BLACKBURN, REGINA L.   "CONSCIOUS AGENTS OF TIME AND SELF:
        THE LIVES AND STYLES OF AFRICAN-AMERICAN WOMEN AS SEEN
        THROUGH THEIR AUTOBIOGRAPHICAL WRITINGS."   PH.D.
        DISSERTATION, UNIVERSITY OF NEW MEXICO, 1978.

16621   BLANKS, WILLIAM D.   "IDEAL AND PRACTICE: A STUDY OF THE

CONCEPTION OF THE CHRISTIAN LIFE IN THE PRESBYTERIAN
CHURCHES OF THE SOUTH DURING THE NINETEENTH CENTURY."
TH.D. DISSERTATION, UNION THEOLOGICAL SEMINARY,
RICHMOND, 1960.

16622 BLASSINGAME, JOHN W. THE SLAVE COMMUNITY: PLANTATION
       LIFE IN THE ANTEBELLUM SOUTH. NEW YORK: OXFORD
       UNIVERSITY PRESS, 1972.

16623 BLAUVELT, MARTHA T. "SLAVES AND GENTLEMEN: RELIGION IN
       THE ANTEBELLUM SOUTH." REVIEWS IN AMERICAN HISTORY, 7
       (SEPTEMBER, 1979): 350-355.

16624 BLIED, BENJAMIN J. CATHOLICS AND THE CIVIL WAR.
       MILWAUKEE: N.P., 1945.

16625 BODO, JOHN R. THE PROTESTANT CLERGY AND PUBLIC ISSUES,
       1812-1848. PRINCETON: PRINCETON UNIVERSITY PRESS,
       1954.

16626 BOLES, JOHN B. RELIGION IN ANTEBELLUM KENTUCKY.
       LEXINGTON: UNIVERSITY PRESS OF KENTUCKY, 1976.

16627 BOLLER, PAUL F. "WASHINGTON, THE QUAKERS, AND SLAVERY."
       JOURNAL OF NEGRO HISTORY, 46 (APRIL, 1961): 83-88.

16628 BOLTON, H. CARRINGTON. "GOMBAY, A FESTAL RITE OF
       BERMUDIAN NEGROES." JOURNAL OF AMERICAN FOLKLORE, 3
       (JULY-SEPTEMBER, 1890): 222-226.

16629 BOLTON, S.C. "SOUTH CAROLINA AND THE REVEREND DOCTOR
       FRANCIS LE JAU: SOUTHERN SOCIETY AND THE CONSCIENCE
       OF AN ANGLICAN MISSIONARY." HISTORICAL MAGAZINE OF
       THE PROTESTANT EPISCOPAL CHURCH, 40 (MARCH, 1971):
       63-79.

16630 BOOTHE, CHARLES O. THE CYCLOPEDIA OF THE COLORED BAPTIST
       OF ALABAMA. BIRMINGHAM: BIRMINGHAM PUBLISHING
       COMPANY, 1895.

16631 BOURGUIGNON, ERIKA. "RITUAL DISSOCIATION AND POSSESSION
       BELIEF IN CARIBBEAN NEGRO RELIGION." IN WHITTEN,
       NORMAN E., JR. AND SZWED, JOHN (EDS.). AFRO-AMERICAN
       ANTHROPOLOGY. NEW YORK: FREE PRESS, 1970, PP. 87-101.

16632 BOWEN, MICHAEL L. "SLAVERY AMONG THE BRETHREN." M.A.
       THESIS, WESTERN CAROLINA UNIVERSITY, 1975.

16633 BOYD, JESSE L. A POPULAR HISTORY OF THE BAPTISTS IN
       MISSISSIPPI. JACKSON: BAPTIST PRESS, 1930.

16634 BOYD, WILLIAM K. "DOCUMENTS AND COMMENTS ON BENEFIT OF
       CLERGY AS APPLIED TO SLAVES." JOURNAL OF NEGRO
       HISTORY, 8 (OCTOBER, 1923): 443-447.

16635   BRADLEY, DAVID H.   "FRANCIS ASBURY AND THE DEVELOPMENT OF
        AFRICAN CHURCHES IN AMERICA."   METHODIST HISTORY, 10
        (OCTOBER, 1971):   3-29.

16636   BRADLEY, DAVID H.   A HISTORY OF THE A.M.E. ZION CHURCH,
        1796-1872.   NASHVILLE: PARTHENON PRESS, 1956.

16637   BRADLEY, L. RICHARD.   "THE CURSE OF CANAAN AND THE
        AMERICAN NEGRO."   CONCORDIA IDEOLOGICAL MONTHLY, 42
        (FEBRUARY, 1971):   100-110.

16638   BRADLEY, L. RICHARD.   "THE LUTHERAN CHURCH AND SLAVERY."
        CONCORDIA HISTORICAL INSTITUTE QUARTERLY, 44
        (FEBRUARY, 1971):   32-41.

16639   BRADLEY, MICHAEL R.   "THE ROLE OF THE BLACK CHURCH IN THE
        COLONIAL SLAVE SOCIETY."   LOUISIANA STUDIES, 14
        (WINTER, 1975):   413-421.

16640   BRADWELL, JAMES B.   VALIDITY OF SLAVE MARRIAGES.
        CHICAGO: E.B. MYERS & CHANDLER, 1866.

16641   BRAGG, GEORGE F.   FIRST NEGRO PRIEST ON SOUTHERN SOIL.
        BALTIMORE: CHURCH ADVOCATE PRESS, 1909.

16642   BRAGG, GEORGE F.   HISTORY OF THE AFRO-AMERICAN GROUP OF
        THE EPISCOPAL CHURCH.   BALTIMORE: CHURCH ADVOCATE
        PRESS, 1922.

16643   BRATTON, MARY J.   "JOHN JASPER OF RICHMOND: FROM SLAVE
        PREACHER TO COMMUNITY LEADER."   VIRGINIA CAVALCADE, 29
        (SUMMER, 1979):   32-39.

16644   BRAWLEY, JAMES P.   TWO CENTURIES OF METHODIST CONCERN:
        BONDAGE, FREEDOM, AND EDUCATION OF BLACK PEOPLE.   NEW
        YORK: VANTAGE PRESS, 1974.

16645   BREATHETT, GEORGE.   "CATHOLIC MISSIONARY ACTIVITY AND THE
        NEGRO SLAVE IN HAITI."   PHYLON, 23 (FALL, 1962):
        278-285.

16646   BREATHETT, GEORGE.   "RELIGIOUS PROTECTIONISM AND THE
        SLAVE IN HAITI."   CATHOLIC HISTORICAL REVIEW, 55
        (APRIL, 1969):   26-39.

16647   BREEDEN, JAMES O.   JOSEPH JONES, M.D.:   SCIENTIST OF THE
        OLD SOUTH.   LEXINGTON: UNIVERSITY PRESS OF KENTUCKY,
        1975.

16648   BRENNAN, EDWARD J.   "IDEOLOGY OF IMPERIALISM: SPANISH
        DEBATES REGARDING THE CONQUEST OF AMERICA, 1511-1551."
        STUDIES, 47 (SPRING, 1958):   66-82.

16649   BREWER, JOHN M.   "NEGRO PREACHER TALES FROM THE TEXAS
        'BRAZOS BOTTOMS.'"   M.A. THESIS, INDIANA UNIVERSITY,

1241

1949.

16650   A BRIEF SKETCH OF THE SCHOOLS FOR BLACK PEOPLE, AND THEIR
        DESCENDANTS, ESTABLISHED BY THE RELIGIOUS SOCIETY OF
        FRIENDS, IN 1770. PHILADELPHIA: FRIENDS' BOOK STORE,
        1867.

16651   BRINGHURST, NEWELL G. "FORGOTTEN MORMON PERSPECTIVES:
        SLAVERY, RACE, AND THE BLACK MAN AS ISSUES AMONG
        NON-UTAH LATTER-DAY SAINTS, 1844-1873." MICHIGAN
        HISTORY, 61 (WINTER, 1977): 353-370.

16652   BRINGHURST, NEWELL G. "A SERVANT OF SERVANTS . . .
        CURSED AS PERTAINING TO THE PRIESTHOOD: MORMON
        ATTITUDES TOWARD SLAVERY AND THE BLACK MAN,
        1830-1880." PH.D. DISSERTATION, UNIVERSITY OF
        CALIFORNIA, DAVIS, 1975.

16653   BROOKS, WALTER H. "THE EVOLUTION OF THE NEGRO BAPTIST
        CHURCH." JOURNAL OF NEGRO HISTORY, 7 (JANUARY, 1922):
        11-22.

16654   BROOKS, WALTER H. "THE PRIORITY OF THE SILVER BLUFF
        CHURCH AND ITS PROMOTERS." JOURNAL OF NEGRO HISTORY,
        7 (APRIL, 1922): 172-196.

16655   BROWN, BEVERLY. "GEORGE LIELE: BLACK BAPTIST AND
        PAN-AFRICANIST, 1750-1826." SAVACOU, 11-12
        (SEPTEMBER, 1975): 58-67.

16656   BROWN, CHARLES S. AND CHAPPELLE, YVONNE R. "AFRICAN
        RELIGIONS AND THE QUEST FOR AFRO-AMERICAN HERITAGE."
        IN BOOTH, NEWELL S., JR. (ED.). AFRICAN RELIGIONS: A
        SYMPOSIUM. NEW YORK: NOK PUBLISHERS, 1977, PP.
        241-254.

16657   BROWN, LARRY. "HISTORIC ROLES OF CHRISTIANITY DURING
        SLAVERY." TRANSITION, 1 (1973): 182-192.

16658   BRUCE, DICKSON D., JR. "RELIGION, SOCIETY AND CULTURE IN
        THE OLD SOUTH: A COMPARATIVE VIEW." AMERICAN
        QUARTERLY, 26 (OCTOBER, 1974): 399-416.

16659   BRUNER, CLARENCE V. AN ABSTRACT OF THE RELIGIOUS
        INSTRUCTION OF THE SLAVES IN THE ANTEBELLUM SOUTH.
        NASHVILLE: GEORGE PEABODY COLLEGE FOR TEACHERS, 1933.

16660   BRUNER, CLARENCE V. "ABSTRACT OF THE RELIGIOUS
        INSTRUCTION OF THE SLAVES IN THE ANTEBELLUM SOUTH."
        PEABODY JOURNAL OF EDUCATION, 11 (NOVEMBER, 1933):
        117-121.

16661   BRUNER, CLARENCE V. "RELIGIOUS INSTRUCTION OF THE SLAVES
        IN THE ANTEBELLUM SOUTH." PH.D. DISSERTATION, GEORGE
        PEABODY COLLEGE FOR TEACHERS, 1933.

16662   BURGER, NASH K.   "THE DIOCESE OF MISSISSIPPI AND THE
        CONFEDERACY."   HISTORICAL MAGAZINE OF THE PROTESTANT
        EPISCOPAL CHURCH, 9 (MARCH, 1940):   52-77.

16663   BURGER, NASH K.   "A SIDE-LIGHT ON AN ANTE-BELLUM
        PLANTATION CHAPEL."   HISTORICAL MAGAZINE OF THE
        PROTESTANT EPISCOPAL CHURCH, 12 (MARCH, 1943):   69-73.

16664   BURRIS, SHIRLEY W.   "'EXERCISING GODLY DISCIPLINE' IN
        SOUTHWEST MISSISSIPPI CHURCHES."   MID-SOUTH FOLKLORE,
        2 (SPRING, 1974):   7-18.

16665   BUSH, LESTER E.   "MORMONISM'S NEGRO DOCTRINE; AN
        HISTORICAL OVERVIEW."   DIALOGUE: A JOURNAL OF MORMON
        THOUGHT, 8 (1973):   11-86.

16666   BUSS, ELIZABETH.   "THE ATTITUDE OF FIVE PROTESTANT
        CHURCHES TOWARDS SLAVERY."   M.A. THESIS, UNIVERSITY OF
        WASHINGTON, 1928.

16667   BUSWELL, JAMES O.   SLAVERY, SEGREGATION AND SCRIPTURE.
        GRAND RAPIDS: WILLIAM B. EERDMANS PUBLISHING COMPANY,
        1964.

16668   BUTLER, ALFLOYD.   THE AFRICANIZATION OF AMERICAN
        CHRISTIANITY.   NEW YORK: CARLTON PRESS, 1980.

16669   BUTLER, ALFLOYD.   "THE BLACKS' CONTRIBUTION OF ELEMENTS
        OF AFRICAN RELIGION TO CHRISTIANITY IN AMERICA: A
        CASE STUDY OF THE GREAT AWAKENING IN SOUTH CAROLINA."
        PH.D. DISSERTATION, NORTHWESTERN UNIVERSITY, 1975.

16670   BUTSCH, JOSEPH.   "CATHOLICS AND THE NEGRO."   JOURNAL OF
        NEGRO HISTORY, 2 (OCTOBER, 1917):   393-410.

16671   BUTSCH, JOSEPH.   "NEGRO CATHOLICS IN THE UNITED STATES."
        CATHOLIC HISTORICAL REVIEW, 3 (APRIL, 1917):   33-51.

16672   BYERS, JAMES F.   "VOODOO: TROPICAL PHARMACOLOGY OR
        PSYCHOSOMATIC PSYCHOLOGY?"   NEW YORK FOLKLORE
        QUARTERLY, 26 (DECEMBER, 1970):   305-312.

16673   BYRNE, BARBARA A.   "CHARLES C. JONES AND THE INTELLECTUAL
        CRISIS OF THE ANTEBELLUM SOUTH."   SOUTHERN STUDIES, 19
        (FALL, 1980):   274-285.

16674   CADBURY, HENRY J.   "COLONIAL QUAKER ANTECEDENTS TO
        BRITISH ABOLITION OF SLAVERY."   FRIENDS' QUARTERLY
        EXAMINER, (JULY, 1933):   260-275.

16675   CAIN, JERRY B.   "THE THOUGHT AND ACTION OF SOME EARLY
        TEXAS BAPTISTS CONCERNING THE NEGRO."   EAST TEXAS
        HISTORICAL JOURNAL, 13 (SPRING, 1975):   3-12.

16676   CALAM, JOHN.   PARSONS AND PEDAGOGUES: THE S.P.G.

ADVENTURE IN AMERICAN EDUCATION. NEW YORK: COLUMBIA
UNIVERSITY PRESS, 1971.

16677 CALDWELL, JOHN H. SLAVERY AND SOUTHERN METHODISM: TWO
SERMONS PREACHED IN THE METHODIST CHURCH IN NEWMAN,
GEORGIA. NEWMAN, GA: THE AUTHOR, 1865.

16678 CALICO, FORREST. HISTORY OF GARRARD COUNTY, KENTUCKY,
AND ITS CHURCHES. NEW YORK: HOBSON BOOK PRESS, 1947.

16679 CAMERON, RICHARD M. METHODISM AND SOCIETY IN HISTORICAL
PERSPECTIVE. NEW YORK: ABINGDON PRESS, 1961.

16680 CARAVAGLIOS, MARIA G. THE AMERICAN CATHOLIC CHURCH AND
THE NEGRO PROBLEM IN THE XVIII-XIX CENTURIES. ROME:
MARIA GENDINO CARAVAGLIOS, 1974.

16681 CARAVAGLIOS, MARIA G. "A ROMAN CRITIQUE OF THE
PRO-SLAVERY VIEWS OF BISHOP MARTIN OF NATCHITOCHES,
LOUISIANA." RECORDS OF THE AMERICAN CATHOLIC
HISTORICAL SOCIETY OF PHILADELPHIA, 83 (JUNE, 1972):
67-81.

16682 CARMAN, RAYMOND S. "AMERICAN CHURCHES AND SLAVERY,
1565-1865." M.A. THESIS, UNIVERSITY OF ROCHESTER,
1911.

16683 CARNEIRO, E. "THE STRUCTURE OF AFRICAN CULTS IN BAHIA."
JOURNAL OF AMERICAN FOLKLORE, 53 (OCTOBER-DECEMBER,
1940): 271-278.

16684 CARROLL, J.M. HISTORY OF TEXAS BAPTISTS. DALLAS:
BAPTIST STANDARD PUBLISHING COMPANY, 1923.

16685 CARROLL, KENNETH L. "MARYLAND QUAKERS AND SLAVERY."
MARYLAND HISTORICAL MAGAZINE, 45 (SEPTEMBER, 1950):
215-225.

16686 CASTELLANOS, ISABEL M. "THE USE OF LANGUAGE IN
AFRO-CUBAN RELIGION." PH.D. DISSERTATION, GEORGETOWN
UNIVERSITY, 1977.

16687 CATHERALL, G.A. "BRITISH BAPTIST INVOLVEMENT IN JAMAICA
(1783-1865)." PH.D. DISSERTATION, UNIVERSITY OF
KEELE, 1971.

16688 "CATHOLIC TEACHING ON RACE, SLAVERY." CATHOLIC
MESSENGER, 30 (JUNE 7, 1962): 8.

16689 CAVIN, SUSAN. "MISSING WOMEN: ON THE VOODOO TRAIL OF
JAZZ." JOURNAL OF JAZZ STUDIES, 3 (FALL, 1975): 4-27.

16690 CHAPLIN, ROBERT F. "THE USE OF THE BIBLE IN THE SLAVERY
CONTROVERSY PRIOR TO THE WAR BETWEEN THE STATES."
B.D. THESIS, EMORY UNIVERSITY, 1951.

16691   CHATTINGIUS, HANS. BISHOPS AND SOCIETIES: A STUDY OF
        ANGLICAN COLONIAL AND MISSIONARY EXPANSION, 1698-1850.
        LONDON: S.P.C.K., 1952.

16692   CHEVANNES, BARRY. "JAMAICAN LOWER CLASS RELIGION."
        M.SC. THESIS, UNIVERSITY OF THE WEST INDIES, 1971.

16693   CHREITZBURG, ABEL M. EARLY METHODISM IN THE CAROLINAS.
        NASHVILLE: PUBLISHING HOUSE OF THE METHODIST
        EPISCOPAL CHURCH, SOUTH, 1897.

16694   CHRISTIANO, DAVID. "SYNOD AND SLAVERY, 1855." NEW
        JERSEY HISTORY, 90 (SPRING, 1972): 27-42.

16695   CHRISTOPHER, STEFAN C. "THE NEGRO CHURCH IN THE U.S.A."
        ORGANON, 2 (1971): 4-12.

16696   CLARK, ELMER T. HEALING OURSELVES, THE FIRST TASK OF THE
        CHURCH IN AMERICA. NASHVILLE: COKESBURY PRESS, 1924.

16697   CLARK, ELMER T. THE NEGRO AND HIS RELIGION. NASHVILLE:
        COKESBURY PRESS, 1924.

16698   CLARK, JOHN. THE VOICE OF JUBILEE: A NARRATIVE OF THE
        BAPTIST MISSION, JAMAICA, FROM ITS COMMENCEMENT.
        LONDON: JOHN SNOW, 1865.

16699   CLARKE, ERSKINE. "AN EXPERIMENT IN PATERNALISM:
        PRESBYTERIANS AND SLAVES IN CHARLESTON, SOUTH
        CAROLINA." JOURNAL OF PRESBYTERIAN HISTORY, 53 (FALL,
        1975): 223-238.

16700   CLARKE, ERSKINE. WRESTLIN' JACOB: A PORTRAIT OF
        RELIGION IN THE OLD SOUTH. ATLANTA: JOHN KNOX PRESS,
        1979.

16701   CLARKE, JOHN. MEMORIALS OF BAPTIST MISSIONARIES IN
        JAMAICA, INCLUDING A SKETCH OF THE LABOURS OF EARLY
        RELIGIOUS INSTRUCTORS IN JAMAICA. LONDON: YATES &
        ALEXANDER, 1869.

16702   CLEAGE, ALBERT B. THE BLACK MESSIAH. NEW YORK: SHEED
        AND WARD, 1968.

16703   CLIFTON, DENZIL T. "ANGLICANISM AND NEGRO SLAVERY IN
        COLONIAL AMERICA." HISTORICAL MAGAZINE OF THE
        PROTESTANT EPISCOPAL CHURCH, 39 (MARCH, 1970): 29-70.

16704   COAN, JOSEPHUS R. "DANIEL COKER: 19TH CENTURY BLACK
        CHURCH ORGANIZER, EDUCATOR AND MISSIONARY." JOURNAL
        OF THE INTERDENOMINATIONAL THEOLOGICAL CENTER, 3
        (FALL, 1975): 17-31.

16705   COBB, JIMMY G. "A STUDY OF WHITE PROTESTANTS' ATTITUDES
        TOWARD NEGROES IN CHARLESTON, SOUTH CAROLINA,

1790-1845." PH.D. DISSERTATION, BAYLOR UNIVERSITY, 1977.

16706   COLEMAN, J. WINSTON JR. "THE KENTUCKY COLONIZATION SOCIETY." REGISTER OF THE KENTUCKY HISTORICAL SOCIETY, 39 (JANUARY, 1941): 1-9.

16707   CONE, JAMES H. "BLACK CONSCIOUSNESS AND THE BLACK CHURCH: A HISTORICAL-THEOLOGICAL INTERPRETATION." ANNALS OF THE AMERICAN ACADEMY OF POLITICAL AND SOCIAL SCIENCE, 387 (JANUARY, 1970): 49-55.

16708   CONE, JAMES H. "BLACK SPIRITUALS: A THEOLOGICAL INTERPRETATION." THEOLOGY TODAY, 29 (APRIL, 1972): 54-69.

16709   CONE, JAMES H. BLACK THEOLOGY AND BLACK POWER. NEW YORK: SEABURY PRESS, 1969.

16710   CONE, JAMES H. A BLACK THEOLOGY OF LIBERATION. PHILADELPHIA: J.B. LIPPINCOTT, 1970.

16711   CONE, JAMES H. THE SPIRITUALS AND THE BLUES: AN INTERPRETATION. NEW YORK: SEABURY PRESS, 1972.

16712   CONE, JAMES H. "STORY CONTEXT OF BLACK THEOLOGY." THEOLOGY TODAY, 32 (JULY, 1975): 144-150.

16713   COOPER, WILLIAM A. THE ATTITUDE OF THE SOCIETY OF FRIENDS TOWARDS SLAVERY. CAMDEN: CAMDEN COUNTY HISTORICAL SOCIETY, 1929.

16714   CORNELIUS, JANET D. "GOD'S SCHOOLMASTERS: SOUTHERN EVANGELISTS TO THE SLAVES, 1830-1860." PH.D. DISSERTATION, UNIVERSITY OF ILLINOIS, 1977.

16715   CORWIN, CHARLES E. "EFFORTS OF THE DUTCH COLONIAL PASTORS FOR THE CONVERSION OF THE NEGROES." JOURNAL OF THE PRESBYTERIAN HISTORICAL SOCIETY, 12 (APRIL, 1927): 425-435.

16716   COULTER, E. MERTON. THOMAS SPALDING OF SAPELO. UNIVERSITY, LA: LOUISIANA STATE UNIVERSITY PRESS, 1940.

16717   COUNCILL, WILLIAM H. SYNOPSIS OF THREE ADDRESSES: 1. BUILDING THE SOUTH, 2. THE CHILDREN OF THE SOUTH, 3. NEGRO RELIGION AND CHARACTER: NO APOLOGY. NORMAL, AL: N.P., 1900.

16718   CRATON, MICHAEL J. "CHRISTIANITY AND SLAVERY IN THE BRITISH WEST INDIES, 1750-1865." HISTORICAL REFLECTIONS, 5 (WINTER, 1978): 141-160.

16719   CREEL, MARGARET W. "ANTEBELLUM RELIGION AMONG THE

GULLAHS: A STUDY OF SLAVE CONVERSION AND RELIGIOUS CULTURE IN THE SOUTH CAROLINA SEA ISLANDS." PH.D. DISSERTATION, UNIVERSITY OF CALIFORNIA, DAVIS, 1980.

16720 CROMWELL, JOHN W. "FIRST NEGRO CHURCHES IN THE DISTRICT OF COLUMBIA." JOURNAL OF NEGRO HISTORY, 7 (JANUARY, 1922): 64-106.

16721 CROSS, JASPER W. (ED.). "JOHN MILLER'S MISSIONARY JOURNAL, 1816-1817; RELIGIOUS CONDITIONS IN THE SOUTH AND MIDWEST." JOURNAL OF PRESBYTERIAN HISTORY, 47 (SEPTEMBER, 1969): 226-261.

16722 CROUCH, ARCHIE. "RACIAL-ETHNIC MINISTRY POLICIES: AN HISTORICAL OVERVIEW." JOURNAL OF PRESBYTERIAN HISTORY, 57 (FALL, 1979): 272-312.

16723 CRUDEN, ROBERT. THE NEGRO IN RECONSTRUCTION. ENGLEWOOD CLIFFS: PRENTICE-HALL, 1969.

16724 CULVERHOUSE, PATRICIA. "BLACK RELIGION; FOLK OR CHRISTIAN?" FOUNDATIONS, 13 (OCTOBER-DECEMBER, 1970): 295-315.

16725 CUMMINGS, A.D. "THE SOUTHERN MINISTRY AND SECESSION." M.A. THESIS, UNIVERSITY OF TEXAS, 1938.

16726 CUNNINGHAM, C.E. "VOODOOS AND OBEAHS IN THE WEST INDIES." M.A. THESIS, UNIVERSITY OF TEXAS, SAN ANTONIO, 1977.

16727 DANIEL, W. HARRISON. "ENGLISH PRESBYTERIANS, SLAVERY AND THE AMERICAN CRISIS OF THE 1860S." JOURNAL OF PRESBYTERIAN HISTORY, 58 (SPRING, 1980): 50-63.

16728 DANIEL, W. HARRISON. "FRONTIER BAPTIST ACTIVITIES, 1780-1803, BEING A STUDY OF SOME ASPECTS OF FRONTIER BAPTIST ACTIVITIES, 1780-1803." M.A. THESIS, VANDERBILT UNIVERSITY, 1947.

16729 DANIEL, W. HARRISON. "THE METHODIST EPISCOPAL CHURCH AND THE NEGRO IN THE EARLY NATIONAL PERIOD." METHODIST HISTORY, 11 (JANUARY, 1973): 40-53.

16730 DANIEL, W. HARRISON. "SOUTHERN PRESBYTERIANS AND THE NEGRO IN THE EARLY NATIONAL PERIOD." JOURNAL OF NEGRO HISTORY, 58 (JULY, 1973): 291-312.

16731 DANIEL, W. HARRISON. "SOUTHERN PROTESTANTISM AND SLAVERY IN THE REVOLUTIONARY GENERATION." VIRGINIA SOCIAL SCIENCE JOURNAL, 14 (NOVEMBER, 1979): 36-43.

16732 DANIEL, W. HARRISON. "SOUTHERN PROTESTANTISM AND THE NEGRO, 1860-1865." NORTH CAROLINA HISTORICAL REVIEW, 41 (SUMMER, 1964): 338-359.

16733   DANIEL, W. HARRISON.   "VIRGINIA BAPTISTS AND THE NEGRO IN
        THE ANTEBELLUM ERA."   JOURNAL OF NEGRO HISTORY, 56
        (JANUARY, 1971):   1-16.

16734   DANIEL, W. HARRISON.   "VIRGINIA BAPTISTS AND THE NEGRO IN
        THE EARLY REPUBLIC."   VIRGINIA MAGAZINE OF HISTORY AND
        BIOGRAPHY, 80 (JANUARY, 1972):   60-69.

16735   DARROW, CLARENCE.   "THE RELIGION OF THE AMERICAN NEGRO."
        CRISIS, 40 (JUNE, 1931):   190.

16736   DAVIS, DAVID B.   "THE EMERGENCE OF IMMEDIATISM IN BRITISH
        AND AMERICAN ANTISLAVERY THOUGHT."   IN MULDER, JOHN M.
        AND WILSON, JOHN F. (EDS.).   RELIGION IN AMERICAN
        HISTORY: INTERPRETIVE ESSAYS.   ENGLEWOOD CLIFFS:
        PRENTICE-HALL, 1978, PP. 236-253.

16737   DAVIS, DAVID B.   THE PROBLEM OF SLAVERY IN THE AGE OF
        REVOLUTION, 1770-1823.   ITHACA: CORNELL UNIVERSITY
        PRESS, 1975.

16738   DAVIS, DAVID B.   "SLAVERY AND THE IDEA OF PROGRESS."
        BULLETIN OF THE CENTER FOR THE STUDY OF SOUTHERN
        CULTURE AND RELIGION, 3 (JUNE, 1979):   1-9.

16739   DAVIS, GERALD L.   "THE PERFORMED AFRICAN-AMERICAN
        SERMON."   PH.D. DISSERTATION, UNIVERSITY OF
        PENNSYLVANIA, 1978.

16740   DAVIS, HENDERSON S.   "THE RELIGIOUS EXPERIENCE UNDERLYING
        THE NEGRO SPIRITUAL."   PH.D. DISSERTATION, BOSTON
        UNIVERSITY, 1950.

16741   DAVIS, J. TREADWELL.   "THE PRESBYTERIANS AND THE
        SECTIONAL CONFLICT."   SOUTHERN QUARTERLY, 8 (JANUARY,
        1970):   117-133.

16742   DAVIS, JOHN W.   "GEORGE LIELE AND ANDREW BRYAN, PIONEER
        NEGRO BAPTIST PREACHERS."   JOURNAL OF NEGRO HISTORY, 3
        (APRIL, 1918):   119-127.

16743   DE BEET, CHRIS AND VAN VELZEN, H.U.E. THODEN.   "BUSH
        NEGRO PROPHETIC MOVEMENTS: RELIGIONS OF DESPAIR?"
        BIJDRAGEN TOT DE TAAL-, LAND- EN VOLKENKUNDE, 133
        (1977):   100-135.

16744   DE JONG, GERALD F.   "THE DUTCH REFORMED CHURCH AND NEGRO
        SLAVERY IN COLONIAL AMERICA."   CHURCH HISTORY, 40
        (DECEMBER, 1971):   423-436.

16745   DEBOER, CLARA M.   "THE ROLE OF AFRO-AMERICANS IN THE
        ORIGIN AND WORK OF THE AMERICAN MISSIONARY
        ASSOCIATION: 1839-1877."   PH.D. DISSERTATION, RUTGERS
        UNIVERSITY, 1973.

16746 DEL PINO, JULIUS E. "BLACKS IN THE UNITED METHODIST
       CHURCH FROM ITS BEGINNING TO 1968." METHODIST
       HISTORY, 19 (OCTOBER, 1980): 3-20.

16747 DEREN, MAYA. DIVINE HORSEMEN: THE LIVING GODS OF HAITI.
       LONDON: THAMES & HUDSON, 1953.

16748 DESMANGLES, LESLIE G. "THE VODUN WAY OF DEATH: CULTURAL
       SYMBIOSIS OF ROMAN CATHOLICISM AND VODUN IN HAITI."
       JOURNAL OF RELIGIOUS THOUGHT, 36 (SPRING-SUMMER,
       1979): 5-20.

16749 DIGGS, JOHN R.L. "NEGRO CHURCH LIFE." VOICE OF THE
       NEGRO, 1 (FEBRUARY, 1904): 46-50.

16750 DOBBINS, H. LIFE AND LABOR OF REV. FRANK DOBBINS, PASTOR
       OF ZION BAPTIST CHURCH, COLUMBIA, S.C. COLUMBIA, SC:
       N.P., 1872.

16751 "DOCUMENTS CONCERNING THE REV. SAMUEL THOMAS, 1702-1707."
       SOUTH CAROLINA HISTORICAL AND GENEALOGICAL MAGAZINE, 5
       (JANUARY, 1904): 39-47.

16752 DONALD, JAMES M. "BISHOP HOPKINS AND THE REUNIFICATION
       OF THE CHURCH." HISTORICAL MAGAZINE OF THE PROTESTANT
       EPISCOPAL CHURCH, 47 (MARCH, 1978): 73-91.

16753 DOOKHAN, ISAAC. "SLAVERY AND EMANCIPATION." A HISTORY
       OF THE BRITISH VIRGIN ISLANDS, 1672 TO 1970. EPPING,
       ESSEX, ENGLAND: CARIBBEAN UNIVERSITIES PRESS, 1975,
       PP. 71-96.

16754 DOROUGH, CHARLES D. "RELIGION IN THE OLD SOUTH; A
       PATTERN OF BEHAVIOR AND THOUGHT." PH.D. DISSERTATION,
       UNIVERSITY OF TEXAS, 1947.

16755 DORRIS, JONATHAN T. AND DORRIS, MAUD W. GLIMPSES OF
       HISTORIC MADISON COUNTY, KENTUCKY. NASHVILLE:
       WILLIAMS PRINTING COMPANY, 1955.

16756 DOWD, JEROME. "REVEREND MOSES HESTER: SKETCH OF A
       QUAINT NEGRO PREACHER IN NORTH CAROLINA." TRINITY
       ARCHIVE, 9 (FEBRUARY, 1896): 283-296.

16757 DOWD, JEROME. "SERMON OF AN ANTE-BELLUM NEGRO PREACHER."
       SOUTHERN WORKMAN, 30 (NOVEMBER, 1901): 655-658.

16758 DRAKE, RICHARD B. "THE GROWTH OF SEGREGATION IN AMERICAN
       CONGREGATIONALISM IN THE SOUTH." NEGRO HISTORY
       BULLETIN, 21 (MARCH, 1958): 135-138.

16759 DRAKE, THOMAS E. "NORTHERN QUAKERS AND SLAVERY." PH.D.
       DISSERTATION, YALE UNIVERSITY, 1933.

16760 DRAKE, THOMAS E. QUAKERS AND SLAVERY IN AMERICA. NEW

HAVEN: YALE UNIVERSITY PRESS, 1950.

16761 DREWRY, HENRY N. "AFRO-AMERICAN CHURCH." IN KETZ,
LOUISE B. (ED.). DICTIONARY OF AMERICAN HISTORY. 7
VOLS. NEW YORK: CHARLES SCRIBNER'S SONS, 1976, VOL.
1, PP. 23-24.

16762 DUBOIS, W.E.B. THE GIFT OF BLACK FOLK: THE NEGROES IN
THE MAKING OF AMERICA. BOSTON: STRAFFORD, 1924.

16763 DUBOIS, W.E.B. (ED.). THE NEGRO CHURCH. ATLANTA:
ATLANTA UNIVERSITY PRESS, 1903.

16764 DUBOIS, W.E.B. "RELIGION IN THE SOUTH." IN WASHINGTON,
BOOKER T. AND DUBOIS. THE NEGRO IN THE SOUTH.
PHILADELPHIA: GEORGE W. JACOBS AND COMPANY, 1907, PP.
123-191.

16765 DUBOIS, W.E.B. "THE RELIGION OF THE AMERICAN NEGRO."
NEW WORLD, 9 (DECEMBER, 1900): 614-625.

16766 DUCHET, MICHELE. "REACTIONS TO THE PROBLEM OF THE SLAVE
TRADE: AN HISTORICAL AND IDEOLOGICAL STUDY." IN THE
AFRICAN SLAVE TRADE FROM THE FIFTEENTH TO THE
NINETEENTH CENTURY. PARIS: UNITED NATIONS
EDUCATIONAL, SCIENTIFIC AND CULTURAL ORGANIZATION,
1979, PP. 31-54.

16767 DUGGER, DAGUERRELYN J. "NEGRO RELIGION IN SLAVERY AND
FREEDOM." IN JOYNER, CHARLES W. (ED.). BLACK
CAROLINIANS: STUDIES IN THE HISTORY OF SOUTH CAROLINA
NEGROES IN THE NINETEENTH CENTURY. LAURINBURG, NC:
ST. ANDREWS PRESBYTERIAN COLLEGE, 1969, PP. 155-164.

16768 DUMOND, DWIGHT L. "DEMOCRACY AND CHRISTIAN ETHICS."
JOURNAL OF NEGRO HISTORY, 46 (JANUARY, 1961): 1-11.

16769 DUNCAN, HERMAN C. THE DIOCESE OF LOUISIANA: SOME OF ITS
HISTORY, 1838-1888. ALSO SOME OF THE HISTORY OF ITS
PARISHES AND MISSIONS, 1805-1888. NEW ORLEANS: A.W.
HYATT, PRINTER, 1888.

16770 DUNHAM, KATHERINE. ISLAND POSSESSED. GARDEN CITY:
DOUBLEDAY, 1969.

16771 DURDEN, ROBERT F. "THE ESTABLISHMENT OF CALVARY
PROTESTANT EPISCOPAL CHURCH FOR NEGROES IN
CHARLESTON." SOUTH CAROLINA HISTORICAL MAGAZINE, 65
(JANUARY, 1964): 63-84.

16772 DUTSON, ROLDO V. "A STUDY OF THE ATTITUDE OF THE
LATTER-DAY SAINT CHURCH, IN THE TERRITORY OF UTAH,
TOWARD SLAVERY AS IT PERTAINED TO THE INDIAN AS WELL
AS TO THE NEGRO FROM 1847 TO 1865." M.S. THESIS,
BRIGHAM YOUNG UNIVERSITY, 1964.

16773   EARNEST, JOSEPH B.   THE RELIGIOUS DEVELOPMENT OF THE
        NEGRO IN VIRGINIA.   CHARLOTTESVILLE: MICHIE COMPANY,
        1914.

16774   EARNEST, JOSEPH B.   "THE RELIGIOUS DEVELOPMENT OF THE
        NEGRO IN VIRGINIA."   PH.D. DISSERTATION, UNIVERSITY OF
        VIRGINIA, 1914.

16775   EDWARDS, HARRY S.   "IN LIGHTER VEIN: THE GUM SWAMP
        DEBATE."   CENTURY MAGAZINE, N.S., 50 (SEPTEMBER,
        1895):   798-800.

16776   EIGHMY, JOHN L.   "THE BAPTISTS AND SLAVERY: AN
        EXAMINATION OF THE ORIGINS AND BENEFITS OF
        SEGREGATION."   SOCIAL SCIENCE QUARTERLY, 49 (DECEMBER,
        1968):   666-673.

16777   EIGHMY, JOHN L.   CHURCHES IN CULTURAL CAPTIVITY: A
        HISTORY OF THE SOCIAL ATTITUDES OF SOUTHERN BAPTISTS.
        KNOXVILLE: UNIVERSITY OF TENNESSEE PRESS, 1972.

16778   ELKINS, W.F.   STREET PREACHERS, FAITH HEALERS, AND HERB
        DOCTORS IN JAMAICA, 1890-1925.   NEW YORK: REVISIONIST
        PRESS, 1977.

16779   ENGELDER, CONRAD J.   "THE CHURCHES AND SLAVERY: A STUDY
        OF THE ATTITUDES TOWARD SLAVERY OF THE MAJOR
        PROTESTANT DENOMINATIONS."   PH.D. DISSERTATION,
        UNIVERSITY OF MICHIGAN, 1964.

16780   "THE EPISCOPAL CHURCH."   CRISIS, 7 (DECEMBER, 1913):
        83-84.

16781   EPPS, ARCHIE C.   "THE CHRISTIAN DOCTRINE OF SLAVERY: A
        THEOLOGICAL ANALYSIS."   JOURNAL OF NEGRO HISTORY, 46
        (OCTOBER, 1961):   243-249.

16782   ERSKINE, NOEL L.   "BLACK RELIGION AND IDENTITY: A
        JAMAICAN PERSPECTIVE."   PH.D. DISSERTATION, UNION
        THEOLOGICAL SEMINARY, 1978.

16783   ESCOTT, PAUL D.   SLAVERY REMEMBERED: A RECORD OF
        TWENTIETH-CENTURY SLAVE NARRATIVES.   CHAPEL HILL:
        UNIVERSITY OF NORTH CAROLINA PRESS, 1979.

16784   ESSIG, JAMES D.   "A VERY WINTRY SEASON: VIRGINIA
        BAPTISTS AND SLAVERY, 1785-1797."   VIRGINIA MAGAZINE
        OF HISTORY AND BIOGRAPHY, 88 (APRIL, 1980):   170-185.

16785   FAIRLY, JOHN S.   THE NEGRO IN HIS RELATIONS TO THE
        CHURCH: HISTORICAL VIEW.   CHARLESTON: WALKER, EVANS
        AND COGSWELL, 1889.

16786   FAULKNER, WILLIAM J.   "THE INFLUENCE OF FOLKLORE UPON THE
        RELIGIOUS EXPERIENCE OF THE ANTE-BELLUM NEGRO."

JOURNAL OF RELIGIOUS THOUGHT, 24 (AUTUMN-WINTER, 1968): 26-28.

16787   FAUST, DREW G. "EVANGELICALISM AND THE MEANING OF THE PROSLAVERY ARGUMENT: THE REVEREND THORNTON STRINGFELLOW OF VIRGINIA." VIRGINIA MAGAZINE OF HISTORY AND BIOGRAPHY, 35 (JANUARY, 1977): 3-17.

16788   FERRIS, WILLIAM R. "THE NEGRO CONVERSION EXPERIENCE." KEYSTONE FOLKLORE QUARTERLY, 15 (SPRING, 1970): 35-51.

16789   FICKLING, SUSAN M. "CHRISTIANIZATION OF THE NEGRO IN SOUTH CAROLINA, 1830-1860." M.A. THESIS, UNIVERSITY OF SOUTH CAROLINA, 1923.

16790   FICKLING, SUSAN M. "SLAVE-CONVERSION IN SOUTH CAROLINA, 1830-1860." BULLETIN OF THE UNIVERSITY OF SOUTH CAROLINA, NO. 146 (SEPTEMBER 1, 1924): 1-59.

16791   FIFE, ROBERT O. "ALEXANDER CAMPBELL AND THE CHRISTIAN CHURCH IN THE SLAVERY CONTROVERSY." PH.D. DISSERTATION, INDIANA UNIVERSITY, 1960.

16792   FISHER, MILES M. "LOTT CARY, THE COLONIZING MISSIONARY." JOURNAL OF NEGRO HISTORY, 7 (OCTOBER, 1922): 380-418.

16793   FISHER, MILES M. "THE NEGRO CHURCHES." CRISIS, 45 (JULY, 1938): 220, 239, 245.

16794   FITZGERALD, O.P. "THE NEGRO PREACHER IN THE SOUTH BEFORE THE WAR." WESLEYAN METHODIST MAGAZINE, 117 (1894): 165-170.

16795   FOGARTY, GERALD P. "SLAVES, QUAKERS, AND CATHOLIC MARRIAGE IN COLONIAL MARYLAND." JURIST, 35 (SPRING-SUMMER, 1975): 142-161.

16796   FORTENBAUGH, ROBERT. "AMERICAN LUTHERAN SYNODS AND SLAVERY, 1830-1860." JOURNAL OF RELIGION, 13 (JANUARY, 1933): 72-92.

16797   FORTENBAUGH, ROBERT. "THE REPRESENTATIVE LUTHERAN PERIODICAL PRESS AND SLAVERY, 1831-1860." LUTHERAN CHURCH QUARTERLY, 8 (1935): 151-172.

16798   FORTES, MEYER. OEDIPUS AND JOB IN WEST AFRICAN RELIGION. CAMBRIDGE: CAMBRIDGE UNIVERSITY PRESS, 1959.

16799   FOSTER, GEORGE M. "COFRADIA AND COMPADRAZGO IN SPAIN AND SPANISH AMERICA." SOUTHWESTERN JOURNAL OF ANTHROPOLOGY, 9 (SPRING, 1953): 1-28.

16800   FRANCIS, BETTIE G. "THE 'RUMINATIN' OF AUNT PHOEBE." SOUTHERN WORKMAN, 35 (1906): 150-152.

16801   FRANKLIN, JOHN H.   "NEGRO EPISCOPALIANS IN ANTE-BELLUM
        NORTH CAROLINA."   HISTORICAL MAGAZINE OF THE
        PROTESTANT EPISCOPAL CHURCH, 13 (SEPTEMBER, 1944):
        216-234.

16802   FRANKLIN, VINCENT P.   "BIBLIOGRAPHICAL ESSAY: ALONSO DE
        SANDOVAL AND THE JESUIT CONCEPTION OF THE NEGRO."
        JOURNAL OF NEGRO HISTORY, 58 (JULY, 1973):   349-360.

16803   FRAZIER, E. FRANKLIN.   BLACK BOURGEOISIE: THE RISE OF A
        NEW MIDDLE CLASS IN THE UNITED STATES.   NEW YORK:
        FREE PRESS, 1957.

16804   FRAZIER, E. FRANKLIN.   THE NEGRO CHURCH IN AMERICA.   NEW
        YORK: SCHOCKEN BOOKS, 1963.

16805   FRAZIER, E. FRANKLIN.   THE NEGRO FAMILY IN THE UNITED
        STATES.   CHICAGO: UNIVERSITY OF CHICAGO PRESS, 1939.

16806   FREEHLING, WILLIAM W.   PRELUDE TO CIVIL WAR: THE
        NULLIFICATION CONTROVERSY IN SOUTH CAROLINA,
        1816-1836.   NEW YORK: HARPER & ROW, 1966.

16807   FREEMAN, EDWARD A.   "NEGRO BAPTIST HISTORY."   BAPTIST
        HISTORY AND HERITAGE, 4 (JULY, 1969):   89-99.

16808   FULLER, THOMAS O.   HISTORY OF THE NEGRO BAPTISTS OF
        TENNESSEE.   MEMPHIS: HASKINS PRINT, 1936.

16809   FURFEY, PAUL H.   THE RESPECTABLE MURDERERS: SOCIAL EVIL
        AND CHRISTIAN CONSCIENCE.   NEW YORK: HERDER & HERDER,
        1966.

16810   FURLEY, OLIVER W.   "MORAVIAN MISSIONARIES AND SLAVES IN
        THE WEST INDIES."   CARIBBEAN STUDIES, 5 (JULY, 1965):
        3-16.

16811   FURLEY, OLIVER W.   "PROTESTANT MISSIONARIES IN THE WEST
        INDIES: PIONEERS OF A NEW RACIAL SOCIETY."   RACE, 6
        (JANUARY, 1965):   232-242.

16812   GAFFNEY, FLOYD.   "THE FUNCTION AND FORM OF THE RING SHOUT
        AS A RELIGIOUS EXPRESSION: FROM WEST AFRICAN ORIGINS
        THROUGH THE ERA OF SLAVERY IN AMERICA."   M.A. THESIS,
        ADELPHI UNIVERSITY, 1962.

16813   GANNON, MICHAEL V.   REBEL BISHOP: THE LIFE AND ERA OF
        AUGUSTINE VEROT.   MILWAUKEE: BRUCE PUBLISHING
        COMPANY, 1964.

16814   GARBER, P.L.A.   "A CENTENNIAL APPRAISAL OF JAMES HENLEY
        THORNWELL."   IN HENRY, STUART C. (ED.).   A MISCELLANY
        OF AMERICAN CHRISTIANITY: ESSAYS IN HONOR OF H.
        SHELTON SMITH.   DURHAM: DUKE UNIVERSITY PRESS, 1963,
        PP. 95-137.

16815   GARDNER, ROBERT. "A TENTH HOUR APOLOGY FOR SLAVERY."
         JOURNAL OF SOUTHERN HISTORY, 26 (AUGUST, 1960):
         352-367.

16816   GELLERT, LAWRENCE. "DANCING IN CHURCH." NEW THEATRE, 2
         (JULY, 1935): 19-20.

16817   GENOVESE, EUGENE D. "BLACK PLANTATION PREACHERS IN THE
         SLAVE SOUTH." LOUISIANA STUDIES, 11 (FALL, 1972):
         188-214.

16818   GENOVESE, EUGENE D. ROLL, JORDAN, ROLL: THE WORLD THE
         SLAVES MADE. NEW YORK: PANTHEON, 1974.

16819   GEORGE, CAROL V.R. SEGREGATED SABBATHS: RICHARD ALLEN
         AND THE EMERGENCE OF INDEPENDENT BLACK CHURCHES,
         1760-1840. NEW YORK: OXFORD UNIVERSITY PRESS, 1973.

16820   GEWEHR, WESLEY. THE GREAT AWAKENING IN VIRGINIA,
         1740-1790. DURHAM: DUKE UNIVERSITY PRESS, 1930.

16821   GILLARD, JOHN T. COLORED CATHOLICS IN THE UNITED STATES.
         BALTIMORE: THE JOSEPHITE PRESS, 1941.

16822   GILMORE, JOHN T. "THE REV. WILLIAM HARTE AND ATTITUDES
         TO SLAVERY IN EARLY NINETEENTH-CENTURY BARBADOS."
         JOURNAL OF ECCLESIASTICAL HISTORY, 30 (OCTOBER, 1979):
         461-474.

16823   GILTNER, JOHN H. "MOSES STUART AND THE SLAVERY
         CONTROVERSY: A STUDY IN THE FAILURE OF MODERATION."
         JOURNAL OF RELIGIOUS THOUGHT, 18 (WINTER-SPRING,
         1961): 27-40.

16824   GLAZIER, WILLARD W. THE CAPTURE, THE PRISON PEN, AND THE
         ESCAPE. NEW YORK: UNITED STATES PUBLISHING COMPANY,
         1868.

16825   GOLLWITZER, HELMUT. "WHY BLACK THEOLOGY?" UNION
         SEMINARY QUARTERLY REVIEW, 31 (FALL, 1975): 38-58.

16826   GOODWIN, MARY F. "CHRISTIANIZING AND EDUCATING THE NEGRO
         IN COLONIAL VIRGINIA." HISTORICAL MAGAZINE OF THE
         PROTESTANT EPISCOPAL CHURCH, 1 (SEPTEMBER, 1932):
         143-152.

16827   GORDON, ASA H. SKETCHES OF NEGRO LIFE AND HISTORY IN
         SOUTH CAROLINA. HAMMOND, IN: W.B. CONKEY, 1929.

16828   GOSS, CHARLES C. STATISTICAL HISTORY OF THE FIRST
         CENTURY OF AMERICAN METHODISM. NEW YORK: CARLTON &
         PORTER, 1866.

16829   GOVEIA, ELSA. "INFLUENCE OF RELIGION IN THE WEST
         INDIES." IN CONFERENCE ON THE HISTORY OF RELIGION IN

THE NEW WORLD DURING COLONIAL TIMES. WASHINGTON: N.P., 1958, PP. 174-180.

16830 GOVEIA, ELSA V. "INFLUENCE OF RELIGION IN THE WEST INDIES." AMERICAS, 14 (APRIL, 1958): 510-516.

16831 GRANDISON, C.N. "WHAT IS THE INTELLECTUAL AND MORAL STATUS OF THE NEGRO MINISTRY?" SOUTHLAND, 2 (APRIL, 1891): 150-155.

16832 GRANT, MADELINE. "ENEMIES TO CAESAR? SECTARIAN MISSIONARIES IN BRITISH WEST INDIAN SLAVE SOCIETY, 1754-1834." M.A. THESIS, UNIVERSITY OF WATERLOO, 1976.

16833 GRAVELY, WILLIAM. GILBERT HAVEN, METHODIST ABOLITIONIST: A STUDY IN RACE, RELIGION, AND REFORM, 1850-1880. NASHVILLE: ABINGDON PRESS, 1973.

16834 GRAVELY, WILLIAM B. "EARLY METHODISM AND SLAVERY: THE ROOTS OF A TRADITION." DREW GATEWAY, 34 (SPRING, 1964): 150-165.

16835 GRAVELY, WILLIAM B. "EARLY METHODISM AND SLAVERY: THE ROOTS OF A TRADITION." WESLEYAN QUARTERLY REVIEW, 2 (MAY, 1965): 84-100.

16836 GRAVELY, WILLIAM B. "METHODIST PREACHERS, SLAVERY AND CASTE: TYPES OF SOCIAL CONCERN IN ANTEBELLUM AMERICA." DUKE DIVINITY SCHOOL REVIEW, 34 (AUTUMN, 1969): 209-229.

16837 GREENBERG, MICHAEL. "SLAVERY AND THE PROTESTANT ETHIC." LOUISIANA STUDIES, 15 (FALL, 1976): 209-240.

16838 GREGG, CHARLES L. "SOME ASPECTS OF THE RELIGIOUS INSTRUCTION OF SLAVES IN THE ANTE-BELLUM SOUTH." M.A. THESIS, OHIO STATE UNIVERSITY, 1948.

16839 GREGORY, HENRY C. "BLACK BAPTISTS." IN WOOD, JAMES E., JR. (ED.). BAPTISTS AND THE AMERICAN EXPERIENCE. VALLEY FORGE: JUDSON PRESS, 1976, PP. 305-322.

16840 GREIER, WILLIE. "NORTH CAROLINA BAPTISTS AND THE NEGRO, 1727-1877." M.A. THESIS, UNIVERSITY OF NORTH CAROLINA, 1944.

16841 GRENZ, SUZANNA M. "THE BLACK COMMUNITY IN BOONE COUNTY, MISSOURI, 1850-1900." PH.D. DISSERTATION, UNIVERSITY OF MISSOURI, 1979.

16842 GRIAULE, MARCEL. CONVERSATIONS WITH OGOTEMMELI: AN INTRODUCTION TO DOGON RELIGIOUS IDEAS. LONDON: OXFORD UNIVERSITY PRESS, 1965.

16843 GRIER, W.M. "WORK OF SOUTHERN CHRISTIANS AMONG NEGROES

BEFORE THE WAR." EVANGELISTIC REPOSITORY, 68 (1891): 513-520.

16844 GROUT, LEWIS. "THE RELATIONS OF THE CHURCH TO THE COLORED RACE." NEW ENGLANDER, 42 (NOVEMBER, 1883): 723-730.

16845 HALBROOKS, G. THOMAS. "FRANCIS WAYLAND: INFLUENTIAL MEDIATOR IN THE BAPTIST CONTROVERSY OVER SLAVERY." BAPTIST HISTORY AND HERITAGE, 13 (OCTOBER, 1978): 21-35.

16846 HALL, ROBERT L. "THE EVOLUTION OF SLAVE RELIGION." BULLETIN OF THE CENTER FOR THE STUDY OF SOUTHERN CULTURE AND RELIGION, 3 (MARCH, 1979): 14-19.

16847 HALLOWELL, EMILY. CALHOUN PLANTATION SONGS. BOSTON: C.W. THOMPSON, 1901.

16848 HALSTEAD, JACQUELINE J. "THE DELAWARE ASSOCIATION FOR THE MORAL IMPROVEMENT AND EDUCATION OF THE COLORED PEOPLE: PRACTICAL CHRISTIANITY." DELAWARE HISTORY, 15 (APRIL, 1973): 19-40.

16849 HAMILTON, CHARLES V. THE BLACK PREACHER IN AMERICA. NEW YORK: MORROW, 1972.

16850 HANDY, ROBERT T. "NEGRO CHRISTIANITY AND AMERICAN CHURCH HISTORIOGRAPHY." IN BRAUER, JERALD C. (ED.). REINTERPRETATION IN AMERICAN CHURCH HISTORY. CHICAGO: UNIVERSITY OF CHICAGO PRESS, 1968, PP. 91-112.

16851 HARDIN, EDWARD K. "SOUTHERN METHODISM AND THE SLAVE." M.A. THESIS, VANDERBILT UNIVERSITY, 1910.

16852 HARDING, VINCENT. "RELIGION AND RESISTANCE AMONG ANTEBELLUM NEGROES, 1800-1860." IN MEIER, AUGUST AND RUDWICK, ELLIOTT (EDS.). THE MAKING OF BLACK AMERICA: ESSAYS IN NEGRO LIFE & HISTORY. 2 VOLS. NEW YORK: ATHENEUM, 1974, VOL. 1, PP. 179-197.

16853 HARRELL, DAVID E., JR. QUEST FOR A CHRISTIAN AMERICA: THE DISCIPLES OF CHRIST AND AMERICAN SOCIETY TO 1866. NASHVILLE: DISCIPLES OF CHRIST HISTORICAL SOCIETY, 1966.

16854 HARRELL, DAVID E., JR. "A SOCIAL HISTORY OF THE DISCIPLES OF CHRIST TO 1866." PH.D. DISSERTATION, VANDERBILT UNIVERSITY, 1962.

16855 HARRINGTON, MICHAEL L. "EVANGELICALISM AND RACISM IN THE DEVELOPMENT OF SOUTHERN RELIGION." MISSISSIPPI QUARTERLY, 27 (SPRING, 1974): 201-209.

16856 HARRIS, JAY. "STATE WAS BIRTHPLACE OF THE NEGRO CHURCH."

WILMINGTON MORNING NEWS, FEBRUARY 19, 1971.

16857   HARRIS, JOHN. "THE CHURCH AND SLAVERY: A GREAT
        OPPORTUNITY." CHURCH OVERSEAS, 6 (1933): 205-209.

16858   HARRISON, WILLIAM P. THE GOSPEL AMONG THE SLAVES: A
        SHORT ACCOUNT OF MISSIONARY OPERATIONS AMONG THE
        AFRICAN SLAVES OF THE SOUTHERN STATES. NASHVILLE:
        PUBLISHING HOUSE OF THE METHODIST EPISCOPAL CHURCH OF
        THE SOUTH, 1893.

16859   HARVEY, CHARLES D. "THE RELATION OF THE NEGRO TO THE
        PRESBYTERIAN CHURCH IN THE UNITED STATES OF AMERICA AS
        REFLECTED IN THE ACTION OF THE GENERAL ASSEMBLY,
        1789-1861." M.A. THESIS, VANDERBILT UNIVERSITY, 1962.

16860   HASKINS, JAMES. WITCHCRAFT, MYSTICISM AND MAGIC IN THE
        BLACK WORLD. GARDEN CITY: DOUBLEDAY, 1974.

16861   HATCHER, WILLIAM E. JOHN JASPER, THE UNMATCHED NEGRO
        PHILOSOPHER AND PREACHER. NEW YORK: F.H. REVELL
        COMPANY, 1908.

16862   HAYDEN, J. CARLETON. "CONVERSION AND CONTROL: DILEMMA
        OF EPISCOPALIANS IN PROVIDING FOR THE RELIGIOUS
        INSTRUCTION OF SLAVES, CHARLESTON, SOUTH CAROLINA,
        1845-1860." HISTORICAL MAGAZINE OF THE PROTESTANT
        EPISCOPAL CHURCH, 40 (JUNE, 1971): 143-171.

16863   HAYDEN, ROGER. "KETTERING 1792 AND PHILADELPHIA 1814:
        THE INFLUENCE OF ENGLISH BAPTISTS UPON THE FORMATION
        OF AMERICAN BAPTIST FOREIGN MISSIONS, 1790-1814."
        BAPTIST QUARTERLY, 21 (JANUARY, APRIL, 1965): 3-20,
        64-72.

16864   HAYNES, LEONARD L. THE NEGRO COMMUNITY WITHIN AMERICAN
        PROTESTANTISM, 1619-1844. BOSTON: CHRISTOPHER
        PUBLISHING HOUSE, 1953.

16865   HEATHCOTE, CHARLES W. THE LUTHERAN CHURCH AND THE CIVIL
        WAR. NEW YORK: FLEMING H. REVELL AND COMPANY, 1918.

16866   HEFELE, KARL J. "SLAVERY AND CHRISTIANITY." AMERICAN
        PRESBYTERIAN AND THEOLOGICAL REVIEW, 2ND SER., 3
        (OCTOBER, 1965): 601.

16867   HEMPHILL, SUSAN L. "FROM EMANCIPATION TO EVANGELIZATION:
        THE ATTITUDE AND ACTION OF THE METHODIST EPISCOPAL
        CHURCH IN GEORGIA TOWARDS NEGRO SLAVES, 1784-1844."
        B.A. THESIS, EMORY UNIVERSITY, 1966.

16868   HENDERSON, DALE E. "METHODIST MISSIONS TO THE PLANTATION
        SLAVES OF THE SOUTH CAROLINA CONFERENCE." M.A.
        THESIS, OLD DOMINION UNIVERSITY, 1971.

16869   HEPBURN, DAVID. "THE NEGRO CATHOLIC IN NEW ORLEANS."
        OUR WORLD, 5 (APRIL, 1950): 16-32.

16870   HERRICK, E.P. "WITCHCRAFT IN CUBA." SOUTHERN WORKMAN,
        36 (JULY, 1907): 401-404.

16871   HERSKOVITS, MELVILLE J. "AFRICAN GODS AND CATHOLIC
        SAINTS IN NEW WORLD NEGRO BELIEF." AMERICAN
        ANTHROPOLOGIST, 39 (OCTOBER/DECEMBER, 1937): 635-643.

16872   HERSKOVITS, MELVILLE J. "THE PANAN, AN AFRO-BAHIAN
        RELIGIOUS RITE OF TRANSITION." LES AFRO-AMERICAINS,
        NO. 27 (1953): 133-140.

16873   HERSKOVITS, MELVILLE J. "SOME ECONOMIC ASPECTS OF THE
        AFROBAHIAN CANDOMBLE." MISCELLANEA PAUL RIVET, 2
        (1958): 227-247.

16874   HEWETSON, W.T. "THE SOCIAL LIFE OF THE SOUTHERN NEGRO."
        CHAUTAUQUAN, 26 (DECEMBER, 1897): 295-304.

16875   HICKIN, P.E.P. "'SITUATION ETHICS' AND ANTISLAVERY
        ATTITUDES IN THE VIRGINIA CHURCHES." IN BOLES, JOHN
        B. (ED.). AMERICA: THE MIDDLE PERIOD: ESSAYS IN
        HONOR OF BERNARD MAYO. CHARLOTTESVILLE: UNIVERSITY
        PRESS OF VIRGINIA, 1973, PP. 188-215.

16876   HICKS, WILLIAM. HISTORY OF LOUISIANA NEGRO BAPTISTS,
        1804 TO 1914. NASHVILLE: NATIONAL BAPTIST PUBLISHING
        BOARD, 1915.

16877   HIGGINSON, THOMAS W. ARMY LIFE IN A BLACK REGIMENT.
        BOSTON: FIELDS, OSGOOD, 1870.

16878   HILGER, ROTHE. "THE RELIGIOUS EXPRESSION OF THE NEGRO."
        M.A. THESIS, VANDERBILT UNIVERSITY, 1931.

16879   HILL, LAWRENCE W. "REACTION OF THE BAPTIST PRESS TO THE
        SLAVERY ISSUE FROM 1856 TO THE CIVIL WAR." M.A.
        THESIS, LAMAR UNIVERSITY, 1966.

16880   HILL, SAMUEL S., JR. THE SOUTH AND THE NORTH IN AMERICAN
        RELIGION. ATHENS: UNIVERSITY OF GEORGIA PRESS, 1980.

16881   HILTY, HIRAM H. "NORTH CAROLINA QUAKERS AND SLAVERY."
        PH.D. DISSERTATION, DUKE UNIVERSITY, 1969.

16882   HIRSCH, CHARLES B. "THE EXPERIENCES OF THE S.P.G. IN
        EIGHTEENTH CENTURY NORTH CAROLINA." PH.D.
        DISSERTATION, INDIANA UNIVERSITY, 1954.

16883   HODGE, W.J. "THE BLACK CHURCH'S OUTREACH." IN MCCALL,
        EMMANUEL L. (ED.). THE BLACK CHRISTIAN EXPERIENCE.
        NASHVILLE: BROADMAN PRESS, 1972, PP. 73-84.

16884   HOETINK, H.   CARIBBEAN RACE RELATIONS: A STUDY OF TWO
        VARIANTS.   NEW YORK: OXFORD UNIVERSITY PRESS, 1967.

16885   HOETINK, HARRY.   THE TWO VARIANTS IN CARIBBEAN RACE
        RELATIONS: A CONTRIBUTION TO THE SOCIOLOGY OF
        SEGMENTED SOCIETIES.   NEW YORK: OXFORD UNIVERSITY
        PRESS, 1967.

16886   HOGG, DONALD W.   "JAMAICAN RELIGIONS: A STUDY IN
        VARIATIONS."   PH.D. DISSERTATION, YALE UNIVERSITY,
        1964.

16887   HOLIFIELD, E. BROOKS.   THE GENTLEMEN THEOLOGIANS:
        AMERICAN THEOLOGY IN SOUTHERN CULTURE, 1795-1860.
        DURHAM: DUKE UNIVERSITY PRESS, 1978.

16888   HOLLAND, TIMOTHY J.   "THE CATHOLIC CHURCH AND THE NEGRO
        IN THE UNITED STATES PRIOR TO THE CIVIL WAR."   PH.D.
        DISSERTATION, FORDHAM UNIVERSITY, 1950.

16889   HOLMES, EDWARD D.   "GEORGE LIELE: NEGRO SLAVERY'S
        PROPHET OF DELIVERANCE."   FOUNDATIONS, 9
        (OCTOBER-DECEMBER, 1966):   333-345.

16890   HOLMES, EDWARD D.   "GEORGE LIELE; NEGRO SLAVERY'S PROPHET
        OF DELIVERANCE."   BAPTIST QUARTERLY, 20 (OCTOBER,
        1964):   340-351.

16891   HOROWITZ, MICHAEL M.   "A COMPARATIVE STUDY OF SEVERAL
        NEGRO CULTS IN THE NEW WORLD."   M.A. THESIS, COLUMBIA
        UNIVERSITY, 1956.

16892   HORTON, JOSEPH P.   "THE RELIGIOUS AND EDUCATIONAL
        CONTRIBUTION OF THE METHODISTS TO THE SLAVES."   B.D.
        THESIS, SOUTHERN METHODIST UNIVERSITY, 1930.

16893   HORTON, ROBIN.   "AFRICAN CONVERSION."   AFRICA, 41 (1971):
        85-108.

16894   HORTON, ROBIN.   "A HUNDRED YEARS OF CHANGE IN KALABARI
        RELIGION."   IN MIDDLETON, JOHN (ED.).   BLACK AFRICA:
        ITS PEOPLE AND THEIR CULTURE TODAY.   LONDON:
        MACMILLAN COMPANY, 1970, PP. 192-211.

16895   HOSKINS, CHARLES L.   BLACK EPISCOPALIANS IN GEORGIA:
        STRIFE, STRUGGLE, AND SALVATION.   SAVANNAH: HOSKINS,
        1980.

16896   HOSS, E.E.   "AFRICAN SLAVERY AND THE TENNESSEE CONVENTION
        OF 1834."   QUARTERLY REVIEW OF THE M.E. CHURCH, SOUTH,
        N.S., 12 (1892):   118-135.

16897   HOVENKAMP, HERBERT.   "THEOLOGICAL INVERSION IN ANTEBELLUM
        AFRO-AMERICAN RELIGIOUS EXPRESSION."   M.A. THESIS,
        UNIVERSITY OF TEXAS AT EL PASO, 1971.

16898   HOVET, THEODORE R.   "THE CHURCH DISEASED: HARRIET
        BEECHER STOWE'S ATTACK ON THE PRESBYTERIAN CHURCH."
        JOURNAL OF PRESBYTERIAN HISTORY, 52 (SUMMER, 1974):
        167-187.

16899   HOWARD, VICTOR B.   "THE KENTUCKY PRESBYTERIANS IN 1849:
        SLAVERY AND THE KENTUCKY CONSTITUTION."   REGISTER OF
        THE KENTUCKY HISTORICAL SOCIETY, 73 (JULY, 1975):
        217-240.

16900   HUGGINS, WILLIS N.   "THE CONTRIBUTION OF THE CATHOLIC
        CHURCH TO THE PROGRESS OF THE NEGRO IN THE UNITED
        STATES."   PH.D. DISSERTATION, FORDHAM UNIVERSITY, 1932.

16901   HUGHES, JOHN E.   "A HISTORY OF THE SOUTHERN BAPTIST
        CONVENTION'S MINISTRY TO THE NEGRO: 1845-1904."
        TH.D. DISSERTATION, SOUTHERN BAPTIST THEOLOGICAL
        SEMINARY, 1971.

16902   HUMM, P.   "RELIGION AND THE FREEING OF BLACK AMERICA."
        M.PHIL. THESIS, UNIVERSITY OF SUSSEX, 1970.

16903   HURSTON, ZORA N.   "HOODOO IN AMERICA."   JOURNAL OF
        AMERICAN FOLKLORE, 44 (OCTOBER-DECEMBER, 1931):
        317-417.

16904   HYATT, HARRY M.   HOODOO, CONJURATION, WITCHCRAFT,
        ROOTWORK: BELIEFS ACCEPTED BY MANY NEGROES AND WHITE
        PERSONS, THESE BEING ORALLY RECORDED AMONG BLACKS AND
        WHITES.   HANNIBAL, MO: WESTERN PUBLISHING COMPANY,
        1970.

16905   JACKSON, IRENE V.   "MUSIC AMONG BLACKS IN THE EPISCOPAL
        CHURCH: SOME PRELIMINARY CONSIDERATIONS."   HISTORICAL
        MAGAZINE OF THE PROTESTANT EPISCOPAL CHURCH, 49
        (MARCH, 1980):   21-36.

16906   JACKSON, JAMES C.   "THE RELIGIOUS EDUCATION OF THE NEGRO
        IN SOUTH CAROLINA PRIOR TO 1850."   HISTORICAL MAGAZINE
        OF THE PROTESTANT EPISCOPAL CHURCH, 36 (MARCH, 1967):
        35-61.

16907   JACKSON, LUTHER P.   "RELIGIOUS DEVELOPMENT OF THE NEGRO
        IN VIRGINIA FROM 1760 TO 1860."   JOURNAL OF NEGRO
        HISTORY, 16 (APRIL, 1931):   168-239.

16908   JACKSON, LUTHER P.   "RELIGIOUS INSTRUCTION OF NEGROES,
        1830 TO 1860, WITH SPECIFIC REFERENCES TO SOUTH
        CAROLINA."   JOURNAL OF NEGRO HISTORY, 15 (JANUARY,
        1930):   72-114.

16909   JAMES, SYDNEY V.   A PEOPLE AMONG PEOPLES: QUAKER
        BENEVOLENCE IN EIGHTEENTH CENTURY AMERICA.   CAMBRIDGE:
        HARVARD UNIVERSITY PRESS, 1963.

16910   JEANSONNE, GLEN.   "SOUTHERN BAPTIST ATTITUDES TOWARD
        SLAVERY, 1845-1861."   GEORGIA HISTORICAL QUARTERLY, 55
        (WINTER, 1971):   510-522.

16911   JENKINS, ULYSSES D.   ANCIENT AFRICAN RELIGION AND THE
        AFRICAN-AMERICAN CHURCH.   JACKSONVILLE, NC: FLAME
        INTERNATIONAL, 1978.

16912   JENKINS, ULYSSES D.   "REMNANTS OF YORUBA CULTURE WITHIN
        THE AFRICAN-AMERICAN CHURCH."   PH.D. DISSERTATION,
        UNION GRADUATE SCHOOL, MIDWEST, 1976.

16913   JENTZ, JOHN.   "A NOTE ON GENOVESE'S ACCOUNT OF THE
        SLAVES' RELIGION."   CIVIL WAR HISTORY, 23 (JUNE,
        1977):   161-169.

16914   JERNEGAN, MARCUS W.   "SLAVERY AND CONVERSION IN THE
        AMERICAN COLONIES."   AMERICAN HISTORICAL REVIEW, 21
        (APRIL, 1916):   504-527.

16915   JESSE, C.   "RELIGION AMONG THE EARLY SLAVES IN THE FRENCH
        ANTILLES."   JOURNAL OF THE BARBADOS MUSUEM AND
        HISTORICAL SOCIETY, 28 (NOVEMBER, 1960):   4-10.

16916   JOHNSON, CHARLES A.   THE FRONTIER CAMP MEETING:
        RELIGION'S HARVEST TIME.   DALLAS: SOUTHERN METHODIST
        UNIVERSITY PRESS, 1955.

16917   JOHNSON, HENRY M.   "THE METHODIST EPISCOPAL CHURCH AND
        THE EDUCATION OF SOUTHERN NEGROES, 1862-1900."   PH.D.
        DISSERTATION, YALE UNIVERSITY, 1939.

16918   JOHNSON, JAMES K.   "THE NEGRO SPIRITUAL, ITS FORM AND ITS
        USES IN WORSHIP."   M.S.M. THESIS, UNION THEOLOGICAL
        SEMINARY, 1968.

16919   JOHNSON, JAMES R.   "THE USEFULNESS OF RELIGIOUS TRAINING
        ON THE SOUTHERN PLANTATION AS A MEANS OF INCULCATING
        SERVILITY AND A DEEP SENSE OF INFERIORITY IN BLACK
        FOLKS DURING THE THIRTY YEARS PRECEDING THE AMERICAN
        CIVIL WAR."   UNPUBLISHED PAPER, TEACHERS COLLEGE,
        COLUMBIA UNIVERSITY, 1970.

16920   JOHNSON, KENNETH R.   "BLACK AMERICAN RELIGION, FROM
        SLAVERY TO SEGREGATION."   JOURNAL OF MUSCLE SHOALS
        HISTORY, 6 (1978):   49-56.

16921   JOHNSTON, RUBY F.   THE DEVELOPMENT OF NEGRO RELIGION.
        NEW YORK: PHILOSOPHICAL LIBRARY, 1954.

16922   JONES, ALICE M.   "THE NEGRO FOLK SERMON: A STUDY IN THE
        SOCIOLOGY OF FOLK CULTURE."   M.A. THESIS, FISK
        UNIVERSITY, 1942.

16923   JONES, JACQUELINE.   "THE DELAWARE ASSOCIATION FOR THE

MORAL IMPROVEMENT AND EDUCATION OF THE COLORED PEOPLE:
PRACTICAL CHRISTIANITY." B.A. THESIS, UNIVERSITY OF
DELAWARE, 1970.

16924   JONES, JEROME W. "THE ESTABLISHED VIRGINIA CHURCH AND
THE CONVERSION OF NEGROES AND INDIANS." JOURNAL OF
NEGRO HISTORY, 46 (JANUARY, 1961): 12-31.

16925   JONES, LAWRENCE. "THE ORGANIZED CHURCH: ITS HISTORIC
SIGNIFICANCE AND CHANGING ROLE IN CONTEMPORARY BLACK
EXPERIENCE." IN JOHNSON, HARRY A. (ED.). NEGOTIATING
THE MAINSTREAM: A SURVEY OF THE AFRO-AMERICAN
EXPERIENCE. CHICAGO: AMERICAN LIBRARY ASSOCIATION,
1978, PP. 103-140.

16926   JONES, WILLIAM B. "EVANGELICAL CATHOLICISM IN EARLY
COLONIAL MEXICO: AN ANALYSIS OF BISHOP JUAN DE
ZUMARRAGA'S DOCTRINA CRISTIANA." AMERICAS, 23 (APRIL,
1967): 423-432.

16927   JORDAN, LEWIS G. NEGRO BAPTIST HISTORY U.S.A.,
1750-1930. NASHVILLE: SUNDAY SCHOOL PUBLISHING
BOARD, 1930.

16928   JORDAN, MARJORIE W. "MISSISSIPPI METHODISTS AND THE
DIVISION OF THE CHURCH OVER SLAVERY." PH.D.
DISSERTATION, UNIVERSITY OF SOUTHERN MISSISSIPPI, 1972.

16929   JORDAN, ROBERT L. TWO RACES IN ONE FELLOWSHIP. DETROIT:
UNITED CHRISTIAN CHURCH, 1944.

16930   JORDAN, WINTHROP D. THE WHITE MAN'S BURDEN: HISTORICAL
ORIGINS OF RACISM IN THE UNITED STATES. NEW YORK:
OXFORD UNIVERSITY PRESS, 1974.

16931   JORDAN, WINTHROP D. WHITE OVER BLACK: AMERICAN
ATTITUDES TOWARD THE NEGRO, 1550-1812. CHAPEL HILL:
UNIVERSITY OF NORTH CAROLINA PRESS, 1968.

16932   "A JOURNAL AND TRAVELS OF JAMES MEACHAM. PART I, MAY 19
TO AUG. 31, 1789." HISTORICAL PAPERS PUBLISHED BY THE
TRINITY COLLEGE HISTORICAL SOCIETY, 9TH SER., (1912):
66-95.

16933   JULES-ROSETTE, BENNETTA. "CREATIVE SPIRITUALITY FROM
AFRICA TO AMERICA: CROSS-CULTURAL INFLUENCES IN
CONTEMPORARY RELIGIOUS FORMS." WESTERN JOURNAL OF
BLACK STUDIES, 4 (WINTER, 1980): 273-285.

16934   JUSTICE, JOHN M. "THE WORK OF THE SOCIETY FOR THE
PROPAGATION OF THE GOSPEL IN FOREIGN PARTS IN NORTH
CAROLINA." M.A. THESIS, UNIVERSITY OF NORTH CAROLINA,
1939.

16935   KAATRUD, PAUL G. "REVIVALISM AND THE POPULAR SPIRITUAL

SONGS IN MID-NINETEENTH-CENTURY AMERICA: 1830-1870."
PH.D. DISSERTATION, UNIVERSITY OF MINNESOTA, 1977.

16936 KARASCH, MARY. "CENTRAL AFRICAN RELIGIOUS TRADITION IN
RIO DE JANEIRO." JOURNAL OF LATIN AMERICAN LORE, 5
(WINTER, 1979): 233-253.

16937 KEARNEY, BELLE. A SLAVEHOLDER'S DAUGHTER. NEW YORK:
ABBEY PRESS, 1900.

16938 KEENE, CALVIN. "FRIENDS AND NEGRO SLAVERY." FRIENDS
INTELLIGENCER, 109 (JANUARY 19, 1952): 33-34.

16939 KILHAM, ELIZABETH. "SKETCHES IN COLOR." PUTNAM'S
MAGAZINE, 14 (DECEMBER, 1869): 741-746; 15
(JANUARY-MARCH, 1870): 31-38, 205-210, 304-311.

16940 KING, DAVID R. "MISSIONARY VESTRYMAN." HISTORICAL
MAGAZINE OF THE PROTESTANT EPISCOPAL CHURCH, 34
(DECEMBER, 1965): 361-368.

16941 KING, DEARING E. "WORSHIP IN THE BLACK CHURCH." IN
MCCALL, EMMANUEL L. (ED.). THE BLACK CHRISTIAN
EXPERIENCE. NASHVILLE: BROADMAN PRESS, 1972, PP.
32-42.

16942 KING, JOE M. A HISTORY OF SOUTH CAROLINA BAPTISTS.
COLUMBIA: GENERAL BOARD OF THE SOUTH CAROLINA BAPTIST
CONVENTION, 1964.

16943 KIRRANE, JOHN P. "THE ESTABLISHMENT OF NEGRO PARISHES
AND THE COMING OF THE JOSEPHITES (1863-1871)." M.A.
THESIS, CATHOLIC UNIVERSITY OF AMERICA, 1932.

16944 KLEIN, HERBERT S. "ANGLICANISM, CATHOLICISM AND THE
NEGRO SLAVE." COMPARATIVE STUDIES IN SOCIETY AND
HISTORY, 8 (APRIL, 1966): 295-330.

16945 KLEIN, HERBERT S. SLAVERY IN THE AMERICAS: A
COMPARATIVE STUDY OF VIRGINIA AND CUBA. CHICAGO:
UNIVERSITY OF CHICAGO PRESS, 1967.

16946 KLINGBEIL, CHRISTA. THE EVANGELIZATION OF THE NEGRO.
N.P., 1960.

16947 KLINGBERG, FRANK J. "THE AFRICAN IMMIGRANT IN COLONIAL
PENNSYLVANIA AND DELAWARE." HISTORICAL MAGAZINE OF
THE PROTESTANT EPISCOPAL CHURCH, 11 (MARCH, 1942):
126-153.

16948 KLINGBERG, FRANK J. ANGLICAN HUMANITARIANISM IN COLONIAL
NEW YORK. PHILADELPHIA: CHURCH HISTORICAL SOCIETY,
1940.

16949 KLINGBERG, FRANK J. "BRITISH HUMANITARIANISM AT

CODRINGTON." JOURNAL OF NEGRO HISTORY, 23 (OCTOBER, 1938): 451-486.

16950   KLINGBERG, FRANK J. (ED.). CODRINGTON CHRONICLE: AN EXPERIMENT IN ANGLICAN ALTRUISM ON A BARBADOS PLANTATION, 1710-1834. BERKELEY: UNIVERSITY OF CALIFORNIA PRESS, 1949.

16951   KLINGBERG, FRANK J. "THE S.P.G. PROGRAM FOR NEGROES IN COLONIAL NEW YORK." HISTORICAL MAGAZINE OF THE PROTESTANT EPISCOPAL CHURCH, 8 (DECEMBER, 1939): 306-371.

16952   KNOTT, MAURICE F. "THE PROTESTANT CHURCHES OF KENTUCKY AND THE SLAVERY QUESTION." M.A. THESIS, UNIVERSITY OF KENTUCKY, 1951.

16953   KOGER, AZZIE B. HISTORY OF NEGRO BAPTISTS OF MARYLAND. BALTIMORE: JESSE B. CLARKE AND SON, 1936.

16954   KORN, BERTRAM. "JEWS AND NEGRO SLAVERY IN THE OLD SOUTH, 1789-1865." PUBLICATIONS OF THE AMERICAN JEWISH HISTORICAL SOCIETY, 50 (1961): 151-201.

16955   KORN, BERTRAM W. JEWS AND NEGRO SLAVERY IN THE OLD SOUTH, 1789-1865. ELKINS PARK, PA: REFORM CONGREGATION KENESETH ISRAEL, 1961.

16956   KULL, IRVING S. "PRESBYTERIAN ATTITUDES TOWARD SLAVERY." CHURCH HISTORY, 7 (JUNE, 1938): 101-114.

16957   LAFARGE, JOHN. "THE SURVIVAL OF THE CATHOLIC FAITH IN SOUTHERN MARYLAND." CATHOLIC HISTORICAL REVIEW, 21 (APRIL, 1935): 1-20.

16958   LAGUERRE, MICHEL. "THE FAILURE OF CHRISTIANITY AMONG THE SLAVES (IN HAITI)." FREEING THE SPIRIT, 2 (1973): 10-24.

16959   LAGUERRE, MICHEL. "TICOULOUTE AND HIS KINFOLK: THE STUDY OF A HAITIAN EXTENDED FAMILY." IN SHIMKIN, DEMITRI B.; SHIMKIN, EDITH M.; AND FRATE, DENNIS A. (EDS.). THE EXTENDED FAMILY IN BLACK SOCIETIES. THE HAGUE: MOUTON PUBLISHERS, 1978, PP. 407-446.

16960   LAGUERRE, MICHEL S. VOODOO HERITAGE. BEVERLY HILLS: SAGE PUBLICATIONS, 1980.

16961   LANDES, RUTH. "FETISH WORSHIP IN BRAZIL." JOURNAL OF AMERICAN FOLKLORE, 53 (OCTOBER-DECEMBER, 1940): 261-270.

16962   LANDON, FRED. "THE WORK OF THE AMERICAN MISSIONARY ASSOCIATION AMONG NEGRO REFUGEES IN CANADA, 1848-1864." PAPERS AND RECORDS OF THE ONTARIO

HISTORICAL SOCIETY, 21 (1924): 198-205.

16963   LANTERNARI, VITTORIO. RELIGIONS OF THE OPPRESSED. NEW
        YORK: RANDOM HOUSE, 1963.

16964   LATIMER, JAMES. "THE FOUNDATION OF RELIGIOUS EDUCATION
        IN THE BRITISH WEST INDIES." JOURNAL OF NEGRO
        EDUCATION, 34 (FALL, 1965): 435-442.

16965   LATIMER, JAMES. "THE FOUNDATIONS OF RELIGIOUS EDUCATION
        IN THE FRENCH WEST INDIES." JOURNAL OF NEGRO
        EDUCATION, 40 (WINTER, 1971): 91-98.

16966   LATIMER, JAMES. "THE FOUNDATIONS OF RELIGIOUS EDUCATION
        IN THE SPANISH WEST INDIES." JOURNAL OF NEGRO
        EDUCATION, 39 (WINTER, 1970): 70-75.

16967   LATIMER, JAMES. "AN HISTORICAL AND COMPARATIVE STUDY OF
        THE FOUNDATIONS OF EDUCATION IN THE BRITISH, SPANISH
        AND FRENCH WEST INDIES (UP TO THE END OF SLAVERY IN
        THE BRITISH ISLANDS)." PH.D. DISSERTATION, UNIVERSITY
        OF LONDON, 1952.

16968   LAWRENCE, JAMES B. "RELIGIOUS EDUCATION OF THE NEGRO IN
        THE COLONY OF GEORGIA." GEORGIA HISTORICAL QUARTERLY,
        14 (MARCH, 1930): 41-57.

16969   LAWTON, SAMUEL M. "THE RELIGIOUS LIFE OF SOUTH CAROLINA
        COASTAL AND SEA ISLAND NEGROES." PH.D. DISSERTATION,
        GEORGE PEABODY COLLEGE FOR TEACHERS, 1939.

16970   "LETTERS CONCERNING SOME MISSIONS OF THE MISSISSIPPI
        VALLEY, A.D. 1818-1827." RECORDS OF THE AMERICAN
        CATHOLIC HISTORICAL SOCIETY, 14 (1903): 141-216.

16971   "LETTERS SHOWING THE RISE AND PROGRESS OF THE EARLY NEGRO
        CHURCHES OF GEORGIA AND THE WEST INDIES." JOURNAL OF
        NEGRO HISTORY, 1 (JANUARY, 1916): 69-92.

16972   LEVINE, LAWRENCE W. BLACK CULTURE AND BLACK
        CONSCIOUSNESS: AFRO-AMERICAN FOLK THOUGHT FROM
        SLAVERY TO FREEDOM. NEW YORK: OXFORD UNIVERSITY
        PRESS, 1977.

16973   LEWIS, JAMES K. "THE RELIGIOUS LIFE OF FUGITIVE SLAVES
        AND RISE OF COLOURED BAPTIST CHURCHES, 1820-1865, IN
        WHAT IS NOW KNOWN AS ONTARIO." B.D. THESIS, MCMASTER
        UNIVERSITY, 1965.

16974   LEWIS, ROBERT S., JR. "SLAVERY, COTTON MATHER AND 17TH
        CENTURY RELIGIOUS INSTRUCTION." BLACK HERITAGE, 17
        (MAY-JUNE, 1978): 102-113.

16975   LINCOLN, C. ERIC (ED.). THE BLACK EXPERIENCE IN
        RELIGION. GARDEN CITY: ANCHOR PRESS, 1974.

16976   LINCOLN, C. ERIC. "BLACK RELIGION IN NORTH CAROLINA:
        FROM COLONIAL TIMES TO 1900." IN CROW, JEFFREY J. AND
        WINTERS, ROBERT E., JR. (EDS.). THE BLACK PRESENCE IN
        NORTH CAROLINA. RALEIGH: NORTH CAROLINA MUSEUM OF
        HISTORY, 1978, PP. 9-24.

16977   LINCOLN, C. ERIC. "200 YEARS OF BLACK RELIGION:
        'CHRISTIAN' SLAVEHOLDERS BROUGHT 'GOD' TO SLAVES."
        EBONY, 30 (AUGUST, 1975): 34-36.

16978   LINCOLN, CHARLES E. "DEVELOPMENT OF BLACK RELIGION IN
        AMERICA." REVIEW AND EXPOSITOR, 70 (SUMMER, 1973):
        295-308.

16979   LINES, STILES B. "SLAVES AND CHURCHMEN: THE WORK OF THE
        EPISCOPAL CHURCH AMONG SOUTHERN NEGROES, 1830-1860."
        PH.D. DISSERTATION, COLUMBIA UNIVERSITY, 1960.

16980   LIPSCOMB, PATRICK C. "THE CHURCH OF ENGLAND AND THE
        NEGRO SLAVES IN THE WEST INDIES, 1783-1883." M.A.
        THESIS, UNIVERSITY OF TEXAS, 1956.

16981   LITWACK, LEON F. BEEN IN THE STORM SO LONG: THE
        AFTERMATH OF SLAVERY. NEW YORK: ALFRED A. KNOPF,
        1979.

16982   LOGAN, R. LEROY. "THE DISCIPLES OF CHRIST AND SLAVERY."
        B.D. THESIS, BUTLER UNIVERSITY, 1935.

16983   LONG, CHARLES H. "OPPRESSIVE ELEMENTS IN RELIGION AND
        THE RELIGIONS OF THE OPPRESSED." HARVARD THEOLOGICAL
        REVIEW, 69 (JULY-OCTOBER, 1976): 397-412.

16984   LONG, CHARLES H. "PERSPECTIVES FOR A STUDY OF
        AFRO-AMERICAN RELIGION IN THE UNITED STATES." HISTORY
        OF RELIGIONS, 11 (AUGUST, 1971): 54-66.

16985   LONG, CHARLES H. "STRUCTURAL SIMILARITIES AND
        DISSIMILARITIES IN BLACK AND AFRICAN THEOLOGIES."
        JOURNAL OF RELIGIOUS THOUGHT, 32 (FALL-WINTER, 1975):
        9-24.

16986   LONG, DURWARD. "THE METHODIST CHURCH AND NEGRO SLAVERY
        IN AMERICA, 1784-1844." WESLEYAN QUARTERLY REVIEW, 3
        (FEBRUARY, 1966): 3-17.

16987   LONG, NORMAN G. "THE THEOLOGY AND PSYCHOLOGY OF THE
        NEGROES' RELIGION PRIOR TO 1860--AS SHOWN PARTICULARLY
        IN THE SPIRITUALS." M.A. THESIS, OBERLIN COLLEGE,
        1936.

16988   LORING, EDUARD N. "CHARLES C. JONES: MISSIONARY TO
        PLANTATION SLAVES 1831-1847." PH.D. DISSERTATION,
        VANDERBILT UNIVERSITY, 1976.

16989   LOVE, EMANUEL K.   HISTORY OF THE FIRST AFRICAN BAPTIST
        CHURCH FROM ITS ORGANIZATION JANUARY 20, 1788 TO JULY
        1, 1888.   SAVANNAH: MORNING NEWS PRINT, 1888.

16990   LOVEJOY, DAVID S.   "SAMUEL HOPKINS: RELIGION, SLAVERY,
        AND THE REVOLUTION."   NEW ENGLAND QUARTERLY, 40 (JUNE,
        1967):   227-243.

16991   LOVELAND, ANNE C.   SOUTHERN EVANGELICALS AND THE SOCIAL
        ORDER, 1800-1860.   BATON ROUGE: LOUISIANA STATE
        UNIVERSITY PRESS, 1980.

16992   LUCAS, FREDERICK A.   "CHRISTIANITY AND THE MILITANT
        SLAVE."   B.A. THESIS, HARVARD UNIVERSITY, 1972.

16993   LYONS, ADELAIDE A.   "RELIGIOUS DEFENCE OF SLAVERY IN THE
        NORTH."   HISTORICAL PAPERS OF THE TRINITY COLLEGE
        HISTORICAL SOCIETY, 13TH SER., (1919):   5-34.

16994   MADDEX, JACK P.   "FROM THEOCRACY TO SPIRITUALITY: THE
        SOUTHERN PRESBYTERIAN REVERSAL ON CHURCH AND STATE."
        JOURNAL OF PRESBYTERIAN HISTORY, 54 (WINTER, 1976):
        438-457.

16995   MADDEX, JACK P.   "PROSLAVERY MILLENNIALISM: SOCIAL
        ESCHATOLOGY IN ANTEBELLUM SOUTHERN CALVINISM."
        AMERICAN QUARTERLY, 31 (SPRING, 1979):   46-62.

16996   MADDEX, JACK P., JR.   "'THE SOUTHERN APOSTASY' REVISITED:
        THE SIGNIFICANCE OF PROSLAVERY CHRISTIANITY."   MARXIST
        PERSPECTIVES, 2 (FALL, 1979):   132-141.

16997   MADRON, THOMAS W.   "JOHN WESLEY ON RACE: A CHRISTIAN
        VIEW OF EQUALITY."   METHODIST HISTORY, 2 (JULY, 1964):
        24-34.

16998   MALDEN, K.S.   BROKEN BONDS, THE S.P.G. AND THE WEST
        INDIAN SLAVES.   WESTMINSTER: THE SOCIETY FOR THE
        PROPAGATION OF THE GOSPEL IN FOREIGN PARTS, 1933.

16999   MALLARD, ANNIE H.   "RELIGIOUS WORK OF SOUTH CAROLINA
        BAPTISTS AMONG THE SLAVES FROM 1781 TO 1830."   M.A.
        THESIS, UNIVERSITY OF SOUTH CAROLINA, 1946.

17000   MARABLE, MANNING.   "THE MEANING OF FAITH IN THE BLACK
        MIND IN SLAVERY."   ROCKY MOUNTAIN REVIEW OF LANGUAGE
        AND LITERATURE, 30 (AUTUMN, 1976):   248-264.

17001   MARKOE, WILLIAM M.   "CATHOLIC CHURCH AND SLAVERY."
        INTERRACIAL REVIEW, 6 (AUGUST, 1933):   146-147.

17002   MARKOE, WILLIAM M.   "THE CATHOLIC CHURCH AND SLAVERY."
        AMERICA, 28 (FEBRUARY 17, 1923):   415-417.

17003   MARKOE, WILLIAM M.   THE SLAVE OF THE NEGROES.   CHICAGO:

LOYOLA UNIVERSITY PRESS, 1920.

17004   MARTIN, JOHN H. "THE UNITARIAN AND SLAVERY." B.D.
         THESIS, UNIVERSITY OF CHICAGO, 1954.

17005   MARX, GARY T. "RELIGION: OPIATE OR INSPIRATION OF CIVIL
         RIGHTS MILITANCY AMONG NEGROES?" AMERICAN
         SOCIOLOGICAL REVIEW, 32 (FEBRUARY, 1967): 64-72.

17006   MATHEWS, DONALD G. "ANTISLAVERY, PIETY, AND
         INSTITUTIONALISM: THE SLAVERY CONTROVERSIES IN THE
         METHODIST EPISCOPAL CHURCH, 1780 TO 1844." PH.D.
         DISSERTATION, DUKE UNIVERSITY, 1962.

17007   MATHEWS, DONALD G. "CHARLES COLCOCK JONES AND THE
         SOUTHERN EVANGELICAL CRUSADE TO FORM A BIRACIAL
         COMMUNITY." JOURNAL OF SOUTHERN HISTORY, 41 (AUGUST,
         1975): 299-320.

17008   MATHEWS, DONALD G. "THE METHODIST MISSION TO THE SLAVES,
         1829-1844." JOURNAL OF AMERICAN HISTORY, 51 (MARCH,
         1965): 615-631.

17009   MATHEWS, DONALD G. "NORTH CAROLINA METHODISTS IN THE
         NINETEENTH CENTURY: CHURCH AND SOCIETY." IN INGRAM,
         O. KELLY (ED.). METHODISM ALIVE IN NORTH CAROLINA.
         DURHAM: DIVINITY SCHOOL, DUKE UNIVERSITY, 1976, PP.
         59-74.

17010   MATHEWS, DONALD G. "RELIGION AND SLAVERY: THE CASE OF
         THE AMERICAN SOUTH." IN BOLT, CHRISTINE AND DRESCHER,
         SEYMOUR (EDS.). ANTI-SLAVERY, RELIGION, AND REFORM:
         ESSAYS IN MEMORY OF ROGER ANSTEY. HAMDEN, CT: ARCHON
         BOOKS, 1980, PP. 207-232.

17011   MATHEWS, DONALD G. RELIGION IN THE OLD SOUTH. CHICAGO:
         UNIVERSITY OF CHICAGO PRESS, 1977.

17012   MATHEWS, DONALD G. "RELIGION IN THE OLD SOUTH:
         SPECULATION ON METHODOLOGY." SOUTH ATLANTIC
         QUARTERLY, 73 (WINTER, 1974): 34-52.

17013   MATHEWS, DONALD G. SLAVERY AND METHODISM: A CHAPTER IN
         AMERICAN MORALITY, 1780-1845. PRINCETON: PRINCETON
         UNIVERSITY PRESS, 1965.

17014   MAULTSBY, PORTIA K. "AFRO-AMERICAN RELIGIOUS MUSIC,
         1619-1861. PART I--HISTORICAL DEVELOPMENT. PART
         II--COMPUTER ANALYSIS OF ONE HUNDRED SPIRITUALS."
         PH.D. DISSERTATION, UNIVERSITY OF WISCONSIN, 1974.

17015   MAXWELL, JOHN F. "THE DEVELOPMENT OF CATHOLIC DOCTRINE
         CONCERNING SLAVERY." WORLD JUSTICE, 11 (DECEMBER,
         1969, MARCH, 1970): 147-192, 291-324.

17016   MAYERS, JULIUS. "THE PRESBYTERIAN CHURCH AND SLAVERY IN
        THE UNITED STATES." M.A. THESIS, COLUMBIA UNIVERSITY,
        1940.

17017   MAYS, BENJAMIN E. THE NEGRO'S GOD AS REFLECTED IN HIS
        LITERATURE. NEW YORK: RUSSELL AND RUSSELL, 1938.

17018   MAYS, BENJAMIN E. AND NICHOLSON, JOSEPH W. THE NEGRO'S
        CHURCH. NEW YORK: INSTITUTE OF SOCIAL AND RELIGIOUS
        RESEARCH, 1933.

17019   MBITI, JOHN S. NEW TESTAMENT ESCHATOLOGY IN AN AFRICAN
        BACKGROUND. LONDON: OXFORD UNIVERSITY PRESS, 1971.

17020   MCCARROLL, JESSE C. "BLACK INFLUENCE ON SOUTHERN WHITE
        PROTESTANT CHURCH MUSIC DURING SLAVERY." PH.D.
        DISSERTATION, COLUMBIA UNIVERSITY, 1972.

17021   MCGEE, DANIEL B. "RELIGIOUS BELIEFS AND ETHICAL MOTIFS
        OF THE NEGRO SPIRITUALS." M.TH. THESIS, SOUTHEASTERN
        BAPTIST THEOLOGICAL SEMINARY, 1960.

17022   MCGILL, ALEXANDER T. AMERICAN SLAVERY, AS VIEWED AND
        ACTED ON BY THE PRESBYTERIAN CHURCH IN THE UNITED
        STATES OF AMERICA. PHILADELPHIA: PRESBYTERIAN BOARD
        OF PUBLICATION, 1865.

17023   MCGOWAN, RAYMOND A. "THE ROLE OF CATHOLIC CULTURE IN THE
        WEST INDIES." CATHOLIC HISTORICAL REVIEW, 26 (JULY,
        1940): 183-194.

17024   MCGREGOR, PEDRO. JESUS OF THE SPIRITS. NEW YORK: STEIN
        AND DAY, 1967.

17025   MCKINNEY, RICHARD I. "THE BLACK CHURCH; ITS DEVELOPMENT
        AND PRESENT IMPACT." HARVARD THEOLOGICAL REVIEW, 64
        (OCTOBER, 1971): 452-481.

17026   MCLEAN, PATRICIA S. "CONJURE DOCTORS IN EASTERN NORTH
        CAROLINA." NORTH CAROLINA FOLKLORE, 20 (FEBRUARY,
        1972): 21-29.

17027   MCLOUGHLIN, WILLIAM G. "INDIAN SLAVEHOLDERS AND
        PRESBYTERIAN MISSIONARIES, 1337-1861." CHURCH
        HISTORY, 42 (DECEMBER, 1973): 535-551.

17028   MCLOUGHLIN, WILLIAM G. AND JORDAN, WINTHROP D. (EDS.).
        "BAPTISTS FACE THE BARBARITIES OF SLAVERY IN 1710."
        JOURNAL OF SOUTHERN HISTORY, 29 (NOVEMBER, 1963):
        495-501.

17029   MCMASTER, RICHARD K. "LIBERTY OF PROPERTY? THE
        METHODISTS PETITION FOR EMANCIPATION IN VIRGINIA,
        1785." METHODIST HISTORY, 10 (OCTOBER, 1971): 44-55.

17030   METRAUX, ALFRED. VOODOO IN HAITI. NEW YORK: OXFORD
        UNIVERSITY PRESS, 1959.

17031   MICELI, MARY V. "THE INFLUENCE OF THE ROMAN CATHOLIC
        CHURCH ON SLAVERY IN COLONIAL LOUISIANA UNDER FRENCH
        DOMINATION, 1718-1763." PH.D. DISSERTATION, TULANE
        UNIVERSITY, 1979.

17032   MICHAUX, RICHARD R. SKETCHES OF LIFE IN NORTH CAROLINA.
        CUTLER, NC: W.C. PHILLIPS, 1894.

17033   MILLER, HARRIET P. PIONEER COLORED CHRISTIANS.
        CLARKSVILLE, TN: W.P. TITUS, 1911.

17034   MILLER, HASKELL M. "INSTITUTIONAL BEHAVIOR OF THE
        CUMBERLAND PRESBYTERIAN CHURCH, AN AMERICAN PROTESTANT
        RELIGIOUS DENOMINATION." PH.D. DISSERTATION, NEW YORK
        UNIVERSITY, 1940.

17035   MILLER, RANDALL M. "BLACK CATHOLICS IN THE SLAVE SOUTH:
        SOME NEEDS AND OPPORTUNITIES FOR STUDY." RECORDS OF
        THE AMERICAN CATHOLIC HISTORICAL SOCIETY OF
        PHILADELPHIA, 86 (MARCH-DECEMBER, 1975): 93-106.

17036   MILLER, RANDALL M. "THE FAILED MISSION: THE CATHOLIC
        CHURCH AND BLACK CATHOLICS IN THE OLD SOUTH." IN
        MAGDOL, EDWARD AND WAKELYN, JON (EDS.). THE COMMON
        PEOPLE OF THE ANTEBELLUM SOUTH. WESTPORT: GREENWOOD
        PRESS, 1980, PP. 37-54.

17037   MILLER, RICHARD R. SLAVERY AND CATHOLICISM. DURHAM:
        NORTH STATE PUBLISHERS, 1957.

17038   MILLS, GARY B. THE FORGOTTEN PEOPLE: CANE RIVER'S
        CREOLES OF COLOR. BATON ROUGE: LOUISIANA STATE
        UNIVERSITY PRESS, 1977.

17039   MISCH, EDWARDO J. "THE AMERICAN BISHOPS AND THE NEGRO
        FROM THE CIVIL WAR TO THE THIRD PLENARY COUNCIL OF
        BALTIMORE (1865-1884)." PH.D. DISSERTATION, GREGORIAN
        UNIVERSITY, ROME, 1968.

17040   MITCHELL, HENRY H. "BLACK PREACHING." IN MCCALL,
        EMMANUEL L. (ED.). THE BLACK CHRISTIAN EXPERIENCE.
        NASHVILLE: BROADMAN PRESS, 1972, PP. 43-62.

17041   MITCHELL, HENRY H. BLACK PREACHING. NEW YORK: J.B.
        LIPPINCOTT, 1970.

17042   MITCHELL, HENRY H. "THE BLACK RELIGIOUS TRADITION; AN
        EXAMINATION OF THE INTERPRETATION OF CHRISTIANITY BY
        EARLY AMERICAN BLACKS." TH.D. DISSERTATION, SCHOOL OF
        THEOLOGY AT CLAREMONT, 1973.

17043   MITCHELL, HENRY H. "THE GENIUS OF NEGRO PREACHING: A

LINGUISTIC AND STYLISTIC EXAMINATION OF THE
HOMILETICAL TWIN BROTHER TO THE AMERICAN NEGRO
SPIRITUAL, WITH SOME POSSIBLE IMPLICATIONS OF THE
RESULT FOR AMERICAN PROTESTANT WHITE CHURCHES." M.A.
THESIS, FRESNO STATE COLLEGE, 1965.

17044   MITCHELL, JAMES N. "NAT TURNER: SLAVE, PREACHER,
        PROPHET, AND MESSIAH, 1800-1931: A STUDY OF THE CALL
        OF A BLACK SLAVE TO PROPHETHOOD AND TO THE MESSIAHSHIP
        OF THE SECOND COMING OF CHRIST." D.MIN. DISSERTATION,
        VANDERBILT UNIVERSITY, 1975.

17045   MITCHELL, JOSEPH. "TRAVELING PREACHER AND SETTLED
        FARMER." METHODIST HISTORY, 5 (JULY, 1967): 3-14.

17046   MODE, PETER G. "THE CHRISTIANIZATION AND EMANCIPATION OF
        THE NEGRO: COLONIAL PERIOD TO THE CIVIL WAR." SOURCE
        BOOK AND BIBLIOGRAPHICAL GUIDE FOR AMERICAN CHURCH
        HISTORY. MENASHA, WI: GEORGE BANTA PUBLISHING
        COMPANY, 1921, PP. 538-575.

17047   MOORE, EDMUND A. "ROBERT J. BRECKINRIDGE AND THE SLAVERY
        ASPECT OF THE PRESBYTERIAN SCHISM OF 1837." CHURCH
        HISTORY, 4 (DECEMBER, 1935): 282-294.

17048   MOORE, JOSEPH G. "RELIGION OF JAMAICA NEGROES: A STUDY
        OF AFRO-JAMAICAN ACCULTURATION." PH.D. DISSERTATION,
        NORTHWESTERN UNIVERSITY, 1953.

17049   MOORE, JOSEPH G. "RELIGIOUS SYNCRETISM IN JAMAICA."
        PRACTICAL ANTHROPOLOGY, 12 (1965): 63-70.

17050   MOORE, LEROY JR. "THE SPIRITUAL: SOUL OF BLACK
        RELIGION." CHURCH HISTORY, 40 (MARCH, 1971): 79-81.

17051   "MORALITY AND RELIGION IN SLAVERY DAYS." SOUTHERN
        WORKMAN, 26 (OCTOBER, 1897): 210.

17052   "THE MORAVIAN MISSION IN BARBADOS." JOURNAL OF THE
        BARBADOS MUSEUM AND HISTORICAL SOCIETY, 31 (MAY,
        1965): 73-77.

17053   MORRIS, GEORGE E. "THE ANTE-BELLUM RELIGIOUS LIFE OF THE
        RACE." IN PENN, I. GARLAND AND BOWEN, J.W.E. (EDS.).
        THE UNITED NEGRO: HIS PROBLEMS AND HIS PROGRESS.
        ATLANTA: D.E. LUTHER PUBLISHING COMPANY, 1902, PP.
        101-106.

17054   MOULTON, PHILLIPS. "JOHN WOOLMAN'S APPROACH TO SOCIAL
        ACTION--AS EXEMPLIFIED IN RELATION TO SLAVERY."
        CHURCH HISTORY, 35 (DECEMBER, 1966): 399-410.

17055   MOUNGER, DWYN M. "BONDAGE AND BENEVOLENCE: AN
        EVANGELICAL CALVINIST APPROACHES SLAVERY--SAMUEL
        HANSON COX." PH.D. DISSERTATION, UNION THEOLOGICAL

SEMINARY, 1976.

17056   MOYD, OLIN P. "REDEMPTION: A THEOLOGY FROM BLACK
        HISTORY (AN EXAMINATION OF THE MEANING OF REDEMPTION
        AS REFLECTED IN BLACK FOLK EXPRESSIONS)." PH.D.
        DISSERTATION, ST. MARY'S SEMINARY AND UNIVERSITY, 1977.

17057   MULLIN, GERRY. "RELIGION, ACCULTURATION, AND AMERICAN
        NEGRO SLAVE REBELLIONS: GABRIEL'S INSURRECTION." IN
        BRACEY, JOHN H., JR.; MEIER, AUGUST; AND RUDWICK,
        ELLIOTT (EDS.). AMERICAN SLAVERY: THE QUESTION OF
        RESISTANCE. BELMONT, CA: WADSWORTH PUBLISHING
        COMPANY, 1971, PP. 160-178.

17058   MULLIN, MICHAEL. "SLAVE OBEAHMEN AND SLAVEOWNING
        PATRIARCHS IN AN ERA OF WAR AND REVOLUTION
        (1766-1807)." IN RUBIN, VERA AND TUDEN, ARTHUR
        (EDS.). COMPARATIVE PERSPECTIVES ON SLAVERY IN NEW
        WORLD PLANTATION SOCIETIES. NEW YORK: NEW YORK
        ACADEMY OF SCIENCES, 1977, PP. 481-490.

17059   MULVEY, PATRICIA A. "BLACK BROTHERS AND SISTERS:
        MEMBERSHIP IN THE BLACK LAY BROTHERHOODS OF COLONIAL
        BRAZIL." LUSO-BRAZILIAN REVIEW, 17 (WINTER, 1980):
        253-279.

17060   MULVEY, PATRICIA A. "THE BLACK LAY BROTHERHOODS OF
        COLONIAL BRAZIL: A HISTORY." PH.D. DISSERTATION,
        CITY UNIVERSITY OF NEW YORK, 1976.

17061   MURCELL, JEANNE F. "THE RELIGIOUS LIFE OF THE NEGROES
        PORTRAYED IN THEIR SPIRITUALS." M.A. THESIS, BOSTON
        UNIVERSITY, 1953.

17062   MURPHY, JOHN C. "AN ANALYSIS OF THE ATTITUDES OF
        AMERICAN CATHOLICS TOWARD THE IMMIGRANT AND THE NEGRO,
        1825-1925." PH.D. DISSERTATION, CATHOLIC UNIVERSITY
        OF AMERICA, 1941.

17063   MURPHY, JOHN C. AN ANALYSIS OF THE ATTITUDES OF AMERICAN
        CATHOLICS TOWARD THE IMMIGRANT AND THE NEGRO,
        1825-1925. WASHINGTON: CATHOLIC UNIVERSITY OF
        AMERICA PRESS, 1940.

17064   MURPHY, MIRIAM T. "CATHOLIC MISSIONARY WORK AMONG THE
        COLORED PEOPLE OF THE UNITED STATES, 1776-1866."
        RECORDS OF THE AMERICAN CATHOLIC HISTORICAL SOCIETY,
        35 (JUNE, 1924): 101-136.

17065   MURPHY, PATRICIA G. THE MORAVIAN MISSION TO THE AFRICAN
        SLAVES OF THE DANISH WEST INDIES, 1732-1828. ST.
        THOMAS: CARIBBEAN RESEARCH INSTITUTE, COLLEGE OF THE
        VIRGIN ISLANDS, 1969.

17066   MURRAY, ANDREW E. PRESBYTERIANS AND THE NEGRO: A

HISTORY. PHILADELPHIA: PRESBYTERIAN HISTORICAL
SOCIETY, 1966.

17067 MURRAY, WM. "CHRISTIANITY IN THE WEST INDIES." IN
SCHAFF, PHILIP AND PRIME, S.I. EVANGELICAL ALLIANCE
SIXTH GENERAL CONFERENCE. NEW YORK: HARPER &
BROTHERS, 1874, PP. 133-136.

17068 MYERS, ROBERT M. (ED.). A GEORGIAN AT PRINCETON. NEW
YORK: HARCOURT BRACE JOVANOVICH, 1976.

17069 NASH, GARY B. "THE AFRICAN RESPONSE TO SLAVERY." RED,
WHITE AND BLACK: THE PEOPLES OF EARLY AMERICA.
ENGLEWOOD CLIFFS: PRENTICE-HALL, 1974, PP. 183-212.

17070 NELSEN, HART M. AND NELSEN, ANNE K. "THE BLACK CHURCH
BEFORE WORLD WAR I." BLACK CHURCH IN THE SIXTIES.
LEXINGTON: UNIVERSITY PRESS OF KENTUCKY, 1975, PP.
17-35.

17071 NELSEN, HART M.; YOKLEY, RAYTHA L.; AND NELSEN, ANNE K.
(EDS.). THE BLACK CHURCH IN AMERICA. NEW YORK:
BASIC BOOKS, 1971.

17072 NELSON, WILLIAM S. "THE CHRISTIAN CHURCH AND SLAVERY IN
AMERICA." HOWARD REVIEW, 2 (JANUARY, 1925): 41-77.

17073 NERI, PHILIP. "BAPTISM AND MANUMISSION OF NEGRO SLAVES
IN THE EARLY COLONIAL PERIOD." RECORDS OF THE
AMERICAN CATHOLIC HISTORICAL SOCIETY, 51
(SEPTEMBER-DECEMBER, 1940): 220-232.

17074 NEVINS, ALLAN. "SLAVERY, RACE-ADJUSTMENT, AND THE
FUTURE." ORDEAL OF THE UNION. 2 VOLS. NEW YORK:
CHARLES SCRIBNER'S SONS, 1947, VOL. 1, PP. 498-544.

17075 NICHOLSON, LOIS B. "THE RELIGIOUS ATTITUDE OF THE SOUTH
TOWARD SLAVERY AND THE CIVIL WAR." M.A. THESIS,
UNIVERSITY OF CALIFORNIA, 1927.

17076 NICHOLSON, ROY S. WESLEYAN METHODISM IN THE SOUTH.
SYRACUSE: WESLEYAN METHODISM PUBLISHING HOUSE, 1933.

17077 NIDA, EUGENE A. "AFRICAN INFLUENCE IN THE RELIGIOUS LIFE
OF LATIN AMERICA." PRACTICAL ANTHROPOLOGY, 13
(JULY-AUGUST, 1966): 133-138.

17078 NOON, THOMAS R. "EARLY BLACK LUTHERANS IN THE SOUTH."
CONCORDIA HISTORICAL INSTITUTE QUARTERLY, 50 (SUMMER,
1977): 50-63.

17079 NORWOOD, JOHN N. THE SCHISM IN THE METHODIST EPISCOPAL
CHURCH, 1844: A STUDY OF SLAVERY AND ECCLESIASTICAL
POLITICS. ALFRED, NY: ALFRED UNIVERSITY, 1923.

17080   NORWOOD, JOHN N. "THE SLAVERY SCHISM IN THE METHODIST
        EPISCOPAL CHURCH; A STUDY OF SLAVERY AND
        ECCLESIASTICAL POLITICS." PH.D. DISSERTATION, CORNELL
        UNIVERSITY, 1915.

17081   NUESSE, CELESTINE J. THE SOCIAL THOUGHT OF AMERICAN
        CATHOLICS, 1634-1829. WASHINGTON: CATHOLIC
        UNIVERSITY OF AMERICA PRESS, 1945.

17082   OBERG, KALERVO. "AFRO-BRAZILIAN RELIGIOUS CULTS."
        SOCIOLOGIA, 21 (MAY, 1959): 134-141.

17083   O'BRIEN, JOHN T. "FACTORY, CHURCH, AND COMMUNITY:
        BLACKS IN ANTEBELLUM RICHMOND." JOURNAL OF SOUTHERN
        HISTORY, 44 (NOVEMBER, 1973): 509-536.

17084   O'BRIEN, MARY L. "SLAVERY IN LOUISVILLE DURING THE
        ANTEBELLUM PERIOD: 1820-1860. A STUDY OF THE EFFECTS
        OF URBANIZATION ON THE INSTITUTION OF SLAVERY AS IT
        EXISTED IN LOUISVILLE, KENTUCKY." M.A. THESIS,
        UNIVERSITY OF LOUISVILLE, 1979.

17085   OOSTHUIZEN, G.C. AFRO-CHRISTIAN RELIGIONS. LEIDEN:
        E.J. BRILL, 1979.

17086   ORR, HORACE E. "THE TENNESSEE CHURCHES AND SLAVERY; WITH
        SPECIAL REFERENCE TO EAST TENNESSEE." M.A. THESIS,
        UNIVERSITY OF TENNESSEE, 1924.

17087   OSBORNE, WILLIAM. "SLAVERY'S SEQUEL: A FREEMAN'S
        ODYSSEY." JUBILEE, 3 (SEPTEMBER, 1955): 10-23.

17088   OWENS, LESLIE H. THIS SPECIES OF PROPERTY: SLAVE LIFE
        AND CULTURE IN THE OLD SOUTH. NEW YORK: OXFORD
        UNIVERSITY PRESS, 1976.

17089   PALM, REBA W. "PROTESTANT CHURCHES AND SLAVERY IN
        MATAGORDA COUNTY." EAST TEXAS HISTORICAL JOURNAL, 14
        (SPRING, 1976): 3-8.

17090   PARKINSON, RALPH T. "THE RELIGIOUS INSTRUCTION OF
        SLAVES, 1820-1860." M.A. THESIS, UNIVERSITY OF NORTH
        CAROLINA, 1948.

17091   PARRINDER, EDWARD G. AFRICAN TRADITIONAL RELIGION.
        LONDON: HUTCHINSON'S UNIVERSITY LIBRARY, 1954.

17092   PARSONS, DENNIS F. "THE RELIGIOUS DEVELOPMENT OF THE
        NEGRO." M.A. THESIS, VANDERBILT UNIVERSITY, 1921.

17093   PASCOE, CHARLES F. TWO HUNDRED YEARS OF THE S.P.G.: AN
        HISTORICAL ACCOUNT OF THE SOCIETY FOR THE PROPAGATION
        OF THE GOSPEL IN FOREIGN PARTS, 1701-1900. 2 VOLS.
        LONDON: PUBLISHED AT THE SOCIETY'S OFFICE, 1901.

17094 PAXTON, WILLIAM E. A HISTORY OF THE BAPTISTS OF
       LOUISIANA FROM THE EARLIEST TIMES TO THE PRESENT. ST.
       LOUIS: C.R. BARNS PUBLISHING COMPANY, 1888.

17095 PEMBROKE, MACEO D. "BLACK WORSHIP EXPERIENCE IN THE
       UNITED METHODIST CHURCH." RELIGION IN LIFE, 44
       (AUTUMN, 1975): 309-317.

17096 PENDLETON, OTHNIEL A., JR. "SLAVERY AND THE EVANGELICAL
       CHURCHES." JOURNAL OF THE PRESBYTERIAN HISTORICAL
       SOCIETY, 25 (MARCH, JUNE, 1947): 88-112, 153-174.

17097 PENNINGTON, EDGAR L. "THE REVEREND FRANCIS LEJAU'S WORK
       AMONG INDIANS AND NEGRO SLAVES." JOURNAL OF SOUTHERN
       HISTORY, 1 (NOVEMBER, 1935): 442-458.

17098 PENNINGTON, EDGAR L. "THOMAS BRAY'S ASSOCIATES AND THEIR
       WORK AMONG THE NEGROES." PROCEEDINGS OF THE AMERICAN
       ANTIQUARIAN SOCIETY, N.S., 48 (OCTOBER, 1938):
       311-403.

17099 PENNINGTON, EDGAR L. THOMAS BRAY'S ASSOCIATES AND THEIR
       WORK AMONG THE NEGROES. WORCHESTER, MA: AMERICAN
       ANTIQUARIAN SOCIETY, 1939.

17100 PERDUE, CHARLES L., JR.; BARDEN, THOMAS E.; AND PHILLIPS,
       ROBERT K. (EDS.). WEEVILS IN THE WHEAT: INTERVIEWS
       WITH VIRGINIA EX-SLAVES. CHARLOTTESVILLE: UNIVERSITY
       PRESS OF VIRGINIA, 1976.

17101 PERKINS, HAVEN P. "RELIGION FOR SLAVES: DIFFICULTIES
       AND METHODS." CHURCH HISTORY, 10 (SEPTEMBER, 1941):
       228-245.

17102 PERSON, MARY A. "THE RELIGION OF THE NEGRO." SOUTHERN
       WORKMAN, 33 (JULY, 1904): 403-404.

17103 PETERS, ERSKINE. "JUPITER HAMMON: HIS INVOLVEMENT WITH
       HIS 'UNCONVERTED' BRETHREN." MINORITY VOICES, 4
       (SPRING, 1980): 1-10.

17104 PETERSON, WALTER F. "SLAVERY IN THE 1850S: THE
       RECOLLECTIONS OF AN ALABAMA UNIONIST." ALABAMA
       HISTORICAL QUARTERLY, 30 (FALL/WINTER, 1968): 219-227.

17105 PHILLIPS, ULRICH B. AMERICAN NEGRO SLAVERY: A SURVEY OF
       THE SUPPLY, EMPLOYMENT AND CONTROL OF NEGRO LABOR AS
       DETERMINED BY THE PLANTATION REGIME. NEW YORK: D.
       APPLETON, 1918.

17106 PHILLIPS, ULRICH B. LIFE AND LABOR IN THE OLD SOUTH.
       BOSTON: LITTLE, BROWN AND COMPANY, 1929.

17107 PHILLIPS, ULRICH B. "RACIAL PROBLEMS, ADJUSTMENTS AND
       DISTURBANCES." IN RILEY, FRANKLIN L. (ED.). THE

SOUTH IN THE BUILDING OF THE NATION. 12 VOLS.
RICHMOND: SOUTHERN HISTORICAL PUBLICATION SOCIETY,
1909, VOL. 4, PP. 194-241.

17108   PIERCE, B.E. "AFRO-AMERICAN AND CHRISTIAN RELIGIOUS
        SYSTEMS OF LOWER STATUS CREOLES IN PARAMARIBO,
        SURINAM." PAPER PRESENTED AT NORTHEASTERN
        ANTHROPOLOGICAL ASSOCIATION, BUFFALO, NEW YORK, APRIL
        21-23, 1972.

17109   PIERRE, C.E. "THE WORK OF THE SOCIETY FOR THE
        PROPAGATION OF THE GOSPEL IN FOREIGN PARTS AMONG THE
        NEGROES IN THE COLONIES." JOURNAL OF NEGRO HISTORY, 1
        (OCTOBER, 1916): 349-360.

17110   PIERSEN, WILLIAM D. "WHITE CANNIBALS, BLACK MARTYRS:
        FEAR, DEPRESSION, AND RELIGIOUS FAITH AS CAUSES OF
        SUICIDE AMONG NEW SLAVES." JOURNAL OF NEGRO HISTORY,
        62 (APRIL, 1977): 147-159.

17111   PILCHER, GEORGE W. "SAMUEL DAVIES AND THE INSTRUCTION OF
        NEGROES IN VIRGINIA." VIRGINIA MAGAZINE OF HISTORY
        AND BIOGRAPHY, 74 (JULY, 1966): 293-300.

17112   PILCHER, GEORGE W. SAMUEL DAVIES: APOSTLE OF DISSENT IN
        COLONIAL VIRGINIA. KNOXVILLE: UNIVERSITY OF
        TENNESSEE PRESS, 1971.

17113   PILLAR, JAMES J. THE CATHOLIC CHURCH IN MISSISSIPPI,
        1837-1865. NEW ORLEANS: HAUSER, 1964.

17114   PINNINGTON, JOHN E. "THE ANGLICAN STRUGGLE FOR SURVIVAL
        IN JAMAICA IN THE PERIOD OF ABOLITION AND
        EMANCIPATION, 1825-1850." JOURNAL OF RELIGIOUS
        HISTORY, 5 (DECEMBER, 1968): 125-148.

17115   PIPES, WILLIAM H. "OLD-TIME NEGRO PREACHING: AN
        INTERPRETATIVE STUDY." QUARTERLY JOURNAL OF SPEECH,
        31 (FEBRUARY, 1945): 15-21.

17116   PIPES, WILLIAM H. "OLD-TIME NEGRO PREACHING: AN
        INTERPRETIVE STUDY." PH.D. DISSERTATION, UNIVERSITY
        OF MICHIGAN, 1943.

17117   PIPES, WILLIAM H. SAY AMEN, BROTHER! OLD-TIME NEGRO
        PREACHING: A STUDY IN AMERICAN FRUSTRATION. NEW
        YORK: WILLIAM-FREDERICK PRESS, 1951.

17118   PITMAN, F.W. "FETISHISM, WITCHCRAFT AND CHRISTIANITY
        AMONG THE SLAVES." JOURNAL OF NEGRO HISTORY, 11
        (OCTOBER, 1926): 650-668.

17119   POLK, WILLIAM M. LIFE OF LEONIDAS POLK, FIRST PROTESTANT
        EPISCOPAL BISHOP OF LOUISIANA. NEW YORK: LONGMAN,
        GREEN AND COMPANY, 1893.

17120   POOL, FRANK K. "THE SOUTHERN NEGRO IN THE METHODIST
         EPISCOPAL CHURCH." PH.D. DISSERTATION, DUKE
         UNIVERSITY, 1939.

17121   POPE, LISTON. "THE NEGRO AND RELIGION IN AMERICA."
         REVIEW OF RELIGIOUS RESEARCH, 5 (SPRING, 1964):
         152-156.

17122   PORCH, JAMES M. "RELATIONS BETWEEN BLACK AND WHITE
         BAPTISTS IN MISSISSIPPI, 1862-1890." TH.D.
         DISSERTATION, NEW ORLEANS BAPTIST THEOLOGICAL
         SEMINARY, 1974.

17123   POSCOE, C.F. TWO HUNDRED YEARS OF THE SOCIETY FOR THE
         PROPAGATION OF THE GOSPEL: AN HISTORICAL ACCOUNT OF
         THE SOCIETY FOR THE PROPAGATION OF THE GOSPEL IN
         FOREIGN PARTS, 1701-1900. 2 VOLS. LONDON: THE
         SOCIETY, 1901.

17124   POSCOE, CHARLES F. CLASSIFIED DIGEST OF THE RECORDS OF
         THE SOCIETY FOR THE PROPAGATION OF THE GOSPEL IN
         FOREIGN PARTS, 1701-1892, WITH MUCH SUPPLEMENTARY
         INFORMATION. LONDON: PUBLISHED AT THE SOCIETY'S
         OFFICE, 1893.

17125   POSEY, WALTER B. THE BAPTIST CHURCH IN THE LOWER
         MISSISSIPPI VALLEY, 1776-1845. LEXINGTON: UNIVERSITY
         OF KENTUCKY PRESS, 1957.

17126   POSEY, WALTER B. "THE BAPTISTS AND SLAVERY IN THE LOWER
         MISSISSIPPI." JOURNAL OF NEGRO HISTORY, 41 (APRIL,
         1956): 117-130.

17127   POSEY, WALTER B. "THE DEVELOPMENT OF METHODISM IN THE
         OLD SOUTHWEST, 1783-1824." PH.D. DISSERTATION,
         VANDERBILT UNIVERSITY, 1933.

17128   POSEY, WALTER B. THE DEVELOPMENT OF METHODISM IN THE OLD
         SOUTHWEST, 1783-1824. TUSCALOOSA: WEATHERFORD
         PRINTING COMPANY, 1933.

17129   POSEY, WALTER B. FRONTIER MISSION: A HISTORY OF RELIGION
         WEST OF THE SOUTHERN APPALACHIANS TO 1861. LEXINGTON:
         UNIVERSITY OF KENTUCKY PRESS, 1966.

17130   POSEY, WALTER B. "INFLUENCE OF SLAVERY UPON THE
         METHODIST CHURCH IN THE EARLY SOUTH AND SOUTHWEST."
         MISSISSIPPI VALLEY HISTORICAL REVIEW, 17 (MARCH,
         1931): 530-543.

17131   POSEY, WALTER B. THE PRESBYTERIAN CHURCH IN THE OLD
         SOUTHWEST, 1788-1838. RICHMOND: JOHN KNOX PRESS,
         1952.

17132   POSEY, WALTER B. "THE SLAVERY QUESTION IN THE

PRESBYTERIAN CHURCH IN THE OLD SOUTHWEST." JOURNAL OF
SOUTHERN HISTORY, 15 (AUGUST, 1949): 311-324.

17133 PRAYTOR, ROBERT E. "FROM CONCERN TO NEGLECT, ALABAMA
BAPTISTS' RELATIONSHIPS TO THE NEGRO, 1823-1870."
M.A. THESIS, SAMFORD UNIVERSITY, 1971.

17134 "THE PRESBYTERIAN CHURCH IN GEORGIA ON SECESSION AND
SLAVERY." GEORGIA HISTORICAL QUARTERLY, 1 (SEPTEMBER,
1917): 263-265.

17135 PRESBYTERIAN CHURCH IN THE U.S.A. ACTIONS OF THE GENERAL
ASSEMBLY OF THE PRESBYTERIAN CHURCH FOR THE FIRST
EIGHTY YEARS OF ITS HISTORY. N.P., 1865.

17136 PROCTOR, H.H. "FROM THE ADDRESS OF DR. PROCTOR."
AMERICAN MISSIONARY, 59 (NOVEMBER, 1905): 283-287.

17137 PROCTOR, H.H. "THE SONS OF 'UNCLE TOM.'" AMERICAN
MISSIONARY, 48 (JANUARY, 1894): 19-22.

17138 PROCTOR, HENRY H. "THE THEOLOGY OF THE SONGS OF THE
SOUTHERN SLAVE." SOUTHERN WORKMAN, 36 (NOVEMBER,
DECEMBER, 1907): 584-592, 652-656.

17139 PUCKETT, NEWBELL N. "THE NEGRO CHURCH IN THE U.S."
SOCIAL FORCES, 4 (MARCH, 1926): 581-587.

17140 PUCKETT, NEWBELL N. "RELIGIOUS FOLK BELIEFS OF WHITES
AND NEGROES." JOURNAL OF NEGRO HISTORY, 16 (JANUARY,
1931): 9-35.

17141 PURIFOY, LEWIS M. "THE METHODIST ANTI-SLAVERY TRADITION,
1784-1844." METHODIST HISTORY, 4 (JULY, 1966): 3-16.

17142 PURIFOY, LEWIS M. "THE SOUTHERN METHODIST CHURCH AND THE
PROSLAVERY ARGUMENT." JOURNAL OF SOUTHERN HISTORY, 32
(AUGUST, 1966): 325-341.

17143 PURIFOY, LEWIS M., JR. "THE METHODIST EPISCOPAL CHURCH,
SOUTH, AND SLAVERY, 1844-1865." PH.D. DISSERTATION,
UNIVERSITY OF NORTH CAROLINA, 1965.

17144 PUTNAM, MARY B. THE BAPTISTS AND SLAVERY, 1840-1845.
ANN ARBOR: GEORGE WAHR, 1913.

17145 PUTNAM, MARY B. "BAPTISTS AND SLAVERY, 1840-1845."
PH.M. THESIS, UNIVERSITY OF CHICAGO, 1910.

17146 RABOTEAU, ALBERT J. "'THE INVISIBLE INSTITUTION': THE
ORIGINS AND CONDITIONS OF BLACK RELIGION BEFORE
EMANCIPATION." PH.D. DISSERTATION, YALE UNIVERSITY,
1974.

17147 RABOTEAU, ALBERT J. SLAVE RELIGION: THE "INVISIBLE

INSTITUTION" IN THE AMERICAN SOUTH. NEW YORK: OXFORD UNIVERSITY PRESS, 1973.

17148 RAMREKERSINGH, AUGUSTUS. "CHRISTIANITY AND SLAVERY, YESTERDAY AND TODAY." PELICAN ANNUAL, (1968): 19-21.

17149 RANKIN, CHARLES H. "THE RISE OF THE NEGRO BAPTIST CHURCHES IN THE SOUTH THROUGH THE RECONSTRUCTION PERIOD." M.R.E. THESIS, NEW ORLEANS BAPTIST THEOLOGICAL SEMINARY, 1955.

17150 RAWICK, GEORGE P. FROM SUNDOWN TO SUNUP: THE MAKING OF THE BLACK COMMUNITY. WESTPORT: GREENWOOD PRESS, 1972.

17151 RAWICK, GEORGE P. "WEST AFRICAN CULTURE AND NORTH AMERICAN SLAVERY: A STUDY OF CULTURE CHANGE AMONG AMERICAN SLAVES IN THE ANTE-BELLUM SOUTH WITH FOCUS UPON SLAVE RELIGION." IN SPENCER, ROBERT F. (ED.). MIGRATION AND ANTHROPOLOGY. SEATTLE: AMERICAN ETHNOLOGICAL SOCIETY, 1970, PP. 149-164.

17152 RECKORD, MARY. "MISSIONARY ACTIVITY IN JAMAICA BEFORE EMANCIPATION." PH.D. DISSERTATION, UNIVERSITY OF LONDON, 1964.

17153 RECKORD, MARY. "MISSIONS IN JAMAICA BEFORE EMANCIPATION." CARIBBEAN STUDIES, 8 (APRIL, 1968): 69-74.

17154 REED, RICHARD C. A SKETCH OF RELIGIOUS HISTORY OF THE NEGROES IN THE SOUTH. NEW YORK: AMERICAN SOCIETY OF CHURCH HISTORY, 1914.

17155 REED, ROBERT M. "DESTRUCTION OF THE METHODIST CHAPEL AT BRIDGETOWN, BARBADOS, OCTOBER 19, 1823." METHODIST HISTORY, 15 (OCTOBER, 1976): 43-67.

17156 REID, ROBERT D. "RELIGION AND RECREATION AMONG SLAVES IN ANTE-BELLUM ALABAMA." MIDWEST JOURNAL, 2 (WINTER, 1949): 29-36.

17157 REILLY, TIMOTHY. "GENTEEL REFORM VERSUS SOUTHERN ALLEGIANCE: EPISCOPALIAN DILEMMA IN OLD NEW ORLEANS." HISTORICAL MAGAZINE OF THE PROTESTANT EPISCOPAL CHURCH, 44 (DECEMBER, 1975): 437-450.

17158 REILLY, TIMOTHY F. "SLAVERY AND THE SOUTHWESTERN EVANGELIST IN NEW ORLEANS, (1800-1861)." JOURNAL OF MISSISSIPPI HISTORY, 41 (NOVEMBER, 1979): 301-318.

17159 REIMERS, DAVID M. WHITE PROTESTANTISM AND THE NEGRO. NEW YORK: OXFORD UNIVERSITY PRESS, 1965.

17160 REINDERS, ROBERT C. "THE CHURCHES AND THE NEGRO IN NEW ORLEANS, 1850-1860." PHYLON, 22 (FALL, 1961):

241-248.

17161 "RELIGIOUS CULTURE OF THE SLAVES BEFORE THE WAR."
       AMERICAN MISSIONARY MAGAZINE, 39 (MARCH, 1885): 74-75.

17162 RENSHAW, J. PARKE. "AFRICAN RELIGIONS IN BRAZIL."
       INTER-AMERICAN REVIEW OF BIBLIOGRAPHY, 24
       (JULY-SEPTEMBER, 1974): 293-300.

17163 REUTER, EDWARD B. THE AMERICAN RACE PROBLEM: A STUDY OF
       THE NEGRO. NEW YORK: THOMAS Y. CROWELL PUBLISHERS,
       1927.

17164 RIBEIRO, RENE. "RELATIONS OF THE NEGRO WITH CHRISTIANITY
       IN PORTUGUESE AMERICA." AMERICAS, 14 (APRIL, 1958):
       454-484.

17165 RICHARDSON, HARRY VAN BUREN. DARK SALVATION: THE STORY
       OF METHODISM AS IT DEVELOPED AMONG BLACKS IN AMERICA.
       GARDEN CITY: ANCHOR PRESS, 1976.

17166 RICKMAN, CLAUDE R. "WESLEYAN METHODISM IN NORTH
       CAROLINA." M.A. THESIS, UNIVERSITY OF NORTH CAROLINA,
       1952.

17167 RIDDELL, WILLIAM R. "THE BAPTISM OF SLAVES IN PRINCE
       EDWARD ISLAND." JOURNAL OF NEGRO HISTORY, 6 (JULY,
       1921): 307-309.

17168 RILEY, B.F. HISTORY OF THE BAPTISTS IN THE SOUTHERN
       STATES EAST OF THE MISSISSIPPI. PHILADELPHIA:
       AMERICAN BAPTIST PUBLICATION SOCIETY, 1898.

17169 RIVERS, ROBERT H. "THE RELATIONSHIP BETWEEN WHITE AND
       NEGRO BAPTISTS IN THE CHURCHES OF NORTH CAROLINA FROM
       1830 TO 1870." M.A. THESIS, DUKE UNIVERSITY, 1971.

17170 ROBERSON, NANCY C. "THE NEGRO AND THE BAPTISTS OF
       ANTE-BELLUM ALABAMA." M.A. THESIS, UNIVERSITY OF
       ALABAMA, 1954.

17171 ROBERT, JOSEPH C. "EXCOMMUNICATION, VIRGINIA STYLE:
       CHURCH DISCIPLINE AS APPLIED TO NEGRO MEMBERS IN THE
       DAYS OF SLAVERY." SOUTH ATLANTIC QUARTERLY, 40 (JULY,
       1941): 243-258.

17172 ROBERTS, J. DEOTIS. "THE AMERICAN NEGRO'S CONTRIBUTIONS
       TO RELIGIOUS THOUGHT." IN ROUCEK, JOSEPH S. AND
       KIERNAN, THOMAS (EDS.). THE NEGRO IMPACT ON WESTERN
       CIVILIZATION. NEW YORK: PHILOSOPHICAL LIBRARY, 1970,
       PP. 75-108.

17173 RODILES, IGNACIO M. "THE SLAVE TRADE WITH
       AMERICA--NEGROES IN MEXICO." FREEDOMWAYS, 1 (FALL,
       1961): 296-307; 2 (WINTER, 1962): 39-52.

17174   ROGERS, MARGUERITE S.   "DEATH AND BURIAL CUSTOMS AMONG
        AMERICAN PLANTATION NEGROES."   M.A. THESIS, ATLANTA
        UNIVERSITY, 1941.

17175   ROGERS, TOMMY W.   "FREDERICK A. ROSS AND THE PRESBYTERIAN
        DEFENSE OF SLAVERY."   JOURNAL OF PRESBYTERIAN HISTORY,
        45 (JUNE, 1967):   112-124.

17176   ROOKE, PATRICIA T.   "THE CHRISTIANIZATION AND EDUCATION
        OF SLAVES AND APPRENTICES IN THE BRITISH WEST INDIES:
        THE IMPACT OF EVANGELICAL MISSIONARIES (1800-1838)."
        PH.D. DISSERTATION, UNIVERSITY OF ALBERTA, 1977.

17177   ROOKE, PATRICIA T.   "EVANGELICAL MISSIONARIES,
        APPRENTICES, AND FREEDMEN: THE PSYCHOSOCIOLOGICAL
        SHIFTS OF RACIAL ATTITUDES IN THE BRITISH WEST
        INDIES."   CARIBBEAN QUARTERLY, 25 (MARCH-JUNE, 1979):
        1-14.

17178   ROOKE, PATRICIA T.   "THE 'NEW MECHANIC' IN SLAVE SOCIETY:
        SOCIO-PSYCHOLOGICAL MOTIVATIONS AND EVANGELICAL
        MISSIONARIES IN THE BRITISH WEST INDIES."   JOURNAL OF
        RELIGIOUS HISTORY, 11 (JUNE, 1980):   77-94.

17179   ROOKE, PATRICIA T.   "THE PEDAGOGY OF CONVERSION:
        MISSIONARY EDUCATION TO SLAVES IN THE BRITISH WEST
        INDIES, 1800-1838."   PAEDAGOGICA HISTORICA, 18 (1978):
        356-374.

17180   ROSE, WILLIE LEE.   REHEARSAL FOR RECONSTRUCTION: THE
        PORT ROYAL EXPERIMENT.   INDIANAPOLIS: BOBBS-MERRILL,
        1964.

17181   ROSENBERG, BRUCE A.   THE ART OF THE AMERICAN FOLK
        PREACHER.   NEW YORK: OXFORD UNIVERSITY PRESS, 1970.

17182   ROUT, LESLIE B., JR.   "THE 'BLACK BISHOPS' MYSTERY."
        LUSO-BRAZILIAN REVIEW, 9 (JUNE, 1972):   86-92.

17183   RUSSELL-WOOD, A.J.R.   "BLACK AND MULATTO BROTHERHOODS IN
        COLONIAL BRAZIL: A STUDY IN COLLECTIVE BEHAVIOR."
        HISPANIC AMERICAN HISTORICAL REVIEW, 54 (NOVEMBER,
        1974):   567-602.

17184   RYLAND, GARNETT.   THE BAPTISTS OF VIRGINIA, 1699-1926.
        RICHMOND: VIRGINIA BAPTIST BOARD OF MISSIONS AND
        EDUCATION, 1955.

17185   SATTERFIELD, JAMES H.   "THE BAPTISTS AND THE NEGRO PRIOR
        TO 1863."   PH.D. DISSERTATION, SOUTHERN BAPTIST
        THEOLOGICAL SEMINARY, 1919.

17186   SAUL, SUZANNE M.   "KING CHRIST AND KING COTTON; THE
        RECORD OF AN UNHAPPY ALLIANCE."   M.A. THESIS, HOWARD
        UNIVERSITY, 1967.

17187 SCALLY, MARY A. AFRICAN HERITAGE IN THE CATHOLIC CHURCH.
       WASHINGTON: ASSOCIATION FOR THE STUDY OF
       AFRO-AMERICAN LIFE AND HISTORY, 1979.

17188 SCARBOROUGH, WILLIAM K. "HEARTLAND OF THE COTTON
       KINGDOM." IN MCLEMORE, RICHARD A. (ED.). A HISTORY
       OF MISSISSIPPI. 2 VOLS. HATTIESBURG: UNIVERSITY AND
       COLLEGE PRESS OF MISSISSIPPI, 1973, VOL. 1, PP.
       310-351.

17189 SCHERER, LESTER B. SLAVERY AND THE CHURCHES IN EARLY
       AMERICA, 1619-1819. GRAND RAPIDS: WILLIAM B.
       EERDMANS PUBLISHING COMPANY, 1975.

17190 SCHMIDT, CYNTHIA E. "SHANGO CULT MUSIC OF TRINIDAD: THE
       ANNUAL CEREMONY." M.A. THESIS, UNIVERSITY OF
       CALIFORNIA, LOS ANGELES, 1974.

17191 SCHREYER, GEORGE M. "METHODIST WORK AMONG THE PLANTATION
       NEGROES IN THE SOUTH CAROLINA CONFERENCE FROM 1829 TO
       1865." B.D. THESIS, DUKE UNIVERSITY, 1939.

17192 SCHUCHTER, ARNOLD. "SLAVERY AND THE CHURCHES."
       REPARATIONS: THE BLACK MANIFESTO AND ITS CHALLENGE TO
       WHITE AMERICA. PHILADELPHIA: J.B. LIPPINCOTT, 1970,
       PP. 210-239.

17193 SCHULER, MONICA. "AFRO-AMERICAN SLAVE CULTURE."
       HISTORICAL REFLECTIONS, 6 (SUMMER, 1979): 121-137.

17194 SCHULER, MONICA. "MYALISM AND THE AFRICAN RELIGIOUS
       TRADITION IN JAMAICA." IN CRAHAN, MARGARET AND
       KNIGHT, FRANKLIN (EDS.). AFRICA AND THE CARIBBEAN:
       THE LEGACY OF A LINK. BALTIMORE: JOHNS HOPKINS
       UNIVERSITY PRESS, 1979, PP. 65-79.

17195 SEAGA, EDWARD. "CULTS IN JAMAICA." JAMAICA JOURNAL, 3
       (JUNE, 1969): 3-13.

17196 SERENO, RENZO. "OBEAH: MAGIC AND SOCIAL STRUCTURE IN
       THE LESSER ANTILLES." PSYCHIATRY, 11 (FEBRUARY,
       1948): 15-31.

17197 "A SERMON TO SERVANTS." HARPER'S NEW MONTHLY MAGAZINE,
       30 (APRIL, 1865): 664-666.

17198 SERNETT, MILTON C. BLACK RELIGION AND AMERICAN
       EVANGELICALISM: WHITE PROTESTANTS, PLANTATION
       MISSIONS, AND THE FLOWERING OF NEGRO CHRISTIANITY,
       1787-1865. METUCHEN, NJ: SCARECROW PRESS, 1975.

17199 SERNETT, MILTON C. "BLACK RELIGION AND AMERICAN
       EVANGELICALISM: WHITE PROTESTANTS, PLANTATION
       MISSIONS, AND THE INDEPENDENT NEGRO CHURCH,
       1787-1865." PH.D. DISSERTATION, UNIVERSITY OF

DELAWARE, 1972.

17200 SHEA, JOSEPH M. "THE BAPTISTS AND SLAVERY, 1840-1845."
PH.D. DISSERTATION, CLARK UNIVERSITY, 1933.

17201 SHELTON, EDWARD E. "RELIGION: AS EXPRESSED IN THE NEGRO
SPIRITUALS." M.A. THESIS, UNIVERSITY OF PITTSBURGH,
1951.

17202 SHILLER, SAMUEL. "SOME ASPECTS OF RELIGIOUS DEVELOPMENTS
IN THE OLD SOUTH." M.A. THESIS, UNIVERSITY OF
ALABAMA, 1931.

17203 SHOCKLEY, GRANT S. "METHODISM, SOCIETY AND BLACK
EVANGELISM IN AMERICA; RETROSPECT AND PROSPECT."
METHODIST HISTORY, 12 (JULY, 1974): 145-182.

17204 SHORT, K.R.M. "JAMAICAN CHRISTIAN MISSIONS AND THE GREAT
SLAVE REBELLION OF 1831-1832." JOURNAL OF
ECCLESIASTICAL HISTORY, 27 (JANUARY, 1976): 57-72.

17205 SHORT, KENNETH R.M. "ENGLISH BAPTISTS AND AMERICAN
SLAVERY." BAPTIST QUARTERLY, 20 (APRIL, 1964):
243-262.

17206 SHORT, KENNETH R.M. "THE ROAD TO RICHMOND; ENGLISH
BAPTISTS AND AMERICAN SLAVERY, 1834 TO 1837."
FOUNDATIONS, 7 (APRIL, 1964): 111-129.

17207 SIDES, SUDIE D. "SLAVE WEDDINGS AND RELIGION:
PLANTATION LIFE IN THE SOUTHERN STATES BEFORE THE
AMERICAN CIVIL WAR." HISTORY TODAY, 24 (FEBRUARY,
1974): 77-87.

17208 SIMMS, JAMES M. THE FIRST COLORED BAPTIST CHURCH IN
NORTH AMERICA. PHILADELPHIA: J.B. LIPPINCOTT, 1888.

17209 SIMPSON, GEORGE E. "AFRO-AMERICAN RELIGIONS AND
RELIGIOUS BEHAVIOR." CARIBBEAN STUDIES, 12 (JULY,
1972): 5-30.

17210 SIMPSON, GEORGE E. "THE BELIEF SYSTEM OF HAITIAN VODUN."
AMERICAN ANTHROPOLOGIST, 47 (JANUARY-MARCH, 1945):
35-39.

17211 SIMPSON, GEORGE E. BLACK RELIGIONS IN THE NEW WORLD.
NEW YORK: COLUMBIA UNIVERSITY PRESS, 1978.

17212 SIMPSON, GEORGE E. "RELIGIONS OF THE CARIBBEAN." IN
KILSON, MARTIN L. AND ROTBERG, ROBERT I. (EDS.). THE
AFRICAN DIASPORA: INTERPRETIVE ESSAYS. CAMBRIDGE:
HARVARD UNIVERSITY PRESS, 1976, PP. 280-311.

17213 SIMPSON, GEORGE E. RELIGIOUS CULTS OF THE CARIBBEAN:
TRINIDAD, JAMAICA, HAITI, AND ST. LUCIA. RIO PIEDRAS,

1283

PR: INSTITUTE OF CARIBBEAN STUDIES, UNIVERSITY OF
PUERTO RICO, 1965.

17214   SIMS, CHARLES F.   "THE RELIGIOUS EDUCATION OF THE
SOUTHERN NEGROES."   PH.D. DISSERTATION, SOUTHERN
BAPTIST THEOLOGICAL SEMINARY, 1926.

17215   SINGLETON, GEORGE A.   "RELIGIOUS INSTRUCTION OF THE NEGRO
IN THE UNITED STATES BEFORE THE REBELLION."   M.A.
THESIS, UNIVERSITY OF CHICAGO, 1929.

17216   SINGLETON, GEORGE A.   THE ROMANCE OF AFRICAN METHODISM:
A STUDY OF THE AFRICAN METHODIST EPISCOPAL CHURCH.
NEW YORK: EXPOSITION PRESS, 1952.

17217   SLATTERY, J.R.   "THE CATHOLIC CHURCH AND THE NEGRO RACE
IN COLONIAL DAYS."   A.M.E. CHURCH REVIEW, 12 (JULY,
1895):   158-180.

17218   "SLAVE BAPTISM."   IN NUNEZ, BENJAMIN.   DICTIONARY OF
AFRO-LATIN AMERICAN CIVILIZATION.   WESTPORT:
GREENWOOD PRESS, 1980, P. 432.

17219   "SLAVE OR MASTER."   CENTURY MAGAZINE, 25 (APRIL, 1883):
953-954.

17220   "SLAVE PREACHER."   IN NUNEZ, BENJAMIN.   DICTIONARY OF
AFRO-LATIN AMERICAN CIVILIZATION.   WESTPORT:
GREENWOOD PRESS, 1980, PP. 436-437.

17221   "SLAVERY AND THE CHURCH."   CATHOLIC MIND, 39 (OCTOBER 8,
1941):   30.

17222   "SLAVERY AND THE CHURCH IN THE COLONIAL PERIOD (1700'S)."
IN RYWELL, MARTIN (ED.).   AFRO-AMERICAN ENCYCLOPEDIA.
10 VOLS.   NORTH MIAMI: EDUCATIONAL BOOK PUBLISHERS,
1974, VOL. 8, PP. 2472-2473.

17223   SMITH, C.O.   "THE EVANGELICAL LUTHERAN TENNESSEE SYNOD'S
ATTITUDE TOWARD THE NEGRO BOTH AS A SLAVE AND AS
FREEDMAN."   CONCORDIA HISTORICAL INSTITUTE QUARTERLY,
21 (JANUARY, 1949):   145-149.

17224   SMITH, CORTLAND V.   "CHURCH ORGANIZATION AS AN AGENCY OF
SOCIAL CONTROL: CHURCH DISCIPLINE IN NORTH CAROLINA,
1800-1860."   PH.D. DISSERTATION, UNIVERSITY OF NORTH
CAROLINA, 1966.

17225   SMITH, H. SHELTON.   "THE CHURCH AND THE SOCIAL ORDER IN
THE OLD SOUTH AS INTERPRETED BY JAMES H. THORNWELL."
CHURCH HISTORY, 7 (JUNE, 1938):   115-121.

17226   SMITH, H. SHELTON.   IN HIS IMAGE, BUT . . . RACISM IN
SOUTHERN RELIGION.   DURHAM: DUKE UNIVERSITY PRESS,
1972.

17227   SMITH, ROBERT W.   "SLAVERY AND CHRISTIANITY IN THE
        BRITISH WEST INDIES."   CHURCH HISTORY, 19 (SEPTEMBER,
        1950):   171-186.

17228   SMITH, TIMOTHY L.   "SLAVERY AND THEOLOGY: THE EMERGENCE
        OF BLACK CHRISTIAN CONSCIOUSNESS IN NINETEENTH-CENTURY
        AMERICA."   CHURCH HISTORY, 41 (DECEMBER, 1972):
        497-512.

17229   SOBEL, MECHAL.   "'THEY CAN NEVER BOTH PROSPER TOGETHER':
        BLACK AND WHITE BAPTISTS IN NASHVILLE, TENNESSEE."
        TENNESSEE HISTORICAL QUARTERLY, 38 (FALL, 1979):
        296-307.

17230   SOBEL, MECHAL.   TRABELIN' ON: THE SLAVE JOURNEY TO AN
        AFRO-BAPTIST FAITH.   WESTPORT: GREENWOOD PRESS, 1979.

17231   SOLOMON, SUSAN.   "EVANGELISM AND MORALISM IN THE
        EIGHTEENTH-CENTURY SOUTH."   UNPUBLISHED SEMINAR PAPER,
        YALE UNIVERSITY, 1969.

17232   "SOME SLAVE SUPERSTITIONS."   SOUTHERN WORKMAN, 41 (APRIL,
        1912):   246-248.

17233   SOSIS, HOWARD J.   "THE COLONIAL ENVIRONMENT AND RELIGION
        IN HAITI: AN INTRODUCTION TO THE BLACK SLAVE CULTS IN
        EIGHTEENTH-CENTURY SAINT-DOMINGUE."   PH.D.
        DISSERTATION, COLUMBIA UNIVERSITY, 1971.

17234   SOULE, JOSHUA.   "THE METHODIST CHURCH AND SLAVERY."
        METHODIST QUARTERLY REVIEW, 57 (OCTOBER, 1908):
        637-650.

17235   SOUTHALL, EUGENE P.   "THE ATTITUDE OF THE METHODIST
        EPISCOPAL CHURCH, SOUTH, TOWARD THE NEGRO FROM 1844 TO
        1870."   JOURNAL OF NEGRO HISTORY, 16 (OCTOBER, 1931):
        359-370.

17236   STACY, JAMES.   HISTORY OF MIDWAY CONGREGATIONAL CHURCH.
        NEWMAN, GA: S.W. MURRAY, PRINTER, 1899.

17237   STAMPP, KENNETH M.   "THE DAILY LIFE OF THE SOUTHERN
        SLAVE."   IN HUGGINS, NATHAN I.; KILSON, MARTIN; AND
        FOX, DANIEL M. (EDS.).   KEY ISSUES IN THE
        AFRO-AMERICAN EXPERIENCE.   2 VOLS.   NEW YORK:
        HARCOURT BRACE JOVANOVICH, 1971, VOL. 1, PP. 116-137.

17238   STAMPP, KENNETH M.   THE PECULIAR INSTITUTION: SLAVERY IN
        THE ANTE-BELLUM SOUTH.   NEW YORK: ALFRED A. KNOPF,
        1956.

17239   STANFORD, PETER T.   THE TRAGEDY OF THE NEGRO IN AMERICA:
        A CONDENSED HISTORY OF THE ENSLAVEMENT, SUFFERINGS,
        EMANCIPATION, PRESENT CONDITION AND PROGRESS OF THE
        NEGRO RACE IN THE UNITED STATES.   BOSTON: THE AUTHOR,

1897.

17240   STANGE, DOUGLAS C. "'A COMPASSIONATE MOTHER TO HER POOR
        NEGRO SLAVES': THE LUTHERAN CHURCH AND NEGRO SLAVERY
        IN EARLY AMERICA." PHYLON, 29 (FALL, 1968): 272-281.

17241   STANGE, DOUGLAS C. "OUR DUTY TO PREACH THE GOSPEL TO
        NEGROES: SOUTHERN LUTHERANS AND AMERICAN SLAVERY."
        CONCORDIA HISTORICAL INSTITUTE QUARTERLY, 42
        (NOVEMBER, 1969): 171-182.

17242   STANLEY, A. KNIGHTON. THE CHILDREN IS CRYING:
        CONGREGATIONALISM AMONG BLACK PEOPLE. NEW YORK:
        PILGRIM PRESS, 1979.

17243   STEELE, ALGERNON O. "THE CONCEPT OF RELIGION REFLECTED
        IN THE EARLY NEGRO SPIRITUALS." M.A. THESIS,
        NORTHWESTERN UNIVERSITY, 1930.

17244   STEELY, WILL F. "THE ESTABLISHED CHURCHES AND SLAVERY,
        1850-1860." REGISTER OF THE KENTUCKY HISTORICAL
        SOCIETY, 55 (APRIL, 1957): 97-104.

17245   STEIN, STEPHEN J. "GEORGE WHITEFIELD ON SLAVERY: SOME
        NEW EVIDENCE." CHURCH HISTORY, 42 (JUNE, 1973):
        243-256.

17246   STOWE, CHARLES E. "THE RELIGION OF SLAVERY." CRISIS, 5
        (NOVEMBER, 1912): 36-33.

17247   STRICKER, BARRY A. "A CROWN FOR EVERYONE: THE RELIGIOUS
        WORLD OF THE SLAVE COMMUNITY, 1830-1860." B.A.
        THESIS, HARVARD UNIVERSITY, 1979.

17248   STRIPLING, PAUL W. "THE NEGRO EXCISION FROM BAPTIST
        CHURCHES IN TEXAS, 1861-1870." TH.D. DISSERTATION,
        SOUTHWESTERN BAPTIST THEOLOGICAL SEMINARY, 1967.

17249   STROGER, HOWARD. "COROMANTINE OBEAH AND MYALISM." B.A.
        THESIS, RUTGERS UNIVERSITY, 1966.

17250   SUMNERS, BILLY F. "SOUTHERN BAPTISTS AND THE FREEDMEN."
        ESSAYS IN HISTORY: THE E.C. BARKSDALE STUDENT
        LECTURES, 4 (1975): 39-54.

17251   SUTTLES, WILLIAM C., JR. "A TRACE OF SOUL: THE RELIGION
        OF NEGRO SLAVES ON THE PLANTATIONS OF NORTH AMERICA."
        PH.D. DISSERTATION, UNIVERSITY OF MICHIGAN, 1979.

17252   SWALLOW, GEORGE. "SLAVERY AND THE EPISCOPAL CHURCH IN
        THE SOUTH." M.A. THESIS, UNIVERSITY OF NEW ORLEANS,
        1968.

17253   SWANEY, CHARLES B. EPISCOPAL METHODISM AND SLAVERY, WITH
        SIDELIGHTS ON ECCLESIASTICAL POLITICS. BOSTON: R.G.

BADGER, 1926.

17254   SWANEY, CHARLES B. "EPISCOPAL METHODISM AND SLAVERY,
         WITH SIDELIGHTS ON ECCLESIASTICAL POLITICS." PH.D.
         DISSERTATION, NORTHWESTERN UNIVERSITY, 1927.

17255   SWEET, WILLIAM W. (ED.). RELIGION ON THE AMERICAN
         FRONTIER: THE BAPTISTS, 1783-1830: A COLLECTION OF
         SOURCE MATERIAL. CHICAGO: UNIVERSITY OF CHICAGO
         PRESS, 1931.

17256   SWEET, WILLIAM W. "SLAVERY, ATTITUDE OF THE CHURCHES
         TO." IN ADAMS, JAMES T. (ED.). DICTIONARY OF
         AMERICAN HISTORY. 5 VOLS. NEW YORK: CHARLES
         SCRIBNER'S SONS, 1940, VOL. 5, PP. 96-97.

17257   SWEET, WILLIAM W. "SOME RELIGIOUS ASPECTS OF THE KANSAS
         STRUGGLE." JOURNAL OF RELIGION, 7 (OCTOBER, 1927):
         578-595.

17258   SYDNOR, CHARLES S. SLAVERY IN MISSISSIPPI. NEW YORK:
         D. APPLETON-CENTURY COMPANY, 1933.

17259   TALLANT, ROBERT. VOODOO IN NEW ORLEANS. NEW YORK:
         MACMILLAN COMPANY, 1946.

17260   TANNENBAUM, FRANK. SLAVE AND CITIZEN: THE NEGRO IN THE
         AMERICAS. NEW YORK: ALFRED A. KNOPF, 1946.

17261   TAUSSIG, MICHAEL. "BLACK RELIGION AND RESISTANCE IN
         COLOMBIA: THREE CENTURIES OF SOCIAL STRUGGLE IN THE
         CAUCA VALLEY." MARXIST PERSPECTIVES, 2 (SUMMER,
         1979): 84-116.

17262   TAYLOR, HUBERT V. "SLAVERY AND THE DELIBERATIONS OF THE
         PRESBYTERIAN GENERAL ASSEMBLY, 1833-1838." JOURNAL OF
         PRESBYTERIAN HISTORY, 48 (SPRING, 1970): 69-70.

17263   TAYLOR, HUBERT V. "SLAVERY AND THE DELIBERATIONS OF THE
         PRESBYTERIAN GENERAL ASSEMBLY, 1833-1838." PH.D.
         DISSERTATION, NORTHWESTERN UNIVERSITY, 1964.

17264   TAYLOR, OLIVE A. THE PROTESTANT EPISCOPAL CHURCH AND THE
         NEGRO IN WASHINGTON, D.C. ANN ARBOR: UNIVERSITY
         MICROFILMS, 1974.

17265   TAYLOR, ORVILLE W. "BAPTISTS AND SLAVERY IN ARKANSAS:
         RELATIONSHIPS AND ATTITUDES." ARKANSAS HISTORICAL
         QUARTERLY, 38 (AUTUMN, 1979): 199-226.

17266   TEGARDEN, J.B.H. "VOODOOISM." M.A. THESIS, UNIVERSITY
         OF CHICAGO, 1924.

17267   THEOBALD, STEPHEN L. "CATHOLIC MISSIONARY WORK AMONG THE
         COLORED PEOPLE OF THE UNITED STATES (1776-1866)."

RECORDS OF THE AMERICAN CATHOLIC HISTORICAL SOCIETY OF PHILADELPHIA, 35 (1924-1925): 325-356.

17268 THOMAS, ALLEN C. "THE ATTITUDE OF THE SOCIETY OF FRIENDS TOWARD SLAVERY IN THE SEVENTEENTH AND EIGHTEENTH CENTURIES PARTICULARLY IN RELATION TO ITS OWN MEMBERS." PAPERS OF THE AMERICAN SOCIETY OF CHURCH HISTORY, 8 (1897): 263-299.

17269 THOMAS, EDGAR G. THE FIRST AFRICAN BAPTIST CHURCH OF NORTH AMERICA. SAVANNAH: N.P., 1925.

17270 THOMAS, HERMAN E. "TOWARD AN UNDERSTANDING OF RELIGION AND SLAVERY IN J.W.C. PENNINGTON." JOURNAL OF THE INTERDENOMINATIONAL THEOLOGICAL CENTER, 6 (SPRING, 1979): 148-156.

17271 THOMAS, WILLIAM H. "CHARACTERISTICS OF NEGRO CHRISTIANITY." NEGRO, 1 (JULY, 1886): 10-21.

17272 THOMAS, WILLIAM H. "RELIGIOUS CHARACTERISTICS OF THE NEGRO." A.M.E. CHURCH REVIEW, 9 (APRIL, 1893): 388-402.

17273 THOMPSON, EDGAR T. "GOD AND THE SOUTHERN PLANTATION SYSTEM." IN HILL, SAMUEL S., JR. (ED.). RELIGION AND THE SOLID SOUTH. NASHVILLE: ABINGDON PRESS, 1972, PP. 57-91.

17274 THOMPSON, ERNEST T. PRESBYTERIANS IN THE SOUTH, 1607-1972. 3 VOLS. RICHMOND: JOHN KNOX PRESS, 1963-1973.

17275 THOMPSON, HENRY P. INTO ALL LANDS: THE HISTORY OF THE SOCIETY FOR THE PROPAGATION OF THE GOSPEL IN FOREIGN PARTS, 1701-1950. LONDON: S.P.C.K., 1951.

17276 THOMPSON, J. EARL JR. "SLAVERY AND PRESBYTERIANISM IN THE REVOLUTIONARY ERA." JOURNAL OF PRESBYTERIAN HISTORY, 54 (SPRING, 1976): 121-141.

17277 THOMPSON, MARIVINE K. "THE MORAL AND RELIGIOUS TRAINING OF THE SLAVE." M.A. THESIS, SOUTHERN METHODIST UNIVERSITY, 1934.

17278 THOMPSON, PATRICK H. THE HISTORY OF NEGRO BAPTISTS IN MISSISSIPPI. JACKSON: R.W. BAILEY, 1898.

17279 THOMPSON, REBA. "RELIGION AND RELIGIOUS INSTRUCTION AMONG THE SLAVES." M.A. THESIS, UNIVERSITY OF GEORGIA, 1942.

17280 THORPE, EARL E. THE MIND OF THE NEGRO: AN INTELLECTUAL HISTORY OF AFRO-AMERICANS. BATON ROUGE: ORTLIEB PRESS, 1961.

17281   THRIFT, CHARLES T., JR. "THE OPERATIONS OF THE AMERICAN
          HOME MISSIONARY SOCIETY IN THE SOUTH, 1826-1861."
          PH.D. DISSERTATION, UNIVERSITY OF CHICAGO, 1936.

17282   THURMAN, HOWARD. DEEP RIVER: AN INTERPRETATION OF NEGRO
          SPIRITUALS. MILLS COLLEGE, CA: EUCALYPTUS PRESS,
          1945.

17283   THURMAN, HOWARD. JESUS AND THE DISINHERITED. NEW YORK:
          ABINGDON-COKESBURY PRESS, 1949.

17284   TISE, LARRY E. "NORTH CAROLINA METHODISM FROM THE
          REVOLUTION TO THE WAR OF 1812." IN INGRAM, O. KELLY
          (ED.). METHODISM ALIVE IN NORTH CAROLINA. DURHAM:
          DIVINITY SCHOOL, DUKE UNIVERSITY, 1976, PP. 33-48.

17285   TODD, WILLIE G. "NORTH CAROLINA BAPTISTS AND SLAVERY."
          NORTH CAROLINA HISTORICAL REVIEW, 24 (APRIL, 1947):
          135-159.

17286   TODD, WILLIE G. "THE SLAVERY ISSUE AND THE ORGANIZATION
          OF A SOUTHERN BAPTIST CONVENTION." PH.D.
          DISSERTATION, UNIVERSITY OF NORTH CAROLINA, 1964.

17287   TORSTENSON, JOEL S. "THE ATTITUDE OF THE LUTHERAN CHURCH
          TOWARD SLAVERY." M.A. THESIS, UNIVERSITY OF
          MINNESOTA, 1940.

17288   TOUCHSTONE, BLAKE. "VOODOO IN NEW ORLEANS." LOUISIANA
          HISTORY, 13 (FALL, 1972): 371-386.

17289   TOUCHSTONE, DONALD B. "PLANTERS AND SLAVE RELIGION IN
          THE DEEP SOUTH." PH.D. DISSERTATION, TULANE
          UNIVERSITY, 1973.

17290   TOWELL, SHERMAN E. "THE FEATURES OF SOUTHERN BAPTIST
          THOUGHT, 1845-1879." TH.D. DISSERTATION, SOUTHERN
          BAPTIST THEOLOGICAL SEMINARY, 1956.

17291   TRENHOLM, W.L. "THE SOUTH: AN ADDRESS." UNPUBLISHED
          PAPER, APRIL 7, 1869, CHARLESTON LIBRARY SOCIETY.

17292   TRESP, LOTHAR L. "EARLY NEGRO BAPTISMS IN COLONIAL
          GEORGIA BY THE SALZBURGERS AT EBENEZER."
          AMERICANA-AUSTRIACA, 2 (1970): 159-170.

17293   TROY, LEON L. AND MCCALL, EMMANUEL L. "BLACK CHURCH
          HISTORY." IN MCCALL (ED.). THE BLACK CHRISTIAN
          EXPERIENCE. NASHVILLE: BROADMAN PRESS, 1972, PP.
          18-31.

17294   TUCKER, DAVID M. BLACK PASTORS AND LEADERS: MEMPHIS,
          1819-1972. MEMPHIS: MEMPHIS STATE UNIVERSITY PRESS,
          1973.

17295 TUCKER, FRANK C. THE METHODIST CHURCH IN MISSISSIPPI,
       1798-1939. NASHVILLE: PARTHENON PRESS, 1966.

17296 TURNER, MARY. "THE BISHOP OF JAMAICA AND SLAVE
       INSTRUCTION." JOURNAL OF ECCLESIASTICAL HISTORY, 26
       (OCTOBER, 1975): 363-378.

17297 TYMS, JAMES D. THE RISE OF RELIGIOUS EDUCATION AMONG
       NEGRO BAPTISTS: A HISTORICAL CASE STUDY. NEW YORK:
       EXPOSITION PRESS, 1965.

17298 TYNER, WAYNE C. "CHARLES COLCOCK JONES: MISSION TO
       SLAVES." JOURNAL OF PRESBYTERIAN HISTORY, 55 (WINTER,
       1977): 363-380.

17299 UNTERKOEFLER, ERNEST L. (ED.). THE AMERICAN CATHOLIC
       CHURCH AND THE NEGRO PROBLEM IN THE XVIII-XIX
       CENTURIES. CHARLESTON: MARIA G. CARAVAGLIOS, 1974.

17300 USHER, GUY S. "THE ATTITUDES OF THE METHODIST EPISCOPAL
       CHURCH TOWARD ABOLITION AS SEEN IN THE GENERAL
       CONFERENCES OF 1836, 1840, AND 1844." M.A. THESIS,
       VANDERBILT UNIVERSITY, 1937.

17301 VALLETTE, MARC F. "THE CHURCH AND HUMAN SLAVERY IN THE
       TIME OF COLUMBUS." AMERICAN CATHOLIC QUARTERLY
       REVIEW, 42 (JULY, 1917): 353-370.

17302 VAN VELZEN, BONNO T. "BUSH NEGRO REGIONAL CULTS: A
       MATERIALIST EXPLANATION." IN WERBNER, R.P. (ED.).
       REGIONAL CULTS. NEW YORK: ACADEMIC PRESS, 1977, PP.
       101-107.

17303 VAN VELZEN, H.U.E. THODEN. "THE ORIGINS OF GOARI GADU
       MOVEMENT OF THE BUSH NEGROES OF SURINAM." NIEUWE WEST
       INDISCHE GIDS, 25 (1978): 81-130.

17304 VAN VELZEN, H.U.E. AND VAN WETERING, W. "ON THE
       POLITICAL IMPACT OF A PROPHETIC MOVEMENT IN SURINAM."
       IN VAN BEEK, W.E.A. AND SCHERER, J. (EDS.).
       EXPLORATIONS IN ANTHROPOLOGY OF RELIGION, ESSAYS IN
       HONOUR OF JAN VAN BAAL. THE HAGUE: MARTINUS NIJHOFF,
       1975, PP. 215-233.

17305 VANDER VELDE, LEWIS G. THE PRESBYTERIAN CHURCHES AND THE
       FEDERAL UNION, 1861-1869. CAMBRIDGE: HARVARD
       UNIVERSITY PRESS, 1932.

17306 VASSAR, RENA. "WILLIAM KNOX'S DEFENSE OF SLAVERY
       (1768)." PROCEEDINGS OF THE AMERICAN PHILOSOPHICAL
       SOCIETY, 114 (AUGUST, 1970): 310-326.

17307 VIBERT, FAITH. "THE SOCIETY FOR THE PROPAGATION OF THE
       GOSPEL IN FOREIGN PARTS: ITS WORKS FOR THE NEGROES IN
       NORTH AMERICA BEFORE 1783." JOURNAL OF NEGRO HISTORY,

18 (APRIL, 1933):   171-212.

17308   VIVAS SALAS, H.   "CLAVER, PETER, ST."   IN NEW CATHOLIC
        ENCYCLOPEDIA.   15 VOLS.   WASHINGTON: CATHOLIC
        UNIVERSITY OF AMERICA, 1967, VOL. 3, PP. 922-923.

17309   VLACH, JOHN M.   "GRAVEYARDS AND AFRO-AMERICAN ART."
        SOUTHERN EXPOSURE, 5 (SUMMER/FALL, 1977):   161-165.

17310   WADE, RICHARD C.   THE URBAN FRONTIER: THE RISE OF
        WESTERN CITIES, 1790-1830.   CAMBRIDGE: HARVARD
        UNIVERSITY PRESS, 1959.

17311   WADE, RICHARD D.   "CATHOLIC, PROTESTANT AND
        AFRO-CHRISTIAN CULTS IN THE NEW WORLD."   M.A. THESIS,
        TULANE UNIVERSITY, 1976.

17312   WAGNER, CLARENCE M.   PROFILES OF BLACK GEORGIA BAPTISTS:
        TWO HUNDRED AND SIX YEARS OF BLACK GEORGIA BAPTIST
        HISTORY, ONE HUNDRED YEARS OF NATIONAL BAPTIST
        HISTORY.   GAINESVILLE, GA: WAGNER, 1980.

17313   WALKER, JOHN S.   "MORRIS BROWN: CRISIS LEADERSHIP OF THE
        AFRICAN METHODIST EPISCOPAL CHURCH, 1830-1850."
        PERSPECTIVE, 13 (1972):   138-155.

17314   WALKER, SHEILA S.   "AFRICAN GODS IN THE AMERICAS: THE
        BLACK RELIGIOUS CONTINUUM."   BLACK SCHOLAR, 11
        (NOVEMBER/DECEMBER, 1980):   25-36.

17315   WALKER, SHEILA S.   "CEREMONIAL SPIRIT POSSESSION IN
        AFRICA AND AFRO-AMERICA: FORMS, MEANING AND
        FUNCTIONAL SIGNIFICANCE FOR INDIVIDUALS AND SOCIAL
        GROUPS."   M.A. THESIS, UNIVERSITY OF CHICAGO, 1969.

17316   WALSH, RICHARD C.   "CHRISTIANITY AND SLAVERY IN THE
        UNITED STATES."   M.A. THESIS, FORDHAM UNIVERSITY, 1933.

17317   WALTON, FLETCHER.   "WHAT WE DID FOR THE NEGRO BEFORE THE
        WAR."   METHODIST REVIEW, 51 (NOVEMBER-DECEMBER, 1902):
        897-905.

17318   WAMBLE, GASTON H.   "NEGROES AND MISSOURI PROTESTANT
        CHURCHES BEFORE AND AFTER THE CIVIL WAR."   MISSOURI
        HISTORICAL REVIEW, 61 (APRIL, 1967):   321-347.

17319   WARREN, DONALD JR.   "THE NEGRO AND RELIGION IN BRAZIL."
        RACE, 6 (JANUARY, 1965):   199-216.

17320   WASHINGTON, JOSEPH R., JR.   BLACK RELIGION: THE NEGRO AND
        CHRISTIANITY IN THE UNITED STATES.   BOSTON: BEACON
        PRESS, 1964.

17321   WASHINGTON, JOSEPH R., JR.   BLACK SECTS AND CULTS.   NEW
        YORK: ANCHOR BOOKS, 1973.

17322   WASHINGTON, JOSEPH R., JR. "NEGRO SPIRITUALS: VOICES OF
         THE NON-CHRISTIAN CHRISTIANS." UNITARIAN-UNIVERSALIST
         REGISTER-LEADER, 146 (MID-SUMMER, 1964): 5-7.

17323   WASHINGTON, L. BARNWELL. "THE USE OF RELIGION FOR SOCIAL
         CONTROL IN AMERICAN SLAVERY." M.A. THESIS, HOWARD
         UNIVERSITY, 1939.

17324   WATKINS, C.T.H. "PSYCHOLOGICAL CRITERIA OF MYSTICISM AS
         APPLIED TO CERTAIN TYPES AND CULTS OF NEGRO RELIGIOUS
         EXPERIENCE." M.A. THESIS, WITTENBERG UNIVERSITY, 1939.

17325   WATSON, A.P.; RADIN, PAUL; AND JOHNSON, CHARLES S.
         (EDS.). GOD STRUCK ME DEAD: RELIGIOUS CONVERSION
         EXPERIENCES AND AUTOBIOGRAPHIES OF NEGRO EX-SLAVES.
         NASHVILLE: SOCIAL SCIENCE INSTITUTE, FISK UNIVERSITY,
         1945.

17326   WATSON, ANDREW P. "PRIMITIVE RELIGION AMONG NEGROES IN
         TENNESSEE." M.A. THESIS, FISK UNIVERSITY, 1932.

17327   WEATHERFORD, WILLIS D. AMERICAN CHURCHES AND THE NEGRO:
         AN HISTORICAL STUDY FROM EARLY SLAVE DAYS TO THE
         PRESENT. BOSTON: CHRISTOPHER PUBLISHING HOUSE, 1957.

17328   WEBBER, THOMAS L. DEEP LIKE THE RIVERS: EDUCATION IN
         THE SLAVE QUARTER COMMUNITY, 1831-1865. NEW YORK:
         W.W. NORTON, 1978.

17329   WEEKS, STEPHEN B. RELIGIOUS DEVELOPMENT IN THE PROVINCE
         OF NORTH CAROLINA. BALTIMORE: JOHNS HOPKINS PRESS,
         1892.

17330   WEEKS, STEPHEN B. SOUTHERN QUAKERS AND SLAVERY: A STUDY
         IN INSTITUTIONAL HISTORY. BALTIMORE: JOHNS HOPKINS
         PRESS, 1896.

17331   WENDEL, HUGO C.M. "THE ATTITUDE OF THE CHURCH TOWARD
         SLAVERY." LUTHERAN CHURCH REVIEW, 30 (APRIL, 1911):
         352-364.

17332   WEST, ANSON. A HISTORY OF METHODISM IN ALABAMA.
         NASHVILLE: PUBLISHING HOUSE, METHODIST EPISCOPAL
         CHURCH, SOUTH, 1893.

17333   WHITE, EUGENE E. "THE PREACHING OF GEORGE WHITEFIELD
         DURING THE GREAT AWAKENING IN AMERICA." PH.D.
         DISSERTATION, LOUISIANA STATE UNIVERSITY, 1951.

17334   WHITFIELD, THEODORE M. "SOUTHERN METHODISM AND SLAVERY."
         TYLER'S QUARTERLY HISTORICAL AND GENEALOGICAL
         MAGAZINE, 13 (JULY, 1931): 44-50.

17335   WICKENDEN, HOMER E. "HISTORY OF THE CHURCHES OF
         LOUISVILLE WITH SPECIAL REFERENCE TO SLAVERY." M.A.

THESIS, UNIVERSITY OF LOUISVILLE, 1921.

17336   WIGHT, WILLARD E.   "BISHOP VEROT AND THE CIVIL WAR."
        CATHOLIC HISTORICAL REVIEW, 47 (JULY, 1961):   153-163.

17337   WIGHT, WILLARD E.   "CHURCHES IN THE CONFEDERACY."   PH.D.
        DISSERTATION, EMORY UNIVERSITY, 1958.

17338   WILEY, BELL I.   SOUTHERN NEGROES, 1861-1865.   NEW HAVEN:
        YALE UNIVERSITY PRESS, 1938.

17339   WILLEFORD, MARY J.   "NEGRO NEW WORLD RELIGIONS AND
        WITCHCRAFT."   BIM, 12 (JANUARY-JUNE, 1969):   216-222.

17340   WILLIAMS, ERIC.   SOME HISTORICAL REFLECTIONS ON THE
        CHURCH IN THE CARIBBEAN.   PORT-OF-SPAIN: PUBLIC
        RELATIONS DIVISION, OFFICE OF THE PRIME MINISTER, 1973.

17341   WILLIAMS, ETHEL L. AND BROWN, CLIFTON F. (EDS.).   THE
        HOWARD UNIVERSITY BIBLIOGRAPHY OF AFRICAN AND
        AFRO-AMERICAN RELIGIOUS STUDIES.   WILMINGTON:
        SCHOLARLY RESOURCES, INC., 1977.

17342   WILLIAMS, EVAN J.   "THE METHODIST EPISCOPAL CHURCH,
        SOUTH, AND THE NEGRO, 1844-1870."   M.A. THESIS,
        VANDERBILT UNIVERSITY, 1939.

17343   WILLIAMS, MICHAEL P.   "THE BLACK EVANGELICAL MINISTRY IN
        THE ANTEBELLUM BORDER STATES: PROFILES OF ELDERS JOHN
        BERRY MEACHUM AND NOAH DAVIS."   FOUNDATIONS, 21
        (JULY-SEPTEMBER, 1978):   225-241.

17344   WILLIAMS, PAUL V.A.   "EXU: THE MASTER AND THE SLAVE IN
        AFRO-BRAZILIAN RELIGION."   IN WILLIAMS (ED.).   THE
        FOOL AND THE TRICKSTER: STUDIES IN HONOUR OF ENID
        WELSFORD.   TOTOWA, NJ: ROWMAN & LITTLEFIELD, 1977,
        PP. 109-119.

17345   WILLIAMS, THOMAS L.   "THE METHODIST MISSION TO THE
        SLAVES."   PH.D. DISSERTATION, YALE UNIVERSITY, 1943.

17346   WILMETH, MARLYN W. AND WILMETH, J. RICHARD.   "THEATRICAL
        ELEMENTS IN VOODOO: THE CASE FOR DIFFUSION."   JOURNAL
        FOR THE SCIENTIFIC STUDY OF RELIGION, 16 (1977):
        27-37.

17347   WILMORE, GAYRAUD S.   BLACK RELIGION AND BLACK RADICALISM.
        GARDEN CITY, NY: DOUBLEDAY, 1972.

17348   WILMORE, GAYRAUD S. AND CONE, JAMES H.   BLACK THEOLOGY:
        A DOCUMENTARY HISTORY, 1966-1979.   MARYKNOLL, NY:
        ORBIS BOOKS, 1979.

17349   WILSON, G.R.   "THE RELIGION OF THE AMERICAN NEGRO SLAVE:
        HIS ATTITUDE TOWARD LIFE AND DEATH."   JOURNAL OF NEGRO

HISTORY, 8 (JANUARY, 1923): 41-71.

17350   WILSON, GOLD R. "THE RELIGION OF THE AMERICAN NEGRO
        SLAVE." B.D. THESIS, UNIVERSITY OF CHICAGO, 1921.

17351   WINTERS, CLYDE. "A SURVEY OF ISLAM AND THE AFRICAN
        DIASPORA." PAN-AFRICAN JOURNAL, 8 (1975): 425-433.

17352   WOOD, PETER H. BLACK MAJORITY: NEGROES IN COLONIAL
        SOUTH CAROLINA, 1670 TO THE STONO REBELLION. NEW
        YORK: ALFRED A. KNOPF, 1974.

17353   WOOD, PETER H. "'JESUS CHRIST HAS GOT THEE AT
        LAST'--AFRO-AMERICAN CONVERSION AS A FORGOTTEN CHAPTER
        IN EIGHTEENTH-CENTURY SOUTHERN INTELLECTUAL HISTORY."
        BULLETIN OF THE CENTER FOR THE STUDY OF SOUTHERN
        CULTURE AND RELIGION, 3 (NOVEMBER, 1979): 1-7.

17354   WOOD, STEPHEN W. "GRACE AND RACE: THE AMERICAN HOLINESS
        MOVEMENT, SLAVERY, AND RACISM: 1850-1950." M.A.
        THESIS, UNIVERSITY OF NORTH CAROLINA, GREENSBORO, 1980.

17355   WOODSON, CARTER G. HISTORY OF THE NEGRO CHURCH.
        WASHINGTON: ASSOCIATION FOR THE STUDY OF NEGRO LIFE
        AND HISTORY, 1921.

17356   WOOLRIDGE, NANCY B. "THE SLAVE PREACHER--PORTRAIT OF A
        LEADER." JOURNAL OF NEGRO EDUCATION, 14 (WINTER,
        1945): 28-37.

17357   WYATT-BROWN, BERTRAM. "CONSCIENCE AND CAREER: YOUNG
        ABOLITIONISTS AND MISSIONARIES." IN BOLT, CHRISTINE
        AND DRESCHER, SEYMOUR (EDS.). ANTI-SLAVERY, RELIGION,
        AND REFORM: ESSAYS IN MEMORY OF ROGER ANSTEY.
        HAMDEN, CT: ARCHON BOOKS, 1980, PP. 183-206.

17358   YONKER, THOMAS W. "THE NEGRO CHURCH IN NORTH CAROLINA,
        1700-1900." M.A. THESIS, DUKE UNIVERSITY, 1955.

17359   YOUNG, HENRY J. MAJOR BLACK RELIGIOUS LEADERS,
        1755-1940. NASHVILLE: ABINGDON PRESS, 1977.

22.
Slave Culture

GENERAL

17360   ABRAHAMS, ROGER D.   "TRADITIONS OF ELOJJENCE IN
           AFRO-AMERICAN COMMUNITIES." JOURNAL OF INTER-AMERICAN
           STUDIES AND WORLD AFFAIRS, 12 (OCTOBER, 1970):
           505-527.

17361   ABRAHAMS, ROGER D. AND SZWED, JOHN F. (EDS.).
           DISCOVERING AFRO-AMERICA. LEIDEN: E.J. BRILL, 1975.

17362   ABRAHAMS, ROGER D. AND SZWED, JOHN F. "INTRODUCTION."
           JOURNAL OF ASIAN AND AFRICAN STUDIES, 9 (JULY-APRIL,
           1974): 135-138.

17363   ACKERMAN, KENNETH J. "THE CULTURAL STUDY OF AMERICAN
           NEGROES: A HISTORY AND CRITIQUE." M.A. THESIS,
           UNIVERSITY OF PENNSYLVANIA, 1960.

17364   AGUIRRE BELTRAN, GONZALO. "AFRICAN INFLUENCES IN THE
           DEVELOPMENT OF REGIONAL CULTURES IN THE NEW WORLD."
           IN PLANTATION SYSTEMS OF THE NEW WORLD. WASHINGTON:
           PAN AMERICAN UNION, 1959, PP. 64-69.

17365   AMES, MARY. FROM A NEW ENGLAND WOMAN'S DIARY IN DIXIE IN
           1865. NORWOOD, MA: PLIMPTON PRESS, 1906.

17366   ANDERSON, ROBERT. FROM SLAVERY TO AFFLUENCE: MEMOIRS OF
           ROBERT ANDERSON, EX-SLAVE. HEMINGSFORD, NE:
           HEMINGSFORD LEDGER, 1927.

17367   ASCHENBRENNER, JOYCE. "HUMANISM IN BLACK CULTURE." IN
           HENRY, FRANCES (ED.). ETHNICITY IN THE AMERICAS. THE
           HAGUE: MOUTON PUBLISHERS, 1976, PP. 333-346.

17368   AVARY, MYRTA L. DIXIE AFTER THE WAR. NEW YORK:
           DOUBLEDAY, 1906.

17369   AVIRETT, JAMES B. THE OLD PLANTATION: HOW WE LIVED IN
           GREAT HOUSE AND CABIN BEFORE THE WAR. NEW YORK: F.
           TENNYSON NEELY, 1901.

17370   BACON, ALICE M. "PLEA FOR NEGRO FOLK-LORE."
           INDIANAPOLIS FREEMAN, JANUARY 27, 1894.

17371   BAHAM, VENITA M. "MYSTICISM AND THE AFRO-AMERICAN
           RELIGIOUS EXPERIENCE." JOURNAL OF RELIGIOUS THOUGHT,
           35 (SPRING-SUMMER, 1978): 68-77.

17372   BARATZ, JOAN AND BARATZ, STEPHEN. "THE SOCIAL PATHOLOGY
           MODEL: HISTORICAL BASES FOR PSYCHOLOGY'S DENIAL OF

THE EXISTENCE OF NEGRO CULTURE." IN KOCHMAN, THOMAS
(ED.). RAPPIN' AND STYLIN' OUT. URBANA: UNIVERSITY
OF ILLINOIS PRESS, 1972, PP. 3-16.

17373 BARNET, MIGUEL. "THE CULTURE THAT SUGAR CREATED." LATIN
AMERICAN LITERARY REVIEW, 8 (SPRING-SUMMER, 1980):
38-46.

17374 BASKIN, WADE AND RUNES, RICHARD N. DICTIONARY OF BLACK
CULTURE. NEW YORK: PHILOSOPHICAL LIBRARY, 1973.

17375 BECK, HORACE P. "THE RIDDLE OF 'THE FLYING CLOUD.'"
JOURNAL OF AMERICAN FOLKLORE, 66 (APRIL-JUNE, 1953):
123-133.

17376 BECKWITH, MARTHA W. JAMAICA FOLK-LORE. NEW YORK: G.E.
STECHERT, 1928.

17377 BECKWITH, MARTHA W. JAMAICA PROVERBS. POUGHKEEPSIE, NY:
VASSAR COLLEGE, 1925.

17378 BENNETT, LERONE JR. "THE WORLD OF THE SLAVE." EBONY, 26
(FEBRUARY, 1971): 44-56.

17379 BERRY, MARY F. AND BLASSINGAME, JOHN W. "AFRICA,
SLAVERY, AND THE ROOTS OF CONTEMPORARY BLACK CULTURE."
IN HARPER, MICHAEL S. AND STEPTO, ROBERT B. (EDS.).
CHANT OF SAINTS: A GATHERING OF AFRO-AMERICAN
LITERATURE, ART, AND SCHOLARSHIP. URBANA: UNIVERSITY
OF ILLINOIS PRESS, 1977, PP. 241-256.

17380 BERRY, MARY F. AND BLASSINGAME, JOHN W. "AFRICA,
SLAVERY, AND THE ROOTS OF CONTEMPORARY BLACK CULTURE."
MASSACHUSETTS REVIEW, 18 (AUTUMN, 1977): 501-516.

17381 BLACK, CLINTON V. DE B. TALES OF OLD JAMAICA. KINGSTON:
PIONEER PRESS, 1952.

17382 BLACK, ELIZABETH. "A SHOW AT THE QUARTER." THEATER ARTS
MONTHLY, 16 (JUNE, 1932): 493-500.

17383 BLANTON, JOSHUA E. "I SHO BEN LUB DAT BUCKRA." SOUTHERN
WORKMAN, 37 (APRIL, 1908): 242-246.

17384 BLAUNER, ROBERT. "BLACK CULTURE: MYTH OR REALITY?" IN
WHITTEN, NORMAN E. AND SZWED, JOHN (EDS.).
AFRO-AMERICAN ANTHROPOLOGY. NEW YORK: FREE PRESS,
1970, PP. 347-366.

17385 BLAUNER, ROBERT. "THE QUESTION OF BLACK CULTURE." IN
SZWED, JOHN F. (ED.). BLACK AMERICA. NEW YORK:
BASIC BOOKS, 1970, PP. 110-120.

17386 BOGGER, TOMMY L. "THE SLAVE AND FREE BLACK COMMUNITY IN
NORFOLK, 1775-1865." PH.D. DISSERTATION, UNIVERSITY

OF VIRGINIA, 1976.

17387   BOWMAN, JAMES C.   JOHN HENRY, THE RAMBLING BLACK ULYSSES.
        CHICAGO: ALBERT WHITMAN, 1942.

17388   BRAWLEY, BENJAMIN G. (ED.).   EARLY NEGRO AMERICAN
        WRITERS. CHAPEL HILL: UNIVERSITY OF NORTH CAROLINA
        PRESS, 1935.

17389   BROOKES, STELLA B.   JOEL CHANDLER HARRIS: FOLKLORIST.
        ATHENS: UNIVERSITY OF GEORGIA PRESS, 1950.

17390   CARAWAN, GUY AND CARAWAN, CANDIE. AIN'T YOU GOT A RIGHT
        TO THE TREE OF LIFE? THE PEOPLE OF JOHNS ISLAND,
        SOUTH CAROLINA--THEIR FACES, THEIR WORDS AND THEIR
        SONGS. NEW YORK: SIMON & SCHUSTER, 1966.

17391   CAULFIELD, MINA D. "SLAVERY AND THE ORIGINS OF BLACK
        CULTURE: ELKINS REVISITED." IN ROSE, PETER I. (ED.).
        AMERICANS FROM AFRICA: SLAVERY AND ITS AFTERMATH. 2
        VOLS. NEW YORK: ATHERTON PRESS, 1970, VOL. 1, PP.
        171-193.

17392   CHASE, JUDITH W.   AFRO-AMERICAN ART AND CRAFT. NEW YORK:
        VAN NOSTRAND, 1971.

17393   CONRAD, GEORGIA B. "REMINISCENCES OF A SOUTHERN WOMAN."
        SOUTHERN WORKMAN, 30 (FEBRUARY, MARCH, MAY, JUNE,
        JULY, 1901): 77-80, 167-171, 252-257, 357-359,
        409-411.

17394   CORBETT, MICHAEL F. "A PRELIMINARY STUDY OF THE PLANTER
        ARISTOCRACY AS A FOLK LEVEL OF LIFE IN THE OLD SOUTH."
        M.A. THESIS, UNIVERSITY OF NORTH CAROLINA, 1941.

17395   CRUSE, HAROLD W. "AN AFRO-AMERICAN'S CULTURAL VIEWS."
        PRESENCE AFRICAINE, NO. 17 (DECEMBER, 1957-JANUARY,
        1958): 31-45.

17396   CUNLIFFE, MARCUS. "BLACK CULTURE & WHITE AMERICA."
        ENCOUNTER, 34 (JANUARY, 1970): 22-35.

17397   DALBY, DAVID. "AMERICANISMS THAT MAY ONCE HAVE BEEN
        AFRICANISMS." LONDON TIMES, JUNE 19, 1969.

17398   DALBY, DAVID. "ASHANTI SURVIVALS IN THE LANGUAGE AND
        TRADITIONS OF THE WINDWARD MAROONS OF JAMAICA."
        AFRICAN LANGUAGE STUDIES, 12 (1971): 31-51.

17399   DANA, KATHERINE F.   OUR PHIL AND OTHER STORIES. BOSTON:
        HOUGHTON MIFFLIN, 1889.

17400   DANA, MARVIN. "VOODOO: ITS EFFECTS ON THE NEGRO RACE."
        IN DE NEVI, DONALD P. AND HOLMES, DORIS A. (EDS.).
        RACISM AT THE TURN OF THE CENTURY: DOCUMENTARY

PERSPECTIVES 1870-1910. SAN RAFAEL, CA: LESWING PRESS, 1973, PP. 344-354.

17401 DANCE, DARYL C. "TUNING IN THE BOILER ROOM AND THE COTTON PATCH: NEW DIRECTIONS IN THE STUDY OF AFRO-AMERICAN FOLKLORE." CLA JOURNAL, 20 (JUNE, 1977): 547-553.

17402 DANCE, DARYL C. "WIT AND HUMOR IN THE SLAVE NARRATIVES." JOURNAL OF AFRO-AMERICAN ISSUES, 5 (SPRING, 1977): 125-134.

17403 DANIEL, JACK L. (ED.). BLACK COMMUNICATION: DIMENSIONS OF RESEARCH AND INSTRUCTION. NEW YORK: SPEECH COMMUNICATION ASSOCIATION, 1974.

17404 DARK, PHILIP J.C. BUSH NEGRO ART: AN AFRICAN ART IN THE AMERICAS. LONDON: ALEC TIRANTI, 1954.

17405 DARK, PHILIP J.C. "BUSH NEGRO ART: AN AFRICAN ART IN THE AMERICAS." M.PHIL. THESIS, YALE UNIVERSITY, 1950.

17406 DAVIS, JOHN A. "THE INFLUENCE OF AFRICANS ON AMERICAN CULTURE." ANNALS OF THE AMERICAN ACADEMY OF POLITICAL AND SOCIAL SCIENCE, 354 (JULY, 1964): 75-83.

17407 DAVIS, LENWOOD G. AND SIMS, JANET. BLACK ARTISTS IN THE UNITED STATES: AN ANNOTATED BIBLIOGRAPHY OF BOOKS, ARTICLES, AND DISSERTATIONS ON BLACK ARTISTS, 1779-1979. WESTPORT: GREENWOOD PRESS, 1980.

17408 DO NASCIMENTO, ABDIAS. "AFRO-BRAZILIAN CULTURE." BLACK IMAGES, 1 (AUTUMN-WINTER, 1972): 41-46.

17409 DORMON, JAMES H. AND JONES, ROBERT R. THE AFRO-AMERICAN EXPERIENCE: A CULTURAL HISTORY THROUGH EMANCIPATION. NEW YORK: JOHN WILEY & SONS, 1974.

17410 DUBOIS, W.E.B. THE SOULS OF BLACK FOLK: ESSAYS AND SKETCHES. CHICAGO: A.C. MCCLURG & COMPANY, 1903.

17411 DUNDES, ALAN (ED.). MOTHER WIT FROM THE LAUGHING BARREL: READINGS IN THE INTERPRETATION OF AFRO-AMERICAN FOLKLORE. ENGLEWOOD CLIFFS: PRENTICE-HALL, 1973.

17412 EARLE, ALICE M. "PINKSTER DAY." OUTLOOK, 49 (APRIL 28, 1894): 743-744.

17413 ECHEVERRIA, PATRICIA. "FOLLOW THE DRINKING GOURD; PROGRAM IN CREATIVE DRAMATICS." INDIANA SCHOOL BULLETIN, 30 (OCTOBER, 1970): 61-63.

17414 EDWARDS, CHARLES L. BAHAMA SONGS AND STORIES. NEW YORK: HOUGHTON MIFFLIN, 1902.

17415   EDWARDS, CHARLES L. "FOLK-LORE OF THE BAHAMA NEGROES."
        AMERICAN JOURNAL OF PSYCHOLOGY, 2 (AUGUST, 1889):
        519-542.

17416   EDWARDS, CHARLES L. "SOME TALES FROM BAHAMA FOLK-LORE."
        JOURNAL OF AMERICAN FOLKLORE, 4 (JANUARY-MARCH,
        JULY-SEPTEMBER, 1891): 47-54, 247-252.

17417   ELDER, ARLENE A. THE "HINDERED HAND": CULTURAL
        IMPLICATIONS OF EARLY AFRICAN-AMERICAN FICTION.
        WESTPORT: GREENWOOD PRESS, 1978.

17418   "SWAMP VERSUS PLANTATION: SYMBOLIC STRUCTURE IN W.E.B.
        DUBOIS' THE QUEST OF THE SILVER FLEECE." PHYLON, 34
        (DECEMBER, 1973): 358-367.

17419   ELKINS, STANLEY M. "CULTURE CONTACTS AND NEGRO SLAVERY."
        PROCEEDINGS OF THE AMERICAN PHILOSOPHICAL SOCIETY, 107
        (APRIL, 1963): 107-109.

17420   EMERSON, WILLIAM C. STORIES AND SPIRITUALS OF THE NEGRO
        SLAVE. BOSTON: R.G. BADGER AND GORHAM PRESS, 1930.

17421   ESCOTT, PAUL D. SLAVERY REMEMBERED: A RECORD OF
        TWENTIETH-CENTURY SLAVE NARRATIVES. CHAPEL HILL:
        UNIVERSITY OF NORTH CAROLINA PRESS, 1979.

17422   FAIRBANKS, CHARLES H. "ANTHROPOLOGY AND THE SEGREGATION
        PROBLEM: II. CULTURAL CONSIDERATIONS." IN THE NEGRO
        IN AMERICAN SOCIETY. TALLAHASSEE: FLORIDA STATE
        UNIVERSITY, 1958, PP. 7-18.

17423   FARRISON, W. EDWARD. "GEORGE MOSES HORTON: POET FOR
        FREEDOM." CLA JOURNAL, 14 (MARCH, 1971): 227-241.

17424   FERRIS, WILLIAM R. "BLACK DELTA RELIGION." MID-SOUTH
        FOLKLORE, 2 (SPRING, 1974): 27-33.

17425   FERRIS, WILLIAM R. "INTRODUCTION." SOUTHERN FOLKLORE
        QUARTERLY, 42 (1978): 99-107.

17426   FRANKLIN, VINCENT P. "SLAVERY, PERSONALITY, AND BLACK
        CULTURE--SOME THEORETICAL ISSUES." PHYLON, 35 (MARCH,
        1974): 54-63.

17427   FRAZIER, E. FRANKLIN. "THE CULTURAL BACKGROUND OF
        SOUTHERN NEGROES." IN SELECTED PAPERS OF THE
        INSTITUTE ON CULTURAL PATTERNS OF NEWCOMERS. CHICAGO:
        WELFARE COUNCIL OF CHICAGO, 1957, PP. 1-14.

17428   FRAZIER, E. FRANKLIN. THE NEGRO FAMILY IN THE UNITED
        STATES. CHICAGO: UNIVERSITY OF CHICAGO PRESS, 1939.

17429   GENOVESE, EUGENE D. ROLL, JORDAN, ROLL: THE WORLD THE
        SLAVES MADE. NEW YORK: PANTHEON, 1974.

17430   GRANT, GEORGE C. "THE NEGRO IN DRAMATIC ART." JOURNAL
        OF NEGRO HISTORY, 17 (JANUARY, 1932): 19-29.

17431   GRIFFIN, LOUIS G. "AFRO-AMERICAN CULTURAL NATIONALISM
        BEFORE THE CIVIL WAR." M.A. THESIS, TEXAS TECH
        UNIVERSITY, 1972.

17432   GUTMAN, HERBERT G. THE BLACK FAMILY IN SLAVERY AND
        FREEDOM, 1750-1925. NEW YORK: PANTHEON BOOKS, 1976.

17433   GUTMAN, HERBERT G. "SLAVE CULTURE AND SLAVE FAMILY AND
        KIN NETWORK: THE IMPORTANCE OF TIME." IN CENSER,
        JACK R.; STEINERT, N. STEVEN; MCCANDLESS, AMY M.
        (EDS.). SOUTH ATLANTIC URBAN STUDIES, VOLUME 2.
        COLUMBIA: UNIVERSITY OF SOUTH CAROLINA PRESS, 1978,
        PP. 73-88.

17434   GUTMAN, HERBERT AND SUTCH, RICHARD. "SAMBO MAKES GOOD,
        OR WERE SLAVES IMBUED WITH THE PROTESTANT WORK ETHIC?"
        IN DAVID, PAUL A.; GUTMAN; SUTCH; TEMIN, PETER; AND
        WRIGHT, GAVIN (EDS.). RECKONING WITH SLAVERY: A
        CRITICAL STUDY IN THE QUANTITATIVE HISTORY OF AMERICAN
        NEGRO SLAVERY. NEW YORK: OXFORD UNIVERSITY PRESS,
        1976, PP. 55-93.

17435   GUTMAN, HERBERT AND SUTCH, RICHARD. "VICTORIANS ALL?
        THE SEXUAL MORES AND CONDUCT OF SLAVES AND THEIR
        MASTERS." IN DAVID, PAUL A.; GUTMAN; SUTCH; TEMIN,
        PETER; AND WRIGHT, GAVIN (EDS.). RECKONING WITH
        SLAVERY: A CRITICAL STUDY IN THE QUANTITATIVE HISTORY
        OF AMERICAN NEGRO SLAVERY. NEW YORK: OXFORD
        UNIVERSITY PRESS, 1976, PP. 135-164.

17436   HAMBLY, W.D. "NEGRO CULTURE IN GUIANA." FIELD MUSEUM
        NEWS, 6 (1935): 3.

17437   HANNERZ, ULF. "WHAT NEGROES MEAN BY 'SOUL.'"
        TRANS-ACTION, 5 (JULY/AUGUST, 1968): 57-61.

17438   HARRIS, MIDDLETON. THE BLACK BOOK. NEW YORK: RANDOM
        HOUSE, 1974.

17439   JACOBS, H.P. "DIALECT, MAGIC AND RELIGION." IN CARGILL,
        MORRIS (ED.). IAN FLEMING INTRODUCES JAMAICA.
        LONDON: DEUTSCH, 1965, PP. 79-101.

17440   JEREMIAH, MILFORD A. "THE LINGUISTIC RELATEDNESS OF
        BLACK ENGLISH AND ANTIGUAN CREOLE: EVIDENCE FROM THE
        EIGHTEENTH AND NINETEENTH CENTURIES." PH.D.
        DISSERTATION, BROWN UNIVERSITY, 1977.

17441   JOEL, MIRIAM. AFRICAN TRADITIONS IN LATIN AMERICA.
        CUERNAVACA: CIDOC, 1972.

17442   JOHNSON, GUION G. A SOCIAL HISTORY OF THE SEA ISLANDS

WITH SPECIAL REFERENCE TO ST. HELENA ISLAND, SOUTH CAROLINA. CHAPEL HILL: UNIVERSITY OF NORTH CAROLINA PRESS, 1930.

17443 JOHNSON, GUY B. "NEGRO CULTURE." IN ADAMS, JAMES T. (ED.). DICTIONARY OF AMERICAN HISTORY. 5 VOLS. NEW YORK: CHARLES SCRIBNER'S SONS, 1940, VOL. 4, PP. 83-84.

17444 JOHNSON, GUY B. "SOME FACTORS IN THE DEVELOPMENT OF NEGRO SOCIAL INSTITUTIONS IN THE UNITED STATES." AMERICAN JOURNAL OF SOCIOLOGY, 40 (NOVEMBER, 1934): 329-337.

17445 JONES, LEROI. BLUES PEOPLE: THE NEGRO EXPERIENCE IN AMERICA AND THE MUSIC THAT DEVELOPED FROM IT. NEW YORK: MORROW, 1963.

17446 KING, JAMES R. "FACTORS SHAPING AFRICAN SURVIVALS IN AMERICA." PH.D. DISSERTATION, UNIVERSITY OF CALIFORNIA, IRVINE, 1976.

17447 LATROBE, BENJAMIN H. IMPRESSIONS RESPECTING NEW ORLEANS. NEW YORK: COLUMBIA UNIVERSITY PRESS, 1951.

17448 LEVINE, LAWRENCE W. BLACK CULTURE AND BLACK CONSCIOUSNESS: AFRO-AMERICAN FOLK THOUGHT FROM SLAVERY TO FREEDOM. NEW YORK: OXFORD UNIVERSITY PRESS, 1977.

17449 LOMAX, ALAN AND ABDUL, RAOUL (EDS.). 3000 YEARS OF BLACK POETRY. NEW YORK: DODD, MEAD, 1970.

17450 LYMAN, STANFORD M. THE BLACK AMERICAN IN SOCIOLOGICAL THOUGHT. NEW YORK: G.P. PUTNAM'S SONS, 1972.

17451 MAGDOL, EDWARD. "THE LEGACY OF THE SLAVE COMMUNITY." A RIGHT TO THE LAND: ESSAYS ON THE FREEDMEN'S COMMUNITY. WESTPORT: GREENWOOD PRESS, 1977, PP. 16-34.

17452 MARS, JEAN-PRICE. "TRANSATLANTIC AFRICAN SURVIVALS AND THE DYNAMISM OF NEGRO CULTURE." PRESENCE AFRICAINE, NOS. 8-10 (JUNE-NOVEMBER, 1956): 276-284.

17453 MILLER, KELLY. "THE ARTISTIC GIFTS OF THE NEGRO." VOICE OF THE NEGRO, 3 (APRIL, 1906): 252-257.

17454 MINTZ, SIDNEY W. "CREATING CULTURE IN THE AMERICAS." COLUMBIA UNIVERSITY FORUM, 13 (SPRING, 1970): 4-11.

17455 MINTZ, SIDNEY W. "FOREWORD." IN WHITTEN, NORMAN E., JR. AND SZWED, JOHN F. (EDS.). AFRO-AMERICAN ANTHROPOLOGY: CONTEMPORARY PERSPECTIVES. NEW YORK: FREE PRESS, 1970, PP. 1-16.

17456 MOORE, JANIE G. "AFRICANISMS AMONG BLACKS OF THE SEA
       ISLANDS." JOURNAL OF BLACK STUDIES, 10 (JUNE, 1980):
       467-480.

17457 MORGAN, P.D. "AFRO-AMERICAN CULTURAL CHANGE; THE CASE OF
       COLONIAL SOUTH CAROLINA SLAVES." UNPUBLISHED PAPER,
       1979.

17458 MORGAN, PHILIP D. "THE DEVELOPMENT OF SLAVE CULTURE IN
       EIGHTEENTH-CENTURY PLANTATION AMERICA." PH.D.
       DISSERTATION, UNIVERSITY OF LONDON, 1978.

17459 MURPHY, JEANNETTE R. SOUTHERN THOUGHT FOR NORTHERN
       THINKERS. NEW YORK: BANDANNA PUBLISHING COMPANY,
       1904.

17460 NASCIMENTO, ABDIAS D. "AFRO-BRAZILIAN CULTURE." BLACK
       IMAGES, 1 (AUTUMN, WINTER, 1972): 41-46.

17461 NASH, GARY B. "THE AFRICAN RESPONSE TO SLAVERY." RED,
       WHITE AND BLACK: THE PEOPLES OF EARLY AMERICA.
       ENGLEWOOD CLIFFS: PRENTICE-HALL, 1974, PP. 183-212.

17462 OSTENDORF, BERNHARD. "BLACK POETRY, BLUES, AND FOLKLORE:
       DOUBLE CONSCIOUSNESS IN AFRO-AMERICAN ORAL CULTURE."
       AMERIKASTUDIEN, 20 (1975): 209-260.

17463 OSTHAUS, CARL R. FREEDMEN, PHILANTHROPY, AND FRAUD: A
       HISTORY OF THE FREEDMAN'S SAVINGS BANK. URBANA:
       UNIVERSITY OF ILLINOIS PRESS, 1976.

17464 OWENS, LESLIE H. "'THIS SPECIES OF PROPERTY': SLAVE
       PERSONALITY AND BEHAVIOR IN THE OLD SOUTH, 1776-1861."
       PH.D. DISSERTATION, UNIVERSITY OF CALIFORNIA,
       RIVERSIDE, 1973.

17465 PATTERSON, LINDSAY (ED.). THE NEGRO IN MUSIC AND ART.
       NEW YORK: PUBLISHERS COMPANY, 1967.

17466 RAWICK, GEORGE P. "WEST AFRICAN CULTURE AND NORTH
       AMERICAN SLAVERY: A STUDY OF CULTURE CHANGE AMONG
       AMERICAN SLAVES IN THE ANTE-BELLUM SOUTH WITH FOCUS
       UPON SLAVE RELIGION." IN SPENCER, ROBERT F. (ED.).
       MIGRATION AND ANTHROPOLOGY. SEATTLE: AMERICAN
       ETHNOLOGICAL SOCIETY, 1970, PP. 149-164.

17467 REHIN, GEORGE F. "THE DARKER IMAGE: AMERICAN NEGRO
       MINSTRELSY THROUGH THE HISTORIAN'S LENS." JOURNAL OF
       AMERICAN STUDIES, 9 (DECEMBER, 1976): 365-373.

17468 REIDY, JOSEPH P. "'NEGRO ELECTION DAY' & BLACK COMMUNITY
       LIFE IN NEW ENGLAND, 1750-1860." MARXIST
       PERSPECTIVES, 1 (FALL, 1973): 102-117.

17469 ROBINSON, WILLIAM H. (ED.). EARLY BLACK AMERICAN POETS.

DUBUQUE, IA: WM.C. BROWN, 1969.

17470 RODNEY, WALTER. "AFRICA IN EUROPE AND THE AMERICAS." IN
       GRAY, RICHARD (ED.). THE CAMBRIDGE HISTORY OF AFRICA:
       VOLUME 4 FROM C. 1600 TO C. 1790. NEW YORK:
       CAMBRIDGE UNIVERSITY PRESS, 1975, PP. 578-622.

17471 ROEDIGER, DAVID. "THE MEANING OF AFRICA FOR THE AMERICAN
       SLAVE." JOURNAL OF ETHNIC STUDIES, 4 (WINTER, 1977):
       1-16.

17472 RUBIN, VERA. "CULTURAL PERSPECTIVES IN CARIBBEAN
       RESEARCH." IN RUBIN (ED.). CARIBBEAN STUDIES: A
       SYMPOSIUM. SEATTLE: UNIVERSITY OF WASHINGTON PRESS,
       1960, PP. 110-122.

17473 SANDAY, PEGGY R. "AFRICAN SURVIVALS, THE CHAINS OF
       SLAVERY, AND ETHNOCENTRISM: INTRA-CULTURAL VARIATION
       IN U.S. SLAVE CULTURE." UNPUBLISHED PAPER PRESENTED
       AT MSSB—UNIVERSITY OF ROCHESTER CONFERENCE: "TIME ON
       THE CROSS: A FIRST APPRAISAL," OCTOBER 24-26, 1974.

17474 SASS, HERBERT R. "I CAN'T HELP FROM CRYIN'." SATURDAY
       EVENING POST, 215 (OCTOBER 3, 1942): 16-17, 66,
       68-69, 71.

17475 STAMPP, KENNETH M. "THE DAILY LIFE OF THE SOUTHERN
       SLAVE." IN HUGGINS, NATHAN I.; KILSON, MARTIN; AND
       FOX, DANIEL M. (EDS.). KEY ISSUES IN THE
       AFRO-AMERICAN EXPERIENCE. 2 VOLS. NEW YORK:
       HARCOURT BRACE JOVANOVICH, 1971, VOL. 1, PP. 116-137.

17476 SZWED, JOHN F. "AFRICA LIES JUST OFF GEORGIA: SEA
       ISLANDS PRESERVES ORIGINS OF AFRO-AMERICAN CULTURE."
       AFRICA REPORT, 15 (OCTOBER, 1970): 29-31.

17477 TAYLOR, RONALD L. "BLACK ETHNICITY AND THE PERSISTENCE
       OF ETHNOGENESIS." AMERICAN JOURNAL OF SOCIOLOGY, 84
       (MAY, 1979): 1401-1423.

17478 TEILHET, JEHANNE. DIMENSIONS IN BLACK. LA JOLLA, CA:
       LA JOLLA MUSEUM OF ART, 1970.

17479 TURNER, LORENZO D. "AFRICAN SURVIVALS IN THE NEW WORLD
       WITH SPECIAL EMPHASIS ON THE ARTS." IN DAVIS, JOHN A.
       (ED.). AFRICA SEEN BY AMERICAN NEGRO SCHOLARS.
       DIJON, FRANCE: PRESENCE AFRICAINE, 1958, 101-118.

17480 TWINING, MARY A. "AFRICAN-AFRO-AMERICAN ARTISTIC
       CONTINUITY." JOURNAL OF AFRICAN STUDIES, 2 (WINTER,
       1975-1976): 569-578.

17481 TWINING, MARY A. "AN EXAMINATION OF AFRICAN RETENTIONS
       IN THE FOLK CULTURE OF THE SOUTH CAROLINA AND GEORGIA
       SEA ISLANDS." PH.D. DISSERTATION, INDIANA UNIVERSITY,

1977.

17482   TWINING, MARY A. "SOURCES IN THE FOLKLORE AND FOLKLIFE
         OF THE SEA ISLANDS." SOUTHERN FOLKLORE QUARTERLY, 39
         (JUNE, 1975): 135-150.

17483   TWINING, MARY A. AND BAIRD, KEITH E. "INTRODUCTION TO
         SEA ISLAND FOLKLIFE." JOURNAL OF BLACK STUDIES, 10
         (JUNE, 1980): 387-416.

17484   UYA, OKON E. "THE CULTURE OF SLAVERY: BLACK EXPERIENCE
         THROUGH A WHITE FILTER." AFRO-AMERICAN STUDIES, 1
         (JANUARY, 1971): 203-209.

17485   UYA, OKON E. "THE CULTURE OF SLAVERY: BLACK EXPERIENCE
         THROUGH A WHITE FILTER." BLACK LINES, 1 (WINTER,
         1970): 27-33.

17486   UYA, OKON E. "LIFE IN THE SLAVE COMMUNITY."
         AFRO-AMERICAN STUDIES, 1 (APRIL, 1971): 281-290.

17487   WAGLEY, CHARLES AND HARRIS, MARVIN. "THE NEGRO IN THE
         AMERICAS." MINORITIES IN THE NEW WORLD. NEW YORK:
         COLUMBIA UNIVERSITY PRESS, 1958, PP. 87-160.

17488   WHITTEN, NORMAN AND SZWED, JOHN. "NEGROES IN THE NEW
         WORLD." TRANS-ACTION, 5 (JULY/AUGUST, 1968): 49-56.

17489   WORK, MONROE N. "SECRET SOCIETIES AS FACTORS IN THE
         SOCIAL AND ECONOMICAL LIFE OF THE NEGRO." IN
         MCCULLOCH, JAMES E. (ED.). DEMOCRACY IN EARNEST.
         WASHINGTON: SOUTHERN SOCIOLOGICAL CONGRESS, 1918, PP.
         342-350.

17490   WORK, MONROE N. "THE SPIRIT OF NEGRO POETRY." SOUTHERN
         WORKMAN, 37 (FEBRUARY, 1908): 73-75.

17491   WRITERS PROJECT, GEORGIA. DRUMS AND SHADOWS: SURVIVAL
         STUDIES AMONG THE GEORGIA COASTAL NEGROES. ATHENS:
         UNIVERSITY OF GEORGIA PRESS, 1940.

MUSIC

17492   ABRAHAMS, ROGER D. "CHRISTMAS MUMMINGS ON NEVIS." NORTH
         CAROLINA FOLKLORE JOURNAL, 21 (SEPTEMBER, 1973):
         120-131.

17493   ACHILLE, LOUIS T. "NEGRO SPIRITUALS AND THE SPREAD OF
         NEGRO CULTURE." PRESENCE AFRICAINE, NOS. 8-10,
         (JUNE-NOVEMBER, 1956): 230-240.

17494   ACHILLE, LOUIS T. "NEGRO SPIRITUALS." IN COLLOQUIM:
         FUNCTION AND SIGNIFICANCE OF AFRICAN NEGRO ART IN THE
         LIFE OF THE PEOPLE AND FOR THE PEOPLE. PARIS:

PRESENCE AFRICAINE, 1968, PP. 351-367.

17495   ADAMS, EDWARD C.C.   "A SOUTH CAROLINA FOLKSONG."
        SOUTHERN WORKMAN, 54 (DECEMBER, 1925):   568.

17496   ADLER, THOMAS.   "THE PHYSICAL DEVELOPMENT OF THE BANJO."
        NEW YORK FOLKLORE QUARTERLY, 28 (SEPTEMBER, 1972):
        187-208.

17497   ALLEN, G.   "NEGRO'S CONTRIBUTION TO AMERICAN MUSIC."
        CURRENT HISTORY, 26 (MAY, 1927):   245-249.

17498   ALLEN, WILLIAM F.   "FROM THE PREFACE TO SLAVE SONGS OF
        THE UNITED STATES." CHORAL JOURNAL, 17 (1976):   25-27.

17499   ALLEN, WILLIAM F.; WARE, CHARLES P.; AND GARRISON, LUCY
        M. "SLAVE SONGS OF THE UNITED STATES." LIVING AGE, 8
        (JANUARY 25, 1868):   230-242.

17500   ALLEN, WILLIAM F.; WARE, CHARLES P.; AND GARRISON, LUCY
        M. SLAVE SONGS OF THE UNITED STATES. NEW YORK: A.
        SIMPSON & COMPANY, 1867.

17501   ALSTON, CHARLES.   "A CONCEPTUAL ANALYSIS OF TEN NEGRO
        SLAVE SONGS; A STUDY OF SLAVE SONGS BASED ON THE
        DEVELOPMENT OF THE SLAVE'S INDIVIDUAL MEANS OF
        ADJUSTMENT AND HIS SOCIAL MOTIVATIONS." M.A. THESIS,
        PENNSYLVANIA STATE UNIVERSITY, 1963.

17502   AMES, RUSSELL.   "PROTEST AND IRONY IN NEGRO FOLKSONGS."
        SCIENCE AND SOCIETY, 14 (SUMMER, 1950):   193-213.

17503   ANDERSON, HILTON.   "SOME NEGRO SLAVE SONGS FROM AN 1856
        NOVEL." MISSISSIPPI FOLKLORE REGISTER, 8 (FALL,
        1974):   221-226.

17504   ANDREWS, ELIZA F.   THE WAR-TIME JOURNAL OF A GEORGIA
        GIRL, 1864-1865. NEW YORK: D. APPLETON, 1908.

17505   ARMSTRONG, MARY F. AND LUDLOW, HELEN W.   HAMPTON AND ITS
        STUDENTS BY TWO OF ITS TEACHERS. NEW YORK: G.P.
        PUTNAM'S SONS, 1874.

17506   ARROWOOD, MARY D. AND HAMILTON, T.F.   "NINE NEGRO
        SPIRITUALS, 1850-1861, FROM LOWER SOUTH CAROLINA."
        JOURNAL OF AMERICAN FOLKLORE, 41 (OCTOBER-DECEMBER,
        1928):   579-580.

17507   BAKER, DAVID N.   "A PERIODIZATION OF BLACK MUSIC
        HISTORY." IN DE LERMA, DOMINIQUE-RENE (ED.).
        REFLECTIONS ON AFRO-AMERICAN MUSIC. KENT: KENT STATE
        UNIVERSITY PRESS, 1973, PP. 143-160.

17508   BALES, MARY V.   "NEGRO FOLKSONGS IN TEXAS: THEIR
        DEFINITION AND ORIGIN." M.A. THESIS, TEXAS CHRISTIAN

UNIVERSITY, 1927.

17509   BALES, MARY V. "SOME NEGRO FOLK SONGS OF TEXAS." FOLLOW
        DE DRINKIN' GOU'D. AUSTIN: TEXAS FOLK-LORE SOCIETY,
        1928, PP. 85-112.

17510   BALLANTA, N.G.J. ST. HELENA ISLAND SPIRITUALS. NEW
        YORK: G. SCHIRMER, 1925.

17511   "BANJO AND BONES." SATURDAY REVIEW OF POLITICS,
        LITERATURE AND ART, 57 (JUNE 7, 1884): 739-740.

17512   BANNER, ELEANOR. "THE HISTORY OF THE BLACK MAN IN
        NARRATIVE AND SONG." PH.D. DISSERTATION, UNION
        GRADUATE SCHOOL, 1972.

17513   BARRETT, HARRIS. "NEGRO FOLK SONGS." SOUTHERN WORKMAN,
        41 (APRIL, 1912): 238-245.

17514   BARTON, WILLIAM E. "HYMNS OF THE SLAVE AND THE
        FREEDMAN." NEW ENGLAND MAGAZINE, N.S., 19 (JANUARY,
        1899): 609-624.

17515   BARTON, WILLIAM E. OLD PLANTATION HYMNS: A COLLECTION
        OF HITHERTO UNPUBLISHED MELODIES OF THE SLAVE AND THE
        FREEDMAN, WITH HISTORICAL AND DESCRIPTIVE NOTES.
        BOSTON: LAMSON, WOLFFE, 1899.

17516   BARTON, WILLIAM E. "OLD PLANTATION HYMNS." NEW ENGLAND
        MAGAZINE, N.S., 19 (DECEMBER, 1898): 443-465.

17517   BARTON, WILLIAM E. "RECENT NEGRO MELODIES." NEW ENGLAND
        MAGAZINE, N.S., 19 (FEBRUARY, 1899): 707-719.

17518   BASTIN, BRUCE. "BLACK MUSIC IN NORTH CAROLINA." IN
        CROW, JEFFREY J. AND WINTERS, ROBERT E., JR. (EDS.).
        THE BLACK PRESENCE IN NORTH CAROLINA. RALEIGH: NORTH
        CAROLINA MUSEUM OF HISTORY, 1978, PP. 41-52.

17519   BASTIN, BRUCE. "BLACK MUSIC IN NORTH CAROLINA." NORTH
        CAROLINA FOLKLORE JOURNAL, 27 (MAY, 1979): 3-19.

17520   BEASLEY, CECILY R. "CREOLE AND AFRO-CREOLE MUSIC OF
        LOUISIANA: ITS ORIGIN AND INFLUENCE." PH.D.
        DISSERTATION, FLORIDA STATE UNIVERSITY, 1976.

17521   BECKHAM, ALBERT S. "THE PSYCHOLOGY OF NEGRO SPIRITUALS."
        SOUTHERN WORKMAN, 60 (SEPTEMBER, 1931): 391-395.

17522   BEHAGUE, GERARD H. MUSIC IN LATIN AMERICA: AN
        INTRODUCTION. ENGLEWOOD CLIFFS: PRENTICE-HALL, 1979.

17523   BENEDICT, HELEN D. BELAIR PLANTATION MELODIES: EIGHT
        NEGRO FOLKSONGS COLLECTED FROM BELAIR PLANTATION IN
        LOUISIANA. NEW ORLEANS: HELEN D. BENEDICT, 1924.

17524 "BIBLIOGRAPHY." BLACK MUSIC RESEARCH NEWSLETTER, 3
   (SUMMER, 1979): 3-13.

17525 BIEBER, ALBERT A. THE ALBERT A. BIEBER COLLECTION OF
   AMERICAN PLAYS, POETRY AND SONGSTERS. NEW YORK:
   COOPER SQUARE, 1963.

17526 BILLUPS, KENNETH B. "THE OTHER SIDE OF BLACK MUSIC." IN
   MCCUE, GEORGE (ED.). MUSIC IN AMERICAN SOCIETY,
   1776-1976: FROM PURITAN HYMN TO SYNTHESIZER. NEW
   BRUNSWICK: TRANSACTION BOOKS, 1977, PP. 87-94.

17527 BLAUSTEIN, RICHARD. "MORE ON SLAVE FIDDLING." DEVIL'S
   BOX, 16 (FEBRUARY 15, 1972): 11-15.

17528 BLAUSTEIN, RICHARD. "MORE ON SLAVE FIDDLING."
   UNIVERSITY OF MICHIGAN FOLKLORE SOCIETY CALENDAR AND
   NEWSLETTER, 1 (1972): 5-8.

17529 BLESH, RUDI. "ANGEL GOT TWO WINGS." ARTS &
   ARCHITECTURE, 63 (APRIL, 1946): 34-35.

17530 BLUESTEIN, EUGENE. "AMERICA'S FOLK INSTRUMENT: NOTES ON
   THE FIVE STRING BANJO." WESTERN FOLKLORE, 23
   (OCTOBER, 1964): 241-248.

17531 BLUESTEIN, EUGENE. "THE BACKGROUND AND SOURCES OF AN
   AMERICAN FOLKSONG TRADITION." PH.D. DISSERTATION,
   UNIVERSITY OF MINNESOTA, 1960.

17532 BOGOMOLNY, MICHAEL. "A SOCIOLOGICAL INTERPRETATION OF
   THE NEGRO FOLK SONG." M.A. THESIS, OHIO STATE
   UNIVERSITY, 1929.

17533 BORNEMAN, ERNEST. "AFRO-CUBAN MUSIC IS NEARLY 400 YEARS
   OLD." MELODY MAKER, 28 (JULY 12, 1952): 5.

17534 BORNEMAN, ERNEST. "BLACK LIGHT AND WHITE SHADOW; NOTES
   FOR A HISTORY OF AMERICAN NEGRO MUSIC." JAZZ
   RESEARCH, 2 (1970): 24-93.

17535 BORNEMAN, ERNEST. "THE BLUES--A STUDY IN AMBIGUITY." IN
   TRAILL, SINCLAIR AND LASCELLES, GERALD (EDS.). JUST
   JAZZ, 3. LONDON: FOUR SQUARE BOOKS, 1959, PP. 75-91.

17536 BORNEMAN, ERNEST. "JAZZ AND THE CREOLE TRADITION."
   JAZZFORSCHUNG, 1 (1969): 99-112.

17537 BOURGUIGNON, ERIKA E. "SYNCRETISM AND AMBIVALENCE IN
   HAITI: AN ETHNOHISTORIC STUDY." PH.D. DISSERTATION,
   NORTHWESTERN UNIVERSITY, 1951.

17538 BOWEN, ELBERT R. "NEGRO MINSTRELS IN EARLY RURAL
   MISSOURI." MISSOURI HISTORICAL REVIEW, 47 (JANUARY,
   1953): 103-109.

17539   BOYER, CLARENCE H. "THE GOSPEL SONG: A HISTORICAL AND ANALYTICAL STUDY." M.A. THESIS, EASTMAN SCHOOL OF MUSIC, UNIVERSITY OF ROCHESTER, 1964.

17540   BOYNTON, MADGE B. "AN EVALUATION OF THE SLAVE SONGS AS A HISTORICAL SOURCE." M.A. THESIS, TEXAS WOMAN'S UNIVERSITY, 1970.

17541   BRAGG, JOHN. "A CANTOMETRIC ANALYSIS OF FOLK MUSIC IN A SEA ISLAND COMMUNITY." NORTH CAROLINA FOLKLORE JOURNAL, 26 (NOVEMBER, 1978): 157-163.

17542   BRIGHT, ALFRED L. "THE BLACK ARTIST IN COLONIAL AMERICA." IN BRIGHT; CLARK, SARAH B.; AMADI, LAWRENCE E.; COOPER, SYRETHA; BARNES, CLARENCE; AND O'NEILL, DANIEL J. AN INTERDISCIPLINARY INTRODUCTION TO BLACK STUDIES. DUBUQUE: KENDALL/HUNT PUBLISHING COMPANY, 1977, PP. 121-124.

17543   BROOKS, TILFORD. "THE BLACK MUSICIAN IN AMERICAN SOCIETY." MISSOURI JOURNAL OF RESEARCH IN MUSIC EDUCATION, 2 (1970): 18-29.

17544   BROUCEK, JACK W. "EIGHTEENTH CENTURY MUSIC IN SAVANNAH, GEORGIA." ED.D. DISSERTATION, FLORIDA STATE UNIVERSITY, 1963.

17545   BROWN, JOHN M. "SONGS OF THE SLAVE." LIPPINCOTT'S MAGAZINE, 2 (DECEMBER, 1868): 617-623.

17546   BROWN, STERLING. "SPIRITUALS." IN BONTEMPS, ARNA W. AND HUGHES, LANGSTON (EDS.). THE BOOK OF NEGRO FOLKLORE. NEW YORK: DODD, MEAD, 1958, PP. 279-288.

17547   BRYANT, MELVILLE C., JR. "DERIVATION AND DEVELOPMENT OF AMERICAN NEGRO GOSPEL SONGS." PH.D. DISSERTATION, INDIANA UNIVERSITY, 1963.

17548   BRYCE, C.A. "DUSKY 'FIDDLERS' OF OLDEN DAYS TENDERLY RECALLED. . . ." RICHMOND TIMES-DISPATCH, MAY 22, 1921.

17549   BURLIN, NATALIE C. "BLACK SINGERS AND PLAYERS." MUSICAL QUARTERLY, 5 (OCTOBER, 1919): 499-504.

17550   BURLIN, NATALIE C. "FOLK MUSIC OF AMERICA." CRAFTSMAN, 21 (JANUARY, 1912): 414-420.

17551   BURLIN, NATALIE C. NEGRO FOLK SONGS--HAMPTON SERIES, BOOKS I, II, III AND IV. NEW YORK: G. SCHIRMER, 1918-1919.

17552   BURLIN, NATALIE C. "NEGRO MUSIC AT BIRTH." MUSICAL QUARTERLY, 5 (JANUARY, 1919): 86-89.

17553   BURLIN, NATALIE C.   SONGS AND TALES FROM THE DARK
        CONTINENT. NEW YORK: G. SCHIRMER, 1921.

17554   BURNIM, MELLONEE V. "THE BLACK GOSPEL MUSIC TRADITION:
        SYMBOL OF ETHNICITY." PH.D. DISSERTATION, INDIANA
        UNIVERSITY, 1980.

17555   BURTON, WILLIAM. "THE HISTORY OF THE NEGRO SPIRITUAL AND
        ITS CONTRIBUTION TO SACRED MUSIC." M.A. THESIS, SAN
        FRANCISCO THEOLOGICAL SEMINARY, 1943.

17556   BUTCHER, MARGARET T. "THE EARLY FOLK GIFTS: MUSIC,
        DANCE, FOLKLORE." THE NEGRO IN AMERICAN CULTURE. NEW
        YORK: ALFRED A. KNOPF, 1972, PP. 40-56.

17557   BUTCHER, MARGARET T. "NEGRO MUSIC AND DANCE: FORMAL
        RECOGNITION AND RECONSTRUCTION." THE NEGRO IN
        AMERICAN CULTURE. NEW YORK: ALFRED A. KNOPF, 1972,
        PP. 57-97.

17558   CABLE, GEORGE W. "CREOLE SLAVE SONGS." CENTURY
        MAGAZINE, 31 (APRIL, 1886): 807-828.

17559   "CANNED NEGRO MELODIES." LITERARY DIGEST, 52 (MAY 27,
        1916): 1556, 1558-1559.

17560   CARAWAN, GUY AND CARAWAN, CANDIE. "JOHN'S ISLAND." SING
        OUT, 16 (1966): 25-30.

17561   CARLISLE, NATALIE T. "OLD-TIME DARKY PLANTATION
        MELODIES." PUBLICATIONS OF THE TEXAS FOLKLORE
        SOCIETY, 5 (1926): 137-143.

17562   CARRATELLO, JOHN D. "AN ECLECTIC CHORAL METHODOLOGY AND
        ITS EFFECT ON THE UNDERSTANDING, INTERPRETATION, AND
        PERFORMANCE OF BLACK SPIRITUALS." M.A. THESIS,
        CALIFORNIA STATE UNIVERSITY, FULLERTON, 1976.

17563   CARTER, ALBERT E. "THE LOUISIANA NEGRO AND HIS MUSIC."
        M.M. THESIS, NORTHWESTERN UNIVERSITY, 1947.

17564   CAVE, RODERICK. "FOUR SLAVE SONGS FROM ST. BARTHOLOMEW."
        CARIBBEAN QUARTERLY, 25 (MARCH-JUNE, 1979): 85-90.

17565   CAVIN, SUSAN. "MISSING WOMEN: ON THE VOODOO TRAIL OF
        JAZZ." JOURNAL OF JAZZ STUDIES, 3 (FALL, 1975): 4-27.

17566   CHASE, GILBERT. AMERICA'S MUSIC FROM THE PILGRIMS TO THE
        PRESENT. NEW YORK: MCGRAW-HILL, 1955.

17567   CHASE, GILBERT. "A NOTE ON NEGRO SPIRITUALS." CIVIL WAR
        HISTORY, 4 (SEPTEMBER, 1958): 261-268.

17568   CHASE, GILBERT. "SOME NOTES ON AFRO-CUBAN MUSIC AND
        DANCING." INTER-AMERICAN, 1 (DECEMBER, 1942): 32-33.

17569   CHASE, GILBERT C. "EDITOR'S OUTLOOK: AFRO-AMERICAN
        ANTHROPOLOGY AND BLACK MUSIC." YEARBOOK FOR
        INTERAMERICAN MUSICAL RESEARCH, 7 (1971): 117-124.

17570   CHEEKS, GERTRUDE D. "THE HISTORICAL BACKGROUND AND
        DEVELOPMENT OF THE NEGRO AND HIS SONGS." M.A. THESIS,
        MILLIKIN UNIVERSITY, 1949.

17571   CIMBALA, PAUL A. "FORTUNATE BONDSMEN: BLACK
        'MUSICIANERS' AND THEIR ROLE AS AN ANTEBELLUM SOUTHERN
        PLANTATION ELITE." SOUTHERN STUDIES, 18 (FALL, 1979):
        291-303.

17572   CIMBALA, PAUL A. "FORTUNATE BONDSMEN: BLACK MUSICIANERS
        IN THE ANTEBELLUM SOUTHERN UNITED STATES." M.A.
        THESIS, EMORY UNIVERSITY, 1977.

17573   CLARK, EDGAR R. "NEGRO FOLK MUSIC IN AMERICA." JOURNAL
        OF AMERICAN FOLKLORE, 64 (JULY/SEPTEMBER, 1951):
        281-287.

17574   CLARK, ROY L. "A FANTASY THEME ANALYSIS OF NEGRO
        SPIRITUALS." PH.D. DISSERTATION, SOUTHERN ILLINOIS
        UNIVERSITY, 1979.

17575   CLARKE, JOE E.L. "COMMUNAL ORIGINS OF SONG AMONG THE
        NEGROES." M.A. THESIS, WASHINGTON UNIVERSITY, 1926.

17576   CLIFFORD, CARRIE. "SORROW SONGS." CRISIS, 34 (JUNE,
        1927): 123.

17577   COAD, ORAL S. "SONGS AMERICA USED TO SING." JOURNAL OF
        THE RUTGERS UNIVERSITY LIBRARY, 31 (1968): 33-45.

17578   COGDELL, JACQUELINE. "AN ANALYTICAL STUDY OF THE
        SIMILARITIES AND DIFFERENCES IN THE AMERICAN BLACK
        SPIRITUAL AND GOSPEL SONG FROM THE SOUTHWEST REGION OF
        GEORGIA." M.A. THESIS, UNIVERSITY OF CALIFORNIA, LOS
        ANGELES, 1972.

17579   COHEN, HENNIG. "CAROLINE GILMAN AND NEGRO BOATMEN'S
        SONGS." SOUTHERN FOLKLORE QUARTERLY, 20 (JUNE, 1956):
        116-117.

17580   CONE, JAMES H. "BLACK SPIRITUALS: A THEOLOGICAL
        INTERPRETATION." THEOLOGY TODAY, 29 (APRIL, 1972):
        54-69.

17581   CONE, JAMES H. THE SPIRITUALS AND THE BLUES: AN
        INTERPRETATION. NEW YORK: SEABURY PRESS, 1972.

17582   CONLEY, DOROTHY L. "ORIGIN OF THE NEGRO SPIRITUALS."
        NEGRO HISTORY BULLETIN, 25 (MAY, 1962): 179-183.

17583   CONRAD, EARL. "GENERAL TUBMAN, COMPOSER OF SPIRITUALS,

AMAZING FIGURE IN AMERICAN FOLK MUSIC." ETUDE, 60
(MAY, 1942): 305, 344.

17584 CONWAY, EUGENIA C. "THE AFRO-AMERICAN TRADITIONS OF THE
FOLK BANJO." PH.D. DISSERTATION, UNIVERSITY OF NORTH
CAROLINA, 1980.

17585 COOMBS, JOSHUA. FOLK SONGS OF THE SOUTHERN UNITED
STATES. AUSTIN: UNIVERSITY OF TEXAS PRESS, 1967.

17586 COPPIN, L.J. "SOUL CULTURE IN SONG." A.M.E. CHURCH
REVIEW, 29 (JULY, 1912): 40-47.

17587 COURLANDER, HAROLD. HAITI SINGING. CHAPEL HILL:
UNIVERSITY OF NORTH CAROLINA PRESS, 1939.

17588 COURLANDER, HAROLD. NEGRO FOLK MUSIC, U.S.A. NEW YORK:
COLUMBIA UNIVERSITY PRESS, 1963.

17589 COURLANDER, HAROLD. "NEGRO SONGS FROM ALABAMA." WESTERN
FOLKLORE, 21 (1962): 144-145.

17590 COURLANDER, HAROLD. A TREASURY OF AFRO-AMERICAN
FOLKLORE. NEW YORK: CROWN PUBLISHERS, 1976.

17591 COUTINHO, J. DE SIQUEIRA. "BRAZILIAN MUSIC AND
MUSICIANS." BULLETIN OF THE PAN AMERICAN UNION, 54
(NOVEMBER, 1930): 1119-1125.

17592 COWELL, HENRY. "THE SONGS OF CUBA." MODERN MUSIC, 8
(1931): 45-47.

17593 CRAY, ED. "AN ACCULTURATIVE CONTINUUM FOR NEGRO FOLK
SONG IN THE UNITED STATES." ETHNOMUSICOLOGY, 5
(JANUARY, 1961): 10-15.

17594 CREED, RUTH. "AFRICAN INFLUENCE ON LATIN AMERICAN
MUSIC." M.M. THESIS, NORTHWESTERN UNIVERSITY, 1947.

17595 CRESSWELL, NICHOLAS. JOURNAL OF NICHOLAS CRESSWELL,
1774-1777. NEW YORK: L. MACVEAGH, DIAL PRESS, 1924.

17596 CUNEY-HARE, MAUD. "HISTORY AND SONG IN THE VIRGIN
ISLANDS." CRISIS, 40 (APRIL, 1933): 83-84, 108, 118.

17597 CUNEY-HARE, MAUD. NEGRO MUSICIANS AND THEIR MUSIC.
WASHINGTON: ASSOCIATED PUBLISHERS, 1936.

17598 CURTIS, NATALIE. "THE NEGRO'S CONTRIBUTION TO THE MUSIC
OF AMERICA: THE LARGER OPPORTUNITY OF THE COLORED MAN
OF TODAY." CRAFTSMAN, 23 (1913): 660-669.

17599 DAVIS, HENDERSON S. "THE RELIGIOUS EXPERIENCE UNDERLYING
THE NEGRO SPIRITUAL." PH.D. DISSERTATION, BOSTON
UNIVERSITY, 1950.

17600   DAVIS, MARTHA E. "AFRO-DOMINICAN RELIGIOUS BROTHERHOODS:
        STRUCTURE, RITUAL, AND MUSIC." PH.D. DISSERTATION,
        UNIVERSITY OF ILLINOIS, 1976.

17601   DE LERMA, DOMINIQUE-RENE. THE BLACK-AMERICAN MUSICAL
        HERITAGE: A PRELIMINARY BIBLIOGRAPHY. N.P.: MUSIC
        LIBRARY ASSOCIATION, 1969.

17602   DE LERMA, DOMINIQUE-RENE (ED.). REFLECTIONS ON
        AFRO-AMERICAN MUSIC. KENT: KENT STATE UNIVERSITY
        PRESS, 1973.

17603   DETT, ROBERT N. RELIGIOUS FOLK-SONGS OF THE NEGRO AS
        SUNG AT HAMPTON INSTITUTE. HAMPTON, VA: HAMPTON
        INSTITUTE PRESS, 1927.

17604   DOUGLASS, FREDERICK. "THE NEGRO IN AMERICA, HIS LIFE &
        TIMES; BLUES 1860? AS A SLAVE SAW IT (WRITTEN IN
        1845)." BLUES, NO. 64 (JULY, 1969): 7-8.

17605   DOWER, CATHERINE A. "THE AFRO-CARIBBEAN MUSICAL LEGACY,
        PART ONE: THE MUSIC OF PUERTO RICO." MUSART, 26
        (SPRING, 1974): 52-56.

17606   DUBOIS, W.E.B. THE GIFT OF BLACK FOLK: THE NEGROES IN
        THE MAKING OF AMERICA. BOSTON: STRAFFORD, 1924.

17607   DUBOIS, W.E.B. "THE NEGRO IN LITERATURE AND ART."
        ANNALS OF THE AMERICAN ACADEMY OF POLITICAL AND SOCIAL
        SCIENCE, 49 (SEPTEMBER, 1913): 233-238.

17608   DUBOIS, W.E.B. THE SOULS OF BLACK FOLK: ESSAYS AND
        SKETCHES. CHICAGO: A.C. MCCLURG & COMPANY, 1903.

17609   DUNCAN, JOHN. "NEGRO SPIRITUALS--ONCE MORE." NEGRO
        HISTORY BULLETIN, 10 (JANUARY, 1947): 80-82, 95.

17610   DUNDES, ALAN (ED.). MOTHER WIT FROM THE LAUGHING BARREL:
        READINGS IN THE INTERPRETATION OF AFRO-AMERICAN
        FOLKLORE. ENGLEWOOD CLIFFS: PRENTICE-HALL, 1973.

17611   DVORAK, ANTON. "MUSIC IN AMERICA." HARPER'S NEW MONTHLY
        MAGAZINE, 90 (FEBRUARY, 1895): 428-434.

17612   EAKLOR, VICKI L. "MUSIC IN THE AMERICAN ANTISLAVERY
        MOVEMENT, 1830-1860." M.A. THESIS, WASHINGTON
        UNIVERSITY, 1979.

17613   EAKLOR, VICKI L. "THE SONGS OF THE EMANCIPATION CAR:
        VARIATIONS ON AN ABOLITIONIST THEME." BULLETIN OF THE
        MISSOURI HISTORICAL SOCIETY, 36 (JANUARY, 1980):
        92-102.

17614   EDET, EDNA M. "BLACK PROTEST MUSIC." AFRO-AMERICAN
        STUDIES, 2 (SEPTEMBER, 1971): 107-116.

17615 EDET, EDNA M. (ED.). THE GRIOT SINGS: SONGS FROM THE
       BLACK WORLD. BROOKLYN: MEDGAR EVERS COLLEGE PRESS,
       1979.

17616 EDET, EDNA M. "ONE HUNDRED YEARS OF BLACK PROTEST
       MUSIC." BLACK SCHOLAR, 7 (JULY-AUGUST, 1976): 38-48.

17617 EKWUEME, LAZARUS E.N. "THE AFRICAN HERITAGE IN AMERICAN
       MUSIC." IN WINKS, ROBIN W. (ED.). OTHER VOICES,
       OTHER VIEWS: AN INTERNATIONAL COLLECTION OF ESSAYS
       FROM THE BICENTENNIAL. WESTPORT: GREENWOOD PRESS,
       1978, PP. 376-392.

17618 EKWUEME, LAZARUS E.N. "AFRICAN-MUSIC RETENTIONS IN THE
       NEW WORLD." BLACK PERSPECTIVE IN MUSIC, 2 (FALL,
       1974): 128-144.

17619 EKWUEME, LAZARUS E.N. "AFRICAN SOURCES IN NEW WORLD
       BLACK MUSIC." BLACK IMAGES, 1 (AUTUMN, WINTER, 1972):
       3-11.

17620 ELDER, J.D. "COLOR, MUSIC, AND CONFLICT: A STUDY OF
       AGGRESSION IN TRINIDAD WITH REFERENCE TO THE ROLE OF
       TRADITIONAL MUSIC." ETHNOMUSICOLOGY, 8 (MAY, 1964):
       128-136.

17621 ELDER, JACOB D. "EVOLUTION OF THE TRADITIONAL CALYPSO OF
       TRINIDAD AND TOBAGO: A SOCIO-HISTORICAL ANALYSIS OF
       CHANGE IN A NEGRO POPULAR FOLKSONG." PH.D.
       DISSERTATION, UNIVERSITY OF PENNSYLVANIA, 1967.

17622 "EMANCIPATED SLAVES." GLOBE, MAY 7, 1873.

17623 ENGEL, CARL. AN INTRODUCTION TO THE STUDY OF NATIONAL
       MUSIC. LONDON: LONGMANS, GREEN, READER, AND DYER,
       1866.

17624 EPSTEIN, DENA J. "AFRICAN MUSIC IN BRITISH AND FRENCH
       AMERICA." MUSICAL QUARTERLY, 59 (JANUARY, 1973):
       61-91.

17625 EPSTEIN, DENA J. "DOCUMENTING THE HISTORY OF BLACK FOLK
       MUSIC IN THE UNITED STATES: A LIBRARIAN'S ODYSSEY."
       FONTE ARTIS MUSICAE, 23 (OCTOBER/DECEMBER, 1976):
       151-157.

17626 EPSTEIN, DENA J. "THE FOLK BANJO: A DOCUMENTARY
       HISTORY." ETHNOMUSICOLOGY, 19 (SEPTEMBER, 1975):
       347-371.

17627 EPSTEIN, DENA J. "THE LIBRARIAN AS DETECTIVE: THE
       SEARCH FOR BLACK MUSIC'S AFRICAN ROOTS." UNIVERSITY
       OF CHICAGO MAGAZINE, 66 (JULY/AUGUST, 1973): 18-24.

17628 EPSTEIN, DENA J. SINFUL TUNES AND SPIRITUALS: BLACK

FOLK MUSIC TO THE CIVIL WAR. URBANA: UNIVERSITY OF
ILLINOIS PRESS, 1977.

17629 EPSTEIN, DENA J. "SLAVE MUSIC IN THE UNITED STATES
BEFORE 1860: A SURVEY OF SOURCES." MUSIC LIBRARY
ASSOCIATION NOTES, 20 (SPRING, SUMMER, 1963):
195-212, 377-390.

17630 EVANS, ARTHUR L. "THE DEVELOPMENT OF THE NEGRO SPIRITUAL
AS CHORAL ART MUSIC BY AFRO-AMERICAN COMPOSERS WITH AN
ANNOTATED GUIDE TO THE PERFORMANCE OF SELECTED
SPIRITUALS." CHORAL JOURNAL, 15 (1974): 16-17.

17631 EVANS, DAVID. "AFRO-AMERICAN ONE-STRINGED INSTRUMENTS."
WESTERN FOLKLORE, 29 (OCTOBER, 1970): 229-245.

17632 EVANS, DAVID H. "AFRICA AND THE BLUES." LIVING BLUES,
NO. 10 (AUTUMN, 1972): 27-29.

17633 EVANS, DAVID H. "THE ROOTS OF AFRO-AMERICAN GOSPEL
MUSIC." JAZZ RESEARCH, 8 (1976): 119-135.

17634 EVANS, DAVID H. "TRADITION AND CREATIVITY IN THE FOLK
BLUES." PH.D. DISSERTATION, UNIVERSITY OF CALIFORNIA,
LOS ANGELES, 1976.

17635 EVANS, MARGUERITE. "SLAVERY'S LAMENT LEAVENS AMERICA'S
SONG." M.M. THESIS, WESTMINSTER CHOIR COLLEGE, 1943.

17636 FENNER, T.P. RELIGIOUS FOLK-SONGS OF THE AMERICAN NEGRO.
HAMPTON: HAMPTON INSTITUTE PRESS, 1924.

17637 FENNER, THOMAS P. CABIN AND PLANTATION SONGS AS SUNG BY
THE HAMPTON STUDENTS. NEW YORK: G.P. PUTNAM, 1877.

17638 FERRIS, WILLIAM. BLUES FROM THE DELTA. GARDEN CITY:
ANCHOR PRESS/DOUBLEDAY, 1978.

17639 FIELD, CHRISTOPHER D.S. "MUSICAL OBSERVATIONS FROM
BARBADOS, 1647-1650." MUSICAL TIMES, 115 (JULY,
1974): 565.

17640 FINCK, JULIA N. "MAMMY'S SONG: A NEGRO MELODY." MUSIC,
13 (MARCH, 1898): 604-605.

17641 FISHER, MILES M. "THE EVOLUTION OF SLAVE SONGS IN THE
UNITED STATES." PH.D. DISSERTATION, UNIVERSITY OF
CHICAGO, 1949.

17642 FISHER, MILES M. NEGRO SLAVE SONGS IN THE UNITED STATES.
ITHACA: CORNELL UNIVERSITY PRESS, 1953.

17643 FORBES, GEORGE W. "AFRO-AMERICAN FOLK-SONGS ONLY BASIS
FOR A NATIONAL MUSIC." A.M.E. CHURCH REVIEW, 31
(JULY, 1914): 85-87.

17644 FOSTER, WILLIAM P. "THE INFLUENCE OF THE NEGRO ON MUSIC
       IN AMERICA." M.A. THESIS, WAYNE STATE UNIVERSITY,
       1950.

17645 FRANCA, EURICO N. "THE NEGRO IN BRAZILIAN MUSIC."
       AFROBEAT, 1 (MAY, 1967): 6-7, 11.

17646 FRANKLIN, H. BRUCE. "SONGS OF AN IMPRISONED PEOPLE."
       MELUS, 6 (SPRING, 1979): 6-22.

17647 FRANKLIN, M. THERESA. "GOD'S VELVET SHADOWS: MODERN
       DANCE COMPOSITION AND STUDY OF THE NEGRO SPIRITUAL."
       M.A. THESIS, NEW YORK UNIVERSITY, 1966.

17648 GABER, DEBORAH R. "NEGRO SPIRITUALS AND RECENT BLACK
       SOUL MUSIC: A COMPARATIVE STUDY." M.A. THESIS,
       INDIANA UNIVERSITY, 1972.

17649 GARRETT, ROMEO B. "AFRICAN SURVIVALS IN AMERICAN
       CULTURE." JOURNAL OF NEGRO HISTORY, 51 (OCTOBER,
       1966): 239-245.

17650 GAUL, HARVEY. "NEGRO SPIRITUALS." CHURCH MUSIC REVIEW,
       17 (APRIL, 1918): 147-151.

17651 GELLERT, LAWRENCE. "NEGRO SONGS OF PROTEST." IN CUNARD,
       NANCY (ED.). NEGRO ANTHOLOGY. LONDON: WISHART,
       1934, PP. 366-377.

17652 GEORGE, ZELMA. "A GUIDE TO NEGRO MUSIC; AN ANNOTATED
       BIBLIOGRAPHY OF NEGRO FOLK MUSIC, AND ART MUSIC BY
       NEGRO COMPOSERS OR BASED ON NEGRO THEMATIC MATERIAL."
       ED.D. DISSERTATION, NEW YORK UNIVERSITY, 1953.

17653 GEORGE, ZELMA. "NEGRO MUSIC IN AMERICAN LIFE." IN
       DAVIS, JOHN P. (ED.). THE AMERICAN NEGRO REFERENCE
       BOOK. ENGLEWOOD CLIFFS: PRENTICE-HALL, 1966, PP.
       731-758.

17654 GILLIS, FRANK AND MERRIAM, ALAN P. ETHNOMUSICOLOGY AND
       FOLK MUSIC: AN INTERNATIONAL BIBLIOGRAPHY OF
       DISSERTATIONS AND THESES. MIDDLETOWN, CT: WESLEYAN
       UNIVERSITY PRESS, 1966.

17655 GLAZER, IRVING W. "NEGRO MUSIC IN EARLY AMERICA, FROM
       1619 TO THE CIVIL WAR." M.A. THESIS, NEW YORK
       UNIVERSITY, 1945.

17656 GOINES, LEONARD. "THE AFRICAN IN THE AMERICAS."
       ALLEGRO, 70 (JUNE, 1971): 4, 29.

17657 GOINES, LEONARD. "AFRO-AMERICAN MUSIC." ALLEGRO, 70
       (APRIL, 1971): 14, 19.

17658 GOINES, LEONARD. "AFRO-AMERICAN MUSIC: THE SPIRITUAL."

ALLEGRO, 70 (AUGUST, 1971): 4, 15.

17659 GOINES, LEONARD. "BLACK MUSIC OF LATIN AMERICA AND THE
       CARIBBEAN." IN SHAPIRO, LINN (ED.). BLACK PEOPLE AND
       THEIR CULTURE: SELECTED WRITINGS FROM THE AFRICAN
       DIASPORA. WASHINGTON: SMITHSONIAN INSTITUTION, 1976,
       PP. 88-98.

17660 GOINES, LEONARD. "EARLY AFRO-AMERICAN MUSIC IN THE
       UNITED STATES—SACRED AND SECULAR." ALLEGRO, 70
       (JULY, 1971): 11, 15.

17661 GOINES, LEONARD. "SLAVE NARRATIVES." ALLEGRO, 73
       (DECEMBER, 1973): 4; 74 (JANUARY, 1974): 4.

17662 GOINES, LEONARD. "'WALK OVER': MUSIC IN THE SLAVE
       NARRATIVES." SING-OUT, 24 (JANUARY-FEBRUARY, 1976):
       6-11.

17663 GOODRICH, W.H. "SLAVE SONGS." AMERICAN MISSIONARY
       MAGAZINE, 16 (JANUARY, 1872): 19-20.

17664 GORDON, R.W. "PALMETTOS FOLKSONGS OF GEORGIA NEGROES."
       GOLDEN BOOK MAGAZINE, 9 (MAY, 1929): 76-77.

17665 GORDON, ROBERT W. "FOLK SONGS OF AMERICA: NEGRO
       'SHOUTS.'" NEW YORK TIMES MAGAZINE, (APRIL 24, 1927):
       4, 22.

17666 GRAHAM, ALICE. "ORIGINAL PLANTATION MELODIES AS ONE
       RARELY HEARS THEM." ETUDE, 40 (1922): 744.

17667 GREENE, BARBARA J. "AFRICAN MUSICAL SURVIVALS IN THE
       SONGS OF THE NEGRO IN HAITI, JAMAICA AND THE UNITED
       STATES." M.A. THESIS, UNIVERSITY OF CHICAGO, 1948.

17668 GREENWAY, JOHN. "AMERICAN FOLKSONGS OF SOCIAL AND
       ECONOMIC PROTEST." PH.D. DISSERTATION, UNIVERSITY OF
       PENNSYLVANIA, 1951.

17669 GREENWAY, JOHN. "NEGRO SONGS OF PROTEST." AMERICAN
       FOLKSONGS OF PROTEST. PHILADELPHIA: UNIVERSITY OF
       PENNSYLVANIA PRESS, 1953, PP. 67-120.

17670 GRIFFIN, GEORGE H. "THE SLAVE MUSIC OF THE SOUTH."
       AMERICAN MISSIONARY, 36 (MARCH, 1882): 70-72.

17671 GRIFFITH, BENJAMIN W. "A LONGER VERSION OF 'GUINEA NEGRO
       SONG': FROM A GEORGIA FRONTIER SONGSTER." SOUTHERN
       FOLKLORE QUARTERLY, 28 (1964): 116-118.

17672 GROVER, CARRIE B. A HERITAGE OF SONGS. NORWOOD, PA:
       NORWOOD EDITIONS, 1973.

17673 GUZMAN, PABLO. "BLACK MUSIC: AMERICAN MUSIC; FROM THE

SLAVE SHIP TO THE WORLD." VILLAGE VOICE, 24 (APRIL 16, 1979): 61-62.

17674 H.G.S. "MISCELLANEOUS." CHRISTIAN EXAMINER, N.S., 5 (JANUARY, 1868): 121-122.

17675 H., N. "NEGROES AND NEGRO MELODIES: THE REAL NEGRO MUSIC IS TO BE FOUND AT A CAMP MEETING OR REVIVAL." AMERICAN ART JOURNAL, 62 (MARCH 24, 1894): 477-478.

17676 HADEL, RICHARD. "BLACK CARIB FOLK MUSIC." CARIBBEAN QUARTERLY, 22 (JUNE/SEPTEMBER, 1976): 84-96.

17677 HALL, FREDERICK. "THE NEGRO SPIRITUAL." LITERARY DIGEST, 98 (SEPTEMBER 22, 1928): 34.

17678 HALL, FREDERICK. "THE NEGRO SPIRITUAL." MIDWEST JOURNAL, 1 (SUMMER, 1949): 27-32.

17679 HALLOWELL, EMILY. CALHOUN PLANTATION SONGS. BOSTON: C.W. THOMPSON, 1901.

17680 HAMMOND, STELLA L. "CONTRIBUTION OF THE AMERICAN INDIAN AND THE NEGRO TO THE FOLK MUSIC OF AMERICA." M.A. THESIS, WAYNE STATE UNIVERSITY, 1936.

17681 HANDLER, JEROME S. AND FRISBIE, CHARLOTTE J. "ASPECTS OF SLAVE LIFE IN BARBADOS: MUSIC AND ITS CULTURAL CONTEXT." CARIBBEAN STUDIES, 11 (JANUARY, 1972): 5-46.

17682 HARDEE, CHARLES S.H. "REMINISCENCES OF CHARLES SETON HENRY HARDEE." GEORGIA HISTORICAL QUARTERLY, 12 (JUNE, 1928): 158-176.

17683 HARE, MAUD C. NEGRO MUSICIANS AND THEIR MUSIC. WASHINGTON: ASSOCIATED PUBLISHERS, 1936.

17684 HARRISON, R.C. "THE NEGRO AS INTERPRETER OF HIS OWN FOLK-SONGS." PUBLICATIONS OF THE TEXAS FOLKLORE SOCIETY, 5 (1926): 144-153.

17685 HARSHAW, D.A. "PHILOSOPHY OF THE NEGRO SPIRITUAL." HOMILETIC REVIEW, 95 (MARCH, 1928): 184-186.

17686 HASKELL, MARION A. "NEGRO SPIRITUALS." CENTURY MAGAZINE, 58 (AUGUST, 1899): 577-581.

17687 HASLAM, GERALD W. "BLACK AND UNKNOWN BARDS: AMERICAN SLAVERY AND ITS LITERARY TRADITION." ETC: A REVIEW OF GENERAL SEMANTICS, 25 (DECEMBER, 1968): 411-419.

17688 HATCHETT, HILLIARY R. "A STUDY OF CURRENT ATTITUDES TOWARD THE NEGRO SPIRITUAL WITH A CLASSIFICATION OF 500 SPIRITUALS BASED ON THEIR RELIGIOUS CONTENT."

M.A. THESIS, OHIO STATE UNIVERSITY, 1946.

17689 HEAPS, WILLARD A. AND HEAPS, PORTER W. "THE NEGRO AND
THE CONTRABAND." IN THE SINGING SIXTIES: THE SPIRIT
OF CIVIL WAR DAYS FROM THE MUSIC OF THE TIMES.
NORMAN: UNIVERSITY OF OKLAHOMA PRESS, 1960, PP.
268-294.

17690 HENTOFF, NAT. "FILLING HOLES IN THE SOUL; NEGRO MUSIC."
REPORTER, 32 (MARCH, 1965): 44.

17691 HERREID, HENRY B. "FOLK MUSIC IN THE UNITED STATES."
M.A. THESIS, UNIVERSITY OF WISCONSIN, 1938.

17692 HERSKOVITS, MELVILLE J. "DRUMS AND DRUMMERS IN
AFRO-BRAZILIAN CULT LIFE." MUSICAL QUARTERLY, 30
(OCTOBER, 1944): 477-492.

17693 HEYWARD, JANIE S. SONGS OF THE CHARLESTON DARKEY.
CHARLESTON: N.P., 1912.

17694 HIGGINSON, T.W. "NEGRO SPIRITUALS." ATLANTIC MONTHLY,
19 (JUNE, 1867): 685-694.

17695 HIGGINSON, THOMAS W. ARMY LIFE IN A BLACK REGIMENT.
BOSTON: FIELDS, OSGOOD, 1870.

17696 HIGGINSON, THOMAS W. "DRUMMER BOYS IN A BLACK REGIMENT."
YOUTH'S COMPANION, 61 (SEPTEMBER 27, 1888): 465.

17697 HILARIAN, MARY. "NEGRO SPIRITUAL." CATHOLIC WORLD, 143
(APRIL, 1939): 80-84.

17698 HINES, JAMES R. "MUSICAL ACTIVITY IN NORFOLK, VIRGINIA,
1680-1973." PH.D. DISSERTATION, UNIVERSITY OF NORTH
CAROLINA, 1974.

17699 "HISTORIAN FINDS THE PAST HIDDEN IN BLACK SONGS."
CHRISTIAN SCIENCE MONITOR, 70 (JANUARY 19, 1978): 12.

17700 HOPPER, LOUIS S. "THE AFRO-AMERICAN FOLK SONG, ITS
ORIGIN AND EVOLUTION." AMERICAN MUSICIAN, 2 (MARCH,
1921): 11-12. 20.

17701 HORNBOSTEL, ERICH M.V. "AMERICAN NEGRO SONGS."
INTERNATIONAL REVIEW OF MISSIONS, 15 (OCTOBER, 1926):
748-753.

17702 HOWARD, JOSEPH H. DRUMS IN THE AMERICAS. NEW YORK: OAK
PUBLICATIONS, 1967.

17703 HOWE, M.A. DEWOLFE. "THE SONG OF CHARLESTON." ATLANTIC
MONTHLY, 146 (JULY, 1930): 108-111.

17704 HOWE, R. WILSON. "THE NEGRO AND HIS SONGS." SOUTHERN

WORKMAN, 51 (AUGUST, 1922): 381-383.

17705   HULEN, RICHARD. "FIDDLING AMONG THE SLAVES IN
        LOUISIANA." DEVIL'S BOX, 9 (JULY 4, 1969): 14.

17706   HURSTON, ZORA N. "DANCE SONGS AND TALES FROM THE
        BAHAMAS." JOURNAL OF AMERICAN FOLKLORE, 43
        (JULY-OCTOBER, 1930): 294-312.

17707   HURSTON, ZORA N. "SPIRITUALS AND NEO-SPIRITUALS." IN
        PATTERSON, LINDSAY (ED.). THE NEGRO IN MUSIC AND ART.
        NEW YORK: PUBLISHERS COMPANY, 1967, PP. 15-17.

17708   "THE HYMNODY OF THE BLACKS." INDEPENDENT, 19 (NOVEMBER
        28, 1867): 2.

17709   JACKSON, EILEEN S. "THE USE OF NEGRO FOLK SONG IN
        SYMPHONIC FORMS." M.A. THESIS, UNIVERSITY OF CHICAGO,
        1941.

17710   JACKSON, GEORGE P. "THE GENESIS OF THE NEGRO SPIRITUAL."
        AMERICAN MISSIONARY, 26 (JUNE, 1932): 243-248.

17711   JACKSON, GEORGE P. "SPIRITUALS." IN BLOM, ERIC (ED.).
        GROVE'S DICTIONARY OF MUSIC AND MUSICIANS. 9 VOLS.
        LONDON: MACMILLAN, 1954, VOL. 8, PP. 8-12.

17712   JACKSON, GEORGE P. WHITE AND NEGRO SPIRITUALS, THEIR
        LIFE SPAN AND KINSHIP, TRACING 200 YEARS OF
        UNTRAMMELED SONG MAKING AND SINGING AMONG OUR COUNTRY
        FOLK. NEW YORK: J.J. AUGUSTIN PUBLISHER, 1943.

17713   JACKSON, GEORGE P. WHITE SPIRITUALS IN THE SOUTHERN
        UPLANDS: THE STORY OF THE FASOLA FOLK, THEIR SONGS,
        SINGINGS, AND "BUCKWHEAT NOTES." CHAPEL HILL:
        UNIVERSITY OF NORTH CAROLINA PRESS, 1933.

17714   JACKSON, IRENE V. "BLACK WOMEN AND AFRO-AMERICAN SONG
        TRADITION." SING OUT, 25 (1976): 10-13.

17715   JACKSON, IRENE V. "BLACK WOMEN AND MUSIC: A SURVEY FROM
        AFRICA TO THE NEW WORLD." MINORITY VOICES, 2 (FALL,
        1978): 15-28.

17716   JACKSON, IRENE V. "MUSIC AMONG BLACKS IN THE EPISCOPAL
        CHURCH: SOME PRELIMINARY CONSIDERATIONS." HISTORICAL
        MAGAZINE OF THE PROTESTANT EPISCOPAL CHURCH, 49
        (MARCH, 1980): 21-36.

17717   JACKSON, IRENE V. "SACRED MUSIC OF THE AFRO-AMERICAN
        HERITAGE." AMERICAN ORGANIST, 13 (1979): 16-17.

17718   JACKSON-BROWN, IRENE V. "AFRO-AMERICAN SACRED SONG IN
        THE NINETEENTH CENTURY: A SURVEY OF A NEGLECTED
        SOURCE." BLACK PERSPECTIVE IN MUSIC, 4 (SPRING,

1976): 22-38.

17719 JAHN, JANHEINZ. MUNTU: AN OUTLINE OF THE NEW AFRICAN
       CULTURE. NEW YORK: GROVE PRESS, 1961.

17720 JEKYLL, WALTER. JAMAICAN SONG AND STORY: ANNANCY
       STORIES, DIGGING SONGS, RING TUNES AND DANCING TUNES.
       LONDON: D. NORTH, 1907.

17721 JENKINS, MILDRED L. "THE IMPACT OF AFRICAN MUSIC UPON
       THE WESTERN HEMISPHERE." M.A. THESIS, BOSTON
       UNIVERSITY, 1942.

17722 JENKS, F.H. "NEGRO MUSIC OF THE UNITED STATES." IN
       COLLES, H.C. (ED.). GROVE'S DICTIONARY OF MUSIC AND
       MUSICIANS. 5 VOLS. NEW YORK: MACMILLAN COMPANY,
       1927, VOL. 3, PP. 611-613.

17723 JERVEY, HUGER W. "NEGRO MUSIC." IN HENNEMAN, JOHN B.
       (ED.). THE SOUTH IN THE BUILDING OF THE NATION. 12
       VOLS. RICHMOND: SOUTHERN HISTORICAL PUBLICATION
       SOCIETY, 1909, VOL. 7, PP. 392-395.

17724 JESSUP, LYNN E. "AFRICAN CHARACTERISTICS FOUND IN
       AFRO-AMERICAN AND ANGLO-AMERICAN MUSIC." M.A. THESIS,
       UNIVERSITY OF WASHINGTON, 1971.

17725 JOHNSON, GUY B. "NEGRO FOLK-SONGS." IN COUCH, W.T.
       (ED.). CULTURE IN THE SOUTH. CHAPEL HILL:
       UNIVERSITY OF NORTH CAROLINA PRESS, 1934, PP. 547-569.

17726 JOHNSON, GUY B. "THE NEGRO SPIRITUAL: A PROBLEM IN
       ANTHROPOLOGY." AMERICAN ANTHROPOLOGIST, 33
       (APRIL-JUNE, 1931): 157-171.

17727 JOHNSON, GUY B. "RECENT CONTRIBUTIONS TO THE STUDY OF
       AMERICAN NEGRO SONGS." SOCIAL FORCES, 4 (JUNE, 1926):
       788-792.

17728 JOHNSON, JAMES K. "THE NEGRO SPIRITUAL, ITS FORM AND ITS
       USES IN WORSHIP." M.S.M. THESIS, UNION THEOLOGICAL
       SEMINARY, 1968.

17729 JOHNSON, JAMES W. THE BOOK OF AMERICAN NEGRO SPIRITUALS.
       NEW YORK: VIKING PRESS, 1925.

17730 JOHNSON, JAMES W. "NEGRO FOLK SONGS AND SPIRITUALS."
       MENTOR, 17 (FEBRUARY, 1929): 50-52.

17731 JOHNSON, JAMES W. THE SECOND BOOK OF NEGRO SPIRITUALS.
       NEW YORK: VIKING PRESS, 1926.

17732 JOHNSTON, THOMAS F. "MUSIC AND BLACKS IN EIGHTEENTH AND
       NINETEENTH CENTURY CANADA." ANTHROPOLOGICAL JOURNAL
       OF CANADA, 18 (1980): 19-21.

17733   JONES, BESSIE AND HAWES, BESS L. STEP IT DOWN: GAMES,
        PLAYS, SONGS, AND STORIES FROM THE AFRO-AMERICAN
        HERITAGE. NEW YORK: HARPER & ROW, 1972.

17734   JONES, GERTRUDE M. OLD MAMMY'S LULLABY SONGS, WITH AN
        INSTRUMENTAL MEDLEY. PHILADELPHIA: PEPPER PUBLISHING
        COMPANY, 1901.

17735   JONES, LEROI. BLUES PEOPLE: THE NEGRO EXPERIENCE IN
        AMERICA AND THE MUSIC THAT DEVELOPED FROM IT. NEW
        YORK: MORROW, 1963.

17736   JONES, SOLOMON AND TANNER, PAUL. "AFRO-AMERICAN MUSIC:
        BLACK MOANS." MUSIC JOURNAL, 28 (MARCH, 1970): 36-37.

17737   JOYNER, CHARLES W. FOLK SONG IN SOUTH CAROLINA.
        COLUMBIA: UNIVERSITY OF SOUTH CAROLINA PRESS, 1971.

17738   JUBILEE AND PLANTATION SONGS. BOSTON: DITSON, 1887.

17739   JULES-ROSETTE, BENNETTA. "CREATIVE SPIRITUALITY FROM
        AFRICA TO AMERICA: CROSS-CULTURAL INFLUENCES IN
        CONTEMPORARY RELIGIOUS FORMS." WESTERN JOURNAL OF
        BLACK STUDIES, 4 (WINTER, 1980): 273-285.

17740   KAATRUD, PAUL G. "REVIVALISM AND THE POPULAR SPIRITUAL
        SONGS IN MID-NINETEENTH-CENTURY AMERICA: 1830-1870."
        PH.D. DISSERTATION, UNIVERSITY OF MINNESOTA, 1977.

17741   KATZ, BERNARD (ED.). THE SOCIAL IMPLICATIONS OF EARLY
        NEGRO MUSIC IN THE UNITED STATES. NEW YORK: ARNO
        PRESS, 1969.

17742   KATZ, BERNARD. "SONGS THAT WILL NOT DIE." NEGRO
        QUARTERLY, 1 (FALL, 1942): 283-288.

17743   KAUFMAN, FREDRICH. THE AFRICAN ROOTS OF JAZZ. SHERMAN
        OAKS, CA: ALFRED PUBLISHING COMPANY, 1979.

17744   KENNEDY, ROBERT E. MELLOWS, A CHRONICLE OF UNKNOWN
        SINGERS. NEW YORK: A. AND C. BONI, 1925.

17745   KENSCELLA, HAZEL G. "SONGS OF THE AMERICAN NEGRO AND
        THEIR INFLUENCE UPON COMPOSED MUSIC." M.A. THESIS,
        COLUMBIA UNIVERSITY, 1934.

17746   KERR, THOMAS H. "A CRITICAL SURVEY OF PRINTED VOCAL
        ARRANGEMENTS OF AFRO-AMERICAN RELIGIOUS FOLK SONGS."
        M.M. THESIS, EASTMAN SCHOOL OF MUSIC, UNIVERSITY OF
        ROCHESTER, 1939.

17747   KINNEY, ESI S. "AFRICANISMS IN MUSIC AND DANCE OF THE
        AMERICAS." IN GOLDSTEIN, RHODA L. (ED.). BLACK LIFE
        AND CULTURE IN THE UNITED STATES. NEW YORK: THOMAS
        Y. CROWELL, 1971, PP. 49-63.

17748   KINSCELLA, HAZEL G. "SONGS OF THE AMERICAN NEGRO AND
         THEIR INFLUENCE UPON COMPOSED MUSIC." M.A. THESIS,
         COLUMBIA UNIVERSITY, 1934.

17749   KMEN, HENRY A. MUSIC IN NEW ORLEANS: THE FORMATIVE
         YEARS, 1791-1841. BATON ROUGE: LOUISIANA STATE
         UNIVERSITY PRESS, 1966.

17750   KMEN, HENRY A. "OLD CORN MEAL: A FORGOTTEN URBAN NEGRO
         FOLKSINGER." JOURNAL OF AMERICAN FOLKLORE, 75
         (JANUARY-MARCH, 1962): 29-34.

17751   KMEN, HENRY A. "THE ROOTS OF JAZZ AND THE DANCE IN PLACE
         CONGO: A REAPPRAISAL." YEARBOOK FOR INTERAMERICAN
         MUSICAL RESEARCH, 8 (1972): 5-16.

17752   KMEN, HENRY A. "SINGING AND DANCING IN NEW ORLEANS--A
         SOCIAL HISTORY OF THE BIRTH AND GROWTH OF BALLS AND
         OPERA, 1791-1841." PH.D. DISSERTATION, TULANE
         UNIVERSITY, 1961.

17753   KOFSKY, FRANK. "AFRO-AMERICAN INNOVATION AND THE FOLK
         TRADITION IN JAZZ: THEIR HISTORICAL SIGNIFICANCE."
         JOURNAL OF ETHNIC STUDIES, 7 (SPRING, 1979): 1-12.

17754   KREHBIEL, HENRY E. AFRO-AMERICAN FOLKSONGS: A STUDY IN
         RACIAL AND NATIONAL MUSIC. NEW YORK: G. SCHIRMER,
         1914.

17755   KREHBIEL, HENRY E. "FOLK MUSIC STUDIES: SLAVE SONGS IN
         AMERICA." NEW YORK TRIBUNE, SEPTEMBER 10, 17, 1899.

17756   LANDECK, BEATRICE. ECHOES OF AFRICA IN FOLK SONGS OF THE
         AMERICAS. NEW YORK: D. MCKAY COMPANY, 1961.

17757   LAUBENSTEIN, PAUL F. "RACE VALUES IN AFRAMERICAN MUSIC."
         MUSICAL QUARTERLY, 16 (JULY, 1930): 378-403.

17758   LEE, AMY. "BLACK MUSIC STUDY TRACES ORIGIN OF
         SPIRITUALS." EDUCATOR, 8 (1976): 10.

17759   LEE, ROBERT C. "THE AFRO-AMERICAN FOUNDATIONS OF THE
         JAZZ IDIOM." JAZZ FORUM, NO. 16 (MARCH-APRIL, 1972):
         74-77.

17760   LEHMANN, THEO. NEGRO SPIRITUALS: GESCHICHTE UND
         THEOLOGIE. BERLIN: ECKART-VERLAG, 1965.

17761   LEKIS, LISA. "THE ORIGIN AND DEVELOPMENT OF ETHNIC
         CARIBBEAN DANCE AND MUSIC." PH.D. DISSERTATION,
         UNIVERSITY OF FLORIDA, 1956.

17762   LEMMON, ALFRED E. "JESUITS AND MUSIC IN THE PROVINCIA
         DEL NUEVO REINO DE GRANADA." ARCHIVUM HISTORICUM
         SOCIETATIS IESU, 48 (1979): 149-160.

17763 LEVINE, LAWRENCE W. BLACK CULTURE AND BLACK
       CONSCIOUSNESS: AFRO-AMERICAN FOLK THOUGHT FROM
       SLAVERY TO FREEDOM. NEW YORK: OXFORD UNIVERSITY
       PRESS, 1977.

17764 LEVINE, LAWRENCE W. "THE CONCEPT OF THE NEW NEGRO AND
       THE REALITIES OF BLACK CULTURE." IN HUGGINS, NATHAN
       I.; KILSON, MARTIN; AND FOX, DANIEL M. (EDS.). KEY
       ISSUES IN THE AFRO-AMERICAN EXPERIENCE. 2 VOLS. NEW
       YORK: HARCOURT BRACE JOVANOVICH, 1971, VOL. 2, PP.
       125-147.

17765 LEVINE, LAWRENCE W. "SLAVE SONGS AND SLAVE
       CONSCIOUSNESS: AN EXPLORATION IN NEGLECTED SOURCES."
       IN HAREVEN, TAMARA K. (ED.). ANONYMOUS AMERICANS:
       EXPLORATIONS IN NINETEENTH-CENTURY SOCIAL HISTORY.
       ENGLEWOOD CLIFFS: PRENTICE-HALL, 1971, PP. 99-130.

17766 LEWIN, OLIVE. "JAMAICAN FOLK MUSIC." CARIBBEAN
       QUARTERLY, 14 (MARCH-JUNE, 1968): 49-56.

17767 LEWIS, ELLISTINE P. "THE E. AZALIA HACKLEY MEMORIAL
       COLLECTION OF NEGRO MUSIC, DANCE, AND DRAMA: A
       CATALOGUE OF SELECTED AFRO-AMERICAN MATERIALS." PH.D.
       DISSERTATION, UNIVERSITY OF MICHIGAN, 1978.

17768 LIST, GEORGE. "AFRICAN INFLUENCES IN THE RHYTHMIC AND
       METRIC ORGANIZATION OF COLOMBIAN COSTENO FOLKSONG AND
       FOLK MUSIC." LATIN AMERICAN MUSIC REVIEW, 1 (SPRING,
       1980): 6-17.

17769 LLOYD, A.L. "THE ORIGIN OF THE SPIRITUALS." KEYNOTE,
       (SPRING, 1946): 4-8.

17770 LOCKE, ALAIN L. "THE NEGRO SPIRITUALS." THE NEW NEGRO.
       NEW YORK: BONI, 1925, PP. 199-213.

17771 LOCKE, ALAIN L. "SPIRITUALS." IN 75 YEARS OF FREEDOM:
       COMMEMORATION OF THE 75TH ANNIVERSARY OF THE 13TH
       AMENDMENT TO THE CONSTITUTION OF THE U.S. WASHINGTON:
       LIBRARY OF CONGRESS, 1943, PP. 7-15.

17772 LOMAX, ALAN. "AFRICANISMS IN NEW WORLD NEGRO MUSIC." IN
       RUBIN, VERA AND SCHAEDEL, RICHARD P. (EDS.). THE
       HAITIAN POTENTIAL: RESEARCH AND RESOURCES OF HAITI.
       NEW YORK: TEACHERS COLLEGE PRESS, COLUMBIA
       UNIVERSITY, 1975, PP. 38-58.

17773 LOMAX, ALAN. "AFRICANISMS IN NEW WORLD NEGRO MUSIC." IN
       SCHAEDEL, RICHARD P. (ED.). PAPERS OF THE CONFERENCE
       ON RESEARCH AND RESOURCES OF HAITI. NEW YORK:
       RESEARCH INSTITUTE FOR THE STUDY OF MAN, 1969, PP.
       118-154.

17774 LOMAX, ALAN. "FOLK SONG STYLE." AMERICAN

ANTHROPOLOGIST, 61 (DECEMBER, 1959): 927-954.

17775 LOMAX, ALAN. _FOLK SONGS OF NORTH AMERICA_. GARDEN CITY: DOUBLEDAY, 1960.

17776 LOMAX, ALAN. "THE HOMOGENEITY OF AFRICAN-AMERICAN MUSICAL STYLE." IN WHITTEN, NORMAN E. AND SZWED, JOHN F. (EDS.). _AFRO-AMERICAN ANTHROPOLOGY: CONTEMPORARY PERSPECTIVES_. NEW YORK: FREE PRESS, 1970, PP. 181-201.

17777 LOMAX, JOHN A. _ADVENTURES OF A BALLAD HUNTER_. NEW YORK: MACMILLAN COMPANY, 1947.

17778 LOMAX, JOHN A. _AMERICAN BALLADS AND FOLK SONGS_. NEW YORK: MACMILLAN COMPANY, 1934.

17779 LOMAX, JOHN A. "SELF-PITY IN NEGRO FOLK SONGS." _NATION_, 105 (AUGUST 9, 1917): 141-145.

17780 LONG, NORMAN G. "THE THEOLOGY AND PSYCHOLOGY OF THE NEGROES' RELIGION PRIOR TO 1860--AS SHOWN PARTICULARLY IN THE SPIRITUALS." M.A. THESIS, OBERLIN COLLEGE, 1936.

17781 LORD, DONALD C. "THE SLAVE SONG AS A HISTORICAL SOURCE." _SOCIAL EDUCATION_, 35 (NOVEMBER, 1971): 763-767, 821.

17782 LOVELL, JOHN JR. _BLACK SONG: THE FORGE AND THE FLAME: THE STORY OF HOW THE AFRO-AMERICAN SPIRITUAL WAS HAMMERED OUT_. NEW YORK: MACMILLAN COMPANY, 1972.

17783 LOVELL, JOHN JR. "REFLECTIONS ON THE ORIGINS OF THE NEGRO SPIRITUAL." _NEGRO AMERICAN LITERATURE FORUM_, 3 (1969): 91-97.

17784 LOVELL, JOHN JR. "THE SOCIAL IMPLICATIONS OF THE NEGRO SPIRITUAL." _JOURNAL OF NEGRO EDUCATION_, 8 (OCTOBER, 1939): 634-643.

17785 LUCAS, JOHN S. "RHYTHMS OF NEGRO MUSIC AND NEGRO POETRY." M.A. THESIS, UNIVERSITY OF MINNESOTA, 1945.

17786 LUEDTKE, JOANNE H. "AN ANALYSIS OF THE LYRICS OF NEGRO FOLK MUSIC AS AN INDICATION OF RESPONSE TO MINORITY GROUP STATUS." B.A. THESIS, MACALESTER COLLEGE, 1959.

17787 LUPER, ALBERT T. _THE MUSIC OF BRAZIL_. WASHINGTON: PAN AMERICAN UNION, 1944.

17788 MACLEOD, BRUCE. "THE ROLE OF FLUTES IN AFRO-AMERICAN MUSIC OF THE U.S." M.A. THESIS, UNIVERSITY OF PITTSBURGH, 1976.

17789 MACLEOD, BRUCE A. "THE MUSICAL INSTRUMENTS OF NORTH

AMERICAN SLAVES." MISSISSIPPI FOLKLORE REGISTER, 11
(SPRING, 1977): 34-49.

17790   MACLEOD, BRUCE A. "QUILLS, FIFES, AND FLUTES BEFORE THE
CIVIL WAR." SOUTHERN FOLKLORE QUARTERLY, 42 (1978):
201-208.

17791   MACON, JOHN A. UNCLE GABE TUCKER; OR, REFLECTION, SONG,
AND SENTIMENT IN THE QUARTERS. PHILADELPHIA:
LIPPINCOTT, 1883.

17792   MALONE, THOMAS H. "ARTISTIC VIRTUE OF NEGRO FOLK-SONGS."
NEW YORK AGE, MAY 4, 1905.

17793   MARKS, MORTON. "UNCOVERING RITUAL STRUCTURE IN
AFRO-AMERICAN MUSIC." IN ZARETSKY, IRVING I. AND
LEONE, MARK P. (EDS.). RELIGIOUS MOVEMENTS IN
CONTEMPORARY AMERICA. PRINCETON: PRINCETON
UNIVERSITY PRESS, 1974, PP. 60-116.

17794   MARR, P. "AN EIGHTEENTH CENTURY MUSICIAN'S INDENTURES."
ORGANISTS REVIEW, 64 (1979): 255.

17795   MARSH, J.B.T. THE STORY OF THE JUBILEE SINGERS, WITH
THEIR SONGS. BOSTON: HOUGHTON MIFFLIN, 1880.

17796   MAULTSBY, PORTIA K. "AFRO-AMERICAN RELIGIOUS MUSIC,
1619-1861. PART I--HISTORICAL DEVELOPMENT. PART
II--COMPUTER ANALYSIS OF ONE HUNDRED SPIRITUALS."
PH.D. DISSERTATION, UNIVERSITY OF WISCONSIN, 1974.

17797   MAULTSBY, PORTIA K. "BLACK SPIRITUALS: AN ANALYSIS OF
TEXTUAL FORMS AND STRUCTURES." BLACK PERSPECTIVE IN
MUSIC, 4 (SPRING, 1976): 54-69.

17798   MAULTSBY, PORTIA K. "INFLUENCES AND RETENTIONS OF WEST
AFRICAN MUSICAL CONCEPTS IN U.S. BLACK MUSIC."
WESTERN JOURNAL OF BLACK STUDIES, 3 (FALL, 1979):
197-215.

17799   MAULTSBY, PORTIA K. "JOHN'S ISLAND, SOUTH CAROLINA: ITS
PEOPLE AND SONGS." JOURNAL OF THE SOCIETY FOR
ETHNOMUSICOLOGY, 18 (JANUARY, 1974): 182.

17800   MAULTSBY, PORTIA K. "MUSIC OF NORTHERN INDEPENDENT BLACK
CHURCHES DURING THE ANTE-BELLUM PERIOD."
ETHNOMUSICOLOGY, 19 (SEPTEMBER, 1975): 401-420.

17801   MAULTSBY, PORTIA K. "SELECTIVE BIBLIOGRAPHY: U.S. BLACK
MUSIC." ETHNOMUSICOLOGY, 19 (SEPTEMBER, 1975):
421-449.

17802   MAYLE, BESSIE H. "HISTORY AND INTERPRETATION OF THE
PRE-REFORMATION CAROL AND THE NEGRO SPIRITUAL." M.A.
THESIS, BOSTON UNIVERSITY, 1932.

17803   MCADAMS, NETTIE F.   "THE FOLKSONGS OF THE AMERICAN NEGRO;
        A COLLECTION OF UNPRINTED TEXTS PRECEDED BY A GENERAL
        SURVEY OF THE TRAITS OF THE NEGRO SONG."   M.A. THESIS,
        UNIVERSITY OF CALIFORNIA, 1923.

17804   MCCARROLL, JESSE C.   "BLACK INFLUENCE ON SOUTHERN WHITE
        PROTESTANT CHURCH MUSIC DURING SLAVERY."   PH.D.
        DISSERTATION, COLUMBIA UNIVERSITY, 1972.

17805   MCGEE, DANIEL B.   "RELIGIOUS BELIEFS AND ETHICAL MOTIFS
        OF THE NEGRO SPIRITUALS."   M.TH. THESIS, SOUTHEASTERN
        BAPTIST THEOLOGICAL SEMINARY, 1960.

17806   MCILHENNY, EDWARD A.   BEFO' DE WAR SPIRITUALS: WORDS AND
        MELODIES COLLECTED BY E.A. MCILHENNY.   BOSTON:
        CHRISTOPHER PUBLISHING HOUSE, 1933.

17807   MCLAUGHLIN, WAYMAN B.   "SYMBOLISM AND MYSTICISM IN THE
        SPIRITUALS."   PHYLON, 24 (SPRING, 1963):   69-78.

17808   MCNEIL, ALBERT J.   "THE SOCIAL FOUNDATIONS OF THE MUSIC
        OF BLACK AMERICANS."   MUSIC EDUCATORS JOURNAL, 60
        (FEBRUARY, 1974):   43-46.

17809   MERRIAM, A.   "THE AFRICAN BACKGROUND: AN ANSWER TO BARRY
        ULANOV."   RECORD CHANGER, 11 (NOVEMBER, 1952):   7-8.

17810   MERRIAM, ALAN P.   "SONGS OF THE AFRO-BAHIAN CULTS: AN
        ETHNOMUSICOLOGICAL ANALYSIS."   PH.D. DISSERTATION,
        NORTHWESTERN UNIVERSITY, 1951.

17811   MERRIAM, ALAN P.   "SONGS OF THE KETU CULT OF BAHIA,
        BRAZIL."   AFRICAN MUSIC, 1 (1954):   53-67.

17812   MERRITT, NANCY G.   "NEGRO SPIRITUALS IN AMERICAN
        COLLECTIONS; A HANDBOOK FOR STUDENTS STUDYING NEGRO
        SPIRITUALS."   M.A. THESIS, HOWARD UNIVERSITY, 1940.

17813   MERWIN, B.W.   "A VOODOO DRUM FROM HAITI."   MUSEUM
        JOURNAL, 8 (1917):   123-125.

17814   METCALFE, RALPH H., JR.   "THE WESTERN AFRICAN ROOTS OF
        AFRO-AMERICAN MUSIC."   BLACK SCHOLAR, 1 (JUNE, 1970):
        16-25.

17815   MEYERS, CHARLES S.   "TRACES OF AFRICAN MELODY IN
        JAMAICA."   IN JEKYLL, WALTER.   SONG AND STORY.
        LONDON: D. NUTT, 1907, PP. 278-285.

17816   MILLER, JAMES W.   SING WITH AFRICA: NEGRO SPIRITUALS
        TAKEN FROM PLANTATION MELODIES.   CHICAGO: RODEHEAVEN
        COMPANY, 1906.

17817   MILLER, KELLY.   "NEGRO'S MUSICAL GIFT."   WASHINGTON POST,
        MAY 10, 1903.

17818   MIMS, A. GRACE. "SOUL: THE BLACK MAN AND HIS MUSIC."
         NEGRO HISTORY BULLETIN, 33 (OCTOBER, 1970): 141-146.

17819   MITCHELL, MRS. M.L. SONGS OF THE CONFEDERACY AND
         PLANTATION MELODIES. CINCINNATI: GEORGE B. JENNINGS
         COMPANY, 1901.

17820   MONTAGUE, J. HAROLD. "A HISTORICAL SURVEY OF NEGRO MUSIC
         AND MUSICIANS AND THEIR INFLUENCE ON TWENTIETH CENTURY
         MUSIC." M.A. THESIS, SYRACUSE UNIVERSITY, 1938.

17821   MOORE, JOHN HAMMOND. "A HYMN OF FREEDOM; SOUTH CAROLINA,
         1813." JOURNAL OF NEGRO HISTORY, 50 (JANUARY, 1965):
         50-53.

17822   MOORE, LEROY JR. "THE SPIRITUAL: SOUL OF BLACK
         RELIGION." AMERICAN QUARTERLY, 23 (DECEMBER, 1971):
         658-676.

17823   MOORE, LEROY JR. "THE SPIRITUAL: SOUL OF BLACK
         RELIGION." CHURCH HISTORY, 40 (MARCH, 1971): 79-81.

17824   THE MOST POPULAR PLANTATION SONGS. NEW YORK: HINDS,
         NOBEL AND ELDREDGE, 1911.

17825   MOTON, ROBERT R. "NEGRO FOLK MUSIC." SOUTHERN WORKMAN,
         44 (JUNE, 1915): 329-330.

17826   MOTON, ROBERT R. RELIGIOUS FOLK-SONGS OF THE NEGRO AS
         SUNG ON THE PLANTATION. HAMPTON: HAMPTON INSTITUTE
         PRESS, 1909.

17827   MURCELL, JEANNE F. "THE RELIGIOUS LIFE OF THE NEGROES
         PORTRAYED IN THEIR SPIRITUALS." M.A. THESIS, BOSTON
         UNIVERSITY, 1953.

17828   MURPHY, JEANNETTE R. "MUST THE TRUE NEGRO MUSIC BECOME
         OBSOLETE?" KUNKLE'S MUSICAL REVIEW, 30 (1905): 10.

17829   MURPHY, JEANNETTE R. "THE SURVIVAL OF AFRICAN MUSIC IN
         AMERICA." POPULAR SCIENCE MONTHLY, 55 (SEPTEMBER,
         1899): 660-672.

17830   MURPHY, JEANNETTE R. "THE TRUE NEGRO MUSIC AND ITS
         DECLINE." INDEPENDENT, 55 (JULY 23, 1903): 1723-1730.

17831   MYERS, C.S. "TRACES OF AFRICAN MELODY IN JAMAICA." IN
         JECKYLL, WALTER (ED.). JAMAICA SONG AND STORY. NEW
         YORK: DOVER PUBLICATIONS, 1966, PP. 279-287.

17832   NATHAN, H. "EARLY BANJO TUNES AND AMERICAN SYNCOPATION."
         MUSICAL QUARTERLY, 42 (OCTOBER, 1956): 455-472.

17833   "NEGRO MINSTRELS." SATURDAY REVIEW, 57 (JUNE 7, 1884):
         739-740.

17834 "THE NEGRO'S CONTRIBUTION TO AMERICAN ART." LITERARY
       DIGEST, 55 (OCTOBER 20, 1917): 26-27.

17835 NETTL, BRUNO. "AFRICAN AND NEW WORLD NEGRO MUSIC." IN
       MUSIC IN PRIMITIVE CULTURE. CAMBRIDGE: HARVARD
       UNIVERSITY PRESS, 1956, PP. 1-166.

17836 NETTL, BRUNO. FOLK AND TRADITIONAL MUSIC OF THE WESTERN
       CONTINENTS. ENGLEWOOD CLIFFS: PRENTICE-HALL, 1965.

17837 NICKERSON, CAMILLE L. "AFRICO-CREOLE MUSIC IN LOUISIANA:
       A THESIS ON THE PLANTATION SONGS CREATED BY THE CREOLE
       NEGROES OF LOUISIANA." M.M. THESIS, OBERLIN COLLEGE,
       1932.

17838 NKETIA, J.H.K. "AFRICAN ROOTS OF MUSIC IN THE
       AMERICAS--AN AFRICAN VIEW." JAMAICA JOURNAL, 43
       (MARCH, 1979): 12-17.

17839 NKETIA, J.H.K. "THE STUDY OF AFRICAN AND AFRO-AMERICAN
       MUSIC." BLACK PERSPECTIVE IN MUSIC, 1 (SPRING, 1973):
       7-15.

17840 "NOTES LITERARY." NATION, 4 (MAY 30, 1867): 428.

17841 ODUM, HOWARD. "RELIGIOUS FOLK-SONGS OF THE SOUTHERN
       NEGROES." AMERICAN JOURNAL OF RELIGIOUS PSYCHOLOGY
       AND EDUCATION, 3 (JULY, 1909): 265-365.

17842 ODUM, HOWARD W. "FOLK-SONG AND FOLK-POETRY AS FOUND IN
       THE SECULAR SONGS OF THE SOUTHERN NEGROES." JOURNAL
       OF AMERICAN FOLKLORE, 24 (JULY-SEPTEMBER,
       OCTOBER-DECEMBER, 1911): 255-294, 351-396.

17843 ODUM, HOWARD W. "RELIGIOUS FOLK-SONGS OF THE SOUTHERN
       NEGROES." PH.D. DISSERTATION, CLARK UNIVERSITY, 1909.

17844 ODUM, HOWARD W. SOCIAL AND MENTAL TRAITS OF THE NEGRO.
       NEW YORK: COLUMBIA UNIVERSITY, 1910.

17845 ODUM, HOWARD W. AND JOHNSON, GUY B. THE NEGRO AND HIS
       SONGS. CHAPEL HILL: UNIVERSITY OF NORTH CAROLINA
       PRESS, 1925.

17846 ODUM, HOWARD W. AND JOHNSON, GUY B. NEGRO WORKADAY
       SONGS. CHAPEL HILL: UNIVERSITY OF NORTH CAROLINA
       PRESS, 1926.

17847 OLIVER, PAUL. "AFRICAN INFLUENCE AND THE BLUES." LIVING
       BLUES, NO. 8 (SPRING, 1978): 13-17.

17848 OLIVER, PAUL. "ECHOES OF THE JUNGLE?" LIVING BLUES, NO.
       13 (SUMMER, 1973): 29-32.

17849 OLIVER, PAUL. SAVANNAH SYNCOPATORS: AFRICAN RETENTIONS

IN THE BLUES. NEW YORK: STEIN AND DAY, 1970.

17850 OMIBIYI, MOSUNMOLA. "INTERACTION BETWEEN AFRICAN AND
AFRO-AMERICAN MUSIC." ACTES DU XLII CONGRES
INTERNATIONAL DES AMERICANISTES, VOLUME VI. PARIS:
SOCIETE DES AMERICANISTES, 1979, PP. 597-604.

17851 ORTIZ, FERNANDO. "AFRO-CUBAN MUSIC." INTER-AMERICAN
QUARTERLY, 1 (1939): 66-74.

17852 ORTIZ ODERIGO, NESTOR R. "NEGRO RHYTHM IN THE AMERICAS."
AFRICAN MUSIC, 1 (1956): 68-69.

17853 OWEN, MAY W. "NEGRO SPIRITUALS: THEIR ORIGIN,
DEVELOPMENT AND PLACE IN AMERICAN FOLK-SONG." MUSICAL
OBSERVER, 19 (1920): 12-13.

17854 OWENS, WILLIAM A. "TEXAS FOLK SONGS." PH.D.
DISSERTATION, UNIVERSITY OF IOWA, 1941.

17855 PANTALEONI, HEWITT. "THE POSSIBILITY OF OBJECTIVE
RYTHMIC EVIDENCE FOR AFRICAN INFLUENCE IN
AFRO-AMERICAN MUSIC." IN BLAKING, JOHN AND
KEALIINOHOMOKEE, JOANN W. (EDS.). THE PERFORMING
ARTS. THE HAGUE: MOUTON, 1979, PP. 287-291.

17856 PARRISH, LYDIA. "THE PLANTATION SONGS OF OUR OLD NEGRO
SLAVES; WITH SCORES." COUNTRY LIFE, 69 (DECEMBER,
1935): 50-54, 62-64, 75-76.

17857 PARRISH, LYDIA A. SLAVE SONGS OF THE GEORGIA SEA
ISLANDS. NEW YORK: CREATIVE AGE PRESS, 1942.

17858 PARSONS, ELSIE C. "NINE NEGRO SPIRITUALS, 1850-1861,
FROM LOWER SOUTH CAROLINA." JOURNAL OF AMERICAN
FOLKLORE, 41 (OCTOBER, 1928): 479-488.

17859 PATTON, LEILA E. "THE SPIRITUALS OF THE AMERICAN NEGRO."
M.A. THESIS, COLUMBIA UNIVERSITY, 1938.

17860 PEABODY, CHARLES. "NOTES ON NEGRO MUSIC." JOURNAL OF
AMERICAN FOLK-LORE, 16 (JULY-SEPTEMBER, 1903):
148-152.

17861 PERDUE, CHARLES L., JR.; BARDEN, THOMAS E.; AND PHILLIPS,
ROBERT K. (EDS.). WEEVILS IN THE WHEAT: INTERVIEWS
WITH VIRGINIA EX-SLAVES. CHARLOTTESVILLE: UNIVERSITY
PRESS OF VIRGINIA, 1976.

17862 PERKINS, A.E. "NEGRO SPIRITUALS FROM THE FAR SOUTH."
JOURNAL OF AMERICAN FOLK-LORE, 35 (APRIL-JUNE, 1922):
223-249.

17863 PHENIX, GEORGE P. "RELIGIOUS FOLK-SONGS OF THE NEGRO."
SOUTHERN WORKMAN, 56 (APRIL, 1927): 151-152.

17864   PHILLIPS, R.E.   PLANTATION MELODIES OLD AND NEW.   NEW
        YORK: G. SCHIRMER, 1901.

17865   PICKETT, ANDREW M.   "THE USE OF BLACK AMERICAN SLAVE FOLK
        SONGS IN THE SOCIAL STUDIES CURRICULUM."   PH.D.
        DISSERTATION, UNIVERSITY OF ILLINOIS, 1977.

17866   PING, NANCY R.   "MUSIC IN ANTEBELLUM WILMINGTON AND THE
        LOWER CAPE FEAR OF NORTH CAROLINA."   PH.D.
        DISSERTATION, UNIVERSITY OF COLORADO, 1979.

17867   "THE PLANTATION MELODY."   COLORED AMERICAN MAGAZINE, 11
        (JULY, 1906):   59-61.

17868   PLANTATION SONGS AND JUBILEE HYMNS.   NEW YORK: WHITE,
        SMITH & COMPANY, 1881.

17869   POLLAK-ELTZ, ANGELINA.   "THE MARIMBULA: AN AFRO-AMERICAN
        INSTRUMENT."   REVIEW OF ETHNOLOGY, 5 (1978):   28-30.

17870   PORTER, THOMAS J.   "THE SOCIAL ROOTS OF AFRO-AMERICAN
        MUSIC."   FREEDOMWAYS, 11 (1971):   264-271.

17871   POUND, LOUISE.   "ANCESTRY OF A NEGRO-SPIRITUAL."   MODERN
        LANGUAGE NOTES, 33 (FEBRUARY, 1933):   442-444.

17872   PRICE, KATE H.   "SPIRITUALS."   STONE AND WEBSTER JOURNAL,
        48 (SEPTEMBER, 1931):   639-645.

17873   PROCTOR, HENRY H.   BETWEEN BLACK AND WHITE.   BOSTON:
        PILGRIM PRESS, 1925.

17874   PROCTOR, HENRY H.   "THE THEOLOGY OF THE SONGS OF THE
        SOUTHERN SLAVE."   SOUTHERN WORKMAN, 36 (NOVEMBER,
        DECEMBER, 1907):   584-592, 652-656.

17875   PYLES, JOSEPH C.   "MUSIC IN THE BLACK CHURCH."   IN
        MCCALL, EMMANUEL L. (ED.).   THE BLACK CHRISTIAN
        EXPERIENCE.   NASHVILLE: BROADMAN PRESS, 1972, PP.
        63-72.

17876   R.J.H.   "NOTES FROM THE CAPITOL--PERSONAL AND LITERARY."
        NATIONAL ANTI-SLAVERY STANDARD, 28 (DECEMBER 21,
        1867):   3.

17877   RAICHELSON, RICHARD M.   "BLACK RELIGIOUS FOLKSONG: A
        STUDY IN GENERIC AND SOCIAL CHANGE."   PH.D.
        DISSERTATION, UNIVERSITY OF PENNSYLVANIA, 1975.

17878   RALSTON, RICHARD.   "BLACK MUSIC AS HISTORY: EXPLORATIONS
        INTO PAN AFRICANIST TRENDS IN THE CULTURE OF THE BLACK
        MASSES."   PAN-AFRICAN JOURNAL, 6 (AUTUMN, 1973):
        263-283.

17879   RAMSEY, F.   "A STUDY OF THE AFRO-AMERICAN MUSIC OF

ALABAMA, LOUISIANA, AND MISSISSIPPI, 1860-1900."
ETHNO-MUSICOLOGY NEWSLETTER, NO. 8 (SEPTEMBER, 1956):
28-31.

17880   RATHBURN, F.G. "THE NEGRO MUSIC OF THE SOUTH." SOUTHERN
        WORKMAN, 22 (1893): 174.

17881   REAGON, BERNICE. "MUSIC AND THE BLACK EXPERIENCE." IN
        CURRICULUM APPROACHES FROM A BLACK PERSPECTIVE.
        WASHINGTON: BLACK CHILD DEVELOPMENT INSTITUTE, 1973,
        PP. 93-98.

17882   REAGON, BERNICE. "WHY DID THEY TAKE US AWAY?" SING OUT,
        24 (1976): 24.

17883   REID, BARNEY F. "A STUDY IN THE RISE OF DEVOTIONAL
        LITERATURE AMONG AMERICAN NEGROES." M.A. THESIS,
        UNIVERSITY OF CINCINNATI, 1932.

17884   RICKS, GEORGE R. "SOME ASPECTS OF THE RELIGIOUS MUSIC OF
        THE UNITED STATES NEGRO: AN ETHNOMUSICOLOGICAL STUDY
        WITH SPECIAL EMPHASIS ON THE GOSPEL TRADITION." PH.D.
        DISSERTATION, NORTHWESTERN UNIVERSITY, 1960.

17885   RICKS, GEORGE R. "A SUBJECTIVE DESCRIPTION OF THE
        AFRO-BAHIAN CULTS AND THEIR MUSIC." M.M. THESIS,
        NORTHWESTERN UNIVERSITY, 1949.

17886   ROACH, HILDRED. "AFRICAN HERITAGE: AN INFLUENCE IN
        MUSICAL TRADITION." BLACK AMERICAN MUSIC: PAST AND
        PRESENT. BOSTON: CRESCENDO PUBLISHING COMPANY, 1973,
        PP. 8-20.

17887   ROACH, HILDRED. "SLAVE ERA: THE BLACK MAN IN COLONIAL
        AMERICA." BLACK AMERICAN MUSIC: PAST AND PRESENT.
        BOSTON: CRESCENDO PUBLISHING COMPANY, 1973, PP. 3-7.

17888   ROBERTS, HELEN. "SOME DRUMS AND DRUM RHYTHMS OF
        JAMAICA." NATURAL HISTORY, 24 (MARCH-APRIL, 1924):
        241-251.

17889   ROBERTS, HELEN H. "POSSIBLE SURVIVALS OF AFRICAN SONG IN
        JAMAICA." MUSICAL QUARTERLY, 12 (JULY, 1926):
        340-358.

17890   ROBINSON, MABEL L. "AMERICAN NEGRO FOLK MUSIC: THE
        EVOLUTION OF ITS STRUCTURE AND TECHNIQUE." M.A.
        THESIS, BOSTON UNIVERSITY, 1940.

17891   RODEHEAVER, HOMER A. RODEHEAVER'S PLANTATION MELODIES.
        CHICAGO: RODEHEAVER, 1918.

17892   RODNITZKY, JEROME L. "THE EVOLUTION OF THE AMERICAN
        PROTEST SONG." JOURNAL OF POPULAR CULTURE, 3 (SUMMER,
        1969): 35-45.

17893   ROOKMAAKER, H.R.   "LET'S SING THE OLD DR. WATTS: A
        CHAPTER IN THE HISTORY OF NEGRO SPIRITUALS."   GORDON
        REVIEW, 9 (WINTER, 1966):   90-101.

17894   RUSSELL, SYLVESTER.   "MUSIC OF THE SLAVES."   INDIANAPOLIS
        FREEMAN, JULY 30, 1904.

17895   RYDER, CHARLES J.   "THE THEOLOGY OF PLANTATION SONGS."
        AMERICAN MISSIONARY, 46 (JANUARY, 1892):   9-16.

17896   SCARBOROUGH, DOROTHY.   ON THE TRAIL OF NEGRO FOLK SONGS.
        CAMBRIDGE: HARVARD UNIVERSITY PRESS, 1925.

17897   SCHIMMEL, JOHANNES C.   SPIRITUALS AND GOSPEL SONGS.
        GELNHAUSEN: BUCHHARDTSHAUS VERLAG, 1963.

17898   SCHLEIN, I.   "SLAVE SONGS OF THE UNITED STATES."
        INTERNATIONAL FOLK MUSIC COUNCIL JOURNAL, 20 (1968):
        82-83.

17899   SCOTT, MARION G.   "WE SING."   CRISIS, 37 (SEPTEMBER,
        1930):   307.

17900   SEBASTIAN, LINDA J.C.   "SYMBOLISM IN AFRO-AMERICAN SLAVE
        SONGS IN THE PRE-CIVIL WAR SOUTH."   M.S. THESIS, NORTH
        TEXAS STATE UNIVERSITY, 1976.

17901   SEEGER, CHARLES.   "THE AFRO-AMERICAN MUSIC COMMUNITY."
        IN SADIE, STANLEY (ED.).   THE NEW GROVE DICTIONARY OF
        MUSIC AND MUSICIANS.   20 VOLS.   LONDON: MACMILLAN,
        1980, VOL. 19, P. 440.

17902   SHARMA, MOHAN L.   "AFRO-AMERICAN MUSIC AND DANCE."   IN
        ROUCEK, JOSEPH S. AND KIERNAN, THOMAS (EDS.).   THE
        NEGRO IMPACT ON WESTERN CIVILIZATION.   NEW YORK:
        PHILOSOPHICAL LIBRARY, 1970, PP. 139-158.

17903   SHELTON, EDWARD E.   "RELIGION: AS EXPRESSED IN THE NEGRO
        SPIRITUALS."   M.A. THESIS, UNIVERSITY OF PITTSBURGH,
        1951.

17904   SIMMS, DAVID MCD.   "THE NEGRO SPIRITUAL: ORIGINS AND
        THEMES."   JOURNAL OF NEGRO EDUCATION, 35 (WINTER,
        1966):   35-41.

17905   "SLAVE SONGS."   IN BASKIN, WADE AND RUNES, RICHARD N.
        DICTIONARY OF BLACK CULTURE.   NEW YORK: PHILOSOPHICAL
        LIBRARY, 1973, P. 407.

17906   "SLAVE SONGS OF THE UNITED STATES."   FREEDMEN'S RECORD,
        (DECEMBER, 1867):   185-186.

17907   "SLAVE SONGS OF THE UNITED STATES."   LIPPINCOTT'S
        MAGAZINE, 1 (MARCH, 1868):   341-343.

17908   "SLAVE SONGS OF THE UNITED STATES." LIVING AGE, 96
        (JANUARY 25, 1868): 230-242.

17909   "SLAVE SONGS OF THE UNITED STATES." NATION, 5 (NOVEMBER
        21, 1867): 411.

17910   "SLAVE-SONGS OF THE UNITED STATES." NEW YORK CITIZEN,
        NOVEMBER 23, 1867.

17911   "SLAVES: MUSIC AND DANCE FORMS." IN RYWELL, MARTIN
        (ED.). AFRO-AMERICAN ENCYCLOPEDIA. 10 VOLS. NORTH
        MIAMI: EDUCATIONAL BOOK PUBLISHERS, 1974, VOL. 8, PP.
        2493-2494.

17912   SMALL, KATHARINE L. "THE INFLUENCE OF THE GOSPEL SONG ON
        THE NEGRO CHURCH." M.A. THESIS, OHIO STATE
        UNIVERSITY, 1945.

17913   SMITH, HUGH L. "GEORGE W. CABLE AND TWO SOURCES OF
        JAZZ." AFRICAN MUSIC, 2 (1960): 59-62.

17914   SMITH, JOSEPH H. "FOLK-SONGS OF THE AMERICAN NEGRO."
        SEWANEE REVIEW, 32 (APRIL, 1924): 206-224.

17915   SMITH, LUCY H. "NEGRO MUSICIANS AND THEIR MUSIC."
        JOURNAL OF NEGRO HISTORY, 20 (OCTOBER, 1935): 428-437.

17916   SMYTHE, AUGUSTINE T. AND SASS, HERBERT R. THE CAROLINA
        LOW COUNTRY. NEW YORK: MACMILLAN, 1931.

17917   SONGS OF DIXIE: A COLLECTION OF CAMP SONGS, HOME SONGS,
        MARCHING SONGS, PLANTATION SONGS. NEW YORK: S.
        BRAINARD'S SONS, 1890.

17918   SOUTHALL, GENEVA H. "ART MUSIC OF THE BLACKS IN THE
        NINETEENTH CENTURY." IN DE LERMA, DOMINIQUE-RENE
        (ED.). REFLECTIONS ON AFRO-AMERICAN MUSIC. KENT:
        KENT STATE UNIVERSITY PRESS, 1973, PP. 161-179.

17919   SOUTHERN, EILEEN. "AFRO-AMERICAN MUSIC." IN SADIE,
        STANLEY (ED.). THE NEW GROVE DICTIONARY OF MUSIC AND
        MUSICIANS. 20 VOLS. LONDON: MACMILLAN, 1980, VOL.
        19, PP. 448-451.

17920   SOUTHERN, EILEEN. "AFRO-AMERICAN MUSICAL MATERIALS."
        BLACK PERSPECTIVE IN MUSIC, 1 (SPRING, 1973): 24-32.

17921   SOUTHERN, EILEEN. THE MUSIC OF BLACK AMERICANS: A
        HISTORY. NEW YORK: W.W. NORTON, 1971.

17922   SOUTHERN, EILEEN. "AN ORIGIN FOR THE NEGRO SPIRITUAL."
        BLACK SCHOLAR, 3 (SUMMER, 1972): 8-13.

17923   SPEERS, MARY W.F. "THE SPIRITUALS AND RACE RELATIONS."
        CHRISTIAN CENTURY, 48 (FEBRUARY, 1931): 230-231.

17924   STANDIFER, J.A. AND REEDER, B.   SOURCE BOOK OF AFRICAN
        AND AFRO-AMERICAN MATERIALS FOR MUSIC EDUCATORS.
        WASHINGTON: CONTEMPORARY MUSIC PROJECT, MUSIC
        EDUCATORS NATIONAL CONFERENCE, 1972.

17925   STARKS, GEORGE L., JR.   "BLACK MUSIC IN THE SEA ISLANDS
        OF SOUTH CAROLINA: ITS CULTURAL CONTEXT--CONTINUITY
        AND CHANGE."   PH.D. DISSERTATION, WESLEYAN UNIVERSITY,
        1973.

17926   STEARNS, MARSHALL.   THE STORY OF JAZZ.   NEW YORK: OXFORD
        UNIVERSITY PRESS, 1956.

17927   STEELE, ALGERNON O.   "THE CONCEPT OF RELIGION REFLECTED
        IN THE EARLY NEGRO SPIRITUALS."   M.A. THESIS,
        NORTHWESTERN UNIVERSITY, 1930.

17928   STEVENSON, ROBERT.   "AFRO-AMERICAN MUSIC--THE COLONIAL
        PERIOD."   IN SADIE, STANLEY (ED.).   THE NEW GROVE
        DICTIONARY OF MUSIC AND MUSICIANS.   20 VOLS.   LONDON:
        MACMILLAN, 1980, VOL. 10, PP. 522-525.

17929   STEVENSON, ROBERT.   "AMERICA'S FIRST BLACK MUSIC
        HISTORIAN."   JOURNAL OF THE AMERICAN MUSICOLOGICAL
        SOCIETY, 26 (FALL, 1973):   383-404.

17930   STEVENSON, ROBERT.   "NEGRO SPIRITUALS: ORIGINS AND
        PRESENT DAY SIGNIFICANCE."   IN PROTESTANT CHURCH MUSIC
        IN AMERICA: A SHORT SURVEY OF MEN AND MOVEMENTS FROM
        1564 TO THE PRESENT.   NEW YORK: W.W. NORTON, 1966,
        PP. 92-105.

17931   STEVENSON, ROBERT M.   "THE AFRO-AMERICAN MUSICAL LEGACY
        TO 1800."   MUSICAL QUARTERLY, 54 (OCTOBER, 1968):
        475-502.

17932   STEVENSON, ROBERT M.   A GUIDE TO CARIBBEAN MUSIC HISTORY:
        BIBLIOGRAPHIC SUPPLEMENT.   LIMA: EDICIONES CULTURA,
        1975.

17933   STILL, WILLIAM G.   "THE NEGRO MUSICIAN IN AMERICA."
        MUSIC EDUCATORS JOURNAL, 56 (JANUARY, 1970):   100-101,
        167-171.

17934   STODDARD, TOM.   "BLIND TOM--SLAVE GENIUS."   STORYVILLE,
        NO. 28 (1970):   134-138.

17935   STOUTAMIRE, ALBERT.   MUSIC OF THE OLD SOUTH: COLONY TO
        CONFEDERACY.   RUTHERFORD: FAIRLEIGH DICKINSON
        UNIVERSITY PRESS, 1972.

17936   STUCKEY, STERLING.   "THROUGH THE PRISM OF FOLKLORE: THE
        BLACK ETHOS IN SLAVERY."   MASSACHUSETTS REVIEW, 9
        (SUMMER, 1968):   417-437.

17937   SUTTON, JOEL B.   "THE GOSPEL HYMN, SHAPED NOTES, AND THE
        BLACK TRADITION: CONTINUITY AND CHANGE IN AMERICAN
        TRADITIONAL MUSIC."   M.A. THESIS, UNIVERSITY OF NORTH
        CAROLINA, 1976.

17938   SYMMES, E.   "AUNT ELIZA AND HER SLAVES."   NEW ENGLAND
        MAGAZINE, N.S., 15 (JANUARY, 1897):   528-537.

17939   SZWED, JOHN F.   "AFRO-AMERICAN MUSICAL ADAPTATION."   IN
        WHITTEN, NORMAN E. AND SZWED (EDS.).   AFRO-AMERICAN
        ANTHROPOLOGY.   NEW YORK: FREE PRESS, 1970, PP.
        219-228.

17940   SZWED, JOHN F.   "MUSICAL ADAPTATIONS AMONG
        AFRO-AMERICANS."   JOURNAL OF AMERICAN FOLKLORE, 82
        (APRIL-JUNE, 1969):   112-121.

17941   SZWED, JOHN F.   "MUSICAL STYLE AND RACIAL CONFLICT."
        PHYLON, 27 (WINTER, 1966):   358-366.

17942   "A TALENTED AFRICAN."   SOUTHERN WORKMAN, 53 (OCTOBER,
        1924):   438-439.

17943   TALLMADGE, WILLIAM H.   "THE RESPONSORIAL AND ANTIPHONAL
        PRACTICE IN GOSPEL SONG."   ETHNOMUSICOLOGY, 12 (MAY,
        1968):   219-238.

17944   TAYLOR, JOHN E.   "THE SOCIOLOGICAL AND PSYCHOLOGICAL
        IMPLICATIONS OF THE TEXTS OF THE ANTEBELLUM NEGRO
        SPIRITUALS."   ED.D. DISSERTATION, UNIVERSITY OF
        NORTHERN COLORADO, 1971.

17945   TAYLOR, JOHN E.   "SOMETHIN' ON MY MIND: A CULTURAL AND
        HISTORICAL INTERPRETATION OF SPIRITUAL TEXTS."
        ETHNOMUSICOLOGY, 19 (SEPTEMBER, 1975):   387-399.

17946   TAYLOR, MARSHALL W.   PLANTATION MELODIES.   CINCINNATI:
        THE AUTHOR, 1883.

17947   TETRICK, GWENDOLYN G.P.   "NO MORE DRIVER'S LASH FOR ME:
        SONGS OF DISCONTENTED SLAVES."   M.A. THESIS, BALL
        STATE UNIVERSITY, 1974.

17948   THIEME, DARIUS L.   "NEGRO FOLKSONG SCHOLARSHIP IN THE
        UNITED STATES."   AFRICAN MUSIC, 2 (1961):   67-72.

17949   THOMPSON, ELIZABETH A.J.   "THE ORIGIN AND THE
        CONTRIBUTION THAT NEGRO SPIRITUALS HAVE MADE IN THE
        AREA OF FOLK MUSIC."   M.ED. THESIS, ALABAMA STATE
        UNIVERSITY, MONTGOMERY, 1947.

17950   THROWER, SARAH S.   "THE SPIRITUAL OF THE GULLAH NEGRO IN
        SOUTH CAROLINA."   M.M. THESIS, COLLEGE-CONSERVATORY OF
        MUSIC OF CINCINNATI, 1954.

17951   THURMAN, HOWARD. DEEP RIVER: AN INTERPRETATION OF NEGRO
        SPIRITUALS. MILLS COLLEGE, CA: EUCALYPTUS PRESS,
        1945.

17952   THURMAN, HOWARD. THE NEGRO SPIRITUAL SPEAKS OF LIFE AND
        DEATH. NEW YORK: HARPER, 1947.

17953   TINSLEY, VALLIE. "SOME NEGRO SONGS HEARD IN THE HILLS OF
        NORTH LOUISIANA." M.A. THESIS, LOUISIANA STATE
        UNIVERSITY, 1928.

17954   TOCUS, CLARENCE S. "THE NEGRO IDIOM IN AMERICAN MUSICAL
        COMPOSITION." M.M. THESIS, UNIVERSITY OF SOUTHERN
        CALIFORNIA, 1942.

17955   TOWE, JOSEPH. "OLD TIME MUSIC OF THE NEGROES." NEW YORK
        TIMES, JUNE 15, 1875.

17956   TRACEY, H. "TINA'S LULLABY." AFRICAN MUSIC, 2 (1961):
        99-101.

17957   TROTTER, JAMES M. MUSIC AND SOME HIGHLY MUSICAL PEOPLE.
        BOSTON: LEE AND SHEPARD, 1878.

17958   TYLER, ROBERT. "THE MUSICAL CULTURE OF AFRO-AMERICA."
        BLACK SCHOLAR, 3 (SUMMER, 1972):   22-27.

17959   UYA, OKON E. "THE MIND OF SLAVES AS REVEALED IN THEIR
        SONGS: AN INTERPRETIVE ESSAY." CURRENT BIBLIOGRAPHY
        ON AFRICAN AFFAIRS, 5 (JANUARY, 1972):   3-10.

17960   VAN DAM, THEODORE. "THE INFLUENCE OF THE WEST AFRICAN
        SONGS OF DERISION IN THE NEW WORLD." AFRICAN MUSIC, 1
        (1954):   53-56.

17961   VAN DAM, THEODORE. "THE INFLUENCE OF THE WEST AFRICAN
        SONGS OF DERISION IN THE NEW WORLD." RECORD CHANGER,
        13 (APRIL, MAY, 1954):   4.

17962   VAN VECHTEN, CARL. "THE FOLK SONGS OF THE AMERICAN
        NEGRO." VANITY FAIR, 24 (JULY, 1925):   52, 92.

17963   VEGA-DROUET, HECTOR. "HISTORICAL AND ETHNOLOGICAL SURVEY
        ON PROBABLE AFRICAN ORIGINS OF THE PUERTO RICAN BOMBA,
        INCLUDING A DESCRIPTION OF SANTIAGO APOSTOL
        FESTIVITIES AT LOIZA ALDEA." PH.D. DISSERTATION,
        WESLEYAN UNIVERSITY, 1979.

17964   VEGA-DROUET, HECTOR. "SOME MUSICAL FORMS OF AFRICAN
        DESCENDANTS IN PUERTO RICO: BOMBA, PLENA, AND ROSARIO
        FRANCES." M.A. THESIS, HUNTER COLLEGE, 1969.

17965   WALDEN, JEAN E. "THE HISTORY, DEVELOPMENT AND
        CONTRIBUTIONS OF THE NEGRO FOLK SONG." M.M. THESIS,
        NORTHWESTERN UNIVERSITY, 1945.

17966 WALKER, WYATT T. "THE MUSICAL TRADITION OF
       AFRO-AMERICANS AND ITS RELATIONSHIP TO AND INFLUENCES
       ON SOCIAL CHANGE." D.MIN. DISSERTATION,
       COLGATE-ROCHESTER DIVINITY SCHOOL, 1975.

17967 WARDER, VELMA G. "SINGING TO ESCAPE." MUSIC JOURNAL, 38
       (SEPTEMBER-OCTOBER, 1930): 18.

17968 WASHINGTON, BOOKER T. "SING THE OLD SONGS." CHARACTER
       BUILDING. NEW YORK: DOUBLEDAY, PAGE AND COMPANY,
       1902, PP. 251-257.

17969 WASHINGTON, JOSEPH R., JR. BLACK SECTS AND CULTS. NEW
       YORK: ANCHOR BOOKS, 1973.

17970 WASHINGTON, JOSEPH R., JR. "NEGRO SPIRITUALS: VOICES OF
       THE NON-CHRISTIAN CHRISTIANS." UNITARIAN-UNIVERSALIST
       REGISTER-LEADER, 146 (MID-SUMMER, 1964): 5-7.

17971 WASHINGTON, MARGARET J.M. "THE SONGS OF OUR FATHERS."
       COLORED AMERICAN MAGAZINE, 8 (MAY, 1905): 245-253.

17972 WATERMAN, RICHARD A. "AFRICAN INFLUENCE ON THE MUSIC OF
       THE AMERICAS." IN TAX, SOL (ED.). ACCULTURATION IN
       THE AMERICAS. CHICAGO: UNIVERSITY OF CHICAGO PRESS,
       1952, PP. 207-218.

17973 WATERMAN, RICHARD A. "AFRICAN PATTERNS IN TRINIDAD NEGRO
       MUSIC." PH.D. DISSERTATION, NORTHWESTERN UNIVERSITY,
       1943.

17974 WATERMAN, RICHARD A. "ON FLOGGING A DEAD HORSE: LESSONS
       LEARNED FROM THE AFRICANISMS CONTROVERSY."
       ETHNOMUSICOLOGY, 7 (MAY, 1963): 83-87.

17975 WATKINS, PATRICIA D. "ORIGINS OF AND INFLUENCES UPON
       BLACK SLAVE SPIRITUALS (THE VALIDITY OF TWO SCHOOLS OF
       THOUGHT)." BA SHIRU, 2 (FALL, 1970): 94-102.

17976 WATSON, JACK M. "NEGRO FOLK MUSIC IN EASTERN SOUTH
       CAROLINA." M.M. THESIS, UNIVERSITY OF SOUTHERN
       CALIFORNIA, 1940.

17977 WEBBER, THOMAS L. DEEP LIKE THE RIVERS: EDUCATION IN
       THE SLAVE QUARTER COMMUNITY, 1831-1865. NEW YORK:
       W.W. NORTON, 1978.

17978 WEEDEN, HOWARD. SONGS OF THE OLD SOUTH: VERSES AND
       DRAWINGS. NEW YORK: DOUBLEDAY, PAGE AND COMPANY,
       1900.

17979 WELCH, DAVID. "WEST AFRICAN CULT MUSIC RETENTIONS IN
       HAITIAN URBAN VANDOU: A PRELIMINARY REPORT." ESSAYS
       FOR A HUMANIST. SPRING VALLEY, NY: TOWN HOUSE PRESS,
       1977, PP. 337-349.

17980   WESLEY, CHARLES H.   "THE FOLK-SONG FROM THE HISTORICAL
        POINT OF VIEW." HOWARD UNIVERSITY RECORD, 19 (MAY,
        1919): 226-231.

17981   "WEST INDIAN NEGROES' NATIVE MUSIC GIVES BRITISH CUTS A
        NEW DISK--'BLUE BEAT.'" VARIETY, 233 (FEBRUARY 5,
        1964): 48.

17982   WHIPPLE, EMORY C. "MUSIC OF THE BLACK CARIBS OF BRITISH
        HONDURAS." M.M. THESIS, UNIVERSITY OF TEXAS, 1971.

17983   WHITE, LILLIAN O. "THE FOLKSONGS OF THE AMERICAN NEGRO
        AND THEIR VALUE TODAY." M.A. THESIS, UNIVERSITY OF
        IDAHO, 1925.

17984   WHITE, NEWMAN I. AMERICAN NEGRO FOLK SONGS. CAMBRIDGE:
        HARVARD UNIVERSITY PRESS, 1928.

17985   WHITE, NEWMAN I. "RACIAL TRAITS IN THE NEGRO SONG."
        SEWANEE REVIEW, 28 (JULY, 1920): 396-404.

17986   WHITE, NEWMAN I. "THE WHITE MAN IN THE WOODPILE: SOME
        INFLUENCES ON NEGRO SECULAR FOLK-SONGS." AMERICAN
        SPEECH, 4 (FEBRUARY, 1929): 207-215.

17987   "WHO ORIGINATED OUR AMERICAN SLAVE SONGS?" NASHVILLE, 7
        (JANUARY, 1980): 36.

17988   WILGUS, D.K. ANGLO-AMERICAN FOLKSONG SCHOLARSHIP SINCE
        1898. NEW BRUNSWICK: RUTGERS UNIVERSITY PRESS, 1959.

17989   WILLIAMS, MARIE B. "A NIGHT WITH THE VOUDOUS."
        APPLETON'S JOURNAL, 13 (MARCH 27, 1875): 403-404.

17990   WILLIAMS, ROBERT. "PRESERVATION OF THE ORAL TRADITION OF
        SINGING HYMNS IN NEGRO RELIGIOUS MUSIC." PH.D.
        DISSERTATION, FLORIDA STATE UNIVERSITY, 1973.

17991   WILLIAMS, THELMA A. "ORIGIN AND ANALYSIS OF NEGRO
        FOLK-SONG." M.S. THESIS, WAYNE STATE UNIVERSITY, 1938.

17992   WILLIAMS-JONES, PEARL. "AFRO-AMERICAN GOSPEL MUSIC: A
        CRYSTALLIZATION OF THE BLACK AESTHETIC."
        ETHNOMUSICOLOGY, 19 (SEPTEMBER, 1975): 373-385.

17993   WILSON, OLLY W. "THE SIGNIFICANCE OF THE RELATIONSHIP
        BETWEEN AFRO-AMERICAN MUSIC AND WEST AFRICAN MUSIC."
        BLACK PERSPECTIVE IN MUSIC, 2 (SPRING, 1974): 3-22.

17994   WINSLOW, HENRY F. "A NEW FURROW." CRISIS, 61 (NOVEMBER,
        1954): 573-574.

17995   WISE, JENNINGS C. YE KINGDOME OF ACCOMACKE; OR, THE
        EASTERN SHORE OF VIRGINIA IN THE SEVENTEENTH CENTURY.
        RICHMOND: BELL BOOK, 1911.

17996   WOOD, HENRY C.   "NEGRO CAMP-MEETING MELODIES."   NEW
        ENGLAND MAGAZINE, 6 (MARCH, 1892):   60-64.

17997   WOODRUFF, MARGUERITE E.   "NEGRO FOLK-SONGS: THEIR ORIGIN
        AND DVORAK'S USE OF THEM."   M.A. THESIS, COLUMBIA
        UNIVERSITY, 1920.

17998   WORK, JOHN W.   AMERICAN NEGRO SONGS.   NEW YORK: HOWELL,
        SOSKIN, 1940.

17999   WORK, JOHN W.   "CHANGING PATTERNS IN NEGRO FOLKSONGS."
        JOURNAL OF AMERICAN FOLKLORE, 62 (APRIL-JUNE, 1949):
        136-144.

18000   WORK, JOHN W.   FOLK SONG OF THE AMERICAN NEGRO.
        NASHVILLE: FISK UNIVERSITY PRESS, 1915.

18001   WORK, JOHN W.   "THE FOLK SONGS OF THE AMERICAN NEGRO."
        M.A. THESIS, COLUMBIA UNIVERSITY, 1931.

18002   WORK, JOHN W.   "THE SONGS OF THE SOUTHLAND."   VOICE OF
        THE NEGRO, 4 (JANUARY-FEBRUARY, 1907):   51-54.

18003   WRIGHT, NATHAN J.   "THE BLACK SPIRITUALS: A TESTAMENT OF
        HOPE FOR OUR TIMES?"   JOURNAL OF RELIGIOUS THOUGHT, 33
        (SPRING-SUMMER, 1976):   87-100.

18004   YATES, NORRIS W.   "FOUR PLANTATION SONGS NOTED BY WILLIAM
        CULLEN BRYANT."   SOUTHERN FOLKLORE QUARTERLY, 15
        (SEPTEMBER, 1951):   251-253.

18005   YOUNG, AURELIA.   "BLACK FOLK MUSIC."   MISSISSIPPI
        FOLKLORE REGISTER, 6 (1972):   1-4.

FOLKLORE

18006   ABRAHAMS, ROGER D.   "THE CHANGING CONCEPT OF THE NEGRO
        HERO."   IN BOATRIGHT, MODY C.; HUDSON, WILSON M.; AND
        MAXWELL, ALLEN. (EDS.).   THE GOLDEN LOG.   DALLAS:
        SOUTHERN METHODIST UNIVERSITY PRESS, 1962, PP. 119-134.

18007   ABRAHAMS, ROGER D.   "THE NEGRO STEREOTYPE: NEGRO
        FOLKLORE AND THE RIOTS."   JOURNAL OF AMERICAN
        FOLKLORE, 83 (APRIL-JUNE, 1970):   229-249.

18008   ABRAHAMS, ROGER D.   "THE SHAPING OF FOLKLORE TRADITIONS
        IN THE BRITISH WEST INDIES."   JOURNAL OF
        INTER-AMERICAN STUDIES, 9 (JULY, 1967):   456-480.

18009   ADAMS, EDWARD C.L.   CONGAREE SKETCHES.   SCENES FROM NEGRO
        LIFE IN THE SWAMPS OF THE CONGAREE AND TALES BY TAD
        AND SCIP OF HEAVEN AND HELL WITH OTHER MISCELLANY.
        CHAPEL HILL: UNIVERSITY OF NORTH CAROLINA PRESS, 1927.

18010   ADAMS, EDWARD C.L.   NIGGER_TO_NIGGER.   NEW YORK:
        SCRIBNER'S, 1928.

18011   AGOSTO MUNOZ, NELIDA. "HAITIAN VOODOO: SOCIAL CONTROL
        OF THE UNCONSCIOUS." CARIBBEAN_REVIEW, 4
        (JULY-SEPTEMBER, 1972): 6-10.

18012   AIMES, HUBERT H.S. "AFRICAN INSTITUTIONS IN AMERICA."
        JOURNAL_OF_AMERICAN_FOLKLORE, 18 (JANUARY-MARCH,
        1905): 15-32.

18013   AMOR, ROSE T. "AFRO-CUBAN FOLK TALES AS INCORPORATED
        INTO THE LITERARY TRADITION OF CUBA." PH.D.
        DISSERTATION, COLUMBIA UNIVERSITY, 1969.

18014   ANDERSON, IZETT AND CUNDALL, FRANK (EDS.). JAMAICA_NEGRO
        PROVERBS_AND_SAYINGS. KINGSTON, JAMAICA: THE
        INSTITUTE OF JAMAICA, 1910.

18015   ANDERSON, JOHN Q. "OLD JOHN AND THE MASTER." SOUTHERN
        FOLKLORE_QUARTERLY, 25 (SEPTEMBER, 1961): 195-197.

18016   ANDREWS, WILLIAM L. THE_LITERARY_CAREER_OF_CHARLES_W.
        CHESNUTT. BATON ROUGE: LOUISIANA STATE UNIVERSITY
        PRESS, 1980.

18017   ANDREWS, WILLIAM L. "THE SIGNIFICANCE OF CHARLES W.
        CHESNUTT'S 'CONJURE STORIES.'" SOUTHERN_LITERARY
        JOURNAL, 7 (FALL, 1974): 78-99.

18018   ARGUEDES, JEANNE. "VARIOUS SUPERSTITIONS KNOWN IN NEW
        ORLEANS AND BELIEVED BY THE OLD COLORED PEOPLE
        DESCENDANTS OF SLAVES, EMPLOYED IN THE OLD CREOLE
        FAMILIES." UNPUBLISHED MANUSCRIPT, N.D., TULANE
        UNIVERSITY LIBRARY.

18019   ARMSTRONG, ORLAND K. OLD_MASSA'S_PEOPLE:_THE_SLAVES_TELL
        THEIR_STORY. INDIANAPOLIS: BOBBS-MERRILL, 1931.

18020   ARMSTRONG, ROBERT P. "PATTERNS IN THE STORIES OF THE
        DAKOTA INDIANS AND THE NEGROES OF PARAMARIBO, DUTCH
        GUIANA." PH.D. DISSERTATION, NORTHWESTERN UNIVERSITY,
        1957.

18021   AUBERT, ALVIN. "BLACK AMERICAN POETRY, ITS LANGUAGE, AND
        THE FOLK TRADITION." BLACK_ACADEMY_REVIEW, 2 (1971):
        71-80.

18022   AUSTIN, H. "WORSHIP OF THE SNAKE: VOODOOISM IN HAITI
        TODAY." NEW_ENGLAND_MAGAZINE, N.S., 47 (JUNE, 1912):
        170-182.

18023   BACKUS, EMMA M. "FOLK-TALES FROM GEORGIA." JOURNAL_OF
        AMERICAN_FOLK-LORE, 13 (JANUARY-MARCH, 1900): 19-32.

18024   BACKUS, EMMA M.   "TALES OF THE RABBIT FROM GEORGIA
        NEGROES."   JOURNAL OF AMERICAN FOLK-LORE, 12
        (APRIL-JUNE, 1899):   108-115.

18025   BACON, ALICE M.   "CONJURING AND CONJURE-DOCTORS."
        SOUTHERN WORKMAN, 24 (NOVEMBER, DECEMBER, 1895):
        193-194, 209-211.

18026   BACON, ALICE M.   "WORK AND METHODS OF THE HAMPTON
        FOLK-LORE SOCIETY."   JOURNAL OF AMERICAN FOLK-LORE, 11
        (JANUARY-MARCH, 1898):   17-21.

18027   BACON, ALICE M. AND PARSONS, ELSIE C.   "FOLKLORE FROM
        ELIZABETH CITY COUNTY, VIRGINIA."   JOURNAL OF AMERICAN
        FOLKLORE, 35 (APRIL-JUNE, 1922):   250-327.

18028   BAKER, HOUSTON A., JR.   "BLACK FOLKLORE AND THE BLACK
        AMERICAN LITERARY TRADITION."   IN LONG BLACK SONG:
        ESSAYS IN BLACK AMERICAN LITERATURE AND CULTURE.
        CHARLOTTESVILLE: UNIVERSITY PRESS OF VIRGINIA, 1972,
        PP. 18-41.

18029   BARRETT, LEONARD E.   THE SUN AND THE DRUM: AFRICAN ROOTS
        IN JAMAICAN FOLK TRADITION.   KINGSTON: HEINEMANN
        EDUCATIONAL BOOKS, 1976.

18030   BASCOM, WILLIAM.   "AFRICAN FOLKTALES IN AMERICA, VIII:
        DEER'S HOOF AND EAR; IX, DOG AND DOG HEAD."   RESEARCH
        IN AFRICAN LITERATURES, 11 (SUMMER, 1980):   175-186.

18031   BASCOM, WILLIAM.   "AFRICAN FOLKTALES IN AMERICA; X:
        HOLDING THE ROCK."   RESEARCH IN AFRICAN LITERATURES,
        11 (WINTER, 1980):   479-510.

18032   BATES, WILLIAM C.   "CREOLE FOLK-LORE FROM JAMAICA."
        JOURNAL OF AMERICAN FOLK-LORE, 9 (JANUARY-MARCH,
        1896):   38-42, 121-126.

18033   BENNETT, PATRICK R.   "REMARKS ON A LITTLE-KNOWN
        AFRICANISM."   BA SHIRU, 6 (1974):   69-71.

18034   BERGEN, F.D.   "UNCLE REMUS AND FOLKLORE."   OUTLOOK, 48
        (SEPTEMBER 2, 1893):   427-428.

18035   BERGEN, FANNY D.   "ON THE EASTERN SHORE."   JOURNAL OF
        AMERICAN FOLK-LORE, 2 (OCTOBER-DECEMBER, 1899):
        295-300.

18036   BLACKBURN, M.J.   FOLKLORE FROM MAMMY DAYS.   BOSTON:
        WALTER H. BAKER COMPANY, 1924.

18037   BLASSINGAME, JOHN W.   THE SLAVE COMMUNITY: PLANTATION
        LIFE IN THE ANTEBELLUM SOUTH.   NEW YORK: OXFORD
        UNIVERSITY PRESS, 1972.

18038 BONTEMPS, ARNA W. AND HUGHES, LANGSTON (EDS.). THE BOOK OF NEGRO FOLKLORE. NEW YORK: DODD, MEAD, 1958.

18039 BOTKIN, B.A. (ED.). A CIVIL WAR TREASURY. NEW YORK: RANDOM HOUSE, 1960.

18040 BOTKIN, B.A. "FOLK AND FOLKLORE." IN COUCH, W.T. (ED.). CULTURE IN THE SOUTH. CHAPEL HILL: UNIVERSITY OF NORTH CAROLINA PRESS, 1935, PP. 570-593.

18041 BOTKIN, B.A. (ED.). LAY MY BURDEN DOWN: A FOLK HISTORY OF SLAVERY. CHICAGO: UNIVERSITY OF CHICAGO PRESS, 1945.

18042 BOTUME, ELIZABETH H. FIRST DAYS AMONGST THE CONTRABANDS. BOSTON: LEE AND SHEPHERD, 1893.

18043 BRADLEY, A.G. "SOME PLANTATION MEMORIES." BLACKWOOD'S MAGAZINE, 161 (MARCH, 1897): 331-341.

18044 BRAKE, ROBERT. "THE LION ACT IS OVER: PASSIVE/AGGRESSIVE PATTERNS OF COMMUNICATIONS IN AMERICAN NEGRO HUMOR." JOURNAL OF POPULAR CULTURE, 9 (WINTER, 1975): 549-560.

18045 BRATHWAITE, EDWARD K. "COMMENTARY." HISTORICAL REFLECTIONS, 6 (SUMMER, 1979): 150-156.

18046 BRATHWAITE, EDWARD K. CONTRADICTORY OMENS: CULTURAL DIVERSITY AND INTEGRATION IN THE CARIBBEAN. MONA, JAMAICA: SAVACOU PUBLICATIONS, 1974.

18047 BRATHWAITE, EDWARD K. FOLK CULTURE OF THE SLAVES IN JAMAICA. LONDON: NEW BEACON BOOKS, 1970.

18048 BRAY, J.C. "MORE MAMMY STORIES." NEW ENGLAND MAGAZINE, N.S., 45 (FEBRUARY, 1912): 594-606.

18049 BREWER, J. MASON (ED.). AMERICAN NEGRO FOLKLORE. CHICAGO: QUADRANGLE BOOKS, 1968.

18050 BREWER, J. MASON. "AMERICAN NEGRO FOLKLORE." PHYLON, 6 (FOURTH QUARTER, 1945): 354-361.

18051 BREWER, J. MASON. "HUMOROUS FOLKTALES OF THE SOUTH CAROLINA NEGRO." PUBLICATIONS OF THE SOUTH CAROLINA FOLKLORE GUILD, NO. 1 (1945): 1-64.

18052 BREWER, J. MASON. "JOHN TALES." PUBLICATIONS OF THE TEXAS FOLKLORE SOCIETY, 21 (1946): 81-104.

18053 BREWER, J. MASON. "JUNETEENTH." IN BOATRIGHT, MODY C.; HUDSON, WILSON M.; AND MAXWELL, ALLEN. TEXAS FOLK AND FOLKLORE. DALLAS: SOUTHERN METHODIST UNIVERSITY PRESS, 1954, PP. 55-66.

18054   BREWER, J. MASON. "JUNETEENTH." PUBLICATIONS OF THE
        TEXAS FOLKLORE SOCIETY, 10 (1932): 12-54.

18055   BREWER, J. MASON. "SLAVE TALES AS A TYPE." PUBLICATIONS
        OF THE TEXAS FOLK-LORE SOCIETY, 10 (1932): 9-11.

18056   BREWER, J. MASON. "TALES FROM JUNETEENTH." IN
        ABERNETHY, FRANCIS E. (ED.). THE FOLKLORE OF TEXAN
        CULTURES. AUSTIN: ENCINO PRESS, 1974, PP. 115-117.

18057   BREWER, JOHN M. "NEGRO PREACHER TALES FROM THE TEXAS
        'BRAZOS BOTTOMS.'" M.A. THESIS, INDIANA UNIVERSITY,
        1949.

18058   BREWER, JOHN M. "OLD-TIME NEGRO PROVERBS." PUBLICATIONS
        OF THE TEXAS FOLKLORE SOCIETY, 11 (1933): 101-105.

18059   BREWER, JOHN MASON. "SLAVERY AND ITS LEGACY." DOG
        GHOSTS AND OTHER TEXAS NEGRO FOLK TALES. AUSTIN:
        UNIVERSITY OF TEXAS PRESS, 1958, PP. 7-24.

18060   "BRIDGE OF THE SLAVES." PAN AMERICAN MAGAZINE, 37
        (NOVEMBER, 1924): 461-463.

18061   BRITT, DAVID. "CHESNUTT'S CONJURE TALES: 'WHAT YOU SEE
        IS WHAT YOU GET.'" CLA JOURNAL, 15 (MARCH, 1972):
        266-283.

18062   BROWN, STERLING A. "BACKGROUND OF FOLKLORE IN NEGRO
        LITERATURE." JACKSON COLLEGE BULLETIN, 2 (SEPTEMBER,
        1953): 26-30.

18063   BROWN, STERLING A. "NEGRO FOLK EXPRESSION: SPIRITUALS,
        SECULARS, BALLADS AND WORK SONGS." PHYLON, 14
        (OCTOBER, 1953): 45-61.

18064   BROWN, WILLIAM W. MY SOUTHERN HOME; OR, THE SOUTH AND
        ITS PEOPLE. BOSTON: A.G. BROWN, 1880.

18065   BRUCE, DICKSON D., JR. "THE 'JOHN AND OLD MASTER'
        STORIES AND THE WORLD OF SLAVERY: A STUDY IN
        FOLKTALES AND HISTORY." PHYLON, 35 (WINTER, 1974):
        418-429.

18066   BULLOCK, MRS. WALLER R. "THE COLLECTION OF MARYLAND
        FOLK-LORE." JOURNAL OF AMERICAN FOLK-LORE, 11
        (JANUARY-MARCH, 1898): 7-16.

18067   BUTCHER, MARGARET T. "THE EARLY FOLK GIFTS: MUSIC,
        DANCE, FOLKLORE." THE NEGRO IN AMERICAN CULTURE. NEW
        YORK: ALFRED A. KNOPF, 1972, PP. 40-56.

18068   BUTLER, ALFLOYD. "THE BLACKS' CONTRIBUTION OF ELEMENTS
        OF AFRICAN RELIGION TO CHRISTIANITY IN AMERICA: A
        CASE STUDY OF THE GREAT AWAKENING IN SOUTH CAROLINA."

PH.D. DISSERTATION, NORTHWESTERN UNIVERSITY, 1975.

18069   BYRD, JAMES W.   "ZORA NEALE HURSTON: A NOVEL
        FOLKLORIST."   BULLETIN OF THE TENNESSEE FOLKLORE
        SOCIETY, 21 (1955):   37-41.

18070   BYRD, JAMES W.   "ZORA NEALE HURSTON, NOVELIST AND
        FOLKLORIST."   PHYLON, 4 (SECOND QUARTER, 1943):
        153-159.

18071   BYRD, MABEL.   "PLANTATION PROVERBS OF 'UNCLE REMUS.'"
        CRISIS, 27 (JANUARY, 1924):   118-119.

18072   CAMERON, VIVIAN.   "FOLK BELIEFS PERTAINING TO HEALTH OF
        THE SOUTHERN NEGRO."   M.A. THESIS, NORTHWESTERN
        UNIVERSITY, 1930.

18073   CAMPBELL, THEOPHINE M.   "AFRICAN AND AFRO-AMERICAN
        PROVERB PARALLELS."   M.A. THESIS, UNIVERSITY OF
        CALIFORNIA, 1975.

18074   CAREW, JAN.   "THE FUSION OF AFRICAN AND AMERINDIAN FOLK
        MYTHS."   CARIBBEAN QUARTERLY, 23 (MARCH, 1977):   7-21.

18075   CARRADINE, B.   MISSISSIPPI STORIES.   CHICAGO: CHRISTIAN
        WITNESS COMPANY, 1904.

18076   CARRIGAN, JO ANN.   "EARLY NINETEENTH CENTURY FOLK
        REMEDIES."   LOUISIANA FOLKLORE MISCELLANY, 1 (1960):
        43-61.

18077   CARROLL, F.J.   "MYSTICISM AMONG THE NEGROES."   NEW YORK
        MEDICAL JOURNAL, 71 (APRIL 21, 1900):   594-596.

18078   CARTER, DORIS D.   "REFUSING TO RELINQUISH THE STRUGGLES:
        THE SOCIAL ROLE OF THE BLACK WOMAN IN LOUISIANA
        HISTORY."   IN MACDONALD, ROBERT R.; KEMP, JOHN R.; AND
        HAAS, EDWARD F. (EDS.).   LOUISIANA'S BLACK HERITAGE.
        NEW ORLEANS: LOUISIANA STATE MUSEUM, 1979, PP.
        163-189.

18079   CARVALHO-NETO, PAULO DE.   "FOLKLORE OF THE BLACK STRUGGLE
        IN LATIN AMERICA."   LATIN AMERICAN PERSPECTIVES, 5
        (SPRING, 1978):   53-88.

18080   "CERTAIN BELIEFS AND SUPERSTITIONS OF THE NEGRO."
        ATLANTIC MONTHLY, 68 (AUGUST, 1891):   286-288.

18081   CHAMBERLAIN, A.F.   "RECORD OF NEGRO FOLK-LORE: BRAZIL."
        JOURNAL OF AMERICAN FOLK-LORE, 21 (APRIL-SEPTEMBER,
        1908):   263-267.

18082   CHAMBERLAIN, ALEXANDER F.   "HYPNOTISM AND SUGGESTION."
        JOURNAL OF AMERICAN FOLK-LORE, 17 (JANUARY-MARCH,
        1904):   78.

18083   CHESNUTT, CHARLES W. "SUPERSTITIONS AND FOLK-LORE OF THE
        SOUTH." MODERN CULTURE, (MAY, 1901): 231-235.

18084   CHESTER, GREVILLE J. TRANSATLANTIC SKETCHES IN THE WEST
        INDIES, SOUTH AMERICA, CANADA, AND THE UNITED STATES.
        LONDON: SMITH, ELDER AND COMPANY, 1869.

18085   CHRISTENSEN, ABIGAL M.H. AFRO-AMERICAN FOLK LORE, TOLD
        ROUND CABIN FIRES ON THE SEA ISLANDS OF SOUTH
        CAROLINA. BOSTON: J.G. CUPPLES, 1892.

18086   CLARK, J.H. "WEST INDIAN SUPERSTITIONS." CHAMBER'S
        JOURNAL, 7TH SER., 8 (AUGUST 17, 1918): 603-605.

18087   CLARK, SARAH B. "AFRO-AMERICAN LITERATURE: ORIGINS."
        IN BRIGHT, ALFRED L.; CLARK; AMADI, LAWRENCE E.;
        COOPER, SYRETHA; BARNES, CLARENCE; AND O'NEILL, DANIEL
        J. AN INTERDISCIPLINARY INTRODUCTION TO BLACK
        STUDIES. DUBUQUE: KENDALL/HUNT PUBLISHING COMPANY,
        1977, PP. 125-128.

18088   CLAVEL, M. "ITEMS OF FOLK-LORE FROM BAHAMA NEGROES."
        JOURNAL OF AMERICAN FOLKLORE, 17 (JANUARY-MARCH,
        1904): 36-38.

18089   CLEARE, W.T. "FOUR FOLK-TALES FROM FORTUNE ISLAND,
        BAHAMAS." JOURNAL OF AMERICAN FOLK-LORE, 30
        (APRIL-JUNE, 1917): 228-229.

18090   COMBES, JOHN D. "ETHNOGRAPHY, ARCHAEOLOGY AND BURIAL
        PRACTICES AMONG COASTAL SOUTH CAROLINA BLACKS."
        CONFERENCE ON HISTORIC SITE ARCHAEOLOGY PAPERS, NO. 7
        (1972): 52-61.

18091   "CONCERNING NEGRO SORCERY IN THE UNITED STATES." JOURNAL
        OF AMERICAN FOLK-LORE, 3 (OCTOBER-DECEMBER, 1890):
        281-287.

18092   COTHRAN, KAY L. "OLMSTED'S CONTRIBUTIONS TO FOLKLIFE
        RESEARCH." IN WHITE, DANA F. AND KRAMER, VICTOR A.
        (EDS.). OLMSTED SOUTH: OLD SOUTH CRITIC/NEW SOUTH
        PLANNER. WESTPORT: GREENWOOD PRESS, 1979, PP. 59-66.

18093   COURLANDER, HAROLD. THE AFRICAN. NEW YORK: CROWN, 1967.

18094   COURLANDER, HAROLD. "AFRICA'S MARK IN THE WESTERN
        HEMISPHERE." A TREASURY OF AFRO-AMERICAN FOLKLORE.
        NEW YORK: CROWN PUBLISHERS, 1976, PP. 1-7.

18095   COURLANDER, HAROLD. THE DRUM AND THE HOE: LIFE AND LORE
        OF THE HAITIAN. BERKELEY: UNIVERSITY OF CALIFORNIA
        PRESS, 1960.

18096   COURLANDER, HAROLD. A TREASURY OF AFRO-AMERICAN
        FOLKLORE. NEW YORK: CROWN PUBLISHERS, 1976.

18097   CRANE, THOMAS F.   "PLANTATION FOLK-LORE." POPULAR
         SCIENCE MONTHLY, 18 (APRIL, 1881): 824-833.

18098   CROSBY, CONSTANCE AND EMERSON, MATHEW C. "IDENTIFYING
         AFRO-AMERICAN MORTUARY CUSTOMS: AN EXAMPLE FROM THE
         PARTING WAYS SETTLEMENT, PLYMOUTH, MASSACHUSETTS."
         UNPUBLISHED PAPER PRESENTED AT MEETING OF SOCIETY FOR
         HISTORICAL ARCHAEOLOGY, NASHVILLE, TENNESSEE, 1979.

18099   CROSS, T.P. "FOLK-LORE FROM THE SOUTHERN STATES."
         JOURNAL OF AMERICAN FOLK-LORE, 22 (APRIL, 1909):
         251-255.

18100   CROWLEY, DANIEL J. (ED.). AFRICAN FOLKLORE IN THE NEW
         WORLD. AUSTIN: UNIVERSITY OF TEXAS PRESS, 1977.

18101   CROWLEY, DANIEL J. "AFRICAN FOLKTALES IN AFRO-AMERICA."
         IN SZWED, JOHN F. (ED.). BLACK AMERICA. NEW YORK:
         BASIC BOOKS, 1970, PP. 179-189.

18102   CROWLEY, DANIEL J. I COULD TALK OLD-STORY GOOD:
         CREATIVITY IN BAHAMIAN FOLKLORE. BERKELEY:
         UNIVERSITY OF CALIFORNIA PRESS, 1966.

18103   CROWLEY, DANIEL J. "NEGRO FOLKLORE: AN AFRICANIST'S
         VIEW." TEXAS QUARTERLY, 5 (AUTUMN, 1962): 65-71.

18104   CROWLEY, DANIEL J. "TRADITION AND INDIVIDUAL CREATIVITY
         IN BAHAMIAN FOLKTALES." PH.D. DISSERTATION,
         NORTHWESTERN UNIVERSITY, 1956.

18105   CULBERTSON, ANNE V. AT THE BIG HOUSE: WHERE AUNT NANCY
         AND AUNT 'PHRONY HELD FORTH ON THE ANIMAL FOLKS.
         INDIANAPOLIS: BOBBS-MERRILL, 1904.

18106   CULIN, STEWART. "CONCERNING NEGRO SORCERY IN THE UNITED
         STATES." JOURNAL OF AMERICAN FOLKLORE, 3
         (OCTOBER-DECEMBER, 1890): 281-287.

18107   CULLINS, ELLA W. "ORIGIN OF AMERICAN NEGRO FOLKWAYS."
         M.A. THESIS, BOSTON UNIVERSITY, 1942.

18108   CUNDALL, FRANK. "FOLK-LORE OF THE NEGROES OF JAMAICA."
         FOLKLORE, 15 (MARCH, JUNE, DECEMBER, 1904): 87-94,
         206-214, 450-456; 16 (MARCH, 1905): 68-77.

18109   CUNNINGHAM, C.E. "VOODOOS AND OBEAHS IN THE WEST
         INDIES." M.A. THESIS, UNIVERSITY OF TEXAS, SAN
         ANTONIO, 1977.

18110   DANCE, DARYL C. "IN THE BEGINNING: A NEW VIEW OF BLACK
         AMERICAN ETHNOLOGICAL TALES." SOUTHERN FOLKLORE
         QUARTERLY, 41 (1977): 53-64.

18111   DARBY, LORAINE. "RING GAMES FROM GEORGIA." JOURNAL OF

AMERICAN FOLK-LORE, 30 (APRIL, 1917): 218-221.

18112 DAVIS, DANIEL W. "ECHOES FROM A PLANTATION PARTY."
       SOUTHERN WORKMAN, 28 (FEBRUARY, 1899): 54-59.

18113 DAVIS, HENRY C. "NEGRO FOLK-LORE IN SOUTH CAROLINA."
       JOURNAL OF AMERICAN FOLKLORE, 27 (JULY-SEPTEMBER,
       1914): 241-254.

18114 DE COSTA, MIRIAM. "THE USE OF AFRICAN FOLKLORE IN
       HISPANIC LITERATURE." CARIBBEAN QUARTERLY, 23 (MARCH,
       1977): 22-30.

18115 DIRKS, ROBERT. "JOHN CANOE: ETHNOHISTORICAL AND
       COMPARATIVE ANALYSIS OF A CARIB DANCE." ACTES DU XLII
       CONGRES INTERNATIONAL DES AMERICANISTES, VOLUME VI.
       PARIS: SOCIETE DES AMERICANISTES, 1979, PP. 487-501.

18116 DIRKS, ROBERT. "SLAVES' HOLIDAY." NATURAL HISTORY, 84
       (DECEMBER, 1975): 82-84, 87-88, 90.

18117 DIXON, MELVIN. "THE TELLER AS FOLK TRICKSTER IN
       CHESNUTT'S THE CONJURE WOMAN." CLA JOURNAL, 18
       (DECEMBER, 1974): 186-197.

18118 DORSON, RICHARD M. "THE AFRICAN CONNECTION: COMMENTS ON
       'AFRICAN FOLKLORE IN THE NEW WORLD.'" RESEARCH IN
       AFRICAN LITERATURES, 8 (FALL, 1977): 260-265.

18119 DORSON, RICHARD M. AMERICAN NEGRO FOLKTALES. GREENWICH,
       CT: FAWCETT PUBLISHERS, 1956.

18120 DORSON, RICHARD M. "ETHNOHISTORY AND ETHNIC FOLKLORE."
       ETHNOHISTORY, 8 (WINTER, 1961): 12-30.

18121 DORSON, RICHARD M. "NEGRO TALES." WESTERN FOLKLORE, 13
       (APRIL, 1954): 77-97.

18122 DORSON, RICHARD M. "ORIGINS OF AMERICAN NEGRO TALES."
       AMERICAN NEGRO FOLKTALES. GREENWICH, CT: FAWCETT
       PUBLISHERS, 1956, PP. 12-13.

18123 DORSON, RICHARD M. "RHYMING TALES FROM BOLIVAR COUNTY,
       MISSISSIPPI." SOUTHERN FOLKLORE QUARTERLY, 19 (1955):
       104-116.

18124 DOUGLAS, S.W. "DIFFICULTIES AND SUPERSTITIONS
       ENCOUNTERED IN PRACTICE AMONG THE NEGROES." JOURNAL
       OF THE ARKANSAS MEDICAL SOCIETY, 18 (JANUARY, 1922):
       155-158.

18125 DUBOIS, W.E.B. THE SOULS OF BLACK FOLK: ESSAYS AND
       SKETCHES. CHICAGO: A.C. MCCLURG & COMPANY, 1903.

18126 DUNBAR, BARRINGTON. "FACTORS IN CULTURAL BACKGROUNDS OF

THE BRITISH WEST INDIAN NEGRO AND THE AMERICAN
SOUTHERN NEGRO THAT CONDITION THEIR ADJUSTMENTS IN
HARLEM." M.A. THESIS, COLUMBIA UNIVERSITY, 1936.

18127   DUNDES, ALAN. "AFRICAN AND AFRO-AMERICAN TALES." IN
        CROWLEY, DANIEL J. (ED.). AFRICAN FOLKLORE IN THE NEW
        WORLD. AUSTIN: UNIVERSITY OF TEXAS PRESS, 1977, PP.
        35-53.

18128   DUNDES, ALAN. "AFRICAN TALES AMONG THE NORTH AMERICAN
        INDIANS." SOUTHERN FOLKLORE QUARTERLY, 29 (SEPTEMBER,
        1965): 207-219.

18129   DUNDES, ALAN. FOLKLORE THESES AND DISSERTATIONS IN THE
        UNITED STATES. AUSTIN: UNIVERSITY OF TEXAS PRESS,
        1976.

18130   DUNDES, ALAN (ED.). MOTHER WIT FROM THE LAUGHING BARREL:
        READINGS IN THE INTERPRETATION OF AFRO-AMERICAN
        FOLKLORE. ENGLEWOOD CLIFFS: PRENTICE-HALL, 1973.

18131   DWYER-SHICK, SUSAN. "THE DEVELOPMENT OF FOLKLORE AND
        FOLKLIFE RESEARCH IN THE FEDERAL WRITERS' PROJECT,
        1935-1943." KEYSTONE FOLKLORE, 20 (FALL, 1975): 5-31.

18132   EBY, CECIL D., JR. "CLASSICAL NAMES AMONG SOUTHERN NEGRO
        SLAVES." AMERICAN SPEECH, 36 (MAY, 1961): 140-141.

18133   EDWARDS, JAY D. THE AFRO-AMERICAN TRICKSTER TALE AND ITS
        ANTECEDENTS: A STRUCTURAL ANALYSIS. BUFFALO: CONCH
        MAGAZINE, 1980.

18134   ELDER, J.D. "SONG GAMES FROM TRINIDAD AND TOBAGO."
        PUBLICATIONS OF THE AMERICAN FOLKLORE SOCIETY, 16
        (1965): 3-119.

18135   ELDER, JACOB D. MA ROSE POINT: AN ANTHOLOGY OF RARE
        LEGENDS AND FOLK TALES FROM TRINIDAD AND TOBAGO. PORT
        OF SPAIN: NATIONAL CULTURAL COUNCIL OF TRINIDAD AND
        TOBAGO, 1972.

18136   ELLIS, A.B. "EVOLUTION IN FOLKLORE: SOME WEST AFRICAN
        PROTOTYPES OF THE UNCLE REMUS STORIES." POPULAR
        SCIENCE MONTHLY, 48 (NOVEMBER, 1895): 93-104.

18137   ELLIS, A.B. "ON VODU WORSHIP." POPULAR SCIENCE MONTHLY,
        38 (MARCH, 1891): 651-663.

18138   EMMONS, MARTHA. "DYIN' EASY." PUBLICATIONS OF THE TEXAS
        FOLKLORE SOCIETY, 10 (1932): 55-61.

18139   EVANS, DAVID K.; RICE, DON S.; AND PARTIN, JOANNE K.
        "PARALLELS IN WEST AFRICAN, WEST INDIAN, AND NORTH
        CAROLINA FOLKLORE." NORTH CAROLINA FOLKLORE, 17
        (NOVEMBER, 1969): 77-84.

18140   FAULKNER, WILLIAM J. THE DAYS WHEN THE ANIMALS TALKED:
        BLACK AMERICAN FOLKTALES AND HOW THEY CAME TO BE.
        CHICAGO: FOLLETT PUBLISHING COMPANY, 1977.

18141   FAULKNER, WILLIAM J. "THE INFLUENCE OF FOLKLORE UPON THE
        RELIGIOUS EXPERIENCE OF THE ANTE-BELLUM NEGRO."
        JOURNAL OF RELIGIOUS THOUGHT, 24 (AUTUMN-WINTER,
        1968): 26-28.

18142   FAUSET, ARTHUR H. "AMERICAN NEGRO FOLK LITERATURE." IN
        LOCKE, ALAIN (ED.). THE NEW NEGRO. NEW YORK: BONI,
        1925, PP. 238-249.

18143   FAUSET, ARTHUR H. "NEGRO FOLKTALES FROM THE SOUTH
        (ALABAMA, MISSISSIPPI, LOUISIANA)." JOURNAL OF
        AMERICAN FOLK-LORE, 40 (JULY-SEPTEMBER, 1927):
        213-303.

18144   FERGUS, HOWARD A. AND GRELL, V. JANE (EDS.). THE SEA
        GULL AND OTHER STORIES. PLYMOUTH, MONTSERRAT:
        ALLIOUAGANA COMMUNE, 1976.

18145   FERRIS, WILLIAM R. MISSISSIPPI BLACK FOLKLORE: A
        RESEARCH BIBLIOGRAPHY AND DISCOGRAPHY. HATTIESBURG:
        UNIVERSITY AND COLLEGE PRESS OF MISSISSIPPI, 1971.

18146   FERRIS, WILLIAM R., JR. "BLACK FOLKLORE FROM THE
        MISSISSIPPI DELTA." PH.D. DISSERTATION, UNIVERSITY OF
        PENNSYLVANIA, 1969.

18147   FERRIS, WILLIAM R., JR. "FOLKLORE AND RACISM." JOURNAL
        OF THE FOLKLORE SOCIETY OF GREATER WASHINGTON, 4
        (SPRING, 1973): 1-5.

18148   FISHWICK, MARSHALL. "UNCLE REMUS VS. JOHN HENRY: FOLK
        TENSION." WESTERN FOLKLORE, 20 (1961): 77-85.

18149   FISK UNIVERSITY, SOCIAL SCIENCE INSTITUTE. RACIAL
        ATTITUDES. NASHVILLE: FISK UNIVERSITY SOCIAL SCIENCE
        SOURCE DOCUMENTS NO. 3, 1946.

18150   FITCHETT, E. HORACE. "SUPERSTITION IN SOUTH CAROLINA."
        CRISIS, 43 (DECEMBER, 1936): 360-361, 370.

18151   FLUSCHE, MICHAEL. "JOEL CHANDLER HARRIS AND THE FOLKLORE
        OF SLAVERY." JOURNAL OF AMERICAN STUDIES, 9
        (DECEMBER, 1975): 347-363.

18152   "FOLK-LORE SCRAP-BOOK." JOURNAL OF AMERICAN FOLK-LORE,
        10 (JULY-SEPTEMBER, 1897): 240-241.

18153   "FOLK-TALES FROM STUDENTS IN TUSKEGEE INSTITUTE,
        ALABAMA." JOURNAL OF AMERICAN FOLK-LORE, 32
        (JULY-SEPTEMBER, 1919): 397-401.

18154   FORTIER, ALCEE. "CUSTOMS AND SUPERSTITIONS IN
        LOUISIANA." JOURNAL OF AMERICAN FOLKLORE, 1
        (JULY-SEPTEMBER, 1888): 136-140.

18155   FORTIER, ALCEE. LOUISIANA FOLK-TALES. BOSTON:
        HOUGHTON, MIFFLIN AND COMPANY, 1895.

18156   FOX, GRACE I. "RING GAMES AND OTHER GAMES OF THE FLORIDA
        NEGRO." PH.D. DISSERTATION, INDIANA UNIVERSITY, 1951.

18157   FRARY, MARYANN T.D. "ANIMAL TRICKSTER TALES OF THE NEGRO
        IN THE NEW WORLD AND AFRICA." M.A. THESIS, UNIVERSITY
        OF OREGON, 1949.

18158   FRUIT, J.P. "UNCLE REMUS IN PHONETIC SPELLING." DIALECT
        NOTES, 1 (1896): 196-198.

18159   FRY, GLADYS-MARIE. "'THE NIGHT RIDERS': A STUDY IN THE
        SOCIAL CONTROL OF THE NEGRO." PH.D. DISSERTATION,
        INDIANA UNIVERSITY, 1967.

18160   FRY, GLADYS-MARIE. NIGHT RIDERS IN BLACK FOLK HISTORY.
        KNOXVILLE: UNIVERSITY OF TENNESSEE PRESS, 1975.

18161   FUNKHOUSER, MYRTLE. "FOLK-LORE OF THE AMERICAN NEGRO: A
        BIBLIOGRAPHY." BULLETIN OF BIBLIOGRAPHY, 16 (JANUARY,
        1937-JANUARY, 1939): 28-29, 49-51, 72-73, 108-110,
        136-137, 159-160.

18162   GANNETT, W.C. "THE FREEDMEN AT PORT ROYAL." NORTH
        AMERICAN REVIEW, 101 (JULY, 1865): 1-28.

18163   GERBER, ADOLF. "UNCLE REMUS TRACED TO THE OLD WORLD."
        JOURNAL OF AMERICAN FOLKLORE, 6 (OCTOBER-DECEMBER,
        1893): 245-257.

18164   GIELOW, MARTHA S. OLD PLANTATION DAYS. NEW YORK:
        RUSSELL, 1902.

18165   GOLDSBOROUGH, EDMUND K. OLE MARS AN' OLE MISS.
        WASHINGTON: NATIONAL PUBLISHING COMPANY, 1900.

18166   GONZALES, AMBROSE E. THE BLACK BORDER: GULLAH STORIES OF
        THE CAROLINA COAST. COLUMBIA, SC: STATE COMPANY,
        1922.

18167   GORDON, A.C. AND PAGE, THOMAS N. BEFO' DE WAR: ECHOES
        IN NEGRO DIALECT. NEW YORK: CHARLES SCRIBNER'S SONS,
        1898.

18168   GORN, ELLIOTT J. "'. . . NO WHITE MAN COULD WHIP ME':
        FOLK BELIEFS OF THE SLAVE COMMUNITY." M.A. THESIS,
        UNIVERSITY OF CALIFORNIA, 1975.

18169   GRISE, GEORGE C. "RUNAWAY SLAVES." KENTUCKY FOLKLORE

RECORD, 4 (JULY/SEPTEMBER, 1958): 93-99.

18170   GUTMAN, HERBERT G. THE BLACK FAMILY IN SLAVERY AND
        FREEDOM, 1750-1925. NEW YORK: PANTHEON BOOKS, 1976.

18171   "GUYANA WILL LEGALIZE A FORM OF WITCHCRAFT." NEW YORK
        TIMES, NOVEMBER 4, 1973.

18172   HALL, JULIEN A. "NEGRO CONJURING AND TRICKING." JOURNAL
        OF AMERICAN FOLK-LORE, 10 (JULY-SEPTEMBER, 1897):
        241-243.

18173   HAMILTON, RUSSELL G. "AFRO-BRAZILIAN CULTS IN THE NOVELS
        OF JORGE AMADO." HISPANIA, 50 (MAY, 1967): 242-252.

18174   HAMLETT, JAMES A. "THE FOLKLORE OF THE FRENCH-SPEAKING
        NEGRO OF EVANGELINE PARISH." M.A. THESIS, LOUISIANA
        STATE UNIVERSITY, 1954.

18175   HANDY, SARA M. "NEGRO SUPERSTITIONS." LIPPINCOTT'S
        MAGAZINE, 48 (DECEMBER, 1891): 735-739.

18176   HANSEN, TERENCE L. "THE TYPES OF FOLKTALE IN CUBA,
        PUERTO RICO, THE DOMINICAN REPUBLIC, AND SPANISH SOUTH
        AMERICA." PH.D. DISSERTATION, STANFORD UNIVERSITY,
        1952.

18177   HARRIS, JOEL C. BALAAM AND HIS MASTER, AND OTHER
        SKETCHES AND STORIES. BOSTON: HOUGHTON MIFFLIN
        COMPANY, 1891.

18178   HARRIS, JOEL C. DADDY JAKE THE RUNAWAY, AND SHORT
        STORIES TOLD AFTER DARK. NEW YORK: CENTURY COMPANY,
        1889.

18179   HARRIS, JOEL C. FREE JOE, AND OTHER GEORGIA SKETCHES.
        NEW YORK: CHARLES SCRIBNER'S SONS, 1887.

18180   HARRIS, JOEL C. MINGO, AND OTHER SKETCHES IN BLACK AND
        WHITE. BOSTON: JAMES R. OSGOOD & COMPANY, 1884.

18181   HARRIS, JOEL C. "THE NEGRO AS THE SOUTH SEES HIM I: THE
        OLD-TIME DARKY." SATURDAY EVENING POST, 176 (JANUARY
        2, 1904): 1-2, 23.

18182   HARRIS, JOEL C. NIGHTS WITH UNCLE REMUS, MYTHS AND
        LEGENDS OF THE OLD PLANTATION. BOSTON: HOUGHTON,
        1881.

18183   HARRIS, JOEL C. ON THE PLANTATION. NEW YORK: D.
        APPLETON & COMPANY, 1892.

18184   HARRIS, JOEL C. PLANTATION PAGEANTS. BOSTON: HOUGHTON
        MIFFLIN AND COMPANY, 1899.

18185   HARRIS, JOEL C.   TOLD BY UNCLE REMUS: NEW STORIES OF THE
        OLD PLANTATION.   NEW YORK: MCCLURE, PHILLIPS &
        COMPANY, 1905.

18186   HARRIS, JOEL C.   UNCLE REMUS AND BRER RABBIT.   NEW YORK:
        FREDERICK A. STOKES, 1906.

18187   HARRIS, JOEL C.   UNCLE REMUS AND HIS FRIENDS: OLD
        PLANTATION STORIES, SONGS AND BALLADS, WITH SKETCHES
        OF NEGRO CHARACTER.   BOSTON: HOUGHTON, MIFFLIN, 1892.

18188   HARRIS, JOEL C.   UNCLE REMUS AND THE LITTLE BOY.   BOSTON:
        SMALL, MAYNARD & COMPANY, 1910.

18189   HARRIS, JOEL C.   UNCLE REMUS: HIS SONGS AND HIS SAYINGS:
        THE FOLK LORE OF THE OLD PLANTATION.   NEW YORK: D.
        APPLETON & COMPANY, 1880.

18190   HARRIS, JOEL C.   UNCLE REMUS RETURNS.   BOSTON: HOUGHTON
        MIFFLIN COMPANY, 1918.

18191   HARRISON, LOWELL H.   "THE FOLKLORE OF SOME KENTUCKY
        SLAVES."   KENTUCKY FOLKLORE RECORD, 17 (APRIL-JUNE,
        JULY-SEPTEMBER, 1971):   25-30, 53-60.

18192   HARVEY, EMILY N.   "A BR'ER RABBIT STORY."   JOURNAL OF
        AMERICAN FOLK-LORE, 32 (JULY-SEPTEMBER, 1919):
        443-444.

18193   HASKELL, JOSEPH A.   "SACRIFICIAL OFFERINGS AMONG NORTH
        CAROLINA NEGROES."   JOURNAL OF AMERICAN FOLKLORE, 4
        (JULY-SEPTEMBER, 1891):   267-269.

18194   HEARN, LAFCADIO.   "NEW ORLEANS SUPERSTITIONS."   HARPER'S
        WEEKLY, 30 (DECEMBER 25, 1886):   343.

18195   HERRICK, E.P.   "WITCHCRAFT IN CUBA."   SOUTHERN WORKMAN,
        36 (JULY, 1907):   401-404.

18196   HERRON, LEONORA.   "CONJURING AND CONJURE-DOCTORS."
        SOUTHERN WORKMAN, 24 (JULY, 1895):   117-118.

18197   HERSKOVITS, MELVILLE J.   "SOME ECONOMIC ASPECTS OF THE
        AFROBAHIAN CANDOMBLE."   MISCELLANEA PAUL RIVET, 2
        (1958):   227-247.

18198   HERSKOVITS, MELVILLE J. AND HERSKOVITS, FRANCES S.   "THE
        NEGROES OF BRAZIL."   YALE REVIEW, 32 (DECEMBER, 1942):
        263-279.

18199   HERSKOVITS, MELVILLE J. AND HERSKOVITS, FRANCES S.
        SURINAME FOLKLORE.   NEW YORK: COLUMBIA UNIVERSITY
        PRESS, 1936.

18200   HILL, MILDRED A.   "COMMON FOLKLORE FEATURES IN AFRICAN

AND AFRICAN AMERICAN LITERATURE." SOUTHERN FOLKLORE
QUARTERLY, 39 (JUNE, 1975): 111-133.

18201 "THE HOG THIEF." SOUTHERN WORKMAN, 26 (APRIL, 1897): 79.

18202 HOVET, THEODORE R. "CHESNUTT'S 'THE GOOPHERED GRAPEVINE'
       AS SOCIAL CRITICISM." NEGRO AMERICAN LITERATURE
       FORUM, 7 (FALL, 1973): 86-88.

18203 HUCKS, J. JENKINS. PLANTATION NEGRO SAYINGS ON THE COAST
       OF SOUTH CAROLINA IN THEIR OWN VERNACULAR.
       GEORGETOWN, SC: CHARLES W. ROUSE, 1899.

18204 HUGHES, LANGSTON AND BONTEMPS, ARNA (EDS.). THE BOOK OF
       NEGRO FOLKLORE. NEW YORK: DODD, MEAD, 1958.

18205 HURSTON, ZORA N. DUST TRACKS ON A ROAD. PHILADELPHIA:
       J.B. LIPPINCOTT COMPANY, 1942.

18206 HURSTON, ZORA N. MULES AND MEN: NEGRO FOLKTALES AND
       VOODOO PRACTICES IN THE SOUTH. NEW YORK: HARPER AND
       ROW, 1935.

18207 HYATT, HARRY M. HOODOO, CONJURATION, WITCHCRAFT,
       ROOTWORK: BELIEFS ACCEPTED BY MANY NEGROES AND WHITE
       PERSONS, THESE BEING ORALLY RECORDED AMONG BLACKS AND
       WHITES. HANNIBAL, MO: WESTERN PUBLISHING COMPANY,
       1970.

18208 HYPPOLITE, MICHELSON P. A STUDY OF HAITIAN FOLKLORE.
       PORT-AU-PRINCE: IMPR. DE L'ETAT, 1954.

18209 JACKSON, BRUCE (ED.). THE NEGRO AND HIS FOLKLORE IN
       NINETEENTH-CENTURY PERIODICALS. AUSTIN: UNIVERSITY
       OF TEXAS PRESS AND THE AMERICAN FOLKLORE SOCIETY, 1967.

18210 JACKSON, MARGARET Y. "FOLKLORE IN SLAVE NARRATIVES
       BEFORE THE CIVIL WAR." NEW YORK FOLKLORE QUARTERLY,
       11 (SPRING, 1955): 5-19.

18211 JAKOSKI, HELEN. "POWER UNEQUAL TO MAN: THE SIGNIFICANCE
       OF CONJURE IN WORKS BY FIVE AFRO-AMERICAN AUTHORS."
       SOUTHERN FOLKLORE QUARTERLY, 38 (JUNE, 1974): 91-108.

18212 JARREAU, LAFAYETTE. "CREOLE FOLKLORE OF POINT COUPEE
       PARISH." M.A. THESIS, LOUISIANA STATE UNIVERSITY,
       1931.

18213 JOHNSON, E.D. "CONJURE WOMAN." IN ROLLER, DAVID C. AND
       TWYMAN, ROBERT W. (EDS.). THE ENCYCLOPEDIA OF
       SOUTHERN HISTORY. BATON ROUGE: LOUISIANA STATE
       UNIVERSITY PRESS, 1979, P. 288.

18214 JOHNSON, F. ROY. THE FABLED DOCTOR JIM JORDAN: A STORY
       OF CONJURE. MURFREESBORO, NC: JOHNSON, 1963.

18215   JOHNSON, F. ROY. TALES FROM OLD CAROLINA. MURFREESBORO,
        NC: JOHNSON, 1965.

18216   JOHNSON, GUION G. A SOCIAL HISTORY OF THE SEA ISLANDS
        WITH SPECIAL REFERENCE TO ST. HELENA ISLAND, SOUTH
        CAROLINA. CHAPEL HILL: UNIVERSITY OF NORTH CAROLINA
        PRESS, 1930.

18217   JOHNSON, GUY B. FOLK CULTURE ON ST. HELENA ISLAND, SOUTH
        CAROLINA. CHAPEL HILL: UNIVERSITY OF NORTH CAROLINA
        PRESS, 1930.

18218   JOHNSON, JOHN H. "FOLKLORE FROM ANTIGUA, BRITISH WEST
        INDIES." JOURNAL OF AMERICAN FOLKLORE, 34 (JANUARY,
        1921): 40-88.

18219   JONES, ALICE M. "THE NEGRO FOLK SERMON: A STUDY IN THE
        SOCIOLOGY OF FOLK CULTURE." M.A. THESIS, FISK
        UNIVERSITY, 1942.

18220   JONES, BESSIE. "A DESCRIPTIVE AND ANALYTICAL STUDY OF
        THE AMERICAN NEGRO FOLKTALE." PH.D. DISSERTATION,
        GEORGE PEABODY COLLEGE FOR TEACHERS, 1967.

18221   JONES, BESSIE AND HAWES, BESS L. STEP IT DOWN: GAMES,
        PLAYS, SONGS, AND STORIES FROM THE AFRO-AMERICAN
        HERITAGE. NEW YORK: HARPER & ROW, 1972.

18222   JONES, CHARLES C., JR. NEGRO MYTHS FROM THE GEORGIA
        COAST TOLD IN THE VERNACULAR. NEW YORK: HOUGHTON,
        MIFFLIN, 1888.

18223   JONES, SAMUEL B. "THE BRITISH WEST INDIAN NEGRO:
        CUSTOMS, MANNERS, AND SUPERSTITIONS." SOUTHERN
        WORKMAN, 40 (APRIL, JUNE, OCTOBER, 1911): 201-205,
        330-335, 580-589.

18224   JOYNER, CHARLES W. "THE CREOLIZATION OF SLAVE FOLKLIFE:
        ALL-SAINTS PARISH, SOUTH CAROLINA, AS A TEST CASE."
        HISTORICAL REFLECTIONS, 6 (WINTER, 1979): 435-453.

18225   JOYNER, CHARLES W. "SLAVE FOLKLIFE ON THE WACCAMAW NECK:
        ANTEBELLUM BLACK CULTURE IN THE SOUTH CAROLINA
        LOWCOUNTRY." PH.D. DISSERTATION, UNIVERSITY OF
        PENNSYLVANIA, 1977.

18226   JOYNER, CHARLES W. "SOUTHERN FOLKLORE AS A KEY TO
        SOUTHERN IDENTITY." SOUTHERN HUMANITIES REVIEW, 1
        (FALL, 1967): 211-220.

18227   JULES-ROSETTE, BENNETTA. "CREATIVE SPIRITUALITY FROM
        AFRICA TO AMERICA: CROSS-CULTURAL INFLUENCES IN
        CONTEMPORARY RELIGIOUS FORMS." WESTERN JOURNAL OF
        BLACK STUDIES, 4 (WINTER, 1980): 273-285.

18228   KILLION, RONALD G. AND WALLER, CHARLES T. A TREASURY OF
        GEORGIA FOLKLORE. ATLANTA: CHEROKEE PUBLISHING
        COMPANY, 1972.

18229   KLIPPLE, MAY A. "AFRICAN FOLK TALES WITH FOREIGN
        ANALOGUES." PH.D. DISSERTATION, INDIANA UNIVERSITY,
        1938.

18230   KUNA, RALPH R. "HOODOO: THE INDIGENOUS MEDICINE AND
        PSYCHIATRY OF THE BLACK AMERICAN." EIHNOMEDIZIN, 3
        (1974-1975): 273-294.

18231   LACY, JAMES M. "FOLKLORE OF THE SOUTH AND RACIAL
        DISCRIMINATION." IN BOATRIGHT, MODY C.; HUDSON,
        WILSON M.; AND MAXWELL, ALLEN (EDS.). A GOOD TALE AND
        A BONNIE TUNE. DALLAS: SOUTHERN METHODIST UNIVERSITY
        PRESS, 1964, PP. 101-111.

18232   LAGUERRE, MICHAEL. "THE PLACE OF VOODOO IN THE SOCIAL
        STRUCTURE OF HAITI." CARIBBEAN QUARTERLY, 19
        (SEPTEMBER, 1973): 36-50.

18233   LAGUERRE, MICHEL S. VOODOO HERITAGE. BEVERLY HILLS:
        SAGE PUBLICATIONS, 1980.

18234   LEACOCK, SETH AND LEACOCK, RUTH. SPIRITS OF THE DEEP: A
        STUDY OF AN AFRO-BRAZILIAN CULT. GARDEN CITY, NY:
        DOUBLEDAY, 1972.

18235   LEE, FLORENCE W. "CHRISTMAS IN VIRGINIA BEFORE THE WAR."
        SOUTHERN WORKMAN, 37 (DECEMBER, 1908): 686-689.

18236   LEON, JULIO ANTONIO. "AFRO-CUBAN POETRY: AN UNPUBLISHED
        TREASURE." AMERICAS, 9 (SEPTEMBER, 1977): 28-32.

18237   LEVINE, LAWRENCE W. BLACK CULTURE AND BLACK
        CONSCIOUSNESS: AFRO-AMERICAN FOLK THOUGHT FROM
        SLAVERY TO FREEDOM. NEW YORK: OXFORD UNIVERSITY
        PRESS, 1977.

18238   LEVINE, LAWRENCE W. "THE CONCEPT OF THE NEW NEGRO AND
        THE REALITIES OF BLACK CULTURE." IN HUGGINS, NATHAN
        I.; KILSON, MARTIN; AND FOX, DANIEL M. (EDS.). KEY
        ISSUES IN THE AFRO-AMERICAN EXPERIENCE. 2 VOLS. NEW
        YORK: HARCOURT BRACE JOVANOVICH, 1971, VOL. 2, PP.
        125-147.

18239   LEVINE, LAWRENCE W. "'SOME GO UP AND SOME GO DOWN': THE
        MEANING OF THE SLAVE TRICKSTER." IN ELKINS, STANLEY
        AND MCKITRICK, ERIC (EDS.). THE HOFSTADTER AEGIS: A
        MEMORIAL. NEW YORK: ALFRED A. KNOPF, 1974, PP.
        94-124.

18240   LEWISOHN, FLORENCE. ST. CROIX UNDER SEVEN FLAGS.
        HOLLYWOOD, FL: DUKANE PRESS, 1970.

18241   LONG, RICHARD A.   "THE UNCLE REMUS DIALECT: A
         PRELIMINARY LINGUISTIC VIEW."   PAPER PRESENTED AT
         SOUTHEASTERN CONFERENCE ON LINGUISTICS, 1969.

18242   MACLEOD, W.C.   "'JUMPING OVER' FROM WEST ARICA TO SOUTH
         AMERICA."   AMERICAN ANTHROPOLOGIST, 30 (JANUARY-MARCH,
         1928):   107-111.

18243   MAGALHAES, BASILIO DE.   FOLK-LORE IN BRAZIL.   RIO DE
         JANEIRO: IMPRENSA NACIONAL, 1945.

18244   MAJOR, CLARENCE (ED.).   DICTIONARY OF AFRO-AMERICAN
         SLANG.   NEW YORK: INTERNATIONAL PUBLISHING COMPANY,
         1970.

18245   MARSH, VIVIAN C.O.   "TYPES AND DISTRIBUTION OF NEGRO
         FOLK-LORE IN AMERICA."   M.A. THESIS, UNIVERSITY OF
         CALIFORNIA, 1922.

18246   MCBRIDE, JOHN M., JR.   "BR'ER RABBIT IN THE FOLKTALES OF
         THE NEGRO AND OTHER RACES."   SEWANEE REVIEW, 19
         (APRIL, 1911):   185-206.

18247   MCCLOUD, VELMA.   LAUGHTER IN CHAINS.   NEW YORK: LENOX
         PRESS, 1901.

18248   MCCLURE, AROZENA L.   "FOLKLORE OF THE NEGROES AS REVEALED
         IN THE 'UNCLE REMUS' STORIES."   M.A. THESIS, STEPHEN
         F. AUSTIN STATE TEACHERS COLLEGE, 1942.

18249   MCCLURG, ALEXANDER C.   "OLD TIME PLANTATION LIFE: ON THE
         PLANTATION."   DIAL, 13 (JUNE, 1892):   46-49.

18250   MCILHENNY, EDWARD A.   BEED' DE WAR SPIRITUALS: WORDS AND
         MELODIES COLLECTED BY E.A. MCILHENNY.   BOSTON:
         CHRISTOPHER PUBLISHING HOUSE, 1933.

18251   MCMILLAN, FAY C.   "MAJOR THEMES IN SOUTHERN NEGRO
         FOLKLORE."   M.A. THESIS, EAST TENNESSEE STATE
         UNIVERSITY, 1961.

18252   MICKLE, ROBINA.   "SOME CUSTOMS AND SUPERSTITIONS OF THE
         SOUTHERN NEGRO."   M.A. THESIS, COLUMBIA UNIVERSITY,
         1916.

18253   MILLER, KELLY.   RACE ADJUSTMENT: ESSAYS ON THE NEGRO IN
         AMERICA.   NEW YORK: NEALE PUBLISHING COMPANY, 1908.

18254   MITCHELL, HENRY H.   BLACK BELIEF: FOLK BELIEFS OF BLACKS
         IN AMERICA AND WEST AFRICA.   NEW YORK: HARPER & ROW,
         1975.

18255   MODERWELL, HIRAM K.   "THE EPIC OF THE BLACK MAN."
         AMERICAN MISSIONARY, 72 (APRIL, 1918):   43-45.

18256   MONTELL, WILLIAM L.   "A FOLK HISTORY OF THE COE RIDGE
         NEGRO COLONY." 2 VOLS. PH.D. DISSERTATION, INDIANA
         UNIVERSITY, 1964.

18257   MONTELL, WILLIAM L.   THE SAGA OF COE RIDGE: A STUDY IN
         ORAL HISTORY. KNOXVILLE: UNIVERSITY OF TENNESSEE
         PRESS, 1970.

18258   MONTELL, WILLIAM L.   "SUPERNATURAL TALES COLLECTED FROM
         NEGROES AND WHITES IN MONROE AND CUMBERLAND COUNTIES,
         KENTUCKY." M.A. THESIS, INDIANA UNIVERSITY, 1963.

18259   MONTERO BASCOM, BERTA.   "SEVEN AFROCUBAN MYTHS." ACTES
         DU XLII CONGRES INTERNATIONAL DES AMERICANISTES,
         VOLUME VI. PARIS: SOCIETE DES AMERICANISTES, 1979,
         PP. 605-613.

18260   "MORALITY AND RELIGION IN SLAVERY DAYS." SOUTHERN
         WORKMAN, 26 (OCTOBER, 1397): 210.

18261   MORGAN, KATHRYN L.   "CADDY BUFFERS: LEGENDS OF A MIDDLE
         CLASS NEGRO FAMILY IN PHILADELPHIA." KEYSTONE
         FOLKLORE QUARTERLY, 11 (SUMMER, 1966): 67-88.

18262   MORGAN, KATHRYN L.   "THE EX-SLAVE NARRATIVE AS A SOURCE
         FOR FOLK HISTORY." PH.D. DISSERTATION, UNIVERSITY OF
         PENNSYLVANIA, 1970.

18263   MOYD, OLIN P.   "REDEMPTION: A THEOLOGY FROM BLACK
         HISTORY (AN EXAMINATION OF THE MEANING OF REDEMPTION
         AS REFLECTED IN BLACK FOLK EXPRESSIONS)." PH.D.
         DISSERTATION, ST. MARY'S SEMINARY AND UNIVERSITY, 1977.

18264   MUFFETT, D.J.M.   "UNCLE REMUS WAS A HAUSAMAN?" SOUTHERN
         FOLKLORE QUARTERLY, 39 (JUNE, 1975): 151-166.

18265   NASSAU, ROBERT H.   FETICHISM IN WEST AFRICA: FORTY YEARS'
         OBSERVATION OF NATIVE CUSTOMS AND SUPERSTITIONS.
         LONDON: DUCKWORTH & COMPANY, 1904.

18266   "NEGRO SUPERSTITION CONCERNING THE VIOLIN." JOURNAL OF
         AMERICAN FOLKLORE, 5 (OCTOBER-DECEMBER, 1892):
         329-330.

18267   "THE NEGRO'S CONTRIBUTION TO AMERICAN ART." LITERARY
         DIGEST, 55 (OCTOBER 20, 1917): 26-27.

18268   NEWELL, W.W.   "REPORTS OF VOODOO WORSHIP IN HAYTI AND
         LOUISIANA." JOURNAL OF AMERICAN FOLK-LORE, 2
         (JANUARY-MARCH, 1889): 41-47.

18269   NEWELL, W. WILLIAM.   "MYTH OF VOODOO WORSHIP AND CHILD
         SACRIFICE IN HAYTI." JOURNAL OF AMERICAN FOLK-LORE, 1
         (APRIL-JUNE, 1888): 16-30.

18270   NOLL, ARTHUR H.   "THE FOLK-LORE OF THE SOUTH."   IN
        HENNEMAN, JOHN B. (ED.).   THE SOUTH IN THE BUILDING OF
        THE NATION.   12 VOLS.   RICHMOND: SOUTHERN HISTORICAL
        PUBLICATION SOCIETY, 1909, VOL. 7, PP. 55-70.

18271   NORRIS, THADDEUS.   "NEGRO SUPERSTITIONS."   LIPPINCOTT'S
        MAGAZINE, 6 (JULY, 1870):   90-95.

18272   O'DEA, MICHAEL.   "THE NEGRO GOVERNORS."   AMERICAN HISTORY
        ILLUSTRATED, 15 (JULY, 1980):   22-25, 48.

18273   OERTEL, HANNS.   "NOTES ON SIX NEGRO MYTHS FROM THE
        GEORGIA COAST."   JOURNAL OF AMERICAN FOLK-LORE, 2
        (OCTOBER-DECEMBER, 1889):   309.

18274   O'REILLY, AICA T.   "THE SURVIVAL OF AFRICAN FOLKTALES IN
        THE NEW WORLD."   PASS: A JOURNAL OF THE BLACK
        EXPERIENCE AND PAN-AFRICAN ISSUES, 1 (WINTER, 1975):
        103-113.

18275   OSOFSKY, GILBERT.   "A NOTE ON THE USEFULNESS OF
        FOLKLORE."   IN OSOFSKY (ED.).   PUTTIN' ON OLE MASSA:
        THE SLAVE NARRATIVES OF HENRY BIBB, WILLIAM WELLS
        BROWN, AND SOLOMAN NORTHUP.   NEW YORK: HARPER & ROW,
        1969, PP. 45-48.

18276   OSTER, HARRY C.   "NEGRO HUMOR: JOHN AND OLD MARSTER."
        JOURNAL OF THE FOLKLORE INSTITUTE, 5 (JUNE, 1968):
        42-57.

18277   OWEN, MARY A.   OLE RABBIT'S PLANTATION STORIES AS TOLD
        AMONG THE NEGROES OF THE SOUTHWEST.   PHILADELPHIA:
        N.P., 1898.

18278   OWEN, MARY A.   VOODOO TALES AS TOLD AMONG THE NEGROES OF
        THE SOUTHWEST.   NEW YORK: N.P., 1893.

18279   OWENS, WILLIAM.   "FOLK-LORE OF THE SOUTHERN NEGROES."
        LIPPINCOTT'S MAGAZINE, 20 (DECEMBER, 1877):   748-755.

18280   OWENS, WILLIAM A.   "RETURN TO PIN HOOK."   IN ABERNETHY,
        FRANCIS E. (ED.).   OBSERVATIONS & REFLECTIONS ON TEXAS
        FOLKLORE.   AUSTIN: ENCINO PRESS, 1972, PP. 31-34.

18281   PALMER, COLIN A.   "RELIGION AND MAGIC IN MEXICAN SLAVE
        SOCIETY, 1570-1650."   IN ENGERMAN, STANLEY L. AND
        GENOVESE, EUGENE D. (EDS.).   RACE AND SLAVERY IN THE
        WESTERN HEMISPHERE: QUANTITATIVE STUDIES.   PRINCETON:
        PRINCETON UNIVERSITY PRESS, 1975, PP. 311-328.

18282   PARRINDER, GEOFFREY.   WITCHCRAFT: EUROPEAN AND AFRICAN.
        NEW YORK: BARNES & NOBLE, 1963.

18283   PARSONS, ELSIE C.   "ASHANTI INFLUENCE IN JAMAICA."
        JOURNAL OF AMERICAN FOLKLORE, 47 (OCTOBER-DECEMBER,

1934):   391-395.

18284   PARSONS, ELSIE C.   "FOLK-LORE FROM AIKEN, S.C."   JOURNAL
        OF AMERICAN FOLK-LORE, 34 (JANUARY-MARCH, 1921):   1-39.

18285   PARSONS, ELSIE C.   FOLK-LORE OF THE ANTILLES, FRENCH AND
        ENGLISH.   3 VOLS.   NEW YORK: AMERICAN FOLK-LORE
        SOCIETY, 1933-1943.

18286   PARSONS, ELSIE C.   FOLK-LORE OF THE SEA ISLANDS, SOUTH
        CAROLINA.   NEW YORK: AMERICAN FOLKLORE SOCIETY, 1923.

18287   PARSONS, ELSIE C.   FOLK-TALES OF ANDROS ISLAND, BAHAMAS.
        NEW YORK: AMERICAN FOLKLORE SOCIETY, 1918.

18288   PARSONS, ELSIE C.   "JOEL CHANDLER HARRIS AND NEGRO
        FOLKLORE."   DIAL, 66 (MAY 17, 1919):   491-493.

18289   PARSONS, ELSIE C.   "THE PROVENIENCE OF CERTAIN NEGRO
        FOLK-TALES."   FOLK-LORE, 28 (DECEMBER 31, 1917):
        408-414; 29 (SEPTEMBER 30, 1918):   206-218; 30
        (SEPTEMBER 30, 1919):   227-234.

18290   PARSONS, ELSIE C.   "TALES FROM GUILFORD COUNTY, NORTH
        CAROLINA."   JOURNAL OF AMERICAN FOLK-LORE, 30
        (APRIL-JUNE, 1917):   168-200.

18291   PARSONS, ELSIE C.   "TEN FOLK TALES FROM THE CAPE VERDE
        ISLANDS."   JOURNAL OF AMERICAN FOLK-LORE, 30
        (APRIL-JUNE, 1917):   230-238.

18292   PENDLETON, LOUIS.   "NOTES ON NEGRO FOLK-LORE AND
        WITCHCRAFT IN THE SOUTH."   JOURNAL OF AMERICAN
        FOLK-LORE, 3 (JULY-SEPTEMBER, 1890):   201-207.

18293   PERDUE, CHARLES L., JR.; BARDEN, THOMAS E.; AND PHILLIPS,
        ROBERT K. (EDS.).   AN ANNOTATED LISTING OF FOLKLORE
        COLLECTED BY WORKERS OF THE VIRGINIA WRITERS' PROJECT,
        WORKS PROJECTS ADMINISTRATION: HELD IN THE
        MANUSCRIPTS DEPARTMENT AT ALDERMAN LIBRARY OF THE
        UNIVERSITY OF VIRGINIA.   NORWOOD, PA: NORWOOD
        EDITIONS, 1979.

18294   PERDUE, CHARLES L., JR.; BARDEN, THOMAS E.; AND PHILLIPS,
        ROBERT K. (EDS.).   WEEVILS IN THE WHEAT: INTERVIEWS
        WITH VIRGINIA EX-SLAVES.   CHARLOTTESVILLE: UNIVERSITY
        PRESS OF VIRGINIA, 1976.

18295   PERDUE, CHUCK.   "I SWEAR TO GOD IT'S THE TRUTH IF I EVER
        TOLD IT!"   KEYSTONE FOLKLORE QUARTERLY, 14 (SPRING,
        1969):   1-56.

18296   PERROW, E.C.   "SONGS AND RHYMES FROM THE SOUTH."   JOURNAL
        OF AMERICAN FOLKLORE, 28 (APRIL-JUNE, 1915):   129-190.

18297   PETERKIN, JULIA AND ULMANN, DORIS. ROLL, JORDAN, ROLL.
        NEW YORK: ROBERT O. BALLOU, 1933.

18298   PICKETT, L.C. "UNCLE REMUS." LIPPINCOTT'S MONTHLY
        MAGAZINE, 89 (APRIL, 1912): 572-578.

18299   PIERSEN, WILLIAM D. "AN AFRICAN BACKGROUND FOR AMERICAN
        NEGRO FOLKTALES?" JOURNAL OF AMERICAN FOLKLORE, 84
        (APRIL/JUNE, 1971): 204-214.

18300   PIERSEN, WILLIAM D. "AFRO-AMERICAN CULTURE IN
        EIGHTEENTH-CENTURY NEW ENGLAND: A COMPARATIVE
        EXAMINATION." PH.D. DISSERTATION, INDIANA UNIVERSITY,
        1975.

18301   PIERSEN, WILLIAM D. "PUTTIN' DOWN OLE MASSA: AFRICAN
        SATIRE IN THE NEW WORLD." IN CROWLEY, DANIEL J.
        (ED.). AFRICAN FOLKLORE IN THE NEW WORLD. AUSTIN:
        UNIVERSITY OF TEXAS PRESS, 1977, PP. 20-34.

18302   PITMAN, F.W. "FETISHISM, WITCHCRAFT AND CHRISTIANITY
        AMONG THE SLAVES." JOURNAL OF NEGRO HISTORY, 11
        (OCTOBER, 1926): 650-668.

18303   PUCKETT, NEWBELL N. FOLK BELIEFS OF THE SOUTHERN NEGRO.
        CHAPEL HILL: UNIVERSITY OF NORTH CAROLINA PRESS, 1926.

18304   PUCKETT, NEWBELL N. "FOLK-BELIEFS OF THE SOUTHERN
        NEGRO." PH.D. DISSERTATION, YALE UNIVERSITY, 1925.

18305   PUCKETT, NEWBELL N. "RACE-PRIDE AND FOLKLORE."
        OPPORTUNITY, 4 (MARCH, 1926): 82-84.

18306   PURCHAS-TULLOCH, JEAN A. "JAMAICA ANASI: A SURVIVAL OF
        THE AFRICAN ORAL TRADITION." PH.D. DISSERTATION,
        HOWARD UNIVERSITY, 1976.

18307   RABOTEAU, ALBERT J. SLAVE RELIGION: THE "INVISIBLE
        INSTITUTION" IN THE AMERICAN SOUTH. NEW YORK: OXFORD
        UNIVERSITY PRESS, 1978.

18308   RICH, CARROLL Y. "BORN WITH THE VEIL: BLACK FOLKLORE IN
        LOUISIANA." JOURNAL OF AMERICAN FOLKLORE, 89
        (JULY-SEPTEMBER, 1976): 328-330.

18309   RICHARDSON, CLEMENT. "SOME SLAVE SUPERSTITIONS."
        SOUTHERN WORKMAN, 41 (APRIL, 1912): 246-248.

18310   RICKS, GEORGE R. "A SUBJECTIVE DESCRIPTION OF THE
        AFRO-BAHIAN CULTS AND THEIR MUSIC." M.M. THESIS,
        NORTHWESTERN UNIVERSITY, 1949.

18311   BLAKE, ROBERT. "THE LION ACT IS OVER:
        PASSIVE/AGGRESSIVE PATTERNS OF COMMUNICATION IN
        AMERICAN NEGRO HUMOR." JOURNAL OF POPULAR CULTURE, 9

(1975): 549-560.

18312   ROBERTS, JAMES D. "FOLKLORE AND RELIGION: THE BLACK
        EXPERIENCE." JOURNAL OF RELIGIOUS THOUGHT, 37
        (SUMMER, 1970): 5-15.

18313   ROBERTS, JOHN W. "SLAVE PROVERBS: A PERSPECTIVE."
        CALLALOO, 1 (OCTOBER, 1978): 129-140.

18314   RODENBAUGH, JEAN. "THE MAGIC SINDER SEED AND OTHER
        MATTERS." NORTH CAROLINA FOLKLORE, 19 (NOVEMBER,
        1971): 180-184.

18315   RODMAN, SELDON. "AFRICAN BRAZIL AND ITS CULTS: BATUQUE,
        CANDOMBLE AND UMBANDA." AMERICAS, 27 (JUNE, 1975):
        6-13.

18316   ROGERS, MARGUERITE S. "DEATH AND BURIAL CUSTOMS AMONG
        AMERICAN PLANTATION NEGROES." M.A. THESIS, ATLANTA
        UNIVERSITY, 1941.

18317   RUTLEDGE, ARCHIBALD. OLD PLANTATION DAYS. NEW YORK:
        FREDERICK A. STOKES, 1921.

18318   SAXON, LYLE. "VOODOO." NEW REPUBLIC, 50 (MARCH 23,
        1927): 135-139.

18319   SAXON, LYLE; DREYER, EDWARD; AND TALLANT, ROBERT. GUMBO
        YA-YA: A COLLECTION OF LOUISIANA FOLK TALES. BOSTON:
        HOUGHTON MIFFLIN, 1945.

18320   SCARBOROUGH, W.S. "NEGRO FOLK-LORE." ARENA, 17
        (JANUARY, 1897): 186-192.

18321   SCHERMERHORN, R.A. THESE OUR PEOPLE: MINORITIES IN
        AMERICAN CULTURE. BOSTON: D.C. HEATH AND COMPANY,
        1949.

18322   SCOTT, PATRICIA B. "BLACK FOLKLORE IN TENNESSEE: A
        WORKING BIBLIOGRAPHY." TENNESSEE FOLKLORE SOCIETY
        BULLETIN, 44 (1978): 130-133.

18323   SEALE, LEA AND SEALE, MARIANNA. "EASTER ROCK: A
        LOUISIANA NEGRO CEREMONY." JOURNAL OF AMERICAN
        FOLKLORE, 55 (OCTOBER-DECEMBER, 1942): 212-218.

18324   SELJAN, ZORA. "NEGRO POPULAR POETRY IN BRAZIL." AFRICAN
        FORUM, 11 (SPRING, 1967): 54-77.

18325   SERENO, RENZO. "OBEAH: MAGIC AND SOCIAL STRUCTURE IN
        THE LESSER ANTILLES." PSYCHIATRY, 11 (FEBRUARY,
        1948): 15-31.

18326   SHEPARD, ELI. "SUPERSTITIONS OF THE NEGRO."
        COSMOPOLITAN, 5 (MARCH, 1888): 47-50.

18327 SHERLOCK, P.M. "JAMAICA SUPERSTITIONS." LIVING AGE, 323
       (DECEMBER 6, 1924): 529-534.

18328 SHOWERS, SUSAN. "A WEDDIN' AND A BURYIN' IN THE BLACK
       BELT." NEW ENGLAND MAGAZINE, 18 (MARCH-AUGUST, 1898):
       478-483.

18329 SIMMONS, DONALD C. "POSSIBLE WEST AFRICAN SOURCES FOR
       THE AMERICAN NEGRO 'DOZENS.'" JOURNAL OF AMERICAN
       FOLKLORE, 76 (OCTOBER-DECEMBER, 1963): 339-340.

18330 SIMMS, MARION. "BLACK MAGIC IN NEW ORLEANS." TRAVEL, 81
       (JULY, 1943): 18-19, 32.

18331 SIMPSON, GEORGE E. BLACK RELIGIONS IN THE NEW WORLD.
       NEW YORK: COLUMBIA UNIVERSITY PRESS, 1978.

18332 SIMPSON, GEORGE E. "THE VODUN SERVICE IN NORTHERN
       HAITI." AMERICAN ANTHROPOLOGIST, 42 (APRIL-JUNE,
       1940): 236-254.

18333 SINGLETON, A.H. "FOLKLORE OF THE NEGROES OF JAMAICA."
       FOLK-LORE, 15 (MARCH, JUNE, DECEMBER, 1904): 94,
       206-214, 450-453.

18334 SISK, GLENN. "FUNERAL CUSTOMS IN THE ALABAMA BLACK BELT,
       1870-1910." SOUTHERN FOLKLORE QUARTERLY, 23
       (SEPTEMBER, 1959): 169-171.

18335 "SLAVE FUNERAL." IN NUNEZ, BENJAMIN. DICTIONARY OF
       AFRO-LATIN AMERICAN CIVILIZATION. WESTPORT:
       GREENWOOD PRESS, 1980, P. 435.

18336 SMETZER, BARBARA. "AN ANNOTATED COLLECTION OF NEGRO
       FOLKTALES FROM HARNETT COUNTY, NORTH CAROLINA." M.A.
       THESIS, INDIANA UNIVERSITY, 1962.

18337 SMILEY, PORTIA. "FOLK-LORE FROM VIRGINIA, SOUTH
       CAROLINA, GEORGIA, ALABAMA, AND FLORIDA." JOURNAL OF
       AMERICAN FOLK-LORE, 32 (JULY, 1919): 357-383.

18338 SMITH, ROBERT A. "A NOTE ON THE FOLKTALES OF CHARLES W.
       CHESNUTT." CLA JOURNAL, 5 (MARCH, 1962): 229-232.

18339 SMYTHE, AUGUSTINE T. AND SASS, HERBERT R. THE CAROLINA
       LOW COUNTRY. NEW YORK: MACMILLAN, 1931.

18340 SNOW, LOUDELL F. "VOODOO ILLNESS IN THE BLACK
       POPULATION." IN CULTURE, CURERS AND CONTAGION.
       NOVATO, CA: CHANDLER & SHARP, 1979, PP. 179-184.

18341 "SOME SLAVE SUPERSTITIONS." SOUTHERN WORKMAN, 41 (APRIL,
       1912): 246-248.

18342 SPALDING, HENRY D. (ED.). ENCYCLOPEDIA OF BLACK FOLKLORE

AND HUMOR. MIDDLE VILLAGE, NY: JONATHAN DAVID
PUBLISHERS, 1972.

18343 SPECK, FRANK G. "A COMPARATIVE STUDY OF THE NATIVE
MYTHOLOGY OF THE SOUTH-EASTERN UNITED STATES." M.A.
THESIS, COLUMBIA UNIVERSITY, 1905.

18344 STAFFORD, A.O. "FOLK LITERATURE OF THE NEGRO." CRISIS,
10 (OCTOBER, 1915): 296-299.

18345 STANSBERRY, FREDDYE B. "FOLKLORE AND ITS EFFECTS UPON
BLACK HISTORY." MISSISSIPPI FOLKLORE REGISTER, 7
(WINTER, 1973): 115-122.

18346 STEINER, ROLAND. "OBSERVATIONS ON THE PRACTICE OF
CONJURING IN GEORGIA." JOURNAL OF AMERICAN FOLK-LORE,
14 (JULY-SEPTEMBER, 1901): 173-180.

18347 STERLING, PHILIP (ED.). LAUGHING ON THE OUTSIDE: THE
INTELLIGENT WHITE READER'S GUIDE TO NEGRO TALES AND
HUMOR. NEW YORK: GROSSET AND DUNLAP, 1965.

18348 STEWART, SADIE E. "SEVEN FOLK TALES FROM THE SEA
ISLANDS, SOUTH CAROLINA." JOURNAL OF AMERICAN
FOLK-LORE, 32 (JULY-SEPTEMBER, 1919): 394-396.

18349 STOCKARD, JANICE L. "THE ROLE OF THE AMERICAN BLACK
WOMAN IN FOLKTALES: AN INTERDISCIPLINARY STUDY OF
IDENTIFICATION AND INTERPRETATION." PH.D.
DISSERTATION, TULANE UNIVERSITY, 1980.

18350 STODDARD, FLORENCE J. AS OLD AS THE MOON: CUBAN
LEGENDS: FOLKLORE OF THE ANTILLES. NEW YORK:
DOUBLEDAY, 1909.

18351 STUCKEY, STERLING. "SLAVE RESISTANCE AS SEEN THROUGH
SLAVE FOLKLORE." IN REID, INEZ S. (ED.). THE BLACK
PRISM: PERSPECTIVES ON THE BLACK EXPERIENCE.
BROOKLYN: SUMMER INSTITUTE ON AFRO-AMERICAN STUDIES,
BROOKLYN COLLEGE, CITY UNIVERSITY OF NEW YORK, 1969,
PP. 51-60.

18352 STUCKEY, STERLING. "THROUGH THE PRISM OF FOLKLORE: THE
BLACK ETHOS IN SLAVERY." MASSACHUSETTS REVIEW, 9
(SUMMER, 1968): 417-437.

18353 SULLIVAN, PHILLIP E. "BUH RABBIT: GOING THROUGH THE
CHANGES." STUDIES IN BLACK LITERATURE, 4 (SUMMER,
1973): 28-32.

18354 SULLIVAN, T.P. PLANTATION AND UP-TO-DATE HUMOROUS NEGRO
STORIES. CHICAGO: M.A. DONAHUE AND COMPANY, 1905.

18355 SWART, P.D. "THE DIFFUSION OF THE FOLKTALE: WITH
SPECIAL NOTES ON AFRICA." MIDWEST FOLKLORE, 7

(SUMMER, 1957):   69-84.

18356   SYKES, REVECCA M.   "TURE, AJAPA AND WAKALULU: THREE
        DIVERSE AFRICAN TRICKSTERS."   B.A. THESIS, HARVARD
        UNIVERSITY, 1973.

18357   SZWED, JOHN F. AND ABRAHAMS, ROGER D.   "AFTER THE MYTH:
        STUDYING AFRO-AMERICAN CULTURAL PATTERNS IN THE
        PLANTATION LITERATURE."   IN CROWLEY, DANIEL J. (ED.).
        AFRICAN FOLKLORE IN THE NEW WORLD.   AUSTIN:
        UNIVERSITY OF TEXAS PRESS, 1977, PP. 65-86.

18358   SZWED, JOHN F. AND ABRAHAMS, ROGER D.   "AFTER THE MYTH:
        STUDYING AFRO-AMERICAN CULTURAL PATTERNS IN THE
        PLANTATION LITERATURE."   RESEARCH IN AFRICAN
        LITERATURES, 7 (FALL, 1976):   211-232.

18359   "TALES OF OLD BARBADOS."   JOURNAL OF THE BARBADOS MUSEUM
        AND HISTORICAL SOCIETY, 12 (AUGUST, 1945):   171-178.

18360   TALLEY, THOMAS W.   NEGRO FOLK RHYMES: WISE AND
        OTHERWISE.   NEW YORK: MACMILLAN COMPANY, 1922.

18361   TALLEY, THOMAS W.   "THE ORIGIN OF NEGRO TRADITIONS."
        PHYLON, 3 (FOURTH QUARTER, 1942):   371-376; 4 (FIRST
        QUARTER, 1943):   30-37.

18362   TALLMAN, MARJORIE.   "CONJURING LODGE."   DICTIONARY OF
        AMERICAN FOLKLORE.   NEW YORK: PHILOSOPHICAL LIBRARY,
        1959, P. 71.

18363   TAYLOR, CELIA B.   "CHEROKEE AND CREEK FOLKLORE ELEMENTS
        IN THE UNCLE REMUS STORIES."   M.A. THESIS, AUBURN
        UNIVERSITY, 1959.

18364   TEGARDEN, J.B.H.   "VOODOOISM."   M.A. THESIS, UNIVERSITY
        OF CHICAGO, 1924.

18365   THOMAS, DAVID H.; SOUTH, STANLEY; AND LARSEN, CLARK S.
        "RICH MAN, POOR MEN: OBSERVATIONS ON THREE ANTEBELLUM
        BURIALS FROM THE GEORGIA COAST."   ANTHROPOLOGICAL
        PAPERS OF THE AMERICAN MUSEUM OF NATURAL HISTORY, 54
        (1977):   397-420.

18366   THORP, WILLARD.   "SOUTHERN LITERATURE AND SOUTHERN
        SOCIETY."   IN THOMPSON, EDGAR T. (ED.).   PERSPECTIVES
        ON THE SOUTH: AGENDA FOR RESEARCH.   DURHAM: DUKE
        UNIVERSITY PRESS, 1967, PP. 95-108.

18367   TOLL, ROBERT C.   "FROM FOLKTYPE TO STEREOTYPE: IMAGES OF
        SLAVES IN ANTEBELLUM MINSTRELSY."   JOURNAL OF THE
        FOLKLORE INSTITUTE, 8 (JUNE, 1971):   38-47.

18368   TOOR, FRANCES.   A TREASURY OF MEXICAN FOLKWAYS.   NEW
        YORK: CROWN PUBLISHING COMPANY, 1947.

18369   TORIAN, SARAH (ED.). "ANTE-BELLUM AND WAR MEMORIES OF
         MRS. TELFAIR HODGSON." GEORGIA HISTORICAL QUARTERLY,
         27 (SEPTEMBER, 1943): 350-356.

18370   TROWBRIDGE, ADA W. "NEGRO CUSTOMS AND FOLK-STORIES OF
         JAMAICA." JOURNAL OF AMERICAN FOLK-LORE, 9
         (OCTOBER-DECEMBER, 1896): 279-287.

18371   TUBB, HILDA. "CHARACTERISTICS OF NEGROES AND ANIMALS IN
         THE UNCLE REMUS STORIES." M.A. THESIS, GEORGE PEABODY
         COLLEGE FOR TEACHERS, 1925.

18372   TURNER, DARWIN. "DADDY JOEL HARRIS AND HIS OLD-TIME
         DARKIES." SOUTHERN LITERARY JOURNAL, 1 (DECEMBER,
         1968): 20-41.

18373   TURNER, FREDERICK W. "BADMEN, BLACK AND WHITE: THE
         CONTINUITY OF AMERICAN FOLK TRADITIONS." PH.D.
         DISSERTATION, UNIVERSITY OF PENNSYLVANIA, 1965.

18374   UDAL, J.S. "OBEAH IN THE WEST INDIES." FOLK-LORE, 26
         (SEPTEMBER, 1915): 255-295.

18375   VALDES-CRUZ, ROSA. "AFRICAN HERITAGE IN CUBAN
         FOLKTALES." IN DIMIC, MILAN V. AND FERRATE, JUAN
         (EDS.). ACTES DU VIIE CONGRES DE L'ASSOCIATION
         INTERNATIONALE DE LITTERATURE COMPAREE. I:
         LITTERATURES AMERICAINES: DEPENDANCE, INDEPENDANCE,
         INTERDEPENDANCE. STUTTGART: BIEBER, 1979, PP.
         327-330.

18376   VAN BLARCOM, CAROLYN C. "RAT PIE AMONG THE BLACK
         MIDWIVES OF THE SOUTH." HARPER'S MAGAZINE, 160
         (FEBRUARY, 1930): 322-332.

18377   VANCE, ROBERT L.J. "PLANTATION FOLK-LORE." OPEN COURT,
         2 (1888): 1029-1032, 1074-1076, 1092-1095.

18378   VOORHOEVE, JAN AND LICHTVELD, URSY M. (EDS.). CREOLE
         DRUM: AN ANTHOLOGY OF CREOLE LITERATURE IN SURINAM.
         NEW HAVEN: YALE UNIVERSITY PRESS, 1975.

18379   WADE, MALVIN. THROUGH TO RABBIT'S EYE: CRITICAL
         PERSPECTIVES ON AFRICAN-AMERICAN FOLK CULTURE OF THE
         NINETEENTH CENTURY. AUSTIN: AFRICAN AND
         AFRO-AMERICAN STUDIES & RESEARCH CENTER, UNIVERSITY OF
         TEXAS, 1977.

18380   WALTON, DAVID W. "JOEL CHANDLER HARRIS AS FOLKLORIST: A
         REASSESSMENT." KEYSTONE FOLKLORE QUARTERLY, 11
         (SPRING, 1966): 21-26.

18381   WARING, MARY A. "MORTUARY CUSTOMS AND BELIEFS OF SOUTH
         CAROLINA NEGROES." JOURNAL OF AMERICAN FOLKLORE, 7
         (OCTOBER-DECEMBER, 1894): 318-319.

18382   WARING, MARY A.   "NEGRO SUPERSTITIONS IN SOUTH CAROLINA."
        JOURNAL OF AMERICAN FOLKLORE, 8 (JULY-SEPTEMBER,
        1895):   251-252.

18383   WARNER, CHARLES D.   STUDIES IN THE SOUTH AND WEST, WITH
        COMMENTS ON CANADA.   HARTFORD: AMERICAN PUBLISHING
        COMPANY, 1904.

18384   WATERMAN, RICHARD A. AND BASCOM, WILLIAM R.   "AFRICAN AND
        NEW WORLD FOLKLORE."   IN LEACH, MARIA (ED.).   FUNK &
        WAGNALLS STANDARD DICTIONARY OF FOLKLORE, MYTHOLOGY,
        AND LEGEND.   2 VOLS.   NEW YORK: FUNK AND WAGNALLS
        COMPANY, 1949, VOL. 1, PP. 18-24.

18385   WATSON, LAURA S.   "NEGRO FOLK-LORE OF THE CAROLINAS."
        M.A. THESIS,   STETSON UNIVERSITY, 1937.

18386   WEIL, DOROTHY.   "FOLKLORE MOTIFS IN ARNA BONTEMPS' BLACK
        THUNDER."   SOUTHERN FOLKLORE QUARTERLY, 35 (MARCH,
        1971):   1-14.

18387   WEISS, DANIEL.   "WILLIAM FAULKNER AND THE RUNAWAY SLAVE."
        NORTHWEST REVIEW, 6 (SUMMER, 1963):   71-79.

18388   WELDON, FRED O.   "NEGRO FOLK HEROES."   M.A. THESIS,
        UNIVERSITY OF TEXAS, 1958.

18389   WELDON, FRED O.   "NEGRO FOLKTALE HEROES."   PUBLICATIONS
        OF THE TEXAS FOLKLORE SOCIETY, 29 (1959):   170-189.

18390   WHALEY, MARCELLUS S.   THE OLD TYPES PASS--GULLAH SKETCHES
        OF THE CAROLINA SEA ISLANDS.   BOSTON: CHRISTOPHER
        PUBLISHING HOUSE, 1925.

18391   WHIPPLE, EMORY C.   "CARIB MUSIC, DANCE AND FOLKLORE."
        ACTES DU XLII CONGRES INTERNATIONAL DES AMERICANISTES,
        VOLUME VI.   PARIS: SOCIETE DES AMERICANISTES, 1979,
        PP. 503-512.

18392   WHITTEN, NORMAN E., JR.   "CONTEMPORARY PATTERNS OF MALIGN
        OCCULTISM AMONG NEGROES IN NORTH CAROLINA."   JOURNAL
        OF AMERICAN FOLKLORE, 65 (OCTOBER-DECEMBER, 1962):
        311-325.

18393   WHITTEN, NORMAN E., JR.   "RITUAL ENACTMENT OF SEX ROLES
        IN THE PACIFIC LOWLANDS OF ECUADOR-COLOMBIA."   IN
        PESCATELLO, ANN M. (ED.).   OLD ROOTS IN NEW LANDS:
        HISTORICAL AND ANTHROPOLOGICAL PERSPECTIVES ON BLACK
        EXPERIENCES IN THE AMERICAS.   WESTPORT: GREENWOOD
        PRESS, 1977, PP. 243-262.

18394   WIGGINS, WILLIAM H.   "'FREE AT LAST!':   A STUDY OF
        AFRO-AMERICAN EMANCIPATION DAY CELEBRATIONS."   PH.D.
        DISSERTATION, INDIANA UNIVERSITY, 1974.

18395   WIGGINS, WILLIAM H., JR. "JANUARY 1: THE
        AFRO-AMERICAN'S 'DAY OF DAYS.'" IN SALZMAN, JACK
        (ED.). PROSPECTS 4. NEW YORK: BURT FRANKLIN, 1979,
        PP. 331-354.

18396   WILLEFORD, MARY J. "NEGRO NEW WORLD RELIGIONS AND
        WITCHCRAFT." BIM, 12 (JANUARY-JUNE, 1969): 216-222.

18397   WILLIAMS, ALFRED M. "A MIRACLE-PLAY IN THE WEST INDIES."
        JOURNAL OF AMERICAN FOLKLORE, 9 (JANUARY-MARCH, 1896):
        117-120.

18398   WILLIAMS, JOSEPH J. VOODOOS AND OBEAHS: PHASES OF WEST
        INDIAN WITCHCRAFT. NEW YORK: DIAL PRESS, 1932.

18399   WINFIELD, ARTHUR A., JR. "SLAVE HOLIDAYS AND FESTIVITIES
        IN THE U.S." M.A. THESIS, ATLANTA UNIVERSITY, 1941.

18400   WINSLOW, DAVID J. "A NEGRO CORN-SHUCKING." JOURNAL OF
        AMERICAN FOLKLORE, 86 (JANUARY-MARCH, 1973): 61-62.

18401   WIPPLER, MIGENE G. SANTERIA: AFRICAN MAGIC IN LATIN
        AMERICA. NEW YORK: JULIAN PRESS, 1973.

18402   WOLFE, BERNARD. "UNCLE REMUS AND THE MALEVOLENT RABBIT:
        'TAKES A LIMBER-TOE GEMMUN FER TER JUMP JIM CROW.'"
        COMMENTARY, 8 (JULY, 1949): 31-41.

18403   WONA. A SELECTION OF ANANCY STORIES. KINGSTON, JAMAICA:
        GARDNER & COMPANY, 1899.

18404   WORK, M.N. "SOME GEECHEE FOLK-LORE." SOUTHERN WORKMAN,
        34 (NOVEMBER, DECEMBER, 1905): 633, 696.

18405   WRIGHT, RICHARD. TWELVE MILLION BLACK VOICES: A FOLK
        HISTORY OF THE NEGRO IN THE UNITED STATES. NEW YORK:
        VIKING, 1941.

18406   WRITERS' PROGRAM, SOUTH CAROLINA. SOUTH CAROLINA FOLK
        TALES: STORIES OF ANIMALS AND SUPERNATURAL BEINGS.
        COLUMBIA: BULLETIN OF THE UNIVERSITY OF SOUTH
        CAROLINA, 1941.

18407   WRITERS PROJECT, GEORGIA. DRUMS AND SHADOWS: SURVIVAL
        STUDIES AMONG THE GEORGIA COASTAL NEGROES. ATHENS:
        UNIVERSITY OF GEORGIA PRESS, 1940.

18408   WYATT, EMMA O. "NEGRO FOLKLORE FROM ALABAMA." M.A.
        THESIS, UNIVERSITY OF IOWA, 1943.

18409   YATES, IRENE. "CONJURES AND CURES IN THE NOVELS OF JULIA
        PETERKIN." SOUTHERN FOLKLORE QUARTERLY, 10 (1946):
        137-149.

DANCE

18410 ADAMS, EDWARD C.L. CONGAREE SKETCHES. SCENES FROM NEGRO
       LIFE IN THE SWAMPS OF THE CONGAREE AND TALES BY TAD
       AND SCIP OF HEAVEN AND HELL WITH OTHER MISCELLANY.
       CHAPEL HILL: UNIVERSITY OF NORTH CAROLINA PRESS, 1927.

18411 ALLEN, ZITA. "THE GREAT AMERICAN 'BLACK DANCE' MYSTERY."
       FREEDOMWAYS, 20 (1980): 233-290.

18412 ANDERSON, JOHN Q. "THE NEW ORLEANS VOODOO RITUAL DANCE
       AND ITS TWENTIETH-CENTURY SURVIVALS." SOUTHERN
       FOLKLORE QUARTERLY, 24 (JUNE, 1960): 135-143.

18413 ARVEY, VERNA. "NEGRO DANCE AND ITS INFLUENCE ON NEGRO
       MUSIC." IN DELERMA, DOMINIQUE-RENE (ED.). BLACK
       MUSIC IN OUR CULTURE. KENT: KENT STATE UNIVERSITY
       PRESS, 1970, PP. 79-92.

18414 BARROW, DAVID C. "A GEORGIA CORN SHUCKING." CENTURY
       MAGAZINE, 24 (OCTOBER, 1882): 373-378.

18415 BASTIN, BRUCE. "BLACK MUSIC IN NORTH CAROLINA." NORTH
       CAROLINA FOLKLORE JOURNAL, 27 (MAY, 1979): 3-19.

18416 BELIZ, ANEL E. "LOS CONGOS: AFRO-PANAMANIAN DANCE
       DRAMA." AMERICAS, 16 (NOVEMBER, 1959): 31-33.

18417 BOURGUIGNON, ERIKA E. "SYNCRETISM AND AMBIVALENCE IN
       HAITI: AN ETHNOHISTORIC STUDY." PH.D. DISSERTATION,
       NORTHWESTERN UNIVERSITY, 1951.

18418 BOWLES, PAUL. "CALYPSO-MUSIC OF THE ANTILLES." MODERN
       MUSIC, 17 (JANUARY-FEBRUARY, 1940): 154-159.

18419 BROWN, CECELIA R. "THE AFRO-AMERICAN CONTRIBUTION TO
       DANCE IN THE UNITED STATES, 1619-1965." NEGRO
       HERITAGE, 14 (1975): 63-71.

18420 BUTCHER, MARGARET T. "THE EARLY FOLK GIFTS: MUSIC,
       DANCE, FOLKLORE." THE NEGRO IN AMERICAN CULTURE. NEW
       YORK: ALFRED A. KNOPF, 1972, PP. 40-56.

18421 BUTCHER, MARGARET T. "NEGRO MUSIC AND DANCE: FORMAL
       RECOGNITION AND RECONSTRUCTION." THE NEGRO IN
       AMERICAN CULTURE. NEW YORK: ALFRED A. KNOPF, 1972,
       PP. 57-97.

18422 CABLE, GEORGE W. "CREOLE SLAVE DANCES: THE DANCE IN
       PLACE CONGO." CENTURY MAGAZINE, 31 (FEBRUARY, 1886):
       517-532.

18423 CARVALHO-NETO, PAULO DE. "THE CANDOMBE, A DRAMATIC DANCE
       FROM AFRO-URUGUAYAN FOLKLORE." ETHNOMUSICOLOGY, 6
       (SEPTEMBER, 1962): 164-174.

18424 CHASE, GILBERT. "SOME NOTES ON AFRO-CUBAN MUSIC AND
       DANCING." INTER-AMERICAN, 1 (DECEMBER, 1942): 32-33.

18425 CHILKOVSKY, NADIA. "ANALYSIS AND NOTATION OF BASIC
       AFRO-AMERICAN MOVEMENTS." IN STEARNS, MARSHALL AND
       STEARNS, JEAN (EDS.). JAZZ DANCE: THE STORY OF
       AMERICAN VERNACULAR DANCE. NEW YORK: MACMILLAN,
       1968, PP. 421-449.

18426 COURLANDER, HAROLD. A TREASURY OF AFRO-AMERICAN
       FOLKLORE. NEW YORK: CROWN PUBLISHERS, 1976.

18427 DE LABAN, JUANA. "SELECTED BIBLIOGRAPHIC SOURCES FOR
       COURSES IN AMERICAN DANCE." REVIEW OF ETHNOLOGY, 4
       (1974): 105-110.

18428 DIMOCK, ANNE. "CAPOEIRA ANGOLA." IN SHAPIRO, LINN
       (ED.). BLACK PEOPLE AND THEIR CULTURE: SELECTED
       WRITINGS FROM THE AFRICAN DIASPORA. WASHINGTON:
       SMITHSONIAN INSTITUTION, 1976, PP. 123-126.

18429 DIRKS, ROBERT. "JOHN CANOE: ETHNOHISTORICAL AND
       COMPARATIVE ANALYSIS OF A CARIB DANCE." ACTES DU XLII
       CONGRES INTERNATIONAL DES AMERICANISTES, VOLUME VI.
       PARIS: SOCIETE DES AMERICANISTES, 1979, PP. 487-501.

18430 DORYK, ELINOR. "STUDY OF HISTORICAL AND PRESENT DAY
       DANCE IN THE AMERICAN VIRGIN ISLANDS." M.A. THESIS,
       NEW YORK UNIVERSITY, 1951.

18431 DREWAL, MARGARET AND JACKSON, GLORIANNE. SOURCES ON
       AFRICAN AND AFRICAN-RELATED DANCE. NEW YORK:
       AMERICAN DANCE GUILD, 1974.

18432 DUBOIS, W.E.B. THE SOULS OF BLACK FOLK: ESSAYS AND
       SKETCHES. CHICAGO: A.C. MCCLURG & COMPANY, 1903.

18433 DUNHAM, KATHERINE. "THE DANCES OF HAITI." ACTA
       ANTHROPOLOGICA, 2 (NOVEMBER, 1947): 1-60.

18434 DUNHAM, KATHERINE. "THE NEGRO DANCE." IN BROWN,
       STERLING A.; DAVIS, ARTHUR P.; AND LEE, ULYSSES
       (EDS.). THE NEGRO CARAVAN. NEW YORK: DRYDEN PRESS,
       1941, PP. 990-1000.

18435 EMERY, LEONORE L. "BLACK DANCE IN THE UNITED STATES,
       FROM 1619 TO 1970." PH.D. DISSERTATION, UNIVERSITY OF
       SOUTHERN CALIFORNIA, 1971.

18436 EMERY, LYNNE F. "BLACK DANCE OF THE CARIBBEAN,
       1518-1900." BLACK DANCE IN THE UNITED STATES FROM
       1619 TO 1970. PALO ALTO: NATIONAL PRESS BOOKS, 1972,
       PP. 15-79.

18437 EMERY, LYNNE F. "DANCE IN THE NORTH, ON THE LEVEE, AND

IN NEW ORLEANS." BLACK DANCE IN THE UNITED STATES
FROM 1619 TO 1970. PALO ALTO: NATIONAL PRESS BOOKS,
1972, PP. 139-178.

18438   EMERY, LYNNE F.   "DANCE ON THE PLANTATIONS."   BLACK DANCE
        IN THE UNITED STATES FROM 1619 TO 1970.   PALO ALTO:
        NATIONAL PRESS BOOKS, 1972, PP. 80-138.

18439   GAFFNEY, FLOYD.   "THE FUNCTION AND FORM OF THE RING SHOUT
        AS A RELIGIOUS EXPRESSION: FROM WEST AFRICAN ORIGINS
        THROUGH THE ERA OF SLAVERY IN AMERICA."   M.A. THESIS,
        ADELPHI UNIVERSITY, 1952.

18440   GELLERT, LAWRENCE.   "DANCING IN CHURCH."   NEW THEATRE, 2
        (JULY, 1935):   19-20.

18441   GOINES, LEONARD.   "'WALK OVER':   MUSIC IN THE SLAVE
        NARRATIVES."   SING-OUT, 24 (JANUARY-FEBRUARY, 1976):
        6-11.

18442   GOINES, MARGARETTA B.   "AFRICAN RETENTIONS IN THE DANCE
        OF THE AMERICAS."   DANCE RESEARCH MONOGRAPH ONE,
        1971-72.   NEW YORK: CORD, 1973, PP. 209-229.

18443   HANNA, JUDITH L.   "AFRICANA DANCE RESEARCH: PAST,
        PRESENT, AND FUTURE."   AFRICANA JOURNAL, 11 (1980):
        33-52.

18444   HANNA, JUDITH L.   "THE STATUS OF AFRICAN DANCE STUDIES."
        AFRICA, 36 (JULY, 1966):   303-307.

18445   HANNA, JUDITH L.   "WHAT IS AFRICAN DANCE?"   NEW AFRICAN
        LITERATURE AND THE ARTS, NO. 2 (FALL, 1966):   64-67.

18446   HANSEN, CHADWICK.   "JENNY'S TOE: NEGRO SHAKING DANCES IN
        AMERICA."   AMERICAN QUARTERLY, 19 (FALL, 1967):
        554-563.

18447   HENRY, BESSIE M.   "A YANKEE SCHOOLMISTRESS DISCOVERS
        VIRGINIA."   ESSEX INSTITUTE HISTORICAL COLLECTIONS,
        101 (APRIL, 1965):   121-132.

18448   HOBSON, ANNE.   IN OLD ALABAMA: BEING THE CHRONICLES OF
        MISS MOUSE, THE LITTLE BLACK MERCHANT.   NEW YORK:
        DOUBLEDAY, PAGE, 1903.

18449   IDESON, JULIA AND HIGGINBOTHAM, SANFORD W. (EDS.).   "A
        TRADING TRIP TO NATCHEZ AND NEW ORLEANS, 1822:   DIARY
        OF THOMAS S. TEAS."   JOURNAL OF SOUTHERN HISTORY, 7
        (AUGUST, 1941):   378-399.

18450   JOHNSTON, THOMAS F.   "MUSIC AND BLACKS IN EIGHTEENTH AND
        NINETEENTH CENTURY CANADA."   ANTHROPOLOGICAL JOURNAL
        OF CANADA, 18 (1980):   19-21.

18451   KEALIINOHOMOKU, JOANN W.   "A COMPARATIVE STUDY OF DANCE
        AS A CONSTELLATION OF MOTOR BEHAVIORS AMONG AFRICAN
        AND UNITED STATES NEGROES."   M.A. THESIS, NORTHWESTERN
        UNIVERSITY, 1965.

18452   KINNEY, ESI S.   "AFRICANISMS IN MUSIC AND DANCE OF THE
        AMERICAS."   IN GOLDSTEIN, RHODA L. (ED.).   BLACK LIFE
        AND CULTURE IN THE UNITED STATES.   NEW YORK: THOMAS
        Y. CROWELL, 1971, PP. 49-63.

18453   KMEN, HENRY A.   "THE ROOTS OF JAZZ AND THE DANCE IN PLACE
        CONGO: A REAPPRAISAL."   YEARBOOK FOR INTERAMERICAN
        MUSICAL RESEARCH, 8 (1972):   5-16.

18454   KMEN, HENRY A.   "SINGING AND DANCING IN NEW ORLEANS--A
        SOCIAL HISTORY OF THE BIRTH AND GROWTH OF BALLS AND
        OPERA, 1791-1841."   PH.D. DISSERTATION, TULANE
        UNIVERSITY, 1961.

18455   KOFSKY, FRANK.   "AFRO-AMERICAN INNOVATION AND THE FOLK
        TRADITION IN JAZZ: THEIR HISTORICAL SIGNIFICANCE."
        JOURNAL OF ETHNIC STUDIES, 7 (SPRING, 1979):   1-12.

18456   KURATH, GERTRUDE P.   "AFRICAN INFLUENCES ON AMERICAN
        DANCE."   FOCUS ON DANCE, 3 (1965):   34-50.

18457   KURATH, GERTRUDE P. (ED.).   "SPECIAL BIBLIOGRAPHY: FILMS
        OF DANCE, PART II."   ETHNOMUSICOLOGY, 7 (MAY, 1963):
        125-126.

18458   KURATH, GERTRUDE P.   "STYLISTIC BLENDS IN AFRO-AMERICAN
        DANCE CULTS OF CATHOLIC ORIGIN."   PAPERS OF THE
        MICHIGAN ACADEMY OF SCIENCE, ARTS, AND LETTERS, 48
        (1963):   577-581.

18459   KURATH, GERTRUDE P. AND CHILKOVSKY, NADIA.   "JAZZ
        CHOREOLOGY."   IN WALLACE, ANTHONY F.C. (ED.).   MEN AND
        CULTURES.   PHILADELPHIA: UNIVERSITY OF PENNSYLVANIA
        PRESS, 1956, PP. 152-160.

18460   LEKIS, LISA.   "THE ORIGIN AND DEVELOPMENT OF ETHNIC
        CARIBBEAN DANCE AND MUSIC."   PH.D. DISSERTATION,
        UNIVERSITY OF FLORIDA, 1956.

18461   MCCOY, JAMES A.   "THE BOMBA AND AGUINALDO OF PUERTO RICO
        AS THEY HAVE EVOLVED FROM INDIGENOUS, AFRICAN, AND
        EUROPEAN CULTURES."   PH.D. DISSERTATION, FLORIDA STATE
        UNIVERSITY, 1968.

18462   "NEGRO DANCES IN ARKANSAS."   JOURNAL OF AMERICAN
        FOLK-LORE, 1 (APRIL-JUNE, 1888):   83.

18463   OESTERLEY, W.O.E.   THE SACRED DANCE.   BROOKLYN: DANCE
        HORIZONS, N.D.

18464   PRIMUS, PEARL E. "PRIMITIVE AFRICAN DANCE (AND ITS
         INFLUENCE ON THE CHURCHES OF THE SOUTH)." IN CHUJOY,
         ANATOLE AND MANCHESTER, P.W. (EDS.). THE DANCE
         ENCYCLOPEDIA. NEW YORK: A.S. BARNES, 1949, PP.
         387-389.

18465   RAFFE, WALTER G. "NEGRO DANCING IN USA." DICTIONARY OF
         THE DANCE. NEW YORK: A.S. BARNES, 1964, PP. 349-350.

18466   RAVENEL, HENRY W. "RECOLLECTIONS OF SOUTHERN PLANTATION
         LIFE." YALE REVIEW, 25 (JUNE, 1936): 748-777.

18467   RUMMONDS, F. "AFRICAN INFLUENCE ON BRAZILIAN FOLK
         DANCING." VILTIS, 25 (1966): 6-7.

18468   RYMAN, CHERYL. "THE JAMAICAN HERITAGE IN DANCE."
         JAMAICA JOURNAL, NO. 44 (JUNE, 1980): 2-13.

18469   SCHERMERHORN, R.A. THESE OUR PEOPLE: MINORITIES IN
         AMERICAN CULTURE. BOSTON: D.C. HEATH AND COMPANY,
         1949.

18470   SHARMA, MOHAN L. "AFRO-AMERICAN MUSIC AND DANCE." IN
         ROUCEK, JOSEPH S. AND KIERNAN, THOMAS (EDS.). THE
         NEGRO IMPACT ON WESTERN CIVILIZATION. NEW YORK:
         PHILOSOPHICAL LIBRARY, 1970, PP. 139-158.

18471   SHEDD, MARGARET. "CARIB DANCE PATTERNS." THEATRE ARTS
         MONTHLY, 17 (JANUARY, 1933): 65-77.

18472   "SLAVES: MUSIC AND DANCE FORMS." IN RYWELL, MARTIN
         (ED.). AFRO-AMERICAN ENCYCLOPEDIA. 10 VOLS. NORTH
         MIAMI: EDUCATIONAL BOOK PUBLISHERS, 1974, VOL. 8, PP.
         2493-2494.

18473   STEARNS, MARSHALL AND STEARNS, JEAN. JAZZ DANCE: THE
         STORY OF AMERICAN VERNACULAR DANCE. NEW YORK:
         MACMILLAN PUBLISHING COMPANY, 1968.

18474   THOMPSON, ROBERT F. "AN AESTHETIC OF THE COOL: WEST
         AFRICAN DANCE." AFRICAN FORUM, 2 (FALL, 1966):
         85-102.

18475   TODD, ARTHUR. "AMERICAN NEGRO DANCE: A NATIONAL
         TREASURE." IN HASKELL, ARNOLD AND CLARKE, MARY
         (EDS.). THE BALLET ANNUAL 1962. LONDON: ADAM AND
         CHARLES BLACK, 1961, PP. 92-105.

18476   TODD, ARTHUR. "FOUR CENTURIES OF AMERICAN DANCE: DANCE
         BEFORE THE AMERICAN REVOLUTION--1734-1775." DANCE
         MAGAZINE, 24 (MARCH, 1950): 20-21, 35.

18477   TODD, ARTHUR. "FOUR CENTURIES OF AMERICAN DANCE: THE
         NEGRO FOLK DANCE IN AMERICA." DANCE MAGAZINE, 24
         (JANUARY, 1950): 14-15, 41.

18478   WHARTON, LINDA F. AND DANIEL, JACK L. "BLACK DANCE: ITS
        AFRICAN ORIGINS AND CONTINUITY." MINORITY VOICES, 1
        (FALL, 1977): 73-80.

18479   WHIPPLE, EMORY C. "CARIB MUSIC, DANCE AND FOLKLORE."
        ACTES DU XLII CONGRES INTERNATIONAL DES AMERICANISTES,
        VOLUME VI. PARIS: SOCIETE DES AMERICANISTES, 1979,
        PP. 503-512.

18480   WIGGINS, DAVID K. "SPORT AND POPULAR PASTIMES IN THE
        PLANTATION COMMUNITY: THE SLAVE EXPERIENCE." PH.D.
        DISSERTATION, UNIVERSITY OF MARYLAND, 1979.

18481   WIGGINS, DAVID K. "SPORT AND POPULAR PASTIMES: SHADOW
        OF THE SLAVEQUARTER." CANADIAN JOURNAL OF THE HISTORY
        OF SPORT AND PHYSICAL EDUCATION, 11 (1980): 61-88.

18482   YOUNG, AURELIA. "BLACK FOLK MUSIC." MISSISSIPPI
        FOLKLORE REGISTER, 6 (1972): 1-4.

MATERIAL CULTURE

18483   ABBITT OUTLAW, MERRY; BOGLEY, BEVERLY A.; AND OUTLAW,
        ALAIN C. "RICH MAN, POOR MAN: STATUS DEFINITION IN
        TWO SEVENTEENTH-CENTURY CERAMIC ASSEMBLAGES FROM
        KINGSMILL." UNPUBLISHED PAPER PRESENTED AT MEETING OF
        SOCIETY FOR HISTORICAL ARCHAEOLOGY, OTTAWA, ONTARIO,
        1977.

18484   ADAMS, WILLIAM H.; MARTIN, DALE L.; BARTON, DAVID L.; AND
        BARTOVIES, ALBERT F. HISTORICAL ARCHAEOLOGY OF THE
        BAY SPRINGS MILL COMMUNITY. INTERIM REPORT. REPORT
        SUBMITTED TO THE INTERAGENCY ARCHAEOLOGICAL SERVICES,
        ATLANTA. BLOOMINGTON: SOIL SYSTEMS, 1979.

18485   ADAMS, WILLIAM H.; MARTIN, DALE L.; ELLIOTT, JACK D.,
        JR.; AND ADAMS, JAMES E. INTERIM REPORT: TEST
        EXCAVATIONS AT WAVERLY FERRY, CLAY COUNTY,
        MISSISSIPPI. SUBMITTED TO INTERAGENCY ARCHAEOLOGICAL
        SERVICES-ATLANTA. BLOOMINGTON: SOIL SYSTEMS, INC.,
        1979.

18486   ADLER, THOMAS. "THE PHYSICAL DEVELOPMENT OF THE BANJO."
        NEW YORK FOLKLORE QUARTERLY, 28 (SEPTEMBER, 1972):
        187-208.

18487   "THE AFRO-AMERICAN TRADITION IN DECORATIVE ARTS." BLACK
        HERITAGE, 19 (SEPTEMBER-OCTOBER, 1979): 11-18.

18488   ASCHER, ROBERT AND FAIRBANKS, CHARLES H. "EXCAVATION OF
        A SLAVE CABIN: GEORGIA, USA." HISTORICAL
        ARCHAEOLOGY, 5 (1971): 3-17.

18489   BAKER, VERNON G. "ARCHAEOLOGICAL VISIBILITY OF

AFRO-AMERICAN CULTURE: AN EXAMPLE FROM BLACK LUCY'S
GARDEN, ANDOVER, MASSACHUSETTS." IN SCHUYLER, ROBERT
L. (ED.). ARCHAEOLOGICAL PERSPECTIVES ON ETHNICITY IN
AMERICA. FARMINGDALE, NY: BAYWOOD PUBLISHING
COMPANY, 1980, PP. 29-37.

18490   BAKER, VERNON G. "HISTORICAL ARCHAEOLOGY AT BLACK LUCY'S
        GARDEN, ANDOVER, MASSACHUSETTS: CERAMICS FROM THE
        SITE OF A NINETEENTH CENTURY AFRO-AMERICAN." PAPERS
        OF THE ROBERT S. PEABODY FOUNDATION FOR ARCHAEOLOGY.
        ANDOVER, MA: PHILLIPS ACADEMY, 1977.

18491   BARFIELD, RODNEY. "NORTH CAROLINA BLACK MATERIAL
        CULTURE: A RESEARCH OPPORTUNITY." NORTH CAROLINA
        FOLKLORE JOURNAL, 27 (NOVEMBER, 1979): 61-66.

18492   BINGHAM, ALFRED M. "SQUATTER SETTLEMENTS OF FREED SLAVES
        IN NEW ENGLAND." CONNECTICUT HISTORICAL SOCIETY
        BULLETIN, 41 (JULY, 1976): 65-80.

18493   BOLTON, H. CARRINGTON. "DECORATION OF NEGRO GRAVES IN
        SOUTH CAROLINA." JOURNAL OF AMERICAN FOLKLORE, 4
        (JULY-SEPTEMBER, 1891): 214.

18494   BRIGHT, ALFRED L. "THE BLACK ARTIST IN COLONIAL
        AMERICA." IN BRIGHT; CLARK, SARAH B.; AMADI, LAWRENCE
        E.; COOPER, SYRETHA; BARNES, CLARENCE; AND O'NEILL,
        DANIEL J. AN INTERDISCIPLINARY INTRODUCTION TO BLACK
        STUDIES. DUBUQUE: KENDALL/HUNT PUBLISHING COMPANY,
        1977, PP. 121-124.

18495   BULLEN, A.K. AND BULLEN, R.P. "BLACK LUCY'S GARDEN."
        BULLETIN OF THE MASSACHUSETTS ARCHAEOLOGICAL SOCIETY,
        6 (1945): 17-28.

18496   BURRISON, JOHN. "EDGEFIELD DISTRICT, SOUTH CAROLINA."
        GEORGIA JUG MAKERS: A HISTORY OF SOUTHERN FOLK
        POTTERY. ANN ARBOR: UNIVERSITY MICROFILMS, 1973, PP.
        228-234.

18497   BURRISON, JOHN A. "AFRO-AMERICAN FOLK POTTERY IN THE
        SOUTH." SOUTHERN FOLKLORE QUARTERLY, 42 (1978):
        175-200.

18498   CHASE, JUDITH W. AFRO-AMERICAN ART AND CRAFT. NEW YORK:
        VAN NOSTRAND, 1971.

18499   CHASE, JUDITH W. "AMERICAN HERITAGE FROM ANTE-BELLUM
        BLACK CRAFTSMEN." SOUTHERN FOLKLORE QUARTERLY, 42
        (1978): 135-158.

18500   CONNELL, NEVILLE. "FURNITURE AND FURNISHINGS IN BARBADOS
        DURING THE 17TH CENTURY." JOURNAL OF THE BARBADOS
        MUSEUM AND HISTORICAL SOCIETY, 24 (1957): 102-121.

18501   CRAFTMANSHIP: A TRADITION IN BLACK AMERICA. NEW YORK:
        RCA CORPORATION, 1976.

18502   CRESSEY, PAMELA J. "AN ENDURING AFRO-AMERICAN
        NEIGHBORHOOD: AN ARCHAEOLOGICAL PERSPECTIVE FROM
        ALEXANDRIA, VIRGINIA." BLACK HERITAGE, 20
        (SEPTEMBER-OCTOBER, 1980): 1-10.

18503   CUREAN, HAROLD G. "THE HISTORIC ROLES OF BLACK AMERICAN
        ARTISTS: A PROFILE OF STRUGGLE." BLACK SCHOLAR, 9
        (NOVEMBER, 1977): 2-13.

18504   DAVIS, GERALD L. "AFRO-AMERICAN COIL BASKETRY IN
        CHARLESTON COUNTY, SOUTH CAROLINA: AFFECTIVE
        CHARACTERISTICS OF A ARTISTIC CRAFT IN SOCIAL
        CONTEXT." IN YODER, DON (ED.). AMERICAN FOLKLIFE.
        AUSTIN: UNIVERSITY OF TEXAS PRESS, 1976, PP. 151-184.

18505   DEETZ, JAMES. "BLACK SETTLEMENT AT PLYMOUTH."
        ARCHAEOLOGY, 29 (1976): 207.

18506   DEETZ, JAMES. IN SMALL THINGS FORGOTTEN. NEW YORK:
        DOUBLEDAY, 1977.

18507   DOW, GEORGE F. THE ARTS AND CRAFTS IN NEW ENGLAND,
        1704-1775. TOPSFIELD, MA: WAYSIDE PRESS, 1927.

18508   DRUCKER, LESLEY M. "SPIERS LANDING: A SOCIOECONOMIC
        STUDY OF AN UNDOCUMENTED LATE EIGHTEENTH CENTURY SITE
        IN BERKELEY COUNTY, SOUTH CAROLINA." UNPUBLISHED
        PAPER DELIVERED AT MEETING OF SOCIETY FOR HISTORICAL
        ARCHAEOLOGY, NASHVILLE, TENNESSEE, 1979.

18509   DRUCKER, LESLEY M. AND ANTHONY, RONALD W. THE SPIERS
        LANDING SITE: ARCHAEOLOGICAL INVESTIGATIONS IN
        BERKELEY COUNTY, SOUTH CAROLINA. COLUMBIA: CAROLINA
        ARCHAEOLOGICAL SERVICES, 1979.

18510   DUBOIS, W.E.B. (ED.). THE NEGRO ARTISAN. ATLANTA:
        ATLANTA UNIVERSITY PRESS, 1902.

18511   DUBOIS, W.E.B. THE SOULS OF BLACK FOLK: ESSAYS AND
        SKETCHES. CHICAGO: A.C. MCCLURG & COMPANY, 1903.

18512   DUBOIS, W.E.B. AND DILL, AUGUSTUS G. (EDS.). THE NEGRO
        AMERICAN ARTISAN. ATLANTA: ATLANTA UNIVERSITY
        PUBLICATIONS, 1912.

18513   FAGG, WILLIAM. "NOTES ON SOME WEST AFRICAN AMERICANA."
        MAN, 52 (AUGUST, 1952): 119-122.

18514   FAIRBANKS, CHARLES H. "THE KINGSLEY SLAVE CABINS IN
        DUVAL COUNTY, FLORIDA, 1968." THE CONFERENCE ON
        HISTORIC SITE ARCHAEOLOGY PAPERS, 1972, NO. 7 (1974):
        62-93.

18515   FAIRBANKS, CHARLES H. "SPANIARDS, PLANTERS, SHIPS, AND
        SLAVES: HISTORICAL ARCHAEOLOGY IN FLORIDA AND
        GEORGIA." ARCHAEOLOGY, 29 (JULY, 1976): 164-172.

18516   FERGUSON, LELAND G. "AFRO-AMERICAN SLAVERY AND THE
        'INVISIBLE' ARCHAEOLOGICAL RECORD OF SOUTH CAROLINA."
        UNPUBLISHED PAPER PRESENTED AT THE CONFERENCE ON
        HISTORIC SITE ARCHAEOLOGY, ST. AUGUSTINE, FLORIDA,
        1979.

18517   FERGUSON, LELAND G. "LOOKING FOR THE 'AFRO' IN
        COLONO-INDIAN POTTERY." IN SCHUYLER, ROBERT L. (ED.).
        ARCHAEOLOGICAL PERSPECTIVES ON ETHNICITY IN AMERICA:
        AFRO-AMERICAN AND ASIAN CULTURE HISTORY. FARMINGDALE,
        NY: BAYWOOD PUBLISHING COMPANY, 1980, PP. 14-28.

18518   FRAZIER, HERBERT L. "BASKET WEAVING TRACED TO ANCIENT
        AFRICAN CRAFT." CHARLESTON NEWS AND COURIER,
        SEPTEMBER 4, 1972.

18519   FRY, GLADYS-MARIE. "HARRIET POWERS: PORTRAIT OF A BLACK
        QUILTER." IN WADSWORTH, ANNA (ED.). MISSING PIECES:
        GEORGIA FOLK ART, 1770-1976. ATLANTA: GEORGIA
        COUNCIL FOR THE ARTS AND HUMANITIES, 1976, PP. 16-23.

18520   GLASSIE, HENRY. "THE NATURE OF THE NEW WORLD ARTIFACT:
        THE INSTANCE OF THE DUGOUT CANOE." IN ESCHER, WALTER;
        GANTNER, THEO; AND TRUMPY, HANS (EDS.). FESTSCHRIFT
        FUR ROBERT WILDHABER ZUM 70. BASEL: G. KREBS, 1973,
        PP. 153-179.

18521   GLASSIE, HENRY. PATTERN IN THE MATERIAL FOLK CULTURE OF
        THE EASTERN UNITED STATES. PHILADELPHIA: UNIVERSITY
        OF PENNSYLVANIA MONOGRAPHS IN FOLKLORE AND FOLKLIFE,
        NO. 1, 1968.

18522   GOTTESMAN, RITA S. THE ARTS AND CRAFTS IN NEW YORK:
        ADVERTISEMENTS AND NEWS ITEMS FROM NEW YORK CITY
        NEWSPAPERS. NEW YORK: NEW-YORK HISTORICAL SOCIETY,
        1938.

18523   GOTTESMAN, RITA S. THE ARTS AND CRAFTS IN NEW YORK,
        1777-1799. NEW YORK: NEW-YORK HISTORICAL SOCIETY,
        1954.

18524   GOTTESMAN, RITA S. THE ARTS AND CRAFTS IN NEW YORK,
        1800-1864. NEW YORK: NEW-YORK HISTORICAL SOCIETY,
        1965.

18525   GYRISCO, GEOFFREY M. AND SALWEN, BERT. "ARCHAEOLOGY OF
        BLACK AMERICAN CULTURE: AN ANNOTATED BIBLIOGRAPHY."
        IN SCHUYLER, ROBERT L. (ED.). ARCHAEOLOGICAL
        PERSPECTIVES ON ETHNICITY IN AMERICA: AFRO-AMERICAN
        AND ASIAN CULTURE HISTORY. FARMINGDALE, NY: BAYWOOD
        PUBLISHING COMPANY, 1980, PP. 76-35.

18526   HAMILTON, JENNIFER M. "EARLY HISTORY AND EXCAVATION OF
        THE LE CONTE WOODMANSTON PLANTATION." M.A. THESIS,
        UNIVERSITY OF FLORIDA, 1980.

18527   HANDLER, JEROME S. "AN ARCHAEOLOGICAL INVESTIGATION OF
        THE DOMESTIC LIFE OF PLANTATION SLAVES IN BARBADOS."
        JOURNAL OF THE BARBADOS MUSEUM AND HISTORICAL SOCIETY,
        34 (MAY, 1972): 64-72.

18528   HANDLER, JEROME S. "A HISTORICAL SKETCH OF POTTERY
        MANUFACTURE IN BARBADOS." JOURNAL OF THE BARBADOS
        MUSEUM AND HISTORICAL SOCIETY, 30 (NOVEMBER, 1963):
        1-24.

18529   HANDLER, JEROME S. AND LANGE, F.W. "PLANTATION SLAVERY
        ON BARBADOS, WEST INDIES." ARCHAEOLOGY, 32 (JULY,
        1979): 45-52.

18530   HANDLER, JEROME S.; LANGE, FREDERICK W.; AND ORSER, C.
        "CARNELIAN BEADS IN NECKLACES FROM A SLAVE CEMETERY IN
        BARBADOS." ORNAMENT: A QUARTERLY OF JEWELRY &
        PERSONAL ADORNMENT, 4 (1979): 15-18.

18531   HANDLER, JEROME S.; LANGE, FREDERICK W.; AND RIORDAN,
        ROBERT V. PLANTATION SLAVERY IN BARBADOS: AN
        ARCHAEOLOGICAL AND HISTORICAL INVESTIGATION.
        CAMBRIDGE: HARVARD UNIVERSITY PRESS, 1978.

18532   HARRIS, MARK. "BEST BUY IN CHARLESTON." NEGRO DIGEST, 8
        (JULY, 1950): 42-44.

18533   HARRIS, MIDDLETON. THE BLACK BOOK. NEW YORK: RANDOM
        HOUSE, 1974.

18534   HIGMAN, BARRY W. "A REPORT ON EXCAVATIONS AT MONTPELIER
        AND ROEHAMPTON." JAMAICA JOURNAL, 8 (1974): 40-45.

18535   HOFFMAN, CHARLES A. "ARCHAEOLOGICAL INVESTIGATIONS ON
        ST. KITTS, W.I." CARIBBEAN JOURNAL OF SCIENCE, 13
        (DECEMBER, 1973): 237-252.

18536   KELSO, WILLIAM M. "CAPTAIN JONES' WORMSLOW: A
        HISTORICAL, ARCHAEOLOGICAL, AND ARCHITECTURAL STUDY OF
        AN EIGHTEENTH-CENTURY PLANTATION SITE NEAR SAVANNAH,
        GEORGIA." PH.D. DISSERTATION, EMORY UNIVERSITY, 1971.

18537   KELSO, WILLIAM M. CAPTAIN JONES'S WORMSLOW: A
        HISTORICAL, ARCHAEOLOGICAL, AND ARCHITECTURAL STUDY OF
        AN EIGHTEENTH-CENTURY PLANTATION SITE NEAR SAVANNAH,
        GEORGIA. ATHENS: UNIVERSITY OF GEORGIA PRESS, 1979.

18538   KELSO, WILLIAM M. "THE COLONIAL SILENT MAJORITY:
        TENANT, SERVANT AND SLAVE SETTLEMENT SITES AT
        KINGSMILL, VIRGINIA." UNPUBLISHED PAPER PRESENTED AT
        MEETING OF AMERICAN ANTHROPOLOGICAL ASSOCIATION,

WASHINGTON, 1976.

18539   LANGE, FREDERICK W.   "SLAVE MORTUARY PRACTICES, BARBADOS,
        WEST INDIES."   IN ACTAS DEL XLI CONGRESSO
        INTERNACIONAL DE AMERICANISTAS. 3 VOLS. MEXICO:
        COMISION DE PUBLICACION DE LAS ACTAS Y MEMORIAS, 1976,
        VOL. 2, PP. 477-483.

18540   LARRABEE, EDWARD M.   "HISTORIC SITE ARCHAEOLOGY IN
        RELATION TO OTHER ARCHAEOLOGY."   HISTORICAL
        ARCHAEOLOGY, 3 (1969): 67-74.

18541   LEWIS, KENNETH E.   "EXCAVATING A COLONIAL RICE
        PLANTATION."   EARLY MAN, (AUTUMN, 1979): 13-17.

18542   LORNELL, KIP.   "BLACK MATERIAL FOLK CULTURE."   SOUTHERN
        FOLKLORE QUARTERLY, 42 (1978): 287-294.

18543   MACLEOD, BRUCE A.   "THE MUSICAL INSTRUMENTS OF NORTH
        AMERICAN SLAVES."   MISSISSIPPI FOLKLORE REGISTER, 11
        (SPRING, 1977): 34-49.

18544   MACLEOD, BRUCE A.   "QUILLS, FIFES, AND FLUTES BEFORE THE
        CIVIL WAR."   SOUTHERN FOLKLORE QUARTERLY, 42 (1978):
        201-208.

18545   MATHEWS, FLEMING W.   "PRELUDE TO AFRO-AMERICAN
        ARCHAEOLOGY: EXCAVATIONS AT CEDER HILL."   M.A.
        THESIS, HOWARD UNIVERSITY, 1976.

18546   MATHEWSON, R. DUNCAN.   "ARCHAEOLOGICAL ANALYSIS OF
        MATERIAL CULTURE AS A REFLECTION OF SUBCULTURAL
        DIFFERENTIATION IN EIGHTEENTH-CENTURY JAMAICA."   IN
        PROCTOR, SAMUEL (ED.).   EIGHTEENTH-CENTURY FLORIDA AND
        THE CARIBBEAN. GAINESVILLE: UNIVERSITY PRESSES OF
        FLORIDA, 1976, PP. 75-37.

18547   MATHEWSON, R. DUNCAN.   "ARCHAEOLOGICAL ANALYSIS OF
        MATERIAL CULTURE AS A REFLECTION OF SUBCULTURAL
        DIFFERENTIATION IN 18TH CENTURY JAMAICA."   JAMAICA
        JOURNAL, 7 (1973): 25-29.

18548   MATHEWSON, R. DUNCAN.   "HISTORY FROM THE EARTH:
        ARCHAEOLOGICAL EXCAVATIONS AT OLD KING'S HOUSE."
        JAMAICA JOURNAL, 6 (1972): 3-11.

18549   MATHEWSON, R. DUNCAN.   "JAMAICAN CERAMICS: AN
        INTRODUCTION TO 18TH CENTURY FOLK POTTERY IN WEST
        AFRICAN TRADITION."   JAMAICA JOURNAL, 6 (1972): 54-56.

18550   MCFARLANE, SUZANNE S.   "THE ETHNOHISTORY OF A SLAVE
        COMMUNITY: THE COUPER PLANTATION SITE."   M.A. THESIS,
        UNIVERSITY OF FLORIDA, 1975.

18551   MULLINS, SUE A.   "THE SOUTHERN COASTAL PLANTATION: VIEW

FROM ST. SIMON'S ISLAND, GEORGIA." UNPUBLISHED PAPER
PRESENTED AT MEETING OF SOCIETY FOR HISTORICAL
ARCHAEOLOGY, NASHVILLE, TENNESSEE, 1979.

18552   MULLINS-MOORE, SUE. "THE ANTEBELLUM PLANTATION: IN
        SEARCH OF AN ARCHAEOLOGICAL PATTERN." PH.D.
        DISSERTATION, UNIVERSITY OF FLORIDA, 1980.

18553   MYERS, BETTY. "GULLAH BASKETRY." CRAFT HORIZONS, 36
        (JUNE, 1976): 30-31, 81.

18554   NEWTON, JAMES E. "SLAVE ARTISANS AND CRAFTSMEN: THE
        ROOTS OF AFRO-AMERICAN ART." BLACK SCHOLAR, 9
        (NOVEMBER, 1977): 35-42.

18555   NEWTON, JAMES E. AND LEWIS, RONALD L. (EDS.). THE OTHER
        SLAVES: MECHANICS, ARTISANS AND CRAFTSMEN. BOSTON:
        G.K. HALL, 1978.

18556   NOEL HUME, IVOR. A GUIDE TO ARTIFACTS OF COLONIAL
        AMERICA. NEW YORK: ALFRED A. KNOPF, 1970.

18557   OTTO, JOHN S. "ARTIFACTS AND STATUS DIFFERENCES--A
        COMPARISON OF CERAMICS FROM PLANTER, OVERSEER, AND
        SLAVE SITES ON AN ANTEBELLUM PLANTATION." IN SOUTH,
        STANLEY (ED.). RESEARCH STRATEGIES IN HISTORICAL
        ARCHEOLOGY. NEW YORK: ACADEMIC PRESS, 1977, PP.
        91-118.

18558   OTTO, JOHN S. "CANNON'S POINT PLANTATION AND THE HARDY
        BANKS FARM: MATERIAL LIVING CONDITIONS OF OLD SOUTH
        SLAVES." UNPUBLISHED PAPER PRESENTED AT MEETING OF
        SOCIETY FOR HISTORICAL ARCHAEOLOGY, NASHVILLE,
        TENNESSEE, 1979.

18559   OTTO, JOHN S. "A NEW LOOK AT SLAVE LIFE." NATURAL
        HISTORY, 88 (JANUARY, 1979): 8, 16, 20, 22, 24, 30.

18560   OTTO, JOHN S. "RACE AND CLASS ON ANTEBELLUM
        PLANTATIONS." IN SCHUYLER, ROBERT L. (ED.).
        ARCHAEOLOGICAL PERSPECTIVES ON ETHNICITY IN AMERICA.
        NEW YORK: BAYWOOD PUBLISHING COMPANY, 1980, PP. 3-13.

18561   OTTO, JOHN S. "STATUS DIFFERENCES AND THE ARCHEOLOGICAL
        RECORD--A COMPARISON OF PLANTER, OVERSEER, AND SLAVE
        SITES FROM CANNON'S POINT PLANTATION (1794-1861), ST.
        SIMON'S ISLAND, GEORGIA." PH.D. DISSERTATION,
        UNIVERSITY OF FLORIDA, 1975.

18562   PARKS, MALCOM. "1712 MANOR HOUSE IN WALKILL VALLEY IS
        TRIBUTE TO WORKMANSHIP OF SLAVES." NEW YORK SUN, JULY
        23, 1938.

18563   PEEK, PHIL. "AFRO-AMERICAN MATERIAL CULTURE AND THE
        AFRO-AMERICAN CRAFTSMAN." SOUTHERN FOLKLORE

QUARTERLY, 42 (1978):   109-134.

18564   PERDUE, ROBERT E., JR.   "'AFRICAN' BASKETS IN SOUTH
        CAROLINA."   ECONOMIC BOTANY, 22 (JULY-SEPTEMBER,
        1968):   289-292.

18565   PETO, FLORENCE.   AMERICAN COVERLETS AND QUILTS.   NEW
        YORK: CHANTICLEER, 1949.

18566   POLLAK-ELTZ, ANGELINA.   "THE CHUAO DEVILS--BANTU MASKS IN
        VENEZUELA."   REVIEW OF ETHNOLOGY, 5 (1978):   25-28.

18567   POLLAK-ELTZ, ANGELINA.   "THE MARIMBULA: AN AFRO-AMERICAN
        INSTRUMENT."   REVIEW OF ETHNOLOGY, 5 (1978):   28-30.

18568   PRIME, ALFRED C. (ED.).   THE ARTS & CRAFTS IN
        PHILADELPHIA, MARYLAND AND SOUTH CAROLINA.   TOPSFIELD,
        MA: WALPOLE SOCIETY, 1929.

18569   ROBERTS, HELEN.   "SOME DRUMS AND DRUM RHYTHMS OF
        JAMAICA."   NATURAL HISTORY, 24 (MARCH-APRIL, 1924):
        241-251.

18570   ROBERTS, NANCY.   "GULLAH BASKETS: REMNANTS OF THE OLD
        SOUTH."   AMERICANA, 7 (MARCH/APRIL, 1979):   38-41.

18571   SALWEN, BERT AND GYRISCO, GEOFFREY M.   "AN ANNOTATED
        BIBLIOGRAPHY: ARCHEOLOGY OF BLACK AMERICAN CULTURE."
        11593, VOL. 3, SUPPLEMENT (FEBRUARY-MARCH, 1978):   1-4.

18572   SCHUYLER, ROBERT L.   "HISTORICAL AND HISTORIC SITES
        ARCHAEOLOGY AS ANTHROPOLOGY."   HISTORICAL ARCHAEOLOGY,
        4 (1970):   83-89.

18573   SINGLETON, THERESA A.   "THE ARCHAEOLOGY OF AFRO-AMERICAN
        SLAVERY IN COASTAL GEORGIA: A REGIONAL PERCEPTION OF
        SLAVE HOUSEHOLD AND COMMUNITY PATTERNS."   PH.D.
        DISSERTATION, UNIVERSITY OF FLORIDA, 1980.

18574   SINGLETON, THERESA A.   "SLAVES AND EX-SLAVE SITES IN
        COASTAL GEORGIA."   UNPUBLISHED PAPER PRESENTED AT
        MEETING OF SOCIETY FOR HISTORICAL ARCHAEOLOGY,
        NASHVILLE, TENNESSEE, 1979.

18575   "SLAVE ART."   AMERICAN HERITAGE, 27 (OCTOBER, 1976):
        102-103.

18576   SMITH, SAMUEL D.   "PLANTATION ARCHAEOLOGY AT THE
        HERMITAGE: SOME SUGGESTED PATTERNS."   TENNESSEE
        ANTHROPOLOGIST, 2 (1977):   152-163.

18577   THOMPSON, ROBERT F.   "AFRICAN INFLUENCE ON THE ART OF THE
        UNITED STATES."   IN ROBINSON, ARMSTEAD L.; FOSTER,
        CRAIG C.; AND OGILIVIE, DONALD H. (EDS.).   BLACK
        STUDIES IN THE UNIVERSITY: A SYMPOSIUM.   NEW YORK:

YALE UNIVERSITY PRESS, 1969, PP. 122-170.

18578   TUCKER, HELEN A.   "NEGRO CRAFTSMEN IN AFRICA AND THE
        SOUTH."   SOUTHERN WORKMEN, 36 (NOVEMBER, 1907):
        613-615.

18579   TWINING, MARY.   "HARVESTING AND HERITAGE: A COMPARISON
        OF AFRO-AMERICAN AND AFRICAN BASKETRY."   SOUTHERN
        FOLKLORE QUARTERLY, 42 (1978): 159-174.

18580   VLACH, JOHN M.   THE AFRO-AMERICAN TRADITION IN DECORATIVE
        ARTS.   CLEVELAND: CLEVELAND MUSEUM OF ART, 1978.

18581   VLACH, JOHN M.   "ARRIVAL AND SURVIVAL: THE MAINTENANCE
        OF AN AFRO-AMERICAN TRADITION IN FOLK ART AND CRAFT."
        IN QUIMBY, IAN M.G. AND SWANK, SCOTT T. (EDS.).
        PERSPECTIVES ON AMERICAN FOLK ART.   NEW YORK: W.W.
        NORTON, 1980, PP. 177-217.

18582   VLACH, JOHN M.   "GRAVEYARDS AND AFRO-AMERICAN ART."
        SOUTHERN EXPOSURE, 5 (SUMMER/FALL, 1977): 161-165.

18583   VLACH, JOHN M.   "PHILLIP SIMMONS: AFRO-AMERICAN
        BLACKSMITH."   FOLKLORE STUDENTS ASSOCIATION PREPRINT
        SERIES, (1973): 1-22.

18584   VLACH, JOHN M.   "PHILLIP SIMMONS: AFRO-AMERICAN
        BLACKSMITH."   IN SHAPIRO, LINN (ED.).   BLACK PEOPLE
        AND THEIR CULTURE: SELECTED WRITINGS FROM THE AFRICAN
        DIASPORA.   WASHINGTON: SMITHSONIAN INSTITUTION, 1976,
        PP. 35-57.

18585   VLACH, JOHN M.   "THE SHOTGUN HOUSE: AN AFRICAN
        ARCHITECTURAL LEGACY."   PIONEER AMERICA, 8 (JANUARY,
        JULY, 1976): 47-56, 57-70.

18586   VLACH, JOHN M.   "SLAVE POTTERS."   CERAMICS MONTHLY, 26
        (SEPTEMBER, 1978): 66-69.

18587   WAHLMAN, MAUDE.   "THE ART OF AFRO-AMERICAN QUILTMAKING:
        ORIGINS, DEVELOPMENT AND SIGNIFICANCE."   PH.D.
        DISSERTATION, YALE UNIVERSITY, 1980.

18588   WAHLMAN, MAUDE AND SCULLY, JOHN.   BLACK QUILTERS.   NEW
        HAVEN: YALE ART AND ARCHITECTURE GALLERY, 1979.

18589   WOOD, PETER H.   "WHETTING, SETTING AND LAYING
        TIMBERS--BLACK BUILDERS IN THE EARLY SOUTH."   SOUTHERN
        EXPOSURE, 8 (SPRING, 1980): 3-8.

18590   WOODFORD, JOHN.   "THE ARTIFACTS OF SLAVERY."   FORD TIMES,
        71 (JANUARY, 1978): 36-40.

18591   ZELINSKY, WILBUR.   "THE LOG HOUSE IN GEORGIA."
        GEOGRAPHICAL REVIEW, 43 (APRIL, 1953): 173-193.

SLAVE ART

18592   AFRICANS IN THE COLONIAL AMERICAS: AN EXHIBITION OF
        BOOKS AND PRINTS. PROVIDENCE: JOHN CARTER BROWN
        LIBRARY, 1970.

18593   "AFRO-AMERICAN ART: 1800-1950." EBONY, 23 (FEBRUARY,
        1968): 116-118, 120-122.

18594   "THE AFRO-AMERICAN TRADITION IN DECORATIVE ARTS." BLACK
        HERITAGE, 19 (SEPTEMBER-OCTOBER, 1979): 11-18.

18595   ALEXANDER, LETITIA H. "LIFE PATTERNS IN BLACK AND
        WHITE." ANTIQUES, 25 (JANUARY, 1934): 11-13.

18596   ASHTON, DORE. "AFRICAN AND AFRO-AMERICAN ART: THE
        TRANS-ATLANTIC TRADITION AT THE MUSEUM OF PRIMITIVE
        ART." STUDIO, 176 (NOVEMBER, 1968): 202-203.

18597   BLACK ARTISTS IN HISTORICAL PERSPECTIVE. N.P.: BLACK
        DIMENSIONS IN ART, INC., 1976.

18598   BOLTON, H. CARRINGTON. "DECORATION OF NEGRO GRAVES IN
        SOUTH CAROLINA." JOURNAL OF AMERICAN FOLKLORE, 4
        (JULY-SEPTEMBER, 1891): 214.

18599   BOWDOIN COLLEGE MUSEUM OF ARTS. THE PORTRAYAL OF THE
        NEGRO IN AMERICAN PAINTING. BRUNSWICK, ME: BOWDOIN
        COLLEGE MUSEUM OF ARTS, 1964.

18600   BRIGHT, ALFRED L. "THE BLACK ARTIST IN COLONIAL
        AMERICA." IN BRIGHT; CLARK, SARAH B.; AMADI, LAWRENCE
        E.; COOPER, SYRETHA; BARNES, CLARENCE; AND O'NEILL,
        DANIEL J. AN INTERDISCIPLINARY INTRODUCTION TO BLACK
        STUDIES. DUBUQUE: KENDALL/HUNT PUBLISHING COMPANY,
        1977, PP. 121-124.

18601   CHASE, JUDITH W. AFRO-AMERICAN ART AND CRAFT. NEW YORK:
        VAN NOSTRAND, 1971.

18602   CHASE, JUDITH W. "AMERICAN HERITAGE FROM ANTE-BELLUM
        BLACK CRAFTSMEN." SOUTHERN FOLKLORE QUARTERLY, 42
        (1978): 135-158.

18603   COLEMAN, FLOYD W. "PERSISTENCE AND DISCONTINUITY OF
        TRADITIONAL AFRICAN PERCEPTION IN AFRO-AMERICAN ART."
        PH.D. DISSERTATION, UNIVERSITY OF GEORGIA, 1975.

18604   CORDWELL, JUSTINE M. "AFRICAN ART." IN BASCOM, WILLIAM
        R. AND HERSKOVITS, MELVILLE J. (EDS.). CONTINUITY AND
        CHANGE IN AFRICAN CULTURES. CHICAGO: UNIVERSITY OF
        CHICAGO PRESS, 1959, PP. 28-45.

18605   CRAFTMANSHIP: A TRADITION IN BLACK AMERICA. NEW YORK:
        RCA CORPORATION, 1976.

18606   CRAIG, JAMES H.   THE ARTS AND CRAFTS IN NORTH CAROLINA,
        1699-1840.   WINSTON-SALEM: MUSEUM OF EARLY SOUTHERN
        DECORATIVE ARTS, 1965.

18607   "CREATIVE ART OF THE AMERICAN NEGRO."   BALTIMORE MUSEUM
        OF ART NEWS, 3 (SEPTEMBER, 1941):   50.

18608   CUREAN, HAROLD G.   "THE HISTORIC ROLES OF BLACK AMERICAN
        ARTISTS: A PROFILE OF STRUGGLE."   BLACK SCHOLAR, 9
        (NOVEMBER, 1977):   2-13.

18609   DARK, PHILIP J.C.   BUSH NEGRO ART: AN AFRICAN ART IN THE
        AMERICAS.   LONDON: ALEC TIRANTI, 1954.

18610   DAVIS, LENWOOD G. AND SIMS, JANET.   BLACK ARTISTS IN THE
        UNITED STATES: AN ANNOTATED BIBLIOGRAPHY OF BOOKS,
        ARTICLES, AND DISSERTATIONS ON BLACK ARTISTS,
        1779-1979.   WESTPORT: GREENWOOD PRESS, 1980.

18611   DAY, GREGORY.   "AFRO-CAROLINIAN ART: TOWARDS THE HISTORY
        OF A SOUTHERN EXPRESSIVE TRADITION."   CONTEMPORARY
        ART/SOUTHEAST, 1 (JANUARY-FEBRUARY, 1978):   10-21.

18612   DEAS, ALSTON.   "CHARLESTON ORNAMENTAL IRONWORK."   IN
        ANTIQUES OF CHARLESTON.   CHARLESTON: HISTORIC
        CHARLESTON FOUNDATION, 1970, PP. 748-751.

18613   DOVER, CEDRIC.   AMERICAN NEGRO ART.   GREENWICH, CT: NEW
        YORK GRAPHIC SOCIETY, 1960.

18614   DOW, GEORGE F.   THE ARTS AND CRAFTS IN NEW ENGLAND,
        1704-1775.   TOPSFIELD, MA: WAYSIDE PRESS, 1927.

18615   DOZIER, RICHARD K.   "A HISTORICAL SURVEY: BLACK
        ARCHITECTS AND CRAFTSMEN."   BLACK WORLD, 23 (MAY,
        1974):   4-15.

18616   DRISKELL, DAVID C.   TWO CENTURIES OF BLACK AMERICAN ART.
        NEW YORK: ALFRED A. KNOPF, 1976.

18617   DUBOIS, W.E.B.   THE GIFT OF BLACK FOLK: THE NEGROES IN
        THE MAKING OF AMERICA.   BOSTON: STRAFFORD, 1924.

18618   DUBOIS, W.E.B. (ED.).   THE NEGRO ARTISAN.   ATLANTA:
        ATLANTA UNIVERSITY PRESS, 1902.

18619   DUBOIS, W.E.B.   THE SOULS OF BLACK FOLK: ESSAYS AND
        SKETCHES.   CHICAGO: A.C. MCCLURG & COMPANY, 1903.

18620   DUBOIS, W.E.B. AND DILL, AUGUSTUS G. (EDS.).   THE NEGRO
        AMERICAN ARTISAN.   ATLANTA: ATLANTA UNIVERSITY
        PUBLICATIONS, 1912.

18621   DURHAM, JOHN S.   "THREE GROWTHS."   A.M.E. CHURCH REVIEW,
        14 (JULY, 1897):   120-130.

18622   ERDMAN, DAVID V. "BLAKE'S VISION OF SLAVERY." JOURNAL
        OF THE WARBURG AND COURTAULD INSTITUTES, 15 (JULY,
        1952): 242-252.

18623   FAX, ELTON C. SEVENTEEN BLACK ARTISTS. NEW YORK: DODD,
        MEAD, 1971.

18624   FERRIS, WILLIAM. "IF YOU AIN'T GOT IT IN YOUR HEAD, YOU
        CAN'T DO IT IN YOUR HAND; JAMES THOMAS; MISSISSIPPI
        DELTA FOLK SCULPTOR." STUDIES IN THE LITERARY
        IMAGINATION, 3 (APRIL, 1970): 89-101.

18625   FINE, ELSA H. THE AFRO-AMERICAN ARTIST: A SEARCH FOR
        IDENTITY. NEW YORK: HOLT, RINEHART & WINSTON, 1973.

18626   FORD, AUSBRA. "THE INFLUENCE OF AFRICAN ART ON
        AFRICAN-AMERICAN ART." IN CORDWELL, JUSTINE M. (ED.).
        THE VISUAL ARTS: PLASTIC AND GRAPHIC. THE HAGUE:
        MOUTON, 1979, PP. 513-534.

18627   FOX, JAMES E. "ICONOGRAPHY OF THE BLACK IN AMERICAN ART
        (1710-1900)." PH.D. DISSERTATION, UNIVERSITY OF NORTH
        CAROLINA, 1979.

18628   FRAZIER, HERBERT L. "BASKET WEAVING TRACED TO ANCIENT
        AFRICAN CRAFT." CHARLESTON NEWS AND COURIER,
        SEPTEMBER 4, 1972.

18629   GREENE, CARROLL JR. "AFRO-AMERICAN ARTISTS: YESTERDAY
        AND NOW." HUMBLE WAY, 7 (THIRD QUARTER, 1968): 10-15.

18630   GREGORY, MARIAN E. "NEGRO ART IN AFRICA AND THE UNITED
        STATES." M.A. THESIS, WESTERN RESERVE UNIVERSITY,
        1941.

18631   GRIGSBY, J. EUGENE JR. ART AND ETHNIC: BACKGROUND FOR
        TEACHING YOUTH IN A PLURALISTIC SOCIETY. DUBUQUE, IA:
        WILLIAM C. BROWN COMPANY, 1977.

18632   H.I.B. "NEGRO'S ART LIVES IN HIS WROUGHT IRON." NEW
        YORK TIMES MAGAZINE, (AUGUST 8, 1926): 14-15.

18633   HARRIS, MARK. "BEST BUY IN CHARLESTON." NEGRO DIGEST, 8
        (JULY, 1950): 42-44.

18634   HARRIS, MIDDLETON. THE BLACK BOOK. NEW YORK: RANDOM
        HOUSE, 1974.

18635   HAYES, CHARLES F. "BUSH NEGRO ART OF DUTCH GUIANA."
        MUSEUM SERVICE, 37 (1964): 78-81.

18636   HERSKOVITS, MELVILLE J. "AFRO-AMERICAN ART." IN
        ENCYCLOPEDIA OF WORLD ART. 15 VOLS. NEW YORK:
        MCGRAW-HILL, 1959, VOL. 1, PP. 150-158.

18637   HERSKOVITS, MELVILLE J.   "AFRO-AMERICAN ART."   IN WILDER,
        E. (ED.).   STUDIES IN LATIN AMERICAN ART.   WASHINGTON:
        AMERICAN COUNCIL OF LEARNED SOCIETIES, 1949, PP. 58-64.

18638   HERSKOVITS, MELVILLE J.   "ART AND VALUE."   IN ASPECTS OF
        PRIMITIVE ART: THE MUSEUM OF PRIMITIVE ART LECTURE
        SERIES NUMBER ONE.   NEW YORK: THE MUSEUM OF PRIMITVE
        ART, 1959, PP. 41-68, 95-97.

18639   HERSKOVITS, MELVILLE J. AND HERSKOVITS, FRANCES S.
        "BUSH-NEGRO ART."   ARTS, 17 (OCTOBER, 1930): 25-37,
        48-49.

18640   HUNTER, WILBUR H., JR.   "JOSHUA JOHNSTON: 18TH CENTURY
        NEGRO ARTIST."   AMERICAN COLLECTOR, 17 (FEBRUARY,
        1948):   6-8.

18641   INGERSOLL, ERNEST.   "DECORATION OF NEGRO GRAVES."
        JOURNAL OF AMERICAN FOLKLORE, 5 (JANUARY-MARCH, 1892):
        68-69.

18642   LANE, JAMES W.   "AFRO-AMERICAN ART ON BOTH CONTINENTS;
        THE GREAT CONTRIBUTION OF THE ARTISTIC NEGRO."   ART
        NEWS, 40 (OCTOBER 15, 1941):   25.

18643   LEWIS, SAMELLA S.   ART: AFRICAN AMERICAN.   NEW YORK:
        HARCOURT BRACE JOVANOVICH, 1978.

18644   LOCKE, ALAIN L.   "THE AMERICAN NEGRO AS ARTIST."
        AMERICAN MAGAZINE OF ART, 23 (SEPTEMBER, 1931):
        210-220.

18645   LOCKE, ALAIN L.   "NEGRO ART IN AMERICA."   DESIGN, 44
        (DECEMBER, 1942):   12-13.

18646   LOCKE, ALAIN L.   NEGRO ART: PAST AND PRESENT.
        WASHINGTON: ASSOCIATES IN NEGRO FOLK EDUCATION, 1936.

18647   LOCKE, ALAIN L.   "THE NEGRO IN ART."   ASSOCIATION OF
        AMERICAN COLLEGES BULLETIN, 17 (NOVEMBER, 1931):
        359-364.

18648   LOCKE, ALAIN L. (ED.).   THE NEGRO IN ART: A PICTORIAL
        RECORD OF NEGRO ARTISTS AND THE NEGRO THEME IN ART.
        WASHINGTON: ASSOCIATES IN NEGRO FOLK EDUCATION, 1940.

18649   MACLEOD, BRUCE A.   "THE MUSICAL INSTRUMENTS OF NORTH
        AMERICAN SLAVES."   MISSISSIPPI FOLKLORE REGISTER, 11
        (SPRING, 1977):   34-49.

18650   MACLEOD, BRUCE A.   "QUILLS, FIFES, AND FLUTES BEFORE THE
        CIVIL WAR."   SOUTHERN FOLKLORE QUARTERLY, 42 (1978):
        201-208.

18651   MADE OF IRON.   HOUSTON: UNIVERSITY OF ST. THOMAS ART

DEPARTMENT, 1966.

18652   MURRAY, FREEMAN H.M.   THE EMANCIPATED AND FREED IN
        AMERICAN SCULPTURE.   A STUDY IN INTERPRETATION.
        WASHINGTON: MURRAY BROTHERS, 1916.

18653   MUSEUM OF ART, RALEIGH.   AFRO-AMERICAN ARTISTS, NORTH
        CAROLINA, USA. NORTH CAROLINA MUSEUM OF ART, NOVEMBER
        9-DECEMBER 31, 1980.   RALEIGH: RALEIGH MUSEUM OF ART,
        1980.

18654   MYERS, BETTY.   "GULLAH BASKETRY."   CRAFT HORIZONS, 36
        (JUNE, 1976):   30-31, 81.

18655   NASCIMENTO, ABDIAS D.   "AFRICAN CULTURE IN BRAZILIAN
        ART."   JOURNAL OF BLACK STUDIES, 8 (JUNE, 1978):
        389-422.

18656   NASCIMENTO, ABDIAS D.   "AFRO-BRAZILIAN ART: A LIBERATING
        SPIRIT."   BLACK ART, 1 (FALL, 1976):   54-62.

18657   NEWTON, JAMES E.   "SLAVE ARTISANS AND CRAFTSMEN: THE
        ROOTS OF AFRO-AMERICAN ART."   BLACK SCHOLAR, 9
        (NOVEMBER, 1977):   35-42.

18658   NEWTON, JAMES E.   "SLAVE ARTISANS AND CRAFTSMEN: THE
        ROOTS OF AFRO-AMERICAN ART."   IN NEWTON AND LEWIS,
        RONALD L. (EDS.).   THE OTHER SLAVES: MECHANICS,
        ARTISANS, AND CRAFTSMEN.   BOSTON: G.K. HALL, 1978,
        PP. 233-241.

18659   NEWTON, JAMES E. AND LEWIS, RONALD L. (EDS.).   THE OTHER
        SLAVES: MECHANICS, ARTISANS AND CRAFTSMEN.   BOSTON:
        G.K. HALL, 1978.

18660   PARKER, PATRICIA.   "TWO CENTURIES OF BLACK AMERICAN ART."
        BLACK COLLEGIAN, 8 (SEPTEMBER/OCTOBER, 1977):   50-51.

18661   PARRY, ELLWOOD.   THE IMAGE OF THE INDIAN AND BLACK MAN IN
        AMERICAN ART: 1590-1900.   NEW YORK: GEORGE
        BRAZILLER, 1974.

18662   PERRY, REGENIA.   SELECTIONS OF NINETEENTH-CENTURY
        AFRO-AMERICAN ART.   NEW YORK: METROPOLITAN MUSEUM OF
        ART, 1976.

18663   PHILADELPHIA MUSEUM OF ART.   IMPACT AFRICA: AFRICAN ART
        AND THE WEST.   PHILADELPHIA: PHILADELPHIA MUSEUM OF
        ART, 1969.

18664   PIERCE, PONCHITTA.   "BLACK ART IN AMERICA."   READERS
        DIGEST, 112 (JUNE, 1978):   176-185.

18665   PINCHBECK, RAYMOND B.   THE VIRGINIA NEGRO ARTISAN AND
        TRADESMAN.   RICHMOND: WILLIAM BYRD PRESS, 1926.

18666   PLEASANTS, J. HALE. "JOSHUA JOHNSTON: THE FIRST
        AMERICAN NEGRO PORTRAIT PAINTER." MARYLAND HISTORICAL
        MAGAZINE, 37 (JUNE, 1942): 1-29, 77.

18667   PORTER, JAMES A. "FOUR PROBLEMS IN THE HISTORY OF NEGRO
        ART." JOURNAL OF NEGRO HISTORY, 27 (JANUARY, 1942):
        9-36.

18668   PORTER, JAMES A. MODERN NEGRO ART. NEW YORK: DRYDEN
        PRESS, 1943.

18669   PORTER, JAMES A. "NEGRO CRAFTSMEN AND ARTISTS OF
        PRE-CIVIL WAR DAYS." IN NEWTON, JAMES E. AND LEWIS,
        RONALD L. (EDS.). THE OTHER SLAVES: MECHANICS,
        ARTISANS, AND CRAFTSMEN. BOSTON: G.K. HALL, 1978,
        PP. 209-220.

18670   PORTER, JAMES A. "ONE HUNDRED AND FIFTY YEARS OF
        AFRO-AMERICAN ART." IN THE NEGRO IN AMERICAN ART.
        LOS ANGELES: UCLA ART GALLERIES, 1966, PP. 5-12.

18671   PORTER, JAMES A. TEN AFRO-AMERICAN ARTISTS OF THE
        NINETEENTH CENTURY. WASHINGTON: GALLERY OF ART,
        HOWARD UNIVERSITY, 1967.

18672   PORTER, JAMES A. "VERSATILE INTERESTS OF THE EARLY NEGRO
        ARTIST: A NEGLECTED CHAPTER OF AMERICAN ART HISTORY."
        ART IN AMERICA AND ELSEWHERE, 24 (JANUARY, 1936):
        16-27.

18673   PRICE, RICHARD. "SARAMAKA WOODCARVING: THE DEVELOPMENT
        OF AN AFROAMERICAN ART." MAN, N.S., 5 (SEPTEMBER,
        1970): 363-378.

18674   PRICE, RICHARD AND PRICE, SALLY. "KAMMBA: THE
        ETHNOHISTORY OF AN AFRO-AMERICAN ART." ANTROPOLOGICA,
        32 (1972): 3-27.

18675   PRICE, RICHARD AND PRICE, SALLY. "THE LEGACY OF AFRICA
        IN THE ARTS OF THE SURINAME MAROONS." UNPUBLISHED
        PAPER, 1980.

18676   PRICE, SALLY AND PRICE, RICHARD. AFRO-AMERICAN ARTS OF
        THE SURINAME RAIN FOREST. BERKELEY: UNIVERSITY OF
        CALIFORNIA PRESS, 1980.

18677   PRICE, SALLY AND PRICE, RICHARD. "THE ARTS OF THE
        SURINAME MAROONS." MEDEDELINGEN DER SURINAAMS MUSEA,
        31 (1980): 17-35.

18678   PRICE, SALLY AND PRICE, RICHARD. "EXOTICA AND COMMODITY:
        THE ARTS OF THE SURINAME MAROONS." CARIBBEAN REVIEW,
        9 (1980): 12-17, 47.

18679   PRIME, ALFRED C. (ED.). THE ARTS & CRAFTS IN

PHILADELPHIA, MARYLAND AND SOUTH CAROLINA. TOPSFIELD,
MA: WALPOLE SOCIETY, 1929.

18680 RUTLEDGE, ANNA W. "ARTISTS IN THE LIFE OF CHARLESTON
THROUGH COLONY AND STATE FROM RESTORATION TO
RECONSTRUCTION." TRANSACTIONS OF THE AMERICAN
PHILOSOPHICAL SOCIETY, N.S., 39 (NOVEMBER, 1949):
101-260.

18681 SHAW, JOANN N. AFRICAN ART OF THE TWO CONTINENTS
SELECTED FROM THE HERSKOVITS COLLECTION. EVANSTON:
NORTHWESTERN UNIVERSITY LIBRARY, 1973

18682 STAVISKY, LEONARD. "THE ORIGINS OF NEGRO CRAFTSMANSHIP
IN COLONIAL AMERICA." JOURNAL OF NEGRO HISTORY, 32
(JULY, 1947): 417-429.

18683 STAVISKY, LEONARD P. "THE NEGRO ARTISAN IN THE SOUTH
ATLANTIC STATES, 1800-1860: A STUDY OF STATUS AND
ECONOMIC OPPORTUNITY WITH SPECIAL REFERENCE TO
CHARLESTON." PH.D. DISSERTATION, COLUMBIA UNIVERSITY,
1958.

18684 STAVISKY, LEONARD P. "NEGRO CRAFTSMANSHIP IN EARLY
AMERICA." AMERICAN HISTORICAL REVIEW, 54 (JANUARY,
1949): 315-325.

18685 TEILHET, JEHANNE. DIMENSIONS IN BLACK. LA JOLLA, CA:
LA JOLLA MUSEUM OF ART, 1970.

18686 THOMPSON, ROBERT F. AFRICAN ART AND AFRO-AMERICAN ART:
THE TRANS-ATLANTIC TRADITION. NEW YORK: MCGRAW-HILL,
1968.

18687 THOMPSON, ROBERT F. AFRICAN ART IN MOTION: ICON AND ACT
IN THE COLLECTION OF KATHERINE CORYTON WHITE. LOS
ANGELES: UNIVERSITY OF CALIFORNIA PRESS, 1974.

18688 THOMPSON, ROBERT F. "AFRICAN INFLUENCE ON THE ART OF THE
UNITED STATES." IN ROBINSON, ARMSTEAD L.; FOSTER,
CRAIG C.; AND OGILIVIE, DONALD H. (EDS.). BLACK
STUDIES IN THE UNIVERSITY: A SYMPOSIUM. NEW YORK:
YALE UNIVERSITY PRESS, 1969, PP. 122-170.

18689 THOMPSON, ROBERT F. "FROM AFRICA." YALE ALUMNI
MAGAZINE, 34 (NOVEMBER, 1970): 16-21.

18690 THOMPSON, ROBERT F. "AN INTRODUCTION TO TRANSATLANTIC
BLACK ART HISTORY: REMARKS IN ANTICIPATION OF A
COMING GOLDEN AGE OF AFRO-AMERICANA." JOURNAL OF
ASIAN AND AFRICAN STUDIES, 9 (APRIL, JULY, 1974):
193-201.

18691 THURM, MARCELLA. "ARTISTS AND CRAFTSMEN." EXPLORING
BLACK AMERICA: A HISTORY AND GUIDE. NEW YORK:

ATHENEUM, 1975, PP. 211-246.

18692   VLACH, JOHN M.   THE AFRO-AMERICAN TRADITION IN DECORATIVE
        ARTS.   CLEVELAND: CLEVELAND MUSEUM OF ART, 1978.

18693   VLACH, JOHN M.   "ARRIVAL AND SURVIVAL: THE MAINTENANCE
        OF AN AFRO-AMERICAN TRADITION IN FOLK ART AND CRAFT."
        IN QUIMBY, IAN M.G. AND SWANK, SCOTT T. (EDS.).
        PERSPECTIVES ON AMERICAN FOLK ART.   NEW YORK: W.W.
        NORTON, 1980, PP. 177-217.

18694   VLACH, JOHN M.   "BLACK CREATIVITY IN MISSISSIPPI:
        ORIGINS AND HORIZONS."   IN BLACK, PATTI (ED.).   MADE
        BY HAND: MISSISSIPPI FOLK ART.   JACKSON: MISSISSIPPI
        DEPARTMENT OF ARCHIVES AND HISTORY, 1980, PP. 28-32.

18695   VLACH, JOHN M.   "GRAVEYARDS AND AFRO-AMERICAN ART."
        SOUTHERN EXPOSURE, 5 (SUMMER/FALL, 1977):   161-165.

18696   VLACH, JOHN M.   "PHILLIP SIMMONS: AFRO-AMERICAN
        BLACKSMITH."   FOLKLORE STUDENTS ASSOCIATION PREPRINT
        SERIES, (1973):   1-22.

18697   VLACH, JOHN M.   "PHILLIP SIMMONS: AFRO-AMERICAN
        BLACKSMITH."   IN SHAPIRO, LINN (ED.).   BLACK PEOPLE
        AND THEIR CULTURE: SELECTED WRITINGS FROM THE AFRICAN
        DIASPORA.   WASHINGTON: SMITHSONIAN INSTITUTION, 1976,
        PP. 35-57.

18698   WADSWORTH, ANNA (ED.).   MISSING PIECES: GEORGIA FOLK
        ART, 1770-1976.   ATLANTA: GEORGIA COUNCIL FOR THE
        ARTS AND HUMANITIES, 1976.

18699   ZABRISKIE, GEORGE A.   "JOHN BROWN: SAINT OR SINNER?"
        NEW YORK HISTORICAL SOCIETY QUARTERLY, 33 (JANUARY,
        1949):   30-38.

GENERAL

18700   AFRO-AMERICAN HISTORY SERIES. 10 VOLS. WILMINGTON:
        SCHOLARLY RESOURCES, 1972.

18701   ALFORD, TERRY. PRINCE AMONG SLAVES. NEW YORK: HARCOURT
        BRACE JOVANOVICH, 1977.

18702   BAKER, HOUSTON A., JR. "COMPLETELY WELL: ONE VIEW OF
        BLACK AMERICAN CULTURE." IN HUGGINS, NATHAN I.;
        KILSON, MARTIN; AND FOX, DANIEL M. (EDS.). KEY ISSUES
        IN THE AFRO-AMERICAN EXPERIENCE. 2 VOLS. NEW YORK:
        HARCOURT BRACE JOVANOVICH, 1971, VOL. 1, PP. 20-33.

18703   BATTLE, KEMP P. "GEORGE HORTON, SLAVE POET." NORTH
        CAROLINA UNIVERSITY MAGAZINE, 7 (1888): 229-232.

18704   BRATHWAITE, EDWARD K. "CREATIVE LITERATURE OF THE
        BRITISH WEST INDIES DURING THE PERIOD OF SLAVERY."
        SAVACOU, 1 (JUNE, 1970): 46-74.

18705   BRAWLEY, BENJAMIN G. "THREE NEGRO POETS: HORTON, MRS.
        HARPER AND WHITMAN." JOURNAL OF NEGRO HISTORY, 2
        (OCTOBER, 1917): 384-392.

18706   BREWER, J. MASON. "SLAVE TALES AS A TYPE." PUBLICATIONS
        OF THE TEXAS FOLK-LORE SOCIETY, 10 (1932): 9-11.

18707   BROWN, STERLING A. "A CENTURY OF NEGRO PORTRAITURE IN
        AMERICAN LITERATURE." MASSACHUSETTS REVIEW, 7
        (WINTER, 1966): 73-96.

18708   BROWN, STERLING A. THE NEGRO IN AMERICAN FICTION.
        WASHINGTON: ASSOCIATES IN NEGRO FOLK EDUCATION, 1937.

18709   BROWN, STERLING A.; DAVIS, ARTHUR P.; AND LEE, ULYSSES
        (EDS.). THE NEGRO CARAVAN. NEW YORK: CITADEL, 1941.

18710   BRYANT, BUNYAN. "AFRICA IN AFRO-AMERICAN THOUGHT,
        1800-1861." B.A. THESIS, HARVARD UNIVERSITY, 1971.

18711   CAMPBELL, RANDOLPH B. AND PICKENS, DONALD K. "'MY DEAR
        HUSBAND': A TEXAS SLAVE'S LOVE LETTER, 1862."
        JOURNAL OF NEGRO HISTORY, 65 (FALL, 1980): 361-364.

18712   CARLSON, LEWIS H. "THE NEGRO IN SCIENCE." IN ROUCEK,
        JOSEPH S. AND KIERNAN, THOMAS (EDS.). THE NEGRO
        IMPACT ON WESTERN CIVILIZATION. NEW YORK:
        PHILOSOPHICAL LIBRARY, 1970, PP. 51-74.

18713   CARROLL, WILLIAM. "NAKED GENIUS: THE POETRY OF GEORGE
         MOSES HORTON, SLAVE BARD OF NORTH CAROLINA,
         1797(?)-1883." PH.D. DISSERTATION, UNIVERSITY OF
         NORTH CAROLINA, 1978.

18714   CAULFIELD, MINA D. "SLAVERY AND THE ORIGINS OF BLACK
         CULTURE: ELKINS REVISITED." IN ROSE, PETER I. (ED.).
         AMERICANS FROM AFRICA: SLAVERY AND ITS AFTERMATH. 2
         VOLS. NEW YORK: ATHERTON PRESS, 1970, VOL. 1, PP.
         171-193.

18715   CLARK, JAMES W., JR. "THE FUGITIVE SLAVE AS HUMORIST."
         STUDIES IN AMERICAN HUMOR, 1 (OCTOBER, 1974): 73-78.

18716   DAVIS, CHARLES S. (ED.). "LIBERIAN LETTERS." GEORGIA
         HISTORICAL QUARTERLY, 24 (SEPTEMBER, 1940): 253-255.

18717   DAVIS, THOMAS J. "SLAVE TESTIMONY: A REVIEW ESSAY AND A
         BIBLIOGRAPHY." AFRO-AMERICANS IN NEW YORK LIFE AND
         HISTORY, 3 (JANUARY, 1979): 73-85.

18718   DIXON, MELVIN W. "HISTORICAL VISION AND PERSONAL WITNESS
         IN AMERICAN SLAVE LITERATURE." PH.D. DISSERTATION,
         BROWN UNIVERSITY, 1975.

18719   DUBOIS, W.E.B. THE GIFT OF BLACK FOLK: THE NEGROES IN
         THE MAKING OF AMERICA. BOSTON: STRAFFORD, 1924.

18720   DUBOIS, W.E.B. THE SOULS OF BLACK FOLK: ESSAYS AND
         SKETCHES. CHICAGO: A.C. MCCLURG & COMPANY, 1903.

18721   GENOVESE, EUGENE D. "'RATHER BE A NIGGER THAN A POOR
         WHITE MAN': SLAVE PERCEPTIONS OF SOUTHERN YEOMEN AND
         POOR WHITES." IN TREFOUSSE, HANS L. (ED.). TOWARD A
         NEW VIEW OF AMERICA: ESSAYS IN HONOR OF ARTHUR C.
         COLE. NEW YORK: BURT FRANKLIN, 1977, PP. 79-96.

18722   GOLDMAN, MORRIS. "THE SOCIOLOGY OF NEGRO HUMOR." PH.D.
         DISSERTATION, NEW SCHOOL FOR SOCIAL RESEARCH, 1960.

18723   HASLAM, GERALD W. "BLACK AND UNKNOWN BARDS: AMERICAN
         SLAVERY AND ITS LITERARY TRADITION." ETC: A REVIEW
         OF GENERAL SEMANTICS, 25 (DECEMBER, 1968): 411-419.

18724   JENSEN, MARILYN. "BOSTON'S POETIC SLAVE." NEW-ENGLAND
         GALAXY, 18 (1977): 22-29.

18725   KARDINER, ABRAM AND OVESEY, LIONEL. "THE SOCIAL
         ENVIRONMENT OF THE NEGRO." IN WEBSTER, STATEN W.
         (ED.). THE DISADVANTAGED LEARNER: KNOWING,
         UNDERSTANDING, EDUCATING. SAN FRANCISCO: CHANDLER
         PUBLISHING COMPANY, 1966, PP. 141-160.

18726   MILLER, RANDALL M. (ED.). "DEAR MASTER": LETTERS OF A
         SLAVE FAMILY. ITHACA: CORNELL UNIVERSITY PRESS, 1978.

18727   MOORE, JOHN HEBRON. "A LETTER FROM A FUGITIVE SLAVE."
        JOURNAL OF MISSISSIPPI HISTORY, 24 (APRIL, 1962):
        99-101.

18728   NICHOLLS, MICHAEL L. (ED.). "NEWS FROM MONROVIA,
        1834-1836: THE LETTERS OF PEYTON SKIPWITH TO JOHN
        HARTWELL COCKE." VIRGINIA MAGAZINE OF HISTORY AND
        BIOGRAPHY, 85 (JANUARY, 1977): 65-85.

18729   SETTLE, E. OPHELIA. "SOCIAL ATTITUDES DURING THE SLAVE
        REGIME: HOUSE SERVANTS VERSUS FIELD HANDS."
        PUBLICATIONS OF THE AMERICAN SOCIOLOGICAL SOCIETY, 28
        (MAY, 1934): 95-98.

18730   STAFFORD, A.O. "THE MIND OF THE AFRICAN NEGRO AS
        REFLECTED IN HIS PROVERBS." JOURNAL OF NEGRO HISTORY,
        1 (JANUARY, 1916): 42-48.

18731   THORPE, EARL E. "AFRICA IN THE THOUGHT OF NEGRO
        AMERICANS." NEGRO HISTORY BULLETIN, 23 (OCTOBER,
        1959): 5-10.

18732   WEEKS, STEPHEN B. "GEORGE MOSES HORTON: SLAVE POET."
        SOUTHERN WORKMAN, 43 (OCTOBER, 1914): 571-577.

18733   WEGELIN, OSCAR. JUPITER HAMMON, AMERICAN NEGRO POET.
        NEW YORK: C.F. HEARTMAN COMPANY, 1915.

18734   "WHAT THE NEGRO WAS THINKING DURING THE EIGHTEENTH
        CENTURY; ESSAY ON NEGRO SLAVERY." JOURNAL OF NEGRO
        HISTORY, 1 (JANUARY, 1916): 49-68.

18735   WOODSON, CARTER G. (ED.). THE MIND OF THE NEGRO AS
        REFLECTED IN LETTERS WRITTEN DURING THE CRISIS,
        1800-1860. WASHINGTON: ASSOCIATION FOR THE STUDY OF
        NEGRO LIFE AND HISTORY, 1926.

SLAVE PERSONALITY

18736   ALSTON, CHARLES. "A CONCEPTUAL ANALYSIS OF TEN NEGRO
        SLAVE SONGS; A STUDY OF SLAVE SONGS BASED ON THE
        DEVELOPMENT OF THE SLAVE'S INDIVIDUAL MEANS OF
        ADJUSTMENT AND HIS SOCIAL MOTIVATIONS." M.A. THESIS,
        PENNSYLVANIA STATE UNIVERSITY, 1963.

18737   ANDERSON, JAMES D. "POLITICAL AND SCHOLARLY INTERESTS IN
        THE 'NEGRO PERSONALITY': A REVIEW OF THE SLAVE
        COMMUNITY." IN GILMORE, AL-TONY (ED.). REVISITING
        BLASSINGAME'S THE SLAVE COMMUNITY: THE SCHOLARS
        RESPOND. WESTPORT: GREENWOOD PRESS, 1978, PP.
        123-134.

18738   BAUGHMAN, E. EARL. BLACK AMERICANS. NEW YORK: ACADEMIC
        PRESS, 1971.

18739   BLACKBURN, REGINA L.   "CONSCIOUS AGENTS OF TIME AND SELF:
        THE LIVES AND STYLES OF AFRICAN-AMERICAN WOMEN AS SEEN
        THROUGH THEIR AUTOBIOGRAPHICAL WRITINGS."   PH.D.
        DISSERTATION, UNIVERSITY OF NEW MEXICO, 1978.

18740   BLASSINGAME, JOHN W.   "SAMBOS AND REBELS: THE CHARACTER
        OF THE SOUTHERN SLAVE."   IN WILLIAMS, LORRAINE A.
        (ED.).   AFRICA AND THE AFRO-AMERICAN EXPERIENCE.
        WASHINGTON: HOWARD UNIVERSITY PRESS, 1977, PP.
        149-166.

18741   BLASSINGAME, JOHN W.   SAMBOS AND REBELS: THE CHARACTER
        OF THE SOUTHERN SLAVE.   WASHINGTON: DEPARTMENT OF
        HISTORY, HOWARD UNIVERSITY, 1972.

18742   BLASSINGAME, JOHN W.   THE SLAVE COMMUNITY: PLANTATION
        LIFE IN THE ANTEBELLUM SOUTH.   NEW YORK: OXFORD
        UNIVERSITY PRESS, 1972.

18743   BRYCE-LAPORTE, ROY S.   "SLAVES AS INMATES, SLAVES AS MEN:
        A SOCIOLOGICAL DISCUSSION OF ELKINS' THESIS."   IN
        LANE, ANN J. (ED.).   THE DEBATE OVER SLAVERY: STANLEY
        ELKINS AND HIS CRITICS.   URBANA: UNIVERSITY OF
        ILLINOIS PRESS, 1971, PP. 269-272.

18744   CAMPBELL, ALBERT A.   ST. THOMAS NEGROES--A STUDY OF
        PERSONALITY AND CULTURE.   EVANSTON, IL: THE AMERICAN
        PSYCHOLOGICAL ASSOCIATION, 1943.

18745   CINEL, DINO.   "TOWARD THE DISCOVERY OF THE BLACK
        PERSONALITY."   UNPUBLISHED PAPER, STANFORD UNIVERSITY,
        1973.

18746   COMER, JAMES P.   "INDIVIDUAL DEVELOPMENT AND BLACK
        REBELLION: SOME PARALLELS."   MIDWAY, 9 (1968):   33-48.

18747   COX, OLIVER C.   "THE NEGRO SLAVE PERSONALITY."   IN RACE
        RELATIONS: ELEMENTS AND SOCIAL DYNAMICS.   DETROIT:
        WAYNE STATE UNIVERSITY PRESS, 1976, PP. 33-36.

18748   CRUMMELL, ALEXANDER.   "THE ACQUISITIVE PRINCIPLE IN THE
        NEGRO RACE."   SOUTHERN WORKMAN, 27 (OCTOBER, 1898):
        196-197.

18749   DAVIS, ALLISON.   CHILDREN OF BONDAGE: THE PERSONALITY
        DEVELOPMENT OF NEGRO YOUTH IN THE URBAN SOUTH.
        WASHINGTON: AMERICAN COUNCIL ON EDUCATION, 1940.

18750   DEW, CHARLES B.   "THE SAMBO AND NAT TURNER IN EVERY
        SLAVE: A REVIEW OF ROLL, JORDAN, ROLL."   CIVIL WAR
        HISTORY, 21 (SEPTEMBER, 1975):   261-268.

18751   ELKINS, STANLEY.   "SLAVERY AND PERSONALITY."   IN KAPLAN,
        BERT (ED.).   STUDYING PERSONALITY CROSS-CULTURALLY.
        EVANSTON: ROW, PETERSON, 1961, PP. 243-267.

18752   ELKINS, STANLEY M.   SLAVERY: A PROBLEM IN AMERICAN
        INSTITUTIONAL AND INTELLECTUAL LIFE.   CHICAGO:
        UNIVERSITY OF CHICAGO PRESS, 1959.

18753   ELKINS, STANLEY M.   "SLAVERY: A PROBLEM IN AMERICAN
        INSTITUTIONAL AND INTELLECTUAL LIFE." PH.D.
        DISSERTATION, COLUMBIA UNIVERSITY, 1959.

18754   FORTUNE, T. THOMAS. "'GOOD INDIANS' AND 'GOOD NIGGERS.'"
        INDEPENDENT, 51 (JUNE 22, 1899): 1689-1690.

18755   FRANKLIN, VINCENT P.   "SLAVERY, PERSONALITY, AND BLACK
        CULTURE--SOME THEORETICAL ISSUES." PHYLON, 35 (MARCH,
        1974): 54-63.

18756   FREDRICKSON, GEORGE M. AND LASCH, CHRISTOPHER.
        "RESISTANCE TO SLAVERY." CIVIL WAR HISTORY, 13
        (DECEMBER, 1967): 315-329.

18757   FRY, GLADYS-MARIE. "'THE NIGHT RIDERS': A STUDY IN THE
        SOCIAL CONTROL OF THE NEGRO." PH.D. DISSERTATION,
        INDIANA UNIVERSITY, 1967.

18758   FRY, GLADYS-MARIE. NIGHT RIDERS IN BLACK FOLK HISTORY.
        KNOXVILLE: UNIVERSITY OF TENNESSEE PRESS, 1975.

18759   GARCIA, MIKEL M. "REACTIONS TO THE 'PECULIAR
        INSTITUTION': ALTERNATIVE TO THE SAMBO STEREOTYPE."
        M.A. THESIS, CALIFORNIA STATE UNIVERSITY, LONG BEACH,
        1973.

18760   GENOVESE, EUGENE D. "REBELLIOUSNESS AND DOCILITY IN THE
        NEGRO SLAVE: A CRITIQUE OF THE ELKINS THESIS." CIVIL
        WAR HISTORY, 13 (DECEMBER, 1967): 293-314.

18761   GUTERMAN, STANLEY S. "ALTERNATIVE THEORIES IN THE STUDY
        OF SLAVERY, THE CONCENTRATION CAMP, AND PERSONALITY."
        BRITISH JOURNAL OF SOCIOLOGY, 26 (JUNE, 1975):
        186-202.

18762   JONES, REGINALD L. (ED.). BLACK PSYCHOLOGY. NEW YORK:
        HARPER AND ROW, 1972.

18763   JOYNER, CHARLES W. "SOUL FOOD AND THE SAMBO STEREOTYPE:
        FOODLORE IN THE SLAVE NARRATIVE COLLECTION." KEYSTONE
        FOLKLORE QUARTERLY, 16 (1971): 171-178.

18764   KARDINER, ABRAM AND OVESEY, LIONEL. THE MARK OF
        OPPRESSION: EXPLORATIONS IN THE PERSONALITY OF THE
        AMERICAN NEGRO. NEW YORK: WORLD PUBLISHING COMPANY,
        1951.

18765   KARON, BERTRAM P. BLACK SCARS. NEW YORK: SPRINGER
        PUBLISHING COMPANY, 1975.

18766   LEWIS, MARY A.   "SLAVERY AND PERSONALITY: A FURTHER
        COMMENT."   AMERICAN QUARTERLY, 19 (SPRING, 1967):
        114-121.

18767   MARABLE, MANNING.   "THE MEANING OF FAITH IN THE BLACK
        MIND IN SLAVERY."   ROCKY MOUNTAIN REVIEW OF LANGUAGE
        AND LITERATURE, 30 (AUTUMN, 1976):   248-264.

18768   MCKENZIE, ROBERT H.   "SHELBY IRON COMPANY: A NOTE ON
        SLAVE PERSONALITY AFTER THE CIVIL WAR."   JOURNAL OF
        NEGRO HISTORY, 58 (JULY, 1973):   341-348.

18769   MOHR, CLARENCE L.   "SAMBOIZATION: A CASE STUDY."
        RESEARCH STUDIES, 38 (JUNE, 1970):   152-154.

18770   OWENS, LESLIE H.   "'THIS SPECIES OF PROPERTY':   SLAVE
        PERSONALITY AND BEHAVIOR IN THE OLD SOUTH, 1776-1861."
        PH.D. DISSERTATION, UNIVERSITY OF CALIFORNIA,
        RIVERSIDE, 1973.

18771   PETTIGREW, THOMAS F.   "NEGRO AMERICAN PERSONALITY: WHY
        ISN'T MORE KNOWN?"   JOURNAL OF SOCIAL FORCES, 20
        (APRIL, 1964):   4-23.

18772   POLE, J.R.   "SLAVERY, RACE, AND THE DEBATE ON
        PERSONALITY."   PATHS TO THE AMERICAN PAST.   NEW YORK:
        OXFORD UNIVERSITY PRESS, 1979, PP. 189-219.

18773   POLLARD, EDWARD.   "THE ROMANCE OF THE NEGRO."   AMERICAN
        MISSIONARY, 15 (NOVEMBER, 1871):   242-248.

18774   "THE QUESTION OF 'SAMBO.'"   NEWBERRY LIBRARY BULLETIN, 5
        (DECEMBER, 1958):   14-40.

18775   RASTEGAR, CAROL C.   "THE SAMBO IMAGE: MYTH OR REALITY."
        M.A. THESIS, UNIVERSITY OF CALIFORNIA, LOS ANGELES,
        1968.

18776   RAWICK, GEORGE.   "THE HISTORICAL ROOTS OF BLACK
        LIBERATION."   RADICAL AMERICA, 2 (JULY-AUGUST, 1968):
        1-13.

18777   SHARPLEY, ROBERT H.   "A PSYCHOHISTORICAL PERSPECTIVE OF
        THE NEGRO."   AMERICAN JOURNAL OF PSYCHIATRY, 126
        (NOVEMBER, 1969):   645-650.

18778   SHARPLEY, ROBERT H.   "A PSYCHOHISTORICAL PERSPECTIVE OF
        THE NEGRO."   IN REINHARDT, ADINA M. AND QUINN, MILDRED
        D. (EDS.).   FAMILY-CENTERED COMMUNITY NURSING: A
        SOCIOLOGICAL FRAMEWORK.   SAINT LOUIS: C.V. MOSBY
        COMPANY, 1973, PP. 78-94.

18779   STAMPP, KENNETH M.   "REBELS AND SAMBOS: THE SEARCH FOR
        THE NEGRO'S PERSONALITY IN SLAVERY."   JOURNAL OF
        SOUTHERN HISTORY, 37 (AUGUST, 1971):   367-392.

18780   STEIN, SHELDON M.   THE BLACK RESPONSE TO ENSLAVEMENT:
        REINTERPRETATIONS OF THE BEHAVIOR AND PERSONALITY OF
        AMERICAN SLAVES.   WASHINGTON: UNIVERSITY PRESS OF
        AMERICA, 1976.

18781   TAXEL, JOEL.   "CHARLES WADDELL CHESNUTT'S SAMBO: MYTH
        AND REALITY."   NEGRO AMERICAN LITERATURE FORUM, 9
        (WINTER, 1975):   105-108.

18782   THORPE, EARL E.   "CHATTEL SLAVERY AND CONCENTRATION
        CAMPS."   NEGRO HISTORY BULLETIN, 25 (MAY, 1962):
        171-176.

18783   THORPE, EARL E.   EROS AND FREEDOM IN SOUTHERN LIFE AND
        THOUGHT.   DURHAM: SEEMAN PRINTERY, 1967.

18784   THORPE, EARL E.   THE OLD SOUTH: A PSYCHOHISTORY.
        WESTPORT: GREENWOOD PRESS, 1979.

18785   THORPE, EARL E.   "THE SLAVE COMMUNITY: STUDIES OF
        SLAVERY NEED FREUD AND MARX."   IN GILMORE, AL-TONY
        (ED.).   REVISITING BLASSINGAME'S THE SLAVE COMMUNITY:
        THE SCHOLARS RESPOND.   WESTPORT: GREENWOOD PRESS,
        1978, PP. 42-60.

18786   WALKER, MARY T.   "THE EFFECT OF SLAVERY IN THE UNITED
        STATES ON THE PERSONALITY OF THE AMERICAN NEGRO: AN
        HISTORIOGRAPHICAL ESSAY, SINCE 1945."   M.A. THESIS,
        UNIVERSITY OF HOUSTON, 1969.

18787   WILLIAMS, WALTER L.   "THE 'SAMBO' DECEPTION: THE
        EXPERIENCE OF JOHN MCELROY IN ANDERSONVILLE PRISON."
        PHYLON, 39 (FALL, 1978):   261-263.

18788   WILLIAMSON, JOEL R.   "BLACK SELF-ASSERTION BEFORE AND
        AFTER EMANCIPATION."   IN HUGGINS, NATHAN I.; KILSON,
        MARTIN; AND FOX, DANIEL M. (EDS.).   KEY ISSUES IN THE
        AFRO-AMERICAN EXPERIENCE.   2 VOLS.   NEW YORK:
        HARCOURT BRACE JOVANOVICH, 1971, VOL. 1, PP. 213-239.

18789   WINETROUB, HEDDA G.   "AN EXAMINATION OF THE CONTROVERSY
        OVER THE SLAVE PERSONALITY QUESTION."   M.A. THESIS,
        UNIVERSITY OF MISSOURI, KANSAS CITY, 1976.

18790   YETMAN, NORMAN R.   "THE SLAVE PERSONALITY: A TEST OF THE
        'SAMBO' HYPOTHESIS."   PH.D. DISSERTATION, UNIVERSITY
        OF PENNSYLVANIA, 1969.

18791   YETMAN, NORMAN R.   "SLAVERY AND PERSONALITY: A PROBLEM
        IN THE STUDY OF MODAL PERSONALITY IN HISTORICAL
        POPULATIONS."   IN HAGUE, JOHN A. (ED.).   AMERICAN
        CHARACTER AND CULTURE IN A CHANGING WORLD: SOME
        TWENTIETH-CENTURY PERSPECTIVES.   WESTPORT: GREENWOOD
        PRESS, 1979, PP. 349-366.

AUTOBIOGRAPHICAL WRITINGS

18792   ADAMS, JOHN Q.   NARRATIVE OF THE LIFE OF JOHN QUINCY
         ADAMS, WHEN IN SLAVERY AND NOW AS A FREEMAN.
         HARRISBURG: THE AUTHOR, 1972.

18793   ALBERT, OCTAVIA V.R.   THE HOUSE OF BONDAGE: OR,
         CHARLOTTE BROOKS AND OTHER SLAVES.   NEW YORK: HUNT
         AND EATON, 1890.

18794   ALECKSON, SAM.   BEFORE THE WAR, AND AFTER THE UNION: AN
         AUTOBIOGRAPHY.   BOSTON: GOLD MIND PUBLISHING COMPANY,
         1929.

18795   ALEXANDER, ARCHER.   THE STORY OF ARCHER ALEXANDER, FROM
         SLAVERY TO FREEDOM, MARCH 30, 1863.   BOSTON: CUPPLES,
         UPHAM, AND COMPANY, 1885.

18796   ALSTON, PRIMUS P.   "UP FROM SLAVERY."   SPIRIT OF
         MISSIONS, 72 (MAY, 1907):   375-373.

18797   ANDERSON, ROBERT.   FROM SLAVERY TO AFFLUENCE: MEMOIRS OF
         ROBERT ANDERSON, EX-SLAVE.   HEMINGSFORD, NE:
         HEMINGSFORD LEDGER, 1927.

18798   ANDERSON, ROBERT.   THE LIFE OF REV. ROBERT ANDERSON.
         MACON: J.W. BURKE, 1891.

18799   ARMSTRONG, ORLAND K.   OLD MASSA'S PEOPLE: THE SLAVES TELL
         THEIR STORY.   INDIANAPOLIS: BOBBS-MERRILL, 1931.

18800   ARTER, JARED M.   ECHOES FROM A PIONEER LIFE.   ATLANTA:
         A.B. CALDWELL PUBLISHING COMPANY, 1922.

18801   "AUTOBIOGRAPHY OF OMAR IBN SAID, SLAVE IN NORTH CAROLINA,
         1831."   AMERICAN HISTORICAL REVIEW, 30 (JULY, 1925):
         787-795.

18802   BAILEY, DAVID T.   "A DIVIDED PRISM: TWO SOURCES OF BLACK
         TESTIMONY ON SLAVERY."   JOURNAL OF SOUTHERN HISTORY,
         46 (AUGUST, 1980):   381-404.

18803   BANNER, ELEANOR.   "THE HISTORY OF THE BLACK MAN IN
         NARRATIVE AND SONG."   PH.D. DISSERTATION, UNION
         GRADUATE SCHOOL, 1972.

18804   BARAKA, AMIRI.   "AFRO-AMERICAN LITERATURE & CLASS
         STRUGGLE."   BLACK AMERICAN LITERATURE FORUM, 14
         (SPRING, 1980):   5-14.

18805   BARNET, MIGUEL (ED.).   THE AUTOBIOGRAPHY OF A RUNAWAY
         SLAVE: ESTABAN MONTEJO.   NEW YORK: PANTHEON BOOKS,
         1968.

18806   BAYLISS, JOHN F. (ED.).   BLACK SLAVE NARRATIVES.   NEW

YORK: MACMILLAN PUBLISHING COMPANY, 1970.

18807 BAYLISS, JOHN F. "SLAVE AND CONVICT NARRATIVES: A DISCUSSION OF AMERICAN AND AUSTRALIAN WRITING." JOURNAL OF COMMONWEALTH LITERATURE, NO. 8 (DECEMBER, 1969): 142-149.

18808 BEAR, JAMES A., JR. (ED.). JEFFERSON AT MONTICELLO: MEMOIRS OF A MONTICELLO SLAVE AS DICTATED TO CHARLES CAMPBELL BY ISAAC. CHARLOTTESVILLE: UNIVERSITY PRESS OF VIRGINIA, 1967.

18809 BEAVER, HAROLD. "RUN, NIGGER, RUN: ADVENTURES OF HUCKLEBERRY FINN AS A FUGITIVE SLAVE NARRATIVE." JOURNAL OF AMERICAN STUDIES, 8 (DECEMBER, 1974): 339-362.

18810 BERWANGER, EUGENE H. AS THEY SAW SLAVERY. MINNEAPOLIS: WINSTON PRESS, 1973.

18811 BLAIR, NORVEL. LIFE OF NORVEL BLAIR, A NEGRO CITIZEN OF MORRIS, GRUNDY COUNTY, ILLINOIS. JOLIET, IL: JOLIET DAILY RECORD STEAM PRINT, 1880.

18812 BLASSINGAME, JOHN W. (ED.). SLAVE TESTIMONY: TWO CENTURIES OF LETTERS, SPEECHES, INTERVIEWS, AND AUTOBIOGRAPHIES. BATON ROUGE: LOUISIANA STATE UNIVERSITY PRESS, 1977.

18813 BLASSINGAME, JOHN W. "USING THE TESTIMONY OF EX-SLAVES: APPROACHES AND PROBLEMS." IN GILMORE, AL-TONY (ED.). REVISITING BLASSINGAME'S THE SLAVE COMMUNITY: THE SCHOLARS RESPOND. WESTPORT: GREENWOOD PRESS, 1978, PP. 169-194.

18814 BLASSINGAME, JOHN W. "USING THE TESTIMONY OF EX-SLAVES: APPROACHES AND PROBLEMS." JOURNAL OF SOUTHERN HISTORY, 41 (NOVEMBER, 1975): 473-492.

18815 BONTEMPS, ARNA (ED.). FIVE BLACK LIVES: THE AUTOBIOGRAPHIES OF VENTURE SMITH, JAMES MARS, WILLIAM GRIMES, THE REV. G.W. OFFLEY AND JAMES L. SMITH. MIDDLETOWN, CT: WESLEYAN UNIVERSITY PRESS, 1971.

18816 BONTEMPS, ARNA. GREAT SLAVE NARRATIVES. BOSTON: BEACON PRESS, 1969.

18817 BONTEMPS, ARNA. "THE SLAVE NARRATIVE: AN AMERICAN GENRE." GREAT SLAVE NARRATIVES. BOSTON: BEACON PRESS, 1969, PP. VII-XIX.

18818 BOTKIN, B.A. (ED.). LAY MY BURDEN DOWN: A FOLK HISTORY OF SLAVERY. CHICAGO: UNIVERSITY OF CHICAGO PRESS, 1945.

18819   BRADFORD, SARAH. HARRIET TUBMAN: THE MOSES OF HER
        PEOPLE. NEW YORK: THE AUTHOR, 1885.

18820   BRAND, NORMAN E. "POWER IN THE BLOOD: THE POLEMICS OF
        THE FUGITIVE SLAVE NARRATIVE." PH.D. DISSERTATION,
        ARIZONA STATE UNIVERSITY, 1972.

18821   BRATTON, MARY J. (ED.). "FIELDS'S OBSERVATIONS: THE
        SLAVE NARRATIVE OF A NINETEENTH-CENTURY VIRGINIAN."
        VIRGINIA MAGAZINE OF HISTORY AND BIOGRAPHY, 88
        (JANUARY, 1980): 75-93.

18822   BREWER, J. MASON (ED.). AMERICAN NEGRO FOLKLORE.
        CHICAGO: QUADRANGLE BOOKS, 1968.

18823   BRIGNANO, RUSSELL C. BLACK AMERICANS IN AUTOBIOGRAPHY:
        AN ANNOTATED BIBLIOGRAPHY OF AUTOBIOGRAPHIES AND
        AUTOBIOGRAPHICAL BOOKS WRITTEN SINCE THE CIVIL WAR.
        DURHAM: DUKE UNIVERSITY PRESS, 1974.

18824   BROWN, CLARENCE. "REFLECTIONS ON 119 YEARS OF LIVING."
        JET, 46 (JULY 4, 1974): 22-25.

18825   BROWN, HALLIE Q. HOMESPUN HEROINES AND OTHER WOMEN OF
        DISTINCTION. XENIA, OH: THE AEDINE PUBLISHING
        COMPANY, 1926.

18826   BROWN, WILLIAM W. MY SOUTHERN HOME: OR, THE SOUTH AND
        ITS PEOPLE. BOSTON: A.G. BROWN, 1880.

18827   BRUCE, HENRY C. THE NEW MAN: TWENTY-NINE YEARS A SLAVE,
        TWENTY-NINE YEARS A FREE MAN: RECOLLECTIONS OF H.C.
        BRUCE. YORK, PA: P. ANSTADT AND SONS, 1895.

18828   BRUCHAC, JOSEPH. "BLACK AUTOBIOGRAPHY IN AFRICA AND
        AMERICA." BLACK ACADEMY REVIEW, 2 (SPRING-SUMMER,
        1971): 61-70.

18829   BRUNER, PETER. A SLAVE'S ADVENTURES TOWARD FREEDOM: NOT
        FICTION, BUT THE TRUE STORY OF A STRUGGLE. OXFORD,
        OH: N.P., 1918.

18830   BURGER, MARY W. "BLACK AUTOBIOGRAPHY--A LITERATURE OF
        CELEBRATION." PH.D. DISSERTATION, WASHINGTON
        UNIVERSITY, 1973.

18831   BURTON, ANNIE L. MEMORIES OF CHILDHOOD'S SLAVERY DAYS.
        BOSTON: ROSS PUBLISHING COMPANY, 1909.

18832   BURTON, THOMAS W. WHAT EXPERIENCE HAS TAUGHT ME.
        CINCINNATI: PRESS OF JENNINGS & GRAHAM, 1910.

18833   BUTTERFIELD, STEPHEN. BLACK AUTOBIOGRAPHY IN AMERICA.
        AMHERST: UNIVERSITY OF MASSACHUSETTS PRESS, 1974.

18834   BUTTERFIELD, STEPHEN T. "BLACK AUTOBIOGRAPHY: THE
         DEVELOPMENT OF IDENTIFICATION, LANGUAGE AND VIEWPOINT
         FROM DOUGLASS TO JACKSON." PH.D. DISSERTATION,
         UNIVERSITY OF MASSACHUSETTS, 1972.

18835   BUTTERFIELD, STEPHEN. "LANGUAGE AND THE SLAVE
         EXPERIENCE." BLACK AUTOBIOGRAPHY IN AMERICA.
         AMHERST: UNIVERSITY OF MASSACHUSETTS PRESS, 1974, PP.
         32-46.

18836   BUTTERFIELD, STEPHEN. "POINT OF VIEW IN THE SLAVE
         NARRATIVES." BLACK AUTOBIOGRAPHY IN AMERICA.
         AMHERST: UNIVERSITY OF MASSACHUSETTS PRESS, 1974, PP.
         11-31.

18837   BUTTERFIELD, STEPHEN T. "THE USE OF LANGUAGE IN THE
         SLAVE NARRATIVES." NEGRO AMERICAN LANGUAGE FORUM, 6
         (FALL, 1972): 72-78.

18838   CALLCOTT, GEORGE H. "OMAR IBN SAID, A SLAVE, WHO WROTE
         AN AUTOBIOGRAPHY IN ARABIC." JOURNAL OF NEGRO
         HISTORY, 39 (JANUARY, 1954): 58-62.

18839   CALLCOTT, GEORGE H. "OMAR IBN SAID'S UNIQUE
         AUTOBIOGRAPHY." STATE MAGAZINE, (APRIL 19, 1953):
         14-15.

18840   CAPEHART, L.C. REMINISCENCES OF ISAAC AND SUKEY, SLAVES
         OF B.F. MOORE, OF RALEIGH, N.C. RALEIGH: EDWARDS AND
         BROUGHTON PRINTING COMPANY, 1907.

18841   CHAPMAN, ABRAHAM (ED.). STEAL AWAY: STORIES OF THE
         RUNAWAY SLAVES. NEW YORK: PRAEGER, 1971.

18842   CLARK, SARAH B. "AFRO-AMERICAN LITERATURE: ORIGINS."
         IN BRIGHT, ALFRED L.; CLARK; AMADI, LAWRENCE E.;
         COOPER, SYRETHA; BARNES, CLARENCE; AND O'NEILL, DANIEL
         J. AN INTERDISCIPLINARY INTRODUCTION TO BLACK
         STUDIES. DUBUQUE: KENDALL/HUNT PUBLISHING COMPANY,
         1977, PP. 125-128.

18843   CLARK, SARAH B. "LITERARY EXPRESSION OF RESISTANCE OF
         BLACKS IN THE UNITED STATES FROM 1800 TO 1940." IN
         BRIGHT, ALFRED L.; CLARK; AMADI, LAWRENCE E.; COOPER,
         SYRETHA; BARNES, CLARENCE; AND O'NEILL, DANIEL J. AN
         INTERDISCIPLINARY INTRODUCTION TO BLACK STUDIES.
         DUBUQUE: KENDALL/HUNT PUBLISHING COMPANY, 1977, PP.
         132-135.

18844   CLEMENT, SAMUEL S. MEMOIRS OF SAMUEL SPOTFORD CLEMENT:
         RELATING INTERESTING EXPERIENCES IN DAYS OF SLAVERY
         AND FREEDOM. STEUBENVILLE, OH: HERALD PRINTING
         COMPANY, 1908.

18845   CLEVELAND, LEN G. "LETTER FROM A FORMER ALABAMA SLAVE TO

HIS OLD MASTER." _ALABAMA REVIEW_, 28 (APRIL, 1975): 151-152.

18846 COFFIN, LEVI. _REMINISCENCES OF LEVI COFFIN, THE REPUTED PRESIDENT OF THE UNDERGROUND RAILROAD_. CINCINNATI: WESTERN TRACT SOCIETY, 1876.

18847 CORTADA, RAFAEL L. "THE SLAVE NARRATIVES: LIVING INDICTMENTS OF AMERICAN HISTORIOGRAPHY." _CURRENT BIBLIOGRAPHY ON AFRICAN AFFAIRS_, 4 (NOVEMBER, 1971): 419-423.

18848 COTT, NANCY F. (ED.). "NARRATIVES FROM ESCAPED SLAVES." _ROOTS OF BITTERNESS: DOCUMENTS OF THE SOCIAL HISTORY OF AMERICAN WOMEN_. NEW YORK: DUTTON, 1972, PP. 186-193.

18849 CROSS, CORA M. "UNCLE JOHN HICKMAN, OLDTIME DARKY, MORE THAN A CENTURY OLD, TALKS ABOUT THE THINGS HE HAS SEEN." _TEXAS MONTHLY_, 4 (OCTOBER, 1929): 380-393.

18850 CUNNINGHAM, EILEEN S. AND SCHNEIDER, MABEL A. "A SLAVE'S AUTOBIOGRAPHY RETOLD." _WESTERN ILLINOIS REGIONAL STUDIES_, 2 (1979): 109-126.

18851 CURTIN, PHILIP D. (ED.). _AFRICA REMEMBERED: NARRATIVES BY WEST AFRICANS FROM THE ERA OF THE SLAVE TRADE_. MADISON: UNIVERSITY OF WISCONSIN PRESS, 1967.

18852 CURTIS, ANNA L. _STORIES OF THE UNDERGROUND_. NEW YORK: ISLAND WORKSHOP PRESS CO-OPERATIVE, 1941.

18853 DANCE, DARYL C. "WIT AND HUMOR IN THE SLAVE NARRATIVES." _JOURNAL OF AFRO-AMERICAN ISSUES_, 5 (SPRING, 1977): 125-134.

18854 DELANEY, LUCY A. _FROM THE DARKNESS COMETH THE LIGHT OR, STRUGGLE FOR FREEDOM_. SAINT LOUIS: J.T. SMITH, 1891.

18855 DORMIGOLD, KATE. _A SLAVE GIRL'S STORY, THE AUTOBIOGRAPHY OF KATE DORMIGOLD_. BROOKLYN: N.P., 1898.

18856 DOUGLASS, FREDERICK. _THE LIFE AND TIMES OF FREDERICK DOUGLASS_. HARTFORD: CONNECTICUT PARK PUBLISHING COMPANY, 1881.

18857 DOWNS, ROBERT B. "FREDERICK DOUGLASS'S _NARRATIVE OF THE LIFE OF FREDERICK DOUGLASS, AN AMERICAN SLAVE WRITTEN BY HIMSELF_." IN _BOOKS THAT CHANGED THE SOUTH_. TOTOWA: LITTLEFIELD, ADAMS, AND COMPANY, 1977, PP. 92-102.

18858 DOYLE, MARY E. "JOSIAH HENSON'S NARRATIVE: BEFORE AND AFTER." _NEGRO AMERICAN LITERATURE FORUM_, 8 (SPRING, 1974): 176-182.

18859   DUNGY, J.A.   A NARRATIVE OF THE REV. JOHN DUNGY, WHO WAS
        BORN A SLAVE. WRITTEN BY HIS DAUGHTER. ROCHESTER:
        N.P., 1866.

18860   DYER, STANFORD P.   "A BLACK VIEW OF MISSISSIPPI
        RECONSTRUCTION." M.A. THESIS, LOUISIANA TECH
        UNIVERSITY, 1974.

18861   EDELSTEIN, TILDEN G. (ED.).   THE REFUGEE: A NORTH-SIDE
        VIEW OF SLAVERY BY BENJAMIN DREW. READING, MA:
        ADDISON-WESLEY, 1969.

18862   EDWARDS, J. LOYD JR.   THE EX-SLAVE EXTRA. THE LIVING
        VOICE AND AUTOBIOGRAPHY OF AN EX-SLAVE IN BICENTENNIAL
        HISTORY. CHATTANOOGA: COSMOPOLITAN COMMUNITY CHURCH,
        1976.

18863   EDWARDS, PAUL (ED.).   EQUIANO'S TRAVELS: THE INTERESTING
        NARRATIVE OF THE LIFE OF OLAUDAH EQUIANO, OR GUSTAVUS,
        THE AFRICAN. NEW YORK: FREDERICK A. PRAEGER, 1966.

18864   ELIZABETH, A COLORED MINISTER OF THE GOSPEL, BORN IN
        SLAVERY. PHILADELPHIA: TRACT ASSOCIATION OF FRIENDS,
        1889.

18865   FELDSTEIN, STANLEY.   ONCE A SLAVE: THE SLAVES' VIEW OF
        SLAVERY. NEW YORK: WILLIAM MORROW AND COMPANY, 1970.

18866   FELDSTEIN, STANLEY.   "THE SLAVES' VIEW OF SLAVERY."
        PH.D. DISSERTATION, NEW YORK UNIVERSITY, 1969.

18867   FEREBEE, LONDON R.   BRIEF HISTORY OF THE SLAVE LIFE OF
        REV. L.R. FEREBEE. RALEIGH: EDWARDS & BROUGHTON,
        1882.

18868   FISHER, ELIJAH J.   THE MASTER SLAVE, ELIJAH JOHN FISHER.
        PHILADELPHIA: JUDSON PRESS, 1922.

18869   FIVE SLAVE NARRATIVES: A COMPENDIUM. NEW YORK: ARNO
        PRESS, 1968.

18870   FOSTER, FRANCES S.   "BRITON HAMMON'S NARRATIVE: SOME
        INSIGHTS INTO BEGINNINGS." CLA JOURNAL, 21 (DECEMBER,
        1977):   179-186.

18871   FOSTER, FRANCES S.   "SLAVE NARRATIVES: TEXT AND SOCIAL
        CONTEXT." PH.D. DISSERTATION, UNIVERSITY OF
        CALIFORNIA, SAN DIEGO, 1976.

18872   FOSTER, FRANCES S.   "ULTIMATE VICTIMS: BLACK WOMEN IN
        SLAVE NARRATIVES." JOURNAL OF AMERICAN CULTURE, 1
        (WINTER, 1978):   845-854.

18873   FOSTER, FRANCES S.   WITNESSING SLAVERY: THE DEVELOPMENT
        OF ANTE-BELLUM SLAVE NARRATIVES. WESTPORT: GREENWOOD

PRESS, 1979.

18874 FRANKLIN, HENRY. A SKETCH OF HENRY FRANKLIN AND FAMILY.
       PHILADELPHIA: COLLINS PRINTING HOUSE, 1887.

18875 FRANKLIN, JOHN H. (ED.). REMINISCENCES OF AN ACTIVE
       LIFE: THE AUTOBIOGRAPHY OF JOHN ROY LYNCH. CHICAGO:
       UNIVERSITY OF CHICAGO PRESS, 1970.

18876 FREDERICK, FRANCIS. AUTOBIOGRAPHY OF REVEREND FRANCIS
       FREDERICK, OF VIRGINIA. BALTIMORE: J.W. WOODS, 1869.

18877 FURMAN, MARVA J. "THE SLAVE NARRATIVE: PROTOTYPE OF THE
       EARLY AFRO-AMERICAN NOVEL." PH.D. DISSERTATION,
       FLORIDA STATE UNIVERSITY, 1979.

18878 GARA, LARRY (ED.). NARRATIVE OF WILLIAM W. BROWN, A
       FUGITIVE SLAVE. READING, MA: ADDISON-WESLEY, 1969.

18879 GATEWOOD, WILLARD B., JR. (ED.). SLAVE AND FREEMAN: THE
       AUTOBIOGRAPHY OF GEORGE L. KNOX. LEXINGTON:
       UNIVERSITY OF KENTUCKY PRESS, 1979.

18880 GIBBS, MIFFLIN W. SHADOW AND LIGHT: AN AUTOBIOGRAPHY
       WITH REMINISCENCES OF THE LAST AND PRESENT CENTURY.
       WASHINGTON: N.P., 1902.

18881 GOINES, LEONARD. "SLAVE NARRATIVES." ALLEGRO, 73
       (DECEMBER, 1973): 4; 74 (JANUARY, 1974): 4.

18882 GREEN, JOHN P. FACT STRANGER THAN FICTION: SEVENTY-FIVE
       YEARS OF A BUSY LIFE. CLEVELAND: RIEHL PRINTING
       COMPANY, 1920.

18883 GREEN, THOMAS L. "THE VOYAGE OF THE SABLE VENUS--BLACK
       WOMEN IN SLAVE NARRATIVES." IN JOHNSON, WILLA D. AND
       GREEN (EDS.). PERSPECTIVES ON AFRO-AMERICAN WOMEN.
       WASHINGTON: EDUCATIONAL COMMUNITY COUNSELORS
       ASSOCIATES, INC., 1975, PP. 11-21.

18884 GRIMES, WILLIAM W. THIRTY-THREE YEARS' EXPERIENCE OF AN
       ITINERANT MINISTER OF THE A.M.E. CHURCH. LANCASTER:
       E.S. SPEAKER, 1887.

18885 HALE, EDWARD E. (ED.). JAMES FREEMAN CLARKE:
       AUTOBIOGRAPHY, DIARY, AND CORRESPONDENCE. BOSTON:
       HOUGHTON, MIFFLIN AND COMPANY, 1891.

18886 HALL, SAMUEL. FORTY-SEVEN YEARS A SLAVE: A BRIEF STORY
       OF HIS LIFE AS A SLAVE AND AFTER FREEDOM. WASHINGTON,
       GA: N.P., 1912.

18887 HAMILTON, JEFF AND HUNT, LENOIR. "MY MASTER": THE
       INSIDE STORY OF SAM HOUSTON AND HIS TIMES. DALLAS:
       MANFRED VAN NORT, 1940.

18888   HARRIS, JOEL C. THE CHRONICLES OF AUNT MINERVY ANN. NEW
        YORK: SCRIBNER'S, 1899.

18889   HEDIN, RAYMOND. "PATERNAL AT LAST: BOOKER T. WASHINGTON
        AND THE SLAVE NARRATIVE TRADITION." CALLALOO, 2
        (OCTOBER, 1979): 95-102.

18890   HEERMANCE, J. NOEL. "NARRATIVE OF WILLIAM W. BROWN, A
        FUGITIVE SLAVE." WILLIAM WELLS BROWN AND CLOTELLE: A
        PORTRAIT OF THE ARTIST IN THE FIRST NEGRO NOVEL.
        HAMDEN, CT: ARCHON BOOKS, 1969, PP. 119-132.

18891   HEERMANCE, J. NOEL. "SLAVE NARRATIVES AS A GENRE:
        FREDERICK DOUGLASS AS PROTOTYPE." WILLIAM WELLS BROWN
        AND CLOTELLE: A PORTRAIT OF THE ARTIST IN THE FIRST
        NEGRO NOVEL. HAMDEN, CT: ARCHON BOOKS, 1969, PP.
        76-90.

18892   HEERMANCE, J. NOEL. "SLAVE NARRATIVES CONTINUED: UNIQUE
        PERSONALITIES AND PURPOSES." WILLIAM WELLS BROWN AND
        CLOTELLE: A PORTRAIT OF THE ARTIST IN THE FIRST
        AMERICAN NOVEL. HAMDEN, CT: ARCHON BOOKS, 1969, PP.
        91-118.

18893   HENRY, GEORGE. LIFE OF GEORGE HENRY; TOGETHER WITH A
        BRIEF HISTORY OF THE COLORED PEOPLE OF AMERICA. N.P.:
        THE AUTHOR, 1894.

18894   HENRY, THOMAS W. AUTOBIOGRAPHY OF REV. THOMAS W. HENRY,
        OF THE A.M.E. CHURCH. BALTIMORE: N.P., 1872.

18895   HENSON, JOSIAH. AN AUTOBIOGRAPHY OF THE REVEREND JOSIAH
        HENSON. LONDON: "CHRISTIAN AGE" OFFICE, 1878.

18896   HENSON, JOSIAH. "TRUTH IS STRONGER THAN FICTION." AN
        AUTOBIOGRAPHY OF THE REV. JOSIAH HENSON. BOSTON:
        B.B. RUSSELL & COMPANY, 1379.

18897   HENSON, JOSIAH. "UNCLE TOM'S STORY OF HIS LIFE": AN
        AUTOBIOGRAPHY OF THE REV. JOSIAH HENSON (MRS. HARRIET
        BEECHER STOWE'S "UNCLE TOM") FROM 1789 TO 1876.
        LONDON: "CHRISTIAN AGE" OFFICE, 1876.

18898   HERRING, MABEN D. "THE DEFINED SELF IN BLACK
        AUTOBIOGRAPHY." PH.D. DISSERTATION, UNIVERSITY OF
        NOTRE DAME, 1974.

18899   HOLSEY, LUCIUS H. AUTOBIOGRAPHY, SERMONS, ADDRESSES AND
        ESSAYS. ATLANTA: THE AUTHOR, 1898.

18900   HUGHES, LOUIS. THIRTY YEARS A SLAVE. FROM BONDAGE TO
        FREEDOM. THE INSTITUTION OF SLAVERY AS SEEN ON THE
        PLANTATION AND IN THE HOME OF THE PLANTER. MILWAUKEE:
        SOUTH SIDE PRINTING COMPANY, 1897.

18901   HURSTON, ZORA N.   DUST TRACKS ON A ROAD.   PHILADELPHIA:
         J.B. LIPPINCOTT COMPANY, 1942.

18902   JACKSON, MARGARET Y.   "FOLKLORE IN SLAVE NARRATIVES
         BEFORE THE CIVIL WAR."   NEW YORK FOLKLORE QUARTERLY,
         11 (SPRING, 1955):   5-19.

18903   JACKSON, MARGARET Y.   "AN INVESTIGATION OF BIOGRAPHIES
         AND AUTOBIOGRAPHIES OF AMERICAN SLAVES PUBLISHED
         BETWEEN 1840 AND 1860:   BASED UPON THE CORNELL SPECIAL
         SLAVERY COLLECTION."   PH.D. DISSERTATION, CORNELL
         UNIVERSITY, 1954.

18904   JACKSON, MARGARET Y.   THE STRUGGLE FOR FREEDOM, PHASE I:
         AS REVEALED IN SLAVE NARRATIVES OF THE PRE-CIVIL WAR
         PERIOD, 1840-1860.   CHICAGO: ADAMS PRESS, 1976.

18905   JACKSON, RICHARD L.   "SLAVE POETRY AND SLAVE NARRATIVE:
         JUAN FRANCISCO MANZANO AND BLACK AUTOBIOGRAPHY."
         BLACK WRITERS IN LATIN AMERICA.   ALBUQUERQUE:
         UNIVERSITY OF NEW MEXICO PRESS, 1979, PP. 25-35.

18906   JAHN, JANHEINZ.   "THE ACCOUNTS OF ESCAPED SLAVES."
         NEO-AFRICAN LITERATURE: A HISTORY OF BLACK WRITING.
         NEW YORK: GROVE, 1969, PP. 125-128.

18907   JAMES, THOMAS.   LIFE OF REVEREND THOMAS JAMES, BY
         HIMSELF.   ROCHESTER: POST EXPRESS PRINTING COMPANY,
         1886.

18908   JAMISON, MONROE F.   AUTOBIOGRAPHY AND WORK OF BISHOP M.F.
         JAMISON.   NASHVILLE: THE AUTHOR, 1912.

18909   JETER, HENRY N.   JETER'S TWENTY-FIVE YEARS' EXPERIENCE
         WITH THE SHILOH BAPTIST CHURCH AND HER HISTORY.
         PROVIDENCE: REMINGTON PRINTING COMPANY, 1901.

18910   "JOHANNA P. MOORE, 1832-1916:   AN AUTOBIOGRAPHY."
         CRISIS, 12 (AUGUST, 1916):   177-178.

18911   JOHNSON, AUGUSTA J.   "AN INTRODUCTION TO THE
         AUTOBIOGRAPHY OF GUSTAVUS VASSA."   M.A. THESIS,
         ATLANTA UNIVERSITY, 1936.

18912   JOHNSON, CHARLES B.   "AN OLD EX-SLAVE."   CRISIS, 22
         (JULY, 1921):   120.

18913   JOHNSON, PAUL D.   "'GOODBY TO SAMBO':   THE CONTRIBUTION
         OF THE BLACK SLAVE NARRATIVES TO THE ABOLITION
         MOVEMENT."   NEGRO AMERICAN LITERATURE FORUM, 6 (FALL,
         1972):   79-84.

18914   JOHNSON, THOMAS L.   AFRICA FOR CHRIST: TWENTY-EIGHT
         YEARS A SLAVE.   LONDON: ALEXANDER & SHEPHEARD, 1892.

18915 JOHNSON, THOMAS L. TWENTY-EIGHT YEARS A SLAVE; OR, THE STORY OF MY LIFE IN THREE CONTINENTS. BOURNEMOUTH, ENGLAND: W. MATE & SONS, 1909.

18916 JONES, THOMAS H. THE EXPERIENCES OF THOMAS H. JONES, WHO WAS A SLAVE FOR FORTY-THREE YEARS. NEW BEDFORD, MA: E. ANTHONY AND SONS, 1871.

18917 JORDAN, LEWIS G. ON TWO HEMISPHERES: BITS FROM THE LIFE OF LEWIS G. JORDAN, AS TOLD BY HIMSELF. N.P., 1935.

18918 KECKLEY, ELIZABETH. BEHIND THE SCENES BY ELIZABETH KECKLEY, FORMERLY A SLAVE, BUT MORE RECENTLY MODISTE, AND FRIEND TO MRS. ABRAHAM LINCOLN; OR, THIRTY YEARS A SLAVE, AND FOUR YEARS IN THE WHITE HOUSE. NEW YORK: G.W. CARLTON AND COMPANY, 1868.

18919 KENNERLY, KAREN. THE SLAVE WHO BOUGHT HIS FREEDOM: EQUIANO'S STORY. NEW YORK: DUTTON, 1971.

18920 KNEEBONE, JOHN T. "SAMBO AND THE SLAVE NARRATIVES: A NOTE ON SOURCES." ESSAYS IN HISTORY, 19 (1975): 7-24.

18921 LANE, ISAAC. AUTOBIOGRAPHY OF BISHOP ISAAC LANE, LL.D.,: WITH A SHORT HISTORY OF THE C.M.E. CHURCH IN AMERICA AND OF METHODISM. NASHVILLE: M.E. CHURCH, SOUTH, 1916.

18922 LANGSTON, JOHN M. FROM THE VIRGINIA PLANTATION TO THE NATIONAL CAPITOL. HARTFORD: AMERICAN PUBLISHING COMPANY, 1894.

18923 LANTZ, HERMAN R. "FAMILY AND KIN AS REVEALED IN THE NARRATIVES OF EX-SLAVES." SOCIAL SCIENCE QUARTERLY, 60 (MARCH, 1980): 667-675.

18924 LEE, ROSA F. "UNCLE JIM AND AUNT MEG." SOUTHERN WORKMAN, 36 (1907): 97-104.

18925 LEE, WILLIAM M. HISTORY OF THE LIFE OF REV. WILLIAM MACK LEE, BODY SERVANT OF GENERAL ROBERT E. LEE, THROUGH THE CIVIL WAR, COOK FROM 1861 TO 1865; STILL LIVING UNDER THE PROTECTION OF THE SOUTHERN STATES. NORFOLK: VIRGINIA SMITH PRINT COMPANY, 1918.

18926 LESTER, JULIUS. TO BE A SLAVE. NEW YORK: DIAL PRESS, 1968.

18927 "LETTER FROM AMBROSE HEADEN." AMERICAN MISSIONARY, 32 (DECEMBER, 1878): 388-389.

18928 "LETTER FROM MARTHA N. FORREST." AMERICAN MISSIONARY, N.S., 3 (JUNE, 1868): 420.

18929 LEWIS, JOSEPH V. OUT OF THE DITCH: A TRUE STORY OF AN

EX-SLAVE. HOUSTON: REIN AND COMPANY, 1910.

18930 LIEBMAN, ARTHUR. "PATTERNS AND THEMES IN AFRO-AMERICAN
LITERATURE." ENGLISH RECORD, 20 (FEBRUARY, 1970):
2-12.

18931 LOBB, JOHN (ED.). AN AUTOBIOGRAPHY OF THE REV. JOSIAH
HENSON FROM 1789 TO 1876. LONDON: CHRISTIAN AGE,
1877.

18932 LOGAN, RAYFORD W. (ED.). MEMOIRS OF A MONTICELLO SLAVE,
AS DICTATED TO CHARLES CAMPBELL IN THE 1840'S BY
ISAAC, ONE OF THOMAS JEFFERSON'S SLAVES.
CHARLOTTESVILE: UNIVERSITY OF VIRGINIA PRESS, 1951.

18933 LOGAN, RAYFORD W. (ED.). "MEMOIRS OF A MONTICELLO SLAVE,
AS DICTATED TO CHARLES CAMPBELL IN THE 1840'S BY
ISAAC, ONE OF THOMAS JEFFERSON'S SLAVES." WILLIAM AND
MARY QUARTERLY, 3RD SER., 8 (OCTOBER, 1951): 561-582.

18934 LOGGINS, VERNON. THE NEGRO AUTHOR: HIS DEVELOPMENT IN
AMERICA. NEW YORK: COLUMBIA UNIVERSITY PRESS, 1931.

18935 LOMAX, ELIZABETH. "SLAVES." DIRECTION, 1 (FEBRUARY,
1938): 88-90.

18936 LOVE, NAT. THE LIFE AND ADVENTURES OF NAT LOVE, BETTER
KNOWN IN THE CATTLE COUNTRY AS "DEADWOOD DICK." LOS
ANGELES: WAYSIDE PRESS, 1907.

18937 LUDLOW, HELEN. "THE HAMPTON NORMAL AND AGRICULTURAL
INSTITUTE." HARPER'S MAGAZINE, 47 (OCTOBER, 1873):
672-675.

18938 MAHAN, BRUCE E. "THE PASSING OF A SLAVE." PALIMPSEST, 3
(JULY, 1922): 227-230.

18939 "MAINE SLAVE STILL REMEMBERS WHIPPING HE RECEIVED IN
1853." BRIDGEPORT FARMER, MARCH 9, 1917.

18940 MARGOLIES, EDWARD. "ANTE-BELLUM SLAVE NARRATIVES: THEIR
PLACE IN AMERICAN LITERARY HISTORY." STUDIES IN BLACK
LITERATURE, 4 (AUTUMN, 1973): 1-8.

18941 MARRS, ELIJAH P. LIFE AND HISTORY OF THE REVEREND ELIJAH
P. MARRS. LOUISVILLE: BRADLEY & GILBERT, 1885.

18942 MARS, JAMES. LIFE OF JAMES MARS, A SLAVE, BORN AND SOLD
IN CONNECTICUT. WRITTEN BY HIMSELF. HARTFORD: CASE,
LOCKWOOD AND COMPANY, 1866.

18943 MARTIN, JOHN S. "SELLA MARTIN." GOOD WORDS, 8 (MAY 1,
JUNE 1, 1867): 314-321, 393-399.

18944 MASA, JORGE O. THE ANGEL IN EBONY: OR, THE LIFE AND

MESSAGE OF SAMMY MORRIS. UPLAND, IN: TAYLOR
UNIVERSITY PRESS, 1928.

18945   MASON, ISAAC. LIFE OF ISAAC MASON AS A SLAVE.
WORCESTER, MA: THE AUTHOR, 1893.

18946   MATLACK, JAMES. "THE AUTOBIOGRAPHIES OF FREDERICK
DOUGLASS." PHYLON, 40 (MARCH, 1979): 15-28.

18947   MICKLES, ALEXANDER. LIFE OF ALEXANDER MICKLES, ONE
HUNDRED YEARS OLD; FIFTY-FOUR YEARS A SLAVE; FORTY-SIX
YEARS A FREE MAN; THE OLDEST DARKEY IN MISSISSIPPI.
JACKSON, MS: TUCKER PRINTING HOUSE, 1911.

18948   MILLER, RANDALL M. "WHEN LIONS WRITE HISTORY: SLAVE
TESTIMONY AND THE HISTORY OF AMERICAN SLAVERY."
RESEARCH STUDIES, 44 (MARCH, 1976): 13-23.

18949   MILLER, RUTH AND KATOPES, PETER J. "SLAVE NARRATIVES."
IN INGE, M. THOMAS; DUKE, MAURICE; AND BRYER, JACKSON
R. (EDS.). BLACK AMERICAN WRITERS: BIBLIOGRAPHICAL
ESSAYS, VOL. 1. NEW YORK: ST. MARTIN'S PRESS, 1978,
PP. 21-46.

18950   MINTER, DAVID. "CONCEPTS OF SELF IN BLACK SLAVE
NARRATIVES." AMERICAN TRANSCENDENTAL QUARTERLY, 24
(FALL, 1974): 62-68.

18951   MOORE, GEORGE W. "AFTER FORTY-FIVE YEARS." AMERICAN
MISSIONARY, 63 (DECEMBER, 1909): 812-815.

18952   MOORE, GEORGE W. BONDAGE AND FREEDOM: THE STORY OF A
LIFE. NEW YORK: AMERICAN MISSIONARY ASSOCIATION, N.D.

18953   MORGAN, KATHRYN L. "THE EX-SLAVE NARRATIVE AS A SOURCE
FOR FOLK HISTORY." PH.D. DISSERTATION, UNIVERSITY OF
PENNSYLVANIA, 1970.

18954   MOTON, ROBERT . FINDING A WAY OUT: AN AUTOBIOGRAPHY.
GARDEN CITY: DOUBLEDAY, PAGE AND COMPANY, 1920.

18955   MOTON, ROBERT R. "A NEGRO'S UPHILL CLIMB." WORLD'S
WORK, 13 (APRIL, MAY, AUGUST, 1907): 8739-8743,
8915-8918, 9198-9201.

18956   MOTT, ABIGAIL F. AND WOOD, S.M. NARRATIVES OF COLORED
AMERICANS. NEW YORK: BROWNE AND COMPANY, 1882.

18957   MOTT, ALEXANDER. NARRATIVES OF COLORED AMERICANS. NEW
YORK: LINDLEY MURRAY ESTATE, 1875.

18958   "MY MASTER." THE INSIDE STORY OF SAM HOUSTON AND HIS
TIMES, BY HIS FORMER SLAVE, JEFF HAMILTON, AS TOLD TO
LENOIR HUNT. DALLAS: MANFRED, VAN NORT, AND COMPANY,
1940.

18959   "'MY 112 YEARS OF LIFE,' BY A FORMER MISSOURI SLAVE."
        ST. LOUIS POST DISPATCH, JANUARY 4, 1920.

18960   NICHOLS, CHARLES H. (ED.).   BLACK MEN IN CHAINS:
        NARRATIVES BY ESCAPED SLAVES. NEW YORK: LAWRENCE
        HILL AND COMPANY, 1972.

18961   NICHOLS, CHARLES H.   MANY THOUSAND GONE: THE EX-SLAVES'
        ACCOUNT OF THEIR BONDAGE AND FREEDOM. LEIDEN,
        NETHERLANDS: E.J. BRILL, 1963.

18962   NICHOLS, CHARLES H.   "WHO READ THE SLAVE NARRATIVES?"
        PHYLON, 20 (JUNE, 1959):   149-152.

18963   NICHOLS, CHARLES H., JR.   "IN FREEDOM'S HELP."   IN
        TILLMAN, NATHANIEL (ED.).   SUMMARIES OF RESEARCH
        PROJECTS, 1947-1952, ATLANTA UNIVERSITY CENTER AND
        ASSOCIATED COLLEGES. ATLANTA: ATLANTA UNIVERSITY,
        1953, PP. 43-44.

18964   NICHOLS, CHARLES H., JR.   "SLAVE NARRATIVES."   NEGRO
        HISTORY BULLETIN, 15 (MARCH, 1952):   107-114.

18965   NICHOLS, CHARLES H., JR.   "SLAVE NARRATIVES AND THE
        PLANTATION LEGEND." PHYLON, 10 (THIRD QUARTER, 1949):
        201-210.

18966   NICHOLS, CHARLES H., JR.   "A STUDY OF THE SLAVE
        NARRATIVE." PH.D. DISSERTATION, BROWN UNIVERSITY,
        1949.

18967   NICHOLS, WILLIAM W. "SLAVE NARRATIVES: DISMISSED
        EVIDENCE IN THE WRITING OF SOUTHERN HISTORY." PHYLON,
        32 (WINTER, 1971):   403-409.

18968   OMEALLY, R.G. "FREDERICK DOUGLASS' 1845 NARRATIVE: THE
        TEXT WAS MEANT TO BE PREACHED." IN FISHER, D. AND
        STEPTO, R.B. (EDS.).   AFRO-AMERICAN LITERATURE: THE
        RECONSTRUCTION OF INSTRUCTION. NEW YORK: MODERN
        LANGUAGE ASSOCIATION, 1978, PP. 192-211.

18969   OSOFSKY, GILBERT (ED.).   PUTTIN' ON OLE MASSA: THE SLAVE
        NARRATIVES OF HENRY BIBB, WILLIAM WELLS BROWN, AND
        SOLOMON NORTHUP. NEW YORK: HARPER & ROW, 1969.

18970   OSOFSKY, GILBERT. "THE SIGNIFICANCE OF SLAVE
        NARRATIVES." IN OSOFSKY (ED.).   PUTTIN' ON OLD MASSA:
        THE SLAVE NARRATIVES OF HENRY BIBB, WILLIAM WELLS
        BROWN, AND SOLOMON NORTHUP. NEW YORK: HARPER & ROW,
        1969, PP. 9-44.

18971   PARKER, ALLEN. RECOLLECTIONS OF SLAVERY TIMES.
        WORCESTER, MA: CHARLES W. BURBANK & COMPANY, 1895.

18972   PARKER, WILLIAM. "THE FREEDMAN'S STORY." ATLANTIC

MONTHLY, 17 (FEBRUARY, MARCH, 1866): 152-166, 276-295.

18973 PAYNE, DANIEL A. RECOLLECTIONS OF SEVENTY YEARS.
NASHVILLE: PUBLISHING HOUSE OF THE A.M.E. SUNDAY
SCHOOL UNION, 1888.

18974 PEASE, JANE H. AND PEASE, WILLIAM H. (EDS.). AUSTIN
STEWARD: TWENTY-TWO YEARS A SLAVE AND FORTY YEARS A
FREEMAN. READING, MA: ADDISON-WESLEY, 1969.

18975 PIPER, HENRY D. "THE PLACE OF FREDERICK DOUGLASS'S
NARRATIVE OF THE LIFE OF AN AMERICAN SLAVE IN THE
DEVELOPMENT OF A NATIVE AMERICAN PROSE STYLE."
JOURNAL OF AFRO-AMERICAN ISSUES, 5 (SPRING, 1977):
183-191.

18976 POLSKY, MILTON. "THE AMERICAN SLAVE NARRATIVE: DRAMATIC
RESOURCE MATERIAL FOR THE CLASSROOM." JOURNAL OF
NEGRO EDUCATION, 45 (SPRING, 1976): 166-178.

18977 POLSKY, MILTON. "THE AMERICAN SLAVE NARRATIVE: EXCITING
RESOURCE MATERIAL FOR THE CLASSROOM." NEGRO
EDUCATIONAL REVIEW, 26 (JANUARY, 1975): 22-36.

18978 POLSKY, MILTON E. "OH, FREEDOM: THEORETICAL AND
PRACTICAL PROBLEMS IN THE TRANSFORMATION OF THREE
AMERICAN SLAVE NARRATIVES INTO ORIGINAL PLAYS FOR
YOUNG PEOPLE." PH.D. DISSERTATION, NEW YORK
UNIVERSITY, 1973.

18979 PRIMEAU, RONALD. "SLAVE NARRATIVE TURNING MIDWESTERN:
DEADWOOD DICK RIDES INTO DIFFICULTIES." MIDAMERICA, 1
(1974): 16-35.

18980 QUARLES, BENJAMIN. BLACK ABOLITIONISTS. NEW YORK:
OXFORD UNIVERSITY PRESS, 1969.

18981 RANDOLPH, PETER. FROM SLAVE CABIN TO THE PULPIT: THE
AUTOBIOGRAPHY OF REV. PETER RANDOLPH: THE SOUTHERN
QUESTION ILLUSTRATED, AND SKETCHES OF SLAVE LIFE.
BOSTON: J.H. EARLE, 1893.

18982 RAY, EMMA. TWICE SOLD, TWICE RANSOMED: AUTOBIOGRAPHY OF
MR. AND MRS. L.P. RAY. CHICAGO: FREE METHODIST
PUBLISHING HOUSE, 1926.

18983 ROBINSON, AVIS P. "SOCIAL CONDITIONS OF SLAVERY AS TAKEN
FROM SLAVE NARRATIVES." M.A. THESIS, HOWARD
UNIVERSITY, 1938.

18984 ROBINSON, WILLIAM H. FROM LOG CABIN TO THE PULPIT: OR,
FIFTEEN YEARS IN SLAVERY. EAU CLAIRE, WI: JAMES H.
TIFFT, 1913.

18985 ROSS, ALEXANDER. RECOLLECTIONS AND EXPERIENCES OF AN

ABOLITIONIST: FROM 1355 TO 1865. TORONTO: ROWSELL
AND HUTCHINSON, 1876.

18986 ROWLAND, REGINALD. AN AMBITIOUS SLAVE. BUFFALO: PETER
       PAUL BOOK COMPANY, 1897.

18987 SADLER, ROBERT. THE EMANCIPATION OF ROBERT SADLER.
       MINNEAPOLIS: BETHANY FELLOWSHIP, 1975.

18988 "SAINT WITHOUT PRIESTHOOD: THE COLLECTED TESTIMONIES OF
       EX-SLAVE SAMUEL D. CHAMBERS." DIALOGUE: A JOURNAL OF
       MORMON THOUGHT, 12 (SUMMER, 1979): 13-21.

18989 SHEPPARD. A SHORT SKETCH OF THE LIFE OF MR. SHEPPARD
       WHILE HE WAS IN SLAVERY, TOGETHER WITH SEVERAL OF THE
       SONGS SUNG DURING THE EVENING OF THE JUBILEE CLUB.
       BELLEVILLE, ONTARIO: STEAM PRESS, N.D.

18990 SINGLETON, WILLIAM H. RECOLLECTIONS OF MY SLAVERY DAYS
       BY WILLIAM HENRY SINGLETON. PEEKSKILL, NY: HIGHLAND
       DEMOCRAT COMPANY, 1922.

18991 "SLAVE NARRATIVES." IN BASKIN, WADE AND RUNES, RICHARD
       N. DICTIONARY OF BLACK CULTURE. NEW YORK:
       PHILOSOPHICAL LIBRARY, 1973, P. 406.

18992 "SLAVE NARRATIVES." IN RYWELL, MARTIN (ED.).
       AFRO-AMERICAN ENCYCLOPEDIA. 10 VOLS. NORTH MIAMI:
       EDUCATIONAL BOOK PUBLISHERS, 1974, VOL. 8, PP.
       2494-2495.

18993 SMITH, AMANDA B. AN AUTOBIOGRAPHY: THE STORY OF THE
       LORD'S DEALINGS WITH MRS. AMANDA SMITH THE COLORED
       EVANGELIST, CONTAINING AN ACCOUNT OF HER LIFE WORK OF
       FAITH, HER TRAVELS IN AMERICA, ENGLAND, SCOTLAND,
       INDIA, AND AFRICA AS AN INDEPENDENT MISSIONARY.
       CHICAGO: MEYER AND BROTHER, 1893.

18994 SMITH, DAVID. BIOGRAPHY OF REV. DAVID SMITH, OF THE
       A.M.E. CHURCH. XENIA, OH: XENIA GAZETTE OFFICE, 1881.

18995 SMITH, HARRY. FIFTY YEARS OF SLAVERY IN THE UNITED
       STATES OF AMERICA. GRAND RAPIDS: WESTERN MICHIGAN
       PRINTING COMPANY, 1891.

18996 SMITH, JAMES L. AUTOBIOGRAPHY OF JAMES L. SMITH,
       INCLUDING ALSO, REMINISCENCES OF SLAVE LIFE,
       RECOLLECTIONS OF THE WAR, EDUCATION OF THE FREEDMEN,
       CAUSES OF THE EXODUS, ETC. NORWICH: PRESS OF THE
       BULLETIN COMPANY, 1881.

18997 SMITH, SIDONIE. WHERE I'M BOUND: PATTERNS OF SLAVERY
       AND FREEDOM IN BLACK AMERICAN AUTOBIOGRAPHY.
       WESTPORT: GREENWOOD PRESS, 1974.

18998   SMITH, SIDONIE A.   "PATTERNS OF SLAVERY AND FREEDOM IN
        BLACK AMERICAN AUTOBIOGRAPHY." PH.D. DISSERTATION,
        CASE WESTERN RESERVE UNIVERSITY, 1971.

18999   SMITH, VENTURE. A NARRATIVE OF THE LIFE AND ADVENTURES
        OF VENTURE, A NATIVE OF AFRICA, BUT RESIDENT ABOVE
        SIXTY YEARS IN THE UNITED STATES OF AMERICA.
        MIDDLETOWN, CT: J.S. STEWART, 1896.

19000   STARLING, MARION W.   THE SLAVE NARRATIVE: ITS PLACE IN
        AMERICAN LITERARY HISTORY. NEW YORK: NEW YORK
        UNIVERSITY PRESS, 1949.

19001   STARLING, MARION.W.   "THE SLAVE NARRATIVE: ITS PLACE IN
        AMERICAN LITERARY HISTORY." PH.D. DISSERTATION, NEW
        YORK UNIVERSITY, 1946.

19002   STAROBIN, ROBERT.   BLACKS IN BONDAGE: LETTERS OF
        AMERICAN SLAVES. NEW YORK: NEW VIEWPOINTS, 1974.

19003   STAROBIN, ROBERT S.   "PRIVILEGED BONDSMEN AND THE PROCESS
        OF ACCOMMODATION: THE ROLE OF HOUSESERVANTS AND
        DRIVERS AS SEEN IN THEIR OWN LETTERS." JOURNAL OF
        SOCIAL HISTORY, 5 (FALL, 1971):   46-70.

19004   STEPTO, R.B.   "NARRATION, AUTHENTICATION, AND AUTHORICAL
        CONTROL IN FREDERICK DOUGLASS'S NARRATIVE OF 1845."
        IN FISHER, D. AND STEPTO (EDS.). AFRO-AMERICAN
        LITERATURE: THE RECONSTRUCTION OF INSTRUCTION. NEW
        YORK: MODERN LANGUAGE ASSOCIATION, 1978, PP. 178-191.

19005   STEPTO, ROBERT B.   FROM BEHIND THE VEIL: A STUDY OF
        AFRO-AMERICAN NARRATIVE. URBANA: UNIVERSITY OF
        ILLINOIS PRESS, 1979.

19006   STEWART, CHARLES.   "MY LIFE AS A SLAVE." HARPER'S NEW
        MONTHLY MAGAZINE, 69 (OCTOBER, 1884):   730-738.

19007   STILL, JAMES.   EARLY RECOLLECTIONS AND LIFE OF DR. JAMES
        STILL. PHILADELPHIA: J.B. LIPPINCOTT AND COMPANY,
        1877.

19008   STONE, ALBERT E.   "IDENTITY AND ART IN FREDERICK
        DOUGLASS'S 'NARRATIVE.'" CLA JOURNAL, 17 (DECEMBER,
        1973):   192-213.

19009   STROYER, JACOB.   SKETCHES OF MY LIFE IN THE SOUTH.
        SALEM, MA: SALEM PRESS, 1879.

19010   TAYLOR, JIMMIE.   UNCLE JIMMIE, THE TRUE STORY OF A
        SLAVE'S LIFE, AS DICTATED TO HIS TEN-YEAR-OLD DAUGHTER
        TWO YEARS AFTER THE CIVIL WAR. NASHVILLE: A.M.E.S.
        SUNDAY SCHOOL UNION, 1948.

19011   TAYLOR, O.C.W.   "THE MARTYR." CRISIS, 15 (MARCH, 1918):

224-226.

19012 TAYLOR, SUSIE K. REMINISCENCES OF MY LIFE IN CAMP WITH
       THE 33RD UNITED STATES COLORED TROOPS LATE 1ST S.C.
       VOLUNTEERS. BOSTON: THE AUTHOR, 1902.

19013 TELLER, WALTER. "INTRODUCTION." IN CHILD, L. MARIA
       (ED.). INCIDENTS IN THE LIFE OF A SLAVE GIRL. NEW
       YORK: HARCOURT BRACE JOVANOVICH, 1973, PP. IX-X.

19014 TIFFANY, NINA M. "STORIES OF THE FUGITIVE SLAVES." NEW
       ENGLAND MAGAZINE, N.S., 2 (MAY, JUNE, JULY, 1890):
       280-283, 385-388, 569-576.

19015 TRAIL, WILLIAM JR. "THE STORY OF A SLAVE IN INDIANA."
       INDIANIAN, 3 (1899): 257-262.

19016 TRUTH, SOJOURNER. NARRATIVE OF SOJOURNER TRUTH: A
       BONDSWOMAN OF OLDEN TIME, EMANCIPATED BY THE NEW YORK
       LEGISLATURE IN THE EARLY PART OF THE PRESENT CENTURY.
       BOSTON: THE AUTHOR, 1875.

19017 TURNER, LORENZO D. AFRICANISMS IN THE GULLAH DIALECT.
       CHICAGO: UNIVERSITY OF CHICAGO PRESS, 1949.

19018 TWINING, M.A. "AN ANTHROPOLOGICAL LOOK AT AFRO-AMERICAN
       FOLK NARRATIVE." CLA JOURNAL, 14 (SEPTEMBER, 1970):
       57-61.

19019 VAN DEBURG, WILLIAM L. "SLAVE DRIVERS AND SLAVE
       NARRATIVES: A NEW LOOK AT THE 'DEHUMANIZED ELITE.'"
       HISTORIAN, 39 (AUGUST, 1977): 717-732.

19020 VAN DEBURG, WILLIAM L. THE SLAVE DRIVERS: BLACK
       AGRICULTURAL LABOR SUPERVISORS IN THE ANTEBELLUM
       SOUTH. WESTPORT: GREENWOOD PRESS, 1979.

19021 VENEY, BETHANY. THE NARRATIVE OF BETHANY VENEY, A SLAVE
       WOMAN. WORCESTER, MA: GEORGE H. ELLIS, 1889.

19022 WALKER, THOMAS C. THE HONEY-POD TREE: THE LIFE STORY OF
       THOMAS CALHOUN WALKER. NEW YORK: JOHN DAY, 1958.

19023 WALLER, RUBEN. "HISTORY OF A SLAVE WRITTEN BY HIMSELF AT
       THE AGE OF 89 YEARS." IN LYNAM, ROBERT (ED.). THE
       BEECHER ISLAND ANNUAL. WRAY, CO: BEECHER ISLAND
       BATTLE MEMORIAL ASSOCIATION, 1930, PP. 115-119.

19024 WALTERS, ALEXANDER. MY LIFE AND WORK. NEW YORK:
       FLEMING H. REVELL, 1917.

19025 WASHINGTON, BOOKER T. THE STORY OF MY LIFE AND WORK.
       NAPERVILLE, IL: J.L. NICHOLS AND COMPANY, 1900.

19026 WASHINGTON, BOOKER T. UP FROM SLAVERY. BOSTON:

1413

HOUGHTON MIFFLIN, 1901.

19027   WATSON, A.P.; RADIN, PAUL; AND JOHNSON, CHARLES S.
        (EDS.). GOD STRUCK ME DEAD: RELIGIOUS CONVERSION
        EXPERIENCES AND AUTOBIOGRAPHIES OF NEGRO EX-SLAVES.
        NASHVILLE: SOCIAL SCIENCE INSTITUTE, FISK UNIVERSITY,
        1945.

19028   WEBB, WILLIAM. HISTORY OF WILLIAM WEBB, COMPOSED BY
        HIMSELF. DETROIT: E. HOKSTRA, 1873.

19029   WELLS, IDA B. CRUSADE FOR JUSTICE: THE AUTOBIOGRAPHY OF
        IDA B. WELLS. CHICAGO: UNIVERSITY OF CHICAGO PRESS,
        1970.

19030   WILLIAMS, ISSAC D. SUNSHINE AND SHADOW OF SLAVE LIFE:
        REMINISCENCES AS TOLD BY ISSAC D. WILLIAMS. EAST
        SAGINAW, MI: EVENING NEWS PRINTING AND BINDING HOUSE,
        1885.

19031   WILLIAMS, JAMES. LIFE AND ADVENTURES OF JAMES WILLIAMS,
        A FUGITIVE SLAVE, WITH A FULL DESCRIPTION OF THE
        UNDERGROUND RAILROAD. SAN FRANCISCO: WOMEN'S UNION
        PRINT, 1873.

19032   WINKS, ROBIN W. (ED.). AN AUTOBIOGRAPHY OF THE REVEREND
        JOSIAH HENSON. READING, MA: ADDISON-WESLEY, 1969.

19033   WINKS, ROBIN W. (ED.). FOUR FUGITIVE SLAVES NARRATIVES.
        READING, MA: ADDISON-WESLEY, 1969.

19034   WOODS, DANIEL G. "SLAVE HISTORY FROM SLAVE TESTIMONY, A
        CRITIQUE." M.A. THESIS, UNIVERSITY OF GEORGIA, 1979.

19035   YETMAN, NORMAN R. (ED.). VOICES FROM SLAVERY. NEW YORK:
        HOLT, RINEHART AND WINSTON, 1970.

19036   ZACHARIAS, DIANNA. "AN INTERPRETATION OF THE FLORIDA
        EX-SLAVES' MEMORIES OF SLAVERY AND THE CIVIL WAR."
        M.A. THESIS, WESTERN KENTUCKY UNIVERSITY, 1976.

19037   ZEMP, FRANCIS L. "UNCLE TOM'S CABIN AND THE SLAVE
        NARRATIVE TRADITION." M.A. THESIS, UNIVERSITY OF
        NORTH CAROLINA, 1964.

INTERVIEWS

19038   "ANDREW EVANS." ST. LOUIS GLOBE-DEMOCRAT, JULY 31, 1932.

19039   BAILEY, DAVID T. "A DIVIDED PRISM: TWO SOURCES OF BLACK
        TESTIMONY ON SLAVERY." JOURNAL OF SOUTHERN HISTORY,
        46 (AUGUST, 1980): 381-404.

19040   BLACK, FREDERICK R. "BIBLIOGRAPHICAL ESSAY: BENJAMIN

DREW'S REFUGEE AND THE BLACK FAMILY." JOURNAL OF NEGRO HISTORY, 57 (JULY, 1972): 28+-289.

19041 BLASSINGAME, JOHN W. (ED.). SLAVE TESTIMONY: TWO CENTURIES OF LETTERS, SPEECHES, INTERVIEWS, AND AUTOBIOGRAPHIES. BATON ROUGE: LOUISIANA STATE UNIVERSITY PRESS, 1977.

19042 BOTKIN, B.A. (ED.). LAY MY BURDEN DOWN: A FOLK HISTORY OF SLAVERY. CHICAGO: UNIVERSITY OF CHICAGO PRESS, 1945.

19043 BOTKIN, B.A. "THE SLAVE AS HIS OWN INTERPRETER." LIBRARY OF CONGRESS QUARTERLY JOURNAL OF CURRENT ACQUISITIONS, 2 (NOVEMBER, 1944): 37-63.

19044 BOTKIN, B.A. "WE CALLED IT LIVING LORE." NEW YORK FOLKLORE QUARTERLY, 14 (FALL, 1958): 189-201.

19045 BREWER, JEUTONNE P. "THE VERB 'BE' IN EARLY BLACK ENGLISH: A STUDY BASED ON THE WPA EX-SLAVE NARRATIVES." PH.D. DISSERTATION, UNIVERSITY OF NORTH CAROLINA, 1974.

19046 CADE, JOHN B. "OUT OF THE MOUTH OF EX-SLAVES." JOURNAL OF NEGRO HISTORY, 20 (JULY, 1935): 294-337.

19047 "CHARLES C. SKINNER." BRIDGEPORT (CT) FARMER, MARCH 9, 1917.

19048 COOK, CHARLES O. AND POTEET, JAMES M. (EDS.). "'DEM WAS BLACK TIMES, SURE 'NOUGH': THE SLAVE NARRATIVES OF LYDIA JEFFERSON AND STEPHEN WILLIAMS." LOUISIANA HISTORY, 20 (SUMMER, 1979): 281-292.

19049 COPPIN, LEVI J. "AARON J. ROBINSON." A.M.E. CHURCH REVIEW, 6 (JULY, 1889): 104.

19050 COPPIN, LEVI J. "ELBERT HEAD." A.M.E. CHURCH REVIEW, 6 (JULY, 1889): 104-106.

19051 COPPIN, LEVI J. "MAJOR NELSON." A.M.E. CHURCH REVIEW, 5 (APRIL, 1889): 432-435.

19052 CRAWFORD, STEPHEN C. "QUANTIFIED MEMORY: A STUDY OF THE WPA AND FISK UNIVERSITY SLAVE NARRATIVE COLLECTIONS." PH.D. DISSERTATION, UNIVERSITY OF CHICAGO, 1980.

19053 DAVIS, K.E. "THE OLD BUTLER FARM." SOUTHERN WORKMAN, 34 (1905): 86-91.

19054 DRAKE, MIKE. "SIGNED: A PERSON WHO LOVES THIS CHURCH." FOXFIRE, 10 (1976): 211-215.

19055 DWYER-SHICK, SUSAN. "THE DEVELOPMENT OF FOLKLORE AND

FOLKLIFE RESEARCH IN THE FEDERAL WRITERS' PROJECT, 1935-1943." KEYSTONE FOLKLORE, 20 (FALL, 1975): 5-31.

19056 EATON, CLEMENT. "THE MIND OF THE SOUTHERN NEGRO: THE REMARKABLE INDIVIDUALS." THE MIND OF THE OLD SOUTH. BATON ROUGE: LOUISIANA STATE UNIVERSITY PRESS, 1967, PP. 170-199.

19057 EGYPT, OPHELIA S.; MASUOKA, J.; AND JOHNSON, CHARLES S. UNWRITTEN HISTORY OF SLAVERY: AUTOBIOGRAPHICAL ACCOUNTS OF NEGRO EX-SLAVES. NASHVILLE: SOCIAL SCIENCE INSTITUTE, FISK UNIVERSITY, 1945.

19058 ERIKSEN, GARY H. "PROBLEMS AND PROSPECTS IN QUANTIFYING THE WPA SLAVE NARRATIVES." UNPUBLISHED PAPER, UNIVERSITY OF CHICAGO, 1973.

19059 ESCOTT, PAUL D. "THE ART AND SCIENCE OF READING WPA SLAVE NARRATIVES." UNPUBLISHED PAPER, 1980.

19060 ESCOTT, PAUL D. SLAVERY REMEMBERED: A RECORD OF TWENTIETH-CENTURY SLAVE NARRATIVES. CHAPEL HILL: UNIVERSITY OF NORTH CAROLINA PRESS, 1979.

19061 FEDERAL WRITERS' PROGRAM, LOUISIANA. GUMBO YA-YA. BOSTON: HOUGHTON MIFFLIN COMPANY, 1945.

19062 FEDERAL WRITERS' PROJECT. AMERICAN STUFF: AN ANTHOLOGY OF PROSE & VERSE. NEW YORK: VIKING PRESS, 1937.

19063 FEDERAL WRITERS' PROJECT. "SLAVE NARRATIVES; A FOLK HISTORY OF SLAVERY IN THE UNITED STATES FROM INTERVIEWS WITH FORMER SLAVES." UNPUBLISHED TYPESCRIPT RECORDS PREPARED BY THE FEDERAL WRITERS' PROJECT, 1936-1938. ASSEMBLED BY THE LIBRARY OF CONGRESS PROJECT, WORKS PROJECTS ADMINISTRATION FOR THE DISTRICT OF COLUMBIA. SPONSORED BY THE LIBRARY OF CONGRESS. 17 VOLS. WASHINGTON: LIBRARY OF CONGRESS, 1941.

19064 FERRIS, WILLIAM R. "THE NEGRO CONVERSION EXPERIENCE." KEYSTONE FOLKLORE QUARTERLY, 15 (SPRING, 1970): 35-51.

19065 GENOVESE, EUGENE D. "GETTING TO KNOW THE SLAVES." NEW YORK REVIEW OF BOOKS, 19 (SEPTEMBER 21, 1972): 16-19.

19066 GEORGIA WRITERS' PROJECT. DRUMS AND SHADOWS: SURVIVAL STUDIES AMONG THE GEORGIA COASTAL NEGROES. ATHENS: UNIVERSITY OF GEORGIA PRESS, 1940.

19067 GLOVER, R.W. ". . . I'M HERE YIT." CHRONICLES OF SMITH COUNTY, TEXAS, 13 (SUMMER, 1974): 28-39.

19068 GOINES, LEONARD. "'WALK OVER': MUSIC IN THE SLAVE NARRATIVES." SING-OUT, 24 (JANUARY-FEBRUARY, 1976):

1416

6-11.

19069   GOODMAN, W.D.   GILBERT ACADEMY AND AGRICULTURAL COLLEGE:
        SKETCHES AND INCIDENTS.   NEW YORK: N.P., 1893.

19070   GOODSON, MARTIA G.   "AN INTRODUCTORY ESSAY AND SUBJECT
        INDEX TO SELECTED INTERVIEWS FROM THE SLAVE NARRATIVE
        COLLECTION."   PH.D. DISSERTATION, UNION GRADUATE
        SCHOOL, MIDWEST, 1977.

19071   GOODSON, MARTIA G.   "THE SLAVE NARRATIVE COLLECTION: A
        TOOL FOR RECONSTRUCTING AFRO-AMERICAN WOMEN'S
        HISTORY."   WESTERN JOURNAL OF BLACK STUDIES, 3
        (SUMMER, 1979):   116-122.

19072   HALL, ROBERT L.   "SLAVE TESTIMONIES."   BULLETIN OF THE
        CENTER FOR THE STUDY OF SOUTHERN CULTURE AND RELIGION,
        3 (NOVEMBER, 1979):   13-15.

19073   HARRISON, LOWELL H.   "MEMORIES OF SLAVERY DAYS IN
        KENTUCKY."   FILSON CLUB HISTORY QUARTERLY, 47 (JULY,
        1973):   242-257.

19074   HARRISON, LOWELL H.   "RECOLLECTIONS OF SOME TENNESSEE
        SLAVES."   TENNESSEE HISTORICAL QUARTERLY, 33 (SUMMER,
        1974):   175-190.

19075   HIRSCH, JERROLD.   "READING AND COUNTING."   REVIEWS IN
        AMERICAN HISTORY, 8 (SEPTEMBER, 1980):   312-317.

19076   HUMPHREY, BARBARA.   "JACK TURNER."   JUNCTION CITY (KS)
        UNION, FEBRUARY 16, 1934.

19077   HURSTON, ZORA N.   "CUDJO'S OWN STORY OF THE LAST AFRICAN
        SLAVER."   JOURNAL OF NEGRO HISTORY, 12 (OCTOBER,
        1927):   648-663.

19078   "ISRAEL JEFFERSON."   PIKE COUNTY (OH) REPUBLICAN,
        DECEMBER 25, 1873.

19079   "JOHN ANDREW JACKSON."   ROCHESTER UNION AND ADVERTISER,
        AUGUST 9, 1893.

19080   "JOHN JACKSON."   ST. LOUIS POST-DISPATCH, JANUARY 4, 1920.

19081   JOHNSON, CHARLES S.   SHADOW OF THE PLANTATION.   CHICAGO:
        UNIVERSITY OF CHICAGO PRESS, 1934.

19082   JOHNSON, GERRI.   "MARYLAND ROOTS: AN EXAMINATION OF THE
        FREE STATE'S WPA EX-SLAVE NARRATIVES."   FREE STATE
        FOLKLORE, 4 (SPRING, 1977):   18-34.

19083   JONES, J. RALPH AND LANDESS, TOM (EDS.).   "PORTRAITS OF
        GEORGIA SLAVES."   GEORGIA REVIEW, 21 (SPRING-WINTER,
        1967):   126-132, 268-273, 407-411, 521-525; 22

(SPRING-SUMMER, 1968): 125-127, 254-257.

19084 JONES, MRS. LAWRENCE C. "THE DESIRE FOR FREEDOM."
PALIMPSEST, 8 (MAY, 1927): 153-163.

19085 JOYNER, CHARLES W. "SOUL FOOD AND THE SAMBO STEREOTYPE:
FOODLORE IN THE SLAVE NARRATIVE COLLECTION." KEYSTONE
FOLKLORE QUARTERLY, 16 (1971): 171-178.

19086 KILLION, R.G. "REMINISCENCES OF THE 'PECULIAR
INSTITUTION.'" SANDLAPPER, 5 (OCTOBER, 1972): 49-54,
68.

19087 KILLION, RONALD G. AND WALLER, CHARLES (EDS.). SLAVERY
TIME WHEN I WAS CHILLUN DOWN ON MARSTER'S PLANTATION:
INTERVIEWS WITH GEORGIA SLAVES. SAVANNAH: BEEHIVE
PRESS, 1973.

19088 LANGHORNE, ORRA. "PARKE JOHNSTON." SOUTHERN WORKMAN, 10
(FEBRUARY, 1881): 14.

19089 LAWRENCE, KEN. "ORAL HISTORY OF SLAVERY." SOUTHERN
EXPOSURE, 1 (WINTER, 1974): 84-86.

19090 LESTER, JULIUS. TO BE A SLAVE. NEW YORK: DIAL PRESS,
1968.

19091 "LETTER FROM JONATHAN WATSON." FREEDMEN'S RECORD, 1
(MARCH, 1866): 12.

19092 "LETTER FROM S.E. FOSTER." FREEDMEN'S RECORD, 1
(JANUARY, 1865): 4.

19093 "LETTER FROM S.F. GOODELL." AMERICAN MISSIONARY, N.S.,
10 (APRIL, 1866): 75-76.

19094 LEWIS, ROSCOE E. "THE LIFE OF MARK THRASH." PHYLON, 20
(WINTER, 1959): 389-403.

19095 MACROBERT, MARION C. "GEORGE ANDERSON." TRENTON STATE
GAZETTE, APRIL 6, 1925.

19096 "MADISON HEMMINGS." PIKE COUNTY (OH) REPUBLICAN, MARCH
13, 1873.

19097 MANGIONE, JERRE. THE DREAM AND THE DEAL: THE FEDERAL
WRITERS PROJECT, 1935-1943. MIAMI: BANYAN BOOKS,
1972.

19098 MERCER, P.M. "TAPPING THE SLAVE NARRATIVE COLLECTION FOR
THE RESPONSE OF BLACK SOUTH CAROLINIANS TO
EMANCIPATION AND RECONSTRUCTION." AUSTRALIAN JOURNAL
OF POLITICS AND HISTORY, 25 (AUGUST, 1979): 358-374.

19099 MILLER, RANDALL M. "WHEN LIONS WRITE HISTORY: SLAVE

TESTIMONY AND THE HISTORY OF AMERICAN SLAVERY."
RESEARCH STUDIES, 44 (MARCH, 1976): 13-23.

19100   MINTER, DAVID. "CONCEPTS OF SELF IN BLACK SLAVE
        NARRATIVES." AMERICAN TRANSCENDENTAL QUARTERLY, 24
        (FALL, 1974): 62-68.

19101   "MISSOURI FORMER SLAVES." PHILADELPHIA SUNDAY ITEM, JULY
        24, 1892.

19102   MYRICK, SUSAN. "CATHERINE BEALE." MACON TELEGRAPH,
        FEBRUARY 10, 1929.

19103   "NANCY BELL." CINCINNATI TRIBUNE, JUNE 17, 1923.

19104   NEAL, WILLARD. "CICERO FINCH." ATLANTA JOURNAL, MARCH
        3, 1929.

19105   OVINGTON, MARY W. "SLAVES' REMINISCENCES OF SLAVERY."
        INDEPENDENT, 68 (MAY 26, 1910): 1131-1136.

19106   PATTON, FLORENCE. "JENNIE HILL." WICHITA EAGLE,
        FEBRUARY 26, 1933.

19107   PENKOWER, MONTY N. THE FEDERAL WRITERS' PROJECT: A
        STUDY IN GOVERNMENT PATRONAGE OF THE ARTS. URBANA:
        UNIVERSITY OF ILLINOIS PRESS, 1977.

19108   PERDUE, CHARLES L., JR. "SLAVE LIFE STYLES IN EARLY
        VIRGINIA." PROCEEDINGS OF THE PIONEER AMERICA
        SOCIETY, 2 (1973): 54-58.

19109   PERDUE, CHARLES L., JR.; BARDEN, THOMAS E.; AND PHILLIPS,
        ROBERT K. (EDS.). WEEVILS IN THE WHEAT: INTERVIEWS
        WITH VIRGINIA EX-SLAVES. CHARLOTTESVILLE: UNIVERSITY
        PRESS OF VIRGINIA, 1976.

19110   "PHILIP COLEMAN." PROVIDENCE JOURNAL, MAY 25, 1924.

19111   PIKE, GUSTAVUS D. THE JUBILEE SINGERS, AND THEIR
        CAMPAIGN FOR TWENTY THOUSAND DOLLARS. BOSTON: LEE
        AND SHEPARD, 1873.

19112   "PRIMUS SMITH." KANSAS CITY (MO) TIMES, MAY 13, 1938.

19113   RAWICK, GEORGE P. (ED.). THE AMERICAN SLAVE: A
        COMPOSITE AUTOBIOGRAPHY. 19 VOLS. WESTPORT:
        GREENWOOD PRESS, 1972.

19114   RAWICK, GEORGE P. (ED.). THE AMERICAN SLAVE: A
        COMPOSITE AUTOBIOGRAPHY: SUPPLEMENT, SERIES 1.   12
        VOLS. WESTPORT: GREENWOOD PRESS, 1977.

19115   RAWICK, GEORGE P. (ED.). THE AMERICAN SLAVE: A
        COMPOSITE AUTOBIOGRAPHY: SUPPLEMENT, SERIES 2.   10

VOLS. WESTPORT: GREENWOOD PRESS, 1979.

19116 RAWICK, GEORGE P. "TOWARDS A METHODOLOGY FOR THE USE OF
SLAVE NARRATIVES." UNPUBLISHED PAPER PRESENTED AT
INSTITUTE FOR AFRO-AMERICAN CULTURE CONFERENCE ON
"SLAVE NARRATIVES," UNIVERSITY OF IOWA, JUNE 18, 1974.

19117 ROSENGARTEN, THEODORE. ALL GOD'S DANGERS: THE LIFE OF
NATE SHAW. NEW YORK: ALFRED A. KNOPF, 1974.

19118 SALKEY, ANDREW. "INTERVIEW WITH ESTEBAN MONTEJO." IN
HAVANA JOURNAL. LONDON: PENGUIN, 1969, PP. 166-185.

19119 "SAMUEL BALLTON." BROOKLYN EAGLE, SEPTEMBER 8, 1910.

19120 SETTLE, E. OPHELIA. "SOCIAL ATTITUDES DURING THE SLAVE
REGIME: HOUSE SERVANTS VERSUS FIELD HANDS."
PUBLICATIONS OF THE AMERICAN SOCIOLOGICAL SOCIETY, 28
(MAY, 1934): 95-98.

19121 SOAPES, THOMAS F. "THE FEDERAL WRITERS' PROJECT SLAVE
INTERVIEWS: USEFUL DATA OR MISLEADING SOURCE." ORAL
HISTORY REVIEW, (1977): 33-38.

19122 "STORIES OF RUNAWAY SLAVES." DETROIT NEWS-TRIBUNE, JULY
22, 1894.

19123 TOUBES, SARAH. "ADELINE HENDERSON." DES MOINES
REGISTER, MARCH 16, 1925.

19124 TYLER, RONNIE C. AND MURPHY, LAWRENCE R. (EDS.). THE
SLAVE NARRATIVES OF TEXAS. AUSTIN: ENCINO PRESS,
1974.

19125 "UNCLE MOREAU (OMAR IBN SAID)." AFRICAN REPOSITORY, 45
(JUNE, 1869): 173-176.

19126 VAN DEBURG, WILLIAM L. "SLAVE DRIVERS AND SLAVE
NARRATIVES: A NEW LOOK AT THE 'DEHUMANIZED ELITE.'"
HISTORIAN, 39 (AUGUST, 1977): 717-732.

19127 VAN DEBURG, WILLIAM L. THE SLAVE DRIVERS: BLACK
AGRICULTURAL LABOR SUPERVISORS IN THE ANTEBELLUM
SOUTH. WESTPORT: GREENWOOD PRESS, 1979.

19128 VAN DEBURG, WILLIAM L. "THE SLAVE DRIVERS OF ARKANSAS:
A NEW VIEW FROM THE NARRATIVES." ARKANSAS HISTORICAL
QUARTERLY, 35 (AUTUMN, 1976): 231-245.

19129 WALTERS, BETH. "ADELINE HENDERSON AND JOHN WALKER." DES
MOINES TRIBUNE-CAPITOL, FEBRUARY 12, 1930.

19130 "WASH DRIVER." MEMPHIS COMMERCIAL APPEAL, APRIL 18, 1926.

19131 WATSON, A.P.; RADIN, PAUL; AND JOHNSON, CHARLES S.

(EDS.). GOD_STRUCK_ME_DEAD:_RELIGIOUS_CONVERSION
EXPERIENCES_AND_AUTOBIOGRAPHIES_OF_NEGRO_EX-SLAVES.
NASHVILLE: SOCIAL SCIENCE INSTITUTE, FISK UNIVERSITY,
1945.

19132   WILLIAMS, JANE. "CHARLES WHITESIDE." MANSFIELD (OH)
        NEWS_JOURNAL, MARCH 15, 1935.

19133   WILSON, L.W. "REMINISCENCES OF JIM TOMM." CHRONICLES_OF
        OKLAHOMA, 44 (AUTUMN, 1966): 290-306.

19134   WOODS, DANIEL G. "SLAVE HISTORY FROM SLAVE TESTIMONY, A
        CRITIQUE." M.A. THESIS, UNIVERSITY OF GEORGIA, 1979.

19135   WOODWARD, C. VANN. "HISTORY FROM SLAVE SOURCES."
        AMERICAN_HISTORICAL_REVIEW, 79 (APRIL, 1974): 470-481.

19136   WRITERS' PROGRAM, VIRGINIA. THE_NEGRO_IN_VIRGINIA. NEW
        YORK: HASTINGS HOUSE, 1940.

19137   YETMAN, NORMAN R. "THE BACKGROUND OF THE SLAVE NARRATIVE
        COLLECTION." AMERICAN_QUARTERLY, 19 (FALL, 1967):
        534-553.

19138   YETMAN, NORMAN R. (ED.). LIFE_UNDER_THE_"PECULIAR
        INSTITUTION":_SELECTIONS_FROM_THE_SLAVE_NARRATIVE
        COLLECTION. NEW YORK: HOLT, RINEHART AND WINSTON,
        1970.

SLAVE_EDUCATION

19139   ALBANESE, ANTHONY G. "THE PLANTATION AS A SCHOOL: THE
        SEA-ISLANDS OF GEORGIA AND SOUTH CAROLINA, A TEST
        CASE, 1800-1860." ED.D. DISSERTATION, RUTGERS
        UNIVERSITY, 1970.

19140   ALBANESE, ANTHONY G. THE_PLANTATION_SCHOOL. NEW YORK:
        VANTAGE PRESS, 1976.

19141   AMES, SUSIE M. READING,_WRITING_AND_ARITHMETIC_IN
        VIRGINIA,_1607-1699. WILLIAMSBURG: HISTORICAL
        BOOKLET NUMBER 15, 1957.

19142   ARMSTRONG, WARREN B. "THE ORGANIZATION, FUNCTION, AND
        CONTRIBUTION OF THE CHAPLAINCY IN THE UNITED STATES
        ARMY, 1861-1865." PH.D. DISSERTATION, UNIVERSITY OF
        MICHIGAN, 1964.

19143   ARMSTRONG, WARREN B. "UNION CHAPLAINS AND THE EDUCATION
        OF THE FREEDMEN." JOURNAL_OF_NEGRO_HISTORY, 52
        (APRIL, 1967): 104-115.

19144   ARROWOOD, CHARLES F. "THE EDUCATION OF AMERICAN
        PLANTATION SLAVES." SCHOOL_AND_SOCIETY, 54 (SEPTEMBER

13, 1941): 175-184.

19145 BAHNEY, ROBERT S. "GENERALS AND NEGROES: EDUCATION OF
       NEGROES BY THE UNION ARMY, 1861-1865." PH.D.
       DISSERTATION, UNIVERSITY OF MICHIGAN, 1965.

19146 BALLARD, ALLEN. THE EDUCATION OF BLACK FOLK: THE
       AFRO-AMERICAN STRUGGLE FOR KNOWLEDGE IN WHITE AMERICA.
       NEW YORK: HARPER & ROW, 1973.

19147 BEARD, AUGUSTUS F. A CRUSADE OF BROTHERHOOD: THE
       HISTORY OF THE AMERICAN MISSIONARY ASSOCIATION. NEW
       YORK: PILGRIM PRESS, 1909.

19148 BELLAMY, DONNIE D. "THE EDUCATION OF BLACKS IN MISSOURI
       PRIOR TO 1861." JOURNAL OF NEGRO HISTORY, 59 (APRIL,
       1974): 143-157.

19149 BIRNEY, CATHERINE H. THE GRIMKE SISTERS: SARA AND
       ANGELINA GRIMKE, THE FIRST AMERICAN WOMEN ADVOCATES OF
       ABOLITION AND WOMAN'S RIGHTS. BOSTON: LEE & SHEPARD,
       1885.

19150 BIRNIE, C.W. "THE EDUCATION OF THE NEGRO IN CHARLESTON,
       SOUTH CAROLINA, BEFORE THE CIVIL WAR." JOURNAL OF
       NEGRO HISTORY, 12 (JANUARY, 1927): 13-21.

19151 BLOUET, OLWYN M. "EDUCATION AND EMANCIPATION IN
       BARBADOS, 1823-1846; A STUDY IN CULTURAL
       TRANSFERENCE." PH.D. DISSERTATION, UNIVERSITY OF
       NEBRASKA, 1977.

19152 BLOUET, OLWYN M. "TO MAKE SOCIETY SAFE FOR FREEDOM,
       SLAVE EDUCATION IN BARBADOS, 1823-1833." JOURNAL OF
       NEGRO HISTORY, 65 (SPRING, 1980): 126-134.

19153 BOND, H.M. "HORACE MANN IN NEW ORLEANS: A NOTE ON THE
       DECLINE OF HUMANITARIANISM IN AMERICAN EDUCATION,
       1837-1937." SCHOOL AND SOCIETY, 45 (MAY 1, 1937):
       607-611.

19154 BOND, HORACE M. NEGRO EDUCATION IN ALABAMA: A STUDY IN
       COTTON AND STEEL. WASHINGTON: ASSOCIATED PUBLISHERS,
       1939.

19155 BRIGHAM, R.I. "NEGRO EDUCATION IN ANTE-BELLUM MISSOURI."
       JOURNAL OF NEGRO HISTORY, 30 (OCTOBER, 1945): 405-420.

19156 BROGLEY, AGNES DE SALES. "THE EDUCATIONAL STATUS OF THE
       NEGRO IN PENNSYLVANIA, 1682-1834." M.A. THESIS,
       CATHOLIC UNIVERSITY OF AMERICA, 1950.

19157 BROOKS, ALBERT N.D. "EDUCATION OF THE NEGRO IN VIRGINIA
       PRIOR TO 1861." M.A. THESIS, HOWARD UNIVERSITY, 1938.

19158   BUCK, JAMES R.   "THE EDUCATION OF THE NEGRO IN THE SOUTH
         PRIOR TO 1861." M.A. THESIS, FISK UNIVERSITY, 1938.

19159   BULLOCK, HENRY A.   "A HIDDEN PASSAGE IN THE SLAVE
         REGIME." IN CURTIS, JAMES C. AND GOULD, LEWIS L.
         (EDS.). THE BLACK EXPERIENCE IN AMERICA. AUSTIN:
         UNIVERSITY OF TEXAS PRESS, 1970, PP. 3-32.

19160   BULLOCK, HENRY A.   A HISTORY OF NEGRO EDUCATION IN THE
         SOUTH: FROM 1619 TO THE PRESENT. NEW YORK: PRAEGER,
         1967.

19161   BURROWS, EDWARD F.   "THE LITERARY EDUCATION OF NEGROES IN
         ANTE-BELLUM VIRGINIA, NORTH CAROLINA, SOUTH CAROLINA,
         AND GEORGIA, WITH SPECIAL REFERENCE TO REGULATORY AND
         PROHIBITIVE LAWS." M.A. THESIS, DUKE UNIVERSITY, 1940.

19162   BUTCHART, RONALD E.   NORTHERN SCHOOLS, SOUTHERN BLACKS,
         AND RECONSTRUCTION: FREEDMAN'S EDUCATION, 1862-1875.
         WESTPORT: GREENWOOD PRESS, 1980.

19163   CALAM, JOHN.   PARSONS AND PEDAGOGUES: THE S.P.G.
         ADVENTURE IN AMERICAN EDUCATION. NEW YORK: COLUMBIA
         UNIVERSITY PRESS, 1971.

19164   COHEN, SHELDON S.   "ELIAS NEAU, 1662-1722, INSTRUCTOR TO
         NEW YORK'S SLAVES." NEW-YORK HISTORICAL SOCIETY
         QUARTERLY, 55 (JANUARY, 1972): 7-27.

19165   CORNELIUS, JANET D.   "GOD'S SCHOOLMASTERS: SOUTHERN
         EVANGELISTS TO THE SLAVES, 1830-1860." PH.D.
         DISSERTATION, UNIVERSITY OF ILLINOIS, 1977.

19166   DABNEY, CHARLES W.   UNIVERSAL EDUCATION IN THE SOUTH.   2
         VOLS. CHAPEL HILL: UNIVERSITY OF NORTH CAROLINA
         PRESS, 1936.

19167   DAVIS, RICHARD B.   INTELLECTUAL LIFE IN THE COLONIAL
         SOUTH, 1585-1763. 3 VOLS. KNOXVILLE: UNIVERSITY OF
         TENNESSEE PRESS, 1978.

19168   DAVIS, THOMAS J.   "EDUCATION IN THE SLAVE QUARTER
         COMMUNITY." JOURNAL OF NEGRO EDUCATION, 48 (FALL,
         1979): 550-552.

19169   DAVIS, WILLIAM R.   THE DEVELOPMENT AND PRESENT STATUS OF
         NEGRO EDUCATION IN EAST TEXAS. NEW YORK: COLUMBIA
         UNIVERSITY PRESS, 1934.

19170   DEBOER, CLARA M.   "THE ROLE OF AFRO-AMERICANS IN THE
         ORIGIN AND WORK OF THE AMERICAN MISSIONARY
         ASSOCIATION: 1839-1877." PH.D. DISSERTATION, RUTGERS
         UNIVERSITY, 1973.

19171   DICKERMAN, G.S.   "OLD-TIME NEGRO EDUCATION IN THE SOUTH."

SOUTHERN WORKMAN, 32 (OCTOBER, 1903): 500-503.

19172 DICKERMAN, GEORGE S. "THE EARLY TEACHING OF SLAVES." IN
       NEGRO EDUCATION: A STUDY OF THE PRIVATE AND HIGHER
       SCHOOLS FOR COLORED PEOPLE IN THE UNITED STATES. 2
       VOLS. WASHINGTON: DEPARTMENT OF THE INTERIOR, BUREAU
       OF EDUCATION BULLETIN, 1915, NO. 38, 1917, VOL. 1, PP.
       245-246.

19173 DJOKHAN, ISAAC. "SLAVERY AND EMANCIPATION." A HISTORY
       OF THE BRITISH VIRGIN ISLANDS, 1672 TO 1970. EPPING,
       ESSEX, ENGLAND: CARIBBEAN UNIVERSITIES PRESS, 1975,
       PP. 71-96.

19174 EATON, CLEMENT. "THE MIND OF THE SOUTHERN NEGRO: THE
       REMARKABLE INDIVIDUALS." THE MIND OF THE OLD SOUTH.
       BATON ROUGE: LOUISIANA STATE UNIVERSITY PRESS, 1967,
       PP. 170-199.

19175 "EDUCATION OF THE COLORED POPULATION OF LOUISIANA."
       HARPER'S NEW MONTHLY MAGAZINE, 33 (JULY, 1866):
       244-250.

19176 FEN, SING-NAN. "NOTES ON THE EDUCATION OF NEGROES AT
       NORFOLK AND PORTSMOUTH, VIRGINIA, DURING THE CIVIL
       WAR." PHYLON, 28 (SUMMER, 1967): 197-208.

19177 FEN, SING-NAN. "NOTES ON THE EDUCATION OF NEGROES IN
       NORTH CAROLINA DURING THE CIVIL WAR." JOURNAL OF
       NEGRO EDUCATION, 36 (WINTER, 1967): 24-31.

19178 FLEMING, JOHN E. "BLACK EFFORTS TO ACQUIRE AN EDUCATION
       DURING THE AGE OF SLAVERY." THE LENGTHENING SHADOW OF
       SLAVERY. WASHINGTON: HOWARD UNIVERSITY PRESS, 1976,
       PP. 1-31.

19179 FREEHLING, WILLIAM W. PRELUDE TO CIVIL WAR: THE
       NULLIFICATION CONTROVERSY IN SOUTH CAROLINA,
       1816-1836. NEW YORK: HARPER & ROW, 1966.

19180 FUKE, RICHARD P. "THE BALTIMORE ASSOCIATION FOR THE
       MORAL AND EDUCATIONAL IMPROVEMENT OF THE COLORED
       PEOPLE, 1864-1870." MARYLAND HISTORICAL MAGAZINE, 66
       (WINTER, 1971): 369-404.

19181 GARDNER, BETTYE. "ANTE-BELLUM BLACK EDUCATION IN
       BALTIMORE." MARYLAND HISTORICAL MAGAZINE, 71 (FALL,
       1976): 360-366.

19182 GILMORE, JOHN T. "THE REV. WILLIAM HARTE AND ATTITUDES
       TO SLAVERY IN EARLY NINETEENTH-CENTURY BARBADOS."
       JOURNAL OF ECCLESIASTICAL HISTORY, 30 (OCTOBER, 1979):
       461-474.

19183 GOODWIN, MARY F. "CHRISTIANIZING AND EDUCATING THE NEGRO

IN COLONIAL VIRGINIA." _HISTORICAL MAGAZINE OF THE PROTESTANT EPISCOPAL CHURCH_, 1 (SEPTEMBER, 1932): 143-152.

19184   GREEN, FLETCHER M.   "NORTHERN MISSIONARY ACTIVITIES IN THE SOUTH, 1846-1861."   _JOURNAL OF SOUTHERN HISTORY_, 21 (MAY, 1955):   147-172.

19185   GREGG, CHARLES L.   "SOME ASPECTS OF THE RELIGIOUS INSTRUCTION OF SLAVES IN THE ANTE-BELLUM SOUTH."   M.A. THESIS, OHIO STATE UNIVERSITY, 1948.

19186   HALL, CLYDE W.   "A SURVEY OF INDUSTRIAL EDUCATION FOR NEGROES IN THE UNITED STATES UP TO 1917."   ED.D. DISSERTATION, BRADLEY UNIVERSITY, 1953.

19187   HART, ALBERT B.   _SLAVERY AND ABOLITION, 1831-1841_.   NEW YORK: HARPER AND BROTHERS, 1906.

19188   HAVILAND, LAURA S.   _A WOMAN'S LIFE-WORK: LABORS AND EXPERIENCES OF LAURA S. HAVILAND_.   CINCINNATI: WALDEN & STOWE, 1881.

19189   HOLT, CHERRYL C.   "NEGRO EDUCATION IN SLAVERY AND FREEDOM."   IN JOYNER, CHARLES W. (ED.).   _BLACK CAROLINIANS: STUDIES IN THE HISTORY OF SOUTH CAROLINA NEGROES_.   LAURINBURG, NC: ST. ANDREWS PRESBYTERIAN COLLEGE, 1969, PP. 144-154.

19190   HORST, SAMUEL L.   "EDUCATION FOR MANHOOD: THE EDUCATION OF BLACKS IN VIRGINIA DURING THE CIVIL WAR."   PH.D. DISSERTATION, UNIVERSITY OF VIRGINIA, 1977.

19191   HORTON, JOSEPH P.   "THE RELIGIOUS AND EDUCATIONAL CONTRIBUTION OF THE METHODISTS TO THE SLAVES."   B.D. THESIS, SOUTHERN METHODIST UNIVERSITY, 1930.

19192   JACKSON, JAMES C.   "THE RELIGIOUS EDUCATION OF THE NEGRO IN SOUTH CAROLINA PRIOR TO 1850."   _HISTORICAL MAGAZINE OF THE PROTESTANT EPISCOPAL CHURCH_, 36 (MARCH, 1967): 35-61.

19193   JACKSON, LUTHER P.   "RELIGIOUS INSTRUCTION OF NEGROES, 1830 TO 1860, WITH SPECIFIC REFERENCES TO SOUTH CAROLINA."   _JOURNAL OF NEGRO HISTORY_, 15 (JANUARY, 1930):   72-114.

19194   JERNEGAN, MARCUS W.   _LABORING AND DEPENDENT CLASSES IN COLONIAL AMERICA, 1607-1783: STUDIES OF THE ECONOMIC, EDUCATIONAL, AND SOCIAL SIGNIFICANCE OF SLAVES, SERVANTS, APPRENTICES, AND POOR FOLK_.   CHICAGO: UNIVERSITY OF CHICAGO PRESS, 1931.

19195   JOHNSON, HENRY M.   "THE METHODIST EPISCOPAL CHURCH AND THE EDUCATION OF SOUTHERN NEGROES, 1862-1900."   PH.D.

DISSERTATION, YALE UNIVERSITY, 1939.

19196   JONES, JACQUELINE. "THE DELAWARE ASSOCIATION FOR THE
         MORAL IMPROVEMENT AND EDUCATION OF THE COLORED PEOPLE:
         PRACTICAL CHRISTIANITY." B.A. THESIS, UNIVERSITY OF
         DELAWARE, 1970.

19197   JONES, JACQUELINE. "THE 'GREAT OPPORTUNITY': NORTHERN
         TEACHERS AND THE GEORGIA FREEDMEN, 1865-1873." PH.D.
         DISSERTATION, UNIVERSITY OF WISCONSIN, 1976.

19198   JONES, JACQUELINE. SOLDIERS OF LIGHT AND LOVE: NORTHERN
         TEACHERS AND GEORGIA BLACKS, 1865-1873. CHAPEL HILL:
         UNIVERSITY OF NORTH CAROLINA PRESS, 1980.

19199   JONES, REGINALD L. "RACISM, MENTAL HEALTH, AND THE
         SCHOOLS." IN WILLIE, CHARLES V.; KRAMER, BERNARD M.;
         AND BROWN, BERTRAM S. (EDS.). RACISM AND MENTAL
         HEALTH: ESSAYS. PITTSBURGH: UNIVERSITY OF
         PITTSBURGH PRESS, 1973, PP. 319-352.

19200   JORDAN, WINTHROP D. THE WHITE MAN'S BURDEN: HISTORICAL
         ORIGINS OF RACISM IN THE UNITED STATES. NEW YORK:
         OXFORD UNIVERSITY PRESS, 1974.

19201   JORDAN, WINTHROP D. WHITE OVER BLACK: AMERICAN
         ATTITUDES TOWARD THE NEGRO, 1550-1812. CHAPEL HILL:
         UNIVERSITY OF NORTH CAROLINA PRESS, 1968.

19202   KASSEL, CHARLES. "EDUCATING THE SLAVE; A FORGOTTEN
         CHAPTER OF CIVIL WAR HISTORY." OPEN COURT, 41 (APRIL,
         1927): 239-256.

19203   KIMBALL, PHILIP C. "FREEDOM'S HARVEST: FREEDMEN'S
         SCHOOLS IN KENTUCKY AFTER THE CIVIL WAR." FILSON CLUB
         HISTORY QUARTERLY, 54 (JULY, 1980): 272-288.

19204   LATIMER, JAMES. "THE FOUNDATION OF RELIGIOUS EDUCATION
         IN THE BRITISH WEST INDIES." JOURNAL OF NEGRO
         EDUCATION, 34 (FALL, 1965): 435-442.

19205   LATIMER, JAMES. "THE FOUNDATIONS OF RELIGIOUS EDUCATION
         IN THE FRENCH WEST INDIES." JOURNAL OF NEGRO
         EDUCATION, 40 (WINTER, 1971): 91-98.

19206   LATIMER, JAMES. "THE FOUNDATIONS OF RELIGIOUS EDUCATION
         IN THE SPANISH WEST INDIES." JOURNAL OF NEGRO
         EDUCATION, 39 (WINTER, 1970): 70-75.

19207   LATIMER, JAMES. "AN HISTORICAL AND COMPARATIVE STUDY OF
         THE FOUNDATIONS OF EDUCATION IN THE BRITISH, SPANISH
         AND FRENCH WEST INDIES (UP TO THE END OF SLAVERY IN
         THE BRITISH ISLANDS)." PH.D. DISSERTATION, UNIVERSITY
         OF LONDON, 1952.

19208 LAWRENCE, JAMES B. "RELIGIOUS EDUCATION OF THE NEGRO IN
THE COLONY OF GEORGIA." GEORGIA HISTORICAL QUARTERLY,
14 (MARCH, 1930): 41-57.

19209 LONG, CLARAMAE B. "HISTORY OF NEGRO EDUCATION IN NEW
YORK CITY (1701-1853)." M.S. THESIS, CITY COLLEGE OF
NEW YORK, 1935.

19210 LOVELAND, ANNE C. SOUTHERN EVANGELICALS AND THE SOCIAL
ORDER, 1800-1860. BATON ROUGE: LOUISIANA STATE
UNIVERSITY PRESS, 1980.

19211 MARTIN, JOSEPHINE W. "THE EDUCATIONAL EFFORTS OF THE
MAJOR FREEDMEN'S AID SOCIETIES AND THE FREEDMEN'S
BUREAU IN SOUTH CAROLINA: 1862-1870." PH.D.
DISSERTATION, UNIVERSITY OF SOUTH CAROLINA, 1971.

19212 MCGEE, LEO. "EARLY EFFORTS TOWARD EDUCATING THE BLACK
ADULT." NEGRO HISTORY BULLETIN, 34 (APRIL, 1971):
88-90.

19213 MESSNER, WILLIAM F. "BLACK EDUCATION IN LOUISIANA,
1863-1865." CIVIL WAR HISTORY, 22 (MARCH, 1976):
41-59.

19214 MONTGOMERY, WINFIELD S. HISTORICAL SKETCH OF EDUCATION
FOR THE COLORED RACE IN THE DISTRICT OF COLUMBIA,
1807-1905. WASHINGTON: SMITH BROTHERS, PRINTERS,
1907.

19215 MULVEY, PATRICIA A. "BLACK BROTHERS AND SISTERS:
MEMBERSHIP IN THE BLACK LAY BROTHERHOODS OF COLONIAL
BRAZIL." LUSO-BRAZILIAN REVIEW, 17 (WINTER, 1980):
253-279.

19216 MULVEY, PATRICIA A. "THE BLACK LAY BROTHERHOODS OF
COLONIAL BRAZIL: A HISTORY." PH.D. DISSERTATION,
CITY UNIVERSITY OF NEW YORK, 1976.

19217 MURPHY, PATRICIA G. "THE EDUCATION OF THE NEW WORLD
BLACKS IN THE DANISH WEST INDIES/U.S. VIRGIN ISLANDS:
A CASE STUDY OF SOCIAL TRANSITION." PH.D.
DISSERTATION, UNIVERSITY OF CONNECTICUT, 1977.

19218 "NEGRO EDUCATION IN VIRGINIA IN THE EIGHTEENTH CENTURY."
VIRGINIA MAGAZINE OF HISTORY AND BIOGRAPHY, 2 (APRIL,
1895): 429.

19219 O'BRIEN, MARY L. "SLAVERY IN LOUISVILLE DURING THE
ANTEBELLUM PERIOD: 1820-1860. A STUDY OF THE EFFECTS
OF URBANIZATION ON THE INSTITUTION OF SLAVERY AS IT
EXISTED IN LOUISVILLE, KENTUCKY." M.A. THESIS,
UNIVERSITY OF LOUISVILLE, 1979.

19220 PAYNE, DANIEL A. RECOLLECTIONS OF SEVENTY YEARS.

NASHVILLE: PUBLISHING HOUSE OF THE A.M.E. SUNDAY
SCHOOL UNION, 1888.

19221 PERDUE, CHARLES L., JR.; BARDEN, THOMAS E.; AND PHILLIPS,
ROBERT K. (EDS.). WEEVILS IN THE WHEAT: INTERVIEWS
WITH VIRGINIA EX-SLAVES. CHARLOTTESVILLE: UNIVERSITY
PRESS OF VIRGINIA, 1976.

19222 PIERRE, C.E. "THE WORK OF THE SOCIETY FOR THE
PROPAGATION OF THE GOSPEL IN FOREIGN PARTS AMONG THE
NEGROES IN THE COLONIES." JOURNAL OF NEGRO HISTORY, 1
(OCTOBER, 1916): 349-360.

19223 PILCHER, GEORGE W. SAMUEL DAVIES: APOSTLE OF DISSENT IN
COLONIAL VIRGINIA. KNOXVILLE: UNIVERSITY OF
TENNESSEE PRESS, 1971.

19224 PINCKNEY, ELISE (ED.). THE LETTERBOOK OF ELIZA LUCAS
PINCKNEY, 1739-1762. CHAPEL HILL: UNIVERSITY OF
NORTH CAROLINA PRESS, 1972.

19225 PORTER, BETTY. "THE HISTORY OF NEGRO EDUCATION IN
LOUISIANA." LOUISIANA HISTORICAL QUARTERLY, 25 (JULY,
1942): 728-821.

19226 PORTER, BETTY. "THE HISTORY OF NEGRO EDUCATION IN
LOUISIANA." M.A. THESIS, LOUISIANA STATE UNIVERSITY,
1938.

19227 "A QUESTION IN CASUISTRY." INDEPENDENT, 67 (OCTOBER 28,
1909): 995-996.

19228 RANSOM, ROGER L. AND SUTCH, RICHARD. ONE KIND OF
FREEDOM: THE ECONOMIC CONSEQUENCES OF EMANCIPATION.
CAMBRIDGE: CAMBRIDGE UNIVERSITY PRESS, 1977.

19229 RICHARDSON, ARCHIE G. THE DEVELOPMENT OF NEGRO EDUCATION
IN VIRGINIA, 1831-1970. RICHMOND: RICHMOND VIRGINIA
CHAPTER, PHI DELTA KAPPA, 1976.

19230 RICHARDSON, JOE M. "FREEDMEN'S SCHOOLS." IN ROLLER,
DAVID C. AND TWYMAN, ROBERT W. (EDS.). THE
ENCYCLOPEDIA OF SOUTHERN HISTORY. BATON ROUGE:
LOUISIANA STATE UNIVERSITY PRESS, 1979, PP. 490-491.

19231 ROOKE, PATRICIA T. "THE CHRISTIANIZATION AND EDUCATION
OF SLAVES AND APPRENTICES IN THE BRITISH WEST INDIES:
THE IMPACT OF EVANGELICAL MISSIONARIES (1800-1838)."
PH.D. DISSERTATION, UNIVERSITY OF ALBERTA, 1977.

19232 ROOKE, PATRICIA T. "EVANGELICAL MISSIONARIES,
APPRENTICES, AND FREEDMEN: THE PSYCHOSOCIOLOGICAL
SHIFTS OF RACIAL ATTITUDES IN THE BRITISH WEST
INDIES." CARIBBEAN QUARTERLY, 25 (MARCH-JUNE, 1979):
1-14.

19233   ROOKE, PATRICIA T. "THE 'NEW MECHANIC' IN SLAVE SOCIETY:
        SOCIO-PSYCHOLOGICAL MOTIVATIONS AND EVANGELICAL
        MISSIONARIES IN THE BRITISH WEST INDIES." JOURNAL OF
        RELIGIOUS HISTORY, 11 (JUNE, 1980): 77-94.

19234   ROOKE, PATRICIA T. "THE PEDAGOGY OF CONVERSION:
        MISSIONARY EDUCATION TO SLAVES IN THE BRITISH WEST
        INDIES, 1800-1838." PAEDAGOGICA HISTORICA, 18 (1978):
        356-374.

19235   ROUNDTREE, JOHN G. "EDUCATION AND THE NEGRO." NEGRO
        HISTORY BULLETIN, 27 (FEBRUARY, 1964): 106-108, 110.

19236   SCOTT, OSBORNE. "PRE- AND POST-EMANCIPATION SCHOOLS."
        URBAN REVIEW, 9 (WINTER, 1976): 234-241.

19237   SERNETT, MILTON C. "BLACK RELIGION AND AMERICAN
        EVANGELICALISM: WHITE PROTESTANTS, PLANTATION
        MISSIONS, AND THE INDEPENDENT NEGRO CHURCH,
        1787-1865." PH.D. DISSERTATION, UNIVERSITY OF
        DELAWARE, 1972.

19238   SHERER, ROBERT G. "LET US MAKE MAN: NEGRO EDUCATION IN
        NINETEENTH CENTURY ALABAMA." PH.D. DISSERTATION,
        UNIVERSITY OF NORTH CAROLINA, 1970.

19239   SIMPKINS, PATRICK L. "NORTH CAROLINA QUAKERS AND BLACKS:
        EDUCATION AND MEMBERSHIP." NEGRO HISTORY BULLETIN, 35
        (NOVEMBER, 1972): 160-162.

19240   "SLAVE EDUCATION (1674-1859)." IN RYWELL, MARTIN (ED.).
        AFRO-AMERICAN ENCYCLOPEDIA. 10 VOLS. NORTH MIAMI:
        EDUCATIONAL BOOK PUBLISHERS, 1974, VOL.8, PP.
        2476-2482.

19241   "SNATCHING LEARNING IN FORBIDDEN FIELDS." NEGRO HISTORY
        BULLETIN, 3 (NOVEMBER, 1939): 21.

19242   STEPHENSON, MARY A. "NOTES ON THE NEGRO SCHOOL IN
        WILLIAMSBURG, 1760-1774." UNPUBLISHED PAPER, N.D.,
        COLONIAL WILLIAMSBURG, INC.

19243   STERLING, DOROTHY. BLACK FOREMOTHERS: THREE LIVES. OLD
        WESTBURY, NY: FEMINIST PRESS, 1979.

19244   THOMPSON, ERNEST T. PRESBYTERIANS IN THE SOUTH,
        1607-1972. 3 VOLS. RICHMOND: JOHN KNOX PRESS,
        1963-1973.

19245   THOMPSON, MARION M.T. THE EDUCATION OF NEGROES IN NEW
        JERSEY. NEW YORK: BUREAU OF PUBLICATIONS, TEACHERS
        COLLEGE, COLUMBIA UNIVERSITY, 1941.

19246   THOMPSON, MARIVINE K. "THE MORAL AND RELIGIOUS TRAINING
        OF THE SLAVE." M.A. THESIS, SOUTHERN METHODIST

UNIVERSITY, 1934.

19247   TIMBERLAKE, C.L. "THE EARLY STRUGGLE FOR EDUCATION OF
        THE BLACKS IN THE COMMONWEALTH OF KENTUCKY." REGISTER
        OF THE KENTUCKY HISTORICAL SOCIETY, 71 (JULY, 1973):
        225-252.

19248   TIMMONS, ROBERT. "AGED EX-SLAVES GATHER AT HOME OF OLD
        MASTER." IN PARKS, WILLIS B. THE POSSIBILITIES OF
        THE NEGRO IN SYMPOSIUM. ATLANTA: FRANKLIN PUBLISHING
        COMPANY, 1904, PP. 69-73.

19249   TURNER, MARY. "THE BISHOP OF JAMAICA AND SLAVE
        INSTRUCTION." JOURNAL OF ECCLESIASTICAL HISTORY, 26
        (OCTOBER, 1975): 363-378.

19250   WALTON, FLETCHER. "WHAT WE DID FOR THE NEGRO BEFORE THE
        WAR." METHODIST REVIEW, 51 (NOVEMBER-DECEMBER, 1902):
        897-905.

19251   WARGNY, FRANK O. "EDUCATION OF THE FREEDMEN BY
        PHILADELPHIA AND BALTIMORE QUAKERS DURING THE CIVIL
        WAR PERIOD." M.A. THESIS, JOHNS HOPKINS UNIVERSITY,
        1947.

19252   WASHINGTON, BOOKER T. "SIGNS OF PROGRESS AMONG THE
        NEGROES." CENTURY MAGAZINE, 59 (JANUARY, 1900):
        472-478.

19253   WEBBER, THOMAS L. DEEP LIKE THE RIVERS: EDUCATION IN
        THE SLAVE QUARTER COMMUNITY, 1831-1865. NEW YORK:
        W.W. NORTON, 1978.

19254   WEBBER, THOMAS L. "THE EDUCATION OF THE SLAVE QUARTER
        COMMUNITY: WHITE TEACHING AND BLACK LEARNING ON THE
        ANTEBELLUM PLANTATION." PH.D. DISSERTATION, COLUMBIA
        UNIVERSITY, 1976.

19255   WILEY, BELL I. SOUTHERN NEGROES, 1861-1865. NEW HAVEN:
        YALE UNIVERSITY PRESS, 1938.

19256   WILLEY, NATHAN. "EDUCATION OF THE COLORED POPULATION OF
        LOUISIANA." HARPER'S NEW MONTHLY MAGAZINE, 33 (JULY,
        1866): 244-250.

19257   WOODSON, C.G. "EARLY NEGRO EDUCATION IN WEST VIRGINIA."
        JOURNAL OF NEGRO HISTORY, 7 (JANUARY, 1922): 23-63.

19258   WOODSON, CARTER G. THE EDUCATION OF THE NEGRO PRIOR TO
        1861: A HISTORY OF THE EDUCATION OF THE COLORED PEOPLE
        OF THE UNITED STATES FROM THE BEGINNING OF SLAVERY TO
        THE CIVIL WAR. NEW YORK: PUTNAM, 1915.

19259   WRIGHT, MARION M.T. "THE EDUCATION OF NEGROES IN NEW
        JERSEY." PH.D. DISSERTATION, COLUMBIA UNIVERSITY,

1940.

SLAVE LANGUAGE

19260　ADELAIDE, JACQUES. "DEMOGRAPHY AND NAMES OF SLAVES OF LE
　　　　MAULE 1845 TO MAY 1848." IN MARSHALL, WOODVILLE K.
　　　　(ED.). PAPERS PRESENTED AT THE THIRD CONFERENCE OF
　　　　CARIBBEAN HISTORIANS. N.P., 1971, PP. 86-90.

19261　AGHEYISI, REBECCA. "WEST AFRICAN PIDGIN ENGLISH:
　　　　SIMPLIFICATION AND SIMPLICITY." PH.D. DISSERTATION,
　　　　STANFORD UNIVERSITY, 1971.

19262　ALLEN, WILLIAM F. "THE NEGRO DIALECT." NATION, 1
　　　　(DECEMBER 14, 1865): 744-745.

19263　ALLEYNE, MERVYN. "LANGUAGE AND SOCIETY IN ST. LUCIA."
　　　　CARIBBEAN STUDIES, 1 (APRIL, 1961): 1-10.

19264　ALLEYNE, MERVYN. "THE LINGUISTIC CONTINUITY OF AFRICA IN
　　　　THE CARIBBEAN." BLACK ACADEMY REVIEW, 1 (WINTER,
　　　　1970): 3-16.

19265　ALLEYNE, MERVYN C. "COMPARATIVE AFRO-AMERICAN (AN
　　　　HISTORICAL COMPARATIVE STUDY OF SOME AFRO-AMERICAN
　　　　DIALECTS OF THE NEW WORLD)." UNPUBLISHED MANUSCRIPT,
　　　　N.D.

19266　ALLEYNE, MERVYN C. COMPARATIVE AFRO-AMERICAN: AN
　　　　HISTORICAL-COMPARATIVE STUDY OF ENGLISH-BASED
　　　　AFRO-AMERICAN DIALECTS OF THE NEW WORLD. ANN ARBOR:
　　　　KAROMA PUBLISHERS, 1980.

19267　"AMERICAN SPEECHWAYS." CRISIS, 55 (JUNE, 1948): 186-187.

19268　BAILEY, BERYL L. "CREOLE LANGUAGES OF THE CARIBBEAN
　　　　AREA." M.A. THESIS, COLUMBIA UNIVERSITY, 1953.

19269　BAILEY, BERYL L. JAMAICAN CREOLE SYNTAX: A
　　　　TRANSFORMATIONAL APPROACH. CAMBRIDGE: CAMBRIDGE
　　　　UNIVERSITY PRESS, 1966.

19270　BAILEY, BERYL L. "TOWARDS A NEW PERSPECTIVE ON NEGRO
　　　　ENGLISH DIALECTOLOGY." AMERICAN SPEECH, 40 (OCTOBER,
　　　　1965): 171-177.

19271　BAIRD, KEITH E. "GUY B. JOHNSON REVISITED: ANOTHER LOOK
　　　　AT GULLAH." JOURNAL OF BLACK STUDIES, 10 (JUNE,
　　　　1980): 425-435.

19272　BAMBARA, TONI C. "BLACK ENGLISH." IN CURRICULUM
　　　　APPROACHES FROM A BLACK PERSPECTIVE. WASHINGTON:
　　　　BLACK CHILD DEVELOPMENT INSTITUTE, 1973, PP. 77-91.

19273   BANKS, MARY R.   BRIGHT DAYS IN THE OLD PLANTATION TIME.
         BOSTON: LEE AND SHEPARD, 1882.

19274   BARKER, HOWARD F.   "THE FAMILY NAMES OF AMERICAN
         NEGROES." AMERICAN SPEECH, 14 (OCTOBER, 1939):
         163-174.

19275   BARNETT, A.C.   "COLONIAL SURVIVALS IN BUSH NEGRO SPEECH."
         AMERICAN SPEECH, 7 (AUGUST, 1932): 393-397.

19276   BARROW, DAVID C.   "MY GRANDMOTHER'S KEY BASKET."
         BULLETIN OF THE UNIVERSITY OF GEORGIA, 17 (1916):
         1-16.

19277   BEERS, H. DWIGHT.   "AFRICAN NAMES AND NAMING PRACTICES:
         A SELECTED LIST OF REFERENCES IN ENGLISH." LIBRARY OF
         CONGRESS INFORMATION BULLETIN, 36 (MARCH 25, 1977):
         206-207.

19278   BENNETT, JOHN.   "GULLAH: A NEGRO PATOIS." SOUTH
         ATLANTIC QUARTERLY, 7 (OCTOBER, 1908): 332-347.

19279   BICKERTON, DEREK AND ESCALANTE, AQUILES.   "PALENQUERO: A
         SPANISH-BASED CREOLE OF NORTHERN COLOMBIA." LINGUA,
         24 (FEBRUARY, 1970): 254-267.

19280   BLOK, H.P.   "ANNOTATIONS TO MR. L.D. TURNER'S AFRICANISMS
         IN THE GULLAH DIALECT." LINGUA, 8 (SEPTEMBER, 1959):
         306-321.

19281   BOLINGER, DWIGHT L.   "BOZO." AMERICAN SPEECH, 14
         (OCTOBER, 1939): 238-239.

19282   BOURGUIGNON, ERIKA E.   "SYNCRETISM AND AMBIVALENCE IN
         HAITI: AN ETHNOHISTORIC STUDY." PH.D. DISSERTATION,
         NORTHWESTERN UNIVERSITY, 1951.

19283   BRASCH, WALTER M.   "BLACK ENGLISH AND THE MASS MEDIA."
         PH.D. DISSERTATION, OHIO UNIVERSITY, 1974.

19284   BREWER, JEUTONNE P.   "THE VERB 'BE' IN EARLY BLACK
         ENGLISH: A STUDY BASED ON THE WPA EX-SLAVE
         NARRATIVES." PH.D. DISSERTATION, UNIVERSITY OF NORTH
         CAROLINA, 1974.

19285   BRINTON, DANIEL G.   "ON CERTAIN SUPPOSED NANTICOKE WORDS,
         SHOWN TO BE AFRICAN." AMERICAN ANTIQUARIAN AND
         ORIENTAL JOURNAL, 9 (NOVEMBER, 1887): 350-354.

19286   BRONSARD, JAMES F.   LOUISIANA CREOLE DIALECT. BATON
         ROUGE: LOUISIANA STATE UNIVERSITY PRESS, 1942.

19287   BUTLER, MELVIN A.   "AFRICAN LINGUISTIC REMNANTS IN THE
         SPEECH OF BLACK LOUISIANANS." BLACK EXPERIENCE: A
         SOUTHERN UNIVERSITY JOURNAL, 55 (JUNE, 1969): 45-52.

19288   BUTTERFIELD, STEPHEN. "LANGUAGE AND THE SLAVE
        EXPERIENCE." BLACK AUTOBIOGRAPHY IN AMERICA.
        AMHERST: UNIVERSITY OF MASSACHUSETTS PRESS, 1974, PP.
        32-46.

19289   BUTTERFIELD, STEPHEN T. "THE USE OF LANGUAGE IN THE
        SLAVE NARRATIVES." NEGRO AMERICAN LANGUAGE FORUM, 6
        (FALL, 1972): 72-78.

19290   CASSIDY, FREDERIC G. JAMAICA TALK: THREE HUNDRED YEARS
        OF THE ENGLISH LANGUAGE IN JAMAICA. LONDON:
        MACMILLAN, 1961.

19291   CASSIDY, FREDERIC G. "MULTIPLE ETYMOLOGIES IN JAMAICAN
        CREOLE." AMERICAN SPEECH, 41 (OCTOBER, 1966):
        211-215.

19292   CASSIDY, FREDERIC G. "THE PLACE OF GULLAH." AMERICAN
        SPEECH, 55 (SPRING, 1980): 3-16.

19293   CASSIDY, FREDERIC G. "SOME NEW LIGHT ON OLD
        JAMAICANISMS." AMERICAN SPEECH, 42 (OCTOBER, 1967):
        190-192.

19294   CASTELLANOS, ISABEL M. "THE USE OF LANGUAGE IN
        AFRO-CUBAN RELIGION." PH.D. DISSERTATION, GEORGETOWN
        UNIVERSITY, 1977.

19295   CHAMBERLAIN, A.F. "GOOBER, A NEGRO WORD FOR PEANUTS."
        AMERICAN NOTES AND QUERIES, 2 (JANUARY 5, 1889): 120.

19296   CHAMBERLAIN, A.F. "NEGRO DIALECT." SCIENCE, 12 (JULY
        13, 1888): 23-24.

19297   CHANDLER, JOHN. "PLANTATION FIELD NAMES IN BARBADOS."
        JOURNAL OF THE BARBADOS MUSEUM AND HISTORICAL SOCIETY,
        32 (MAY, 1968): 133-142.

19298   CHAPPELL, NAOMI C. "NEGRO NAMES." AMERICAN SPEECH, 4
        (APRIL, 1929): 272-275.

19299   CHRISTIE, CHRISTINA. "AFRICAN INFLUENCE IN THE BRAZILIAN
        PORTUGUESE LANGUAGE AND LITERATURE." HISPANIA, 26
        (OCTOBER, 1943): 259-266.

19300   CLAERBAUT, DAVID. BLACK JARGON IN WHITE AMERICA. GRAND
        RAPIDS: EERDMANS, 1972.

19301   COHEN, HENNIG. "SLAVE NAMES IN COLONIAL SOUTH CAROLINA."
        AMERICAN SPEECH, 27 (MAY, 1952): 102-107.

19302   COURLANDER, HAROLD. A TREASURY OF AFRO-AMERICAN
        FOLKLORE. NEW YORK: CROWN PUBLISHERS, 1976.

19303   CROWLEY, DANIEL J. "THE CREOLIZATION OF AFRICANISMS."

UNPUBLISHED PAPER PRESENTED AT MEETING OF AMERICAN
ANTHROPOLOGICAL ASSOCIATION, 1967.

19304   CUNNINGHAM, IRMA. "A SYNTACTIC ANALYSIS OF SEA ISLAND
        CREOLE ('GULLAH')." PH.D. DISSERTATION, UNIVERSITY OF
        MICHIGAN, 1970.

19305   DALBY, DAVID. "THE AFRICAN ELEMENT IN AMERICAN ENGLISH."
        IN KOCHMAN, T. (ED.). RAPPIN' AND STYLIN' OUT:
        COMMUNICATION IN URBAN BLACK AMERICA. URBANA:
        UNIVERSITY OF ILLINOIS PRESS, 1972, PP. 170-186.

19306   DALBY, DAVID. "ASHANTI SURVIVALS IN THE LANGUAGE AND
        TRADITIONS OF THE WINDWARD MAROONS OF JAMAICA."
        AFRICAN LANGUAGE STUDIES, 12 (1971): 31-51.

19307   DALBY, DAVID. BLACK THROUGH WHITE: PATTERNS OF
        COMMUNICATION IN AFRICA AND THE NEW WORLD.
        BLOOMINGTON: AFRICAN STUDIES PROGRAM, INDIANA
        UNIVERSITY, 1970.

19308   DALBY, DAVID. "BLACK THROUGH WHITE: PATTERNS OF
        COMMUNICATION IN AFRICA AND THE NEW WORLD." IN
        WOLFRAM, WALT AND CLARKE, NONA H. (EDS.). BLACK-WHITE
        SPEECH RELATIONSHIPS. WASHINGTON: CENTER FOR APPLIED
        LINGUISTICS, 1971, PP. 99-133.

19309   DALBY, DAVID. "REFLECTIONS ON THE HISTORICAL DEVELOPMENT
        OF AFRO-AMERICAN LANGUAGES: A DISCUSSION OF MERVYN C.
        ALLEYNE'S PAPER 'THE LINGUISTIC CONTINUITY OF AFRICA
        IN THE CARIBBEAN.'" UNPUBLISHED PAPER PRESENTED AT
        SYMPOSIUM ON CONTINUITIES AND DISCONTINUITIES IN
        AFRO-AMERICAN SOCIETIES AND CULTURES, MONA, JAMAICA,
        APRIL 25, 1970.

19310   DANA, MARVIN. "VOODOO, ITS EFFECTS ON THE NEGRO RACE."
        METROPOLITAN MAGAZINE, 28 (AUGUST, 1908): 529-538.

19311   DAVIS, DANIEL W. 'WEH DOWN SOUF. CLEVELAND:
        HELMAN-TAYLOR, 1897.

19312   DAVIS, LAWRENCE M. "DIALECT RESEARCH: MYTHOLOGY VS.
        REALITY." ORBIS, 18 (DECEMBER, 1969): 332-337.

19313   DE GRANDA, GERMAN. "MATERIALS FOR THE SOCIO-HISTORICAL
        STUDY OF THE AFRO-AMERICN LINGUISTIC ELEMENTS IN
        SPANISH-SPEAKING AREAS." CARIBBEAN STUDIES, 13
        (APRIL, 1973): 110-130.

19314   DECAMP, DAVID. "AFRICAN DAY-NAMES IN JAMAICA."
        LANGUAGE, 43 (MARCH, 1967): 139-149.

19315   DECAMP, DAVID. "INTRODUCTION: THE STUDY OF PIDGIN AND
        CREOLE LANGUAGES." IN HYMES, DELL (ED.).
        PIDGINIZATION AND CREOLIZATION OF LANGUAGES:

PROCEEDINGS OF A CONFERENCE HELD AT THE UNIVERSITY OF
THE WEST INDIES, MONA, JAMAICA, APRIL, 1968.
CAMBRIDGE: CAMBRIDGE UNIVERSITY PRESS, 1971, PP.
13-39.

19316 DILLARD, J.L. "AFRO-AMERICAN, SPANGLISH, AND SOMETHING
       ELSE: ST. CRUZAN NAMING PRACTICES." NAMES, 20
       (DECEMBER, 1972): 225-230.

19317 DILLARD, J.L. "BLACK ENGLISH." IN LAMAR, HOWARD R.
       (ED.). THE READER'S ENCYCLOPEDIA OF THE AMERICAN
       WEST. NEW YORK: THOMAS Y. CROWELL, 1977, PP. 100-101.

19318 DILLARD, J.L. BLACK ENGLISH: ITS HISTORY AND USAGE IN
       THE UNITED STATES. NEW YORK: RANDOM HOUSE, 1972.

19319 DILLARD, J.L. "CREOLE STUDIES AND AMERICAN
       DIALECTOLOGY." CARIBBEAN STUDIES, 12 (JANUARY, 1973):
       76-91.

19320 DILLARD, J.L. "THE HISTORY OF BLACK ENGLISH IN NOVA
       SCOTIA--A FIRST STEP." REVISTA/REVIEW INTERAMERICANA,
       2 (WINTER, 1973): 507-520.

19321 DILLARD, J.L. "ON THE BEGINNINGS OF BLACK ENGLISH IN THE
       NEW WORLD." ORBIS, 21 (1972): 523-536.

19322 DILLARD, J.L. "ON THE GRAMMAR OF AFRO-AMERICAN NAMING
       PRACTICES." NAMES, 16 (SEPTEMBER, 1968): 230-237.

19323 DILLARD, J.L. "PIDGIN TRANSMISSION PROBLEMS AND THE
       TRANSITIVIZER." ACTA SYMBOLICA, 2 (1971): 44-50.

19324 DILLARD, J.L. "THE WEST AFRICAN DAY-NAMES IN
       NOVA-SCOTIA." NAMES, 19 (SEPTEMBER, 1971): 257-261.

19325 DILLARD, J.L. "THE WRITINGS OF HERSKOVITS AND THE STUDY
       OF THE LANGUAGE OF THE NEGRO IN THE NEW WORLD."
       CARIBBEAN STUDIES, 4 (JULY, 1964): 35-41.

19326 EBY, CECIL D., JR. "CLASSICAL NAMES AMONG SOUTHERN NEGRO
       SLAVES." AMERICAN SPEECH, 36 (MAY, 1961): 140-141.

19327 ELAM, WILLIAM C. "LINGO IN LITERATURE." LIPPINCOTT'S
       MONTHLY MAGAZINE, 55 (FEBRUARY, 1899): 286-288.

19328 FASOLD, RALPH AND WOLFRAM, WALT. "SOME LINGUISTIC
       FEATURES OF NEGRO DIALECT." IN FASOLD AND SHUY, ROGER
       (EDS.). TEACHING STANDARD ENGLISH IN THE INNER CITY.
       WASHINGTON: CENTER FOR APPLIED LINGUISTICS, 1970, PP.
       41-86.

19329 FORTIER, ALCEE. LOUISIANA STUDIES. NEW ORLEANS:
       HANSELL, 1894.

19330   FOSTER, CHARLES W.   "THE REPRESENTATION OF NEGRO DIALECT
        IN CHARLES W. CHESNUTT'S THE CONJURE WOMAN."   PH.D.
        DISSERTATION, UNIVERSITY OF ALABAMA, 1968.

19331   FRUIT, J.P.   "UNCLE REMUS IN PHONETIC SPELLING."   DIALECT
        NOTES, 1 (1896):   196-198.

19332   FUNK, HENRY E.   "THE FRENCH CREOLE DIALECT OF MARTINIQUE,
        ITS HISTORICAL BACKGROUND, VOCABULARY, SYNTAX,
        PROVERBS AND LITERATURE; WITH A GLOSSARY."   PH.D.
        DISSERTATION, UNIVERSITY OF VIRGINIA, 1953.

19333   GENOVESE, EUGENE D.   "THE LANGUAGE OF CLASS AND NATION."
        URBAN REVIEW, 8 (1975):   39-47.

19334   GENOVESE, EUGENE D.   ROLL, JORDAN, ROLL: THE WORLD THE
        SLAVES MADE.   NEW YORK: PANTHEON, 1974.

19335   GIELOW, MARTHA S.   MAMMY'S REMINISCENCES, AND OTHER
        SKETCHES.   NEW YORK: A.S. BARNES AND COMPANY, 1893.

19336   GLENN, ROBERT W.   BLACK RHETORIC: A GUIDE TO
        AFRO-AMERICAN COMMUNICATION.   METUCHEN, NJ: SCARECROW
        PRESS, 1976.

19337   GREENBERG, JOSEPH H.   "AN APPLICATION OF NEW WORLD
        EVIDENCE TO AN AFRICAN LINGUISTIC PROBLEM."   LES
        AFRO-AMERICAINS, NO. 27 (1953):   129-131.

19338   GUTMAN, HERBERT G.   THE BLACK FAMILY IN SLAVERY AND
        FREEDOM, 1750-1925.   NEW YORK: PANTHEON BOOKS, 1976.

19339   HAIR, P.E.H.   "BLACK AFRICAN SLAVES AT VALENCIA,
        1482-1516:   AN ONOMASTIC INQUIRY."   HISTORY IN AFRICA,
        7 (1980):   119-139.

19340   HAIR, P.E.H.   "SIERRA LEONE ITEMS IN THE GULLAH DIALECT
        OF AMERICAN ENGLISH."   SIERRA LEONE LANGUAGE REVIEW, 4
        (1965):   79-84.

19341   HALL, BEVERLY.   "DIALECT VARIATION IN THE DOMINICAN
        REPUBLIC."   M.A. THESIS, UNIVERSITY OF THE WEST
        INDIES, 1970.

19342   HALL, ROBERT A., JR.   "AFRICAN SUBSTRATUM IN NEGRO
        ENGLISH."   AMERICAN SPEECH, 25 (FEBRUARY, 1950):
        51-54.

19343   HALL, ROBERT A., JR.   PIDGIN AND CREOLE LANGUAGES.
        ITHACA: CORNELL UNIVERSITY PRESS, 1965.

19344   HANCOCK, IAN F.   "A DOMESTIC ORIGIN FOR THE
        ENGLISH-DERIVED ATLANTIC CREOLES."   FLORIDA FL
        REPORTER, 10 (SPRING/FALL, 1972):   7-8, 52.

19345   HANCOCK, IAN F. "GULLAH AND BARBADIAN--ORIGINS AND
        RELATIONSHIPS." AMERICAN SPEECH, 55 (SPRING, 1980):
        17-35.

19346   HANCOCK, IAN F. "THE RELATIONSHIP OF BLACK VERNACULAR
        ENGLISH TO THE ATLANTIC CREOLES." WORKING PAPER OF
        THE AFRICAN AND AFRO-AMERICAN STUDIES AND RESEARCH
        CENTER. AUSTIN: UNIVERSITY OF TEXAS PRESS, 1978.

19347   HANCOCK, IAN F. "WEST AFRICA AND THE ATLANTIC CREOLES."
        IN SPENCER, JOHN (ED.). THE ENGLISH LANGUAGE IN WEST
        AFRICA. LONDON: LONGMAN, 1971, PP. 113-122.

19348   HARRISON, CARL H. AND MONOD, VICTOR P. "THE PARTICLE
        T'AH IN SLAVERY DISCOURSE." WORKPAPERS OF THE SUMMER
        INSTITUTE OF LINGUISTICS, UNIVERSITY OF NORTH DAKOTA,
        22 (1978): 48-53.

19349   HAU, KATHLEEN. "AFRICAN WRITING IN THE NEW WORLD."
        BULLETIN DE L'INSTITUT FONDAMENTAL D'AFRIQUE NOIRE, 40
        (1978): 28-48.

19350   HELLER, MURRAY (ED.). BLACK NAMES IN AMERICA: A GUIDE
        TO THEIR HISTORY AND MEANING. CLEVELAND: CLEVELAND
        PUBLIC LIBRARY, 1974.

19351   HELLER, MURRAY (ED.). BLACK NAMES IN AMERICA: ORIGINS
        AND USAGE COLLECTED BY NEWBELL NILES PUCKETT. BOSTON:
        G.K. HALL, 1974.

19352   HIGGINSON, THOMAS W. ARMY LIFE IN A BLACK REGIMENT.
        BOSTON: FIELDS, OSGOOD, 1870.

19353   HUCKS, J. JENKINS. PLANTATION NEGRO SAYINGS ON THE COAST
        OF SOUTH CAROLINA IN THEIR OWN VERNACULAR.
        GEORGETOWN, SC: CHARLES W. ROUSE, 1899.

19354   HUDSON, ARTHUR P. "SOME CURIOUS NEGRO NAMES." SOUTHERN
        FOLKLORE QUARTERLY, 2 (DECEMBER, 1938): 179-193.

19355   HUTTAR, GEORGE L. "A COMPARATIVE WORD LIST FOR DJUKA."
        IN GRIMES, JOSEPH E. (ED.). LANGUAGES OF THE GUIANAS.
        NORMAN: SUMMER INSTITUTE OF LINGUISTICS, UNIVERSITY
        OF OKLAHOMA, 1972, PP. 12-21.

19356   JARREAU, LAFAYETTE. "CREOLE FOLKLORE OF POINT COUPEE
        PARISH." M.A. THESIS, LOUISIANA STATE UNIVERSITY,
        1931.

19357   JEFFREYS, MERVYN D.W. "NAMES OF AMERICAN NEGRO SLAVES."
        AMERICAN ANTHROPOLOGIST, 50 (JULY, 1948): 571-573.

19358   JEREMIAH, MILFORD A. "THE LINGUISTIC RELATEDNESS OF
        BLACK ENGLISH AND ANTIGUAN CREOLE: EVIDENCE FROM THE
        EIGHTEENTH AND NINETEENTH CENTURIES." PH.D.

DISSERTATION, BROWN UNIVERSITY, 1977.

19359 JOHNSON, GUY B. "THE SPEECH OF THE NEGRO." FOLK=SAY, 2
       (1930): 346=358.

19360 JONES=JACKSON, PATRICIA A. "GULLAH: ON THE QUESTION OF
       AFRO=AMERICAN LANGUAGE." ANTHROPOLOGICAL LINGUISTICS,
       20 (DECEMBER, 1978): 422=429.

19361 KANE, ELISHA K. "THE NEGRO DIALECTS ALONG THE SAVANNAH
       RIVER." DIALECT NOTES, 5 (1925): 354=361.

19362 KLOE, DONALD R. "BUDDY QUAW: AN ANONYMOUS POEM IN
       GULLAH=JAMAICAN DIALECT WRITTEN CIRCA 1800." SOUTHERN
       FOLKLORE QUARTERLY, 38 (JUNE, 1974): 81=90.

19363 KOCHER, MARGARET. "ANNOTATED BIBLIOGRAPHY." IN
       CULLINAN, BERNICE E. (ED.). BLACK DIALECTS AND
       READING. URBANA, IL: NATIONAL COUNCIL OF TEACHERS OF
       ENGLISH, 1974, PP. 155=189.

19364 KOCHMAN, THOMAS. "TOWARD AN ETHNOGRAPHY OF BLACK
       AMERICAN SPEECH BEHAVIOR." TRANS=ACTION, 6 (FEBRUARY,
       1969): 26=34.

19365 KRAPP, GEORGE P. "THE ENGLISH OF THE NEGRO." AMERICAN
       MERCURY, 2 (JUNE, 1924): 190=195.

19366 LEE, RUTH A. "GULLAH ROOTS IN THE SEA ISLANDS." ENCORE,
       7 (OCTOBER 16, 1978): 38=39.

19367 LEPAGE, ROBERT B. JAMAICAN CREOLE: AN HISTORICAL
       INTRODUCTION TO JAMAICAN CREOLE. NEW YORK: ST.
       MARTIN'S PRESS, 1960.

19368 LEVINE, LAWRENCE W. BLACK CULTURE AND BLACK
       CONSCIOUSNESS: AFRO=AMERICAN FOLK THOUGHT FROM
       SLAVERY TO FREEDOM. NEW YORK: OXFORD UNIVERSITY
       PRESS, 1977.

19369 LONG, RICHARD A. "'MAN' AND 'EVIL' IN AMERICAN NEGRO
       SPEECH." AMERICAN SPEECH, 34 (DECEMBER, 1959):
       305=306.

19370 LONG, RICHARD A. "THE UNCLE REMUS DIALECT: A
       PRELIMINARY LINGUISTIC VIEW." PAPER PRESENTED AT
       SOUTHEASTERN CONFERENCE ON LINGUISTICS, 1969.

19371 MAJOR, CLARENCE (ED.). DICTIONARY OF AFRO=AMERICAN
       SLANG. NEW YORK: INTERNATIONAL PUBLISHING COMPANY,
       1970.

19372 MATHEWS, MITFORD M. "AFRICANISMS IN THE PLANTATION
       VOCABULARY." SOME SOURCES OF SOUTHERNISMS.
       UNIVERSITY, AL: UNIVERSITY OF ALABAMA PRESS, 1948,

PP. 86-129.

19373   MCDAVID, RAVEN I., JR.   "HISTORICAL, REGIONAL, AND SOCIAL
        VARIATION." JOURNAL OF ENGLISH LINGUISTICS, 1 (1967):
        24-40.

19374   MCDAVID, RAVEN I., JR. AND MCDAVID, VIRGINIA G.   "THE
        RELATIONSHIP OF THE SPEECH OF AMERICAN NEGROES TO THE
        SPEECH OF THE WHITES." AMERICAN SPEECH, 26 (FEBRUARY,
        1951):   3-17.

19375   MCDOWELL, TREMAINE.   "NOTES ON NEGRO DIALECT IN THE
        AMERICAN NOVEL TO 1821." AMERICAN SPEECH, 5 (APRIL,
        1930):   291-296.

19376   MCDOWELL, TREMAINE.   "THE USE OF NEGRO DIALECT BY HARRIET
        BEECHER STOWE." AMERICAN SPEECH, 6 (JUNE, 1931):
        322-326.

19377   MINTZ, SIDNEY W.   "THE SOCIO-HISTORICAL BACKGROUND OF
        PIDGINIZATION AND CREOLIZATION." IN HYMES, DELL
        (ED.). PIDGINIZATION AND CREOLIZATION OF LANGUAGES.
        CAMBRIDGE: CAMBRIDGE UNIVERSITY PRESS, 1971, PP.
        481-496.

19378   MINTZ, SIDNEY W.   "TOWARD AN AFRO-AMERICAN HISTORY."
        CAHIERS D'HISTOIRE MONDIALE, 8 (1971):   317-332.

19379   MITTELSDORF, SIBYLLE.   "AFRICAN RETENTIONS IN JAMAICAN
        CREOLE: A REASSESSMENT." PH.D. DISSERTATION,
        NORTHWESTERN UNIVERSITY, 1978.

19380   MORRIS, JOHN A.   "GULLAH IN THE STORIES AND NOVELS OF
        WILLIAM GILMORE SIMMS." AMERICAN SPEECH, 22
        (FEBRUARY, 1947):   46-53.

19381   MORSE, J. MITCHELL.   "THE SHUFFLING SPEECH OF SLAVERY:
        BLACK ENGLISH." COLLEGE ENGLISH, 34 (MARCH, 1973):
        834-843.

19382   MORSE, J. MITCHELL.   "THE SHUFFLING SPEECH OF SLAVERY:
        BLACK ENGLISH." THE IRRELEVANT ENGLISH TEACHER.
        PHILADELPHIA: TEMPLE UNIVERSITY PRESS, 1972, PP.
        81-95.

19383   NICHOLS, PATRICIA C.   "LINGUISTIC CHANGE IN GULLAH: SEX,
        AGE, AND MOBILITY." PH.D. DISSERTATION, STANFORD
        UNIVERSITY, 1976.

19384   OGUNSANYA, EBUN.   "THE YORUBA DIALECT IN BAHIAN
        PORTUGUESE." B.A. THESIS, RADCLIFFE COLLEGE, 1971.

19385   OKE, DAVID O.   "ON THE GENESIS OF NEW WORLD BLACK
        ENGLISH." CARIBBEAN QUARTERLY, 23 (MARCH, 1977):
        61-79.

1439

19386   "OLD SLAVE NAMES." ATLANTIC MONTHLY, 66 (SEPTEMBER, 1890): 428.

19387   PARDOE, T. EARL. "A HISTORICAL AND PHONETIC STUDY OF NEGRO DIALECT." PH.D. DISSERTATION, LOUISIANA STATE UNIVERSITY, 1937.

19388   PEDERSON, LEE. "NEGRO SPEECH IN THE ADVENTURES OF HUCKLEBERRY FINN." MARK TWAIN JOURNAL, 13 (SUMMER, 1966): 1-4.

19389   PLATT, JAMES JR. "THE NEGRO ELEMENT IN ENGLISH." ATHENAEUM, 3801 (SEPTEMBER 1, 1900): 283.

19390   PRICE, RICHARD AND PRICE, SALLY. "SECRET PLAY LANGUAGES IN SARAMAKA: LINGUISTIC DISGUISE IN A CARIBBEAN CREOLE." IN KIRSHENBLATT-GIMBLETT, BARBARA (ED.). SPEECH PLAY. PHILADELPHIA: UNIVERSITY OF PENNSYLVANIA PRESS, 1976, PP. 37-50.

19391   PUCKETT, NEWBELL N. "AMERICAN NEGRO NAMES." JOURNAL OF NEGRO HISTORY, 23 (JANUARY, 1938): 35-48.

19392   PUCKETT, NEWBELL N. "NAMES OF AMERICAN NEGRO SLAVES." IN MURDOCK, GEORGE P. (ED.). STUDIES IN THE SCIENCE OF SOCIETY PRESENTED TO ALBERT GALLOWAY KELLER IN CELEBRATION OF HIS COMPLETION OF THIRTY YEARS AS PROFESSOR OF SOCIETY IN YALE UNIVERSITY. NEW HAVEN: YALE UNIVERSITY PRESS, 1937, PP. 471-494.

19393   PUCKETT, NEWBELL N. AND HELLER, MURRAY. BLACK NAMES IN AMERICA: ORIGINS AND USAGE. BOSTON: G.K. HALL, 1975.

19394   RAMCHAND, KENNETH. "THE NEGRO AND THE ENGLISH LANGUAGE IN THE WEST INDIES." SAVACOU, 1 (JUNE, 1970): 33-45.

19395   READ, A.W. "SPEECH DEFECTS AND MANNERISMS AMONG SLAVES AND SERVANTS IN COLONIAL AMERICA." QUARTERLY JOURNAL OF SPEECH, 24 (OCTOBER, 1938): 397-401.

19396   READ, ALLEN W. "EIGHTEENTH CENTURY SLAVES AS ADVERTISED BY THEIR MASTERS." JOURNAL OF NEGRO HISTORY, 1 (APRIL, 1916): 163-216.

19397   READ, ALLEN W. "THE SPEECH OF NEGROES IN COLONIAL AMERICA." JOURNAL OF NEGRO HISTORY, 24 (JULY, 1939): 247-258.

19398   READ, WILLIAM A. LOUISIANA-FRENCH. BATON ROUGE: LOUISIANA STATE UNIVERSITY PRESS, 1931.

19399   REINECKE, JOHN E. "MARGINAL LANGUAGES: A SOCIOLOGICAL SURVEY OF THE CREOLE LANGUAGES AND TRADE JARGONS." PH.D. DISSERTATION, YALE UNIVERSITY, 1937.

19400 REINECKE, JOHN E. "TRADE JARGON AND CREOLE DIALECTS AS
       MARGINAL LANGUAGES." SOCIAL FORCES, 13 (OCTOBER,
       1933): 107-118.

19401 BLAKE, ROBERT. "THE LION ACT IS OVER:
       PASSIVE/AGGRESSIVE PATTERNS OF COMMUNICATION IN
       AMERICAN NEGRO HUMOR." JOURNAL OF POPULAR CULTURE, 9
       (1975): 549-560.

19402 ROBERTSON, IAN A. "DUTCH CREOLE LANGUAGES IN GUAYANA."
       BOLETIN DE ESTUDIOS LATINOAMERICANOS Y DEL CARIBE, 23
       (DECEMBER, 1977): 61-68.

19403 RUSSELL-WOOD, A.J.R. "THE BLACK FAMILY IN THE AMERICAS."
       JAHRBUCH FUR GESCHICHTE VON STAAT, WIRTSCHAET UND
       GESELLSCHAFT LATEINAMERIKAS, 16 (1979): 267-309.

19404 SANDERS, ISAIAH S. "SOME PHASES OF NEGRO ENGLISH." M.A.
       THESIS, UNIVERSITY OF CHICAGO, 1926.

19405 SCARBOROUGH, W.S. "THE NEGRO ELEMENT IN FICTION."
       PROCEEDINGS OF THE AMERICAN PHILOLOGICAL ASSOCIATION,
       21 (JULY, 1890): XLII-XLIV.

19406 SCARBOROUGH, W.S. "NOTES ON THE FUNCTION OF MODERN
       LANGUAGES IN AFRICA." PROCEEDINGS OF THE AMERICAN
       PHILOLOGICAL ASSOCIATION, 27 (JULY, 1896):
       XLVI-XLVIII.

19407 SCHNEIDER, GILBERT D. CAMEROONS CREOLE DICTIONARY.
       BAMENDA: CAMEROON BAPTIST MISSION, 1960.

19408 SEIDLEMAN, MORTON. "SURVIVALS IN NEGRO VOCABULARY."
       AMERICAN SPEECH, 12 (OCTOBER, 1937): 231-232.

19409 SINGLER, JOHN V. "LANGUAGE IN LIBERIA IN THE NINETEENTH
       CENTURY: THE SETTLERS' PERSPECTIVE." LIBERIAN
       STUDIES JOURNAL, 7 (1976-1977): 73-86.

19410 "SLAVE NAME." IN NUNEZ, BENJAMIN. DICTIONARY OF
       AFRO-LATIN AMERICAN CIVILIZATION. WESTPORT:
       GREENWOOD PRESS, 1980, P. 436.

19411 "SLAVES, NAMING OF." IN RYWELL, MARTIN (ED.).
       AFRO-AMERICAN ENCYCLOPEDIA. 10 VOLS. NORTH MIAMI:
       EDUCATIONAL BOOK PUBLISHERS, 1974, VOL. 8, P. 2493.

19412 SMITH, ARTHUR L. "SOCIO-HISTORICAL PERSPECTIVES OF BLACK
       ORATORY." QUARTERLY JOURNAL OF SPEECH, 56 (OCTOBER,
       1970): 264-269.

19413 SMITH, R.B. SOCIOLOGICAL ASPECTS OF BLACK ENGLISH
       DIALECTS IN THE U.S. LANGUAGE AND SOCIETY. THE HAGUE:
       MOUTON, 1979.

19414   SMITH, REED. GULLAH: DEDICATED TO THE MEMORY OF AMBROSE
        E. GONZALES. COLUMBIA: BULLETIN OF THE UNIVERSITY OF
        SOUTH CAROLINA NO. 190, 1926.

19415   STANLEY, OMA. "NEGRO SPEECH IN EAST TEXAS." AMERICAN
        SPEECH, 16 (FEBRUARY, 1941): 3-16.

19416   STEWART, WILLIAM A. "ACCULTURATIVE PROCESSES AND THE
        LANGUAGE OF THE AMERICAN NEGRO." IN GAGE, WILLIAM A.
        (ED.). LANGUAGE IN ITS SOCIAL SETTING. WASHINGTON:
        ANTHROPOLOGICAL SOCIETY OF WASHINGTON, 1974, PP. 1-46.

19417   STEWART, WILLIAM A. "CONTINUITY AND CHANGE IN AMERICAN
        NEGRO DIALECTS." FLORIDA FL REPORTER, 6 (SPRING,
        1968): 3-4, 14-16, 18.

19418   STEWART, WILLIAM A. "FACTS AND ISSUES CONCERNING BLACK
        DIALECT." ENGLISH RECORD, 21 (APRIL, 1971): 121-135.

19419   STEWART, WILLIAM A. "HISTORICAL AND STRUCTURAL BASES FOR
        THE RECOGNITION OF NEGRO DIALECT." IN ALATIS, JAMES
        E. (ED.). REPORT OF THE TWENTIETH ANNUAL ROUND TABLE
        MEETING ON LINGUISTICS AND LANGUAGE STUDIES.
        WASHINGTON: GEORGETOWN UNIVERSITY PRESS, 1969, PP.
        239-247.

19420   STEWART, WILLIAM A. "MORE ON BLACK-WHITE SPEECH
        RELATIONSHIPS." FLORIDA FL REPORTER, 11 (SPRING/FALL,
        1973): 35-40.

19421   STEWART, WILLIAM A. "NONSTANDARD SPEECH PATTERNS."
        BALTIMORE BULLETIN OF EDUCATION, 43 (1966-1967): 2-4,
        52-65.

19422   STEWART, WILLIAM A. "SOCIOLINGUISTIC FACTORS IN THE
        HISTORY OF AMERICAN NEGRO DIALECTS." FLORIDA FL
        REPORTER, 5 (SPRING, 1967): 11, 22, 24, 26, 30.

19423   STEWART, WILLIAM A. "SOCIOLINGUISTIC FACTORS IN THE
        HISTORY OF AMERICAN NEGRO DIALECTS." IN ABRAHAMS,
        ROGER D. AND TROIKE, RUDOLPH C. (EDS.). LANGUAGE AND
        CULTURAL DIVERSITY IN AMERICAN EDUCATION. ENGLEWOOD
        CLIFFS: PRENTICE-HALL, 1972, PP. 219-224.

19424   STODDARD, ALBERT H. "ORIGIN, DIALECT, BELIEFS, AND
        CHARACTERISTICS OF THE NEGROES OF SOUTH CAROLINA AND
        GEORGIA COASTS." GEORGIA HISTORICAL QUARTERLY, 28
        (SEPTEMBER, 1944): 186-195.

19425   STONEY, SAMUEL G. BLACK GENESIS: A CHRONICLE. NEW YORK:
        MACMILLAN, 1930.

19426   SULLIVAN, ALLEN R. "AFRO-ANGLO COMMUNICATION IN AMERICA:
        SOME EDUCATIONAL IMPLICATIONS." PAN-AFRICAN JOURNAL,
        5 (SPRING, 1972): 231-238.

19427 TAYLOR, CLYDE. "THE LANGUAGE OF HIP: FROM AFRICA TO
       WHAT'S HAPPENING NOW." FIRST WORLD: AN INTERNATIONAL
       JOURNAL OF BLACK THOUGHT, 1 (JANUARY/FEBRUARY, 1977):
       25-40.

19428 TAYLOR, DOUGLAS M. "NEW LANGUAGES FOR OLD IN THE WEST
       INDIES." COMPARATIVE STUDIES IN SOCIETY AND HISTORY,
       3 (1960-1961): 277-288.

19429 TAYLOR, DOUGLAS M. "THE ORIGIN OF WEST INDIAN CREOLE
       LANGUAGES: EVIDENCE FROM GRAMMATICAL CATEGORIES."
       AMERICAN ANTHROPOLOGIST, 65 (AUGUST, 1965): 800-814.

19430 THOMAS, WILLIAM J. "LOUISIANA CREOLE FRENCH, BLACK OR
       WHITE?" WICHITA STATE UNIVERSITY BULLETIN, 49
       (FEBRUARY, 1973): 15-26.

19431 TIDWELL, J.M. "MARK TWAIN'S REPRESENTATION OF NEGRO
       SPEECH." AMERICAN SPEECH, 17 (OCTOBER, 1942):
       174-176.

19432 TILLER, LESSIE. "GULLAH IN AMERICAN LITERATURE." M.A.
       THESIS, UNIVERSITY OF SOUTH CAROLINA, 1923.

19433 TROUBRIDGE, ST. VINCENT. "NOTES ON DAE: NEGROES AND
       SLAVERY." AMERICAN SPEECH, 26 (FEBRUARY, 1951):
       27-28.

19434 TURNER, LORENZO D. AFRICANISMS IN THE GULLAH DIALECT.
       CHICAGO: UNIVERSITY OF CHICAGO PRESS, 1949.

19435 TURNER, LORENZO D. "AFRICANISMS IN THE PLANTATION
       VOCABULARY." IN MATHEWS, M.M. (ED.). SOME SOURCES OF
       SOUTHERNISMS. UNIVERSITY, AL: UNIVERSITY OF ALABAMA
       PRESS, 1948, PP. 86-129.

19436 TURNER, LORENZO D. AN ANTHOLOGY OF KRIO FOLKLORE AND
       LITERATURE. CHICAGO: DEPARTMENT OF ENGLISH,
       ROOSEVELT UNIVERSITY, N.D.

19437 TURNER, LORENZO D. "LINGUISTIC RESEARCH AND AFRICAN
       SURVIVALS." BULLETIN OF THE AMERICAN COUNCIL OF
       LEARNED SOCIETIES, NO. 32 (1941): 68-89.

19438 TURNER, LORENZO D. "PROBLEMS CONFRONTING THE
       INVESTIGATOR OF GULLAH." PUBLICATION OF THE AMERICAN
       DIALECT SOCIETY, NO. 9 (APRIL, 1948): 74-84.

19439 VAN SERTIMA, IVAN. "AFRICAN LINGUISTIC AND MYTHOLOGICAL
       STRUCTURES IN THE NEW WORLD." IN GOLDSTEIN, RHODA L.
       (ED.). BLACK LIFE AND CULTURE IN THE UNITED STATES.
       NEW YORK: CROWELL, 1971, PP. 12-35.

19440 WALKER, SAUNDERS E. "A DICTIONARY OF THE FOLK SPEECH OF
       THE EAST ALABAMA NEGRO." PH.D. DISSERTATION, WESTERN

RESERVE UNIVERSITY, 1956.

19441 WHINNOM, KEITH. "THE ORIGIN OF EUROPEAN-BASED CREOLES
AND PIDGINS." ORBIS, 14 (DECEMBER, 1965): 511-526.

19442 WHITNEY, ANNIE W. "NEGRO AMERICAN DIALECTS."
INDEPENDENT, 53 (AUGUST 22, 29, 1901): 1979-1981,
2039-2042.

19443 WILKINSON, LUPTON A. "GULLAH VERSUS GRAMMAR." NORTH
AMERICAN REVIEW, 236 (DECEMBER, 1933): 539-542.

19444 WILLEFORD, MARY JO. "AFRICANISMS IN THE BAJAN DIALECT."
BIM, 12 (JANUARY-JUNE, 1968): 90-97.

19445 WILLIAMS, DARNELL. "AN INVESTIGATION OF POSSIBLE GULLAH
SURVIVALS IN THE SPEECH AND CULTURAL PATTERNS OF BLACK
MISSISSIPPIANS." PH.D. DISSERTATION, OHIO STATE
UNIVERSITY, 1973.

19446 WILLIAMS, GEORGE W. "SLAVE NAMES IN ANTE-BELLUM SOUTH
CAROLINA." AMERICAN SPEECH, 33 (DECEMBER, 1958):
294-295.

19447 WOOD, PETER H. BLACK MAJORITY: NEGROES IN COLONIAL
SOUTH CAROLINA, 1670 TO THE STONO REBELLION. NEW
YORK: ALFRED A. KNOPF, 1974.

19448 "WORD SHADOWS." ATLANTIC MONTHLY, 67 (JANUARY, 1891):
143-144.

24.
Slave Resistance

GENERAL

19449   ABZUG, ROBERT H.   "THE INFLUENCE OF GARRISONIAN
        ABOLITIONISTS' FEARS OF SLAVE VIOLENCE ON THE
        ANTISLAVERY ARGUMENT." JOURNAL OF NEGRO HISTORY, 55
        (JANUARY, 1970): 15-28.

19450   ADAMS, SAMUEL H.   "A SLAVE IN THE FAMILY." NEW YORKER,
        23 (DECEMBER 13, 1947): 32-36.

19451   ALILUNAS, LEO. "FUGITIVE SLAVE CASES IN OHIO PRIOR TO
        1850." OHIO ARCHAEOLOGICAL AND HISTORICAL QUARTERLY,
        49 (APRIL-JUNE, 1940): 160-184.

19452   AMES, RUSSELL. "PROTEST AND IRONY IN NEGRO FOLKSONGS."
        SCIENCE AND SOCIETY, 14 (SUMMER, 1950): 193-213.

19453   ANDERSON, ALAN B.   "RECENT ACCULTURATION OF BUSH NEGROES
        IN SURINAM AND FRENCH GUIANA." ANTHROPOLOGICA, N.S.,
        22 (1980): 61-84.

19454   APTHEKER, HERBERT. "ADDITIONAL DATA ON AMERICAN
        MAROONS." JOURNAL OF NEGRO HISTORY, 32 (OCTOBER,
        1947): 452-460.

19455   APTHEKER, HERBERT. AND WHY NOT EVERY MAN? DOCUMENTARY
        STORY OF THE FIGHT AGAINST SLAVERY IN THE U.S.
        BERLIN: SEVEN SEAS PUBLISHERS, 1961.

19456   APTHEKER, HERBERT. "BUYING FREEDOM." TO BE FREE:
        PIONEERING STUDIES IN AFRO-AMERICAN HISTORY. NEW
        YORK: INTERNATIONAL PUBLISHERS, 1948, PP. 31-40.

19457   APTHEKER, HERBERT. "MAROONS WITHIN THE PRESENT LIMITS OF
        THE UNITED STATES." JOURNAL OF NEGRO HISTORY, 24
        (APRIL, 1939): 167-184.

19458   APTHEKER, HERBERT. THE NEGRO IN THE ABOLITION MOVEMENT.
        NEW YORK: INTERNATIONAL PUBLISHERS, 1941.

19459   APTHEKER, HERBERT. "SLAVE RESISTANCE IN THE UNITED
        STATES." IN HUGGINS, NATHAN I.; KILSON, MARTIN; AND
        FOX, DANIEL M. (EDS.). KEY ISSUES IN THE
        AFRO-AMERICAN EXPERIENCE. 2 VOLS. NEW YORK:
        HARCOURT BRACE JOVANOVICH, 1971, VOL.1, PP. 161-173.

19460   APTHEKER, HERBERT. "THEY BEGAN THE FIGHT ON SLAVERY."
        OPPORTUNITY, 17 (AUGUST, 1939): 243-244.

19461   ARMSTRONG, HANNIBAL. "HOW I HID A UNION SPY." JOURNAL

OF NEGRO HISTORY, 9 (JANUARY, 1924): 34-40.

19462   ARNOLD, I.C. "AN UNDERGROUND STATION IN DRUMORE
        TOWNSHIP." LANCASTER COUNTY HISTORICAL SOCIETY
        PAPERS, 55 (1951): 186-188.

19463   BAADE, ANNE A. "SLAVE INDEMNITIES: A GERMAN COAST
        RESPONSE, 1795." LOUISIANA HISTORY, 20 (WINTER,
        1979): 102-109.

19464   BAILEY, WILLIAM S. "THE UNDERGROUND RAILROAD IN SOUTHERN
        CHAUTAUQUA COUNTY." NEW YORK HISTORY, 16 (JANUARY,
        1935): 53-63.

19465   BASLER, ROY P. "'BEEF! BEEF! BEEF!' LINCOLN AND JUDGE
        ROBERTSON." ABRAHAM LINCOLN QUARTERLY, 6 (SEPTEMBER,
        1951): 400-407.

19466   BAUGHMAN, A.J. "THE 'UNDERGROUND RAILWAY.'" OHIO
        ARCHAEOLOGICAL AND HISTORICAL SOCIETY PUBLICATIONS, 15
        (APRIL, 1906): 189-191.

19467   BEARSE, AUSTIN. REMINISCENCES OF FUGITIVE-SLAVE LAW DAYS
        IN BOSTON. BOSTON: W. RICHARDSON, 1880.

19468   BEATTIE, JESSIE L. BLACK MOSES, THE REAL UNCLE TOM.
        TORONTO: RYERSON PRESS, 1957.

19469   BELL, HOWARD H. "EXPRESSIONS OF NEGRO MILITANCY IN THE
        NORTH, 1840-1860." JOURNAL OF NEGRO HISTORY, 45
        (JANUARY, 1960): 11-20.

19470   BELL, HOWARD H. "NATIONAL NEGRO CONVENTIONS OF THE
        MIDDLE 1840S: MORAL SUASION VS. POLITICAL ACTION."
        JOURNAL OF NEGRO HISTORY, 42 (OCTOBER, 1957): 247-260.

19471   BJORNSON, MARION L. "UNDERGROUND RAILROAD IN DELAWARE."
        M.A. THESIS, UNIVERSITY OF PENNSYLVANIA, 1928.

19472   BLACKETT, R.J.M. "'FREEDOM, OR THE MARTYR'S GRAVE':
        BLACK PITTSBURGH'S AID TO THE FUGITIVE SLAVE."
        WESTERN PENNSYLVANIA HISTORICAL MAGAZINE, 61 (APRIL,
        1978): 117-134.

19473   BLACKETT, R.J.M. "FUGITIVE SLAVES IN BRITAIN: THE
        ODYSSEY OF WILLIAM AND ELLEN CRAFT." JOURNAL OF
        AMERICAN STUDIES, 12 (APRIL, 1978): 41-62.

19474   BLAKE, RICHARD A. "HUMANITY AGAINST ITSELF; ROOTS AND
        THE FIGHT AGAINST SLAVERY IN TELEVISION SERIES."
        AMERICA, 136 (JANUARY 15, 1977): 34-35.

19475   BLANCHARD, FOREST I. "FUGITIVE SLAVES IN OHIO."
        NORTHWEST OHIO HISTORICAL SOCIETY QUARTERLY BULLETIN,
        9 (1937): 1-14.

19476   BLASSINGAME, JOHN W. SAMBOS AND REBELS: THE CHARACTER
        OF THE SOUTHERN SLAVE. WASHINGTON: DEPARTMENT OF
        HISTORY, HOWARD UNIVERSITY, 1972.

19477   BLAZER, O.N. "THE HISTORY OF THE UNDERGROUND RAILROAD OF
        MCDONOUGH COUNTY, ILLINOIS." JOURNAL OF THE ILLINOIS
        STATE HISTORICAL SOCIETY, 15 (OCTOBER, 1922): 579-591.

19478   BOLES, JOHN B. "TENSION IN A SLAVE SOCIETY: THE TRIAL
        OF THE REVEREND JACOB GRUBER." SOUTHERN STUDIES, 18
        (SUMMER, 1979): 179-198.

19479   BONEY, F.N. "NATHANIEL FRANCIS, REPRESENTATIVE
        ANTEBELLUM SOUTHERNER." PROCEEDINGS OF THE AMERICAN
        PHILOSOPHICAL SOCIETY, 118 (OCTOBER, 1974): 449-458.

19480   BOTSFORD, DAVID P. "SOME ESSEX COUNTY, ONTARIO,
        FAMILIES." THE DETROIT SOCIETY FOR GENEALOGICAL
        RESEARCH MAGAZINE, 14 (JUNE, 1951): 127-133.

19481   BRACEY, JOHN H., JR.; MEIER, AUGUST; AND RUDWICK, ELLIOTT
        (EDS.). AMERICAN SLAVERY: THE QUESTION OF
        RESISTANCE. BELMONT, CA: WADSWORTH PUBLISHING
        COMPANY, 1971.

19482   BRACEY, JOHN H., JR.; MEIER, AUGUST; AND RUDWICK, ELLIOTT
        (EDS.). BLACKS IN THE ABOLITION MOVEMENT. BELMONT,
        CA: WADSWORTH PUBLISHING COMPANY, 1971.

19483   BRADFORD, SARAH E. SCENES IN THE LIFE OF HARRIET TUBMAN.
        AUBURN, NY: W.J. MOSES, 1869.

19484   BREYFOGLE, WILLIAM A. MAKE FREE: THE STORY OF THE
        UNDERGROUND RAILROAD. PHILADELPHIA: J.B. LIPPINCOTT,
        1958.

19485   BRIDNER, ELWOOD L., JR. "THE FUGITIVE SLAVES OF
        MARYLAND." MARYLAND HISTORICAL MAGAZINE, 66 (SPRING,
        1971): 33-50.

19486   BROWIN, FRANCES W. "BUT WE HAVE NO COUNTRY." QUAKER
        HISTORY, 57 (AUTUMN, 1968): 84-95.

19487   BRUBAKER, MARIANNA G. "THE UNDERGROUND RAILROAD."
        LANCASTER COUNTY HISTORICAL SOCIETY PAPERS, 15 (APRIL,
        1911): 95-119.

19488   BRUCE, DICKSON D., JR. "SLAVERY AND VIOLENCE: THE
        SLAVES' VIEW." VIOLENCE AND CULTURE IN THE ANTEBELLUM
        SOUTH. AUSTIN: UNIVERSITY OF TEXAS PRESS, 1979, PP.
        137-160.

19489   BRUMBAUGH, RODERICK. "BLACK MAROONS IN FLORIDA,
        1800-1830." UNPUBLISHED PAPER PRESENTED AT MEETING OF
        ORGANIZATION OF AMERICAN HISTORIANS, BOSTON, 1975.

19490   BUCKMASTER, HENRIETTA. LET MY PEOPLE GO: THE STORY OF
        THE UNDERGROUND RAILROAD AND THE GROWTH OF THE
        ABOLITION MOVEMENT. NEW YORK: HARPER & BROTHERS,
        1941.

19491   BUCKMASTER, HENRIETTA. "THE UNDERGROUND RAILROAD."
        NORTH AMERICAN REVIEW, 246 (AUTUMN, 1938): 142-149.

19492   BURNS, E. BRADFORD. "CULTURES IN CONFLICT: THE
        IMPLICATION OF MODERNIZATION IN NINETEENTH-CENTURY
        LATIN AMERICA." IN BURNS AND GRAHAM, RICHARD.
        ELITES, MASSES, AND MODERNIZATION IN LATIN AMERICA,
        1850-1930. AUSTIN: UNIVERSITY OF TEXAS PRESS, 1979,
        PP. 11-78.

19493   BURROUGHS, WILBUR G. "OBERLIN'S PART IN THE SLAVERY
        CONFLICT." OHIO ARCHAEOLOGICAL AND HISTORICAL
        PUBLICATIONS, 20 (APRIL, 1911): 269-334.

19494   CAMPBELL, STANLEY W. "ENFORCEMENT OF THE FUGITIVE SLAVE
        LAW, 1850-1860." PH.D. DISSERTATION, UNIVERSITY OF
        NORTH CAROLINA, 1967.

19495   CAMPBELL, STANLEY W. THE SLAVE CATCHERS: ENFORCEMENT OF
        THE FUGITIVE SLAVE LAW, 1850-1860. CHAPEL HILL:
        UNIVERSITY OF NORTH CAROLINA PRESS, 1968.

19496   "CANADIAN HOME OF THE ORIGINAL UNCLE TOM." CRISIS, 54
        (MARCH, 1947): 81.

19497   CARNOCHAN, JANET. "A SLAVE RESCUE IN NIAGARA SIXTY YEARS
        AGO." NIAGARA HISTORICAL SOCIETY PUBLICATIONS, 2
        (1897): 8-17.

19498   CARROLL, PATRICK J. "MANDINGA: THE EVOLUTION OF A
        MEXICAN RUNAWAY SLAVE COMMUNITY, 1735-1827."
        COMPARATIVE STUDIES IN SOCIETY AND HISTORY, 19
        (OCTOBER, 1977): 488-505.

19499   "THE CASE OF SIMS, 1851." PROCEEDINGS OF THE
        MASSACHUSETTS HISTORICAL SOCIETY, 45 (1912): 623-626.

19500   "CASPAR HANWAY AND THE FUGITIVE SLAVE LAW." MAGAZINE OF
        HISTORY, 21 (OCTOBER, 1915): 148-150.

19501   CHAMPION, THOMAS E. "THE UNDERGROUND RAILWAY AND ONE OF
        ITS OPERATORS." CANADIAN MAGAZINE, 5 (1895): 9-16.

19502   CHAPMAN, ABRAHAM (ED.). STEAL AWAY: STORIES OF THE
        RUNAWAY SLAVES. NEW YORK: PRAEGER, 1971.

19503   CHEEK, WILLIAM F. (ED.). BLACK RESISTANCE BEFORE THE
        CIVIL WAR. BEVERLY HILLS: GLENCOE PRESS, 1970.

19504   CHITTENDEN, ELIZABETH F. PROFILES IN BLACK AND WHITE:

STORIES OF MEN AND WOMEN WHO FOUGHT AGAINST SLAVERY.
NEW YORK: CHARLES SCRIBNER'S SONS, 1973.

19505   CHRISTY, SARAH R. "FUGITIVE SLAVES IN INDIANA COUNTY."
        WESTERN PENNSYLVANIA HISTORICAL MAGAZINE, 18 (1935):
        278-288.

19506   CLAIBORNE, WILLIAM B. "RUNAWAY SLAVES IN VIRGINIA."
        M.A. THESIS, VIRGINIA STATE UNIVERSITY, 1978.

19507   CLARK, JAMES W., JR. "THE FUGITIVE SLAVE AS HUMORIST."
        STUDIES IN AMERICAN HUMOR, 1 (OCTOBER, 1974): 73-78.

19508   CLARK, SARAH B. "LITERARY EXPRESSION OF RESISTANCE OF
        BLACKS IN THE UNITED STATES FROM 1800 TO 1940." IN
        BRIGHT, ALFRED L.; CLARK; AMADI, LAWRENCE E.; COOPER,
        SYRETHA; BARNES, CLARENCE; AND O'NEILL, DANIEL J. AN
        INTERDISCIPLINARY INTRODUCTION TO BLACK STUDIES.
        DUBUQUE: KENDALL/HUNT PUBLISHING COMPANY, 1977, PP.
        132-135.

19509   CLEVEN, N. ANDREW. "THE CONVENTION BETWEEN SPAIN AND
        HOLLAND REGULATING THE RETURN OF DESERTERS AND
        FUGITIVE SLAVES IN THEIR AMERICAN COLONIES." JOURNAL
        OF NEGRO HISTORY, 14 (JULY, 1929): 341-344.

19510   COATES, HOWARD N. "THE KIDNAPPING OF RACHEL AND
        ELIZABETH PARKER." LANCASTER COUNTY HISTORICAL
        SOCIETY PAPERS, 33 (MARCH, 1928): 31-39.

19511   COCHRANE, WILLIAM C. THE WESTERN RESERVE AND THE
        FUGITIVE SLAVE LAW: A PRELUDE TO THE CIVIL WAR.
        CLEVELAND: WESTERN RESERVE HISTORICAL SOCIETY
        PUBLICATION NO. 101, 1920.

19512   COCKRUM, WILLIAM M. HISTORY OF THE UNDERGROUND RAILROAD
        AS IT WAS CONDUCTED BY THE ANTI-SLAVERY LEAGUE.
        OAKLAND CITY, IN: J.W. COCKRUM, 1915.

19513   COFFIN, LEVI. REMINISCENCES OF LEVI COFFIN, THE REPUTED
        PRESIDENT OF THE UNDERGROUND RAILROAD. CINCINNATI:
        WESTERN TRACT SOCIETY, 1876.

19514   COLE, JOHNETTA. "MILITANT BLACK WOMEN IN EARLY U.S.
        HISTORY." BLACK SCHOLAR, 9 (APRIL, 1978): 38-44.

19515   COLLEY, VERNA. "ILLINOIS AND THE UNDERGROUND RAILROAD TO
        CANADA." TRANSACTIONS OF THE ILLINOIS STATE
        HISTORICAL SOCIETY FOR THE YEAR 1917, (1918): 76-98.

19516   CONKLIN, JULIA S. "THE UNDERGROUND RAILROAD IN INDIANA."
        INDIANA MAGAZINE OF HISTORY, 6 (JUNE, 1910): 63-74.

19517   COOPER, JOHN I. "THE MISSION OF THE FUGITIVE SLAVES AT
        LONDON." ONTARIO HISTORY, 46 (1954): 133-139.

19518   CROMWELL, JOHN W.   "THE EARLY NEGRO CONVENTION MOVEMENT."
         THE AMERICAN NEGRO ACADEMY OCCASIONAL PAPERS NO. 9.
         WASHINGTON: THE ACADEMY, 1904.

19519   CROW, JEFFREY J.   THE BLACK EXPERIENCE IN REVOLUTIONARY
         NORTH CAROLINA.   RALEIGH: NORTH CAROLINA DEPARTMENT
         OF CULTURAL RESOURCES, 1977.

19520   CROW, JEFFREY J.   "SLAVE REBELLIOUSNESS AND SOCIAL
         CONFLICT IN NORTH CAROLINA, 1775 TO 1802."   WILLIAM
         AND MARY QUARTERLY, 3RD SER., 37 (JANUARY, 1980):
         79-102.

19521   CRUZAT, HELOISE H.   "TRIAL AND SENTENCE CF BIRON, RUNAWAY
         NEGRO SLAVE, BEFORE THE SUPERIOR COUNCIL OF LOUISIANA,
         1728."   LOUISIANA HISTORICAL QUARTERLY, 8 (JANUARY,
         1925):   23-27.

19522   CURTIS, ANNA L.   STORIES OF THE UNDERGROUND.   NEW YORK:
         ISLAND WORKSHOP PRESS CO-OPERATIVE, 1941.

19523   DE FERARI, CARLO M.   "STEVEN SPENCER HILL, FUGITIVE FROM
         LABOR."   TUOLUMNE COUNTY HISTORICAL SOCIETY QUARTERLY,
         5 (JANUARY-MARCH, 1966):   162-164.

19524   DEMARIS, OVID.   AMERICA THE VIOLENT.   NEW YORK: COWLES
         BOOK COMPANY, 1970.

19525   DEWOLF, CALVIN.   "A FUGITIVE SLAVE IN CHICAGO."   CHICAGO
         HISTORY, 2 (SUMMER, 1951):   364-366.

19526   DICKMAN, JOSEPH C., JR.   "THE UNDERGROUND RAILROAD IN
         ILLINOIS: A STUDY IN PRACTICAL ABOLITIONISM."   M.A.
         THESIS, OHIO STATE UNIVERSITY, 1971.

19527   DIGGS, IRENE.   "THE CRAFTY SLAVE."   CRISIS, 60 (JANUARY,
         1953):   21-22.

19528   DIN, GILBERT C.   "CIMARRONES AND THE SAN MALO BAND IN
         SPANISH LOUISIANA."   LOUISIANA HISTORY, 21 (SUMMER,
         1980):   237-262.

19529   "DISPATCHES OF SPANISH OFFICIALS BEARING ON THE FREE
         NEGRO SETTLEMENT OF GRACIA REAL DE SANTA TERESA DE
         MOSE, FLORIDA."   JOURNAL OF NEGRO HISTORY, 9 (APRIL,
         1924):   144-195.

19530   DONALD, CLEVELAND JR.   "SLAVE RESISTANCE AND ABOLITIONISM
         IN BRAZIL: THE CAMPISTA CASE, 1879-1888."
         LUSO-BRAZILIAN REVIEW, 13 (WINTER, 1976):   182-193.

19531   DOVAN, EDWIN.   "THE MAROONS IN THE EIGHTEENTH CENTURY."
         CARIBBEAN QUARTERLY, 8 (1962):   25-27.

19532   DROTNING, PHILLIP T.   BLACK HEROES IN OUR NATION'S PAST.

NEW YORK: COWLES BOOK COMPANY, 1969.

19533   DUBOIS, W.E.B.   "THE LIE OF HISTORY AS IT IS TAUGHT
        TODAY." NEW YORK NATIONAL GUARDIAN, JULY 25, 1960.

19534   DUBOIS, W.E.B. THE SOULS OF BLACK FOLK: ESSAYS AND
        SKETCHES. CHICAGO: A.C. MCCLURG & COMPANY, 1903.

19535   EAKLOR, VICKI L. "MUSIC IN THE AMERICAN ANTISLAVERY
        MOVEMENT, 1830-1860." M.A. THESIS, WASHINGTON
        UNIVERSITY, 1979.

19536   EAKLOR, VICKI L. "THE SONGS OF THE EMANCIPATION CAR:
        VARIATIONS ON AN ABOLITIONIST THEME." BULLETIN OF THE
        MISSOURI HISTORICAL SOCIETY, 36 (JANUARY, 1980):
        92-102.

19537   EATON, CLEMENT. "THE MIND OF THE SOUTHERN NEGRO: THE
        REMARKABLE INDIVIDUALS." THE MIND OF THE OLD SOUTH.
        BATON ROUGE: LOUISIANA STATE UNIVERSITY PRESS, 1967,
        PP. 170-199.

19538   EDET, EDNA M. "BLACK PROTEST MUSIC." AFRO-AMERICAN
        STUDIES, 2 (SEPTEMBER, 1971):   107-116.

19539   EDET, EDNA M. "ONE HUNDRED YEARS OF BLACK PROTEST
        MUSIC." BLACK SCHOLAR, 7 (JULY-AUGUST, 1976):   38-48.

19540   EUSEBIJS, MARY. "A MODERN MOSES: HARRIET TUBMAN."
        JOURNAL OF NEGRO EDUCATION, 19 (WINTER, 1950):   16-27.

19541   FAIRCHILD, JAMES H. UNDERGROUND RAILROAD. CLEVELAND:
        WESTERN RESERVE HISTORICAL SOCIETY, 1877.

19542   FAREWELL, J.W. "THE ANDERSON CASE." CANADIAN LAW TIMES
        AND REVIEW, 32 (MARCH, 1912):   256-262.

19543   FARRELL, JOHN K.A. "SCHEMES FOR THE TRANSPLANTING OF
        REFUGEE AMERICAN NEGROES FROM UPPER CANADA IN THE
        1840'S." ONTARIO HISTORY, 52 (DECEMBER, 1960):
        245-250.

19544   FINGER, JOEL L. "VIRGINIA FUGITIVES OF THE 1850'S."
        M.A. THESIS, UNIVERSITY OF VIRGINIA, 1969.

19545   FONER, PHILIP S. "A PLEA AGAINST REENSLAVEMENT."
        PENNSYLVANIA HISTORY, 39 (APRIL, 1972):   239-241.

19546   FONER, PHILIP S. "THE TWO TRIALS OF JOHN READ: A
        FUGITIVE SLAVE WHO RESISTED REENSLAVEMENT." ESSAYS IN
        AFRO-AMERICAN HISTORY. PHILADELPHIA: TEMPLE
        UNIVERSITY PRESS, 1978, PP. 6-18.

19547   FORBES, DAVID R. A TRUE STORY OF THE CHRISTIANA RIOT.
        QUARRYVILLE, PA: SUN PRINTING HOUSE, 1898.

19548 FORTUNE, T. THOMAS. THE NEGRO IN POLITICS. NEW YORK:
       OGILVIE & ROWNTREE PUBLISHERS, 1886.

19549 FRANKLIN, JOHN H. THE MILITANT SOUTH, 1800-1861.
       CAMBRIDGE: HARVARD UNIVERSITY PRESS, 1956.

19550 FRANKLIN, JOHN H. "SLAVERY AND THE MARTIAL SOUTH."
       JOURNAL OF NEGRO HISTORY, 37 (JANUARY, 1952): 36-53.

19551 FRAZEE, GEORGE. "THE IOWA FUGITIVE SLAVE CASE." ANNALS
       OF IOWA, 4 (JULY, 1899): 118-137.

19552 FRAZEE, GEORGE. "AN IOWA FUGITIVE SLAVE CASE--1850."
       ANNALS OF IOWA, 6 (APRIL, 1903): 9-45.

19553 FREDRICKSON, GEORGE M. AND LASCH, CHRISTOPHER.
       "RESISTANCE TO SLAVERY." CIVIL WAR HISTORY, 13
       (DECEMBER, 1967): 315-329.

19554 FRIEDMAN, LAWRENCE J. THE WHITE SAVAGE: RACIAL
       FANTASIES IN THE POSTBELLUM SOUTH. ENGLEWOOD CLIFFS:
       PRENTICE-HALL, 1970.

19555 FRIEDMAN, TOM. "THE MINISTER WITH THE 35,000 LASHES."
       MOTHER JONES, 2 (MAY, 1977): 68-69.

19556 GAITHER, FRANCES O. THE RED COCK CROWS. NEW YORK:
       MACMILLAN COMPANY, 1944.

19557 GALPIN, W. FREEMAN. "THE JERRY RESCUE." NEW YORK
       HISTORY, 26 (JANUARY, 1945): 19-34.

19558 GARA, LARRY. "FRIENDS AND THE UNDERGROUND RAILROAD."
       QUAKER HISTORY, 51 (SPRING, 1962): 3-19.

19559 GARA, LARRY. "THE FUGITIVE SLAVE LAW IN THE EASTERN OHIO
       VALLEY." OHIO HISTORY, 72 (APRIL, 1963): 116-128.

19560 GARA, LARRY. THE LIBERTY LINE: THE LEGEND OF THE
       UNDERGROUND RAILROAD. LEXINGTON: UNIVERSITY OF
       KENTUCKY PRESS, 1961.

19561 GARA, LARRY. "THE PROFESSIONAL FUGITIVE IN THE ABOLITION
       MOVEMENT." WISCONSIN MAGAZINE OF HISTORY, 48 (SPRING,
       1965): 196-204.

19562 GARA, LARRY. "THE UNDERGROUND RAILROAD: A
       RE-EVALUATION." OHIO HISTORICAL QUARTERLY, 69 (JULY,
       1960): 217-230.

19563 GARA, LARRY. "THE UNDERGROUND RAILROAD IN ILLINOIS."
       JOURNAL OF THE ILLINOIS STATE HISTORICAL SOCIETY, 56
       (AUTUMN, 1963): 508-528.

19564 GARA, LARRY. "THE UNDERGROUND RAILROAD: LEGEND OR

REALITY?" PROCEEDINGS OF THE AMERICAN PHILOSOPHICAL
SOCIETY, 105 (JUNE, 1961): 334-339.

19565 GARA, LARRY. "WILLIAM STILL AND THE UNDERGROUND
RAILROAD." PENNSYLVANIA HISTORY, 28 (JANUARY, 1961):
33-44.

19566 GARDNER, THEODORE. "AN EPISODE IN KANSAS HISTORY: THE
DOY RESCUE." KANSAS STATE HISTORICAL SOCIETY
COLLECTIONS, 17 (1928): 851-855.

19567 GARRETSON, O.A. "TRAVELLING ON THE UNDERGROUND RAILROAD
IN IOWA." IOWA JOURNAL OF HISTORY AND POLITICS, 22
(JULY, 1924): 418-453.

19568 GASPAR, D. BARRY. "SLAVE RESISTANCE AND SOCIAL CONTROL
IN ANTIGUA, 1700-1763." PH.D. DISSERTATION, JOHNS
HOPKINS UNIVERSITY, 1974.

19569 GASPAR, DAVID B. "THE ANTIGUA SLAVE CONSPIRACY OF 1736:
A CASE STUDY OF THE ORIGINS OF COLLECTIVE RESISTANCE."
WILLIAM AND MARY QUARTERLY, 3RD SER., 35 (APRIL,
1978): 308-324.

19570 GELLERT, LAWRENCE. "NEGRO SONGS OF PROTEST." IN CUNARD,
NANCY (ED.). NEGRO ANTHOLOGY. LONDON: WISHART,
1934, PP. 366-377.

19571 GENOVESE, EUGENE D. "REBELLIOUSNESS AND DUCILITY IN THE
NEGRO SLAVE: A CRITIQUE OF THE ELKINS THESIS." CIVIL
WAR HISTORY, 13 (DECEMBER, 1967): 293-314.

19572 GERLACH, DON R. "BLACK ARSON IN ALBANY, NEW YORK,
NOVEMBER, 1793." JOURNAL OF BLACK STUDIES, 7 (MARCH,
1977): 301-312.

19573 GORDON, ASA H. SKETCHES OF NEGRO LIFE AND HISTORY IN
SOUTH CAROLINA. HAMMOND, IN: W.B. CONKEY, 1929.

19574 GORDON, ASA H. "THE SLAVES' STRUGGLE FOR FREEDOM IN
SOUTH CAROLINA." M.A. THESIS, COLUMBIA UNIVERSITY,
1932.

19575 GORN, ELLIOTT J. "'. . . NO WHITE MAN COULD WHIP ME':
FOLK BELIEFS OF THE SLAVE COMMUNITY." M.A. THESIS,
UNIVERSITY OF CALIFORNIA, 1975.

19576 GRANADE, RAY. "SLAVE UNREST IN FLORIDA." FLORIDA
HISTORICAL QUARTERLY, 55 (JULY, 1976): 18-36.

19577 GRANT, JOANNE (ED.). BLACK PROTEST: HISTORY, DOCUMENTS,
AND ANALYSES, 1619 TO THE PRESENT. NEW YORK: FAWCETT
WORLD LIBRARY, 1968.

19578 GRAU, RICHARD. "THE CHRISTIANA RIOT OF 1851: A

REAPPRAISAL." JOURNAL OF THE LANCASTER COUNTY
HISTORICAL SOCIETY, 68 (1964): 147-175.

19579 GREENWAY, JOHN. "NEGRO SONGS OF PROTEST." AMERICAN
       FOLKSONGS OF PROTEST. PHILADELPHIA: UNIVERSITY OF
       PENNSYLVANIA PRESS, 1953, PP. 67-120.

19580 GRIEST, ELLWOOD. JOHN AND MARY; OR, THE FUGITIVE SLAVES,
       A TALE OF SOUTH-EASTERN PENNSYLVANIA. LANCASTER, PA:
       LANCASTER INQUIRER, 1873.

19581 GRIMKE, ARCHIBALD H. "PREJUDICE, PREPARING, ERUPTION."
       NEW YORK AGE, NOVEMBER 30, 1905.

19582 HAGGARD, JUAN V. "THE NEUTRAL GROUND BETWEEN LOUISIANA
       AND TEXAS, 1806-1821." PH.D. DISSERTATION, UNIVERSITY
       OF TEXAS, 1942.

19583 HALASZ, NICHOLAS. THE RATTLING CHAINS; SLAVE UNREST AND
       REVOLT IN THE ANTE-BELLUM SOUTH. NEW YORK: D. MCKAY
       COMPANY, 1966.

19584 HALE, FRANK W. "BLACK PROTEST: PAST AND PRESENT--TWO
       HUNDRED YEARS OF BLACK RESISTANCE TO OPPRESSION."
       NEGRO EDUCATIONAL REVIEW, 27 (JULY/OCTOBER, 1976):
       182-206.

19585 HARDING, VINCENT. "RELIGION AND RESISTANCE AMONG
       ANTEBELLUM NEGROES, 1800-1860." IN MEIER, AUGUST AND
       RUDWICK, ELLIOTT (EDS.). THE MAKING OF BLACK AMERICA:
       ESSAYS IN NEGRO LIFE & HISTORY. 2 VOLS. NEW YORK:
       ATHENEUM, 1974, VOL. 1, PP. 179-197.

19586 HATFIELD, EDWIN F. HISTORY OF ELIZABETH, NEW JERSEY;
       INCLUDING THE EARLY HISTORY OF UNION COUNTY. NEW
       YORK: CARLTON & LANAHAN, 1868.

19587 HEARD, PATRICIA L. AND HODSON, FLORENCE T. "THE NORTH
       STAR ROUTE THROUGH SANDWICH." ANNUAL EXCURSION OF THE
       SANDWICH HISTORICAL ASSOCIATION, 56 (1975): 3-8.

19588 HELPLER, MORRIS K. "NEGROES AND CRIME IN NEW ORLEANS,
       1850-1861." M.A. THESIS, TULANE UNIVERSITY, 1960.

19589 HENSEL, WILLIAM U. "AFTERMATH SUPPLEMENTARY TO HISTORY
       OF THE CHRISTIANA RIOT, 1851." LANCASTER COUNTY
       HISTORICAL SOCIETY PAPERS, 16 (1912): 133-141.

19590 HENSEL, WILLIAM U. THE CHRISTIANA RIOT AND THE TREASON
       TRIALS OF 1851: AN HISTORICAL SKETCH. LANCASTER, PA:
       NEW ERA PRINTING COMPANY, 1911.

19591 HERRICK, J.P. "STORY OF A NOBLE LIFE: REV. CALVIN
       FAIRBANK AND HIS WORK FOR THE SLAVE." HISTORICAL
       WYOMING, 1 (JULY, 1948): 79-82.

19592   HEWITT, JOHN H. "THE STORY OF CINJJE THE SLAVE." NEGRO
        DIGEST, 13 (JULY, 1964): 71-74.

19593   HICKS, GRANVILLE. "DR. CHANNING AND THE CREOLE CASE."
        AMERICAN HISTORICAL REVIEW, 37 (APRIL, 1932): 516-525.

19594   HIGGINSON, THOMAS W. TRAVELLERS AND OUTLAWS: EPISODES IN
        AMERICAN HISTORY. BOSTON: LEE AND SHEPARD, 1889.

19595   HILL, JUDITH A.R. "FEDERAL FUGITIVE SLAVE POLICY:
        APPREHENSION TO EMANCIPATION (THE ROLE OF MILITARY
        CONDITIONS IN FORCING THE ISSUE OF EMANCIPATION)."
        M.A. THESIS, CALIFORNIA STATE UNIVERSITY, FULLERTON,
        1974.

19596   HINE, DARLENE C. "FEMALE SLAVE RESISTANCE: THE
        ECONOMICS OF SEX." WESTERN JOURNAL OF BLACK STUDIES,
        3 (SUMMER, 1979): 123-127.

19597   HINSHAW, IDRIS E. "FUGITIVE SLAVES IN INDIANA." M.A.
        THESIS, COLUMBIA UNIVERSITY, 1931.

19598   HITE, ROGER W. "VOICES OF A FUGITIVE: HENRY BIBB AND
        ANTEBELLUM BLACK SEPARATISM." JOURNAL OF BLACK
        STUDIES, 5 (MARCH, 1974): 269-284.

19599   HOSTETTER, ALBERT K. "THE NEWSPAPERS AND THE CHRISTIANA
        RIOT." LANCASTER COUNTY HISTORICAL SOCIETY PAPERS, 15
        (1911): 296-308.

19600   HOWE, BENNIE W. "THE FUGITIVE SLAVE PROBLEM IN SOUTH
        CAROLINA AND FLORIDA, 1670-1763: A CONTRAST IN
        ATTITUDES." M.A. THESIS, OHIO STATE UNIVERSITY, 1962.

19601   HUTCHINSON, LOUISE D. OUT OF AFRICA: FROM WEST AFRICAN
        KINGDOMS TO COLONIZATION. WASHINGTON: SMITHSONIAN
        INSTITUTION PRESS, 1979.

19602   "AN IMPORTANT FUGITIVE SLAVE CASE." INDIANA MAGAZINE OF
        HISTORY, 7 (MARCH, 1911): 23-24.

19603   "AN IOWA FUGITIVE SLAVE CASE." ANNALS OF IOWA, 2
        (OCTOBER, 1896): 531-539.

19604   JENSEN, CAROL. "HISTORY OF THE NEGRO COMMUNITY IN ESSEX
        COUNTY, 1850-1860." M.A. THESIS, UNIVERSITY OF
        WINDSOR, 1966.

19605   JOHNSON, AUGUSTA J. "AN INTRODUCTION TO THE
        AUTOBIOGRAPHY OF GUSTAVUS VASSA." M.A. THESIS,
        ATLANTA UNIVERSITY, 1936.

19606   JOHNSON, F. ROY. TALES FROM OLD CAROLINA. MURFREESBORO,
        NC: JOHNSON, 1965.

19607 JOHNSON, HOMER U. FROM DIXIE TO CANADA, ROMANCES AND
       REALITIES OF THE UNDERGROUND RAILROAD. BUFFALO:
       CHARLES WELLS MOULTON, 1894.

19608 JONES, RHETT S. "THE TRANSFORMATION OF MAROON IDENTITY
       IN JAMAICA, 1738-1795." IN B.O.P. (BLACKS ON PAPER).
       PROVIDENCE: BROWN UNIVERSITY, AFRO-AMERICAN STUDIES,
       1975, PP. 94-100.

19609 JONES, RHETT S. "WHITE SETTLERS, BLACK REBELS: JAMAICA
       IN THE ERA OF THE FIRST MAROON WAR, 1655-1738." PH.D.
       DISSERTATION, BROWN UNIVERSITY, 1976.

19610 KAPLAN, SIDNEY. "THE 'DOMESTIC INSURRECTIONS' OF THE
       DECLARATION OF INDEPENDENCE." JOURNAL OF NEGRO
       HISTORY, 61 (OCTOBER, 1976): 243-255.

19611 KATZ, JONATHAN. RESISTANCE AT CHRISTIANA: THE FUGITIVE
       SLAVE REBELLION, CHRISTIANA, PENNSYLVANIA, SEPTEMBER
       11, 1851: A DOCUMENTARY ACCOUNT. NEW YORK: THOMAS Y.
       CROWELL, 1974.

19612 KATZ, WILLIAM L. "BLACK AND INDIAN COOPERATION AND
       RESISTANCE TO SLAVERY." FREEDOMWAYS, 17 (THIRD
       QUARTER, 1977): 164-174.

19613 KETCHUM, ALTON. "THE AMERICAN CIVIL WAR." AMERICAN
       REVIEW, 1 (SPRING, 1961): 32-48.

19614 KNABENSHUE, S.S. "THE UNDERGROUND RAILROAD." OHIO
       ARCHAEOLOGICAL AND HISTORICAL QUARTERLY, 14 (1905):
       397-404.

19615 KOCH, FELIX J. "MARKING THE OLD 'ABOLITION HOLES.'"
       OHIO ARCHAEOLOGICAL AND HISTORICAL QUARTERLY, 22
       (APRIL, 1913): 308-318.

19616 KOLCHIN, PETER. "THE PROCESS OF CONFRONTATION: PATTERNS
       OF RESISTANCE TO BONDAGE IN NINETEENTH-CENTURY RUSSIA
       AND THE UNITED STATES." JOURNAL OF SOCIAL HISTORY, 11
       (SUMMER, 1978): 457-490.

19617 LANDON, FRED. "AGRICULTURE AMONG THE NEGRO REFUGEES IN
       UPPER CANADA." JOURNAL OF NEGRO HISTORY, 21 (JULY,
       1936): 304-312.

19618 LANDON, FRED. "AMHERSTBURG, TERMINUS OF THE UNDERGROUND
       RAILROAD." JOURNAL OF NEGRO HISTORY, 10 (JANUARY,
       1925): 1-9.

19619 LANDON, FRED. "THE ANDERSON FUGITIVE CASE." JOURNAL OF
       NEGRO HISTORY, 7 (JULY, 1922): 233-242.

19620 LANDON, FRED. "ANTHONY BURNS IN CANADA." PAPERS AND
       RECORDS OF THE ONTARIO HISTORICAL SOCIETY, 22 (1925):

162-166.

19621 LANDON, FRED. "THE ANTI-SLAVERY SOCIETY OF CANADA."
JOURNAL OF NEGRO HISTORY, 4 (JANUARY, 1919): 33-40.

19622 LANDON, FRED. "THE BUXTON SETTLEMENT IN CANADA."
JOURNAL OF NEGRO HISTORY, 3 (OCTOBER, 1918): 360-367.

19623 LANDON, FRED. "CANADA AND THE UNDERGROUND RAILROAD."
REPORTS AND PROCEEDINGS OF THE KINGSTON HISTORICAL
SOCIETY, (1923): 17-31.

19624 LANDON, FRED. "CANADA'S PART IN FREEING THE SLAVE."
PAPERS AND RECORDS OF THE ONTARIO HISTORICAL SOCIETY,
17 (1919): 74-84.

19625 LANDON, FRED. "THE CANADIAN ANTI-SLAVERY GROUP BEFORE
THE CIVIL WAR." UNIVERSITY MAGAZINE, 18 (DECEMBER,
1918): 540-547.

19626 LANDON, FRED. "CANADIAN NEGROES AND THE JOHN BROWN
RAID." JOURNAL OF NEGRO HISTORY, 6 (APRIL, 1921):
174-182.

19627 LANDON, FRED. "A DARING CANADIAN ABOLITIONIST."
MICHIGAN HISTORY MAGAZINE, 5 (JULY-OCTOBER, 1921):
364-373.

19628 LANDON, FRED. "THE FUGITIVE SLAVE IN CANADA."
UNIVERSITY MAGAZINE, 18 (APRIL, 1919): 270-279.

19629 LANDON, FRED. "FUGITIVE SLAVES IN LONDON, ONTARIO BEFORE
1860." TRANSACTIONS OF THE LONDON AND MIDDLESEX
HISTORICAL SOCIETY, 10 (1919): 25-38.

19630 LANDON, FRED. "FUGITIVE SLAVES IN ONTARIO." NORTHWEST
OHIO HISTORICAL SOCIETY QUARTERLY BULLETIN, 8 (1936):
1-12.

19631 LANDON, FRED. "HENRY BIBB, A COLONIZER." JOURNAL OF
NEGRO HISTORY, 5 (OCTOBER, 1920): 437-447.

19632 LANDON, FRED. "THE NEGRO MIGRATION TO CANADA AFTER THE
PASSING OF THE FUGITIVE SLAVE ACT." JOURNAL OF NEGRO
HISTORY, 5 (JANUARY, 1920): 22-36.

19633 LANDON, FRED. "OVER LAKE ERIE TO FREEDOM." NORTHWEST
OHIO HISTORICAL QUARTERLY, 17 (1945): 132-138.

19634 LANDON, FRED. "THE RELATION OF CANADA TO THE
ANTI-SLAVERY AND ABOLITION MOVEMENTS IN THE UNITED
STATES." M.A. THESIS, UNIVERSITY OF WESTERN ONTARIO,
1919.

19635 LANDON, FRED. "THE UNDERGROUND RAILROAD ALONG THE

DETROIT RIVER." MICHIGAN HISTORY, 39 (MARCH, 1955):
63-68.

19636 LAPP, RUDOLPH M. ARCHY LEE, A CALIFORNIA FUGITIVE SLAVE
CASE. SAN FRANCISCO: BOOK CLUB OF CALIFORNIA, 1969.

19637 LAPP, RUDOLPH M. "NEGRO RIGHTS ACTIVITIES IN GOLD RUSH
CALIFORNIA." CALIFORNIA HISTORICAL SOCIETY QUARTERLY,
45 (MARCH, 1966): 3-20.

19638 LARA, BRUNO D. "RESISTANCE TO SLAVERY: FROM AFRICA TO
BLACK AMERICA." IN RUBIN, VERA AND TUDEN, ARTHUR
(EDS.). COMPARATIVE PERSPECTIVES ON SLAVERY IN NEW
WORLD PLANTATION SOCIETIES. NEW YORK: NEW YORK
ACADEMY OF SCIENCES, 1977, PP. 464-480.

19639 LAWRENCE, JACOB. HARRIET AND THE PROMISED LAND. NEW
YORK: WINDMILL BOOKS, 1968.

19640 LEASK, J. MACKENZIE. "JESSE HAPPY, A FUGITIVE SLAVE FROM
KENTUCKY." ONTARIO HISTORY, 54 (JUNE, 1962): 87-98.

19641 LEDBETTER, BILLY D. "SLAVE UNREST AND WHITE PANIC: THE
IMPACT OF BLACK REPUBLICANISM IN ANTE-BELLUM TEXAS."
TEXANA, 10 (1972): 335-350.

19642 LEE, B.F., JR. "NEGRO ORGANIZATIONS." ANNALS OF THE
AMERICAN ACADEMY OF POLITICAL AND SOCIAL SCIENCE, 49
(SEPTEMBER, 1913): 129-137.

19643 LESLIE, WILLIAM R. "THE PENNSYLVANIA FUGITIVE SLAVE ACT
OF 1826." JOURNAL OF SOUTHERN HISTORY, 18 (NOVEMBER,
1952): 429-445.

19644 LEVERING, WILLIAM J. "PENNSYLVANIA AND THE FUGITIVE
SLAVE ISSUE IN THE EARLY 1850S." M.A. THESIS,
UNIVERSITY OF MARYLAND, 1970.

19645 LEVY, LEONARD W. "THE 'ABOLITION RIOT': BOSTON'S FIRST
SLAVE RESCUE." NEW ENGLAND QUARTERLY, 25 (MARCH,
1952): 85-92.

19646 LEVY, LEONARD W. "SIMS' CASE: THE FUGITIVE SLAVE LAW IN
BOSTON." JOURNAL OF NEGRO HISTORY, 35 (JANUARY,
1950): 49-74.

19647 LEWIS, G. MALCOLM. "GEOGRAPHICAL ASPECTS OF RACE-RELATED
VIOLENCE IN THE UNITED STATES." IN WATSON, J. WREFORD
AND O'RIORDAN, TIMOTHY (EDS.). THE AMERICAN
ENVIRONMENT: PERCEPTIONS AND POLICIES. LONDON: JOHN
WILEY, 1976, PP. 115-136.

19648 LEWIS, JAMES K. "THE RELIGIOUS LIFE OF FUGITIVE SLAVES
AND RISE OF COLOURED BAPTIST CHURCHES, 1820-1865, IN
WHAT IS NOW KNOWN AS ONTARIO." B.D. THESIS, MCMASTER

UNIVERSITY, 1965.

19649　LEWIS, JAMES K.　"RELIGIOUS LIFE OF FUGITIVE SLAVES AND
　　　　　RISE OF COLOURED BAPTIST CHURCHES, 1820-1865, IN WHAT
　　　　　IS NOW KNOWN AS ONTARIO."　M.A. THESIS, MCMASTER
　　　　　DIVINITY COLLEGE, 1965.

19650　LEWIS, JAMES K.　RELIGIOUS LIFE OF FUGITIVE SLAVES AND
　　　　　RISE OF COLOURED BAPTIST CHURCHES, 1820-1865, IN WHAT
　　　　　IS NOW KNOWN AS ONTARIO.　NEW YORK:　ARNO PRESS, 1980.

19651　LEWIS, JAMES K.　"RELIGIOUS NATURE OF THE EARLY NEGRO
　　　　　MIGRATION TO CANADA AND THE AMHERSTBURG BAPTIST
　　　　　ASSOCIATION."　ONTARIO HISTORY, 58 (JUNE, 1966):
　　　　　117-132.

19652　LOGSDON, JOSEPH.　"DIARY OF A SLAVE:　RECOLLECTION AND
　　　　　PROPHECY."　IN SHADE, WILLIAM G. AND HERRENKOHL, ROY
　　　　　C. (EDS.).　SEVEN ON BLACK:　REFLECTIONS ON THE NEGRO
　　　　　EXPERIENCE IN AMERICA.　PHILADELPHIA:　J.B.
　　　　　LIPPINCOTT, 1969, PP. 24-49.

19653　LOVE, EDGAR F.　"NEGRO RESISTANCE TO SPANISH RULE IN
　　　　　COLONIAL MEXICO."　JOURNAL OF NEGRO HISTORY, 52
　　　　　(APRIL, 1967):　89-103.

19654　LUCAS, FREDERICK A.　"CHRISTIANITY AND THE MILITANT
　　　　　SLAVE."　B.A. THESIS, HARVARD UNIVERSITY, 1972.

19655　LUDLOW, FITZHUGH.　"IF MASSA PUT GUNS INTO OUR HAN'S."
　　　　　ATLANTIC MONTHLY, 15 (APRIL, 1865):　504-512.

19656　LUMPKIN, KATHERINE D.　"'THE GENERAL PLAN WAS FREEDOM':
　　　　　A NEGRO SECRET ORDER ON THE UNDERGROUND RAILROAD."
　　　　　PHYLON, 28 (SPRING, 1967):　63-77.

19657　MAGEE, DAVID F.　"THE CHRISTIANA RIOT:　ITS CAUSES AND
　　　　　EFFECTS FROM A SOUTHERN STANDPOINT."　LANCASTER COUNTY
　　　　　HISTORICAL SOCIETY PAPERS, 15 (1911):　193-208.

19658　MAGILL, EDWARD H.　"WHEN MEN WERE SOLD; REMINISCENCES OF
　　　　　THE UNDERGROUND RAILROAD IN BUCKS COUNTY AND ITS
　　　　　MANAGERS."　BUCKS COUNTY HISTORICAL SOCIETY
　　　　　COLLECTIONS, 2 (1909):　493-520.

19659　MAGINNES, DAVID R.　"THE POINT OF HONOR:　THE RENDITION
　　　　　OF THE FUGITIVE SLAVE ANTHONY BURNS, BOSTON, 1854."
　　　　　PH.D. DISSERTATION, COLUMBIA UNIVERSITY, 1973.

19660　MALEHORN, W.M.　"FUGITIVE SLAVE LAW OF 1850:　ITS
　　　　　ENFORCEMENT IN OHIO."　M.A. THESIS, OHIO STATE
　　　　　UNIVERSITY, 1928.

19661　MANN, CHARLES W.　THE CHICAGO COMMON COUNCIL AND THE
　　　　　FUGITIVE SLAVE LAW OF 1850.　CHICAGO:　CHICAGO

HISTORICAL SOCIETY, 1903.

19662   MANN, KENNETH E. "NINETEENTH CENTURY BLACK MILITANT:
        HENRY HIGHLAND GARNET'S ADDRESS TO THE SLAVES."
        SOUTHERN SPEECH JOURNAL, 36 (FALL, 1970): 11-21.

19663   MARTIN, GRAHAM E. "THE UNDERGROUND RAILROAD IN INDIANA."
        M.A. THESIS, HOWARD UNIVERSITY, 1942.

19664   MCCLURE, STANLEY W. "THE UNDERGROUND RAILROAD IN
        SOUTH-CENTRAL OHIO." M.A. THESIS, OHIO STATE
        UNIVERSITY, 1932.

19665   MCDOUGALL, MARIAN G. "FUGITIVE SLAVES." ACADEMY, 42
        (NOVEMBER 5, 1892): 410.

19666   MCDOUGALL, MARIAN G. FUGITIVE SLAVES, 1619-1865.
        BOSTON: GINN & COMPANY, 1891.

19667   MCDOUGALL, MARION G. "FUGITIVE SLAVES (1619-1865)." FAY
        HOUSE MONOGRAPHS, NO. 3 (1891): III-150.

19668   MCGOVERN, ANN. RUNAWAY SLAVE: THE STORY OF HARRIET
        TUBMAN. NEW YORK: FOUR WINDS PRESS, 1965.

19669   MCKINNON, WILLIAM. "NEIGHBORS: A ROUTE OF THE
        UNDERGROUND RAILROAD, PENNSYLVANIA AND NEW YORK." NEW
        YORK FOLKLORE QUARTERLY, 8 (AUTUMN, 1952): 227-229.

19670   MEADERS, DANIEL E. "SOUTH CAROLINA FUGITIVES AS VIEWED
        THROUGH LOCAL COLONIAL NEWSPAPERS WITH EMPHASIS ON
        RUNAWAY NOTICES, 1732-1801." JOURNAL OF NEGRO
        HISTORY, 60 (APRIL, 1975): 288-319.

19671   MEREDITH, WILLIAM J. "THE NEGRO IN THE ANTI-SLAVERY
        MOVEMENT." M.A. THESIS, OHIO STATE UNIVERSITY, 1930.

19672   MERKEL, BENJAMIN G. "THE UNDERGROUND RAILROAD AND THE
        MISSOURI BORDERS, 1840-1860." MISSOURI HISTORICAL
        REVIEW, 37 (APRIL, 1943): 271-285.

19673   MINICK, ALICE A. "THE UNDERGROUND RAILWAY IN NEBRASKA."
        PROCEEDINGS AND COLLECTIONS OF THE NEBRASKA STATE
        HISTORICAL SOCIETY, 7 (1893): 70-79.

19674   MINTZ, SIDNEY W. "TOWARD AN AFRO-AMERICAN HISTORY."
        CAHIERS D'HISTOIRE MONDIALE, 8 (1971): 317-332.

19675   MONEY, CHARLES H. "THE FUGITIVE SLAVE LAW IN INDIANA."
        INDIANA MAGAZINE OF HISTORY, 17 (JUNE, SEPTEMBER,
        1921): 159-198, 257-297.

19676   MOOREN, ROBERT L. "THE SLAVE TRADE AND FUGITIVE SLAVES
        DURING THE CIVIL WAR." M.A. THESIS, UNIVERSITY OF
        WISCONSIN, 1949.

19677   MORRILL, RICHARD L. AND DONALDSON, D. FRED.
         "GEOGRAPHICAL PERSPECTIVES ON THE HISTORY OF BLACK
         AMERICA." IN ERNST, ROBERT T. AND HUGG, LAWRENCE
         (EDS.). BLACK AMERICA: GEOGRAPHIC PERSPECTIVES.
         GARDEN CITY: ANCHOR PRESS/DOUBLEDAY, 1976, PP. 9-33.

19678   MORSBERGER, ROBERT E. "SLAVERY AND THE SANTA FE TRAIL,
         OR, JOHN BROWN ON HOLLYWOOD'S SOUR APPLE TREE."
         AMERICAN STUDIES, 18 (FALL, 1977): 87-98.

19679   MURAPA, RUKUDZO. "MAROONS: MAU MAU PREDECESSORS."
         BLACK WORLD, 19 (JULY, 1970): 33-38.

19680   MURDOCK, WILLIAM J. "SLAVE SAVER." NEGRO DIGEST, 7
         (JANUARY, 1949): 64-66.

19681   MUTUNHJ, TENDAI. "TOMPKINS COUNTY: AN UNDERGROUND
         RAILROAD TRANSIT IN CENTRAL NEW YORK." AFRO-AMERICANS
         IN NEW YORK LIFE AND HISTORY, 3 (JULY, 1979): 15-33.

19682   NASH, RODERICK. "THE CHRISTIANA RIOT: AN EVALUATION OF
         ITS NATIONAL SIGNIFICANCE." JOURNAL OF THE LANCASTER
         COUNTY HISTORICAL SOCIETY, 65 (SPRING, 1961): 65-91.

19683   NASH, RODERICK W. "WILLIAM PARKER AND THE CHRISTIANA
         RIOT." JOURNAL OF NEGRO HISTORY, 46 (JANUARY, 1961):
         24-31.

19684   "THE NEGRO IN CANADA." NEGRO HISTORY BULLETIN, 12
         (OCTOBER, 1948): 19-22.

19685   NOGEE, JOSEPH L. "FUGITIVE SLAVERY IN THE NORTHEASTERN
         STATES, 1842-1850." M.A. THESIS, UNIVERSITY OF
         CHICAGO, 1951.

19686   NOGEE, JOSEPH L. "THE PRIGG CASE AND FUGITIVE SLAVERY,
         1842-1850." JOURNAL OF NEGRO HISTORY, 39 (JULY,
         1954): 185-205.

19687   NORCROSS, GRENVILLE H. "GEORGE LATIMER." MASSACHUSETTS
         HISTORICAL SOCIETY PROCEEDINGS, 56 (1923): 170-171.

19688   OFARI, EARL. "LET YOUR MOTTO BE RESISTANCE": THE LIFE
         AND THOUGHT OF HENRY HIGHLAND GARNET. BOSTON: BEACON
         PRESS, 1972.

19689   OFARI, EARL. "THE ROOTS OF BLACK RADICALISM." NEGRO
         DIGEST, 18 (AUGUST, 1969): 18-21, 70.

19690   OHLINE, HOWARD A. "GEORGETOWN, SOUTH CAROLINA: RACIAL
         ANXIETIES AND MILITANT BEHAVIOR, 1802." SOUTH
         CAROLINA HISTORICAL MAGAZINE, 73 (JULY, 1972):
         130-140.

19691   "OLD PASSAGES OF BOSTON'S UNDERGROUND RAILROAD."

MAGAZINE OF HISTORY, 31 (1926): 31-43.

19692 OWENS, LESLIE H. THIS SPECIES OF PROPERTY: SLAVE LIFE
AND CULTURE IN THE OLD SOUTH. NEW YORK: OXFORD
UNIVERSITY PRESS, 1976.

19693 PALMER, GERTRUDE E. "HARRIET TUBMAN: MOSES OF THE
AMERICAN NEGRO." M.A. THESIS, ST. JOHN'S UNIVERSITY,
1946.

19694 PANTLE, ALBERTA (ED.). "THE STORY OF A KANSAS FREEDMAN."
KANSAS HISTORICAL QUARTERLY, 11 (NOVEMBER, 1942):
341-369.

19695 PARISH, JOHN C. "AN EARLY FUGITIVE SLAVE CASE WEST OF
THE MISSISSIPPI RIVER." IOWA JOURNAL OF HISTORY AND
POLITICS, 6 (JANUARY, 1908): 88-95.

19696 PARKER, FREDDIE L. "SLAVE PROTEST IN NORTH CAROLINA,
1775-1835." M.A. THESIS, NORTH CAROLINA CENTRAL
UNIVERSITY, 1976.

19697 PAYNTER, JOHN H. "THE FUGITIVES OF THE PEARL." JOURNAL
OF NEGRO HISTORY, 1 (JULY, 1916): 243-264.

19698 PAYNTER, JOHN H. FUGITIVES OF THE PEARL. WASHINGTON:
ASSOCIATED PUBLISHERS, 1930.

19699 PEASE, JANE H. AND PEASE, WILLIAM H. THE FUGITIVE SLAVE
LAW AND ANTHONY BURNS: A PROBLEM IN ENFORCEMENT.
PHILADELPHIA: J.B. LIPPINCOTT, 1975.

19700 PEASE, JANE H. AND PEASE, WILLIAM H. THEY WHO WOULD BE
FREE: BLACKS' SEARCH FOR FREEDOM, 1830-1861. NEW
YORK: ATHENEUM, 1974.

19701 PEASE, WILLIAM H. AND PEASE, JANE H. "OPPOSITION TO THE
FOUNDING OF THE ELGIN SETTLEMENT." CANADIAN
HISTORICAL REVIEW, 38 (SEPTEMBER, 1957): 202-218.

19702 PEEKS, EDWARD. THE LONG STRUGGLE FOR BLACK POWER. NEW
YORK: CHARLES SCRIBNER'S SONS, 1971.

19703 PETRY, ANN. HARRIET TUBMAN: CONDUCTOR OF THE
UNDERGROUND RAILROAD. NEW YORK: CROWELL, 1955.

19704 PETTIT, EBER M. SKETCHES IN THE HISTORY OF THE
UNDERGROUND RAILROAD. FREDONIA, NY: W. MCKINSTRY,
1879.

19705 PHILLIPS, ULRICH B. "SLAVE CRIME IN VIRGINIA." AMERICAN
HISTORICAL REVIEW, 20 (JANUARY, 1915): 336-340.

19706 PIERCE, BESSIE L. A HISTORY OF CHICAGO, 1673-1848. NEW
YORK: A.A. KNOPF, 1937.

19707 PIERSEN, WILLIAM D. "WHITE CANNIBALS, BLACK MARTYRS:
       FEAR, DEPRESSION, AND RELIGIOUS FAITH AS CAUSES OF
       SUICIDE AMONG NEW SLAVES." JOURNAL OF NEGRO HISTORY,
       62 (APRIL, 1977): 147-159.

19708 PILTON, JAMES W. "EARLY NEGRO SETTLEMENT IN VICTORIA."
       B.A. THESIS, UNIVERSITY OF BRITISH COLUMBIA, 1949.

19709 PILTON, JAMES W. "NEGRO SETTLEMENT IN BRITISH COLUMBIA,
       1853-1871." M.A. THESIS, UNIVERSITY OF BRITISH
       COLUMBIA, 1951.

19710 PORTER, KENNETH W. "FLORIDA SLAVES AND FREE NEGROES IN
       THE SEMINOLE WAR, 1835-1842." JOURNAL OF NEGRO
       HISTORY, 28 (OCTOBER, 1943): 390-421.

19711 PORTER, KENNETH W. "JOHN CAESAR: A FORGOTTEN HERO OF
       THE SEMINOLE WAR." JOURNAL OF NEGRO HISTORY, 28
       (JANUARY, 1943): 53-65.

19712 PORTER, KENNETH W. "JOHN CAESAR: SEMINOLE NEGRO
       PARTISAN." JOURNAL OF NEGRO HISTORY, 31 (APRIL,
       1946): 190-207.   .

19713 PORTER, KENNETH W. "LOUIS PACHECO: THE MAN AND THE
       MYTH." JOURNAL OF NEGRO HISTORY, 28 (JANUARY, 1943):
       65-72.

19714 PORTER, KENNETH W. "NEGRO GUIDES AND INTERPRETERS IN THE
       EARLY STAGES OF THE SEMINOLE WAR, DECEMBER 28,
       1835-MARCH 6, 1837." JOURNAL OF NEGRO HISTORY, 35
       (APRIL, 1950): 174-183.

19715 PORTER, KENNETH W. "NEGROES AND THE SEMINOLE WAR,
       1817-1818." JOURNAL OF NEGRO HISTORY, 36 (JULY,
       1951): 249-280.

19716 PRESTON, E. DELORUS. "THE UNDERGROUND RAILROAD IN
       NORTHWEST OHIO." JOURNAL OF NEGRO HISTORY, 17
       (OCTOBER, 1932): 409-436.

19717 PRESTON, E. DELORUS JR. "THE GENESIS OF THE UNDERGROUND
       RAILROAD." JOURNAL OF NEGRO HISTORY, 18 (APRIL,
       1933): 144-170.

19718 PRINCE, BENJAMIN F. "THE RESCUE CASE OF 1857." OHIO
       STATE ARCHAEOLOGICAL AND HISTORICAL QUARTERLY, 16
       (JULY, 1907): 292-309.

19719 PRUSSING, EUGENE E. CHICAGO'S FIRST GREAT LAWSUIT.
       MADISON: STATE HISTORICAL SOCIETY OF WISCONSIN, 1915.

19720 PRUSSING, EUGENE E. "CHICAGO'S FIRST GREAT LAWSUIT."
       PROCEEDINGS OF THE WISCONSIN STATE HISTORICAL SOCIETY,
       63 (1916): 124-139.

19721　PURTEE, EDWARD O.　"THE UNDERGROUND RAILROAD FROM
　　　　SOUTHWESTERN OHIO TO LAKE ERIE."　PH.D. DISSERTATION,
　　　　OHIO STATE UNIVERSITY, 1933.

19722　QUARLES, BENJAMIN.　"ABOLITION'S DIFFERENT DRUMMER:
　　　　FREDERICK DOUGLASS."　IN DUBERMAN, MARTIN (ED.).　THE
　　　　ANTISLAVERY VANGUARD:　NEW ESSAYS ON THE
　　　　ABOLITIONISTS.　PRINCETON:　PRINCETON UNIVERSITY
　　　　PRESS, 1965, PP. 123-134.

19723　QUARLES, BENJAMIN.　BLACK ABOLITIONISTS.　NEW YORK:
　　　　OXFORD UNIVERSITY PRESS, 1969.

19724　QUARLES, BENJAMIN.　"THE BLACK UNDERGROUND."　NEGRO
　　　　DIGEST, 18 (FEBRUARY, 1969):　4-12.

19725　QUARLES, BENJAMIN.　FREDERICK DOUGLASS.　WASHINGTON:
　　　　ASSOCIATION FOR THE STUDY OF NEGRO LIFE AND HISTORY,
　　　　1948.

19726　QUARLES, BENJAMIN.　"FREEDOM'S BLACK VANGUARD."　IN
　　　　HUGGINS, NATHAN I.; KILSON, MARTIN; AND FOX, DANIEL M.
　　　　(EDS.).　KEY ISSUES IN THE AFRO-AMERICAN EXPERIENCE.
　　　　2 VOLS.　NEW YORK:　HARCOURT BRACE JOVANOVICH, 1971,
　　　　VOL. 1, PP. 174-190.

19727　"A QUESTION IN CASUISTRY."　INDEPENDENT, 67 (OCTOBER 28,
　　　　1909):　995-996.

19728　RACHLEFF, MARSHALL.　"BIG JOE, LITTLE JOE, BILL, AND
　　　　JACK:　AN EXAMPLE OF SLAVE RESISTANCE IN ALABAMA."
　　　　ALABAMA REVIEW, 32 (APRIL, 1979):　141-146.

19729　RAPPAPORT, STANLEY.　"SLAVE STRUGGLES FOR FREEDOM."
　　　　CRISIS, 43 (SEPTEMBER, 1936):　264-265, 274, 284-286.

19730　RAWICK, GEORGE.　"THE HISTORICAL ROOTS OF BLACK
　　　　LIBERATION."　RADICAL AMERICA, 2 (JULY-AUGUST, 1968):
　　　　1-13.

19731　REED, HARRY A.　"THE SLAVE AS ABOLITIONIST:　HENRY
　　　　HIGHLAND GARNET'S ADDRESS TO THE SLAVES OF THE UNITED
　　　　STATES OF AMERICA."　CENTENNIAL REVIEW, 20 (FALL,
　　　　1976):　385-394.

19732　REED, MARION L.B.　"THE UNDERGROUND RAILROAD IN
　　　　DELAWARE."　M.A. THESIS, UNIVERSITY OF PENNSYLVANIA,
　　　　1928.

19733　REYNOLDS, HELEN W.　"JOHN A. BOLDING, FUGITIVE SLAVE."
　　　　DUTCHESS COUNTY HISTORICAL SOCIETY YEAR BOOK, 20
　　　　(1935):　51-55.

19734　RICHARDSON, MARTIN D.　"SLAVE GUIDE FINDS FREEDOM."
　　　　NEGRO DIGEST, 8 (SEPTEMBER, 1950):　74-78.

19735   RIDDELL, WILLIAM R.   "ANDERSON'S CASE--AN EARLY
        EXTRADITION CONTROVERSY."   ST. LOUIS LAW REVIEW, 19
        (1934):   178-182.

19736   ROBBOY, STANLEY J. AND ROBBOY, ANITA W.   "LEWIS HAYDEN:
        FROM FUGITIVE SLAVE TO STATESMAN."   NEW ENGLAND
        QUARTERLY, 46 (DECEMBER, 1973):   591-613.

19737   ROBINSON, CAREY.   THE FIGHTING MAROONS OF JAMAICA.
        KINGSTON: WILLIAM COLLINS AND SANGSTER, 1969.

19738   ROBINSON, CEDRIC.   "A CRITIQUE OF W.E.B. DUBOIS' BLACK
        RECONSTRUCTION."   BLACK SCHOLAR, 8 (MAY, 1977):   44-50.

19739   RODILES, IGNACIO M.   "THE SLAVE TRADE WITH
        AMERICA--NEGROES IN MEXICO."   FREEDOMWAYS, 1 (FALL,
        1961):   296-307; 2 (WINTER, 1962):   39-52.

19740   ROEDIGER, DAVID R.   "ELMA STUCKEY: A POET LAUREATE OF
        BLACK HISTORY."   NEGRO HISTORY BULLETIN, 40
        (MARCH-APRIL, 1977):   690-691.

19741   ROSE, WILLIE LEE.   "THE IMPACT OF THE AMERICAN REVOLUTION
        ON THE BLACK POPULATION."   IN GERLACH, LARRY R.;
        DOLPH, JAMES A.; AND NICHOLLS, MICHAEL L. (EDS.).
        LEGACIES OF THE AMERICAN REVOLUTION.   LOGAN, UT: UTAH
        STATE UNIVERSITY, 1978, PP. 133-198.

19742   ROSSBACH, JEFFREY S.   "THE SECRET SIX: A STUDY OF THE
        CONSPIRACY BEHIND JOHN BROWN'S RAID."   PH.D.
        DISSERTATION, UNIVERSITY OF MASSACHUSETTS, 1974.

19743   ROTBERG, ROBERT I.   HAITI: THE POLITICS OF SQUALOR.
        BOSTON: HOUGHTON MIFFLIN COMPANY, 1971.

19744   RUSSELL, MARION J.   "AMERICAN SLAVE DISCONTENT IN RECORDS
        OF THE HIGH COURTS."   JOURNAL OF NEGRO HISTORY, 31
        (OCTOBER, 1946):   411-434.

19745   SADLER, LYNN B.   "DR. STEPHEN GRAHAM'S NARRATION OF THE
        'DUPLIN INSURRECTION':   ADDITIONAL EVIDENCE OF THE
        IMPACT OF NAT TURNER."   JOURNAL OF AMERICAN STUDIES,
        12 (DECEMBER, 1978):   359-367.

19746   SAVAGE, W. SHERMAN.   BLACKS IN THE WEST.   WESTPORT:
        GREENWOOD PRESS, 1976.

19747   SCHMIDT, O.L.   "ILLINOIS UNDERGROUND RAILROAD."   JOURNAL
        OF THE ILLINOIS STATE HISTORICAL SOCIETY, 18 (OCTOBER,
        1925):   703-717.

19748   SCHOR, JOEL.   HENRY HIGHLAND GARNET: A VOICE OF BLACK
        RADICALISM IN THE NINETEENTH CENTURY.   WESTPORT:
        GREENWOOD PRESS, 1977.

19749   SCHOR, JOEL A.   "THE ANTI-SLAVERY AND CIVIL RIGHTS ROLE
         OF HENRY HIGHLAND GARNET, 1850-1865."   PH.D.
         DISSERTATION, HOWARD UNIVERSITY, 1973.

19750   SCHWARTZ, HAROLD.   "FUGITIVE SLAVE DAYS IN BOSTON."   NEW
         ENGLAND QUARTERLY, 27 (JUNE, 1954):   191-212.

19751   SCHWARTZ, ROSALIE.   ACROSS THE RIO TO FREEDOM: U.S.
         NEGROES IN MEXICO.   EL PASO: TEXAS WESTERN PRESS,
         UNIVERSITY OF TEXAS, EL PASO, 1974.

19752   SCHWARTZ, ROSALIE.   "ACROSS THE RIO TO FREEDOM: U.S.
         NEGROES IN MEXICO."   SOUTHWESTERN STUDIES, 44 (1975):
         3-64.

19753   SCHWARTZ, STUART B.   "THE MOCAMBO: SLAVE RESISTANCE IN
         COLONIAL BAHIA."   JOURNAL OF SOCIAL HISTORY, 3
         (SUMMER, 1970):   313-333.

19754   SCHWARTZ, STUART B.   "RESISTANCE AND ACCOMMODATION IN
         EIGHTEENTH-CENTURY BRAZIL: THE SLAVES' VIEW OF
         SLAVERY."   HISPANIC AMERICAN HISTORICAL REVIEW, 57
         (FEBRUARY, 1977):   69-81.

19755   SCHWENINGER, LOREN.   "A FUGITIVE NEGRO IN THE PROMISED
         LAND, JAMES RAPIER IN CANADA, 1856-1864."   ONTARIO
         HISTORY, 67 (JUNE, 1975):   91-104.

19756   SCOTT, VIRGINIA.   "AN EARLY EPISODE OF BLACK RESISTANCE."
         PAN-AFRICAN JOURNAL, 3 (SUMMER, 1970):   203-208.

19757   SCRUGGS, OTEY.   "THE MEANING OF HARRIET TUBMAN."   IN
         GEORGE, CAROL V.R. (ED.).   "REMEMBER THE LADIES":   NEW
         PERSPECTIVES ON WOMEN IN AMERICAN HISTORY--ESSAYS IN
         HONOR OF NELSON MANFRED BLAKE.   SYRACUSE: SYRACUSE
         UNIVERSITY PRESS, 1975, PP. 110-121.

19758   SEXSMITH, W.N.   "SOME NOTES ON THE BUXTON SETTLEMENT,
         RALEIGH, KENT COUNTY."   KENT HISTORICAL SOCIETY
         PAPERS, 4 (1919):   40-44.

19759   SHALER, NATHANIEL S.   "THE NEGRO PROBLEM."   ATLANTIC
         MONTHLY, 54 (NOVEMBER, 1884):   696-709.

19760   SHAPIRO, SAMUEL.   "THE RENDITION OF ANTHONY BURNS."
         JOURNAL OF NEGRO HISTORY, 44 (JANUARY, 1959):   43-51.

19761   SHARP, WILLIAM F.   "MANUMISSION, LIBRES, AND BLACK
         RESISTANCE: THE COLOMBIAN CHOCO 1680-1810."   IN
         TOPLIN, ROBERT B. (ED.).   SLAVERY AND RACE RELATIONS
         IN LATIN AMERICA.   WESTPORT: GREENWOOD PRESS, 1974,
         PP. 89-111.

19762   "SHE WHO WOULD BE FREE.   RESISTANCE (THE NEGRO WOMAN IN
         SLAVERY, IN THE CIVIL WAR AND RECONSTRUCTION)."

FREEDOMWAYS, 2 (WINTER, 1962): 60-70.

19763   SHELDON, A. "REMINISCENCES OF UNDERGROUND RAILROADS."
        FIRELANDS PIONEER, N.S., 17 (1909): 1429-1434.

19764   SHELDON, JANE M. "SEMINOLE ATTACKS NEAR NEW SMYRNA,
        1835-1856." FLORIDA HISTORICAL QUARTERLY, 8 (APRIL,
        1930): 188-196.

19765   SHELE DE VERE, M.R.B. "THE FREEDMAN'S STORY." HARPER'S
        MONTHLY MAGAZINE, 33 (OCTOBER, 1866): 647.

19766   SHERWIN, OSCAR. "SONS OF OTIS AND HANCOCK." NEW ENGLAND
        QUARTERLY, 19 (JUNE, 1946): 212-223.

19767   SHIFFRIN, STEVEN H. "THE RHETORIC OF BLACK VIOLENCE IN
        THE ANTEBELLUM PERIOD: HENRY HIGHLAND GARNET."
        JOURNAL OF BLACK STUDIES, 2 (SEPTEMBER, 1971): 45-56.

19768   SIEBERT, WILBUR H. "BEGINNINGS OF THE UNDERGROUND
        RAILROAD IN OHIO." OHIO ARCHAEOLOGICAL AND HISTORICAL
        QUARTERLY, 56 (1947): 70-93.

19769   SIEBERT, WILBUR H. "LIGHT ON THE UNDERGROUND RAILROAD."
        AMERICAN HISTORICAL REVIEW, 1 (APRIL, 1896): 455-463.

19770   SIEBERT, WILBUR H. THE MYSTERIES OF OHIO'S UNDERGROUND
        RAILROADS. COLUMBUS: LONG'S COLLEGE BOOK COMPANY,
        1951.

19771   SIEBERT, WILBUR H. "OHIO'S AID TO FUGITIVE SLAVES AS A
        CONTRIBUTING CAUSE OF THE CIVIL WAR." OHIO SOCIAL
        SCIENCE JOURNAL, 4 (1932): 5-13.

19772   SIEBERT, WILBUR H. "A QUAKER SECTION OF THE UNDERGROUND
        RAILROAD IN NORTHERN OHIO." OHIO ARCHAEOLOGICAL AND
        HISTORICAL QUARTERLY, 39 (JULY, 1930): 479-502.

19773   SIEBERT, WILBUR H. "THE UNDERGROUND RAILROAD." NEW
        ENGLAND MAGAZINE, 33 (JANUARY, 1903): 565-578.

19774   SIEBERT, WILBUR H. THE UNDERGROUND RAILROAD FROM SLAVERY
        TO FREEDOM. NEW YORK: MACMILLAN, 1898.

19775   SIEBERT, WILBUR H. "THE UNDERGROUND RAILROAD IN
        MASSACHUSETTS." NEW ENGLAND QUARTERLY, 9 (SEPTEMBER,
        1936): 447-467.

19776   SIEBERT, WILBUR H. "THE UNDERGROUND RAILROAD IN
        MASSACHUSETTS." PROCEEDINGS OF THE AMERICAN
        ANTIQUARIAN SOCIETY, 45 (APRIL, 1935): 25-100.

19777   SIEBERT, WILBUR H. "THE UNDERGROUND RAILROAD IN
        MICHIGAN." DETROIT HISTORICAL MONTHLY, 1 (MARCH,
        1923): 10.

19778   SILVERMAN, JASON H. "THE AMERICAN FUGITIVE SLAVE IN
        CANADA: MYTHS AND REALITIES." SOUTHERN STUDIES, 19
        (FALL, 1980): 215-227.

19779   SILVERMAN, JASON H. "KENTUCKY, CANADA, AND EXTRADITION:
        THE JESSE HAPPY CASE." FILSON CLUB HISTORY QUARTERLY,
        54 (JANUARY, 1980): 50-60.

19780   SLOANE, RUSH R. "THE UNDERGROUND RAILROAD OF THE
        FIRELANDS." MAGAZINE OF WESTERN HISTORY, 8 (MAY,
        1888): 32-57.

19781   SMEDLEY, ROBERT C. HISTORY OF THE UNDERGROUND RAILROAD
        IN CHESTER AND THE NEIGHBORING COUNTIES OF
        PENNSYLVANIA. LANCASTER, PA: OFFICE OF THE JOURNAL,
        1883.

19782   SMITH, DORIS W. "TROUBLESOME PROPERTY: FUGITIVES,
        SABOTEURS, AND MALINGERERS." IN JOYNER, CHARLES W.
        (ED.). BLACK CAROLINIANS: STUDIES IN THE HISTORY OF
        SOUTH CAROLINA NEGROES. LAURINBURG, NC: ST. ANDREWS
        PRESBYTERIAN COLLEGE, 1969, PP. 43-49.

19783   SMITH, HENRY L. "THE UNDERGROUND RAILROAD IN MONROE
        COUNTY." INDIANA MAGAZINE OF HISTORY, 13 (SEPTEMBER,
        1917): 288-297.

19784   SMITH, JOSEPH H. "SOME ASPECTS OF THE UNDERGROUND
        RAILWAY IN THE COUNTIES OF SOUTHEASTERN PENNSYLVANIA."
        MONTGOMERY COUNTY HISTORICAL SOCIETY BULLETIN, 3
        (1941): 3-19.

19785   SMYRL, FRANK H. "UNIONISM, ABOLITIONISM, AND VIGILANTISM
        IN TEXAS, 1856-1865." M.A. THESIS, UNIVERSITY OF
        TEXAS, 1961.

19786   "SNATCHING LEARNING IN FORBIDDEN FIELDS." NEGRO HISTORY
        BULLETIN, 3 (NOVEMBER, 1939): 21.

19787   SPERRY, EARL E. THE JERRY RESCUE, OCTOBER 1, 1851.
        SYRACUSE: ONONDAGA HISTORICAL ASSOCIATION, 1924.

19788   STAMPP, KENNETH M. THE PECULIAR INSTITUTION: SLAVERY IN
        THE ANTE-BELLUM SOUTH. NEW YORK: ALFRED A. KNOPF,
        1956.

19789   STAROBIN, ROBERT. BLACKS IN BONDAGE: LETTERS OF
        AMERICAN SLAVES. NEW YORK: NEW VIEWPOINTS, 1974.

19790   STAROBIN, ROBERT S. INDUSTRIAL SLAVERY IN THE OLD SOUTH.
        NEW YORK: OXFORD UNIVERSITY PRESS, 1970.

19791   STERLING, DOROTHY. FREEDOM TRAIN: THE STORY OF HARRIET
        TUBMAN. NEW YORK: DOUBLEDAY, 1954.

19792   STERLING, PHILIP AND LOGAN, RAYFORD. FOUR TOOK FREEDOM.
         NEW YORK: DOUBLEDAY AND COMPANY, 1967.

19793   STEVENS, CHARLES E. ANTHONY BURNS, A HISTORY. BOSTON:
         JOHN P. JEWELL AND COMPANY, 1881.

19794   STILES, CASSIUS C. "JOHN ROSS MILLER." ANNALS OF IOWA,
         3RD SER., 19 (JULY, 1934): 384-386.

19795   STILL, WILLIAM. THE UNDERGROUND RAILROAD. A RECORD OF
         FACTS, AUTHENTIC NARRATIVES, LETTERS, ETC.
         PHILADELPHIA: PORTER AND COATES, 1872.

19796   STONE, LUCIE P. (ED.). "A SOUVENIR OF THE DAYS OF THE
         'UNDERGROUND RAILROAD.'" JOURNAL OF AMERICAN HISTORY,
         6 (JULY-SEPTEMBER, 1912): 613-615.

19797   STROTHER, HORATIO T. THE UNDERGROUND RAILROAD IN
         CONNECTICUT. MIDDLETOWN, CT: WESLEYAN UNIVERSITY
         PRESS, 1966.

19798   STROTHER, HORATIO T. "THE UNDERGROUND RAILROAD IN
         CONNECTICUT FROM 1830-1850." M.A. THESIS, UNIVERSITY
         OF CONNECTICUT, 1957.

19799   "THE STRUGGLE OF THE NEGRO AGAINST BONDAGE." NEGRO
         HISTORY BULLETIN, 1 (FEBRUARY, 1938): 2-3.

19800   STRUHS, JAMES F. "CANADA, A HAVEN FOR FUGITIVE SLAVES,
         1820-1861." M.S. THESIS, ILLINOIS STATE UNIVERSITY,
         1972.

19801   STUCKEY, STERLING. "SLAVE RESISTANCE AS SEEN THROUGH
         SLAVE FOLKLORE." IN REID, INEZ S. (ED.). THE BLACK
         PRISM: PERSPECTIVES ON THE BLACK EXPERIENCE.
         BROOKLYN: SUMMER INSTITUTE ON AFRO-AMERICAN STUDIES,
         BROOKLYN COLLEGE, CITY UNIVERSITY OF NEW YORK, 1969,
         PP. 51-60.

19802   STUCKEY, STERLING. "THROUGH THE PRISM OF FOLKLORE: THE
         BLACK ETHOS IN SLAVERY." MASSACHUSETTS REVIEW, 9
         (SUMMER, 1968): 417-437.

19803   SYDNOR, CHARLES S. "PURSUING FUGITIVE SLAVES." SOUTH
         ATLANTIC QUARTERLY, 28 (APRIL, 1929): 152-164.

19804   TANNER, EARL C. (ED.). "THE EARLY CAREER OF EDWIN T.
         JENCKES: A FLORIDA PIONEER OF THE 1830'S." FLORIDA
         HISTORICAL QUARTERLY, 30 (JANUARY, 1952): 270-275.

19805   TAUSSIG, MICHAEL. "BLACK RELIGION AND RESISTANCE IN
         COLOMBIA: THREE CENTURIES OF SOCIAL STRUGGLE IN THE
         CAUCA VALLEY." MARXIST PERSPECTIVES, 2 (SUMMER,
         1979): 84-116.

19806 TAYLOR, RICH L. "RESISTANCE TO SLAVERY IN THE NORTHERN
COAST OF SOUTH AMERICA." M.A. THESIS, UNIVERSITY OF
FLORIDA, 1975.

19807 TAYLOR, S.A.G. "THE GENESIS OF THE LEEWARD MAROONS."
BULLETIN OF THE JAMAICA HISTORICAL SOCIETY, 4
(DECEMBER, 1968): 301-304.

19808 TEAKLE, THOMAS. "THE RENDITION OF BARCLAY COPPOC." IOWA
JOURNAL OF HISTORY AND POLITICS, 10 (OCTOBER, 1912):
503-566.

19809 TELFORD, MARGARET J.A. "SLAVE RESISTANCE IN TEXAS."
M.A. THESIS, SOUTHERN METHODIST UNIVERSITY, 1975.

19810 TEPASKE, JOHN J. "THE FUGITIVE SLAVE: INTERCOLONIAL
RIVALRY AND SPANISH SLAVE POLICY, 1687-1764." IN
PROCTOR, SAMUEL (ED.). EIGHTEENTH-CENTURY FLORIDA AND
ITS BORDERLANDS. GAINESVILLE: UNIVERSITY PRESSES OF
FLORIDA, 1975, PP. 1-12.

19811 TETRICK, GWENDOLYN G.P. "NO MORE DRIVER'S LASH FOR ME:
SONGS OF DISCONTENTED SLAVES." M.A. THESIS, BALL
STATE UNIVERSITY, 1974.

19812 THORNBROUGH, EMMA L. "INDIANA AND FUGITIVE SLAVE
LEGISLATION." INDIANA MAGAZINE OF HISTORY, 50
(SEPTEMBER, 1954): 201-228.

19813 THORNE, IRENE. "THE ANTI-SLAVERY MOVEMENT IN OHIO AS
ILLUSTRATED BY THE ABOLITION MOVEMENT AND THE
UNDERGROUND RAILROAD." M.A. THESIS, KENT STATE
UNIVERSITY, 1942.

19814 TOPLIN, ROBERT B. "PETER STILL VERSUS THE PECULIAR
INSTITUTION." CIVIL WAR HISTORY, 13 (DECEMBER, 1967):
340-349.

19815 TURLEY, DAVID M. "'FREE AIR' AND FUGITIVE SLAVES:
BRITISH ABOLITIONISTS VERSUS GOVERNMENT OVER AMERICAN
FUGITIVES, 1834-1861." IN BOLT, CHRISTINE AND
DRESCHER, SEYMOUR (EDS.). ANTI-SLAVERY, RELIGION, AND
REFORM: ESSAYS IN MEMORY OF ROGER ANSTEY. HAMDEN,
CT: ARCHON BOOKS, 1980, PP. 163-182.

19816 TURNER, EDWARD R. "THE UNDERGROUND RAILROAD IN
PENNSYLVANIA." PENNSYLVANIA MAGAZINE OF HISTORY AND
BIOGRAPHY, 36 (JULY, 1912): 309-318.

19817 TURTON, CECIL M. "THE UNDERGROUND RAILROAD IN KANSAS,
NEBRASKA, AND IOWA." M.A. THESIS, OHIO STATE
UNIVERSITY, 1935.

19818 TUTTLE, W.M., JR. (ED.). "35 YEARS OVERDUE: NOTE ON A
BELATED UP FROM SLAVERY." LABOR HISTORY, 15 (WINTER,

1974):   86-88.

19819   TWOMBLY, ROBERT C.   "BLACK RESISTANCE TO SLAVERY IN
        MASSACHUSETTS."   IN O'NEILL, WILLIAM L. (ED.).
        INSIGHT AND PARALLELS: PROBLEMS AND ISSUES OF
        AMERICAN SOCIAL HISTORY.   MINNEAPOLIS: BURGESS
        PUBLISHING COMPANY, 1973, PP. 41-53.

19820   TYLER, RONNIE.   "FUGITIVE SLAVES IN MEXICO."   JOURNAL OF
        NEGRO HISTORY, 57 (JANUARY, 1972):   1-12.

19821   TYLER, RONNIE C.   "THE CALLAHAN EXPEDITION OF 1855:
        INDIANS OR NEGROES?"   SOUTHWESTERN HISTORICAL
        QUARTERLY, 70 (APRIL, 1967):   574-585.

19822   TYLER, RONNIE C.   "SLAVE OWNERS AND RUNAWAY SLAVES IN
        TEXAS."   M.A. THESIS, TEXAS CHRISTIAN UNIVERSITY, 1966.

19823   "UNDERGROUND RAILROAD."   IN SCHAPSMEIER, EDWARD L. AND
        SCHAPSMEIER, FREDERICK.   ENCYCLOPEDIA OF AMERICAN
        AGRICULTURAL HISTORY.   WESTPORT: GREENWOOD PRESS,
        1975, P. 357.

19824   VAN EK, JACOB.   "UNDERGROUND RAILROAD IN IOWA."
        PALIMPSEST, 2 (MAY, 1921):   129-143.

19825   VERGER, PIERRE.   "NIGERIA, BRAZIL AND CUBA."   NIGERIA
        MAGAZINE, NO. 66 (OCTOBER, 1960):   113-123.

19826   WALKER, GEORGE.   "BLACK RESISTANCE TO THE FUGITIVE SLAVE
        LAW OF 1850, 1850-1856."   M.A. THESIS, COLUMBIA
        UNIVERSITY, 1971.

19827   WALKER, JAMES W. ST. G.   THE BLACK LOYALISTS: THE SEARCH
        FOR A PROMISED LAND IN NOVA SCOTIA AND SIERRA LEONE,
        1783-1870.   NEW YORK: AFRICANA PUBLISHING COMPANY,
        1976.

19828   WALKER, JAMES W. ST. G.   "BLACKS AS AMERICAN LOYALISTS:
        THE SLAVES' WAR FOR INDEPENDENCE."   HISTORICAL
        REFLECTIONS, 2 (SUMMER, 1975):   51-68.

19829   WARNER, MARY C.   "AN INCIDENT OF THE CORBIT MANSION IN
        THE DAYS OF SLAVERY BEFORE THE WAR OF 1861-1864."
        UNPUBLISHED PAPER, N.D., SLAVERY COLLECTION, DELAWARE
        HISTORICAL SOCIETY.

19830   WARREN, STANLEY JR.   "PALMARES: A NEGRO STATE IN
        COLONIAL BRAZIL."   NEGRO HISTORY BULLETIN, 28
        (JANUARY, 1965):   79-80.

19831   WATERS, WILLIAM A.   "THE UNDERGROUND RAILROAD IN
        MASSACHUSETTS."   M.A. THESIS, OHIO STATE UNIVERSITY,
        1935.

19832   WATRISS, WENDY. "CELEBRATE FREEDOM: JUNETEENTH."
        SOUTHERN EXPOSURE, 5 (1977): 80-87.

19833   WATTS, RALPH M. "HISTORY OF THE UNDERGROUND RAILROAD IN
        MECHANICSBURG." OHIO ARCHAEOLOGICAL AND HISTORICAL
        QUARTERLY, 43 (1934): 209-254.

19834   WERNER, RANDOLPH. "AN INQUIRY INTO SOME ASPECTS OF NAT
        TURNER'S REBELLION." M.A. THESIS, COLLEGE OF WILLIAM
        AND MARY, 1971.

19835   WESLEY, CHARLES H. "THE NEGRO IN THE ORGANIZATION OF
        ABOLITION." PHYLON, 2 (AUTUMN, 1941): 223-235.

19836   "WHITE SLAVERY: A FRAGMENT OF AMERICAN HISTORY." A.M.E.
        CHURCH REVIEW, 17 (OCTOBER, 1900): 130-142.

19837   WHITING, HELEN A. "SLAVE ADVENTURES." NEGRO HISTORY
        BULLETIN, 19 (FEBRUARY-MAY, 1955): 109-111, 138, 164,
        190; 20 (NOVEMBER-DECEMBER, 1956): 47, 67-69.

19838   WHITMAN, KAREN. "RE-EVALUATING JOHN BROWN'S RAID AT
        HARPER'S FERRY." WEST VIRGINIA HISTORY, 34 (OCTOBER,
        1972): 46-84.

19839   WHITSON, THOMAS. "WILLIAM PARKER, THE HERO OF THE
        CHRISTIANA RIOT." LANCASTER COUNTY HISTORICAL SOCIETY
        PAPERS, 1 (1896): 27-34.

19840   WIGGINS, WILLIAM H., JR. "'LIFT EVERY VOICE': A STUDY
        OF AFRO-AMERICAN EMANCIPATION CELEBRATIONS." JOURNAL
        OF ASIAN AND AFRICAN STUDIES, 9 (JULY, APRIL, 1974):
        180-191.

19841   WILCOX, D. RAY. "THE REFORMED PRESBYTERIAN CHURCH AND
        THE ANTI-SLAVERY MOVEMENT." M.A. THESIS, COLORADO
        STATE COLLEGE OF EDUCATION, GREELEY, 1948.

19842   WILEY, BELL I. SOUTHERN NEGROES, 1861-1865. NEW HAVEN:
        YALE UNIVERSITY PRESS, 1938.

19843   WILLIAMS, HELEN. "LITTLETON, A STATION OF THE
        UNDERGROUND RAILROAD." RECORD, 4 (FALL, 1914): 10-11.

19844   WILLIAMS, JOSEPH J. "THE MAROONS OF JAMAICA."
        ANTHROPOLOGICAL SERIES OF THE BOSTON COLLEGE GRADUATE
        SCHOOL, 3 (DECEMBER, 1938): 379-471.

19845   WILLIGAN, J. DENNIS. "SANCTUARY; A COMMUNITARIAN FORM OF
        COUNTER-CULTURE." UNION SEMINARY QUARTERLY REVIEW, 25
        (SUMMER, 1970): 517-541.

19846   WILSON, BENJAMIN C. "KENTUCKY KIDNAPPERS, FUGITIVES, AND
        ABOLITIONISTS IN ANTEBELLUM CASS COUNTY MICHIGAN."
        MICHIGAN HISTORY, 60 (WINTER, 1976): 339-358.

19847 WINDERS, GERTRUDE H. HARRIET TUBMAN: FREEDOM GIRL. NEW
       YORK: BOBBS-MERRILL, 1969.

19848 WINDLEY, LATHAN A. "FLIGHT AND REBELLION: A CASE OF
       HYPERBOLIC EXAGGERATION." NEGRO HISTORY BULLETIN, 41
       (SEPTEMBER-OCTOBER, 1978): 895.

19849 WINDLEY, LATHAN A. "A PROFILE OF RUNAWAY SLAVES IN
       VIRGINIA AND SOUTH CAROLINA FROM 1730 THROUGH 1787."
       PH.D. DISSERTATION, UNIVERSITY OF IOWA, 1974.

19850 WITHROW, W.H. "THE UNDERGROUND RAILROAD." TRANSACTIONS
       OF THE ROYAL SOCIETY OF CANADA, 2ND SER., 8 (1902):
       49-78.

19851 WOODWARD, C. VANN. "JOHN BROWN'S PRIVATE WAR." IN
       AARON, DANIEL (ED.). AMERICA IN CRISIS: FOURTEEN
       CRUCIAL EPISODES IN AMERICAN HISTORY. NEW YORK:
       ALFRED A. KNOPF, 1952, PP. 109-130.

19852 WRIGHT, MRS. FLORENCE B. "A STATION ON THE UNDERGROUND
       RAILROAD." OHIO ARCHAEOLOGICAL AND HISTORICAL
       QUARTERLY, 14 (1905): 164-169.

19853 YANUCK, JULIUS. "THE GARNER FUGITIVE SLAVE CASE."
       MISSISSIPPI VALLEY HISTORICAL REVIEW, 40 (JUNE, 1953):
       47-66.

19854 YEIGH, FRANK. "FAMOUS CANADIAN TRIALS: ANDERSON, THE
       FUGITIVE SLAVE." CANADIAN MAGAZINE, 45 (SEPTEMBER,
       1915): 397-401.

19855 YETMAN, NORMAN R. "FUGITIVE SLAVES." IN ROLLER, DAVID
       C. AND TWYMAN, ROBERT W. (EDS.). THE ENCYCLOPEDIA OF
       SOUTHERN HISTORY. BATON ROUGE: LOUISIANA STATE
       UNIVERSITY PRESS, 1979, P. 1115.

19856 ZORN, ROMAN J. "AN ARKANSAS FUGITIVE SLAVE INCIDENT AND
       ITS INTERNATIONAL REPERCUSSIONS." ARKANSAS HISTORICAL
       QUARTERLY, 16 (SUMMER, 1957): 139-149.

19857 ZURLO, JOHN A. "BLACK ODYSSEY." CRISIS, 84 (OCTOBER,
       1977): 409-410.

REVOLTS/INSURRECTIONS

19858 ABBOTT, ALBERT. "STONO SLAVE CONSPIRACY." IN ROLLER,
       DAVID C. AND TWYMAN, ROBERT W. (EDS.). THE
       ENCYCLOPEDIA OF SOUTHERN HISTORY. BATON ROUGE:
       LOUISIANA STATE UNIVERSITY PRESS, 1979, P. 1164.

19859 ADAMS, HERBERT B. "MR. FREEMAN'S VISIT TO BALTIMORE."
       JOHNS HOPKINS UNIVERSITY STUDIES IN HISTORICAL AND
       POLITICAL SCIENCE, 1 (1882): 5-12.

19860   ADDINGTON, WENDELL G. "SLAVE INSURRECTIONS IN TEXAS."
        JOURNAL OF NEGRO HISTORY, 35 (OCTOBER, 1950): 408-434.

19861   ALEXIS, STEPHEN. BLACK LIBERATOR: THE LIFE OF TOUSSAINT
        LOUVERTURE. NEW YORK: MACMILLAN COMPANY, 1949.

19862   ANDERSON, ALICE L. "THE CREOLE AFFAIR: CLIMAX OF THE
        BRITISH-AMERICAN FUGITIVE SLAVE CONTROVERSY,
        1831-1842." M.A. THESIS, OLD DOMINION UNIVERSITY,
        1970.

19863   APTHEKER, HERBERT. AMERICAN NEGRO SLAVE REVOLTS. NEW
        YORK: COLUMBIA UNIVERSITY PRESS, 1943.

19864   APTHEKER, HERBERT. "AMERICAN NEGRO SLAVE REVOLTS."
        PH.D. DISSERTATION, COLUMBIA UNIVERSITY, 1944.

19865   APTHEKER, HERBERT. "AMERICAN NEGRO SLAVE REVOLTS."
        SCIENCE AND SOCIETY, 1 (SUMMER, 1937): 512-538.

19866   APTHEKER, HERBERT. "MORE ON AMERICAN NEGRO SLAVE
        REVOLTS." SCIENCE AND SOCIETY, 2 (SPRING, 1938):
        386-391.

19867   APTHEKER, HERBERT. "NAT TURNER'S REVOLT: THE
        ENVIRONMENT, THE EVENT, THE EFFECTS." M.A. THESIS,
        COLUMBIA UNIVERSITY, 1937.

19868   APTHEKER, HERBERT. NAT TURNER'S SLAVE REBELLION. NEW
        YORK: HUMANITIES PRESS, 1966.

19869   APTHEKER, HERBERT. "NEGRO SLAVE REVOLTS IN THE UNITED
        STATES, 1526-1860." ESSAYS IN THE HISTORY OF THE
        AMERICAN NEGRO. NEW YORK: INTERNATIONAL PUBLISHERS,
        1945, PP. 1-70, 209-210.

19870   APTHEKER, HERBERT. NEGRO SLAVE REVOLTS IN THE UNITED
        STATES, 1526-1860. NEW YORK: INTERNATIONAL
        PUBLISHERS, 1939.

19871   APTHEKER, HERBERT. "NOTES ON SLAVE CONSPIRACIES IN
        CONFEDERATE MISSISSIPPI." JOURNAL OF NEGRO HISTORY,
        29 (JANUARY, 1944): 75-79.

19872   APTHEKER, HERBERT. "SLAVE GUERRILLA WARFARE." TO BE
        FREE: PIONEERING STUDIES IN AFRO-AMERICAN HISTORY.
        NEW YORK: INTERNATIONAL PUBLISHERS, 1948, PP. 11-30.

19873   BALDWIN, SIMEON E. "THE CAPTIVES OF THE AMISTAD."
        PAPERS OF THE NEW HAVEN COLONY HISTORICAL SOCIETY, 4
        (1888): 331-370.

19874   BARALT, GUILLERMO A. "SLAVE CONSPIRACIES AND UPRISINGS
        IN PUERTO RICO, 1796-1848." PH.D. DISSERTATION,
        UNIVERSITY OF CHICAGO, 1977.

19875 BARNEY, WILLIAM L. THE SECESSIONIST IMPULSE: ALABAMA
AND MISSISSIPPI IN 1860. PRINCETON: PRINCETON
UNIVERSITY PRESS, 1974.

19876 BARTLETT, ELLEN S. "THE AMISTAD CAPTIVES." NEW ENGLAND
MAGAZINE, N.S., 22 (MARCH, 1900): 72-89.

19877 BAUR, JOHN E. "INTERNATIONAL REPERCUSSIONS OF THE
HAITIAN REVOLUTION." AMERICAS, 26 (APRIL, 1970):
394-418.

19878 BEEMAN, RICHARD R. THE OLD DOMINION AND THE NEW NATION,
1788-1801. LEXINGTON: UNIVERSITY PRESS OF KENTUCKY,
1972.

19879 BEEMAN, RICHARD R. "THE OLD DOMINION AND THE NEW NATION,
1788-1801." PH.D. DISSERTATION, UNIVERSITY OF
CHICAGO, 1968.

19880 BELLEGARDE-SMITH, PATRICK. "HAITIAN SOCIAL THOUGHT IN
THE NINETEENTH CENTURY: CLASS FORMATION AND
WESTERNIZATION." CARIBBEAN STUDIES, 20 (MARCH, 1980):
5-34.

19881 BENNETT, LERONE JR. "SLAVE REVOLTS AND INSURRECTIONS."
EBONY, 17 (FEBRUARY, 1962): 82-86.

19882 BERLIN, IRA (ED.). "AFTER NAT TURNER: A LETTER FROM THE
NORTH." JOURNAL OF NEGRO HISTORY, 55 (APRIL, 1970):
144-152.

19883 BLAKE, NELSON M. "WAS NAT TURNER RIGHT? VIOLENCE IN
AMERICAN HISTORY." IN HAGUE, JOHN A. (ED.). AMERICAN
CHARACTER AND CULTURE IN A CHANGING WORLD: SOME
TWENTIETH-CENTURY PERSPECTIVES. WESTPORT: GREENWOOD
PRESS, 1979, PP. 185-195.

19884 BLASSINGAME, JOHN W. THE SLAVE COMMUNITY: PLANTATION
LIFE IN THE ANTEBELLUM SOUTH. NEW YORK: OXFORD
UNIVERSITY PRESS, 1972.

19885 BONEY, F.N. "THE BLUE LIZARD: ANOTHER VIEW OF NAT
TURNER'S COUNTRY ON THE EVE OF REBELLION." PHYLON, 31
(WINTER, 1970): 351-358.

19886 BONTEMPS, ARNA. BLACK THUNDER. NEW YORK: MACMILLAN,
1936.

19887 BOOTH, SALLY S. SEEDS OF ANGER: REVOLTS IN AMERICA,
1607-1771. NEW YORK: HASTINGS HOUSE, 1977.

19888 BRATHWAITE, EDWARD K. "CALIBAN, ARIEL, AND UNPROSPERO IN
THE CONFLICT OF CREOLOZATION: A STUDY OF THE SLAVE
REVOLT IN JAMAICA IN 1831-1832." IN RUBIN, VERA AND
TUDEN, ARTHUR (EDS.). COMPARATIVE PERSPECTIVES ON

SLAVERY IN NEW WORLD PLANTATION SOCIETIES. NEW YORK: NEW YORK ACADEMY OF SCIENCES, 1977, PP. 41-62.

19889 BRATHWAITE, EDWARD K. "CREOLIZATION AND THE SLAVE REVOLT IN JAMAICA, 1831-1832." UNPUBLISHED PAPER PRESENTED AT CONFERENCE ON SLAVE PEASANT SOCIETIES, INSTITUTE FOR THE STUDY OF MAN, NEW YORK, 1976.

19890 BRATHWAITE, EDWARD K. "SLAVE REVOLTS AND MARONAGE IN THE CARIBBEAN." UNPUBLISHED PAPER PRESENTED AT REUNION D'EXPERTS SUR LA TRAITE NEGRIERE, PORT-AU-PRINCE, 1978.

19891 BRATTON, MARY J. "CREOLE SLAVE CASE (1841)." IN ROLLER, DAVID C. AND TWYMAN, ROBERT W. (EDS.). THE ENCYCLOPEDIA OF SOUTHERN HISTORY. BATON ROUGE: LOUISIANA STATE UNIVERSITY PRESS, 1979, PP. 310-311.

19892 BRITT, JAMES W. "HISTORICAL REACTION TO NAT TURNER'S REBELLION, 1900-1970." M.A. THESIS, NORTH CAROLINA CENTRAL UNIVERSITY, 1976.

19893 BRONNER, F.L. "THE HISTORIAN AND WILLIAM STYRON; REVIEW OF CONFESSIONS OF NAT TURNER." NEW YORK STATE EDUCATION, 55 (JANUARY, 1968): 34.

19894 BROWN, RICHARD M. "THE HISTORY OF VIGILANTISM IN AMERICA." IN ROSENBAUM, H. JON AND SEDERBERG, PETER C. (EDS.). VIGILANTE POLITICS. PHILADELPHIA: UNIVERSITY OF PENNSYLVANIA PRESS, 1976, PP. 79-109.

19895 BURNHAM, FORBES. ADDRESS BY THE LEADER OF THE PEOPLE'S NATIONAL CONGRESS, PRIME MINISTER COMRADE FORBES BURNHAM, AT THE UNVEILING OF THE 1763 MONUMENT ON MAY 23, 1976. GEORGETOWN: OFFICE OF THE PRIME MINISTER, 1976.

19896 BURNS, E. BRADFORD. "CULTURES IN CONFLICT: THE IMPLICATION OF MODERNIZATION IN NINETEENTH-CENTURY LATIN AMERICA." IN BURNS AND GRAHAM, RICHARD. ELITES, MASSES, AND MODERNIZATION IN LATIN AMERICA, 1850-1930. AUSTIN: UNIVERSITY OF TEXAS PRESS, 1979, PP. 11-78.

19897 BUTTERFIELD, ROGER. "NAT TURNER WAS A GRIM AGENT OF REVOLT." LIFE, 65 (NOVEMBER 22, 1968): 98-99.

19898 CABLE, GEORGE W. "A WEST INDIAN SLAVE INSURRECTION." SCRIBNER'S MAGAZINE, 12 (DECEMBER, 1892): 709-720.

19899 CABLE, MARY. BLACK ODYSSEY: THE CASE OF THE SLAVE SHIP AMISTAD. NEW YORK: VIKING PRESS, 1971.

19900 CALLAWAY, CAROLYN. "THE RUNAWAY SCRAPE: AN EPISODE OF THE TEXAS REVOLUTION." M.A. THESIS, UNIVERSITY OF TEXAS, 1942.

19901   CAREY, ROBINSON. THE FIGHTING MAROONS OF JAMAICA.
         KINGSTON: W. COLLINS AND SANGSTER, 1969.

19902   CARROLL, JOSEPH C. SLAVE INSURRECTIONS IN THE UNITED
         STATES, 1800-1865. BOSTON: CHAPMAN AND GRIMES, 1938.

19903   CARROLL, JOSEPH C. "SLAVE INSURRECTIONS IN THE UNITED
         STATES, 1800-1865." PH.D. DISSERTATION, OHIO STATE
         UNIVERSITY, 1937.

19904   CARTER, HOLLIE E. "NEGRO INSURRECTIONS IN AMERICAN
         HISTORY, 1639-1860." M.A. THESIS, HOWARD UNIVERSITY,
         1936.

19905   CASE, H.G. "A CLAIM FOR THE SLAVE SHIP AMISTAD." LONG
         ISLAND FORUM, 35 (1972): 238-241.

19906   CHIPHE, LEPPAINE. "THE DENMARK VESEY PLOT: A YOUNG
         BLACK VIEW." IN JOYNER, CHARLES W. (ED.). BLACK
         CAROLINIANS: STUDIES IN THE HISTORY OF SOUTH CAROLINA
         NEGROES IN THE NINETEENTH CENTURY. LAURINBURG, NC:
         ST. ANDREWS PRESBYTERIAN COLLEGE, 1969, PP. 50-60.

19907   CLARKE, JOHN H. "AFRICAN CULTURAL CONTINUITY AND SLAVE
         REVOLTS IN THE NEW WORLD." BLACK SCHOLAR, 8
         (SEPTEMBER, OCTOBER-NOVEMBER, 1976): 2-9, 41-49.

19908   CLARKE, JOHN H. THE INFLUENCE OF AFRICAN CULTURAL
         CONTINUITY ON THE SLAVE REVOLTS IN SOUTH AMERICA AND
         IN THE CARIBBEAN ISLANDS. ATLANTA: ATLANTA
         UNIVERSITY CENTER FOR AFRICAN AND AFRICAN-AMERICAN
         STUDIES OCCASIONAL PAPER NO. 14, 1973.

19909   CLARKE, JOHN H. "SLAVE REVOLT IN THE CARIBBEAN." BLACK
         WORLD, 22 (FEBRUARY, 1973): 12-25.

19910   CLARKE, JOHN H. "SLAVE REVOLTS IN THE CARIBBEAN
         ISLANDS." PRESENCE AFRICAINE, NO. 34 (1972): 117-130.

19911   CLARKE, JOHN H. (ED.). WILLIAM STYRON'S NAT TURNER: TEN
         BLACK WRITERS RESPOND. BOSTON: BEACON PRESS, 1968.

19912   CLARKE, T. WOOD. "THE NEGRO PLOT OF 1741." NEW YORK
         HISTORY, 25 (APRIL, 1944): 167-181.

19913   COFFIN, CHARLES C. OLD TIMES IN THE COLONIES. NEW YORK:
         HARPER, 1880.

19914   COLES, ROBERT. "THE TURNER THESIS." PARTISAN REVIEW, 35
         (SUMMER, 1968): 412-414.

19915   "THE CONFESSION, TRIAL AND EXECUTION OF NAT TURNER, THE
         NEGRO INSURGENT, ALSO A LIST OF PERSONS KILLED."
         AMERICAN NEGRO MONOGRAPHS, 1 (1910): 1-15.

19916   COOK, FRED J.   "THE SLAVE SHIP REBELLION."   AMERICAN
        HERITAGE, 8 (FEBRUARY, 1957):   60-64, 104-106.

19917   CORE, GEORGE.   "THE CONFESSIONS OF NAT TURNER AND THE
        BURDEN OF THE PAST."   SOUTHERN LITERARY JOURNAL, 2
        (SPRING, 1970):   117-134.

19918   COULTER, E. MERTON.   "CUDJO FYE'S INSURRECTION."   GEORGIA
        HISTORICAL QUARTERLY, 38 (SEPTEMBER, 1954):   213-226.

19919   COWLEY, CHARLES.   THE ROMANCE OF HISTORY IN "THE BLACK
        COUNTY," AND THE ROMANCE OF WAR IN THE CAREER OF GEN.
        ROBERT SMALLS, "THE HERO OF THE PLANTER."   LOWELL, MA:
        N.P., 1882.

19920   CRATON, MICHAEL J.   "THE PASSION TO EXIST: SLAVE
        REBELLIONS IN THE BRITISH WEST INDIES, 1650-1832."
        JOURNAL OF CARIBBEAN HISTORY, 13 (SUMMER, 1980):   1-20.

19921   CRATON, MICHAEL J.   "PROTO-PEASANT REVOLTS?   THE LATE
        SLAVE REBELLIONS IN THE BRITISH WEST INDIES,
        1816-1832."   PAST & PRESENT, 85 (NOVEMBER, 1979):
        99-125.

19922   CROMWELL, JOHN W.   "THE AFTERMATH OF NAT TURNER'S
        INSURRECTION."   JOURNAL OF NEGRO HISTORY, 5 (APRIL,
        1920):   208-234.

19923   CROUCHETT, LAWRENCE.   "TOUSSAINT L'OUVERTURE: BLACK
        LIBERATOR."   NEGRO DIGEST, 19 (FEBRUARY, 1970):   16-20.

19924   CROW, JEFFREY J.   THE BLACK EXPERIENCE IN REVOLUTIONARY
        NORTH CAROLINA.   RALEIGH: NORTH CAROLINA DEPARTMENT
        OF CULTURAL RESOURCES, 1977.

19925   CUTLER, JAMES E.   LYNCH-LAW: AN INVESTIGATION INTO THE
        HISTORY OF LYNCHING IN THE UNITED STATES.   NEW YORK:
        LONGMANS, GREEN, 1905.

19926   DABNEY, VIRGINIUS.   "GABRIEL'S INSURRECTION."   AMERICAN
        HISTORY ILLUSTRATED, 11 (JULY, 1976):   24-32.

19927   DALY, P.H.   REVOLUTION TO REPUBLIC.   GEORGETOWN, GUYANA:
        DAILY CHRONICLE, 1970.

19928   DAVIS, OSSIE.   "NAT TURNER: HERO RECLAIMED."
        FREEDOMWAYS, 8 (SUMMER, 1968):   230-234.

19929   DAVIS, THOMAS J. (ED.).   THE NEW YORK CONSPIRACY BY
        DANIEL HORSMANDEN.   BOSTON: BEACON PRESS, 1971.

19930   DAVIS, THOMAS J.   "THE NEW YORK SLAVE CONSPIRACY OF 1741
        AS BLACK PROTEST."   JOURNAL OF NEGRO HISTORY, 56
        (JANUARY, 1971):   17-30.

19931   DEGLER, CARL N.   NEITHER BLACK NOR WHITE: SLAVERY AND
        RACE RELATIONS IN BRAZIL AND THE UNITED STATES.   NEW
        YORK: MACMILLAN COMPANY, 1971.

19932   DEGLER, CARL N.   THE OTHER SOUTH: SOUTHERN DISSENTERS IN
        THE NINETEENTH CENTURY.   NEW YORK: HARPER & ROW, 1974.

19933   DEW, CHARLES B.   "BLACK IRONWORKERS AND THE SLAVE
        INSURRECTION PANIC OF 1856."   JOURNAL OF SOUTHERN
        HISTORY, 16 (AUGUST, 1975):   321-338.

19934   DIGGS, IRENE.   "LUMBI AND THE REPUBLIC OF OS PALMARES."
        PHYLON, 14 (FIRST QUARTER, 1953):   62-70.

19935   DINSMORE, CHARLES A.   "INTERESTING SKETCHES OF THE
        AMISTAD CAPTIVES."   YALE UNIVERSITY LIBRARY GAZETTE, 9
        (JANUARY, 1935):   51-55.

19936   DOMINGUEZ, JORGE I.   INSURRECTION OR LOYALTY: THE
        BREAKDOWN OF THE SPANISH AMERICAN EMPIRE.   CAMBRIDGE:
        HARVARD UNIVERSITY PRESS, 1980.

19937   DOOKHAN, ISAAC.   "PLANTATION AGRICULTURE DURING SLAVERY."
        A HISTORY OF THE VIRGIN ISLANDS OF THE UNITED STATES.
        EPPING, ESSEX, ENGLAND: CARIBBEAN UNIVERSITIES PRESS,
        1974, PP. 69-86.

19938   DOOKHAN, ISAAC.   "SLAVERY AND EMANCIPATION."   A HISTORY
        OF THE BRITISH VIRGIN ISLANDS, 1672 TO 1970.   EPPING,
        ESSEX, ENGLAND: CARIBBEAN UNIVERSITIES PRESS, 1975,
        PP. 71-96.

19939   DORF, ANNETTE.   "THE SLAVE CONSPIRACY OF 1741."   M.A.
        THESIS, COLUMBIA UNIVERSITY, 1958.

19940   DORMON, JAMES H.   "THE PERSISTENT SPECTER: SLAVE
        REBELLION IN TERRITORIAL LOUISIANA."   LOUISIANA
        HISTORY, 18 (FALL, 1977):   389-404.

19941   DOUGLASS, FREDERICK.   "THE HEROIC SLAVE."   MASSES AND
        MAINSTREAM, 8 (FEBRUARY, 1955):   46-55.

19942   DREWRY, HENRY N.   "SLAVE INSURRECTIONS."   IN KETZ, LOUISE
        B. (ED.).   DICTIONARY OF AMERICAN HISTORY.   7 VOLS.
        NEW YORK: CHARLES SCRIBNER'S SONS, 1976, VOL. 6, PP.
        303-304.

19943   DREWRY, WILLIAM S.   "SLAVE INSURRECTIONS IN VIRGINIA
        (1830-1865)."   PH.D. DISSERTATION, JOHNS HOPKINS
        UNIVERSITY, 1900.

19944   DREWRY, WILLIAM S.   THE SOUTHAMPTON INSURRECTION.
        WASHINGTON: NEALE COMPANY, 1900.

19945   DUBOIS, W.E.B.   JOHN BROWN.   PHILADELPHIA: G.W. JACOBS &

COMPANY, 1909.

19946   DUFF, JOHN B. AND MITCHELL, PETER M. (EDS.).   THE NAT
        TURNER REBELLION: THE HISTORICAL EVENT AND THE MODERN
        CONTROVERSY.   NEW YORK: HARPER & ROW, 1971.

19947   EATON, CLEMENT.   "THE FEAR OF SERVILE INSURRECTION."   THE
        FREEDOM-OF-THOUGHT STRUGGLE IN THE OLD SOUTH.   NEW
        YORK: HARPER & ROW, 1964, PP. 89-117.

19948   EATON, CLEMENT.   THE MIND OF THE OLD SOUTH.   BATON ROUGE:
        LOUISIANA STATE UNIVERSITY PRESS, 1954.

19949   EDGAR, WALTER B. (ED.).   THE LETTERBOOK OF ROBERT
        PRINGLE.   2 VOLS.   COLUMBIA: UNIVERSITY OF SOUTH
        CAROLINA PRESS, 1972.

19950   ELLIOTT, ROBERT N.   "THE NAT TURNER INSURRECTION AS
        REPORTED IN THE NORTH CAROLINA PRESS."   NORTH CAROLINA
        HISTORICAL REVIEW, 38 (JANUARY, 1961): 1-18.

19951   ERNST, WILLIAM J.   "GABRIEL'S REVOLT: BLACK FREEDOM,
        WHITE FEAR."   M.A. THESIS, UNIVERSITY OF VIRGINIA,
        1968.

19952   FARLEY, M. FOSTER.   "THE FEAR OF NEGRO SLAVE REVOLTS IN
        SOUTH CAROLINA, 1690-1865."   AFRO-AMERICAN STUDIES, 3
        (DECEMBER, 1972): 199-207.

19953   FARLEY, M. FOSTER.   "A HISTORY OF NEGRO SLAVE REVOLTS IN
        SOUTH CAROLINA."   AFRO-AMERICAN STUDIES, 3 (SEPTEMBER,
        1972): 97-102.

19954   FARRAR, WILLIAM L.   "THE NAT TURNER REBELLION: THE
        IMPACT OF A SLAVE REVOLT ON SOUTHERN THOUGHT AND
        LEGISLATION, 1831-1832."   M.A. THESIS, SOUTHERN
        ILLINOIS UNIVERSITY, 1964.

19955   FERGUS, HOWARD A. AND GRELL, V. JANE (EDS.).   THE SEA
        GULL AND OTHER STORIES.   PLYMOUTH, MONTSERRAT:
        ALLIOUAGANA COMMUNE, 1976.

19956   FICK, CAROLYN E.   "BLACK MASSES IN THE SAN DOMINGO
        REVOLUTION: 1791-1803."   PH.D. DISSERTATION,
        CONCORDIA UNIVERSITY, 1980.

19957   "FIGHTING SLAVE."   NEGRO DIGEST, 1 (JUNE, 1943): 66-68.

19958   FILLER, LOUIS.   THE CRUSADE AGAINST SLAVERY, 1830-1860.
        NEW YORK: HARPER & ROW, 1960.

19959   FISHER, MILES M.   "NAT TURNER, A HUNDRED YEARS
        AFTERWARDS."   CRISIS, 38 (SEPTEMBER, 1931): 305.

19960   FLEMING, G. JAMES.   "WITH TORCH AND TOMAHAWK TO FREEDOM."

CRISIS, 41 (JULY, 1934): 203-210.

19961   FLEMING, JOHN E.   "THE STONO RIVER REBELLION AND ITS
         IMPACT ON THE SOUTH CAROLINA SLAVE CODE." NEGRO
         HISTORY BULLETIN, 42 (JULY-AUGUST-SEPTEMBER, 1979):
         66-68.

19962   FONER, ERIC (ED.). NAT TURNER. ENGLEWOOD CLIFFS:
         PRENTICE-HALL, 1971.

19963   FORDHAM, MONROE. "NINETEENTH-CENTURY BLACK THOUGHT IN
         THE UNITED STATES: SOME INFLUENCES OF THE SANTO
         DOMINGO REVOLUTION." JOURNAL OF BLACK STUDIES, 6
         (DECEMBER, 1975): 115-126.

19964   FOX, P.C. "AN EXAMINATION AND COMPARISON OF THE REVOLTS
         LED BY NAT TURNER AND JOHN CHILEMBWE." M.SC. THESIS,
         UNIVERSITY OF BRISTOL, 1971.

19965   FREEHLING, WILLIAM W. PRELUDE TO CIVIL WAR: THE
         NULLIFICATION CONTROVERSY IN SOUTH CAROLINA,
         1816-1836. NEW YORK: HARPER & ROW, 1966.

19966   FRESNEAU, MME. ARMAND. THERESA AT SAN DOMINGO, A TALE OF
         THE NEGRO INSURRECTION OF 1791. CHICAGO: A.C.
         MCCLURG, 1889.

19967   GASTMANN, ALBERT. "SLAVE REBELLIONS." HISTORICAL
         DICTIONARY OF THE FRENCH AND NETHERLANDS ANTILLES.
         METUCHEN, NJ: SCARECROW PRESS, 1978, P. 24.

19968   GELLERT, LAWRENCE. "TWO SONGS ABOUT NAT TURNER." WORKER
         MAGAZINE, (JUNE 12, 1949): 8.

19969   GENOVESE, EUGENE D. FROM REBELLION TO REVOLUTION:
         AFRO-AMERICAN SLAVE REVOLTS IN THE MAKING OF THE
         MODERN WORLD. BATON ROUGE: LOUISIANA STATE
         UNIVERSITY PRESS, 1979.

19970   GENOVESE, EUGENE D. ROLL, JORDAN, ROLL: THE WORLD THE
         SLAVES MADE. NEW YORK: PANTHEON, 1974.

19971   GORDON, ASA H. SKETCHES OF NEGRO LIFE AND HISTORY IN
         SOUTH CAROLINA. HAMMOND, IN: W.B. CONKEY, 1929.

19972   GRAHAM, HARRY. "THE NAPOLEON OF SAN DOMINGO." DUBLIN
         REVIEW, 153 (JULY-OCTOBER, 1913): 86-110.

19973   "GREAT MEN IN NEGRO HISTORY: SON OF MENDI CHIEF LED
         REVOLT ABOARD SHIP." SEPIA, 7 (SEPTEMBER, 1959): 51.

19974   GREEN, CHARLES. "THE SECOND AMERICAN REVOLUTION." NEGRO
         HISTORY BULLETIN, 27 (FEBRUARY, 1964): 103-105.

19975   GREENE, LORENZO J. "MUTINY ON THE SLAVE SHIPS." PHYLON,

5 (FOURTH QUARTER, 1944): 340-354.

19976 GREGORIE, ANNE K. "VESEY, DENMARK." IN DICTIONARY OF
       AMERICAN BIOGRAPHY. 26 VOLS. NEW YORK: CHARLES
       SCRIBNER'S SONS, 1927-1980, VOL. 19, PP. 258-259.

19977 GRIMKE, ARCHIBALD H. "RIGHT ON THE SCAFFOLD, OR THE
       MARTYR OF 1822." AMERICAN NEGRO ACADEMY OCCASIONAL
       PAPERS NO. 7. WASHINGTON: THE ACADEMY, 1901.

19978 GRIMSHAW, ALLEN D. "LAWLESSNESS AND VIOLENCE IN AMERICA
       AND THEIR SPECIAL MANIFESTATIONS IN CHANGING
       NEGRO-WHITE RELATIONSHIPS." JOURNAL OF NEGRO HISTORY,
       44 (JANUARY, 1959): 52-72.

19979 GROOT, SILVIA W. DE. DJUKA SOCIETY AND SOCIAL CHANGE.
       ASSEN: VAN GORCUM, 1969.

19980 GROSS, SEYMOUR L. AND BENDER, EILEEN. "HISTORY, POLITICS
       AND LITERATURE: THE MYTH OF NAT TURNER." AMERICAN
       QUARTERLY, 23 (OCTOBER, 1971): 437-518.

19981 GWINN, JANE W. "THE GEORGETOWN SLAVE INSURRECTION OF
       1829." IN JOYNER, CHARLES W. (ED.). BLACK
       CAROLINIANS: STUDIES IN THE HISTORY OF SOUTH CAROLINA
       NEGROES IN THE NINETEENTH CENTURY. LAURINBURG, NC:
       ST. ANDREWS PRESBYTERIAN COLLEGE, 1969, PP. 72-76.

19982 HALASZ, NICHOLAS. THE RATTLING CHAINS: SLAVE UNREST AND
       REVOLT IN THE ANTE-BELLUM SOUTH. NEW YORK: D. MCKAY
       COMPANY, 1966.

19983 HALL, GWENDOLYN M. "BLACK RESISTANCE IN COLONIAL HAITI."
       NEGRO DIGEST, 17 (FEBRUARY, 1968): 40-48.

19984 HALL, GWENDOLYN M. "WHAT TOUSSAINT L'OUVERTURE CAN TEACH
       US." BLACK WORLD, 21 (FEBRUARY, 1972): 46-48.

19985 HAMILTON, JOSEPH G. DE R. "TURNER, NAT." IN DICTIONARY
       OF AMERICAN BIOGRAPHY. 26 VOLS. NEW YORK: CHARLES
       SCRIBNER'S SONS, 1927-1980, VOL. 19, PP. 69-70.

19986 HARDING, VINCENT. "INTIMATIONS OF THINGS TO COME."
       BLACK-WORLD-VIEW, 1 (1976): 4-7.

19987 HARTRIDGE, WALTER C. "THE REFUGEES FROM THE ISLAND OF
       ST. DOMINGO IN MARYLAND." MARYLAND HISTORICAL
       MAGAZINE, 38 (JUNE, 1943): 103-122.

19988 HARTSINCK, J.J. "THE STORY OF THE SLAVE REBELLION IN
       BERBICE, 1762." JOURNAL OF THE BRITISH GUIANA MUSEUM
       AND ZOO OF THE ROYAL AGRICULTURAL AND COMMERCIAL
       SOCIETY, NOS. 20-27 (DECEMBER, 1958-SEPTEMBER, 1960):
       35-42, 37-45, 45-54, 43-51, 49-57, 55-64, 59-68, 61-70.

19989   HEADLEY, JOEL T.   THE GREAT RIOTS OF NEW YORK:
         1712-1873. NEW YORK: E.B. TREAT, 1873.

19990   HEALY, MARY A. "CONTRIBUTIONS OF TOUSSAINT L'OUVERTURE
         TO THE INDEPENDENCE OF THE AMERICAN REPUBLICS,
         1776-1826." AMERICAS, 9 (APRIL, 1953): 413-451.

19991   HERRICK, E.P. "UPRISING OF CUBA'S NEGROES." SOUTHERN
         WORKMAN, 42 (FEBRUARY, 1913): 95-99.

19992   HIGGINSON, THOMAS W.   TRAVELLERS AND OUTLAWS: EPISODES IN
         AMERICAN HISTORY. BOSTON: LEE AND SHEPARD, 1889.

19993   HILL, LESLIE P.   TOUSSAINT L'OUVERTURE, A DRAMATIC
         HISTORY. BOSTON: CHRISTOPHER PUBLISHING HOUSE, 1928.

19994   HINTON, RICHARD J.   JOHN BROWN AND HIS MEN, WITH SOME
         ACCOUNTS OF THE ROADS THEY TRAVELLED TO REACH HARPER'S
         FERRY. NEW YORK: FUNK & WAGNALLS, 1894.

19995   HODGE, W.J. "THE BLACK CHURCH'S OUTREACH." IN MCCALL,
         EMMANUEL L. (ED.).   THE BLACK CHRISTIAN EXPERIENCE.
         NASHVILLE: BROADMAN PRESS, 1972, PP. 73-84.

19996   HOES, ROSWELL R. "THE NEGRO PLOT OF 1712." NEW YORK
         GENEALOGICAL AND BIOGRAPHICAL RECORD, 21 (OCTOBER,
         1890): 162-163.

19997   HOEY, EDWIN. "TERROR IN NEW YORK--1741." AMERICAN
         HERITAGE, 25 (JUNE, 1974): 72-77.

19998   HOLLON, W. EUGENE.   FRONTIER VIOLENCE: ANOTHER LOOK.
         NEW YORK: OXFORD UNIVERSITY PRESS, 1974.

19999   HOLMES, JACK D.L. "THE ABORTIVE SLAVE REVOLT AT POINTE
         COUPEE, LOUISIANA, 1795." LOUISIANA HISTORY, 11
         (FALL, 1970): 341-362.

20000   HOLUB, NORMAN. "THE BRAZILIAN SABINADA (1837-1838):
         REVOLT OF THE NEGRO MASSES." JOURNAL OF NEGRO
         HISTORY, 54 (JULY, 1969): 275-283.

20001   HOPE, CORRIE S. "THE SOCIAL PSYCHOLOGICAL DETERMINANTS
         OF MINORITY UPRISING: A COMPARISON OF THE NAT TURNER
         SLAVE REBELLION (1831) AND THE NEWARK RIOT (1967)."
         PH.D. DISSERTATION, UNIVERSITY OF MASSACHUSETTS, 1975.

20002   HORTON, J. "THE HAPPY BLACK HOOKER." SEPIA, 21
         (DECEMBER, 1972): 26-28.

20003   HOWLAND, JOSEPH A. "THE AMISTAD CAPTIVES." PROCEEDINGS
         OF THE WORCESTER SOCIETY OF ANTIQUITY FOR 1886.
         WORCESTER: THE SOCIETY, 1887, PP. 61-75.

20004   HUNT, ALFRED N. "THE INFLUENCE OF HAITI ON THE

ANTEBELLUM SOUTH, 1791-1865." PH.D. DISSERTATION, UNIVERSITY OF TEXAS, 1975.

20005   INABINET, L. GLEN.   "'THE JULY FOURTH INCIDENT' OF 1816: AN INSURRECTION PLOTTED BY SLAVES IN CAMDEN, SOUTH CAROLINA."   IN JOHNSON, HERBERT A. (ED.).   SOUTH CAROLINA LEGAL HISTORY.   COLUMBIA: SOUTHERN STUDIES PROGRAM, UNIVERSITY OF SOUTH CAROLINA, 1980, PP. 209-221.

20006   INGERSOLL, HENRY H.   "THE NEW YORK NEGRO PLOT OF 1741."   GREEN BAG, 20 (JANUARY, 1908):   130-138.

20007   IVERSON, PETER J.   "THE AMISTAD AFRICANS AND AMERICA; A STUDY IN RESPONSE."   M.A. THESIS, UNIVERSITY OF WISCONSIN, 1967.

20008   JACKSON, MARGARET Y.   "MELVILLE'S USE OF A REAL SLAVE MUTINY IN 'BENITO CERENO.'"   CLA JOURNAL, 4 (DECEMBER, 1960):   79-93.

20009   JAMES, C.L.R.   THE BLACK JACOBINS: TOUSSAINT L'OUVERTURE AND THE SAN DOMINGO REVOLUTION.   NEW YORK: DIAL PRESS, 1938.

20010   JAMES, C.L.R.   A HISTORY OF NEGRO REVOLT.   LONDON: FACT LIMITED, 1938.

20011   JENKINS, H.J.K.   "GUADELOUPE, 1799-1803:   A HAITI MANQUE."   HISTORY TODAY, 30 (APRIL, 1980):   13-16.

20012   JEROME, YVES J.   TOUSSAINT L'OUVERTURE.   NEW YORK: VANTAGE PRESS, 1978.

20013   JERVEY, EDWARD D. AND HUBER, C. HAROLD.   "THE CREOLE AFFAIR."   JOURNAL OF NEGRO HISTORY, 65 (SUMMER, 1980):   196-211.

20014   JERVEY, THEODORE D.   ROBERT Y. HAYNE AND HIS TIMES.   NEW YORK: MACMILLAN, 1909.

20015   JETER, JEREMIAH B.   THE RECOLLECTIONS OF A LONG LIFE.   RICHMOND: RELIGIOUS HERALD COMPANY, 1891.

20016   JOHNSON, CLIFTON H.   "THE CREOLE AFFAIR."   CRISIS, 78 (OCTOBER, 1971):   248-250.

20017   JOHNSON, F. ROY.   THE NAT TURNER STORY: HISTORY OF THE SOUTH'S MOST IMPORTANT SLAVE REVOLT.   MURFREESBORO, NC: JOHNSON PUBLISHING COMPANY, 1970.

20018   JOHNSON, FRANK R.   THE NAT TURNER SLAVE INSURRECTION.   MURFREESBORO, NC: JOHNSON PUBLISHING COMPANY, 1966.

20019   JOHNSTON, JAMES H.   "THE PARTICIPATION OF WHITE MEN IN

VIRGINIA NEGRO INSURRECTIONS." JOURNAL OF NEGRO
HISTORY, 16 (APRIL, 1931): 158-167.

20020 JOHNSTON, STANLEY. "PEARL OF THE NEW WORLD." NEGRO
       DIGEST, 4 (FEBRUARY, 1946): 69-72.

20021 JONES, HOWARD. "THE PECULIAR INSTITUTION AND NATIONAL
       HONOR: THE CASE OF THE CREOLE SLAVE REVOLT." CIVIL
       WAR HISTORY, 21 (MARCH, 1975): 28-50.

20022 JORDAN, WINTHROP D. THE WHITE MAN'S BURDEN: HISTORICAL
       ORIGINS OF RACISM IN THE UNITED STATES. NEW YORK:
       OXFORD UNIVERSITY PRESS, 1974.

20023 JORDAN, WINTHROP D. WHITE OVER BLACK: AMERICAN
       ATTITUDES TOWARD THE NEGRO, 1550-1812. CHAPEL HILL:
       UNIVERSITY OF NORTH CAROLINA PRESS, 1968.

20024 JUNKINS, ENDA. "SLAVE PLOTS, INSURRECTIONS, AND ACTS OF
       VIOLENCE IN THE STATE OF TEXAS, 1828-1865." M.A.
       THESIS, BAYLOR UNIVERSITY, 1969.

20025 KAPLAN, SIDNEY (ED.). "BLACK MUTINY ON THE 'AMISTAD.'"
       MASSACHUSETTS REVIEW, 10 (SUMMER, 1969): 493-532.

20026 KENNEDY, MELVIN D. "THE BISSETTE AFFAIR AND THE FRENCH
       COLONIAL QUESTION." JOURNAL OF NEGRO HISTORY, 45
       (JANUARY, 1960): 1-10.

20027 KENT, R.K. "AFRICAN REVOLT IN BAHIA: 24-25 JANUARY,
       1835." JOURNAL OF SOCIAL HISTORY, 3 (SUMMER, 1970):
       334-356.

20028 KILLENS, JOHN O. GREAT GETTIN' UP MORNING: A BIOGRAPHY
       OF DENMARK VESEY. NEW YORK: DOUBLEDAY, 1972.

20029 KILLENS, JOHN O. (ED.). THE TRIAL RECORD OF DENMARK
       VESEY. BOSTON: BEACON PRESS, 1970.

20030 KILSON, MARION D. DE B. "TOWARDS FREEDOM: AN ANALYSIS
       OF SLAVE REVOLTS IN THE UNITED STATES." PHYLON, 25
       (SUMMER, 1964): 175-187.

20031 KIMBALL, WILLIAM J. "THE GABRIEL INSURRECTION OF 1800."
       NEGRO HISTORY BULLETIN, 34 (NOVEMBER, 1971): 153-156.

20032 KING, ETHEL. "THE NEW YORK NEGRO PLOT OF 1741." UNITED
       STATES CATHOLIC HISTORICAL SOCIETY RECORDS AND
       STUDIES, 20 (1931): 173-180.

20033 KLEINMAN, MAX L. "DENMARK VESEY CONSPIRACY: AN
       HISTORIOGRAPHICAL STUDY." NEGRO HISTORY BULLETIN, 37
       (FEBRUARY-MARCH, 1974): 225-229.

20034 KNIGHT, FRANKLIN W. "EUGENE GENOVESE ON AMERICAN SLAVE

REVOLTS."   REVIEWS IN AMERICAN HISTORY, 8 (SEPTEMBER,
1980):   309-311.

20035   KOPYTOFF, BARBARA K.   "GUERRILLA WARFARE IN EIGHTEENTH
CENTURY JAMAICA."   EXPEDITION, 19 (WINTER, 1977):
20-26.

20036   KORNGOLD, RALPH.   CITIZEN TOUSSAINT.   BOSTON: LITTLE,
BROWN, 1944.

20037   KORNGOLD, RALPH.   "CITIZEN TOUSSAINT."   NEGRO DIGEST, 3
(NOVEMBER, 1944):   91-98.

20038   KORT, WESLEY A.   "THE CONFESSIONS OF NAT TURNER AND THE
DYNAMIC OF REVOLUTION."   IN SHRIVEN SELVES: RELIGIOUS
PROBLEMS IN RECENT AMERICAN FICTION.   PHILADELPHIA:
FORTRESS PRESS, 1972, PP. 116-140.

20039   LANE, CARL A.   "CONCERNING JAMAICA'S 1760 SLAVE
REBELLION."   JAMAICA JOURNAL, 7 (DECEMBER, 1973):   2-4.

20040   LARA, ORUNO D.   "NEGRO RESISTANCE TO SLAVERY AND THE
ATLANTIC SLAVE TRADE FROM AFRICA TO BLACK AMERICA."
IN THE AFRICAN SLAVE TRADE FROM THE FIFTEENTH TO THE
NINETEENTH CENTURY.   PARIS: UNITED NATIONS
EDUCATIONAL, SCIENTIFIC AND CULTURAL ORGANIZATION,
1979, PP. 101-114.

20041   LAUNITZ-SCHURER, LEOPOLD S., JR.   "SLAVE RESISTANCE IN
COLONIAL NEW YORK: AN INTERPRETATION OF DANIEL
HORSMANDEN'S NEW YORK CONSPIRACY."   PHYLON, 41 (JUNE,
1980):   137-152.

20042   LAWSON, ELIZABETH.   "AFTER NAT TURNER'S REVOLT."   NEW
YORK DAILY WORKER, AUGUST 21, 1936.

20043   LEVENTHAL, HERBERT.   IN THE SHADOW OF THE ENLIGHTENMENT:
OCCULTISM AND RENAISSANCE IN EIGHTEENTH CENTURY
AMERICA.   NEW YORK: NEW YORK UNIVERSITY PRESS, 1976.

20044   LEVINE, ROBERT M.   "SLAVE INSURRECTION OF 1522."   RACE
AND ETHNIC RELATIONS IN LATIN AMERICA AND THE
CARIBBEAN.   METUCHEN, NJ: SCARECROW PRESS, 1980, P.
127.

20045   LEVINE, ROBERT M.   "SLAVE REVOLTS."   RACE AND ETHNIC
RELATIONS IN LATIN AMERICA AND THE CARIBBEAN.
METUCHEN, NJ: SCARECROW PRESS, 1980, P. 127.

20046   LEWIS, ALONZO N.   "RECOLLECTIONS OF THE AMISTAD SLAVE
CASE."   CONNECTICUT MAGAZINE, 11 (JANUARY, 1907):
125-129.

20047   LINCOLN, C. ERIC.   THE BLACK MUSLIMS IN AMERICA.   BOSTON:
BEACON PRESS, 1961.

20048   LITTLEFIELD, DANIEL F., JR. AND UNDERHILL, LONNIE E.
        "SLAVE 'REVOLT' IN THE CHEROKEE NATION, 1842."
        AMERICAN INDIAN QUARTERLY, 3 (SUMMER, 1977): 121-133.

20049   LOFTON, JOHN. INSURRECTION IN SOUTH CAROLINA: THE
        TURBULENT WORLD OF DENMARK VESEY. YELLOW SPRINGS, OH:
        ANTIOCH PRESS, 1964.

20050   LOFTON, JOHN. "NEGRO INSURRECTIONIST." ANTIOCH REVIEW,
        18 (SUMMER, 1958): 183-196.

20051   LOFTON, JOHN M. "SLAVERY IN THE TIME AND LANDS OF
        DENMARK VESEY'S CAPTIVITY." M.A. THESIS, UNIVERSITY
        OF PITTSBURGH, 1956.

20052   LOFTON, JOHN M., JR. "DENMARK VESEY'S CALL TO ARMS."
        JOURNAL OF NEGRO HISTORY, 33 (OCTOBER, 1948): 395-417.

20053   LOGAN, RAYFORD W. "THE NEGRO IN SPANISH AMERICA." IN
        WESLEY, CHARLES H. (ED.). THE NEGRO IN THE AMERICAS.
        WASHINGTON: THE GRADUATE SCHOOL, HOWARD UNIVERSITY,
        1940, PP. 24-35.

20054   LUX, WILLIAM. "SLAVE INSURRECTION." HISTORICAL
        DICTIONARY OF THE BRITISH CARIBBEAN. METUCHEN, NJ:
        SCARECROW PRESS, 1975, P. 186.

20055   MANIGAT, LESLIE F. "THE RELATIONSHIP BETWEEN MARRONAGE
        AND SLAVE REVOLTS AND REVOLUTION IN ST.
        DOMINGUE-HAITI." IN RUBIN, VERA AND TUDEN, ARTHUR
        (EDS.). COMPARATIVE PERSPECTIVES ON SLAVERY IN NEW
        WORLD PLANTATION SOCIETIES. NEW YORK: NEW YORK
        ACADEMY OF SCIENCES, 1977, PP. 420-438.

20056   MARABLE, MANNING. "REVOLT AND FAITH: NAT TURNER AND
        SISYPHUS." CLAFLIN COLLEGE REVIEW, 2 (DECEMBER,
        1977): 30-37.

20057   MARR, WARREN. "EVOLUTION OF AMISTAD." JOURNAL OF
        INTERGROUP RELATIONS, 2 (1972): 32-36.

20058   MARSZALEK, JOHN F. "BATTLE FOR FREEDOM--GABRIEL'S
        INSURRECTION." NEGRO HISTORY BULLETIN, 39 (MARCH,
        1976): 540-543.

20059   MARSZALEK, JOHN F. "GABRIEL'S INSURRECTION." IN ROLLER,
        DAVID C. AND TWYMAN, ROBERT W. (EDS.). THE
        ENCYCLOPEDIA OF SOUTHERN HISTORY. BATON ROUGE:
        LOUISIANA STATE UNIVERSITY PRESS, 1979, P. 502.

20060   MARTIN, BERT E. "FREEDOM AND THE PURITAN CONSCIENCE:
        AMERICAN DESTINY AND THE DEFENDERS OF THE AMISTAD
        AFRICANS." PH.D. DISSERTATION, BAYLOR UNIVERSITY,
        1979.

20061   MARTIN, CHRISTOPHER. THE AMISTAD AFFAIR. LONDON:
        ABELARD-SCHUMAN, 1970.

20062   MATTHEWSON, TIMOTHY M. "GEORGE WASHINGTON'S POLICY
        TOWARD THE HAITIAN REVOLUTION." DIPLOMATIC HISTORY, 3
        (SUMMER, 1979): 321-336.

20063   MCCLENDON, R. EARL. "THE AMISTAD CLAIMS:
        INCONSISTENCIES OF POLICY." POLITICAL SCIENCE
        QUARTERLY, 48 (SEPTEMBER, 1933): 386-412.

20064   MCCOLLEY, ROBERT. "SLAVE INSURRECTIONS." IN ROLLER,
        DAVID C. AND TWYMAN, ROBERT W. (EDS.). THE
        ENCYCLOPEDIA OF SOUTHERN HISTORY. BATON ROUGE:
        LOUISIANA STATE UNIVERSITY PRESS, 1979, P. 1109.

20065   MCGILL, WILLIAM J. "WILLIAM STYRON'S NAT TURNER AND
        RELIGION." SOUTH ATLANTIC QUARTERLY, 79 (WINTER,
        1980): 75-81.

20066   MCKIBBEN, DAVIDSON B. "NEGRO SLAVE INSURRECTIONS IN
        MISSISSIPPI, 1800-1865." JOURNAL OF NEGRO HISTORY, 34
        (JANUARY, 1949): 73-90.

20067   MEACHAM, GLORIA H. "SELECTED NINETEENTH CENTURY
        INTERPRETATIONS OF ORGANIZED SLAVE RESISTANCE: BLACK
        CHARACTER AND CONSCIOUSNESS AS REPRESENTED IN THE
        FICTIONAL WORKS OF HARRIET BEECHER STOWE, HERMAN
        MELVILLE, AND MARTIN ROBINSON DELANY AND RELATED
        HISTORICAL SOURCES." PH.D. DISSERTATION, CORNELL
        UNIVERSITY, 1980.

20068   MEADER, J.R. "SOME NEGRO INSURRECTIONS." AMERICANA, 6
        (AUGUST, 1911): 744-752.

20069   MILES, EDWIN A. "THE MISSISSIPPI SLAVE INSURRECTION
        SCARE OF 1835." JOURNAL OF NEGRO HISTORY, 42
        (JANUARY, 1957): 48-60.

20070   MILLER, BEVERLY. "THE FORCIBLE LIBERATION OF AMERICAN
        SLAVES IN BRITISH COLONIAL PORTS, 1830-1855." M.A.
        THESIS, UNIVERSITY OF CHICAGO, 1952.

20071   MILLIGAN, JOHN D. "SLAVE REBELLIOUSNESS AND THE FLORIDA
        MAROON." PROLOGUE, 6 (SPRING, 1974): 4-18.

20072   MINTZ, SIDNEY W. "TOWARD AN AFRO-AMERICAN HISTORY."
        CAHIERS D'HISTOIRE MONDIALE, 3 (1971): 317-332.

20073   MITCHELL, JAMES N. "NAT TURNER: SLAVE, PREACHER,
        PROPHET, AND MESSIAH, 1800-1931: A STUDY OF THE CALL
        OF A BLACK SLAVE TO PROPHETHOOD AND TO THE MESSIAHSHIP
        OF THE SECOND COMING OF CHRIST." D.MIN. DISSERTATION,
        VANDERBILT UNIVERSITY, 1975.

20074   MOORE, JOHN HAMMOND. "A HYMN OF FREEDOM; SOUTH CAROLINA,
        1813." JOURNAL OF NEGRO HISTORY, 50 (JANUARY, 1965):
        50-53.

20075   MOORE, ROBERT J. "SLAVE REBELLIONS IN GUYANA." PAPERS
        PRESENTED AT THE THIRD ANNUAL CONFERENCE OF CARIBBEAN
        HISTORIANS, APRIL 15-17, 1971. GEORGETOWN:
        UNIVERSITY OF GUYANA, 1971, PP. 62-74.

20076   MOORE, W.K. "AN ABORTIVE SLAVE UPRISING." MISSOURI
        HISTORICAL REVIEW, 52 (JANUARY, 1958): 123-126.

20077   MORRILL, RICHARD L. AND DONALDSON, O. FRED.
        "GEOGRAPHICAL PERSPECTIVES ON THE HISTORY OF BLACK
        AMERICA." IN ERNST, ROBERT T. AND HUGG, LAWRENCE
        (EDS.). BLACK AMERICA: GEOGRAPHIC PERSPECTIVES.
        GARDEN CITY: ANCHOR PRESS/DOUBLEDAY, 1976, PP. 9-33.

20078   MORRIS, CHARLES E. "PANIC AND REPRISAL: REACTION IN
        NORTH CAROLINA TO THE NAT TURNER INSURRECTION." M.A.
        THESIS, NORTH CAROLINA STATE UNIVERSITY, 1979.

20079   MORRIS, RICHARD B. "'NEGRO PLOT OF 1741.'" IN KETZ,
        LOUISE B. (ED.). DICTIONARY OF AMERICAN HISTORY. 7
        VOLS. NEW YORK: CHARLES SCRIBNER'S SONS, 1976, VOL.
        5, P. 32.

20080   MORSBERGER, ROBERT E. "SLAVERY AND THE SANTA FE TRAIL,
        OR, JOHN BROWN ON HOLLYWOOD'S SOUR APPLE TREE."
        AMERICAN STUDIES, 18 (FALL, 1977): 87-98.

20081   MOSSELL, CHARLES W. TOUSSAINT L'OUVERTURE, THE HERO OF
        SAINT DOMINGO: SOLDIER, STATESMAN, MARTYR. NEW YORK:
        WARD & COBB, 1890.

20082   MULLIN, GERALD W. FLIGHT AND REBELLION: SLAVE
        RESISTANCE IN EIGHTEENTH CENTURY VIRGINIA. NEW YORK:
        OXFORD UNIVERSITY PRESS, 1972.

20083   MULLIN, GERALD W. "GABRIEL'S INSURRECTION." IN ROSE,
        PETER I. (ED.). AMERICANS FROM AFRICA. 2 VOLS. NEW
        YORK: ATHERTON PRESS, 1970, VOL. 2, PP. 53-73.

20084   MULLIN, GERALD W., JR. "PATTERNS OF SLAVE BEHAVIOR IN
        EIGHTEENTH-CENTURY VIRGINIA." PH.D. DISSERTATION,
        UNIVERSITY OF CALIFORNIA, 1968.

20085   MULLIN, GERRY. "RELIGION, ACCULTURATION, AND AMERICAN
        NEGRO SLAVE REBELLIONS: GABRIEL'S INSURRECTION." IN
        BRACEY, JOHN H., JR.; MEIER, AUGUST; AND RUDWICK,
        ELLIOTT (EDS.). AMERICAN SLAVERY: THE QUESTION OF
        RESISTANCE. BELMONT, CA: WADSWORTH PUBLISHING
        COMPANY, 1971, PP. 160-178.

20086   NASH, GARY B. "THE AFRICAN RESPONSE TO SLAVERY." RED,

WHITE AND BLACK: THE PEOPLES OF EARLY AMERICA.
ENGLEWOOD CLIFFS: PRENTICE-HALL, 1974, PP. 183-212.

20087 "NEGRO INSURRECTIONS." CENTURY MAGAZINE, N.S., 26
       (OCTOBER, 1884): 865-867.

20088 "NEGRO PLOT IN NEW YORK IN 1741." NATIONAL MAGAZINE, 18
       (APRIL, 1903): 128-131.

20089 NEIL, SARA E. "THE GREAT FEAR: WHITE REACTIONS TO SLAVE
       REBELLIONS." IN JOYNER, CHARLES W. (ED.). BLACK
       CAROLINIANS: STUDIES IN THE HISTORY OF SOUTH CAROLINA
       NEGROES IN THE NINETEENTH CENTURY. LAURINBURG, NC:
       ST. ANDREWS PRESBYTERIAN COLLEGE, 1969, PP. 77-87.

20090 NEWTON, JAMES. "DELAWARE'S REACTION TO THE NAT TURNER
       REBELLION." NEGRO HISTORY BULLETIN, 38 (DECEMBER,
       1974-JANUARY, 1975): 328-329.

20091 NEWTON, JAMES E. "DELAWARE'S REACTION TO THE NAT TURNER
       REBELLION." CRISIS, 81 (AUGUST/SEPTEMBER, 1974):
       240-241.

20092 NORTHCOTT, CECIL. SLAVERY'S MARTYR: JOHN SMITH OF
       DEMERARA AND THE EMANCIPATION MOVEMENT, 1817-1824.
       LONDON: EPWORTH PRESS, 1976.

20093 NORTON, WESLEY. "THE METHODIST EPISCOPAL CHURCH AND THE
       CIVIL DISTURBANCES IN NORTH TEXAS IN 1859 AND 1860."
       SOUTHWESTERN HISTORICAL QUARTERLY, 68 (JANUARY, 1965):
       317-341.

20094 NYE, RUSSEL B. "FREEDOM ROAD: NAT TURNER." A BAKER'S
       DOZEN: THIRTEEN UNUSUAL AMERICANS. EAST LANSING:
       MICHIGAN STATE UNIVERSITY PRESS, 1956, PP. 233-253.

20095 NYE, RUSSEL B. "FREEDOM ROAD: NAT TURNER." CENTENNIAL
       REVIEW, 1 (SUMMER, 1957): 242-263.

20096 OATES, STEPHEN B. "CHILDREN OF DARKNESS." AMERICAN
       HERITAGE, 24 (OCTOBER, 1973): 42-47, 89-91.

20097 OATES, STEPHEN B. THE FIRES OF JUBILEE: NAT TURNER'S
       FIERCE REBELLION. NEW YORK: HARPER & ROW, 1975.

20098 OATES, STEPHEN B. "TURNER'S REBELLION." IN ROLLER,
       DAVID C. AND TWYMAN, ROBERT W. (EDS.). THE
       ENCYCLOPEDIA OF SOUTHERN HISTORY. BATON ROUGE:
       LOUISIANA STATE UNIVERSITY PRESS, 1975, P. 1255.

20099 O'CONNELL, SHAUN. "STYRON'S NAT TURNER. . . ." NATION,
       205 (OCTOBER 16, 1967): 373-374.

20100 O'CONNELL, SHAUN V. "THE CONTEXTS OF WILLIAM STYRON'S
       'THE CONFESSIONS OF NAT TURNER.'" PH.D. DISSERTATION,

1490

UNIVERSITY OF MASSACHUSETTS, 1970.

20101   OLSEN, PETER.   "THE NEGRO AND THE SEA; BLACK RESISTANCE
        TO SLAVERY."   NEGRO HISTORY BULLETIN, 35 (FEBRUARY,
        1972):   40-44.

20102   OTT, THOMAS O.   THE HAITIAN REVOLUTION, 1789-1804.
        KNOXVILLE: UNIVERSITY OF TENNESSEE PRESS, 1973.

20103   "OUT OF THE FILES; SLAVE UPRISING IN CARACAS."   AMERICAS,
        2 (NOVEMBER, 1950):   33-34.

20104   OVIEDO Y BANOS, JOSE DE.   "REVOLT AND CORONATION OF THE
        NEGRO MIGUEL."   IN DEONIS, HARRIET W. (ED.).   THE
        GOLDEN LAND: AN ANTHOLOGY OF LATIN AMERICAN FOLKLORE
        IN LITERATURE.   NEW YORK: ALFRED A. KNOPF, 1948, PP.
        81-84.

20105   OWENS, WILLIAM A.   SLAVE MUTINY: THE REVOLT ON THE
        SCHOONER AMISTAD.   NEW YORK: J. DAY COMPANY, 1953.

20106   PARKER, WILLIAM H.   "THE NAT TURNER INSURRECTION."   OLD
        VIRGINIA YARNS, 1 (JANUARY, 1893):   14-29.

20107   PARKS, H.B.   "FOLLOW THE DRINKING GOURD."   PUBLICATIONS
        OF THE TEXAS FOLKLORE SOCIETY, 7 (1928):   81-84.

20108   PARRAMORE, THOMAS C.   "CONSPIRACY AND REVIVALISM IN 1802:
        A DIREFUL SYMBIOSIS."   NEGRO HISTORY BULLETIN, 43
        (APRIL-MAY-JUNE, 1980):   28-31.

20109   PARRAMORE, THOMAS C.   "THE GREAT SLAVE CONSPIRACY."   THE
        STATE, 39 (AUGUST 15, 1971):   7-10, 19.

20110   PARRAMORE, THOMAS C.   SOUTHAMPTON COUNTY, VIRGINIA.
        CHARLOTTESVILLE: UNIVERSITY PRESS OF VIRGINIA, 1978.

20111   PATTERSON, ORLANDO.   "SLAVERY AND SLAVE REVOLTS: A
        SOCIO-HISTORICAL ANALYSIS OF THE FIRST MAROON WAR,
        JAMAICA, 1655-1740."   SOCIAL AND ECONOMIC STUDIES, 19
        (SEPTEMBER, 1970):   289-325.

20112   PERRIN, LESTER W.   "THE SLAVE PLOT OF 1734."   UNPUBLISHED
        PAPER, FAR HILLS, NEW JERSEY, 1958.

20113   PHILLIPS, ULRICH B.   AMERICAN NEGRO SLAVERY: A SURVEY OF
        THE SUPPLY, EMPLOYMENT AND CONTROL OF NEGRO LABOR AS
        DETERMINED BY THE PLANTATION REGIME.   NEW YORK: D.
        APPLETON, 1918.

20114   PHILLIPS, ULRICH B.   "RACIAL PROBLEMS, ADJUSTMENTS AND
        DISTURBANCES."   IN RILEY, FRANKLIN L. (ED.).   THE
        SOUTH IN THE BUILDING OF THE NATION.   12 VOLS.
        RICHMOND: SOUTHERN HISTORICAL PUBLICATION SOCIETY,
        1909, VOL. 4, PP. 194-241.

20115   PHILLIPS, ULRICH B. "THE SLAVE LABOR PROBLEM IN THE
        CHARLESTON DISTRICT." POLITICAL SCIENCE QUARTERLY, 22
        (SEPTEMBER, 1907): 415-439.

20116   PICKENS, DONALD K. "UNCLE TOM BECOMES NAT TURNER: A
        COMMENTARY ON TWO AMERICAN HEROES." NEGRO AMERICAN
        LITERATURE FORUM, 3 (SUMMER, 1969): 45-48.

20117   POLLAK-ELTZ, ANGELINA. "SLAVE REVOLTS IN VENEZUELA." IN
        RUBIN, VERA AND TUDEN, ARTHUR (EDS.). COMPARATIVE
        PERSPECTIVES ON SLAVERY IN NEW WORLD PLANTATION
        SOCIETIES. NEW YORK: NEW YORK ACADEMY OF SCIENCES,
        1977, PP. 439-445.

20118   POOL, GAIL R. "JAMAICAN SLAVERY AND SLAVE REVOLTS."
        M.A. THESIS, MCMASTER UNIVERSITY, 1972.

20119   POOLE, WILLIAM J. "THE CREOLE CASE." M.A. THESIS,
        LOUISIANA STATE UNIVERSITY, NEW ORLEANS, 1970.

20120   POTTER, DAVID M. THE IMPENDING CRISIS, 1848-1861. NEW
        YORK: HARPER & ROW, 1976.

20121   PRICE, RICHARD (ED.). "AFTERWORD." MAROON SOCIETIES:
        REBEL SLAVE COMMUNITIES IN THE AMERICAS. BALTIMORE:
        JOHNS HOPKINS UNIVERSITY PRESS, 1979, PP. 417-431.

20122   PRICE, RICHARD (ED.). MAROON SOCIETIES: REBEL SLAVE
        COMMUNITIES IN THE AMERICAS. GARDEN CITY:
        ANCHOR-DOUBLEDAY, 1973.

20123   PRINCE, HOWARD M. "SLAVE REBELLION IN BAHIA, 1807-1835."
        PH.D. DISSERTATION, COLUMBIA UNIVERSITY, 1972.

20124   PRINCE, WALTER F. "NEW YORK 'NEGRO PLOT' OF 1741." NEW
        HAVEN SATURDAY CHRONICLE, JUNE 28, AUGUST 23, 1902.

20125   "PUNISHMENT FOR A NEGRO REBEL." WILLIAM AND MARY COLLEGE
        QUARTERLY, 10 (1902): 177-178.

20126   QUARLES, BENJAMIN. "THE ABDUCTION OF THE 'PLANTER.'"
        CIVIL WAR HISTORY, 4 (MARCH, 1958): 5-10.

20127   RAPER, DENNIS L. "THE EFFECTS OF DAVID WALKER'S APPEAL
        AND NAT TURNER'S INSURRECTION ON NORTH CAROLINA."
        M.A. THESIS, UNIVERSITY OF NORTH CAROLINA, 1969.

20128   RAPPAPORT, STANLEY. "SLAVE STRUGGLES FOR FREEDOM."
        CRISIS, 43 (SEPTEMBER, 1936): 264-265, 274, 284-286.

20129   RAWICK, GEORGE P. FROM SUNDOWN TO SUNUP: THE MAKING OF
        THE BLACK COMMUNITY. WESTPORT: GREENWOOD PRESS, 1972.

20130   RECKORD, MARY. "THE JAMAICA SLAVE REBELLION OF 1831."
        IN FRUCHT, RICHARD (ED.). BLACK SOCIETY IN THE NEW

WORLD]. NEW YORK: RANDOM HOUSE, 1971, PP. 50-66.

20131   RECKORD, MARY. "THE JAMAICA SLAVE REBELLION OF 1831."
        PAST & PRESENT, NO. 40 (JULY, 1968): 108-125.

20132   RECKORD, MARY. "THE SLAVE REBELLION OF 1831." JAMAICA
        JOURNAL, 3 (JUNE, 1969): 25-31.

20133   REIS, JOAO J. "BLACK REVOLTS IN BAHIA, 1807-1335." M.A.
        THESIS, UNIVERSITY OF MINNESOTA, 1978.

20134   REYNOLDS, C. ROY. "TACKY AND THE GREAT SLAVE REBELLION
        OF 1760." JAMAICA JOURNAL, 6 (JUNE, 1972): 5-8.

20135   REYNOLDS, DONALD E. "SMITH COUNTY AND ITS NEIGHBORS
        DURING THE SLAVE INSURRECTION PANIC OF 1860."
        CHRONICLES OF SMITH COUNTY, TEXAS, 10 (FALL, 1971):
        1-8.

20136   RODNEY, WALTER AND AUGUSTUS, EARL. "THE NEGRO SLAVE."
        CARIBBEAN QUARTERLY, 10 (MARCH, 1964): 40-47.

20137   ROSBROW, JAMES M. "THE 'ABDUCTION' OF THE PLANTER."
        CRISIS, 56 (APRIL, 1949): 106-107.

20138   ROSE, LISLE A. "A COMMUNICATION." WILLIAM AND MARY
        QUARTERLY, 3RD SER., 26 (JANUARY, 1969): 162-164.

20139   ROUT, LESLIE B. THE AFRICAN EXPERIENCE IN SPANISH
        AMERICA, 1502 TO THE PRESENT DAY. CAMBRIDGE:
        CAMBRIDGE UNIVERSITY PRESS, 1976.

20140   RUCKER, ALVIN. "THE STORY OF SLAVE UPRISING IN
        OKLAHOMA." OKLAHOMA CITY DAILY OKLAHOMAN, OCTOBER 30,
        1932.

20141   RUKEYSER, M. "AMISTAD MUTINY." IN MOON, BUCKLIN (ED.).
        PRIMER FOR WHITE FOLKS. NEW YORK: DOUBLEDAY, 1945,
        PP. 23-50.

20142   SADLER, LYNN B. "DR. STEPHEN GRAHAM'S NARRATION OF THE
        'DUPLIN INSURRECTION': ADDITIONAL EVIDENCE OF THE
        IMPACT OF NAT TURNER." JOURNAL OF AMERICAN STUDIES,
        12 (DECEMBER, 1978): 359-367.

20143   "THE SAGA OF L'AMISTAD." PHYLON, 2 (FIRST QUARTER,
        1941): 2-4.

20144   SCHAFER, DANIEL L. "THE MAROONS OF JAMAICA; AFRICAN
        SLAVE REBELS IN THE CARIBBEAN." PH.D. DISSERTATION,
        UNIVERSITY OF MINNESOTA, 1973.

20145   SCHAFER, JUDITH K. "THE IMMEDIATE IMPACT OF NAT TURNER'S
        INSURRECTION ON NEW ORLEANS." LOUISIANA HISTORY, 21
        (FALL, 1980): 361-376.

20146   SCHERMAN, KATHARINE. *THE SLAVE WHO FREED HAITI: THE STORY OF TOUSSAINT LOUVERTURE*. NEW YORK: RANDOM HOUSE, 1954.

20147   SCHULER, MONICA. "AKAN SLAVE REBELLIONS IN THE BRITISH CARIBBEAN." *SAVACOU*, 1 (JUNE, 1970): 8-31.

20148   SCHULER, MONICA. "ETHNIC SLAVE REBELLIONS IN THE CARIBBEAN AND THE GUIANAS." *JOURNAL OF SOCIAL HISTORY*, 3 (SUMMER, 1970): 374-385.

20149   SCOTT, KENNETH. "THE SLAVE INSURRECTION IN NEW YORK IN 1712." *NEW YORK HISTORICAL SOCIETY QUARTERLY*, 45 (JANUARY, 1961): 43-74.

20150   SHEPPARD, JILL. "THE SLAVE CONSPIRACY THAT NEVER WAS." *JOURNAL OF THE BARBADOS MUSEUM AND HISTORICAL SOCIETY*, 34 (MARCH, 1974): 190-197.

20151   SHERIDAN, RICHARD B. "THE JAMAICAN SLAVE INSURRECTION SCARE OF 1776 AND THE AMERICAN REVOLUTION." *JOURNAL OF NEGRO HISTORY*, 61 (JULY, 1976): 290-310.

20152   SIMMONS, WILLIAM J. "INSURRECTIONIST." *MEN OF MARK: EMINENT, PROGRESSIVE AND RISING*. CLEVELAND: REWELL PUBLISHING COMPANY, 1887, P. 1035.

20153   SINGHAM, ARCHIE. "C.L.R. JAMES ON THE BLACK JACOBIN REVOLUTION IN SAN DOMINGO." *SAVACOU*, 1 (JUNE, 1970): 82-97.

20154   SIRES, RONALD V. "THE JAMAICA SLAVE INSURRECTION LOAN, 1832-1863." *JOURNAL OF NEGRO HISTORY*, 27 (JULY, 1942): 295-319.

20155   SKEMER, DON C. "NEW EVIDENCE ON BLACK UNREST IN COLONIAL NEW YORK." *JOURNAL OF LONG ISLAND HISTORY*, 12 (FALL, 1975): 46-49.

20156   "SLAVE INSURRECTIONS." IN RYWELL, MARTIN (ED.). *AFRO-AMERICAN ENCYCLOPEDIA*. 10 VOLS. NORTH MIAMI: EDUCATIONAL BOOK PUBLISHERS, 1974, VOL. 8, P. 2507.

20157   "SLAVE INSURRECTIONS." IN WEBB, WALTER P. (ED.). *THE HANDBOOK OF TEXAS*. 2 VOLS. AUSTIN: TEXAS STATE HISTORICAL ASSOCIATION, 1952, VOL. 2, PP. 618-619.

20158   "A SLAVE MUTINY, 1764." *CONNECTICUT HISTORICAL SOCIETY BULLETIN*, 31 (JANUARY, 1966): 30-32.

20159   "SLAVE REVOLTS." IN BASKIN, WADE AND RUNES, RICHARD N. *DICTIONARY OF BLACK CULTURE*. NEW YORK: PHILOSOPHICAL LIBRARY, 1973, P. 406.

20160   "SLAVE UPRISING IN NEW YORK (1712)." IN RYWELL, MARTIN

(ED.). AFRO-AMERICAN ENCYCLOPEDIA. 10 VOLS. NORTH MIAMI: EDUCATIONAL BOOK PUBLISHERS, 1974, VOL. 8, PP. 2506-2507.

20161 "SLAVERY IN THE AMERICAS." IN PLOSKI, HARRY A. AND MARR, WARREN (EDS.). THE NEGRO ALMANAC: A REFERENCE WORK ON THE AFRO-AMERICAN. NEW YORK: BELLWETHER PUBLISHING COMPANY, 1976, PP. 1049-1064.

20162 SLOAN, RUTH C.M. "FEAR OF INSURRECTION IN THE ANTE BELLUM SOUTH." M.A. THESIS, WESTERN RESERVE UNIVERSITY, 1935.

20163 SMITH, JULIA F. "RACIAL ATTITUDES IN THE OLD SOUTHWEST." IN ELLSWORTH, LUCIUS F. (ED.). THE AMERICANIZATION OF THE GULF COAST, 1803-1850. PENSACOLA: HISTORIC PENSACOLA PRESERVATION BOARD, 1972, PP. 68-77.

20164 SNAVLEY, LARRY M. "VESEY PLOT (1821-1822)." IN ROLLER, DAVID C. AND TWYMAN, ROBERT W. (EDS.). THE ENCYCLOPEDIA OF SOUTHERN HISTORY. BATON ROUGE: LOUISIANA STATE UNIVERSITY PRESS, 1979, P. 1272.

20165 STAMPP, KENNETH M. THE PECULIAR INSTITUTION: SLAVERY IN THE ANTE-BELLUM SOUTH. NEW YORK: ALFRED A. KNOPF, 1956.

20166 STAROBIN, ROBERT. BLACKS IN BONDAGE: LETTERS OF AMERICAN SLAVES. NEW YORK: NEW VIEWPOINTS, 1974.

20167 STAROBIN, ROBERT S. (ED.). DENMARK VESEY: THE SLAVE CONSPIRACY OF 1822. ENGLEWOOD CLIFFS: PRENTICE-HALL, 1970.

20168 STAROBIN, ROBERT S. "DENMARK VESEY'S SLAVE CONSPIRACY OF 1822: A STUDY IN REBELLION AND REPRESSION." IN BRACEY, JOHN H., JR.; MEIER, AUGUST; AND RUDWICK, ELLIOTT (EDS.). AMERICAN SLAVERY: THE QUESTION OF RESISTANCE. BELMONT, CA: WADSWORTH PUBLISHING COMPANY, 1971, PP. 142-157.

20169 STEGMAIER, MARK J. "MARYLAND'S FEAR OF INSURRECTION AT THE TIME OF BRADDOCK'S DEFEAT." MARYLAND HISTORICAL MAGAZINE, 71 (WINTER, 1976): 467-483.

20170 STERLING, DOROTHY. CAPTAIN OF THE PLANTER: THE STORY OF ROBERT SMALLS. GARDEN CITY: DOUBLEDAY AND COMPANY, 1958.

20171 STEVENS, N. "THE 100TH ANNIVERSARY OF THE NAT TURNER REVOLT." COMMUNIST, 10 (AUGUST, 1931): 737-743.

20172 STEWARD, THEOPHILUS G. HAITIAN REVOLUTION, 1791 TO 1804: OR, SIDELIGHTS ON THE FRENCH REVOLUTION. NEW YORK: NEALE PUBLISHING COMPANY, 1914.

1495

20173   STODDARD, THEODORE L.   THE FRENCH REVOLUTION IN SAN
        DOMINGO.   BOSTON: HOUGHTON MIFFLIN COMPANY, 1914.

20174   STODDARD, THEODORE L.   "THE FRENCH REVOLUTION IN SAN
        DOMINGO."   PH.D. DISSERTATION, HARVARD UNIVERSITY,
        1914.

20175   STRINE, MARY S.   "THE CONFESSIONS OF NAT TURNER:
        STYRON'S MEDITATION ON HISTORY AS RHETORICAL ACT."
        QUARTERLY JOURNAL OF SPEECH, 64 (OCTOBER, 1978):
        246-266.

20176   STUCKEY, STERLING.   "REMEMBERING DENMARK VESEY."   NEGRO
        DIGEST, 15 (FEBRUARY, 1966):   23-41.

20177   "SUMMARY OF TRIAL PROCEEDINGS OF THOSE ACCUSED OF
        PARTICIPATING IN THE SLAVE UPRISING OF JANUARY 9,
        1811."   LOUISIANA HISTORY, 18 (FALL, 1977):   472-473.

20178   SUTTLES, WILLIAM C., JR.   "AFRICAN RELIGIOUS SURVIVALS AS
        FACTORS IN AMERICAN SLAVE REVOLTS."   JOURNAL OF NEGRO
        HISTORY, 56 (APRIL, 1971):   97-104.

20179   SYNNOTT, ANTHONY.   "SLAVE REVOLTS IN GUYANA AND TRINIDAD:
        A HISTORY AND COMPARATIVE ANALYSIS."   UNPUBLISHED
        MANUSCRIPT, SIR GEORGE WILLIAMS UNIVERSITY, 1971.

20180   SYNNOTT, ANTHONY J.   "SLAVE REVOLTS IN THE CARIBBEAN."
        PH.D. DISSERTATION, UNIVERSITY OF LONDON, 1976.

20181   SZASZ, FERENC M.   "THE NEW YORK SLAVE REVOLT OF 1741:   A
        RE-EXAMINATION."   NEW YORK HISTORY, 48 (JULY, 1967):
        215-230.

20182   TATUM, GEORGIA L.   DISLOYALTY IN THE CONFEDERACY.   CHAPEL
        HILL: UNIVERSITY OF NORTH CAROLINA PRESS, 1934.

20183   TAYLOR, ROSSER H.   "SLAVE CONSPIRACIES IN NORTH
        CAROLINA."   NORTH CAROLINA HISTORICAL REVIEW, 5
        (JANUARY, 1928):   20-34.

20184   TERRY, GEORGE D.   "A STUDY OF THE IMPACT OF THE FRENCH
        REVOLUTION AND THE INSURRECTIONS IN SAINT-DOMINGUE
        UPON SOUTH CAROLINA: 1790-1805."   M.A. THESIS,
        UNIVERSITY OF SOUTH CAROLINA, 1975.

20185   TEULON, ALAN.   "THE WINDWARD MAROONS."   BULLETIN OF THE
        JAMAICA HISTORICAL SOCIETY, 4 (DECEMBER, 1968):
        304-309.

20186   THELWELL, MIKE.   "THE TURNER THESIS."   PARTISAN REVIEW,
        35 (SUMMER, 1968):   403-412.

20187   TRAGLE, HENRY I.   NAT TURNER'S SLAVE REVOLT--1831.   NEW
        YORK: GROSSMAN, 1972.

1

20188   TRAGLE, HENRY I.   "SOUTHAMPTON SLAVE REVOLT." AMERICAN
         HISTORY ILLUSTRATED, 6 (NOVEMBER, 1971):   4-11, 44-47.

20189   TRAGLE, HENRY I.   "THE SOUTHAMPTON SLAVE REVOLT."   PH.D.
         DISSERTATION, UNIVERSITY OF MASSACHUSETTS, 1971.

20190   TRAGLE, HENRY I.   THE SOUTHAMPTON SLAVE REVOLT OF 1831:
         A COMPILATION OF SOURCE MATERIAL.   AMHERST:
         UNIVERSITY OF MASSACHUSETTS PRESS, 1971.

20191   TURNER, BLAIR P.   "DENMARK VESEY ON TRIAL."   ST. ANDREWS
         REVIEW, 1 (SUMMER, 1971):   17-21.

20192   TURNER, BLAIR P.   "THE TRIAL OF DENMARK VESEY."   IN
         JOYNER, CHARLES W. (ED.).   BLACK CAROLINIANS: STUDIES
         IN THE HISTORY OF SOUTH CAROLINA NEGROES.   LAURINBURG,
         NC: ST. ANDREWS PRESBYTERIAN COLLEGE, 1969, PP. 61-71.

20193   TURNER, LUCY M.   "THE FAMILY OF NAT TURNER, 1831 TO
         1954."   NEGRO HISTORY BULLETIN, 18 (MARCH, 1955):
         127-132, 145-146, 155-158.

20194   "TURNER, NAT."   IN SCHAPSMEIER, EDWARD L. AND
         SCHAPSMEIER, FREDERICK.   ENCYCLOPEDIA OF AMERICAN
         AGRICULTURAL HISTORY.   WESTPORT: GREENWOOD PRESS,
         1975, P. 354.

20195   "TURNER REBELLION."   IN SCHAPSMEIER, EDWARD L. AND
         SCHAPSMEIER, FREDERICK.   ENCYCLOPEDIA OF AMERICAN
         AGRICULTURAL HISTORY.   WESTPORT: GREENWOOD PRESS,
         1975, P. 355.

20196   UYA, OKON E.   "SLAVE REVOLTS OF THE MIDDLE PASSAGE: A
         NEGLECTED THEME."   CALABAR HISTORICAL JOURNAL, 1
         (JUNE, 1976):   65-88.

20197   VALENTINE, D.T.   MANUAL OF THE CORPORATION OF THE CITY OF
         NEW YORK, 1865.   NEW YORK: COMMON COUNCIL, 1865.

20198   "VESEY, DENMARK."   IN SCHAPSMEIER, EDWARD L. AND
         SCHAPSMEIER, FREDERICK.   ENCYCLOPEDIA OF AMERICAN
         AGRICULTURAL HISTORY.   WESTPORT: GREENWOOD PRESS,
         1975, P. 361.

20199   "VESEY REBELLION."   IN SCHAPSMEIER, EDWARD L. AND
         SCHAPSMEIER, FREDERICK.   ENCYCLOPEDIA OF AMERICAN
         AGRICULTURAL HISTORY.   WESTPORT: GREENWOOD PRESS,
         1975, P. 361.

20200   WADE, RICHARD C.   THE URBAN FRONTIER: THE RISE OF
         WESTERN CITIES, 1790-1830.   CAMBRIDGE: HARVARD
         UNIVERSITY PRESS, 1959.

20201   WADE, RICHARD C.   "THE VESEY PLOT: A RECONSIDERATION."
         JOURNAL OF SOUTHERN HISTORY, 30 (MAY, 1964):   143-161.

20202   WALKER, DENNIS. "BLACK ISLAMIC SLAVE REVOLTS OF SOUTH
        AMERICA." ISLAMIC REVIEW, 53 (OCTOBER/NOVEMBER,
        1970): 9-11.

20203   WALTON, PERRY. "THE MYSTERIOUS CASE OF THE LONG, LOW,
        BLACK SCHOONER." NEW ENGLAND QUARTERLY, 6 (JUNE,
        1933): 353-361.

20204   WATSON, ALAN D. "IMPULSE TOWARD INDEPENDENCE:
        RESISTANCE AND REBELLION AMONG NORTH CAROLINA SLAVES,
        1750-1755." JOURNAL OF NEGRO HISTORY, 63 (FALL,
        1978): 317-328.

20205   WAX, DAROLD D. "NEGRO RESISTANCE TO THE EARLY AMERICAN
        SLAVE TRADE." JOURNAL OF NEGRO HISTORY, 51 (JANUARY,
        1966): 1-15.

20206   WAXMAN, PERCY. THE BLACK NAPOLEON: THE STORY OF
        TOUSSAINT LOUVERTURE. NEW YORK: HARCOURT, BRACE,
        1931.

20207   WEEKS, STEPHEN B. "THE SLAVE INSURRECTION IN VIRGINIA,
        1831, KNOWN AS 'OLD NAT'S WAR.'" MAGAZINE OF AMERICAN
        HISTORY, 25 (JUNE, 1891): 448-458.

20208   WERNER, RANDOLPH. "AN INQUIRY INTO SOME ASPECTS OF NAT
        TURNER'S REBELLION." M.A. THESIS, COLLEGE OF WILLIAM
        AND MARY, 1971.

20209   WESTERGAARD, WALDEMAR. "ACCOUNT OF THE NEGRO REBELLION
        ON ST. CROIX, DANISH WEST INDIES, 1759." JOURNAL OF
        NEGRO HISTORY, 11 (JANUARY, 1926): 50-61.

20210   WHITE, LAURA A. "SLAVE INSURRECTIONS." IN ADAMS, JAMES
        T. (ED.). DICTIONARY OF AMERICAN HISTORY. 5 VOLS.
        NEW YORK: CHARLES SCRIBNER'S SONS, 1940, VOL. 5, P.
        90.

20211   WHITE, WILLIAM W. "THE TEXAS SLAVE INSURRECTION OF
        1860." SOUTHWESTERN HISTORICAL QUARTERLY, 52
        (JANUARY, 1949): 259-285.

20212   WILEY, BELL I. SOUTHERN NEGROES, 1861-1865. NEW HAVEN:
        YALE UNIVERSITY PRESS, 1938.

20213   WISH, HARVEY. "AMERICAN SLAVE INSURRECTIONS BEFORE
        1861." JOURNAL OF NEGRO HISTORY, 22 (JULY, 1937):
        299-320.

20214   WISH, HARVEY. "THE SLAVE INSURRECTION PANIC OF 1856."
        JOURNAL OF SOUTHERN HISTORY, 5 (MAY, 1939): 206-222.

20215   WOOD, PETER H. BLACK MAJORITY: NEGROES IN COLONIAL
        SOUTH CAROLINA, 1670 TO THE STONO REBELLION. NEW
        YORK: ALFRED A. KNOPF, 1974.

20216   WOODSON, CARTER G. "ROBERT SMALLS AND HIS DESCENDANTS."
        NEGRO HISTORY BULLETIN, 11 (NOVEMBER, 1947): 27-33.

20217   ZEUGNER, JOHN. "A NOTE ON MARTIN DELANY'S BLAKE, AND
        BLACK MILITANCY." PHYLON, 32 (SPRING, 1971): 98-105.

20218   ZILVERSMIT, ARTHUR. THE FIRST EMANCIPATION: THE
        ABOLITION OF SLAVERY IN THE NORTH. CHICAGO:
        UNIVERSITY OF CHICAGO PRESS, 1967.

DAY-TO-DAY RESISTANCE

20219   APTHEKER, HERBERT. "ADDITIONAL DATA ON AMERICAN
        MAROONS." JOURNAL OF NEGRO HISTORY, 32 (OCTOBER,
        1947): 452-460.

20220   BALOGH, JOSEPH. "CRIME." IN ROLLER, DAVID C. AND
        TWYMAN, ROBERT W. (EDS.). THE ENCYCLOPEDIA OF
        SOUTHERN HISTORY. BATON ROUGE: LOUISIANA STATE
        UNIVERSITY PRESS, 1979, PP. 311-312.

20221   BANCROFT, FREDERIC. "SOME UNDISTINGUISHED NEGROES."
        JOURNAL OF NEGRO HISTORY, 5 (OCTOBER, 1920): 476-480.

20222   BARADELL, WILLIAM L. "RUNAWAY SLAVES IN MISSISSIPPI."
        M.A. THESIS, UNIVERSITY OF SOUTHERN MISSISSIPPI, 1974.

20223   BAUER, RAYMOND A. AND BAUER, ALICE H. "DAY TO DAY
        RESISTANCE TO SLAVERY." JOURNAL OF NEGRO HISTORY, 27
        (OCTOBER, 1942): 388-419.

20224   BISHOP, PATRICIA A. "RUNAWAY SLAVES IN JAMAICA,
        1740-1807: A STUDY BASED ON NEWSPAPER ADVERTISEMENTS
        PUBLISHED DURING THAT PERIOD FOR RUNAWAYS." M.A.
        THESIS, UNIVERSITY OF THE WEST INDIES, 1972.

20225   BLAKE, RUSSELL. "SLAVE RUNAWAYS IN COLONIAL SOUTH
        CAROLINA." UNPUBLISHED PAPER, UNIVERSITY OF MICHIGAN,
        1972.

20226   BLASSINGAME, JOHN W. THE SLAVE COMMUNITY: PLANTATION
        LIFE IN THE ANTEBELLUM SOUTH. NEW YORK: OXFORD
        UNIVERSITY PRESS, 1972.

20227   BLASSINGAME, JOHN W. "STATUS AND SOCIAL STRUCTURE IN THE
        SLAVE COMMUNITY: EVIDENCE FROM NEW SOURCES." IN
        OWENS, HARRY P. (ED.). PERSPECTIVES AND IRONY IN
        AMERICAN SLAVERY. JACKSON: UNIVERSITY PRESS OF
        MISSISSIPPI, 1976, PP. 137-152.

20228   BRUCE, DICKSON D., JR. "SLAVERY AND VIOLENCE: THE
        SLAVES' VIEW." VIOLENCE AND CULTURE IN THE ANTEBELLUM
        SOUTH. AUSTIN: UNIVERSITY OF TEXAS PRESS, 1979, PP.
        137-160.

20229   BUKER, GEORGE E.   SWAMP SAILORS: RIVERINE WARFARE IN THE
        EVERGLADES, 1835-1842.   GAINESVILLE: UNIVERSITY
        PRESSES OF FLORIDA, 1975.

20230   CAREY, ROBINSON.   THE FIGHTING MAROONS OF JAMAICA.
        KINGSTON: W. COLLINS AND SANGSTER, 1969.

20231   CONRAD, EARL.   HARRIET TUBMAN: NEGRO SOLDIER AND
        ABOLITIONIST.   NEW YORK: INTERNATIONAL PRESS, 1942.

20232   COTT, NANCY F. (ED.).   "NARRATIVES FROM ESCAPED SLAVES."
        ROOTS OF BITTERNESS: DOCUMENTS OF THE SOCIAL HISTORY
        OF AMERICAN WOMEN.   NEW YORK: DUTTON, 1972, PP.
        186-193.

20233   CROW, JEFFREY J.   THE BLACK EXPERIENCE IN REVOLUTIONARY
        NORTH CAROLINA.   RALEIGH: NORTH CAROLINA DEPARTMENT
        OF CULTURAL RESOURCES, 1977.

20234   CUNDALL, FRANK AND ANDERSON, IZETT.   JAMAICA NEGRO
        PROVERBS AND SAYINGS.   KINGSTON: INSTITUTE OF
        JAMAICA, 1927.

20235   DAVIDSON, DAVID M.   "NEGRO SLAVE CONTROL AND RESISTANCE
        IN COLONIAL MEXICO, 1519-1650."   HISPANIC AMERICAN
        HISTORICAL REVIEW, 46 (AUGUST, 1966):   235-253.

20236   DOUGLASS, FREDERICK.   "MY ESCAPE FROM SLAVERY."   CENTURY
        MAGAZINE, 1 (NOVEMBER, 1881):   124-131.

20237   DUBOIS, W.E.B.   "THE NEGRO AND THE CIVIL WAR."   SCIENCE
        AND SOCIETY, 25 (DECEMBER, 1961):   347-352.

20238   "EIGHTEENTH CENTURY SLAVES AS ADVERTISED BY THEIR
        MASTERS."   JOURNAL OF NEGRO HISTORY, 1 (APRIL, 1916):
        163-216.

20239   EPSTEIN, SAM AND EPSTEIN, BERYL.   HARRIET TUBMAN: GUIDE
        TO FREEDOM.   CHAMPAIGN: GARRARD, 1968.

20240   ERVIN, EDDIE M.   "RUNAWAY SLAVES IN ANTE-BELLUM NORTH
        CAROLINA."   M.A. THESIS, NORTH CAROLINA CENTRAL
        UNIVERSITY, 1946.

20241   "ESCAPE OF VALUABLE SLAVE."   NEGRO HISTORY BULLETIN, 26
        (APRIL, 1963):   216-218.

20242   FARRISON, WILLIAM E.   "A FLIGHT ACROSS OHIO: THE ESCAPE
        OF WILLIAM WELLS BROWN FROM SLAVERY."   OHIO STATE
        ARCHAEOLOGICAL AND HISTORICAL QUARTERLY, 61 (JULY,
        1952):   272-282.

20243   FITTS, JAMES.   "THE NEGRO IN BLUE."   GALAXY, 3 (FEBRUARY
        1, 1867):   249-255.

20244   GASPAR, DAVID B.   "RUNAWAYS IN SEVENTEENTH-CENTURY
        ANTIGUA, WEST INDIES."   BOLETIN DE ESTUDIOS
        LATINOAMERICANOS Y DEL CARIBE, 26 (JUNE, 1979):   3-14.

20245   GEGGUS, DAVID P.   "THE SLAVES OF BRITISH-OCCUPIED SAINT
        DOMINGUE: AN ANALYSIS OF THE WORKFORCES OF 197
        ABSENTEE PLANTATIONS, 1796-1797."   CARIBBEAN STUDIES,
        18 (APRIL-JULY, 1978):   5-42.

20246   GENOVESE, EUGENE D.   ROLL, JORDAN, ROLL: THE WORLD THE
        SLAVES MADE. NEW YORK: PANTHEON, 1974.

20247   GORDON, A.H.   "THE STRUGGLE OF THE NEGRO SLAVE FOR
        PHYSICAL FREEDOM."   JOURNAL OF NEGRO HISTORY, 13
        (JANUARY, 1928):   22-35.

20248   GREEN, EDWARD.   "THE MATAWAI MAROONS: AN ACCULTURATING
        AFRO-AMERICAN SOCIETY."   PH.D. DISSERTATION, CATHOLIC
        UNIVERSITY OF AMERICA, 1974.

20249   GREENE, LORENZO J.   "THE NEW ENGLAND NEGRO AS SEEN IN
        ADVERTISEMENTS FOR RUNAWAY SLAVES."   JOURNAL OF NEGRO
        HISTORY, 29 (APRIL, 1944):   125-146.

20250   GREY, MARTIN.   "SLAVE FUGITIVES AND SLAVE COMMUNITY:
        PATTERNS OF FLIGHT IN SOUTHERN MARYLAND, 1745-1800."
        UNPUBLISHED PAPER, JOHNS HOPKINS UNIVERSITY, 1975.

20251   GUTMAN, HERBERT G.   THE BLACK FAMILY IN SLAVERY AND
        FREEDOM, 1750-1925. NEW YORK: PANTHEON BOOKS, 1976.

20252   HALASZ, NICHOLAS.   THE RATTLING CHAINS: SLAVE UNREST AND
        REVOLT IN THE ANTE-BELLUM SOUTH. NEW YORK: D. MCKAY
        COMPANY, 1966.

20253   HARPER, ROBERT W.   "SOUTH JERSEY'S ANGEL TO RUNAWAY
        SLAVES."   SOUTH JERSEY LIVING, JUNE 15, 1975.

20254   HART, ALBERT B.   SLAVERY AND ABOLITION, 1831-1841.   NEW
        YORK: HARPER AND BROTHERS, 1906.

20255   HAWKINS, MARJORIE B.   "RUNAWAY SLAVES IN TEXAS,
        1830-1860."   M.A. THESIS, PRAIRIE VIEW AGRICULTURAL
        AND MECHANICAL COLLEGE, 1952.

20256   HAY, ROBERT P.   "AND TEN DOLLARS EXTRA, FOR EVERY HUNDRED
        LASHES ANY PERSON WILL GIVE HIM, TO THE AMOUNT OF
        THREE HUNDRED: A NOTE ON ANDREW JACKSON'S RUNAWAY
        SLAVE AD OF 1804 AND ON THE HISTORIAN'S USE OF
        EVIDENCE."   TENNESSEE HISTORICAL QUARTERLY, 36
        (WINTER, 1977):   468-473.

20257   HEARD, GEORGE A.   "ST. SIMON'S ISLAND DURING THE WAR
        BETWEEN THE STATES."   GEORGIA HISTORICAL QUARTERLY, 22
        (SEPTEMBER, 1938):   249-272.

20258   HELPLER, MORRIS K.   "NEGROES AND CRIME IN NEW ORLEANS,
        1850-1861."   M.A. THESIS, TULANE UNIVERSITY, 1960.

20259   JUNKINS, ENDA.   "SLAVE PLOTS, INSURRECTIONS, AND ACTS OF
        VIOLENCE IN THE STATE OF TEXAS, 1828-1865."   M.A.
        THESIS, BAYLOR UNIVERSITY, 1969.

20260   KNIGHT, MICHAEL.   IN CHAINS TO LOUISIANA.   NEW YORK:
        DUTTON, 1971.

20261   LARA, ORUNO D.   "NEGRO RESISTANCE TO SLAVERY AND THE
        ATLANTIC SLAVE TRADE FROM AFRICA TO BLACK AMERICA."
        IN THE AFRICAN SLAVE TRADE FROM THE FIFTEENTH TO THE
        NINETEENTH CENTURY.   PARIS: UNITED NATIONS
        EDUCATIONAL, SCIENTIFIC AND CULTURAL ORGANIZATION,
        1979, PP. 101-114.

20262   LEAMING, HUGO P.   "HIDDEN AMERICANS: MAROONS OF VIRGINIA
        AND THE CAROLINAS."   PH.D. DISSERTATION, UNIVERSITY OF
        ILLINOIS, CHICAGO CIRCLE, 1979.

20263   LENOIR, JOHN D.   "THE PARAMAKA MAROONS: A STUDY IN
        RELIGIOUS ACCULTURATION."   PH.D. DISSERTATION, NEW
        SCHOOL FOR SOCIAL RESEARCH, 1973.

20264   LESLIE, WILLIAM R.   "THE PENNSYLVANIA FUGITIVE SLAVE ACT
        OF 1826."   JOURNAL OF SOUTHERN HISTORY, 18 (NOVEMBER,
        1952):   429-445.

20265   LITWACK, LEON F.   BEEN IN THE STORM SO LONG: THE
        AFTERMATH OF SLAVERY.   NEW YORK: ALFRED A. KNOPF,
        1979.

20266   MANIGAT, LESLIE F.   "THE RELATIONSHIP BETWEEN MARRONAGE
        AND SLAVE REVOLTS AND REVOLUTION IN ST.
        DOMINGUE-HAITI."   IN RUBIN, VERA AND TUDEN, ARTHUR
        (EDS.).   COMPARATIVE PERSPECTIVES ON SLAVERY IN NEW
        WORLD PLANTATION SOCIETIES.   NEW YORK: NEW YORK
        ACADEMY OF SCIENCES, 1977, PP. 420-438.

20267   "THE MAROONS IN THE 18TH CENTURY: A NOTE ON INDIRECT
        RULE IN JAMAICA."   CARIBBEAN QUARTERLY, 8 (JANUARY,
        1962):   25-27.

20268   MARSHALL, BERNARD A.   "MAROONAGE IN SLAVE PLANTATION
        SOCIETIES: A CASE STUDY OF DOMINICA, 1785-1815."
        CARIBBEAN QUARTERLY, 22 (JUNE-SEPTEMBER, 1976):   26-32.

20269   MEADERS, DANIEL E.   "SOUTH CAROLINA FUGITIVES AS VIEWED
        THROUGH LOCAL COLONIAL NEWSPAPERS WITH EMPHASIS ON
        RUNAWAY NOTICES, 1732-1801."   JOURNAL OF NEGRO
        HISTORY, 60 (APRIL, 1975):   288-319.

20270   MORRIS, RICHARD B.   "LABOR CONTROLS IN MARYLAND IN THE
        NINETEENTH CENTURY."   JOURNAL OF SOUTHERN HISTORY, 14

(AUGUST, 1948):   385-400.

20271   MULLIN, MICHAEL.   "BRITISH CARIBBEAN AND NORTH AMERICAN
        SLAVES IN AN ERA OF WAR AND REVOLUTION, 1775-1807."
        IN CROW, JEFFREY J. AND TISE, LARRY E. (EDS.).   THE
        SOUTHERN EXPERIENCE IN THE AMERICAN REVOLUTION.
        CHAPEL HILL: UNIVERSITY OF NORTH CAROLINA PRESS,
        1978, PP. 235-267.

20272   MURDOCH, RICHARD K.   "THE RETURN OF RUNAWAY SLAVES,
        1790-1794."   FLORIDA HISTORICAL QUARTERLY, 38
        (OCTOBER, 1959):   96-113.

20273   MURRAY, ALEXANDER L.   "EXTRADITION OF FUGITIVE SLAVES
        FROM CANADA: A REEVALUATION."   CANADIAN HISTORICAL
        REVIEW, 43 (DECEMBER, 1962):   298-314.

20274   NASH, A.E. KEIR.   "DRAPETOMANIA."   IN ROLLER, DAVID C.
        AND TWYMAN, ROBERT W. (EDS.).   THE ENCYCLOPEDIA OF
        SOUTHERN HISTORY.   BATON ROUGE: LOUISIANA STATE
        UNIVERSITY PRESS, 1979, P. 369.

20275   NASH, GARY.   "THE FORGOTTEN EXPERIENCE: INDIANS, BLACKS,
        AND THE AMERICAN REVOLUTION."   IN FOWLER, WILLIAM M.,
        JR. AND COYLE, WALLACE (EDS.).   THE AMERICAN
        REVOLUTION: CHANGING PERSPECTIVES.   BOSTON:
        NORTHEASTERN UNIVERSITY PRESS, 1979, PP. 27-46.

20276   NELSON, WILLIAM.   "THE AMERICAN NEWSPAPER OF THE
        EIGHTEENTH CENTURY AS SOURCES OF HISTORY."   ANNUAL
        REPORT OF THE AMERICAN HISTORICAL ASSOCIATION FOR THE
        YEAR 1908.   2 VOLS.   WASHINGTON: GOVERNMENT PRINTING
        OFFICE, 1909, VOL. 1, PP. 211-222.

20277   NELSON, WILLIAM N.   "BLOOD-HOUNDS AND SLAVES."   CENTURY
        MAGAZINE, 39 (MARCH, 1890):   796-797.

20278   NICHOLS, CHARLES H., JR.   "THE CASE OF WILLIAM GRIMES,
        THE RUNAWAY SLAVE."   WILLIAM AND MARY QUARTERLY, 3RD
        SER., 8 (OCTOBER, 1951):   552-560.

20279   OWENS, LESLIE H.   THIS SPECIES OF PROPERTY: SLAVE LIFE
        AND CULTURE IN THE OLD SOUTH.   NEW YORK: OXFORD
        UNIVERSITY PRESS, 1976.

20280   PEDTTER, E.J.G.   "THE RUNAWAY SLAVES OF DUTCH GUIANA.
        THE STRANGE DESCENDANTS OF RUNAWAY SLAVES--THE HOUSE
        OF THE MAGICIAN—CURIOUS CUSTOMS AT BIRTH."   TRAVEL,
        47 (JULY, 1926):   17-19, 46.

20281   PERDUE, CHARLES L., JR.; BARDEN, THOMAS E.; AND PHILLIPS,
        ROBERT K. (EDS.).   WEEVILS IN THE WHEAT: INTERVIEWS
        WITH VIRGINIA EX-SLAVES.   CHARLOTTESVILLE: UNIVERSITY
        PRESS OF VIRGINIA, 1976.

1503

20282 PHILLIPS, JAMES R. "ESCAPE OF VALUABLE SLAVE." NEGRO
HISTORY BULLETIN, 26 (APRIL, 1963): 215.

20283 PHILLIPS, ULRICH B. LIFE AND LABOR IN THE OLD SOUTH.
BOSTON: LITTLE, BROWN AND COMPANY, 1929.

20284 PORTER, KENNETH W. "'MAROONS' IN MASSACHUSETTS: FELIX
CUFF AND HIS FRIENDS." JOURNAL OF NEGRO HISTORY, 28
(JANUARY, 1943): 51-53.

20285 PORTER, KENNETH W. "NEGROES ON THE FRONTIER." IN LAMAR,
HOWARD R. (ED.). THE READER'S ENCYCLOPEDIA OF THE
AMERICAN WEST. NEW YORK: THOMAS Y. CROWELL, 1977,
PP. 814-821.

20286 PORTER, KENNETH W. "NEGROES ON THE SOUTHERN FRONTIER,
1670-1763." JOURNAL OF NEGRO HISTORY, 33 (JANUARY,
1948): 53-78.

20287 PORTER, KENNETH W. "SEMINOLE FLIGHT FROM FORT MARION."
FLORIDA HISTORICAL QUARTERLY, 22 (JANUARY, 1944):
112-133.

20288 RAPPAPORT, STANLEY. "SLAVE STRUGGLES FOR FREEDOM."
CRISIS, 43 (SEPTEMBER, 1936): 264-265, 274, 284-286.

20289 RAWICK, GEORGE P. FROM SUNDOWN TO SUNUP: THE MAKING OF
THE BLACK COMMUNITY. WESTPORT: GREENWOOD PRESS, 1972.

20290 READ, ALLEN W. "EIGHTEENTH CENTURY SLAVES AS ADVERTISED
BY THEIR MASTERS." JOURNAL OF NEGRO HISTORY, 1
(APRIL, 1916): 163-216.

20291 REMINI, ROBERT V. ANDREW JACKSON AND THE COURSE OF
AMERICAN EMPIRE, 1767-1821. NEW YORK: HARPER & ROW,
PUBLISHERS, 1977.

20292 RODNEY, WALTER AND AUGUSTUS, EARL. "THE NEGRO SLAVE."
CARIBBEAN QUARTERLY, 10 (MARCH, 1964): 40-47.

20293 "A RUNAWAY SLAVE IN MASSACHUSETTS." HISTORICAL MAGAZINE,
9 (NOVEMBER, 1865): 339.

20294 SCARBOROUGH, WILLIAM K. THE OVERSEER: PLANTATION
MANAGEMENT IN THE OLD SOUTH. BATON ROUGE: LOUISIANA
STATE UNIVERSITY PRESS, 1966.

20295 SCHULER, MONICA. "DAY-TO-DAY RESISTANCE TO SLAVERY IN
THE CARIBBEAN DURING THE EIGHTEENTH CENTURY."
BULLETIN OF THE AFRICAN STUDIES ASSOCIATION OF THE
WEST INDIES, 6 (DECEMBER, 1973): 57-75.

20296 SCHWARTZ, STUART B. "BURACO DE TATU: THE DESTRUCTION OF
A BAHIAN QUILOMBO." IN VERHANDLUNGEN DES XXXVIII.
INTERNATIONALEN AMERIKANISTENKONGRESS. 4 VOLS.

STUTTGART-MUNCHEN: KOMMISSIONSVERLAG KLAUS RENNER, 1971, VOL. 3, PP. 429-438.

20297 "SLAVE-CATCHING IN IOWA." ANNALS OF IOWA, 3RD SER., 4 (JULY, 1899): 154-155.

20298 "SLAVE HUNTING DOGS." IN NUNEZ, BENJAMIN. DICTIONARY OF AFRO-LATIN AMERICAN CIVILIZATION. WESTPORT: GREENWOOD PRESS, 1980, P. 435.

20299 "SLAVES, RUNAWAY." IN RYWELL, MARTIN (ED.). AFRO-AMERICAN ENCYCLOPEDIA. 10 VOLS. NORTH MIAMI: EDUCATIONAL BOOK PUBLISHERS, 1974, VOL. 8, PP. 2496-2498.

20300 SMITH, DORIS W. "TROUBLESOME PROPERTY: FUGITIVES, SABOTEURS, AND MALINGERERS." IN JOYNER, CHARLES W. (ED.). BLACK CAROLINIANS: STUDIES IN THE HISTORY OF SOUTH CAROLINA NEGROES. LAURINBURG, NC: ST. ANDREWS PRESBYTERIAN COLLEGE, 1969, PP. 43-49.

20301 STAMPP, KENNETH M. THE PECULIAR INSTITUTION: SLAVERY IN THE ANTE-BELLUM SOUTH. NEW YORK: ALFRED A. KNOPF, 1956.

20302 STAROBIN, ROBERT. BLACKS IN BONDAGE: LETTERS OF AMERICAN SLAVES. NEW YORK: NEW VIEWPOINTS, 1974.

20303 SWIFT, HILDEGARDE H. RAILROAD TO FREEDOM. NEW YORK: HARCOURT BRACE JOVANOVICH, 1932.

20304 SZASZ, THOMAS S. "THE SANE SLAVE: AN HISTORICAL NOTE ON THE USE OF MEDICAL DIAGNOSIS AS JUSTIFICATORY RHETORIC." AMERICAN JOURNAL OF PSYCHOTHERAPY, 25 (APRIL, 1971): 228-239.

20305 THIRSK, RICHARD. "OBEAH IN THE WEST INDIES: ILLUSTRATIONS OF NEGRO WITCHCRAFT." CHAMBERS' JOURNAL, 7 (MARCH 17, 1917): 247-250.

20306 THOMPSON, ALVIN O. SOME PROBLEMS OF SLAVE DESERTION IN GUYANA, C. 1750-1814. CAVE HILL, BARBADOS: UNIVERSITY OF THE WEST INDIES, INSTITUTE OF SOCIAL AND ECONOMIC RESEARCH, 1976.

20307 "THE THRILLING ESCAPE OF WILLIAM AND ELLEN CRAFT." NEGRO HISTORY BULLETIN, 1 (OCTOBER, 1937): 5.

20308 TRAYNOR, MARTIN J. "RUNAWAY SLAVES IN COLONIAL AMERICA, SOUTH CAROLINA, 1750-1776." M.A. THESIS, ROOSEVELT UNIVERSITY, 1970.

20309 "TRIAL AND SENTENCE OF BIRON, RUNAWAY NEGRO SLAVE, BEFORE THE SUPERIOR COUNCIL OF LOUISIANA, 1728." LOUISIANA HISTORICAL QUARTERLY, 8 (JANUARY, 1925): 23-27.

20310 VAN NESS, JAMES S. "ECONOMIC DEVELOPMENT, SOCIAL AND
       CULTURAL CHANGES: 1800-1850." IN WALSH, RICHARD AND
       FOX, WILLIAM L. (EDS.). MARYLAND: A HISTORY,
       1632-1974. BALTIMORE: MARYLAND HISTORICAL SOCIETY,
       1974, PP. 151-238.

20311 WATSON, ALAN D. "IMPULSE TOWARD INDEPENDENCE:
       RESISTANCE AND REBELLION AMONG NORTH CAROLINA SLAVES,
       1750-1755." JOURNAL OF NEGRO HISTORY, 63 (FALL,
       1978): 317-328.

20312 "WHEN ESCAPING SLAVES WERE HUNTED LIKE WILD BEASTS OF THE
       FOREST." TIFFIN (OH) TRIBUNE, JANUARY 2, 1920.

20313 WHITE, ELAIN. "THE MAROON WARRIORS OF JAMAICA AND THEIR
       SUCCESSFUL RESISTANCE TO ENSLAVEMENT." PAN-AFRICAN
       JOURNAL, 6 (1973): 297-312.

20314 WILEY, BELL I. SOUTHERN NEGROES, 1861-1865. NEW HAVEN:
       YALE UNIVERSITY PRESS, 1938.

20315 WINDLEY, LATHAN A. "A PROFILE OF RUNAWAY SLAVES IN
       VIRGINIA AND SOUTH CAROLINA FROM 1730 THROUGH 1787."
       PH.D. DISSERTATION, UNIVERSITY OF IOWA, 1974.

20316 WINDLEY, LATHAN A. (ED.). "RUNAWAY SLAVE ADVERTISEMENTS
       OF GEORGE WASHINGTON AND THOMAS JEFFERSON." JOURNAL
       OF NEGRO HISTORY, 63 (FALL, 1978): 373-374.

20317 WISH, HARVEY. "SLAVE DISLOYALTY UNDER THE CONFEDERACY."
       JOURNAL OF NEGRO HISTORY, 23 (OCTOBER, 1938): 435-450.

20318 WOOD, PETER H. BLACK MAJORITY: NEGROES IN COLONIAL
       SOUTH CAROLINA, 1670 TO THE STONO REBELLION. NEW
       YORK: ALFRED A. KNOPF, 1974.

20319 WRIGHT, PHILIP. "WAR AND PEACE WITH THE MAROONS,
       1730-1739." CARIBBEAN QUARTERLY, 16 (MARCH, 1970):
       5-27.

25.
Slavery and
the Civil War

GENERAL

20320   ALEXANDER, N.D.   "THE COTTON TRADE BETWEEN THE LINES
        DURING THE CIVIL WAR."   M.A. THESIS, OHIO STATE
        UNIVERSITY, 1932.

20321   ANDERSON, GALUSHA.   THE STORY OF A BORDER CITY DURING THE
        CIVIL WAR.   BOSTON: LITTLE, BROWN & COMPANY, 1908.

20322   ANDREWS, MATTHEW P.   THE WOMEN OF THE SOUTH IN WAR TIMES.
        BALTIMORE: NORMAN, REMINGTON, 1920.

20323   APTHEKER, HERBERT.   THE AMERICAN CIVIL WAR.   NEW YORK:
        INTERNATIONAL PUBLISHERS, 1961.

20324   APTHEKER, HERBERT.   "THE NEGRO IN THE CIVIL WAR."   ESSAYS
        IN THE HISTORY OF THE AMERICAN NEGRO.   NEW YORK:
        INTERNATIONAL PUBLISHERS, 1945, PP. 161-208.

20325   APTHEKER, HERBERT.   THE NEGRO IN THE CIVIL WAR.   NEW
        YORK: INTERNATIONAL PUBLISHERS, 1938.

20326   AUGHEY, JOHN H.   TUPELO.   LINCOLN, NE: STATE JOURNAL
        COMPANY, 1888.

20327   BADER, CARL G., JR.   "MILITARY USE OF NEGROES IN THE
        AMERICAN CIVIL WAR."   M.A. THESIS, UNIVERSITY OF
        NEBRASKA, 1950.

20328   BARNEY, WILLIAM L.   FLAWED VICTORY: A NEW PERSPECTIVE ON
        THE CIVIL WAR.   NEW YORK: PRAEGER, 1975.

20329   BARRON, ELWYN A.   "SHADOWY MEMORIES OF NEGRO-LORE."
        FOLKLORIST, 1 (1892):   46-53.

20330   BLACKLEDGE, CHARLES H.   "PHASES OF BLACK NATIONALISM AND
        EMIGRATION TO HAITI, 1860-1862."   M.A. THESIS,
        UNIVERSITY OF SOUTH ALABAMA, 1977.

20331   BONEKEMPER, EDWARD H.   "NEGRO OWNERSHIP OF REAL PROPERTY
        IN HAMPTON AND ELIZABETH CITY COUNTY, VIRGINIA,
        1860-1870."   JOURNAL OF NEGRO HISTORY, 55 (JULY,
        1970):   165-181.

20332   BOTKIN, B.A. (ED.).   A CIVIL WAR TREASURY.   NEW YORK:
        RANDOM HOUSE, 1960.

20333   BRAUER, KINLEY J.   "THE SLAVERY PROBLEM IN THE DIPLOMACY
        OF THE AMERICAN CIVIL WAR."   PACIFIC HISTORICAL
        REVIEW, 46 (AUGUST, 1977):   439-469.

20334   BREMNER, ROBERT H.   THE PUBLIC GOOD: PHILANTHROPY AND WELFARE IN THE CIVIL WAR ERA. NEW YORK: ALFRED A. KNOPF, 1980.

20335   BURKETT, E. VANN. "AN INVESTIGATION OF UNION AND CONFEDERATE ARMY DOCUMENTS ADVOCATING THE USE OF THE NEGRO IN OCCUPATIONAL PURSUITS, 1861-1865." M.A. THESIS, TENNESSEE STATE UNIVERSITY, 1968.

20336   BUTCHART, RONALD E.   NORTHERN SCHOOLS, SOUTHERN BLACKS, AND RECONSTRUCTION: FREEDMAN'S EDUCATION, 1862-1875. WESTPORT: GREENWOOD PRESS, 1980.

20337   CAMEJO, PETER.   RACISM, REVOLUTION, REACTION, 1861-1877: THE RISE AND FALL OF RADICAL RECONSTRUCTION. NEW YORK: MONAD PRESS, 1976.

20338   CLARK, CHARLES B.   POLITICS IN MARYLAND DURING THE CIVIL WAR. CHESTERTOWN, MD: N.P., 1952.

20339   CLARK, CHARLES B. "POLITICS IN MARYLAND DURING THE CIVIL WAR." MARYLAND HISTORICAL MAGAZINE, 36 (SEPTEMBER, DECEMBER, 1941):   239-262, 331-393; 37 (JUNE, DECEMBER, 1942):   171-192, 378-399; 38 (SEPTEMBER, 1943):   230-260; 39 (JUNE, DECEMBER, 1944):   149-161, 315-331; 40 (SEPTEMBER, DECEMBER, 1945):   233-241, 295-309; 41 (JUNE, 1946):   132-158.

20340   COFFIN, CHARLES C.   PERSONAL OBSERVATIONS WITH THE ARMY AND NAVY FROM THE FIRST BATTLE OF BULL RUN TO THE FALL OF RICHMOND. BOSTON: TICKNOR-FIELDS, 1866.

20341   COLVIN, SARAH.   A REBEL IN THOUGHT. NEW YORK: ISLAND PRESS, 1944.

20342   COUCH, WILLIAM JR. "THE IMAGE OF THE BLACK SOLDIER IN SELECTED AMERICAN NOVELS." CLA JOURNAL, 20 (DECEMBER, 1976):   176-184.

20343   COULTER, E. MERTON. "COMMERCIAL RELATIONS OF KENTUCKY, 1860-1870." PH.D. DISSERTATION, UNIVERSITY OF WISCONSIN, 1917.

20344   COX, EARNEST S.   LINCOLN'S NEGRO POLICY. RICHMOND: THE AUTHOR, 1972.

20345   CRAVEN, AVERY O. "SLAVERY AND THE CIVIL WAR." SOUTHERN REVIEW, 4 (AUTUMN, 1938):   243-255.

20346   CRUDEN, ROBERT.   THE WAR THAT NEVER ENDED: THE AMERICAN CIVIL WAR. ENGLEWOOD CLIFFS: PRENTICE-HALL, 1973.

20347   CURRY, LEONARD P.   BLUEPRINT FOR MODERN AMERICA: NONMILITARY LEGISLATION OF THE FIRST CIVIL WAR CONGRESS. NASHVILLE: VANDERBILT UNIVERSITY PRESS,

1968.

20348   DANIEL, W. HARRISON. "RESPONSE OF THE CHURCH OF ENGLAND
        TO THE CIVIL WAR AND RECONSTRUCTION IN AMERICA."
        HISTORICAL MAGAZINE OF THE PROTESTANT EPISCOPAL
        CHURCH, 47 (MARCH, 1978): 51-72.

20349   DUGANNE, A.J.H. CAMPS AND PRISONS: 20 MONTHS IN THE
        DEPARTMENT OF THE GULF. NEW YORK: J.P. ROBENS, 1865.

20350   ENGS, ROBERT F. FREEDOM'S FIRST GENERATION: BLACK
        HAMPTON, VIRGINIA, 1861-1890.. PHILADELPHIA:
        UNIVERSITY OF PENNSYLVANIA PRESS, 1979.

20351   FLEMING, WALTER L. "SLAVE-HOLDING INDIANS IN THE CIVIL
        WAR." DIAL, 59 (SEPTEMBER 16, 1915): 216-218.

20352   FONT, FREDERICK. THE DARK DAYS OF THE CIVIL WAR, 1861 TO
        1865. ST. LOUIS: WAGENFUEHR, 1904.

20353   FRANKLIN, JOHN H. THE EMANCIPATION PROCLAMATION. GARDEN
        CITY: DOUBLEDAY, 1963.

20354   GARNET, HENRY H. A MEMORIAL DISCOURSE. PHILADELPHIA:
        J.M. WILSON, 1865.

20355   "GENERAL SHERMAN'S 'THOUSAND SLAVES.'" HARPER'S WEEKLY,
        9 (JANUARY 21, 1865): 34.

20356   GLAZIER, WILLARD W. THE CAPTURE, THE PRISON PEN, AND THE
        ESCAPE. NEW YORK: UNITED STATES PUBLISHING COMPANY,
        1865.

20357   HALLOWELL, NORWOOD P. SELECTED LETTERS AND PAPERS.
        PETERBOROUGH, NH: R.R. SMITH COMPANY, 1963.

20358   HATCH, CARL E. "NEGRO MIGRATION AND NEW JERSEY--1863."
        NEW JERSEY HISTORY, 87 (WINTER, 1969): 233-244.

20359   HEAPS, WILLARD A. AND HEAPS, PORTER W. "THE NEGRO AND
        THE CONTRABAND." IN THE SINGING SIXTIES: THE SPIRIT
        OF CIVIL WAR DAYS FROM THE MUSIC OF THE TIMES.
        NORMAN: UNIVERSITY OF OKLAHOMA PRESS, 1960, PP.
        268-294.

20360   HEDLEY, FENWICK Y. MARCHING THROUGH GEORGIA. PEN
        PICTURES OF EVERY-DAY LIFE IN GENERAL SHERMAN'S ARMY.
        CHICAGO: DONOHUE, HENNEBERRY, 1884.

20361   HYMAN, HAROLD M. A MORE PERFECT UNION: THE IMPACT OF
        THE CIVIL WAR AND RECONSTRUCTION ON THE CONSTITUTION.
        NEW YORK: ALFRED A. KNOPF, 1973.

20362   IRVIS, K. LEROY. "THE NEGRO IN THE CIVIL WAR SONG
        BALLADS." M.A. THESIS, NEW YORK STATE COLLEGE FOR

TEACHERS, 1939.

20363 JONES, CHARLES C., JR. "NEGRO SLAVES DURING THE CIVIL
       WAR." MAGAZINE OF AMERICAN HISTORY, 16 (AUGUST,
       1886): 168-175.

20364 "JOURNAL OF ARTHUR BRAILSFORD WESCOAT, 1863, 1864."
       SOUTH CAROLINA HISTORICAL AND GENEALOGICAL MAGAZINE,
       55 (APRIL, 1954): 71-102.

20365 KAPLAN, SIDNEY. "THE MISCEGENATION ISSUE IN THE ELECTION
       OF 1864." JOURNAL OF NEGRO HISTORY, 34 (JULY, 1949):
       274-343.

20366 KETCHUM, ALTON. "THE AMERICAN CIVIL WAR." AMERICAN
       REVIEW, 1 (SPRING, 1961): 32-48.

20367 KINCAID, LARRY. "TWO STEPS FORWARD, ONE STEP BACK:
       RACIAL ATTITUDES DURING THE CIVIL WAR AND
       RECONSTRUCTION." IN NASH, GARY B. AND WEISS, RICHARD
       (EDS.). THE GREAT FEAR: RACE IN THE MIND OF AMERICA.
       NEW YORK: HOLT, RINEHART AND WINSTON, 1970, PP. 45-70.

20368 KLEMENT, FRANK L. THE LIMITS OF DISSENT: CLEMENT L.
       VALLANDIGHAM & THE CIVIL WAR. LEXINGTON: UNIVERSITY
       PRESS OF KENTUCKY, 1970.

20369 KNAPP, CHARLES M. NEW JERSEY DURING THE PERIOD OF THE
       CIVIL WAR AND RECONSTRUCTION. GENEVA, NY: W.F.
       HUMPHREY, 1924.

20370 KORN, BERTRAM W. "THE RABBIS AND THE SLAVERY QUESTION."
       AMERICAN JEWRY AND THE CIVIL WAR. PHILADELPHIA:
       JEWISH PUBLICATION SOCIETY OF AMERICA, 1951, PP. 15-31.

20371 LANE, ANN J. "THE CIVIL WAR, RECONSTRUCTION, AND THE
       AFRO-AMERICAN." IN GOLDSTEIN, RHODA L. (ED.). BLACK
       LIFE AND CULTURE IN THE UNITED STATES. NEW YORK:
       THOMAS Y. CROWELL, 1971, PP. 131-152.

20372 LATHROP, BARNES F. "THE PUGH PLANTATIONS, 1860-1865: A
       STUDY OF LIFE IN LOWER LOUISIANA." PH.D.
       DISSERTATION, UNIVERSITY OF TEXAS, 1945.

20373 LINDSEY, DAVID. AMERICANS IN CONFLICT: THE CIVIL WAR
       AND RECONSTRUCTION. BOSTON: HOUGHTON MIFFLIN
       COMPANY, 1974.

20374 LITWACK, LEON F. BEEN IN THE STORM SO LONG: THE
       AFTERMATH OF SLAVERY. NEW YORK: ALFRED A. KNOPF,
       1979.

20375 LIVERMORE, MARY A. MY STORY OF THE WAR: A WOMAN'S
       NARRATIVE OF FOUR YEARS PERSONAL EXPERIENCE AS NURSE
       IN THE UNION ARMY. HARTFORD: A.D. WORTHINGTON, 1887.

20376   LONN, ELLA.   DESERTION DURING THE CIVIL WAR.   NEW YORK:
        CENTURY COMPANY, 1928.

20377   MANAKEE, HAROLD R.   MARYLAND IN THE CIVIL WAR.
        BALTIMORE: MARYLAND HISTORICAL SOCIETY, 1961.

20378   MARRS, ELIJAH P.   LIFE AND HISTORY OF THE REVEREND ELIJAH
        P. MARRS.   LOUISVILLE: BRADLEY & GILBERT, 1885.

20379   MCCAGUE, JAMES.   THE SECOND REBELLION: THE STORY OF THE
        NEW YORK CITY DRAFT RIOTS OF 1863.   NEW YORK: DIAL
        PRESS, 1968.

20380   MCMAHON, ADRIAN M.   "THE CONCEPT OF FREEDOM AND THE
        RADICAL ABOLITIONISTS, 1860-1870."   PH.D.
        DISSERTATION, UNIVERSITY OF TEXAS, 1970.

20381   MCPHERSON, JAMES M.   "ABOLITIONIST AND NEGRO OPPOSITION
        TO COLONIZATION DURING THE CIVIL WAR."   PHYLON, 26
        (WINTER, 1965):   391-399.

20382   MCPHERSON, JAMES M.   "ABOLITIONISTS AND THE NEGRO IN THE
        CIVIL WAR AND RECONSTRUCTION."   PH.D. DISSERTATION,
        JOHNS HOPKINS UNIVERSITY, 1963.

20383   MCPHERSON, JAMES M.   "A BRIEF FOR EQUALITY: THE
        ABOLITIONIST REPLY TO THE RACIST MYTH, 1860-1865."   IN
        DUBERMAN, MARTIN (ED.).   THE ANTISLAVERY VANGUARD:
        NEW ESSAYS ON THE ABOLITIONISTS.   PRINCETON:
        PRINCETON UNIVERSITY PRESS, 1965, PP. 156-177.

20384   MCPHERSON, JAMES M.   "THE CIVIL WAR AND RECONSTRUCTION:
        A REVOLUTION OF RACIAL EQUALITY?"   IN SHADE, WILLIAM
        G. AND HERRENKOHL, ROY C. (EDS.).   SEVEN ON BLACK:
        REFLECTIONS ON THE NEGRO EXPERIENCE IN AMERICA.
        PHILADELPHIA: J.B. LIPPINCOTT, 1969, PP. 49-72.

20385   MCPHERSON, JAMES M.   MARCHING TOWARD FREEDOM: THE NEGRO
        IN THE CIVIL WAR, 1861-1865.   NEW YORK: ALFRED A.
        KNOPF, 1967.

20386   MCPHERSON, JAMES M.   THE NEGRO'S CIVIL WAR: HOW AMERICAN
        NEGROES FELT AND ACTED DURING THE WAR FOR THE UNION.
        NEW YORK: PANTHEON BOOKS, 1965.

20387   MCPHERSON, JAMES M.   THE STRUGGLE FOR EQUALITY:
        ABOLITIONISTS AND THE NEGRO IN THE CIVIL WAR AND
        RECONSTRUCTION.   PRINCETON: PRINCETON UNIVERSITY
        PRESS, 1964.

20388   MOOREN, ROBERT L.   "THE SLAVE TRADE AND FUGITIVE SLAVES
        DURING THE CIVIL WAR."   M.A. THESIS, UNIVERSITY OF
        WISCONSIN, 1949.

20389   MORGAN, THOMAS J.   THE NEGRO IN AMERICA, AND THE IDEAL

AMERICAN REPUBLIC. PHILADELPHIA: AMERICAN BAPTIST
PUBLICATION SOCIETY, 1898.

20390 MYERS, ROBERT (ED.). THE CHILDREN OF PRIDE: A TRUE
       STORY OF GEORGIA AND THE CIVIL WAR. NEW HAVEN: YALE
       UNIVERSITY PRESS, 1971.

20391 NEELY, MARK E., JR. "ABRAHAM LINCOLN AND BLACK
       COLONIZATION: BENJAMIN BUTLER'S SPURIOUS TESTIMONY."
       CIVIL WAR HISTORY, 25 (MARCH, 1979): 77-83.

20392 "THE NEGRO QUESTION." SOUTHERN HISTORICAL SOCIETY
       PAPERS, 1 (APRIL, 1876): 317.

20393 NEVINS, ALLAN. "UNDER THE TRAMPLING ARMIES: THE TRAGIC
       LOT OF THE FREEDMEN." THE WAR FOR THE UNION. 4 VOLS.
       NEW YORK: CHARLES SCRIBNER'S SONS, 1960-1971, VOL. 3,
       PP. 413-444.

20394 NOYES, EDWARD. "WHITE OPPOSITION TO BLACK MIGRATION INTO
       CIVIL-WAR WISCONSIN." LINCOLN HERALD, 73 (FALL,
       1971): 181-191.

20395 O'CONNOR, THOMAS H. THE DISUNITED STATES: THE ERA OF
       THE CIVIL WAR AND RECONSTRUCTION. NEW YORK: DODD,
       MEAD & COMPANY, 1972.

20396 PARSONS, LLOYD C. "THE PLACE OF THE NEGRO IN THE WAR OF
       THE REBELLION." M.A. THESIS, VANDERBILT UNIVERSITY,
       1927.

20397 PEABODY, FRANCIS G. "THE NEGRO IN THE CIVIL WAR
       (1861-1865)." EDUCATION FOR LIFE: THE STORY OF
       HAMPTON INSTITUTE. GARDEN CITY, NY: DOUBLEDAY, PAGE
       & COMPANY, 1918, PP. 3-25.

20398 PIERCE, EDWARD L. ENFRANCHISEMENT AND CITIZENSHIP:
       ADDRESSES AND PAPERS. BOSTON: ROBERTS BROTHERS, 1896.

20399 POWELL, LAWRENCE N. NEW MASTERS: NORTHERN PLANTERS
       DURING THE CIVIL WAR AND RECONSTRUCTION. NEW HAVEN:
       YALE UNIVERSITY PRESS, 1980.

20400 QUARLES, BENJAMIN. THE NEGRO IN THE CIVIL WAR. BOSTON:
       LITTLE, BROWN AND COMPANY, 1953.

20401 RANDALL, JAMES G. AND DONALD, DAVID. THE CIVIL WAR AND
       RECONSTRUCTION. BOSTON: D.C. HEATH AND COMPANY, 1961.

20402 RANKIN, DAVID C. "THE POLITICS OF CASTE: FREE COLORED
       LEADERSHIP IN NEW ORLEANS DURING THE CIVIL WAR." IN
       MACDONALD, ROBERT R.; KEMP, JOHN R.; AND HAAS, EDWARD
       F. (EDS.). LOUISIANA'S BLACK HERITAGE. NEW ORLEANS:
       LOUISIANA STATE MUSEUM, 1979, PP. 107-146.

20403   REED, JOHN C.   THE BROTHERS' WAR.   BOSTON: LITTLE, BROWN
        AND COMPANY, 1905.

20404   RIPLEY, C. PETER.   "THE BLACK FAMILY IN TRANSITION:
        LOUISIANA, 1860-1865."   JOURNAL OF SOUTHERN HISTORY,
        41 (AUGUST, 1975):   369-380.

20405   RIPLEY, C. PETER.   SLAVES AND FREEDMEN IN CIVIL WAR
        LOUISIANA.   BATON ROUGE: LOUISIANA STATE UNIVERSITY
        PRESS, 1976.

20406   ROY, JOSEPH E.   "OUR INDEBTEDNESS TO THE NEGROES FOR
        THEIR CONDUCT DURING THE WAR."   NEW ENGLANDER, 51
        (NOVEMBER, 1889):   353-364.

20407   SERAILE, WILLIAM.   "AFRO-AMERICAN EMIGRATION TO HAITI
        DURING THE AMERICAN CIVIL WAR."   AMERICAS, 35
        (OCTOBER, 1978):   185-200.

20408   SHAW, JAMES.   OUR LAST CAMPAIGN AND SUBSEQUENT SERVICE IN
        TEXAS.   PROVIDENCE: THE SOCIETY, 1905.

20409   SHERMAN, WILLIAM T.   "OLD SHADY WITH A MORAL."   NORTH
        AMERICAN REVIEW, 147 (OCTOBER, 1888):   361.

20410   "SLAVERY AND ITS CONTRADICTIONS."   TYLER'S QUARTERLY
        HISTORICAL AND GENEALOGICAL MAGAZINE, 11 (JULY, 1929):
        67-68.

20411   SMITH, EDWARD C.   THE BORDERLAND IN THE CIVIL WAR.   NEW
        YORK: MACMILLAN, 1927.

20412   SMITH, GEORGE W. AND JUDAH, CHARLES.   "THE NEGRO'S
        PLACE."   LIFE IN THE NORTH DURING THE CIVIL WAR: A
        SOURCE HISTORY.   ALBUQUERQUE: UNIVERSITY OF NEW
        MEXICO PRESS, 1966, PP. 129-162.

20413   SMITH, GREENVILLE.   "EMANCIPATION DURING THE CIVIL WAR."
        M.A. THESIS, INDIANA UNIVERSITY, 1933.

20414   SMITH, HAROLD S.   "NEGRO COLONIZATION DURING THE CIVIL
        WAR."   M.A. THESIS, UNIVERSITY OF WISCONSIN, 1941.

20415   SMITH, JAMES M.   "THE 'SEPARATE BUT EQUAL' DOCTRINE: AN
        ABOLITIONIST DISCUSSES RACIAL SEGREGATION AND
        EDUCATIONAL POLICY DURING THE CIVIL WAR, A DOCUMENT."
        JOURNAL OF NEGRO HISTORY, 41 (APRIL, 1956):   138-147.

20416   SPRAGGINS, TINSLEY L.   "ECONOMIC ASPECTS OF NEGRO
        COLONIZATION DURING THE CIVIL WAR."   PH.D.
        DISSERTATION, AMERICAN UNIVERSITY, 1957.

20417   STAMPP, KENNETH M.   INDIANA POLITICS DURING THE CIVIL
        WAR.   INDIANAPOLIS: INDIANA HISTORICAL BUREAU, 1949.

20418   STEARNS, FRANK P. THE LIFE AND PUBLIC SERVICE OF GEORGE
        LUTHER STEARNS. PHILADELPHIA: J.B. LIPPINCOTT
        COMPANY, 1907.

20419   STILLMAN, RACHEL B. "EDUCATION IN THE CONFEDERATE STATES
        OF AMERICA, 1861-1865." PH.D. DISSERTATION,
        UNIVERSITY OF ILLINOIS, 1972.

20420   SUTHERLAND, G.E. "THE NEGRO IN THE LATE WAR." IN
        MILITARY ORDER OF THE LOYAL LEGION OF THE UNITED
        STATES, WISCONSIN COMMANDERY, WAR PAPERS I.
        MILWAUKEE: THE COMMANDERY, 1891, PP. 164-188.

20421   SYNNESTVEDT, SIG. "SLAVERY AND RECONSTRUCTION." THE
        WHITE RESPONSE TO BLACK EMANCIPATION. NEW YORK:
        MCMILLAN COMPANY, 1972, PP. 7-35.

20422   TAYLOR, RICHARD. DESTRUCTION AND RECONSTRUCTION: MY
        PERSONAL EXPERIENCES IN THE LATE WAR. NEW YORK: D.
        APPLETON AND COMPANY, 1879.

20423   "TEEN-AGE CIVIL WAR NURSE: SUSIE KING TAYLOR." EBONY,
        25 (FEBRUARY, 1970): 96-93, 100-102.

20424   THOMPSON, WILLIAM F., JR. "PICTORIAL IMAGES OF THE NEGRO
        DURING THE CIVIL WAR." WISCONSIN MAGAZINE OF HISTORY,
        48 (SUMMER, 1965): 282-294.

20425   TURNER, HENRY M. THE NEGRO IN SLAVERY, WAR, AND PEACE.
        PHILADELPHIA: N.P., 1913.

20426   TURNER, JOHN J. AND D'INNOCENZO, MICHAEL. "THE PLACE OF
        BLACKS IN AMERICAN SOCIETY: A CASE OF THREE
        NEWSPAPERS IN NEW YORK CITY DURING THE CIVIL WAR,
        1860-1865." PAN AFRICAN JOURNAL, 5 (WINTER, 1972):
        429-443.

20427   VLOCK, LAUREL F. AND LEVITCH, JOEL A. CONTRABAND OF WAR:
        THE STORY OF WILLIAM HENRY SINGLETON: SLAVE AND
        SOLDIER IN THE CIVIL WAR. NEW YORK: FUNK AND
        WAGNALLS, 1970.

20428   VOEGELI, JACQUE. "THE NORTHWEST AND THE RACE ISSUE,
        1861-1862." MISSISSIPPI VALLEY HISTORICAL REVIEW, 50
        (SEPTEMBER, 1963): 235-251.

20429   VOEGELI, V. JACQUE. FREE BUT NOT EQUAL: THE MIDWEST AND
        THE NEGRO DURING THE CIVIL WAR. CHICAGO: UNIVERSITY
        OF CHICAGO PRESS, 1967.

20430   VOEGELI, VICTOR J. "THE NORTHWEST AND THE NEGRO DURING
        THE CIVIL WAR." PH.D. DISSERTATION, TULANE
        UNIVERSITY, 1965.

20431   WEINTRAUB, ANDREW. "THE ECONOMICS OF LINCOLN'S PROPOSAL

FOR COMPENSATED EMANCIPATION." AMERICAN JOURNAL OF
ECONOMICS AND SOCIOLOGY, 33 (APRIL, 1973): 171-177.

20432 WELDON, M.C. "THE SOCIAL ASPECTS OF NEGRO SLAVERY DURING
THE PERIOD OF THE CIVIL WAR." M.A. THESIS, OHIO STATE
UNIVERSITY, 1929.

20433 WESLEY, CHARLES H. "THE CIVIL WAR AND THE NEGRO-
AMERICAN." JOURNAL OF NEGRO HISTORY, 47 (APRIL,
1962): 77-96.

20434 WESLEY, CHARLES H. AND ROMERO, PATRICIA W. NEGRO
AMERICANS IN THE CIVIL WAR: FROM SLAVERY TO
CITIZENSHIP. NEW YORK: PUBLISHERS COMPANY, 1967.

20435 WHALEY, H. "SLAVERY AND THE CIVIL WAR." MOODY MONTHLY,
(MAY, 1976): 78.

20436 WILBUR, HENRY W. PRESIDENT LINCOLN'S ATTITUDE TOWARDS
SLAVERY AND EMANCIPATION: WITH A REVIEW OF EVENTS
BEFORE AND SINCE THE CIVIL WAR. PHILADELPHIA: W.H.
JENKINS, 1914.

20437 WILEY, BELL I. THE LIFE OF BILLY YANK: THE COMMON
SOLDIER OF THE UNION. INDIANAPOLIS: BOBBS-MERRILL,
1952.

20438 WILEY, BELL I. SOUTHERN NEGROES, 1861-1865. NEW HAVEN:
YALE UNIVERSITY PRESS, 1938.

20439 WILEY, BELL I. "THE WAR'S IMPACT ON SLAVERY." CIVIL WAR
TIMES ILLUSTRATED, 9 (APRIL, 1970): 36-48.

20440 WILLIAMS, T. HARRY. "GENERAL BANKS AND THE RADICAL
REPUBLICANS IN THE CIVIL WAR." NEW ENGLAND QUARTERLY,
12 (JUNE, 1939): 268-280.

20441 WILLIAMS, T. HARRY. "LINCOLN AND THE RADICALS: AN ESSAY
IN CIVIL WAR HISTORY AND HISTORIOGRAPHY." IN
MCWHINEY, GRADY (ED.). GRANT, LEE, LINCOLN AND THE
RADICALS: ESSAYS ON CIVIL WAR LEADERSHIP. EVANSTON:
NORTHWESTERN UNIVERSITY PRESS, 1964, PP. 92-117.

20442 WILLIAMSON, JOEL. AFTER SLAVERY: THE NEGRO IN SOUTH
CAROLINA DURING RECONSTRUCTION, 1861-1877. CHAPEL
HILL: UNIVERSITY OF NORTH CAROLINA PRESS, 1965.

20443 WOLF, HAZEL C. "THE CIVIL WAR GOVERNORS AND
EMANCIPATION." M.A. THESIS, UNIVERSITY OF WISCONSIN,
1941.

20444 ZOELLNER, ROBERT H. "NEGRO COLONIZATION: THE CLIMATE OF
OPINION SURROUNDING LINCOLN, 1860-1865." MID-AMERICA,
42 (JULY, 1960): 131-150.

20445 ZORN, ROMAN J. "ABOLITIONISM DURING THE CIVIL WAR, 1860-1865." PH.M. THESIS, UNIVERSITY OF WISCONSIN, 1940.

20446 ZORNOW, WILLIAM F. "THE OHIO DEMOCRATS AND THE AFRICANIZATION ISSUE IN 1862." NEGRO HISTORY BULLETIN, 11 (JUNE, 1943): 211-214.

SLAVES AND THE CONFEDERACY

20447 ALEXANDER, THOMAS B. AND BERINGER, RICHARD E. THE ANATOMY OF THE CONFEDERATE CONGRESS. NASHVILLE: VANDERBILT UNIVERSITY PRESS, 1972.

20448 ANDREWS, ELIZA F. THE WAR-TIME JOURNAL OF A GEORGIA GIRL, 1864-1865. NEW YORK: D. APPLETON, 1908.

20449 APTHEKER, HERBERT. "NOTES ON SLAVE CONSPIRACIES IN CONFEDERATE MISSISSIPPI." JOURNAL OF NEGRO HISTORY, 29 (JANUARY, 1944): 75-79.

20450 ARMSTRONG, HANNIBAL. "HOW I HID A UNION SPY." JOURNAL OF NEGRO HISTORY, 9 (JANUARY, 1924): 34-40.

20451 AVARY, MYRTA L. (ED.). A VIRGINIA GIRL IN THE CIVIL WAR, 1861-1865. NEW YORK: APPLETON, 1903.

20452 BAKER, VAUGHAN (ED.). "GLIMPSES OF IBERIA IN THE CIVIL WAR." ATTAKAPAS GAZETTE, 6 (SEPTEMBER, 1971): 73-94.

20453 BARBER, JAMES G. "ALEXANDRIA IN THE CIVIL WAR, 1861-1865." M.A. THESIS, VIRGINIA POLYTECHNIC INSTITUTE AND STATE UNIVERSITY, 1977.

20454 BASSETT, JOHN S. (ED.). THE WESTOVER JOURNAL OF JOHN A. SELDEN, ESQUIRE, 1858-1862. NORTHAMPTON, MA: SMITH COLLEGE STUDIES IN HISTORY, 1921.

20455 BAYLOR, GEORGE. "THE ARMY NEGRO." SOUTHERN HISTORICAL SOCIETY PAPERS, 31 (JANUARY-DECEMBER, 1903): 365-369.

20456 BAYLOR, GEORGE. "THE ARMY NEGRO, HIS AFFECTION AND FIDELITY--MASTER AND SLAVE CONGENIAL." PUBLICATIONS OF THE SOUTHERN HISTORY ASSOCIATION, 8 (NOVEMBER, 1904): 484.

20457 BEARSS, EDWIN C. (ED.). A LOUISIANA CONFEDERATE: DIARY OF FELIX PIERRE POCHE. NATCHITOCHES: LOUISIANA STUDIES INSTITUTE, NORTHWESTERN STATE UNIVERSITY, 1972.

20458 BERRY, MARY F. "NEGRO TROOPS IN BLUE AND GRAY: THE LOUISIANA NATIVE GUARDS, 1861-1863." LOUISIANA HISTORY, 8 (SPRING, 1967): 165-190.

20459   BERRY, THOMAS F.   FOUR YEARS WITH MORGAN AND FORREST.
        OKLAHOMA CITY: HARLOW-RATLIFF COMPANY, 1914.

20460   BERWANGER, EUGENE H.   "ARMING OF SLAVES."   IN ROLLER,
        DAVID C. AND TWYMAN, ROBERT W. (EDS.).   THE
        ENCYCLOPEDIA OF SOUTHERN HISTORY.   BATON ROUGE:
        LOUISIANA STATE UNIVERSITY PRESS, 1979, P. 79.

20461   BETTERSWORTH, JOHN K.   CONFEDERATE MISSISSIPPI: THE
        PEOPLE AND POLICIES IN A COTTON STATE IN WARTIME.
        BATON ROUGE: LOUISIANA STATE UNIVERSITY PRESS, 1943.

20462   BIGELOW, MARTHA M.   "VICKSBURG: EXPERIMENT IN FREEDOM."
        JOURNAL OF MISSISSIPPI HISTORY, 26 (FEBRUARY, 1964):
        28-44.

20463   BLACK, BLANTON E.   "DECLINE OF PLANTATION AGRICULTURE IN
        COASTAL GEORGIA."   NEGRO EDUCATION REVIEW, 5
        (JULY-OCTOBER, 1954):   108-115.

20464   BLACK, IRVING D.   "A CONFEDERATE PLAN FOR ARMING THE
        SLAVES."   SOUTHERN HISTORICAL SOCIETY PAPERS, 29
        (1901):   173-174.

20465   BLACK, ROBERT C.   THE RAILROADS OF THE CONFEDERACY.
        CHAPEL HILL: UNIVERSITY OF NORTH CAROLINA PRESS, 1952.

20466   BRANSCOME, JAMES L.   "IMPRESSMENT IN THE STATE OF
        VIRGINIA DURING THE CIVIL WAR."   M.A. THESIS, WAKE
        FOREST UNIVERSITY, 1976.

20467   BRASSEAUX, CARL A. (ED.).   "THE GLORY DAYS: E.T. KING
        RECALLS THE CIVIL WAR YEARS."   ATTAKAPAS GAZETTE, 11
        (SPRING, 1976):   3-33.

20468   BREWER, JAMES H.   THE CONFEDERATE NEGRO: VIRGINIA'S
        CRAFTSMEN AND MILITARY LABORERS, 1861-1865.   DURHAM:
        DUKE UNIVERSITY PRESS, 1969.

20469   BROWN, MAUD M.   "THE WAR COMES TO COLLEGE HILL."   JOURNAL
        OF MISSISSIPPI HISTORY, 16 (JANUARY, 1954):   22-30.

20470   BRUCE, PHILIP A.   "PLANTATION MEMORIES OF THE CIVIL WAR."
        SOUTH ATLANTIC QUARTERLY, 14 (JANUARY, 1915):   28-46.

20471   BRYAN, THOMAS C.   CONFEDERATE GEORGIA.   ATHENS:
        UNIVERSITY OF GEORGIA PRESS, 1953.

20472   BUCK, IRVING A.   CLEBURNE AND HIS COMMAND.   JACKSON, TN:
        MCCOWAT-MERCER PRESS, 1959.

20473   BUCK, IRVING A.   "NEGROES IN OUR ARMY."   SOUTHERN
        HISTORICAL SOCIETY PAPERS, 31 (JANUARY-DECEMBER,
        1903):   215-228.

20474 BURGER, NASH K. "THE DIOCESE OF MISSISSIPPI AND THE CONFEDERACY." HISTORICAL MAGAZINE OF THE PROTESTANT EPISCOPAL CHURCH, 9 (MARCH, 1940): 52-77.

20475 BUTLER, PIERCE. "STATUS OF SLAVERY." IN RILEY, FRANKLIN L. (ED.). THE SOUTH IN THE BUILDING OF THE NATION. 12 VOLS. RICHMOND: SOUTHERN HISTORICAL PUBLICATION SOCIETY, 1909, VOL. 4, PP. 489-491.

20476 CAMPBELL, RANDOLPH B. AND PICKENS, DONALD K. "'MY DEAR HUSBAND': A TEXAS SLAVE'S LOVE LETTER, 1862." JOURNAL OF NEGRO HISTORY, 65 (FALL, 1980): 361-364.

20477 CANDLER, MYRTIE L. "REMINISCENCES OF LIFE IN GEORGIA DURING THE 1850S AND 1860S." GEORGIA HISTORICAL QUARTERLY, 33 (MARCH, JUNE, SEPTEMBER, DECEMBER, 1949): 36-48, 110-123, 218-227, 303-313; 34 (MARCH, 1950): 10-13.

20478 CASH, WILLIAM M. AND HOWORTH, LUCY S. (EDS.). MY DEAR NELLIE: THE CIVIL WAR LETTERS OF WILLIAM L. NUGENT TO ELEANOR SMITH NUGENT. JACKSON: UNIVERSITY PRESS OF MISSISSIPPI, 1977.

20479 CAUTHEN, CHARLES E. SOUTH CAROLINA GOES TO WAR, 1860-1865. CHAPEL HILL: UNIVERSITY OF NORTH CAROLINA PRESS, 1950.

20480 CHANNING, STEVEN A. "THE DIVIDED SOUTH: CONTINUITY AND CHANGE IN RACE AND CLASS RELATIONS, 1861-1865, A PRELIMINARY REPORT." UNPUBLISHED PAPER, AMERICAN HISTORY SEMINAR, JOHNS HOPKINS UNIVERSITY, APRIL 28, 1971.

20481 CHANNING, STEVEN A. "SLAVERY AND CONFEDERATE SURVIVAL: THE DEBATE ON ARMING AND FREEING THE SLAVES." REVIEWS IN AMERICAN HISTORY, 1 (SEPTEMBER, 1973): 400-405.

20482 CLAIBORNE, J.F.H. "REMINISCENCES OF THE LATE WAR." NEW ORLEANS DAILY PICAYUNE, JULY 5, 1883.

20483 COLEMAN, KENNETH. CONFEDERATE ATHENS. ATHENS: UNIVERSITY OF GEORGIA PRESS, 1967.

20484 "THE CONFEDERATE PLAN FOR ARMING THE SLAVES." SOUTHERN WORKMAN, 30 (SEPTEMBER, 1901): 475-476.

20485 CONYNGHAM, DAVID P. SHERMAN'S MARCH THROUGH THE SOUTH. NEW YORK: SHELDON AND COMPANY, 1865.

20486 CORNISH, DUDLEY T. "THE NEGRO." IN NEVINS, ALLAN; ROBERTSON, JAMES I., JR.; AND WILEY, BELL I. (EDS.). CIVIL WAR BOOKS: A CRITICAL BIBLIOGRAPHY. 2 VOLS. BATON ROUGE: LOUISIANA STATE UNIVERSITY PRESS, 1967, VOL. 1, PP. 207-216.

20487   COULTER, E. MERTON.   THE CONFEDERATE STATES OF AMERICA,
        1861-1865.   BATON ROUGE: LOUISIANA STATE UNIVERSITY
        PRESS, 1950.

20488   COULTER, E. MERTON.   "THE MOVEMENT FOR AGRICULTURAL
        REORGANIZATION IN THE COTTON SOUTH DURING THE CIVIL
        WAR."   NORTH CAROLINA HISTORICAL REVIEW, 4 (JANUARY,
        1927):   22-36.

20489   COULTER, E. MERTON.   "PLANTER'S WANTS IN THE DAYS OF THE
        CONFEDERACY."   GEORGIA HISTORICAL QUARTERLY, 12
        (MARCH, 1928):   38-52.

20490   COULTER, E. MERTON.   "SLAVERY AND FREEDOM IN ATHENS,
        GEORGIA, 1860-1866."   GEORGIA HISTORICAL QUARTERLY, 49
        (SEPTEMBER, 1965):   264-293.

20491   CRABTREE, BETH G. AND PATTON, JAMES W. (EDS.).   "JOURNAL
        OF A SECESH LADY":   THE DIARY OF CATHERINE DEVEREUX
        EDMONDSTON, 1860-1866.   RALEIGH: NORTH CAROLINA
        DIVISION OF ARCHIVES AND HISTORY, 1979.

20492   CUMMINGS, FRANK L.   "SLAVERY LEGISLATION OF THE
        CONFEDERATE GOVERNMENT."   M.A. THESIS, UNIVERSITY OF
        CHICAGO, 1911.

20493   CURRIE, JAMES T.   ENCLAVE: VICKSBURG AND HER
        PLANTATIONS, 1863-1870.   JACKSON: UNIVERSITY PRESS OF
        MISSISSIPPI, 1980.

20494   DANIEL, W. HARRISON.   "SOUTHERN PROTESTANTISM AND THE
        NEGRO, 1860-1865."   NORTH CAROLINA HISTORICAL REVIEW,
        41 (SUMMER, 1964):   333-359.

20495   DAVIS, WILLIAM W.   THE CIVIL WAR AND RECONSTRUCTION IN
        FLORIDA.   NEW YORK: COLUMBIA UNIVERSITY PRESS, 1913.

20496   DEBERRY, JOHN H.   "CONFEDERATE TENNESSEE."   PH.D.
        DISSERTATION, UNIVERSITY OF KENTUCKY, 1967.

20497   DEW, CHARLES B.   IRONMAKER TO THE CONFEDERACY: JOSEPH R.
        ANDERSON AND THE TREDEGAR IRON WORKS.   NEW HAVEN:
        YALE UNIVERSITY PRESS, 1966.

20498   DINKINS, JAMES.   "THE NEGROES AS SLAVES."   NEW ORLEANS
        PICAYUNE, OCTOBER 13, 1907.

20499   DONNELLY, RALPH W.   "THE BARTOW COUNTY CONFEDERATE
        SALTPETRE WORKS."   GEORGIA HISTORICAL QUARTERLY, 54
        (FALL, 1970):   305-319.

20500   DOUGAN, MICHAEL B.   CONFEDERATE ARKANSAS: THE PEOPLE AND
        POLICIES OF A FRONTIER STATE IN WARTIME.   UNIVERSITY,
        AL: UNIVERSITY OF ALABAMA PRESS, 1976.

20501　DRAGO, EDMUND L.　"HOW SHERMAN'S MARCH THROUGH GEORGIA AFFECTED THE SLAVES."　GEORGIA HISTORICAL QUARTERLY, 57 (FALL, 1973):　361-375.

20502　DUBOIS, W.E.B.　"THE NEGRO AND THE CIVIL WAR."　SCIENCE AND SOCIETY, 25 (DECEMBER, 1961):　347-352.

20503　DURDEN, ROBERT F.　THE GRAY AND THE BLACK: THE CONFEDERATE DEBATE ON EMANCIPATION.　BATON ROUGE: LOUISIANA STATE UNIVERSITY PRESS, 1972.

20504　EATON, CLEMENT.　A HISTORY OF THE SOUTHERN CONFEDERACY.　NEW YORK:　FREE PRESS, 1954.

20505　ECKENRODE, H.J.　"NEGROES IN RICHMOND IN 1864."　VIRGINIA MAGAZINE OF HISTORY AND BIOGRAPHY, 46 (JULY, 1938):　193-200.

20506　ELLSWORTH, LOIS C.　"SAN ANTONIO DURING THE CIVIL WAR."　M.A. THESIS, UNIVERSITY OF TEXAS, 1938.

20507　ESCOTT, PAUL D.　"THE CONTEXT OF FREEDOM:　GEORGIA'S SLAVES DURING THE CIVIL WAR."　GEORGIA HISTORICAL QUARTERLY, 58 (SPRING, 1974):　79-104.

20508　EVANS, W. MCKEE.　BALLOTS AND FENCE RAILS: RECONSTRUCTION ON THE LOWER CAPE FEAR.　CHAPEL HILL: UNIVERSITY OF NORTH CAROLINA PRESS, 1966.

20509　FARMER, H.H.　VIRGINIA BEFORE AND DURING THE WAR.　HENDERSON, KY:　THE AUTHOR, 1892.

20510　FARNOWSKI, MARY S.　"NATCHITOCHES DURING THE CIVIL WAR AND RECONSTRUCTION PERIOD."　M.A. THESIS, CATHOLIC UNIVERSITY OF AMERICA, 1951.

20511　FLEMING, WALTER L.　CIVIL WAR AND RECONSTRUCTION IN ALABAMA.　NEW YORK:　COLUMBIA UNIVERSITY PRESS, 1905.

20512　FLEMING, WALTER L.　"THE LABOR FORCE AND LABOR CONDITIONS, 1861-1865."　IN BALLAGH, JAMES C. (ED.). THE SOUTH IN THE BUILDING OF THE NATION.　12 VOLS. RICHMOND:　SOUTHERN HISTORICAL PUBLICATION SOCIETY, 1909, VOL. 5, PP. 146-151.

20513　FONER, JACK D.　BLACKS AND THE MILITARY IN AMERICAN HISTORY: A NEW PERSPECTIVE.　NEW YORK:　PRAEGER PUBLISHERS, 1974.

20514　FONTENOT, ELFA L.　"SOCIAL AND ECONOMIC LIFE IN LOUISIANA, 1861-1865, AS RECORDED BY CONTEMPORARIES."　M.A. THESIS, LOUISIANA STATE UNIVERSITY, 1933.

20515　FURLOW, HENRY J.　"THE LEGAL CONTROL OF THE NEGRO IN GEORGIA DURING THE CIVIL WAR."　M.A. THESIS, ATLANTA

UNIVERSITY, 1952.

20516   GATELL, FRANK O. (ED.). "THE SLAVEHOLDER AND THE
         ABOLITIONIST: BINDING UP A FAMILY'S WOUNDS." JOURNAL
         OF SOUTHERN HISTORY, 27 (AUGUST, 1961): 368-391.

20517   GATES, PAUL W. AGRICULTURE AND THE CIVIL WAR. NEW YORK:
         ALFRED A. KNOPF, 1965.

20518   "GENERAL LEE'S VIEWS ON ENLISTING THE NEGROES." CENTURY
         MAGAZINE, 36 (AUGUST, 1888): 599-600.

20519   "GENERAL R. E. LEE ON CONSCRIPTING SLAVES." CIVIL WAR
         TIMES ILLUSTRATED, 9 (JULY, 1970): 18-19.

20520   GHOLSON, THOMAS S. SPEECH OF HON. THOS. S. GHOLSON, OF
         VIRGINIA, ON THE POLICY OF EMPLOYING NEGRO TROOPS, AND
         THE DUTY OF ALL CLASSES TO AID IN THE PROSECUTION OF
         THE WAR. RICHMOND: G.P. EVANS & COMPANY, 1865.

20521   GOLDMANN, PAULINE S. "LETTERS FROM THREE MEMBERS OF
         TERRY'S TEXAS RANGERS, 1861-1865." M.A. THESIS,
         UNIVERSITY OF TEXAS, 1930.

20522   GONZALES, WILLIAM E. "THE NEGRO SLAVES." IN CHANDLER,
         JULIAN A.C. (ED.). THE SOUTH IN THE BUILDING OF THE
         NATION. 12 VOLS. RICHMOND: SOUTHERN HISTORICAL
         PUBLICATION SOCIETY, 1909, VOL. 2, PP. 90-91.

20523   HAGGARD, J. VILLSANA. "A BRIEF STUDY OF THE IMPRESSMENT
         OF SLAVE LABOR IN TEXAS, 1861-1865." M.A. THESIS,
         UNIVERSITY OF TEXAS, 1938.

20524   HAGUE, PARTHENIA A. A BLOCKADED FAMILY: LIFE IN
         SOUTHERN ALABAMA DURING THE CIVIL WAR. BOSTON:
         HOUGHTON, MIFFLIN, 1888.

20525   HARDEE, W.H. "BIOGRAPHICAL SKETCH OF MAJOR-GENERAL P.R.
         CLEBURNE." SOUTHERN HISTORICAL SOCIETY PAPERS, 31
         (JANUARY-DECEMBER, 1903): 151-164.

20526   HAY, THOMAS R. "THE SOUTH AND THE ARMING OF THE SLAVES."
         MISSISSIPPI VALLEY HISTORICAL REVIEW, 6 (JUNE, 1919):
         34-73.

20527   HEARD, GEORGE A. "ST. SIMON'S ISLAND DURING THE WAR
         BETWEEN THE STATES." GEORGIA HISTORICAL QUARTERLY, 22
         (SEPTEMBER, 1938): 249-272.

20528   HOUSE, ALBERT V., JR. (ED.). "DETERIORATION OF A GEORGIA
         RICE PLANTATION DURING FOUR YEARS OF CIVIL WAR."
         JOURNAL OF SOUTHERN HISTORY, 9 (FEBRUARY, 1943):
         98-113.

20529   JAMES, D. CLAYTON. "MISSISSIPPI AGRICULTURE, 1861-1865."

JOURNAL OF MISSISSIPPI HISTORY, 24 (MAY, 1962):
129-141.

20530   JERVEY, SUSAN R. AND RAVENEL, CHARLOTTE ST. J.   TWO
          DIARIES FROM MIDDLE ST. JOHN'S BERKELEY, SOUTH
          CAROLINA, FEBRUARY-MAY, 1865.   PINOPOLIS, SC: ST.
          JOHN'S HUNTING CLUB, 1921.

20531   JOHNS, JOHN E.   FLORIDA DURING THE CIVIL WAR.
          GAINESVILLE: UNIVERSITY OF FLORIDA PRESS, 1963.

20532   JOHNSON, R.M.   "NEGROES IN GEORGIA, BEFORE, DURING AND
          SINCE THE WAR."   AMERICAN CATHOLIC QUARTERLY REVIEW, 6
          (APRIL, 1881):   353.

20533   JONES, CHARLES C., JR.   "NEGRO SLAVES DURING THE CIVIL
          WAR."   MAGAZINE OF AMERICAN HISTORY, 16 (AUGUST,
          1886):   168-175.

20534   JORDAN, ERVIN L.   "A PAINFUL CASE: THE WRIGHT-SANBORN
          INCIDENT IN NORFOLK, VIRGINIA, JULY-OCTOBER, 1863."
          M.A. THESIS, OLD DOMINION UNIVERSITY, 1979.

20535   JORDAN, GLADYS E.W.   "THE NEGRO IN RICHMOND DURING THE
          CIVIL WAR AS DEPICTED BY THE RICHMOND WHIG."   M.A.
          THESIS, VIRGINIA STATE COLLEGE, 1967.

20536   JORDAN, WEYMOUTH T. (ED.).   "'SYSTEM OF FARMING AT BEAVER
          BEND,' ALABAMA, 1862."   JOURNAL OF SOUTHERN HISTORY, 7
          (FEBRUARY, 1941):   76-34.

20537   KERBY, ROBERT L.   KIRBY SMITH'S CONFEDERACY: THE
          TRANS-MISSISSIPPI SOUTH, 1863-1865.   NEW YORK:
          COLUMBIA UNIVERSITY PRESS, 1972.

20538   KIRKPATRICK, ARTHUR R.   "MISSOURI, THE TWELFTH
          CONFEDERATE STATE."   PH.D. DISSERTATION, UNIVERSITY OF
          MISSOURI, 1954.

20539   KRAMER, EDWARD M.   "ALABAMA NEGROES, 1861-1865."   M.A.
          THESIS, AUBURN UNIVERSITY, 1955.

20540   LATHROP, BARNES F.   "THE LAFOURCHE DISTRICT IN 1862:
          CONFEDERATE REVIVAL."   LOUISIANA HISTORY, 1 (FALL,
          1960):   300-319.

20541   LATHROP, BARNES F.   "THE LAFOURCHE DISTRICT IN 1862:
          INVASION."   LOUISIANA HISTORY, 2 (SPRING, 1961):
          175-201.

20542   LEE, WILLIAM M.   HISTORY OF THE LIFE OF REV. WILLIAM MACK
          LEE, BODY SERVANT OF GENERAL ROBERT E. LEE, THROUGH
          THE CIVIL WAR, COOK FROM 1861 TO 1865; STILL LIVING
          UNDER THE PROTECTION OF THE SOUTHERN STATES.   NORFOLK:
          VIRGINIA SMITH PRINT COMPANY, 1918.

20543   LEWIS, RONALD L. "BLACK LABOR IN THE EASTERN VIRGINIA
        COAL FIELD, 1765-1865." IN NEWTON, JAMES E. AND LEWIS
        (EDS.). THE OTHER SLAVES: MECHANICS, ARTISANS AND
        CRAFTSMEN. BOSTON: G.K. HALL, 1978, PP. 87-108.

20544   LEWIS, RONALD L. COAL, IRON, AND SLAVES: INDUSTRIAL
        SLAVERY IN MARYLAND AND VIRGINIA, 1715-1865.
        WESTPORT: GREENWOOD PRESS, 1979.

20545   LEWIS, RONALD L. "'THE DARKEST ABODE OF MAN'--BLACK
        MINERS IN THE FIRST SOUTHERN COAL FIELD, 1780-1865."
        VIRGINIA MAGAZINE OF HISTORY AND BIOGRAPHY, 87 (APRIL,
        1979): 190-202.

20546   LITWACK, LEON F. BEEN IN THE STORM SO LONG: THE
        AFTERMATH OF SLAVERY. NEW YORK: ALFRED A. KNOPF,
        1979.

20547   LOVETT, BOBBY L. "THE NEGRO IN TENNESSEE, 1861-1866: A
        SOCIO-MILITARY HISTORY OF THE CIVIL WAR ERA." PH.D.
        DISSERTATION, UNIVERSITY OF ARKANSAS, 1978.

20548   LOVETT, BOBBY L. "THE NEGRO'S CIVIL WAR IN TENNESSEE,
        1861-1865." JOURNAL OF NEGRO HISTORY, 61 (JANUARY,
        1976): 36-50.

20549   LUKE, JOSEPHINE. "FROM SLAVERY TO FREEDOM IN LOUISIANA,
        1862-1865." M.A. THESIS, TULANE UNIVERSITY, 1939.

20550   LURAGHI, RAIMONDO. "THE CIVIL WAR AND THE MODERNIZATION
        OF AMERICAN SOCIETY: SOCIAL STRUCTURE AND INDUSTRIAL
        REVOLUTION IN THE OLD SOUTH BEFORE AND DURING THE
        WAR." CIVIL WAR HISTORY, 18 (SEPTEMBER, 1972):
        230-250.

20551   MARSZALEK, JOHN F. THE DIARY OF MISS EMMA HOLMES:
        1861-1866. BATON ROUGE: LOUISIANA STATE UNIVERSITY
        PRESS, 1979.

20552   MASSEY, MARY E. BONNET BRIGADES. NEW YORK: ALFRED A.
        KNOPF, 1966.

20553   MCPHERSON, JAMES M. "NEGRO TROOPS IN THE CIVIL WAR." IN
        ROLLER, DAVID C. AND TWYMAN, ROBERT W. (EDS.). THE
        ENCYCLOPEDIA OF SOUTHERN HISTORY. BATON ROUGE:
        LOUISIANA STATE UNIVERSITY PRESS, 1979, PP. 892-893.

20554   MCPHERSON, JAMES M. THE NEGRO'S CIVIL WAR: HOW AMERICAN
        NEGROES FELT AND ACTED DURING THE WAR FOR THE UNION.
        NEW YORK: PANTHEON BOOKS, 1965.

20555   MEGEE, JONNIE M. "CONFEDERATE IMPRESSMENT ACTS IN THE
        TRANS-MISSISSIPPI DEPARTMENT." M.A. THESIS,
        UNIVERSITY OF TEXAS, 1915.

20556   MESSNER, WILLIAM F. "BLACK VIOLENCE AND WHITE RESPONSE:
        LOUISIANA, 1862." JOURNAL OF SOUTHERN HISTORY, 41
        (FEBRUARY, 1975): 19-38.

20557   MIERS, EARL S. (ED.). WHEN THE WORLD ENDED: THE DIARY
        OF EMMA LECONTE. NEW YORK: OXFORD UNIVERSITY PRESS,
        1957.

20558   MILLER, RANDALL M. "'DEAR MASTER': LETTERS FROM
        NASHVILLE, 1862." TENNESSEE HISTORICAL QUARTERLY, 33
        (SPRING, 1974): 85-92.

20559   MILLER, RANDALL M. "'IT IS GOOD TO BE RELIGIOUS': A
        LOYAL SLAVE ON GOD, MASTERS, AND THE CIVIL WAR."
        NORTH CAROLINA HISTORICAL REVIEW, 54 (WINTER, 1977):
        66-71.

20560   MILLS, GARY B. "CANE RIVER COUNTRY, 1860-1866."
        PROCEEDINGS OF THE SEVENTEENTH ANNUAL GENEALOGICAL
        INSTITUTE. BATON ROUGE: LOUISIANA GENEALOGICAL AND
        HISTORICAL SOCIETY, 1974, PP. 1-12.

20561   MILLS, GARY B. "PATRIOTISM FRUSTRATED: THE NATIVE
        GUARDS OF CONFEDERATE NATCHITOCHES." LOUISIANA
        HISTORY, 18 (FALL, 1977): 437-452.

20562   MOBLEY, JOE A. "FLUSH TIMES, WAR, AND RECONSTRUCTION IN
        A SOUTHERN TOWN, MOBILE, 1850-1867." M.A. THESIS,
        NORTH CAROLINA STATE UNIVERSITY, 1976.

20563   MOHR, CLARENCE L. "BEFORE SHERMAN: GEORGIA BLACKS AND
        THE UNION WAR EFFORT, 1861-1864." JOURNAL OF SOUTHERN
        HISTORY, 45 (AUGUST, 1979): 331-352.

20564   MOHR, CLARENCE L. "GEORGIA BLACKS DURING SECESSION AND
        CIVIL WAR, 1859-1865." PH.D. DISSERTATION, UNIVERSITY
        OF GEORGIA, 1975.

20565   MOHR, CLARENCE L. "SLAVERY IN OGLETHORPE COUNTY,
        GEORGIA, 1773-1865." PHYLON, 33 (SPRING, 1972): 4-21.

20566   MOHR, CLARENCE L. "SOUTHERN BLACKS IN THE CIVIL WAR: A
        CENTURY OF HISTORIOGRAPHY." JOURNAL OF NEGRO HISTORY,
        59 (APRIL, 1974): 177-195.

20567   MOORE, ALBERT B. CONSCRIPTION AND CONFLICT IN THE
        CONFEDERACY. NEW YORK: MACMILLAN COMPANY, 1924.

20568   MORRIS, GEORGE G. "CONFEDERATE LYNCHBURG, 1861-1865."
        M.A. THESIS, VIRGINIA POLYTECHNIC INSTITUTE AND STATE
        UNIVERSITY, 1977.

20569   MOSER, HAROLD D. "REACTION IN NORTH CAROLINA TO THE
        EMANCIPATION PROCLAMATION." M.A. THESIS, WAKE FOREST
        UNIVERSITY, 1963.

20570   MOSER, HAROLD D.   "REACTION IN NORTH CAROLINA TO THE
        EMANCIPATION PROCLAMATION."   NORTH CAROLINA HISTORICAL
        REVIEW, 44 (JANUARY, 1967):   53-71.

20571   "NEGRO CONFEDERATE BURIED WITH HONORS."   ATLANTA
        CONSTITUTION, OCTOBER 19, 1915.

20572   "NEGROES IN OUR ARMY."   RICHMOND DISPATCH, AUGUST 5, 1904.

20573   "NEGROES IN OUR ARMY."   SOUTHERN HISTORICAL SOCIETY
        PAPERS, 31 (JANUARY-DECEMBER, 1903):   215-228.

20574   NELSON, B.H.   "SOME ASPECTS OF NEGRO LIFE IN NORTH
        CAROLINA DURING THE CIVIL WAR."   NORTH CAROLINA
        HISTORICAL REVIEW, 25 (APRIL, 1948):   143-166.

20575   NELSON, BERNARD H.   "CONFEDERATE SLAVE IMPRESSMENT
        LEGISLATION, 1861-1865."   JOURNAL OF NEGRO HISTORY, 31
        (OCTOBER, 1946):   392-410.

20576   NELSON, BERNARD H.   "LEGISLATIVE CONTROL OF THE SOUTHERN
        FREE NEGRO, 1861-1865."   CATHOLIC HISTORICAL REVIEW,
        32 (APRIL, 1946):   28-45.

20577   OLSON, CARL I.   "THE NEGRO AND CONFEDERATE MORALE."   M.A.
        THESIS, UNIVERSITY OF MISSISSIPPI, 1951.

20578   ORREN, G.G.   "THE HISTORY OF HOPKINS COUNTY."   M.A.
        THESIS, EAST TEXAS STATE TEACHERS COLLEGE, 1938.

20579   PARISH, PETER J.   THE AMERICAN CIVIL WAR.   NEW YORK:
        HOLMES & MEIER PUBLISHERS, 1975.

20580   PORTER, DAVID D.   INCIDENTS AND ANECDOTES OF THE CIVIL
        WAR.   NEW YORK: D. APPLETON AND COMPANY, 1885.

20581   PREISSER, THOMAS M.   "THE VIRGINIA DECISION TO USE NEGRO
        SOLDIERS IN THE CIVIL WAR, 1864-1865."   VIRGINIA
        MAGAZINE OF HISTORY AND BIOGRAPHY, 33 (JANUARY, 1975):
        98-113.

20582   PRICHARD, WALTER.   "THE EFFECTS OF THE CIVIL WAR ON THE
        LOUISIANA SUGAR INDUSTRY."   JOURNAL OF SOUTHERN
        HISTORY, 5 (AUGUST, 1939):   315-332.

20583   QUARLES, BENJAMIN.   THE NEGRO IN THE CIVIL WAR.   BOSTON:
        LITTLE, BROWN AND COMPANY, 1953.

20584   RAMSAY, ARCHIBALD S.   "COTTON AND THE CONFEDERACY."   M.A.
        THESIS, PENNSYLVANIA STATE UNIVERSITY, 1952.

20585   RANSON, A.R.H.   "DICK."   HARPER'S MONTHLY REVIEW, 123
        (JULY, 1911):   300-302.

20586   REDWOOD, A.C.   "THE COOK OF THE CONFEDERATE ARMY."

SCRIBNER'S MONTHLY, 18 (AUGUST, 1879): 560-568.

20587 REID, BILL G. "CONFEDERATE OPPONENTS OF ARMING THE
       SLAVES, 1861-1865." JOURNAL OF MISSISSIPPI HISTORY,
       22 (OCTOBER, 1960): 249-270.

20588 REID, GURNEY H. "THE NEGRO IN RICHMOND ON THE EVE OF AND
       DURING THE CIVIL WAR." M.A. THESIS, COLLEGE OF
       WILLIAM AND MARY, 1936.

20589 REID, ROBERT D. "THE NEGRO IN ALABAMA DURING THE CIVIL
       WAR." JOURNAL OF NEGRO HISTORY, 35 (JULY, 1950):
       265-288.

20590 "RELATION OF SOUTHERN MASTERS TO SLAVES." CONFEDERATE
       VETERAN, 5 (JANUARY, 1897): 21-22.

20591 RIPLEY, C. PETER. SLAVES AND FREEDMEN IN CIVIL WAR
       LOUISIANA. BATON ROUGE: LOUISIANA STATE UNIVERSITY
       PRESS, 1976.

20592 RIPLEY, CHARLES P. "BLACK, BLUE AND GRAY: SLAVES AND
       FREEDMEN IN CIVIL WAR LOUISIANA." PH.D. DISSERTATION,
       FLORIDA STATE UNIVERSITY, 1973.

20593 ROARK, JAMES L. MASTERS WITHOUT SLAVES: SOUTHERN
       PLANTERS IN THE CIVIL WAR AND RECONSTRUCTION. NEW
       YORK: W.W. NORTON, 1977.

20594 ROARK, JAMES L. "MASTERS WITHOUT SLAVES: SOUTHERN
       PLANTERS IN THE CIVIL WAR AND RECONSTRUCTION." PH.D.
       DISSERTATION, STANFORD UNIVERSITY, 1973.

20595 ROBINSON, ARMSTEAD L. "DAY OF JUBLIO: CIVIL WAR AND THE
       DEMISE OF SLAVERY IN THE MISSISSIPPI VALLEY,
       1861-1865." PH.D. DISSERTATION, UNIVERSITY OF
       ROCHESTER, 1977.

20596 ROBINSON, ARMSTEAD L. "IN THE SHADOW OF OLD JOHN BROWN:
       INSURRECTION ANXIETY AND CONFEDERATE MOBILIZATION,
       1861-1863." JOURNAL OF NEGRO HISTORY, 65 (FALL,
       1980): 279-297.

20597 ROLAND, CHARLES P. THE CONFEDERACY. CHICAGO:
       UNIVERSITY OF CHICAGO PRESS, 1960.

20598 ROLAND, CHARLES P. "DIFFICULTIES OF CIVIL WAR SUGAR
       PLANTING IN LOUISIANA." LOUISIANA HISTORICAL
       QUARTERLY, 38 (OCTOBER, 1955): 40-62.

20599 ROLAND, CHARLES P. LOUISIANA SUGAR PLANTATIONS DURING
       THE AMERICAN CIVIL WAR. LEIDEN: E.J. BRILL, 1957.

20600 ROLAND, CHARLES P. "LOUISIANA SUGAR PLANTATIONS DURING
       THE CIVIL WAR." PH.D. DISSERTATION, LOUISIANA STATE

UNIVERSITY, 1951.

20601   ROSBROW, JAMES M.   "THE 'ABDUCTION' OF THE PLANTER."
        CRISIS, 56 (APRIL, 1949):   106-107.

20602   RUBY, BARBARA C.   "GENERAL PATRICK CLEBURNE'S PROPOSAL TO
        ARM SOUTHERN SLAVES."   ARKANSAS HISTORICAL QUARTERLY,
        30 (AUTUMN, 1971):   193-212.

20603   RUFFIN, EDWARD.   "CONDUCT OF THE NEGROES DURING THE WAR,
        1861-1865:   EXTRACTS FROM THE DIARY OF EDWARD RUFFIN."
        WILLIAM AND MARY COLLEGE QUARTERLY, 1ST SER., 22
        (APRIL, 1914):   258-262.

20604   SCARBOROUGH, WILLIAM K.   THE OVERSEER: PLANTATION
        MANAGEMENT IN THE OLD SOUTH.   BATON ROUGE: LOUISIANA
        STATE UNIVERSITY PRESS, 1966.

20605   SCHNEIDER, TRACY W.   "THE INSTITUTION OF SLAVERY IN NORTH
        CAROLINA, 1860-1865."   PH.D. DISSERTATION, DUKE
        UNIVERSITY, 1979.

20606   SHUGG, ROGER W.   ORIGINS OF CLASS STRUGGLE IN LOUISIANA:
        A SOCIAL HISTORY OF WHITE FARMERS AND LABORERS DURING
        SLAVERY AND AFTER, 1840-1875.   UNIVERSITY, LA:
        LOUISIANA STATE UNIVERSITY PRESS, 1939.

20607   SILVER, JAMES W.   CONFEDERATE MORALE & CHURCH PROPAGANDA.
        TUSCALOOSA: CONFEDERATE PUBLISHING COMPANY, 1957.

20608   SMITH, JOHN DAVID.   "CONFEDERATE REACTIONS TO PROPOSALS
        FOR ARMING THE NEGROES, 1864-1865."   B.A. THESIS,
        BALDWIN-WALLACE COLLEGE, 1971.

20609   SOMMERS, RICHARD J.   "THE DUTCH GAP AFFAIR: MILITARY
        ATROCITIES AND THE RIGHTS OF NEGRO SOLDIERS."   CIVIL
        WAR HISTORY, 21 (MARCH, 1975):   51-64.

20610   SOWLE, PATRICK M.   "THE CONFEDERACY, SLAVERY, AND
        EMANCIPATION, 1860-1865."   M.A. THESIS, DUKE
        UNIVERSITY, 1961.

20611   SPRAGGINS, TINSLEY L.   "MOBILIZATION OF NEGRO LABOR FOR
        THE DEPARTMENT OF VIRGINIA AND NORTH CAROLINA,
        1861-1865."   NORTH CAROLINA HISTORICAL REVIEW, 24
        (APRIL, 1947):   160-197.

20612   STAMPP, KENNETH M.   "THE SOUTHERN ROAD TO APPOMATTOX."
        COTTON MEMORIAL PAPERS NO. 4.   EL PASO: TEXAS WESTERN
        PRESS, UNIVERSITY OF TEXAS, EL PASO, 1969.

20613   STEPHENSON, NATHANIEL W.   "THE QUESTION OF ARMING THE
        SLAVES."   AMERICAN HISTORICAL REVIEW, 18 (JANUARY,
        1913):   295-308.

20614   STERKX, H.E.   PARTNERS IN REBELLION: ALABAMA WOMEN IN
        THE CIVIL WAR. RUTHERFORD: FAIRLEIGH DICKINSON
        UNIVERSITY PRESS, 1970.

20615   STOCKHOLM, RICHARD J. "ALABAMA IRON FOR THE CONFEDERACY:
        THE SELMA IRON WORKS." ALABAMA REVIEW, 21 (JULY,
        1968): 163-172.

20616   TATUM, GEORGIA L. DISLOYALTY IN THE CONFEDERACY. CHAPEL
        HILL: UNIVERSITY OF NORTH CAROLINA PRESS, 1934.

20617   TAYLOR, JOE G. "SLAVERY IN LOUISIANA DURING THE CIVIL
        WAR." LOUISIANA HISTORY, 8 (WINTER, 1967): 27-34.

20618   THOMAS, DAVID Y. ARKANSAS IN WAR AND RECONSTRUCTION,
        1861-1874. LITTLE ROCK: UNITED DAUGHTERS OF THE
        CONFEDERACY, 1926.

20619   THOMAS, EMORY M. THE CONFEDERACY AS A REVOLUTIONARY
        EXPERIENCE. ENGLEWOOD CLIFFS: PRENTICE-HALL, 1971.

20620   THOMAS, EMORY M. THE CONFEDERATE NATION, 1861-1865. NEW
        YORK: HARPER & ROW, 1979.

20621   THOMAS, PERCIAL M. "PLANTATIONS IN TRANSITION: A STUDY
        OF FOUR VIRGINIA PLANTATIONS, 1860-1870." PH.D.
        DISSERTATION, UNIVERSITY OF VIRGINIA, 1979.

20622   TREXLER, HARRISON A. "THE OPPOSITION OF PLANTERS TO THE
        EMPLOYMENT OF SLAVES AS LABORERS BY THE CONFEDERACY."
        MISSISSIPPI VALLEY HISTORICAL REVIEW, 27 (SEPTEMBER,
        1940): 211-224.

20623   TYLER, RONNIE C. "THE AGE OF COTTON: SANTIAGO VIDAURRI
        AND THE CONFEDERACY, 1861-1864." PH.D. DISSERTATION,
        TEXAS CHRISTIAN UNIVERSITY, 1968.

20624   "U.C.V. TO HONOR WARTIME SLAVES." NEW YORK AGE, APRIL
        18, 1914.

20625   "UP THE EDISTO." ATLANTIC MONTHLY, 20 (AUGUST, 1867):
        157-165.

20626   VAN DEBURG, WILLIAM L. "ELITE SLAVE BEHAVIOR DURING THE
        CIVIL WAR: BLACK DRIVERS AND FOREMEN IN
        HISTORIOGRAPHICAL PERSPECTIVE." SOUTHERN STUDIES, 16
        (FALL, 1977): 253-269.

20627   VANDIVER, FRANK. REBEL BRASS: THE CONFEDERATE COMMAND
        SYSTEM. BATON ROUGE: LOUISIANA STATE UNIVERSITY
        PRESS, 1956.

20628   VANDIVER, FRANK E. "THE SHELBY IRON COMPANY IN THE CIVIL
        WAR: A STUDY OF A CONFEDERATE INDUSTRY." ALABAMA
        REVIEW, 1 (JANUARY, 1948): 12-26.

20629   VANDIVER, FRANK E.   "THE SHELBY IRON WORKS: A STUDY IN
        CONFEDERATE INDUSTRY."   ALABAMA REVIEW, 1 (JULY,
        1948):   203-217.

20630   VANDIVER, FRANK E.   THEIR TATTERED FLAGS: THE EPIC OF
        THE CONFEDERACY.   NEW YORK: HARPER'S MAGAZINE PRESS,
        1970.

20631   VINCENT, CHARLES.   "BLACK LOUISIANIANS DURING THE CIVIL
        WAR AND RECONSTRUCTION: ASPECTS OF THEIR STRUGGLES
        AND ACHIEVEMENTS."   IN MACDONALD, ROBERT R.; KEMP,
        JOHN R.; AND HAAS, EDWARD F. (EDS.).   LOUISIANA'S
        BLACK HERITAGE.   NEW ORLEANS: LOUISIANA STATE MUSEUM,
        1979, PP. 85-106.

20632   "A VISIT TO THE CITIES AND CAMPS OF THE CONFEDERATE
        STATES, 1863-64."   BLACKWOOD'S EDINBURGH MAGAZINE, 97
        (JANUARY, 1865):   26-48.

20633   WALLACE, JAMES D.   "SAN ANTONIO DURING THE CIVIL WAR."
        M.A. THESIS, ST. MARY'S UNIVERSITY, SAN ANTONIO, 1940.

20634   WALLER, RUBEN.   "HISTORY OF A SLAVE WRITTEN BY HIMSELF AT
        THE AGE OF 89 YEARS."   IN LYNAM, ROBERT (ED.).   THE
        BEECHER ISLAND ANNUAL.   WRAY, CO: BEECHER ISLAND
        BATTLE MEMORIAL ASSOCIATION, 1930, PP. 115-119.

20635   WELLS, TOM H.   THE CONFEDERATE NAVY: A STUDY IN
        ORGANIZATION.   UNIVERSITY, AL: UNIVERSITY OF ALABAMA
        PRESS, 1971.

20636   WESLEY, CHARLES H.   THE COLLAPSE OF THE CONFEDERACY.
        WASHINGTON: ASSOCIATED PUBLISHERS, INC., 1937.

20637   WESLEY, CHARLES H.   "THE EMPLOYMENT OF NEGROES AS
        SOLDIERS IN THE CONFEDERATE ARMY."   JOURNAL OF NEGRO
        HISTORY, 4 (JULY, 1919):   239-253.

20638   WESLEY, CHARLES H.   "THE NEGRO SOLDIER IN THE CONFEDERATE
        ARMY."   ADDRESS PRESENTED AT SECOND BIENNIAL MEETING
        OF THE ASSOCIATION FOR THE STUDY OF NEGRO LIFE AND
        HISTORY, JUNE 17-18, 1919.

20639   WHARTON, VERNON L.   "SLAVERY AND THE NEGRO IN 1865."   THE
        NEGRO IN MISSISSIPPI, 1865-1890.   CHAPEL HILL:
        UNIVERSITY OF NORTH CAROLINA PRESS, 1947, PP. 9-22.

20640   WHITTINGTON, G.P. (ED.).   "CONCERNING THE LOYALTY OF
        SLAVES IN NORTH LOUISIANA IN 1862."   LOUISIANA
        HISTORICAL QUARTERLY, 14 (OCTOBER, 1931):   487-502.

20641   WIENER, JONATHAN M.   "FEMALE PLANTERS AND PLANTERS' WIVES
        IN CIVIL WAR AND RECONSTRUCTION: ALABAMA, 1850-1870."
        ALABAMA REVIEW, 30 (APRIL, 1977):   135-149.

20642   WIGHT, WILLARD E.   "CHURCHES IN THE CONFEDERACY."   PH.D.
        DISSERTATION, EMORY UNIVERSITY, 1958.

20643   WILEY, BELL I.   THE LIFE OF JOHNNY REB: THE COMMON
        SOLDIER OF THE CONFEDERACY.   INDIANAPOLIS:
        BOBBS-MERRILL, 1943.

20644   WILEY, BELL I.   "THE MOVEMENT TO HUMANIZE THE INSTITUTION
        OF SLAVERY DURING THE CONFEDERACY."   EMORY UNIVERSITY
        QUARTERLY, 5 (DECEMBER, 1949):   207-220.

20645   WILEY, BELL I.   "THE NEGRO IN THE CONFEDERACY."   PH.D.
        DISSERTATION, YALE UNIVERSITY, 1933.

20646   WILEY, BELL I.   THE PLAIN PEOPLE OF THE CONFEDERACY.
        BATON ROUGE: LOUISIANA STATE UNIVERSITY PRESS, 1943.

20647   WILEY, BELL I.   SOUTHERN NEGROES, 1861-1865.   NEW HAVEN:
        YALE UNIVERSITY PRESS, 1938.

20648   WILLIAMS, BEN A. (ED.).   A DIARY FROM DIXIE.   BOSTON:
        HOUGHTON MIFFLIN, 1949.

20649   WINTERS, JOHN D.   THE CIVIL WAR IN LOUISIANA.   BATON
        ROUGE: LOUISIANA STATE UNIVERSITY PRESS, 1963.

20650   WISH, HARVEY.   "SLAVE DISLOYALTY UNDER THE CONFEDERACY."
        JOURNAL OF NEGRO HISTORY, 23 (OCTOBER, 1938):   435-450.

20651   WOODS, WILLIAM L.   "THE TRAVAIL OF FREEDOM: MISSISSIPPI
        BLACKS, 1862-1870."   PH.D. DISSERTATION, PRINCETON
        UNIVERSITY, 1979.

20652   WOODWARD, JOSEPH H.   "ALABAMA IRON MANUFACTURING,
        1860-1865."   ALABAMA REVIEW, 7 (JULY, 1954):   199-207.

20653   WORLEY, TED R. (ED.).   "AT HOME IN CONFEDERATE ARKANSAS:
        LETTERS FROM PULASKI COUNTIANS, 1861-1865."   PULASKI
        COUNTY HISTORICAL SOCIETY BULLETIN, 2 (DECEMBER,
        1955):   36-42.

20654   WRIGHT, MRS. D. GIRAND.   A SOUTHERN GIRL IN '61:   THE
        WAR-TIME MEMORIES OF A CONFEDERATE SENATOR'S DAUGHTER.
        NEW YORK: DOUBLEDAY, PAGE, 1905.

20655   YEARNS, WILFRED B.   THE CONFEDERATE CONGRESS.   ATHENS:
        UNIVERSITY OF GEORGIA PRESS, 1960.

SLAVES AND THE UNION

20656   ABBOTT, ABIAL R.   "THE NEGRO IN THE WAR OF THE
        REBELLION."   IN MILITARY ESSAYS AND RECOLLECTIONS.
        PAPERS READ BEFORE THE COMMANDERY OF THE STATE OF
        ILLINOIS, MILITARY ORDER OF THE LOYAL LEGION OF THE

UNITED STATES. VOL. III. CHICAGO: DIAL PRESS, 1899, PP. 373-384.

20657 ABBOTT, MARTIN. "FREE LAND, FREE LABOR, AND THE FREEDMEN'S BUREAU." AGRICULTURAL HISTORY, 30 (OCTOBER, 1956): 150-156.

20658 ABBOTT, MARTIN. THE FREEDMEN'S BUREAU IN SOUTH CAROLINA: 1865-1877. CHAPEL HILL: UNIVERSITY OF NORTH CAROLINA PRESS, 1967.

20659 ABBOTT, MARTIN. "VOICES OF FREEDOM: THE RESPONSE OF SOUTHERN FREEDMEN TO LIBERTY." PHYLON, 34 (DECEMBER, 1973): 399-405.

20660 ABBOTT, MARTIN L. "THE FREEDMEN'S BUREAU IN SOUTH CAROLINA, 1865-1872." PH.D. DISSERTATION, EMORY UNIVERSITY, 1954.

20661 ABBOTT, RICHARD H. "MASSACHUSETTS AND THE RECRUITMENT OF SOUTHERN NEGROES, 1863-1865." CIVIL WAR HISTORY, 14 (SEPTEMBER, 1968): 197-210.

20662 ADAMS, DAVID W. "ILLINOIS SOLDIERS AND THE EMANCIPATION PROCLAMATION." JOURNAL OF THE ILLINOIS STATE HISTORICAL SOCIETY, 67 (SEPTEMBER, 1974): 407-421.

20663 ADDEMAN, J.M. "REMINISCENCES OF TWO YEARS WITH THE COLORED TROOPS." PERSONAL NARRATIVES OF EVENTS IN THE WAR OF THE REBELLION, BEING PAPERS READ BEFORE THE RHODE ISLAND SOLDIERS AND SAILORS HISTORICAL SOCIETY, SECOND SERIES, NO. 7. PROVIDENCE: N. BANGS WILLIAM AND COMPANY, 1880.

20664 AKERS, FRANK H., JR. "BLACKS IN THE CIVIL WAR: THEY FOUGHT FOR THE UNION AND EQUALITY." ARMY, 25 (1975): III, 47-51.

20665 ALDERSON, WILLIAM T., JR. "THE FREEDMEN'S BUREAU AND NEGRO EDUCATION IN VIRGINIA." NORTH CAROLINA HISTORICAL REVIEW, 29 (JANUARY, 1952): 64-90.

20666 AMES, SUSIE M. "FEDERAL POLICY TOWARD THE EASTERN SHORE OF VIRGINIA IN 1861." VIRGINIA MAGAZINE OF HISTORY AND BIOGRAPHY, 69 (OCTOBER, 1961): 432-459.

20667 ANDERSON, CHARLES W. "THE TRUE STORY OF FORT PILLOW." CONFEDERATE VETERAN, 3 (NOVEMBER, 1895): 322-323.

20668 ANDERSON, RUBY J. "THE PROBLEM OF COMPENSATED EMANCIPATION DURING THE CIVIL WAR." M.A. THESIS, DUKE UNIVERSITY, 1945.

20669 ANDREWS, CHRISTOPHER C. "MY OBSERVATIONS OF COLORED TROOPS IN THE CIVIL WAR." UNPUBLISHED PAPER, NOVEMBER

22, 1903, CHRISTOPHER C. ANDREWS PAPERS, MINNESOTA
HISTORICAL SOCIETY, ST. PAUL.

20670   APPLETON, MARY E. "THE EMANCIPATION PROCLAMATION AS AN
        INTEGRAL PART OF LINCOLN'S POLICY." M.A. THESIS,
        CORNELL UNIVERSITY, 1931.

20671   APTHEKER, HERBERT. "THE EMANCIPATION PROCLAMATION."
        POLITICAL AFFAIRS, 34 (FEBRUARY, 1955): 56-65.

20672   APTHEKER, HERBERT. "NEGRO CASUALTIES IN THE CIVIL WAR."
        JOURNAL OF NEGRO HISTORY, 32 (JANUARY, 1947): 10-80.

20673   APTHEKER, HERBERT. "THE NEGRO IN THE UNION NAVY."
        JOURNAL OF NEGRO HISTORY, 32 (APRIL, 1947): 169-200.

20674   ARMSTRONG, HANNIBAL. "HOW I HID A UNION SPY." JOURNAL
        OF NEGRO HISTORY, 9 (JANUARY, 1924): 34-40.

20675   ARMSTRONG, WARREN B. "THE ORGANIZATION, FUNCTION, AND
        CONTRIBUTION OF THE CHAPLAINCY IN THE UNITED STATES
        ARMY, 1861-1865." PH.D. DISSERTATION, UNIVERSITY OF
        MICHIGAN, 1964.

20676   ARMSTRONG, WARREN B. "UNION CHAPLAINS AND THE EDUCATION
        OF THE FREEDMEN." JOURNAL OF NEGRO HISTORY, 52
        (APRIL, 1967): 104-115.

20677   ARMSTRONG, WILLIAM H. "THE NEGRO AS A SOLDIER." IN WAR
        PAPERS OF THE INDIANA COMMANDERY, MILITARY ORDER OF
        THE LOYAL LEGION OF THE UNITED STATES. INDIANAPOLIS:
        INDIANA COMMANDERY, 1898, PP. 316-333.

20678   ARNOLD, PAUL T. "NEGRO SOLDIERS IN THE UNITED STATES
        ARMY." MAGAZINE OF HISTORY, 10 (AUGUST-NOVEMBER,
        1909): 61-70, 123-129, 185-193, 247-255; 11
        (JANUARY-MARCH, 1910): 1-12, 119-125.

20679   BAHNEY, ROBERT S. "GENERALS AND NEGROES: EDUCATION OF
        NEGROES BY THE UNION ARMY, 1361-1865." PH.D.
        DISSERTATION, UNIVERSITY OF MICHIGAN, 1965.

20680   BANGS, ISAAC S. "THE ULLMAN BRIGADE." IN WAR PAPERS OF
        THE MAINE COMMANDERY, MILITARY ORDER OF THE LOYAL
        LEGION OF THE UNITED STATES. 2 VOLS. PORTLAND:
        MAINE COMMANDERY, 1902, VOL. 2, PP. 290-310.

20681   BARNES, ELINOR AND BARNES, JAMES A. (EDS.). NAVAL
        SURGEON: BLOCKADING THE SOUTH, 1862-1866.
        BLOOMINGTON: INDIANA UNIVERSITY PRESS, 1963.

20682   BASFORD, MRS. GERTHA B. "FEDERAL ADMINISTRATION OF
        ABANDONED PLANTATIONS AND NEGRO LABOR DURING THE CIVIL
        WAR, 1862-1865." M.A. THESIS, UNIVERSITY OF TEXAS,
        1931.

20683   BEJACH, LOIS D. (ED.). "THE JOURNAL OF A CIVIL WAR
        'COMMANDO'--DEWITT CLINTON FORT." WEST TENNESSEE
        HISTORICAL SOCIETY PAPERS, 2 (1948): 5-32.

20684   BELZ, HERMAN. EMANCIPATION AND EQUAL RIGHTS: POLITICS
        AND CONSTITUTIONALISM IN THE CIVIL WAR ERA. NEW YORK:
        W.W. NORTON, 1978.

20685   BELZ, HERMAN. "THE FREEDMEN'S BUREAU ACT OF 1865 AND THE
        PRINCIPLE OF NO DISCRIMINATION ACCORDING TO COLOR."
        CIVIL WAR HISTORY, 21 (SEPTEMBER, 1975): 197-217.

20686   BELZ, HERMAN. "LAW, POLITICS, AND RACE IN THE STRUGGLE
        FOR EQUAL PAY DURING THE CIVIL WAR." CIVIL WAR
        HISTORY, 22 (SEPTEMBER, 1976): 197-213.

20687   BELZ, HERMAN. A NEW BIRTH OF FREEDOM: THE REPUBLICAN
        PARTY AND FREEDMEN'S RIGHTS 1861 TO 1866. WESTPORT:
        GREENWOOD PRESS, 1977.

20688   BELZ, HERMAN. "PROTECTION OF PERSONAL LIBERTY IN
        REPUBLICAN EMANCIPATION LEGISLATION OF 1862." JOURNAL
        OF SOUTHERN HISTORY, 42 (AUGUST, 1976): 385-400.

20689   BELZ, HERMAN J. "RECONSTRUCTING THE UNION: CONFLICTS OF
        THEORY AND POLICY DURING THE CIVIL WAR." PH.D.
        DISSERTATION, UNIVERSITY OF WASHINGTON, 1966.

20690   BENSON, ANDREW M. "MY CAPTURE, PRISON LIFE AND ESCAPE."
        IN CIVIL WAR PAPERS, MILITARY ORDER OF THE LOYAL
        LEGION, MASSACHUSETTS COMMANDERY, VOL. 1. BOSTON:
        THE COMMANDERY, 1900, PP. 107-138.

20691   BENTLEY, GEORGE R. A HISTORY OF THE FREEDMEN'S BUREAU.
        PHILADELPHIA: UNIVERSITY OF PENNSYLVANIA, 1955.

20692   BERRY, MARY F. "THE HISTORY OF THE 73RD REGIMENT AND
        75TH UNITED STATES COLORED INFANTRY REGIMENTS." M.A.
        THESIS, HOWARD UNIVERSITY, 1962.

20693   BERRY, MARY F. "LINCOLN AND CIVIL RIGHTS FOR BLACKS."
        PAPERS OF THE ABRAHAM LINCOLN ASSOCIATION, 2 (1980):
        46-57.

20694   BERRY, MARY F. MILITARY NECESSITY AND CIVIL RIGHTS
        POLICY: BLACK CITIZENSHIP AND THE CONSTITUTION,
        1861-1868. PORT WASHINGTON, NY: KENNIKAT PRESS, 1977.

20695   BERRY, MARY F. "THE NEGRO SOLDIER MOVEMENT AND THE
        ADOPTION OF NATIONAL CONSCRIPTION, 1652-1865." PH.D.
        DISSERTATION, UNIVERSITY OF MICHIGAN, 1966.

20696   BERRY, MARY F. "NEGRO TROOPS IN BLUE AND GRAY: THE
        LOUISIANA NATIVE GUARDS, 1861-1863." LOUISIANA
        HISTORY, 8 (SPRING, 1967): 165-190.

20697 BETHEL, ELIZABETH. "THE FREEDMEN'S BUREAU IN ALABAMA."
       JOURNAL OF SOUTHERN HISTORY, 14 (FEBRUARY, 1948):
       49-92.

20698 BIGELOW, MARTHA M. "FREEDMEN OF THE MISSISSIPPI VALLEY,
       1862-1865." CIVIL WAR HISTORY, 8 (MARCH, 1962):
       38-47.

20699 BIGELOW, MARTHA M. (ED.). "PLANTATION LESSEE PROBLEMS IN
       1864." JOURNAL OF SOUTHERN HISTORY, 27 (AUGUST,
       1961): 354-367.

20700 BIGELOW, MARTHA M. "THE SIGNIFICANCE OF MILLIKEN'S BEND
       IN THE CIVIL WAR." JOURNAL OF NEGRO HISTORY, 45
       (JULY, 1960): 156-163.

20701 BILLINGTON, RAY A. (ED.). THE JOURNAL OF CHARLOTTE
       FORTEN. NEW YORK: DRYDEN PRESS, 1953.

20702 BILLINGTON, RAY A. "A SOCIAL EXPERIMENT: THE PORT ROYAL
       JOURNAL OF CHARLOTTE L. FORTEN, 1862-1863." JOURNAL
       OF NEGRO HISTORY, 35 (JULY, 1950): 233-264.

20703 BINDER, FREDERICK M. "PENNSYLVANIA'S NEGRO REGIMENTS IN
       THE CIVIL WAR." JOURNAL OF NEGRO HISTORY, 37
       (OCTOBER, 1952): 383-417.

20704 BINDER, FREDERICK M. "PHILADELPHIA'S FREE MILITARY
       SCHOOL." PENNSYLVANIA HISTORY, 17 (JULY, 1950):
       281-291.

20705 BIRNEY, WILLIAM. GENERAL WILLIAM BIRNEY'S ANSWER TO
       LIBELS CLANDESTINELY CIRCULATED BY JAMES SHAW, JR.,
       COLLECTOR OF THE PORT, PROVIDENCE, R.I., WITH A REVIEW
       OF THE MILITARY RECORD OF THE SAID JAMES SHAW, JR.,
       LATE COLONEL OF THE SEVENTH U.S. COLORED TROOPS.
       WASHINGTON: N.P., 1878.

20706 BISSELL, J.W. "THE WESTERN ORGANIZATION OF COLORED
       PEOPLE FOR FURNISHING INFORMATION TO UNITED STATES
       TROOPS IN THE SOUTH." IN NEILL, EDWARD D. (ED.).
       GLIMPSES OF THE NATION'S STRUGGLE. SECOND SERIES. A
       SERIES OF PAPERS READ BEFORE THE MINNESOTA COMMANDERY
       OF THE MILITARY ORDER OF THE LOYAL LEGION OF THE
       UNITED STATES, 1887-1889. ST. PAUL: ST. PAUL BOOK
       AND STATIONARY COMPANY, 1890, PP. 314-321.

20707 "THE BLACK TROOPERS." LEISURE HOUR, 19 (1876): 353-417.

20708 BLACKBURN, GEORGE M. (ED.). "THE NEGRO AS VIEWED BY A
       MICHIGAN CIVIL WAR SOLDIER: LETTERS OF JOHN C.
       BUCHANAN." MICHIGAN HISTORY, 47 (MARCH, 1963): 75-84.

20709 BLACKISTON, HARRY S. "LINCOLN'S EMANCIPATION PLAN."
       JOURNAL OF NEGRO HISTORY, 7 (JULY, 1922): 257-277.

20710   BLASSINGAME, JOHN W.   "NEGRO CHAPLAINS IN THE CIVIL WAR."
        NEGRO HISTORY BULLETIN, 26 (OCTOBER, 1963):   23-24.

20711   BLASSINGAME, JOHN W.   "THE ORGANIZATION AND USE OF NEGRO
        TROOPS IN THE UNION ARMY, 1863-1865."   M.A. THESIS,
        HOWARD UNIVERSITY, 1961.

20712   BLASSINGAME, JOHN W.   "THE RECRUITMENT OF COLORED TROOPS
        IN KENTUCKY, MARYLAND AND MISSOURI: 1863-1865."
        HISTORIAN, 29 (AUGUST, 1967):   533-545.

20713   BLASSINGAME, JOHN W.   "THE RECRUITMENT OF NEGRO TROOPS IN
        MARYLAND."   MARYLAND HISTORICAL MAGAZINE, 58 (MARCH,
        1963):   20-29.

20714   BLASSINGAME, JOHN W.   "RECRUITMENT OF NEGRO TROOPS IN
        MISSOURI DURING THE CIVIL WAR."   MISSOURI HISTORICAL
        REVIEW, 58 (APRIL, 1964):   326-338.

20715   BLASSINGAME, JOHN W.   "THE SELECTION OF OFFICERS AND
        NON-COMMISSIONED OFFICERS OF NEGRO TROOPS IN THE UNION
        ARMY, 1863-1865."   NEGRO HISTORY BULLETIN, 30
        (JANUARY, 1967):   8-11.

20716   BLASSINGAME, JOHN W.   "THE UNION ARMY AS AN EDUCATIONAL
        INSTITUTION FOR NEGROES, 1862-1865."   JOURNAL OF NEGRO
        EDUCATION, 34 (SPRING, 1965):   152-159.

20717   BODINE, GEORGE (ED.).   "FORT PILLOW 'MASSACRE':
        OBSERVATIONS OF A MINNESOTAN."   MINNESOTA HISTORY, 43
        (SPRING, 1973):   186-190.

20718   BONEY, F.N. (ED.).   A UNION SOLDIER IN THE LAND OF THE
        VANQUISHED.   UNIVERSITY, AL: UNIVERSITY OF ALABAMA
        PRESS, 1969.

20719   BOWEN, DON R.   "GUERRILLA WAR IN WESTERN MISSOURI,
        1862-1865:   HISTORICAL EXTENSIONS OF THE RELATIVE
        DEPRIVATION HYPOTHESIS."   COMPARATIVE STUDIES IN
        SOCIETY AND HISTORY, 19 (JANUARY, 1977):   30-51.

20720   BOYD, WILLIAM L.   "KANSAS NEGRO TROOPS IN THE CIVIL WAR."
        M.A. THESIS, KANSAS STATE TEACHERS COLLEGE, PITTSBURG,
        1951.

20721   BOYD, WILLIS D.   "NEGRO COLONIZATION IN THE NATIONAL
        CRISIS: 1860-1870."   PH.D. DISSERTATION, UNIVERSITY
        OF CALIFORNIA, LOS ANGELES, 1953.

20722   BRADFORD, J.H.   "A TRIBUTE TO TOM; OR THE 'SERVANT
        QUESTION' AMONG THE VOLUNTEERS."   MILITARY ORDER OF
        THE LOYAL LEGION OF THE UNITED STATES, COMMANDERY OF
        THE DISTRICT OF COLUMBIA, NO. 21 (1895):   1-16.

20723   BRADFORD, M.E.   "LINCOLN LEGACY: A LONG VIEW."   MODERN

AGE, 24 (FALL, 1980): 355-363.

20724 BRICELAND, ALAN V. "ABRAHAM LINCOLN IN THE WAR YEARS: HIS GOALS AND THE THINKING BEHIND THEM." B.A. HONORS THESIS, COLLEGE OF WILLIAM AND MARY, 1961.

20725 BRIDGMAN, ROBERT W. "ANTECEDENTS OF THE FREEDMEN'S BUREAU." M.A. THESIS, UNIVERSITY OF WISCONSIN, 1912.

20726 BRIGGS, WALTER D.B. _CIVIL WAR SURGEON IN A COLORED REGIMENT_. BERKELEY: N.P., 1960.

20727 BRINGER, GLADYS S. "TRANSITION FROM SLAVE TO FREE LABOR IN LOUISIANA AFTER THE CIVIL WAR." M.A. THESIS, TULANE UNIVERSITY, 1927.

20728 BROCKETT, LINUS P. _THE CAMP, THE BATTLE FIELD, AND THE HOSPITAL: OR, LIGHTS AND SHADOWS OF THE GREAT REBELLION_. PHILADELPHIA: NATIONAL PUBLISHING COMPANY, 1866.

20729 BRONSON, LOUIS H. "THE FREEDMEN'S BUREAU: A PUBLIC POLICY ANALYSIS." D.S.W. DISSERTATION, UNIVERSITY OF SOUTHERN CALIFORNIA, 1970.

20730 BROOKS, NOAH. _ABRAHAM LINCOLN AND THE DOWNFALL OF AMERICAN SLAVERY_. NEW YORK: PUTNAM, 1894.

20731 BROWN, WILLIAM W. _THE BLACK MAN, HIS ANTECEDENTS, HIS GENIUS, AND HIS ACHIEVEMENTS_. BOSTON: R.F. WALLCUT, 1865.

20732 BROWN, WILLIAM W. _THE NEGRO IN THE AMERICAN REBELLION: HIS HEROISM AND HIS FIDELITY_. BOSTON: LEE & SHEPARD, 1867.

20733 BROWNE, FREDERICK W. _MY SERVICE IN THE U.S. COLORED CAVALRY_. CINCINNATI: OHIO COMMANDERY OF THE LOYAL LEGION, 1908.

20734 BROWNE, JUNIUS H. _FOUR YEARS IN SECESSIA_. HARTFORD: O.D. CASE AND COMPANY, 1865.

20735 BRYAN, CHARLES F., JR. "THE CIVIL WAR IN EAST TENNESSEE: A SOCIAL, POLITICAL, AND ECONOMIC STUDY." PH.D. DISSERTATION, UNIVERSITY OF TENNESSEE, 1978.

20736 BRYANT, WILLIAM C. (ED.). "A YANKEE SOLDIER LOOKS AT THE NEGRO." _CIVIL WAR HISTORY_, 7 (JUNE, 1961): 133-148.

20737 BUICE, SAMMY D. "THE CIVIL WAR AND THE FIVE CIVILIZED TRIBES--A STUDY IN FEDERAL-INDIAN RELATIONS." PH.D. DISSERTATION, UNIVERSITY OF OKLAHOMA, 1970.

20738 BURCHARD, PETER. _ONE GALLANT RUSH: ROBERT GOULD SHAW_

AND HIS BRAVE BLACK REGIMENT. NEW YORK: ST. MARTIN'S PRESS, 1965.

20739   BUTLER, BENJAMIN. BUTLER'S BOOK. BOSTON: A.M. THAYER AND COMPANY, 1892.

20740   BUTLER, BENJAMIN. MAJOR GEN. BUTLER AT HOME. N.P., N.D.

20741   CALEY, G.C. "THE ATTITUDE OF CLEVELAND, OHIO TOWARD SLAVERY AS EXPRESSED THROUGH ITS LEADING NEWSPAPERS DURING THE CIVIL WAR." M.A. THESIS, OHIO STATE UNIVERSITY, 1926.

20742   CALIFF, JOSEPH M. RECORD OF THE SERVICES OF THE SEVENTH REGIMENT, U.S. COLORED TROOPS, FROM SEPTEMBER, 1863, TO NOVEMBER, 1866. PROVIDENCE: L.L. FREEMAN AND COMPANY, 1878.

20743   CALIFF, JOSEPH M. TO THE EX-MEMBERS AND FRIENDS OF THE U.S.C.T. FORT HAMILTON, NY: N.P., 1878.

20744   CAPERS, GERALD M. OCCUPIED CITY: NEW ORLEANS UNDER THE FEDERALS, 1862-1865. LEXINGTON: UNIVERSITY OF KENTUCKY PRESS, 1965.

20745   "CAPTURE OF FORT PILLOW--VINDICATION OF GENERAL CHALMERS BY A FEDERAL OFFICER." SOUTHERN HISTORICAL SOCIETY PAPERS, 7 (OCTOBER, 1879): 439-441.

20746   CARMICHAEL, MAUDE S. "FEDERAL EXPERIMENTS WITH NEGRO LABOR ON ABANDONED PLANTATIONS IN ARKANSAS: 1862-1865." ARKANSAS HISTORICAL QUARTERLY, 1 (MARCH, 1942): 101-116.

20747   CARPENTER, JOHN A. SWORD AND OLIVE BRANCH: OLIVER OTIS HOWARD. PITTSBURGH: UNIVERSITY OF PITTSBURGH PRESS, 1964.

20748   CARPENTER, W. SPENCER. "THE NEGRO SOLDIER'S CONTRIBUTION IN THE WARS OF THE UNITED STATES." A.M.E. CHURCH REVIEW, 29 (JANUARY, 1913): 215-224.

20749   CARTER, SOLON A. "FOURTEEN MONTHS' SERVICE WITH COLORED TROOPS." CIVIL WAR PAPERS, VOLUME 1. BOSTON: MILITARY ORDER OF LOYAL LEGION, MASSACHUSETTS COMMANDERY, 1900, PP. 155-179.

20750   CASTEL, ALBERT. "CIVIL WAR KANSAS AND THE NEGRO." JOURNAL OF NEGRO HISTORY, 51 (APRIL, 1966): 125-138.

20751   CASTEL, ALBERT. "THE FORT PILLOW MASSACRE: A FRESH EXAMINATION OF THE EVIDENCE." CIVIL WAR HISTORY, 4 (MARCH, 1958): 37-50.

20752   CASTEL, ALBERT. "FORT PILLOW: VICTORY OR MASSACRE?"

AMERICAN HISTORY ILLUSTRATED, 9 (APRIL, 1974): 4-10, 46-48.

20753 CHASE, J.J. THE CHARGE AT DAY-BREAK: SCENES AND INCIDENTS AT THE BATTLE OF THE MINE EXPLOSION. LEWISTON, ME: LEWIS JOURNAL, 1875.

20754 CHENAULT, JOHN C. OLD CANE SPRINGS: A STORY OF THE WAR BETWEEN THE STATES IN MADISON COUNTY, KENTUCKY. LOUISVILLE: STANDARD PRINTING COMPANY, 1937.

20755 CHENERY, WILLIAM. THE FOURTEENTH REGIMENT RHODE ISLAND HEAVY ARTILLERY (COLORED) IN THE WAR TO PRESERVE THE UNION, 1861-1865. PROVIDENCE: SNOW AND FARNHAM, 1898.

20756 CHETLAIN, AUGUSTUS L. RECOLLECTIONS OF SEVENTY YEARS. GALENA, IL: GAZETTE PUBLISHING COMPANY, 1899.

20757 CHRISTENSEN, MIKE. "HISTORIAN FIGHTS TO COMMEMORATE CIVIL WAR'S UNSUNG BLACK HEROES." ATLANTA JOURNAL AND CONSTITUTION, MAY 11, 1980.

20758 CIMPRICH, JOHN. "THE BEGINNING OF THE BLACK SUFFRAGE MOVEMENT IN TENNESSEE, 1863-1865." JOURNAL OF NEGRO HISTORY, 65 (SUMMER, 1980): 185-195.

20759 CIMPRICH, JOHN. "MILITARY GOVERNOR JOHNSON AND TENNESSEE BLACKS, 1862-1865." TENNESSEE HISTORICAL QUARTERLY, 39 (WINTER, 1980): 459-470.

20760 CIMPRICH, JOHN V. "THE DEVELOPMENT OF JOHN SHERMAN'S VIEWS ON SLAVERY AND THE FREEDMAN, 1861-1867." M.A. THESIS, OHIO STATE UNIVERSITY, 1973.

20761 CIMPRICH, JOHN V., JR. "SLAVERY AMIDST THE CIVIL WAR IN TENNESSEE: THE DEATH OF AN INSTITUTION." PH.D. DISSERTATION, OHIO STATE UNIVERSITY, 1977.

20762 CLAY, GREEN. "OLD CANE SPRINGS--A BORDER-LAND TALE OF THE CIVIL WAR." REGISTER OF THE KENTUCKY HISTORICAL SOCIETY, 29 (APRIL, JULY, 1931): 184-196, 246-277.

20763 CLAYTON, RONNIE W. "THE FEDERAL WRITERS' PROJECT FOR BLACKS IN LOUISIANA." LOUISIANA HISTORY, 19 (SUMMER, 1978): 327-335.

20764 COCHRANE, JOHN. ARMING THE SLAVES IN THE WAR FOR THE UNION. NEW YORK: ROGERS AND SHERWOOD, 1875.

20765 COCHRANE, WILLIAM G. "FREEDOM WITHOUT EQUALITY: A STUDY OF NORTHERN OPINION AND THE NEGRO ISSUE, 1861-1870." PH.D. DISSERTATION, UNIVERSITY OF MINNESOTA, 1957.

20766 COFFIN, CHARLES C. THE BOYS OF '61: OR, FOUR YEARS OF FIGHTING. BOSTON: ESTES AND LAURIAT, 1881.

20767 COLE, ARTHUR C. THE ERA OF THE CIVIL WAR, 1848-1870. SPRINGFIELD: ILLINOIS CENTENNIAL COMMISSION, 1919.

20768 CONNOR, SELDON. "THE COLORED TROOPS." IN WAR PAPERS READ BEFORE THE COMMANDERY OF THE STATE OF MAINE, MILITARY ORDER OF THE LOYAL LEGION OF THE UNITED STATES VOLUME III. PORTLAND: LEFAVOR-TOWER COMPANY, 1908, PP. 61-82.

20769 COONEY, CHARLES F. "I WAS . . . EAGER TO BECOME A SOLDIER." MANUSCRIPTS, 26 (FALL, 1974): 280-282.

20770 CORNISH, DUDLEY T. "KANSAS NEGRO REGIMENTS IN THE CIVIL WAR." KANSAS HISTORICAL QUARTERLY, 20 (MAY, 1952): 417-429.

20771 CORNISH, DUDLEY T. "THE NEGRO." IN NEVINS, ALLAN; ROBERTSON, JAMES I., JR.; AND WILEY, BELL I. (EDS.). CIVIL WAR BOOKS: A CRITICAL BIBLIOGRAPHY. 2 VOLS. BATON ROUGE: LOUISIANA STATE UNIVERSITY PRESS, 1967, VOL. 1, PP. 207-216.

20772 CORNISH, DUDLEY T. "NEGRO TROOPS IN THE UNION ARMY, 1861-1865." PH.D. DISSERTATION, UNIVERSITY OF COLORADO, 1950.

20773 CORNISH, DUDLEY T. THE SABLE ARM: NEGRO TROOPS IN THE UNION ARMY, 1861-1865. NEW YORK: LONGMANS, GREEN AND COMPANY, 1956.

20774 CORNISH, DUDLEY T. "THE UNION ARMY AS A SCHOOL FOR NEGROES." JOURNAL OF NEGRO HISTORY, 37 (OCTOBER, 1952): 368-382.

20775 COULTER, E. MERTON. THE CIVIL WAR AND READJUSTMENT IN KENTUCKY. CHAPEL HILL: UNIVERSITY OF NORTH CAROLINA PRESS, 1926.

20776 COULTER, E. MERTON. "SOME REASONS FOR KENTUCKY'S POSITION IN THE CIVIL WAR." M.A. THESIS, UNIVERSITY OF WISCONSIN, 1915.

20777 COUSINS, PHYLLIS M. "A HISTORY OF THE THIRTY-THIRD UNITED STATES COLORED TROOPS." M.A. THESIS, HOWARD UNIVERSITY, 1961.

20778 COWDEN, ROBERT. A BRIEF SKETCH OF THE ORGANIZATION AND SERVICES OF THE FIFTY-NINTH REGIMENT OF UNITED STATES COLORED INFANTRY AND BIOGRAPHICAL SKETCHES. DAYTON: UNITED BRETHREN PUBLISHING HOUSE, 1883.

20779 COWDREY, ALBERT E. "SLAVE INTO SOLDIER: THE ENLISTMENT BY THE NORTH OF RUNAWAY SLAVES." HISTORY TODAY, 20 (OCTOBER, 1970): 704-715.

20780   COWEN, RUTH C.   "CIVIL WAR AND POLITICS IN MISSOURI,
        1863." M.A. THESIS, WASHINGTON UNIVERSITY, 1954.

20781   COX, JOHN H. AND COX, LAWANDA. "GENERAL O.O. HOWARD AND
        THE 'MISREPRESENTED BUREAU.'" JOURNAL OF SOUTHERN
        HISTORY, 19 (NOVEMBER, 1953): 427-456.

20782   COX, LAWANDA. "PROMISE OF LAND FOR THE FREEDMEN."
        MISSISSIPPI VALLEY HISTORICAL REVIEW, 45 (DECEMBER,
        1958): 413-440.

20783   CRAIN, JOHN W. "THE ORIGINS OF THE THIRTEENTH AMENDMENT:
        EMANCIPATION IN THE SENATE AND HOUSE OF
        REPRESENTATIVES, 1863-1865." M.A. THESIS, SOUTHWEST
        TEXAS STATE UNIVERSITY, 1970.

20784   CRESTO, KATHLEEN M. "SHERMAN AND SLAVERY." CIVIL WAR
        TIMES ILLUSTRATED, 17 (NOVEMBER, 1978): 12-21.

20785   CURRIE, JAMES T. "BENJAMIN MONTGOMERY AND THE DAVIS BEND
        COLONY." PROLOGUE, 10 (SPRING, 1978): 5-21.

20786   CURRY, LEONARD P. BLUEPRINT FOR MODERN AMERICA:
        NONMILITARY LEGISLATION OF THE FIRST CIVIL WAR
        CONGRESS. NASHVILLE: VANDERBILT UNIVERSITY PRESS,
        1968.

20787   DAVIS, RONALD L.F. "THE J.S. ARMY AND THE ORIGINS OF
        SHARECROPPING IN THE NATCHEZ DISTRICT--A CASE STUDY."
        JOURNAL OF NEGRO HISTORY, 62 (JANUARY, 1977): 60-80.

20788   DE FOREST, JOHN W. A VOLUNTEER'S ADVENTURES: A UNION
        CAPTAIN'S RECORD OF THE CIVIL WAR. NEW HAVEN: YALE
        UNIVERSITY PRESS, 1946.

20789   D'EHTREMONT, JOHN P. "WHITE OFFICERS AND BLACK TROOPS,
        1863-1865." M.A. THESIS, UNIVERSITY OF VIRGINIA, 1974.

20790   DENNETT, GEORGE M. HISTORY OF THE NINTH U.S.C. TROOPS,
        FROM ITS ORGANIZATION TILL MUSTER OUT, WITH LIST OF
        NAMES OF ALL OFFICERS AND ENLISTED MEN, WHO HAVE EVER
        BELONGED TO THE REGIMENT. PHILADELPHIA: KING AND
        BAIRD, PRINTERS, 1866.

20791   DICKERMAN, GEORGE S. "THE EARLY TEACHING OF SLAVES." IN
        NEGRO EDUCATION: A STUDY OF THE PRIVATE AND HIGHER
        SCHOOLS FOR COLORED PEOPLE IN THE UNITED STATES. 2
        VOLS. WASHINGTON: DEPARTMENT OF THE INTERIOR, BUREAU
        OF EDUCATION BULLETIN, 1916, NO. 38, 1917, VOL. 1, PP.
        245-246.

20792   DOMINICK, CHARLES A. "THE RACIAL VIEWS OF LINCOLN'S
        CABINET." M.A. THESIS, OHIO STATE UNIVERSITY, 1969.

20793   DOUGLAS, WILLIAM O. MR. LINCOLN AND THE NEGROES: THE

LONG ROAD TO EQUALITY. NEW YORK: ATHENEUM, 1963.

20794 DRAKE, RICHARD B. "THE AMERICAN MISSIONARY ASSOCIATION AND THE SOUTHERN NEGRO, 1861-1888." PH.D. DISSERTATION, EMORY UNIVERSITY, 1957.

20795 DUBOIS, W.E.B. BLACK RECONSTRUCTION. NEW YORK: HARCOURT, BRACE AND COMPANY, 1935.

20796 DUNCAN, RICHARD. "THE SOCIAL AND ECONOMIC IMPACT OF THE CIVIL WAR IN MARYLAND." PH.D. DISSERTATION, OHIO STATE UNIVERSITY, 1963.

20797 DUNCAN, RICHARD R. "THE ERA OF THE CIVIL WAR." IN WALSH, RICHARD AND FOX, WILLIAM L. (EDS.). MARYLAND: A HISTORY, 1632-1974. BALTIMORE: MARYLAND HISTORICAL SOCIETY, 1974, PP. 300-395.

20798 DYER, BRAINERD. "THE TREATMENT OF COLORED UNION TROOPS BY THE CONFEDERATES, 1861-1865." JOURNAL OF NEGRO HISTORY, 20 (JULY, 1935): 273-286.

20799 DYER, FREDERICK H. COMPENDIUM OF THE WAR OF THE REBELLION, COMPILED AND ARRANGED FROM OFFICIAL RECORDS OF THE FEDERAL AND CONFEDERATE ARMIES, REPORTS OF THE ADJUTANT GENERALS OF THE SEVERAL STATES, THE ARMY REGISTERS, AND OTHER RELIABLE DOCUMENTS AND SOURCES. DES MOINES: DYER PUBLISHING COMPANY, 1908.

20800 EATON, JOHN. GRANT, LINCOLN AND THE FREEDMEN. NEW YORK: LONGMANS, GREEN & COMPANY, 1907.

20801 EBERSTADT, CHARLES. "LINCOLN'S EMANCIPATION PROCLAMATION." NEW COLOPHON, (1950): 312-356.

20802 EDELSTEIN, TILDEN G. STRANGE ENTHUSIASM: A LIFE OF THOMAS WENTWORTH HIGGINSON. NEW HAVEN: YALE UNIVERSITY PRESS, 1968.

20803 EDMONDS, FLORENCE. "THOMAS ELLIOTT BRAMLETTE." M.A. THESIS, WESTERN KENTUCKY STATE TEACHERS COLLEGE, 1935.

20804 EGGLESTON, G.K. "THE WORK OF RELIEF SOCIETIES DURING THE CIVIL WAR." JOURNAL OF NEGRO HISTORY, 14 (JULY, 1929): 272-299.

20805 EGGLESTON, GEORGE K. "THE NUMBER, CARE, AND DISPOSITION OF THE NEGROES BY THE UNION FORCES DURING THE CIVIL WAR." PH.D. DISSERTATION, UNIVERSITY OF WISCONSIN, 1929.

20806 EGGLESTON, GEORGE K. "THE NUMBER OF THE SLAVES FREED IN THE SOUTH, THEIR DISPOSITION BY THE FEDERAL FORCES DURING THE CIVIL WAR." M.A. THESIS, UNIVERSITY OF WISCONSIN, 1922.

20807   ELLIOTT, CLAUDE. "THE FREEDMEN'S BUREAU IN TEXAS."
        SOUTHWESTERN HISTORICAL QUARTERLY, 56 (JULY, 1952):
        1-24.

20808   ELLIOTT, MARY E. "EFFECTS OF PRESIDENT LINCOLN'S
        PRELIMINARY PROCLAMATION OF EMANCIPATION." M.A.
        THESIS, UNIVERSITY OF NEBRASKA, 1913.

20809   ELMORE, JOYCE A. "BLACK NURSES: THEIR SERVICE AND THEIR
        STRUGGLE." AMERICAN JOURNAL OF NURSING, 76 (MARCH,
        1976): 435-437.

20810   EMILIO, LUIS F. HISTORY OF THE FIFTY-FOURTH REGIMENT OF
        THE MASSACHUSETTS VOLUNTEER INFANTRY, 1863-1865.
        BOSTON: BOSTON BOOK COMPANY, 1891.

20811   ENGLESMAN, JOHN C. "THE FREEDMEN'S BUREAU IN LOUISIANA."
        LOUISIANA HISTORICAL QUARTERLY, 32 (JANUARY, 1949):
        145-224.

20812   ESSERT, VICTOR A. "CONGRESSIONAL LEGISLATION ON SLAVERY
        DURING THE CIVIL WAR." M.A. THESIS, CREIGHTON
        UNIVERSITY, 1958.

20813   EVERETT, DONALD E. "BEN BUTLER AND THE LOUISIANA NATIVE
        GUARDS, 1861-1862." JOURNAL OF SOUTHERN HISTORY, 24
        (MAY, 1958): 202-217.

20814   EVERETT, DONALD E. "DEMANDS OF THE NEW ORLEANS FREE
        COLORED POPULATION FOR POLITICAL EQUALITY, 1862-1865."
        LOUISIANA HISTORICAL QUARTERLY, 38 (APRIL, 1955):
        43-64.

20815   EVERLY, ELAINE C. "THE FREEDMEN'S BUREAU IN THE NATIONAL
        CAPITAL." PH.D. DISSERTATION, GEORGE WASHINGTON
        UNIVERSITY, 1972.

20816   EVERLY, ELAINE C. "MARRIAGE REGISTERS OF FREEDMEN."
        PROLOGUE, 5 (FALL, 1973): 150-154.

20817   FEHRENBACHER, DON E. "ONLY HIS STEPCHILDREN: LINCOLN
        AND THE NEGRO." CIVIL WAR HISTORY, 20 (DECEMBER,
        1974): 293-310.

20818   FEN, SING-NAN. "NOTES ON THE EDUCATION OF NEGROES AT
        NORFOLK AND PORTSMOUTH, VIRGINIA, DURING THE CIVIL
        WAR." PHYLON, 28 (SUMMER, 1967): 197-208.

20819   FEN, SING-NAN. "NOTES ON THE EDUCATION OF NEGROES IN
        NORTH CAROLINA DURING THE CIVIL WAR." JOURNAL OF
        NEGRO EDUCATION, 36 (WINTER, 1967): 24-31.

20820   FIELDS, BARBARA J. "THE MARYLAND WAY FROM SLAVERY TO
        FREEDOM." PH.D. DISSERTATION, YALE UNIVERSITY, 1978.

20821   FIERCE, MILFRED C.   "BLACK STRUGGLE FOR LAND DURING
        RECONSTRUCTION."   BLACK SCHOLAR, 5 (FEBRUARY, 1974):
        13-18.

20822   FISHER, MIKE.   "THE FIRST KANSAS COLORED--MASSACRE AT
        POISON SPRINGS."   KANSAS HISTORY: A JOURNAL OF THE
        CENTRAL PLAINS, 2 (SUMMER, 1979): 121-128.

20823   FITTS, JAMES.   "THE NEGRO IN BLUE."   GALAXY, 3 (FEBRUARY
        1, 1867): 249-255.

20824   FLEETWOOD, CHRISTIAN A.   THE NEGRO AS A SOLDIER.
        WASHINGTON: HOWARD UNIVERSITY PRINT, 1895.

20825   FONER, JACK D.   BLACKS AND THE MILITARY IN AMERICAN
        HISTORY: A NEW PERSPECTIVE. NEW YORK: PRAEGER
        PUBLISHERS, 1974.

20826   FONER, PHILIP S.   "THE FIRST NEGRO MEETING IN MARYLAND."
        MARYLAND HISTORICAL MAGAZINE, 46 (SPRING, 1971):
        60-67.

20827   FOX, C.B.   RECORD OF THE SERVICE OF THE FIFTY-FIFTH
        MASSACHUSETTS VOLUNTEER INFANTRY. CAMBRIDGE:
        REGIMENTAL ASSOCIATION, 1868.

20828   FOX, WILLIAM F.   "THE CHANCES OF BEING HIT IN BATTLE, A
        STUDY OF REGIMENTAL LOSSES IN THE CIVIL WAR."   CENTURY
        MAGAZINE, 14 (MAY, 1888): 93-133.

20829   FRANKLIN, JOHN H. (ED.).   THE DIARY OF JAMES T. AYERS,
        CIVIL WAR RECRUITER. SPRINGFIELD, IL: STATE OF
        ILLINOIS, 1947.

20830   FRANKLIN, JOHN H.   THE EMANCIPATION PROCLAMATION. GARDEN
        CITY: DOUBLEDAY, 1963.

20831   FRANKLIN, JOHN H.   "JAMES T. AYERS: CIVIL WAR
        RECRUITER."   JOURNAL OF THE ILLINOIS STATE HISTORICAL
        SOCIETY, 40 (SEPTEMBER, 1947): 267-297.

20832   FREDRICKSON, GEORGE M.   THE BLACK IMAGE IN THE WHITE
        MIND: THE DEBATE ON AFRO-AMERICAN CHARACTER AND
        DESTINY, 1817-1914. NEW YORK: HARPER & ROW, 1971.

20833   FREDRICKSON, GEORGE M.   THE INNER CIVIL WAR: NORTHERN
        INTELLECTUALS AND THE CRISIS OF THE UNION. NEW YORK:
        HARPER & ROW, 1965.

20834   FREDRICKSON, GEORGE M.   "A MAN BUT NOT A BROTHER:
        ABRAHAM LINCOLN AND RACIAL EQUALITY."   JOURNAL OF
        SOUTHERN HISTORY, 41 (FEBRUARY, 1975): 39-58.

20835   FREEMAN, HENRY V.   "A COLORED BRIGADE IN THE CAMPAIGN AND
        BATTLE OF NASHVILLE."   IN MILITARY ESSAYS AND

RECOLLECTIONS. PAPERS READ BEFORE COMMANDERY OF THE
STATE OF ILLINOIS, MILITARY ORDER OF THE LOYAL LEGION
OF THE UNITED STATES. 2 VOLS. CHICAGO: A.C. MCCLURG
AND COMPANY, 1894, VOL. 2, PP. 399-422.

20836   FRENCH, ROBERT. COL. ROBERT G. SHAW. BOSTON: N.P.,
        1904.

20837   FUKE, RICHARD P. "A REFORM MENTALITY: FEDERAL POLICY
        TOWARD BLACK MARYLANDERS, 1364-1868." CIVIL WAR
        HISTORY, 22 (SEPTEMBER, 1976): 214-235.

20838   FURNESS, WILLIAM E. "THE NEGRO AS A SOLDIER." IN
        MILITARY ESSAYS AND RECOLLECTIONS. PAPERS READ BEFORE
        THE COMMANDERY OF THE STATE OF ILLINOIS, MILITARY
        ORDER OF THE LOYAL LEGION OF THE UNITED STATES. 2
        VOLS. CHICAGO: A.C. MCCLURG AND COMPANY, 1894, VOL.
        2, PP. 457-487.

20839   GALPIN, MARION C. "NATIONAL MEASURES ENACTED FOR THE
        ABOLITION OF SLAVERY 1861 TO 1865." M.A. THESIS,
        UNIVERSITY OF NEBRASKA, 1914.

20840   GANNETT, W.C. "FIVE YEARS OF FREEDMEN'S EDUCATION AS
        SEEN IN THE BUREAU REPORTS." FREEDMEN'S RECORD, 5
        (JANUARY, 1871): 91-95.

20841   GANNETT, W.C. "WHAT THE FREEDMEN'S AID SOCIETY DO FOR
        RECONSTRUCTION." FREEDMEN'S RECORD, 3 (SEPTEMBER,
        1867): 141-144.

20842   GANUS, CLIFTON L., JR. "THE FREEDMEN'S BUREAU IN
        MISSISSIPPI." PH.D. DISSERTATION, TULANE UNIVERSITY,
        1953.

20843   GERTEIS, LOUIS S. "FROM CONTRABAND TO FREEDMAN: FEDERAL
        POLICY TOWARD SOUTHERN BLACKS, 1861-1865." PH.D.
        DISSERTATION, UNIVERSITY OF WISCONSIN, 1969.

20844   GERTEIS, LOUIS S. FROM CONTRABAND TO FREEDMAN: FEDERAL
        POLICY TOWARD SOUTHERN BLACKS, 1861-1865. WESTPORT:
        GREENWOOD PRESS, 1973.

20845   GERTEIS, LOUIS S. "SALMON P. CHASE, RADICALISM, AND THE
        POLITICS OF EMANCIPATION, 1861-1864." JOURNAL OF
        AMERICAN HISTORY, 60 (JUNE, 1973): 42-62.

20846   GIBBS, C.R. "BLACKS IN THE UNION NAVY." NEGRO HISTORY
        BULLETIN, 36 (OCTOBER, 1973): 137-139.

20647   GILES, HENRY L. "THE MILITARY CONTRIBUTION OF THE NEGRO
        TO THE UNITED STATES DURING THE PERIOD OF THE CIVIL
        WAR." M.A. THESIS, OHIO STATE UNIVERSITY, 1937.

20848   GILLIS, KATHERINE A. "THE PERFORMANCE OF THE BLACK UNION

1544

SOLDIER IN MISSISSIPPI." M.A. THESIS, MISSISSIPPI
UNIVERSITY FOR WOMEN, 1978.

20849 GOODMAN, M.H. "THE BLACK TAR: THE BLACK ENLISTED MAN IN
THE UNION NAVY, 1861-1365." PH.D. DISSERTATION,
UNIVERSITY OF NOTTINGHAM, 1976.

20850 GREENE, LARRY A. "THE EMANCIPATION PROCLAMATION IN NEW
JERSEY AND THE PARANOID STYLE." NEW JERSEY HISTORY,
91 (SUMMER, 1973): 108-124.

20851 GREENE, ROBERT E. BLACK DEFENDERS OF AMERICA:
1775-1973: A REFERENCE AND PICTORIAL HISTORY.
CHICAGO: JOHNSON PUBLISHING COMPANY, 1974.

20852 GREGG, JOHN C. LIFE IN THE ARMY, IN THE DEPARTMENTS OF
VIRGINIA, AND THE GULF, INCLUDING OBSERVATIONS IN NEW
ORLEANS. PHILADELPHIA: PERKINPINE & HIGGINS, 1866.

20853 GRIGSBY, MELVIN. THE SMOKED YANK. SIOUX FALLS: DAKOTA
BELL PUBLISHING COMPANY, 1888.

20854 GUNTHER, LENWORTH A. "WHITE MAN'S BURDEN: NORTHERN
BLACK POLITICAL ACTIVITY IN THE RECONSTRUCTION OF
SOUTH CAROLINA, 1862-1872." M.A. THESIS, COLUMBIA
UNIVERSITY, 1971.

20855 GUTHRIE, JAMES M. CAMP-FIRES OF THE AFRO-AMERICAN: OR,
THE COLORED MAN AS A PATRIOT, SOLDIER, SAILOR, AND
HERO IN THE CAUSE OF FREE AMERICA. PHILADELPHIA:
AFRO-AMERICAN PUBLISHING COMPANY, 1899.

20856 HALL, DAN. "BLACK SOLDIERS FROM STATE HAD MAJOR CIVIL
WAR ROLE." GREENWICH (CT) TIMES, DECEMBER 1, 1978.

20857 HALL, E.H. "LETTERS OF DR. SETH ROGERS, 1862, 1863."
MASSACHUSETTS HISTORICAL SOCIETY PROCEEDINGS, 43
(FEBRUARY, 1910): 337-398.

20858 HALLOWELL, N.P. THE NEGRO AS A SOLDIER IN THE WAR OF THE
REBELLION. BOSTON: LITTLE, BROWN & COMPANY, 1897.

20859 HALLOWELL, NORWOOD P. RECORD OF THE FIFTY-FIFTH REGIMENT
OF THE MASSACHUSETTS VOLUNTEER INFANTRY. BOSTON:
N.P., 1868.

20860 HALPERIN, BERNARD S. "ANDREW JOHNSON, THE RADICALS, AND
THE NEGRO, 1865-1866." PH.D. DISSERTATION, FLORIDA
STATE UNIVERSITY, 1966.

20861 HAMBLIN, THOMAS D. "DRIVE THE LAST NAIL: JOHN M. PALMER
AND THE BLACKS IN ILLINOIS AND KENTUCKY." M.A.
THESIS, SOUTHERN ILLINOIS UNIVERSITY, 1976.

20862 HANCHETT, WILLIAM. "YANKEE LAW AND THE NEGRO IN NEVADA,

1861-1869." WESTERN HUMANITIES REVIEW, 10 (SUMMER, 1956): 241-249.

20863 HANCOCK, RICHARD R. HANCOCK'S DIARY. NASHVILLE: BRANDON PRINTING COMPANY, 1887.

20864 HARDING, LEONARD L. "THE CINCINNATI RIOTS OF 1862." BULLETIN OF THE CINCINNATI HISTORICAL SOCIETY, 25 (OCTOBER, 1967): 229-239.

20865 HARDING, LEONARD L. "THE NEGRO IN CINCINNATI, 1860-1870; A DEMOGRAPHIC STUDY OF A TRANSITIONAL DECADE." M.A. THESIS, UNIVERSITY OF CINCINNATI, 1967.

20866 HARRINGTON, FRED H. FIGHTING POLITICIAN: MAJOR GENERAL N.P. BANKS. PHILADELPHIA: UNIVERSITY OF PENNSYLVANIA PRESS, 1948.

20867 HARRINGTON, FRED H. "THE FORT JACKSON MUTINY." JOURNAL OF NEGRO HISTORY, 27 (OCTOBER, 1942): 420-431.

20868 HARRIS, ALFRED G. "THE DISTRICT EMANCIPATION LAW." LINCOLN HERALD, 53 (SPRING, 1951): 11-18, 33.

20869 HARRIS, ALFRED G. "THE ENFORCEMENT OF THE DISTRICT EMANCIPATION ACT." LINCOLN HERALD, 54 (SPRING, 1952): 12-21.

20870 HARRIS, ALFRED G. "SLAVERY AND EMANCIPATION IN THE DISTRICT OF COLUMBIA, 1801-1862." PH.D. DISSERTATION, OHIO STATE UNIVERSITY, 1947.

20871 HARVEY, MRS. GOVERNOR. MY STORY OF WAR: A WOMAN'S NARRATIVE OF LIFE AND WORK IN UNION HOSPITALS. NEW YORK: LONGMAN, GREEN & COMPANY, 1885.

20872 HATCH, CARL E. (ED.). DEAREST SUSIE: A CIVIL WAR INFANTRYMAN'S LETTERS TO HIS SWEETHEART. NEW YORK: EXPOSITION PRESS, 1971.

20873 HAWKINS, HUBERT H. "CIVIL WAR POLITICS IN KENTUCKY, 1861-1863." M.A. THESIS, WESTERN RESERVE UNIVERSITY, 1940.

20874 HAWKS, JOHN M. "THE FIRST FREEDMEN TO BECOME SOLDIERS." SOUTHERN WORKMAN, 38 (FEBRUARY, 1909): 107-109.

20875 HAY, THOMAS R. "NEGRO SOLDIERS." IN ADAMS, JAMES T. (ED.). DICTIONARY OF AMERICAN HISTORY. 5 VOLS. NEW YORK: CHARLES SCRIBNER'S SONS, 1940, VOL. 4, PP. 84-85.

20876 HEAPS, WILLARD A. AND HEAPS, PORTER W. "THE NEGRO AND THE CONTRABAND." IN THE SINGING SIXTIES: THE SPIRIT OF CIVIL WAR DAYS FROM THE MUSIC OF THE TIMES.

NORMAN: UNIVERSITY OF OKLAHOMA PRESS, 1960, PP. 268-294.

20877 HECKMAN, OLIVER S. "NORTHERN CHURCH PENETRATION OF THE SOUTH, 1860-1880." PH.D. DISSERTATION, DUKE UNIVERSITY, 1939.

20878 HELLER, CHARLES E. "THE 54TH MASSACHUSETTS." CIVIL WAR TIMES ILLUSTRATED, 11 (APRIL, 1972): 32-41.

20879 HENDRICKS, GEORGE L. "UNION ARMY OCCUPATION OF THE SOUTHERN SEABOARD, 1861-1865." PH.D. DISSERTATION, COLUMBIA UNIVERSITY, 1954.

20880 HERMANN, JANET S. "THE BLACK COMMUNITY AT DAVIS BEND: THE PURSUIT OF A DREAM." PH.D. DISSERTATION, UNIVERSITY OF CALIFORNIA, 1979.

20881 HESSELTINE, WILLIAM B. LINCOLN'S PLAN OF RECONSTRUCTION. TUSCALOOSA: CONFEDERATE PUBLISHING COMPANY, 1960.

20882 HESSELTINE, WILLIAM B. "THE UNDERGROUND RAILROAD FROM CONFEDERATE PRISONS TO EAST TENNESSEE." EAST TENNESSEE HISTORICAL SOCIETY PUBLICATIONS, 2 (1930): 55-69.

20883 HIGGINSON, THOMAS W. ARMY LIFE IN A BLACK REGIMENT. BOSTON: FIELDS, OSGOOD, 1870.

20884 HIGGINSON, THOMAS W. "COLORED TROOPS UNDER FIRE." CENTURY MAGAZINE, 54 (JUNE, 1897): 194-200.

20885 HIGGINSON, THOMAS W. "DRUMMER BOYS IN A BLACK REGIMENT." YOUTH'S COMPANION, 61 (SEPTEMBER 27, 1888): 465.

20886 HIGGINSON, THOMAS W. "THE FIRST BLACK REGIMENT." OUTLOOK, 59 (JULY 2, 1898): 521-531.

20887 HIGGINSON, THOMAS W. "UP THE ST. JOHN'S." ATLANTIC MONTHLY, 16 (SEPTEMBER, 1865): 312-325.

20888 HIGGINSON, THOMAS W. "UP THE ST. MARY'S." ATLANTIC MONTHLY, 15 (APRIL, 1865): 422-436.

20889 HIGHSMITH, WILLIAM E. "LOUISIANA LANDHOLDING DURING WAR AND RECONSTRUCTION." LOUISIANA HISTORICAL QUARTERLY, 38 (JANUARY, 1955): 39-54.

20890 HILL, JUDITH A.R. "FEDERAL FUGITIVE SLAVE POLICY: APPREHENSION TO EMANCIPATION (THE ROLE OF MILITARY CONDITIONS IN FORCING THE ISSUE OF EMANCIPATION)." M.A. THESIS, CALIFORNIA STATE UNIVERSITY, FULLERTON, 1974.

20891 HOBART, EDWIN L. SEMI-HISTORY OF A BOY-VETERAN OF THE

TWENTY-EIGHTH REGIMENT ILLINOIS INFANTRY VOLUNTEERS,
IN A BLACK REGIMENT. DENVER: THE AUTHOR, 1909.

20892 HOLLAND, RUPERT S. (ED.). LETTERS AND DIARY OF LAURA M.
TOWNE: WRITTEN FROM THE SEA ISLANDS OF SOUTH CAROLINA,
1862-1884. CAMBRIDGE: RIVERSIDE PRESS, 1912.

20893 HOOD, JAMES L. "THE UNION AND SLAVERY: CONGRESSMAN
BRUTUS J. CLAY OF THE BLUEGRASS." REGISTER OF THE
KENTUCKY HISTORICAL SOCIETY, 75 (JULY, 1977): 214-221.

20894 HOOPER, ERNEST W. "MEMPHIS, TENNESSEE: FEDERAL
OCCUPATION AND RECONSTRUCTION, 1862-1870." PH.D.
DISSERTATION, UNIVERSITY OF NORTH CAROLINA, 1957.

20895 HOROWITZ, MURRAY M. "BEN BUTLER AND THE NEGRO:
'MIRACLES ARE OCCURRING.'" LOUISIANA HISTORY, 17
(SPRING, 1976): 159-186.

20896 HORST, SAMUEL L. "EDUCATION FOR MANHOOD: THE EDUCATION
OF BLACKS IN VIRGINIA DURING THE CIVIL WAR." PH.D.
DISSERTATION, UNIVERSITY OF VIRGINIA, 1977.

20897 HOWARD, O.O. "THE FREEDMAN DURING THE WAR." NEW
PRINCETON REVIEW, 1 (1866): 373-385.

20898 HUBBELL, JOHN T. "ABRAHAM LINCOLN AND THE RECRUITMENT OF
BLACK SOLDIERS." PAPERS OF THE ABRAHAM LINCOLN
ASSOCIATION, 2 (1980): 6-21.

20899 HUCH, RONALD K. "FORT PILLOW MASSACRE: THE AFTERMATH OF
PADUCAH." JOURNAL OF THE ILLINOIS STATE HISTORICAL
SOCIETY, 66 (SPRING, 1973): 62-70.

20900 HUGHES, JOHN S. "LAFAYETTE COUNTY AND THE AFTERMATH OF
SLAVERY, 1861-1870." MISSOURI HISTORICAL REVIEW, 75
(OCTOBER, 1980): 51-63.

20901 HUNT, SANFORD B. "THE NEGRO AS A SOLDIER." QUARTERLY
JOURNAL OF PSYCHOLOGICAL MEDICINE AND MEDICAL
JURISPRUDENCE, 1 (OCTOBER, 1867): 161-186.

20902 HUNT, SANFORD B. "THE NEGRO AS A SOLDIER."
ANTHROPOLOGICAL REVIEW, 7 (JANUARY, 1869): 40-54.

20903 HYMAN, HAROLD. "LINCOLN AND EQUAL RIGHTS FOR NEGROES:
THE IRRELEVANCY OF THE 'WADSWORTH LETTER.'" CIVIL WAR
HISTORY, 12 (SEPTEMBER, 1966): 258-292.

20904 HYMAN, HAROLD M. LINCOLN'S RECONSTRUCTION: NEITHER
FAILURE OF VISION NOR VISION OF FAILURE. FORT WAYNE:
LOUIS A. WARREN LINCOLN LIBRARY AND MUSEUM, 1980.

20905 IANNI, JUAN B. "THE DESPOT'S HEEL: FEDERAL MILITARY
POLICY IN MARYLAND DURING THE OPENING MONTHS OF THE

CIVIL WAR, INCLUDING A COMPARISON WITH THE POLICIES
PURSUED IN MISSOURI AND KENTUCKY." M.A. THESIS,
GEORGE MASON UNIVERSITY, 1977.

20906 JACKSON, GEORGE F. "BLACK HEROINE FREEDOM FIGHTERS IN
       THE CIVIL WAR." BLACK WOMEN, MAKERS OF HISTORY: A
       PORTRAIT. SACRAMENTO: FONG & FONG, 1977, PP. 65-76.

20907 JACKSON, LUTHER P. "THE EDUCATIONAL EFFORTS OF THE
       FREEDMEN'S BUREAU AND FREEDMEN'S AID SOCIETIES IN
       SOUTH CAROLINA, 1862-1872." JOURNAL OF NEGRO HISTORY,
       8 (JANUARY, 1923): 1-40.

20908 JACKSON, W. SHERMAN. "THE COLLAPSE OF THE PECULIAR
       INSTITUTION THROUGH MILITARY AND LEGAL ACTION." OHIO
       HISTORY, 83 (SUMMER, 1974): 183-191.

20909 JAFFA, HARRY V. "THE EMANCIPATION PROCLAMATION." IN
       GOLDWIN, ROBERT A. (ED.). 100 YEARS OF EMANCIPATION.
       CHICAGO: PUBLIC AFFAIRS CONFERENCE CENTER, UNIVERSITY
       OF CHICAGO, 1963, PP. 1-24.

20910 JAMES, ALFRED P. "THE BATTLE OF THE CRATER." JOURNAL OF
       THE AMERICAN MILITARY HISTORY FOUNDATION, 2 (SPRING,
       1938): 3-25.

20911 JAMES, FELIX. "THE ATTITUDES TOWARD THE RECRUITMENT OF
       BLACK TROOPS IN OHIO, 1862-1863." JOURNAL OF
       AFRO-AMERICAN ISSUES, 2 (FEBRUARY, 1974): 49-58.

20912 JAMES, FELIX. "THE ESTABLISHMENT OF FREEDMAN'S VILLAGE
       IN ARLINGTON, VIRGINIA." NEGRO HISTORY BULLETIN, 33
       (APRIL, 1970): 90-93.

20913 JOHNSON, LUDWELL. "LINCOLN AND EQUAL RIGHTS: A REPLY."
       CIVIL WAR HISTORY, 13 (MARCH, 1967): 66-73.

20914 JOHNSON, LUDWELL. "LINCOLN AND EQUAL RIGHTS: THE
       AUTHENTICITY OF THE WADSWORTH LETTER." JOURNAL OF
       SOUTHERN HISTORY, 32 (FEBRUARY, 1966): 83-87.

20915 JOHNSTON, ELIZABETH B. CHRISTMAS IN KENTUCKY, 1862.
       WASHINGTON: GIBSON BROTHERS, 1892.

20916 JONES, HOWARD J. "LETTERS IN PROTEST OF RACE PREJUDICE
       IN THE ARMY DURING THE AMERICAN CIVIL WAR." JOURNAL
       OF NEGRO HISTORY, 61 (JANUARY, 1976): 97-98.

20917 JORDAN, JOHN L. "WAS THERE A MASSACRE AT FORT PILLOW?"
       TENNESSEE HISTORICAL QUARTERLY, 6 (JUNE, 1947):
       99-133.

20918 JORDAN, WEYMOUTH T. "THE FREEDMEN'S BUREAU IN
       TENNESSEE." EAST TENNESSEE HISTORICAL SOCIETY
       PUBLICATIONS, NO. 11 (1939): 47-61.

20919 KALIEBE, JOHN E. "THE LETTERS OF THOMAS SCOTT JOHNSON; HIS WORK AMONG THE NEGRO AS CHRISTIAN COMMISSION DELEGATE AND CHAPLAIN, 1864-1866." M.S. THESIS, UNIVERSITY OF WISCONSIN, 1965.

20920 KERBY, ROBERT L. KIRBY SMITH'S CONFEDERACY: THE TRANS-MISSISSIPPI SOUTH, 1863-1865. NEW YORK: COLUMBIA UNIVERSITY PRESS, 1972.

20921 KILMER, GEORGE L. "THE DASH INTO THE CRATER." CENTURY MAGAZINE, 12 (SEPTEMBER, 1887): 774-776.

20922 KNIGHT, WESLEY B. "FORTY ACRES AND A MULE AND A SPELLER." HISTORY OF EDUCATION JOURNAL, 8 (SUMMER, 1957): 113-127.

20923 KNOX, THOMAS W. CAMP-FIRE AND COTTON-FIELD: SOUTHERN ADVENTURE IN TIME OF WAR. LIFE WITH THE UNION ARMIES AND A RESIDENCE ON A LOUISIANA PLANTATION. NEW YORK: BLELOCK, 1865.

20924 KOELLING, HARRY C. "THE CIVIL WAR IN MISSOURI DURING 1861." M.A. THESIS, WASHINGTON UNIVERSITY, 1937.

20925 KIGER, A. BRISCOE. THE MARYLAND NEGRO IN OUR WARS. BALTIMORE: CLARKE, 1942.

20926 KREBS, SYLVIA H. "WILL THE FREEDMEN WORK? WHITE ALABAMIANS ADJUST TO FREE BLACK LABOR." ALABAMA HISTORICAL QUARTERLY, 36 (SUMMER, 1974): 151-163.

20927 KURILEC, ROBERT E. "THE IMPACT OF THE PERFORMANCE OF NEGRO SOLDIERS IN THE UNION ARMY ON WHITE OFFICERS AND GOVERNMENT OFFICIALS, 1862-1865." M.A. THESIS, CATHOLIC UNIVERSITY OF AMERICA, 1967.

20928 LAIDLEY, W.S. HISTORY OF CHARLESTON AND KANAWHA COUNTY, WEST VIRGINIA, AND REPRESENTATIVE CITIZENS. CHICAGO: RICHMOND-ARNOLD PUBLISHING COMPANY, 1911.

20929 LEACOCK, STEPHEN. LINCOLN FREES THE SLAVES. NEW YORK: PUTNAM, 1934.

20930 LEAVENS, F. PATRICK. "L'UNION AND THE NEW ORLEANS TRIBUNE AND LOUISIANA RECONSTRUCTION." M.A. THESIS, LOUISIANA STATE UNIVERSITY, 1966.

20931 LEDOUX, LOUIS H. "THE CIVIL WAR IN MISSOURI IN 1862." M.A. THESIS, WASHINGTON UNIVERSITY, 1949.

20932 LEE, BILL R. "MISSOURI'S FIGHT OVER EMANCIPATION." MISSOURI HISTORICAL REVIEW, 45 (APRIL, 1951): 256-274.

20933 LEFKOWITZ, ABRAHAM. "HISTORY OF THE LEGISLATIVE AND EXECUTIVE ATTEMPTS AT EMANCIPATION FROM MARCH 4, 1861

TO JANUARY 1, 1863." PH.D. DISSERTATION, NEW YORK
UNIVERSITY, 1914.

20934 LEVSTIK, FRANK. "THE TOLEDO RIOT OF 1862: A STUDY OF
MIDWEST NEGROPHOBIA." NORTHWEST OHIO QUARTERLY, 44
(FALL, 1972): 100-106.

20935 LEVSTIK, FRANK R. (ED.). "FROM SLAVERY TO FREEDOM: TWO
WARTIME LETTERS OF ONE OF THE CONFLICT'S FEW BLACK
MEDAL WINNERS." CIVIL WAR TIMES ILLUSTRATED, 11
(NOVEMBER, 1972): 10-15.

20936 LEVSTIK, FRANK R. (ED.). "A JOURNEY AMONG THE
CONTRABANDS: THE DIARY OF WALTER TOTTEN CARPENTER."
INDIANA MAGAZINE OF HISTORY, 73 (SEPTEMBER, 1977):
204-222.

20937 LEVSTIK, FRANK R. "ROBERT A. PINN: COURAGEOUS BLACK
SOLDIER." NEGRO HISTORY BULLETIN, 37
(OCTOBER-NOVEMBER, 1974): 304-305.

20938 LEWIS, VIRGIL A. "COLORED SOLDIERS IN THE UNITED STATES
SERVICE ACCREDITED TO WEST VIRGINIA." THIRD BIENNIAL
REPORT OF THE WEST VIRGINIA DEPARTMENT OF ARCHIVES AND
HISTORY. CHARLESTON: NEWS-MAIL COMPANY, 1911, P. 222.

20939 LITWACK, LEON F. BEEN IN THE STORM SO LONG: THE
AFTERMATH OF SLAVERY. NEW YORK: ALFRED A. KNOPF,
1979.

20940 LITWACK, LEON F. "FREE AT LAST." IN HAREVEN, TAMARA K.
(ED.). ANONYMOUS AMERICANS: EXPLORATIONS IN
NINETEENTH CENTURY SOCIAL HISTORY. ENGLEWOOD CLIFFS:
PRENTICE-HALL, 1971, PP. 131-171.

20941 LOFTON, WILLISTON H. "NORTHERN LABOR AND THE NEGRO
DURING THE CIVIL WAR." JOURNAL OF NEGRO HISTORY, 34
(JULY, 1949): 251-273.

20942 LORD, FRANCIS A. "THE FEDERAL VOLUNTEER SOLDIER IN THE
AMERICAN CIVIL WAR, 1861-1865." PH.D. DISSERTATION,
UNIVERSITY OF MICHIGAN, 1949.

20943 LOVETT, BOBBY L. "BLACKS IN THE BATTLE OF NASHVILLE."
BULLETIN: THE FACULTY JOURNAL OF TENNESSEE STATE
UNIVERSITY, (1975-1976): 39-46.

20944 LOVETT, BOBBY L. "THE NEGRO IN TENNESSEE, 1861-1866: A
SOCIO-MILITARY HISTORY OF THE CIVIL WAR ERA." PH.D.
DISSERTATION, UNIVERSITY OF ARKANSAS, 1978.

20945 LOVETT, BOBBY L. "THE NEGRO'S CIVIL WAR IN TENNESSEE,
1861-1865." JOURNAL OF NEGRO HISTORY, 61 (JANUARY,
1976): 36-50.

20946 LOVETT, BOBBY L. "THE WEST TENNESSEE COLORED TROOPS IN CIVIL WAR COMBAT." PAPERS OF THE WEST TENNESSEE HISTORICAL SOCIETY, 34 (OCTOBER, 1980): 53-70.

20947 LOW, W.A. "THE FREEDMEN'S BUREAU AND CIVIL RIGHTS IN MARYLAND." JOURNAL OF NEGRO HISTORY, 37 (JULY, 1952): 221-276.

20948 LOW, W.A. "THE FREEDMEN'S BUREAU AND CIVIL RIGHTS IN MARYLAND." MARYLAND HISTORICAL MAGAZINE, 47 (MARCH, 1952): 29-39.

20949 LOW, W.A. "THE FREEDMEN'S BUREAU IN THE BORDER STATES." IN CURRY, RICHARD O. (ED.). RADICALISM, RACISM, AND PARTY REALIGNMENT: THE BORDER STATES DURING RECONSTRUCTION. BALTIMORE: JOHNS HOPKINS UNIVERSITY PRESS, 1969, PP. 245-264.

20950 LUCIE, PATRICIA A. "FREEDOM AND FEDERALISM, CONGRESS AND COURTS, 1861-1866." PH.D. DISSERTATION, UNIVERSITY OF GLASGOW, 1972.

20951 LUKE, JOSEPHINE. "FROM SLAVERY TO FREEDOM IN LOUISIANA, 1862-1865." M.A. THESIS, TULANE UNIVERSITY, 1939.

20952 MABE, PHILIP M. "RACIAL IDEOLOGY IN THE NEW ORLEANS PRESS, 1862-1877." PH.D. DISSERTATION, UNIVERSITY OF SOUTHWESTERN LOUISIANA, 1977.

20953 MAGUIRE, EDWARD J. "NORTHERN MERCHANT OPINION AND THE CIVIL WAR." HISTORICAL BULLETIN, 28 (MARCH, 1950): 51-52.

20954 MAIN, ED M. THE STORY OF THE MARCHES, BATTLES, AND INCIDENTS OF THE THIRD UNITED STATES COLORED CAVALRY, A FIGHTING REGIMENT IN THE WAR OF THE REBELLION. LOUISVILLE: GLOBE PRINTING COMPANY, 1908.

20955 MALLORY, WILLIAM. OLD PLANTATION DAYS. N.P., 1902.

20956 MAN, ALBON P., JR. "LABOR COMPETITION AND THE NEW YORK DRAFT RIOTS OF 1863." JOURNAL OF NEGRO HISTORY, 36 (OCTOBER, 1951): 375-405.

20957 MARSZALEK, JOHN F., JR. "THE BLACK MAN IN MILITARY HISTORY." NEGRO HISTORY BULLETIN, 36 (OCTOBER, 1973): 122-125.

20958 MARTIN, JOSEPHINE W. "THE EDUCATIONAL EFFORTS OF THE MAJOR FREEDMEN'S AID SOCIETIES AND THE FREEDMEN'S BUREAU IN SOUTH CAROLINA: 1862-1870." PH.D. DISSERTATION, UNIVERSITY OF SOUTH CAROLINA, 1971.

20959 MASLOWSKI, PETER. TREASON MUST BE MADE ODIOUS: MILITARY OCCUPATION AND WARTIME RECONSTRUCTION IN NASHVILLE,

TENNESSEE, 1862-1865. MILLWOOD, NY: KRAUS-THOMSON
ORGANIZATION, 1978.

20960 MASLOWSKI, PETER. "'TREASON MUST BE MADE ODIOUS':
MILITARY OCCUPATION AND WARTIME RECONSTRUCTION IN
NASHVILLE, TENNESSEE, 1862-1865." PH.D. DISSERTATION,
OHIO STATE UNIVERSITY, 1972.

20961 MASON, ETHEL O. "THE NEGRO AND THE UNION ARMY IN WAR
TIME." SOUTHERN WORKMAN, 34 (OCTOBER, 1905): 546-554.

20962 MASON, JANIE C. "THE CIVIL WAR IN MISSOURI, 1864-1865."
M.A. THESIS, WASHINGTON UNIVERSITY, 1937.

20963 MATSON, DAN. "THE COLORED MAN IN THE CIVIL WAR." WAR
SKETCHES AND INCIDENTS. 2 VOLS. DES MOINES: KENYON
PRESS, 1893, VOL. 1, PP. 235-254.

20964 MAY, J. THOMAS. "CONTINUITY AND CHANGE IN THE LABOR
PROGRAM OF THE UNION ARMY AND THE FREEDMEN'S BUREAU."
CIVIL WAR HISTORY, 17 (SEPTEMBER, 1971): 245-254.

20965 MAY, J. THOMAS. "THE FREEDMEN'S BUREAU AT THE LOCAL
LEVEL: A STUDY OF A LOUISIANA AGENT." LOUISIANA
HISTORY, 9 (WINTER, 1963): 5-19.

20966 MAY, J. THOMAS. "THE LOUISIANA NEGRO IN TRANSITION: AN
APPRAISAL OF THE MEDICAL ACTIVITIES OF THE FREEDMEN'S
BUREAU." BULLETIN OF THE TULANE UNIVERSITY MEDICAL
FACULTY, 26 (FEBRUARY, 1967): 29-36.

20967 MAY, J. THOMAS. "A 19TH CENTURY MEDICAL CARE PROGRAM FOR
BLACKS: THE CASE OF THE FREEDMEN'S BUREAU."
ANTHROPOLOGICAL QUARTERLY, 46 (JULY, 1973): 160-171.

20968 MAY, JUDE T. "THE MEDICAL CARE OF BLACKS IN LOUISIANA
DURING OCCUPATION AND RECONSTRUCTION, 1862-1868: ITS
SOCIAL AND POLITICAL BACKGROUND." PH.D. DISSERTATION,
TULANE UNIVERSITY, 1971.

20969 MCCALL, MARIE E. "GENERAL BENJAMIN F. BUTLER AND THE
NEGRO, 1861-1865." M.A. THESIS, CATHOLIC UNIVERSITY
OF AMERICA, 1966.

20970 MCCONNELL, ROLAND C. "CONCERNING THE PROCUREMENT OF
NEGRO TROOPS IN THE SOUTH DURING THE CIVIL WAR."
JOURNAL OF NEGRO HISTORY, 35 (JULY, 1950): 315-319.

20971 MCCONNELL, ROLAND C. "LOUISIANA'S BLACK MILITARY
HISTORY, 1729-1865." IN MACDONALD, ROBERT R.; KEMP,
JOHN R.; AND HAAS, EDWARD F. (EDS.). LOUISIANA'S
BLACK HERITAGE. NEW ORLEANS: LOUISIANA STATE MUSEUM,
1979, PP. 32-62.

20972 MCCRARY, JAMES P. "MODERATION IN A REVOLUTIONARY WORLD:

LINCOLN AND THE FAILURE OF RECONSTRUCTION IN
LOUISIANA." PH.D. DISSERTATION, PRINCETON UNIVERSITY,
1972.

20973   MCCRARY, PEYTON. ABRAHAM LINCOLN AND RECONSTRUCTION:
THE LOUISIANA EXPERIMENT. PRINCETON: PRINCETON
UNIVERSITY PRESS, 1978.

20974   MCDOWELL, A.W. "HOSPITAL OBSERVATIONS UPON NEGRO
SOLDIERS." AMERICAN PRACTITIONER, 10 (1874): 155-158.

20975   MCFEELY, WILLIAM S. "THE FREEDMEN'S BUREAU: A STUDY IN
BETRAYAL." PH.D. DISSERTATION, YALE UNIVERSITY, 1966.

20976   MCFEELY, WILLIAM S. YANKEE STEPFATHER: GENERAL O.O.
HOWARD AND THE FREEDMEN. NEW HAVEN: YALE UNIVERSITY
PRESS, 1968.

20977   MCKENZIE, ROBERT H. "THE ECONOMIC IMPACT OF FEDERAL
OPERATIONS IN ALABAMA DURING THE CIVIL WAR." ALABAMA
HISTORICAL QUARTERLY, 38 (SPRING, 1976): 51-68.

20978   MCMURRAY, JOHN. RECOLLECTIONS OF A COLORED TROOP. N.P.,
1916.

20979   MCPHERSON, JAMES M. "NEGRO TROOPS IN THE CIVIL WAR." IN
ROLLER, DAVID C. AND TWYMAN, ROBERT W. (EDS.). THE
ENCYCLOPEDIA OF SOUTHERN HISTORY. BATON ROUGE:
LOUISIANA STATE UNIVERSITY PRESS, 1979, PP. 892-893.

20980   MCPHERSON, JAMES M. THE NEGRO'S CIVIL WAR: HOW AMERICAN
NEGROES FELT AND ACTED DURING THE WAR FOR THE UNION.
NEW YORK: PANTHEON BOOKS, 1965.

20981   MELDER, KEITH E. "ANGEL OF MERCY IN WASHINGTON:
JOSEPHINE GRIFFING AND THE FREEDMEN, 1864-1872."
RECORDS OF THE COLUMBIA HISTORICAL SOCIETY OF
WASHINGTON, 33-35 (1963-1965): 243-272.

20982   MERCER, P.M. "TAPPING THE SLAVE NARRATIVE COLLECTION FOR
THE RESPONSE OF BLACK SOUTH CAROLINIANS TO
EMANCIPATION AND RECONSTRUCTION." AUSTRALIAN JOURNAL
OF POLITICS AND HISTORY, 25 (AUGUST, 1979): 358-374.

20983   MESSMER, CHARLES K. "CITY IN CONFLICT: A HISTORY OF
LOUISVILLE, 1860-1865." M.A. THESIS, UNIVERSITY OF
KENTUCKY, 1953.

20984   MESSMER, CHARLES K. "THE END OF AN ERA: LOUISVILLE IN
1865." FILSON CLUB HISTORY QUARTERLY, 54 (JULY,
1980): 239-271.

20985   MESSNER, WILLIAM F. "BLACK EDUCATION IN LOUISIANA,
1863-1865." CIVIL WAR HISTORY, 22 (MARCH, 1976):
41-59.

20986   MESSNER, WILLIAM F. "THE FEDERAL ARMY AND BLACKS IN THE
        GULF DEPARTMENT, 1862-1865." PH.D. DISSERTATION,
        UNIVERSITY OF WISCONSIN, 1972.

20987   MESSNER, WILLIAM F. FREEDMEN AND THE IDEOLOGY OF FREE
        LABOR: LOUISIANA, 1862-1865. LAFAYETTE, LA:
        UNIVERSITY OF SOUTHWESTERN LOUISIANA HISTORY SERIES,
        1978.

20988   MESSNER, WILLIAM F. "THE VICKSBURG CAMPAIGN OF 1862: A
        CASE STUDY IN THE FEDERAL UTILIZATION OF BLACK LABOR."
        LOUISIANA HISTORY, 16 (FALL, 1975): 371-382.

20989   MEYER, HOWARD N. COLONEL OF THE BLACK REGIMENT: THE
        LIFE OF THOMAS WENTWORTH HIGGINSON. NEW YORK: W.W.
        NORTON, 1967.

20990   MICKLEY, JEREMIAH M. THE FORTY-THIRD REGIMENT UNITED
        STATES COLORED TROOPS. GETTYSBURG: J.E. WIBLE, 1866.

20991   MILLER, RANDALL M. "FREEDOM TIME, 1865--AN EX-SLAVE
        WRITES HOME." NEGRO HISTORY BULLETIN, 38 (APRIL-MAY,
        1975): 382-383.

20992   MILLER, RANDALL M. AND ZOPHY, JON. "UNWELCOME ALLIES:
        BILLY YANK AND THE BLACK SOLDIER." PHYLON, 39
        (SEPTEMBER, 1978): 234-240.

20993   MONTGOMERY, HORACE. "A UNION OFFICER'S RECOLLECTIONS OF
        THE NEGRO AS A SOLDIER." PENNSYLVANIA HISTORY, 28
        (APRIL, 1961): 156-186.

20994   MOORE, ROSE H. "SOCIAL AND ECONOMIC CONDITIONS IN
        MISSISSIPPI DURING RECONSTRUCTION." PH.D.
        DISSERTATION, DUKE UNIVERSITY, 1938.

20995   MOORHEAD, JAMES H. AMERICAN APOCALYPSE: YANKEE
        PROTESTANTS AND THE CIVIL WAR, 1860-1869. NEW HAVEN:
        YALE UNIVERSITY PRESS, 1978.

20996   MORGAN, THOMAS J. "REMINISCENCES OF SERVICE WITH COLORED
        TROOPS IN THE ARMY OF THE CUMBERLAND, 1863-1865."
        PERSONAL NARRATIVES. 3 VOLS. PROVIDENCE: SOLDIERS
        AND SAILORS HISTORICAL SOCIETY OF RHODE ISLAND, 1885,
        VOL. 3, PP. 1-52.

20997   MORTON, RICHARD L. (ED.). "'CONTRABANDS' AND QUAKERS IN
        THE VIRGINIA PENINSULA, 1862-1869." VIRGINIA MAGAZINE
        OF HISTORY AND BIOGRAPHY, 61 (OCTOBER, 1953): 419-429.

20998   MORTON, RICHARD L. (ED.). "LIFE IN VIRGINIA, BY A
        'YANKEE TEACHER,' MARGARET NEWBOLD THORPE." VIRGINIA
        MAGAZINE OF HISTORY AND BIOGRAPHY, 64 (APRIL, 1956):
        180-207.

20999 MULLEN, ROBERT W. BLACKS IN AMERICA'S WARS. NEW YORK: MONAD PRESS, 1973.

21000 MURDOCK, EUGENE C. ONE MILLION MEN: THE CIVIL WAR DRAFT IN THE NORTH. MADISON: STATE HISTORICAL SOCIETY OF WISCONSIN, 1971.

21001 MURRAY, ROBERT K. "GENERAL SHERMAN, THE NEGRO, AND SLAVERY: THE STORY OF AN UNRECOGNIZED REBEL." NEGRO HISTORY BULLETIN, 22 (MARCH, 1959): 125-130.

21002 MURRAY, ROBERT K. "SHERMAN: SLAVERY AND THE SOUTH." M.A. THESIS, OHIO STATE UNIVERSITY, 1947.

21003 MYERS, JOHN B. "BLACK HUMAN CAPITAL: THE FREEDMEN AND THE RECONSTRUCTION OF LABOR IN ALABAMA, 1860-1880." PH.D. DISSERTATION, FLORIDA STATE UNIVERSITY, 1974.

21004 MYERS, WILLIAM S. THE MARYLAND CONSTITUTION OF 1864. BALTIMORE: JOHNS HOPKINS PRESS, 1901.

21005 NASH, HOWARD P., JR. "GENERAL BUTLER'S FUGITIVE SLAVE WAR." NEGRO DIGEST, 13 (APRIL, 1964): 19-23.

21006 NEAL, JULIA. BY THEIR FRUITS: THE STORY OF SHAKERISM IN SOUTH UNION, KENTUCKY. CHAPEL HILL: UNIVERSITY OF NORTH CAROLINA PRESS, 1947.

21007 NEELY, MARK E., JR. "LINCOLN AND SLAVERY: AN OVERVIEW." LINCOLN LORE, NO. 1703 (JANUARY, 1980): 1-4.

21008 NELSON, EARL J. "MISSOURI SLAVERY, 1861-1865." MISSOURI HISTORICAL REVIEW, 28 (JULY, 1934): 260-274.

21009 NELSON, LARRY E. "BLACK LEADERS AND THE PRESIDENTIAL ELECTION OF 1864." JOURNAL OF NEGRO HISTORY, 63 (JANUARY, 1978): 42-58.

21010 NEVINS, ALLAN. "SHAPE OF REVOLUTION: CHATTELS NO MORE." THE WAR FOR THE UNION. 4 VOLS. NEW YORK: CHARLES SCRIBNER'S SONS, 1960-1971, VOL. 2, PP. 512-529.

21011 NEVINS, ALLAN. "UNDER THE TRAMPLING ARMIES: THE TRAGIC LOT OF THE FREEDMEN." THE WAR FOR THE UNION. 4 VOLS. NEW YORK: CHARLES SCRIBNER'S SONS, 1960-1971, VOL. 3, PP. 413-444.

21012 NEWTON, ALEXANDER H. OUT OF THE BRIARS: AN AUTOBIOGRAPHY AND SKETCH OF THE TWENTY-NINTH REGIMENT, CONNECTICUT VOLUNTEERS. PHILADELPHIA: A.M.E. BOOK CONCERN, 1910.

21013 NIEMAN, DONALD G. "FREEDMEN'S BUREAU." IN ROLLER, DAVID C. AND TWYMAN, ROBERT W. (EDS.). THE ENCYCLOPEDIA OF SOUTHERN HISTORY. BATON ROUGE: LOUISIANA STATE

1556

UNIVERSITY PRESS, 1979, PP. 489-490.

21014   NIEMAN, DONALD G. "THE FREEDMEN'S BUREAU AND THE
        MISSISSIPPI BLACK CODE." JOURNAL OF MISSISSIPPI
        HISTORY, 40 (MAY, 1978): 91-118.

21015   NIEMAN, DONALD G. TO SET THE LAW IN MOTION: THE
        FREEDMEN'S BUREAU AND THE LEGAL RIGHTS OF BLACKS,
        1865-1868. MILLWOOD, NY: KTO PRESS, 1979.

21016   NIEMAN, DONALD G. "TO SET THE LAW IN MOTION: THE
        FREEDMEN'S BUREAU AND THE LEGAL RIGHTS OF BLACKS,
        1865-1868." PH.D. DISSERTATION, RICE UNIVERSITY, 1975.

21017   NIVEN, JOHN. CONNECTICUT FOR THE UNION: THE ROLE OF THE
        STATE IN THE CIVIL WAR. NEW HAVEN: YALE UNIVERSITY
        PRESS, 1965.

21018   NORTON, HENRY A. "COLORED TROOPS IN THE WAR OF THE
        REBELLION." GLIMPSES OF THE NATION'S STRUGGLE. 5
        VOLS. ST. PAUL: REVIEW PUBLISHING COMPANY, 1903,
        VOL. 5, PP. 59-73.

21019   NOYES, EDWARD. "THE NEGRO IN WISCONSIN'S CIVIL WAR
        EFFORT." LINCOLN HERALD, 69 (SUMMER, 1967): 70-82.

21020   OAKES, JAMES. "A FAILURE OF VISION: THE COLLAPSE OF THE
        FREEDMEN'S BUREAU COURTS." CIVIL WAR HISTORY, 25
        (MARCH, 1979): 66-76.

21021   OATES, STEPHEN B. "'THE MAN OF OUR REDEMPTION': ABRAHAM
        LINCOLN AND THE EMANCIPATION OF THE SLAVES."
        PRESIDENTIAL STUDIES QUARTERLY, 9 (WINTER, 1979):
        15-25.

21022   OUBRE, CLAUDE F. FORTY ACRES AND A MULE: THE FREEDMEN'S
        BUREAU AND BLACK LAND OWNERSHIP. BATON ROUGE:
        LOUISIANA STATE UNIVERSITY PRESS, 1978.

21023   OUBRE, CLAUDE F. "THE FREEDMEN'S BUREAU AND NEGRO LAND
        OWNERSHIP." M.A. THESIS, UNIVERSITY OF SOUTHWESTERN
        LOUISIANA, 1970.

21024   OUBRE, CLAUDE F. "THE FREEDMEN'S BUREAU AND NEGRO LAND
        OWNERSHIP." PH.D. DISSERTATION, UNIVERSITY OF
        SOUTHWESTERN LOUISIANA, 1973.

21025   PALMER, JOHN M. PERSONAL RECOLLECTIONS OF JOHN M.
        PALMER: THE STORY OF AN EARNEST LIFE. CINCINNATI: R.
        CLARKE COMPANY, 1901.

21026   PALUDAN, PHILLIP S. A COVENANT WITH DEATH: THE
        CONSTITUTION, LAW AND EQUALITY IN THE CIVIL WAR ERA.
        URBANA: UNIVERSITY OF ILLINOIS PRESS, 1975.

21027 PALUDAN, PHILLIP S. "LAW AND EQUAL RIGHTS: THE CIVIL
       WAR ENCOUNTER--A STUDY OF LEGAL MURDER IN THE CIVIL
       WAR ERA." PH.D. DISSERTATION, UNIVERSITY OF ILLINOIS,
       1968.

21028 PARISH, PETER J. THE AMERICAN CIVIL WAR. NEW YORK:
       HOLMES & MEIER PUBLISHERS, 1975.

21029 PARKER, E.K. "'THE BRAVEST DEED I EVER KNEW'; THE NEGRO
       BOY AT THE EMBRASURE." CENTURY MAGAZINE, N.S., 48
       (MAY, 1911): 122-124.

21030 PARMELEE, JULIUS H. "FREEDMEN'S AID SOCIETIES,
       1861-1871." IN NEGRO EDUCATION: A STUDY OF THE
       PRIVATE AND HIGHER SCHOOLS FOR COLORED PEOPLE IN THE
       UNITED STATES. 2 VOLS. WASHINGTON: DEPARTMENT OF
       THE INTERIOR, BUREAU OF EDUCATION BULLETIN, 1916, NO.
       38, 1917, VOL. 1, PP. 268-301.

21031 PARMET, ROBERT D. "SCHOOLS FOR THE FREEDMEN." NEGRO
       HISTORY BULLETIN, 34 (OCTOBER, 1971): 128-132.

21032 PARRISH, WILLIAM E. TURBULENT PARTNERSHIP: MISSOURI AND
       THE UNION, 1861-1865. COLUMBIA: UNIVERSITY OF
       MISSOURI PRESS, 1965.

21033 PEARCE, LARRY W. "THE AMERICAN MISSIONARY ASSOCIATION
       AND THE FREEDMEN IN ARKANSAS, 1863-1867." ARKANSAS
       HISTORICAL QUARTERLY, 30 (SUMMER, 1971): 123-144.

21034 PEARSON, ELIZABETH W. (ED.). LETTERS FROM PORT ROYAL
       WRITTEN AT THE TIME OF THE CIVIL WAR. BOSTON: W.B.
       CLARKE COMPANY, 1906.

21035 PEASE, WILLIAM H. "THREE YEARS AMONG THE FREEDMEN:
       WILLIAM C. GANNETT AND THE PORT ROYAL EXPERIMENT."
       JOURNAL OF NEGRO HISTORY, 42 (APRIL, 1957): 98-117.

21036 PEIRCE, PAUL S. "THE FREEDMEN'S BUREAU." BULLETIN OF
       THE STATE UNIVERSITY OF IOWA, N.S., 74 (MARCH, 1904):
       III-200.

21037 PERKINS, FRANCES B. "TWO YEARS WITH A COLORED REGIMENT,
       A WOMAN'S EXPERIENCE." NEW ENGLAND MAGAZINE, N.S., 17
       (JANUARY, 1898): 533-543.

21038 PERMAN, MICHAEL. REUNION WITHOUT COMPROMISE: THE SOUTH
       AND RECONSTRUCTION, 1865-1868. LONDON: CAMBRIDGE
       UNIVERSITY PRESS, 1973.

21039 PETRINE, STEVEN F. "BENJAMIN BUTLER AND THE BUREAU OF
       NEGRO AFFAIRS IN TIDEWATER, VIRGINIA, 1861-1865."
       M.A. THESIS, OLD DOMINION UNIVERSITY, 1975.

21040 PHILLIPS, PAUL D. "A HISTORY OF THE FREEDMEN'S BUREAU IN

TENNESSEE." PH.D. DISSERTATION, VANDERBILT
UNIVERSITY, 1964.

21041 PHILLIPS, PAUL D. "WHITE REACTION TO THE FREEDMEN'S
BUREAU IN TENNESSEE." TENNESSEE HISTORICAL QUARTERLY,
24 (MARCH, 1966): 50-62.

21042 PIROWSKI, GLORIA J. "LINCOLN'S USE OF THE SLAVERY ISSUE
AS A POLITICAL EXPEDIENT." M.A. THESIS, UNIVERSITY OF
ARIZONA, 1948.

21043 PORTER, KENNETH W. "NEGROES ON THE FRONTIER." IN LAMAR,
HOWARD R. (ED.). THE READER'S ENCYCLOPEDIA OF THE
AMERICAN WEST. NEW YORK: THOMAS Y. CROWELL, 1977,
PP. 814-821.

21044 POWELL, LAWRENCE N. "NEW MASTERS: NORTHERN PLANTERS
DURING THE CIVIL WAR AND RECONSTRUCTION." PH.D.
DISSERTATION, YALE UNIVERSITY, 1976.

21045 QUALLS, YOURA T. "FRIEND AND FREEDMEN: THE WORK OF THE
ASSOCIATION OF FRIENDS OF PHILADELPHIA AND ITS
VICINITY FOR THE RELIEF AND EDUCATION OF FREEDMEN
DURING THE CIVIL WAR AND RECONSTRUCTION, 1862-1872."
PH.D. DISSERTATION, HARVARD UNIVERSITY, 1955.

21046 QUARLES, BENJAMIN. LINCOLN AND THE NEGRO. NEW YORK:
OXFORD UNIVERSITY PRESS, 1962.

21047 QUARLES, BENJAMIN. THE NEGRO IN THE CIVIL WAR. BOSTON:
LITTLE, BROWN AND COMPANY, 1953.

21048 RAMPP, LARY C. "NEGRO TROOP ACTIVITY IN INDIAN
TERRITORY, 1863-1865." CHRONICLES OF OKLAHOMA, 47
(SPRING, 1969): 531-559.

21049 RANDALL, JAMES G. CONSTITUTIONAL PROBLEMS UNDER LINCOLN.
NEW YORK: D. APPLETON AND COMPANY, 1926.

21050 RAWICK, GEORGE P. FROM SUNDOWN TO SUNUP: THE MAKING OF
THE BLACK COMMUNITY. WESTPORT: GREENWOOD PRESS, 1972.

21051 RECORD OF THE FIFTY-FIFTH REGIMENT OF MASSACHUSETTS
VOLUNTEER INFANTRY. CAMBRIDGE: N.P., 1868.

21052 REDDICK, L.D. "THE NEGRO POLICY OF THE UNITED STATES
ARMY, 1775-1945." JOURNAL OF NEGRO HISTORY, 34
(JANUARY, 1949): 9-29.

21053 REED, H. CLAY. "LINCOLN'S COMPENSATED EMANCIPATION PLAN
AND ITS RELATION TO DELAWARE." DELAWARE NOTES, 7
(1931): 27-78.

21054 RICE, ELIZABETH G. "A YANKEE TEACHER IN THE SOUTH, AN
EXPERIENCE IN THE EARLY DAYS OF RECONSTRUCTION."

CENTURY MAGAZINE, 62 (MAY, 1901): 151-154.

21055   RICHARDS, CHANNING. "DEALING WITH SLAVERY." IN
        CHAMBERLIN, W.H. (ED.). SKETCHES OF WAR HISTORY,
        1861-1865. PAPERS PREPARED FOR THE OHIO COMMANDERY OF
        THE MILITARY ORDER OF THE LOYAL LEGION OF THE UNITED
        STATES, VOLUME IV. CINCINNATI: ROBERT CLARKE
        COMPANY, 1896, PP. 315-326.

21056   RICHARDSON, JOE M. "THE AMERICAN MISSIONARY ASSOCIATION
        AND BLACK EDUCATION IN CIVIL WAR MISSOURI." MISSOURI
        HISTORICAL REVIEW, 69 (JULY, 1975): 433-448.

21057   RICHARDSON, JOE M. "THE AMERICAN MISSIONARY ASSOCIATION
        AND BLACK EDUCATION IN LOUISIANA, 1862-1878." IN
        MACDONALD, EDWARD F.; KEMP, JOHN R.; AND HAAS, EDWARD
        F. (EDS.). LOUISIANA'S BLACK HERITAGE. NEW ORLEANS:
        LOUISIANA STATE MUSEUM, 1979, PP. 147-162.

21058   RICHARDSON, JOE M. "THE EVOLUTION OF THE FREEDMEN'S
        BUREAU IN FLORIDA." FLORIDA HISTORICAL QUARTERLY, 41
        (JANUARY, 1963): 223-238.

21059   RICHARDSON, JOE M. "'WE ARE TRULY DOING MISSIONARY
        WORK': LETTERS FROM AMERICAN MISSIONARY ASSOCIATION
        TEACHERS IN FLORIDA, 1364-1874." FLORIDA HISTORICAL
        QUARTERLY, 54 (OCTOBER, 1975): 178-195.

21060   RICKARD, JAMES H. "SERVICES WITH COLORED TROOPS IN
        BURNSIDE'S CORPS." PERSONAL NARRATIVES OF EVENTS IN
        THE WAR OF THE REBELLION, BEING PAPERS READ BEFORE THE
        RHODE ISLAND SOLDIERS AND SAILORS HISTORICAL SOCIETY,
        SERIES 5, NO. 1. PROVIDENCE: THE SOCIETY, 1894, PP.
        1-43.

21061   RIPLEY, C. PETER. SLAVES AND FREEDMEN IN CIVIL WAR
        LOUISIANA. BATON ROUGE: LOUISIANA STATE UNIVERSITY
        PRESS, 1976.

21062   RIPLEY, CHARLES P. "BLACK, BLUE AND GRAY: SLAVES AND
        FREEDMEN IN CIVIL WAR LOUISIANA." PH.D. DISSERTATION,
        FLORIDA STATE UNIVERSITY, 1973.

21063   ROBBINS, GERALD. "THE RECRUITING AND ARMING OF NEGROES
        IN THE SOUTH CAROLINA SEA ISLANDS--1862-1865." NEGRO
        HISTORY BULLETIN, 28 (APRIL, 1965): 150-151.

21064   ROBERTSON, JAMES I., JR. "NEGRO SOLDIERS IN THE CIVIL
        WAR." CIVIL WAR TIMES ILLUSTRATED, 7 (OCTOBER, 1968):
        21-33.

21065   ROBINSON, ARMSTEAD L. "DAY OF JUBLIO: CIVIL WAR AND THE
        DEMISE OF SLAVERY IN THE MISSISSIPPI VALLEY,
        1861-1865." PH.D. DISSERTATION, UNIVERSITY OF
        ROCHESTER, 1977.

21066   ROLLIN, FRANK A.   LIFE AND PUBLIC SERVICES OF MARTIN R.
         DELANY, SUB-ASSISTANT COMMISSIONER, BUREAU RELIEF OF
         REFUGEES, FREEDMEN, AND OF ABANDONED LANDS, AND LATE
         MAJOR 104TH U.S. COLORED TROOPS. BOSTON: LEE AND
         SHEPARD, 1868.

21067   ROMEYN, HENRY.   WITH COLORED TROOPS IN THE ARMY OF THE
         CUMBERLAND. WASHINGTON: MILITARY ORDER OF THE LOYAL
         LEGION OF THE UNITED STATES, COMMANDERY OF THE
         DISTRICT OF COLUMBIA WAR PAPERS, 1904.

21068   ROSE, WILLIE LEE.   "'ICONOCLASM HAS HAD ITS DAY':
         ABOLITIONISTS AND FREEDMEN IN SOUTH CAROLINA."   IN
         DUBERMAN, MARTIN (ED.).   THE ANTISLAVERY VANGUARD:
         NEW ESSAYS ON THE ABOLITIONISTS. PRINCETON:
         PRINCETON UNIVERSITY PRESS, 1965, PP. 178-205.

21069   ROSE, WILLIE LEE.   "JUBILEE & BEYOND: WHAT WAS FREEDOM?"
         IN SANSING, DAVID G. (ED.).   WHAT WAS FREEDOM'S PRICE?
         JACKSON: UNIVERSITY PRESS OF MISSISSIPPI, 1978, PP.
         3-20.

21070   ROSE, WILLIE LEE.   "MASTERS WITHOUT SLAVES."   PAPER
         PRESENTED AT MEETING OF AMERICAN HISTORICAL
         ASSOCIATION, NEW YORK, DECEMBER, 1966.

21071   ROSE, WILLIE LEE.   REHEARSAL FOR RECONSTRUCTION: THE
         PORT ROYAL EXPERIMENT. INDIANAPOLIS: BOBBS-MERRILL,
         1964.

21072   ROSE, WILLIE LEE.   "REHEARSAL FOR RECONSTRUCTION: THE
         PORT ROYAL EXPERIMENT." PH.D. DISSERTATION, JOHNS
         HOPKINS UNIVERSITY, 1962.

21073   ROSEBOOM, EUGENE H.   THE CIVIL WAR ERA, 1850-1873.
         COLUMBUS: OHIO STATE ARCHAEOLOGICAL AND HISTORICAL
         SOCIETY, 1944.

21074   ROSS, STEVEN J.   "FREED SOIL, FREED LABOR, FREED MEN:
         JOHN EATON AND THE DAVIS BEND EXPERIMENT."   JOURNAL OF
         SOUTHERN HISTORY, 44 (MAY, 1978):   213-232.

21075   ROY, JOSEPH E.   "OUR INDEBTEDNESS TO THE NEGROES FOR
         THEIR CONDUCT DURING THE WAR."   NEW ENGLANDER, 51
         (NOVEMBER, 1889):   353-364.

21076   SEARS, CYRUS.   PAPERS OF CYRUS SEARS, LATE LIEUT. COL. OF
         THE 49TH U.S. COLORED INFANTRY VOLS. OF AFRICAN
         DESCENT--ORIGINALLY 11TH LOUISIANA VOL. INFANTRY--A.D.
         OF HARPSTER, OHIO. COLUMBUS: THE F.J. HEER PRINTING
         COMPANY, 1909.

21077   SERAILE, WILLIAM.   "NEW YORK'S BLACK REGIMENTS DURING THE
         CIVIL WAR." PH.D. DISSERTATION, CITY UNIVERSITY OF
         NEW YORK, 1977.

21078   SERAILE, WILLIAM. "THE STRUGGLE TO RAISE BLACK REGIMENTS
        IN NEW YORK STATE, 1861-1864." NEW YORK HISTORICAL
        SOCIETY QUARTERLY, 58 (JULY, 1974): 215-233.

21079   SHANNON, FRED A. "THE FEDERAL GOVERNMENT AND THE NEGRO
        SOLDIER, 1861-1865." JOURNAL OF NEGRO HISTORY, 11
        (OCTOBER, 1926): 563-583.

21080   SHANNON, FRED A. THE ORGANIZATION AND ADMINISTRATION OF
        THE UNION ARMY, 1861-1865. 2 VOLS. CLEVELAND:
        ARTHUR H. CLARK COMPANY, 1928.

21081   SHANNON, FRED A. "ORGANIZATION AND ADMINISTRATION OF THE
        UNION ARMY, 1861-1865." PH.D. DISSERTATION,
        UNIVERSITY OF IOWA, 1924.

21082   SHERMAN, GEORGE R. THE NEGRO AS A SOLDIER. PROVIDENCE:
        SOLDIERS AND SAILORS HISTORICAL SOCIETY OF RHODE
        ISLAND, 7TH SER., NO. 7, 1913.

21083   SIMON, JOHN Y. AND JAMES, FELIX. "ANDREW JOHNSON AND THE
        FREEDMEN." LINCOLN HERALD, 79 (SUMMER, 1977): 71-75.

21084   SING-NAN, FEN. "NOTES ON THE EDUCATION OF NEGROES AT
        NORFOLK AND PORTSMOUTH, VIRGINIA DURING THE CIVIL
        WAR." PHYLON, 28 (SUMMER, 1967): 197-207.

21085   SLAUGHTER, LINDA W. THE FREEDMEN OF THE SOUTH.
        CINCINNATI: ELM STREET PRINTING COMPANY, 1869.

21086   SMALL, SANDRA E. "THE YANKEE SCHOOLMARM IN FREEDMEN'S
        SCHOOLS: AN ANALYSIS OF ATTITUDES." JOURNAL OF
        SOUTHERN HISTORY, 45 (AUGUST, 1979): 381-402.

21087   SMALL, SANDRA E. "THE YANKEE SCHOOLMARM IN SOUTHERN
        FREEDMEN'S SCHOOLS, 1861-1971: THE CAREER OF A
        STEREOTYPE." PH.D. DISSERTATION, WASHINGTON STATE
        UNIVERSITY, 1976.

21088   SMEDLEY, KATHERINE. "THE NORTHERN TEACHER ON THE SOUTH
        CAROLINA SEA ISLANDS." M.A. THESIS, UNIVERSITY OF
        NORTH CAROLINA, 1932.

21089   SMITH, GEORGE W. AND JUDAH, CHARLES. "THE NEGRO'S
        PLACE." LIFE IN THE NORTH DURING THE CIVIL WAR: A
        SOURCE HISTORY. ALBUQUERQUE: UNIVERSITY OF NEW
        MEXICO PRESS, 1966, PP. 129-162.

21090   SMITH, JOHN DAVID. "THE RECRUITMENT OF NEGRO SOLDIERS IN
        KENTUCKY, 1863-1865." REGISTER OF THE KENTUCKY
        HISTORICAL SOCIETY, 72 (OCTOBER, 1974): 364-390.

21091   SMITH, JOHN DAVID AND COOPER, WILLIAM JR. (EDS.). WINDOW
        ON THE WAR: FRANCES DALLAM PETER'S LEXINGTON CIVIL
        WAR DIARY. LEXINGTON: LEXINGTON-FAYETTE COUNTY

HISTORIC COMMISSION, 1976.

21092 SMITH, LESLIE S. AROUND MUHLENBERG COUNTY, KENTUCKY: A
BLACK HISTORY. EVANSVILLE: UNIGRAPHIC, INC., 1979.

21093 SMITH, PHILIP R., JR. "THE NEGRO'S ARMY HERITAGE." ARMY
DIGEST, 23 (JULY, 1968): 13-21.

21094 SMITH, THOMAS H. "OHIO QUAKERS AND MISSISSIPPI
FREEDMEN--A FIELD OF LABOR." OHIO HISTORY, 78
(SUMMER, 1969): 159-171.

21095 SOMMERS, RICHARD J. "THE DUTCH GAP AFFAIR: MILITARY
ATROCITIES AND THE RIGHTS OF NEGRO SOLDIERS." CIVIL
WAR HISTORY, 21 (MARCH, 1975): 51-64.

21096 SPENCER, JAYME R. "ABRAHAM LINCOLN AND THE NEGRO
COLONIZATION: THE ILE A VACHE, HAYTI EXPERIENCE,
1862-1864." M.A. THESIS, COLLEGE OF WILLIAM AND MARY,
1971.

21097 SPROAT, JOHN G. "BLUEPRINT FOR RADICAL RECONSTRUCTION."
JOURNAL OF SOUTHERN HISTORY, 23 (FEBRUARY, 1957):
25-44.

21098 STANLEY, A. KNIGHTON. THE CHILDREN IS CRYING:
CONGREGATIONALISM AMONG BLACK PEOPLE. NEW YORK:
PILGRIM PRESS, 1979.

21099 STAPLES, THOMAS S. RECONSTRUCTION IN ARKANSAS,
1862-1874. NEW YORK: COLUMBIA UNIVERSITY PRESS, 1923.

21100 STEINER, PAUL E. MEDICAL HISTORY OF A CIVIL WAR
REGIMENT: DISEASE IN THE SIXTY-FIFTH UNITED STATES
COLORED INFANTRY. CLAYTON, MO: INSTITUTE OF CIVIL
WAR STUDIES, 1977.

21101 STEWARD, THEOPHILUS G. THE COLORED REGULARS IN THE
UNITED STATES ARMY. PHILADELPHIA: A.M.E. BOOK
CONCERN, 1904.

21102 STONE, HENRY. "HOOD'S INVASION ON TENNESSEE." CENTURY
MAGAZINE, 12 (AUGUST, 1887): 597-616.

21103 SWINT, HENRY L. (ED.). DEAR ONES AT HOME: LETTERS FROM
CONTRABAND CAMPS. NASHVILLE: VANDERBILT UNIVERSITY
PRESS, 1966.

21104 SWINT, HENRY L. THE NORTHERN TEACHER IN THE SOUTH,
1862-1870. NASHVILLE: VANDERBILT UNIVERSITY PRESS,
1941.

21105 SWINT, HENRY L. "THE NORTHERN TEACHER IN THE SOUTH,
1862-1870." PH.D. DISSERTATION, VANDERBILT
UNIVERSITY, 1939.

21106   SYNNESTVEDT, SIG (ED.). "'THE EARTH SHOOK AND
        QUIVERED.'" CIVIL WAR TIMES ILLUSTRATED, 11
        (DECEMBER, 1972): 30-37.

21107   TALBOTT, FORREST. "SOME LEGISLATIVE AND LEGAL ASPECTS OF
        THE NEGRO QUESTION IN WEST VIRGINIA DURING THE CIVIL
        WAR AND RECONSTRUCTION." M.A. THESIS, UNIVERSITY OF
        MINNESOTA, 1942.

21108   TALBOTT, FORREST. "SOME LEGISLATIVE AND LEGAL ASPECTS OF
        THE NEGRO QUESTION IN WEST VIRGINIA DURING THE CIVIL
        WAR AND RECONSTRUCTION." WEST VIRGINIA HISTORY, 24
        (OCTOBER, 1962, JANUARY, APRIL, 1963): 1-31, 110-133,
        211-247.

21109   TAPP, HAMBLETON AND KLOTTER, JAMES C. (EDS.). THE UNION,
        THE CIVIL WAR, AND JOHN W. TUTTLE. FRANKFORT:
        KENTUCKY HISTORICAL SOCIETY, 1980.

21110   TAYLOR, JOSEPH H. THE AMERICAN NEGRO SOLDIER IN THE
        CIVIL WAR: A PICTORIAL DOCUMENTARY. DURHAM: J.S.C. &
        A. PUBLISHERS, 1960.

21111   TAYLOR, S.R. REMINISCENCES OF MY LIFE IN CAMP WITH THE
        33RD U.S. COLORED TROOPS, LATE 1ST SOUTH CAROLINA
        VOLUNTEERS. BOSTON: THE AUTHOR, 1902.

21112   TAYLOR, SUSIE K. REMINISCENCES OF MY LIFE IN CAMP WITH
        THE 33RD UNITED STATES COLORED TROOPS LATE 1ST S.C.
        VOLUNTEERS. BOSTON: THE AUTHOR, 1902.

21113   TEAMOH, R.T. SKETCH OF THE LIFE AND DEATH OF COL. ROBERT
        GOULD SHAW. BOSTON: THE AUTHOR, 1904.

21114   TENNESSEANS IN THE CIVIL WAR: A MILITARY HISTORY OF
        CONFEDERATE AND UNION UNITS WITH AVAILABLE ROSTERS OF
        PERSONNEL. 2 VOLS. NASHVILLE: CIVIL WAR CENTENNIAL
        COMMISSION OF TENNESSEE, 1964.

21115   TERRELL, W.H.H. INDIANA IN THE WAR OF THE REBELLION:
        REPORT OF THE ADJUTANT GENERAL. INDIANAPOLIS:
        INDIANA HISTORICAL SOCIETY, 1960.

21116   THOMAS, BENJAMIN P. AND HYMAN, HAROLD M. STANTON: THE
        LIFE AND TIMES OF LINCOLN'S SECRETARY OF WAR. NEW
        YORK: ALFRED A. KNOPF, 1962.

21117   THOMAS, HENRY G. "THE COLORED TROOPS AT PETERSBURG."
        CENTURY MAGAZINE, N.S., 12 (SEPTEMBER, 1887): 777-782.

21118   THORNBROUGH, EMMA L. INDIANA IN THE CIVIL WAR ERA,
        1850-1880. INDIANAPOLIS: INDIANA HISTORICAL BUREAU
        AND INDIANA HISTORICAL SOCIETY, 1965.

21119   TOWNE, LAURA M. LETTERS AND DIARY OF LAURA M. TOWNE

WRITTEN FROM THE SEA ISLANDS OF SOUTH CAROLINA,
1862-1884. CAMBRIDGE: PRIVATELY PRINTED, 1912.

21120 TREDWAY, G.R. DEMOCRATIC OPPOSITION TO THE LINCOLN
       ADMINISTRATION IN INDIANA. INDIANAPOLIS: INDIANA
       HISTORICAL BUREAU, 1973.

21121 TREFOUSSE, HANS L. LINCOLN'S DECISION FOR EMANCIPATION.
       PHILADELPHIA: J.B. LIPPINCOTT, 1975.

21122 TREFOUSSE, HANS L. THE RADICAL REPUBLICANS: LINCOLN'S
       VANGUARD FOR RACIAL JUSTICE. NEW YORK: ALFRED A.
       KNOPF, 1969.

21123 TROWBRIDGE, CHARLES T. "SIX MONTHS IN THE FREEDMEN'S
       BUREAU WITH A COLORED REGIMENT." GLIMPSES OF THE
       NATION'S STRUGGLE, VOL. 6. MINNEAPOLIS: AUGUST DAVIS
       PUBLISHER, 1909, PP. 198-222.

21124 TUNNELL, TED. "FREE NEGROES AND THE FREEDMEN: BLACK
       POLITICS IN NEW ORLEANS DURING THE CIVIL WAR."
       SOUTHERN STUDIES, 19 (SPRING, 1980): 5-28.

21125 TWINING, ALEXANDER C. "PRESIDENT LINCOLN'S PROCLAMATION
       OF FREEDOM TO THE SLAVES." NEW ENGLANDER, 24
       (JANUARY, 1865): 178-186.

21126 ULLMAN, DANIEL. ADDRESS BY DANIEL ULLMAN, LL.D., BEFORE
       THE SOLDIER'S AND SAILOR'S UNION OF THE STATE OF NEW
       YORK, ON THE ORGANIZATION OF COLORED TROOPS AND THE
       REGENERATION OF THE SOUTH, FEBRUARY 5, 1867.
       WASHINGTON: GREAT REPUBLIC OFFICE, 1868.

21127 VALUSKA, DAVID L. "THE NEGRO IN THE UNION NAVY:
       1861-1865." PH.D. DISSERTATION, LEHIGH UNIVERSITY,
       1973.

21128 VAN ALSTYNE, LAWRENCE. DIARY OF AN ENLISTED MAN. NEW
       HAVEN: TUTTLE, MOREHOUSE & TAYLOR, 1910.

21129 VAN GUNDY, MORRIS S. "ABRAHAM LINCOLN'S ADVOCACY OF
       GRADUAL, COMPENSATED EMANCIPATION." M.A. THESIS,
       SOUTHERN METHODIST UNIVERSITY, 1932.

21130 VINCENT, CHARLES. "BLACK LOUISIANANS DURING THE CIVIL
       WAR AND RECONSTRUCTION: ASPECTS OF THEIR STRUGGLES
       AND ACHIEVEMENTS." IN MACDONALD, ROBERT R.; KEMP,
       JOHN R.; AND HAAS, EDWARD F. (EDS.). LOUISIANA'S
       BLACK HERITAGE. NEW ORLEANS: LOUISIANA STATE MUSEUM,
       1979, PP. 85-106.

21131 WAGANDT, CHARLES L. "THE ARMY VERSUS MARYLAND SLAVERY,
       1862-1864." CIVIL WAR HISTORY, 10 (JUNE, 1964):
       141-148.

21132   WAGANDT, CHARLES L. "ELECTION BY SWORD AND BALLOT: THE
        EMANCIPATIONIST VICTORY OF 1863." MARYLAND HISTORICAL
        MAGAZINE, 59 (JUNE, 1964): 143-164.

21133   WAGANDT, CHARLES L. THE MIGHTY REVOLUTION: NEGRO
        EMANCIPATION IN MARYLAND, 1862-1864. BALTIMORE:
        JOHNS HOPKINS UNIVERSITY PRESS, 1964.

21134   WAGANDT, CHARLES L. "REDEMPTION OR REACTION?--MARYLAND
        IN THE POST-CIVIL WAR YEARS." IN CURRY, RICHARD O.
        (ED.). RADICALISM, RACISM, AND PARTY REALIGNMENT:
        THE BORDER STATES DURING RECONSTRUCTION. BALTIMORE:
        JOHNS HOPKINS UNIVERSITY PRESS, 1969, PP. 146-187.

21135   WALKER, CAM. "CORINTH: THE STORY OF A CONTRABAND CAMP."
        CIVIL WAR HISTORY, 20 (MARCH, 1974): 5-22.

21136   WARREN, FRANCIS H. MICHIGAN MANUAL OF FREEDMEN'S
        PROGRESS. DETROIT: N.P., 1915.

21137   WEBSTER, LAURA J. THE OPERATION OF THE FREEDMEN'S BUREAU
        IN SOUTH CAROLINA. NORTHAMPTON, MA: SMITH COLLEGE,
        1916.

21138   WEIXLMANN, JOE. "POLITICS, PIRACY AND OTHER GAMES:
        SLAVERY AND LIBERATION IN FLIGHT TO CANADA." MELUS, 6
        (FALL, 1979): 41-50.

21139   WELCH, ELOISE T. "THE BACKGROUND AND DEVELOPMENT OF THE
        AMERICAN MISSIONARY ASSOCIATION'S DECISION TO EDUCATE
        FREEDMEN IN THE SOUTH, WITH SUBSEQUENT REPERCUSSIONS
        FOR HIGHER EDUCATION." PH.D. DISSERTATION, BRYN MAWR
        COLLEGE, 1976.

21140   WELLS, ANNA M. DEAR PRECEPTOR: THE LIFE AND TIMES OF
        THOMAS WENTWORTH HIGGINSON. BOSTON: HOUGHTON MIFFLIN
        COMPANY, 1963.

21141   WENZEL, CAROL N. "FREEDMEN'S FARM LETTERS OF SAMUEL AND
        LOUISA MALLORY TO 'OUR ABSENT BUT EVER REMEMBERED BOY'
        IN MCHENRY COUNTY, ILLINOIS." JOURNAL OF THE ILLINOIS
        STATE HISTORICAL SOCIETY, 73 (AUTUMN, 1980): 162-176.

21142   WESLEY, CHARLES H. OHIO NEGROES IN THE CIVIL WAR.
        COLUMBUS: OHIO STATE UNIVERSITY PRESS, 1962.

21143   WESTIN, RICHARD B. "THE STATE AND SEGREGATED SCHOOLS:
        NEGRO PUBLIC EDUCATION IN NORTH CAROLINA, 1863-1923."
        PH.D. DISSERTATION, DUKE UNIVERSITY, 1966.

21144   WHARTON, VERNON L. "SLAVERY AND THE NEGRO IN 1865." THE
        NEGRO IN MISSISSIPPI, 1865-1890. CHAPEL HILL:
        UNIVERSITY OF NORTH CAROLINA PRESS, 1947, PP. 9-22.

21145   WHITE, HOWARD A. THE FREEDMEN'S BUREAU IN LOUISIANA.

BATON ROUGE: LOUISIANA STATE UNIVERSITY PRESS, 1970.

21146 WHITE, HOWARD A. "THE FREEDMEN'S BUREAU IN LOUISIANA."
PH.D. DISSERTATION, TULANE UNIVERSITY, 1956.

21147 WHITE, HOWARD A. "THE FREEDMEN'S BUREAU IN NEW ORLEANS."
M.A. THESIS, TULANE UNIVERSITY, 1950.

21148 WHYTE, JAMES H. "MARYLAND'S NEGRO REGIMENTS." CIVIL WAR
TIMES ILLUSTRATED, 1 (JULY, 1962): 41-45.

21149 WILDER, BURT G. THE FIFTY-FIFTH MASSACHUSETTS VOLUNTEER
INFANTRY, COLORED, JUNE, 1863-SEPTEMBER, 1865.
BROOKLINE, MA: BROOKLINE HISTORICAL SOCIETY, 1914.

21150 WILEY, BELL I. "BILLY YANK AND THE BLACK FOLK." JOURNAL
OF NEGRO HISTORY, 36 (JANUARY, 1951): 35-52.

21151 WILEY, BELL I. KINGDOM COMING: THE EMANCIPATION
PROCLAMATION OF SEPTEMBER 22, 1862. CHICAGO: CHICAGO
HISTORICAL SOCIETY, 1963.

21152 WILEY, BELL I. THE LIFE OF BILLY YANK: THE COMMON
SOLDIER OF THE UNION. INDIANAPOLIS: BOBBS-MERRILL,
1952.

21153 WILEY, BELL I. SOUTHERN NEGROES, 1861-1865. NEW HAVEN:
YALE UNIVERSITY PRESS, 1938.

21154 WILEY, BELL I. "VICISSITUDES OF EARLY RECONSTRUCTION
FARMING IN THE LOWER MISSISSIPPI VALLEY." JOURNAL OF
SOUTHERN HISTORY, 3 (NOVEMBER, 1937): 441-452.

21155 WILLIAMS, GEORGE W. HISTORY OF THE NEGRO TROOPS IN THE
WAR OF THE REBELLION, 1861-1865. NEW YORK: HARPER
AND BROTHERS, 1888.

21156 WILLIAMS, HESSIE S. "A COMPARATIVE ANALYSIS OF EX-SLAVE
THOUGHTS CONCERNING THEIR MASTERS, THE UNITED STATES
ARMY, AND FREEDOM." M.A. THESIS, UNIVERSITY OF NORTH
CAROLINA, 1969.

21157 WILLIAMS, R.K. DISSENTING OPINION OF JUDGE R.K.
WILLIAMS, OF THE APPELLATE COURT OF KENTUCKY.
FRANKFORT: OSBORNE AND COMPANY, 1865.

21158 WILLIAMS, T. HARRY. LINCOLN AND THE RADICALS. MADISON:
UNIVERSITY OF WISCONSIN PRESS, 1960.

21159 WILSON, JOSEPH T. THE BLACK PHALANX: A SHORT HISTORY OF
THE NEGRO SOLDIERS OF THE UNITED STATES. HARTFORD:
AMERICAN PUBLISHING COMPANY, 1887.

21160 WOOD, FORREST G. BLACK SCARE: THE RACIST RESPONSE TO
EMANCIPATION AND RECONSTRUCTION. BERKELEY:

UNIVERSITY OF CALIFORNIA PRESS, 1968.

21161   WOOD, FORREST G.   "RACE DEMAGOGUERY DURING THE CIVIL WAR
        AND RECONSTRUCTION."   PH.D. DISSERTATION, UNIVERSITY
        OF CALIFORNIA, 1965.

3893, 3909, 4592, 4652, 4658,
4664, 4665, 4666, 4669, 4670,
4671, 4674, 4677, 4678, 4680,
4686, 4687, 4688, 4693, 4700,
4701, 4702, 4707, 4712, 4714,
4716, 4717, 4719, 4720, 4723,
4728, 4729, 4730, 4731, 4732,
4737, 4740, 4741, 4745, 4747,
4748, 4750, 4751, 4755, 4756,
4757, 4761, 4762, 4767, 4768,
4773, 4774, 4775, 4776, 4777,
4779, 4780, 4781, 4782, 4789,
4792, 4797, 4799, 4801, 4802,
4804, 4805, 4808, 4809, 4811,
4815, 4816, 4817, 4818, 4824,
4825, 4827, 4829, 4832, 4834,
4840, 4841, 4842, 4843, 4845,
4846, 4848, 4849, 4851, 4853,
4855, 4856, 4858, 4859, 4860,
4861, 4862, 4863, 4864, 4865,
4866, 4867, 4868, 4871, 4872,
4873, 4877, 4878, 4879, 4881,
4882, 4884, 4885, 4886, 4887,
4891, 4893, 4894, 4898, 4900,
4902, 4904, 4909, 4910, 4911,
4912, 4913, 4914, 4915, 4916,
4917, 4922, 4924, 4927, 4928,
4929, 4931, 4932, 4933, 4935,
4937, 4938, 4940, 4941, 4942,
4943, 4944, 4945, 4946, 4947,
4948, 4958, 4963, 4966, 4967,
4968, 4969, 4970, 4971, 4972,
4973, 4974, 4976, 4977, 4978,
4980, 4981, 4982, 4985, 4987,
4988, 4989, 4991, 4993, 4995,
4996, 4997, 4999, 5000, 5001,
5003, 5004, 5006, 5008, 5009,
5010, 5011, 5013, 5014, 5015,
5016, 5017, 5018, 5019, 5020,
5021, 5022, 5023, 5024, 5025,
5026, 5027, 5028, 5029, 5030,
5031, 5033, 5034, 5035, 5039,
5040, 5041, 5042, 5043, 5045,
5047, 5049, 5050, 5053, 5054,
5055, 5056, 5057, 5058, 5059,
5061, 5062, 5064, 5065, 5066,
5067, 5069, 5070, 5072, 5073,
5075, 5076, 5077, 5078, 5080,
5082, 5085, 5086, 5087, 5088,
5089, 5090, 5091, 5092, 5093,
5094, 5095, 5096, 5099, 5100,
5101, 5102, 5103, 5104, 5105,
5106, 5107, 5108, 5109, 5110,
5113, 5114, 5116, 5118, 5119,
5120, 5121, 5122, 5125, 5126,

5127, 5128, 5130, 5131, 5132,
5133, 5134, 5136, 5137, 5138,
5140, 5141, 5142, 5143, 5144,
5145, 5146, 5147, 5148, 5149,
5151, 5338, 5435, 5462, 5507,
5841, 6053, 6060, 6220, 6856,
6922, 6989, 7034, 7107, 7127,
7138, 7200, 7201, 7237, 7238,
7239, 7241, 7321, 7452, 7552,
7634, 7641, 7886, 7938, 7964,
7987, 8011, 8018, 8128, 8134,
8135, 8138, 8168, 8421, 13128,
13136, 13971, 15542, 15559,
15586, 15809, 15839, 15849,
16105, 16162, 16243, 16249,
17019, 17147, 17309, 17314,
17315, 17321, 17444, 17479,
17519, 17600, 17631, 17768,
17815, 17831, 17849, 17855,
17869, 17955, 17960, 17961,
17964, 17972, 17979, 18005,
18324, 18375, 18384, 18401,
18464, 18474, 18478, 18581,
19017, 19287, 19302, 19303,
19337, 19426, 19435, 19436,
19437, 19439, 19443, 19488,
20292

AFRICAN IMPORTATION CASE, 1820
  5938

AFRICAN METHODIST EPISCOPAL CHURCH
  17216, 17313

AFRICAN MUSIC   13971

AFRICAN RELIGION   4709, 4955, 4969,
  4970, 5019

AFRICAN SQUADRON, UNITED STATES
  5237, 5358, 5814

AFRICANISMS   86, 379, 405, 862,
  947, 1670, 1679, 1685, 1970,
  2548, 2647, 3441, 3473, 3523,
  4592, 4664, 4682, 4696, 4704,
  4708, 4709, 4711, 4718, 4719,
  4723, 4741, 4758, 4764, 4770,
  4771, 4779, 4780, 4782, 4787,
  4788, 4791, 4799, 4804, 4807,
  4811, 4819, 4826, 4828, 4854,
  4857, 4863, 4866, 4877, 4889,
  4896, 4897, 4906, 4911, 4918,
  4919, 4920, 4933, 4944, 4946,
  4947, 4952, 4953, 4954, 4959,

4965, 4966, 4978, 4981, 4987,
4995, 4996, 4997, 5003, 5013,
5014, 5018, 5019, 5020, 5026,
5027, 5029, 5030, 5031, 5034,
5040, 5041, 5045, 5047, 5049,
5055, 5056, 5057, 5073, 5076,
5080, 5082, 5086, 5087, 5088,
5091, 5093, 5094, 5096, 5098,
5105, 5106, 5107, 5108, 5110,
5119, 5120, 5126, 5127, 5131,
5137, 5140, 6157, 6218, 6220,
6238, 6242, 6302, 6378, 6410,
6444, 6529, 6627, 6839, 6922,
6955, 6989, 7034, 7107, 7127,
7195, 7200, 7237, 7238, 7239,
7241, 7261, 7306, 7321, 7452,
7456, 7611, 7634, 7641, 7675,
7681, 7872, 7886, 7888, 7938,
7964, 7987, 8011, 8128, 8134,
8135, 8138, 8168, 11410, 13128,
13136, 13971, 14831, 15224,
15542, 15559, 15586, 15737,
15839, 16105, 16249, 16586,
16812, 16933, 17070, 17147,
17309, 17314, 17315, 17321,
17444, 17468, 17473, 17476,
17479, 17519, 17617, 17633,
17743, 17768, 17798, 17815,
17829, 17831, 17849, 17850,
17855, 17869, 17942, 17955,
17960, 17961, 17964, 17972,
17979, 18005, 18012, 18033,
18136, 18139, 18259, 18306,
18324, 18384, 18401, 18442,
18456, 18464, 18474, 18478,
18581, 18603, 18720, 19017,
19287, 19302, 19303, 19305,
19314, 19316, 19337, 19355,
19372, 19379, 19398, 19426,
19427, 19435, 19437, 19439,
19443

AFRICANS' SCHOOL, PHILADELPHIA
9592

AGE 14235

AGRARIANS 2006

AGRICULTURAL IMPLEMENTS AND
MACHINERY 14243

AGRICULTURAL REFORMERS 3304, 7591,
11731, 12121, 14140, 14147,
14159, 14240

AGRICULTURAL REORGANIZATION 20488

AGRICULTURE 2416, 3292, 4989,
7593, 7861, 8619, 10329, 11380,
11384, 11560, 11993, 12071,
12087, 12132, 12342, 12590,
12679, 12680, 12713, 13022,
13448, 13536, 13672, 14081,
14104, 14109, 14110, 14136,
14147, 14234, 14243, 14325,
14379, 14395, 14435, 14451,
14466, 14532, 14536, 14544,
15226, 21154

AIME, VALCOUR 12214

AJA COASTAL STATES 5163

AKAN 4755

ALABAMA 2755, 8855, 9440, 10072,
10073, 10155, 11265, 11676,
11678, 11679, 11680, 11681,
11682, 11683, 11685, 11636,
11689, 11692, 11693, 11694,
11695, 11696, 11697, 11698,
11699, 11700, 11701, 11702,
11703, 11704, 11705, 11706,
11707, 11708, 11710, 11712,
11713, 11714, 11715, 11716,
11717, 11718, 11719, 11721,
11722, 11723, 11724, 11725,
11726, 11728, 11730, 11731,
11732, 11733, 11734, 11735,
11736, 11737, 11738, 11739,
11740, 11741, 11742, 11746,
11747, 11748, 11749, 11750,
11751, 11753, 11754, 11755,
11756, 11757, 11758, 11759,
11761, 11762, 11763, 11764,
11765, 11766, 11768, 11772,
11773, 11775, 11777, 11778,
11780, 11781, 11782, 11784,
11785, 11786, 11788, 11790,
11791, 11792, 11793, 11794,
11795, 11796, 11797, 11798,
11799, 11800, 11801, 11802,
11803, 11806, 12093, 12529,
14355, 14759, 14760, 14812,
14923, 15006, 15042, 15328,
16630, 17156, 17170, 17589,
19238, 19728, 19875, 20511,
20524, 20539, 20589, 20652,
20926, 21003

ALBANY, NY 10708, 19572

ALEA, GUTIERREZ 7248

ALECKSON, SAM 12834

ALEXANDER, ARCHER 11568, 18795

ALEXANDER, JOHN B. 2490, 3790,
    16536, 20001

ALEXANDRIA, LA 9832

ALEXANDRIA, VA 13806

ALL SAINTS PARISH, SC 18224

ALLEN, RICHARD 3545, 3956, 4558,
    16819

ALLEN, WILLIAM F. 1795, 1796,
    1797, 1798, 1799, 13066

ALLEYNE, MERVYN C. 894

ALLSTON, F.W. 12907, 12908, 15099

AMADO, JORGE 7641, 7886

AMAZON BASIN 7976

AMAZONIA 7630

A.M.E. ZION CHURCH 16636

AMELIA COUNTY, VA 8389

AMERICAN ANTISLAVERY SOCIETY
    9693

AMERICAN COLONIZATION SOCIETY
    343, 2251, 2262, 2283, 2373,
    2397, 2414, 2493, 2887, 2899,
    3575, 3576, 9844, 9874
    (SEE ALSO COLONIZATION)

AMERICAN FREEDMEN'S INQUIRY
    COMMISSION 21083, 21097

AMERICAN HOLINESS MOVEMENT 17354

AMERICAN HOME BAPTIST MISSION
    SOCIETY 16604, 18643

AMERICAN HOME MISSIONARY SOCIETY
    10837, 17281

AMERICAN MISSIONARY ASSOCIATION
    3045, 3046, 3820, 9639, 11360,
    11628, 11940, 12318, 13076,
    16745, 17242, 19147, 20794,
    21033, 21057, 21059, 21139

AMERICAN REVOLUTION 421, 2602,
    2603, 2693, 4649, 6287, 8273,
    8274, 8276, 8277, 8278, 8280,
    8281, 8282, 8290, 8291, 8296,
    8304, 8309, 8310, 8311, 8316,
    8318, 8320, 8323, 8328, 8330,
    8331, 8341, 8342, 8345, 8347,
    8376, 8377, 8380, 8383, 8384,
    8385, 8387, 8388, 8398, 8400,
    8403, 8404, 8406, 8407, 8409,
    8410, 8415, 8417, 8418, 8424,
    8432, 8433, 8434, 8451, 8458,
    8504, 8508, 8510, 8511, 8513,
    8519, 8522, 8531, 8549, 8555,
    8578, 8581, 8584, 8585, 8586,
    8588, 8592, 8596, 8604, 8608,
    8610, 8613, 8614, 8615, 8616,
    8622, 8623, 8624, 8629, 8631,
    8632, 8634, 8636, 8646, 8648,
    8649, 8651, 8653, 8655, 8667,
    8669, 8672, 8673, 8678, 8682,
    8683, 8684, 8697, 8709, 8715,
    8722, 8723, 8724, 8730, 8731,
    8732, 8735, 8736, 8848, 8849,
    9140, 9439, 9780, 9964, 10121,
    10317, 10804, 11656, 11972,
    13013, 13145, 13744, 16243,
    19827, 20513

AMISTAD 5082, 5278, 6066, 9062,
    19873, 19876, 19905, 19935,
    20003, 20007, 20025, 20046,
    20057, 20060, 20061, 20105,
    20141, 20143

ANDERSON (SLAVE) 19854

ANDERSON, JOSEPH R. 13475, 13594,
    13595, 19790

ANDERSON, JOURDAN 3049

ANDERSON, ROBERT (EX-SLAVE,
    1843-1930) 11261

ANDERSON'S CASE 8879, 9179, 19854

ANDERSONVILLE PRISON 12204

ANDOYAGE 6754

ANDREWS, STEPHEN P. 4325

ANGLICAN CHURCH 1177, 6303, 6793,
  6978, 16703, 16752, 16944,
  17147, 17306, 20348

ANGLO-AMERICAN RELATIONS 5975,
  5976

ANGLO-TEXAS DIPLOMACY 13304,
  13337

ANGOLA 1503, 4985, 5636, 5744,
  5745, 5746, 6029

ANGUILLA 6588

ANNEKE, MATHILDE 2961

ANSTEY, ROGER 903

ANTHROPOMETRY 2433

ANTI-SLAVERY IDEOLOGY 8848, 8849,
  19671

ANTIGUA 6485, 6487, 6553, 6588,
  6934, 6975, 7091, 7094, 7095,
  7097, 17440, 18218, 19569,
  20054

ANTIGUA SLAVE CONSPIRACY, 1736
  19569

APPALACHIA 4559, 8646, 11398

APTHEKER, HERBERT 662

ARAM, MARIE (SLAVE) 10007

ARCHAEOLOGY, SLAVE HABITATION
  499, 2699, 6569, 6579, 6636,
  6649, 6836, 6837, 6838, 6839,
  7038, 8469, 10424, 10425, 10751,
  11240, 12045, 12136, 12137,
  12138, 12140, 12175, 12176,
  12899, 12900, 12918, 13270,
  13271, 13581, 15220, 15466,
  15469, 15482, 15506, 15510,

15512, 15549, 15806, 18365,
18484, 18485, 18517, 18525,
18526, 18536, 18537, 18539,
18540, 18551, 18572

ARCHITECTURE 5127, 15541, 15542,
  15543
  (SEE ALSO HOUSING)

ARCHY CASE 8905, 19636

ARGENTINA 7320, 7321, 7322, 7404,
  7411, 7441, 7477, 7513, 7615,
  7709, 7710, 7711, 7712, 8074,
  8105, 8189, 15785, 16309

ARGYLE ISLAND, GA 122

ARIEL 761

ARKANSAS 2637, 8764, 8804, 9301,
  11119, 11809, 11810, 11812,
  11813, 11814, 11815, 11816,
  11817, 11818, 11819, 11820,
  11822, 11823, 11824, 11825,
  11826, 11827, 11828, 11830,
  11831, 11833, 11834, 11835,
  11836, 11837, 11838, 11839,
  11842, 11844, 11845, 11846,
  11847, 11848, 11852, 11853,
  11854, 11855, 12137, 14855,
  14895, 16089, 17265, 20182,
  20500

ARMFIELD, JOHN 15116

ARNOLD, RICHARD D. 15801

ARSON 19572

ART 688, 4792, 4804, 4815, 4837,
  4935, 4949, 5026, 5105, 5106,
  5107, 5108, 7676, 7872, 7873,
  7956, 7957, 8304, 8670, 13787,
  14771, 14806, 15541, 17309,
  17438, 17478, 17606, 18501,
  18507, 18532, 18554, 18568,
  18581, 18593, 18595, 18597,
  18599, 18603, 18606, 18607,
  18611, 18612, 18613, 18616,
  18622, 18623, 18624, 18625,
  18627, 18629, 18631, 18632,
  18635, 18636, 18637, 18638,
  18640, 18645, 18646, 18647,
  18651, 18652, 18660, 18661,

BAHIA 2807, 2914, 6032, 6055,
7335, 7433, 7664, 7698, 7739,
7804, 7842, 7843, 7929, 7930,
7932, 7933, 7984, 8017, 8038,
8040, 8116, 8136, 9826, 10106,
14321, 14346, 15850, 18197,
19384, 19753, 20123, 20296

BAJAN DIALECT 7261

BALAFO 17519

BALDWIN COUNTY, GA 9219

BALDWIN, LOAMMI 14484

BALLAGH, JAMES C. 535, 1165, 1818

BALLY (SLAVE) 20478

BALTIMORE 2959, 3193, 11411,
11413, 11429, 11443, 11454,
15180, 15952, 19180, 19181

BAMBOULA 19302

BANCROFT, FREDERIC 621, 846, 847,
848, 983, 1989, 11598, 11599

BANJO 4692, 17496, 17511, 17519,
17584, 17626, 17832

BANKS, NATHANIEL P. 20440, 20866

BANNEKER, BENJAMIN 3090

BANTU MASKS 7938

BAPTISM 8587, 10288, 12192, 17147,
17218

BAPTIST CHURCH 4530, 5086, 6295,
6296, 6297, 6307, 6310, 7214,
8373, 12198, 12324, 12532,
13020, 13207, 13313, 13586,
16653, 16684, 16728, 16733,
16742, 16776, 16777, 16807,
16839, 16845, 16879, 16901,
16910, 16927, 16942, 16989,
16999, 17010, 17094, 17122,
17125, 17126, 17144, 17145,
17147, 17149, 17168, 17169,
17170, 17184, 17185, 17200,
17205, 17206, 17248, 17250,
17255, 17265, 17269, 17285,

17286, 17290, 17297

BAPTIST MISSIONARY SOCIETY 6964

BARBADOS 251, 253, 424, 2568,
2849, 5416, 5499, 5904, 6185,
6187, 6188, 6189, 6205, 6206,
6224, 6272, 6300, 6309, 6323,
6380, 6382, 6387, 6418, 6419,
6504, 6531, 6533, 6543, 6545,
6562, 6565, 6566, 6567, 6568,
6569, 6571, 6572, 6573, 6574,
6575, 6576, 6577, 6579, 6587,
6599, 6607, 6611, 6658, 6663,
6672, 6697, 6722, 6772, 6779,
6780, 6781, 6829, 6899, 6988,
6997, 6998, 7018, 7078, 7079,
7085, 7113, 7114, 7116, 7155,
7182, 7183, 7212, 7242, 7261,
7285, 7296, 8552, 9564, 10059,
14118, 15380, 15670, 17595,
17639, 18359, 18528, 18530,
18539, 20271

BARBUDA 6553, 6588, 6807

BARRACOONS 6068

BARRINGER, PAUL B. 648, 1549,
1818, 12646

BARROW, BENNET H. 12272, 12274,
12275

BARTRAM, JOHN 11965

BASKETS 5106, 15541, 18564, 18570,
18579, 18654

BASKETS, SLAVE 4815, 15541, 17392,
18504

BASSETT, JOHN S. 535, 863, 1856,
1857

BATH, JONAS M. 6277, 6278

BATON ROUGE 12213, 12283, 12385,
12437

BATTLE OF NEW ORLEANS 3881, 9433

BATTLE, JAMES S. 8761

1575

BATUQUE 7996

BAUTISTA PINO, DON PEDRO 2467

BEADS 5812, 18530

BEARD, CHARLES A. 1442

BECKFORD, WILLIAM 7093

BEDFORD COUNTY, VA 13486, 13552

BEDSPREADS 17438

BEES 14730

BEHN, APHRA 7708

BELIZE 7365, 7366, 7367, 7410,
7516, 7636, 7637, 7648
(SEE ALSO BRITISH HONDURAS)

BENEZET, ANTHONY 3278

BENIN 4677, 4831, 4832

BENJAMIN, JUDAH P. 9315

BENNEHAN, RICHARD 12776

BENTON, THOMAS H. 13440

BERBICE 7662

BERGEN COUNTY, NJ 10529, 10547

BERKS COUNTY, PA 10755

BERLIN, IRA 1348, 1397, 1689,
2018, 2021

BERMUDA 6132, 6207, 6354, 6942,
7131, 7132, 7258, 7259, 7260,
7298, 16469

BEVERLY, JOHN W. 1767

BEVERLY, MA 10455

BIBB, HENRY 18969, 19598, 19631

BIBLE 2535, 8456, 17147, 20022

BIGHT OF BENIN 4960, 4961, 5901,
5933, 6055

BIGHT OF BIAFRA 4999, 5783

BIRMINGHAM, AL 15945

BIRNEY, JAMES G. 11264, 11265,
11715

BIRON (SLAVE) 8837, 9299

BIRTH RATES 14901, 15015, 15821

BISLAND, JOHN 12478

BISSETTE, CYRILLE-CHARLES-AUGUSTE
20026

BLACK BELT 12529

BLACK CARIBS 6541, 6542, 7187,
7345, 7459, 7471, 7631, 7636,
8075, 8098, 17982, 18115, 18479

BLACK LAWS 2124, 8838, 9071, 9072
9372, 9480, 15805

BLACK MATRIARCHY, MYTH OF 16384

BLACK NATIONALISM 268, 1120, 1130
2387, 9690, 20330

BLACK SOLDIERS, RECRUITMENT OF
135, 820, 2123, 10023, 10130,
10142, 10199, 11307, 12251,
12368, 12439, 13013, 13065,
19352, 20327, 20347, 20429,
20458, 20460, 20473, 20484,
20513, 20525, 20553, 20587,
20595, 20637, 20656, 20661,
20678, 20686, 20692, 20695,
20711, 20712, 20713, 20714,
20715, 20716, 20732, 20756,
20767, 20770, 20772, 20773,
20774, 20777, 20778, 20779,
20789, 20797, 20802, 20829,
20831, 20843, 20844, 20847,
20855, 20858, 20874, 20886,
20898, 20911, 20938, 20946,
20964, 20970, 20989, 21000,
21019, 21025, 21064, 21077,
21078, 21079, 21080, 21115,
21118, 21126, 21142, 21148,
21159
(SEE ALSO UNION ARMY, U.S.
ARMY, U.S. COLORED TROOPS)

BLACK TONGUE 15704

BLACKMORE, BETTIE R. 13277

BLACKNESS 2535, 8456, 20022

BLACKSMITHS, SLAVE 13136, 13136,
    14235, 14730, 15541, 17438,
    18583, 19790

BLAIR, MONTGOMERY 11513

BLAKE, JANE (SLAVE) 11404

BLAKE, WILLIAM 18622

BLASSINGAME, JOHN W. 654, 716,
    830, 1011, 1152, 1164, 1318,
    1589, 1680, 1874, 1913, 5131

BLEDSOE, ALBERT T. 2118, 2254

BLOW FAMILY 8792

BLUES 16711, 17634

BLYD, CORNELIUS W. 8144

BLYDEN, EDWARD W. 3921

BOAS, FRANZ 708

BOATBUILDING 15541

BODY SERVANTS 14873, 19842

BOLAND, ROBERT J. 3681

BOLDING, JOHN A. 19733

BOLIVIA 7666

BOLIVIAN CONFEDERATION 7358, 7513

BOLLAERT, WILLIAM 13364

BONAPARTE, NAPOLEON 353, 6950

BOND, SCOTT 4260

BONGA, GEORGE 9650

BONTEMPS, ARNA 18386

BOON, JAMES 9519

BOONE COUNTY, KY 11274

BOONE COUNTY, MO 11532, 11581,
    11598, 11599

BOOTH, KATE 9971

BOSTOCK, ROBERT 5535

BOSTON 8777, 9595, 10438, 10451,
    15893

BOUGHTON, WILLIS 1321

BOULLE, PIERRE H. 1004

BOWEN, J.W.E. 1812

BOWRING, JOHN 4469

BRACKETT, JEFFREY R. 535, 840,
    1233

BRADDOCK, EDWARD 11518

BRAMLETTE, THOMAS E. 11296

BRATHWAITE, EDWARD K. 797

BRAY, THOMAS 17098, 17099

BRAZIL 90, 133, 169, 190, 315,
    346, 440, 448, 579, 753, 802,
    1181, 1267, 1319, 1418, 1692,
    1693, 1724, 1793, 1794, 1846,
    1921, 2038, 2105, 2107, 2227,
    2256, 2356, 2390, 2403, 2454,
    2459, 2499, 2594, 2646, 2795,
    2807, 2817, 2850, 2914, 3377,
    4487, 4718, 4813, 4828, 4912,
    4913, 5103, 5246, 5376, 5611,
    5632, 5639, 5641, 5700, 5705,
    6006, 6032, 6055, 6064, 6681,
    7019, 7229, 7244, 7299, 7304,
    7305, 7313, 7314, 7315, 7318,
    7319, 7323, 7327, 7328, 7329,
    7335, 7337, 7338, 7347, 7352,
    7353, 7360, 7361, 7362, 7363,
    7378, 7380, 7382, 7398, 7399,
    7403, 7409, 7415, 7417, 7418,
    7419, 7421, 7427, 7431, 7433,
    7439, 7449, 7451, 7458, 7463,
    7465, 7466, 7467, 7468, 7469,

7470, 7475, 7476, 7483, 7485,
7487, 7499, 7500, 7501, 7502,
7506, 7509, 7512, 7515, 7521,
7522, 7528, 7531, 7535, 7536,
7537, 7540, 7541, 7551, 7552,
7557, 7558, 7559, 7560, 7561,
7562, 7566, 7567, 7568, 7570,
7571, 7578, 7579, 7580, 7581,
7582, 7583, 7584, 7585, 7586,
7587, 7590, 7591, 7592, 7593,
7594, 7595, 7598, 7601, 7612,
7616, 7617, 7619, 7620, 7621,
7630, 7635, 7638, 7641, 7642,
7650, 7659, 7664, 7671, 7673,
7674, 7675, 7677, 7688, 7689,
7690, 7696, 7697, 7698, 7699,
7707, 7719, 7721, 7728, 7729,
7732, 7734, 7735, 7736, 7737,
7738, 7739, 7740, 7741, 7742,
7743, 7756, 7760, 7767, 7774,
7777, 7781, 7782, 7783, 7784,
7804, 7808, 7809, 7814, 7817,
7818, 7821, 7822, 7824, 7825,
7831, 7839, 7840, 7842, 7843,
7844, 7855, 7862, 7863, 7864,
7869, 7870, 7872, 7873, 7874,
7877, 7878, 7879, 7882, 7884,
7886, 7888, 7892, 7900, 7908,
7909, 7914, 7915, 7920, 7929,
7930, 7931, 7932, 7933, 7934,
7940, 7942, 7943, 7945, 7964,
7965, 7966, 7968, 7969, 7970,
7971, 7972, 7973, 7974, 7978,
7979, 7980, 7982, 7983, 7984,
7987, 7988, 7990, 7993, 7996,
7998, 7999, 8006, 8007, 8011,
8012, 8015, 8016, 8017, 8018,
8019, 8020, 8021, 8025, 8027,
8028, 8029, 8030, 8035, 8038,
8040, 8056, 8061, 8063, 8064,
8065, 8071, 8073, 8077, 8078,
8079, 8081, 8082, 8083, 8084,
8100, 8109, 8113, 8114, 8115,
8116, 8118, 8119, 8122, 8135,
8136, 8138, 8147, 8152, 8155,
8156, 8157, 8174, 8175, 8182,
8183, 8184, 8899, 9826, 10183,
10186, 13357, 14346, 14482,
14485, 14511, 15711, 15850,
16309, 16483, 17024, 17591,
17645, 17787, 18081, 18082,
18197, 18234, 18324, 19215,
19216, 19302, 19530, 19753,
20123, 20296

BRAZOS COUNTY, TX   13358

BRECKINRIDGE, JOHN   11312, 11313

BRECKINRIDGE, LUCY G.   13812

BRECKINRIDGE, ROBERT J.   8979,
    11373, 11375, 17047

BRENT, LINDA (SLAVE)   19013

BRESSA, CESARE   12398

BREWER, J. MASON   791

BRICKMAKERS   11497, 19790

BRIGGS, WALTER D.B.   20726

BRISTOL, ENGLAND   5695, 5696, 5749,
    5753, 5860, 5865, 5869, 5870,
    5871, 5919, 10093

BRISTOL, RI   15115

BRITISH ARMY   8616

BRITISH COLUMBIA   10265

BRITISH EAST INDIA COMPANY   4950

BRITISH GUIANA   1244, 1245, 5279,
    5681, 6815, 7233, 7300, 7301,
    7302, 7303, 7402, 7437, 7442,
    7481, 7488, 7489, 7490, 7553,
    7554, 7555, 7564, 7622, 7754,
    7823, 7841, 7852, 7885, 7992,
    8002, 8032, 8041, 8068, 8069,
    8151, 8153, 8158, 8177, 8185,
    10114, 14991
    (SEE ALSO GUYANA)

BRITISH GUIANA SLAVE UPRISING OF
    1823   7885

BRITISH HONDURAS   6810, 7365, 7366,
    7367, 7410, 7516, 7636, 7637,
    8098, 8145, 8167, 17982
    (SEE ALSO BELIZE)

BRITISH NAVY   5243, 5898, 6106,
    8616

BRITISH WEST AFRICA SQUADRON
    6106

BRITISH WEST INDIA REGIMENTS
6264, 6298, 6439

BRITISH WEST INDIES   464, 465, 466,
   869, 1180, 1275, 1699, 1902,
   1951, 2543, 5274, 5424, 5534,
   5645, 5657, 5668, 5691, 5726,
   5935, 5971, 6026, 6091, 6093,
   6123, 6124, 6136, 6168, 6256,
   6267, 6268, 6269, 6271, 6275,
   6287, 6297, 6298, 6301, 6303,
   6325, 6337, 6338, 6341, 6344,
   6346, 6348, 6374, 6401, 6420,
   6421, 6439, 6445, 6460, 6503,
   6517, 6518, 6521, 6526, 6528,
   6530, 6544, 6547, 6548, 6551,
   6557, 6564, 6570, 6630, 6631,
   6634, 6637, 6640, 6656, 6689,
   6719, 6721, 6723, 6724, 6762,
   6766, 6769, 6772, 6810, 6811,
   6812, 6813, 6826, 6828, 6829,
   6840, 6841, 6844, 6860, 6869,
   6892, 6909, 6916, 6917, 6933,
   6935, 6947, 6948, 6979, 6980,
   6981, 6982, 7006, 7008, 7025,
   7029, 7030, 7031, 7045, 7073,
   7080, 7087, 7089, 7094, 7095,
   7097, 7098, 7103, 7106, 7121,
   7136, 7137, 7140, 7141, 7146,
   7168, 7169, 7185, 7190, 7191,
   7192, 7206, 7216, 7227, 7236,
   7245, 7257, 7263, 7269, 7270,
   7271, 7273, 7274, 7281, 7284,
   7287, 8311, 8372, 8417, 8484,
   8485, 8648, 8649, 8680, 8920,
   10143, 10173, 14194, 14468,
   15800, 16309, 16832, 16998,
   17176, 17177, 17179, 17196,
   17360, 18084, 19204, 19249,
   20054, 20147

BRODIE, FAWN M.   773, 1387

BROOKLYN   7346

BROOKS, CHARLOTTE   11976

BROWN, ALBERT G.   4197

BROWN, ANDREW   14766

BROWN, JOHN   3440, 3674, 4281,
   9779, 10041, 11583, 19626,
   19742, 19838, 19851, 19994

BROWN, MORRIS   17313

BROWN, SAMUEL   11308

BROWN, WILLIAM J.   10785

BROWN, WILLIAM W.   837, 1029, 1258,
   1591, 4509, 9492, 18969, 20242

BROWNLOW, WILLIAM G.   1866, 13196

BROWNSON, ORESTES A.   2567

BRUCE, HENRY C.   11547

BRUCE, PHILIP A.   1643, 1733, 1777,
   1778, 1779

BRYAN, ANDREW   16742

BRYANT, WILLIAM C.   18004

BU ALLAH (SLAVE)   14831

BUCHANAN, JAMES   4141, 4198, 5275,
   5371, 5372, 8751

BUCHANAN, JOHN C.   2133, 3803

BUENOS AIRES   7320, 7321, 7615,
   7709, 7710, 7711, 7712, 8074,
   16309

BUILDING MATERIALS   15508

BUREAU OF NEGRO AFFAIRS   21039

BURIAL PRACTICES   10435, 12088,
   12847, 12882, 16933, 17174,
   17232, 17309, 18328, 18334,
   18335, 18365, 18381, 18539

BURKE COUNTY, GA   11983

BURKE COUNTY, NC   12709, 12766

BURKE, EDMUND   5972

BURNS, ANTHONY   9300, 19620, 19659,
   19699, 19760, 19793

BURNSIDE, JOHN   14557

BURROUGHS PLANTATION, VA   13489,
   13716

BUSH NEGROES   4959, 6619, 7317,
   7482, 7491, 7492, 7498, 7611,
   7676, 7681, 7723, 7725, 7726,
   7753, 7785, 7951, 8124, 8129,
   8130, 8131, 8132, 18635, 19275
   (SEE ALSO MAROONS)

BUSHNELL, HORACE   4541

BUSTILL, CYRUS   10728

BUTLER, BENJAMIN F.   20739, 20740,
   20813, 20895, 20969, 21005,
   21039

BUTLER, THOMAS   12276

BYRD, WILLIAM   126, 6111, 13723,
   13901

BYRD, WILLIAM II   13632

CABINS   5127, 12168, 15482, 15542,
   15543
   (SEE ALSO HOUSING)

CABLE, GEORGE W.   788, 892, 1725,
   1928, 2214, 3686, 4470, 9387,
   17913

CAESAR (SLAVE DENTIST)   15648,
   15649

CAESAR (SLAVE)   10695

CAESAR, JOHN   11926, 19712

CAIRNES, JOHN E.   1296, 14367

CALDWELL, WILSON   12657

CALHOUN, JOHN C.   3153, 4611,
   12878

CALIBAN   761, 5257

CALIFORNIA   2124, 8769, 8905,
   11031, 11069, 11070, 11071,
   11073, 11074, 11075, 11076,
   11077, 11079, 11080, 11081,
   11082, 11083, 11085, 11086,
   11087, 11088, 11090, 11091,
   11093, 11094, 11095, 11096,
   11098, 11099, 11100, 11119,
   19746

CALLAWAY COUNTY, MO   9345, 11633,
   11634

CALLENDER, JAMES   2559

CALVINISM   16995

CAMDEN INSURRECTION (1816)   19971

CAMDEN, SC   19971, 20005

CAMERON, PAUL C.   12642

CAMEROON   4674

CAMPBELL, ALEXANDER   3500, 16791

CAMPBELL, ROBERT   9399

CAMPISTA CASE   19530

CANADA   42, 241, 303, 329, 479,
   566, 587, 684, 3199, 3806, 7028
   8323, 8381, 8398, 8431, 9796,
   10226, 10227, 10230, 10231,
   10233, 10234, 10236, 10237,
   10239, 10240, 10241, 10243,
   10244, 10245, 10248, 10249,
   10250, 10252, 10253, 10254,
   10255, 10256, 10257, 10258,
   10261, 10262, 10263, 10264,
   10265, 10268, 10269, 10270,
   10271, 10272, 10273, 10274,
   10275, 10276, 10277, 10278,
   10279, 10280, 10281, 10282,
   10284, 10285, 10286, 10287,
   10288, 10289, 10290, 10292,
   10293, 10295, 10296, 10297,
   10298, 10299, 10300, 10301,
   10302, 10303, 10304, 10306,
   10307, 10308, 10309, 10310,
   10311, 10312, 10314, 10315,
   10317, 10319, 10320, 10321,
   10322, 10323, 10324, 10325,
   10326, 19480, 19634, 19827

CANALS   19790

CANDOMBLE   7433, 7641, 18423

CANE-BINDERS   14235

CANNON, PATTY   15138

CANNON'S POINT PLANTATION 12137,
    12140

CANOE 13520

CANOT, THEODORE 5544, 5625

CAPE FEAR REGION, NC 8499, 12669,
    12816

CAPE OF GOOD HOPE 4700, 4772

CAPELL, ELI J. 12621

CAPERS, WILLIAM 4360

CAPITAL 14377

CAPITALISM 1705, 2390, 5198,
    11717, 14598

CAPOEIRA 15850

CARACAS 7364, 7893

CAREY, LOTT 9836
    (SEE ALSO CARY, LOTT)

CARIBBEAN 73, 82, 83, 147, 768,
    912, 933, 1127, 1244, 1245,
    1275, 1515, 1648, 2390, 2612,
    2985, 2987, 3441, 4704, 5243,
    5250, 5580, 5600, 5935, 6139,
    6141, 6156, 6167, 6171, 6174,
    6175, 6176, 6177, 6181, 6182,
    6193, 6201, 6209, 6217, 6218,
    6221, 6222, 6223, 6226, 6229,
    6241, 6243, 6250, 6251, 6256,
    6264, 6266, 6267, 6268, 6270,
    6273, 6284, 6304, 6312, 6313,
    6317, 6318, 6322, 6324, 6335,
    6336, 6358, 6368, 6399, 6408,
    6409, 6412, 6414, 6441, 6443,
    6451, 6470, 6471, 6472, 6475,
    6476, 6477, 6479, 6516, 6522,
    6537, 6539, 6555, 6596, 6597,
    6604, 6624, 6626, 6630, 6634,
    6652, 6653, 6662, 6671, 6678,
    6693, 6701, 6710, 6729, 6748,
    6759, 6767, 6776, 6783, 6784,
    6785, 6787, 6792, 6793, 6794,
    6802, 6805, 6806, 6814, 6832,
    6848, 6859, 6862, 6868, 6873,
    6876, 6878, 6879, 6880, 6889,
    6896, 6897, 6912, 6914, 6918,
    6921, 6954, 6958, 6966, 6975,
    6984, 6989, 6991, 6999, 7007,
    7009, 7011, 7020, 7024, 7027,
    7036, 7039, 7041, 7051, 7054,
    7057, 7061, 7063, 7089, 7096,
    7107, 7110, 7111, 7119, 7126,
    7130, 7133, 7139, 7149, 7174,
    7204, 7223, 7224, 7226, 7233,
    7234, 7240, 7246, 7256, 7263,
    7264, 7265, 7272, 7276, 7277,
    7919, 8032, 8267, 8311, 8417,
    9159, 14482, 16166, 16655,
    17196, 20122, 20271, 20292

CARIBBEAN, DANISH 6135, 6761,
    6786, 6906, 6907, 6918, 6967,
    6972, 7153, 7184, 7205, 7249,
    7250, 7251, 7252, 9557, 9646

CARIBBEAN, DUTCH 271, 1190, 5467,
    6489, 6491, 6512, 6918, 6928,
    6986

CARIBBEAN, FRENCH 2457, 2543,
    5467, 5983, 5984, 5986, 6356,
    6426, 6435, 6484, 6488, 6489,
    6491, 6602, 6603, 6676, 6677,
    6699, 6764, 6766, 6855, 6867,
    6918, 6950, 6994, 6995, 7000,
    7028, 7035, 7158, 7160, 7161,
    7243, 16309

CARIBBEAN, SPANISH 2290, 6137,
    6274, 6765, 6766, 6918, 6965

CARIBBEE 5260

CARLOG 12548

CARLYLE, THOMAS 2522, 4006

CAROLINA CORPS 7217

CAROLINE COUNTY, MD 9992

CARPENTERS 14730, 15226
    (SEE ALSO CRAFTSMEN)

CARRIACOU 6251, 19302

CARSON, JAMES G. 12219, 12432

CARTAGENA 6056

CARTER, LANDON   8399

CARTER, ROBERT   8566, 13898, 14875

CARTWRIGHT, SAMUEL A.   2428, 15728

CARUTHERS, ELI   4467

CARY, LOTT   3547, 9498, 9649, 9760
   (SEE ALSO CAREY, LOTT)

CASH, WILBUR J.   1336

CASKEY, T.W.   11057

CASS COUNTY, MI   9924

CASTILLO, JAMES   5797

CASTLEREAGH, LORD   5699

CAT HAULING   15370

CATAHOULA PARISH, LA   12260

CATHOLIC CHURCH   202, 1177, 2665,
   4218, 4219, 6246, 6393, 6859,
   7641, 7720, 8652, 11584, 12245,
   16591, 16592, 16624, 16662,
   16670, 16671, 16680, 16688,
   16821, 16869, 16888, 16900,
   16944, 16957, 17001, 17002,
   17015, 17031, 17035, 17036,
   17037, 17039, 17062, 17064,
   17081, 17113, 17147, 17173,
   17267, 17299, 17301, 17311,
   18458

CATTO, OCTAVIUS V.   9851

CAUCA VALLEY   8095, 8096

CELIA   9342, 9344, 9345

CEMETERY MARKERS   8536, 18641

CEMETERY, SLAVE   18530, 18539

CENTRAL AMERICA   2740, 3929, 7345,
   7563, 7572, 7631, 7648, 7811,
   7936, 8001, 8049, 8050, 8051,
   8164, 14992

CERAMICS   5106, 6839, 10429, 10447,
   12136, 12140, 15466, 18497,

18517, 18586, 19856

CHAMBERS, JORDAN   12717

CHAMBERS, SAMUEL D.   18988

CHAMPION, RICHARD   5752

CHANNING, EDWARD   1349, 1350, 135.

CHAPLAINS, UNION ARMY   19143

CHARCOAL IRON INDUSTRY   13510

CHARLES COUNTY, MD   8698, 11526

CHARLESTON SLAVE CONSPIRACY, 1797
   20138

CHARLESTON, SC   8419, 8420, 8531,
   8699, 8735, 8995, 9003, 9163,
   9290, 9499, 9500, 9501, 9502,
   12869, 12875, 12893, 12897,
   12911, 12935, 12979, 13054,
   13059, 13063, 13068, 13069,
   13084, 13136, 13138, 13152,
   14805, 14806, 15522, 15829,
   15978, 16066, 16771, 18612,
   20138

CHARLESTON, WV   16075

CHARLOTTESVILLE   13593

CHASE-RIBOUD, BARBARA   1478

CHASE, SALMON P.   3667, 3808,
   10045

CHATTANOOGA   13197

CHAVIS, JOHN   3164, 9596, 9632,
   9838, 9895, 9917, 12698, 12778
   14865

CHEROKEE COUNTY, TX   13365

CHEROKEES   1495, 11126, 11129,
   12116, 12160, 13929, 13936,
   13937, 13945, 13954, 13959,
   13961, 13963, 13966, 13967,
   13972, 13987, 13989, 13998,
   14000, 14007, 14010, 14013,
   14015, 14016, 14017, 14018,
   14029, 14031, 14032, 14042,

1582

14043, 14049, 14055, 14058

CHESAPEAKE 1494, 1894, 5843, 8238, 8245, 8487, 8490, 8521, 8565, 8666, 8698, 11178, 11418, 11465, 11474, 11476, 11492, 11510, 13708, 14325, 14751, 14752, 15007, 15136, 15786, 18520, 20271

CHESHIRE 5923

CHESNUTT, CHARLES W. 656, 696, 769, 936, 1028, 1262, 1573, 1895, 1957, 2461, 2769, 3559, 12728, 16234, 18016, 18017, 18117, 18202, 18211, 18338, 19330

CHESTER COUNTY, PA 8686

CHEVES, LANGDON 12964

CHICKASAWS 13979, 13988, 14044, 14060

CHILDREN, SLAVE 1679, 2855, 7766, 11512, 12395, 12396, 14220, 14844, 14894, 14975, 14976, 15015, 15025, 15058, 15332, 15528, 15789, 15876, 16114, 16129, 16173, 16224, 16225, 16319, 19488

CHILE 1289, 6404, 7432, 8026, 15785

CHLOTILDE 5564

CHOCTAWS 13922, 13939, 13940, 13979, 13999, 14001, 14039, 14060

CHOLERA 12109, 15647, 15715

CHRISTIANA, PA RIOT 8923, 19486, 19547, 19589, 19590, 19599, 19611, 19657, 19682, 19683, 19839

CHRISTIANITY 1224, 6338, 17072, 19654

CHRISTMAS CUSTOMS 6405, 11762, 12558, 13060, 13702, 15846,

15858, 15860, 17238

CHURCH, ROBERT R. 13187, 13257

CIMARRONES 8000, 20053

CINCINNATI 9372, 9566, 9586, 9675, 20864

CINQUE, JOSEPH 5082, 19592

CIRCUIT RIDERS 3129

CIVIL RIGHTS 2122, 17005

CIVIL WAR 135, 377, 1525, 1940, 1978, 2122, 2123, 2133, 2196, 2287, 2628, 2629, 3021, 4038, 4510, 8530, 8770, 9284, 9285, 9484, 9794, 9978, 10003, 10017, 10037, 10042, 10045, 10055, 10056, 10057, 10059, 10060, 10065, 10081, 10127, 10130, 10142, 10146, 10167, 10172, 10190, 10197, 10199, 10216, 10225, 11108, 11122, 11214, 11276, 11288, 11307, 11320, 11368, 11369, 11374, 11421, 11422, 11432, 11430, 11523, 11542, 11556, 11585, 11586, 11613, 11624, 11628, 11812, 11848, 12004, 12041, 12051, 12084, 12099, 12133, 12236, 12244, 12439, 12446, 12507, 12577, 12596, 12607, 12748, 12757, 12805, 13158, 13183, 13188, 13189, 13190, 13213, 13232, 13233, 13235, 13236, 13241, 13321, 13334, 13517, 13607, 13614, 13680, 13753, 13792, 13912, 14355, 14873, 15385, 15960, 16047, 16272, 16824, 18925, 19023, 19142, 19190, 19352, 19613, 19842, 20182, 20237, 20243, 20317, 20320, 20322, 20323, 20324, 20325, 20326, 20327, 20328, 20331, 20337, 20340, 20341, 20344, 20345, 20346, 20347, 20349, 20352, 20354, 20357, 20360, 20362, 20363, 20364, 20369, 20371, 20373, 20375, 20376, 20382, 20385, 20387, 20388, 20392, 20393, 20395, 20396, 20398, 20399, 20401,

20408, 20410, 20411, 20414,
20416, 20417, 20419, 20420,
20421, 20423, 20424, 20426,
20429, 20430, 20432, 20434,
20435, 20436, 20439, 20440,
20450, 20451, 20455, 20456,
20458, 20460, 20461, 20479,
20495, 20507, 20512, 20513,
20516, 20519, 20524, 20525,
20526, 20535, 20537, 20539,
20553, 20567, 20572, 20573,
20584, 20585, 20587, 20595,
20596, 20598, 20600, 20603,
20607, 20608, 20611, 20613,
20617, 20622, 20631, 20637,
20645, 20656, 20664, 20666,
20672, 20673, 20677, 20682,
20686, 20689, 20690, 20692,
20695, 20698, 20700, 20706,
20710, 20713, 20718, 20722,
20728, 20731, 20732, 20733,
20734, 20735, 20738, 20739,
20740, 20741, 20742, 20749,
20751, 20752, 20753, 20755,
20756, 20764, 20766, 20770,
20772, 20773, 20774, 20776,
20784, 20789, 20790, 20798,
20804, 20805, 20806, 20810,
20812, 20813, 20829, 20831,
20835, 20836, 20837, 20838,
20840, 20841, 20843, 20844,
20846, 20848, 20851, 20852,
20853, 20859, 20863, 20867,
20871, 20876, 20877, 20882,
20895, 20893, 20905, 20910,
20911, 20912, 20919, 20921,
20924, 20925, 20928, 20930,
20931, 20941, 20946, 20954,
20957, 20963, 20969, 20986,
20988, 20996, 21000, 21005,
21007, 21010, 21017, 21025,
21034, 21035, 21037, 21039,
21040, 21042, 21045, 21046,
21048, 21055, 21060, 21064,
21067, 21068, 21069, 21073,
21075, 21076, 21079, 21080,
21081, 21082, 21084, 21089,
21091, 21101, 21102, 21103,
21104, 21105, 21110, 21111,
21114, 21117, 21132, 21135,
21138, 21150, 21155

CIVIL WAR DIPLOMACY 5515, 20333

CLARK, JAMES F. 18885

CLARKSON, JOHN 4604

CLARKSON, THOMAS 5487

CLAVER, PETER 8121, 17003, 17308

CLAY EATING 15822

CLAY, BRUTUS J. 11320

CLAY, CASSIUS M. 11310, 11365

CLAY, HENRY 2397, 3241, 10191,
    11254, 11266, 11285, 11295,
    11340

CLEBURNE, PATRICK R. 16064, 2046
    20472, 20525, 20572, 20573,
    20602, 20608

CLIOMETRICS 502, 1058, 1471
    (SEE ALSO ECONOMETRICS)

CLOTHING 1679, 2959, 9159, 12554
    14894, 15106, 15147, 15224,
    15229, 15409, 15553, 15554,
    15555, 15559, 15564, 15565,
    15573, 15574, 15575, 15576,
    16319, 16546, 16565, 19108,
    20276

COAL 11473, 13568, 13694, 13704,
    13802, 14747

COCKE, JOHN H. 13575, 18728

CODRINGTON PLANTATIONS 6185, 618
    6188, 6721, 6722, 7086

CODRINGTON, CHRISTOPHER 6625

COE RIDGE NEGRO COLONY 11350,
    11351, 11352

COFFEE PLANTATIONS 7688, 7689,
    7822, 7839, 7840, 8081, 8082,
    14235·

COFFEE, JOHN 11697

COFFIN, LEVI 18846

COHOON, JOHN C., JR.   13655

COKER, DANIEL   16704

COLE COUNTY, MO   11578, 11579

COLEMAN, J. WINSTON   621, 838

COLEMAN, JOHN W.   11281

COLERIDGE, SAMUEL T.   4132

COLES, EDWARD   10858, 10884, 13634

COLES, ROBERT   1900

COLOMBIA   2867, 5022, 5730, 6056,
   7324, 7497, 7597, 7610, 7657,
   7658, 7694, 7748, 7769, 7835,
   7836, 7868, 7905, 7912, 7926,
   7961, 7995, 8000, 8022, 8024,
   8045, 8046, 8047, 8095, 8096,
   8121, 8161, 8163, 8172, 8173,
   9837, 14467, 15785, 17003,
   17308, 17768

COLONIALISM   2612

COLONIZATION   174, 343, 377, 2093,
   2112, 2162, 2163, 2183, 2215,
   2216, 2315, 2334, 2345, 2395,
   2397, 2493, 2638, 2666, 2695,
   2697, 2713, 2735, 2741, 2779,
   2814, 2832, 2834, 2835, 2837,
   2842, 2846, 2872, 2886, 2887,
   2977, 3095, 3202, 3865, 3989,
   4047, 4116, 4165, 4249, 4320,
   4321, 4322, 4477, 4547, 4581,
   8484, 8485, 9370, 9382, 9399,
   9423, 9513, 9520, 9572, 9638,
   9685, 9689, 9698, 9797, 9843,
   11180, 11514, 12154, 12456,
   12760, 18728, 19932, 20381,
   20391, 20414, 20416, 20444,
   20721

COLONIZATIONISTS AND SLAVERY
   343, 848, 2112, 2116, 2117,
   2151, 2362, 2394, 2396, 2397,
   2566, 2638, 2695, 2697, 2814,
   2886, 2887, 2965, 2977, 3149,
   3202, 3552, 3785, 3842, 4322,
   4477, 9365, 9400, 9452, 9460,
   9513, 9649, 9698, 9843, 11260,
   11536, 12154, 12760, 16706,

20444, 20721

COLORADO   11101, 11102, 11103,
   11104, 11105, 19746

COLTON, CALVIN   2230

COLYAR, ARTHUR S.   3367

COMBE, GEORGE   2413

COMMUNAL DEPRIVATION   16112

COMPANY OF ROYAL ADVENTURERS
   6117, 6118, 6119

COMPANY OF THE INDIES   8348

COMPARATIVE SLAVERY   137, 216, 423,
   537, 640, 907, 950, 962, 964,
   997, 1097, 1124, 1174, 1227,
   1261, 1323, 1344, 1437, 1449,
   1530, 1593, 1651, 1724, 1771,
   1786, 1921, 1975, 2038, 2060,
   2276, 2290, 2331, 2356, 2361,
   2390, 2442, 2454, 2560, 2562,
   2593, 2682, 2731, 2759, 2785,
   2852, 2948, 2954, 2991, 3113,
   3146, 3148, 3202, 3237, 3322,
   3358, 3377, 3385, 3416, 3435,
   3449, 3451, 3457, 3468, 3538,
   3539, 3540, 3541, 3542, 3573,
   3641, 3657, 3659, 3678, 3720,
   3721, 3897, 3939, 3941, 3944,
   3945, 3964, 4021, 4123, 4259,
   4295, 4297, 4347, 4392, 4393,
   4447, 4485, 4504, 4533, 4562,
   4566, 4571, 4575, 4590, 4613,
   4651, 4734, 4833, 5040, 5103,
   5376, 5585, 5637, 6082, 6100,
   6150, 6389, 6422, 6436, 6508,
   6534, 6559, 6560, 6634, 6719,
   6766, 6874, 6890, 6921, 6945,
   6962, 6975, 7114, 7137, 7138,
   7151, 7173, 7186, 7207, 7315,
   7325, 7329, 7347, 7762, 7775,
   7776, 7921, 7943, 8077, 8113,
   8182, 8183, 8475, 8545, 8578,
   8621, 8848, 8849, 8967, 9077,
   9097, 9145, 9171, 9184, 9248,
   9273, 9326, 9347, 9991, 10071,
   10145, 10217, 10218, 12370,
   12582, 13046, 13148, 13149,
   14118, 14171, 14194, 14202,
   14249, 14281, 14294, 14337,

14338, 14403, 14424, 14433,
14473, 14493, 14569, 14977,
15204, 15224, 15321, 15452,
15526, 15817, 15899, 16060,
16152, 16308, 16309, 16319,
16891, 18126, 18200, 19616,
19964, 19969, 20271, 20304

COMPROMISE OF 1850   4087, 9193,
11054

CONDITIONS OF SLAVE LIFE   1485,
3410, 3415, 4777, 6341, 8337,
8557, 8854, 10058, 11337, 12033,
12227, 12712, 12743, 13377,
13864, 14220, 15194, 15195,
15197, 15198, 15199, 15200,
15203, 15211, 15212, 15216,
15219, 15221, 15222, 15223,
15225, 15231, 15232, 15233,
15243, 15247, 15249, 15252,
15253, 15263, 15272, 15275,
15289, 15336, 15559, 16048,
16105, 17237, 18770, 18865,
18866, 19108, 19117
(SEE ALSO SLAVE TREATMENT)

CONFEDERACY   135, 377, 820, 1525,
1940, 8798, 8839, 8864, 9122,
9123, 9701, 10004, 10023, 10117,
10130, 10142, 10172, 11588,
11754, 11792, 11793, 11795,
11848, 11854, 11985, 12003,
12008, 12038, 12084, 12128,
12129, 12388, 12440, 12459,
12507, 12596, 12639, 12690,
12757, 12780, 12925, 12974,
13131, 13183, 13350, 134C7,
13447, 13517, 13749, 13753,
13865, 13936, 14632, 14663,
14812, 15226, 15359, 15385,
16047, 16063, 16064, 16662,
17337, 18925, 19023, 19842,
20137, 20182, 20237, 20317,
20322, 20419, 20447, 20450,
20454, 20457, 20459, 20460,
20464, 20469, 20472, 20473,
20478, 20480, 20482, 20483,
20484, 20485, 20487, 20489,
20496, 20498, 20500, 20504,
20512, 20513, 20518, 20519,
20520, 20525, 20526, 20535,
20537, 20540, 20541, 20551,
20553, 20555, 20557, 20567,
20570, 20571, 20572, 20573,

20580, 20582, 20584, 20586,
20587, 20589, 20594, 20596,
20597, 20602, 20603, 20607,
20608, 20611, 20612, 20613,
20614, 20617, 20622, 20623,
20624, 20627, 20630, 20631,
20632, 20635, 20636, 20637,
20638, 20643, 20645, 20646,
20648, 20649, 20652, 20654,
20655, 20798, 21095, 21144

CONFEDERATION PERIOD   8397

CONFISCATION   9976, 9977, 10177,
20347

CONGO   5745

CONGO COAST   5261

CONGAREE RIVER   12830

CONGREGATIONALIST CHURCH   2300,
4299, 17242

CONJURE   5101, 15589, 15677, 1817
18211, 18213, 18214, 18346,
18409, 18462, 19575

CONNECTICUT   508, 8284, 8508, 866
8715, 8809, 10381, 10382, 1038
10387, 10388, 10391, 10392,
10393, 10394, 10396, 10397,
10398, 10399, 10400, 10401,
10402, 10404, 10405, 10407,
10408, 10411, 10412, 10413,
10414, 10417, 10699, 10810,
17468, 18999

CONRAD, ALFRED H. AND MEYER, JOHN
R.   1053, 1416, 1523

CONSPICUOUS CONSUMPTION   14404

CONTRABAND CAMPS   19172, 19842,
20537, 20681, 20897, 20936
(SEE ALSO UNION ARMY, U.S. AR

CONVENTION MOVEMENT, NEGRO   3093,
3094, 3096, 9381, 9540, 9546,
9746, 19518

CONVERSION   8439, 12885, 16751,
17147, 17179, 17293, 17306,
17325, 17353

(SEE ALSO RELIGION)

CONVICT LEASE SYSTEM 3453

CONWAY, JAMES S. 14895

COOKS 14235, 20586

COOPER, ANNA J. 6699

COOPER, JAMES F. 2873

COOPERS 18606

COPPOC, BARCLAY 19808

COBA 5495, 5546

CORINTH, MS 21135

CORN 14315, 15411, 15412, 15413,
15416

CORN-SHUCKING 15880

CORNELL UNIVERSITY SPECIAL SLAVERY
COLLECTION 15235

CORO REVOLT, 1795 6404

CORPORATE SLAVERY 10706

CORWIN, ARTHUR F. 1509

COSTA RICA 7480, 7889, 7890, 7891

COTTON 1721, 4458, 11673, 11718,
11947, 11951, 11998, 12697,
13280, 13287, 13288, 13361,
13451, 14120, 14128, 14162,
14167, 14222, 14223, 14238,
14243, 14275, 14276, 14277,
14308, 14329, 14373, 14375,
14376, 14401, 14419, 14422,
14452, 14498, 14509, 14516,
14543, 14550, 14551, 14552,
14560, 14564, 20584

COTTON FACTOR 11951, 13361, 14282,
14283, 14498

COTTON GIN 11998, 14172, 14373,
14460

COTTON GINNING 14062

COULTER, E. MERTON 624, 2044,
2045

COUPER PLANTATION SITE 15510

COUPER, JAMES H. 12109

COURTS, SLAVE 8580, 8948, 8949,
9108, 9109, 9110, 9111, 9112,
9115, 9117, 9119, 9219, 9228,
9234, 13040

COURTSHIP 1679, 9523, 16087,
16245, 16537

COWAN, JACOB 11768

COWBOYS 7784, 9474, 11010, 11011,
11012, 13433

COX, SAMUEL H. 17055

CRAFT, ELLEN 19243, 20307

CRAFT, WILLIAM 19473, 20307

CRAFTSMEN 395, 3464, 3465, 5106,
7709, 8304, 8670, 8699, 9519,
9579, 9964, 11473, 11474, 11476,
11516, 12096, 12125, 12704,
12790, 13136, 13708, 13787,
14630, 14669, 14676, 14694,
14696, 14701, 14702, 14703,
14704, 14710, 14751, 14752,
14753, 14757, 14771, 14774,
14777, 14796, 14800, 14806,
14816, 14826, 15224, 15541,
16010, 17238, 17309, 17392,
17438, 18499, 18501, 18554,
18563, 18575, 18581, 18590,
18629, 18654, 18658, 18667,
18668, 18669, 18682, 18691,
19789, 19842
(SEE ALSO CARPENTERS, COOPERS,
FURNITURE, MATERIAL CULTURE,
SKILLED SLAVES)

CRANDALL, PRUDENCE 2382, 9436,
9528, 9678

CRAVEN, AVERY O. 15007

CRAWFORD COUNTY, GA 12066

CREEKS 11125, 11133, 13930, 13938,
13985, 14034, 14040

CREOLE 493, 4664, 6627, 6777,
11864, 12243, 12316, 12401,
17440, 18212, 19268, 19269,
19286, 19302, 19315, 19319,
19347, 19377, 19379, 19399,
19400, 19422, 19429

CREOLE 5293, 5455, 15080, 15120,
15121, 19593, 19862, 19941,
20021, 20119

CREOLIZATION 761, 6166, 6232,
6233, 6234, 7422, 18224, 19343,
19377

CRESSWELL, NICHOLAS 17595

CRIME 3362, 8753, 9127, 9339,
9340, 9575, 9964, 10373, 13784,
15195, 15925, 20220

CROMWELL, OLIVER 7189

CRUMMELL, ALEXANDER 1956

CRUSE, HAROLD 1120

CUBA 726, 753, 2060, 2253, 2390,
2613, 4966, 5160, 5453, 5626,
5627, 5630, 5637, 6017, 6120,
6127, 6128, 6130, 6131, 6146,
6151, 6160, 6161, 6162, 6199,
6208, 6274, 6294, 6302, 6329,
6330, 6331, 6361, 6362, 6404,
6425, 6459, 6464, 6480, 6508,
6540, 6557, 6559, 6560, 6613,
6614, 6615, 6634, 6654, 6665,
6704, 6705, 6709, 6711, 6715,
6727, 6728, 6731, 6732, 6733,
6734, 6736, 6758, 6774, 6775,
6817, 6834, 6850, 6866, 6896,
6910, 6931, 6936, 6938, 6944,
6945, 6996, 7011, 7019, 7052,
7060, 7077, 7099, 7127, 7128,
7129, 7170, 7195, 7221, 7225,
7229, 7290, 8475, 9633, 14482,
14950, 16309, 16398, 17373,
17592, 17851, 18013, 18259,
18350, 18375, 19302

CUFF, FELIX 10481

CUFFE, PAUL 4271, 4319, 9573,
9844

CULTS, AFRICAN 7642, 8084, 16891,
17233, 17311

CULTURE, SLAVE 1534, 1936, 2783,
4689, 4777, 4898, 4965, 5049,
5069, 5119, 6064, 6433, 7054,
7515, 8561, 8562, 9523, 10629,
12112, 12835, 12859, 13129,
16010, 16083, 16105, 16179,
16243, 17237, 17363, 17372,
17373, 17374, 17379, 17384,
17385, 17391, 17395, 17396,
17403, 17419, 17420, 17422,
17425, 17426, 17427, 17431,
17444, 17450, 17453, 17454,
17455, 17463, 17465, 17468,
17474, 17476, 17477, 17479,
17485, 17488, 17637, 18720

CURACAO 2484, 5476, 6645, 6963

CURRICULUM UNITS, SLAVE 63, 260,
481, 594, 17881

CURSE OF HAM 20022

CURTIN, PHILIP D. 779, 890, 1311,
1313, 1315

CUSTIS, G.W.P. 13809

D'ABBADIE, JEAN-JACQUES-BLAISE
12235

D'IBERVILLE, PIERRE LEMOYNE 12235

DAHOMEY 4659, 4660, 4661, 4864,
4939, 4993, 5024, 5034, 5595,
5612, 5897, 8118

DALLAS COUNTY, AL 11805

DALZEL, ARCHIBALD 5164

DANCE 86, 163, 177, 331, 646,
1226, 4701, 4703, 4920, 6302,
6407, 6416, 6441, 6776, 7059,
7349, 8011, 10263, 12241, 1305,
15854, 15855, 15877, 16105,
16812, 16816, 17557, 17751,

17753, 17902, 17911, 18005,
18067, 18115, 18321, 18412,
18413, 18414, 18419, 18423,
18425, 18434, 18435, 18442,
18444, 18445, 18446, 18447,
18448, 18449, 18451, 18456,
18458, 18459, 18462, 18463,
18464, 18465, 18471, 18473,
18474, 18475, 18476, 18477,
18478, 18479, 18481, 18720,
19302

DANVERS, MA   10477, 10478

DARBY (SLAVE)   10426

DARWIN, CHARLES   2248, 3477

DAVE (SLAVE)   18496

DAVENPORT, WILLIAM   5871

DAVIDSON COUNTY, NC   12777

DAVIDSON COUNTY, TN   13244

DAVIDSON, BASIL   1314

DAVIDSON, JAMES D.   15124

DAVIES, SAMUEL   19223

DAVIS BEND COLONY, MS   10003,
12566, 12570, 12607

DAVIS, CHARLES S.   1210

DAVIS, DAVID B.   1397, 2018, 2020

DAVIS, HUGH   11735

DAVIS, JEFFERSON   11013, 12547,
12549, 12550, 12551, 12574

DAVIS, JOSEPH   10003

DAVIS, NOAH   9941

DAY, THOMAS   26, 9366, 9374, 9552,
9553, 9579, 9947, 18691

DE ALBURQUERQUE, KLAUS   8122

DE ALVARADO, DON PEDRO   8048

DE BOW, J.D.B.   3463, 4334

DE SA, SALVADOR   5248

DE SANDOVAL, ALONSO   1094, 7926

DE TOCQUEVILLE, ALEXIS   2770, 4373,
14250

DEBIEN, GABRIEL   1178

DECLARATION OF INDEPENDENCE   2989,
8394, 8459, 8656, 9202

DECLARATION OF THE RIGHTS OF MAN
6375

DECORATIVE ARTS   15541, 18487
(SEE ALSO ART, BASKETS, SLAVE;
FURNITURE, MATERIAL CULTURE)

DEERFIELD, MA   10488

DEGLER, CARL N.   786, 962, 1537

DELANE, BEN   13082

DELANY, MARTIN R.   1487, 4479,
9399, 9549, 9670, 9694, 20217,
21066

DELAWARE   473, 8575, 9129, 9173,
9561, 9591, 10740, 11185, 11186,
11188, 11189, 11190, 11191,
11192, 11193, 11194, 11195,
11196, 11197, 11201, 11202,
11203, 11204, 11205, 11207,
11208, 11209, 11210, 11214,
11217, 11218, 11219, 11220,
11222, 11224, 14926, 15286,
19196, 20090

DELAWARE ASSOCIATION FOR THE MORAL
IMPROVEMENT AND EDUCATION OF
THE COLORED PEOPLE   19196

DEMOGRAPHY   120, 363, 548, 549,
749, 887, 1003, 1061, 1062,
1064, 1520, 1947, 2454, 2487,
2978, 4370, 5072, 5635, 5769,
5783, 5791, 5840, 6029, 6251,
6324, 6418, 6419, 6631, 6634,
6638, 6639, 6640, 6705, 6719,
6945, 6988, 7029, 7030, 7031,
7032, 7158, 7247, 7248, 7297,

7432, 7768, 7772, 8061, 8358,
8460, 8461, 8541, 8543, 8552,
8594, 8727, 9163, 9457, 9566,
9624, 9846, 9949, 9963, 10624,
11257, 11465, 11802, 11803,
12733, 12812, 13046, 13064,
13300, 13318, 13378, 13452,
13608, 13655, 13876, 13943,
14194, 14235, 14335, 14369,
14382, 14489, 14494, 14495,
14901, 14903, 14904, 14907,
14910, 14911, 14914, 14923,
14926, 14928, 14931, 14932,
14935, 14936, 14938, 14942,
14943, 14947, 14949, 14950,
14952, 14956, 14957, 14967,
14977, 14980, 14984, 14991,
14992, 14994, 15002, 15006,
15007, 15009, 15010, 15015,
15018, 15023, 15025, 15029,
15031, 15032, 15035, 15039,
15041, 15042, 15046, 15047,
15048, 15051, 15053, 15058,
15064, 15065, 15068, 15178,
15771, 15821, 15839, 16557,
19260

DENT, JOHN H.   11685, 11727, 11743,
11749, 19976

DENTISTRY   15528, 15648, 15649

DEPARTMENT OF THE GULF   20986

DESSALINES, JEAN J.   6183, 6898

DETROIT   10293, 10953, 10954

DEVEREUX, JULIEN S.   13455

DEW, THOMAS R.   3946, 4383, 13504,
13640

DIALECT   327, 766, 4664, 7261,
18167, 19265, 19270, 19311,
19312, 19319, 19333, 19335,
19340, 19361, 19375, 19376,
19387, 19418, 19423, 19442
(SEE ALSO LANGUAGE)

DICKENS, CHARLES   2514, 3032

DICKSON COUNTY, TN   13193, 13194,
13195

DICKSON, DAVID   14159

DIET   499, 1679, 2548, 2959, 5136
6172, 6710, 6745, 6952, 8648,
9159, 11750, 12137, 12138,
12140, 12272, 12398, 12899,
12900, 13324, 14220, 14630,
14844, 14894, 14975, 14976,
15106, 15147, 15224, 15253,
15372, 15392, 15393, 15400,
15405, 15409, 15411, 15412,
15413, 15414, 15415, 15416,
15417, 15418, 15419, 15420,
15421, 15429, 15434, 15443,
15446, 15451, 15452, 15453,
15454, 15455, 15457, 15461,
15482, 15528, 15554, 15559,
15574, 15704, 16225, 16319,
16546, 16565, 17084, 17238,
18525
(SEE ALSO NUTRITION)

DIPLOMACY   3908, 4039, 4094, 5293
5419, 5655, 5674, 5675, 5747,
5748, 5795, 5846, 5847, 5970,
5975, 5976, 6047, 6094, 6852,
9062, 9140, 9311, 10290, 13402
15080

DIRT EATING   12398, 15528

DISCIPLES OF CHRIST   3714, 16853,
16854, 16929, 16982

DISEASE   2548, 2549, 4932, 5088,
5536, 5927, 6710, 14235, 14844
15206, 15362, 15528, 15613,
15640, 15647, 15687, 15704,
15720, 15723, 15747, 15754,
15766, 15768, 15774, 15776,
15780, 15787, 15828, 15839
(SEE ALSO MEDICINE, SUDDEN
INFANT DEATH SYNDROME,
TREPONEMATOSIS, TUBERCULOSIS)

DISSECTION   2492

DISTILLERS   14235

DISTRICT OF COLUMBIA   9421, 9422,
9450, 9643, 9771, 9795, 9939,
10055, 10056, 10057, 10067,
10077, 10108, 10171, 11225,
11227, 11228, 11229, 11230,
11231, 11232, 11236, 11238,

11240, 11241, 11243, 11244,
11246, 11248, 11249, 11251,
11252, 11253, 11254, 11255,
11257, 11258, 17264, 20815,
20981

DIXON, THOMAS JR.   1703, 2139

DJUKA   7681, 19355, 19979

DOCUMENTS   364, 7453, 11856
   (SEE ALSO SOURCE MATERIALS)

DODD, WILLIAM E.   871, 2000

DOGTROT HOUSE   15470, 15498

DOLBEN, SIR WILLIAM   5916, 10857

DOMINICA   6827, 6995, 7187, 8312

DOMINICAN REPUBLIC   947, 6642,
   17600, 19341

DORCHESTER COUNTY, MD   9992

DORMIGOLD, KATE   18855

DOUGLAS COUNTY, IL   10394

DOUGLAS, STEPHEN A.   3698, 4192,
   11036

DOUGLASS, FREDERICK   958, 1259,
   1433, 1576, 1812, 2406, 3141,
   3566, 3602, 3625, 3651, 3746,
   3952, 4210, 4583, 9526, 9542,
   9691, 9722, 9748, 9783, 11240,
   11502, 11521, 13658, 13846,
   15149, 15223, 16319, 18211,
   18856, 18946, 18975, 19004,
   19008, 19722, 19725, 20236

DOW, LORENZO   3158

DOWLAND, KAYE   6924

DRAKE, RICHARD   5397

DRAPETOMANIA   15749

DRED SCOTT CASE   641, 8741, 8751,
   8792, 8811, 8812, 8823, 8824,
   8830, 8857, 8867, 8868, 8869,
   8870, 8871, 8878, 8890, 8971,

9015, 9027, 9029, 9077, 9078,
   9207, 9260, 9268, 9269, 9279,
   9292

DREW, BENJAMIN   19040

DREWRY, WILLIAM S.   1922

DRIED BEEF INDUSTRY   7399

DRINKER, JOSEPH   9470

DRUMS   7033, 7671, 8130, 17519,
   17696, 17813
   (SEE ALSO MUSICAL INSTRUMENTS)

DUBOIS, SILVIA   16443, 16499

DUBOIS, WILLIAM E.B.   15, 425, 535,
   669, 682, 772, 832, 1092, 1280,
   1433, 1667, 1701, 1705, 1729,
   1811, 1812, 1813, 1829, 1875,
   1919, 1981, 1932, 2003, 2632,
   17418

DUKE, BASIL W.   2311

DUNBAR, PAUL L.   2202

DUNCAN, STEVEN (EX-SLAVE)   19069

DUNCANSON, ROBERT S.   9742

DUNMORE, LORD   8281, 8615, 19827

DUNNING, WILLIAM A.   1540

DUPLIN INSURRECTION   12775

DURHAM, JAMES   4164

DUTCH GUIANA   458, 1244, 1245,
   1648, 6619, 7233, 7482, 7491,
   7492, 7564, 7565, 7611, 7640,
   7662, 7723, 7725, 7726, 7753,
   7823, 7895, 7899, 7951, 7986,
   8032, 8128, 8129, 8130, 14991,
   16259, 17108, 18635, 19355,
   20280
   (SEE ALSO SURINAM)

DUTCH REFORMED CHURCH   8360

DUTCH WEST INDIA COMPANY   18, 5342,
   10611

DUTCH WEST INDIES 173
  (SEE ALSO CARIBBEAN, DUTCH)

DUTCHESS COUNTY, NY 8623

DVORAK, ANTON 17997

DWIGHT, THEODORE 3579

DYOTT, WILLIAM 6672

EARL, AR 11838

EAST FELICIANA PARISH 12422

EAST FLORIDA ANNEXATION PLOT
  11931

EAST INDIA COMPANY 5824

EASTERN STATE HOSPITAL 13584

EATON, JOHN 12607, 20787

ECONOMETRICS 842, 897, 14220,
  14558
  (SEE ALSO CLIOMETRICS)

ECONOMIC GROWTH, SLAVERY AND
  1416, 6168, 6547, 14143, 14171,
  14220, 14228, 14231, 14244,
  14377, 14396, 14456

ECONOMICS OF SCALE 1647, 14162,
  14363, 14463, 14570

ECONOMICS OF SLAVERY 260, 436,
  730, 768, 781, 789, 803, 842,
  899, 940, 1008, 1012, 1114,
  1127, 1188, 1198, 1332, 1400,
  1510, 1575, 1599, 1720, 1722,
  2048, 2049, 2148, 2390, 3717,
  3825, 3873, 3972, 5450, 5575,
  6167, 6399, 6443, 6498, 6554,
  6715, 6874, 6890, 7098, 7263,
  7264, 7269, 7767, 7781, 7839,
  7979, 7980, 8061, 8100, 8218,
  8277, 8308, 8314, 8316, 8372,
  8438, 8522, 8680, 9159, 9163,
  10046, 10143, 10156, 11384,
  11481, 11600, 11706, 11980,
  12020, 12121, 12306, 12370,
  12454, 12461, 12467, 12469,
  12554, 12720, 12843, 12861,
  12863, 12874, 13046, 13069,

13092, 13250, 13319, 13608,
13690, 13760, 14065, 14071,
14078, 14079, 14081, 14090,
14091, 14099, 14100, 14102,
14106, 14107, 14108, 14112,
14115, 14120, 14124, 14133,
14136, 14139, 14143, 14144,
14146, 14148, 14150, 14151,
14154, 14158, 14162, 14164,
14169, 14170, 14172, 14173,
14174, 14175, 14176, 14177,
14178, 14182, 14186, 14187,
14189, 14192, 14193, 14194,
14195, 14196, 14197, 14198,
14199, 14200, 14201, 14203,
14204, 14207, 14208, 14210,
14211, 14213, 14215, 14220,
14222, 14223, 14227, 14228,
14229, 14230, 14231, 14232,
14233, 14242, 14243, 14244,
14245, 14249, 14250, 14253,
14258, 14260, 14261, 14266,
14268, 14269, 14270, 14277,
14284, 14288, 14290, 14295,
14298, 14299, 14303, 14307,
14312, 14313, 14314, 14321,
14324, 14329, 14331, 14334,
14336, 14340, 14343, 14349,
14352, 14355, 14356, 14362,
14363, 14365, 14366, 14367,
14369, 14373, 14374, 14377,
14384, 14385, 14387, 14388,
14389, 14390, 14391, 14393,
14395, 14396, 14397, 14398,
14403, 14404, 14407, 14408,
14411, 14412, 14413, 14415,
14416, 14419, 14420, 14422,
14425, 14427, 14433, 14435,
14436, 14442, 14444, 14448,
14449, 14453, 14454, 14456,
14458, 14461, 14464, 14465,
14466, 14468, 14471, 14472,
14473, 14475, 14476, 14480,
14481, 14484, 14485, 14488,
14491, 14493, 14494, 14495,
14496, 14497, 14499, 14501,
14506, 14507, 14508, 14509,
14510, 14511, 14512, 14513,
14514, 14515, 14516, 14521,
14527, 14528, 14530, 14531,
14533, 14534, 14535, 14539,
14540, 14541, 14542, 14543,
14544, 14545, 14551, 14553,
14554, 14555, 14556, 14558,
14559, 14560, 14564, 14565,

14566, 14568, 14569, 14570,
14571, 14574, 14578, 14579,
14580, 14581, 14582, 14590,
14595, 14596, 14624, 14630,
14649, 15010, 15106, 15146,
15147, 15280, 15281, 15662,
15918, 19971

ECUADOR 5730, 7748, 7836, 8169,
8171, 8172, 15785

EDGECOMBE COUNTY, NC 12802, 12803

EDMONDSON FAMILY 19697, 19698

EDUCATION 914, 2156, 6205, 6206,
6504, 6764, 6765, 6766, 6906,
7045, 8497, 8582, 8796, 9384,
9762, 10070, 10592, 10600,
10618, 10657, 10723, 11244,
11316, 11377, 11545, 11571,
11689, 11975, 12289, 12382,
12414, 12508, 12735, 12833,
12844, 13468, 13526, 13532,
14630, 15379, 15554, 16319,
16565, 16676, 16714, 16826,
16844, 16892, 16906, 16917,
16991, 17084, 17109, 17176,
17177, 17179, 17277, 17317,
18973, 19142, 19143, 19144,
19145, 19146, 19147, 19149,
19158, 19159, 19160, 19162,
19166, 19167, 19169, 19171,
19172, 19176, 19177, 19178,
19179, 19180, 19181, 19186,
19189, 19190, 19193, 19197,
19198, 19199, 19202, 19204,
19212, 19215, 19216, 19223,
19224, 19229, 19230, 19235,
19236, 19237, 19238, 19240,
19241, 19243, 19244, 19249,
19251, 19252, 19254, 19257,
19258, 19727, 19842, 20716,
20774, 20998

EFFICIENCY OF SLAVERY 899, 1249,
1251, 14150, 14151, 14214,
14215, 14216, 14219, 14442,
14484, 14561, 14590, 14595,
14601, 14610, 14639, 14652,
15106

ELBERT COUNTY, GA 8831

ELDERLY SLAVES 150, 3724, 4639,
15013, 15289, 16331

ELITES, SLAVE 1940, 3754, 3938,
6600, 8595, 14235, 19003, 19126,
19789
(SEE ALSO HOUSE SERVANTS,
OVERSEERS, BLACK; SLAVE DRIVERS)

ELIZABETH CITY COUNTY, VA 13659,
13660

ELKINS, STANLEY M. 783, 995, 1043,
1102, 1140, 1143, 1174, 1318,
1394, 1404, 1425, 1524, 1567,
1869, 2054, 2256, 5131, 17391,
18767

ELLETSON, ROGER H. 484

ELLIOT, STEPHEN 11985

ELLIS, RICHARD 13312

ELLIS, ROBERT 5615, 10775

EMANCIPATION 141, 238, 377, 466,
606, 1275, 2114, 2977, 3393,
4212, 5190, 5668, 6032, 6138,
6205, 6268, 6334, 6401, 6405,
6526, 6629, 6723, 6781, 6815,
6840, 6841, 6867, 6889, 6917,
6964, 6972, 7025, 7137, 7168,
7169, 7184, 7192, 7208, 7245,
7257, 7288, 7453, 7455, 7688,
7689, 7742, 7743, 7895, 8109,
8114, 8281, 8367, 8615, 8664,
8848, 8849, 9045, 9052, 9155,
9298, 9459, 9468, 9585, 9794,
9799, 9964, 9968, 9970, 9971,
9972, 9973, 9974, 9976, 9977,
9979, 9980, 9982, 9984, 9985,
9986, 9989, 9995, 9997, 10000,
10001, 10002, 10003, 10004,
10007, 10008, 10010, 10017,
10019, 10020, 10023, 10027,
10029, 10036, 10037, 10043,
10045, 10046, 10049, 10053,
10054, 10055, 10056, 10057,
10058, 10059, 10060, 10065,
10067, 10070, 10071, 10072,
10073, 10074, 10075, 10076,
10077, 10078, 10079, 10080,
10081, 10082, 10086, 10087,
10088, 10089, 10094, 10099,

1098, 1167, 1202, 1209, 1243,
1265, 1371, 1408, 1445, 1459,
1465, 1520, 1700, 1727, 1731,
1737, 1761, 1988, 1993, 2043,
2052, 2309, 2472, 2645, 2758,
3123, 3938, 4668, 4782, 4813,
4918, 4996, 4997, 5045, 6308,
6337, 6468, 6609, 6610, 6620,
6627, 6632, 6635, 6637, 6754,
6814, 6849, 6959, 7141, 7422,
7529, 7621, 7929, 8069, 8173,
8175, 8594, 9397, 9432, 9523,
9771, 9964, 10166, 10387, 10724,
11210, 11461, 11462, 11474,
11598, 11599, 11857, 12230,
12784, 12933, 13037, 13076,
13184, 14630, 14844, 14854,
14936, 15025, 15112, 15253,
15355, 15559, 15673, 15717,
15839, 16076, 16079, 16081,
16083, 16084, 16086, 16089,
16090, 16094, 16095, 16096,
16097, 16099, 16105, 16106,
16107, 16111, 16113, 16114,
16115, 16121, 16122, 16123,
16130, 16134, 16135, 16136,
16138, 16146, 16148, 16149,
16152, 16154, 16157, 16158,
16161, 16162, 16163, 16164,
16166, 16167, 16169, 16170,
16172, 16173, 16174, 16177,
16178, 16184, 16185, 16196,
16200, 16202, 16203, 16204,
16207, 16210, 16211, 16212,
16216, 16218, 16220, 16228,
16233, 16234, 16237, 16240,
16243, 16249, 16251, 16254,
16258, 16259, 16261, 16264,
16269, 16270, 16272, 16273,
16278, 16280, 16282, 16283,
16285, 16286, 16289, 16290,
16291, 16292, 16296, 16298,
16302, 16303, 16304, 16305,
16306, 16308, 16309, 16310,
16311, 16312, 16313, 16314,
16317, 16318, 16319, 16320,
16326, 16328, 16331, 16401,
16402, 16418, 17237, 17238,
17896, 18749, 19040, 20163

FARQUHARSON, CHARLES 6449

FARRAND, MAX 3206

FATHERS 16319

FAULKNER, WILLIAM 954, 1529, 2136,
    2784, 2822, 2930, 2958, 2968,
    3686, 4007, 4471, 18387

FAYETTEVILLE, NC 8786

FEDERAL WRITERS' PROJECT, WORKS
    PROGRESS ADMINISTRATION 365,
    467, 468, 469, 1018, 1679, 1822,
    13899, 14854, 19055, 19107

FEDERALIST PARTY 4361

FEE, JOHN G. 11268, 11298, 11300,
    11331

FEREBEE, LONDON R. 12708

FERRIES 19790

FERTILITY 6635, 6719, 12876,
    14220, 14235, 14947, 15068,
    15717

FIDDLES 12332, 17527, 17528,
    17548
    (SEE ALSO MUSICAL INSTRUMENTS)

FIELD HANDS 3529, 15228, 16264,
    17238, 18729

FIFTEENTH AMENDMENT 2318, 2319

FIFTY-NINTH U.S. COLORED INFANTRY
    20778

FIFTY-SEVENTH U.S. COLORED TROOPS
    20669

FILIBUSTERS 4429, 6853, 6854,
    7152, 7222, 7223

FILLMORE, MILLARD 4049

FILM, SLAVERY IN 2080, 2145, 2259,
    2260, 2261, 2551, 2569, 2610,
    2667, 2685, 19678

FIRST MAROON WAR 6960

FISHER, ELIJAH J. 3544, 18868

FISK UNIVERSITY 467, 468, 469

FITZHUGH, GEORGE 2293, 2390, 2996,
    2997, 3007, 3964, 4603, 4617,
    4633

FITZHUGH, WILLIAM 13591

FITZPATRICK, JOHN 12265

FIVE CIVILIZED TRIBES 11122,
    11124, 13942, 13952, 13953,
    14014

FIXED CAPITAL 14231

FLEMING, TERRELL 11558

FLEMING, WALTER L. 1860

FLORIDA 235, 437, 633, 2833, 5334,
    5626, 5942, 8263, 8427, 8442,
    8669, 8731, 8759, 8760, 8917,
    8993, 9334, 9468, 9767, 11722,
    11856, 11857, 11858, 11863,
    11864, 11867, 11868, 11869,
    11870, 11871, 11872, 11873,
    11874, 11875, 11876, 11878,
    11880, 11882, 11883, 11886,
    11887, 11890, 11891, 11892,
    11893, 11894, 11895, 11897,
    11898, 11899, 11900, 11902,
    11904, 11907, 11908, 11909,
    11910, 11911, 11912, 11914,
    11915, 11916, 11917, 11918,
    11919, 11921, 11923, 11924,
    11926, 11929, 11930, 11931,
    11932, 11933, 11934, 11935,
    11936, 11937, 11938, 11939,
    11940, 11941, 11942, 11943,
    11946, 11947, 11948, 11949,
    11950, 11951, 11952, 11953,
    11954, 11955, 11956, 11957,
    11960, 11961, 11962, 11964,
    11965, 11967, 11968, 11969,
    11971, 11972, 11973, 12045,
    13996, 15482, 15752, 19489,
    19712, 19713, 19764, 19810,
    20229, 20495

FLUTE 17788

ELY 6107

FOGEL, ROBERT W. AND ENGERMAN,
    STANLEY L. 635, 665, 670, 690,
    691, 737, 799, 834, 896, 897,
    938, 953, 971, 992, 1048, 1054,
    1109, 1145, 1170, 1188, 1201,
    1203, 1204, 1222, 1229, 1250,
    1251, 1265, 1238, 1293, 1298,
    1305, 1337, 1397, 1407, 1408,
    1413, 1422, 1557, 1558, 1586,
    1607, 1611, 1625, 1675, 1687,
    1689, 1719, 1722, 1743, 1773,
    1774, 1838, 1850, 1882, 1884,
    1886, 1917, 1962, 1984, 2007,
    2018, 2027, 2036, 2042, 2053,
    2056, 5131, 15374

FOLK HEALING 15711
    (SEE ALSO DISEASE, MEDICINE)

FOLK REPRESSION 18255

FOLKLORE 225, 357, 398, 431, 491,
    511, 769, 862, 866, 1033, 1049,
    1472, 1582, 1598, 1623, 1877,
    1930, 1952, 1966, 2227, 2564,
    4742, 4743, 4771, 4777, 4826,
    4946, 4991, 5013, 5020, 5030,
    5080, 6123, 6157, 6166, 6235,
    6314, 6315, 6359, 6360, 6366,
    6430, 6431, 6434, 6615, 6689,
    6955, 7311, 7634, 7641, 7677,
    7679, 7814, 7993, 7996, 8172,
    8595, 8611, 9432, 11311, 11350,
    11351, 11352, 11445, 11886,
    12031, 12211, 12220, 12300,
    12301, 12314, 12452, 12543,
    12830, 12849, 12852, 12890,
    12978, 13306, 13307, 13409,
    13702, 13947, 14041, 15446,
    15559, 15591, 15609, 15612,
    15677, 15711, 15825, 15848,
    15849, 15879, 15830, 15997,
    16020, 16105, 16511, 16565,
    16726, 16786, 16904, 16922,
    17051, 17056, 17118, 17147,
    17174, 17196, 17266, 17360,
    17361, 17362, 17369, 17370,
    17375, 17383, 17387, 17399,
    17401, 17402, 17411, 17413,
    17420, 17509, 17625, 17628,
    17753, 17764, 17916, 18007,
    18010, 18011, 18013, 18015,
    18016, 18019, 18021, 18022,
    18023, 18024, 18026, 18027,
    18028, 18030, 18031, 18034,

18035, 18036, 18038, 18039,
18040, 18041, 18048, 18049,
18050, 18052, 18053, 18054,
18056, 18058, 18060, 18062,
18063, 18064, 18065, 18066,
18067, 18071, 18074, 18075,
18077, 18080, 18081, 18082,
18083, 18084, 18085, 18086,
18091, 18092, 18099, 18103,
18105, 18107, 18110, 18111,
18115, 18117, 18118, 18119,
18120, 18121, 18122, 18124,
18126, 18127, 18133, 18135,
18136, 18138, 18139, 18140,
18142, 18143, 18146, 18147,
18148, 18149, 18150, 18152,
18153, 18157, 18158, 18162,
18163, 18164, 18166, 18169,
18172, 18175, 18176, 18177,
18178, 18179, 18180, 18182,
18183, 18184, 18185, 18186,
18187, 18188, 18189, 18190,
18192, 18194, 18197, 18200,
18201, 18204, 18206, 18208,
18209, 18211, 18212, 18213,
18215, 18218, 18220, 18221,
18222, 18224, 18225, 18226,
18228, 18229, 18233, 18234,
18236, 18240, 18241, 18242,
18244, 18245, 18246, 18247,
18248, 18250, 18251, 18252,
18253, 18254, 18255, 18259,
18261, 18264, 18266, 18268,
18269, 18270, 18271, 18273,
18276, 18277, 18278, 18279,
18281, 18282, 18284, 18285,
18286, 18287, 18290, 18291,
18292, 18295, 18296, 18297,
18303, 18304, 18305, 18306,
18308, 18309, 18311, 18312,
18314, 18317, 18318, 18320,
18321, 18323, 18324, 18326,
18327, 18328, 18332, 18333,
18334, 18335, 18336, 18337,
18338, 18340, 18342, 18344,
18345, 18346, 18347, 18348,
18350, 18353, 18354, 18355,
18356, 18357, 18358, 18359,
18360, 18361, 18362, 18363,
18365, 18366, 18367, 18368,
18369, 18370, 18371, 18373,
18375, 18377, 18381, 18382,
18383, 18384, 18385, 18386,
18387, 18388, 18389, 18390,
18392, 18394, 18395, 18396,

18397, 18398, 18401, 18402,
18403, 18404, 18405, 18406,
18408, 18409, 18423, 18479,
18497, 18720, 18842, 18901,
19055, 19302, 19575, 19801,
19955, 20234, 20305

FOOD--SEE DIET

FORD, TIMOTHY   12839

FORREST, NATHAN B.   15113

FORT JACKSON MUTINY   20867

FORT PILLOW, TN   20667, 20683,
   20717, 20745, 20751, 20752,
   20899, 20917

FORTEN, CHARLOTTE   9665, 20701,
   20702

FORTEN, JAMES   9398

FORTUNE, AMOS   10379

FORTUNE, T. THOMAS   3219

FORTUNETELLER, SLAVE   18066

FORTY-THIRD REGIMENT, U.S. COLORED
   TROOPS   20990

FORWOOD, WILLIAM S.   2172

FOSTER, STEPHEN   2675, 3209

FOURTEENTH AMENDMENT   2286, 4444,
   8752

FOWLER, FRED (EX-SLAVE)   20221

FRANCE   2226, 2385, 2405, 4292,
   5152, 5846, 5847, 6950, 6994,
   6995, 18366

FRANCIS, NATHANIEL   13503

FRANKLIN & ARMFIELD COMPANY   15033

FRANKLIN COUNTY, VA   13486, 13552

FRANKLIN, BENJAMIN   3043, 3238,
   3301, 10739

FRANKLIN, ISAAC 15083, 15170

FRANKLIN, JOHN H. 1083, 1256,
1294, 1444, 2012

FRAZIER, E. FRANKLIN 991, 1167,
1202, 1949, 2322, 5131

FREDERICK DOUGLASS HOUSE 11240

FREDERICK, FRANCIS 11302

FREE BLACKS 156, 224, 250, 273,
300, 407, 560, 1093, 1217, 1343,
1717, 2148, 2382, 2393, 2535,
2745, 2753, 2804, 2849, 2959,
3093, 3096, 3881, 3981, 3987,
4144, 4357, 4391, 5090, 6280,
6318, 6335, 6415, 6575, 6645,
6731, 6768, 6792, 6802, 6825,
7000, 7065, 7113, 7114, 7217,
7245, 7375, 7555, 7756, 7760,
7766, 8015, 8116, 8259, 8304,
8456, 8530, 8636, 8893, 8929,
8943, 8986, 8987, 8998, 8999,
9123, 9159, 9167, 9170, 9186,
9213, 9217, 9290, 9364, 9365,
9366, 9367, 9368, 9369, 9370,
9371, 9372, 9374, 9375, 9376,
9377, 9378, 9380, 9381, 9382,
9385, 9387, 9388, 9389, 9390,
9394, 9396, 9398, 9399, 9402,
9403, 9404, 9405, 9407, 9408,
9409, 9410, 9411, 9412, 9413,
9415, 9416, 9420, 9421, 9422,
9423, 9424, 9425, 9426, 9427,
9428, 9429, 9431, 9432, 9433,
9434, 9435, 9436, 9437, 9438,
9439, 9440, 9441, 9443, 9444,
9445, 9446, 9448, 9449, 9450,
9451, 9453, 9454, 9455, 9456,
9457, 9459, 9460, 9463, 9464,
9465, 9466, 9467, 9469, 9470,
9472, 9474, 9475, 9476, 9477,
9478, 9479, 9480, 9481, 9482,
9483, 9484, 9485, 9486, 9487,
9488, 9489, 9491, 9492, 9493,
9494, 9496, 9497, 9498, 9499,
9500, 9501, 9502, 9503, 9504,
9505, 9506, 9507, 9508, 9509,
9510, 9511, 9512, 9513, 9514,
9515, 9516, 9517, 9518, 9519,
9520, 9522, 9523, 9525, 9526,
9527, 9528, 9531, 9532, 9533,
9535, 9536, 9537, 9538, 9540,
9543, 9544, 9546, 9549, 9550,
9551, 9552, 9553, 9555, 9556,
9557, 9558, 9562, 9564, 9565,
9568, 9569, 9570, 9571, 9572,
9573, 9574, 9575, 9576, 9577,
9579, 9580, 9581, 9582, 9583,
9584, 9586, 9590, 9591, 9592,
9593, 9594, 9595, 9601, 9603,
9604, 9605, 9606, 9609, 9610,
9611, 9615, 9617, 9620, 9621,
9623, 9624, 9625, 9626, 9627,
9631, 9633, 9635, 9636, 9637,
9638, 9640, 9641, 9643, 9644,
9646, 9648, 9649, 9650, 9651,
9652, 9653, 9654, 9656, 9657,
9658, 9659, 9661, 9662, 9665,
9669, 9670, 9671, 9672, 9673,
9675, 9676, 9677, 9678, 9679,
9680, 9682, 9685, 9686, 9688,
9689, 9690, 9691, 9692, 9693,
9694, 9696, 9698, 9699, 9700,
9701, 9702, 9703, 9704, 9705,
9706, 9707, 9710, 9711, 9712,
9713, 9714, 9715, 9716, 9717,
9718, 9719, 9720, 9722, 9723,
9724, 9727, 9729, 9730, 9731,
9732, 9735, 9736, 9737, 9738,
9739, 9740, 9741, 9742, 9743,
9744, 9745, 9746, 9747, 9748,
9749, 9750, 9753, 9754, 9755,
9759, 9760, 9761, 9762, 9763,
9764, 9765, 9766, 9767, 9769,
9771, 9772, 9773, 9775, 9776,
9777, 9778, 9779, 9780, 9781,
9782, 9783, 9784, 9788, 9789,
9790, 9791, 9792, 9793, 9794,
9796, 9797, 9799, 9800, 9801,
9802, 9803, 9804, 9806, 9808,
9809, 9810, 9812, 9813, 9815,
9818, 9819, 9820, 9821, 9823,
9824, 9825, 9826, 9827, 9828,
9831, 9832, 9833, 9834, 9836,
9837, 9838, 9839, 9840, 9842,
9844, 9845, 9846, 9847, 9848,
9849, 9850, 9851, 9852, 9856,
9858, 9859, 9862, 9863, 9864,
9865, 9866, 9868, 9869, 9870,
9871, 9874, 9875, 9876, 9877,
9879, 9880, 9881, 9882, 9883,
9885, 9886, 9888, 9889, 9891,
9892, 9895, 9896, 9899, 9900,
9904, 9909, 9912, 9913, 9914,
9915, 9916, 9917, 9918, 9920,
9921, 9922, 9923, 9924, 9926,
9927, 9928, 9929, 9930, 9931,

9932, 9933, 9934, 9935, 9937,
9938, 9939, 9942, 9943, 9944,
9945, 9946, 9947, 9948, 9949,
9950, 9952, 9953, 9954, 9955,
9956, 9957, 9958, 9959, 9960,
9961, 9962, 9963, 9993, 10089,
10199, 10319, 10331, 10334,
10352, 10353, 11180, 11257,
11369, 11416, 12526, 13136,
13138, 13263, 13264, 13345,
13449, 13864, 14408, 14894,
14926, 15041, 15138, 15283,
15354, 15916, 15949, 15950,
16136, 16170, 16316, 16328,
16565, 17238, 17386, 17468,
18882, 19196, 19469, 19827,
19842, 19932, 19998, 20022,
20026, 20285, 20631, 20782,
21124

FREE BLACKS, KIDNAPPING OF 9696,
9848, 15138

FREE TRADE 14267

FREE WILL 4395

FREEDMAN'S AID SOCIETIES 13076,
20841, 20907, 21030

FREEDMAN'S VILLAGE, VA 20912

FREEDMEN 2487, 2511, 2641, 3193,
3251, 8942, 9647, 9977, 10086,
10195, 12384, 12440, 12494,
12607, 12700, 13011, 13076,
13906, 14632, 14873, 15779,
15780, 16309, 19842, 20334,
20393, 20659, 20747, 20800,
20806, 20866, 20897, 20922,
20936, 20981, 21003, 21031,
21033, 21035, 21085, 21086,
21087, 21088, 21094, 21141

FREEDMEN'S BUREAU 144, 4100, 4266,
9729, 10195, 11725, 12826,
12827, 12862, 13011, 13076,
13209, 14873, 19162, 20657,
20665, 20685, 20691, 20697,
20725, 20729, 20747, 20781,
20807, 20811, 20815, 20840,
20841, 20842, 20907, 20918,
20947, 20948, 20949, 20964,
20965, 20966, 20967, 20975,
21013, 21014, 21015, 21016,

21020, 21022, 21023, 21024,
21036, 21040, 21041, 21058,
21066, 21123, 21137, 21145,
21146, 21147

FREEDOM'S JOURNAL 4035

FREEMASONRY 9551, 9704, 9716,
9923

FRENCH AND INDIAN WAR 8294

FRENCH ANTILLES 5617, 6168, 6357,
6488, 6674, 6676, 6677, 6764,
6918, 6950, 6995, 7000
(SEE ALSO CARIBBEAN, FRENCH)

FRENCH GUIANA 7317, 7625, 8031

FRENCH REVOLUTION 2452, 3851,
4430, 5850, 6305, 6484, 7000,
7165, 7166, 7167, 9290, 13120

FREUD, SIGMUND 1913

FREYRE, GILBERTO 1225, 1246, 1470,
1793, 2038, 2256, 8063, 8079

FRONTIER 9457

FROUDE, JAMES A. 912, 1902

FUGITIVE SLAVE LAW 3844, 3845,
8749, 8777, 8797, 8803, 8806,
8807, 8808, 8813, 8847, 8852,
8880, 8885, 8907, 8908, 8912,
8913, 8914, 8997, 9006, 9024,
9031, 9032, 9049, 9057, 9153,
9166, 9255, 9259, 9264, 9286,
9322, 9338, 9356, 19451, 19500,
19511, 19632, 19636, 19646,
19661, 19684, 19746, 19826

FUGITIVE SLAVES 4091, 4309, 8326,
8777, 8795, 8852, 8879, 8906,
8908, 8912, 8990, 9024, 9030,
9033, 9049, 9063, 9064, 9104,
9131, 9153, 9166, 9293, 9329,
9357, 9362, 10060, 10281, 10304,
11085, 11409, 11449, 11902,
12591, 14327, 14873, 16973,
18715, 18820, 18895, 19464,
19467, 19472, 19473, 19475,
19497, 19505, 19510, 19517,
19525, 19543, 19544, 19545,

19546, 19547, 19551, 19552,
19582, 19589, 19590, 19597,
19598, 19599, 19602, 19607,
19620, 19622, 19623, 19624,
19626, 19628, 19629, 19630,
19632, 19636, 19640, 19644,
19646, 19649, 19650, 19651,
19659, 19667, 19669, 19670,
19682, 19683, 19684, 19685,
19697, 19698, 19703, 19729,
19746, 19750, 19751, 19752,
19755, 19771, 19778, 19782,
19800, 19803, 19810, 19815,
19820, 19839, 19846, 19848,
19849, 19854, 19855, 19857,
20297, 20303, 20347, 20388,
21005

FUNERALS   12408, 15443, 17147,
17595, 18334, 18335, 18539

FUR TRADE   10845

FURNITURE   26, 6323, 8304, 14894
(SEE ALSO HOUSING, MATERIAL
CULTURE)

FYE, CUDJO   19918

GABRIEL'S REVOLT   5082, 6623,
13494, 13724, 13725, 13756,
17057, 19729, 19859, 19878,
19926, 19951, 19974, 20031

GAG RULE   4195

GALLATIN COUNTY, IL   10886

GALT, JAMES   13648

GALT, WILLIAM JR.   13648, 13649

GALVEZ, JOSE DE   6316

GAMA, LUIZ   7855

GAMBIA   3174

GANNETT, WILLIAM C.   13076, 21035

GARDEN, ALEXANDER   13143

GARNER FUGITIVE SLAVE CASE   9357

GARNET, HENRY H.   3165, 9670, 9671,
19662, 19688, 19731, 19748,
19749, 19767

GARRISON, LUCY M.   1017, 1795,
1796, 1797, 1798, 1799

GARRISON, WILLIAM L.   1990, 19449

GATRELL, LUCIUS J.   232

GENEALOGY   488, 592, 604, 10387,
16184, 16185, 16254, 16258,
16282
(SEE ALSO FAMILY, SLAVE)

GENETICS   2978, 5134

GENOVESE, EUGENE D.   651, 672, 739,
906, 939, 953, 961, 992, 1162,
1188, 1189, 1325, 1334, 1367,
1383, 1384, 1397, 1459, 1483,
1486, 1551, 1610, 1631, 1653,
1681, 1689, 1757, 1808, 1825,
1837, 1838, 1849, 1850, 1882,
1962, 2018, 2022, 11660, 16069,
18767

GEOGRAPHIC INFLUENCES ON SLAVERY
3980, 6862, 7297, 8421, 8546,
9963, 11042, 11043, 11722,
11802, 11803, 12079, 12427,
13393, 14186, 14382, 14387,
14399, 14529, 14923, 15522

GEORGETOWN COUNTY, SC   12997,
13064, 13071

GEORGETOWN, SC   12934, 13042,
13064, 13070

GEORGIA   122, 277, 435, 1253, 1750
2394, 2396, 2701, 8196, 8221,
8228, 8313, 8328, 8335, 8351,
8352, 8453, 8497, 8506, 8549,
8550, 8574, 8619, 8620, 8692,
8705, 8717, 8733, 8818, 8820,
8831, 8834, 8840, 8865, 8866,
9073, 9154, 9160, 9210, 9219,
9273, 9575, 10200, 11764, 11980
11982, 11983, 11984, 11986,
11988, 11989, 11990, 11991,
11992, 11993, 11994, 11996,
11997, 11998, 12000, 12003,
12006, 12007, 12008, 12009,

12010, 12013, 12016, 12017,
12019, 12020, 12023, 12024,
12025, 12027, 12028, 12029,
12031, 12033, 12037, 12038,
12039, 12040, 12041, 12042,
12044, 12045, 12046, 12047,
12048, 12049, 12050, 12051,
12052, 12054, 12055, 12056,
12057, 12058, 12059, 12060,
12061, 12063, 12065, 12066,
12067, 12068, 12069, 12070,
12071, 12072, 12075, 12076,
12077, 12078, 12079, 12080,
12083, 12084, 12085, 12087,
12088, 12089, 12090, 12091,
12092, 12093, 12094, 12095,
12097, 12098, 12099, 12100,
12101, 12103, 12104, 12105,
12108, 12110, 12112, 12113,
12114, 12116, 12118, 12119,
12120, 12121, 12123, 12125,
12128, 12129, 12130, 12132,
12133, 12134, 12135, 12136,
12137, 12138, 12139, 12140,
12141, 12144, 12145, 12146,
12147, 12150, 12152, 12154,
12155, 12157, 12158, 12159,
12160, 12161, 12163, 12164,
12165, 12166, 12167, 12168,
12169, 12170, 12172, 12174,
12175, 12176, 12178, 12179,
12180, 12181, 12182, 12186,
12187, 12189, 12191, 12192,
12196, 12198, 12202, 12204,
12205, 12206, 12207, 12208,
12209, 12210, 12211, 12786,
12961, 13046, 13108, 13128,
13129, 13998, 14120, 14690,
14727, 14831, 14851, 15006,
15179, 15243, 15485, 15510,
15604, 15842, 16317, 16742,
17134, 17504, 18024, 18222,
18365, 19012, 19017, 20463,
20483, 20507

GERMANS 13301

GERSTACKER, FRIEDRICH 4629, 4630

GHANA 4972, 5360, 5434

GHOLSON, THOMAS S. 20520

GIDEON WILL CASE 232

GLASGOW EMANCIPATION SOCIETY
2129

GLAZER, NATHAN 676

GLOUCESTER COUNTY, VA 8435, 9612

GLOUCESTER, NJ 10588

GLYNN COUNTY, GA 12139

GODFREY, GUSSA 16540

GODPARENTHOOD 6754

GOLD COAST 4757, 5053, 5062, 5128,
6013

GOLD MINING 12065, 12718, 14690

GOLDSBOROUGH, CHARLES 11447

GOMBAY 6207

GOOD HOPE PLANTATION 12933

GOYENS, WILLIAM 9776

GRAHAM, STEPHEN 12775

GRAHAM, WILLIAM 2782

GRAIN 13690

GRAMSCI, ANTONIO 1134, 16069

GRANITEVILLE COMPANY 13012

GRANT, HUGH F. 277, 12085

GRANT, RICHARD (SLAVE) 12811

GRAVEYARD DECORATIONS 15541,
17309
(SEE ALSO FUNERALS)

GRAY, LEWIS C. 1133, 1376, 1481,
1528

GRAY, SIMON 14768

GRAYSON, WILLIAM J. 4603

GREAT AWAKENING 4709, 13624,
17293

GREELEY, HORACE   4437

GREELEY, JULIA   16477

GREENE, LORENZO J.   1890

GREENER, RICHARD T.   1812

GREGG, WILLIAM   13012

GRENADA   6335, 6611, 7286

GRIMES, WILLIAM   20278

GRIMKE, ANGELINA   19149

GRIMKE, ARCHIBALD H.   1811

GRIMKE, FRANCIS J.   4628

GRIMKE, SARA   19149

GROCE, JARED E.   13302

GROG AND GROCERY SHOPS   2959,
   16316

GROTON, MA   10453, 10454

GROUP IDENTIFICATION, SLAVE   4246

GROVE, JUNE (EX-SLAVE)   10935

GROVE, WILLIAM H.   5990

GRUBER, REV. JACOB   19478

GUADELOUPE   6574, 6994

GUATEMALA   7770, 8051, 8075, 8165,
   14992

GUERILLA WAR   6743, 11542

GUERILLA WARFARE   19872

GUIGNARD FAMILY   2803, 12864

GUILFORD COUNTY, NC   12660, 12706

GUILT   3758, 16673

GUINEA COAST   4845, 5059, 5061,
   5064, 5066, 5231, 5491, 5792,
   5889, 5893

GULLAH   6292, 12999, 18166, 18390,
   18654, 19017, 19271, 19280,
   19304, 19340, 19360, 19380,
   19414, 19425, 19432, 19443,
   19445

GULLAH NEGROES   4681, 12885, 19017,
   19278, 19383

GUNNISON, WILLIAM   3198

GURNEY, JOSEPH J.   4199

GUTMAN, HERBERT G.   652, 701, 1098,
   1520, 1526, 1700, 1737, 1761,
   2043, 5131, 6983, 16148, 16269

GUYANA   1707, 5691, 6634, 7143,
   7173, 7233, 7414, 7607, 7608,
   7634, 7885, 8104, 19402, 20075
   (SEE ALSO BRITISH GUIANA)

HAITI   790, 1386, 1559, 2163, 2488,
   2680, 3908, 4581, 4701, 5041,
   5537, 5538, 5864, 6165, 6183,
   6246, 6248, 6256, 6320, 6332,
   6333, 6355, 6385, 6392, 6393,
   6406, 6416, 6417, 6423, 6529,
   6556, 6601, 6605, 6617, 6660,
   6670, 6674, 6747, 6750, 6751,
   6752, 6753, 6754, 6788, 6796,
   6800, 6822, 6830, 6851, 6865,
   6898, 6911, 6925, 6939, 6949,
   6968, 7021, 7047, 7048, 7068,
   7081, 7108, 7112, 7165, 7166,
   7167, 7176, 7218, 7244, 7612,
   9290, 15542, 15711, 17233,
   17346, 17813, 17979, 18011,
   18022, 18233, 18332, 19302,
   19409, 19880, 20037, 20330,
   20407

HAITIAN REVOLUTION   1783, 6169,
   6196, 6247, 6670, 6822, 6851

HALE COUNTY, AL   11757

HALEY, ALEX   636, 685, 942, 1026,
   1255, 1616, 1761, 1763, 1791,
   1844, 1968, 1995, 2792

HALL, EDWIN   13623

HALL, PRINCE   9923

HALL, SAMUEL   3490

HAMILTON, JEFF   7627, 13399

HAMILTON, THOMAS   11990

HAMMON, BRITON   18870

HAMMON, JUPITER   16529, 17103,
   18733

HAMMOND, JAMES H.   3525, 4000,
   4468, 4495, 12986, 13030, 13124

HAMPTON FOLK-LORE SOCIETY   18026

HAMPTON INSTITUTE   3832, 17505,
   17603

HAMPTON, VA   13607

HANAWAY, CASPAR   19500

HANNON, HENRY (EX-SLAVE)   11514

HAPPY, JESSE   19640, 19779

HARDEE, CHARLES S.H.   17682

HARDIN, WILLIAM J.   9394

HARMON, GARLAND D.   14860

HARRIS, JOEL C.   717, 775, 1049,
   1050, 1238, 1472, 1545, 1598,
   1623, 1914, 1915, 1930, 1966,
   9387, 17511, 18241, 18264,
   18371

HARRISON COUNTY, TX   98, 13314,
   13316, 13318

HARRISON, RICHARD   9971

HART, ALBERT B.   535, 695

HARVEST CUSTOMS   13703

HATCHER, JORDAN   13610

HAUSALAND   4881

HAVILAND, LAURA S.   11316

HAWAII   2911, 2912, 9769

HAWKINS, JOHN   5214, 5831, 6043

HAWTHORNE, NATHANIEL   2582

HAYDEN, LEWIS   19736

HAYNE, ROBERT Y.   12975

HAYNES, LEMUEL   9710

HEALTH--SEE MEDICINE

HEIGHT   6634, 14220, 14938, 15035

HELPER, HINTON R.   2087, 2576,
   3075, 4140, 4603, 4617

HELYAR, CARY   6186

HEMINGS, SALLY   1451, 1478, 16392

HEMINGS, MADISON   1451

HEMP   8415, 8416, 11281, 11321,
   11322, 11353, 11567, 14296

HENDERSON, F.H.   3387

HENRY, HOWELL M.   535, 1817, 20138

HENRY, JOHN   17387, 18148

HENSON, JOSIAH   1608, 3660, 3705,
   3933, 4117, 4506, 11358, 11431,
   18858, 18895, 18896, 18897,
   18931, 19496

HERBERT, HILARY A.   15328

HERDER, JOHANN G.   2341

HERNDON, WILLIAM H.   7976

HERO, NEGRO   13006

HERSKOVITS, MELVILLE J.   396, 764,
   944, 1492, 1496, 1497, 1514,
   1578, 1780, 1876, 5131

HESTER, MOSES   12699

HIBBERT, GEORGE   6477

HURSTON, ZORA N.   792, 793, 1435

IBO   4885, 5121

IDAHO   11056

IGBO   4891, 5000

ILA   5113, 5114, 5115

ILE A VACHE   2093, 2162, 2872

ILLINOIS   1047, 2124, 8763, 8862,
   8893, 8929, 9151, 9158, 9200,
   9211, 9302, 9536, 10290, 10839,
   10855, 10856, 10857, 10858,
   10859, 10861, 10862, 10863,
   10864, 10865, 10866, 10867,
   10872, 10873, 10874, 10875,
   10876, 10877, 10878, 10879,
   10880, 10881, 10882, 10883,
   10884, 10886, 10887, 10888,
   10889, 10891, 10894, 10895,
   10897, 10898, 10899, 10901,
   10987, 11025

IMMUNITIES   2549

IMPERIALISM   3864, 7100

IMPRESSMENT   13511, 13517, 15226,
   16064, 20447, 20537, 20555,
   20627, 20643, 20655

INCENTIVES, SLAVE   12449, 14220,
   15010

INCOME REDISTRIBUTION   14066

INDEMNITIES, SLAVE   8754

INDIAN TERRITORY   11124, 13943,
   13948, 14033

INDIANA   2124, 9158, 10865, 10902,
   10903, 10904, 10905, 10906,
   10908, 10909, 10910, 10911,
   10912, 10913, 10914, 10915,
   10916, 10919, 10920, 10921,
   10922, 10923, 10924, 10987,
   19663

INDIANA COUNTY, PA   19505

INDIANS   310, 462, 1495, 1771,
   2138, 2625, 2626, 2670, 3777,
   3916, 3928, 3929, 3930, 6391,
   7798, 8223, 8239, 8495, 8496,
   8507, 8596, 11121, 11122, 11123,
   11124, 11125, 11126, 11129,
   11133, 11135, 11410, 11596,
   11870, 11881, 11933, 12116,
   12160, 12771, 13160, 13902,
   13903, 13905, 13906, 13907,
   13908, 13909, 13910, 13911,
   13912, 13913, 13914, 13915,
   13916, 13917, 13918, 13919,
   13921, 13922, 13924, 13925,
   13926, 13927, 13928, 13929,
   13930, 13931, 13932, 13933,
   13935, 13936, 13937, 13938,
   13939, 13940, 13941, 13942,
   13943, 13945, 13946, 13947,
   13948, 13949, 13950, 13951,
   13952, 13953, 13955, 13956,
   13957, 13959, 13960, 13961,
   13962, 13963, 13966, 13967,
   13969, 13970, 13971, 13972,
   13973, 13974, 13976, 13977,
   13978, 13979, 13980, 13981,
   13982, 13985, 13986, 13987,
   13988, 13989, 13996, 13998,
   13999, 14000, 14001, 14002,
   14006, 14007, 14008, 14010,
   14012, 14013, 14014, 14015,
   14016, 14017, 14018, 14019,
   14020, 14021, 14023, 14024,
   14025, 14026, 14029, 14031,
   14032, 14033, 14034, 14035,
   14037, 14039, 14040, 14041,
   14042, 14043, 14044, 14045,
   14046, 14048, 14051, 14052,
   14054, 14056, 14057, 14058,
   14059, 14061

INDIGO   8645, 11899, 12020, 12269,
   12883, 14298, 14301, 15691,
   19224

INDIGO NEGROES   15691

INDUSTRIAL REVOLUTION   11450,
   14281, 14336, 14468

INDUSTRIAL SLAVERY   395, 1647,
   2959, 7946, 8085, 8440, 8633,
   8663, 8670, 9217, 9856, 11283,
   11353, 11450, 11473, 11474,
   11476, 11497, 11516, 11517,

11528, 11576, 11718, 11753,
11792, 11793, 12038, 12065,
12096, 12249, 12469, 12718,
12773, 12790, 13012, 13517,
13567, 13594, 13595, 13656,
13704, 13708, 13793, 13811,
13850, 14243, 14375, 14376,
14491, 14658, 14659, 14660,
14683, 14690, 14693, 14694,
14695, 14696, 14702, 14704,
14707, 14717, 14720, 14722,
14723, 14725, 14726, 14727,
14728, 14729, 14733, 14736,
14747, 14751, 14752, 14753,
14756, 14759, 14762, 14767,
14769, 14771, 14772, 14774,
14775, 14776, 14777, 14781,
14785, 14788, 14789, 14796,
14797, 14798, 14800, 14803,
14805, 14806, 14809, 14812,
14813, 14815, 14816, 14819,
14822, 14823, 14826, 14828,
15949, 16316, 18667, 18668,
18682, 19790, 20652

INFANTICIDE 20292

INPUT SUBSTITUTABILITY 14570

INSANITY 15736, 15772, 15773
  (SEE ALSO MENTAL HEALTH)

INSURANCE, SLAVE 13822, 14130,
  14242, 15662

INTEGRATION 2649

INTERNAL MARKETING, SLAVES' ROLE IN
  6882

INTERVIEWS, SLAVE 64, 94, 142,
  162, 204, 365, 467, 468, 469,
  621, 623, 694, 751, 1018, 1019,
  1021, 1125, 1285, 1286, 1411,
  1822, 2055, 5563, 7060, 10106,
  11297, 11314, 11455, 12056,
  12103, 12104, 12294, 13215,
  13446, 13899, 14056, 14854,
  14855, 14865, 15140, 15221,
  15238, 15420, 16010, 16565,
  17325, 17662, 18041, 18149,
  18729, 18926, 19038, 19040,
  19043, 19047, 19049, 19050,
  19051, 19053, 19054, 19055,
  19067, 19069, 19076, 19078,

19079, 19080, 19084, 19088,
19091, 19092, 19093, 19094,
19095, 19096, 19102, 19103,
19104, 19105, 19106, 19107,
19108, 19110, 19111, 19112,
19116, 19117, 19119, 19122,
19123, 19125, 19126, 19129,
19130, 19132, 19138

INVENTIONS 4634, 14656, 14657

IOWA 2124, 8746, 10926, 10928,
  10929, 10930, 10931, 10933,
  10934, 19746

IRON COLLAR 20125

IRONWORKERS 8443, 8633, 11283,
  11473, 11474, 11476, 11517,
  11528, 11557, 11576, 12249,
  12537, 12676, 12790, 13136,
  13509, 13533, 13534, 13535,
  13544, 13567, 13594, 13656,
  13708, 14677, 14679, 14680,
  14694, 14695, 14696, 14709,
  14734, 14743, 14751, 14752,
  14756, 14783, 14812, 14822,
  14823, 15528, 18575, 18583,
  18612, 19842

ISAAC (SLAVE) 12675, 13711, 13712

ISLAM 4669, 4824, 4903, 4948,
  5075, 5111, 5112, 14831

JACKSON COUNTY, IL 9617

JACKSON COUNTY, MO 11549, 11561

JACKSON, ANDREW 1254, 13198,
  13278

JACKSON, HARRY 9369

JACKSONVILLE, FL 11369, 11939

JAILS 15157

JALAPA, MEXICO 14910

JAMAICA 146, 289, 290, 359, 471,
  484, 761, 767, 867, 868, 1290,
  1475, 1684, 2361, 2557, 2849,
  4425, 4799, 4882, 5076, 5276,
  5359, 5494, 5631, 5644, 5797,

JOHNSON, GUY B.   19271

JOHNSON, THOMAS S.   20919

JOHNSON, WILLIAM   273, 9454, 9455,
9456, 9932

JOHNSTON, HARRY H.   104, 813, 1724

JOHNSTON, JOSHUA   9635, 18640

JONAS, BENJAMIN   4294

JONES, CHARLES C.   3111, 3942,
15604, 16673, 16988, 17007,
17298, 18273, 20738

JONES, EDWARD   9444

JONES, GEORGE N.   437

JONES, JEHU   9869

JONES, JOHN   9540

JONES, JOSEPH   15604

JONES, THOMAS H.   18916

JORDAN, EDWARD   9429

JORDAN, WINTHROP D.   702, 1290,
1627, 1629, 1630

JOSEPHITES   16943

JOURNAL OF NEGRO HISTORY   632,
1169

JOYNER, PRISCILLA   16220

JUBILEE SINGERS   17795

JULIAN, GEORGE   3677

JUNETEENTH   19832

JUNKERS   3148

JUNO, MAUMER   4300

KAMMBA   7957

KANAWHA VALLEY   13802

KANSAS   2124, 4527, 10936, 10937,
10938, 10939, 10940, 10941,
10943, 10944, 10945, 10946,
10948, 10949, 11035, 19746,
20750, 20770

KANSAS-NEBRASKA ACT   3718, 10851,
13396

KECKLEY, ELIZABETH   18918

KELLAR, HERBERT A.   536

KELLOGG, EBENEZER   12119

KEMBLE, FRANCES A.   721, 959, 968,
1436, 1750, 1751, 12202

KENDRICKS, FRANCIS P.   3173

KENNEDY, JOHN P.   2791

KENTUCKY   2067, 2116, 8979, 9933,
10191, 11171, 11259, 11262,
11264, 11265, 11266, 11267,
11268, 11269, 11270, 11271,
11272, 11273, 11274, 11275,
11276, 11278, 11280, 11281,
11283, 11284, 11285, 11286,
11288, 11289, 11290, 11291,
11292, 11293, 11294, 11295,
11296, 11297, 11299, 11300,
11301, 11302, 11304, 11305,
11306, 11307, 11308, 11309,
11310, 11311, 11312, 11313,
11314, 11315, 11316, 11317,
11318, 11319, 11320, 11321,
11322, 11323, 11324, 11325,
11326, 11327, 11329, 11331,
11332, 11333, 11334, 11335,
11336, 11337, 11338, 11339,
11340, 11342, 11343, 11344,
11345, 11346, 11347, 11348,
11349, 11350, 11351, 11352,
11353, 11354, 11358, 11359,
11360, 11361, 11363, 11364,
11365, 11367, 11368, 11369,
11370, 11372, 11373, 11374,
11375, 11377, 11378, 11379,
11380, 11382, 11383, 11384,
11385, 11386, 11387, 11388,
11389, 11390, 11391, 11392,
11393, 11395, 11396, 11397,
14638, 15041, 15858, 16706,
17084, 17244, 18941, 18995,

20343, 20776, 20905, 21006, 21007

KENTUCKY NEGRO LAW (1833) 11365

KENYA COAST 4737

KEY, FERNANDO 8286

KIMBER, EDWARD 11434

KING, E.T. 12236

KING, RUFUS 10423

KING, WILLIAM 1608, 3660, 3806, 10315

KINGSLEY SLAVE CABINS 15482

KINGSLEY, ZEPHANIA 11960, 15133

KINSHIP NETWORKS 6959, 8173, 12933, 16173, 16179 (SEE ALSO FAMILY, SLAVE)

KLEIN, HERBERT S. 1177, 1509

KLINGBERG, FRANK 1078

KNIBB, WILLIAM 7142

KNIGHT, FRANKLIN W. 1213, 1509

KNOW NOTHINGS 2108

KNOX, GEORGE L. 13208

KNOX COUNTY, INDIANA TERRITORY 10902, 10913

KNOX, WILLIAM 17306

KOLCHIN, PETER 1466

KUMINA 6238

KURTZ, BENJAMIN 4387

LA VIGERIE, CARDINAL 5303

LABOR 3699, 3944, 3945, 6874, 6884, 6890, 8277, 9730, 14071, 14796

LABOR UTILIZATION, SLAVE 3442, 5208, 8206, 13317, 14068, 14069, 14578

LACTATION PRACTICES 6719

LAFAYETTE COUNTY, MO 11179

LAFAYETTE PARISH, LA 12225

LAFAYETTE, MARQUIS DE 3849, 3370

LAFFAN, SIR JOSEPH DE COUREY 3268

LAFITTE, JEAN 11533

LAFITTE, PIERRE 11533

LAMAR, C.A.L. 5272, 5964, 6083

LANCASHIRE 5923

LANCASHIRE BILL SYSTEM 5175

LANCASTER COUNTY, PA 8686, 10717, 10731, 10778

LAND FERTILITY 14118

LAND POLICIES, COLONIAL 3085, 11984, 12823, 14082, 14084, 14400, 14401

LAND WASTE 14566

LANDON, FRED 29, 684

LANE, ISAAC L. 13174

LANE, LUNSFORD 12778

LANGSTON, JOHN M. 3253, 18922

LANGUAGE 81, 118, 327, 376, 493, 894, 919, 944, 1731, 3516, 4664, 4701, 4718, 4841, 4946, 6290, 6291, 6292, 6293, 6294, 6474, 7007, 7261, 10237, 10238, 11299, 11410, 12999, 13108, 13126, 15839, 16105, 17043, 17440, 18132, 18158, 18203, 18212, 18241, 18244, 18311, 18835, 18837, 19017, 19045, 19261, 19262, 19263, 19265, 19267,

LIBERIA   174, 512, 547, 606, 2334,
   2749, 2835, 2846, 3202, 3989,
   4019, 4261, 4267, 4320, 4321,
   4322, 4478, 4883, 5962, 9513,
   9760, 9849, 10104, 10153, 11285,
   11514, 12154, 12456, 12519,
   13737, 18716, 18728

LIEBER, FRANCIS   3595, 4146

LIELE, GEORGE   16655, 16742, 16839,
   16890

LIFE SPAN   15039, 15771

LIMA   7375, 7596

LIMERICK (SLAVE)   16130

LIMESTONE COUNTY, TX   13324

LINCOLN, ABRAHAM   377, 1547, 1811,
   2061, 2109, 2112, 2119, 2122,
   2151, 2162, 2208, 2292, 2312,
   2339, 2344, 2363, 2444, 2498,
   2563, 2644, 2674, 2713, 2735,
   2741, 2814, 2818, 2842, 2872,
   2977, 3018, 3066, 3082, 3164,
   3225, 3272, 3433, 3616, 3725,
   3747, 3868, 3986, 4043, 4091,
   4159, 4192, 4201, 4277, 4513,
   4515, 4518, 5917, 8815, 8884,
   9060, 9069, 9211, 9323, 9365,
   9967, 9982, 9985, 10014, 10017,
   10021, 10025, 10028, 10037,
   10050, 10078, 10122, 10127,
   10133, 10146, 10190, 10197,
   10221, 10897, 10899, 11022,
   11391, 12369, 19465, 20391,
   20431, 20436, 20441, 20444,
   20724, 20730, 20881, 20898,
   20903, 20913, 20914, 20972,
   21007, 21042, 21046, 21158

LINCOLN, LEVI   8787, 9034

LINGUISTICS   6133, 17043, 17440
   (SEE ALSO LANGUAGE)

LIQUOR   15453, 19179

LISBON   6062

LITERATURE, SLAVERY IN   25, 41, 93,
   298, 344, 491, 541, 578, 580,

612, 696, 711, 758, 794, 835,
917, 936, 949, 954, 1050, 1079
1159, 1207, 1218, 1232, 1252,
1262, 1287, 1357, 1373, 1395,
1487, 1529, 1539, 1543, 1570,
1571, 1574, 1642, 1667, 1676,
1695, 1883, 1887, 1898, 1916,
1957, 1971, 2001, 2002, 2004,
2005, 2041, 2063, 2075, 2128,
2136, 2170, 2187, 2188, 2190,
2199, 2214, 2237, 2247, 2257,
2277, 2369, 2398, 2426, 2427,
2443, 2488, 2489, 2501, 2502,
2503, 2514, 2523, 2554, 2562,
2582, 2584, 2586, 2620, 2639,
2650, 2681, 2719, 2724, 2727,
2769, 2784, 2792, 2815, 2822,
2845, 2862, 2876, 2881, 2882,
2928, 2929, 2930, 2952, 2958,
2968, 3013, 3015, 3016, 3019,
3031, 3067, 3188, 3224, 3240,
3364, 3368, 3386, 3412, 3466,
3472, 3558, 3580, 3581, 3601,
3611, 3612, 3623, 3641, 3650,
3686, 3700, 3758, 3768, 3804,
3839, 3840, 3975, 4007, 4051,
4072, 4080, 4131, 4150, 4193,
4241, 4254, 4258, 4292, 4310,
4374, 4377, 4380, 4394, 4425,
4428, 4439, 4469, 4471, 4472,
4480, 4507, 4531, 4573, 4594,
4607, 4643, 4644, 4722, 4760,
4966, 4981, 5238, 5591, 5625,
6220, 6508, 7147, 7641, 7704,
7706, 7708, 7886, 7966, 8029,
8394, 9378, 9423, 9474, 10030,
11625, 15905, 16404, 16426,
16523, 16614, 17417, 17606,
18013, 18016, 18200, 18211,
18324, 18338, 18366, 18378,
18409, 18842, 18843, 18877,
18930, 18997, 18998, 19000,
19001, 19008, 19037, 19375,
19376, 19380, 19388, 19431,
19432, 20116, 20175, 20217

LITTLE ROCK   16089

LIVERPOOL   501, 5175, 5289, 5568,
   5596, 5654, 5738, 5832, 5870,
   5871, 5882, 5916, 5923, 5998,
   6037, 6095, 6513

LIVESTOCK   14241, 14243

1612

LOG HOUSES 15502, 15550, 15552
  (SEE ALSO HOUSING)

LOGAN, GREENBURY 19998

LONDON 5855

LONG ISLAND 10646

LONG, ALEXANDER 8946

LONGVILLE PLANTATION 6342

LOPEZ, AARON 5223, 5823, 5825

LOTTERY 20053

LOUISIANA 131, 132, 446, 1307,
  1458, 1896, 2343, 2630, 2631,
  2683, 2759, 2765, 5517, 5518,
  5650, 6008, 6945, 8348, 8473,
  8530, 8545, 8689, 8793, 8826,
  8837, 8844, 8846, 8943, 9018,
  9020, 9066, 9145, 9156, 9172,
  9277, 9299, 9337, 9410, 9432,
  9448, 9464, 9472, 9590, 9699,
  9700, 9701, 9731, 9794, 9799,
  9832, 9856, 9946, 9948, 9987,
  10007, 10020, 10044, 10049,
  10074, 11671, 11676, 11899,
  11900, 12213, 12215, 12216,
  12217, 12218, 12219, 12220,
  12223, 12224, 12225, 12228,
  12229, 12230, 12232, 12234,
  12235, 12236, 12240, 12241,
  12242, 12243, 12244, 12248,
  12249, 12250, 12251, 12252,
  12253, 12254, 12258, 12259,
  12260, 12262, 12265, 12268,
  12269, 12272, 12273, 12274,
  12275, 12276, 12277, 12278,
  12280, 12283, 12286, 12289,
  12290, 12292, 12293, 12294,
  12295, 12297, 12298, 12300,
  12301, 12302, 12304, 12305,
  12306, 12307, 12308, 12309,
  12310, 12312, 12316, 12317,
  12318, 12320, 12324, 12325,
  12326, 12327, 12332, 12334,
  12336, 12337, 12338, 12339,
  12340, 12341, 12342, 12343,
  12345, 12346, 12348, 12353,
  12355, 12356, 12357, 12358,
  12359, 12361, 12362, 12363,
  12365, 12368, 12369, 12372,

  12373, 12379, 12380, 12382,
  12383, 12384, 12385, 12387,
  12388, 12391, 12392, 12393,
  12394, 12395, 12396, 12398,
  12399, 12400, 12401, 12404,
  12405, 12408, 12411, 12413,
  12414, 12415, 12416, 12417,
  12418, 12420, 12421, 12422,
  12427, 12428, 12429, 12430,
  12432, 12433, 12434, 12435,
  12436, 12437, 12439, 12440,
  12441, 12442, 12443, 12446,
  12448, 12449, 12450, 12451,
  12452, 12453, 12454, 12456,
  12458, 12459, 12460, 12461,
  12462, 12464, 12465, 12466,
  12467, 12468, 12469, 12470,
  12471, 12473, 12475, 12476,
  12477, 12478, 12479, 12481,
  12483, 12484, 12485, 12487,
  12489, 12490, 12491, 12492,
  12493, 12494, 12497, 12499,
  12500, 12502, 12506, 12507,
  12508, 12510, 12511, 12513,
  12516, 12517, 13148, 13149,
  14168, 14649, 15006, 15191,
  15731, 15870, 15882, 15895,
  15925, 15961, 15972, 15982,
  15985, 16272, 16869, 17031,
  17520, 17563, 18212, 18250,
  19286, 19582, 20458, 20514,
  20582, 20598, 20600, 20617,
  20631, 20649, 20866, 20889,
  20972

LOUISIANA NATIVE GUARDS 9701,
  20813

LOUISIANA TERRITORY 2124, 5650,
  5731, 8545, 8783, 10832, 10835,
  10845, 11915, 12238, 12279,
  12282, 12358, 12360, 12442,
  12472

LOUISIANA, FRENCH 8545, 12442,
  17031

LOUISIANA, SPANISH 2651, 8545,
  9590, 9948, 12345, 12442, 15985

LOUISVILLE 9933, 11349, 11393,
  15945, 17084, 20983

LOUVERTURE, TOUSSAINT 341, 353,
  1386, 6183, 6355, 6598, 6601,

6660, 6670, 6675, 6682, 6747,
6898, 7068, 7218, 7244, 19861,
19972, 19984, 19993, 20037,
20081, 20206

LOVE, NAT 18936

LOVEJOY, ELIJAH P. 3398

LOWENTHAL, DAVID 824

LOYALISTS 8296, 8310, 8311, 8312,
8323, 8431, 8549, 8586, 8592,
8608, 8651, 8732

LOYALTY, SLAVE 3150, 8697, 10317

LUMBER 11714, 11882, 12044, 12911,
14182, 14706, 14707, 14733,
14766, 14768, 14791

LUMPKIN, JOSEPH H. 12182

LUTHERAN CHURCH 4387, 9869, 16638,
16796, 16797, 16865, 17078,
17223, 17240, 17241, 17287,
17331

LYELL, CHARLES 11777

LYNCH, JOHN R. 18875

LYNCHBURG, VA 13749

LYND, STAUGHTON .1150

LYONS-SEWARD TREATY, 1862 5748

MADAGASCAR 5824

MADISON, JAMES 304

MAGRUDER, THOMAS 4117

MAINE 10419

MALARIA 12868, 15602, 15647,
15739, 15786
(SEE ALSO MEDICINE)

MALTHUS, THOMAS 14490, 14554

MALVIN, JOHN 9754

MAMMIES 13564, 16020, 16394,
16407, 16465, 16474, 16480,
16481, 16487, 16497, 16517,
16520, 17640
(SEE ALSO WOMEN, SLAVE)

MANDLE, JAY R. 1513

MAMMY SALLY (SLAVE) 15328

MANIGAULT, CHARLES 12872

MANIGAULT, LOUIS 12084

MANILLAS 5812

MANLY, BASIL 4605

MANN, HORACE 19153

MANSFIELD, LORD 8888, 9331

MANUMISSION 7710, 7729, 7739,
8038, 8045, 8587, 8981, 9014,
9059, 9837, 9936, 9991, 9992,
10063, 10074, 10091, 10094,
10105, 10116, 10162, 10555,
10714, 10715, 12792, 13722,
16130, 16309
(SEE ALSO EMANCIPATION)

MANZANO, JUAN F. 18905

MARAMEC IRON WORKS 11576
(SEE ALSO IRONWORKERS)

MARANHAO 7809

MARIMBULA 17869

MARLBOROUGH, NY 10711

MAROONS 458, 1648, 6192, 6200,
6216, 6241, 6259, 6261, 6281,
6282, 6321, 6378, 6408, 6409,
6478, 6585, 6592, 6593, 6623,
6687, 6688, 6740, 6741, 6742,
6743, 6744, 6746, 6822, 6823,
6960, 6987, 7037, 7067, 7082,
7171, 7188, 7194, 7254, 7279,
7295, 7498, 7612, 7625, 7628,
7629, 7724, 7785, 7786, 7951,
8130, 8342, 10251, 10270, 1031
10481, 11917, 18675, 18677,
18678, 19454, 19457, 19489,

19674, 19679, 19901, 20053,
20122, 20248, 20262, 20271
(SEE ALSO BUSH NEGROES)

MARQUESES DEL VALLE, MEXICO   7334

MARRIAGE RITUALS   16173, 17147

MARRIAGES   203, 1465, 1679, 2613,
   7123, 7799, 8781, 9052, 9432,
   10468, 10492, 10724, 11842,
   14844, 14992, 16173, 16203,
   16289, 16292, 16306, 16542,
   16546, 16556, 16557, 16565,
   16567, 16570, 16571, 16572,
   16576, 16577, 17147, 19243,
   19842

MARS, ELIJAH P.   18941

MARS, JAMES   10396

MARSHALL, JOHN   9144, 9187

MARSHALL, LEVIN R.   15729

MARSHALL, MARTIN   11737, 11738

MARSTON, HENRY   12422

MARTIN, BISHOP   12245

MARTIN, SAMUEL   7097

MARTINEAU, HARRIET   4564

MARTINIQUE   6474, 6603, 6994, 7209,
   7235, 16239, 20026

MARTINSBURG GAZETTE   13740

MARX, KARL   1913, 4437

MARXISM   739, 1009, 1055, 1056,
   1127, 1131

MARYLAND   100, 239, 363, 969, 6597,
   8195, 8238, 8245, 8322, 8325,
   8370, 8379, 8391, 8424, 8445,
   8454, 8460, 8461, 8472, 8487,
   8489, 8490, 8493, 8494, 8521,
   8541, 8543, 8544, 8565, 8607,
   8633, 8644, 8658, 8698, 9068,
   9096, 9438, 9871, 9971, 9992,
   10002, 10033, 11402, 11404,

11405, 11406, 11407, 11408,
11409, 11411, 11413, 11414,
11416, 11418, 11421, 11422,
11424, 11425, 11426, 11427,
11429, 11430, 11431, 11432,
11433, 11434, 11437, 11439,
11440, 11441, 11443, 11446,
11447, 11449, 11450, 11451,
11454, 11455, 11460, 11461,
11462, 11465, 11468, 11473,
11474, 11476, 11430, 11481,
11482, 11483, 11484, 11485,
11486, 11492, 11496, 11497,
11502, 11505, 11506, 11507,
11510, 11511, 11512, 11513,
11514, 11516, 11517, 11518,
11519, 11520, 11521, 11523,
11526, 11527, 11528, 11529,
13046, 13708, 14751, 15007,
15283, 16685, 16957, 18972,
19181, 19725, 20797, 20837,
20905, 20948, 21134

MASON, ISAAC   13945

MASONRY   9637, 14484

MASSACHUSETTS   582, 1801, 4773,
   5374, 5375, 5618, 8523, 8688,
   9045, 9056, 9139, 9964, 10405,
   10420, 10421, 10423, 10426,
   10427, 10429, 10431, 10434,
   10435, 10436, 10437, 10438,
   10439, 10440, 10441, 10442,
   10445, 10447, 10448, 10449,
   10450, 10451, 10452, 10453,
   10454, 10455, 10456, 10457,
   10459, 10463, 10464, 10465,
   10466, 10467, 10468, 10469,
   10470, 10471, 10472, 10473,
   10474, 10476, 10477, 10478,
   10479, 10480, 10481, 10482,
   10484, 10485, 10486, 10487,
   10488, 10490, 10491, 10492,
   10494, 10495, 10496, 10497,
   10498, 10499, 10500, 10502,
   10504, 10505, 10506, 10507,
   10509, 10510, 10615, 15893,
   17468

MAT (SLAVE)   11653

MATAGORDA COUNTY, TX   13424

MATAWAI MAROONS   20248

MATERIAL CULTURE   26, 357, 499,
   2699, 4773, 4815, 5106, 6323,
   6836, 6837, 6838, 6839, 7033,
   8304, 8469, 8590, 10424, 10425,
   10447, 11240, 11485, 12136,
   12137, 12138, 12140, 12175,
   12176, 12899, 12900, 14816,
   14826, 15482, 15512, 15541,
   15542, 15552, 15806, 16400,
   17496, 18484, 18485, 18496,
   18507, 18520, 18522, 18523,
   18524, 18525, 18526, 18528,
   18530, 18536, 18537, 18539,
   18562, 18563, 18564, 18568,
   18583, 18586, 18590
   (SEE ALSO CRAFTSMEN, FURNITURE,
   POTTERY)

MATHER, COTTON   8500, 10345

MATHEWS, EDWARD   10996

MATSON SLAVE CASE   9060, 9069,
   9323

MATSON, ROBERT   9060

MAURITIUS   4708, 4803, 5601

MAZZEI, PHILIP   8525

MCCRAY, MARY F. (SLAVE)   3974

MCDONOGH, JOHN   12218, 12248,
   12340, 12404

MCELROY, JOHN   12204

MCLENNAN COUNTY, TX   13347

MCPHERSON, CHRISTOPHER   9386

MCPHERSON, JAMES M.   902

MEACHAM, JAMES   16932

MEACHUM, JOHN B.   9941

MEDFORD, MA   10437, 10484

MEDICINE   426, 1366, 2285, 2306,
   2436, 2548, 2549, 2904, 2978,
   2980, 4707, 4854, 4856, 4932,

4946, 5088, 5146, 5188, 5291,
5342, 5343, 5348, 5367, 5536,
5562, 5781, 5783, 5924, 5927,
6048, 6049, 6339, 6505, 6539,
6544, 6634, 6710, 6719, 6998,
7517, 7691, 8606, 8635, 9159,
9647, 10109, 11359, 11367,
11737, 11738, 11830, 11990,
12222, 12232, 12285, 12286,
12398, 12867, 13076, 13149,
13150, 13212, 13584, 14242,
14844, 14894, 14901, 14967,
15010, 15015, 15147, 15206,
15224, 15233, 15341, 15362,
15392, 15405, 15413, 15528,
15583, 15584, 15585, 15586,
15592, 15593, 15594, 15595,
15596, 15599, 15601, 15602,
15603, 15604, 15605, 15606,
15608, 15609, 15612, 15613,
15614, 15615, 15616, 15620,
15623, 15626, 15627, 15628,
15635, 15636, 15639, 15640,
15641, 15642, 15643, 15646,
15647, 15648, 15649, 15650,
15652, 15653, 15654, 15655,
15664, 15666, 15671, 15673,
15676, 15677, 15680, 15682,
15683, 15686, 15691, 15692,
15695, 15698, 15700, 15701,
15702, 15704, 15711, 15712,
15713, 15715, 15716, 15719,
15720, 15723, 15724, 15726,
15727, 15728, 15729, 15730,
15731, 15732, 15733, 15734,
15736, 15737, 15739, 15742,
15743, 15745, 15747, 15749,
15752, 15754, 15761, 15762,
15763, 15764, 15766, 15768,
15769, 15770, 15771, 15772,
15773, 15774, 15775, 15776,
15779, 15780, 15781, 15783,
15786, 15787, 15789, 15791,
15794, 15795, 15797, 15800,
15802, 15803, 15804, 15805,
15806, 15809, 15810, 15812,
15813, 15817, 15818, 15819,
15820, 15821, 15822, 15825,
15826, 15827, 15828, 15829,
15830, 15831, 15836, 15837,
15838, 15839, 15840, 15841,
16225, 16565, 17084, 17110,
17238, 19677, 19790, 20304,
20966, 20967
(SEE ALSO SUDDEN INFANT DEATH

SYNDROME, TREPONEMATOSIS,
TUBERCULOSIS)

MELVILLE, HERMAN 1487, 2002, 2350,
 2540, 2541, 2542, 2582, 2815,
 2845, 2952, 3015, 3019, 3031,
 3368, 3572, 3610, 3623, 3840,
 3935, 4080, 5679, 8928, 15988,
 20008

MEMPHIS 13180, 13187, 13221,
 13257, 13260, 13261, 15606,
 17294

MENARCHE 15821

MENDE 4651

MENTAL HEALTH 2285, 15365, 15366,
 15736, 15761, 15762, 15769,
 15775, 15783, 15838, 17110
 (SEE ALSO INSANITY)

MENTAL HOSPITALS 15666

MERCANTILISM 3717

MERCHANT MARINE 14744

MERCIER, HENRI 2225

MESOPOTAMIA, JAMAICA 6422

METHODIST CHURCH 2605, 2750, 3845,
 9006, 11025, 12076, 12649,
 16619, 16644, 16677, 16679,
 16693, 16729, 16746, 16833,
 16834, 16835, 16836, 16851,
 16868, 16892, 16917, 16928,
 16986, 17006, 17008, 17009,
 17010, 17013, 17029, 17076,
 17079, 17080, 17095, 17120,
 17127, 17128, 17130, 17143,
 17165, 17191, 17203, 17234,
 17235, 17284, 17295, 17300,
 17334, 17342, 17345

METOYER, AUGUSTIN 12391

MEXICAN WAR 11664, 11665

MEXICO 2649, 2740, 4487, 5716,
 5785, 6056, 6324, 6404, 7307,
 7308, 7309, 7310, 7312, 7330,
 7331, 7334, 7344, 7368, 7388,

7389, 7390, 7391, 7393, 7394,
7395, 7396, 7434, 7436, 7443,
7448, 7450, 7453, 7473, 7478,
7493, 7494, 7529, 7532, 7533,
7623, 7624, 7633, 7643, 7660,
7661, 7701, 7702, 7720, 7768,
7775, 7776, 7798, 7799, 7800,
7826, 7827, 7828, 7829, 7830,
7896, 7898, 7921, 7925, 7944,
7946, 7994, 8004, 8054, 8066,
8067, 8085, 13323, 13325, 14910,
15377, 15785, 17173, 18281,
19302, 19820, 20053

MEXICO CITY 7375, 7632, 7799

MIAMI VALLEY 250

MICHIGAN 8877, 10950, 10951,
 10954, 10955, 10956, 10957,
 10958, 10959, 10960, 10961,
 10962

MICKLES, ALEXANDER 18947

MIDDELBURG COMMERCE COMPANY 5924

MIDDLETOWN, NJ 10553

MILITARY OCCUPATIONS, SLAVE 9122,
 11873, 11874, 13183

MILK 15392

MILL, JOHN S. 2522, 4542

MILLEDGEVILLE, GA 12150

MILLER, JOHN 16721

MILLER, JOHN R. (SLAVE) 19794

MILLER, KELLY 1490, 1703, 1812

MINERS 7394, 7822, 7826, 7827,
 7828, 7995, 8020, 8045, 8150,
 8161, 8162, 9837, 11051, 11552,
 11575, 11590, 11640, 13517,
 13802, 14467, 14667, 14828,
 19842, 20235

MINNESOTA 542, 563, 10845, 10963,
 10964, 10965, 10968, 10969,
 10970, 10971, 10973

MINOR, WILLIAM J. 12467, 12468,
    12638

MINSTRELSY 2295, 2332, 2417, 2496,
    2675, 2746, 2812, 2903, 2933,
    2998, 17467, 18367

MISCEGENATION 548, 1694, 2075,
    2106, 2150, 2306, 2307, 2362,
    2404, 2454, 2486, 2516, 2517,
    2518, 2519, 2535, 2539, 2552,
    2553, 2586, 2614, 2643, 2645,
    2651, 2655, 2745, 2766, 2774,
    2780, 2786, 2828, 2829, 2836,
    2849, 2870, 2895, 2897, 2910,
    2914, 2919, 3003, 3005, 3938,
    5537, 5538, 6638, 7483, 8456,
    8752, 9324, 13854, 13921, 14873,
    14910, 14992, 15058, 16058,
    16309, 16565, 19932, 20022,
    20365
    (SEE ALSO MULATTOES)

MISSIONARIES 6476, 6656, 7045,
    7079, 7105, 7142, 7220, 14002,
    16832, 16968, 17003, 17064,
    17176, 17177, 17179, 17198,
    17267, 17308, 17345, 19184,
    19237

MISSISSIPPI 480, 535, 8841, 9007,
    9025, 9048, 9080, 9190, 9274,
    9409, 9455, 9932, 10004, 11676,
    11722, 11764, 11766, 11809,
    12219, 12519, 12520, 12524,
    12526, 12528, 12529, 12531,
    12532, 12533, 12534, 12536,
    12537, 12543, 12544, 12545,
    12546, 12548, 12549, 12550,
    12551, 12552, 12554, 12555,
    12557, 12558, 12559, 12560,
    12561, 12563, 12564, 12565,
    12566, 12568, 12569, 12570,
    12571, 12572, 12573, 12574,
    12575, 12577, 12581, 12584,
    12585, 12588, 12589, 12590,
    12591, 12592, 12593, 12594,
    12595, 12596, 12597, 12605,
    12607, 12609, 12610, 12611,
    12613, 12614, 12615, 12616,
    12617, 12618, 12619, 12620,
    12621, 12623, 12624, 12625,
    12628, 12630, 12631, 12632,
    12633, 12634, 12635, 12638,
    12639, 12640, 13046, 14449,

14722, 14864, 14894, 15006,
15039, 15096, 15316, 15325,
15729, 16264, 16662, 17113,
17278, 17295, 18075, 18947,
19307, 19308, 19871, 19875,
20461, 20469, 20994

MISSISSIPPI VALLEY 8317, 10840,
    10841, 11675, 11809, 17125,
    17126, 20595, 20698

MISSOURI 500, 2114, 2235, 8774,
    8879, 8901, 9013, 9090, 9137,
    9138, 9174, 9200, 9314, 9343,
    9344, 9345, 9384, 9538, 10024,
    10079, 10080, 10699, 10946,
    11179, 11531, 11532, 11534,
    11538, 11542, 11543, 11544,
    11545, 11547, 11549, 11550,
    11551, 11552, 11553, 11554,
    11556, 11557, 11558, 11560,
    11561, 11562, 11563, 11564,
    11565, 11567, 11568, 11569,
    11571, 11573, 11574, 11575,
    11576, 11577, 11578, 11579,
    11580, 11581, 11582, 11583,
    11584, 11585, 11586, 11587,
    11588, 11590, 11591, 11593,
    11595, 11596, 11597, 11598,
    11599, 11601, 11602, 11603,
    11605, 11606, 11609, 11610,
    11611, 11612, 11613, 11614,
    11615, 11618, 11619, 11620,
    11621, 11622, 11623, 11624,
    11625, 11627, 11628, 11629,
    11633, 11634, 11635, 11637,
    11638, 11639, 11640, 11643,
    11644, 11645, 11646, 11648,
    11649, 11653, 11654, 11655,
    15140, 15280, 15281, 19672,
    20905, 20924, 20931

MISSOURI COMPROMISE 9090

MISSOURI TERRITORY 11643

MISTRESS, PLANTATION 3266

MITCHELL, DAVID B. 5938

MOBILE, AL 2959, 5968, 9170,
    11726, 11754, 11780, 15042

MOBS, ANTI-ABOLITION 2317, 2425,
    2465, 2546, 2975

1618

MONONGALIA COUNTY, VA   9266

MONROE COUNTY, MO   11625

MONROE COUNTY, MS   12605

MONTANA   11056

MONTEJO, ESTABAN   6151, 7060

MONTESQUIEU, BARON DE   4574

MONTGOMERY COUNTY, AL   11785,
   11786

MONTGOMERY RACE CONFERENCE   2432

MONTGOMERY, BENJAMIN   10003, 12613

MONTSERRAT   6451, 6553, 19955,
   20054

MOORE, B.F.   12675

MOORE, MARIA L.   9574

MOORMAN, CLARK T.   4283

MORALITY, SLAVE   2185, 11842,
   14983, 15025, 15039, 17277

MORAVIAN CHURCH   6475, 6899, 6907,
   12659

MORELOS   7335

MORMON CHURCH   2177, 2178, 2813,
   11155, 11162, 11163, 11164,
   11165

MORRIS COUNTY, NJ   10595

MORTALITY, SLAVE   549, 1064, 2978,
   5072, 5367, 5639, 5640, 5641,
   5840, 6342, 6571, 7484, 14901,
   14947, 15015, 15789, 15800,
   15827, 17238, 19677

MOSS, WILLIAM   12060

MOTIVATIONS, SLAVE   17501

MOTON, ROBERT R.   18954, 18955

MOUNT AIRY, VA   6422

MOYNIHAN, DANIEL P.   1200, 2758,
   16099, 16161

MOZAMBIQUE   4388, 6116

MULATTOES   1072, 2063, 2128, 2199,
   2255, 2355, 2402, 2530, 2578,
   2634, 2635, 2774, 2897, 2937,
   3016, 5537, 6731, 8746, 11780,
   13921, 14844, 15058, 15354,
   16289
   (SEE ALSO MISCEGENATION)

MULES   14323

MULLIN, GERALD   5131

MURRAY, AMELIA M.   3711, 11977

MUSIC--SEE SONGS, SLAVE AND
   SPIRITUALS

MUSICAL INSTRUMENTS   4933, 7200,
   12332, 15541, 17496, 17519,
   17527, 17548, 17584, 17631,
   17788, 17789, 17790, 17813,
   17869, 19302
   (SEE ALSO DRUMS, FIDDLES)

MUSICIANS   7671, 17543, 17548,
   17549, 17571, 17572, 17597,
   17683, 17789, 17790

MUSLIMS   8152

MYRDAL, GUNNAR   1851

NABUCO, JOAQUIM   7869

NAMES, SLAVE   2, 1731, 2914, 3074,
   4110, 4570, 4841, 6300, 7959,
   10238, 10405, 11299, 12835,
   13379, 16091, 16173, 16311,
   18132, 19260, 19274, 19276,
   19298, 19301, 19314, 19316,
   19318, 19322, 19350, 19351,
   19354, 19357, 19386, 19391,
   19392, 19393, 19410, 19411,
   19446

NANSEMOND COUNTY, VA   13655

10570, 10571, 10572, 10573,
10575, 10576, 10577, 10578,
10579, 10580, 10583, 10586,
10588, 10589, 10590, 10591,
10592, 10593, 10594, 10595,
10597, 10598, 10600, 10603,
10606, 10607, 10619, 10660,
10699, 16443, 20253

NEW JERSEY SLAVE PLOT, 1734   10556

NEW MADRID, MO   11627, 11637

NEw MEXICO   2124, 2467, 7661,
   11110, 11111, 11114, 11115,
   11116, 11117, 11118, 11119,
   11120

NEW NATION   3023, 4125

NEW NETHERLAND   8659, 10611, 10706

NEW ORLEANS, LA   1458, 2343, 2598,
   2683, 2765, 2959, 7222, 7223,
   9485, 9487, 9488, 9681, 9688,
   9717, 9724, 9791, 9792, 9793,
   9794, 9799, 9800, 9946, 9948,
   10074, 12220, 12230, 12244,
   12248, 12250, 12261, 12287,
   12292, 12298, 12302, 12308,
   12316, 12320, 12337, 12338,
   12339, 12340, 12346, 12347,
   12348, 12349, 12399, 12413,
   12428, 12429, 12430, 12433,
   12434, 12435, 12453, 12460,
   12476, 12491, 12513, 15153,
   15484, 15613, 15646, 15870,
   15882, 15886, 15895, 15925,
   15939, 15945, 15961, 15972,
   15982, 15985, 16316, 17259,
   17288, 17749, 17751, 18383,
   18412, 21147

NEW SPAIN   759, 7326, 7369, 7944,
   7946, 8000, 8054, 8154, 8162,
   20663

NEW WORLD FRONTIER   3298

NEW YORK   2492, 8324, 8358, 8359,
   8478, 8479, 8512, 8602, 8623,
   8627, 8659, 8720, 8918, 8955,
   9092, 9093, 9094, 9135, 9143,
   9744, 10337, 10576, 10590,
   10591, 10608, 10609, 10610,

10611, 10612, 10613, 10614,
10615, 10617, 10618, 10619,
10620, 10621, 10622, 10624,
10626, 10627, 10629, 10630,
10631, 10632, 10636, 10638,
10641, 10642, 10643, 10645,
10646, 10648, 10649, 10650,
10654, 10655, 10656, 10657,
10659, 10660, 10661, 10662,
10663, 10664, 10665, 10666,
10667, 10668, 10672, 10673,
10675, 10676, 10677, 10678,
10680, 10681, 10682, 10684,
10686, 10687, 10689, 10693,
10694, 10695, 10696, 10697,
10699, 10702, 10703, 10704,
10705, 10706, 10709, 10710,
10711, 10713, 10714, 10715,
16948, 19572, 20149

NEW YORK CITY   8359, 9135, 9446,
   9753, 10617, 10627, 10634,
   10635, 10649, 10667, 10672,
   10694, 10708

NEW YORK CITY DRAFT RIOTS   9673

NEW YORK MANUMISSION SOCIETY
   10116

NEW YORK NEGRO PLOT, 1741   9964,
   10617, 10650, 10702, 10705,
   20079, 20124

NEW YORK SLAVE REVOLT, 1712   10697,
   20149

NEWPORT, RI   5330, 5823, 5825,
   5826, 5856, 5905, 5929, 5973,
   6014, 10800

NEWSPAPERS   333, 2765, 3498, 4253,
   4465, 4498, 5918, 12261, 13152,
   15343, 19950, 20426

NEWTON, JOHN   5239, 5500, 5806

NICKOLLS, ROBERT   5598

NIEBOER, H.J.   1290

NIGER DELTA   4776, 5167

NIGERIA   4654, 4656, 4675, 4729,
   4806, 4878, 4967, 4974, 4994,

5001, 5121, 5599, 5971, 7138,
7229, 8119

NIGHTINGALE 5213

NITER MINING 12038

NON-SLAVEHOLDING WHITES 1173,
2189, 2389, 2621, 2623, 4086,
4551, 14243, 14248, 14455,
14632

NORFOLK, VA 10064, 13618, 13680,
14484, 17386

NORTH CAROLINA 26, 393, 2169,
2229, 8305, 8327, 8343, 8344,
8423, 8464, 8499, 8546, 8606,
8660, 8702, 8703, 8708, 8758,
8761, 8779, 8786, 8791, 8799,
8801, 8816, 8817, 8886, 8961,
8974, 9035, 9065, 9086, 9148,
9164, 9288, 9358, 9424, 9435,
9570, 10117, 10699, 12363,
12641, 12643, 12644, 12647,
12649, 12650, 12651, 12652,
12656, 12657, 12658, 12659,
12660, 12662, 12664, 12665,
12666, 12668, 12669, 12675,
12676, 12677, 12679, 12680,
12681, 12682, 12686, 12687,
12690, 12694, 12695, 12696,
12697, 12699, 12700, 12701,
12702, 12703, 12704, 12705,
12706, 12708, 12709, 12712,
12713, 12714, 12715, 12716,
12717, 12718, 12719, 12723,
12726, 12727, 12730, 12731,
12732, 12733, 12735, 12736,
12739, 12740, 12743, 12745,
12746, 12748, 12750, 12751,
12753, 12754, 12755, 12756,
12757, 12758, 12759, 12760,
12761, 12764, 12766, 12768,
12769, 12771, 12773, 12775,
12776, 12777, 12778, 12780,
12782, 12783, 12784, 12785,
12786, 12787, 12790, 12791,
12792, 12795, 12797, 12799,
12801, 12802, 12803, 12804,
12805, 12806, 12808, 12810,
12812, 12816, 12818, 12819,
12820, 13811, 13822, 14515,
14534, 14723, 14797, 14798,
15291, 15826, 16283, 16840,

17166, 17169, 17285, 17358,
18606, 18971, 20078, 20127,
20262, 20311, 20485

NORTH CAROLINA MANUMISSION SOCIET
589

NORTH, SLAVERY IN 915, 8363, 840
8402, 8537, 8551, 8664, 10327,
10337, 10338, 10369, 10374,
10377, 10380

NORTHAMPTON COUNTY, PA 10757

NORTHUP, SOLOMON 18969

NORTHWEST TERRITORY 2124, 2753,
3242, 8514, 8877, 8891, 9158,
9784, 10825, 10827, 10833,
10834, 10836, 10837, 10838,
10839, 10843, 10916, 10953,
10957, 10963, 10937, 11676

NOTT, JOSIAH C. 2166, 15593

NOVA SCOTIA 6261, 8323, 10121,
10226, 10236, 10237, 10240,
10244, 10251, 10255, 10256,
10270, 10277, 10278, 10279,
10311, 10317, 10319, 10324,
10326, 19827

NOVELS, SLAVERY IN 765, 2090,
2095, 2175, 2201, 2207, 3070,
3157, 3178, 6221, 6222, 6223,
7329, 18707, 18708

NULLIFICATION CONTROVERSY 13036,
19179

NURSES 20809

NUTRITION 6710, 14975, 14976,
15405
(SEE ALSO DIET)

O'NEAL, WILLIAM 4108

O'NEALL, JOHN B. 13040

OBEAH 7219, 7634, 8573, 15711,
16726, 17196, 17249, 18398,
19302, 20305

1622

OBEAHMEN 8573

OBRAJES 7400, 7623, 7624, 7946, 8085

OCCUPATIONS, SLAVE 14483, 14630, 16316

OFF TIME 19674

OGLETHORPE COUNTY, GA 12130

OGLETHORPE, JAMES E. 12179

OHIO 156, 2117, 2124, 2753, 8838, 8908, 9043, 9049, 9158, 9296, 9583, 9584, 9585, 9784, 9944, 9945, 10979, 10980, 10982, 10987, 19451

OHIO COUNTY, KY 11338

OHIO VALLEY 10817

OHY SYSTEM OF SLAVERY 4885

OKLAHOMA 564, 11121, 11122, 11123, 11124, 11125, 11126, 11129, 11132, 11133, 11134, 11135, 13950, 13962, 13966, 13967, 14002, 14033, 14039, 14046

OLD BEN (EX-SLAVE) 15328

OLD NORTHWEST--SEE NORTHWEST TERRITORY

OLD SLAVE HOUSE, JUNCTION, IL 10863

OLD SLAVE MART MUSEUM 18532

OLMSTED, FREDERICK L. 545, 1395, 1396, 1519, 1715, 1744, 1984, 2016, 14374, 15479, 18092

OMENS 6229

ONONDAGA STANDARD 3498

ONSLOW COUNTY, NC 12658

ONTARIO 3806, 10231, 10233, 10304, 10320, 10321, 10324, 19630

OPELOUSAS COUNTY, LA 12417

OPELOUSAS, LA 2630

OPOTHLEYOHOLO 13912

ORAL HISTORY 867, 868

ORAL TRADITION 10, 17990

ORANGE COUNTY, NC 12719

OREGON 159, 351, 2124, 9038, 9203, 9401, 11032, 11137, 11138, 11140, 11141, 11145, 11146, 11147, 11149, 11151, 11152, 19746

ORIGINS OF SLAVERY 746, 1843, 2156, 2157, 2386, 2506, 2531, 2535, 2587, 2662, 2686, 2885, 3456, 6690, 6693, 7276, 8198, 8199, 8207, 8210, 8211, 8214, 8215, 8216, 8219, 8224, 8225, 8226, 8228, 8229, 8238, 8239, 8241, 8242, 8244, 8245, 8246, 8247, 8252, 8257, 8259, 8261, 8262, 8263, 8266, 8267, 8269, 8445, 8456, 8553, 8556, 15354, 20022

OSBORN, ROBERT 6621

OSBORNE, SAMUEL 6658

OSCEOLA 11935

OUACHITA PARISH, LA 12229

OVERLAYING 15789 (SEE ALSO SMOTHERING)

OVERSEERS 85, 1720, 9356, 11446, 11658, 11727, 12136, 12140, 12334, 12405, 12592, 12795, 12819, 13803, 14839, 14854, 14858, 14860, 14862, 14864, 14865, 14875, 14879, 14886, 14887, 14894, 14895, 15106, 15147, 15203, 15791, 16565, 17238, 18346, 19789, 19842

OVERSEERS, BLACK 14854

1623

OWEN, NICHOLAS   5719

OWEN, THOMAS 4.   278, 1861

OWSLEY, FRANK L.   1759

OYO   4938, 5762

PACHEO, LUIS   11924, 19713

PACIFIC NORTHWEST   155, 9578, 11028

PAGE COUNTY, VA   13699

PAGE, THOMAS N.   1297, 2844, 3686

PALMARES   7446, 7512, 7551, 7738, 8157

PALMER, JOHN M.   11307, 21025

PANAMA   5730, 7349, 7359, 7716, 7748, 7836, 8000, 15586

PARAGUAY   7474, 7513, 7766, 8178, 8179, 8180, 8181, 15785

PARAMAKA MAROONS   7786

PARHAM, HAROLD   17430, 19054

PARKER, ELIZABETH   19510

PARKER, JOHN P.   9915

PARKER, RACHEL   19510

PARKER, WILLIAM   19683, 19839

PARLIAMENT   6630

PARTICLE T'AH   19348

PASSES, SLAVE   9249

PATENT LAWS   8900

PATERNALISM   1126, 1772, 2390, 2511, 2604, 2760, 2945, 2946, 9159, 11660, 12869, 13783, 13836, 14873, 15013, 15328, 15333, 15353, 15364, 15559, 16037, 16038, 16066, 16173, 17237

PATRIARCHAL IDEOLOGY   12979

PATTERSON, H. ORLANDO   1517

PATTERSON, WILLIAM   10575

PAYNE, DANIEL A.   9868

PEACH POINT PLANTATION   14509

PEARL DIVERS, SLAVE   15785

PEASANTRIES   6889

PECK, JOHN M.   10878

PEEDEE RIVER   12854

PELLAGRA   15704

PELLETIER, ANTONIO   5244

PEMBERTON, CAROLINE H.   1068

PENAL SYSTEMS   4297, 9212, 13266

PENDLETON, JAMES M.   11323

PENNINGTON, J.W.C.   17270

PENNSYLVANIA   6072, 8340, 8579, 8588, 8626, 8686, 8687, 8720, 9023, 9167, 9177, 9580, 9581, 10576, 10660, 10717, 10718, 10719, 10720, 10721, 10722, 10723, 10724, 10726, 10727, 10728, 10729, 10730, 10731, 10734, 10739, 10740, 10744, 10746, 10743, 10749, 10750, 10754, 10755, 10757, 10758, 10760, 10761, 10762, 10764, 10765, 10768, 10770, 10771, 10774, 10775, 10778, 10779, 14822, 14823, 15187, 15188

PENSACOLA   11873, 11874

PENSIONS, SLAVE   3551

PEONAGE   3229, 8843, 9136, 11205

PERCY, CHARLES   12560

PERNAMBUCO   802, 6032, 7541, 7542, 7543, 7544, 7551, 7594, 7595,

7978, 7982

PERRY COUNTY, AL 11606

PERSONAL LIBERTY LAWS 8797, 9011,
9022, 9098, 9188, 9247

PERSONALITY 654, 939, 997, 1143,
1199, 1420, 1524, 1634, 1662,
1674, 1677, 1836, 1895, 1909,
1913, 1960, 3127, 6436, 12204,
15365, 15366, 16105, 16163,
17426, 18733, 18740, 18745,
18746, 18747, 18748, 18749,
18751, 18759, 18762, 18764,
18765, 18767, 18768, 18770,
18771, 18773, 18780, 18783,
18784, 18788, 18789, 18790,
18791

PERU 1289, 1385, 2213, 5628, 7368,
7372, 7376, 7394, 7424, 7426,
7484, 7507, 7596, 7762, 7791,
7851, 7867, 7923, 14907, 15716,
15785, 20053

PETERKIN, JULIA 18409

PETERS, THOMAS 10121

PETERSBURG, VA 3488, 9605, 20910

PETIGRU, JAMES L. 16066

PETRIE, GEORGE 1859

PETTIGREW, EBENEZER 12808, 14534,
14535, 15826

PETTUS, JOHN JONES 12544, 12545

PEUKERT, WERNER 5595

PHILADELPHIA 433, 9580, 9581,
9644, 10708

PHILIPS, MARTIN W. 12533

PHILLIPPO, JAMES M. 7220

PHILLIPS, ULRICH B. 332, 457, 535,
536, 621, 776, 860, 871, 874,
957, 960, 974, 994, 1034, 1036,
1043, 1058, 1148, 1153, 1154,
1184, 1202, 1220, 1292, 1370,

1398, 1399, 1402, 1423, 1467,
1556, 1622, 1641, 1681, 1711,
1712, 1713, 1714, 1734, 1749,
1782, 1813, 1815, 1818, 1819,
1833, 1837, 1854, 1863, 1864,
1865, 1942, 1984, 2006, 2011,
2022, 2035, 2388, 2604

PHOTOGRAPHS OF SLAVES 12858,
13062

PICKERING, TIMOTHY 2206

PIDGINIZATION 19315, 19323, 19377

PIKE, JAMES S. 2313

PINCKNEY, ELIZA L. 12883, 19224

PINN, ROBERT A. 20769, 20937

PITT, WILLIAM 1428, 5676

PITTSBURGH 9942

PLANTATION CHAPELS 16663

PLANTATION RECORDS 536, 549

PLANTATION SYSTEM 569, 713, 929,
990, 1006, 1617, 2390, 2416,
2760, 2922, 2923, 2924, 3200,
3428, 4022, 4116, 4284, 4400,
4621, 5201, 6175, 6177, 6534,
6535, 6536, 6735, 7234, 7501,
7669, 7762, 7988, 8568, 8593,
8693, 9159, 11481, 11657, 11685,
11708, 11809, 11813, 12023,
12024, 12155, 12136, 12280,
12881, 12932, 13783, 13865,
14115, 14117, 14168, 14209,
14268, 14316, 14328, 14344,
14345, 14363, 14395, 14409,
14413, 14419, 14422, 14424,
14425, 14427, 14428, 14432,
14452, 14459, 14512, 14517,
14518, 14520, 14544, 14566,
14624, 15147, 15210, 16112,
16173, 17273, 20463, 20470,
20699

PLANTATIONS, ABANDONED 11812

PLANTER 13106, 19919, 20126,
20137

PLANTER ARISTOCRACY 1173, 3911, 3913, 6528, 12887, 13633, 14449, 14632, 15364, 17394, 20594

PLEASANT, MARY E. 16347, 16421

PLEASANTS, ROBERT 9937

PLYMOUTH, MA 4773

PO, FERNANDO 3059, 5273

POCHE, FELIX P. 20457

POCOCK, NICHOLAS 5752

POE, EDGAR A. 2212, 2582, 4010

POETRY 83, 2202, 3370, 3579, 4486, 4607, 6224, 6236, 6288, 9378, 12677, 16354, 16502, 16529, 17469, 17490, 18236, 18703, 18705, 18733, 19740

POINTE COUPEE, LA 12328

POLANYI, KARL 1378, 5595

POLITICS 1409, 3184, 3279, 3759, 3977, 4095, 4149, 4195, 4226, 4229, 4230, 4330, 4331, 4332, 4366, 4404, 5217, 9099, 9100, 9246, 9269, 11053, 13494, 19878, 20120, 20368, 20441

POLK, JAMES K. 3950

POLK, LEONIDAS 17119

POOLE, CAROLINE B. 12408

POOR WHITES 2198

POPE, JOHN 15713

POPULAR SOVEREIGNTY 10846, 11036

POPULATION, BLACK 6425, 8541, 14369, 14932, 14933, 14952, 15029

PORK 1769, 6745, 15411, 15412, 15413, 15414, 15415, 15416

PORT ROYAL ISLAND 15574, 21035, 21072

PORTER, ALEXANDER 12475

PORTUGAL 2817, 4274, 8018

PORTUGUESE COMPANY 5772

PORTUGUESE SLAVERY 2160, 4274, 5247, 5407, 5408, 7377, 7379, 7383, 7509, 7584, 7818, 7825, 7943, 8020, 15785

POSTERS, CIVIL WAR 15150

POTTER, DAVID M. 1139

POTTERS 18496, 18586, 18606

POTTERY 26, 5106, 6839, 8304, 10429, 10447, 15541, 18496, 18497, 18517, 18528, 18586

POWERS, HARRIET 16400

PRATT, DANIEL 11753

PRE-COLUMBIAN ORIGINS OF AMERICAN BLACKS 4725, 4726, 4727

PREACHERS 4946, 12698, 12699, 14873, 15559, 16565, 16595, 16757, 16794, 16817, 16849, 16861, 16941, 17040, 17041, 17043, 17044, 17115, 17116, 17117, 17131, 17220, 17356, 17951
(SEE ALSO RELIGION)

PRESBYTERIAN CHURCH 2579, 2666, 3772, 8681, 11324, 12869, 14001, 16589, 16593, 16594, 16596, 16609, 16621, 16730, 16741, 16859, 16956, 16994, 17010, 17016, 17022, 17034, 17047, 17066, 17131, 17132, 17134, 17135, 17175, 17262, 17263, 17270, 17305, 17647, 19244, 19841

PRICE, CHARLES 6347

PRICE, JOSEPH C. 1965

PRICE, RICHARD 1513

PRIGG V. PENNSYLVANIA 8889, 9131

PRINCE GEORGE'S COUNTY, MD 8489,
  8490, 11482, 11483

PRINCESS ANNE COUNTY, VA 8491,
  13837, 13838

PRINCIPIO COMPANY 8633, 11528

PRINGLE, ROBERT 19949

PRIVATEERING 5876

PROBATE RECORDS 363

PROCTOR, HENRY H. 1327

PROFITABILITY MODEL 14649

PROFITABILITY OF SLAVERY 843, 844,
  899, 956, 1058, 1416, 1555,
  1768, 2025, 3471, 5738, 6140,
  6638, 8046, 9159, 9163, 9964,
  10156, 12348, 12506, 13046,
  13148, 14076, 14077, 14150,
  14151, 14172, 14220, 14243,
  14385, 14398, 14408, 14411,
  14420, 14442, 14454, 14456,
  14458, 14483, 14489, 14568,
  14571, 14580, 14581, 14595,
  14596, 14598, 14600, 14601,
  14602, 14624, 14630, 14632,
  14637, 14638, 14645, 14646,
  14647, 14649, 14652, 15010,
  15106, 15147, 15289, 17238,
  19790

PROGRESSIVE ERA 535, 1812, 1813,
  1818

PROGRESSIVE HISTORIANS 1442, 1552

PROLETERIAT 6874, 6890

PROPERTY OWNERS, BLACK 8301

PROSLAVERY ARGUMENT 787, 935, 937,
  1051, 1431, 1543, 1561, 1812,
  1813, 1818, 2071, 2102, 2118,
  2131, 2159, 2165, 2172, 2191,
  2222, 2224, 2241, 2246, 2254,
  2263, 2285, 2293, 2336, 2338,
  2346, 2362, 2368, 2381, 2428,
  2432, 2476, 2505, 2560, 2579,
  2599, 2604, 2659, 2660, 2661,
  2663, 2673, 2702, 2717, 2750,
  2754, 2782, 2793, 2809, 2816,
  2840, 2841, 2844, 2869, 2881,
  2901, 2908, 2909, 2918, 2931,
  2932, 2939, 2953, 2964, 2965,
  2984, 2991, 2995, 2996, 2997,
  3004, 3007, 3039, 3087, 3153,
  3170, 3186, 3193, 3207, 3208,
  3230, 3270, 3274, 3281, 3334,
  3409, 3412, 3461, 3463, 3494,
  3638, 3655, 3656, 3670, 3737,
  3743, 3800, 3878, 3910, 3964,
  3966, 3969, 3973, 3982, 4000,
  4104, 4119, 4231, 4261, 4264,
  4286, 4294, 4334, 4360, 4363,
  4386, 4389, 4428, 4468, 4495,
  4496, 4571, 4603, 4605, 4617,
  4619, 4633, 4638, 5109, 5357,
  6477, 8859, 8889, 8936, 9159,
  11035, 11723, 12581, 12616,
  12929, 12931, 13640, 15199,
  15248, 15272, 15316, 15346,
  15623, 15702, 15818, 16003,
  16037, 16038, 16048, 16617,
  16673, 16995, 16996, 17175,
  18246, 20409, 20585

PROSSER, GABRIEL 5082, 13725,
  15900, 19995, 19998

PROSTITUTION 4485, 7915

PROTESTANT CHURCHES 11335, 16666,
  16732, 16779

PROTESTANT EPISCOPAL CHURCH 17264

PROTESTANT ETHIC 3052, 14272,
  16837

PROVERBS 15446, 18073, 18730

PROVIDENCE AFRICAN SOCIETY 2183

PROVINCIAL FREEMAN 10273, 10274

PROVISIONS, SLAVE 6882

PSYCHODYNAMICS OF SLAVERY 731

PUCKETT, NEWBELL N. 1991

PUEBLA, MEXICO 7344

PUERTO RICO 238, 2617, 5126, 5537,
   5538, 6120, 6142, 6149, 6372,
   6394, 6395, 6450, 6508, 6856,
   6866, 6872, 6875, 6881, 6884,
   6885, 6887, 6926, 6996, 7001,
   7065, 7066, 7163, 7164, 7247,
   7612, 17964

PUGH PLANTATIONS 12355

PULASKI COUNTY, AR 11837, 11839

PURCELL, JOHN B. 2287

PURITANS 10367, 10373

PURVIS, ROBERT 2152

QUAKERS 1105, 4211, 4313, 4456,
   5456, 5466, 5583, 5714, 6998,
   7285, 8448, 8679, 9426, 9470,
   9964, 10603, 10833, 11439,
   12660, 12723, 12745, 12746,
   12758, 12759, 12782, 12785,
   12799, 13630, 15188, 16598,
   16627, 16650, 16674, 16685,
   16713, 16759, 16760, 16909,
   16938, 17330, 19251, 19558,
   21045

QUARLES, BENJAMIN 1488, 1612

QUARRYING 19790

QUEBEC 10275, 10276

QUERINO, MANUEL 7418

QUIER, JOHN 6505

QUILOMBO 20296

QUILTS 15541, 16400, 17438, 18565,
   18587, 18588

QUINN, DAVID 2754

QUITMAN, JOHN A. 12581

QUITO 7923

QUOK WALKER CASE 10436, 10494

RACE 259, 533, 548, 636, 662, 674,
   702, 746, 747, 748, 771, 818,
   880, 890, 917, 921, 933, 937,
   1072, 1094, 1216, 1236, 1307,
   1339, 1340, 1344, 1532, 1552,
   1554, 1694, 1724, 1792, 1818,
   1900, 1918, 2040, 2061, 2062,
   2063, 2065, 2066, 2069, 2070,
   2071, 2072, 2074, 2075, 2077,
   2078, 2079, 2080, 2081, 2082,
   2083, 2084, 2085, 2086, 2087,
   2089, 2091, 2093, 2094, 2096,
   2100, 2101, 2102, 2103, 2104,
   2106, 2109, 2113, 2114, 2118,
   2120, 2121, 2122, 2125, 2126,
   2127, 2128, 2129, 2130, 2132,
   2133, 2134, 2135, 2136, 2137,
   2139, 2140, 2141, 2142, 2143,
   2144, 2145, 2147, 2150, 2152,
   2157, 2158, 2159, 2161, 2162,
   2163, 2165, 2166, 2167, 2168,
   2171, 2172, 2174, 2176, 2180,
   2182, 2183, 2184, 2185, 2186,
   2187, 2188, 2189, 2190, 2191,
   2193, 2194, 2196, 2197, 2199,
   2200, 2204, 2205, 2206, 2207,
   2208, 2209, 2210, 2211, 2212,
   2213, 2214, 2215, 2216, 2217,
   2218, 2220, 2221, 2223, 2224,
   2227, 2228, 2229, 2230, 2231,
   2233, 2234, 2236, 2237, 2238,
   2240, 2241, 2242, 2244, 2245,
   2246, 2247, 2248, 2249, 2250,
   2251, 2252, 2253, 2254, 2255,
   2256, 2257, 2258, 2259, 2260,
   2261, 2262, 2264, 2266, 2268,
   2269, 2272, 2273, 2275, 2276,
   2277, 2283, 2284, 2285, 2286,
   2288, 2289, 2290, 2291, 2292,
   2293, 2294, 2295, 2296, 2297,
   2298, 2299, 2300, 2301, 2302,
   2303, 2304, 2305, 2306, 2309,
   2310, 2311, 2312, 2313, 2315,
   2316, 2318, 2319, 2320, 2321,
   2322, 2323, 2324, 2325, 2326,
   2327, 2328, 2329, 2330, 2331,
   2332, 2333, 2334, 2335, 2338,
   2339, 2340, 2341, 2342, 2344,
   2345, 2347, 2350, 2351, 2353,
   2354, 2355, 2359, 2360, 2361,
   2362, 2363, 2364, 2365, 2366,
   2369, 2370, 2371, 2372, 2375,
   2376, 2377, 2378, 2379, 2380,
   2381, 2382, 2384, 2386, 2388,
   2390, 2391, 2392, 2395, 2397,

2398, 2400, 2401, 2402, 2403,
2404, 2405, 2406, 2407, 2408,
2409, 2410, 2411, 2412, 2414,
2415, 2416, 2417, 2418, 2419,
2420, 2421, 2422, 2424, 2425,
2426, 2427, 2430, 2432, 2433,
2434, 2436, 2437, 2438, 2439,
2440, 2441, 2442, 2443, 2444,
2445, 2446, 2447, 2449, 2450,
2452, 2454, 2456, 2457, 2458,
2459, 2460, 2461, 2462, 2463,
2464, 2465, 2467, 2468, 2469,
2470, 2471, 2473, 2474, 2475,
2476, 2478, 2480, 2482, 2484,
2486, 2487, 2490, 2491, 2492,
2493, 2495, 2496, 2498, 2499,
2500, 2502, 2503, 2504, 2506,
2507, 2508, 2509, 2510, 2511,
2512, 2514, 2515, 2516, 2517,
2518, 2519, 2520, 2521, 2522,
2523, 2525, 2527, 2528, 2529,
2531, 2535, 2536, 2537, 2539,
2540, 2541, 2542, 2544, 2545,
2546, 2547, 2548, 2550, 2551,
2552, 2553, 2554, 2555, 2556,
2557, 2559, 2560, 2561, 2562,
2563, 2564, 2565, 2567, 2568,
2569, 2570, 2571, 2572, 2573,
2574, 2575, 2576, 2577, 2579,
2580, 2581, 2582, 2583, 2584,
2585, 2586, 2587, 2590, 2591,
2592, 2593, 2594, 2595, 2596,
2597, 2598, 2600, 2601, 2602,
2603, 2604, 2606, 2607, 2608,
2609, 2610, 2611, 2612, 2613,
2614, 2615, 2616, 2617, 2618,
2619, 2620, 2621, 2622, 2623,
2624, 2625, 2626, 2627, 2628,
2629, 2630, 2631, 2632, 2633,
2634, 2635, 2636, 2637, 2638,
2639, 2640, 2641, 2642, 2643,
2644, 2645, 2646, 2647, 2648,
2649, 2650, 2651, 2654, 2655,
2657, 2658, 2659, 2660, 2661,
2662, 2663, 2664, 2665, 2666,
2667, 2668, 2669, 2670, 2671,
2672, 2673, 2674, 2675, 2677,
2680, 2681, 2682, 2683, 2684,
2685, 2686, 2687, 2688, 2689,
2690, 2692, 2693, 2694, 2695,
2696, 2697, 2698, 2699, 2700,
2701, 2702, 2703, 2704, 2705,
2706, 2707, 2710, 2711, 2712,
2713, 2714, 2715, 2716, 2717,
2718, 2719, 2720, 2721, 2722,

2723, 2724, 2725, 2727, 2728,
2730, 2731, 2734, 2735, 2737,
2739, 2740, 2741, 2742, 2743,
2744, 2745, 2746, 2747, 2748,
2749, 2750, 2751, 2753, 2754,
2755, 2757, 2758, 2759, 2760,
2761, 2762, 2763, 2764, 2765,
2766, 2768, 2769, 2770, 2773,
2774, 2775, 2776, 2777, 2778,
2779, 2780, 2781, 2782, 2783,
2784, 2785, 2786, 2787, 2789,
2790, 2791, 2792, 2793, 2794,
2795, 2797, 2798, 2799, 2800,
2801, 2802, 2803, 2804, 2807,
2809, 2810, 2811, 2812, 2813,
2814, 2815, 2816, 2817, 2818,
2819, 2820, 2822, 2823, 2824,
2825, 2826, 2827, 2828, 2829,
2830, 2831, 2832, 2833, 2834,
2835, 2836, 2838, 2839, 2840,
2841, 2842, 2843, 2844, 2845,
2847, 2849, 2850, 2852, 2853,
2855, 2856, 2857, 2860, 2861,
2862, 2866, 2867, 2869, 2870,
2872, 2873, 2874, 2875, 2876,
2878, 2879, 2880, 2882, 2883,
2884, 2885, 2886, 2887, 2889,
2890, 2891, 2892, 2893, 2894,
2895, 2896, 2897, 2898, 2899,
2900, 2901, 2902, 2903, 2904,
2906, 2907, 2908, 2909, 2910,
2911, 2912, 2913, 2914, 2915,
2917, 2918, 2919, 2920, 2921,
2922, 2923, 2924, 2925, 2926,
2927, 2928, 2929, 2930, 2931,
2932, 2933, 2934, 2936, 2937,
2938, 2939, 2940, 2942, 2943,
2944, 2945, 2946, 2947, 2948,
2949, 2950, 2951, 2952, 2953,
2954, 2958, 2959, 2960, 2961,
2962, 2963, 2964, 2965, 2966,
2967, 2968, 2969, 2970, 2971,
2972, 2973, 2974, 2975, 2976,
2977, 2978, 2979, 2980, 2982,
2983, 2984, 2985, 2986, 2987,
2989, 2990, 2991, 2992, 2993,
2994, 2995, 2996, 2997, 2998,
3003, 3004, 3005, 3006, 3007,
3008, 3009, 3011, 3012, 3013,
3014, 3015, 3016, 3018, 3019,
3021, 3220, 3222, 3313, 3383,
3414, 3661, 4261, 5376, 5538,
5863, 6557, 6638, 6646, 6749,
7113, 7323, 7338, 7377, 7427,
7483, 7694, 7783, 7860, 7934,

8018, 8027, 8063, 8209, 8216,
8456, 8553, 8848, 8849, 8902,
8959, 9159, 9217, 9290, 9324,
9514, 9528, 9582, 9611, 9781,
9812, 9993, 10334, 10373, 10568,
11180, 11514, 11625, 11805,
12282, 12456, 12859, 12875,
13783, 13915, 13921, 14012,
14088, 14106, 14198, 15041,
15058, 15354, 15522, 15836,
15839, 15972, 15998, 16270,
16289, 16688, 17177, 17354,
18661, 18720, 19179, 19932,
20022, 20163, 20304, 20365,
20368, 20379, 20394, 20426,
20428, 20429, 20430, 20444,
20685, 20686, 20721, 20741,
20864, 21160, 21161

RADICAL REPUBLICANS   3008, 20860,
21122

RAILROADS   1620, 13873, 14407,
14416, 14427, 14663

RALPH (SLAVE)   9281, 20297

RAMSAY, JAMES   5251, 7106

RANCHES   13433

RANDALL, JAMES G.   1547, 8580

RANDOLPH COUNTY, VA   13549

RANDOLPH, JOHN   9058, 9585

RANDOLPH, JOHN H.   12415, 12416

RANTOUL, ROBERT   784

RAPE   2609, 9000, 10373, 15195,
15212, 16359

RAPIER, JAMES T.   9494, 13263,
13264, 19755

RAPIER, JOHN H., SR.   9831

RAWICK, GEORGE P.   623, 693, 1518

RAY, FRANCIS M.   13454

RAY, L.P.   18982

READ, JOHN   19546

RECIPES   13212

RECONSTRUCTION   710, 1093, 2205,
2498, 2641, 2716, 3008, 3437,
3462, 3738, 4461, 7186, 8942,
9546, 9793, 9987, 10072, 10073
10106, 10195, 11392, 11755,
11941, 11942, 12040, 12141,
12291, 12318, 12326, 12369,
12492, 12494, 12570, 12635,
12697, 12703, 12806, 12856,
13096, 13158, 13159, 13235,
13236, 13260, 13273, 13279,
13432, 13718, 14146, 14345,
15041, 16062, 16068, 16723,
19162, 20334, 20689, 20781,
20821, 20854, 20866, 20881,
20926, 20930, 20949, 20972,
20994, 20998, 21003, 21014,
21015, 21016, 21038, 21054,
21070, 21097, 21099, 21122,
21134, 21144

RECREATION   2959, 6400, 6441, 859
10401, 10405, 11762, 11886,
15842, 15843, 15844, 15845,
15846, 15854, 15855, 15858,
15860, 15870, 15872, 15874,
15875, 15876, 15877, 15879,
15880, 17156, 17468, 18111,
18221, 18481

REDPATH, JAMES   2163

REDWOOD, ABRAHAM   10784

REEVE, LYMAS   10709

RELATIVE DEPRIVATION HYPOTHESIS
11542

RELIEF SOCIETIES   20804

RELIGION   455, 610, 736, 790, 109
1224, 1236, 1325, 1462, 1468,
1679, 1684, 1910, 2168, 2336,
2665, 2861, 3132, 4679, 4705,
4809, 4861, 4882, 4894, 4895,
4912, 4946, 4955, 4969, 4970,
5019, 5049, 5076, 5086, 5138,
6153, 6209, 6294, 6306, 6392,
6417, 6446, 6504, 6514, 6516,
6653, 6677, 6721, 6752, 6754,

1630

6760, 6764, 6765, 6766, 6894,
6895, 6899, 6922, 6978, 7009,
7014, 7018, 7045, 7075, 7083,
7105, 7108, 7110, 7111, 7146,
7272, 7348, 7433, 7498, 7574,
7673, 7742, 7774, 7888, 7987,
7990, 8007, 8012, 8095, 8129,
8131, 8132, 8133, 8155, 8184,
8297, 8347, 8360, 8423, 8439,
8497, 8500, 8509, 8573, 8587,
8652, 8679, 8681, 8848, 8849,
9159, 9334, 9498, 9523, 9699,
9933, 9941, 10288, 10521, 10619,
10649, 10654, 10740, 11155,
11180, 11189, 11197, 11230,
11267, 11275, 11649, 11762,
11765, 11985, 12076, 12192,
12198, 12324, 12428, 12430,
12532, 12613, 12662, 12699,
12723, 12740, 12869, 12870,
12875, 12885, 12920, 12941,
13020, 13076, 13207, 13530,
13599, 13600, 13653, 13664,
14002, 14831, 14844, 14873,
14894, 15147, 15354, 15554,
15559, 15565, 15604, 15740,
15839, 15949, 15961, 16010,
16026, 16105, 16243, 16270,
16309, 16316, 16319, 16418,
16568, 16582, 16583, 16584,
16585, 16586, 16587, 16590,
16596, 16599, 16601, 16602,
16603, 16614, 16617, 16619,
16621, 16625, 16634, 16635,
16636, 16638, 16641, 16642,
16644, 16650, 16653, 16654,
16657, 16658, 16659, 16660,
16661, 16662, 16663, 16664,
16666, 16667, 16668, 16670,
16671, 16673, 16676, 16677,
16679, 16682, 16688, 16689,
16690, 16693, 16695, 16696,
16697, 16702, 16703, 16704,
16707, 16709, 16710, 16711,
16712, 16713, 16714, 16721,
16722, 16723, 16724, 16725,
16726, 16727, 16735, 16739,
16740, 16742, 16749, 16750,
16751, 16752, 16754, 16757,
16761, 16763, 16764, 16765,
16767, 16768, 16769, 16775,
16777, 16778, 16779, 16780,
16781, 16785, 16786, 16788,
16789, 16793, 16794, 16800,
16804, 16807, 16809, 16812,

16813, 16814, 16815, 16816,
16817, 16819, 16821, 16823,
16824, 16825, 16826, 16828,
16831, 16833, 16834, 16836,
16839, 16840, 16842, 16843,
16844, 16845, 16846, 16849,
16851, 16852, 16853, 16854,
16857, 16858, 16859, 16860,
16861, 16863, 16864, 16865,
16866, 16869, 16878, 16879,
16880, 16887, 16888, 16889,
16890, 16891, 16892, 16894,
16895, 16896, 16897, 16898,
16902, 16903, 16904, 16905,
16906, 16916, 16917, 16918,
16920, 16921, 16924, 16925,
16927, 16928, 16929, 16932,
16933, 16934, 16935, 16939,
16941, 16942, 16943, 16944,
16946, 16948, 16953, 16956,
16957, 16969, 16970, 16971,
16973, 16975, 16977, 16978,
16979, 16982, 16983, 16984,
16987, 16988, 16989, 16991,
16993, 16994, 16995, 16996,
16999, 17001, 17002, 17003,
17004, 17005, 17006, 17007,
17008, 17009, 17011, 17013,
17015, 17016, 17017, 17018,
17019, 17021, 17024, 17025,
17029, 17031, 17032, 17033,
17034, 17035, 17036, 17037,
17039, 17040, 17041, 17042,
17043, 17045, 17046, 17050,
17051, 17053, 17054, 17055,
17056, 17057, 17061, 17062,
17064, 17067, 17068, 17070,
17071, 17072, 17075, 17076,
17078, 17079, 17080, 17081,
17084, 17085, 17086, 17087,
17089, 17090, 17092, 17093,
17094, 17095, 17096, 17097,
17098, 17101, 17102, 17103,
17108, 17109, 17110, 17111,
17113, 17115, 17116, 17117,
17118, 17119, 17120, 17121,
17122, 17123, 17125, 17126,
17127, 17128, 17129, 17130,
17131, 17132, 17134, 17135,
17136, 17137, 17138, 17139,
17140, 17141, 17143, 17144,
17145, 17146, 17147, 17149,
17154, 17156, 17159, 17161,
17165, 17166, 17168, 17169,
17170, 17171, 17172, 17173,

17174, 17175, 17175, 17177,
17179, 17181, 17184, 17185,
17186, 17187, 17189, 17190,
17191, 17192, 17196, 17197,
17198, 17200, 17201, 17202,
17203, 17205, 17206, 17208,
17209, 17211, 17214, 17215,
17216, 17213, 17219, 17220,
17221, 17222, 17223, 17224,
17225, 17228, 17229, 17231,
17233, 17234, 17235, 17236,
17237, 17239, 17240, 17241,
17242, 17243, 17244, 17245,
17246, 17247, 17248, 17249,
17250, 17251, 17252, 17253,
17254, 17255, 17256, 17257,
17259, 17262, 17263, 17264,
17265, 17266, 17267, 17269,
17270, 17271, 17272, 17273,
17275, 17277, 17278, 17279,
17281, 17283, 17284, 17285,
17286, 17287, 17288, 17289,
17290, 17291, 17293, 17294,
17295, 17297, 17298, 17299,
17300, 17301, 17305, 17307,
17308, 17309, 17311, 17313,
17314, 17315, 17316, 17317,
17320, 17321, 17322, 17323,
17324, 17325, 17326, 17327,
17329, 17330, 17331, 17332,
17333, 17334, 17337, 17341,
17342, 17345, 17346, 17347,
17348, 17349, 17350, 17353,
17354, 17355, 17356, 17357,
17358, 17359, 17424, 17606,
17793, 17951, 17990, 18197,
18214, 18233, 18396, 18720,
18767, 19179, 19185, 19193,
19196, 19204, 19215, 19216,
19223, 19237, 19244, 19249,
19352, 19654, 19842, 19971,
19995

RELIGIOUS PROTECTIONISM 6248

REMOND, SARAH P.   9766

REPARATIONS 3119, 3273, 3605,
  4082, 4083, 4084, 4418, 4505,
  4585, 5310, 5444, 5819, 8983,
  14124, 14341

REPUBLICAN PARTY 3560, 10076

RESISTANCE--SEE SLAVE RESISTANCE

RHODE ISLAND 5386, 5388, 5621,
  5845, 8331, 8629, 9879, 9964,
  10699, 10782, 10783, 10784,
  10786, 10787, 10791, 10792,
  10793, 10794, 10795, 10796,
  10798, 10799, 10800, 10801,
  10804, 10807, 10808, 17468

RHODES, JAMES F.   535, 657, 698,
  699, 880, 881, 882, 1440, 1441,
  1853, 2008, 2009

RICE 122, 277, 4143, 8222, 8693,
  11980, 12013, 12019, 12079,
  12083, 12084, 12085, 12168,
  12168, 12205, 12359, 12687,
  12816, 12838, 12854, 12863,
  12866, 12867, 12872, 12876,
  12895, 12907, 12908, 12951,
  12993, 12997, 13070, 13078,
  13093, 13101, 13113, 13148,
  13149, 13150, 14337, 14338,
  14356, 14441, 14506, 14507,
  14851, 15099, 15506, 15839

RICHARDS, FANNIE M.   9574

RICHARDSON, DAVID   1004

RICHMOND WHIG   20535

RICHMOND, VA 2959, 8700, 8864,
  9217, 13494, 13818, 13864,
  15900, 15945, 15949, 15950,
  15960, 16316, 19878, 20535

RILEY, FRANKLIN 1116, 1827

RING SHOUT 15812, 18111
  (SEE ALSO DANCE)

RIO CLARA   7501

RIO DE JANEIRO 4912, 4913, 5632,
  5639, 5641, 6032, 7728, 7729,
  7732, 16309

RIO DE LA PLATA 7513, 7837

ROANOKE, VA   13508

ROBIDOUX, JOSEPH   11533

ROBINSON, WILLIAM H.   18984

ROCKLAND COUNTY, NY   10675

RODNEY, WALTER   766, 801, 1421

RODRIGUES, JOSE H.   1470

ROGERS, J.A.   1738, 5916

ROGERS, SETH   20857

ROGERS, THOMAS   6078

ROSE, WILLIE LEE   902

ROSS, ALEXANDER   18935

ROSS, DAVID   14695

ROSS, FREDERICK A.   17175

ROUSSEAU, J. JACQUES   4574

ROW HOUSE   15470

ROYAL AFRICAN COMPANY   5274, 5311,
   5312, 5313, 5369, 5479, 5548,
   5619, 8306

RUFFIN, EDMUND   14147, 14461

RUFFIN, THOMAS   2169, 9358

RUGGLES, DAVID   9763

RUNAWAY SLAVES   614, 1254, 6197,
   6487, 7254, 7317, 8104, 8288,
   8343, 8369, 8380, 8837, 9031,
   9032, 9096, 9104, 9131, 9159,
   9236, 9299, 9781, 10121, 10343,
   10481, 10487, 11449, 11919,
   11936, 12075, 12279, 12524,
   12613, 12701, 13123, 13355,
   13445, 13557, 13989, 14023,
   14235, 14844, 14873, 15147,
   15283, 15354, 15749, 15791,
   15839, 16372, 16565, 17238,
   18169, 18346, 18841, 19122,
   19396, 19397, 19454, 19613,
   19620, 19657, 19658, 19659,
   19670, 19684, 19685, 19697,
   19698, 19733, 19766, 19782,
   19789, 19794, 19820, 19827,
   19849, 19900, 20053, 20107,
   20221, 20229, 20236, 20237,
   20241, 20243, 20247, 20253,
   20260, 20262, 20271, 20276,
   20277, 20278, 20280, 20282,
   20291, 20292, 20296, 20299,
   20303, 20304, 20307, 20311,
   20312, 20779
   (SEE ALSO FUGITIVE SLAVES)

RUPPIUS, OTTO   4629, 4630

RUSH, BENJAMIN   4164, 15763, 15764

RUSSIAN SERFDOM   2560, 3416, 3457,
   19616

RUTLING, THOMAS (EX-SLAVE)   19111

SABINE LAKE, TX   15077

SACO, JOSE ANTONIO   852

SADLER, ROBERT   18987

SAFFIN, JOHN   10340

SAID, OMAR IBN   12644, 18838,
   18839, 19125

SAINT DOMINGUE, BRITISH OCCUPIED
   14235

SAINT-DOMINGUE   6183, 6266, 6375,
   6559, 6560, 6675, 6994, 9556,
   13120, 17233, 19880, 20081
   (SEE ST. DOMINGUE)

SALEM COMMUNITY, NC   12641

SALEM, MA   5252

SALT INDUSTRY   10863, 13850, 14809

SALT LAKE CITY, UT   11158

SAM (SLAVE)   20125

SAMBO PERSONALITY   747, 748, 939,
   1382, 1524, 1662, 1674, 1836,
   2158, 12204, 15420, 18740,
   18759, 18790, 18913

SAN ANTONIO   13326, 13334, 13447

1633

SAN DOMINGO 1783, 6454, 7166,
7167, 19966, 19972
(SEE SANTO DOMINGO)

SAN FRANCISCO 9451

SAN JOSE DE PARRAL 7826, 7827,
7828

SAN LORENZO 8171

SANDBURG, CARL 9060

SANDERSON, JEREMIAH B. 9641

SANITARY CONDITIONS 15528

SANTA CRUZ 19898

SANTIAGO DE GUATEMALA 14992

SANTO DOMINGO 5452, 6255, 6670,
6994, 7213, 9290, 20138
(SEE SAN DOMINGO)

SAO PAULO, BRAZIL 7500, 7688,
7689, 7863, 7864, 8114, 14321

SARAMAKA 7953, 7954, 7955, 7956,
7959, 19390

SARGEANT, NATHANIEL P. 10421

SATIRE 5031

SAVANNAH, GA 2959, 9575, 9615,
9647, 10200, 11989, 12000,
12004, 12005, 12147, 12206,
15945, 16316, 16317

SAVITT, TODD L. 1366

SCARBOROUGH, WILLIAM K. 1720

SCHLESINGER, ARTHUR M. 1342

SCHLESINGER, ARTHUR M., JR. 1342

SCHOELCHER, VICTOR 2974

SCHOMBURG, ARTHUR A. 269, 827,
1352

SCHURZ, CARL 4391

SCOTT, DRED 4424, 8792, 8976

SCOTT, GEORGE 5929

SCULPTURE 4911, 5106, 8304, 18624
18652

SEA ISLANDS 12135, 12144, 12885,
12962, 13128, 13129, 17476,
17483, 19017, 20702, 21072,
21088

SEAMAN ACTS 8940, 8941, 8994,
9170, 9261, 9290, 9413, 12984,
13004, 19179

SEAMEN 3877, 14744

SEARS, CYRUS 21076

SEASONING 15267, 15615, 16374

SECESSION 6096, 12017, 12097,
12098, 12228, 12261, 12523,
12544, 12859, 12860, 14087,
16725

SECRET SOCIETIES 17489, 18082

SEGREGATION 1554, 2343, 2353,
2362, 2585, 2630, 2669, 2677,
3009, 7860, 8902, 12297, 12298,
15041, 16316, 16776, 21143

SEIGNEURIALISM 2390, 7733

SELF CONCEPTS, SLAVE 391

SELF-DEFENSE 9329, 19674

SELF-PURCHASE 6915, 9059, 9599,
9984, 10058, 10064, 11579,
11763, 16201, 19971

SEMINOLE WAR (1817-1818) 11932,
11973

SEMINOLE WAR (1835-1842) 9767,
11926, 11930, 11933, 13926,
13996, 14048, 19712, 19713,
20229

SEMINOLES 6506, 9767, 11881,
11933, 13905, 13957, 13982,
13986, 13996, 14021, 19712,

19713, 19764, 20229

SENEGAL 3174, 4747

SENEGAMBIA 4748, 4752, 4925, 5043

SERMONS 3710, 16739, 16922

SEWARD, WILLIAM H. 3313, 3752,
4135

SEXUAL PRACTICES 2613, 6468, 7915,
8173, 11842, 14235, 15058,
15452, 16162, 16173, 16182,
16211, 16292, 16414

SHAKERS 21006

SHALER, NATHANIEL S. 1216

SHARECROPPING 14153, 14310, 14438,
14505, 20787

SHARP, GRANVILLE 5659

SHAW, ROBERT G. 20836, 21113

SHELBY IRON COMPANY 11792, 11793,
18768

SHENANDOAH VALLEY 8409, 13561

SHEPARD, ELLA (EX-SLAVE) 19111

SHEPPARD 18989

SHERMAN, JOHN 20760

SHERMAN, WILLIAM T. 2668, 12041,
20355, 20360, 20784, 21002

SHINGLETON, ROYCE 15415

SHIP MANIFESTS 15123

SHOTGUN HOUSE 5127, 15470, 15493,
15494, 15505, 15542, 15543
(SEE ALSO HOUSING)

SHOUTS 17665
(SEE ALSO DANCE)

SHUGG, ROGER W. 1924

SICKLE-CELL TRAIT 2980, 15839

SIERRA LEONE 2183, 4604, 4650,
4651, 4844, 4883, 5941, 8342,
8722, 9573, 10317, 19340, 19827

SIERRA LEONE COMPANY 8722, 10226

SILK RAISING 7370

SILVER 7826, 7827, 7828

SIMMS, WILLIAM G. 2201, 2791,
3737, 4394, 4464, 4496, 4531,
19380

SINGLETON, WILLIAM H. 12786,
12805

SKILLED SLAVES 7399, 8663, 13257,
14730, 14753, 14757
(SEE ALSO CRAFTSMEN)

SKIPWITH, PEYTON 18728

SLANG 18244

SLAVE BRANDING IRON 6789

SLAVE BREEDING 6807, 14335, 14503,
14504, 15071, 15162, 15183,
16565

SLAVE BURNING 10420, 10456, 10457,
10507, 20043

SLAVE CHILD MORTALITY 6710, 14975,
14976, 15015
(SEE ALSO MORTALITY, SLAVE)

SLAVE COAST 6013

SLAVE CODES--SEE LAW

SLAVE COMMUNITY 1164, 1679, 3590,
4246, 6405, 11883, 12175, 12176,
12916, 14854, 15228, 15242,
15510, 16114, 16137, 16319,
17237, 17247, 17486, 17951,
19488, 19575

SLAVE DRIVERS 1940, 14235, 14839,
14840, 14841, 14843, 14844,
14847, 14848, 14851, 14854,
14855, 14856, 14865, 15106,

19620, 19622, 19623, 19624,
19625, 19628, 19629, 19631,
19633, 19638, 19640, 19642,
19644, 19645, 19646, 19647,
19654, 19655, 19656, 19657,
19658, 19662, 19664, 19670,
19674, 19677, 19678, 19679,
19680, 19681, 19682, 19683,
19684, 19687, 19691, 19693,
19697, 19698, 19699, 19700,
19702, 19703, 19704, 19706,
19708, 19709, 19716, 19717,
19718, 19719, 19720, 19722,
19724, 19725, 19727, 19728,
19729, 19731, 19732, 19733,
19734, 19740, 19742, 19746,
19747, 19748, 19749, 19750,
19751, 19752, 19756, 19757,
19758, 19759, 19760, 19763,
19764, 19765, 19766, 19767,
19768, 19769, 19770, 19771,
19772, 19773, 19774, 19775,
19776, 19777, 19778, 19779,
19782, 19783, 19784, 19787,
19789, 19791, 19792, 19794,
19795, 19796, 19799, 19800,
19801, 19808, 19810, 19813,
19814, 19815, 19817, 19818,
19820, 19821, 19823, 19824,
19826, 19827, 19829, 19831,
19832, 19834, 19836, 19837,
19838, 19839, 19845, 19846,
19847, 19849, 19850, 19851,
19852, 19854, 19855, 19856,
19857, 19882, 19919, 19957,
19960, 19963, 19971, 19978,
20010, 20037, 20095, 20101,
20107, 20108, 20163, 20221,
20223, 20237, 20243, 20247,
20260, 20278, 20280, 20282,
20307, 20317, 20388, 20450
(SEE ALSO FUGITIVE SLAVES,
RUNAWAY SLAVES, SLAVE REVOLTS,
UNDERGROUND RAILROAD)

SLAVE REVOLTS   761, 839, 913, 1102,
    1143, 1380, 1392, 1477, 1487,
    1648, 1679, 1783, 1900, 1922,
    3440, 4719, 5082, 5096, 5278,
    5481, 5658, 6066, 6149, 6232,
    6241, 6312, 6313, 6344, 6346,
    6355, 6404, 6405, 6454, 6489,
    6597, 6614, 6623, 6660, 6670,
    6674, 6682, 6756, 6822, 6851,
    6869, 6939, 6960, 6985, 7012,

7013, 7016, 7023, 7057, 7068,
7086, 7115, 7165, 7166, 7167,
7173, 7174, 7194, 7249, 7414,
7416, 7452, 7489, 7512, 7662,
7690, 7885, 7893, 7894, 7939,
7984, 8152, 8292, 8324, 8343,
8649, 8898, 9009, 9062, 9128,
9159, 9277, 9303, 9304, 9964,
10566, 10621, 10622, 10627,
10642, 10643, 10645, 10650,
10673, 10696, 10697, 10702,
10705, 11518, 11609, 11768,
11917, 12282, 12328, 12453,
12584, 12589, 12775, 12797,
12825, 12912, 12913, 12934,
13003, 13004, 13005, 13006,
13033, 13106, 13120, 13138,
13286, 13373, 13429, 13453,
13494, 13596, 13597, 13676,
13724, 13725, 13756, 13776,
13777, 13868, 13869, 13989,
14033, 14694, 15080, 15120,
15121, 15354, 15554, 15839,
16105, 16243, 16316, 17044,
17057, 17238, 19179, 19455,
19481, 19533, 19583, 19674,
19677, 19678, 19729, 19789,
19834, 19851, 19859, 19861,
19863, 19864, 19865, 19866,
19869, 19870, 19873, 19875,
19878, 19880, 19881, 19886,
19894, 19898, 19900, 19902,
19903, 19904, 19905, 19906,
19915, 19916, 19918, 19922,
19926, 19932, 19935, 19941,
19942, 19947, 19949, 19950,
19955, 19962, 19964, 19966,
19969, 19971, 19972, 19973,
19974, 19976, 19979, 19985,
19993, 19994, 19995, 19998,
20001, 20002, 20003, 20005,
20007, 20015, 20017, 20018,
20021, 20025, 20026, 20030,
20031, 20042, 20043, 20044,
20045, 20046, 20047, 20053,
20054, 20056, 20060, 20061,
20064, 20068, 20075, 20079,
20082, 20084, 20087, 20089,
20093, 20094, 20095, 20096,
20097, 20098, 20105, 20109,
20119, 20120, 20122, 20123,
20124, 20125, 20126, 20127,
20135, 20137, 20138, 20141,
20143, 20147, 20149, 20152,
20156, 20158, 20159, 20162,

5641, 5644, 5645, 5646, 5648,
5649, 5650, 5651, 5652, 5653,
5654, 5655, 5657, 5658, 5659,
5660, 5661, 5662, 5663, 5664,
5667, 5668, 5669, 5670, 5671,
5672, 5673, 5674, 5675, 5676,
5677, 5678, 5679, 5680, 5681,
5682, 5683, 5686, 5687, 5688,
5689, 5690, 5693, 5694, 5695,
5696, 5697, 5698, 5699, 5701,
5704, 5706, 5710, 5711, 5712,
5713, 5714, 5716, 5717, 5718,
5719, 5720, 5721, 5722, 5723,
5726, 5728, 5731, 5732, 5733,
5735, 5736, 5737, 5738, 5739,
5741, 5742, 5743, 5744, 5745,
5746, 5747, 5748, 5749, 5750,
5751, 5752, 5753, 5754, 5757,
5758, 5759, 5760, 5762, 5763,
5764, 5765, 5766, 5767, 5769,
5770, 5771, 5772, 5773, 5774,
5776, 5777, 5778, 5780, 5781,
5783, 5785, 5787, 5788, 5789,
5790, 5793, 5794, 5795, 5797,
5798, 5800, 5801, 5802, 5803,
5804, 5805, 5806, 5807, 5809,
5810, 5811, 5812, 5814, 5815,
5816, 5819, 5822, 5823, 5824,
5825, 5826, 5827, 5831, 5832,
5833, 5834, 5835, 5836, 5837,
5838, 5839, 5840, 5841, 5842,
5843, 5845, 5846, 5847, 5849,
5850, 5853, 5854, 5855, 5856,
5857, 5858, 5859, 5860, 5862,
5863, 5864, 5865, 5866, 5867,
5868, 5869, 5870, 5871, 5873,
5874, 5876, 5879, 5880, 5881,
5882, 5883, 5884, 5889, 5891,
5893, 5895, 5896, 5897, 5898,
5899, 5900, 5901, 5902, 5904,
5905, 5906, 5907, 5910, 5911,
5913, 5914, 5916, 5917, 5918,
5919, 5920, 5921, 5922, 5923,
5924, 5925, 5927, 5928, 5929,
5930, 5931, 5932, 5933, 5934,
5935, 5936, 5937, 5938, 5939,
5940, 5941, 5942, 5943, 5945,
5946, 5947, 5948, 5949, 5950,
5951, 5952, 5953, 5954, 5955,
5956, 5957, 5958, 5959, 5960,
5961, 5962, 5963, 5964, 5965,
5966, 5967, 5968, 5970, 5971,
5972, 5973, 5974, 5975, 5976,
5977, 5978, 5979, 5980, 5981,
5983, 5984, 5986, 5990, 5992,

5995, 5996, 5997, 5998, 5999,
6000, 6003, 6006, 6007, 6008,
6009, 6010, 6011, 6012, 6013,
6014, 6016, 6017, 6018, 6020,
6021, 6024, 6025, 6026, 6027,
6028, 6029, 6031, 6032, 6033,
6034, 6035, 6036, 6037, 6038,
6039, 6040, 6043, 6045, 6047,
6048, 6049, 6050, 6053, 6056,
6057, 6058, 6061, 6062, 6063,
6064, 6065, 6066, 6068, 6069,
6070, 6071, 6072, 6077, 6078,
6079, 6080, 6081, 6082, 6083,
6084, 6085, 6086, 6087, 6088,
6089, 6091, 6093, 6094, 6095,
6096, 6097, 6098, 6099, 6101,
6102, 6103, 6105, 6106, 6107,
6108, 6110, 6111, 6112, 6114,
6116, 6117, 6118, 6119, 6316,
6513, 6927, 7158, 7160, 7161,
7201, 7264, 8136, 8260, 8336,
8342, 8364, 8419, 8420, 8425,
8452, 8456, 8505, 8520, 8527,
8578, 8616, 8626, 9062, 9309,
9311, 9964, 10445, 10659, 10771,
12320, 13807, 14235, 14496,
14528, 14977, 14983, 14984,
15146, 15187, 15354, 15599,
16309, 17110, 17173, 19677,
20022, 20196, 20205

SLAVE TRADE, BRAZILIAN 579, 5155,
5218, 5219, 5220, 5221, 5247,
5248, 5336, 5530, 5611, 5632,
5639, 5641, 5673, 5700, 5705,
7351, 7465, 7808, 8136, 17668

SLAVE TRADE, BRITISH 1475, 5054,
5175, 5179, 5183, 5196, 5197,
5206, 5207, 5224, 5246, 5267,
5274, 5281, 5286, 5289, 5296,
5306, 5312, 5313, 5326, 5420,
5421, 5431, 5466, 5543, 5554,
5565, 5631, 5648, 5652, 5668,
5670, 5681, 5686, 5687, 5695,
5696, 5697, 5698, 5699, 5701,
5720, 5721, 5726, 5732, 5733,
5737, 5738, 5739, 5742, 5749,
5750, 5753, 5754, 5766, 5767,
5768, 5769, 5770, 5776, 5778,
5780, 5824, 5832, 5833, 5835,
5849, 5853, 5855, 5858, 5859,
5860, 5863, 5865, 5866, 5867,
5868, 5869, 5870, 5871, 5873,
5874, 5882, 5884, 5898, 5919,

17147, 17275, 17293, 17307

SOIL 14120

SOIL EXHAUSTION 11427, 14118,
14238, 14243, 14273, 15007

SOMERSET, NJ 8538, 10517, 10555,
10586

SOMERSETT'S CASE 8762, 8888, 9107,
9331

SONGS, SLAVE 53, 79, 164, 201,
229, 299, 307, 345, 356, 371,
405, 439, 491, 546, 551, 1025,
1070, 1206, 1252, 1302, 1309,
1331, 1365, 1468, 1564, 1795,
1796, 1797, 1798, 1799, 1867,
1877, 1970, 1972, 2013, 4701,
4741, 4787, 4788, 4819, 4893,
4896, 4905, 4920, 4934, 4946,
4952, 4953, 4954, 4978, 4995,
5055, 5087, 5126, 5137, 6122,
6208, 6299, 6302, 6370, 6410,
6434, 6444, 6529, 6576, 6673,
6776, 6782, 7241, 7612, 7842,
7843, 7993, 8304, 9676, 9863,
10263, 11543, 12000, 12144,
12242, 12341, 12347, 12401,
12477, 12653, 13033, 16319,
16430, 16431, 16565, 16689,
16711, 16847, 16905, 16933,
16987, 17020, 17021, 17043,
17050, 17061, 17138, 17201,
17243, 17321, 17322, 17411,
17420, 17495, 17497, 17498,
17499, 17500, 17501, 17502,
17503, 17507, 17508, 17509,
17510, 17511, 17512, 17513,
17514, 17515, 17516, 17517,
17519, 17521, 17522, 17523,
17526, 17531, 17532, 17534,
17535, 17536, 17539, 17541,
17543, 17545, 17546, 17547,
17548, 17549, 17550, 17551,
17552, 17553, 17554, 17557,
17559, 17560, 17561, 17563,
17566, 17567, 17569, 17570,
17571, 17572, 17573, 17575,
17576, 17579, 17585, 17586,
17588, 17589, 17591, 17592,
17593, 17595, 17597, 17598,
17600, 17602, 17603, 17604,
17606, 17607, 17609, 17611,

17612, 17613, 17614, 17615,
17616, 17617, 17621, 17622,
17623, 17625, 17626, 17628,
17635, 17636, 17637, 17638,
17639, 17640, 17641, 17642,
17644, 17645, 17646, 17650,
17651, 17653, 17655, 17656,
17657, 17660, 17661, 17662,
17663, 17664, 17665, 17666,
17669, 17670, 17671, 17672,
17673, 17675, 17676, 17678,
17680, 17682, 17683, 17684,
17685, 17686, 17688, 17690,
17691, 17693, 17694, 17696,
17697, 17698, 17699, 17700,
17702, 17703, 17704, 17706,
17707, 17709, 17710, 17711,
17712, 17713, 17717, 17719,
17722, 17723, 17725, 17726,
17730, 17734, 17736, 17737,
17738, 17741, 17745, 17746,
17748, 17749, 17750, 17751,
17753, 17754, 17755, 17757,
17758, 17759, 17760, 17762,
17764, 17768, 17770, 17771,
17774, 17775, 17777, 17778,
17779, 17782, 17783, 17784,
17785, 17786, 17789, 17790,
17791, 17792, 17793, 17794,
17795, 17797, 17798, 17799,
17802, 17803, 17807, 17808,
17809, 17812, 17815, 17816,
17817, 17818, 17819, 17820,
17822, 17824, 17825, 17826,
17828, 17829, 17830, 17831,
17832, 17833, 17836, 17840,
17841, 17842, 17843, 17844,
17845, 17846, 17847, 17848,
17849, 17850, 17851, 17852,
17853, 17854, 17856, 17859,
17860, 17862, 17863, 17864,
17866, 17867, 17868, 17870,
17871, 17872, 17873, 17875,
17876, 17877, 17878, 17879,
17880, 17881, 17882, 17883,
17884, 17890, 17891, 17892,
17893, 17894, 17895, 17896,
17897, 17898, 17899, 17900,
17901, 17902, 17904, 17905,
17911, 17912, 17913, 17914,
17915, 17916, 17917, 17918,
17919, 17920, 17921, 17922,
17923, 17925, 17930, 17931,
17935, 17937, 17938, 17940,
17941, 17942, 17944, 17945,

17946, 17947, 17948, 17949,
17950, 17951, 17952, 17953,
17954, 17955, 17956, 17957,
17960, 17961, 17962, 17964,
17965, 17966, 17967, 17968,
17971, 17972, 17976, 17978,
17979, 17980, 17981, 17982,
17983, 17984, 17985, 17987,
17988, 17989, 17990, 17991,
17992, 17995, 17996, 17997,
17998, 17999, 18000, 18001,
18002, 18003, 18004, 18005,
18067, 18221, 18250, 18267,
19302, 19352, 20876
(SEE ALSO SPIRITUALS)

SOPHIA, CATHARINA 7772

SORCERY, NEGRO 18106
(SEE ALSO WITCHCRAFT)

SOULE, SILASS 10943

SOURCE MATERIALS 2, 8, 13, 16, 22,
79, 80, 98, 100, 115, 119, 120,
123, 143, 144, 152, 171, 172,
173, 175, 176, 177, 183, 188,
191, 201, 203, 204, 232, 235,
270, 273, 304, 310, 318, 324,
333, 340, 345, 348, 352, 355,
356, 359, 368, 375, 381, 389,
391, 398, 407, 424, 436, 437,
443, 444, 445, 456, 464, 465,
467, 468, 469, 479, 480, 484,
488, 501, 513, 536, 548, 560,
582, 583, 587, 589, 606, 614,
619, 621, 623, 625, 626, 628,
1021, 1382, 1561, 1583, 1822,
1922, 1984, 2055, 4052, 6574,
7091, 8374, 9009, 10023, 10749,
11297, 12336, 12592, 18700,
18961, 18969, 19040, 19138,
20648
(SEE ALSO DOCUMENTS)

SOUTH AFRICA 2361, 2954

SOUTH AMERICA 136, 997, 1127,
1212, 1648, 2204, 2390, 2654,
2852, 3441, 4857, 5624, 5895,
6318, 6414, 6436, 6479, 6896,
6900, 6901, 6914, 7024, 7027,
7224, 7234, 7316, 7342, 7555,
7692, 7746, 7747, 7834, 7875,
7881, 7947, 7953, 7954, 7955,

7957, 7959, 7975, 8028, 8101,
8139, 8159, 8168, 8170, 9168,
20122

SOUTH CAROLINA 326, 577, 728, 864,
1553, 1758, 1817, 2205, 2364,
2466, 2591, 2789, 3130, 3910,
4709, 4987, 5107, 5140, 5253,
5268, 5773, 6000, 6420, 6607,
8288, 8319, 8364, 8366, 8367,
8376, 8377, 8400, 8413, 8419,
8420, 8421, 8480, 8505, 8506,
8507, 8531, 8532, 8533, 8534,
8549, 8561, 8621, 8642, 8645,
8650, 8660, 8668, 8678, 8693,
8699, 8718, 8726, 8727, 8728,
8729, 8735, 8898, 8940, 8941,
8948, 8949, 8950, 8951, 8963,
8966, 8967, 8968, 8969, 8970,
8984, 9163, 9213, 9214, 9290,
9339, 9340, 9788, 9889, 9986,
10106, 11902, 12020, 12079,
12103, 12168, 12825, 12829,
12830, 12835, 12836, 12837,
12838, 12841, 12842, 12843,
12844, 12849, 12852, 12853,
12854, 12855, 12856, 12858,
12859, 12860, 12862, 12863,
12864, 12865, 12866, 12867,
12868, 12869, 12871, 12872,
12873, 12874, 12875, 12876,
12877, 12878, 12879, 12881,
12882, 12883, 12885, 12886,
12887, 12888, 12890, 12892,
12893, 12894, 12895, 12896,
12899, 12900, 12907, 12908,
12909, 12912, 12913, 12916,
12917, 12918, 12920, 12925,
12928, 12929, 12931, 12933,
12934, 12935, 12936, 12940,
12950, 12951, 12961, 12962,
12964, 12965, 12969, 12971,
12974, 12975, 12976, 12977,
12978, 12979, 12981, 12984,
12986, 12987, 12989, 12991,
12993, 12995, 12997, 12999,
13000, 13003, 13004, 13005,
13006, 13007, 13008, 13010,
13011, 13012, 13014, 13020,
13021, 13022, 13023, 13025,
13026, 13027, 13029, 13030,
13031, 13033, 13034, 13036,
13037, 13040, 13041, 13042,
13043, 13046, 13048, 13050,
13051, 13053, 13054, 13058,

13059, 13060, 13062, 13063,
13064, 13065, 13066, 13067,
13068, 13069, 13070, 13071,
13072, 13073, 13076, 13077,
13078, 13080, 13082, 13084,
13088, 13091, 13092, 13093,
13094, 13096, 13098, 13100,
13106, 13107, 13108, 13110,
13111, 13113, 13115, 13116,
13117, 13120, 13121, 13122,
13123, 13124, 13126, 13127,
13128, 13129, 13131, 13132,
13133, 13136, 13138, 13139,
13140, 13141, 13143, 13144,
13145, 13147, 13148, 13149,
13150, 13151, 13152, 13153,
13154, 13157, 13158, 13159,
13160, 13161, 13162, 13171,
13563, 14112, 14298, 14741,
14743, 14805, 14806, 14851,
15099, 15341, 15521, 15522,
15574, 15639, 15676, 15774,
15839, 15848, 15880, 15978,
15992, 16066, 16587, 16629,
16751, 16771, 16789, 16868,
16906, 16942, 16969, 16999,
17191, 17737, 18224, 18225,
18504, 18586, 18973, 19009,
19017, 19179, 19193, 19224,
19301, 19574, 19782, 19849,
19949, 19971, 20005, 20138,
20262, 20271, 20479, 20802,
20907, 21034, 21072

SOUTHAMPTON COUNTY, VA 13777

SOUTHERN AID SOCIETY 3774

SOUTHERN CULTIVATOR 13332

SOUTHERN HISTORICAL COLLECTION,
   UNIVERSITY OF NORTH CAROLINA
   188

SOUTHEY, ROBERT 4131, 4132

SPAIN 2718, 2992, 6316, 6331,
   7128, 7129, 7574, 7901, 7903,
   8326, 15735, 19810

SPALDING, THOMAS 12135, 14831

SPANISH AMERICA 77, 322, 413, 753,
   754, 759, 919, 1212, 1535, 1731,
   2454, 2718, 5622, 5623, 5624,

5628, 6211, 6581, 6582, 6583,
   6606, 6708, 6717, 7390, 7392,
   7400, 7401, 7407, 7408, 7413,
   7455, 7548, 7574, 7613, 7651,
   7652, 7746, 7747, 7780, 7790,
   7806, 7811, 7813, 7847, 7860,
   7861, 7901, 7903, 7919, 7922,
   7923, 8042, 8090, 8191, 9997,
   11047, 14992, 15716, 18176,
   20053

SPANISH EXPLORATION 3190, 3191,
   3201, 3696, 3745, 6606, 7652,
   7847, 8190, 11026, 11047, 1112

SPARKS, JARED 13034

SPARTANBURG COUNTY, SC 8948, 894
   13008

SPEECH 19412
   (SEE ALSO LANGUAGE)

SPEECH DEFECTS, SLAVE 19395

SPIRIT MEDIUMSHIP 6173

SPIRITUALS 307, 491, 586, 630,
   1252, 1468, 1867, 1972, 4946,
   12477, 16708, 16711, 16740,
   16918, 16935, 16987, 17020,
   17021, 17050, 17061, 17138,
   17147, 17201, 17321, 17420,
   17493, 17494, 17506, 17519,
   17521, 17526, 17529, 17554,
   17555, 17562, 17574, 17577,
   17578, 17582, 17583, 17609,
   17611, 17630, 17633, 17648,
   17658, 17675, 17677, 17685,
   17688, 17697, 17698, 17707,
   17710, 17711, 17712, 17726,
   17729, 17730, 17731, 17736,
   17737, 17758, 17760, 17769,
   17770, 17771, 17782, 17783,
   17784, 17793, 17797, 17802,
   17807, 17812, 17816, 17822,
   17853, 17858, 17859, 17862,
   17871, 17872, 17873, 17875,
   17877, 17883, 17884, 17893,
   17904, 17912, 17922, 17923,
   17930, 17933, 17934, 17939,
   17943, 17944, 17945, 17949,
   17951, 17952, 17966, 17986,
   17990, 17998, 18003, 18250
   (SEE ALSO SONGS, SLAVE)

SPLIT LABOR MARKETS   2148, 14106,
   14107

SPOONER, LYSANDER   3038

SPOTSYLVANIA COUNTY, VA   8436

SPRING PLANTATION   6683

ST. BARTHOLOMEW   6299

ST. CROIX   6987, 7249, 7250, 9646

ST. CRUZAN   6986, 19316

ST. DOMINGUE   6481, 6496, 6598,
   6798, 6822, 6852, 9506
   (SEE SAINT-DOMINGUE)

ST. EUSTATIA   6748

ST. HELENA ISLAND   12932, 12977,
   12978, 17510

ST. INIGOES MANOR   11400

ST. KITTS   6335, 6472, 6473, 6553,
   6649, 6862, 6923, 7049, 7203

ST. LANDRY PARISH, LA   9731, 12234

ST. LOUIS   9459, 11538, 11553,
   11584, 11587, 11596, 11600,
   11638, 15140, 15280, 15281,
   16316

ST. LUCIA   6358, 19263

ST. MARTIN   6748

ST. SIMON'S ISLAND, GA   12140

ST. TAMMANY PARISH, LA   9337

ST. THOMAS   6748

ST. VINCENT   6541, 6542, 6829

STAG HARBOR CORRECTOR   4498

STAMPP, KENNETH M.   1043, 1102,
   1567, 1850, 1926, 1984, 2037

STANUP, RICHARD   13803

STARR, CHESTER G.   931

STARR, FREDERICK   11540

STATUS, SLAVE   15205

STEARNS, GEORGE L.   20418

STEELE, RICHARD   6201

STEPHEN, JAMES   6159, 6726, 10173

STEPHENS, ALEXANDER H.   11009

STEPHENSON, WENDELL H.   823, 16668

STEVENS, THADDEUS   3061, 4434

STEVENS, THOMAS   11991

STEWART, CHARLES   19006

STILL, JAMES   19007

STILL, PETER   10554, 19814

STILL, WILLIAM   9732, 19565

STOCKTON, ROBERT F.   2749, 5410

STONE CUTTERS, SLAVE   14484

STONE, ALFRED HOLT   973, 1810

STONO REBELLION   8898, 12825,
   15839

STORM TOWERS   12855

STORY, JOSEPH   9144

STOWE, HARRIET B.   344, 758, 1287,
   1395, 1459, 1487, 1521, 1522,
   1608, 1969, 2004, 2005, 2575,
   2640, 2778, 2792, 3188, 3240,
   3466, 3467, 3627, 3660, 3768,
   3769, 3882, 4117, 4250, 4469,
   4507, 4542, 15224, 16898, 18897,
   19037, 19376

STRADER V. GRAHAM   11303

STRAYER, JACOB   19009

TAPIA Y RIVERA, ALEJANDRO   6508

TARIFFS   3343, 3411, 12506, 14291

TARKARS   5039

TASK SYSTEM   15791, 20271

TAXATION   8799, 12534, 13344,
   13807, 14537, 14538, 14556,
   20347

TAYLOR, JIMMIE   19010

TAYLOR, JOHN   13477, 14340

TAYLOR, O.C.W.   19011

TAYLOR, SUSIE K.   20423

TAYLOR, WILLIAM B.   15070

TAYLOR, ZACHARY   12553

TEAS, THOMAS S.   18449

TECHNOLOGICAL CHANGE   5471

TEETH   15809

TELEVISION, SLAVERY ON   724, 1995

TENNESSEE   538, 1254, 8952, 8981,
   8987, 9089, 9155, 9298, 9831,
   10008, 10027, 10029, 10113,
   11297, 11319, 13173, 13174,
   13175, 13176, 13178, 13179,
   13180, 13182, 13184, 13185,
   13186, 13188, 13189, 13190,
   13191, 13192, 13193, 13194,
   13195, 13196, 13197, 13198,
   13200, 13201, 13202, 13206,
   13207, 13209, 13210, 13211,
   13213, 13214, 13215, 13218,
   13220, 13221, 13222, 13224,
   13226, 13227, 13228, 13229,
   13232, 13233, 13234, 13235,
   13236, 13238, 13239, 13240,
   13241, 13244, 13245, 13246,
   13247, 13250, 13251, 13252,
   13253, 13255, 13256, 13257,
   13258, 13259, 13260, 13261,
   13263, 13264, 13266, 13267,
   13270, 13271, 13273, 13274,
   13275, 13277, 13278, 13279,

13280, 13281, 13282, 13283,
13284, 14638, 15006, 15211,
15713, 15806, 17086, 17223,
18921, 20496, 20735

TENNESSEE VALLEY   14336

TERRITORIES, SLAVERY IN   2124,
   2127, 2763, 4091, 7660, 7661,
   8770, 8800, 9047, 9087, 9099,
   9100, 9125, 9395, 10823, 10828,
   10830, 10844, 10846, 10847,
   10848, 10853, 10854, 10942,
   11002, 11009, 11013, 11018,
   11019, 11022, 11023, 11036,
   11037, 11042, 11043, 11044,
   11053, 11054, 11055, 11061,
   11062, 11068, 14402

TESTIMONY, SLAVE   64, 162, 236,
   410, 467, 468, 469, 606, 621,
   623, 694, 734, 735, 1021, 1125,
   1215, 1560, 1561, 1563, 2055,
   11297, 12033, 13737, 13899,
   14056, 15559, 16010, 16409,
   17325, 17662, 18935, 18960,
   18961, 18962, 19003, 19035,
   19040, 19116, 19138, 19789
   (SEE ALSO AUTOBIOGRAPHIES,
   INTERVIEWS, LETTERS, NARRATIVES)

TEXAS   98, 144, 625, 626, 2571,
   2572, 2781, 4272, 5192, 5200,
   5282, 5449, 5789, 5879, 5880,
   8066, 8067, 8954, 9037, 9112,
   9117, 9512, 9713, 9776, 9846,
   9957, 11065, 11119, 11176,
   13285, 13286, 13287, 13288,
   13289, 13290, 13294, 13295,
   13296, 13297, 13298, 13299,
   13300, 13301, 13302, 13304,
   13305, 13306, 13308, 13309,
   13310, 13311, 13312, 13313,
   13314, 13316, 13317, 13318,
   13319, 13320, 13321, 13323,
   13324, 13325, 13326, 13328,
   13329, 13330, 13331, 13332,
   13333, 13334, 13335, 13336,
   13337, 13338, 13339, 13340,
   13343, 13344, 13345, 13346,
   13347, 13348, 13349, 13350,
   13352, 13353, 13354, 13355,
   13356, 13358, 13360, 13361,
   13362, 13364, 13365, 13367,
   13368, 13369, 13371, 13373,

13374, 13377, 13378, 13379,
13381, 13384, 13385, 13387,
13388, 13389, 13390, 13391,
13392, 13393, 13394, 13395,
13396, 13397, 13399, 13402,
13403, 13405, 13407, 13408,
13409, 13411, 13412, 13413,
13414, 13415, 13417, 13418,
13419, 13420, 13424, 13426,
13428, 13429, 13430, 13431,
13432, 13433, 13436, 13437,
13438, 13439, 13440, 13441,
13443, 13445, 13446, 13447,
13448, 13449, 13450, 13451,
13452, 13453, 13454, 13455,
13456, 13457, 13458, 13462,
13463, 13464, 14339, 14509,
14739, 15077, 15117, 15860,
15937, 16684, 17089, 19582,
19998, 20093, 20135

TEXTBOOKS, SLAVERY IN 3, 4, 12,
17, 101, 243, 259, 362, 432,
439, 463, 498, 552, 594, 1160,
1839, 1855, 1980, 2377, 2378,
15342

TEXTILES 1647, 7344, 7389, 7400,
7623, 7624, 8085, 8566, 11450,
11718, 11753, 12995, 14243,
14375, 14376, 14380, 14700,
14723, 14726, 14727, 14728,
14741, 14759, 14760, 14762,
14767, 14769, 14788, 14797,
14798, 14813, 14815, 14819,
14829, 15785, 16400, 17438,
19790

THARP ESTATE 6342

THAYER, A.J. 2857

THELWELL, MICHAEL 839

THIRD SEMINOLE WAR 11870

THIRTEENTH AMENDMENT 9206, 9976,
9977, 9979, 10000, 10001, 10006,
10031, 10053, 10054

THIRTY-THIRD U.S. COLORED TROOPS
20777, 20857

THOMAS COUNTY, GA 8818, 12110

THOMAS, JAMES P. 9828, 15870

THOMAS, JESSE B. 2901

THOMAS, WILLIAM H. 732, 861, 133
1958

THOMPSON, EDGAR T. 1390

THOMPSON, LEWIS 12464

THOREAU, HENRY D. 3606, 4480

THORNTON, WILLIAM 3785

THORNWELL, JAMES H. 2131, 2165,
2579, 16814, 17225

THORPE, EARL E. 731

THRASH, MARK 19094

THURMAN, JACK (SLAVE) 18496

TIME FACTOR 16173, 16179

TIMEHRI 6243

TINSMITH 18606

TOBACCO 5843, 5899, 6936, 7019,
7657, 7658, 7804, 8489, 8490,
11294, 11328, 11425, 11426,
11482, 11483, 11492, 12686,
12773, 12804, 13525, 13552,
13602, 13690, 13793, 13811,
14303, 14325, 14522, 14638,
14671, 14736, 14772, 14783,
14785, 15007

TOBAGO 6434, 6924, 7058, 7268,
7612, 17621, 18135

TOGO 4994

TOMM, JIM 14056

TONY (SLAVE) 10426

TORONTO 10227, 10257, 10258

TOYNBEE, ARNOLD 1113

TRANS-MISSISSIPPI WEST 616, 617,
11065

TRANSCENDENTALISTS 4438

TRANSPORTATION, USE OF SLAVES IN
19790

TRAVELERS' ACCOUNTS 119, 510, 543,
1296, 1395, 1396, 1984, 2195,
3107, 3108, 3112, 3497, 3588,
3622, 3662, 3735, 3899, 4001,
4055, 4106, 4199, 4265, 4290,
4324, 4373, 4452, 4460, 4550,
4564, 7431, 7879, 8077, 11563,
11701, 11777, 12531, 12727,
13077, 13623, 14854, 15194,
15285, 15479, 15899, 15964,
18092

TRAYLOR, ROBERT (EX-SLAVE) 3885

TREATY OF GHENT 4039

TREDEGAR IRON WORKS 13595, 19790

TREPONEMATOSIS 15754

TREXLER, HARRISON A. 535

TRIALS, SLAVE 7637, 8580, 8831,
8837, 8896, 9073, 9108, 9109,
9110, 9111, 9112, 9115, 9117,
9119, 13040, 13222, 14894
(SEE ALSO COURTS, SLAVE)

TRIANGULAR TRADE 5163, 5417, 5738,
5739, 5754, 5798, 5992
(SEE ALSO SLAVE TRADE, ATLANTIC)

TRIANGULAR TRADE MYTH 5798

TRICKSTER 4946, 18239
(SEE ALSO FOLKLORE)

TRINIDAD 1290, 2174, 5537, 5538,
5681, 6204, 6277, 6278, 6279,
6433, 6434, 6467, 6482, 6510,
6620, 6627, 6632, 6634, 6641,
6768, 6815, 6849, 6870, 6913,
6941, 7058, 7151, 7173, 7208,
7237, 7238, 7239, 7241, 7268,
7288, 7612, 9428, 14118, 17190,
17621, 18135

TROLLOPE, ANTHONY 2522

TROLLOPE, F.M. 4290

TROTTER, JAMES M. 1867

TRUCK PATCHES 7121, 14730

TRUTH, SOJOURNER 3882, 9493, 9743,
10632, 19016

TUBERCULOSIS 15740, 15772, 15820
(SEE ALSO DISEASE, MEDICINE)

TUBMAN, EMILY 2396

TUBMAN, HARRIET 3379, 16372,
16391, 16445, 16461, 17583,
18819, 19483, 19540, 19693,
19703, 19737, 19791, 19847

TUCKER, BEVERLY 3196

TURNER, FREDERICK J. 1324, 1442,
1618, 1919, 9956, 9957

TURNER, HENRY M. 2474

TURNER, JAMES MILTON 9636, 9637,
9705, 11554

TURNER, LORENZO D. 944, 19280,
19342

TURNER, MAJOR SQUIRE 14169

TURNER, NAT 678, 679, 680, 681,
711, 770, 831, 839, 853, 913,
978, 1079, 1133, 1163, 1196,
1207, 1218, 1232, 1357, 1373,
1392, 1477, 1570, 1571, 1642,
1823, 1879, 1883, 1898, 1899,
1900, 1922, 1923, 1976, 2001,
5082, 6623, 8882, 9128, 12453,
12775, 13502, 13596, 13597,
13776, 13868, 13869, 17044,
19179, 19834, 19867, 19868,
19883, 19897, 19915, 19922,
19925, 19932, 19950, 19959,
19962, 19964, 19968, 19974,
19985, 19986, 19995, 19998,
20001, 20015, 20017, 20018,
20042, 20056, 20078, 20090,
20094, 20095, 20097, 20098,
20116, 20127, 20152, 20171,
20175, 20188, 20193, 20194,
20155, 20207, 20213

TURPENTINE   12628, 14775, 14776

TUSCALOOSA COUNTY, AL   9833, 11724

TWAIN, MARK   2069, 2110, 2111,
   2115, 2190, 2349, 2443, 2489,
   2723, 2724, 2725, 2727, 2883,
   2891, 3014, 4258, 9387, 11625,
   19388, 19431

TYLER, JULIA J.   13794

TYLER, ROYALL   3048

TYPHOID FEVER   15604

U.S. ARMY   12517, 20513, 20703,
   20704, 20711, 20726, 20750,
   20757, 20799, 20835, 20910,
   21052, 21081, 21116, 21117,
   21144, 21149

U.S. COLORED TROOPS   377, 9727,
   10142, 12363, 15734, 17696,
   19012, 20347, 20513, 20669,
   20672, 20677, 20680, 20692,
   20703, 20704, 20705, 20711,
   20713, 20720, 20726, 20743,
   20748, 20757, 20768, 20769,
   20773, 20790, 20798, 20827,
   20828, 20836, 20856, 20857,
   20859, 20872, 20875, 20878,
   20884, 20886, 20887, 20888,
   20891, 20898, 20902, 20910,
   20921, 20943, 20970, 20978,
   20990, 20992, 21010, 21051,
   21064, 21066, 21076, 21081,
   21095, 21100, 21106, 21110,
   21111, 21113, 21116, 21117,
   21123, 21128, 21149
   (SEE ALSO BLACK TROOPS,
   RECRUITMENT OF; UNION ARMY)

U.S. CONGRESS   5736, 9088, 20812

U.S. CONSTITUTION, SLAVERY AND
   1444, 2498, 2536, 3206, 3923,
   4330, 4331, 8395, 8745, 8747,
   8813, 9141, 9223, 9244, 9322,
   9683, 10062, 15075

U.S. NAVY   5156, 5264, 5410, 5505,
   5506, 5704, 5814, 6068, 8275,
   14484, 14744, 20229, 20673,
   20846, 20849, 21127

UMBANDA   7996, 15711

UNDERGROUND RAILROAD   1115, 3619,
   9781, 10995, 11218, 18846,
   18852, 19462, 19464, 19466,
   19471, 19477, 19484, 19487,
   19490, 19491, 19501, 19512,
   19515, 19516, 19526, 19540,
   19541, 19555, 19553, 19562,
   19563, 19554, 19565, 19567,
   19607, 19614, 19618, 19623,
   19635, 19656, 19658, 19663,
   19664, 19672, 19673, 19677,
   19681, 19691, 19704, 19716,
   19717, 19721, 19732, 19747,
   19763, 19768, 19769, 19770,
   19771, 19772, 19773, 19774,
   19775, 19776, 19777, 19780,
   19783, 19784, 19791, 19795,
   19796, 19797, 19798, 19813,
   19816, 19817, 19823, 19824,
   19829, 19831, 19833, 19841,
   19843, 19847, 19850, 19852
   (SEE ALSO SLAVE RESISTANCE)

UNION ARMY   377, 2521, 9976, 9977,
   10142, 10199, 11367, 11368,
   11395, 11523, 11613, 12439,
   12440, 13065, 13076, 13183,
   13235, 13236, 13753, 14873,
   15688, 17242, 17696, 19352,
   19842, 20237, 20243, 20285,
   20344, 20429, 20513, 20553,
   20595, 20656, 20663, 20672,
   20703, 20704, 20706, 20707,
   20710, 20711, 20713, 20715,
   20722, 20733, 20738, 20739,
   20740, 20742, 20749, 20750,
   20753, 20755, 20764, 20768,
   20789, 20790, 20798, 20805,
   20810, 20822, 20824, 20835,
   20838, 20843, 20844, 20847,
   20848, 20852, 20858, 20867,
   20874, 20884, 20886, 20899,
   20902, 20911, 20927, 20935,
   20937, 20938, 20942, 20946,
   20954, 20957, 20961, 20963,
   20964, 20969, 20986, 20993,
   20996, 20999, 21013, 21022,
   21023, 21024, 21025, 21029,
   21037, 21046, 21048, 21055,
   21060, 21064, 21067, 21076,
   21079, 21080, 21082, 21084,
   21091, 21093, 21095, 21100,
   21101, 21103, 21104, 21110,

21111, 21126, 21128, 21135,
21136, 21148, 21155, 21159
(SEE ALSO BLACK SOLDIERS,
RECRUITMENT OF; U.S. COLORED
TROOPS)

UNITARIANS 3380, 9264, 17004

UNIVERSITY OF NORTH CAROLINA
12657

UPPER CANADA 479, 9638, 10233,
10292, 10296, 10299, 10300,
10301

URBAN SLAVERY 781, 1138, 1458,
2959, 4008, 8302, 8359, 8531,
8735, 8864, 9003, 9159, 9217,
9391, 9575, 9624, 9788, 10667,
10672, 11225, 11243, 11429,
11587, 11600, 11753, 11780,
12178, 12250, 12292, 12337,
12338, 12339, 12340, 12413,
12434, 12435, 12460, 12491,
12513, 12563, 12573, 12893,
13054, 13180, 13345, 13470,
13818, 13864, 14717, 14805,
15041, 15105, 15521, 15522,
15652, 15870, 15882, 15886,
15893, 15895, 15899, 15900,
15905, 15910, 15916, 15917,
15918, 15919, 15920, 15921,
15925, 15937, 15938, 15939,
15945, 15952, 15960, 15961,
15964, 15972, 15978, 15979,
15982, 15983, 15985, 16286,
16316, 17084, 19790

UPSHUR, ABEL P. 3670

URUGUAY 11, 7513, 7967, 8186,
15785, 18423

UTAH 157, 158, 2124, 11109, 11153,
11155, 11156, 11157, 11158,
11159, 11160, 11161, 11163,
11164, 11165

VALDES, JOSE M. 7705

VAN BUREN, MARTIN 4528

VAN DEN BERGHE, PIERRE L. 640,
1290

VASSA, GUSTAVUS 19605

VASSALL, HENRY 10426

VASSOURAS 8081, 8082

VAUGHAN, USAN (SLAVE) 12548

VENEY, BETHANY 16521

VENEZUELA 3012, 5730, 6404, 7364,
7499, 7669, 7748, 7751, 7789,
7793, 7794, 7795, 7796, 7836,
7893, 7894, 7938, 7939, 8010,
8062, 15785, 16557, 19302,
20053

VERACRUZ 6056, 7429, 7430, 7434

VERMONT 10810, 10811, 10812,
10813, 10814, 10815, 10816

VEROT, AUGUSTIN 3618, 16813

VESEY, DENMARK 1380, 5082, 6623,
9009, 9163, 9303, 9304, 13003,
13004, 13005, 13006, 13138,
16316, 19179, 19729, 19906,
19971, 19974, 19977, 19995,
20028, 20164, 20167, 20168,
20176, 20198, 20199, 20213

VESUVIUS FURNACE PLANTATION 12790

VICKSBURG 12526, 12528, 12592

VIDAURRI, SANTIAGO 20623

VIGINTAL CROP 15183

VIOLENCE, SLAVE 1543, 2571, 3185,
12383, 13373, 14873, 15988,
15998, 19449, 19488, 19647,
19883, 19978, 19998

VIRGIN ISLANDS 6135, 6276, 6370,
6405, 6407, 6563, 6761, 6786,
6906, 6987, 15554

VIRGINIA 54, 421, 527, 715, 746,
2060, 2182, 2506, 2517, 2518,
2860, 5073, 5619, 5637, 5638,
5990, 5997, 6422, 7347, 8197,
8204, 8205, 8207, 8225, 8238,
8245, 8259, 8266, 8279, 8286,

8294, 8298, 8301, 8303, 8306,
8308, 8309, 8314, 8315, 8316,
8330, 8333, 3334, 8337, 8339,
8353, 8354, 8355, 8373, 8374,
8384, 8389, 8399, 8409, 8414,
8415, 8416, 8426, 8433, 8434,
8435, 8436, 8437, 8441, 8465,
8466, 8469, 8475, 8487, 8491,
8520, 8528, 8529, 8553, 8556,
8557, 8563, 8566, 8567, 8568,
8580, 8581, 8582, 8583, 8589,
8594, 8605, 8609, 8612, 8615,
8617, 8618, 8625, 8637, 8646,
8647, 8675, 8700, 8713, 8755,
8776, 8864, 8930, 8944, 9199,
9208, 9209, 9217, 9265, 9266,
9438, 9612, 9640, 9815, 9871,
9972, 9973, 10064, 10089, 10099,
10188, 11319, 11413, 11427,
11465, 11473, 11474, 11476,
11492, 11558, 13101, 13465,
13466, 13467, 13469, 13471,
13472, 13473, 13477, 13479,
13482, 13484, 13486, 13488,
13491, 13494, 13499, 13502,
13503, 13506, 13508, 13509,
13510, 13511, 13512, 13513,
13517, 13521, 13523, 13525,
13526, 13529, 13530, 13532,
13533, 13534, 13535, 13536,
13540, 13541, 13543, 13544,
13545, 13546, 13547, 13548,
13550, 13551, 13552, 13553,
13555, 13556, 13557, 13559,
13561, 13563, 13564, 13565,
13567, 13568, 13571, 13573,
13575, 13576, 13579, 13581,
13583, 13584, 13586, 13590,
13591, 13592, 13593, 13595,
13596, 13597, 13599, 13600,
13601, 13602, 13604, 13605,
13606, 13607, 13608, 13610,
13612, 13613, 13614, 13615,
13616, 13618, 13619, 13620,
13622, 13623, 13624, 13627,
13628, 13629, 13630, 13632,
13633, 13635, 13638, 13639,
13640, 13643, 13644, 13647,
13648, 13649, 13652, 13653,
13654, 13655, 13656, 13659,
13660, 13661, 13664, 13671,
13672, 13674, 13675, 13676,
13679, 13680, 13684, 13690,
13694, 13696, 13698, 13699,
13702, 13703, 13704, 13708,

13711, 13712, 13713, 13714,
13716, 13718, 13719, 13720,
13721, 13722, 13723, 13724,
13725, 13727, 13729, 13730,
13731, 13732, 13735, 13736,
13738, 13739, 13740, 13741,
13742, 13744, 13746, 13749,
13753, 13756, 13759, 13760,
13765, 13766, 13773, 13774,
13776, 13777, 13780, 13783,
13784, 13787, 13788, 13789,
13790, 13792, 13793, 13794,
13802, 13803, 13804, 13806,
13807, 13809, 13810, 13811,
13812, 13813, 13818, 13822,
13824, 13827, 13829, 13832,
13833, 13936, 13937, 13838,
13839, 13840, 13844, 13845,
13846, 13848, 13850, 13854,
13855, 13858, 13859, 13860,
13862, 13863, 13864, 13865,
13866, 13868, 13869, 13870,
13871, 13872, 13873, 13875,
13876, 13878, 13879, 13880,
13881, 13832, 13883, 13885,
13886, 13867, 13888, 13889,
13891, 13895, 13896, 13897,
13898, 13899, 13900, 13901,
14147, 14434, 14662, 14689,
14717, 14747, 14751, 14752,
14783, 14809, 14875, 15023,
15105, 15147, 15154, 15259,
15260, 15362, 15528, 15594,
15595, 15596, 15789, 15917,
15949, 15950, 15960, 16286,
16565, 16733, 16826, 16924,
17111, 17171, 18027, 18844,
18922, 19138, 19190, 19223,
19257, 19544, 19849, 19878,
20031, 20082, 20084, 20098,
20262, 20271, 20454

VON HOLST, HERMAN E.   1171, 1247,
   1950

VOODOO   790, 4946, 4991, 6393,
   6605, 6751, 6753, 6865, 7048,
   7108, 7112, 12460, 15711, 1573
   15737, 15831, 16689, 16726,
   17259, 17266, 17288, 17400,
   17813, 18011, 18022, 18091,
   18137, 18194, 18268, 18269,
   18278, 18318, 18332, 18340,
   18383, 18398, 18412, 19310

1652

WACCAMAW NECK, SC 18225

WADE, RICHARD C. 1138, 1458,
20168

WADSWORTH LETTER 20903, 20913,
20914

WAGE SLAVERY 14252

WAILES, BENJAMIN L.C. 12625

WALKER COUNTY, TX 13356

WALKER, DAVID 4138, 9609, 11768,
20127

WALKER, ELIZA (EX-SLAVE) 19111

WALKER, QUOK 10510

WALKER, SUSAN 15574

WALKING STICKS 4911, 5106

WALLS, JOSIAH 9631

WALTON, RUFUS (SLAVE) 18986

WANDERER 5254, 5272, 5496, 5578,
5651, 5661, 5662, 5759, 6024,
6084, 6085, 6086

WAR OF 1812 3256, 3881, 4115,
8323, 8585, 11418, 13033, 20513

WARE, CHARLES P. 1795, 1796, 1797,
1798, 1799

WARE, ENOCH R. 5265

WARNER, CHARLES D. 1368, 1609

WASHERWOMAN, SLAVE 16328

WASHINGTON COUNTY, PA 10719

WASHINGTON TERRITORY 10286

WASHINGTON, AUGUSTUS 9930

WASHINGTON, BOOKER T. 535, 609,
1257, 1591, 1811, 1812, 1818,
2057, 2632, 3689, 4408, 4588,
10518, 13638, 13639, 13671,

13716, 18720

WASHINGTON, GEORGE 614, 3889,
6851, 8529, 13803, 16221, 16627

WASHINGTON, LA 2630

WATAUGA COUNTY, NC 12726

WATKINS, BENJAMIN 13854

WATKINS, WILLIAM 9531

WAYLAND, FRANCIS 16845

WAYNE COUNTY, KY 11374

WAYNE, JAMES M. 5474, 6079

WEATHERFORD, WILLIS D. 663

WEBB, ARCHIE P. 9441

WEBB, WILLIAM 19028

WEBSTER-ASHBURTON TREATY 3833,
15080

WEBSTER, DANIEL 5419

WEBSTER, JOHN B. 13377

WEDDINGS 16568, 17147, 18328

WEEKS, STEPHEN B. 1355, 1644

WELD, THEODORE D. 3025, 3328,
4446

WELLER, SYDNEY 12681

WELLS, IDA B. 19029

WESCOAT, ARTHUR B. 20364

WESLEY, JOHN 2605

WEST AFRICA 179, 2066, 2927, 3174,
4651, 4655, 4657, 4659, 4660,
4661, 4665, 4685, 4690, 4759,
4789, 4790, 4809, 4830, 4831,
4901, 4917, 4922, 4926, 4957,
4962, 4976, 4978, 4994, 5012,
5054, 5065, 5067, 5075, 5089,
5103, 5111, 5112, 5167, 5216,

1653

5230, 5233, 5266, 5312, 5435,
5545, 5556, 5571, 5594, 5683,
5684, 5720, 5722, 5723, 5782,
5792, 5883, 5948, 5949, 6050,
9789, 15711, 19347
(SEE ALSO AFRICA)

WEST INDIA REGIMENTS 6262, 6263,
6935, 7216, 7217

WEST INDIES--SEE CARIBBEAN

WEST NEW JERSEY 10583

WEST VIRGINIA 2860, 9266, 9267,
9284, 9285, 13529, 13549, 13550,
13559, 13568, 13576, 13601,
13606, 13638, 13639, 13644,
13694, 13700, 13741, 13742,
13766, 13790, 13832, 13850,
13862, 13870, 14809, 16075,
19257, 20928, 20938

WEST, SLAVERY IN 1, 154, 219,
2124, 2126, 2127, 2879, 9047,
10853, 10854, 11002, 11003,
11005, 11008, 11010, 11011,
11012, 11013, 11015, 11017,
11018, 11025, 11026, 11027,
11029, 11030, 11031, 11033,
11042, 11043, 11045, 11046,
11049, 11050, 11051, 11052,
11053, 11055, 11056, 11057,
11058, 11059, 11060, 11062,
11065, 11066, 11067, 11068,
11094, 11138, 14503, 14504,
18969, 19746

WESTERN RESERVE 19511

WESTFIELD, MA 10431

WESTMORELAND COUNTY, VA 8437

WHALEY, WILLIAM 6190

WHEAT 13069

WHEATLEY, PHILLIS 265, 451, 1161,
1539, 3813, 4223, 4235, 4293,
4545, 4890, 8375, 9378, 10347,
10422, 10486, 10491, 16354,
16362, 16410, 16426, 16458,
16502, 16507, 16529

WHEELER, JOHN W. 2235

WHIG PARTY 4296

WHIPPING 1679, 8854, 9129, 11186
14220, 14854, 16316, 18939,
20125

WHIPPLE, PRINCE 8280

WHIPS 14730

WHITE SERVITUDE 3496, 3814, 4365
7084, 8219, 8222, 8262, 8316,
8346, 8390, 8607, 8988, 9275,
10733, 10735, 11484, 13481

WHITE, ADDISON 19718

WHITEFIELD, GEORGE 17245, 17333

WHITFIELD, RACHEL (SLAVE) 16364

WHITMAN, WALT 4139, 4270, 4473

WHITMORE, CHARLES 12623

WHYDAH 4672

WILBERFORCE, WILLIAM 2091, 5306

WILDER, BURT G. 708

WILL (SLAVE) 8758, 8761

WILLIAM 5244

WILLIAMS, EMPEROR (EX-SLAVE)
19069

WILLIAMS, ERIC 658, 659, 849, 94
1004, 1012, 1179, 1234, 1450,
1476, 1693, 1702, 1892, 1998,
3338

WILLIAMS, FRANCIS 6792

WILLIAMS, GEORGE H. 11152

WILLIAMS, GEORGE W. 788, 1080,
1085, 1086, 1087, 1092, 1550,
1594

WILLIAMS, ISAAC D. 19030

WILLIAMS, JAMES   19031

WILLIAMS, SAMUEL   11326

WILLIAMS, SARAH H.   15291

WILLIAMS, STEPHEN   12257

WILLIAMSBURG, VA   421, 8675, 13855

WILMINGTON, NC   8786, 11768

WILMOT PROVISO   9099, 9100, 11058

WINCHESTER, MA   9056

WINDSOR, ONTARIO   587

WINDWARD ISLANDS   6826, 6828, 7194

WINN PARISH, LA   12418

WISCONSIN   9158, 10993, 10994,
  10995, 10996, 10997, 20394

WITCHCRAFT   6181, 6615, 7634,
  16860, 17118, 17147, 17196,
  18282, 18292, 18396
  (SEE ALSO SORCERY, NEGRO)

WOMEN, AFRICAN   7775, 7776

WOMEN, FREE BLACK   595, 2806, 9821,
  16170, 16387

WOMEN, SLAVE   57, 58, 91, 152, 153,
  340, 352, 383, 494, 515, 516,
  553, 565, 576, 595, 613, 1445,
  1478, 1679, 1804, 1988, 2106,
  2204, 3379, 4924, 6271, 6818,
  6819, 6845, 6846, 6847, 6848,
  7638, 7775, 7776, 7915, 8016,
  8021, 8361, 8588, 8712, 9432,
  9602, 11008, 11327, 14293,
  14844, 14873, 14936, 15196,
  15287, 15641, 16020, 16163,
  16170, 16200, 16283, 16291,
  16304, 16319, 16333, 16335,
  16336, 16337, 16338, 16339,
  16341, 16342, 16344, 16345,
  16346, 16347, 16349, 16350,
  16351, 16352, 16353, 16356,
  16357, 16359, 16361, 16362,
  16364, 16365, 16367, 16368,
  16370, 16371, 16372, 16373,
  16374, 16375, 16376, 16379,
  16381, 16382, 16384, 16385,
  16386, 16387, 16389, 16391,
  16392, 16393, 16394, 16395,
  16397, 16398, 16401, 16402,
  16403, 16404, 16407, 16408,
  16409, 16410, 16411, 16414,
  16416, 16418, 16419, 16421,
  16422, 16423, 16424, 16426,
  16427, 16429, 16430, 16431,
  16433, 16436, 16438, 16439,
  16440, 16443, 16444, 16445,
  16447, 16458, 16459, 16460,
  16461, 16464, 16465, 16466,
  16467, 16468, 16469, 16470,
  16472, 16473, 16474, 16477,
  16478, 16479, 16480, 16483,
  16485, 16487, 16492, 16494,
  16495, 16496, 16497, 16499,
  16506, 16507, 16508, 16511,
  16513, 16516, 16517, 16519,
  16520, 16521, 16522, 16523,
  16525, 16526, 16527, 16531,
  16533, 18824, 18825, 18864,
  18993, 19013, 19243, 20552

WOMEN, WHITE   3266, 3978, 4184,
  4285, 8021, 11795, 16053, 16054,
  16057, 16058, 16422

WOOD, MARY (EX-SLAVE)   18824

WOOD, PETER H.   728, 1932, 5131

WOODCARVING   7956, 15541

WOODSON, CARTER G.   709, 858, 980,
  1117, 1169, 1217, 1264, 1283,
  1381, 1432, 1500, 1686, 1710,
  1741, 1752, 1812, 1875, 1977,
  2014, 2057

WOODWARD, C. VANN   1139, 1568,
  1581, 1712, 1825, 1943, 1975,
  1983

WOOL WEAVING   19053

WOOLFOLK, AUSTIN   15085

WOOLMAN, JOHN   17054

WORDSWORTH, WILLIAM   4132

WORK ETHIC 14630

WORK, MONROE N. 1205, 1284, 1483

WORKS PROGRESS ADMINISTRATION
142, 467, 468, 469, 1018, 1019

WORTHY PARK PLANTATION 6339, 6342,
6351, 6352, 15010

WRIGHT-SANBORN INCIDENT 13680

WRIGHT, FRANCES 10027, 10029,
13202, 13237, 13251, 13255,
13256

WRITING SYSTEMS, SLAVE 4857

WROUGHT IRON 18632

WYETH, JOHN A. 643

WYOMING COUNTY, NY 10639

WYTHE COUNTY, VA 13760

WYTHE, GEORGE 8778

YAO 5174

YATES, WILLIAM 11195

YAWS 15810

YELL COUNTY, AR 11833

YELLOW FEVER 2549, 5600, 15613,
15614, 15647

YOPP, BILL 3992, 4442, 4443

YORK (SLAVE) 11005

YORK, JACK 3791

YORUBA 4658, 4687, 4806, 4828,
4895, 4902, 4994, 5008, 5014,
5085, 5762, 6121, 6161, 6162,
7239, 7299, 8138, 19302

YOUNG COUNTY, TX 13379

YOUNGER, WILLIAMSON 13284

ZACATECAS, MEXICO 7330

ZAMBIA 5114

ZANZIBAR 4662, 4982, 5993

ZARIA 5971, 7138

ZION COMMUNITY 6827, 13220

ZOBEME 4673

ZONG 6081

ZUMARRAGA, JUAN DE 7720

Author Index

A.M.   10420

AARON, EUGENE M.   6143

ABAJIAN, JAMES DE T.   1, 2

ABANIME, EMEKA P.   5152

ABBEY, KATHRYN T.   11856

ABBEY, RICHARD   16582

ABBITT OUTLAW, MERRY   15466

ABBOT, ERNEST H.   16583

ABBOTT, ABIAL R.   20656

ABBOTT, ALBERT   12825

ABBOTT, IRA A.   10421

ABBOTT, MARTIN   3022, 12826, 20657, 20659

ABBOTT, MARTIN L.   12827

ABBOTT, RICHARD H.   20661

ABDUL, RAOUL   17449

ABEL, ANNIE H.   13285, 13902

ABERNETHY, THOMAS P.   3023, 11678, 13173

ABIMBOLA, WANDE   7299

ABRAHAM, ARTHUR   4650, 4651

ABRAHAM, R.C.   6121

ABRAHAM, W.E.   4652, 5153

ABRAHAMS, ROGER D.   562, 6122, 6123, 6124, 13212, 16333, 17360, 17361, 17362, 18006, 18007, 18357, 18358

ABRAMOVA, S.U.   5154

ABRAMOWITZ, JACK   3, 4

ABRAMS, JOSEPHINE S.   15287

ABRAMS, WILLIAM M.   635

ABZUG, ROBERT   16076

ABZUG, ROBERT H.   3024, 3025, 19449

ACHILLE, LOUIS T.   17493, 17494

ACKERMAN, KENNETH J.   17363

ACKERMAN, ROBERT K.   12828, 12829

ADAIR, THOMAS J.   13174

ADAMS, ALICE D.   16584

ADAMS, BRUCE P.   2063

ADAMS, C.F.   8738

ADAMS, DAISY A.   3026

ADAMS, DAVID W.   20662

ADAMS, EDWARD C.C.   17495

ADAMS, EDWARD C.L.   12830, 18010

ADAMS, HERBERT B.   19859

ADAMS, JAMES E.   18485

ADAMS, JAMES T.   8739, 9364

ADAMS, JANE E.   5155

ADAMS, JOHN Q.   18792

ADAMS, MARC D.   9365

ADAMS, MRS. W. CARLETON   3027

ADAMS, ROBERTA E.   354

ADAMS, RUSSELL L.   5, 636

ADAMS, SAMUEL H.   19450

ADAMS, SHERMAN W.   10381

ADAMS, WILLIAM H.   18484, 18485

ADAMSON, ALAN H.   7300, 7301, 7302, 7303

ADAMU, MAHDI   4653

ADDEMAN, J.M.   20663

ADDINGTON, WENDELL G.   13286

ADDO, LINDA D.   6, 16585

ADEFILA, JOHNSON A.   16586

ADELAIDE, JACQUES   19260

ADER, PAUL   9366

ADEWOYE, OMONIYI   5156

ADGER, JOHN B.   16587

ADGER, ROBERT M.   7

ADLER, JOYCE   15988

ADLER, JOYCE S.   3031

ADLER, MORTIMER   8

ADLER, THOMAS   17496

ADRIAN, ARTHUR A.   3032

AERTKER, ROBERT J.   12213

AFIGBO, A.E.   4654

AFRICA, PHILIP   12641

AGASSIZ, ELIZABETH C.   7305

AGASSIZ, LOUIS   7305

AGHEYISI, REBECCA   19261

AGIRI, BABATUNDE   10

AGONITO, JOSEPH   11400

AGOSTO MUNOZ, NELIDA   18011

AGRESTI, BARBARA F.   11857

AGUET, ISABELLE   5159

AGUIRRE BELTRAN, GONZALO   7306, 7307, 7308, 7309, 7310

AHROLD, KYLE   638, 3036

AIKEN, CHARLES S.   14062

AIKEN, JOHN F.   3037

AIME, VALCOUR   12214

AIMES, HUBERT H.S.   5160, 6128, 6130, 6131, 18012

AITKEN, BARBARA   7311

AITKEN, HUGH G.J.   14571

AITON, ARTHUR S.   5161, 7312

AJAYI, J.F. ADE   4657, 4658

AJAYI, J.F.A.   4655, 4656

AKED, CHARLES F.   2065

AKERS, CHARLES W.   10422

AKERS, FRANK H., JR.   20664

AKERS, J.N.   16589

AKIN, WILLIAM E.   639

AKINJOGBIN, I.A.   4659, 4660, 46?, 5163, 5164

AKINOLA, G.A.   4662

AKIWOWO, AKINSOLA   2066

ALAGOA, E.J.   5167

ALBANESE, ANTHONY G.   11975, 123?

ALBARS, MARTH M.   11705

ALBERT, OCTAVIA V.R.   11976

ALBERT, PETER J.   13465

ALBUQUERQUE, KLAUS DE   640

ALCOCK, NATHANIEL 15583

ALDEN, DAURIL 7313, 7314

ALDEN, JOHN R. 8270, 11656, 13903

ALDERMAN, CLIFFORD L. 5168

ALDERSON, WILLIAM T. 13175

ALDERSON, WILLIAM T., JR. 20665

ALDRICH, GENE 11121

ALDRICH, ORLANDO W. 10855, 10856

ALDRIDGE, HAROLD R. 5169

ALECKSON, SAM 12834

ALEXANDER, A. JOHN 3038

ALEXANDER, ARCHER 18795

ALEXANDER, ARTHUR J. 10608

ALEXANDER, CLAUDE H. 11679

ALEXANDER, HERBERT B. 7315

ALEXANDER, JOHN B. 16536

ALEXANDER, LETITIA H. 18595

ALEXANDER, N.D. 20320

ALEXANDER, ROBERTA S. 3039

ALEXANDER, THOMAS B. 641, 14064, 20447

ALEXANDER, WILLIAM T. 3040

ALEXIS, STEPHEN 19861

ALFORD, TERRY 18701

ALFORD, TERRY L. 12519, 12520

ALHO, OLLI 16590

ALILUNAS, LEO 19451

ALISKY, MARVIN 11

ALLAIN, MATHE 12215, 12216, 12217

ALLAN, WILLIAM 12218

ALLEN, CUTHBERT E. 16591, 16592

ALLEN, DIANE L. 642

ALLEN, G. 17497

ALLEN, HEMAN H. 16593

ALLEN, JAMES E. 10609

ALLEN, JAMES S. 14065

ALLEN, JEFFREY B. 2067, 11259, 11260

ALLEN, JOHN W. 10857

ALLEN, LEE N. 643

ALLEN, PAMELA P. 3042

ALLEN, RICHARD H. 3041

ALLEN, ROBERT L. 3042

ALLEN, T.N. 6132

ALLEN, THEODORE 2068

ALLEN, THEODORE W. 644

ALLEN, VAN S. 12

ALLEN, VIRGINIA R. 15584

ALLEN, WALTER R. 645, 16079

ALLEN, WILLIAM F. 17498, 17499, 17500, 19262

ALLEN, ZITA 646

ALLEYNE, MERVYN 6133, 19263

ALLEYNE, MERVYN C. 4664, 19265

ALLIS, FREDERICK S., JR. 8741

ALLISON, JOHN 13176

ALLISON, MATTIE F. 8194

ALPERS, EDWARD A. 5171, 5172, 5173, 5174

ALPERT, JONATHAN L. 8195, 8742

ALSTON, CHARLES 17501

ALSTON, PRIMUS P. 18796

ALTENBERND, LYNN 2069

ALVAREZ, ALONZO 2070

ALVORD, CLARENCE W. 10858

AMACHER, RICHARD E. 3043

AMADI, LAWRENCE E. 4665, 4666

AMADO, JORGE 3044

AMBLER, CHARLES H. 13466, 13467

AMERICA, RICHARD 14066

AMERICAN MISSIONARY ASSOCIATION 3045, 3046

AMERICO DE GALVAL BUENO 7316

AMES, HERMAN V. 3745

AMES, MARY 12835

AMES, RUSSELL 17502

AMES, SUSIE M. 13468, 13469, 20666

AMIS, HARRY D. 650

AMOR, ROSE T. 18013

AMUNDSON, RICHARD J. 14067

ANDERSON, ALAN B. 7317

ANDERSON, ALICE L. 19862

ANDERSON, B.L. 5175

ANDERSON, CHARLES A. 16594

ANDERSON, CHARLES W. 20667

ANDERSON, DAVID D. 2072

ANDERSON, DONALD W. 8747

ANDERSON, GALUSHA 11531

ANDERSON, HILTON 17503

ANDERSON, IZETT 6134, 20234

ANDERSON, JAMES D. 651, 652, 653, 654

ANDERSON, JAN T. 3048

ANDERSON, JEAN 12642

ANDERSON, JERVIS 655

ANDERSON, JOHN L. 6135

ANDERSON, JOHN Q. 12219, 15585, 18015, 18412

ANDERSON, JOHNNY R. 16595

ANDERSON, JOURDON 3049

ANDERSON, MATTHEW 16596

ANDERSON, RALPH V. 14068, 14069, 14231

ANDERSON, ROBERT 11261, 18798

ANDERSON, ROBERT L. 13905

ANDERSON, RUBY J. 9966

ANDERSON, SOLENA 16031

ANDERSON, THORNTON 3817

ANDERSON-GREEN, PAULA H. 656

ANDRADE, MANUEL CORREIA DE OLIVEI 7318

ANDREANO, RALPH L. 14070

ANDREWS, CHARLES M. 657, 6136, 8271, 8272, 10382

ANDREWS, CHRISTOPHER C.   7319,
    20669

ANDREWS, ELIZA F.   17504

ANDREWS, EVANGELINE W.   15194

ANDREWS, GARNETT 15842

ANDREWS, GEORGE R.   7320, 7321,
    7322, 7323

ANDREWS, KENNETH R.   6137

ANDREWS, MATTHEW P.   11402, 20322

ANDREWS, RENA M. 2074

ANDREWS, ROBERT H.   3051

ANDREWS, THOMAS F.   13906

ANDREWS, WILLIAM L. 2075, 18016,
    18017

ANENE, JOSEPH C. 5177

ANGEL, ROBERT 8196

ANGERMULLER, LINNEA A.   15586

ANGUS, DONALD 10935

ANSTEY, ROGER T.   658, 659, 660,
    661, 3052, 5178, 5179, 5180,
    5181, 5182, 5183, 5184

ANTHONY, CARL 15467

ANTHONY, RONALD W.   12900

ANTONE, GEORGE P. 663

ANTWI, SHIRLEY 4668

APOSTLE, RICHARD A.   2078

APPEL, LIVIA 10963

APPLEBY, ANDREW 664

APPLEGARTH, ALBERT C.   3053

APPLETON, MARY E.   9967

APPLEWHITE, JOSEPH D.   12836,
    12837

APPLEWHITE, RIVERS 12523

APPLEYARD, LULA D.K.   11858

APTHEKER, BETTINA 665, 666

APTHEKER, HERBERT 15, 16, 667,
    668, 669, 670, 671, 672, 673,
    674, 675, 676, 677, 678, 679,
    680, 681, 682, 683, 2079, 3054,
    3055, 3056, 3057, 3058, 8273,
    8274, 8275, 8748, 9367, 9368,
    9968, 9969, 9970, 14071, 16336,
    16598, 19454, 19455, 19457,
    19459, 19460, 19863, 19864,
    19865, 19866, 19867, 19868,
    19869, 19870, 19871, 19872,
    20323, 20324, 20325, 20672,
    20673

ARAFAT, W. 4669

ARANA, EUGENIA B.   11887

ARBENA, JOSEPH L.   10423

ARBOLETA, JOSE R.   7324

ARCHDEACON, THOMAS J.   10610

ARCHER, LEONARD C.   2080

ARCHER, WILLIAM 2081

ARCHIBALD, ADAMS G.   10226

ARDERY, JULIA S.   9971

ARENDT, HANNAH 2082

ARGUEDES, JEANNE 12220

ARHIN, KWAME 4670, 4671

ARIEL 2083

ARMSTRONG, CLEATON O.   17

ARMSTRONG, F.H.   10227

ARMSTRONG, FRED 684

ARMSTRONG, HANNIBAL 20450

ARMSTRONG, JIM 15468

ARMSTRONG, LOIS 1968

ARMSTRONG, MARY F. 17505

ARMSTRONG, ORLAND K. 18019

ARMSTRONG, ROBERT P. 7325

ARMSTRONG, THOMAS F. 11980, 13470

ARMSTRONG, WARREN B. 19142, 19143

ARMSTRONG, WILLIAM H. 20677

ARMSTRONG, WILLIAM N. 15070

ARMYTAGE, W.H.G. 13177

ARNETT, ETHEL S. 12643

ARNOLD, B.W., JR. 13471

ARNOLD, I.C. 19462

ARNOLD, PAUL T. 20678

ARNOLD, ROSEMARY 4672, 4673

ARNOLD, S.G. 10327

ARNOLD-FORSTER, MARK 3059

ARONSON, DAVID 8749

ARORA, V.N. 685

ARROWOOD, CHARLES F. 19144

ARROWOOD, MARY D. 17506

ARTEMEL, JANICE 13765

ARTER, JARED M. 18800

ARTHUR, T.S. 13472

ARVEY, VERNA 18413

ASCHENBRENNER, JOYCE 16083

ASCHER, ROBERT 15469

ASH, HARRY C. 13907

ASHBURN, KARL E. 13287, 13288

ASHBURN, PERCY M. 5188

ASHBY, NATHANIEL E. 7326

ASHE, S.A. 636, 3060

ASHER, G.M. 18

ASHFORD, NICHOLAS 687

ASHMORE, HARRY S. 16084

ASHTON, DORE 688

ASHTON, THOMAS S. 5189

ASIEGBU, JOHNSON U. 5190, 6138

ASTRACHAN, ANTHONY 689, 16337

ATHERTON, LEWIS E. 11532

ATKINSON, BERTHA 13289

ATKINSON, EDWARD 15071

ATKINSON, LILLIE E. 13290

ATKINSON, THOMAS P. 14901

ATLEE, BENJAMIN C. 3061

ATMORE, ANTHONY 5010

AUBERT, ALVIN 18021

AUBREY, PHILIP 5191

AUCHAMPAUGH, PHILIP 8751

AUFHAUSER, KEITH 690

AUFHAUSER, R. KEITH 691, 6140, 14076, 14077

AUFHAUSER, ROBERT K. 14078

AUGELLI, JOHN P. 8164

AUGHEY, JOHN H.   20326

AUGUSTUS, EARL   20292

AUPING, JOHN A.   3063

AURENTZ, JANET   5192

AUSTEN, RALPH A.   692, 4674, 5194,
   5195, 5196

AUSTIN, H.   18022

AVANT, GLADYS B.   11680

AVARY, MYRTA L.   17368, 20451

AVERY, ISAAC W.   11982

AVINS, ALFRED   8752

AVIRETT, JAMES B.   17369

AXTELL, JAMES   13908

AYANDELE, EMMANUEL A.   4675

AYERS, EDWARD L.   8753

AYKROYD, WALLACE R.   6141

AYRES, S. EDWARD   13473

AZEVEDO, AUZIO   7327

AZEVEDO, ELIANE S.   2914

AZEVEDO, FERNANDO D.   7328

BAA, ENID M.   19

BAADE, ANNE A.   8754

BABCHUK, NICHOLAS   16086

BABCOCK, THEODORE S.   9972

BABER, ELIZABETH G.   2085

BABIN, MARIA T.   6142

BABUSCIO, JACK   2086

BACH, JULIAN S., JR.   3064

BACHMAN, VAN CLEAF   10611

BACHMANN, FREDERICK W.   11533

BACKUS, EMMA M.   18023, 18024

BACON, ALICE M.   3065, 15589,
   17370, 18026, 18027

BACON, DORIS Y.   12222

BACON, EDGAR M.   6143

BADER, CARL G., JR.   20327

BAGLEY, MARY   693

BAGLEY, WILLIAM C., JR.   14079

BAHAM, VENITA M.   16601

BAHNEY, ROBERT S.   19145

BAILEY, BERYL L.   19268, 19269,
   19270

BAILEY, CLAY   13475

BAILEY, DALE S.   7329

BAILEY, DAVID C.   5197

BAILEY, DAVID T.   694, 16602

BAILEY, E. BRASHER   13178

BAILEY, HUGH C.   2087, 11681,
   11983

BAILEY, KENNETH K.   520, 16603

BAILEY, LYNN R.   13909

BAILEY, MARILYN   10817

BAILEY, MINNIE T.   13910

BAILEY, RAYMOND C.   9369

BAILEY, RONALD W.   5198

BAILEY, THOMAS P.   2088

BAILEY, WILLIAM S.   19464

BAILEY, WILMA R. 6144, 6145

BAILOR, KENNETH M. 13477

BAILY, MARILYN 9370

BAILYN, BERNARD 8276, 8755

BAIN, MILDRED 4676

BAIRD, CAROL F. 695

BAIRD, KEITH E. 17483, 19271

BAIRD, W. DAVID 13911

BAKER, ANTHONY J. 2089

BAKER, BEVERLY A. 3066

BAKER, DAVID N. 17507

BAKER, DONALD G. 2090

BAKER, E.C. 22

BAKER, HENRY E. 14656, 14657

BAKER, HOUSTON A., JR. 3067,
18028, 18702

BAKER, ROBERT A. 16604

BAKER, S.C. 15195

BAKER, THOMAS N. 15196, 16339

BAKER, VAUGHAN 12223, 12224,
12225

BAKER, VERNON G. 10424, 10425

BAKER, WILLIAM 2091

BAKEWELL, DENNIS C. 23

BAKEWELL, PETER J. 7330

BALDUS, BERND 4677

BALDWIN, CLINTON T. 12838

BALDWIN, LEWIS V. 9371

BALDWIN, RICHARD E. 696

BALDWIN, SIMEON E. 19873

BALES, MARY V. 17508, 17509

BALL, TIMOTHY H. 11682

BALL, WILLIAM W. 15992

BALLAGH, JAMES C. 3068, 8197,
8198, 8199, 8277, 13479, 13481,
14081, 14082, 14084, 15197

BALLANTA, N.G.J. 17510

BALLARD, ALLEN 19146

BALLOU, MATURIN M. 6146

BALLWEG, JOHN A. 16036

BALOGH, JOSEPH 20220

BALTIMORE, LESTER B. 3069, 11534

BAMBARA, TONI C. 19272

BAMBERG, ROBERT D. 3070

BAMFORD, PAUL W. 6147

BANCROFT, FREDERIC 698, 699, 700,
2093, 3071, 20221

BANCROFT, FREDERIC A. 3072

BANCROFT, HUBERT H. 7331

BANGS, ISAAC S. 20680

BANKS, ENOCH M. 11584

BANKS, FRANK D. 16087, 16537

BANKS, JAMES A. 24

BANKS, MARY R. 3074

BANKS, MELVIN J. 15074

BANNER, ELEANOR 17512

BANNER, JAMES M. 378

BANNER, JAMES M., JR.   10328

BANNER, MELVIN E.   10950

BANNINGA, JERALD L.   8756.

BANTON, MICHAEL   2094, 6148

BARADELL, WILLIAM L.   12524

BARAKA, AMIRI   18804

BARALT, GUILLERMO A.   6149

BARATZ, JOAN   17372

BARATZ, STEPHEN   17372

BARBEE, DAVID R.   3075

BARBER, JAMES G.   13482

BARBER, NOEL   4678

BARBOUR, JAMES   25

BARDEN, THOMAS E.   431, 16565

BARDOLPH, RICHARD   3076, 3077,
  8757

BARDWELL, J.P.   16341

BAREFIELD, JAMES T.   11657

BAREKMAN, JUNE B.   10902

BARFIELD, RODNEY   26, 9374

BARGAINNIER, EARL F.   2095, 3078

BARKER, A.J.   2096

BARKER, ANTHONY J.   2097

BARKER, DOROTHY M.   15882

BARKER, EUGENE C.   5200, 13294,
  13295, 13296, 13297

BARKER, HOWARD F.   19274

BARKER, MARCUS L.   6150

BARKSDALE, RICHARD K.   15198

BARNARD, HENRY   27

BARNES, CLARENCE   5201

BARNES, ELINOR   20681

BARNES, GILBERT H.   3079

BARNES, JAMES A.   20681

BARNET, MIGUEL   6151, 17373

BARNETT, A.C.   19275

BARNETT, EVELYN B.   701

BARNEY, WILLIAM L.   11683, 14087,
  19875, 20328

BARNHART, JOHN D.   10359, 10903,
  10979, 11262

BARNWELL, JACK   702

BARNWELL, JOSEPH W.   12839

BARNWELL, STEPHEN B.   11985

BARON, HAROLD M.   2100, 14088

BARR, ALWYN   13298, 16089

BARR, RUTH B.   9375

BARRETT, HARRIS   17513

BARRETT, LEONARD E.   4679, 6153,
  6154, 6155, 6156, 6157

BARRETT, WARD J.   6158, 7334, 7335

BARRIFFE, EUGENE   13299

BARRINGER, PAUL B.   12646, 15199,
  15200, 15289, 16090

BARRINGER, R.   14090

BARRON, ELWYN A.   15591

BARRON, T.J.   6159

1665

BARROW, DAVID C.   11986, 18414,
     19276

BARROW, LIONEL C., JR.   3080

BARROW, ROBERT M.   13484

BARROWS, EDITH C.   11916

BARRY, BOUBACAR   5095

BARRY, JAMES P.   10936

BARRY, RICHARD   3081

BARRY, WAYNE E.   9973

BARTLETT, C.L.   5202

BARTLETT, ELLEN S.   19876

BARTLETT, IRVING H.   703, 9376,
     10782, 16342

BARTLETT, JOHN R.   28

BARTON, DAVID L.   18484

BARTON, WILLIAM E.   17514, 17515,
     17516, 17517

BARTOVIES, ALBERT F.   18484

BARZEL, YORAM   14091

BARZELAY, DOUGLAS   704

BARZUN, JACQUES   2101

BASCOM, WILLIAM   705, 4680, 18030,
     18031

BASCOM, WILLIAM R.   4681, 6160,
     6161, 6162, 18384

BASFORD, MRS. GERTHA B.   20682

BASKIN, ANDREW L.   13486

BASKIN, WADE   17374

BASLER, ROY P.   3082, 19465

BASS, BERNIE S.   16609

BASSETT, JOHN S.   1165, 2103, 2104,
     3083, 3084, 3085, 4682, 8758,
     12647, 12649, 12650, 12651,
     12652, 14858, 20454

BASSETT, VICTOR H.   15592

BASTIDE, ROGER   706, 707, 2105,
     2106, 2107, 3086, 6164, 7337,
     7338

BASTIEN, REMY   6165

BASTIN, BRUCE   12653, 17519

BATCHELDER, SAMUEL F.   10426

BATEMAN, FRED   14658, 14659, 14660

BATES, ERNEST S.   3087

BATES, HILARY   29

BATES, RUTH   12227

BATES, THELMA   8759, 8760

BATES, WILLIAM C.   6166

BATHERSFIELD, JOAN P.   16614

BATIE, ROBERT C.   6167, 6168

BATTALIO, RAYMOND C.   12841

BATTLE, CHARLES A.   10783

BATTLE, GEORGE G.   8761

BATTLE, KEMP P.   12656, 12657,
     18703

BATTLE, LORENZO   30

BATTLE, THOMAS C.   31

BAUDET, HENRI   7342

BAUER, ALICE H.   20223

BAUER, CAROL P.   8762

BAUER, RAYMOND A.   20223

BAUGHMAN, A.J. 19466

BAUGHMAN, E. EARL 18738

BAUGHMAN, JAMES P. 14095

BAUMGARTNER, SANDRA A. 8763

BAUR, JOHN E. 6169

BAUSMAN, LOTTIE M. 10717

BAXTER, GARRETT 3088

BAY, EDNA G. 4971

BAYARD, FRANCK 6170

BAYITCH, S.A. 32

BAYLISS, JOHN F. 18806, 18807

BAYLOR, GEORGE 20455, 20456

BAZANT, JAN 7344

BEACH, E. MERRILL 8278

BEACHEY, R.W. 33, 4684, 5204, 5205

BEAL, FRANCES M. 16344

BEALS, CARLETON 6171

BEAN, RICHARD N. 4685, 5206, 5207, 5208, 5209, 6020, 6172

BEAN, WILLIAM B. 15593

BEAN, WILLIAM G. 2108

BEAR, JAMES A., JR. 13488, 13497

BEARD, AUGUSTUS F. 19147

BEARD, EVA 3089

BEARDSLEY, EDWARD H. 708

BEARDSMORE, VALERIE 2109

BEARSE, AUSTIN 19467

BEARSS, EDWIN C. 13489, 13912, 20457

BEASLEY, CECILY R. 17520

BEASLEY, DELILAH L. 11069, 11070

BEASLEY, EDWARD JR. 9974

BEASLEY, JONATHAN 12526

BEATTIE, JESSIE L. 19468

BEATTIE, JOHN 6173

BEATTY, JAMES P. 13490

BEATTY, WILLIAM J. 9377

BEATTY-BROWN, FLORENCE R. 8764

BEAUBIEN, HARRIET F. 8765

BEAUCAGE, PIERRE 7345

BEAUCHAMP, HELEN C. 13491

BEAUCHAMP, VIRGINIA W. 2110

BEAUFORD, G.L. 6174

BEAVER, HAROLD 2111

BECK, HORACE P. 17375

BECK, WARREN A. 2112

BECKER, CARL M. 13179

BECKER, GARY 14099

BECKER, WILLIAM H. 2113

BECKFORD, GEORGE 6175, 6176

BECKFORD, GEORGE L. 6177

BECKHAM, ALBERT S. 17521

BECKWITH, MARTHA W. 6178, 6179, 6180

BEDINI, SILVIO A. 3090

BELL, MICHAEL D.   378

BELL, RAYMOND M.   10719

BELL, RUDOLPH M.   14574

BELL, WHITFIELD J., JR.   3097

BELLAMY, DONNIE D.   2114, 9384,
9385, 11536, 12658

BELLAMY, GLADYS C.   2115

BELL AND HOWELL COMPANY   35, 36,
37, 38, 39

BELLAROSA, JAMES M.   5212, 5213

BELLEGARDE, DANTES   6183

BELLEGARDE, IDA R.   11938

BELLEGARDE-SMITH, PATRICK   19880

BELLER, JACK   11153

BELLINGSHAUSEN, THADDEUS   7351

BELLOC, HILAIRE   5214

BELLOT, LELAND J.   16617

BELSER, THOMAS A., JR.   11685

BELTING, NATALIA   10861

BELTON, BILL   8280, 13913

BELZ, HERMAN   710, 9976, 9977,
9978, 20685, 20686

BELZ, HERMAN J.   20689

BEMER, LEO S.   10904

BENDER, EILEEN   1196

BENDER, FLORENCE R.   15843

BENEDICT, HELEN D.   17523

BENJAMIN, GILBERT G.   13301

BENNERS, ALFRED H.   3099

BEECH, MERVYN W.H.   4686

BEEHLER, W.H.   7346

BEEMAN, RICHARD R.   7347, 8279,
13494, 19878

BEER, GEORGE L.   5210

BEERS, H. DWIGHT   16091

BEERS, HENRY P.   34

BEHAGUE, GERARD H.   7348, 17522

BEHLING, AGNES   709

BEIER, H.U.   4687

BEIGUELMAN, PAULA   3091

BEJACH, LOIS D.   20683

BELIN, H.E.   3092, 12342

BELISLE, JOHN   14100

BELIZ, ANEL E.   7349

BELKNAP, JEREMY   10427

BELL, ALEXANDER K.   10718

BELL, BARBARA L.   40

BELL, BERNARD W.   41, 9378

BELL, DERRICK   8766

BELL, DOROTHY   42

BELL, H.S.   11809

BELL, HERBERT C.   5211

BELL, HESKETH J.   6181

BELL, HOWARD H.   3093, 3094, 3095
3096, 9380, 9381, 9382, 11071,
19469, 19470

BELL, KENNETH N.   6182

BELL, MATTIE   13300

BENNETT, CHARLES R.   2116, 2117

BENNETT, CLIFFORD T.   43

BENNETT, FRANK   7352

BENNETT, J. HARRY   6185, 6186,
   6187, 6188, 6189, 6190, 6191

BENNETT, JOHN   19278

BENNETT, JON B.   2118

BENNETT, LERONE   16345, 16346

BENNETT, LERONE JR.   711, 2119,
   3100, 3101, 3102, 3103, 3104,
   3105, 3106, 9979, 9980, 13914,
   13915, 15203, 16347, 19881

BENNETT, NORMAN R.   4688, 5216

BENNETT, PATRICK R.   18033

BENNETT, ROBERT A.   16618

BENNETT, WILLIAM J.   2316

BENSON, ANDREW M.   20690

BENTLEY, GEORGE R.   20691

BENTLEY, WILLIAM G.   12843

BERG, PHILIP L.   2120

BERGEN, F.D.   18034

BERGEN, FANNY D.   18035

BERGER, MAX   3107, 3108

BERGMAN, MORT N.   44

BERGMAN, PETER M.   44

BERGMANN, LEOLA N.   10926

BERGSTRESSER, REBECCA B.   7353

BERGSTROM, T.   14102

BERINGER, RICHARD E.   20447

BERKELEY, EDMUND JR.   9386

BERKELEY, FRANCIS L., JR.   8281

BERKELEY, KATHLEEN C.   13180

BERKHOFER, ROBERT F.   712

BERKHOFER, ROBERT F., JR.   13916,
   13917

BERKOVE, LAWRENCE I.   9387

BERLIN, IRA   713, 714, 3109, 8282,
   9388, 9389, 9390, 9391, 19882

BERNARD, JESSIE   16094

BERNARD-POWELL, NORMA A.   6192

BERNS, WALTER   15075

BERNSTEIN, BARTON J.   5217

BERREMAN, G.D.   3385, 4026

BERRIGAN, J.R.   3110

BERRY, BENJAMIN D., JR.   45

BERRY, MARY F.   715, 716, 2121,
   2122, 2123, 4689, 17379, 20458,
   20692, 20695

BERRY, THOMAS F.   20459

BERRY, THOMAS S.   14662

BERRY, WILLIAM   3111

BERTHOLD, EUGENIE   11538

BERTLETH, ROSA G.   13302

BERTRAM, WINIFRED E.   11658

BERWANGER, EUGENE H.   2124, 2125,
   2126, 2127, 3112, 8769, 9394,
   20460

BERZON, JUDITH R.   2128

BEST, LLOYD   6193

BESTOR, ARTHUR 8770, 9395

BETHEA, JOSEPH B. 16619

BETHEL, ELIZABETH 20697

BETHELL, ARNOLD T. 6194

BETHELL, LESLIE M. 5218, 5219, 5220, 5221, 5222

BETHKE, ROBERT D. 10720

BETTELHEIM, JUDITH 6195

BETTERSWORTH, JOHN K. 20461

BETTS, EDWIN M. 13497

BEVERLY, JOHN W. 11686

BEYER, RICHARD L. 10612

BICKERTON, DEREK 19279

BICKETT, THOMAS W. 3113

BICKLEY, R. BRUCE JR. 717

BIDDLE, STANTON F. 52

BIDWELL, PERCY W. 10329

BIEBER, ALBERT A. 53

BIERBAUM, MILTON E. 11540

BIERCK, HAROLD A., JR. 7358

BIESANZ, JOHN 7359

BIGELOW, BRUCE M. 5223

BIGELOW, MARTHA M. 12528, 20698, 20699, 20700

BIGHAM, DARREL E. 9396

BIGLEY, A.J. 7360, 7361

BILGER, RICHARD J. 5224

BILLIAS, GEORGE A. 5225

BILLINGS, EDWARD C. 3115

BILLINGS, SYLVIA L. 10823

BILLINGS, WARREN M. 54, 719, 828

BILLINGSLEY, AMY T. 16097

BILLINGSLEY, ANDREW 9397, 16095, 16096, 16097

BILLINGSLEY, R.G. 720

BILLINGTON, RAY A. 9398, 20701, 20702

BILLUPS, KENNETH B. 17526

BIMBA, ANTHONY 3116

BIMS, HAMILTON 16099

BINDER, FREDERICK M. 5226, 20703 20704

BINDER-JOHNSON, HILDEGARD 10721

BINGHAM, ALFRED M. 10331

BINGHAM, R.L. 2129

BINGHAM, ROBERT 2130

BINNING, F. WAYNE 12228

BIRBECK, MORRIS 3117

BIRD, M.B. 6196

BIRD, TIMOTHY 721

BIRKOS, ALEXANDER S. 56

BIRMINGHAM, DAVID 1493, 5227, 5228, 5229

BIRNEY, CATHERINE H. 19149

BIRNEY, JAMES G. 11264

BIRNEY, WILLIAM 11265, 20705

BIRNIE, C.W. 12844

BIRTHA, BECKY   57

BIRTWHISTLE, T.M.   3118

BISHOP, CHARLES C.   2131

BISHOP, PATRICIA A.   6197

BISSELL, J.W.   20706

BITTKER, BORIS I.   3119

BITTLE, WILLIAM E.   13918

BIVINS, JOHN JR.   12659

BJORNSON, MARION L.   19471

BLACK BICENTENNIAL COMMITTEE
   12229

BLACK, BLANTON E.   20463

BLACK, CHARLES L.   9165

BLACK, CLINTON V. DE B.   6198

BLACK, ELIZABETH   15844

BLACK, FREDERICK R.   19040

BLACK, IRVING D.   20464

BLACK, JOHN L.   3121

BLACK, PATTI C.   15470

BLACK, ROBERT C.   14663

BLACKBURN, GEORGE M.   2133, 13064

BLACKBURN, M.J.   18036

BLACKBURN, REGINA L.   16351

BLACKBURN, ROBIN   6199

BLACKETT, R.J.M.·   19472, 19473

BLACKETT, RICHARD   9399

BLACKFORD, L. MINOR   13499

BLACKISTON, HARRY S.   9982

BLACKLAW, A. SCOTT   7362

BLACKLEDGE, CHARLES H.   20330

BLACKWELL, GLORIA   3122

BLACKWELL, JAMES E.   3123

BLACKWELL, VELVELYN   63

BLAIR, HENRY W.   3124

BLAIR, NORVEL   18311

BLAIR, THOMAS L.V.   7363

BLAKE, CLOTILDE   9400

BLAKE, EDITH   6200

BLAKE, J. HERMAN   12969

BLAKE, JANE   11404

BLAKE, JOHN W.   3125, 4690, 5230,
   5231

BLAKE, NELSON M.   19883

BLAKE, RICHARD A.   724

BLAKE, ROBERT   18311

BLAKE, ROBERT R.   2134

BLAKE, RUSSELL   8288

BLAKE, RUSSELL C.   15993

BLALOCK, HUBERT M., JR.   2135

BLANCHARD, FOREST I.   19475

BLANCHARD, RAE   6201

BLAND, LINDA A.   12660

BLANK, STEPHANIE B.   7364

BLANKS, WILLIAM D.   16621

BLANTON, JOSHUA E.   17383

BLANTON, WYNDHAM B.   15594, 15595,
   15596

BLOUET, OLWYN M.   6205, 6206

BLUESTEIN, EUGENE   4692, 17531

BLUESTONE, D.M.   739

BLYDEN, EDWARD W.   4693

BOAHEN, ADU   5233

BOAS, FRANZ   2140, 2141, 2142,
   4694, 4695, 4696, 4697, 4698,
   4699

BOASE, PAUL H.   3129

BOATNER, MARK M.   8290

BODDY, JAMES M.   2143

BODINE, GEORGE   20717

BODO, JOHN R.   16625

BOEDING, MICHAEL A.   11266

BOEHRER, GEORGE C.   68

BOESEKEN, A.J.   4700

BOGART, ERNEST L.   14104

BOGART, JOHN A.   10614

BOGGER, TOMMY L.   17386

BOGGS, JAMES   2144

BOGGS, WILLIAM E.   3130

BOGIN, RUTH   352, 9407

BOGLE, DONALD   2145

BOGLEY, BEVERLY A.   15466

BOGOMOLNY, MICHAEL   17532

BOGT, WALE   8291

BOGUE, WILLIAM W.   8774

BOHANNAN, PAUL   5234

BLASSINGAME, JOHN W.   64, 65, 66,
   725, 726, 727, 728, 729, 730,
   731, 732, 734, 735, 3127, 4689,
   11989, 12230, 15204, 15205,
   15886, 16105, 16106, 16107,
   17379, 18740, 20710, 20711,
   20712, 20713, 20714, 20715,
   20716

BLAUNER, ROBERT   17384, 17385

BLAUSTEIN, ALBERT P.   3128

BLAUSTEIN, RICHARD   17527, 17528

BLAUVELT, MARTHA T.   736

BLAZEK, RON   67

BLAZER, D.N.   19477

BLEBY, HENRY   6203

BLEDSOE, JOHN C.   9401

BLESH, RUDI   17529

BLIED, BENJAMIN J.   16624

BLISS, WILLIAM R.   5232

BLISSARD, THOMASINA   2136

BLIVEN, NAOMI   737

BLOCH, H.   15206

BLOCH, HERMAN D.   2137, 9402, 940
   9404, 9405, 10613

BLOCK, W.T.   15077

BLOCKSON, CHARLES L.   10722

BLOK, H.P.   19280

BLOOM, LEONARD   2138, 13919

BLOOMFIELD, MAXWELL   2139

BLOORE, J. STEPHEN   10862

BLOUET, BRIAN W.   6204

BOHMER, DAVID A. 3131

BOITANI, PIERO 740

BOLES, JOHN B. 3132, 11267, 19478

BOLES, NANCY G. 69

BOLHOUSE, GLADYS E. 10784

BOLINGER, DWIGHT L. 19281

BOLLAND, O. NIGEL 7365, 7366, 7367

BOLLER, PAUL F. 16627

BOLT, CHRISTINE 2147, 3133, 13921

BOLTON, H. CARRINGTON 6207, 12847

BOLTON, H.E. 3134

BOLTON, HERBERT E. 9408

BOLTON, S.C. 16629

BOMAN, MARTHA 9409

BONAICH, EDNA 2148, 14106, 14107, 14108

BOND, H.M. 19153

BOND, HORACE M. 11689

BOND, JOHN W. 11268

BOND, THEODORE 4260

BONE, ROBERT 3135

BONE, ROBERT A. 70

BONEKEMPER, EDWARD H. 8776, 20331

BONEY, F. NASH 742

BONEY, F.N. 741, 2149, 2150, 3136, 3137, 11990, 11991, 13502, 13503, 20718

BONEY, FRANCIS N. 743

BONNER, HYPATIA B. 3139

BONNER, JAMES C. 744, 3140, 11992, 11993, 11994, 14109, 14110, 14860, 15291

BONNIFIELD, PAUL 13922

BONSAL, LEIGH 14904

BONTEMPS, ARNA 71, 745, 3141, 3783, 18204, 18815, 18816, 18817, 19886

BONTEMPS, ARNA W. 3142, 18038

BOGG WATSON, W.N. 15599

BOOKER, GEORGE W. 5236

BOOKER, H. MARSHALL 13504

BOORSTIN, DANIEL J. 3143

BOOTH, ALAN R. 5237

BOOTH, NORMAN E. 11862

BOOTH, SALLY S. 3292

BOOTHE, CHARLES O. 16630

BORAH, WOODROW 5238, 6324, 7368

BORAH, WOODROW W. 7369, 7370

BORCHERT, JAMES 11225

BORELLO, FRANK C. 9410

BORITT, G.S. 2151

BORNEMAN, ERNEST 6208, 17534, 17535, 17536

BOROME, JOSEPH A. 2152

BORUS, DANIEL H. 388

BOSKIN, JOSEPH 746, 747, 748, 2156, 2157, 2158

BOSSY, JOHN 749

BOSTICK, CLYDE M. 12232

BOTKIN, B.A. 750, 751, 18039,
    18040, 18041, 19043

BOTSFORD, DAVID P. 19480

BOTUME, ELIZABETH H. 12849

BOUCHER, CHAUNCEY S. 11002, 14112

BOUCHER, M. 5240

BOUCHER, MORRIS R. 9412

BOUGHTON, WILLIS 3144

BOULLE, PIERRE H. 5241

BOUQUET, MICHAEL R. 5242

BOURGER, LARRY 11185

BOURGUIGNON, ERIKA 6209

BOURGUIGNON, ERIKA E. 4701

BOURNE, ANNIE N. 8293

BOURNE, EDWARD G. 362

BOURNE, RUTH 5243

BOURNE, THEODORE 3145

BOUSFIELD, M.O. 15601

BOUTWELL, GEORGE S. 5244

BOWDEN, EDGAR 3146

BOWDITCH, CHARLES P. 9413

BOWDOIN COLLEGE MUSEUM OF ARTS
    18599

BOWEN, DAVID W. 13181

BOWEN, DON R. 11542

BOWEN, ELBERT R. 11543

BOWEN, GREGORY 2159

BOWEN, J.W.E. 4142, 4702

BOWEN, MICHAEL L. 12662

BOWEN, ROBERT A. 3147

BOWERS, DOUGLAS 14, 15

BOWERS, JAMES C., JR. 13506

BOWLES, PAUL 4703

BOWLING, CHARLES H. 76

BOWMAN, JAMES C. 17387

BOWMAN, LARRY G. 8294

BOWMAN, SHEARER D. 3148

BOWSER, FREDERICK P. 77, 753,
    6211, 7372, 7375, 7376

BOX, MRS. EUGENE 12531

BOXER, C.R. 754

BOXER, CHARLES R. 2160, 5245,
    5246, 5247, 5248, 6213, 6214,
    7377, 7378, 7379, 7380, 7382,
    7383

BOYD, ANTONIO O. 2161

BOYD, GEORGIA 16352

BOYD, JARRITUS 755

BOYD, JESSE L. 12532

BOYD, JULIAN P. 8778

BOYD, MARK F. 11863, 15602

BOYD, MINNIE C. 11692, 11693

BOYD, WILLIAM K. 78, 8779, 12664,
    16634

BOYD, WILLIAM L. 20720

BOYD, WILLIS D. 2162, 2163, 3149,
    20721

BOYD-BOWMAN, PETER 7388, 7389, 7390

BOYER, CLARENCE H. 17539

BOYER, RICHARD 7391

BOYKIN, EUGENE M. 9984

BOYKIN, JAMES H. 12665, 12666

BOYKIN, MARY A. 13304

BOYLE, VIRGINIA F. 3150

BOYLES, WILLIAM J. 5249

BOYNTON, MADGE B. 79

BOZEMAN, THEODORE D. 2165, 3151

BOZEMAN, WILLIAM F. 12533

BRACE, C. LORING 2166

BRACEY, JOHN H., JR. 80, 9415, 9416, 19481

BRACEY, SUSAN L. 13508

BRACKETT, JEFFREY R. 756, 8295, 11405, 11406, 11407

BRACKETT, LOUISA DEB. BACON 1233

BRADFORD, J.H. 20722

BRADFORD, M.E. 757, 2167, 9985

BRADFORD, S. SYDNEY 13509

BRADFORD, SAMUEL S. 13510

BRADFORD, SARAH 18819

BRADFORD, SARAH E. 19483

BRADFORD, SAX 7392

BRADING, D.A. 7393, 7394

BRADLEE, FRANCIS B.C. 5250

BRADLEY, A.G. 18043

BRADLEY, ARTHUR G. 3152, 8296

BRADLEY, BERT E. 3153

BRADLEY, DAVID H. 16635, 16636

BRADLEY, GERALD S., JR. 3154

BRADLEY, IAN 5251

BRADLEY, JOHN L. 9986

BRADLEY, L. RICHARD 2168, 16638

BRADLEY, LAWRENCE J. 5373

BRADLEY, MICHAEL R. 8297

BRADWELL, JAMES B. 8781

BRADY, CYRUS T. 5252

BRADY, KATHLEEN 758

BRADY, P.S. 2169

BRADY, PATRICK S. 5253

BRADY, ROBERT L. 759, 7395, 7396

BRADY, TERENCE 3155

BRAGAW, DONALD H. 11864

BRAGG, GEORGE F. 16641, 16642

BRAGG, GEORGE F., JR. 11408

BRAGG, JOHN 17541

BRAGG, LILLIAN C. 5254

BRAINERD, ALFRED F. 14667

BRAINES, EDGAR F., JR. 3156

BRAKE, ROBERT 18044

BRANCACCIO, PATRICK 740, 2170

BRAND, NORMAN E. 18820

BRANDAO, GUILHERME E. 7398

BRANDFCN, ROBERT 760

BRANDSTADTER, EVAN 3157

BRANDT, LILIAN 5256

BRANNEN, CLAUDE O. 14115

BRANSCOME, JAMES L. 13511

BRANTLEY, WILLIAM H. 11694

BRASCH, ILA W. 81

BRASCH, WALTER M. 81, 19283

BRASSEAUX, CARL A. 8783, 12234, 12235, 12236

BRATHWAITE, EDWARD 6216

BRATHWAITE, EDWARD K. 82, 83, 84, 761, 762, 763, 764, 765, 766, 767, 768, 4704, 5257, 6217, 6218, 6220, 6221, 6222, 6223, 6224, 6226, 6229, 6230, 6232, 6233, 6234, 6235, 6236, 6238, 6241, 6242, 6243, 6244, 6245

BRATTON, MARY J. 13512, 13513, 15080

BRATZEL, JOHN F. 7399

BRAUER, KINLEY J. 20333

BRAVERMAN, HOWARD 2171

BRAWLEY, BENJAMIN 3158, 3159, 16353

BRAWLEY, BENJAMIN G. 3160, 3161, 3162, 17388, 18705

BRAWLEY, JAMES P. 16644

BRAWLEY, JAMES S. 12668

BRAY, J.C. 18048

BRAZIL, BLAS 7400

BREATHETT, GEORGE 6246, 6247, 6248

BREBNER, JOHN B. 10254

BRECKENRIDGE, W.C. 500

BRECKENRIDGE, WILLIAM C. 11544

BRECKINRIDGE, WILLIAM C.P. 3163

BREEDEN, JAMES O. 85, 2172, 156⏄ 15604, 15605

BREEN, T.H. 8204, 8205, 8298, 8299

BREISETH, CHRISTOPHER N. 3164

BREMNER, ROBERT H. 20334

BRENNAN, EDWARD J. 7401

BRENT, JOSEPH L. 2173

BRERETON, BRIDGET 2174

BREWER, J. MASON 12852, 15997, 18049, 18050, 18052, 18053, 18054, 18056

BREWER, JAMES H. 3301, 8786, 12669, 13517

BREWER, JEUTONNE P. 19045

BREWER, JOHN M. 13305, 13306, 18058

BREWER, JOHN MASON 13307

BREWER, PAT B. 2175

BREWER, WILLIAM M. 3165, 14117

BREWSTER, ROBERT W. 3166

BREYFOGLE, WILLIAM A. 19484

BRICELAND, ALAN V. 20724

BRIDENBAUGH, CARL 3167, 5259, 6250, 8302, 8303, 14669, 1635⏄

BRIDENBAUGH, ROBERTA 6250

BRIDGES, CLARENCE A. 13308

BRIDGES, JONATHAN L., JR.   12802

BRIDGMAN, ROBERT W.   20725

BRIDNER, ELWOOD L., JR.   11409

BRIGGS, THOMAS V.   5260

BRIGGS, WALTER D.B.   20726

BRIGHAM, R.I.   11545

BRIGHT, ALFRED L.   8304

BRIGHT, MARGARET D.   13309

BRIGINSHAW, VALERIE A.   86

BRIGNAND, RUSSELL C.   87

BRINGEN, HAROLD L.   2176

BRINGER, GLADYS S.   9987

BRINGHURST, NEWELL G.   2177, 2178

BRINK, WILLIAM   3168

BRINKLEY, FRANCES K.   6251

BRINKMAN, GROVER   10863

BRINN, SUSAN H.   8305

BRINSMADE, R.B.   14113

BRINTON, DANIEL G.   11410

BRITT, DAVID   769

BRITT, JAMES W.   770

BROADHEAD, SUSAN H.   5261

BROCK, H.I.   3169

BROCK, R.A.   3170

BROCK, ROBERT A.   5263, 8306, 13521

BROCK, W.R.   771

BROCK, WILLIAM R.   3171, 3172

BROCKETT, LINUS P.   20728

BROCKHURST, H.V.P.   7402

BRODERICK, FRANCIS L.   772

BRODIE, FAWN M.   773, 2180, 2182, 13523

BRODIE, SYDNEY   8788

BROGLEY, AGNES DE SALES   10723

BROKHAGE, JOSEPH D.   3173

BROMBERG, ALAN B.   13525

BRONNER, F.L.   774

BRONNER, SIMON J.   88

BRONSARD, JAMES F.   19286

BRONSON, E.B.   10386

BRONSON, LOUIS H.   20729

BROOKE, GEORGE M., JR.   5264

BROOKES, STELLA B.   775

BROOKS, ALBERT N.D.   13526

BROOKS, GEORGE E., JR.   2183, 3174, 5216, 5265, 5266

BROOKS, NEAL A.   11411

BROOKS, NOAH   3175, 20730

BROOKS, ROBERT P.   78, 11996, 11997, 11998, 14120

BROOKS, TILFORD   17543

BROOKS, WALTER H.   16653, 16654

BROPHY, LIAM   2184, 2185

BROUCEK, JACK W.   12000

BROUGH, CHARLES H.   12534

BROUGHTON, N.B.   3177

1677

BROUWER, MERLE G.   9419, 10724

BROWER, ELIZABETH E.   15081

BROWIN, FRANCES W.   19486

BROWN, ANNA B.A.   9989

BROWN, B. KATHERINE   8309

BROWN, BARBARA   10404

BROWN, BARBARA W.   10387, 10388

BROWN, BEATRICE J.   776

BROWN, BENNIE D.   5267

BROWN, BEVERLY   16655

BROWN, CARL H.   5268

BROWN, CAROL   89

BROWN, CAROLINE Q.   11269

BROWN, CECELIA R.   18419

BROWN, CECIL M.   777

BROWN, CHARLES S.   4705

BROWN, CHERYL L.   553

BROWN, CLARENCE   18824

BROWN, CLIFTON F.   610, 17341

BROWN, COURTNEY   778

BROWN, DELINDUS R.   9420

BROWN, DOROTHY S.   3178

BROWN, E. ETHELRED   6253

BROWN, ELISABETH D.   8308

BROWN, ELLWOOD W.   8789

BROWN, EVERETT S.   12238

BROWN, GENEVIEVE   5269

BROWN, GEORGE W.   6255

BROWN, GREGORY G.   7403

BROWN, HALLIE Q.   18825

BROWN, HERBERT E.   5270

BROWN, INA C.   3179

BROWN, IRA V.   10726

BROWN, JAMES A.   16111

BROWN, JAN   3180

BROWN, JOHN M.   17545

BROWN, JOHN P.   13924

BROWN, JONATHAN C.   7404

BROWN, KARL   90

BROWN, KENNETH S.   8206

BROWN, LARRY   16657

BROWN, LETITIA W.   9421, 9422,
     11227

BROWN, MARY V.   13529

BROWN, MATTIE   11810

BROWN, MAUD M.   20469

BROWN, MINNIE M.   16356

BROWN, MRS. DOUGLAS   13530

BROWN, PHILIP M.   12853

BROWN, RICHARD D.   3181, 3182,
     3183

BROWN, RICHARD H.   3184

BROWN, RICHARD M.   3185, 13925,
     19894

BROWN, RICHARD W., JR.   10333

BROWN, ROBERT E.   8309

BROWN, ROBERT T. 779, 5272, 5273

BROWN, SARA W. 2186

BROWN, STERLING 2187, 9423, 17546

BROWN, STERLING A. 780, 2188, 3186, 18062, 18063, 18707, 18708, 18709

BROWN, THOMAS I. 12001

BROWN, W.H. 13532

BROWN, W.O. 2189

BROWN, WALLACE 6256, 8310, 8311, 8312

BROWN, WILLIAM G. 11659, 11695

BROWN, WILLIAM H. 10864

BROWN, WILLIAM J. 10785

BROWN, WILLIAM W. 3187, 18064, 20731, 20732

BROWN, WILLIS L. 8790

BROWNE, FREDERICK W. 20733

BROWNE, GARY L. 11413

BROWNE, JUANITA M. 16357

BROWNE, JUNIUS H. 20734

BROWNE, MARGARET A. 3188

BROWNE, PHILIP D. 13310

BROWNE, ROBERT S. 14124

BROWNE, WILLIAM H. 11414

BROWNELL, FRANCIS V. 2190

BROWNELL, JEAN B. 11137

BROWNELL, MARJORIE 3189

BROWNELL, R. 5329

BROWNING, DAVID G. 14907

BROWNING, JAMES B. 3190, 3191, 8791, 9424

BROWNLEE, MARY M. 91

BROWNLEE, W. ELLIOT 91, 781

BROWNMILLER, SUSAN 16359

BRCZEAL, ERNESTINE E. 8313

BRUBAKER, MARIANNA G. 19487

BRUCE, DICKSON D., JR. 2191, 15845, 15998, 16658, 18065, 19488

BRUCE, HENRY C. 11547

BRUCE, JOHN E. 782

BRUCE, KATHLEEN 13533, 13534, 13535, 13536

BRUCE, LINDA L. 6259

BRUCE, PHILIP A. 2193, 3192, 3193, 3194, 3195, 8314, 8315, 8316, 11170, 13540, 15999, 16000, 20470

BRUCE, WILLIAM C. 13541

BRUCHAC, JOSEPH 18828

BRUCHEY, STUART 842, 14128

BRUESCH, S.R. 15606

BRUGGER, ROBERT J. 3196

BRUMBAUGH, RODERICK 19489

BRUNER, CLARENCE V. 16659, 16660, 16661

BRUNER, PETER 11270

BRUNN, STANLEY D. 9924

BRUNS, ROGER 3197, 3198

BRUSER, LAWRENCE 2194

BRYAN, C. BRAXTON 8207

BRYAN, C. HOWARD 5274

BRYAN, CHARLES F., JR. 20735

BRYAN, CORBIN B. 13543

BRYAN, JOHN A. 8792

BRYAN, LEON S. 12854

BRYAN, LOUISE M. 13182

BRYAN, PATRICK 7407, 7408

BRYAN, THOMAS C. 12003

BRYANT, BUNYAN 18710

BRYANT, CHARLES A. 14862

BRYANT, IDA M. 2195

BRYANT, MELVILLE C., JR. 17547

BRYANT, WILLIAM C. 2196

BRYCE, C.A. 17548

BRYCE, EMMA A. 3199

BRYCE, JAMES 2197

BRYCE-LAPORTE, ROY S. 783, 3200, 15210, 16112

BRYDON, G. MACLAREN 13544

BRYDON, GEORGE M. 13545

BRYMNER, D. 6261

BUCHANAN, WILLIAM J. 3201

BUCK, IRVING A. 20472, 20473

BUCK, JAMES R. 19158

BUCK, PAUL H. 2198

BUCKINGHAM, DAVID E. 5275

BUCKLEY, ROBERT D., JR. 784

BUCKLEY, ROGER N. 6262, 6263, 6264

BUCKMASTER, HENRIETTA 19490, 19491

BUCKNER, JANICE 7409

BUECHLER, JOHN 10810

BUEHLER, RICHARD D. 13546

BUELL, RAYMOND L. 3202

BUGBEE, LESTER G. 13311

BUHLER, RICHARD O. 7410

BUICE, SAMMY J. 11122

BUISSERET, DAVID J. 5276

BUKER, GEORGE E. 13926, 20229

BULEY, R. CARLYLE 10825

BULL, ELIAS B. 12855

BULL, JACQUELINE 510

BULL, ROSE W. 1233

BULLEN, A.K. 10429

BULLEN, R.P. 10429

BULLOCK, HENRY A. 19159, 19160

BULLOCK, MRS. WALLER R. 18066

BULLOCK, PENELOPE L. 2199

BUNCE, W.K. 2200

BUNDSCHU, HENRY A. 11549

BURCH, CHARLES E. 2201, 2202

BURCHARD, PETER 20738

BURCHARD, PRESTON C. 2203

BURGER, MARY W.   18830

BURGER, NASH K.   785, 16662, 16663

BURGESS, AMY P.   14129

BURGESS, ANTHONY   3204

BURGESS, DONALD   6266

BURGESS, ERNEST W.   16113

BURGESS, JOHN W.   3205, 15211

BURGIN, MIRON   7411

BURKE, JOSEPH C.   3206, 3207, 3208

BURKE-GAFFNEY, H.J.O.'D   4707

BURKETT, E. VANN   13183

BURKETT, ELINOR C.   2204

BURLIN, NATALIE C.   17549, 17550, 17551, 17552, 17553

BURMA, JOHN H.   7413

BURN, WILLIAM L.   6267, 6268

BURNHAM, DOROTHY   16114, 16361

BURNHAM,-FORBES   7414

BURNIM, MELLONEE V.   17554

BURNS, ALAN   6269

BURNS, ALVIN E.   13312

BURNS, E. BRADFORD   786, 7415, 7416, 7417, 7418, 7419, 7964

BURNS, EDWARD M.   10727

BURNS, FRANCIS P.   8793

BURNS, HAYWOOD   8794

BURNS, LEE   10905

BURR, NELSON R.   92

BURRAGE, HENRY S.   8795

BURRELL, W.P.   10518, 14130

BURRIS, SHIRLEY W.   16664

BURRISON, JOHN   18496

BURRISON, JOHN A.   18497

BURROUGHS, PETER   4708

BURROUGHS, WILBUR G.   19493

BURROWS, EDWARD F.   8796

BURROWS, VINIE   16362

BURT, OLIVE W.   11003

BURT, RICHARD F.   8797

BURTNETT, J.G.   3209

BURTON, ANNIE L.   11696

BURTON, ORVILLE V.   12856

BURTON, RICHARD F.   7421

BURTON, THOMAS W.   11271

BURTON, VERNON   2205, 9425

BURTON, WILLIAM   17555

BURTON, WILLIAM J.   2206

BURWELL, LETITIA M.   13547, 13548

BURWELL, WILLIAM M.   3210, 6270

BUSCHKENS, WILLEM F.L.   7422

BUSER, JOHN E.   787

BUSH, BARBARA M.   6271

BUSH, LESTER E.   11155

BUSS, ELIZABETH   16666

BUSWELL, JAMES O.   16667

BUTCHART, RONALD E.   19162

BUTCHER, MARGARET T.   3211, 17557,
    18067

BUTCHER, PHILIP   93, 788

BUTLER, ALFLOYD   4709, 16668

BUTLER, BENJAMIN   20739, 20740

BUTLER, MELVIN A.   19287

BUTLER, PATRICK H.   5990

BUTLER, PIERCE   8798, 12240

BUTLER, RANDALL R.   3212

BUTLIN, NOEL G.   789

BUTSCH, JOSEPH   16670, 16671

BUTTERFIELD, ROGER   19897

BUTTERFIELD, STEPHEN   18833, 18835,
    18836

BUTTERFIELD, STEPHEN T.   18834,
    18837

BUTTS, DONALD C.   8799

BUXBAUM, MELVIN H.   10728

BUZZELL, L.H.   13549

BYERS, JAMES F.   790

BYERS, S.H.M.   10927

BYERS, SAMUEL H.M.   5277

BYRD, EDWARD L., JR.   3213

BYRD, JAMES W.   791, 792, 793,
    2207

BYRD, MABEL   18071

BYRD, PRATT   11272, 11273

BYRD, SHERMAN C.   3214

BYRNE, BARBARA A.   16673

BYRNE, WILLIAM A.   12004

BYRNE, WILLIAM A., JR.   12005

C.D.   3215

CABLE, GEORGE W.   3216, 12241,
    12242, 12243, 19898

CABLE, MARY   5278

CADBURY, HENRY J.   6272, 9426,
    16674

CADBURY, WILLIAM A.   4710

CADE, JOHN B.   94

CADWALLADER, D.E.   15608

CAIN, JERRY B.   13313

CAIN, KENNETH J.   8800

CAIN, MARVIN R.   2208

CALAM, JOHN   16676

CALDECOTT, ALFRED   6273

CALDERHEAD, WILLIAM L.   15082,
    15083, 15084, 15085

CALDWELL, JOAN P.   12536

CALDWELL, JOHN H.   16677

CALDWELL, JOSHUA W.   3217

CALDWELL, MERRILL S.   11274

CALDWELL, NORMAN W.   8317

CALDWELL, ROBERT G.   6274, 11186

CALEY, G.C.   20741

CALHOON, ROBERT M.   794, 795, 83

CALHOUN, ARTHUR W.   16115

CALHOUN, DANIEL   796

CALHOUN, WILLIAM P. 2209

CALICO, FORREST 11275

CALIFF, JOSEPH M. 20742, 20743

CALKIN, HOMER L. 10928

CALKINS, DAVID L. 95, 9427

CALLAHAN, BENJAMIN F. 8801

CALLAHAN, JAMES M. 13550

CALLAWAY, CAROLYN 19900

CALLAWAY, JAMES E. 12006

CALLAWAY, T.F. 3218

CALLCOTT, GEORGE H. 18838, 18839

CALLENDER, GUY S. 14133

CALLIGARO, LEE 8802

CALLOWAY, INA E. 96

CALLOWAY, J.N. 4711

CALLOWAY, THOMAS J. 14676

CALLOWAY-THOMAS, C. 3219

CAMBOR, C. GLENN 16342

CAMEJO, PETER 20337

CAMERON, NORMAN E. 5279

CAMERON, REBECCA 15846

CAMERON, RICHARD M. 16679

CAMERON, VIVIAN 15609

CAMERON, WILLIAM A. 8803

CAMEROTA, MICHAEL 10431

CAMP, ALONZO D. 8804

CAMPBELL, ALBERT A. 6276

CAMPBELL, CARL 6277, 6278, 6279, 9428

CAMPBELL, DOROTHY W. 97

CAMPBELL, ENA 797

CAMPBELL, ERNEST Q. 2210

CAMPBELL, JAMES B. 2211

CAMPBELL, JANE 798

CAMPBELL, JANET 15893

CAMPBELL, KILLIS 2212

CAMPBELL, LEON G. 2213, 7424

CAMPBELL, LEON G., JR. 7426

CAMPBELL, MAVIS 9429

CAMPBELL, MAVIS C. 799, 3220, 6280, 6281, 6282, 9591

CAMPBELL, MICHAEL L. 2214

CAMPBELL, PENELOPE 2215, 2216

CAMPBELL, RANDOLPH 13384

CAMPBELL, RANDOLPH B. 98, 13314, 13316, 13317, 13318, 13319, 13320, 13321, 13377, 14335

CAMPBELL, REX R. 11550

CAMPBELL, ROBERT F. 3222

CAMPBELL, SIR GEORGE 3223

CAMPBELL, STANLEY W. 8806, 8807, 8808

CAMPBELL, T.E. 13551

CAMPBELL, THEOPHINE M. 18073

CAMPBELL-JOHNSTON, MICHAEL 6284

CANADAY, NICHOLAS JR. 3224

CANARELLA, GIORGIO 14578

CANDLER, MARK A. 12007

CANDLER, MYRTIE L. 12008

CANN, MARVIN L. 8319

CANNIFF, WILLIAM 10233

CANOT, THEODORE 5280

CANSLER, CHARLES W. 13184

CANTOR, MILTON 2217

CAPEHART, L.C. 12675

CAPEN, EDWARD W. 8809

CAPERS, GERALD M. 12244

CAPLAN, G.L. 801

CAPPON, LESTER J. 12676, 14677, 14679, 14680

CAPPONI, JOSEPH B.S. 2218

CARAVAGLIOS, MARIA G. 12245, 16680

CARAWAN, CANDIE 12858, 17560

CARAWAN, GUY 12858, 17560

CARDELL, NICHOLAS 15392

CARDOSC, FERNANDO H. 7427

CARDOSO, GERALD 802

CARDOSO, GERALDC D.S. 7429, 7430

CARDOZO, MANOEL 7431

CARDWELL, GARY L. 13552

CAREW, JAN 2220, 2221, 18074

CAREY, PAUL M. 13553

CAREY, ROBINSON 19901

CARGILL, KATHLEEN 15393, 15405

CARLETTI, GIUSSEPE 3226

CARLILE, PEGGY J. 2222

CARLINE, RICHARD 4712

CARLISLE, NATALIE T. 17561

CARLISLE, WILLIAM T. 99, 803

CARLSON, DONALD A. 5281

CARLSON, LEWIS H. 2223, 18712

CARLSSCN, ROBERT J. 14312

CARLTON, ROBERT L. 9431

CARMAGNANI, MARCELLO 7432

CARMAN, RAYMOND S. 16682

CARMICHAEL, MAUDE S. 11812, 11813, 11814

CARMOUCHE, P.L. 3227

CARNATHAN, W.J. 5282, 5283

CARNATHAN, WILEY J. 8320

CARNEGIE, ANDREW 3228

CARNEIRO, E. 7433

CARNOCHAN, JANET 19497

CAROTHERS, BETTIE S. 100

CARPENTER, ESTHER B. 10786

CARPENTER, JOHN A. 20747

CARPENTER, MARIE E. 101

CARPENTER, W. SPENCER 20748

CARPENTER, W.H. 13472

CARPER, N. GORDON 3229

CARR, LOIS G. 8494, 8544, 11416

CARRADINE, B. 18075

CARRATELLO, JOHN D. 17562

CARREIRA, ANTONIO 102

CARRERA DAMAS, GERMAN 354

CARRICK, JOHN 10615

CARRIER, LYMAN 14136

CARRIGAN, JO ANN 15612, 15613, 15614

CARRINGTON, EVELYN M. 16364

CARRINGTON, S.H.H. 6287

CARPION, ARTURO M. 103

CARROLL, CHARLES 2224, 3230

CARROLL, DANIEL B. 2225

CARROLL, F.J. 18077

CARROLL, J.M. 16684

CARROLL, JOHN M. 3231

CARROLL, JOSEPH C. 19902, 19903

CARROLL, KENNETH L. 9992, 16685

CARROLL, MICHAEL P. 16365

CARROLL, PATRICK 7434

CARROLL, PATRICK J. 7436, 14910

CARROLL, PETER N. 8321

CARROLL, ROSEMARY F. 13185

CARROLL, SHARON A. 3232

CARROLL, WILLIAM 12677

CARROLL, WILLIAM E. 7437

CARSEL, WILFRED 3233

CARSON, CLAY 808

CARSTENSEN, F.V. 15086

CARTER, ALBERT E. 17563

CARTER, DAN T. 809, 9993

CARTER, DORIS D. 9432

CARTER, ELMER A. 3234

CARTER, HOLLIE E. 19904

CARTER, K. 5286

CARTER, KATE B. 11156

CARTER, RALPH D. 810

CARTER, SAMUEL 9433

CARTER, SOLON A. 20749

CARTER, T. 3235

CARTER, WILLIAM T. 2226

CARTEY, WILFRED 6288

CARTWRIGHT, MARGUERITE 811

CARUSO, JOHN A. 3236

CARVALHO-NETO, PAULO DE 2227, 18423

CARVER, JOHN L. 3237

CARY, LORIN L. 8464, 12733

CASADA, JAMES A. 104, 812, 813

CASE, H.G. 19905

CASEY, TERRY 3238

CASEY, THOMAS W. 10234

CASH, W.J. 3239

CASH, WILLIAM M. 20478

CASHMAN, MARC 105

CASS, JOHN E. 2228

CASSARA, ERNEST 3240

CASSEDY, JAMES H.   14911

CASSELL, FRANK A.   11418

CASSERLY, F.L.   6289

CASSIDY, FREDERIC G.   6290, 6291, 6292, 6293

CASSIDY, VINCENT H.   12217

CASSIDY, WILEY L.   3241

CASSIMERE, RAPHAEL JR.   8322

CASSITY, MICHAEL J.   815

CASTEL, ALBERT   11551, 20750, 20751, 20752

CASTEL, ALBERT E.   10937

CASTELLANOS, HENRY C.   15895

CASTELLANOS, ISABEL M.   6294

CASTRO, JOSUE DE   7439

CATE, MARGARET D.   12009, 12010

CATES, GERALD L.   15615

CATHERALL, G.A.   6295, 6296

CATHERALL, GORDON A.   6297

CATHEY, BOYD D.   2229

CATHEY, CLYDE W.   11815, 11816

CATHEY, CORNELIUS O.   12679, 12680, 12681

CATTERALL, HELEN T.   115, 8811

CATTON, BRUCE   816, 5287, 8812

CAULFIELD, J.E.   6298

CAULFIELD, MINA D.   17391

CAUTHEN, CHARLES E.   20479

CAVANAGH, HELEN M.   3242

CAVE, ALFRED A.   2230

CAVE, R.C.   3243

CAVE, RODERICK   6299

CAVIN, SUSAN   16689

CAWTE, L.H.   5288

CAYTON, HORACE R.   9469

CAZENEAU, J.M.   3244

CEDERBERG, HERBERT R.   817

CENSER, JANE T.   12682

CESPEDES, GUILLERMO   7440

CHACE, RUSSELL E., JR.   7441

CHACKCO, SUSAN   867

CHADDOCK, ROBERT E.   10980

CHADWICK, FRENCH E.   3245

CHALMERS, DAVID M.   818

CHAMBERLAIN, A.F.   18081, 19295, 19296

CHAMBERLAIN, ALEX F.   2231

CHAMBERLAIN, ALEXANDER F.   4714, 13927, 13928, 18082

CHAMBERLAIN, E. NOBLE   5289

CHAMBERLAYNE, C.G.   13555

CHAMBERLIN, DAVID   7442

CHAMBERLIN, HARVEY H.   1646

CHAMBERS, HENRY E.   11552

CHAMPION, THOMAS E.   19501

CHAMPLIN, ROBERT   5290

CHANCE, JOHN K.   7443

CHANDLER, ALFRED 842

CHANDLER, BARBARA 3246

CHANDLER, CHARLES 3247

CHANDLER, DAVID L. 819, 5291, 15616

CHANDLER, JOHN 6300

CHANDLER, JULIAN A.C. 5293, 8813

CHANDLER, WILLIAM E. 3248

CHANNING, EDWARD 3249, 10787

CHANNING, STEVEN A. 820, 3250, 12859, 12860, 20480

CHAPLIN, ROBERT F. 16690

CHAPMAN, ABRAHAM 18841

CHAPMAN, ANNE W. 12861

CHAPMAN, BERLIN B. 3251

CHAPMAN, CHARLES E. 7446

CHAPMAN, T.J. 10729

CHAPPELL, GORDON T. 11697, 13186

CHAPPELL, NAOMI C. 19298

CHAPPELLE, YVONNE R. 4705

CHARLTON, K. 6301

CHARTOCK, LEWIS C. 12862

CHASE, CLARENCE 9434

CHASE, GILBERT 6302, 17566, 17567

CHASE, GILBERT C. 17569

CHASE, J.J. 20753

CHASE, JUDITH W. 17392, 18499

CHASE, NELKA S. 2233

CHATELAIN, HELI 4715

CHATHAM, KATHERINE 11867

CHATTINGIUS, HANS 6303

CHAUNU, HUGUETTE 7447

CHAUNU, PIERRE 7447

CHEANEY, HENRY E. 2234

CHECKLAND, SYDNEY G. 6304

CHEEK, WILLIAM F. 3253, 19503

CHEEKS, GERTRUDE D. 17570

CHEE-MOOKE, ROBERT A. 5294

CHENAULT, JOHN C. 11276

CHENERY, WILLIAM 20755

CHERRY, ADA L. 11868

CHERRY, VIRGINIA M. 6305

CHESNUTT, CHARLES W. 4525, 9435, 18083

CHESTER, ARNOT 3254, 9995, 12863

CHESTER, GREVILLE J. 18084

CHESTER, SAMUEL H. 11817, 11818

CHETLAIN, AUGUSTUS L. 20756

CHEVALIER, FRANCOIS 7448

CHEVANNES, BARRY 6306

CHEW, PETER 821

CHEYNEY, E.P. 10730

CHIESA, V. DELLA 683, 822

CHILCOTE, RONALD 4716

CHILCOTE, RONALD H. 7449

CHILD, ALFRED T., JR. 9436

CHILD, LYDIA M.F. 3255

CHILDS, ARNEY R. 12864, 12865, 12866, 13094

CHILDS, ST. JULIEN RAVENEL 12367, 12868

CHILDS, WILLIAM T. 12248

CHILKOVSKY, NADIA 18425, 18459

CHILTON, JOHN 7450

CHILVER, E.M. 5295

CHINWEIZU 4717

CHIPHE, LEPPAINE 19906

CHITTENDEN, ELIZABETH F. 19504

CHREITZBURG, ABEL M. 16693

CHRISTELOW, ALLAN 5296

CHRISTENSEN, ABIGAL M.H. 18085

CHRISTENSEN, JAMES B. 11157, 11158

CHRISTENSEN, LAWRENCE O. 2235, 11553, 11554

CHRISTENSEN, MIKE 20757

CHRISTIAN, ELLA S. 11698, 11699

CHRISTIAN, MARCUS 9437

CHRISTIAN, MARCUS B. 3256, 12249

CHRISTIANO, DAVID 10521

CHRISTIE, CHRISTINA 4718

CHRISTIE, WILLIAM D. 7451

CHRISTOPHE, CLEVELAND A. 8814

CHRISTOPHER, STEFAN C. 16695

CHRISTY, SARAH R. 19505

CHROUST, ANTON-HERMANN 8815

CHURCH, ANNETTE E. 13187

CHURCH, ROBERTA 13187

CIMBALA, PAUL A. 17571, 17572

CIMPRICH, JOHN 13188, 13189

CIMPRICH, JOHN V. 20760

CIMPRICH, JOHN V., JR. 13190

CINEL, DINO 18745

CIPOLLA, CARLO M. 5297

CLAERBAUT, DAVID 118

CLAIBORNE, J.F.H. 20482

CLAIBORNE, JOHN H. 15212, 15620

CLAIBORNE, LOUIS F. 2236.

CLAIBORNE, WILLIAM B. 13557

CLAIRMONT, DONALD H. 8323, 1023

CLAPPERT, ALBERT M. 3257

CLARK, BLANCHE H. 13191

CLARK, CALVIN M. 3258

CLARK, CHARLES B. 9433, 11421, 11422

CLARK, EDGAR R. 17573

CLARK, EDWARD 2237

CLARK, ELMER T. 16696, 16697

CLARK, ERNEST J. 8816

CLARK, ERNEST J., JR. 8817

CLARK, ETHEL R. 16367

CLARK, HORACE S. 8818

CLARK, J.H. 18086

CLARK, JAMES W., JR. 12686, 18715

CLARK, JOHN 6307

CLARK, JOHN G. 2238, 11660, 12250

CLARK, MARTHA B. 10731

CLARK, ROY L. 17574

CLARK, SARAH B. 18842, 18843

CLARK, TERRI 16368

CLARK, THOMAS O. 119, 823, 11171, 11172, 11278, 15088

CLARK, WALTER 9439

CLARKE, COLIN G. 824, 6807

CLARKE, EDITH 6308

CLARKE, ERSKINE 12869, 12870

CLARKE, FORSTER 6309

CLARKE, JAMES F. 3259

CLARKE, JOE E.L. 17575

CLARKE, JOHN 6310

CLARKE, JOHN H. 825, 826, 827, 828, 829, 830, 831, 832, 2240, 3260, 3261, 3262, 4719, 4720, 4722, 4723, 5299, 5300, 5301, 6312, 6313, 7452, 8209, 16121

CLARKE, R.H. 4724

CLARKE, RICHARD F. 5303

CLARKE, ROBERT L. 120, 833

CLARKE, T. WOOD 8324

CLAUSEN, C.A. 2241

CLAVEL, M. 6314

CLAY, EARL C. 13559

CLAY, GREEN 11280

CLAY-CLOPTON, VIRGINIA 12871

CLAYTON, BRUCE 2242

CLAYTON, FRANK 3263

CLAYTON, LOUISE 11819

CLAYTON, RONNIE W. 12251

CLAYTON, VICTORIA H. 11700

CLAYTON, W.W. 13192

CLEAGE, ALBERT B. 16702

CLEARE, W.T. 6315

CLEGG, LEGRAND H. 4725, 4726, 4727

CLEMENCE, STELLA R. 7453

CLEMENS, PAUL G.E. 5304, 8325, 11424, 11425, 11426

CLEMENT, SAMUEL S. 18844

CLEMONS, LULAMAE 3264

CLEMONS, WALTER 834

CLENDENEN, CLARENCE 5409

CLENDENEN, CLARENCE C. 3265

CLEPHANE, WALTER C. 11228

CLEVELAND, GORDON B. 11701

CLEVELAND, HERDMAN F. 11702

CLEVELAND, LEN G. 11703

CLEVEN, N. ANDREW 6316, 7455, 8326, 9997

CLICK, PATRICIA C. 13561

CLIFFORD, CARRIE 17576

CLIFT, MILDRED 10906

CLIFTON, DENZIL T. 16703

CLIFTON, JAMES M. 122, 12013, 12687, 12872

CLINKSCALES, JOHN G. 12873

CLINTON, CATHERINE 3266

CLINTON, GEORGE W. 1106

CLONTS, F.W. 8327

CLOSE, CAROLINE 362

CLOWES, WILLIAM L. 3267

CLOWSE, CONVERSE D. 12874

COAD, ORAL S. 17577

COAN, JOSEPHUS R. 16704

COATES, HOWARD N. 19510

COATSWORTH, JOHN H. 6317

COBB, HENRY 9440

COBB, HENRY E. 4728

COBB, HERSCHEL P. 8820

COBB, JIMMY G. 12875

COBB, MARTHA K. 835, 7456

COBB, NORMAN J. 12016

COBBS, H.A. GRIER 16122

COCHRAN, JOHN P. 11704

COCHRAN, THOMAS C. 123

COCHRAN, THOMAS L. 5306

COCHRANE, JOHN 20764

COCHRANE, WILLIAM C. 19511

COCHRANE, WILLIAM G. 10334

COCKE, MARGARET R.H. 3268

COCKRUM, WILLIAM M. 19512

CODMAN, JOHN 7458

CODY, CHERYLL A. 12876

CODY, P.E. 2244

COELHO, RUY 7459

COFFIN, CHARLES C. 10617, 20340, 20766

COFFIN, GREGORY C. 124

COFFIN, LEVI 18846

COFFIN, NATHAN E. 9441

COGDELL, JACQUELINE 17578

COHEN, ABNER 5307, 5308

COHEN, DAVID S. 10522

COHEN, DAVID W. 6318

COHEN, DE SILVER 16370

COHEN, HAROLD 2245

COHEN, HENNIG 12877, 15848, 175 19301

COHEN, IRVIN S. 3269

COHEN, IRVING S. 3909

COHEN, JOEL E. 8823

COHEN, RONALD 4729, 4730

COHEN, SHELDON S. 10618

COHEN, SYLVESTER JR. 3270

COHEN, WILLIAM 2246, 13562

COHEN, YEHUDI A. 6319

COHN, DAVID L. 3271

COHN, JAN 2247

COHN, M.M. 8824

COHN, MICHAEL 15474

COHN, N. 3385, 4026

COIT, MARGARET 12878

COLBURN, GEORGE H. 2223

COLE, ADRIENNE R. 9443

COLE, ARTHUR C. 3272, 20767

COLE, ARTHUR H. 14139

COLE, ARTHUR J. 12017

COLE, DAVID W. 12879

COLE, FRED C. 14140

COLE, HERBERT M. 4811

COLE, HUBERT 6320

COLE, JOHNETTA 16371

COLEMAN, ANNIE C. 13563

COLEMAN, EDWARD M. 837

COLEMAN, ELIZABETH D. 13564

COLEMAN, FLOYD W. 18603

COLEMAN, J. WINSTON 838

COLEMAN, J. WINSTON JR. 125, 11281, 11282, 11283, 11284, 16706

COLEMAN, JOHN W. 11285, 11286

COLEMAN, KENNETH 8328, 20483

COLEMAN, MAYBELLE 12881

COLEMAN, MRS. GEORGE P. 13565

COLEMAN, P.J. 5309

COLEMAN, RONALD G. 11159, 11160, 11161

COLES, HARRY L., JR. 12252

COLES, ROBERT 839

COLEY, JAMES E. 10391

COLL, BLANCHE D. 840

COLLEY, VERNA 19515

COLLIER, H.C. 6321

COLLINS, BRUCE 841

COLLINS, DAISY G. 3273, 5310

COLLINS, EDWARD D. 5311, 5312, 5313

COLLINS, HERBERT 14683

COLLINS, WINFIELD H. 15092

COLLISTER, PETER 5314

COLOMB, PHILIP H. 5315

COLP, RALPH JR. 2248

COLQUHOUN, ARCHIBALD R. 3274

COLTHARP, ROBERT W. 15297

COLVIN, AUDREY T. 11229

COLVIN, SARAH 20341

COLWELL, PERCY R. 3275

COMAS, JUAN 2249

COMBES, JOHN D. 12882

COMER, JAMES P. 2250, 4731, 4732, 18746

COMETTI, ELIZABETH 8330

COMINGS, L.L. NEWCOMB 11705

COMITAS, LAMBROS 127, 128, 6322

COMMAGER, HENRY S. 3276

COMMONS, JOHN R. 3277

CONDE, ROBERTO C. 129

CONDIT, WILLIAM W. 13567

CONE, JAMES H. 16707, 16708, 16709, 16710, 16711, 16712, 17348

CONKLIN, JULIA S. 19516

CONLEY, DOROTHY L. 17562

CONLEY, PHIL 13568

CONLIN, KATHARINE E. 10811

CONLON, NOEL P. 8331

CONNALLY, ERNEST A. 15475

CONNEAU, THEOPHILE 5317

CONNEAU, THEOPHILUS 5318

CONNELL, NEVILLE 6323

CONNELLY, THOMAS J. 3279

CONNER, ELOISE 11287

CONNER, VALERIE J. 2251

CONNOLLY, JAMES C. 8332

CONNOR, SELDON 20768

CONRAD, ALFRED H. 842, 843, 844, 14143, 14580, 14581, 14582

CONRAD, EARL 2252, 16372, 17583

CONRAD, GEORGIA B. 12019

CONRAD, GLENN R. 131, 132, 12253, 12254

CONRAD, ROBERT 133, 7463, 7465, 7466, 7467, 7468, 7469, 7470

CONSTANTINE, J. ROBERT 5320

CONSTANTINE, JAMES R. 5321, 5322

CONSTANTINE, R.R. 8826

CONTEE, CLARENCE G. 9444

CONWAY, ALAN 845

CONWAY, EUGENIA C. 17584

CONYNGHAM, DAVID P. 20485

CONZIMIUS, E. 7471

COOK, CHARLES O. 12257

COOK, FRED J. 19916

COOK, M. 2253

COOK, MARGARET C. 10434

COOK, PHILLIP C. 12258

COOK, SAMUEL D. 3282

COOK, SHERBURNE F. 6324, 7473

COOKE, ALISTAIR 3283

COOKE, J.W. 2254

COOKE, JACOB E. 846, 847, 848

COOKE, RAYMOND M. 349

COOLEY, HENRY S. 10524, 10525

COOLEY, ROSSA B. 15476

COOLING, B. FRANKLIN 134

COOMBS, JOSHUA 17585

COOMBS, NORMAN 3284

COOMBS, ORDE 2255, 3736, 6325

COON, DAVID L. 12883

COONEY, CHARLES F. 20769

COONEY, JERRY W. 7474

COOPER, ANNA J. 3285, 8828

COOPER, CLAYTON S. 7475

COOPER, FREDERICK 850, 1493, 4734, 4735, 4736, 4737, 9445

COOPER, GUY E. 5323

COOPER, JOHN I. 19517

COOPER, MADIE 13323

COOPER, WILLIAM A. 16713

COOPER, WILLIAM J., JR. 3286, 14144

COOPER, WILLIAM JR. 21091

COPE, ROBERT S. 8333, 8334

COPELAND, J. ISAAC 240

COPENHAUSER, J.E. 12020

COPLAND, S. 6326

COPPIN, L.J. 851, 17586

COPPIN, LEVI J. 19049, 19050, 19051

CORBETT, MICHAEL F. 17394

CORBIN, FRANCIS 13571

CORBITT, DUVON C. 852, 5324

CORCORAN, JOHN JR. 9446

CORDWELL, JUSTINE M. 4738

CORE, GEORGE 853

CORKRAN, DAVID H. 13929, 13930

CORLEW, ROBERT E. 13193, 13194, 13195

CORLEY, DANIEL 3. 12259

CORNELIUS, JANET D. 16714

CORNISH, DUDLEY T. 135, 20770, 20772, 20773, 20774

CORREA DO LAGO, LUIZ A. 7476

CORRIGAN, PHILIP 3287

CORRUCCINI, R. 15670

CORRY, JOHN P. 8335, 13931, 13932

CORSON, EUGENE R. 15623

CORTADA, JAMES W. 6329

CORTADA, RAFAEL L. 136, 137, 138, 854, 855, 856

CORWIN, ARTHUR F. 2256, 6330, 6331, 8829

CORWIN, CHARLES E. 10619

CORWIN, EDWARD S. 8830

CORY, CHARLES E. 10938

COSTA, LUIZ E.A. 7477

COSTELLO, RICHARD D. 3288

COSTON, WILLIAM H. 3289

COTHRAN, KAY L. 13092

COTT, NANCY F. 16373

COTTER, JOHN L. 14689

COTTERILL, ROBERT S. 3290, 3291, 13933

COTTON, BARBARA R. 139, 11869

COTTON, ROLAND M. 12260

COTTON, ROOSEVELT C. 358

COTTON, SOLOMON R. 10365

COTTON, WALTER 13324

COTTRELL, DANNELL G. 13325

COTTROL, ROBERT J. 15899

COUCH, WILLIAM JR. 20342

COUGHTRY, JAY A. 5325

COULON, EARL C. 12261

COULTER, CALVIN B., JR. 8336

COULTER, E. MERTON 860, 3292,
    8831, 11288, 12023, 12024,
    12025, 12027, 12028, 12029,
    13196, 14690, 14831, 15918,
    20343, 20487, 20488, 20489,
    20776

COULTER, ROY D. 13197

COULTHARD, G.R. 2257

COUNCILL, W.H. 861, 3293, 3294,
    3295

COUNCILL, WILLIAM H. 3296, 16717

COUPLAND, R.W. 5326

COUPLAND, REGINALD 5327

COURLANDER, HAROLD 862, 6332,
    6333, 12031, 17588, 17589,
    19302

COUSINS, LEONE B. 5328

COUSINS, PHYLLIS M. 20777

COUSINS, W.M. 6334

COUSINS, WINIFRED M. 16123

COUTINHO, J. DE SIQUEIRA 17591

COUTURIER, EDITH 7478

COVER, ROBERT M. 8832

COVINGTON, JAMES W. 11870

COWAN, ZELIDE 6011, 6012

COWARD, JERRY L. 863

COWARD, JOAN W. 11289, 11290

COWDEN, JOANNA D. 3328

COWDEN, ROBERT 20778

COWDREY, ALBERT E. 20779

COWELL, HENRY 17592

COWEN, RUTH C. 11556

COWLEY, CHARLES 19919

COWLEY, M. 5329

COWLEY, MALCOLM 5712, 5713

COX, EARNEST S. 20344

COX, EDWARD L. 864, 6335

COX, HAROLD E. 13573

COX, JOHN H. 10000, 20781

COX, LAWANDA 10000, 20781, 20782

COX, LAWANDA F. 14146

COX, OLIVER C. 2258, 18747

COX, STEPHEN L. 3297

COY, OWEN C. 11074

COYLE, BETTY W. 8337

COYNER, MARTIN B., JR. 13575

COZZENS, ARTHUR B. 11557

CRABTREE, BETH G. 12690

CRADDOCK, EMMIE 3298

CRAGAR, WALDO E. 3299

CRAHAN, MARGARET E. 6336

CRAIG, GERALD M. 865

CRAIG, JAMES H. 18606

CRAIGHEAD, JAMES B. 3300

CRAIK, ELMER L. 10939

CRAIN, JOHN W. 10001

CRANE, ELAINE F. 5330

CRANE, THOMAS F. 866

CRANE, VERNER W. 3301, 3302, 5331

CRAPSEY, ALGERNON S. 13576

CRATON, MICHAEL 141, 867

CRATON, MICHAEL J. 868, 869, 3303,
    5332, 6337, 6338, 6339, 6340,
    6341, 6342, 6343, 6344, 6346,
    6347, 6348, 6351, 6352

CRAVEN, AVERY O. 870, 871, 3304,
    3305, 3306, 3307, 11427, 12262,
    14147, 20345

CRAVEN, WESLEY F. 6354, 8210,
    8211, 8338, 8339, 13579

CRAVENS, JOHN N. 9448

CRAWFORD, JEWELL R. 8834

CRAWFORD, MARGO 16374

CRAWFORD, OSWALD 4740

CRAWFORD, PAUL 8340

CRAWFORD, STEPHEN C. 142

CRAY, ED 17593

CREASE, SOPHIA 11834

CREED, RUTH 4741

CREEDMAN, THEODORE S. 7480

CREEL, MARGARET W. 873, 1806,
    12885

CREMER, HENRY 143

CREMONY, F.C. 5335

CRESSEY, PAMELA J. 13581

CRESSWELL, NICHOLAS 17595

CRESTO, KATHLEEN M. 8341, 20784

CREYKE, PETER 6461

CRIPPS, THOMAS 2259, 2260

CRIPPS, THOMAS R. 2261

CROCKER, LES 12537

CROCKER, RUTH H. 874

CROCKETT, NORMAN L. 11123

CROFT, Q. MICHAEL 2262

CROGMAN, W.H. 3308, 3309, 3634

CROGMAN, WILLIAM H. 3635, 3861

CROMWELL, JOHN W. 3310, 9449,
    11230, 19518, 19922

CROOK, CARLAND E. 13326

CROOKS, JOHN J. 8342

CROSBY, ALFRED W. 3311, 15626,
    15627

CROSBY, CONSTANCE 10435

CROSBY, ERNEST 3312

CROSS, CORA M. 18849

CROSS, HARRY E. 7394

CROSS, JASPER W. 16721

CROSS, MARY E. 3313

CROSS, S.C. 3314

CROSS, SAMUEL C. 3315

CROSS, T.P. 18099

CROSS, WILLIAM E., JR. 875

CROSSMAN, LELAND E. 2263

CROUCH, ARCHIE 16722

CROUCH, BARRY A. 144, 8836

CROUCHETT, LAWRENCE 6355

CROUSE, NELLIS M. 6356, 6357

CROW, JEFFREY J. 8343, 8344, 8345, 12694

CROWDER, RALPH L. 876, 15628, 16540

CROWE, CHARLES 877, 878, 879, 13935

CROWL, JOHN A. 10002

CROWLEY, DANIEL J. 4742, 4743, 6358, 6359, 6360, 18103, 19303

CRUDEN, ROBERT 880, 881, 16723, 20346

CRUDEN, ROBERT L. 882

CRUICKSHANK, J. GRAHAM 7481

CRUM, MASON 12886

CRUMMELL, ALEXANDER 3316, 3317, 3318, 3319, 18748

CRUSE, HAROLD W. 17395

CRUZAT, HELOISE H. 8837

CUBAN ANTI-SLAVERY COMMITTEE 6362

CUBAN, LARRY 883

CULBERTSON, ANNE V. 18105

CULIN, STEWART 18106

CULLEN, JOSEPH P. 8346

CULLINS, ELLA W. 18107

CULMER, FREDERIC A. 11558

CULP, DANIEL W. 3320

CULPEPPER, BETTY M. 8838

CULVERHOUSE, PATRICIA 16724

CUMMINGS, A.D. 16725

CUMMINGS, DOROTHY A. 5336

CUMMINGS, FRANK L. 8839

CUMMINS, D. DUANE 3321

CUMPER, G.E. 6363

CUNARD, NANCY 6364

CUNDALL, FRANK 146, 147, 6134, 6366, 6367, 6368, 20234

CUNDALL, FRANK C. 6369

CUNEY-HARE, MAUD 6370, 17597

CUNLIFFE, MARCUS 3322, 17396

CUNNINGHAM, C.E. 16726

CUNNINGHAM, EILEEN S. 12033

CUNNINGHAM, IRMA 19304

CUNNINGHAM, RUTH R. 8840

CUREAN, HAROLD G. 18503

CURET, JOSE 6372

CURLEE, ABIGAIL 13328, 13329, 13330

CURRIE, JAMES T. 8841, 10003, 10004

CURRIER, CHARLES F.A. 362

CURRIER, CHARLES W. 7482

CURRY, J.L.M. 3323, 3324, 3325, 3326, 8842

CURRY, JABEZ L.M. 3327

CURRY, LEONARD P. 20347

CURRY, OLIVIA B. 7483

CURRY, RICHARD O. 884, 3328

CURTIN, P.D.   5337

CURTIN, PHILIP   5234

CURTIN, PHILIP D.   886, 887, 888,
   889, 2264, 3329, 3330, 4744,
   4745, 4747, 4748, 4750, 4751,
   4752, 4753, 4754, 5338, 5341,
   5342, 5343, 5345, 5346, 5347,
   5348, 6373, 6374, 6375, 6376,
   6377

CURTIS, AGNES B.   10620

CURTIS, ANNA L.   18852

CURTIS, JAMES C.   3331, 13198

CURTIS, K.D.   11005

CURTIS, L.P.   890

CURTIS, NATALIE   17598

CUSACK, MICHAEL   3332

CUSHING, JOHN D.   10436

CUSHING, WALTER H.   10437

CUSHNER, NICHOLAS P.   7484

CUTLER, JAMES E.   19925

DA COSTA EDUARDO, OCTAVIO   7485

DA COSTA, EMILIA V.   891, 3333

DA VEIGA PINTO, FRANCOISE L.
   5350

DAAKU, KWAME Y.   4755, 4756, 4757

DABBS, SOPHIE M.   3334

DABNEY, CHARLES W.   14148, 19166

DABNEY, LILLIAN G.   9450

DABNEY, R.L.   892

DABNEY, ROBERT L.   13583, 15216

DABNEY, SUSAN   15300

DABNEY, VIRGINIUS   12695, 15900,
   19926

DACEY, RAYMOND   893

DAGET, SERGE   5354, 5355, 5356

DAIN, NORMAN   13584

DAINGERFIELD, HENRIETTA   3335

DALBY, DAVID   894, 4758, 4759,
   6378, 19305, 19307, 19308

DALE, EDWARD E.   13936

DALE, HERBERT P.   5357

DALE, WILLIAM P.   11681

DALLAS, GEORGE M.   5358

DAL-ROSSO, SADI   7487

DALRYMPLE, MARGARET F.   12265

DALTON, HENRY G.   7488

DALTON, LAWRENCE   11820

DALY, P.H.   7489

DAMON, SAMUEL F.   2266

DANA, KATHERINE F.   17399

DANA, MARVIN   17400, 19310

DANA, R.H., JR.   10006

DANCE, CHARLES D.   7490

CANCE, DARYL C.   17401, 17402,
   18110

DANCEY, ROGER   5359

DANCY, JOHN C.   10951

DANGERFIELD, GEORGE   3336

CANIEL, JACK L.   17403, 18478

DANIEL, JOHN W.   3337

DANIEL, L.H.   3338

DANIEL, PETE   3339, 8843

DANIEL, VATTEL E.   3340

DANIEL, W. HARRISON   8347, 13586,
16727, 16728, 16729, 16730,
16732, 16733, 20348

DANIELS, DOUGLAS H.   2268, 9451

DANIELS, JOHN   10438

DANIELS, JONATHAN   15096

DANIELS, O.C. BOBBY   3341

DANIELS, WINTHROP M.   895

DANN, MARTIN E.   3342

DANTZIG, A. VAN   5360

DANTZIG, ALBERT V.   5361

DARBY, LORAINE   18111

DARGAN, JOHN J.   3343

DARK, PHILIP J.C.   7491, 7492

DARROW, CLARENCE   16735

DART, HENRY P.   8348, 8844, 8845,
8846, 10007, 12268, 12269

DASH, J. SYDNEY   6380

DASH, MICHAEL   3345

DATHORNE, O.R.   4760

DATHORNE, OSCAR R.   3346

D'AUVERGNE, EDMUND B.F.   3347

DAVENPORT, F. GARVIN   11291, 14864

DAVENPORT, TIMOTHY W.   11138

DAVID, C.W.A.   8847

DAVID, JAY   16525

DAVID, PAUL A.   896, 897, 898, 899
900, 14150, 14151

DAVID, ROBERT R., JR.   15553

DAVIDSON, BASIL   4761, 4762, 4753,
4764, 4765, 4766, 4767, 4768

DAVIDSON, CHALMERS   12887

DAVIDSON, DAVID M.   7493, 7494

DAVIDSON, JOHN N.   10993, 10994,
10995

DAVIDSON, PHILIP G.   14693

DAVIE, MAURICE R.   3348

DAVIES, AUTUMN   9452

DAVIES, JULIA E.   12888

DAVIES, K.G.   901, 5367

DAVIES, KENNETH G.   5368, 5369,
6382

DAVIES, OLIVER   4769

DAVIES, W.W.H.   9453

DAVIS, ALLISON   2269, 18749

DAVIS, ANGELA   16375

DAVIS, ANGELA Y.   16376

DAVIS, ARCHIBALD K.   12696

DAVIS, ARTHUR P.   18709

DAVIS, BARBARA J.   11706

DAVIS, CHARLES S.   11707, 11708,
18716

DAVIS, D..WEBSTER   3800

DAVIS, DANIEL S.   3349

DAVIS, DANIEL W.   15849, 19311

DAVIS, DAVID B.   902, 903, 904,
905, 906, 907, 908, 909, 2272,

3350, 3351, 3352, 3355, 3357, 3358, 3359, 3360, 8848, 8849, 16736

DAVIS, E.A. 12272

DAVIS, EDWIN A. 273, 9454, 9455, 9456, 12273, 12274, 12275

DAVIS, F. MARSHALL 3361

DAVIS, GEORGE A. 14923

DAVIS, GEORGE T. 10439, 10440, 10441

DAVIS, GERALD L. 16739, 18504

DAVIS, HAROLD E. 8351, 8352

DAVIS, HAROLD P. 6385

DAVIS, HENDERSON S. 16740

DAVIS, HENRY C. 12890

CAVIS, J. TREADWELL 10008, 16741

DAVIS, J.B. 13937

DAVIS, J.E. 8353, 8354, 8355

DAVIS, J.R. 12697

DAVIS, JAMES E. 9457

DAVIS, JESS G. 11871

DAVIS, JOHN A. 3362, 4770

DAVIS, JOHN P. 149

DAVIS, JOHN W. 16742

DAVIS, JOSEPH L. 3363

DAVIS, K.E. 19053

DAVIS, LANCE E. 910

DAVIS, LAWRENCE M. 19312

DAVIS, LENWOOD G. 150, 151, 152, 153, 154, 155, 156, 157, 158, 159, 160

DAVIS, LEONA K. 3364

DAVIS, MARGARET 10009

DAVIS, MARIANNA 12891

DAVIS, MARTHA E. 17600

DAVIS, N. DARNELL 6337

DAVIS, NICHOLAS D. 912

DAVIS, NOAH K. 3365

DAVIS, OLIVIA N. 16129

DAVIS, OSSIE 913

DAVIS, RALPH 5370

DAVIS, RICHARD B. 12892, 13590, 13591, 19167

DAVIS, ROBERT H. 7497

DAVIS, ROBERT R. 161

DAVIS, ROBERT R., JR. 5371, 5372

DAVIS, RONALD 14153

CAVIS, RONALD L.F. 20787

DAVIS, SEARL S. 2273

DAVIS, T. FREDERICK 11872

DAVIS, THOMAS J. 162, 914, 915, 8358, 8359, 10621, 10622, 10624

DAVIS, THOMAS R. 8214, 8215

DAVIS, THOMAS W. 3367

DAVIS, WALTER S. 8852

DAVIS, WILLIAM R. 19169

DAVIS, WILLIAM W. 20495

DAVISSON, WILLIAM I. 5373

DAWES, EMMA L.M. 12276

DAWSON, HENRY B. 9056

DAWSON, SANDRA 10010

DAY, GREGORY 18611

DAY, JUDY 9459

DAY, RICHARD E. 13592

DAYKIN, WALTER L. 917

D'AZEVEDO, WARREN 3368

D'AZEVEDO, WARREN L. 918

DE BEET, CHRIS 7498

DE BERRY, W.N. 3369

DE CHASCA, EDMUND 2275

DE COSTA, BENJAMIN F. 10442

DE COSTA, MIRIAM 3370, 4771

DE FERARI, CARLO M. 11075

DE FOREST, JOHN W. 20788

DE GRANDA, GERMAN 919

DE JONG, GERALD F. 8360, 10626

DE KOCK, VICTOR 4772

DE LABAN, JUANA 163

DE LERMA, DOMINIQUE-RENE 164,
17602

DE REUCK, A.V.S. 3385, 4026

DE REUCK, ANTHONY 2276

DE SLIBE, MORRELLA JIMINEZ 7499

DE TOCQUEVILLE, ALEXIS 3371

DEAKIN, N. 3385

DEAN, DAVID M. 9460

DEAN, DEOLA E. 16379

DEAN, JOHN G. 14926

DEAN, JOHN W. 10812

DEAN, TERESA H. 3373

DEAN, WARREN 920, 7500, 7501,
7502

DEANE, CHARLES 5374, 5375, 10445

DEANE, PAUL C. 2277

DEARBURY, LINDA J. 921

DEAS, ALSTON 18612

DEBERRY, JOHN H. 13200, 20496

DEBO, ANGIE 13938

DEBOER, CLARA M. 16745

DEBOW, J.D.B. 15301

DECAMP, DAVID 19314, 19315

DECANIO, STEPHEN J. 922, 923,
14154

DECORSE, HELEN C. 13593

DEERR, NOEL 6389

DEETZ, JAMES 4773, 10447

DEGLER, CARL 924

DEGLER, CARL N. 925, 926, 927,
928, 929, 930, 931, 932, 3374,
3376, 3377, 5376, 8216, 19932

DEGN, CHRISTIAN 933

DEGRAAF, LAWRENCE B. 934, 11008

DEGRUMMOND, JEWEL L. 12277

D'EHTREMONT, JOHN P. 20789

DEJARNETTE, E.M. 16003

DEJOURNETTE, GLADYS 2283

DEL PINO, JULIUS E.   16746

DELAFOSSE, MAURICE   4774

DELANEY, DEBRA   16381

DELANEY, LUCY A.   16382

DELANGE, JACQUELINE   4944

DELLA, M. RAY JR.   11429, 11430

DELMAR, P. JAY   936

DEMARIS, OVID   19524

DEMMING, DAVID W.   9463

DEMOND, A.L.   3378

DENEVAN, WILLIAM M.   6391

DENEVI, DONALD P.   937

DENMAN, CLARENCE P.   11710

DENNETT, GEORGE M.   20790

DENNEY, JOSEPH E.   8854

DENNIS, CHARLES   3379

DENSON, JOHN V.   8855

DENT, HASTINGS C.   7506

DENTON, CHARLES R.   3380

DEPAUW, LINDA G.   8361, 8362

DEPEW, CHAUNCY M.   3381

DEREN, MAYA   6392

DEROSIER, ARTHUR H.   13939

DEROSIER, ARTHUR H., JR.   13940

DERRICK, JONATHAN   4775

DESAI, M.   14158

DESAI, MEGHNAD   938

DESAUSSURE, NANCY B.   3382

DESCHAMPS, MARGARET B.   12698,
   13201

DESCOLA, JEAN 7507

DESDUNES, RODULPHE L.   9464

DESMANGLES, LESLIE G.   6393

DESTLER, CHESTER M.   14159

DETT, ROBERT N.   17603

DETWEILER, FREDERICK G.   2284

DETWEILER, PHILIP F.   3383

DETWEILER, ROBERT   2885

DEUTSCH, ALBERT   2285

DEVEREUX, MARGARET   3384

DEVEREUX, WILLIAM C.   5378

DEVERS, DE ETTE   8857

DEVOS, G.   4026

DEVOS, GEORGE   3385

DEW, CHARLES B.   939, 940, 13594,
   13595, 14694, 14695, 14696

DEW, JOANNA   3386

DEW, LEE A.   2286

DEWOLF, CALVIN   19525

DEWS, MARGERY P.   3387

DEYE, ANTHONY   2287

DIAZ SOLER, LUIS M.   6394, 6395

DIBBLE, ERNEST F.   11873, 11874

DICK, EVERETT   3388

DICK, ROBERT C.   3389

DICKERMAN, G.S.   12893, 14161, 19171

DICKERMAN, GEORGE S.   19172

DICKERSON, O.M.   8363

DICKEY, G. EDWARD   14162

DICKMAN, JOSEPH C., JR.   19526

DICKSON, HARRIS   3390, 3391, 3392, 15635

DICKSON, MOSES   3393

DICKSON, WARREN C.   11009

DICKY SAM   5379

DIDDLE, A.W.   15636

DIEGUES JUNIOR, MANUEL   169

DIEHL, DIGBY   942

DIETERLEN, G.   4808

DIETRICH, KATHERYN T.   16384

DIFFIE, BAILEY W.   7509

DIGGINS, JOHN P.   2288

DIGGS, IRENE   2289, 3394, 3395, 7511, 7512, 7513

DIGGS, JOHN R.L.   16749

DIKE, K.O.   4776

DILL, AUGUSTUS G.   2309, 14703

DILL, BONNIE T.   16385, 16386

DILL, FLOYD R.   12037

DILLARD, J.L.   170, 944, 10237, 10238, 19316, 19317, 19318, 19319, 19321, 19322, 19323

DILLINGHAM, MCKINLEY   3824

DILLINGHAM, WILLIAM P.   14164

DILLON, J.T.   6396

DILLON, MERTON   3396

DILLON, MERTON L.   945, 946, 3397, 3398, 9465

DIMOCK, ANNE   15850

DIN, GILBERT C.   12279

DINARDO, ANDREW A.   10528

DINKINS, JAMES   3399, 20498

D'INNOCENZO, MICHAEL   20426

DINSMORE, CHARLES A.   19935

DIOUF, SYLVIANE   5381

DIPP, HUGO T.   947

DIRKS, ROBERT   6399, 6400, 18115

DISMUKES, CAMILLUS J.   12894

DIXON, HEIMAN D.   11560

DIXON, MELVIN   18117

DIXON, MELVIN W.   949

DIXON, MRS. ARCHIBALD   3400

DIXON, P.F.   6401

DIXON, SUSAN B.   3401

DO NASCIMENTO, ABDIAS   7515

DOAR, DAVID   12895, 12896

DOBBINS, H.   16750

DOBIE, BERTHA M.   13331

DOBSON, NARDA   7516

DOBYNS, H.F.   7517

DOBYNS, HENRY F.   13941

DOCTOROFF, STEPHEN J.   5383

1702

DODD, DOROTHY 5384, 11875, 11876

DODD, WILLIAM E. 175, 3403, 3404,
    3405

DODGE, DAVID 9467

DODGE, N.S. 12897

DODGE, PETER 2290

DOGGETT, ALLEN B., JR. 3406

DOHERTY, HERBERT J., JR. 9468,
    11878

DOLE, SHARON F. 950

DOLLARD, JOHN 2291

DOMAR, EVSEY D. 3407, 3408

DOMINGUEZ, JORGE I. 6404

DOMINICK, CHARLES A. 2292

DONALD, CLEVELAND JR. 7521, 19530

DONALD, DAVID 3409, 20401

DONALD, DAVID H. 951, 952

DONALD, HENDERSON H. 3410

DONALD, JAMES M. 16752

DONALDSON, O. FRED 14382, 14923,
    19677

DONNAN, ELIZABETH 176, 5386, 5388,
    8364

DONNELL, EZEKIEL J. 3411, 14167

DONNELLY, RALPH W. 12038

DONNER, CHRISTOPHER S. 7522

DONOVAN, FRANK 10014

DOOKHAN, ISAAC 6405, 15554

DORAN, MICHAEL F. 13942, 13943

DORF, ANNETTE 10627

DORFMAN, JOSEPH 2293

DORJAHN, VERNON R. 5390

DORMIGOLD, KATE 18855

DORMON, JAMES H. 953, 2294, 4777,
    12280, 12282, 14168

DORMON, JAMES H., JR. 2295

DOROUGH, CHARLES D. 16754

DORRIS, JONATHAN T. 11292, 11293,
    14169

DORRIS, MAUD W. 11293

DORSETT, LYLE W. 11561

DORSEY, JAMES E. 492, 12039

DORSEY, VIRGINIA F. 3412

DORSINVILLE, MAX H. 6406

DORSON, RICHARD M. 12543, 18118,
    18119, 18120, 18121, 18122

DORYK, ELINOR 6407

DOSTER, WILLIAM C. 954

DOUGAN, MICHAEL B. 20500

DOUGLAS, ELLA D.L. 3413

DOUGLAS, ESQUE 11562

DOUGLAS, MARJORY S. 11880

DOUGLAS, MURIEL L. 12283

DOUGLAS, PAUL H. 14170

DOUGLAS, S.W. 18124

DOUGLAS, WADSWORTH C. 6408

DOUGLAS, WILLIAM L. 15479

DOUGLAS, WILLIAM O. 10017

DOUGLASS, FREDERICK 2296, 3414, 3415, 17604, 18856, 19941, 20236

DOVAN, EDWIN 6409

DOVAN, LOWRY A. 11294

DOVER, CEDRIC 18613

DOVRING, FOLKE 955

DOW, GEORGE F. 5392, 18507

DOW, ROGER 3416

DOWD, DOUGLAS F. 956, 14143, 14171

DOWD, JEROME 3417, 4778, 12699, 14700, 16757

DOWER, CATHERINE A. 5410

DOWNS, R.R. 3418, 4779

DOWNS, ROBERT B. 957, 958, 959

DOWTY, ALAN 15905

DOYLE, BERTRAM W. 2297, 2298, 2299

DOYLE, J.A. 3421

DOYLE, MARY E. 18858

DOYLE, MICHAEL A. 960

DOZIER, RICHARD K. 14701

DRACHLER, JACOB 4780

DRAGO, EDMUND L. 12040, 12041

DRAKE, B.K. 5393, 5394

DRAKE, BRYAN K. 5395

DRAKE, FREDERICK C. 5396

DRAKE, MIKE 19054

DRAKE, RICHARD 5397

DRAKE, RICHARD B. 961, 2300, 20794

DRAKE, ST. CLAIR 2301, 3422, 946

DRAKE, THOMAS E. 9470, 16759, 16760

DRAKE, W.M. 16130

DRAPER, JOHN W. 3425

DRESCHER, SEYMOUR 5393, 5399, 6411

DREWAL, MARGARET 177

DREWERY, R.F. 178

DREWRY, HENRY N. 2302, 3426, 342 3428, 16761, 19942

DREWRY, WILLIAM S. 13596, 13597

DREYER, EDWARD 12452

DRIMMER, MELVIN 179, 962, 963, 964, 965, 967, 2303, 3429, 641 14172

DRISKELL, DAVID C. 18616

DRIVER, LEOTA S. 968

DROKE, JACOBUS D. 3430

DRONAMRAJU, KRISHNA R. 969

DROTNING, PHILLIP T. 19532

DRUCKER, LESLEY M. 12899, 12900

DRUMMOND, HENRY 4781, 5400

DRZYCIMSKI, MARY E. 3431

DUBAY, ROBERT W. 12544, 12545

DUBERMAN, MARTIN 970, 971, 2304

DUBERMAN, MARTIN B. 972, 2305

DUBLIN, LOUIS I. 14928

DUBOIS, W.E. BURGHARDT 4525

DUBOIS, W.E.B. 180, 181, 182, 973,
    974, 975, 976, 2306, 2307, 2308,
    2309, 3433, 3434, 3435, 3436,
    3437, 3438, 3439, 3440, 3441,
    3442, 3443, 3444, 3445, 3446,
    3447, 3448, 3449, 3450, 3451,
    3453, 3454, 3455, 4782, 4784,
    5401, 5403, 5404, 10019, 12042,
    14173, 14174, 14702, 14703,
    15219, 15480, 16134, 16135,
    16136, 16137, 16138, 16387,
    16763, 16764, 16765, 17606,
    17607, 18720, 19533, 20237

DUBOSE, J.W. 11712

DUBOSE, JOHN W. 11713

DUBROCA, ISABELLE C. 10020

DUCAS, GEORGE 8, 183

DUCHET, MICHELE 5406

DUDA, MARGARET B. 11188

DUDEN, GOTTFRIED 11563

DUDLEY, T.U. 2310

DUFF, JOHN B. 978, 3456

DUFFNER, MICHAEL P. 11881

DUFFNER, ROBERT W. 11564

DUFFY, JAMES 5407, 5408, 7528

DUFFY, JOHN 12285, 12286, 15639,
    15640, 15641, 15642, 15643,
    15646

DUFOUR, CHARLES L. 12287

DUGANNE, A.J.H. 20349

DUGAS, L.A. 15647

DUGGER, DAGUERRELYN J. 16767

DUIGNAN, PETER 3265, 5409

DUKE, BASIL W. 2311

DUKE, CATHY 7529

DUKE, DENNIS 328

DUKE, MARVIN L. 5410

DUKES, PAUL 3457

DUMBELL, STANLEY 5411

DUMMETT, CLIFTON O. 15648, 15649

DUMMETT, RAYMOND E. 979

DUMOND, DWIGHT L. 184, 3458, 3459,
    5413, 10021, 16768

DUMONT, L. 3385, 4026

DUNAYEVSKAYA, RAYA 16389

DUNBAR, BARRINGTON 18126

DUNBAR, CHARLES F. 14175

DUNBAR, PAUL L. 4525

DUNBAR-NELSON, ALICE 9472

DUNCAN, ANNIE E. 11431

DUNCAN, H.G. 3461

DUNCAN, HERMAN C. 16769

DUNCAN, JAMES W. 13945

DUNCAN, JOHN 17609

DUNCAN, JOHN D. 8366, 8367

DUNCAN, KENNETH 6414

DUNCAN, OTIS D. 13946

DUNCAN, RICHARD 11432

DUNCAN, RICHARD R. 20797

DUNCAN, WINNIE L. 3461

DUNCKER, SHEILA J. 6415

DUNDES, ALAN   185, 13947, 17411, 18127

DUNGY, J.A.   18859

DUNHAM, KATHERINE   6416, 6417, 18434

DUNIWAY, CLYDE A.   11076

DUNLAP, WILLIAM D.   980

DUNMORE, CHARLOTTE J.   186

DUNN, BALLARD S.   7531

DUNN, CYRIL   981

DUNN, JACOB P.   10827, 10908, 10909, 10910

DUNN, LYNN P.   187

DUNN, RICHARD S.   982, 6418, 6419, 6420, 6421, 6422

DUNNING, WILLIAM A.   983, 3462

DUNSON, A.A.   11565

DUPUY, ALEX   5423

DURAM, JAMES C.   5414, 8982

DURAND, SALLY G.   15555

DURDEN, ROBERT F.   984, 2312, 2313, 3463, 10023, 16771

DURHAM, JOHN S.   3464, 3465, 14704

DURHAM, JOSEPH T.   10866

DURHAM, PHILIP   9474, 11010, 11011, 11012

DURRILL, WAYNE K.   188

DUSENBERRY, WILLIAM H.   7532, 7533

DUTRA, FRANK   190

DUTSON, ROLDO V.   11162

DUVALL, S.P.C.   3466

DUVALL, SEVERN P.C.   3467

DVORAK, ANTON   17611

DWIGHT, HENRY O.   3468

DWIGHT, MARGARET L.   10024, 10867

DWORKIN, RONALD   985

DWYER, PHILIP J.   3469

DWYER-SHICK, SUSAN   19055

DYE, JOHN S.   3470

DYER, BRAINERD   2315, 20798

DYER, FREDERICK H.   20799

DYER, G.W.   3471

DYER, STANFORD P.   12540

DYKES, EVA B.   3472

DZIDZIENYO, ANANI   3473, 7535

E.M.S.   5416

E.Y.E.   10337

EADS, J.K.   7536

EAKIN, PAUL J.   3474

EAKLOR, VICKI L.   17612, 17613

EARLE, ALICE M.   10338, 10339, 10629

EARLE, CARVILLE   3475, 11433, 14176

EARLE, CARVILLE V.   14177

EARLE, STAFFORD   6424

EARLY, JUBAL A.   3476

EARNEST, JOSEPH B.   13599, 13600

EASLEY, E.T. 15650

EASTERBROOK, DAVID L. 192

EASTERBY, JAMES H. 12907, 12908, 12909, 15099

EASTERLIN, RICHARD A. 14178

EASTLAND, TERRY 2316

EASTMAN, ZEBINA 8862

EASTON, CHARLES E. 13601

EATON, CLEMENT 987, 2317, 3477, 3478, 3479, 3480, 3481, 8863, 11174, 11295, 12547, 14833, 14865, 19947, 20504

EATON, JOHN 20800

EATON, MILES W. 11567

EAVES, CHARLES D. 13602

EBERSTADT, CHARLES 10025

EBLEN, JACK 14931

EBLEN, JACK E. 6425, 10828, 14932 14933

EBY, CECIL D., JR. 18132

ECCLES, W.J. 6426

ECHEVERRIA, PATRICIA 17413

ECKENRODE, H.J. 8864

EDEL, MATTHEW 7537

EDELSTEIN, TILDEN G. 3483, 18861, 20802

EDER, DONALD G. 988, 989

EDET, EDNA M. 17614, 17615, 17616

EDGAR, WALTER B. 19949

EDGINGTON, T.B. 2318

EDGINGTON, THOMAS B. 2319

EDMONDS, ANTHONY O. 990

EDMONDS, FLORENCE 11296

EDMONDS, RANDOLPH 2320

EDMONDS, RICHARD H. 3484

EDMONDSON, LOCKSLEY 2321, 3485

EDUARDO, OCTAVIO DA COSTA 7540

EDWARDS, CHARLES L. 6429, 6430, 6431

EDWARDS, EVERETT E. 195, 332

EDWARDS, G. FRANKLIN 991, 2322

EDWARDS, H.S. 3487

EDWARDS, HARRY S. 16775

EDWARDS, J. LOYD JR. 18862

EDWARDS, JAY D. 18133

EDWARDS, JOHN C. 8865, 8866

EDWARDS, JOHN E. 3488

EDWARDS, MARY JO 13332

EDWARDS, PAUL 2323, 18863

EDWARDS, S.J.C. 3489

EGERTON, JOHN 13202

EGGLESTON, G.K. 20804

EGGLESTON, GEORGE C. 13604

EGGLESTON, GEORGE K. 20805, 20806

EGGLESTON, JOSEPH D. 13605

EGNAL, MARC 992, 5417

EGYPT, OPHELIA S. 11297

EHRLICH, WALTER 8867, 8868, 8869, 8870, 8871

EICHHOLZ, ALICE 488

EIGHMY, JOHN L. 16776, 16777

EISENBERG, PETER 7541

EISENBERG, PETER L. 7542, 7543,
7544

EISNER, GISELA 6432

EISTERHOLD, JOHN A. 11714, 11882,
12044, 12911, 14182, 14706,
14707

EKMAN, ERNST 5418

EKWUEME, LAZARUS E.N. 4787, 4788,
17617

ELAM, WILLIAM C. 19327

ELBERT, SARAH 993

ELDEN, GARY 8872

ELDER, ARLENE A. 17417

ELDER, J.D. 6433, 6434

ELDER, JACOB D. 17621, 18135

ELDER, ORVILLE 3490

ELIOT, WILLIAM G. 11568

ELISABETH, LEO 6435

ELITZER, MICHAEL R. 5419

ELKINS, STANLEY 8218, 18751

ELKINS, STANLEY M. 994, 995, 997,
998, 999, 1000, 2324, 3385,
3491, 3492, 3493, 4026, 6436,
8874, 17419

ELKINS, W.F. 16778

ELLEFSON, C. ASHLEY 9476

ELLEFSON, CLINTON A. 8370

ELLER, W.H. 3494

ELLIOT, G.M. 3495

ELLIOT, JOHN H. 6438

ELLIOTT, CLAUDE 20807

ELLIOTT, HELEN 10027

ELLIOTT, JACK D., JR. 18485

ELLIOTT, JOHN 7548

ELLIOTT, MARY E. 10028

ELLIOTT, ROBERT N. 19950

ELLIS, A.B. 3496, 4789, 18136,
18137

ELLIS, ALFRED B. 6439

ELLIS, DAVID M. 10630

ELLIS, GEORGE W. 2325, 2326, 479

ELLIS, HOWARD C. 3497

ELLIS, ISABELLA D.C. 12290

ELLIS, JOHN H. 15652

ELLIS, MARY H. 13333

ELLIS, WALTER J. 3498

ELLISON, RALPH 1001, 2041, 2327

ELLSWORTH, LOIS C. 13334

ELLSWORTH, ROBERT A. 14935

ELMORE, JOYCE A. 20809

ELTIS, DAVID 5420, 5421, 5422,
5423, 5424, 5425, 14197

ELWANG, WILLIAM W. 11569

EMERICK, CHARLES F. 3499

EMERSON, F.V. 14186

EMERSON, MATHEW C. 10435

EMERSON, O.B.   196, 10029

EMERSON, WILLIAM C.   17420

EMERY, LEONORE L.   18435

EMERY, LYNNE F.   6441, 15854, 15855

EMILIO, LUIS F.   20810

EMINHIZER, EARL E.   3500

EMM, MARSHALL   8876

EMMER, DOROTHY   8877

EMMER, PIETER C.   1002, 1508, 5426, 5428, 6051, 8123

EMMERICH, J. OLIVER   3501

EMMERTH, BARBARA L.   13606

EMMONS, MARTHA   18138

ENABULELE, ARLENE B.   197

ENGEL, CARL   17623

ENGELDER, CONRAD J.   16779

ENGELKING, JOHANNA R.   13335

ENGELSMAN, JOHN C.   12291

ENGERMAN, STANLEY   6719

ENGERMAN, STANLEY L.   1003, 1004, 1005, 1006, 1007, 1008, 1009, 1010, 1011, 1012, 1013, 1014, 1062, 1064, 3502, 5640, 5641, 6443, 8371, 8372, 10036, 14064, 14143, 14187, 14189, 14192, 14193, 14194, 14195, 14196, 14197, 14198, 14213, 14214, 14215, 14216, 14217, 14219, 14220, 14590, 14936, 14938, 14947, 14980, 14983

ENGLAND, J. MERTON   9477

ENGLAND, JAMES M.   9478, 9479

ENGLESMAN, JOHN C.   20811

ENGLISH, PHILIP W.   11298

ENGS, ROBERT F.   1015, 13607

ENKVIST, NILS E.   2328

ENNES, ERNESTO   7551

ENNIS, BARBARA S.   12700

ENRIGHT, D.J.   1016

EPPES, MRS. NICHOLAS W.   11883

EPPS, ARCHIE C.   16781

EPPSE, MERL R.   199, 200

EPSTEIN, BERYL   16391

EPSTEIN, DENA J.   201, 1017, 4791, 6444, 17625, 17626, 17628

EPSTEIN, SAM   16391

EQUIANO, OLAUDAH   5430

ERDMAN, DAVID V.   18622

ERICKSON, E. GORDON   6445

ERICKSON, LEONARD   9480

ERIKSEN, GARY H.   1018

ERNO, RICHARD B.   2330

ERNST, ROBERT   9481, 9482

ERNST, WILLIAM J.   13608, 19951

ERSKINE, NOEL L.   6446

ERVIN, EDDIE M.   12701

ERVIN, SAMUEL J.   12702

ESCALANTE, AQUILES   19279

ESCOTT, PAUL D.   1019, 1020, 1021, 1023, 11013, 16010, 20507

ESEDEBE, P. OLISANWUCHE 5431

ESHLERMAN, J. RCSS 16146

ESSERT, VICTOR A. 20812

ESSIEN-UDOM, E.U. 3505

ESSIG, JAMES D. 3506, 8373

ESTEVIZ, FRED 7419

ETHERIDGE, HARRISON M. 13610

EUDY, JOHN C. 12548

EUSEBIUS, MARY 19540

EVANS, ARTHUR L. 17630

EVANS, DAVID 4792, 17631

EVANS, DAVID H. 1025, 17633, 17634

EVANS, DAVID K. 18139

EVANS, ELLIOT A.P. 15481

EVANS, EMORY G. 8374

EVANS, GLADYS C. 15729

EVANS, MARGUERITE 17635

EVANS, MAURICE S. 3507

EVANS, OLIVER 12292

EVANS, ROBERT JR. 14200, 14201, 14202, 14203, 14204

EVANS, ROBLEY D. 13612

EVANS, W. MCKEE 12703

EVANS, W.A. 9483, 15653

EVANS, WILLIAM M. 2331

EVERETT, DONALD E. 9484, 9485, 9486, 9487, 9488, 15654, 20813

EVERETT, FRANK E. 12549

EVERETT, LLOYD T. 3508, 3509

EVERETT, MARY 13336

EVERETT, SUSANNE 3510

EVERLY, ELAINE C. 203, 20815

EWING, ELBERT W.R. 3511, 8878

EYRE, LAWRENCE A. 6447

EZELL, GRETA S. 13941

EZELL, PAUL H. 13941

FABIO, SARAH W. 3516

FABRE, M. 8375

FABRE, MICHEL 1026

FACTOR, ROBERT L. 2333

FADUMA, ORISHATUKEH 3517

FAGE, J.D. 1027, 4793, 4795, 543? 5435, 5438

FAGE, JOHN D. 4797

FAGG, WILLIAM 7552

FAIRBANK, CALVIN 3518, 3519

FAIRBANKS, CHARLES H. 12045, 15220, 15469, 15482, 17422

FAIRCHILD, JAMES H. 19541

FAIRLY, JOHN S. 16785

FALCONER, JOHN I. 10329

FALER, KAREN B. 13337

FALK, LESLIE A. 9489

FALKNER, ROLAND P. 2334

FAREWELL, J.W. 8879

FARISH, HUNTER D. 13613

FARLEY, ENA L. 4799, 8880

FARLEY, M. FOSTER 8376, 8377,
   12912, 12913

FARLEY, RAWLE 7553, 7554, 7555

FARLEY, REYNOLDS 14942, 14943,
   15910

FARLOW, GALE J. 12704

FARMER, H.H. 13614

FARMER, HALLIE 3521, 5440, 9491

FARNAM, HENRY W. 8881

FARNIE, D.A. 5441

FARNOWSKI, MARY S. 12293

FARNSWORTH, ROBERT M. 1028

FARQUHARSON, CHARLES 6449

FARR, KENNETH R. 6450

FARRAND, MAX 5442, 10830

FARRANT, LEDA 4800

FARRAR, WILLIAM L. 8882

FARRELL, JOHN K.A. 2335, 10239,
   19543

FARRELL, NANCIE C. 3522

FARRISON, W. EDWARD 12705, 16392

FARRISON, WILLIAM E. 1029, 9492,
   12706, 20242

FASOLD, RALPH 19328

FASSETT, JAMES 10448

FAULK, ODIE B. 13338, 13339

FAULKNER, WILLIAM J. 16786, 18140

FAUSET, ARTHUR H. 3523, 9493,
   18142, 18143

FAUSET, JESSIE 16393

FAUST, DREW G. 2336, 2338, 3524,
   3525, 12916, 12917

FAWCETT, BILL 11299

FAX, ELTON C. 18623

FAYE, STANLEY 5443

FEDERAL WRITERS' PROGRAM, LOUISIANA
   12294

FEDERAL WRITERS' PROJECT 204,
   15221

FEE, JOHN G. 11300

FEHRENBACH, T.R. 13340

FEHRENBACHER, DON E. 1030, 2339,
   8883, 8884

FEIERMAN, STEVEN 4753

FELD, KENNETH J. 8885

FELDMAN, EUGENE P.R. 9494

FELDMESSER, ROBERT A. 1031

FELDSTEIN, STANLEY 2340, 18865,
   18866

FELT, JEREMY P. 1032

FELTS, JOE M. 8886

FEN, SING-NAN 19176, 19177

FENNELL, JANICE 67

FENNER, T.P. 17636

FENNER, THOMAS P. 17637

FEREBEE, LONDON R. 12708

FERGUS, HOWARD A. 6451, 19955

FERGUSON, ALFRED R. 10030

FERGUSON, C.W. 3526

FERGUSON, J. HALCRO   6452

FERGUSON, LELAND G.   12918, 18517

FERGUSON, XENOPHON F.   6453

FERGUSSON, C. BRUCE   10240

FERMOSELLE LOPEZ, RAFAEL   205

FERNANDES, FLORESTAN   7557, 7558,
   7559, 7560, 7561, 7562

FERRIS, AARON A.   10031

FERRIS, WILLIAM   15470, 17638,
   18624

FERRIS, WILLIAM H.   3527

FERRIS, WILLIAM R.   16788, 17424,
   17425, 18145

FERRIS, WILLIAM R., JR.   1033,
   18146, 18147

FERTIG, JAMES W.   13206

FEUSER, WILLFRIED F.   2341

FICK, CAROLYN E.   6454

FICKLING, SUSAN M.   12920, 16789

FIDDES, EDWARD   8888

FIEHRER, THOMAS   7563

FIEHRER, THOMAS M.   12295

FIELD, CHRISTOPHER D.S.   17639

FIELD, PHINEAS   10449

FIELD, REUBEN   10505

FIELDING, RONALD H.   14205

FIELDS, BARBARA J.   10033

FIELDS, CARL   11301

FIELDS, EMMETT B.   13615

FIERCE, MILFRED C.   5444, 20821

FIFE, ROBERT D.   16791

FIKES, ROBERT   2342

FILLER, LOUIS   207, 1034, 1035,
   1036, 3531, 3532

FINCH, LUCINE   3533, 16394

FINCK, JULIA N.   17640

FINDLAY, RONALD   3534

FINE, ELSA H.   18625

FINGER, JOEL L.   19544

FINK, LEON   16148

FINKELMAN, PAUL   1038, 3536, 888
   8890

FINLASON, WILLIAM F.   6455

FINLEY, M.I.   1039, 1040, 1041,
   3538

FINLEY, MOSES I.   1042, 3539, 35
   3541, 3542

FINLEY, MRS. H.R.   15101

FINN, PETER C.   8379

FINNEY, BERNICE E.   8891

FINNEY, GORDON E.   3543

FINNEY, JAMES E.   208

FIRTH, EDITH G.   10241

FISCHBAUM, MARVIN   14207

FISCHER, DAVID H.   1043

FISCHER, HUGO   8892

FISCHER, LEROY H.   13948

FISCHER, ROGER A.   2343, 12297,
   12298

FISHBACK, MASON M. 8393

FISHBURNE, ANN S. 12921

FISHEL, LESLIE H., JR. 209, 210, 1044

FISHER, ALLAN G.B. 4801

FISHER, EDGAR J. 10530

FISHER, ELIJAH J. 18868

FISHER, HUMPHREY J. 4801

FISHER, J.B. 8380

FISHER, JAMES A. 9496, 9497, 11077

FISHER, JOHN E. 10832

FISHER, MIKE 20822

FISHER, MILES M. 3544, 3545, 9498, 16793, 17641, 17642, 19959

FISHER, RUTH A. 211, 6456

FISHER, WALTER 15655

FISHWICK, MARSHALL 18148

FISHWICK, MARSHALL W. 14709

FISK UNIVERSITY, SOCIAL SCIENCE INSTITUTE 18149

FISKE, JOHN 3546

FITCH, JAMES M. 15484

FITCHETT, E. HORACE 9499, 9500, 9501, 9502, 13150

FITTS, JAMES 20243

FITTS, LEROY 3547

FITZGERALD, O.P. 16794

FITZHUGH, GEORGE 3548, 14208

FLADELAND, BETTY 3549, 11715

FLADELAND, BETTY L. 8394

FLANDERS, JANE 1045

FLANDERS, RALPH B. 3550, 9503, 12046, 12047, 12048, 12049, 14209

FLANIGAN, DANIEL J. 8395, 8896

FLECK, ANNE 7419

FLEETWOOD, CHRISTIAN A. 20824

FLEETWOOD, GEORGE B. 13616

FLEISCHMAN, RICHARD K. 2344

FLEISIG, HAYWOOD 14210

FLEMING, G. JAMES 19960

FLEMING, JOHN E. 8898, 12709, 16395, 19178

FLEMING, ROBERT E. 25

FLEMING, ROY F. 8381

FLEMING, WALTER L. 1046, 1047, 2345, 3551, 3552, 3553, 12550, 12551, 12552, 13949, 14211, 20511, 20512

FLEMING, WILLIAM H. 2346, 3554

FLETCHER, ALAN M. 7564

FLETCHER, JAMES C. 7740

FLINT, JOHN E. 3556, 4802

FLISCH, JULIA A. 14710

FLOAN, HOWARD R. 3558

FLOETHE, LOUISE L. 7565

FLOETHE, RICHARD 7565

FLORY, MARLEEN B. 16149

FLORY, RAE 7567

FLORY, RAE J.D. 7566

FLORY, THOMAS 7568, 7570, 7571, 8899

FLOUD, RODERICK 1064

FLOYD, JENNIE W. 212

FLOYD, M. 15485

FLOYD, SILAS X. 15222

FLOYD, TROY S. 7572

FLUSCHE, MICHAEL 1048, 1049, 1050, 3559, 9504

FLUSCHE, MICHAEL A. 1051

FOGARTY, GERALD P. 11439

FOGEL, ROBERT W. 213, 214, 842, 1014, 1052, 1053, 1054, 1055, 1056, 1058, 1059, 1060, 1061, 1062, 1064, 10036, 14213, 14214, 14215, 14216, 14217, 14219, 14220, 14590, 14947, 15400

FOGG, JOHN S.H. 8382

FOKEER, A.F. 4803

FOLK, RICHARD A. 9505

FOLSOM, JOSEPH F. 10531

FONER, ERIC 215, 1065, 1066, 1067, 2347, 3560, 3561, 11015, 19962

FONER, JACK D. 20513

FONER, LAURA 216, 9506

FONER, PHILIP S. 217, 1068, 3562, 3563, 3564, 3565, 3566, 6459, 8383, 9507, 9508, 19545, 19546, 20826

FONT, FREDERICK 20352

FONTAINE, PIERRE-MICHEL 218

FONTENOT, ELFA L. 20514

FOOTE, JULIA A.J. 9509

FOOTE, TIMOTHY 1069

FORBES, DAVID R. 19547

FORBES, G. 13950

FORBES, GEORGE W. 1070, 1071, 1072, 1073, 15103

FORBES, JACK 219

FORBES, JACK D. 11017

FORD, AUSBRA 4804

FORD, N.A. 2349

FORD, NICK A. 3567

FORD, WILLIAM F. 6460

FORD, WORTHINGTON C. 5447

FORDE, C. DARYLL 4805, 4806

FORDE, CYRIL D. 5448

FORDE, DARYLL 5045

FORDHAM, MONROE 9510, 19963

FOREMAN, GRANT 13951, 13952, 13953

FORMAN, HENRY C. 15487, 15488

FORMISANO, RONALD P. 9511

FORNELL, EARL W. 5449, 5450, 95 13343

FORNESS, NORMAN O. 8900

FORRESTER, ANN 4807

FORRESTER, ANNE M. 220

FORREY, ROBERT 2350

FORSYTHE, DENNIS G. 3570

FORTENBAUGH, ROBERT 16796, 1679

FORTES, M. 4808

FORTES, MEYER 4809

FORTIER, ALCEE 12300, 12301, 19329

FORTUNE, T. THOMAS 2351, 3571, 4525, 14949, 18754, 19548

FOSSIER, ALBERT E. 12302

FOSTER, CHARLES H. 3572

FOSTER, CHARLES I. 9513

FOSTER, CHARLES W. 19330

FOSTER, FRANCES S. 16397, 18870, 18871, 18873

FOSTER, FRANK C. 1075

FOSTER, GEORGE E. 13954

FOSTER, GEORGE M. 7574

FOSTER, HERBERT J. 4810

FOSTER, LAURENCE 3573, 13955, 13956, 13957

FOSTER, PHILLIPS W. 6461

FOSTER, RICHARD B. 11571

FOSTER, WILLIAM P. 17644

FOSTER, WILLIAM Z. 3574

FOUCHARD, JEAN 5452

FOUSHEE, KENNETH 8901

FOUST, JAMES 14658

FOUST, JAMES D. 14222, 14223, 14595, 14659

FOWLER, DAVID 9514

FOWLER, WILLIAM C. 10392, 10393

FOX, C.B. 20827

FOX, DANIEL M. 3780

FOX, DIXON R. 10631

FOX, EARLY L. 3575, 3576

FOX, GEOFFREY E. 16398

FOX, GRACE I. 11886

FOX, JAMES A. 3577

FOX, JAMES E. 18627

FOX, P.C. 19964

FOX, WILLIAM F. 20828

FOX, WILLIAM L. 11527

FOX-GENOVESE, ELIZABETH 1076, 1077, 14249

FOY, FIDELE 2913

FRAGINALS, MANUEL M. 6464, 14950

FRALEY, WILLIAM 3198

FRANCA, EURICO N. 17645

FRANCIS, BETTIE G. 16800

FRANCIS, JAMES P. 12050

FRANCO, JOSE L. 5453

FRANK, WILLARD 8384

FRANKLIN, BENJAMIN V. 3579

FRANKLIN, FRANCES M. 3580

FRANKLIN, H. BRUCE 17646

FRANKLIN, HENRY 18874

FRANKLIN, HOWARD B. 3581

FRANKLIN, JIMMIE L. 1079, 11124

FRANKLIN, JOHN H. 221, 1080, 1081, 1082, 1083, 1084, 1085, 1086, 1087, 1088, 1089, 1090, 1091, 1092, 1093, 2353, 2354, 3582,

3583, 3584, 3585, 3586, 3587, 3588, 8385, 8902, 9515, 9516, 9517, 9518, 9519, 10037, 12711, 12712, 18875, 20829, 20831

FRANKLIN, M. THERESA 17647

FRANKLIN, VINCENT P. 1094, 9520, 17426

FRANKLIN, W. NEIL 12713

FRANKLIN, WILLIAM E. 8905

FRARY, MARYANN T.D. 13157

FRASER, DOUGLAS 4811

FRASER, L.M. 6467

FRATE, DENNIS A. 16286

FRAZEE, GEORGE 8906, 19551, 19552

FRAZIER, E. FRANKLIN 2355, 2356, 2359, 2360, 3589, 3590, 3591, 3592, 4813, 9522, 9523, 16152, 16154, 16157, 16158, 16804, 17427

FRAZIER, HERBERT L. 4815

FRAZIER, THOMAS R. 1095

FREDERICK, FRANCIS 11302

FREDRICKSON, GEORGE M. 1096, 1097, 1098, 1099, 1100, 1101, 1102, 2361, 2362, 2363, 2364, 2365, 2366, 20833

FREEHLING, ALISON H.G. 13619

FREEHLING, WILLIAM W. 8386, 19179

FREEMAN, DOUGLAS S. 13620

FREEMAN, EDWARD A. 16807

FREEMAN, HENRY V. 20835

FREEMAN, LEON H., JR. 2368

FREEMAN, MARCUS A. 13344

FREEMAN, MARIE G. 9526

FREEMAN, RHODA G. 9527

FREIDEL, FRANK 3595

FREILICH, MORRIS 6468

FREIMARCK, VINCENT 2369

FRENCH, CHRISTOPHER J. 5454

FRENCH, MANLY 3596

FRENCH, ROBERT 20836

FRESNEAU, MME. ARMAND 19966

FRETWELL, MARK E. 11887

FREUCHEN, PETER 5455

FREY, SYLVIA R. 8387

FREYRE, GILBERTO 7578, 7579, 75, 7581, 7582, 7583, 7584, 7585, 7586, 7587

FRIED, ALBERT 10041

FRIEDE, JUAN 6469, 6583

FRIEDEL, LAWRENCE M. 2370

FRIEDMAN, LAWRENCE J. 2371, 237 2373, 2375, 2376, 9528

FRIEDMAN, LEE M. 10450

FRIEDMAN, MELVIN J. 1103

FRIEDMAN, TOM 19555

FRIEDMANN, HARRIET 1104

FRIES, ADELAIDE 12714

FRIES, SYLVIA D. 2377, 2378

FRISBIE, CHARLOTTE J. 6576

FRISSELL, HOLLIS B. 3597

FRITZ, HARRY W. 2379

FROST, J. WILLIAM 1105

FROST, WILLIAM G. 1106, 3600

FROUDE, JAMES A. 6470

FRUCHT, RICHARD 1107, 6471, 6472, 6473

FRUIT, J.P. 18158

FRY, GLADYS-MARIE 16014, 16015, 16400

FRY, SYLVIA R. 8388

FRYKMAN, GEORGE A. 1108

FUKE, RICHARD P. 11441, 19180, 20837

FULCHER, JAMES 3601

FULKERSON, HORACE S. 2381, 15316

FULKERSON, RAYMOND G. 3602

FULLER, BERNICE M. 11573

FULLER, EDMUND 2382

FULLER, JOHN D.P. 11664, 11665

FULLER, JUANITA B. 222, 223

FULLER, SARA 224

FULLER, THOMAS O. 3603, 13207

FULLER, WILLIE J. 11716

FULLINWIDER, S.P. 3604

FUNK, ALFRED A. 3606

FUNK, HENRY E. 6474

FUNKE, CAROL N. 8389

FUNKHOUSER, MYRTLE 225

FURET, FRANCOIS 1109

FURFEY, PAUL H. 16809

FURLEY, OLIVER W. 1110, 6475, 6476

FURLOW, HENRY J. 12051

FURMAN, MARVA J. 18877

FURNAS, J.C. 5457, 15224

FURNAS, JOSEPH C. 3607

FURNESS, A.E. 6477, 6478

FURNESS, WILLIAM E. 20838

FURSTENBERG, FRANK F. 16401, 16402

FURTADO, CELSO 6479, 7590

FYFE, CHRISTOPHER 1112, 4816, 4817, 5390, 5458, 5459, 5462

FYNN, J.K. 4818

GABER, DEBORAH R. 17648

GAFFNEY, FLOYD 16812

GAGE, FRANK W. 3609

GAILLARD, S. PALMER 1113

GAILLARD, THEODORE L., JR. 3610

GAINES, ALBERT W. 8911

GAINES, FRANCIS P. 3611, 3612

GAINES, W.J. 3613, 15225

GAITHER, FRANCES O. 19556

GALBREATH, C.B. 8912

GALBREATH, CHARLES B. 3614

GALENSON, DAVID 5463

GALENSON, DAVID W. 1114, 8219, 8390

GALLAGHER, BUELL G. 226

GALLAGHER, J. 5464

GALLAHER, RUTH A. 10929

GALLAWAY, LOWELL E. 14532, 14819

GALLENGA, ANTONIO C.N. 6480

GALLMAN, ROBERT E. 14069, 14226,
   14227, 14228, 14229, 14230,
   14231

GALLOWAY, CHARLES B. 3615

GALLOWAY, J.H. 7591, 7592, 7593,
   7594

GALLOWAY, JOHN H. 7595

GALPIN, MARION C. 10042

GALPIN, W. FREEMAN 19557

GALT, WILLIAM R., JR. 7596

GALVIN, CORINNE B. 10632

GALVIS, ANTONIO J. 7597

GAMBLE, CHARLES F. 6481

GAMBLE, ROBERT S. 13622

GAMBLE, W.H. 6482

GAMBRELL, HERBERT P. 13403

GAMMON, TIM 13959

GANAWAY, LOOMIS M. 11110

GANDY, J.M. 3616

GANNETT, HENRY 3617, 15318

GANNETT, W.C. 18162, 20840, 20841

GANNON, MICHAEL V. 3618, 16813

GANS, HERBERT J. 16161

GANUS, CLIFTON L., JR. 20842

GARA, LARRY 1115, 3619, 3620,
   3621, 8913, 8914, 13623, 18878,
   19558, 19561, 19562, 19563,
   19564, 19565

GARBER, P.L.A. 16814

GARCIA, E.C. 3622

GARCIA, MIKEL M. 18759

GARCIA-ZAMOR, JEANE C. 7598

GARDNER, BETTY 567

GARDNER, BETTYE 19181

GARDNER, BETTYE J. 9531

GARDNER, D.H. 10043

GARDNER, MARY E. 16403

GARDNER, ROBERT 16815

GARDNER, THEODORE 19566

GARDNER, WILLIAM J. 6483

GARLAND, AUGUSTUS H. 8915

GARNER, REUBEN 5465

GARNER, STANTON 3623

GARNET, HENRY H. 20354

GARONZIK, JOSEPH 11443

GARRETSON, O.A. 19567

GARRETT, M.B. 6484

GARRETT, RICHARD D. 14232

GARRETT, ROMEO B. 4819

GARRETT, SUE G. 16162

GARRISON, LUCY M. 17499, 17500

GARVIN, RUSSELL 9532

GARY, A.T. 5466

GARY, EUGENE B. 3624

GASPAR, D. BARRY 6485

GASPAR, DAVID B. 6487, 19569

GASS, W. CONARD 1116

GASSETT, MATTYELU 14233

GASTMANN, ALBERT 5467, 6488, 6439, 6491

GASTON, L. CLIFTON 227

GASTON, LEROY C. 228

GASTON, PAUL M. 2334

GATELL, FRANK O. 596, 597, 598, 10044, 20516

GATES, H.L. 3625

GATES, PAUL W. 14234, 15226

GATEWOOD, WILLARD B., JR. 13208

GAUL, HARVEY 17650

GAULD, CHARLES A. 7601

GAUNT, MARY E.B. 6494

GAVINS, RAYMOND 12715

GAVRONSKY, SERGE 2385

GAY, DOROTHY A. 3626

GAY, EDWIN F. 6495

GAYARRE, CHARLES 2386, 12304, 12305

GEBO, DORA R. 3627

GEEDER, KATHERINE G. 1117

GEGGUS, D.P. 6496

GEGGUS, DAVID P. 14235

GEHRKE, WILLIAM H. 12716

GEIS, GILBERT 13918

GEISER, KARL F. 10733

GEISS, I. 3556

GEIST, CHRISTOPHER D. 13960, 16404

GELLERT, LAWRENCE 16816, 17651, 19968

GEMERY, H.A. 6498

GEMERY, HENRY A. 4821, 5469, 5471, 5472

GENOVESE, EUGENE D. 216, 1014, 1118, 1119, 1120, 1121, 1122, 1123, 1124, 1125, 1126, 1127, 1128, 1129, 1130, 1131, 1132, 1133, 1134, 1135, 1136, 1137, 1138, 1139, 1140, 1141, 1143, 1144, 1145, 1146, 1147, 1148, 1149, 1150, 1151, 1152, 1153, 1154, 1155, 1976, 2387, 2388, 2389, 2390, 3628, 3629, 3630, 3631, 3632, 4008, 9533, 12052, 14198, 14238, 14240, 14241, 14242, 14243, 14244, 14245, 14246, 14248, 14249, 14596, 14598, 15321, 15559, 16163, 16817, 19333, 19969

GEORGE, CAROL V.R. 16819

GEORGE, JAMES Z. 3633

GEORGE, KATHERINE 2391

GEORGE, ZELMA 229, 17653

GEORGEOFF, JOHN 2392

GEORGIA WRITERS' PROJECT 12054, 12055, 12056, 12057, 12058, 12059

GERBEAU, HUBERT 1156

GERBER, ADOLF 18163

GERBER, DAVID A. 2393

GERHARD, PETER 6502

GERLACH, DON R.   19572

GERLACH, RUSSEL L.   11574

GERSHMAN, SALLY   14250

GERSMAN, ELINOR M.   9535

GERTEIS, LOUIS S.   10045, 20843,
    20844

GERTZ, ELMER   9536

GEWDY, SYBIL   1157

GEWEHR, WESLEY   13624

GHOLSON, THOMAS S.   20520

GHORABA, HAMMOUDA   4824

GIBB, HARLEY L.   10953

GIBBS, C.R.   20846

GIBBS, MIFFLIN W.   18880

GIBBS, TYSON   15393, 15405

GIBNEY, HUGH F.   9537

GIBSON, A.E.M.   4825

GIBSON, A.M.   11575

GIBSON, CHARLES   1158, 7605

GIBSON, DONALD B.   1159

GIBSON, EMILY F.   1160

GIBSON, GEORGE H.   12554

GIBSON, JOHN W.   3634, 3635

GIBSON, MARY J.   231

GIBSON, WILLIAM   16164

GIDDENS, PAUL H.   8391

GIDDINGS, FRANKLIN H.   3636

GIDDINGS, PAULA   1161

GIELOW, MARTHA S.   18164, 19335

GIFFORD, JAMES M.   232, 2394, 23
    2396, 2397, 12060, 12061

GILBERT, EUNICE M.   6503

GILBERT, JAMES   1162

GILBERT, JAMES W.   9538

GILBERT, JOHN W.   3637

GILBERT, ROBERT B.   2398

GILBERT, WILLIAM H., JR.   13961

GILES, HENRY L.   20847

GILL, CONRAD   5475

GILLARD, JOHN T.   16821

GILLESPIE, J. DAVID   12717

GILLESPIE, JUDI F.   12717

GILLESPIE, NEAL C.   3638

GILLIAM, ANGELA   2399

GILLIAM, E.W.   2400

GILLIAM, FARLEY M.   8917

GILLIAM, WILL D.   10940

GILLIGAN, FRANCIS J.   3639

GILLIS, D. HUGH   10243

GILLIS, FRANK   233

GILLIS, KATHERINE A.   20848

GILMAN, RICHARD   1163

GILMAN, SANDER L.   2401

GILMER, ALBERT H.   10451

GILMORE, AL-TONY   1164

GILMORE, JOHN T.   6504

GILTNER, JOHN H. 16823

GINSBURG, E. 14143

GIPSON, LAWRENCE H. 8392, 8393

GIRARDIN, J.A. 10954

GITTLEMAN, EDWIN 8394

GLADNEY, LOUISE 12555

GLASCO, LAURENCE A. 2402

GLASGOW, ROY A. 2403, 7607, 7608

GLASRUD, BRUCE A. 13345

GLASS, BENTLEY 2404

GLASSIE, HENRY 4826, 15491, 18520

GLASSON, WILLIAM H. 1165

GLAVIS, ANTONIO J. 7610

GLAZER, IRVING W. 17655

GLAZER, NATHAN 1166, 1167, 1168

GLAZIER, WILLARD W. 16824

GLEAVE, M.B. 4827

GLENN, ROBERT W. 19336

GLIOZZO, CHARLES A. 9540

GLOSTER, JESSE E. 15662

GLOVER, R.W. 19067

GLUNT, JAMES D. 235, 437

GLYNN, WILLIAM A. 2405

GODMAN, INEZ A. 16407

GOEBEL, JULIUS 8918

GOERKE, HEINZ 6505

GOGGIN, JACQUELINE 1169

GOGGIN, JOHN M. 6506

GOINES, LEONARD 7611, 7612, 17656,
17657, 17658, 17660, 17661,
17662

GOINES, MARGARETTA B. 18442

GOLD, ROBERT L. 11890

GOLDBERG, BARRY H. 14252

GOLDEN, DEAN C. 13209

GOLDEN, SOMA 1170

GOLDFIELD, DAVID R. 13627, 15105,
15664, 15916, 15917

GOLDIN, CLAUDIA 14253, 16408

GOLDIN, CLAUDIA D. 10046, 15918,
15919, 15920, 15921

GOLDMAN, ERIC F. 1171

GOLDMAN, HANNAH S. 3641

GOLDMAN, MARTIN S. 1172

GOLDMAN, MORRIS 18722

GOLDMANN, PAULINE S. 13346

GOLDSBOROUGH, EDMUND K. 11445

GOLDSTEIN, LESLIE F. 2406, 9542

GOLDSTEIN, NAOMI F. 2407

GOLDSTEIN, RHODA L. 3642

GOLDSTON, ROBERT 3643

GOLDSTONE, LAWRENCE S. 8395

GOLIBER, THOMAS J. 9543

GOLLWITZER, HELMUT 16825

GONGORA, MARIO 7613

GONZALES, AMBROSE E. 18166

GONZALES, WILLIAM E.   12925

GONZALEZ, ANIBAL   6508

GONZALEZ, NANCIE L.   16166

GOODE, CECIL E.   10734

GOODE, KENNETH G.   3644, 11079

GOODELL, ABNER C.   10340

GOODFRIEND, JOYCE D.   10634, 10635

GOODHART, MORGAN   11018

GOODMAN, M.H.   20849

GOODMAN, PAUL   1173

GOODMAN, S.E.   15086

GOODMAN, W.D.   19069

GOODMAN, WALTER   3645

GOODRICH, W.H.   17663

GOODRIDGE, CECIL A.   6510

GOODSON, MARTIA G.   236, 16409

GOODSTEIN, ANITA S.   13210

GOODWIN, MARY F.   13628, 16826

GOODWIN, MRS. MAUD W.   8396

GOODY, JACK   3646

GORDON, A.C.   18167

GORDON, A.H.   20247

GORDON, ARMISTEAD C.   13629, 14258

GORDON, ASA H.   12063, 19574,
    19971

GORDON, EZEKIEL N.   3647

GORDON, JACOB U.   4828

GORDON, JAMES   3648

GORDON, MAX   10872

GORDON, MICHAEL   16167

GORDON, R.W.   17664

GORDON, RAMSEY J.   13347

GORDON, ROBERT A.   1174

GORDON, ROBERT W.   12928, 17665

GORDON, S.C.   6511

GORDON, WILLIAM   10452

GORDON, WILLIAM A.   11231

GORDON, WILLIAM S.   3649

GORER, GEOFFREY   4829

GORN, ELLIOTT J.   19575

GOSLINGA, CORNELIUS CH   5476, 651

GOSS, CHARLES C.   16828

GOSSETT, THOMAS F.   2408

GOTTESMAN, RITA S.   18522, 18523,
    18524

GOUGH, ROBERT J.   10534

GOULD, CLARENCE P.   11446

GOULD, JOHN J.   6513

GOULD, LEWIS L.   3331

GOURNAY, P.F. DE   9544

GOVAN, THOMAS P.   1175, 1176,
    14260, 14261, 14600

GOVEIA, ELSA   1177, 1178, 6514,
    6515

GOVEIA, ELSA V.   1179, 1180, 6516
    6517, 6518, 6521, 8920

GOWER, HERSCHEL   13211

GRACE, JOHN 4830

GRACY, DAVID B. 13212

GRAEBNER, KARL F. 7615

GRAEBNER, NORMAN A. 8922, 13962

GRAF, HILDEGARDE F. 2409, 2410

GRAFFAGNINO, J. KEVIN 2411

GRAGG, LARRY J. 13630

GRAHAM, ALICE 17666

GRAHAM, DOUGLAS H. 7844

GRAHAM, HARRY 19972

GRAHAM, JAMES D. 4831

GRAHAM, JAMIE R. 237

GRAHAM, MARIA 7616

GRAHAM, MARY E. 3650

GRAHAM, PEARL M. 2412

GRAHAM, PHILIP 13348

GRAHAM, RICHARD D. 1181, 1182,
    4832, 7617, 7619, 7620, 7621

GRAHAM, SHIRLEY 3651, 16410

GRAHAM, STEPHEN 3652

GRANADE, RAY 11891

GRANDISON, C.N. 16831

GRANDPRE, LOUIS E. 8397

GRANT, A. CAMERON 2413

GRANT, DOUGLAS 6522

GRANT, GEORGE C. 17430

GRANT, JOANNE 19577

GRANT, JOHN N. 10244

GRANT, MADELINE 16832

GRANT, MINNIE S. 2414

GRATIOT, A.P. 11303

GRATUS, JACK 2415

GRAU, RICHARD 8923

GRAU, RICHARD P. 3653

GRAVELY, WILLIAM 16833

GRAVELY, WILLIAM B. 16834, 16835,
    16836

GRAY, CLYCE C. 5479

GRAY, LEWIS C. 2416, 14601, 14602,
    15106

GRAY, RALPH 8222

GRAY, RICHARD 5480

GRAY, WOOD 1184

GREAT BRITAIN. PARLIAMENTARY
    PAPERS. 238

GREAVES, IDA C. 10245

GREEN, ALAN W.C. 2417, 2418

GREEN, BARBARA L. 11576, 11577,
    15107

GREEN, CHARLES 19974

GREEN, CONSTANCE M. 11232

GREEN, EDWARD 20248

GREEN, ELISHA W. 11304

GREEN, ERNEST 8398

GREEN, FLETCHER M. 239, 240, 1185,
    3654, 3655, 3656, 8924, 11666,
    12065, 12718, 12719, 15108,
    15109, 19184

GREEN, GEORGE D. 12306

GREEN, HELEN B.   3657, 4833

GREEN, JOHN P.   18882

GREEN, LORAINE R.   2419

GREEN, MITCHELL A.   16169

GREEN, RODNEY D.   14717

GREEN, SAMUEL A.   10453, 10454

GREEN, THOMAS L.   16411

GREEN, THOMAS M.   12066

GREEN, WILLIAM A.   1186, 6526, 6528, 7622

GREENBERG, DOUGLAS   1187, 8926, 10636

GREENBERG, JOSEPH   4834

GREENBERG, JOSEPH H.   19337

GREENBERG, KENNETH S.   12929

GREENBERG, MICHAEL   1188, 1189, 13632, 16837

GREENBERG, MICHAEL S.   13633

GREENBERG, STANLEY B.   11717

GREENE, BARBARA J.   6529

GREENE, CARROLL JR.   18629

GREENE, EVARTS B.   10873, 14952

GREENE, JACK P.   6318, 6530, 8399, 8400, 15324

GREENE, JOHN C.   2420

GREENE, LARRY A.   2421, 3456, 14266

GREENE, LORENZO J.   5481, 8401, 8402, 8403, 8404, 10343, 10344, 11578, 11579, 11580

GREENE, MARTHA C.   9397

GREENE, MURRAY   9546

GREENE, ROBERT E.   20851

GREENE, Z.D.   3658

GREENER, RICHARD T.   2422

GREENFIELD, SIDNEY M.   6531, 6532, 6533, 6534, 6535, 6536

GREENIDGE, CHARLES W.W.   6537

GREENLEAF, RICHARD E.   7623, 7624

GREENOUGH, CHARLES P.   8927

GREEN-PEDERSEN, SVEND E.   1190, 4836, 5482, 5483, 5485, 14606

GREENSTEIN, LEWIS J.   3659

GREENWALD, BRUCE C.N.   12307, 12308

GREENWAY, JOHN   17668, 17669

GREER, HAROLD E., JR.   8700

GREER, JAMES K.   12309

GREGG, CHARLES L.   19185

GREGG, JOHN C.   20852

GREGG, WILLIAM R.   3660

GREGORIE, ANNE K.   19976

GREGOROVICH, ANDREW   241

GREGORY, CHESTER W.   16170

GREGORY, HENRY C.   16839

GREGORY, HIRAM   12310

GREGORY, JAMES P.   11305

GREGORY, MARIAN E.   4837

GREIER, WILLIE   16840

GRELL, V. JANE   19955

GRENANDER, M.E.   8928

GRENZ, SUZANNA M.   11581

GREY, MARTIN   11449

GRIAULE, MARCEL   16842

GRIDER, SYLVIA   15493

GRIDER, SYLVIA A.   15494

GRIDLEY, J.N.   8929

GRIER, W.M.   16343

GRIEST, ELLWOOD   19580

GRIFFIN, A.P.C.   242

GRIFFIN, ALVERIA G.   243

GRIFFIN, APPLETON P.C.   244

GRIFFIN, CHARLES C.   245

GRIFFIN, GEORGE H.   17670

GRIFFIN, JOHN H.   2423

GRIFFIN, LARRY D.   13963

GRIFFIN, LOUIS G.   17431

GRIFFIN, RICHARD   14797, 14798

GRIFFIN, RICHARD W.   11450, 11713,
    14720, 14722, 14723, 14725,
    14726, 14727, 14728

GRIFFIN, SAMUEL F.   13349

GRIFFIS, WILLIAM E.   5486

GRIFFITH, BENJAMIN W.   17671

GRIFFITH, CYNTHIA A.   12720

GRIFFITH, CYRIL E.   9549

GRIFFITH, LUCILLE   15325

GRIFFITH, PATRICK   1192

GRIGGS, EARL L.   5487

GRIGGS, GEORGIA   12931

GRIGSBY, J. EUGENE JR.   18631

GRIGSBY, MELVIN   20853

GRIGSBY, ROBERT W.   10049

GRIMES, JOSEPH   1193

GRIMES, WILLIAM W.   9550

GRIMKE, ARCHIBALD H.   2424, 3661,
    10050, 14729, 19581, 19977

GRIMSHAW, ALLEN D.   19978

GRIMSHAW, WILLIAM H.   9551

GRIMSTED, DAVID   2425

GRINDE, DONALD JR.   8223

GRINNAN, A.G.   13635

GRISE, GEORGE C.   18169

GROB, GERALD N.   15666

GROBMAN, NEIL R.   1194

GRUENE, BERTRAM H.   11892

GROGAN, ELMIRA F.   12067

GROOME, JOHN R.   15809

GROOT, SILVIA W. DE   7625, 7627,
    7628, 7629, 19979

GROPP, ARTHUR E.   246

GROSS, IZHAK   10051

GROSS, JAMES A.   1195

GROSS, SEYMOUR L.   247, 1196, 2426,
    2427

GROSS, SUE A.   7630

GROSSMAN, MITCHELL M.V.N.   8224

1725

GROUT, LEWIS 16844

GROVER, CARRIE B. 17672

GUDEMAN, STEPHEN 1197

GUERRA, FRANCISCO 6539

GUERRA Y SANCHEZ, RAMIRO 6540

GUEYE, MBAYE 4838

GUILD, JUNE P. 8930

GUILD, WALTER 16018

GUILLORY, JAMES D. 2428

GUINN, NANCY C. 11822

GUJER, BRUNO 14267

GULLICK, CHARLES J.M.R. 6541,
   6542, 7631

GUNDER FRANK, ANDRE 14268

GUNDERSON, GERALD 1198, 14269,
   14270

GUNKEL, ALEXANDER 6543

GUNN, VICTORIA R. 12068, 12069

GUNTER, CAROLYN P. 9552, 9553

GUNTER, CHARLES JR. 13213

GUNTHER, LENWORTH 3662

GUNTHER, LENWORTH A. 20854

GUTERMAN, STANLEY S. 1199

GUTHRIE, CHESTER L. 7632, 7633

GUTHRIE, DOUGLAS 6544

GUTHRIE, JAMES M. 20855

GUTHRIE, PATRICIA 12932

GUTMAN, HERBERT 1014, 14272,
   15112, 16172, 16182

GUTMAN, HERBERT G. 896, 897, 120
   1201, 1202, 1203, 1204, 9391,
   12933, 16173, 16174, 16177,
   16178, 16179, 16414

GUZMAN, JESSIE P. 1205

GUZMAN, PABLO 17673

GWINN, JANE W. 12934

GWYNN, AUBREY 6545

GYRISCO, GEOFFREY M. 499, 18525

GYSIN, BRION 10248, 10249, 11306

H., N. 17675

H.B.D. 8406

H.G.S. 1206

H.I.B. 18632

HAAG, LYDIA A. 10941

HAARDT, SARA 3663, 3664

HABERLY, DAVID T. 7635

HACKETT, CHARLES W. 11111

HACKETT, D.L.A. 12312

HACKETT, DEREK 3665

HADAWAY, WILLIAM S. 8407

HADD, DONALD R. 11893

HADEL, RICHARD 17676

HADEL, RICHARD E. 7636, 7637

HADEN, C.J. 3666

HADSKEY, JOHN W. 12557

HAGAN, HORACE H. 8931

HAGGARD, J. VILLSANA 13350

HAGGARD, JUAN V. 19582

HAGOOD, LOUISE W.   13352

HAGUE, PARTHENIA A.   20524

HAHNER, JUNE E.   7638

HAINES, CHARLES G.   8932

HAIR, P.E.H.   661, 4840, 4841,
    4842, 4843, 4844, 4845, 5488,
    5489, 5491, 19340

HAIRSTON, LOYLE   1207

HALASZ, NICHOLAS   19583

HALBROOKS, G. THOMAS   16845

HALE, EDWARD E.   5493, 18885

HALE, FRANK W.   3667, 19584

HALE, LAURA E.   13353

HALE, WILLIAM T.   13214

HALEY, ALEX   1208, 1209, 3668,
    4846, 16184, 16185

HALEY, J. EVETTS   13354

HALEY, JAMES T.   249

HALEY, VIOLET L.   3669

HALL, ARTHUR R.   1210, 14273

HALL, BEVERLY   19341

HALL, CLAUDE H.   3670

HALL, CLYDE W.   19186

HALL, D.G.   6546, 6547

HALL, DAN   20856

HALL, DOUGLAS   6548, 6549, 6551,
    6552, 9555

HALL, DOUGLAS G.   6553, 6554, 6891

HALL, E.H.   20857

HALL, ELLEN J.   3743

HALL, FREDERICK   17677, 17678

HALL, G. STANLEY   2430

HALL, GWENDOLYN M.   1211, 1212,
    1213, 6555, 6556, 6557, 6559,
    6560, 9556, 19984

HALL, HENRY L.   12935

HALL, HILAND   10313

HALL, HINES H.   2432

HALL, JONATHAN L.   3671

HALL, JULIEN A.   18172

HALL, KERMIT L.   8936

HALL, N.A.T.   5494, 9557

HALL, NEVILLE   6562, 6563

HALL, RAYMOND L.   9558

HALL, ROBERT A., JR.   19342, 19343

HALL, ROBERT L.   1215, 16846

HALL, SAMUEL   18836

HALL, WILBURN   5495

HALLAM, LILLIAN G.   10250

HALLER, D.A.   3672

HALLER, JOHN S.   2433

HALLER, JOHN S., JR.   1216, 2434,
    2436, 2437, 2438, 2439, 2440

HALLER, MARK H.   2441

HALLER, STEPHEN E.   250

HALLETT, ROBIN   4848

HALLIBURTON, JANET   11125

HALLIBURTON, R., JR.   1217, 11126,
    11129, 13966, 13967

HALLOWELL, A. IRVING 13969

HALLOWELL, EMILY 16847

HALLOWELL, N.P. 20353

HALLOWELL, NORWOOD P. 20357, 20859

HALPERIN, BERNARD S. 20860

HALPERN, MANFRED 2442

HALSEY, ASHLEY JR. 5496

HALSTEAD, JACQUELINE J. 11189

HALSTED, SARA D. 15327

HAMBLEN, ABIGAIL A. 2443

HAMBLIN, THOMAS D. 11307

HAMBLY, W.D. 7640

HAMER, MARGUERITE B. 12936

HAMER, PHILIP M. 8940, 8941

HAMILL, HOWARD M. 3673

HAMILTON, CHARLES V. 1218, 16849

HAMILTON, H.D. 10053

HAMILTON, HOLMAN 12558

HAMILTON, HOWARD D. 10054

HAMILTON, J.C. 3674, 10251

HAMILTON, J.G. DE R. 1219

HAMILTON, JAMES C. 10252, 10253

HAMILTON, JEFF 18887

HAMILTON, JENNIFER M. 18526

HAMILTON, JOSEPH G. DE R. 3675, 8942, 19985

HAMILTON, PETER J. 3676, 11719

HAMILTON, RUSSELL G. 7641

HAMILTON, RUSSELL G., JR. 7642

HAMILTON, T.F. 17506

HAMILTON, W.B. 12559

HAMILTON, WILLIAM B. 12560

HAMLETT, J. ARTHUR 2444

HAMLETT, JAMES A. 12314

HAMM, TOMMY T. 5497

HAMMERBACK, JOHN C. 3677

HAMMERSCHLAG, CARL A. 3678

HAMMETT, HUGH B. 15323

HAMMOND, ISAAC W. 10511, 10512

HAMMOND, J. 2445

HAMMOND, L.H. 3679

HAMMOND, M.B. 1220, 2446, 14275

HAMMOND, MATTHEW B. 14276, 14277

HAMMOND, PETER B. 3680

HAMMOND, STELLA L. 17680

HAMNETT, BRIAN 7643

HAMSHERE, CYRIL 6564

HANAWALT, LESLIE L. 3681

HANCHETT, WILLIAM 11108

HANCOCK, HAROLD B. 9561, 9562, 11190, 11191, 11192, 11193, 11194, 11195

HANCOCK, IAN F. 19344, 19345, 19346, 19347

HANCOCK, RICHARD R. 20863

HAND, CHARLES R. 5498

HAND, JOHN P. 10374

HANDLER, JEROME S. 251, 253, 5499,
6543, 6565, 6566, 6567, 6568,
6569, 6570, 6571, 6572, 6573,
6574, 6575, 6576, 6577, 6579,
9564, 15670, 18528, 18530

HANDLIN, MARY 1223

HANDLIN, MARY F. 8225

HANDLIN, OSCAR 1221, 1222, 1223,
2447, 8225, 9565

HANDY, ROBERT T. 1224

HANDY, SARA M. 18175

HANKE, LEWIS 1225, 6581, 6582,
6583

HANLEY, JAMES 5500

HANNA, JUDITH L. 1226, 18444,
18445

HANNERZ, ULF 17437

HANNIGAN, D.F. 1227

HANREIDER, BARBARA 3632

HANSEN, CHADWICK 18446

HANSEN, KLAUS J. 1228, 2449

HANSEN, LINDA 1229

HANSEN, MARCUS L. 10254

HANSEN, TERENCE L. 18176

HANSON, CARL A. 254

HARCOURT-SMITH, SIMON 6585

HARDEE, CHARLES S.H. 17682

HARDEE, W.H. 20525

HARDER, LELAND 11196

HARDIE, PETER A. 2450

HARDIN, BAYLESS E. 11308

HARDIN, EDWARD K. 16851

HARDING, COLIN 6414

HARDING, LEONARD L. 9566, 20864

HARDING, VINCENT 1231, 1232, 1976,
3262, 3683, 3684, 16852, 19986

HARDING, W.F. 3685

HARDISON, TERRY M. 3686

HARDWICK, KATHARINE D. 1233

HARDY, ALFRED 7648

HARDY, CHARLES O. 2452

HARDY, JOHN E. 2427

HARDYMAN, J.T. 5501

HARE, MAUD C. 17683

HARE, NATHAN 255

HARE, R.M. 3687

HARGIS, MODESTE 9375

HARGREAVES, JOHN 1234

HARGREAVES, JOHN D. 5502, 5503

HARING, CLARENCE H. 7650, 7651,
7652

HARKINS, JOHN E. 8943

HARKNESS, DONALD R. 3688

HARLAN, A.W. 10930

HARLAN, LOUIS R. 256, 3689, 13638,
13639

HARLEY, ELSIE F. 124

HARLEY, SHARON 9568, 16416

HARLOW, ALVIN F. 9569, 10833

HARLOW, VINCENT T.   6587

HARMON, GEORGE D.   3690

HARMON, JUDD S.   5505, 5506

HARMS, ROBERT   1235

HARMS, ROBERT W.   5507

HARN, JULIA   12070

HAROLD, KATHRYN D.   10911

HARPER, C.W.   15228

HARPER, FRANCIS P.   257

HARPER, LAWRENCE   5508

HARPER, ROBERT W.   20253

HARPER, ROLAND M.   11894, 12071

HARRELL, DAVID E., JR.   15713,
   16853, 16854

HARRELL, ISAAC S.   9570

HARRELL, JAMES A.   9571

HARRINGTON, FRED H.   20866, 20867

HARRINGTON, MICHAEL L.   1236

HARRINGTON, VIRGINIA D.   5509,
   14952

HARRIS, ABRAM L.   14796

HARRIS, ALFRED G.   10055, 10056,
   10057

HARRIS, ALLAN   7653

HARRIS, CHARLES M., JR.   3691

HARRIS, DAVID R.   6588

HARRIS, GEORGE W.   1237

HARRIS, J.S.   4849

HARRIS, JAY   11197

HARRIS, JOEL C.   1238, 1239, 1522
   16020, 18177, 18178, 18179,
   18180, 18182, 18183, 18184,
   18185, 18186, 18187, 18188,
   18189, 18190, 18888

HARRIS, JOHN   3692, 16857

HARRIS, JOHN H.   3693, 3694, 3695,
   4850

HARRIS, JOSEPH E.   1240, 4851,
   5510

HARRIS, LOUIS   3168

HARRIS, MARK   3696, 10058, 18532

HARRIS, MARVIN   2454, 6064, 7235

HARRIS, MICHAEL H.   258

HARRIS, MIDDLETON   17438

HARRIS, N. DWIGHT   10875

HARRIS, NELSON H.   259

HARRIS, NORMAN D.   10876, 10877

HARRIS, P.M.G.   8544

HARRIS, R.L.J.   2456

HARRIS, ROBERT L., JR.   9572

HARRIS, ROSEMARY   1242, 4853

HARRIS, SEALE   15671

HARRIS, SHELDON H.   9573

HARRIS, WILLIAM G.   1243

HARRIS, WILSON   1244, 1245

HARRISON, ALFERDTEEN   2457

HARRISON, CARL H.   19348

HARRISON, DIANA S.   15673

HARRISON, EDITH B.   3698

HARRISON, IRA E. 4854, 15873

HARRISON, JOHN 1246

HARRISON, JOHN P. 7657, 7658

HARRISON, LOWELL H. 11309, 11310, 11311, 11312, 11313, 11314, 11315, 13215, 13640

HARRISON, R.C. 17534

HARRISON, ROYDEN 3699

HARRISON, WILLIAM E. 3700

HARRISON, WILLIAM P. 16858

HARRISSEE, HENRY 3701

HARRO-HARRING, PAUL 7559

HARSHAW, D.A. 17585

HARSHBARGER, EMMETT L. 5513

HART, ALBERT B. 1247, 3702, 3703, 3704, 14730

HART, C.R. DESMOND 11019

HART, CHARLES D. 7660, 7661, 10942, 11022

HART, FREEMAN H. 8409

HART, JEFFREY 757

HART, RICHARD 6592, 6593, 6594, 6595, 6596

HARTDAGEN, GERALD E. 11451

HARTGROVE, W.B. 3705, 8410, 9574

HARTMAN, D.A. 3706, 3707

HARTRIDGE, WALTER C. 6597

HARTSINCK, J.J. 7662

HARTWELL, E.C. 260

HARTWELL, RONALD M. 14281

HARTWIG, GERALD W. 4855, 4856

HARTZ, LOUIS 2458

HARVEY, CECIL 509

HARVEY, CHARLES D. 16859

HARVEY, DIANE 12072

HARVEY, EMILY N. 18192

HARVEY, JAMES R. 11101, 11102

HARVEY, MERIWETHER 11721

HARVEY, MRS. GOVERNOR 20871

HARVIN, ANNA F. 2459

HARVIN, E.L. 11823

HARWOOD, MICHAEL 2460

HARWOOD, THOMAS F. 3708

HASKELL, JOHN D. 261

HASKELL, JOHN G. 11582

HASKELL, JOSEPH A. 14839

HASKELL, MARION A. 17686

HASKELL, THOMAS L. 1249, 1250, 1251

HASKETT, N.D. 3709

HASKINS, EDWARD C. 7664

HASKINS, JAMES 12316, 16860

HASKINS, RALPH W. 14282, 14283

HASLAM, GERALD W. 1252, 2461

HAST, ADELE 8944

HATCH, CARL E. 2462, 2463, 20872

HATCH, JAMES R. 12317

HATCH, TERRY B. 15676

1731

HATCHARD, KEITH A. 10255

HATCHER, WILLIAM E. 16861

HATCHETT, HILLIARY R. 17688

HATFIELD, EDWIN F. 10535

HATHAWAY, PHYLLIS S. 969

HAU, KATHLEEN 4857

HAUGHT, JAMES A. 13643

HAUNTON, RICHARD H. 9575

HAVARD, WILLIAM C. 1253

HAVARD, WILLIAM C., JR. 15231

HAVEN, GILBERT 3710

HAVILAND, LAURA S. 11316

HAWES, BESS L. 18221

HAWES, JOHN 6598

HAWES, LILLA M. 3711

HAWES, RUTH B. 12561

HAWK, EMORY Q. 14284

HAWKES, ALTA M. 15409

HAWKINS, FRANK R. 12940

HAWKINS, HUBERT H. 11317

HAWKINS, MARJORIE B. 13355

HAWKS, JOHN M. 20874

HAWLEY, CHARLES A. 2464

HAWTAYNE, G.H. 6599

HAY, ROBERT P. 1254

HAY, SAMUEL A. 1255

HAY, THOMAS R. 20526, 20875

HAYDEN, J. CARLETON 12941

HAYDEN, ROGER 16863

HAYEN, EBERHARD 3712

HAYES, CHARLES F. 18635

HAYES, DORIS J. 1256

HAYES, FLOYD W. 262

HAYES, FRED E. 11023

HAYGOOD, ATTICUS G. 13331

HAYMAN, BETTIE 13356

HAYMOND, HENRY 13644

HAYNE, COE S. 10878

HAYNES, CHARLES H. 9576

HAYNES, DONALD 263

HAYNES, FRED C. 8226

HAYNES, HENRY W. 10345

HAYNES, LEONARD L. 16864

HAYNES, MRS. ELIZABETH R. 3713

HAYNES, N.S. 3714

HAYNES, ROBERT V. 3715, 11895

HAYNES, ROSE MARY F. 13357

HAYNIE, J.J. 3716

HAYWOOD, C. ROBERT 3717

HAYWOOD, CHARLES 264

HAYWOOD, JACQUELYN S. 12318

HAYWOOD, WILLIAM C. 10996

HAZARD, CAROLINE 10791, 10792

HAZEL, JOHN T., JR. 2465

HAZEL, JOSEPH A.   11722

HEAD, JOSEPH L.   2466

HEADLEY, JOEL T.   10638

HEALY, MARY A.   6601

HEALY, MARY P.   3718

HEAP, JOHN P.   15232

HEAPS, PORTER W.   20876

HEAPS, WILLARD A.   20876

HEARD, GEORGE A.   12075

HEARD, PATRICIA L.   19587

HEARD, WILLIAM H.   3719

HEARN, LAFCADIO   6602, 6603, 6604,
   18194

HEARN, WALTER C.   12563

HEARON, CLEO C.   12564

HEARTMAN, CHARLES F.   265

HEATH, DWIGHT B.   7666

HEATH, JIM F.   2467

HEATH, TRUDY   266

HEATHCOTE, CHARLES W.   16865

HECHT, DAVID   3720

HECHT, J. JEAN   2468

HECHTLINGER, ADELAIDE   8412

HECKMAN, OLIVER S.   20877

HEDIN, RAYMOND   1257

HEDLEY, FENWICK Y.   20360

HEDRICK, CHARLES E.   11318, 11319

HEERMANCE, J. NOEL   1258, 1259,
   1260

HEFELE, KARL J.   16866

HEFFERNAN, WILLIAM   5514

HEIDELBERG, NELL A.   12565

HEIDISH, LOUISE O.S.   8946

HEILLE, RICHARD   1261

HEINEN, HEINZ   3721

HEINL, NANCY G.   6605

HEINL, ROBERT D., JR.   6605

HEISKELL, C.W.   13218

HELLER, CHARLES E.   20878

HELLER, MURRAY   19350, 19351,
   19393

HELLWIG, DAVID J.   9577

HELMER, WINIFRED G.   3722

HELMREICH, WILLIAM B.   267, 268

HELMS, MARY W.   2469

HELPLER, MORRIS K.   15925

HELPS, ARTHUR   6606

HELTON, ALFRED J.   3723

HELWIG, ADELAIDE B.   6607, 8413

HEMENWAY, ROBERT   1262

HEMPHILL, JOHN   8414

HEMPHILL, SUSAN L.   12076

HEMPHILL, W. EDWIN   8947

HEMPSTEAD, FAY   11824

HENDERSON, ARCHIE M.   9578

HENDERSON, CONWAY W.   5515

HENDERSON, DALE E.   16868

1733

HENDERSON, DONALD H.   3724

HENDERSON, DWIGHT F.   12320

HENDERSON, EMMETE L.   2470

HENDERSON, G.W.   3725

HENDERSON, GEORGE   2471

HENDERSON, GEORGE W.   15497

HENDERSON, MAE G.   66

HENDERSON, ROSE   269

HENDERSON, T.W.   1105

HENDERSON, WILLIAM C.   8948, 8949

HENDRICK, ROBERT M.   15332

HENDRICKS, GEORGE L.   20379

HENDPIX, JAMES P.   5517, 5518

HENDRIX, JAMES P., JR.   1263

HENDRIX, LEWELLYN   15717

HENEGAN, HERBERT   3726

HENIGE, DAVID   5519

HENNESSY, ALISTAIR   5608

HENRETTA, JAMES A.   14956

HENRIQUES, E.   3335

HENRIQUES, F.   4026

HENRIQUES, FERNANDO   2472, 6609, 6610, 6611

HENRY, BESSIE M.   13447

HENRY, FRANCES   10256

HENRY, GEORGE   13647

HENRY, HOWELL M.   8950, 8951, 8952

HENRY, ROBERT S.   15113

HENRY, THOMAS W.   18894

HENRY, WILLIE R.   13353

HENSEL, WILLIAM U.   8953, 19589, 19590

HENSHAW, HENRY W.   13970

HENSON, HERBERT H.   3727

HENSON, JOSIAH   18895, 18896, 18897

HENSON, MARGARET S.   8954

HENTOFF, NAT   17690

HEPBURN, A.C.   3728

HEPBURN, DAVID   16869

HERBERG, WILL   2473

HERBERT, HILARY A.   3729, 11723

HERING, JULIA F.   11897, 11898

HERKLOTZ, HILDEGARDE R.   11583

HERMANN, JANET S.   1254, 12566, 15114

HERNDON, DALLAS T.   3730

HERNDON, G. MELVIN   8415, 13648, 13649

HERNDON, GEORGE M.   8416

HERNDON, JANE W.   2474

HERREID, HENRY B.   17691

HERRERO, RAFAEL   7669

HERRICK, CHEESMAN A.   10735

HERRICK, E.P.   6612, 6613, 6614, 6615

HERRICK, J.P.   10639

HERRING, HUBERT   4858

HERRING, JAMES V. 9579

HERRING, MABEN D. 18898

HERRINGTON, ELSIE I. 5520

HERRON, LEONORA 15677

HERRON, STELLA 5521

HERSCH, ROBERT C. 3731

HERSHAW, LAFAYETTE M. 3732

HERSHBERG, THEODORE 1265, 9580,
9581, 16402

HERSHKOWITZ, LEO 8955

HERSKOVITS, FRANCES S. 5523, 6619,
6620, 7676, 7677, 7679

HERSKOVITS, MELVILLE J. 1266,
1267, 1268, 1269, 1271, 1272,
1274, 2475, 3733, 3734, 4859,
4860, 4861, 4862, 4863, 4864,
4865, 4866, 4867, 4368, 4871,
4872, 4873, 4874, 5323, 6617,
6618, 6619, 6620, 7671, 7673,
7674, 7675, 7676, 7677, 7679,
18197, 18636, 18637, 18638

HERTZBERG, STEVEN 12077

HERTZLER, JAMES R. 12078

HERZBERG, LOUIS F. 11724

HERZOG, GEORGE 13971

HESBURGH, THEODORE M. 8956

HESS, ELDORA F. 10975

HESSELTINE, WILLIAM B. 2476,
20881, 20882

HESTON, ALFRED M. 10536, 10537,
10538, 10539

HEUMAN, GAD J. 1275, 6621

HEWES, JENNIE G.R. 11025

HEWETSON, W.T. 16418

HEWETT, DAVID G. 3735

HEWITT, JOHN H. 9582, 19592

HEWITT, M.J. 8417

HEYWARD, DUBOSE 12950

HEYWARD, DUNCAN C. 12951

HEYWARD, JANIE S. 17693

HICKEY, DONALD R. 13652

HICKIN, P.F.P. 13653

HICKIN, PATRICIA 13654, 13765

HICKOK, CHARLES T. 9583, 9584

HICKS, GRANVILLE 4031, 19593

HICKS, NORA L. 16419

HICKS, WILLIAM 12324

HIGGINBOTHAM, A. LEON JR. 2478,
8957, 8958, 8959, 8960

HIGGINBOTHAM, JON 8961, 10059

HIGGINBOTHAM, SANFORD W. 18449

HIGGINS, CHESTER JR. 3736

HIGGINS, FRANK B. 5524

HIGGINS, W. ROBERT 8418, 8419,
8420, 8421, 8963

HIGGINSON, T.W. 17694

HIGGINSON, THOMAS W. 6623, 17695,
19352, 20884, 20886, 20887,
20888

HIGGS, ROBERT 14288

HIGH, JAMES 5527

HIGH, JAMES H. 5528

HIGHAM, C.S.S. 6624, 6625

HIGHAM, CHARLES S.S. 6626

HIGHAM, JOHN 3737

HIGHSAW, MARY W. 13223

HIGHSMITH, WILLIAM E. 12325,
  12326, 20889

HIGHTOWER, MARVIN 7631

HIGMAN, B.W. 1276, 6627, 6629,
  6630, 14957, 16195

HIGMAN, B.W.C. 6631

HIGMAN, BARRY W. 1278, 6632, 6633,
  6634, 6635, 6636, 6637, 6638,
  6639, 6640

HIJIYA, JAMES A. 1279

HILARIAN, MARY 17697

HILGER, ROTHE 16378

HILL, ADELAIDE C. 4877

HILL, CAROLE E. 15680

HILL, CHARLES L. 10455

HILL, D.G. 11140

HILL, D.H. 10284

HILL, DANIEL G. 10257, 10258,
  11103

HILL, DANIEL G., JR. 11141

HILL, ERROL 6641

HILL, FREDERICK T. 8964

HILL, HERBERT 8965

HILL, JAMES D. 14290

HILL, JOSEPH J. 11026

HILL, JUDITH A.R. 10060

HILL, LAWRENCE F. 5530

HILL, LAWRENCE W. 16879

HILL, LEONARD U. 9585

HILL, LESLIE P. 19993

HILL, MILDRED A. 18200

HILL, PATRICIA L. 1280

HILL, POLLY 1281, 4878

HILL, SAMUEL S., JR. 16880

HILL, WALTER B. 3738

HILL, WILLIAM 14291

HILL, WILLIAM H. 1282

HILLIARD, SAM B. 12079, 12080,
  15411, 15412, 15413, 15414,
  15415

HILLIER, SUSAN 5531

HILLIS, NEWELL D. 3739

HILTY, HIRAM H. 12723

HINDUS, MICHAEL S. 8966, 8967,
  8968, 8969, 8970

HINE, CARLENE C. 1283, 14293

HINE, WILLIAM C. 270, 14294

HINES, JAMES R. 17698

HINES, JOSEPH S., JR. 2480

HINES, LINDA E.O. 1284

HINSDALE, B.A. 3740

HINSDALE, BURKE A. 10834

HINSHAW, IDRIS E. 19597

HINTON, E.H. 15333

HINTON, RICHARD J. 19994

1736

HIPPARD, SUE A.   9586

HIRSCH, CHARLES B.   8423

HIRSCH, JERROLD   1285, 1286

HIRSCH, LEO H., JR.   10641

HIRSCH, STEPHEN A.   1287

HIRST, MAURICE H.   5532

HISS, PHILIP H.   271, 3741

HITE, JAMES C.   3743

HITE, ROGER W.   19598

HJEJLE, BENEDICTE   5533

HOBART, EDWIN L.   20891

HOBBS, PHILIP   5534

HOBSBAWM, E.J.   1288, 14295

HOBSON, ANNE   18448

HOBSON, JOHN A.   3744

HOCHMAN, STEVEN H.   1451

HODDER, FRANK H.   8971

HODGE, FREDERICK W.   3745

HODGE, W.J.   19995

HODGES, CARL G.   10879

HODGES, J. ALLISON   15233, 15682, 15683

HODGES, NORMAN E.   4879

HODGKINS, WILLIAM H.   272

HODGSON, JOSEPH   11667

HODSON, FLORENCE T.   19587

HODSON, J.H.   5535

HOEPNER, PAUL H.   14313

HOEPPLI, R.   5536

HOES, ROSWELL R.   10642

HOETINK, H.   1289, 1290, 2482, 5537, 6642, 6645

HOETINK, HARMANNUS   6646

HOETINK, HARRY   1291, 2484, 5538

HOEXTER, CORINNE K.   3746

HOEY, EDWIN   10643

HOFFERT, SYLVIA D.   2486

HOFFMAN, CHARLES A.   6649

HOFFMAN, EDWIN D.   12961

HOFFMAN, FREDERICK L.   2487

HOFFMAN, RICHARD L.   8972

HOFFMAN, RONALD   3475, 8424, 14176

HOFFMANN, LEON-FRANCOIS   2488

HOFSTADTER, RICHARD   1292, 8425

HOGAN, DANIEL M.   11584

HOGAN, WILLIAM R.   273, 9455, 9456, 13360

HOGEN, MILDRED E.   3747

HOGENDORN, J.S.   6498

HOGENDORN, JAN S.   4821, 4881, 4957, 5469, 5471, 5472

HOGG, DONALD W.   4882

HOGG, P.C.   274

HOGG, PETER C.   275, 3748

HOGG, THOMAS C.   3749

HOIG, STAN   10943

HOLBROOK, ABIGAIL C.   13361, 13362

HOLBROOK, ELIZABETH 362

HOLCOMBE, A.R. 3750

HOLDEN, CONSTANCE 1293

HOLDEN, F. 1294

HOLDER, ALAN 1295

HOLDER, RAY 12568

HOLDERFIELD, HORACE M. 11725

HOLDREDGE, HELEN 16421

HOLIFIELD, E. BROOKS 16887

HOLLADAY, HENRY M. 3751

HOLLAND, ANTHONY F. 11580

HOLLAND, C.G. 13655

HOLLAND, FRANCIS R., JR. 13656

HOLLAND, JOHN P. 3752

HOLLAND, LAURENCE B. 378

HOLLAND, REID A. 13972

HOLLAND, RUPERT S. 12962

HOLLAND, TIMOTHY J. 16888

HOLLANDER, A.N.J. DEN 1296

HOLLANDER, BARNETT 8973

HOLLARD, REID 3754

HOLLEY, JOSEPH W. 3755

HOLLIS, D. 5543

HOLLITZ, ERWIN 3264

HOLLON, W. EUGENE 13364, 19998

HOLLOWAY, THOMAS H. 7688, 7689

HOLLOWAY, WILLIAM H. 3756

HOLMAN, C. HUGH 3757, 3758

HOLMAN, HARRIET 1297

HOLMES, DORIS A. 937

HOLMES, EDWARD D. 16889, 16890

HOLMES, JACK 9590, 12327

HOLMES, JACK D.L. 11726, 11899,
   11900, 12328

HOLSEY, LUCIUS H. 18899

HOLSOE, SVEND E. 4883, 5544

HOLT, BRYCE R. 8974

HOLT, CHERRYL C. 19189

HOLT, MICHAEL F. 3759

HOLT, THOMAS 1298

HOLT, THOMAS C. 3760

HOLJB, NORMAN 7690

HOLVERSOTT, L.J. 8975

HOMSEY, ELIZABETH M. 9591

HONEYMAN, A. VAN DOREN 10540

HOOD, A.P. 12569

HOOD, JAMES L. 11320

HOOK, FRANCIS M. 8426

HOOLE, W. STANLEY 11727

HOOPER, ERNEST W. 13221

HOOVER, DWIGHT W. 1299, 13973

HOPE, ASCOTT R. 3764

HOPE, CORRIE S. 20001

HOPKINS, A.G. 1300, 1301

HOPKINS, ANTHONY G. 5545

HOPKINS, JAMES F. 11321, 11322, 14296

HOPKINS, K. 4026

HOPKINS, KEITH 3385

HOPKINS, MARK M. 15392

HOPKINS, VINCENT C. 8976

HOPPE, ANNA 3765

HOPPER, LOUIS S. 17700

HORNBOSTEL, ERICH M.V. 1302

HORNE, LINDA 2489

HORNEY, HELEN 10880

HORNICK, NANCY S. 9592

HORNSBY, ALTON JR. 276

HOROWITZ, DONALD L. 2490

HOROWITZ, HAROLD W. 8977, 8978

HOROWITZ, MICHAEL M. 6652, 16891

HOROWITZ, MURRAY M. 20895

HORST, SAMUEL L. 19190

HORSWELL, CHRISTINE 303

HORTON, FRAZIER R. 12726

HORTON, J. 20002

HORTON, J. BENJAMIN JR. 3766

HORTON, JAMES A. 4884

HORTON, JAMES O. 9593, 9594, 9595

HORTON, JOSEPH P. 16892

HORTON, LOIS E. 9595

HORTON, ROBIN 6653, 16894

HORTON, W.R.G. 4885

HOSKINS, CHARLES L. 16895

HOSMER, JAMES K. 10835

HOSS, E.E. 16896

HOSTETTER, ALBERT K. 19599

HOUGH, S. 253

HOUGHTON, SUSAN A. 3767

HOUSE, A.V. 277

HOUSE, ALBERT V. 12083

HOUSE, ALBERT V., JR. 12084, 12085

HOVENKAMP, HERBERT 16897

HOVET, THEODORE R. 3768, 3769, 16898, 18202

HOWARD, ALLEN 4886

HOWARD, BRYAN C. 5548

HOWARD, CLINTON N. 8427

HOWARD, JAMES H.W. 3770

HOWARD, JOHN C. 14733

HOWARD, JOHN R. 3771

HOWARD, JOSEPH H. 17702

HOWARD, LAWRENCE C. 5549

HOWARD, MILO B., JR. 278

HOWARD, O.O. 20897

HOWARD, RICHARD C. 5550

HOWARD, THOMAS 5551

HOWARD, VICTOR B. 3772, 3773, 3774, 8979, 11323, 11324, 11325

HOWARD, WARREN S. 5552, 5553

HOWAY, F.W. 11080

HOWE, BENNIE W.   11902

HOWE, DANIEL W.   3775

HOWE, GEORGE 5554

HOWE, GEORGE L.   5555

HOWE, JOHN R., JR.   3776

HOWE, M.A. DEWOLFE   15115, 17703

HOWE, MENTAR A.   279

HOWE, R. WILSON   17704

HOWE, RUSSELL W.   5556

HOWELL, ISABEL   15116

HOWELL, KEITH K.   5557

HOWELL, R.C.   5558

HOWIE, DON   2491

HOWINGTON, ARTHUR   13222

HOWINGTON, ARTHUR F.   8981

HOWLAND, JOSEPH A.   20003

HOWORTH, LUCY S.   20478

HOWRY, L.B.   6654

HOYT, EDWIN P.   5559

HUBBARD, G.W.   13224

HUBBARD, GARDINER G.   6655

HUBBARD, GERALDINE H.   280

HUBBART, HENRY C.   11027

HUBBELL, JOHN T.   20898

HUBBS, BARBARA B.   10881

HUBER, C. HAROLD   15120

HUBER, JO ANNE S.   16422

HUCH, RONALD K.   20899

HUCKS, J. JENKINS   18203

HUDSON, ARTHUR P.   19354

HUDSON, CHARLES M.   3777, 13974, 13976

HUDSON, ELLIS H.   15636

HUDSON, GOSSIE H.   281, 1303, 95

HUDSON, J. PAUL   14734

HUDSON, JACK   12458

HUDSON, RANDALL O.   7692, 8982

HUERTAS, THOMAS   14610

HUFF, A.V.   3778

HUFF, ARCHIE V., JR.   12964

HUGER, ALFRED   12965

HUGGINS, NATHAN I.   1304, 1305, 3779, 3780, 13658

HUGGINS, WILLIS N.   16900

HUGHES, CHARLES   15687

HUGHES, G.   8983

HUGHES, H.B.L.   6656

HUGHES, JOHN E.   16901

HUGHES, JOHN S.   11585, 11586

HUGHES, L. ROBERT   6657

HUGHES, LANGSTON   282, 283, 284, 3781, 3782, 3783, 18038, 1820

HUGHES, LOUIS   15334

HUGHES, NATHANIEL C., JR.   1132

HUGHES, RONALD   6658

HUGHES, SARAH S.   13659, 13660

HUGHES, W.A.C. 1106

HUGHES, WILLIAM C. 11411

HUGHSON, SHIRLEY C. 8984

HULAN, RICHARD 15498

HULEN, RICHARD 12332

HULL, RICHARD W. 4887

HULSEY, HAL 8228

HUME, JOHN F. 3784

HUMM, P. 16902

HUMPHREY, BARBARA 19076

HUMPHREY, DAVID C. 2492

HUMPHREY, EDWARD P. 2493

HUMPHREY, N.D. 7694

HUMPHREYS, R.A. 285

HUMPHREYS, ROBERT A. 5560

HUNEYCUTT, DWIGHT J. 14298

HUNNICUTT, GEORGE F. 12087

HUNT, ALFRED N. 6660

HUNT, E.K. 1306

HUNT, E.M. 5561

HUNT, GAILLARD 3785

HUNT, H.F. 13977

HUNT, LENOIR 18887

HUNT, SANFORD B. 15638, 20902

HUNT, SHANE J. 1848

HUNT, WILLIAM A. 14299

HUNT, WILLIAM C. 3786

HUNTER, BEN 1307

HUNTER, FRANCES L. 3737

HUNTER, IRENE P. 13365

HUNTER, JAMES 3788

HUNTER, JOHN M. 5562, 15418, 15687

HUNTER, LLOYD A. 11587

HUNTER, R.M.T. 3789

HUNTER, WILBUR H., JR. 18640

HUNTING, CLAUDINE 2495

HUNTON, ADDIE 16423

HURLEY, CHARLES F. 12727

HURST, D. 12088

HURSTON, ZORA N. 5563, 5564, 16903, 17706, 17707, 18206, 18901

HURWITZ, EDITH F. 1308, 3790, 6661, 8986

HURWITZ, SAMUEL J. 6661, 8986

HUTCHINSON, EDWARD 5565, 5566

HUTCHINSON, H.W. 7696

HUTCHINSON, HARRY 7697

HUTCHINSON, HARRY W. 7698

HUTCHINSON, LOUISE D. 19601

HUTCHINSON, WILLIAM K. 15419

HUTSON, CHARLES W. 15117

HUTTAR, GEORGE L. 19355

HUTTON, LAURENCE 2496

HYATT, HARRY M. 16904

HYDE, ANNE B. 5567

HYDE, FRANCIS E. 5568

HYDE, LAURA H. 8428

HYLTON, JOSEPH G. 2497

HYMAN, HAROLD 20903

HYMAN, HAROLD M. 2498, 10062,
    21116

HYMOWITZ, CAROL 16424

HYNDS, ERNEST C. 12089

HYPPOLITE, MICHELSON P. 18208

HYPPS, IRENE C. 9599

HYZER, MURIEL 3791

IANNI, JUAN B. 20905

IANNI, OCTAVIO 1310, 2499, 7699

IDESON, JULIA 18449

IMES, G. LAKE 5569

IMES, WILLIAM L. 8987, 13226

INABINET, L. GLEN 20005

INGERSOLL, ERNEST 18641

INGERSOLL, HENRY H. 10645

INGLE, EDWARD 3792, 3793, 11236

INGRAHAM, J.H. 13227

INGRAHAM, LEONARD W. 3794

INGRAM, JOHN K. 3795

INGRAM, K.E. 288

INGRAM, K.E.N. 289

INGRAM, KENNETH E. 290

INIKORI, J.E. 1311, 1312, 1313,
    4656, 5571, 5574

INIKORI, JOSEPH E. 5575

INMAN, HENRY F. 11728

INNES, F.C. 6662

INNES, FRANK C. 6663

INNES, STEPHEN 8205

INSTITUTE OF JAMAICA 291

INSTITUTE OF TEXAN CULTURES 1336

IRBY, CHARLES C. 9601

IRELAND, OWEN S. 2500

IRELAND, RALPH R. 10646

IRELAND, ROBERT M. 8991

IRISH, JAMES 6665

IRVIN, HELEN D. 11327

IRVINE, KEITH 292, 5576

IRVIS, K. LEROY 20362

IRWIN, GRAHAM W. 293

IRWIN, LEONARD B. 294

ISAAC, RHYS 1317

ISAACMAN, ALLEN 4888

ISAACMAN, BARBARA 4883

ISAACS, HAROLD R. 3797, 4889

ISANI, MUKHTAR ALI 2501, 4890,
    16426

ISICHEI, ELIZABETH 4891

ISRAEL, J.I. 7701, 7702

ISSEL, WILLIAM 1318

IVERS, LARRY E. 12091

IVERSON, PETER J. 20007

IVY, JAMES W. 1319, 1320

J.A.B. 10513

J.D.B. 10456

J.N. 10457

JACK, I. ALLEN 8431

JACKLE, LYDIA A. 8992

JACKSON, ANDREW S. 5577

JACKSON, BLYDEN 12728, 12729

JACKSON, BRUCE 13209

JACKSON, DONALD 3798

JACKSON, EILEEN S. 17709

JACKSON, ESTHER 832

JACKSON, FLORENCE 3799

JACKSON, GEORGE F. 9602, 16427, 16429

JACKSON, GEORGE P. 17710, 17711, 17712, 17713

JACKSON, GILES B. 3800

JACKSON, GLORIANNE 177

JACKSON, HARVEY H. 8432, 12334

JACKSON, HENRY R. 5578

JACKSON, IRENE V. 295, 16430, 16431, 16905, 17717

JACKSON, JACQUELYNE J. 16200

JACKSON, JAMES C. 16906

JACKSON, JESSE J. 8993

JACKSON, JOHN G. 4892

JACKSON, JUANITA 12969

JACKSON, LUTHER P. 5579, 8433, 8434, 9603, 9604, 9605, 9606,

10063, 10064, 13661, 13664, 19193, 20907

JACKSON, MARGARET Y. 15235, 15236, 18210, 20008

JACKSON, MAURICE J. 12570

JACKSON, MILES M., JR. 296

JACKSON, MRS. F.N. 3801

JACKSON, RICHARD L. 297, 298, 2502, 2503, 2504, 7704, 7705, 18905

JACKSON, SHIRLEY M. 7706, 14840, 14841

JACKSON, SUSAN 12092, 12730, 12971, 13368

JACKSON, W. SHERMAN 1321, 10065

JACKSON-BROWN, IRENE V. 299

JACOB, CARY F. 1322

JACOB, J.R. 3802

JACOBS, ALMA S. 572

JACOBS, DONALD M. 300, 9609, 9610, 9611

JACOBS, GRACE H. 11454

JACOBS, H.P. 6668, 17439

JACOBS, HARRIET 16201

JACOBS, P.M. 301

JACOBSEN, EDWARD C. 3803

JACOBSTEIN, MEYER 11328, 14303

JAFFA, HARRY V. 757, 10066

JAHN, JANHEINZ 302, 3804, 17719, 18906

JAIN, SUSHIL K. 303

JAKOBSSON, STIV 5580

JAKOSKI, HELEN 18211

JAMES, ALFRED P. 20910

JAMES, C.L.R. 3805, 6670, 6671,
     20010

JAMES, D. CLAYTON 12571, 12572

JAMES, DORIS C. 12573

JAMES, EDWARD W. 8435, 8436, 8437,
     9612

JAMES, FELIX 20911, 20912, 21083

JAMES, JACQUELINE 13671

JAMES, JAMES A. 13978

JAMES, SYDNEY V. 10793, 16909

JAMES, THOMAS 18907

JAMESON, J. FRANKLIN 1323

JAMIESON, ANNIE S. 3806

JAMISON, MONROE F. 12093

JANNEY, SAMUEL M. 3807

JANSEN, MARY L. 13672

JANSON, ADRIAN J. 3808

JANUARY, ALAN F. 8994, 8995

JANVIER, THOMAS A. 5582

JARREAU, LAFAYETTE 18212

JEANSONNE, GLEN 16910

JEFFREY, REGINALD W. 6672

JEFFREYS, M.D.W. 3809

JEFFREYS, MERVYN D.W. 19357

JEKYLL, WALTER 6673

JELTZ, WYATT F. 13979

JENKINS, H.J.K. 6674

JENKINS, JOHN H. 13369

JENKINS, MILDRED L. 4893

JENKINS, ULYSSES D. 4894, 4895

JENKINS, WILLIAM S. 2505, 3810

JENKINS, WILLIAM T. 12094

JENKS, F.H. 17722

JENNINGS, ARTHUR H. 8229

JENNINGS, JUDITH 5583

JENNINGS, KATHLEEN 5584

JENNINGS, LAWRENCE 5585

JENNINGS, LAWRENCE C. 5586, 558

JENNINGS, STEPHEN S. 2506

JENNINGS, THELMA 13228

JENSEN, CAROL 10261

JENSEN, JOAN M. 3812

JENSEN, MARILYN 10347

JENSEN, RICHARD 1324

JENSON, MARILYN 3813

JENTZ, JOHN 1325

JEREMIAH, MILFORD A. 17440

JERNEGAN, MARCUS W. 3814, 3815
     8438, 8439, 8440

JEROME, YVES J. 6675

JERVEY, EDWARD D. 15120

JERVEY, HUGER W. 17723

JERVEY, SUSAN R. 12974

1744

JERVEY, THEODORE D. 3816, 12975,
    14307

JESSE, C. 6676, 6677

JESSUP, LYNN E. 4896

JESTER, ANNIE L. 8441

JETER, HENRY N. 13674

JETER, JEREMIAH B. 20015

JILLSON, CALVIN 3817

JOEL, MIRIAM 4897

JOHANNSEN, ROBERT W. 1326, 11028

JOHN, ELIZABETH, A.H. 11029

JOHN, K.R.V. 6678

JOHNS, A. TRENT 1327

JOHNS, JOHN E. 11904

JOHNSON, ALLEN 8997

JOHNSON, ALLEN W. 7707

JOHNSON, AMANDA 12095

JOHNSON, AUGUSTA J. 19605

JOHNSON, C. 14308

JOHNSON, C.A. 12976

JOHNSON, C.B. 3818

JOHNSON, CECIL S. 8442

JOHNSON, CHARLES A. 16916

JOHNSON, CHARLES B. 18912

JOHNSON, CHARLES S. 1328, 2507,
    2508, 2972, 11297, 14736, 15238,
    17325

JOHNSON, CLIFTON H. 305, 1329,
    1330, 3820, 12336, 15121

JOHNSON, DERWOOD 2241

JOHNSON, E.A. 3821

JOHNSON, E.D. 18213

JOHNSON, EDWARD A. 3822

JOHNSON, EDWIN D. 7708

JOHNSON, F. ROY 18214, 18215,
    20017

JOHNSON, FANNY A. 11825

JOHNSON, FRANK R. 20018

JOHNSON, FRANKLIN 8998, 8999

JOHNSON, G.G. 12731

JOHNSON, GEORGIA D. 3823

JOHNSON, GERRI 11455

JOHNSON, GUION G. 2509, 2510,
    2511, 12732, 12977

JOHNSON, GUY B. 182, 1331, 2512,
    4898, 12978, 17444, 17725,
    17726, 17845, 17846, 19359

JOHNSON, HARRY G. 1332

JOHNSON, HENRY M. 16917

JOHNSON, HOMER U. 19607

JOHNSON, ISAAC 11329

JOHNSON, J.G. 12096

JOHNSON, JAMES B. 4900

JOHNSON, JAMES K. 16918

JOHNSON, JAMES P. 307, 308

JOHNSON, JAMES R. 5589, 16026

JOHNSON, JAMES W. 17729, 17730,
    17731

JOHNSON, JERAH 5590

JOHNSON, JOHN H.   18218

JOHNSON, KEACH D.   8443

JOHNSON, KENNETH R.   11730, 16202, 16920

JOHNSON, LEMUEL   2513

JOHNSON, LEMUEL A.   5591

JOHNSON, LEONARD W.   15692

JOHNSON, LOUISE H.   2514

JOHNSON, LUCETTA A.   309

JOHNSON, LUDWELL   20913, 20914

JOHNSON, LULU M.   10262, 10836

JOHNSON, LYMAN L.   7709, 7710, 7711, 7712

JOHNSON, M.D.   8444

JOHNSON, MARION   4901, 4904, 5519, 5593, 5594, 5595

JOHNSON, MICHAEL P.   12097, 12098, 12979

JOHNSON, PAUL D.   18913

JOHNSON, R.M.   12099

JOHNSON, RICHARD   1334

JOHNSON, RICHARD H.   14967

JOHNSON, SAMUEL   4902

JOHNSON, T. BRADFORD   3824

JOHNSON, THAVOLIA G.   14310

JOHNSON, THEODORE W.   2515

JOHNSON, THOMAS L.   13675, 18914

JOHNSON, VERA M.   5596

JOHNSON, WHITTINGTON B.   3825, 8445, 9615

JOHNSON, WILLIAM R.   14739

JOHNSTON, ALLAN J.   10067

JOHNSTON, ELIZABETH B.   15858

JOHNSTON, HARRY H.   5597, 6679, 6681

JOHNSTON, J.H.   4903

JOHNSTON, JAMES H.   310, 1335, 2516, 2517, 2518, 13676

JOHNSTON, JAMES H., JR.   2519

JOHNSTON, RICHARD M.   3826

JOHNSTON, ROBERT D.   3827

JOHNSTON, RUBY F.   16921

JOHNSTON, STANLEY   6682

JOHNSTON, THOMAS F.   10263

JOHNSTON, W. DAWSON   311

JOHNSTON, WILLIAM D.   10794, 107

JULY, LUZ G.   7716

JONAS, ROSALIE M.   3828

JONES, ADAM   4904

JONES, ALICE M.   16922

JONES, ALLEN W.   312

JONES, ARCHER   14312, 14313

JONES, BESSIE   18220, 18221

JONES, BEVERLY W.   1336

JONES, BOBBY F.   9000, 16203

JONES, BRENDA L.   1337

JONES, CHARLES C., JR.   12100, 18222, 20353

JONES, CLYDE V.   13371

JONES, D.K.   6683

JONES, DIONNE J.   197

JONES, E. ALFRED   5598

JONES, ELDRED D.   2520

JONES, ELSIE C.   15123

JONES, EVAN   3155

JONES, EVERETT L.   11010, 11011,
   11012

JONES, F.M.   11331

JONES, FAUSTINE C.   16204

JONES, GEORGE F.   13679

JONES, GERTRUDE M.   17734

JONES, GWILYM I.   5599

JONES, HOWARD   20021

JONES, HOWARD J.   2521

JONES, IVA G.   2522

JONES, J. RALPH   12101

JONES, J.C.   1338

JONES, JACQUELINE   19196, 19197,
   19198

JONES, JEROME W.   16924

JONES, JOHN M.   2523

JONES, JOHNETTA L.   9617

JONES, JOSEPH   5600

JONES, KATHARINE M.   3829

JONES, LAWRENCE   16925

JONES, LEROI   4905

JONES, MARY K.   5601

JONES, MRS. LAWRENCE C.   19084

JONES, MRS. ROBERT L.   3830

JONES, PAULA   16433

JONES, R.C.   6685

JONES, R.L.   3831

JONES, R.M.   8448

JONES, REGINALD L.   18762, 19199

JONES, RHETT S.   313, 1339, 1340,
   2525, 2527, 2528, 2529, 3473,
   4906, 6687, 6688, 8449, 8450,
   8451

JONES, ROBERT B.   1341

JONES, ROBERT H.   8452

JONES, ROBERT R.   4777

JONES, RUBYE M.   8453

JONES, S.B.   15695

JONES, SAMUEL B.   6689, 6690

JONES, SOLOMON   17736

JONES, STUART M.   1342

JONES, THOMAS H.   18916

JONES, THOMAS J.   3832

JONES, W.D.   5603, 7719

JONES, WILBUR J.   3833, 6691

JONES, WILLIAM A.   3834

JONES, WILLIAM B.   7720

JONES-JACKSON, PATRICIA A.   19360

JORDAN, DAVID W.   8454

JORDAN, ERVIN L.   13680

JORDAN, GLADYS E.W.   20535

JORDAN, JAMES W.   10264

JORDAN, JOHN L.   20917

JORDAN, LAYLON W.   9003

JORDAN, LEWIS G.   10955, 16927

JORDAN, MARJORIE W.   16928

JORDAN, PHILLIP D.   3335

JORDAN, ROBERT L.   16929

JORDAN, TERRY G.   11176, 15502

JORDAN, WEYMOUTH T.   11731, 11732,
     11733, 11734, 11735, 11736,
     11737, 11738, 11739, 11740,
     15698, 20918

JORDAN, WINTHROP   1343

JORDAN, WINTHROP D.   1344, 1345,
     1346, 1347, 1839, 2530, 2531,
     2535, 3644, 6693, 8456, 13020,
     20022

JOSEPHSON, HAROLD   11177

JOSEPHY, ALVIN M.   13980

JOSEY, E.J.   314

JOSHI, MANOJ K.   1348

JOSHUA, HEIDI J.   3836

JOYCE, DAVIS D.   1349, 1350, 1351

JOYCE, DONALD F.   1352

JOYCE, FRANKLIN J.   1353

JOYNER, CHARLES W.   1354, 12981,
     15420, 17737, 18224, 18225,
     18226

JUDAH, CHARLES   21089

JUDD, JACOB   5607

JUDGE, M.T.   16028

JUHNKE, WILLIAM E.   10739

JULES-ROSETTE, BENNETTA   16933

JULIAN, G.W.   1355

JULIAN, GEORGE W.   1356

JULY, ROBERT W.   4909, 4910

JUNIOR, MANUEL D.   315, 7721

JUNKINS, ENDA   13373

JURIS, GAIL   328

JUSTICE, JOHN M.   16934

K.   3837

KAATRUD, PAUL G.   16935

KABERRY, P.M.   5295

KACZOROWSKI, R.J.   2536

KAGAN, ALFRED   517

KAGEL, JOHN   12841

KAHN, JOAN M.   13374

KAHN, M.C.   7723

KAHN, MORTON C.   7724, 7725, 772

KAIN, RICHARD M.   2537, 3839

KAISER, ERNEST   441, 332, 1357,
     1358, 1359, 1360

KAISER, JOHN B.   316

KAKE, I.B.   5609

KALCK, PIERRE   5610

KALIEBE, JOHN E.   20919

KAMMEN, MICHAEL   1361, 10648

KAN, MICHAEL   4911

KANE, ELISHA K.   19361

1748

KAPLAN, SIDNEY 2539, 3840, 8458, 8459, 20025, 20365

KARASCH, MARY 1362, 1363, 4912, 7728, 7729

KARASCH, MARY C. 4913, 5611, 7732

KARCHER, CAROLYN L. 2540, 2541, 2542

KARDINER, ABRAM 18725, 18764

KARENGA, MAULANA R. 1364

KARINEN, ARTHUR E. 8460, 8461

KARON, BERTRAM P. 18765

KARST, FREDERICK A. 9620

KARST, KENNETH L. 8978

KASIRIKA, KAIDI 3841

KASSEL, CHARLES 19202

KATES, DON B. 3842

KATOPES, PETER J. 390

KATZ, BERNARD 1365, 17741

KATZ, JONATHAN 19611

KATZ, NAOMI 5612

KATZ, WALLACE 2543

KATZ, WILLIAM L. 317, 318, 319, 11030, 13981

KATZMAN, DAVID M. 10956, 10957, 10958

KAUFMAN, FREDRICH 17743

KAUFMAN, MARTIN 1366

KAY, FREDERICK G. 5614

KAY, MARVIN L.M. 8464, 12733

KAYE, HARVEY J. 1367, 7733

KEAGY, THOMAS J. 6697

KEALIINOHOMOKU, JOANN W. 18451

KEALING, H.T. 1368, 1369, 4525

KEARNEY, BELLE 15565

KEASBEY, A.Q. 10541

KECKLEY, ELIZABETH 18918

KEDRO, M. JAMES 9459

KEECH, MICHAEL R. 12984

KEEN, BENJAMIN 6469, 6583

KEENE, CALVIN 16938

KEESEE, IRENE 11826

KEHL, JAMES A. 5615

KEIFER, JOSEPH W. 3843

KEITH, HENRY H. 4914

KEITH, NELSON 6698

KEITH, NOVELLA 6698

KELL, PATRICIA A. 12575

KELLAR, HERBERT A. 1370, 15124, 15421

KELLER, ALBERT G. 2544, 7734

KELLER, FRANCES R. 6699

KELLER, MARK 11741

KELLER, RALPH A. 3844, 3845, 9006

KELLER, WILLIAM F. 10880

KELLEY, DONALD B. 9007

KELLY, KEVIN P. 8465, 8466

KELLY, PAUL E. 1031

KELSEY, CARL 3846, 3847, 4915

KELSEY, GEORGE D.   2545

KELSEY, VERA   7735

KELSO, C.   14143

KELSO, WILLIAM M.   8469, 18536,
   18537

KEMMERER, DONALD L.   14314, 14315

KENDALL, JOHN   5616

KENDALL, JOHN S.   12337, 12338,
   12339

KENDALL, LANE C.   12340

KENKEL, FREDERICK P.   3848

KENNEDY, JAMES H.   7736

KENNEDY, JAMES HARRISON   9621

KENNEDY, MELVIN D.   3849, 5617,
   20026

KENNEDY, ROBERT E.   12341

KENNEDY, ROBERT M.   12989

KENNERLY, KAREN   18919

KENNICOTT, PATRICK C.   3850, 9623

KENNY, JOHN A.   15700

KENSCELLA, HAZEL G.   17745

KENT, R.K.   7737, 7738

KERBER, LINDA K.   2546

KERBY, ROBERT L.   20537

KERR, GRAHAM B.   4916

KERR, THOMAS H.   17746

KERRI, JAMES N.   320

KERSEY, HARRY A., JR.   13982

KERSHAW, MARY C.   10882

KESSLER, ARNOLD   7739

KESSLER, S.H.   321

KETCHAM, RALPH L.   13684

KETCHUM, ALTON   19613

KETT, JOSEPH F.   1371

KEYS, LINDA D.   12735

KIDDER, DANIEL P.   7740

KIDDER, FREDERIC   5618

KIELY, TERRENCE F.   1372

KIEMEN, MATHIAS C.   7741

KIERNAN, JAMES P.   7742, 7743

KIES, HARRY B.   3851

KIGER, JOSEPH C.   11742

KILGOUR, FREDERICK G.   15701

KILHAM, ELIZABETH   16939

KILIAN, CRAWFORD   10265

KILLEBREW, J.B.   3852, 3853, 143▊

KILLENS, JOHN O.   1373, 9009,
   20028

KILLINGER, CHARLES L.   5619

KILLION, R.G.   12103

KILLION, RONALD G.   12104, 1822▊

KILMAN, GRADY W.   12342, 12343

KILMER, GEORGE L.   20921

KILPATRICK, A.R.   15702

KILSON, MARION D. DE B.   4917,
   9624, 20030

KILSON, MARTIN   3780

KILSON, MARTIN L. 3855

KIMBALL, GERTRUDE S. 5621, 10736

KIMBALL, PHILIP C. 10070

KIMBALL, WILLIAM J. 20031

KIMMEL, MARGARET 6701

KIMMEL, ROBERT E. 12936

KIMMEL, ROSS M. 8472, 9625

KINARD, MARGARET 13229

KINCAID, LARRY 2547

KING, AMEDA R. 8473

KING, CAROLINE O. 12987

KING, CYRUS B. 9626

KING, CAVID R. 10649

KING, DEARING E. 16941

KING, ETHEL 10650

KING, JAMES F. 322, 5622, 5623, 5624, 7746, 7747, 7748, 7749, 7750, 7751, 9627

KING, JAMES R. 4918, 4919

KING, JOE M. 16942

KING, MAE C. 16436

KING, PEARL H.M. 4026

KING, RICHARD H. 1374

KING, RUTH A. 12345

KING, SAMUEL A. 9011

KINGSBURY, ROBERT C. 323

KINGSBURY, SUSAN M. 324

KINGSTCN, JOHN T. 10883

KINNEMAN, JOHN A. 5625

KINNEY, ESI S. 4920

KINDY, ARTHUR 9012

KINSCELLA, HAZEL G. 17748

KIPLE, KENNETH F. 2548, 2549, 5626, 5627, 6704, 6705, 6708, 6709, 6710, 14975, 14976, 15704

KIPLE, VIRGINIA 2548

KIPLE, VIRGINIA H. 2549, 6710, 14975, 14976, 15704

KIRBY, JACK T. 2550, 2551

KIRBY, JOHN B. 1375

KIRK, JAMES 16207

KIRKE, D.B. 7753

KIRKE, EDMUND 3856

KIRKE, HENRY 7754

KIRKENDALL, RICHARD S. 1376

KIRKLAND, THOMAS J. 12989

KIRKLAND, WINIFRED M. 3857

KIRKPATRICK, ARTHUR R. 11588

KIRKPATRICK, JAMES C. 9013

KIRRANE, JOHN P. 16943

KIRWAN, ALBERT D. 1377

KITCHEL, KELSEY P. 16030

KITCHENS, JOHN W. 5628

KITCHENS, JOSEPH H., JR. 8866

KITTLE, WILLIAM 3859, 3860

KITTLER, GLENN D. 5629

KITTREDGE, FRANK E. 11907

KIVEN, ARLINE R.   10798

KLEBANER, BENJAMIN J.   9014

KLEBER, LOUIS C.   9015

KLEIN, A. NORMAN   1378, 1518, 4922

KLEIN, ADA P.   11590

KLEIN, HERBERT S.   5630, 5631,
   5632, 5634, 5635, 5636, 5637,
   5638, 5639, 5640, 5641, 6711,
   6715, 6717, 6719, 7756, 7757,
   7760, 7762, 8475, 14977, 14980,
   14983, 16944

KLEIN, MARTIN   325, 4924

KLEIN, MARTIN A.   4925, 4926, 4927

KLEIN, MILTON M.   8478, 8479

KLEIN, RACHEL   8480

KLEIN, SELMA L.   12346

KLEINMAN, MAX L.   1380

KLEM, MARY J.   11591

KLEMENT, FRANK L.   20368

KLETZING, HENRY F.   3361

KLINE, BURTON   4928

KLINEBERG, OTTO   2552, 2553

KLINGAMAN, DAVID   13690

KLINGAMAN, DAVID C.   14532, 14819

KLINGBEIL, CHRISTA   16946

KLINGBERG, FRANK J.   326, 1381,
   3862, 5644, 5645, 6721, 6722,
   6723, 6724, 10654, 10740, 12991,
   16948

KLINGMAN, PETER D.   9631, 11908

KLIPPLE, MAY A.   18229

KLOE, DONALD R.   19362

KLOOSTERBOER, WILLEMINA   10071

KLOTMAN, PHYLLIS R.   2554

KLOTTER, JAMES C.   2555, 11333,
   11334, 11374

KMEN, HENRY A.   12347, 17749,
   17750, 17751

KNABENSHUE, S.S.   19614

KNAPLUND, PAUL   6726

KNAPP, CHARLES M.   20369

KNEEBONE, JOHN T.   1382

KNIFFEN, FRED B.   15505

KNIFFIN, HARRY A.   10557

KNIGHT, DERRICK   5646

KNIGHT, EDGAR W.   9632

KNIGHT, FRANKLIN W.   1383, 1384,
   1385, 1386, 2556, 3863, 3864,
   3865, 3866, 6336, 6727, 6728,
   6729, 6731, 6732, 6733, 6734,
   6735, 6736, 9633, 14984

KNIGHT, HANNAH D.   11827

KNIGHT, JULIE   2276

KNIGHT, LUCIAN L.   12105

KNIGHT, MICHAEL   20260

KNIGHT, WESLEY B.   20922

KNORR, KLAUS E.   8484, 8485

KNOTT, MAURICE F.   11335

KNOX, A.J. GRAHAM   2557

KNOX, A.J.G.   6737

KNOX, GEORGE L.   3867

KNOX, GRAHAM 6739

KNOX, THOMAS W. 12577

KNUDSON, JERRY 1387

KNUDSON, JERRY W. 2559

KOBAYASHI, NUINOSUKE 3868

KOCH, FELIX J. 11336, 19615

KOCHER, MARGARET 327

KOCHMAN, THOMAS 19364

KOELLING, HARRY C. 20924

KOFSKY, FRANK 17753

KOGER, A. BRISCOE 20925

KOGER, AZZIE B. 11460, 16953

KOHAK, BARBARA A. 5648

KOLCHIN, PETER 1388, 1389, 1390, 2560, 10072, 19616

KOLCHIN, PETER R. 10073

KOLINSKI, CHARLES J. 7766

KOLLMORGEN, WALTER M. 3869

KOMMERS, DONALD P. 1391

KOPYTOFF, BARBARA K. 6740, 6741, 6742, 6743, 6744, 6745, 6746

KOPYTOFF, IGOR 4929, 4983, 5649

KORBIN, DAVID 10655

KORN, BERTRAM 16954

KORN, BERTRAM W. 16955, 20370

KORNGOLD, RALPH 6747, 20037

KORT, WESLEY A. 1392

KOTLIKOFF, LAURENCE J. 10074, 12348, 12349, 14614

KOVAL, B.I. 7767

KOVEL, JOEL 2561

KOYER, KENNETH 9635

KRADITOR, AILEEN S. 1393, 1394

KRAMER, EDWARD M. 20539

KRAMER, ELIZABETH K. 9018

KRAMER, VICTOR A. 1395, 1396

KRAPP, GEORGE P. 19365

KRASH, RONALD 328

KRAUS, MICHAEL 8486, 10075

KREBS, A. 3870

KREBS, SYLVIA H. 20926

KREHBIEL, HENRY E. 17754, 17755

KREMER, GARY R. 9636, 9637, 11580

KRESTENSEN, K. 329

KRIEGEL, LEONARD 2562

KRIEGER, LEONARD 1397

KRONUS, SIDNEY 2870

KRUG, MARK 2563

KRUG, MARK M. 10076

KRUIJER, G.J. 6748

KUBLER, GEORGE 7768

KUETHE, ALLAN J. 7769

KUGLER, RUBEN F. 1398, 1399

KUHNS, FREDERICK I. 10837

KUHR, MANUEL I. 9019

KULIKOFF, ALLAN 1400, 8238, 8487, 8489, 11461, 11462, 11465

KULIKOFF, ALLAN L.   8490

KULL, IRVING S.   10542, 10543, 16956

KUMATZ, TAD   330

KUNA, RALPH R.   15711, 15712

KUNKEL, PAUL A.   9020

KUNKEL, PETER   11831

KUNREUTHER, HOWARD   14565

KUNST, J.   7770

KUPER, ADAM   6749

KUPER, T.F.   9021

KURATH, GERTRUDE P.   331, 18456, 18458, 18459

KURILEC, ROBERT E.   20927

KURODA, TADAHISA   9022

KURTZ, MICHAEL J.   10077

KUSER, ROBERT C.   10544

KUTLER, STANLEY   9023

KUYK, BETTY M.   16210

KUZNESOF, ELIZABETH A.   14321

LA ROCHE, J.H.   15336

LABBE, DOLORES E.   12353

LABINJOH, JUSTIN   16211

LABCON, BRANDT   3871

LABOUISSE, ALICE M.   3872

LABOURET, H.   4931

LACERTE, ROBERT K.   6750

LACHANCE, PAUL F.   5650

LACHIOTTE, ALBERTA M.   12993

LACK, PAUL   15937

LACK, PAUL D.   3873, 15938

LACY, DAN   3874

LACY, JAMES M.   2564

LACY, VIRGINIA J.   15713

LADER, LAWRENCE   3875

LADNER, JOYCE   16438

LADNER, JOYCE A.   16439, 16440

LAFARGE, JOHN   1401, 3876, 11468, 16957

LAGUERRE, MICHAEL   6751

LAGUERRE, MICHEL   6752, 6753, 67

LAGUERRE, MICHEL S.   18233

LAIDLEY, W.S.   20928

LAING, JAMES T.   13694

LAIRD, MARSHALL   4932

LAKE, MARY D.   15860

LALE, MAX S.   13377

LAMAR, CHARLES A.L.   5651

LAMB, D.P.   5652, 5653, 5654

LAMB, ROBERT B.   14323

LAMMERMEIER, PAUL J.   16212

LAMPLUGH, GEORGE R.   2565

LAMUR, HUMPHREY E.   7772

LANCASTER, C.M.   4933

LAND, AUBREY C.   8493, 8494, 11, 14324, 14325

LANDAU, NOAH 3877

LANDECK, BEATRICE 4934

LANDER, ERNEST M. 14741

LANDER, ERNEST M., JR. 12995, 14743

LANDES, RUTH 7774, 7775, 7776

LANDESS, TOM 12101

LANDON, FRED 332, 1402, 2566, 9024, 9638, 9639, 10267, 10268, 10269, 14327, 19618, 19619, 19620, 19621, 19622, 19623, 19624, 19625, 19626, 19627, 19628, 19629, 19630, 19631, 19632, 19633, 19634, 19635

LANDRY, HARRAL E. 5655

LANE, ANN J. 1404, 20371

LANE, CARL A. 6756

LANE, ISAAC 18921

LANE, JAMES W. 4935

LANG, JAMES 7777

LANG, JOHN 4936

LANG, MEREDITH 9025

LANGDON, WILLIAM C. 3878

LANGDON-DAVIES, JOHN 5657

LANGE, F.W. 6577

LANGE, FREDERICK W. 6579, 18530, 18539

LANGHORNE, ELIZABETH 3879

LANGHORNE, ORRA 9640, 13696, 19088

LANGLEY, HAROLD D. 14744

LANGLEY, LESTER D. 6758

LANGRIDGE, LELAND 15715

LANGSTON, JOHN M. 18922

LANNING, JOHN T. 15716

LANNOY, CHARLES DE 6759

LANTERNARI, VITTORIO 6760

LANTZ, HERMAN 15717

LANTZ, HERMAN R. 16216

LAPOMARDA, VINCENT A. 2567

LAPP, RUDOLPH 11081

LAPP, RUDOLPH M. 9641, 11031, 11082, 11083, 11085, 19636

LAPRADE, WILLIAM T. 333, 334, 9643, 11238

LAPSANSKY, EMMA J. 9644

LARA, ORJNO D. 5658, 19638

LARISON, CORNELIUS W. 16443

LARRABEE, EDWARD M. 18540

LARRIE, REGINALD 10959

LARSEN, CLARK S. 18365

LARSEN, JENS PETER M. 6761

LARSON, C.S. 12088

LASCELLES, EDWARD C.P. 5659

LASCH, CHRISTOPHER 1102

LASLETT, PETER 1407, 1408, 16218

LATANE, JOHN H. 13698

LATHAM, A.J.H. 5663, 5664

LATHAM, FRANK B. 9027

LATHAM, JOYCE E. 3990

LATHROP, BARNES F.   12355, 13378,
   20540, 20541

LATIMER, JAMES   6762, 6764, 6765,
   6766, 19204

LATNER, RICHARD B.   1409

LATROBE, BENJAMIN H.   15939

LATTA, MORGAN L.   12736

LATTIMER, CATHERINE   16444

LAUBENSTEIN, PAUL F.   17757

LAUBER, ALMON W.   8495, 8496

LAUNAY, ROBERT   4937

LAUNITZ-SCHURER, LEOPOLD S., JR.
   10656

LAURENCE, K.O.   6767, 6768

LAURENCE, STEPHEN M.   6769

LAW, ROBIN   4938, 4939, 4940

LAWAETZ, EVA   9646

LAWRENCE, GRACE M.   12356

LAWRENCE, HAROLD G.   4941

LAWRENCE, JACOB   16445

LAWRENCE, JAMES B.   8497

LAWRENCE, KEN   1411, 3880

LAWS, C.A.   3881

LAWS, J. BRADFORD   12357

LAWSON, DENNIS T.   12997

LAWSON, ELIZABETH   335, 20042

LAWSON, HAROLD L.   13699

LAWSON, HERBERT H.   13700

LAWSON, JOHN H.   5667

LAWSON, MARY J.   10270

LAWTON, SAMUEL M.   16969

LAYNE, ANTHONY   2568, 6772

LAYNG, ANTHONY   320, 1412

LE RIVEREND BRUSONE, JULIO   6773

LE RIVEREND, JULIO   6774

LEA, HENRY C.   7780

LEAB, DANIEL J.   2569

LEACH, EDMUND   2570

LEACOCK, RUTH   18234

LEACOCK, SETH   18234

LEACOCK, STEPHEN   10078

LEAMING, HUGO P.   20262

LEARD, ROBERT B.   6775

LEASK, J. MACKENZIE   19640

LEATH, G.   336

LEAVENS, F. PATRICK   20930

LEBEDUN, JEAN   3882

LEBERGOTT, STANLEY   1413

LEBRETON, MARIETTA M.   12358

LECKIE, J.D.   4942

LEDBETTER, BARBARA A.   13379

LEDBETTER, BILLY D.   2571, 2572,
   13381

LEDOUX, LOUIS H.   20931

LEDYARD, ERWIN   3883

LEE, AMY   17758

LEE, ANNE S.   9647

LEE, B.F., JR. 19642

LEE, BILL R. 10079

LEE, CARLETON L. 1414

LEE, CHAN 12359

LEE, ELI 2573

LEE, EVERETT S. 9647

LEE, FLORENCE W. 13702, 13703

LEE, FRANCIS B. 10546

LEE, FRANK F. 10394

LEE, GEORGE R. 10080

LEE, JULIET A. 10944

LEE, LAWRENCE 8499

LEE, R. ALTON 9028, 11032

LEE, ROBERT C. 17759

LEE, ROSA F. 18924

LEE, RUTH A. 12999

LEE, SUSAN P. 14329

LEE, THOMAS G. 9029

LEE, THOMAS H. 2574

LEE, ULYSSES 18709

LEE, WALLACE 2575

LEE, WILLIAM M. 18925

LEFF, NATHANIEL H. 7781

LEFFALL, DOLORES C. 337, 338

LEFKOWITZ, ABRAHAM 10081

LEFLER, HUGH T. 2576, 4943, 12739

LEGAN, MARSHALL S. 15719

LEGGETT, JOHN 1415

LEHMANN, THEO 17760

LEIGH, FRANCES B. 12108

LEIGH, JAMES W. 3884

LEIMAN, M.M. 1416

LEIRIS, MICHEL 4944

LEITMAN, SPENCER 7782

LEITMAN, SPENCER L. 7783, 7784

LEKIS, LISA 6776

LEMMER, GEORGE F. 11593

LEMMON, ALFRED E. 17762

LEMOINE, L.M. 10271

LEMON, JOHN W. 3885, 3886

LEMONS, J. STANLEY 2577, 9648

LEMPEL, LEONARD R. 2578

LENNOX, MARY 3887

LENOIR, J.D. 7785

LENOIR, JOHN D. 7786

LEON, JULIO ANTONIO 18236

LEONARD, KATHERINE E. 339

LEONARD, PHILIP 2579

LEPAGE, P.G. 4945

LEPAGE, ROBERT B. 6777

LERCH, KEITH W. 3888

LERNER, EUGENE 14331

LERNER, GERDA 340

LERNER, LAWRENCE 2580

LESLIE, WILLIAM R.   9030, 9031,
   9032, 9033

LESTER, JULIUS   18926

LETCHER, J.H.   15720

LETHEM, GORDON J.   5668

LEVEEN, F. PHILLIP   5669, 5670,
   5671, 5672

LEVENE, H.H.   10879

LEVENTHAL, HERBERT   20043

LEVERING, WILLIAM J.   19644

LEVESQUE, GEORGE A.   2581, 9651,
   9652

LEVI, KATE E.   3890

LEVIN, DAVID   344

LEVIN, HARRY   2582

LEVINE, EDWIN A.   8239

LEVINE, LAWRENCE W.   345, 1839,
   4946, 17764, 13239

LEVINE, ROBERT M.   346, 347, 1418,
   4947, 5673, 16556, 20044, 20045

LEVITCH, JOEL A.   12805

LEVO, JOHN E.   10082

LEVSTIK, FRANK   2583

LEVSTIK, FRANK R.   9653, 20935,
   20936, 20937

LEVY, CLAUDE   6779, 6780, 6781

LEVY, DAVID W.   2584

LEVY, LEONARD W.   2585, 19645,
   19646

LEVY, RONALD   3891

LEWALLEN, KENNETH A.   1419, 11179

LEWIN, OLIVE   6782

LEWINSON, EDWIN R.   9654

LEWIS, ALONZO N.   20046

LEWIS, BERNARD   4948

LEWIS, ELLISTINE P.   348

LEWIS, ELSIE M.   11828

LEWIS, ERWIN   4676

LEWIS, FRANK   6783

LEWIS, G. MALCOLM   19647

LEWIS, GEORGE   12110

LEWIS, GORDON K.   3892, 6784, 678
   6786

LEWIS, J.H.   15723

LEWIS, JAMES K.   16973, 19649,
   19650, 19651

LEWIS, JOSEPH V.   18929

LEWIS, KENNETH E.   15506

LEWIS, M.G.   6787

LEWIS, MARY   11337

LEWIS, MARY A.   1420

LEWIS, NEIL M.   12360

LEWIS, ROBERT S., JR.   8500

LEWIS, ROBERT V.   3893

LEWIS, RONALD L.   217, 3894, 114
   11474, 11476, 13704, 13708,
   14747, 14751, 14752, 14771

LEWIS, ROSCOE   16220

LEWIS, ROSCOE E.   279, 19094

LEWIS, RUPERT   1421

LEWIS, SAMELLA S. 18643

LEWIS, THEODORE H. 3745

LEWIS, VIRGIL A. 20938

LEWIS, W.A. 15724

LEWISOHN, FLORENCE 18240

LEYBURN, JAMES G. 6788

LI, C.C. 2404

LIBRARY COMPANY OF PHILADELPHIA
  349

LICHTMAN, ALAN J. 1422

LICHTVELD, URSY M. 18378

LIDE, ROBERT 3895

LIEBER, TODD M. 1423

LIEBERMAN, HAROLD 3896

LIEBERMAN, LESLIE 15393

LIEBERMAN, LESLIE S. 15405

LIEBMAN, ARTHUR 18930

LIEBMAN, CAROL S. 1424

LIEDEL, DONALD E. 1425, 2586

LIGGIO, LEONARD P. 2587

LIGHTNER, O.C. 3897

LINAKER, R. HYDE 6789

LINCOLN, C. ERIC 284, 3898, 12740
  16975, 16977, 20047

LINCOLN, CHARLES E. 16978

LINCOLN, LEVI 9034

LINDEN, FABIAN 1426, 1427

LINDLEY, CHARLES A. 6790

LINDLEY, HARLOW 10838

LINDLEY, LENORA E. 11338

LINDO, ABRAHAM 6791

LINDO, LOCKSLEY 6792

LINDSAY, ARNETT G. 5674, 5675,
  9656

LINDSAY, CRAWFORD B. 350

LINDSEY, DAVID 20373

LINDSTROM, DIANE L. 14333

LINDUP, VALERIE A. 3899

LINES, STILES B. 16979

LINN, WILLIAM A. 10547

LINS DO REGO, JOSE 7789

LIPSCOMB, ATALANTA B. 8502, 8503

LIPSCOMB, PATRICK 1428

LIPSCOMB, PATRICK C. 5676, 6793

LISENBY, JULIE A. 9657

LIST, GEORGE 17768

LISTON, ROBERT A. 3900

LITTLE, JOHN B. 11746

LITTLE, JOYCE B. 9035

LITTLE, KENNETH 6794

LITTLEFIELD, DANIEL C. 8505

LITTLEFIELD, DANIEL F., JR. 9658,
  13985, 13986, 13987, 13988,
  13989

LITTLEFIELD, MARY ANN 9658

LITWACK, LEON F. 9659, 9661, 9662,
  10086, 10352, 10353, 14873

LIVERMORE, MARY A.   11339, 20375

LIVESAY, HAROLD   11201

LIVESAY, HAROLD C.   11202

LIVINGOOD, JAMES W.   13258

LLOYD, A.L.   17769

LLOYD, ARTHUR Y.   3901, 3902

LLOYD, CHRISTOPHER   5677

LLOYD, R.G.   3241

LOBB, JOHN   18931

LOBER, JERE W.   10550

LOCKE, ALAIN L.   4949, 17770,
   17771, 18644, 18645, 18646,
   18647

LOCKE, HARVEY J.   16113

LOCKE, MARY S.   3903

LOCKEY, JOSEPH B.   11909

LOCKHART, JAMES   7790, 7791

LOCKHART, W.E.   9037

LOCKLEY, FRED   351, 9038

LODWICK, MICHAEL   1430

LOESER, CORNELIUS   8106

LOEWALD, KLAUS G.   8506

LOEWENBERG, BERT J.   352

LOEWENBERG, PETER   2590

LOFTIN, JOSEPH E., JR.   5678

LOFTON, CHARLES R.   9039

LOFTON, JOHN   3904, 13003, 13004

LOFTON, JOHN M.   13005

LUFTON, JOHN M., JR.   8507, 13000

LOFTON, WILLISTON H.   20941

LOGAN, FRENISE A.   1431, 4950

LOGAN, GWENDOLYN E.   8508

LOGAN, JOHN A.   3905, 8242

LOGAN, JOSEPHINE M.   3906

LOGAN, R. LEROY   16982

LOGAN, RAYFORD   19792

LOGAN, RAYFORD W.   1432, 1433,
   3269, 3907, 3908, 3909, 6796,
   9040, 11033, 13711, 13712,
   20053

LOGERFO, JAMES W.   5679

LOGGINS, VERNON   1434

LOGSDON, JOSEPH   12361

LOKEN, GREGORY A.   13713

LOKKE, CARL L.   353, 5680, 6798

LOMAX, ALAN   1435, 4952, 4953,
   4954, 17443, 17774, 17775

LOMAX, ELIZABETH   18935

LOMAX, JOHN A.   17777, 17778,
   17779

LOMBARD, MILDRED E.   1436

LOMBARDI, JOHN V.   354, 1437, 779
   7794, 7795, 7796, 16557

LONG, ANTON V.   6799

LONG, CHARLES H.   4955, 16983,
   16984

LONG, CLARAMAE B.   10657

LONG, DURWARD   16986

LONG, ELLEN C.   11910

LONG, NORMAN G.   16987

LONG, RICHARD A.   1438, 6800,
    18241, 19369

LONGSWORTH, POLLY I.   9665

LONGTON, WILLIAM H.   2591, 3910

LONN, ELLA   20376

LOONEY, LOUISA P.   3911

LOPEZ, AMY K.   6801

LORCH, ROBERT S.   9041

LORD, DONALD C.   355, 356

LORD, FRANCIS A.   20942

LORD, KATHRYN L.   10087

LORIA, A.   14334

LORIMER, DOUGLAS A.   2592

LORIMER, JOYCE   5681

LORING, EDUARD N.   16988

LORING, GEORGE B.   10459

LORNELL, CHRISTOPHER   88

LORNELL, KIP   357

LOTT, AUDREY P.   11911

LOUIE, GLORIA J.   16286

LOVE, EDGAR F.   7798, 7799, 7800

LOVE, EMANUEL K.   16989

LOVE, NAT   18936

LOVE, ROBERT W., JR.   5682

LOVEJOY, DAVID S.   8509

LOVEJOY, PAUL E.   4926, 4957, 5683,
    5684

LOVELAND, ANNE C.   3912, 10088,
    16991

LOVELL, JOHN JR.   17782, 17783,
    17784

LOVETT, BOBBY L.   13232, 13233,
    20943, 20946

LOVETT, HOWARD M.   3913

LOVETT, OTTO A.   9043

LOW, ALFRED M.   3914

LOW, W. AUGUSTUS   359

LOW, W.A.   20947, 20948, 20949

LOWE, RICHARD   13384

LOWE, RICHARD G.   13319, 13320,
    14335

LOWELL, JAMES R.   3915

LOWENTHAL, DAVID   2593, 2594, 2595,
    6322, 6802, 6805, 6806, 6807,
    14991

LOWERY, CHARLES D.   13714

LOWERY, CHARLINE E.   8510

LOWERY, IRVING E.   13007

LOWERY, RALPH J.   5686

LOWERY, WOODBURY   3916

LOWMAN, DAVID ST. CLAIR   10089

LOWRIE, SAMUEL H.   360

LOWRY, RALPH J.   8511

LOWRY, ROBERT   14753

LUBBOCK, BASIL   5687

LUCAS, FREDERICK A.   19654

LUCAS, JOHN S.   17785

LUCIE, PATRICIA 9044

LUCIE, PATRICIA A. 20950

LUCKINGHAM, BRAD 11595

LUCKOCK, BENJAMIN 6809

LUDLOW, FIZHUGH 19655

LUDLOW, HELEN 18937

LUDLOW, HELEN W. 3917, 12112,
17505

LUDMERER, KENNETH M. 2596

LUDWIG, C. 5688

LUEDTKE, JOANNE H. 17786

LUGAR, CATHERINE 7804

LUGARD, LORD 3918

LUKAS, JOHN H. 11086

LUKE, JOSEPHINE 12362

LUMB, JOHN F. 8512

LUMPKIN, KATHARINE D. 12113

LUMPKIN, KATHERINE D. 19656

LUMPKINS, JOSEPHINE 13385

LUNN, ARNOLD H.M. 5689

LUPER, ALBERT T. 17787

LURAGHI, RAIMONDO 3919, 14336,
14337, 14338

LUTTRELL, ANTHONY 5690

LUTZ, CHRISTOPHER H. 14992

LUX, WILLIAM 5691, 6810, 6811,
20054

LYDA, CHESTER H. 8513

LYDA, JOHN W. 10912

LYDON, JAMES G. 5693, 10659

LYMAN, JANE L. 3920

LYMAN, STANFORD M. 17450

LYNCH, HOLLIS R. 3921, 3922, 495

LYNCH, JOHN 7806

LYNCH, JOHN R. 1440, 1441

LYND, STAUGHTON 1442, 1443, 3923
3924, 3925, 8514

LYON, ANNIE L.K. 14339

LYON, EUGENE 11912

LYONS, ADELAIDE A. 16993

LYONS, JOHN F. 2597

LYONS, THOMAS T. 3926

LYTHGOE, DENNIS L. 11163, 11164,
11165

MABBUTT, FRED R. 1444

MABE, PHILIP M. 2598

MABEE, CARLETON 3927, 9669

MABON, ARTHUR F. 10660

MACARTHUR, WILLIAM J. 13008

MACAULAY, THOMAS B. 6812

MACAULAY, ZACHARY 6813

MACCORMACK, CAROL P. 5694

MACCRIMMON, JOHN R. 2599

MACDONALD, JOHN S. 6814

MACDONALD, LEATRICE D. 6814

MACDONALD, WILLIAM 362

MACEACHEREN, ELAINE 9045

MACINNES, C.M. 5695, 5696, 5697

MACINNES, CHARLES M. 5698

MACK, DELORES 1445

MACKENZIE, K. 5699

MACKENZIE-GRIEVE, AVERIL 5700, 5701

MACKINLAY, PETER W. 2600

MACKINTOSH, BARRY 13716

MACLACHLAN, COLIN M. 7808, 7809

MACLEAN, J.R. 6815

MACLEOD, BRUCE 17788

MACLEOD, BRUCE A. 17789, 17790

MACLEOD, D. 2601

MACLEOD, DUNCAN 1446, 14340

MACLEOD, DUNCAN J. 1447, 1448, 2602, 2603

MACLEOD, MURDO J. 7811

MACLEOD, W.C. 18242

MACLEOD, WILLIAM C. 3928, 3929, 3930

MACMASTER, RICHARD K. 5703, 5704, 8519, 8520, 9670, 9671

MACMUNN, GEORGE F. 3931

MACNAUL, WILLARD C. 10839

MACON, JOHN A. 17791

MACRAE, DAVID 3932

MACROBERT, MARION C. 19095

MACTAVISH, NEWTON 3933

MADARIAGA, SALVADOR DE 7813

MADDEN, RICHARD R. 6817

MADDEX, JACK P. 16994, 16995

MADDEX, JACK P., JR. 2604, 13718, 16996

MADDOX, JOLENE 13387

MADRON, THOMAS W. 2605

MAEHLING, JOHN J. 9047

MAGALHAES, BASILIO DE 7814

MAGDOL, EDWARD 3934, 15242

MAGEE, DAVID F. 19657

MAGILL, DENNIS W. 8323, 10236

MAGILL, EDWARD H. 19658

MAGINNES, DAVID R. 19659

MAGNAGHI, RUSSELL M. 11596

MAGOFFIN, DOROTHY S. 12114

MAGOWAN, R. 3935

MAGRUDER, W.W. 9048

MAGUBANE, BERNARD 2606

MAGUIRE, EDWARD J. 20953

MAHAJANI, USHA 1449

MAHAN, BRUCE E. 18938

MAHER, J. 3937

MAHON, JOHN K. 13996

MAIDENBERG, H.J. 4959

MAIN, B.J. 14341

MAIN, ED M. 20954

MAIN, GLORIA L. 363, 8521

MAIN, JACKSON T. 8522, 13719, 13720

MAINGOT, ANTHONY P.   1450, 2607

MAIR, LUCILLE M.   6818, 6819

MAJOR, CLARENCE   18244

MAJOR, GERRI   3938

MALBERG, EDWARD I.   3939

MALCOLM X.   3940

MALDEN, K.S.   16998

MALEHORN, W.M.   9049

MALIN, JAMES C.   11035

MALINO, SARAH   16224

MALLAM, WILLIAM D.   3941

MALLARD, ANNIE H.   16999

MALLARD, ROBERT Q.   3942, 15243

MALLORY, WILLIAM   12363

MALLOY, THOMAS A.   8523

MALONE, DUMAS   1451, 13721

MALONE, HENRY T.   12116, 13998

MALONE, THOMAS H.   17792

MALSCH, S.   2043

MALVIN, JOHN   9672

MAN, ALBON P., JR.   9673

MANAKEE, HAROLD R.   11480

MANCHESTER, ALAN K.   5705, 7817

MANDEL, BERNARD   2608, 3944, 3945, 14343

MANDELBAUM, SEYMOUR   1413

MANDELLER, PHILIP   8972

MANDERSON-JONES, MARLENE   6821

MANDEVILLE, ERNEST W.   10553

MANDLE, JAY R.   1452, 1453, 14344, 14345

MANESS, LONNIE E.   11340

MANGIONE, JERRE   365

MANGUM, CHARLES S.   9051

MANIGAT, LESLIE F.   6822

MANN, CHARLES W.   19661

MANN, CORAMAE R.   2609

MANN, KENNETH E.   19662

MANN, PEGGY   10554

MANNERS, ROBERT A.   7163

MANNING, EDWARD   5706

MANNING, PATRICK   4960, 4961, 49..

MANNIX, DANIEL   5710, 5711

MANNIX, DANIEL P.   5712, 5713

MANSFIELD, STEPHEN S.   3946

MANYONI, JOSEPH   6611

MAPP, EDWARD   2610

MAQUET, JAQUES   4963

MARABLE, MANNING   1454, 18767, 20056

MARABLE, W. MANNING   5714

MARAMBAUD, PIERRE   13723

MARCHAIRT, ALEXANDER N.D.   7818

MARCILIO, MARIA L.   14346

MARGOLIES, EDWARD   367, 368

MARINA, WILLIAM   4561

MARION, ERNESTINE A. 12118

MARK, PETER 2611

MARKETTI, J. 3947

MARKLEY, RICHARD 3948

MARKMAN, SIDNEY D. 369

MARKOE, WILLIAM M. 17001, 17002,
17003

MARKS, BAYLY E. 11481

MARKS, MORTON 17793

MARMOR, THEODORE R. 1456

MARQUES RODILES, IGNACIO 5716

MARR, JOHN C. 13388

MARR, P. 17794

MARR, WARREN 20057

MARRARC, HOWARD R. 8525

MARRINER, SHEILA 5568

MARRS, ELIJAH P. 18941

MARS, JAMES 10396

MARS, JEAN-PRICE 4965

MARSH, HENRY 3949

MARSH, J.B.T. 17795

MARSH, J.O. 15132

MARSH, RICHARD D. 3950

MARSH, VIVIAN C.O. 18245

MARSHALL, BERNARD 6825, 6826

MARSHALL, BERNARD A. 6827, 6828

MARSHALL, CHARLES 9053

MARSHALL, ELMER G. 13339

MARSHALL, MARY L. 15726, 15727,
15728

MARSHALL, PETER 10093

MARSHALL, T.M. 3134

MARSHALL, THEODORA B. 15729

MARSHALL, WOODVILLE K. 1457, 6829

MARSZALEK, JOHN F. 13724, 13725,
20551

MARSZALEK, JOHN F., JR. 13010,
20957

MARTIN, ASA E. 11342, 11343

MARTIN, BERNARD 5717

MARTIN, BERT E. 20060

MARTIN, CHRISTOPHER 20061

MARTIN, DALE L. 18484, 18485

MARTIN, DELLITA L. 4966

MARTIN, DOUGLAS D. 3951

MARTIN, ELMER P. 16226

MARTIN, EVELINE 5718, 5719

MARTIN, EVELINE C. 5720, 5721

MARTIN, GEO 10272

MARTIN, GRAHAM E. 19663

MARTIN, IDA M. 9054

MARTIN, JERRYE L.B. 1458

MARTIN, JOANNEY M. 16226

MARTIN, JOHN E. 1459

MARTIN, JOHN H. 17004

MARTIN, JOHN S. 18943

MARTIN, JOSEPHINE W. 13011

1765

MARTIN, PERCY A. 7821

MARTIN, PHYLLIS M. 5722, 5723

MARTIN, R.F. 6830

MARTIN, SIDNEY W. 11914, 12119

MARTIN, THOMAS P. 13012

MARTIN, TONY 2612, 6832

MARTIN, WALDO E. 3952

MARTINEZ-ALIER, VERENA 2613

MARTINS, ROBERTO B. 7822

MARTINSON, FLOYD M. 16228

MARTYN, BYRON C. 2614

MARVIN, ABIJAH P. 9056

MARX, GARY T. 17005

MASA, JORGE O. 18944

MASFERRER, MARIANNE 6834

MASLOWSKI, PETER 13013, 13235, 13236

MASON, ETHEL U. 20961

MASON, GEORGE 10799

MASON, GEORGE C. 8527, 10800

MASON, ISAAC 18945

MASON, JANIE C. 11597

MASON, M.C.B. 3953

MASON, MARY L. 3954

MASON, MICHAEL 4967

MASON, PHILIP 2615

MASON, SARA E. 11747

MASON, VROMAN 9057

MASSEY, MARY E. 20552

MASTERSON, DANIEL M. 7399

MASTROGIOVANNI, FRANCIS J. 9675

MASUOKA, J. 11297

MATAS, RUDOLPH 15730

MATHER, FREDERIC G. 10661

MATHEUS, JOHN F. 2616

MATHEWS, DONALD G. 1462, 3955, 17006, 17007, 17008, 17009, 17010, 17011, 17013

MATHEWS, FLEMING W. 11240

MATHEWS, MARCIA M. 3956

MATHEWS, MITFORD M. 19372

MATHEWS, THOMAS 1463

MATHEWS, THOMAS G. 1464, 2617, 7823

MATHEWS, WILLIAM 3957

MATHEWSON, R. DUNCAN 6836, 6837, 6838, 6839

MATHIAS, ARTHUR 1465

MATHIAS, FRANK F. 9058, 10094, 11344

MATHIESON, W.L. 6840

MATHIESON, WILLIAM L. 5726, 684 6842, 6844

MATHIS, MARY 11749

MATHIS, RAY 1466, 1467, 11748, 11749

MATHURIN, LUCILLE 6845, 6846, 6847, 6848

MATISON, SUMNER E. 9059

MATLACK, JAMES 18946

MATLOCK, GENE D. 3958

MATSON, DAN 20963

MATSON, R. LYNN 16458

MATTHEWS, ALBERT 8528, 10356, 10463, 13727

MATTHEWS, BASIL 6849

MATTHEWS, CHRISTIAN N. 6850

MATTHEWS, ESSIE C. 12743

MATTHEWS, MIRIAM 370

MATTHEWS, PAUL A. 13237

MATTHEWSON, TIMOTHY M. 6851, 6852

MAULTSBY, PORTIA K. 371, 1468, 9676, 17797, 17798, 17799

MAUNCY, ALBERT C. 15508

MAURER, OSCAR 2618

MAXIMILIAN, I. 7824

MAXWELL, JOHN F. 17015

MAXWELL, KENNETH R. 7825

MAY, ALMA 9677

MAY, EARL C. 14756

MAY, HENRY F. 3959

MAY, J. THOMAS 20964, 20965, 20966, 20967

MAY, JUDE T. 15731

MAY, PHILIP S. 15133

MAY, ROBERT E. 3960, 6853, 6854, 12581

MAY, SAMUEL J. 3963

MAYCOCK, WILLOUGHBY 4117

MAYER, JEAN 15429

MAYER, VINCENT 7826

MAYER, VINCENT V. 7827

MAYER, VINCENT V., JR. 7828

MAYER, WILLIAM 7829

MAYERS, JULIUS 17016

MAYES, SHARON S. 3964

MAYLE, BESSIE H. 17802

MAYO, A.C. 3965

MAYO, A.D. 3966

MAYO, AMORY D. 3967

MAYO, MARION J. 2619

MAYOCK, THOMAS J. 1469

MAYS, BENJAMIN E. 17017, 17018

MAYS, J.T. 15732

MAZRUI, ALI A. 4968

MAZYCK, WALTER H. 8529

MAZZARA, RICHARD A. 1470

MBITI, JOHN S. 4969, 4970, 17019

MCADAMS, NETTIE F. 17803

MCALISTER, L.N. 7830

MCARTHUR, SCOTT 11145

MCBETH, MICHAEL C. 7831

MCBRIDE, DAVID 373

MCBRIDE, JOHN M., JR. 18246

MCCAGUE, JAMES 20379

MCCAIN, JAMES R. 12120

MCCAIN, WILLIAM D. 12560, 12582

MCCALL, DANIEL F. 4971

MCCALL, DAVID 4972

MCCALL, EMMANUEL L. 17293

MCCALL, MARIE E. 20969

MCCANTS, DOROTHEA O. 12365

MCCANTS, E.C. 13014

MCCARDELL, JOHN 3969

MCCARROLL, JESSE C. 17020

MCCARRON, ANNA T. 9678

MCCARTHY, JOHN R. 3970

MCCARTHY, MICHAEL J. 4973

MCCARTHY, TERENCE 14349

MCCAULEY, DONALD 11482

MCCAULEY, DONALD J. 11483

MCCLELLAND, E.M. 3971

MCCLELLAND, PETER D. 1471

MCCLENDON, R. EARL 9062

MCCLOUD, VELMA 18247

MCCLOY, SHELBY T. 6855

MCCLUNG, DENNIS V. 2793

MCCLURE, AROZENA L. 18248

MCCLURE, STANLEY W. 19664

MCCLURG, ALEXANDER C. 1472

MCCOLLEY, ROBERT 1473, 13729, 13730, 20064

MCCOLLEY, ROBERT M. 13731

MCCOMB, DAVID G. 13390

MCCONNELL, JOHN P. 10099

MCCONNELL, ROLAND C. 5728, 8530, 10100, 11915, 12368, 20970

MCCORMAC, EUGENE I. 11484

MCCORMACK, EDWARD M. 13238

MCCORMICK, RICHARD P. 10556

MCCORMICK, V. 16459

MCCOWEN, GEORGE S., JR. 8531

MCCOY, A.D. 3972

MCCOY, AMBROSE 15733

MCCOY, JAMES A. 6856

MCCRADY, EDWARD 8532, 8533, 8534

MCCRADY, EDWARD JR. 3973

MCCRARY, JAMES P. 20972

MCCRARY, PEYTON 12369

MCCRARY, ROYCE C. 12121

MCCRAY, S.J. 3974

MCCULLOCH, SAMUEL C. 1474

MCCULLOUGH, NORMAN V. 3975

MCCUSKER, JOHN J. 14352

MCDANIEL, GEORGE W. 11485

MCDAVID, RAVEN I., JR. 19373, 19374

MCDAVID, VIRGINIA G. 19374

MCDERMOTT, JOHN F. 10840, 10841

MCDONALD, DAVID R. 374

MCDONALD, EARL E. 10913, 10914

MCDONALD, FORREST 14064

MCDONALD, JAMES J. 13732

MCDONALD, LAWRENCE H. 13391

MCDONALD, RODERICK 12370

MCDONALD, RODERICK A. 1475, 1476

MCDONOUGH, JOHN 375

MCDOUGALD, LOIS 10915

MCDOUGALL, MARIAN G. 9063, 9064

MCDOUGALL, MARION G. 19667

MCDOUGLE, IVAN E. 11345, 11346, 11347

MCDOWELL, A.W. 15734

MCDOWELL, GEORGE T. 2620

MCDOWELL, TREMAINE 19375, 19376

MCELROY, BARCLAY M. 2621

MCFARLANE, A. 5730

MCFARLANE, SUZANNE S. 15510

MCFAUL, JOHN M. 3977, 9679

MCFEELY, WILLIAM S. 20975, 20976

MCGANN, C. STEVEN 1931

MCGEACHY, KAHERINE A. 9065

MCGEE, DANIEL B. 17021

MCGEE, HENRY W. 16460

MCGEE, LEO 19212

MCGETTIGAN, JAMES W. 11598

MCGETTIGAN, JAMES W., JR. 11599

MCGILL, ALEXANDER T. 17022

MCGILL, WILLIAM J. 1477

MCGIMSEY, RICHARD 9066

MCGINTY, GARNIE W. 3978

MCGLOTTEN, MILDRED L. 9680

MCGOVERN, ANN 16461

MCGOWAN, EMMA W. 9681

MCGOWAN, JAMES T. 12372, 12373

MCGOWAN, RAYMOND A. 6859

MCGRATH, ROSEMARIE C. 5731

MCGREGOR, PEDRO 7834, 17024

MCGROATY, WILLIAM B. 10101

MCGUE, D.B. 3979

MCGUINN, HENRY J. 9067, 9068, 9682, 11486

MCHENRY, SUSAN 1478

MCILHENNY, EDWARD A. 18250

MCINTIRE, CARL 8536

MCINTOSH, JAMES 15341

MCINTYRE, DUNCAN T. 9069

MCKEAN, KEITH F. 16233

MCKEE, JAY W. 9683

MCKEE, JESSE D. 3980, 13999

MCKEE, SAMUEL 10662

MCKENNA, MICHAEL A. 9648

MCKENZIE, EDNA 3981

MCKENZIE, EDNA C. 14354

MCKENZIE, MARION J. 5732

MCKENZIE, ROBERT H. 14355, 18768

MCKIBBEN, DAVIDSON B. 12584

MCKIE, THOMAS J. 15736

MCKIEVER, CHARLES F. 12745, 12746

MCKINLEY, CARLYLE 2622

MCKINNEY, FRANCES M. 67

MCKINNEY, RICHARD I. 17025

MCKINNEY, WILLIAM K. 10557

MCKINNCN, WILLIAM 19669

MCKITRICK, ERIC 8218, 8874

MCKITRICK, ERIC L. 3982

MCLAGAN, ELIZABETH 11146

MCLAUGHLIN, ANDREW C. 3983

MCLAUGHLIN, TOM L. 2623, 2624,
9685

MCLAUGHLIN, WAYMAN B. 17807

MCLAURIN, MELTON 15342

MCLEAN, MRS. C.F. 8244

MCLEAN, PATRICIA S. 15737

MCLEMORE, WILLIAM P. 9686

MCLOUGHLIN, JAMES J. 9071, 9072

MCLOUGHLIN, WILLIAM G. 2625, 2626,
13020, 14000, 14001, 14002

MCMAHON, ADRIAN M. 20380

MCMAHON, EDWARD 11036

MCMANUS, EDGAR J. 8537, 10663,
10664, 10665, 10666

MCMANUS, MARY P. 1479

MCMASTER, JOHN B. 3984, 3985,
15343

MCMASTER, RICHARD K. 17029

MCMICHAEL, LOIS 12123

MCMILLAN, FAY C. 18251

MCMILLAN, JAMES B. 376

MCMILLAN, LUCY M. 12535

MCMURDY, R. 3986

MCMURRAY, JOHN 20978

MCMURRY, LINDA O. 1480

MCNALL, NEIL A. 1481

MCNEAL, SARAH L.J. 3987

MCNEIL, ALBERT J. 17808

MCNEIL, W.K. 2627

MCNEILL, WILLIAM H. 15738

MCNEILLY, EARL E. 5733

MCNEILLY, JAMES H. 13239, 15344

MCNULTY, ROBERT B. 1482

MCPHERSON, HALLIE M. 13392

MCPHERSON, JAMES M. 377, 378,
1483, 1484, 2628, 2629, 3988,
6860, 20381, 20382, 20385,
20387, 20553

MCPHERSON, JOHN H.T. 3989, 10104

MCPHERSON, ROBERT G. 9073

MCQUEEN, WINI 379

MCRAE, JEAN A. 3990

MCRAE, NORMAN 10960

MCREYNOLDS, EDWIN C. 13957

MCRORY, MARY O. 11916

MCTIGUE, GERALDINE 2630, 9688

MCTIGUE, GERALDINE M. 2631

MCWALTERS, DON 12016

MCWHINEY, GRADY 1485, 1486, 11750 14064

MEACHAM, GLORIA H. 1487

MEADE, ANNA H. 15246

MEADE, GEORGE 3991

MEADE, MELINDA S. 15739

MEADER, J.R. 20068

MEADERS, DANIEL E. 19670

MEBANE, MARY E. 16234

MECKLIN, JOHN M. 9074

MEEK, C.K. 4974

MEEKER, EDWARD 14994

MEGEE, JONNIE M. 20555

MEHLINGER, LOUIS R. 9689

MEIER, AUGUST 80, 786, 1488, 1489, 1490, 1491, 1492, 2632, 3993, 9415, 9416, 9690, 9691, 19481

MEIKLEJOHN, NORMAN A. 7835, 7836

MEILLASSOUX, C. 4975

MEILLASSOUX, CLAUDE 1493, 4976

MEINERS, EVELYN P. 7837

MEINIG, D.W. 13393

MELDEN, CHARLES M. 3994

MELDER, KEITH E. 20981

MELDRUM, GEORGE W. 11087

MELL, PATRICK H. 14356

MELLAFE, ROLANDO 6861

MELLICK, ANDREW D. 8538

MELLO, PEDRO C. DE 7839

MELLO, PEDRO CARVAHLO DE 7840

MELLON, MATTHEW T. 2633

MELLOR, GEORGE R. 5735

MELLOWN, WILLIAM E. 11751

MELNICK, RALPH 13021

MELOM, HALVOR G. 11600

MELTZER, MILTON 282, 283, 284, 380, 3995, 3996

MELVIN, EDWARD J. 9077

MENARD, RUSSELL R. 1114, 1494, 8245, 8540, 8541, 8543, 8544, 11416, 11492

MENARD, W.T. 14757

MENCKE, JOHN G. 2634, 2635

MENCKEN, H.L. 2636

MENDELSON, W. 9078

MENDENHALL, M.S. 13022

MENDENHALL, MARJORIE S. 13023

MENEZES, MARY N. 7841, 8545

MENN, JOSEPH K. 11671, 12379, 12380

MERCER, P.M. 10106

MEREDITH, WILLIAM J. 19671

MERING, NORMA J. 5736

MERIWETHER, COLYER 3998

MERIWETHER, ELIZABETH A. 13240

MERIWETHER, ROBERT L. 13025

MERK, FREDERICK 11037, 13394, 13395

MERKEL, BENJAMIN 11601, 11602

MERKEL, BENJAMIN G. 11603, 19672

MERRELL, JAMES H. 1495

MERRENS, H. ROY 13026

MERRENS, HARRY R. 8546

MERRIAM, A. 17809

MERRIAM, ALAN P. 233, 1496, 1497,
   7842, 7843

MERRIAM, GEORGE S. 3999

MERRICK, GEORGE B. 11605

MERRICK, THOMAS W. 7844

MERRILL, BOYNTON JR. 11348

MERRILL, GORDON C. 6862

MERRILL, LOUIS T. 5737

MERRILL, PIERCE K. 2637

MERRIMAN, ROGER B. 7845

MERRITT, CAROLE 381

MERRITT, ELIZABETH 4000

MERRITT, J.E. 5738, 5739

MERRITT, NANCY G. 17812

MERRYMAN, EUGENE T. 11241

MERWIN, B.W. 17813

MESA-LAGO, CARMELO 6334

MESICK, JANE L. 4001

MESSLER, ABRAHAM 10560

MESSMER, CHARLES K. 11349, 20983

MESSNER, WILLIAM F. 9080, 12382,
   12383, 12384, 20986, 20988

METCALF, GEORGE 6864

METCALFE, JAMES S. 4977, 15247

METCALFE, RALPH H., JR. 4978

METRAUX, ALFRED 6865

METZER, JACOB 14362, 14363

METZGER, JOHN A. 10886

MEULEN, VANDER 15346

MEVIS, RENE 382

MEYER, DOUGLAS K. 9692

MEYER, HARVEY K. 6866

MEYER, HOWARD N. 1499, 1500,
   20989

MEYER, JOHN 1501

MEYER, JOHN R. 843, 844, 14143,
   14580, 14581, 14582

MEYER-HEISELBERG, R. 5741

MEYERS, ALLAN 4979, 4980

MEYERS, CHARLES S. 17815

MEYERS, JOHN L. 9693

MEYERS, MARVIN 13735

MEYERS, ROSE 12385

MEZU, SEBASTIAN O. 4981

MICELI, MARY V. 17031

MICHAEL, MARION C. 196

MICHAUX, RICHARD R. 17032

MICKLE, ROBINA 18252

MICKLES, ALEXANDER 18947

MICKLEY, JEREMIAH M. 20990

MIDAS, ANDRE 6867

MIDDLEKAUFF, ROBERT L. 1839

MIDDLETON, ARTHUR P. 15136

MIDDLETON, JOHN 4982, 6173

MIDGETT, DOUGLAS 6868

MIERS, EARL S. 4002, 20557

MIERS, SUZANNE 4003, 4983, 5649, 5742

MIKELL, I. JENKINS 13027

MILBURN, PAGE 10108

MILES, EDWIN A. 4004, 12588, 12589

MILES, RUTH W. 8246

MILLER, BASIL W. 4005

MILLER, BEVERLY 6869

MILLER, CHARLES A. 9081

MILLER, CHARLES M. 384

MILLER, CLARENCE C. 4006

MILLER, DOUGLAS T. 4007

MILLER, E.E. 1502

MILLER, ELINOR 4008

MILLER, ELIZABETH W. 385

MILLER, FLOYD J. 2638, 9694

MILLER, GEORGE J. 4009

MILLER, HARRIET P. 17033

MILLER, HASKELL M. 17034

MILLER, HELEN D. 8548

MILLER, J.F. 10109, 15740

MILLER, JAMES W. 17816

MILLER, JOHN C. 4010, 13736

MILLER, JOSEPH C. 386, 387, 388, 1503, 4985, 5743, 5744, 5745, 5746

MILLER, KELLY 4011, 4012, 4013, 4014, 4015, 4016, 4017, 4018, 10358, 14364, 15742, 17453, 17817, 18253

MILLER, KENNETH J. 14365

MILLER, LOREN 9082

MILLER, M. SAMMY 9083, 9696, 11203, 11243, 15138

MILLER, MARION M. 14366

MILLER, MARY E.W. 12125

MILLER, RANDALL M. 389, 1504, 2639, 2640, 4019, 8549, 8550, 9698, 10110, 11753, 12748, 13241, 13737, 14759, 14760, 14762, 14843, 17035, 17036, 20992

MILLER, RICHARD R. 17037

MILLER, ROBERT D. 2641

MILLER, RUTH 390

MILLER, RUTH M. 9084

MILLER, WILLIAM D. 10801

MILLER, WILLIAM L. 14367, 14368, 14369

MILLER, ZANE L. 15945

MILLETTE, JAMES 6870

MILLIGAN, JOHN D. 11917

MILLING, CHAPMAN J. 14006

MILLS, BILLIE R. 11606

MILLS, GARY   12387

MILLS, GARY B.   9699, 9700, 9701,
    12388, 12391, 16464

MILNE, A. TAYLOR   5748

MILNE, A.T.   5747

MILTON, GEORGE F.   2642

MIMS, A. GRACE   17818

MINCHINTON, W.E.   5749, 5750, 5751

MINCHINTON, WALTER   6871

MINCHINTON, WALTER E.   1508, 5752,
    5753, 5754

MINICK, ALICE A.   19673

MINOR, CHARLES L.C.   4020, 4021

MINTER, DAVID   391

MINTZ, SIDNEY   6872, 6873, 6874

MINTZ, SIDNEY W.   392, 1509, 1510,
    1511, 1512, 1513, 1514, 1515,
    1516, 1517, 1518, 3385, 4022,
    4023, 4024, 4025, 4026, 6875,
    6876, 6877, 6878, 6879, 6880,
    6881, 6882, 6883, 6884, 6885,
    6886, 6887, 6889, 6890, 6891,
    7163, 16237, 17454, 17455,
    19377, 19674

MIRSKY, JEANETTE   7847, 14373

MISCH, EDWARDO J.   17039

MITCHELL, BROADUS   1519, 14374,
    14375, 14376

MITCHELL, GEORGE W.   4027

MITCHELL, HENRY H.   17040, 17041,
    17042, 17043, 18254

MITCHELL, J.J.R.   4028

MITCHELL, JAMES N.   17044

MITCHELL, JOHN JR.   16034

MITCHELL, JOSEPH   17045

MITCHELL, LOUIS D.   5756

MITCHELL, MARTHA C.   15743

MITCHELL, MARY H.   10397

MITCHELL, MEMORY F.   9085

MITCHELL, MRS. M.L.   17819

MITCHELL, PETER M.   978

MITCHELL, ROBERT D.   13738, 1373

MITCHELL, THORNTON W.   393

MITCHELL, VIRGIL L.   8551

MITGANG, HERBERT   2644

MITTELSDORF, SIBYLLE   19379

MOBLEY, JOE A.   11754

MODE, PETER G.   17046

MODELL, JOHN   1520, 16402

MODERWELL, HIRAM K.   18255

MODEY, YAO F.   9086

MOERMAN, DANIEL E.   13029

MOERS, ELLEN   1521, 1522

MOES, JOHN E.   1523, 14377

MOESCHLER, CLARA M.   5757

MOFFAT, CHARLES H.   4029

MOFFATT, FRED T., JR.   13030

MOFFATT, JOSIAH   13031

MOFFATT, WALTER   11830

MOHR, CLARENCE   395

MOHR, CLARENCE L. 1524, 1525, 12128, 12129, 12130

MOISTER, WILLIAM 6892

MOLEN, PATRICIA A. 8552

MOLLER, HERBERT 2645

MOLLI, GIORGIO 5758

MONEY, CHARLES H. 9087

MONEYPENNY, A. 396

MONICO, FRANCIS W. 13740

MONK, ABRAHAM 2646

MONKKONEN, ERIC 397

MONTAGU, M.S. ASHLEY 2647

MONTAGUE, J. HAROLD 17820

MONTE, ANITA 2648

MONTELL, WILLIAM L. 11350, 11351, 11352

MONTERO BASCOM, BERTA 18259

MONTESANO, PHIL M. 9702

MONTESANO, PHILIP M. 9703

MONTGOMERY, CHARLES J. 5759

MONTGOMERY, DAVID 1526

MONTGOMERY, HORACE 20993

MONTGOMERY, MARGARET L. 11755

MONTGOMERY, WALTER A. 12750

MONTGOMERY, WINFIELD S. 11244

MONTIEL, LUZ MARIA M. 2649

MONUS, VICTOR P. 19348

MOOD, FULMER 4031

MOODY, DAVID W. 10113

MOODY, R.E. 9088

MOODY, V. ALTON 12392

MOODY, VERNIE A. 12393, 12394

MOOHR, MICHAEL 10114

MOON, BUCKLIN 4032

MOONEY, CHASE C. 1527, 9089, 13244, 13245, 13246, 13247

MOONEY, JAMES 14007

MOORE, ALBERT B. 11756, 20567

MOORE, ANTHONY R. 9704

MOORE, BRENT 11353

MOORE, CHARLES L. 13396

MOORE, COUNCIL S. 13397

MOORE, EDMUND A. 17047

MOORE, GEORGE E. 13741, 13742

MOORE, GEORGE H. 10441, 10465, 10466, 10467, 10468, 10469, 10470, 10744

MOORE, GEORGE W. 18951, 18952

MOORE, GLOVER 9090

MOORE, HARRY E. 4033

MOORE, JACK B. 2650

MOORE, JANIE G. 4987

MOORE, JOHN HAMMOND 13033, 13034, 15248

MOORE, JOHN HEBRON 1528, 12590, 12591, 12592, 14379, 14380, 14766, 14767, 14768

MOORE, JOHN P. 7851

MOORE, JOSEPH G. 6894, 6895

MOORE, LEROY JR. 17050, 17822

MOORE, M.H. 16465

MOORE, M.V. 4034

MOORE, N. WEBSTER 9705, 9706

MOORE, NORMAN W. 11204

MOORE, R.J. 7852

MCORE, RACHEL W. 6896

MOORE, ROBERT 6897

MOORE, ROBERT H. 8688, 10471

MOORE, ROBERT J. 20075

MOORE, ROSE H. 20994

MOORE, W.K. 11609

MOORE, WILBERT E. 4035, 4036,
    4037, 4988, 9091

MOORE, ZELBERT L. 7855

MOOREN, ROBERT L. 20388

MOORER, VIRGINIA C. 9707

MOORHEAD, JAMES H. 20995

MORAIS, HERBERT M. 15745

MORAN, CHARLES 6898

MORAN, ROBERT E. 12395, 12396

MORAZAN, RONALD R. 2651

MORDECAI, ELLEN 12751

MOREL, EDMUND D. 5760

MORELAND, AGNES L. 1529

MORGAN, CLAIRE S. 15249

MORGAN, D. 9709

MORGAN, E.V. 10667

MORGAN, EDMUND S. 8553, 8555,
    8556, 8557, 13744, 13746

MORGAN, EDWIN V. 9092, 9093, 90
    10668, 10672

MORGAN, GORDON D. 11831

MORGAN, KATHRYN 16240

MORGAN, KATHRYN L. 398, 18261

MORGAN, MANIE 11610

MORGAN, P.D. 8561

MORGAN, PHILIP 1530

MORGAN, PHILIP D. 8562

MORGAN, THOMAS J. 4038, 20996

MORGAN, TIMOTHY E. 8563

MORISON, SAMUEL E. 4039, 10472

MORNER, MAGNUS 399, 1531, 1532,
    1534, 1535, 2654, 2655, 6900,
    6901, 7860, 10115

MORRELL, W.P. 6182

MORRILL, RICHARD L. 14382, 1967

MORRIS, CHARLES E. 20078

MORRIS, FRANCIS G. 12753

MORRIS, GEORGE E. 17053

MORRIS, GEORGE G. 13749

MORRIS, JOHN A. 19380

MORRIS, OLLIE M. 4040

MORRIS, PHYLLIS M. 12753

MORRIS, RICHARD B. 8564, 9096,
    9097, 11205, 14769, 20079

MORRIS, ROY R. 2657

MORRIS, THOMAS D.   9098

MORRISEY, RICHARD J.   7861

MORRISON, CHAPLAIN W.   9099, 9100

MORRISON, CHARLES E.   13036

MORRISON, LARRY R.   2658, 2659,
   2660, 2661

MORRISS, MARGARET S.   8565

MORROK, RICHARD   2662

MORROW, DECATUR F.   12754

MORROW, LANCE   1536

MORROW, RALPH E.   2663

MORSBERGER, ROBERT E.   19678

MORSE, J. MITCHELL   19381, 19382

MORSE, RICHARD M.   1537, 2664,
   7862, 7863, 7864

MORSE, W.H.   9710

MORTON, JENNIE C.   11354

MORTON, LOUIS   8566, 14875

MORTON, RICHARD L.   8567, 12755,
   13753, 20998

MORTON-WILLIAMS, PETER   5762

MOSCOV, STEPHEN C.   400

MOSELEY, THOMAS V.   10116

MOSER, HAROLD D.   10117, 20570

MOSES, JANET S.   13037

MOSES, MONTROSE J.   4041

MOSES, WILSON J.   1538, 9711,
   16466

MOSLEY, MRS. CHARLES C.   12593

MOSS, CHARLES G.G.   8568

MOSS, SIMEON F.   10561

MOSSELL, CHARLES W.   20081

MOSSELL, MRS. N.F.   4042

MOTHERSHEAD, HARMON   11104

MOTLEY, CONSTANCE B.   10118, 10393

MOTON, ROBERT   18954

MOTON, ROBERT R.   4043, 4044, 4045,
   15747, 17825, 17826, 18955

MOTT, ABIGAIL F.   18956

MOTT, ALEXANDER   18957

MOULTON, PHILLIPS   17054

MOUNGER, DWYN M.   17055

MOUNT, ROBERT L.   5763

MOUSER, BRUCE L.   5764, 5765

MOWAT, CHARLES   11918

MOWRY, D.   4047

MOWRY, DUANE   4048

MOYD, OLIN P.   17056

MPHAHLELE, EZEKIEL   1539

MUDGE, ISADORE G.   311

MUFASSIR, SULAYMAN S.   4050

MUFFETT, D.J.M.   18264

MUGGLESTON, WILLIAM F.   4051

MUIR, ANDREW F.   9712, 9713, 9714,
   9715

MULCASTER, J.G.   10887

MULCASTER, JOHN   10881

MULLEN, ROBERT W.   20999

MULLER, PHILIP R.   1540

MULLIN, GERALD W.   1541, 13756, 20082

MULLIN, GERALD W., JR.   20084

MULLIN, GERRY   17057

MULLIN, MICHAEL   4052, 8573, 20271

MULLING, VICTOR H.   8574

MULLINS, SUE A.   18551

MULLINS-MOORE, SUE   15512

MULLINS-MOORE, SUE A.   15220

MULVEY, PATRICIA A.   19215, 19216

MUNFORD, BEVERLY B.   13759

MUNGEN, DONNA   16467

MUNRO, J. FORBES   5766

MUNRO, WILFRED H.   5767

MUNROE, JOHN A.   8575, 11207, 11208, 11209

MUNROE, ROBERT L.   6905

MUNTU, MAHARIBI   3841

MURAPA, RUKUDZO   19679

MURASKIN, WILLIAM A.   9716

MURCELL, JEANNE F.   17061

MURDOCH, RICHARD K.   11919

MURDOCK, EUGENE C.   21000

MURDOCK, GEORGE P.   4989

MURDOCK, WILLIAM J.   19680

MURPHEE, DENNIS   12594

MURPHY, EDGAR G.   4053

MURPHY, J.M.   9717

MURPHY, JEANNETTE R.   17459, 17, 17829, 17830

MURPHY, JOHN C.   2665, 17062

MURPHY, LARRY G.   9718

MURPHY, LAWRENCE R.   11114, 134

MURPHY, MIRIAM T.   17064

MURPHY, PATRICIA G.   6906, 6907

MURPHY, ROBERT C.   7867, 7868

MURRAL, A.L.   6908

MURRAY, ALBERT   4054

MURRAY, ALEXANDER L.   9104, 102 10274

MURRAY, AMELIA M.   4055

MURRAY, ANDREW E.   2666, 17066

MURRAY, D.J.   6909

MURRAY, D.R.   5768, 5769

MURRAY, DAVID R.   4056, 5770, 6

MURRAY, FREEMAN H.M.   10119, 18

MURRAY, GEORGE W.   10120

MURRAY, GERALD F.   6911

MURRAY, JAMES   2667

MURRAY, PAUL   12132

MURRAY, PAULI   9105, 9106, 1121

MURRAY, PERCY E.   1542

MURRAY, ROBERT K.   2668, 21002

MURRAY, WESTON L.   5771

MURRAY, WM. 17067

MURRY, LINDLEY 4057

MUSCATINE, LISSA 16468

MUSEUM OF ART, RALEIGH 18653

MUSGRAVE, M.E. 1543

MUSSER, CARL W. 13760

MUSSON, NELLIE E. 16469

MUSTACCHI, PIERO 12398

MUSTO, DAVID F. 15775

MUTUNHU, TENDAI 12756, 19681

MUTZ, RONALD L. 5772

MYERS, BETTY 18654

MYERS, C.S. 17831

MYERS, JACOB W. 10888

MYERS, JOHN B. 21003

MYERS, JOHN L. 4058, 9719

MYERS, LENA W. 16470

MYERS, MINNIE W. 11672

MYERS, ROBERT 12133

MYERS, ROBERT M. 17068

MYERS, WILLIAM S. 11496

MYRDAL, GUNNAR 2669, 3385, 4026

MYRICK, SUSAN 19102

NABUCO, CAROLINA 7869

NABUCO, JOAQUIM 7870

NADELHAFT, JEROME 9107

NADELHAFT, JEROME J. 5773

NAIPAUL, V.S. 6912

NAIPAUL, VIDIADHAR S. 6913, 6914

NAISH, F.D.· PRIDEAUX 5774

NAISON, MARK 1544

NAPTON, WILLIAM B. 11612

NASCIMENTO, ABDIAS D. 7872, 7873, 7874

NASCIMENTO, ELISA L. 7875

NASH, A.E. KEIR 9113, 9115, 9116, 9117, 9118, 13040, 15749

NASH, A.E.K. 9108, 9109, 9110, 9111, 9112

NASH, ARNOLD E.K. 9119

NASH, GARY 10121

NASH, GARY B. 2670, 2671, 2672, 8578, 8579, 14008, 16243

NASH, HOWARD P., JR. 21005

NASH, J.V. 1545

NASH, RODERICK 19682

NASH, RODERICK W. 19683

NASH, ROY 7877, 7878

NASSAU, ROBERT H. 4991

NATHAN, H. 17832

NATHANS, SYDNEY 1546

NAU, JOHN F. 12399

NAUGHTON, T. RAYMOND 8918

NAY, ROBERT F. 8580

NEAL, JULIA 21006

NEAL, STEPHEN C. 9720

NEAL, WILLARD 19104

NEARING, SCOTT 4059

NEATBY, HILDA M. 10275

NEBRASKA WRITERS' PROJECT 10977

NEEDHAM, J.B. 15252

NEELY, MARK E., JR. 1547, 10122, 20391, 21007

NEELY, SHARLOTTE 14010

NEFF, JOAN M. 10889

NEIGHBORS, RUBYE G. 11757

NEIL, SARA E. 20089

NEILL, EDWARD D. 8583, 10965

NEILSON, HUBERT 10276

NEKHOM, LISA M. 8189

NELL, WILLIAM C. 8584, 8585

NELSEN, ANNE K. 17070, 17071

NELSEN, HART M. 17070, 17071

NELSON, ALICE D. 12400

NELSON, B.H. 12757

NELSON, BERNARD H. 5776, 9122, 9123

NELSON, EARL J. 11613, 11614

NELSON, GEORGE H. 5777

NELSON, J.H. 4072

NELSON, LARRY E. 9722

NELSON, LEE H. 11497

NELSON, MARGARET V. 7879

NELSON, MARY L. 12595

NELSON, PAUL D. 2674

NELSON, ROBERT E. 13402

NELSON, THOMAS C. 9723

NELSON, TRUMAN 1551

NELSON, WILLIAM 10564, 20276

NELSON, WILLIAM E. 9124

NELSON, WILLIAM H. 8586

NELSON, WILLIAM J., JR. 9724

NELSON, WILLIAM N. 20277

NELSON, WILLIAM S. 17072

NERI, PHILIP 8587

NETHERTON, NAN 13765

NETTELS, CURTIS P. 5778, 14384

NETTL, BRUNO 405, 17836

NEURATH, PETER F. 13766

NEVIN, R.P. 2675

NEVINS, ALLAN 6915, 9125, 11180 14373, 14385, 15253, 20393, 21010

NEVINSON, HENRY W. 4992

NEWBURY, C.N. 4993

NEWBURY, COLIN W. 4994

NEWBY, I.A. 1552, 1553, 2677

NEWBY, IDUS 1554

NEWDING, STANLEY 1555

NEWELL, W. WILLIAM 18269

NEWELL, W.W. 16245, 18268

NEWITT, M.D. 7881

NEWLANDS, H.S.   4075

NEWMAN, DEBORAH L.   407

NEWMAN, DEBRA   8588

NEWMAN, FRANCIS W.   4076, 6916, 6917

NEWMAN, FRED M.   4102

NEWMAN, PHILIP C.   1556

NEWTON, ALEXANDER H.   9727

NEWTON, ARTHUR P.   5780, 6918

NEWTON, EDWARD   1557, 1558

NEWTON, JAMES   20090

NEWTON, JAMES E.   9128, 9129, 14771, 18554, 18658

NEWTON, LEWIS W.   13403

NIANI (DEE BROWN)   7882

NICHOLLS, DAVID   1559, 2680

NICHOLLS, MICHAEL L.   8589, 18728

NICHOLLS, W.H.   14386

NICHOLS, CHARLES H.   2681, 18960, 18961, 18962

NICHOLS, CHARLES H., JR.   410, 1560, 1561, 18963, 20278

NICHOLS, NEWTON D.   4077

NICHOLS, PATRICIA C.   19383

NICHOLS, ROY F.   4078, 4079

NICHOLS, WILLIAM W.   1563

NICHOLSON, JOSEPH W.   17018

NICHOLSON, LOIS B.   17075

NICHOLSON, ROY S.   17076

NICKERSON, CAMILLE L.   12401

NICOL, CHARLES   4080

NICOL, DAVIDSON   6921

NICOLOSI, ANTHONY S.   411

NIDA, EUGENE A.   6922

NIGORIE, DAVID L.   6923, 6924

NIEBOER, HERMAN J.   2682

NIEHAUS, EARL F.   2683

NIELDS, JOHN P.   9130

NIELSEN, LAWRENCE J.   7884

NIEMAN, DONALD G.   9729, 21013, 21014, 21015, 21016

NIEMI, ALBERT W., JR.   14387

NILES, BLAIR   6925

NILON, CHARLES H.   2684

NISTAL-MORET, BENJAMIN   6926

NIVEN, JOHN   21017

NIXON, J.A.   5781

NKETIA, J.H.K.   1564, 4995

NOBLE, DAVID W.   8321

NOBLE, JEANNE   16472, 16473

NOBLE, PETER   2685

NOBLE, WILLIAM A.   12134

NOBLES, WADE W.   4996, 4997, 16249

NOEL, DONALD L.   2686, 2687, 8252

NOEL HUME, IVOR   8590

NOGEE, JOSEPH L.   9131, 19685

NOGGLE, BURL   1565

NOLAN, PARTICK B. 9132

NOLAN, RUSSELL B. 9730

NOLEN, CLAUDE H. 2688, 2689

NOLL, ARTHUR H. 18270

NOLL, MARK A. 8591

NOON, THOMAS R. 17078

NOONAN, JOHN T., JR. 6927

NORCROSS, GRENVILLE H. 19687

NORDIN, KENNETH D. 4085

NORDMANN, C.A. 9731

NORDSTROM, CARL 9135, 10675

NORREGARD, GEORG 5782

NORRIS, THADDEUS 18271

NORTH, DOUGLASS C. 14388

NORTHCOTT, CECIL 7885

NORTHRUP, ANSEL J. 10676, 10677

NORTHRUP, DAVID 4999, 5000, 5001, 5733

NORTHRUP, HERBERT R. 14772

NORTON, DONNIE J. 4086

NORTON, FREDERICK C. 10399

NORTON, HENRY A. 21018

NORTON, HENRY L. 11615

NORTON, L. WESLEY 4087

NORTON, MARY BETH 8592

NORTON, WESLEY 20093

NORWOOD, ALBERTA S. 9732

NORWOOD, JOHN N. 17079, 17080

NORWOOD, THOMAS M. 4088

NOVACK, GEORGE 14389

NOVACK, GEORGE E. 8593, 14390

NOVAK, DANIEL A. 9136

NOVELS, ALPHONSE 6928

NOYES, EDWARD 20394, 21019

NOYES, JAMES O. 14391

NUERMBERGER, RUTH K. 11758, 127

NUESSE, CELESTINE J. 17081

NUGENT, MARIA 6929

NUHRAH, ARTHUR G. 12404

NULL, ALVIN E. 11673

NUNES, MARIA L. 7886

NUNEZ, BENJAMIN 413

NUNN, CHARLES F. 5785

NUNN, FREDERICK M. 2467

NUXOLL, ELIZABETH M. 1566

NWULIA, MOSES D.E. 5002

NYE, RUSSEL B. 4089, 4090, 2009 20095

OAKES, JAMES 21020

OAKS, PRISCILLA 414

OATES, STEPHEN B. 4091, 10127, 20096, 20097, 20098

O'BANION, MAURINE M. 13405

OBATALA, J.K. 5003

OBERG, KALERVO 7888

OBERHOLZER, EMIL 9137, 9138

OBERLIN COLLEGE LIBRARY 415

OBERSEIDER, NANCY L. 8594

OBLINGER, CARL 10748

OBLINGER, CARL D. 10749, 10750

O'BRIEN, DAVID J. 1567

O'BRIEN, JOHN T. 15949, 15950

O'BRIEN, KENNETH P. 2692

O'BRIEN, MARY L. 17084

O'BRIEN, MICHAEL 1568, 1569

O'BRIEN, WILLIAM S.J. 9139

O'CALLAGHAN, EDMUND B. 5787, 5788

O'CONNELL, SHAUN 1570

O'CONNELL, SHAUN V. 1571

O'CONNOR, STELLA 9735

O'CONNOR, THOMAS F. 1572

O'CONNOR, THOMAS H. 20395

O'DEA, MICHAEL 8595

ODELL, ABRABELLA G. 5789

O'DELL, J.H. 332

ODEN, GLORIA C. 1573

O'DONNELL, JAMES H. 8596

ODUM, HOWARD 17841

ODUM, HOWARD W. 4092, 17842, 17843, 17844, 17845, 17846

OEDEL, HOWARD T. 10514, 10515

OEHLRICH, CONRAD 5790

OERTEL, HANNS 18273

OESTERLEY, W.O.E. 18463

OFARI, EARL 19688, 19689

OFONAGORO, WALTER I. 4093

OFOSU-APPIAH, L.H. 5004

OFOSU-APPIAH, LAWRENCE H. 5005

OFUATEY-KODJOE, W. 5006

OGG, FREDERIC A. 4094, 9140, 10843

OGOT, BETHWELL A. 5791

O'GRADY, PATRICIA D. 12135

OGUNSANYA, EBUN 19384

O'HALLORAN, THOMAS P. 417

OHIRI, CHRISTIAN L. 5792

OHLINE, HOWARD A. 4095, 4096, 9141, 13042

OJO, G.J.A. 5008

OKE, DAVID O. 19385

O'KELLY, JAMES J. 6931

OKIGBO, PIUS N.C. 5793

OKINSHEVICH, LEO 418

OKOYE, F. NWABUEZE 2693

OKOYE, FELIX N. 2694

OLBRICH, EMIL 4097

OLDS, VICTORIA M. 4100

O'LEARY, TIMOTHY J. 419

OLENICK, PAUL J. 4101

OLIEN, MICHAEL D. 7889, 7890, 7891

OLIVEIRA LIMA, MANOEL DE 7892

OLIVER, ALBERT G. 2695

OLIVER, CAROLINE 5011

OLIVER, CLINTON F. 1574

OLIVER, DONALD W. 4102

OLIVER, E.S. 4103

OLIVER, P. 10277

OLIVER, PAUL 17847, 17848, 17849

OLIVER, PEARLEEN 10278

OLIVER, ROLAND 5009, 5010, 5011

OLIVER, VERE L. 6933, 6934

OLIVER, W.P. 10279, 10280

OLORUNTIMEHIN, TUNJI 5012

OLSBERG, ROBERT N. 13043

OLSEN, OTTO H. 1575, 4104

OLSEN, PETER 4105, 9737, 20101

OLSHAUSEN, GEORGE 9142

OLSON, CARL I. 12596

OLSON, EDWIN 9143, 10678, 10680

OLSON, FREDERICK 9738

OLSON, LEROY A. 4106

OLTON, ROY 5795

OMEALLY, R.G. 1576

OMIBIYI, MOSUNMOLA 17850

ONEAL, JAMES 4107

O'NEAL, WILLIAM 4108

O'NEIL, MAUD 7079

O'NEILL, CHARLES E. 9739

O'NEILL, DANIEL J. 9740

O'NEILL, WILLIAM L. 10476

ONSTOTT, KYLE 4109

ONWOOD, MAURICE 16035

OOSTHUIZEN, G.C. 17085

OPLER, MORRIS E. 1578

OPOKU, SAMUEL K. 2696

OPPENHEIM, LEONARD 9145

OPPER, PETER K. 2697, 12759, 12760

O'REILLY, AIDA T. 5013

ORMAN, RICHARD A. VAN 617

ORNSTEIN, A.C. 420

OROGE, E. ADENIYI 5014

ORR, G.M. 6935

ORR, HORACE E. 17086

ORREN, G.G. 13407

ORSER, C. 18530

ORTIZ, ADALBERTO 2698

ORTIZ, FERNANDO 6936, 17851

ORTIZ ODERIGO, NESTOR R. 17852

OSBORN, GEORGE C. 12597

OSBORNE, D.F. 9146

OSBORNE, F.J. 5797

OSBORNE, FRED Y. 13403

OSBORNE, JOSEPH A. 421

OSBORNE, WILLIAM 17087

OSGOOD, HERBERT L. 1580

O'SHEEL, PATRICK 1581

OSIEK, BETTY T.   6938

OSOFSKY, GILBERT   422, 1582, 1583, 18969

OSTENDORF, BERNHARD   1584

OSTER, HARRY C.   18276

OSTERWEIS, ROLLIN G.   4110

OSTHAUS, CARL R.   17463

OSTRANDER, GILMAN M.   5798

OTT, ELEANORE   15434

OTT, THOMAS O.   6939

OTTEN, ALLAN L.   1586

OTTENBERG, S.J.   5015

OTTERBEIN, KEITH F.   6940, 16251

OTTLEY, CARLTON R.   6941

OTTLEY, ROI   1587, 4111, 10681, 10682

OTTO, JOHN S.   2699, 11833, 12136, 12137, 12138, 12139, 12140

OUBRE, CLAUDE F.   21022, 21023, 21024

OUTLAW, ALAIN C.   15466

OVERDYKE, W. DARRELL   11618

OVERTON, JACQUELINE   8602

OVESEY, LIONEL   18725, 18764

OVIEDO Y BANOS, JOSE DE   7894

OVINGTON, MARY W.   10684, 19105

OWEN, CHANDLER   4113

OWEN, DANIEL   10916

OWEN, H.T.   13773

OWEN, MARY A.   18277, 18278

OWEN, MAY W.   17853

OWEN, THOMAS M.   4114

OWENS, HARRY P.   1588

OWENS, JAMES L.   12141

OWENS, LESLIE H.   1589, 14844, 18770

OWENS, M. LILLIANA   16477

OWENS, WILLIAM   18279

OWENS, WILLIAM A.   13409, 17854, 20105

OWSLEY, FRANK L.   1590, 13250, 14393, 15006

OWSLEY, FRANK L., JR.   4115

OWSLEY, HARRIET C.   13250, 14393

OXENDINE, PEARL M.   1591

PACKARD, GEORGE   2700

PACKWOOD, CYRIL O.   6942

PADGETT, JAMES A.   9147, 9148, 12408, 12761

PADGUG, ROBERT A.   1592, 1593

PADILLA, ELENA   4116

PAGE, ANNE L.   10477

PAGE, EUGENE T.   2701

PAGE, JOHN T.   4117

PAGE, MELVIN E.   5016, 5799

PAGE, THOMAS N.   2702, 2703, 4118, 4119, 4120, 13774, 16037, 16038, 18167

PAGE, WILBUR A.   1594

PAGLIARO, HAROLD E.   2704

PAINTER, DIANN H.   16478

PAINTER, NELL   9741

PALGRAVE, W.G.   7895

PALM, REBA W.   17089

PALMER, COLIN A.   5800, 7896, 7898, 8604, 18281

PALMER, GERTRUDE E.   19693

PALMER, HENRY E.   11921, 15752

PALMER, JACLYN C.   1595

PALMER, JOHN M.   21025

PALMER, PAUL C.   8605

PALMER, ROBERT L.   8972

PALUDAN, PHILLIP S.   10128, 10129

PAN AMERICAN UNION   6943

PANDAY, R.M.N.   7899

PANG, EUL-SOO   7900

PANTALEONI, HEWITT   17855

PANTLE, ALBERTA   11619

PAPENFUSE, EDWARD C.   8494

PAPENFUSE, EDWARD C., JR.   15007

PAQUETTE, ROBERT L.   6945

PARDOE, T. EARL   19387

PARENTON, VERNON J.   12411

PARES, RICHARD   424, 5801, 6947, 6948

PARHAM, ALTHEA DE P.   6949

PARISH, JOHN C.   9153, 11088

PARISH, PETER J.   4121, 10130

PARK, ANDREW   16479

PARK, JOSEPH H.   4122

PARK, ROBERT E.   2705, 2706, 270(5017

PARKER, ALLEN   18971

PARKER, D.M.   9154

PARKER, E.K.   21029

PARKER, FREDDIE L.   12764

PARKER, GEORGE W.   5018

PARKER, PATRICIA   18660

PARKER, R.H.   5802

PARKER, WILLIAM   18972

PARKER, WILLIAM H.   13776

PARKER, WILLIAM N.   1596, 14395, 14396, 14397

PARKHURST, JESSIE W.   16480

PARKINS, A.E.   14398

PARKINS, ALMON E.   14399

PARKINSON, BRADBURY B.   5568, 5

PARKINSON, CYRIL N.   5804

PARKINSON, RALPH T.   17090

PARKS, EDD W.   13251

PARKS, GORDON E.   11620

PARKS, H.B.   20107

PARKS, JAMES D.   9742

PARKS, MALCOM   18562

PARKS, ROGER N.   10362

PARKS, VALERIE E. 6950

PARMELEE, JULIUS H. 21030

PARMET, ROBERT D. 21031

PARRAMORE, THOMAS C. 8606, 13777, 15754, 20108, 20109

PARRINDER, EDWARD G. 5019

PARRINDER, GEOFFREY 18282

PARRISH, LYDIA 17856

PARRISH, LYDIA A. 12144

PARRISH, THOMAS M. 4123

PARRISH, WILLIAM E. 11621, 11622, 11623, 11624

PARRY, ELLWOOD 18661

PARRY, JOHN 7901

PARRY, JOHN H. 1597, 5805, 6951, 6952, 6953, 6954, 7903

PARSONS, ALBERT W. 5806

PARSONS, DENNIS F. 17092

PARSONS, ELSIE C. 1598, 5020, 6955, 17858, 18027, 18284, 18285, 18286, 18287, 18290, 18291

PARSONS, JAMES J. 7905

PARSONS, LLOYD C. 20396

PARTIN, JOANNE K. 18139

PARTINGTON, PAUL G. 425

PARTON, JAMES 4124

PASCALE, VICTOR 4125

PASCHAL, ANDREW G. 14012

PASCOE, CHARLES F. 17093

PASSELL, PETER 1599, 14400, 14401, 14402

PASSIN, H. 3385

PATRICK, REMBERT W. 2710, 5807

PATRICK, WALTON R. 4126

PATTEE, RICHARD 1600, 7907

PATTEE, RICHARD F. 7908, 7909

PATTERSON, CALEB P. 13252, 13253

PATTERSON, CECIL L. 2711, 2712

PATTERSON, H. ORLANDO 6956, 6957

PATTERSON, HORACE O. 1601

PATTERSON, J. STAHL 15009

PATTERSON, K. DAVID 426, 4856, 5021, 5809

PATTERSON, LINDSAY 17465

PATTERSON, O. 4127

PATTERSON, ORLANDO 427, 428, 1603, 1604, 4128, 5810, 6958, 6959, 6960, 6962, 14403

PATTON, FLORENCE 19106

PATTON, JAMES W. 4129, 9155, 12690

PATTON, JUNE O. 16481

PATTON, LEILA E. 17859

PATTON, WILLIAM W. 4130, 10133

PAUL, WILLIAM G. 15952

PAULA, A.F. 6963

PAUL-EMILE, BARBARA T. 4131, 4132

PAULI, HERTHA E. 9743

PAULLIN, CHARLES O. 429

PAVY, DAVID 5022

PAVY, PAUL D. 7912

PAXSON, FREDERIC L. 429

PAXTON, WILLIAM E. 17094

PAYNE, AARON A. 9744

PAYNE, DANIEL A. 18973

PAYNE, ERNEST A. 6964

PAYNE, PHILIP M. 8607

PAYNE, WALTER A. 2713

PAYNE-GAPOSCHKIN, CECILIA H. 13255

PAYNTER, JOHN H. 19697, 19698

PEABODY, A.P. 4133

PEABODY, CHARLES 17860

PEABODY, FRANCIS G. 20397

PEARCE, HAYWOOD J., JR. 4134

PEARCE, LARRY W. 21033

PEARCE, THOMAS S. 1607

PEARSON, ELIZABETH W. 21034

PEASE, JANE H. 1608, 2714, 4135, 4136, 4137, 4138, 9745, 9746, 9747, 9748, 9749, 10137, 10281, 13256, 14404, 18974, 19699, 19700

PEASE, THEODORE C. 10891

PEASE, WILLIAM H. 1608, 2714, 4136, 4137, 4138, 9745, 9746, 9747, 9748, 9749, 10137, 10281, 13256, 18974, 19699, 19700, 21035

PEAY, SUE C. 11834

PECHIN, PETER 2715

PECK, ROBERT M. 11105

PECOT, SHIRLEY C. 9156

PEDERSON, LEE 19388

PEDRAJA, T. RENE ANDRES DE LA 6965

PEDROSA, MARIO 5023

PEEBLES, JOAN B. 430

PEEBLES, MINNIE K. 16254

PEEK, PHIL 18563

PEEKS, EDWARD 19702

PEEPLES, KEN JR. 4139

PEGGS, A. DEANS 6966

PEIRCE, PAUL S. 21036

PELLEGRIN, ROLAND J. 12411

PELLETREAU, WILLIAM S. 4140

PELZER, LOUIS 10931

PEMBERTON, CAROLINE H. 1609

PEMBROKE, MACEO D. 17095

PENDLETON, LAWSON A. 4141

PENDLETON, LEILA A. 6967

PENDLETON, LOUIS 18292

PENDLETON, OTHNIEL A., JR. 1709

PENEL, J. 5024

PENISTON, GREGORY S. 14774

PENKOWER, MONTY N. 19107

PENN, I. GARLAND 4142, 9750

PENNEKAMP, A.H.C. 2716

PENNINGTON, EDGAR L. 17097, 17
17099

PENNINGTON, PATIENCE 4143

PENNYPACKER, FRANCES W. 12145

PENSON, L. 5311

PENTLAND, H. CLARE 10282

PEOTTER, E.J.G. 20280

PERDUE, CHARLES L., JR. 431, 16565, 19108

PERDUE, CHUCK 18295

PERDUE, ROBERT E. 4144, 12147

PERDUE, ROBERT E., JR. 18564

PERDUE, THEDA 14013, 14014, 14015, 14016, 14017, 14018

PEREDA VALDES, ILDEFONSO 7914

PERINBAUM, B. MARIE 5025

PERKINS, A.E. 17862

PERKINS, A.L. 16039

PERKINS, ERIC 1610

PERKINS, FRANCES B. 21037

PERKINS, HAVEN P. 17101

PERKINS, HOWARD C. 2717

PERKINS, WILLIAM E. 1611, 1932

PERLMAN, DANIEL 9753

PERMAN, MICHAEL 21038

PERRIN, LESTER W. 10566

PERROW, E.C. 18296

PERRY, GEORGIA L. 1612

PERRY, PERCIVAL 14405, 14775, 14776

PERRY, REGENIA 18662

PERRY, T.D. 4145

PERRY, THOMAS S. 4146

PERSON, MARY A. 17102

PERUSSE, ROLAND I. 6968

PESCATELLO, ANN 7915, 16483

PESCATELLO, ANN M. 2718, 4147, 6969, 7919, 7920

PESKIN, ALLAN 9754

PESSEN, EDWARD 1613, 14064

PETERKIN, JULIA 18297

PETERS, ERSKINE 17103

PETERS, MARIE F. 432

PETERS, THELMA P. 8608

PETERS, VIRGINIA B. 14019

PETERSON, B.H. 4148

PETERSON, CHERYL R. 2719

PETERSON, JOHN H., JR. 14020

PETERSON, MENDEL 5812

PETERSON, MERRILL D. 13780

PETERSON, SAMUEL 3257

PETERSON, THOMAS V. 2720, 2721

PETERSON, VICTOR H. 9755

PETERSON, WALTER F. 11761, 11762

PETO, FLORENCE 18565

PETRINE, STEVEN F. 21039

PETRY, ANN 19703

PETTIGREW, THOMAS F. 2722, 18771

PETTIS, JOYCE 1614

PETTIT, ARTHUR G. 2723, 2724, 2725, 2727, 11625

PETTIT, EBER M. 19704

PFAUTZ, JAMES C. 5814

PFISTER, FREDERICK W. 8609

PHELAN, J.L. 7921

PHELAN, JOHN L. 7922, 7923, 7924

PHELAN, RAYMOND V. 9158

PHENIX, GEORGE P. 17863

PHIFER, EDWARD W. 12766

PHILADELPHIA MUSEUM OF ART 5026

PHILBRICK, FRANCIS S. 10844

PHILBRICK, JULIA A. 10478

PHILHOWER, CHARLES A. 10557

PHILLIPPO, JAMES M. 6973

PHILLIPS, ARTHUR 5027

PHILLIPS, DAVID E. 8610

PHILLIPS, GEORGE 1615

PHILLIPS, GLENN I.O. 31

PHILLIPS, GLENN O. 434

PHILLIPS, HARLAN B. 2585

PHILLIPS, IVORY 2728

PHILLIPS, JAMES D. 5815, 5816

PHILLIPS, JAMES R. 20282

PHILLIPS, KEVIN 1616

PHILLIPS, PAUL D. 21040, 21041

PHILLIPS, R.E. 17864

PHILLIPS, ROBERT K. 431, 16565

PHILLIPS, ULRICH B. 435, 436, 4 1617, 1618, 1619, 1620, 1621, 2730, 2731, 4149, 4150, 4151, 4152, 4153, 5028, 5029, 6975, 9159, 9160, 9163, 12150, 1215 13046, 13783, 13784, 14407, 14408, 14409, 14411, 14412, 14413, 14415, 14416, 14419, 14420, 14422, 14424, 14425, 14427, 14624, 15010, 15146, 15147, 15353, 15354

PHILLIPS, W.M., JR. 4154

PHILLIPS, WALDO B. 4155

PHINAZEE, ANNETTE L. 438

PHYFE, J. ESTON 362

PICKARD, KATE E.R. 11763

PICKENS, ANDREW L. 4156

PICKENS, DONALD K. 13321, 20116

PICKENS, FRANCIS W. 10140

PICKENS, WILLIAM 4157, 15355

PICKERING, SAMUEL F., JR. 2734

PICKETT, ALBERT J. 11764

PICKETT, ANDREW M. 437

PICKETT, L.C. 1623

PICKETT, WILLIAM P. 2735

PICON SALAS, MARIANO 7926

PICOT, J. RUPERT 16258

PIERCE, B. EDWARD 7929

PIERCE, B.E. 16259, 17108

PIERCE, BESSIE L. 19706

PIERCE, BURNETT C. 13411

PIERCE, EDWARD L. 20398

1790

PIERCE, MILFRED C.   5319

PIERCE, PONCHITTA   18664

PIERRE, C.E.   17109

PIERSEN, WILLIAM D.   5030, 5031,
   8611, 17110

PIERSON, DONALD   440, 7930, 7931,
   7932, 7933, 7934

PIERSON, HAMILTON W.   15443

PIH, RICHARD W.   9759

PIKE, GUSTAVUS D.   19111

PIKE, RUTH   5821

PILCHER, GEORGE W.   17111, 19223

PILGRIM, E.I.   4158

PILLAR, JAMES J.   17113

PILLSBURY, ALBERT E.   4159

PILTON, JAMES W.   19708, 19709

PIM, BEDFORD C.T.   6977

PINCHBECK, RAYMOND B.   13787,
   14777

PINCKNEY, C.C.   13048

PINCKNEY, ELISE   19224

PINDERHUGHES, CHARLES A.   2737,
   15761, 15762

PINERA, SEBASTIAN E.   14614

PING, NANCY R.   17866

PINGEON, FRANCES D.   10567, 10568,
   10569, 10570, 10571

PINKNEY, ALPHONSO   2739, 4160,
   4161, 16261

PINNEY, ROY   5822

PINNINGTON, JOHN E.   6978

PIPER, HENRY D.   18975

PIPES, DANIEL   5032

PIPES, WILLIAM H.   17115, 17116,
   17117

PIPKIN, JOHN G.   11835

PIROWSKI, GLORIA J.   21042

PI-SUNYER, ORIOL   7925

PITMAN, F.W.   6979, 17118

PITMAN, FRANK W.   6980, 6981, 6982,
   6983

PITT, H.G.   1625

PITT-RIVERS, JULIAN   2740, 7936

PLANCK, GARY R.   2741

PLATT, JAMES JR.   19389

PLATT, ORVILLE H.   10401

PLATT, RAYE   6934

PLATT, VIRGINIA B.   5823, 5824,
   5825, 5826

PLATTER, ALLEN A.   13412

PLEASANTS, J. HALE   18666

PLEASANTS, MARY M.   15257

PLEASANTS, SALLY   13738

PLEAT, GERALDINE R.   10686

PLIMMER, CHARLOTTE   5827

PLIMMER, DENIS   5827

PLIMPTON, GEORGE   1626

PLIMPTON, GEORGE A.   5828

PLOSKI, HARRY   441

1791

PLOTNICOV, LEONARD 5116

PLUMB, J.H. 1627, 1628, 1629, 1630, 4163

PLUMMER, BETTY L. 4164, 15763, 15764

POE, CLARENCE H. 9164

POE, WILLIAM A. 4165, 9760, 12154

POE, WILLIAM B. 4166

POKU, K. 5033

POLANYI, KARL 5034, 5035

POLE, J.R. 1631, 1632, 1633, 1634, 2742, 4167

POLIAKOV, L. 3385, 4026

POLK, LEE R. 13789

POLK, WILLIAM M. 17119

POLK, WILLIAM T. 2743

POLLAK, LOUIS H. 9165

POLLAK-ELTZ, ANGELINA 442, 7938, 7939, 17869

POLLARD, EDWARD 18773

POLLARD, EDWARD A. 4168

POLLARD, LANCASTER 4169

POLLARD, LESLIE J. 15013

POLLITT, RONALD 5831

POLOS, NICHOLAS C. 9761

POLSKY, MILTON 443, 444

POLSKY, MILTON E. 445

POMFRET, JOHN E. 10572

POOL, FRANK K. 17120

POOL, GAIL R. 6985

POOL, WILLIAM C., JR. 13413

POOLE, STAFFORD 6583

POOLE, WILLIAM F. 4170

POOLE, WILLIAM J. 20119

POPE, CLAYNE L. 1064

POPE, D.J. 5832

POPE, LISTON 17121

POPE, PAULINE H. 6986

POPE, POLLY 6987

POPE, THOMAS H. 13050

POPE-HENNESSEY, JAMES 5833

POPKIN, RICHARD H. 2744

POPPINO, ROLLIE E. 7940

PORCH, JAMES M. 17122

PORTEOUS, LAURA L. 446

PORTER, ALICE T. 12413

PORTER, ANTHONY T. 4171

PORTER, BETTY 9762, 12414

PORTER, DALE H. 5834, 5835

PORTER, DAVID D. 20580

PORTER, DOROTHY 447, 4172, 976

PORTER, DOROTHY B. 448, 449, 4 451, 452, 453, 454, 7942, 97 9765, 9766, 10480

PORTER, JAMES A. 18667, 18668, 18669, 18670, 18671, 18672

PORTER, KENNETH W. 4173, 9767, 9769, 10481, 10845, 11923, 11924, 11926, 11929, 11930, 11931, 11932, 11933, 11934,

11935, 11936, 13414, 13415,
14021, 14023, 14024, 14025,
19712, 19713, 20285

PORTER, R. 5036

PORTER, THOMAS J. 17870

POSCOE, C.F. 17123

POSCOE, CHARLES F. 455

POSEY, DARRELL A. 2745

POSEY, THOMAS E. 13790

POSEY, WALTER B. 17125, 17126,
17127, 17128, 17129, 17130,
17131, 17132

POST, KEN 6989

POSTELL, PAUL E. 12415, 12416

POSTELL, W.D. 15766

POSTELL, WILLIAM D. 15015, 15768,
15769, 15770, 15771

POSTMA, JOHANNES 456, 5836, 5837,
5838, 5839, 5840, 5841, 5842

POTEET, JAMES M. 12257

POTTER, DAVID M. 1639, 1640, 1641,
4174, 20120

POTTER, DAVID M., JR. 457, 12155

POTTER, HAROLD H. 10284

POTTER, HUGH O. 11353

POTTER, J. 15018

POTTS, ALMA G. 10987

POTTS, EUGENIA D. 4175

POULTON, HELEN J. 11147

POUND, LOUISE 17871

POUSSAINT, ALVIN F. 1642

POWDERMAKER, HORTENSE 16264

POWELL, ETTA O. 11090

POWELL, FRANCES L.J. 9771

POWELL, HERBERT 2746

POWELL, LAWRENCE N. 20399, 21044

POWELL, PHILIP W. 7944

POWELL, THEOPHILUS O. 15772,
15773

POWELL, VIRGIL S. 13051

POWELL, WILLIAM S. 1643, 1644,
12768

PRADO, CAIO JR. 7945

PRAGER, CAROLYN 2747, 2748

PRATT, ALEXANDER T.M. 9772

PRATT, FRANCIS E. 7946

PRATT-THOMAS, H. RAWLINGS 15774

PRAYTOR, ROBERT E. 11765

PREECE, HAROLD 5039

PREISSER, THOMAS M. 8612, 13792

PREJEAN, HAROLD 12417

PRESBYTERIAN CHURCH IN THE U.S.A.
17135

PRESENCE AFRICAINE 4176

PRESSLY, THOMAS J. 1645, 1646

PRESTON, DAVID 7947

PRESTON, DICKSON J. 11502, 15149

PRESTON, E. DELORUS 19716

PRESTON, E. DELORUS JR. 19717

PRESTON, EMMETT D. 9166

PRESTON, J.T.L.   4177

PRETO-RODAS, RICHARD A.   7948

PREYER, NORRIS W.   1647, 14781

PRICE, CLEMENT A.   10573

PRICE, EDWARD   9773

PRICE, EDWARD J.   9167

PRICE, EDWARD J., JR.   9775

PRICE, EDWARD T.   14026

PRICE, GLENN W.   2749

PRICE, JACOB   5843

PRICE, JACOB M.   13793

PRICE, JOHN A.   4178

PRICE, JOHN M.   12418

PRICE, JOSEPH E.   4179

PRICE, KATE H.   17872

PRICE, M.   16122

PRICE, MARTIN S.   4368

PRICE, RICHARD   392, 458, 459, 460,
   1648, 1649, 1650, 6991, 7951,
   7953, 7954, 7955, 7956, 7957,
   7959, 18675, 18676, 18677,
   18678, 19390, 20122

PRICE, SALLY   460, 7957, 7959,
   18675, 18676, 18677, 18678,
   19390

PRICE, THOMAS J.   4180, 5040, 7961

PRICE, WILLIAM S., JR.   8961,
   12769

PRICE-MARS, JEAN   5041

PRICHARD, WALTER   12420, 12421,
   20582

PRIESTLEY, MARGARET   5042

PRIESTLY, HERBERT I.   6994

PRIME, ALFRED C.   18568

PRIMEAU, RONALD   461, 18979

PRIMUS, PEARL E.   18464

PRINCE, BENJAMIN F.   19718

PRINCE, DIANE E.   9776

PRINCE, H.   9168

PRINCE, HOWARD M.   20123

PRINCE, WALTER F.   20124

PRINGLE, ELIZABETH W.   13053

PRIOR, LINDA T.   4181

PRITCHARD, ALAN   9169

PROCTOR, H.H.   17136, 17137

PROCTOR, HENRY H.   17138, 17873

PROCTOR, WILLIAM G.   12157, 1215
   12159

PROESMANS, R.   6995

PROTHERO, R.M.   4827

PROVIDENCE INSTITUTION FOR SAVIN
   5845

PROVINE, DOROTHY   9777

PRUCHA, FRANCIS P.   462

PRUDHOMME, CHARLES   15775

PRUNTY, MERLE JR.   14432

PRUSSING, EUGENE E.   19719, 1972

PRYOR, F.L.   1651

PSENCIK, LEROY F.   463

PICKETT, ERASTUS P. 9778

PUCKETT, NEWBELL N. 17139, 17140, 18303, 18304, 18305, 19391, 19392, 19393

PUCKREIN, GARY 15776

PUCKREIN, GARY A. 6937

PUGH, EVELYN L. 13794

PULLAN, BRIAN 1652

PULLEY, RICHARD D. 14783

PULWERS, JACOB E. 12422

PURCHAS-TULLOCH, JEAN A. 18306

PURIFOY, LEWIS M. 2750, 17141

PURIFOY, LEWIS M., JR. 17143

PURTEE, EDWARD O. 19721

PUTNAM, EMILY J. 4184

PUTNAM, JAMES W. 10846

PUTNAM, MARY B. 17144, 17145

PUTNEY, MARTHA 5846

PUTNEY, MARTHA S. 5847

PUZZO, DANTE A. 2751

PYBUS, CASSANDRA 1653

PYLES, JOSEPH C. 17875

PYRNELLE, LOUISA-CLARK 11766

QUAIFE, MILO M. 10847, 10848

QUALLS, YOURA T. 21045

QUARLES, BENJAMIN 209, 210, 1654, 1655, 1656, 1657, 1658, 1659, 1660, 1661, 4185, 4187, 4188, 8613, 8614, 8615, 8616, 9779, 9780, 9781, 9782, 10142, 19722, 19724, 19725, 20126, 21046

QUARLES, BENJAMIN A. 9783

QUASHIE, CASTINE I. 6999

QUEAL, WILLIAM G. 4189

QUERINO, MANUEL 7964

QUICK, EDWARD 4191

QUICK, HERBERT 4191

QUILLIN, FRANK U. 2753, 9784

QUINLAN, JOHN 4192, 14433

QUINLAN, JOHN F. 5849

QUINN, ARTHUR H. 4193

QUINN, CHARLOTTE A. 5043

QUINN, DAVID 2754

QUINNEY, VALERIE 5850, 7000

QUINT, HOWARD H. 4194

QUINTERO RIVERA, A.G. 7001

QUINTIN, M. 7965

R.J.H. 17876

RABASSA, GREGORY 7966

RABE, HARRY G. 8617

RABE, STEPHEN G. 3183

RABLE, GEORGE C. 4195

RABOTEAU, ALBERT J. 17146, 17147

RACHLEFF, MARSHALL 9170, 11768, 19728

RACHLEFF, MARSHALL J. 2755

RADCLIFFE-BROWN, ALFRED R. 5045

RADFORD, JOHN P. 9788, 13054, 15521, 15522

RADIN, PAUL   17325

RAFFE, WALTER G.   18465

RAFKY, DAVID M.   2757

RAGATZ, LOWELL J.   464, 465, 466,
  7006, 10143

RAGSDALE, EVALYN   5853

RAHV, PHILIP   1665

RAICHELSON, RICHARD M.   17877

RAINBOLT, JOHN C.   8618

RAINWATER, LEE   2758

RALPH, JULIAN   4196

RALSTON, RICHARD   9789, 17878

RAMA, C.M.   7967

RAMAGE, BURR J.   9171, 12160

RAMCHAND, KENNETH   7007

RAMLACKHANSINGH, G.S.   7008

RAMMELKAMP, JULIAN S.   9790

RAMOS, ARTHUR   7968, 7969, 7970,
  7971

RAMOS, DONALD   7972, 7973, 7974

RAMPERSAD, ARNOLD   1667

RAMPP, LARY C.   21048

RAMREKERSINGH, AUGUSTUS   7009

RAMSAY, ARCHIBALD S.   20584

RAMSDELL, CHARLES W.   1668, 11042,
  11043

RAMSEY, F.   17879

RANCK, JAMES B.   4197, 4198

RAND, LARRY A.   10145

RANDALL, JAMES G.   1669, 10146,
  20401

RANDALL, STANLEY J.   11937

RANDOLPH, PETER   15259

RANGE, WILLARD   8619, 12161

RANGER, T.O.   1670, 1671

RANKIN, CHARLES H.   17149

RANKIN, DAVID C.   2759, 9791, 97
  9793, 9794

RANSFORD, H. EDWARD   2760

RANSFORD, OLIVER   5854

RANSOM, ROGER   2902, 14435, 1450

RANSOM, ROGER L.   1673, 14436,
  14630

RANSON, A.R.H.   15260, 20585

RANTOUL, ROBERT   10482

RAPER, DENNIS L.   20127

RAPHAEL, ALAN   11359

RAPPAPORT, STANLEY   19729

RASTEGAR, CAROL C.   1674

RATCLIFFE, DONALD   1675

RATCLIFFE, ROBERTA M.   13257

RATEKIN, MERVYN   7010

RATHBURN, F.G.   17880

RATNER, LORMAN   2761, 2762

RATNER, MARC L.   1676

RATTNER, SELMA   9795

RATTRAY, ROBERT S.   5047

RAUCH, BASIL   7011

RAULSTON, J. LEONARD 13258

RAVENEL, CHARLOTTE ST. J. 12974

RAVENEL, HENRY W. 13023, 13058

RAVENEL, ROSE P. 13059

RAVITZ, ABE C. 13060

RAWICK, GEORGE 1677, 16269

RAWICK, GEORGE P. 467, 468, 469,
   1679, 1680, 1681, 5049, 19116

RAWLEY, JAMES A. 2763, 4199, 5855,
   10150

RAWLYK, GEORGE A. 9796

RAY, BENJAMIN 5050

RAY, EMMA 18982

RAY, JOHN M. 5856

RAYBECK, JOSEPH G. 11044

RAYMOND 4200

RAYMOND, WILLIAM O. 10285

REA, ROBERT R. 11938

READ, A.W. 19395

READ, ALLEN W. 19396, 19397

READ, BENJAMIN M. 7975

READ, HARLAN E. 5857

READ, MARGARET M. 4201

READ, WILLIAM A. 19398

READY, M.L. 8620

REAGON, BERNICE 17881, 17882

REAT, JAMES L. 10894

RECHTIN, WILLIAM T. 2764

RECKORD, MARY 1634, 4202, 7012,
   7013, 7014, 7016

REDDICK, A.R. 1635

REDDICK, JAMES P., JR. 7976

REDDICK, L.D. 1636, 1687, 1688,
   4203, 21052

REDDICK, LAWRENCE D. 1689, 2765

REDDING, JAY S. 1690, 4204

REDDING, SAUNDERS 472

REDKEY, EDWIN 4205

REDWINE, W.A. 13417, 13418

REDWOOD, A.C. 20586

REED, GERMAINE A. 9172

REED, H. CLAY 473, 9173, 11214

REED, HARRY A. 8621, 9797, 19731

REED, JOHN C. 20403

REED, MARION B. 473

REED, MARION L.B. 19732

REED, PATRICK 13765

REED, RICHARD C. 17154

REED, ROBERT M. 7018

REED, T. EDWARD 2766

REEDER, B. 546

REES, A.M. 5858

REES, GARETH 5859, 5860

REFSELL, OLIVER M. 13419

REGO, WALDELOIR 1692

REHDER, JOHN B. 12427

REHIN, GEORGE F. 17467

REICH, JEROME 5862

REICH, PETER 7419

REICHARD, MAXIMILAN 9174

REICHLIN, ELINOR 13062

REID, BARNEY F. 17883

REID, BILL G. 20587

REID, GURNEY H. 15960

REID, JOHN P. 14029

REID, JOSEPH D. 14438

REID, JULIA M. 5863

REID, ROBERT D. 11772, 17156, 20589

REID, ROBIE L. 10286

REID, WHITELAW 4206

REIDY, JOSEPH P. 17468

REILLY, EDWARD C. 4207

REILLY, TIMOTHY 12428

REILLY, TIMOTHY F. 12429, 12430

REIMERS, DAVID 4483

REIMERS, DAVID M. 2768, 17159

REINDERS, ROBERT C. 9799, 9800, 12432, 12433, 12434, 12435, 15961

REINECKE, JOHN E. 19399, 19400

REIS, J.B.G. 7978

REIS, JAIME 1693, 7979, 7980, 7982, 7983

REIS, JOAO J. 7984

REITZ, ELIZABETH 15405

REIVICH, LOIS 7019

REMINI, ROBERT V. 20291

RENDER, SYLVIA L. 231, 2769, 42 16485

RENS, LUCIEN L.E. 7986

PENSHAW, J. PARKE 7987

RENTON, A. WOOD 7020

REPS, JOHN W. 11627

RESH, RICHARD W. 2770

RESNICK, DANIEL P. 5864

REUBEN, ODELL R. 4211

REUTER, E.B. 1694

REUTER, EDWARD B. 2773, 2774, 16270

REXROTH, KENNETH 1695

REYBURN, ROBERT 4212, 4213, 157 15780, 15781

REYNOLDS, C. ROY 7023

REYNOLDS, DONALD E. 20135

REYNOLDS, EDWARD 5053

REYNOLDS, HELEN W. 8623, 19733

REYNOLDS, MARION H. 11091

REYNOLDS, MARYLEE 11773

REYNOLDS, MICHAEL M. 476

REYNOLDS, TODD A. 11360

REZENDE, GERVASIO C.D. 7988

RHETT, ROBERT G. 13063

RHODES, BESSIE M.L. 124

RHODES, ETHEL C.   11045

RHODES, JAMES F.   1696, 4214,
   15358

RHODES, ROBERT C.   11836

RIACH, D.C.   4215

RIACH, DOUGLAS C.   2775

RIBEIRO, DARCY   7024

RIBEIRO, RENE   7990

RICARDS, SHERMAN L.   13064

RICE, ARNOLD S.   15151

RICE, C. DUNCAN   477, 1698, 1699,
   1700, 2776, 4216, 4217, 7025

RICE, DON S.   18139

RICE, ELIZA G.   10153

RICE, ELIZABETH G.   21054

RICE, MADELEINE H.   4218, 4219

RICE, MARY L.   4220

RICE, OTIS K.   13802

RICH, CARROLL Y.   18308

RICH, E.E.   7027

RICH, EDSON P.   10978

RICHARD, HENRY T.   11181

RICHARDS, A.M.   5865

RICHARDS, CHANNING   21055

RICHARDS, ELAINE C.   8624

RICHARDS, LEONARD L.   2777, 4221

RICHARDS, PAUL   1701

RICHARDS, W.A.   5866, 5867, 5868

RICHARDSON, ARCHIE G.   19229

RICHARDSON, BARBARA A.   11939

RICHARDSON, BENJAMIN H.   15964

RICHARDSON, CLEMENT   10485, 18309

RICHARDSON, CORA L.   14442

RICHARDSON, DAVID   5869, 5870,
   5871

RICHARDSON, DAVID R.   5054

RICHARDSON, E.   9178

RICHARDSON, E.C.   1702

RICHARDSON, EUDORA R.   13804

RICHARDSON, FRANCIS D.   12436

RICHARDSON, HARRY VAN BUREN   17165

RICHARDSON, JOE M.   11628, 11940,
   11941, 11942, 19230, 21057,
   21058, 21059

RICHARDSON, MARILYN   478

RICHARDSON, MARTIN D.   19734

RICHARDSON, PATRICK   4222

RICHARDSON, SAMUEL A.   7992

RICHARDSON, WILLIAM   5873

RICHES, WILLIAM T.M.   8625

RICHMOND, M.A.   4223

RICHTER, WILLIAM L.   12437

RICKARD, CHAUNCEY   10689

RICKARD, JAMES H.   21060

RICKE, DENNIS F.   10895

RICKMAN, CLAUDE R.   17166

RICKS, GEORGE R.   7993, 17884

RIDDELL, WILLIAM R. 479, 4224, 4225, 5874, 5875, 5876, 7028, 8626, 8627, 8628, 9179, 9182, 9184, 10287, 10288, 10289, 10290, 10292, 10293, 10295, 10296, 10297, 10298, 10299, 10300, 10301, 10302, 10303, 10961

RIDER, S.G. 9801

RIDER, SIDNEY S. 8629, 10804

RIDGEWAY, MICHAEL A. 13806

RIES, ADELINE F. 16487

RIETVELD, RONALD D. 4226

RIGGIO, THOMAS P. 2778

RIGGS, ELEANOR 11675

RIGHTS, DOUGLAS L. 12771

RILEY, B.F. 4227, 17168

RILEY, CARROLL L. 11046

RILEY, FRANKLIN L. 480, 2779, 8631

RILEY, G. MICHAEL 7994

RILEY, LLOYD H. 2780

RILEY, PATRICIA M. 9802

RIORDAN, ROBERT V. 6579

RIPLEY, C. PETER 12439, 16272

RIPLEY, CHARLES P. 12440

RIPLEY, ELIZA M.C.H. 12441

RIPLEY, WILLIAM Z. 13807

RIPPY, J. FRED 11047

RISINGER, ROBERT G. 15262

RIVERS, LARRY E. 481

RIVERS, ROBERT H. 17169

ROACH, HILDRED 5055, 8632

ROARK, JAMES L. 14632, 20594

ROBBINS, FRED 5879, 5880

ROBBINS, GERALD 13065, 13066

ROBBINS, HAL 13424

ROBBINS, I.M. 14444

ROBBINS, MICHAEL W. 8633

ROBBINS, PEGGY 13259

ROBBOY, ANITA W. 19736

ROBBOY, STANLEY J. 19736

ROBERSON, NANCY C. 11775, 17170

ROBERT, CHARLES E. 4228

ROBERT, JOSEPH C. 12773, 13809, 13810, 13811, 14785, 17171

ROBERTS, ANDREW 5056

ROBERTS, FRANCES C. 10155

ROBERTS, G.W. 7029, 7030

ROBERTS, GEORGE W. 7031, 7032

ROBERTS, HELEN 7033

ROBERTS, HELEN H. 7034

ROBERTS, J. DEOTIS 5057, 17172

ROBERTS, JAMES D. 18312

ROBERTS, JOHN W. 15446

ROBERTS, MARY E. 11361

ROBERTS, NANCY 18570

ROBERTS, R.O. 5831

ROBERTS, RICHARD L. 5058

ROBERTS, SAMUEL K.   1703

ROBERTS, W. ADOLPHE   7035

ROBERTS, WESLEY A.   1704, 8634

ROBERTSON, IAN A.   19402

ROBERTSON, JAMES A.   7036, 12442

ROBERTSON, JAMES I., JR.   21064

ROBERTSON, MARY D.   13812

ROBERTSON, PETER C.   11550

"ROBIN HOOD"   5882

ROBINSON, ARMSTEAD L.   13260,
    20595, 20596

ROBINSON, AVIS P.   15263

ROBINSON, CAREY   7037

ROBINSON, CEDRIC   1705

ROBINSON, CHARLES   10945

ROBINSON, DAVID J.   14907

ROBINSON, DONALD L.   4229, 4230

ROBINSON, HENRY S.   9803

ROBINSON, JAMES H.   13261

ROBINSON, JEAN W.   8635

ROBINSON, LEIGH   4231

ROBINSON, MABEL L.   17890

ROBINSON, MARY N.   10754

ROBINSON, NINA H.   4232

ROBINSON, RICHARDSON R.   2781

ROBINSON, ROBERT L.   5883

ROBINSON, VICTOR   4233

ROBINSON, W. STITT   4234

ROBINSON, WILLIAM H.   4235, 10486,
    17469, 18984

ROBOTHAM, DON   7038

ROBSON, DAVID W.   2782

ROBSON, ERIC   4236

ROCCA, MARIE L.   7995

ROCHE, EMMA L.   11777, 11778

ROCKEL, ERIC G.   11411

ROCKETT, ROCKY L.   1706

ROCKWELL, TIM O.   13813

RODABAUGH, JAMES H.   9804

RODABOUGH, JOHN E.   12605

RODEFFER, J.D.   482

RODEHEAVER, HOMER A.   17891

RODENBAUGH, JEAN   18314

RODGERS, AVA D.   12163

RODGERS, BETSY   5884

RODILES, IGNACIO M.   17173

RODMAN, SELDON   7996

RODNEY, W.A.   5059

RODNEY, WALTER   1707, 2783, 4237,
    5061, 5062, 5064, 5065, 5066,
    5889, 5891, 5893, 7039, 20292

RODNEY, WALTER A.   5067

RODNITZKY, JEROME L.   17892

RODRIGUES, JOSE H.   7998, 7999

RODRIGUEZ, FREDERICK M.   8000

RODRIQUEZ, MARIO   8001

RODWAY, JAMES   7041, 8002

ROEDIGER, DAVID 5069

ROEDIGER, DAVID R. 19740

ROESSINGH, M.P.H. 483

ROETHLER, MICHAEL D. 14031

ROGERS, DOUGLAS G. 2784

ROGERS, GEORGE C. 13067

ROGERS, GEORGE C., JR. 13068,
   13069, 13070, 13071, 13072

ROGERS, J.A. 1708

ROGERS, J.G. 15783

ROGERS, J.S. 485

ROGERS, JAMES A. 2785

ROGERS, JOEL A. 2786, 5070

ROGERS, JOHN R. 2787

ROGERS, JOSEPH M. 4238

ROGERS, MARGUERITE S. 17174

ROGERS, TOMMY W. 4239, 12443,
   17175

ROGERS, W. MCDOWELL 9186

ROGERS, WILLIAM W. 11947, 12164

ROHLEHR, GORDON 1709

ROHRBOUGH, MALCOLM J. 11676

ROKELA 4240

ROLAND, CHARLES P. 12446, 20597,
   20598, 20600

ROLAND, HAROLD 13073

ROLLER, DAVID C. 486

ROLLIN, FRANK A. 21066

ROLLINS, ALICE W. 15526

ROLLINS, HYDER E. 4241

ROLLO, VERA A.F. 11505

ROLLO, VERA F. 11506

ROMAN, C.V. 4242, 4243, 16273

ROMAN, CHARLES V. 4244

ROMERO, FERNANDO 5895

ROMERO, PATRICIA 5896

ROMERO, PATRICIA W. 487, 1710,
   20434

ROMEYN, HENRY 21067

RONCAL, JOAQUIN 8004

RONEN, DOV 5897

ROOKE, PATRICIA T. 7045, 17176,
   17177, 17179

ROOKMAAKER, H.R. 17893

ROOKS, MILTON P. 9806

ROPER, DONALD M. 9187

ROPER, JOHN A. 2789

ROPER, JOHN H. 1711, 1712, 1713,
   1714

ROPER, LAURA W. 1715

ROPPOLO, JOSEPH P. 15153

ROSBROW, JAMES M. 20137

ROSE, ALAN H. 2790, 2791

ROSE, ARNOLD M. 1716, 4245, 424

ROSE, F. HOLLAND 5898

ROSE, JAMES 488, 10404

ROSE, LISLE A. 20138

ROSE, LOUIS A. 10156

ROSE, PETER I. 4247

ROSE, WILLIE LEE 489, 1717, 1718, 2792, 8636, 13076, 21068, 21069, 21070, 21072

ROSEBOOM, EUGENE H. 21073

ROSEN, BRUCE 4249

ROSENBAUM, JANE A. 4250

ROSENBERG, BRUCE A. 17181

ROSENBERG, LEONARD B. 10575

ROSENBERG, MORTON M. 2793

ROSENBERG, NEIL V. 2794

ROSENBERG, NORMAN L. 9188

ROSENBLATT, SAMUEL M. 5899

ROSENDALE, NANCY D. 4251

ROSENGARTEN, THEODORE 19117

ROSENTHAL, BERNARD 2369, 10367

ROSENTHAL, ERIC 5900

ROSEWATER, VICTOR 10158

ROSIN, WILBERT H. 11629

ROSS, ALEXANDER 18985

ROSS, DAVID A. 5901

ROSS, EDYTH L. 4252

ROSS, FITZGERALD 15359

ROSS, MARGARET S. 9808

ROSS, MELVIN L., JR. 11780

ROSS, RAYMOND A. 4253

ROSS, STEVEN J. 12607

ROSSBACH, JEFFREY S. 19742

ROSSELOT, GERALD S. 4254

ROTBERG, ROBERT 4255

ROTBERG, ROBERT I. 3855, 7047, 7048

ROTHGERY, MICHAEL F. 9809

ROTHMAN, DAVID 1719

ROTHSEIDEN, JEANE L. 16060

ROTHSTEIN, MORTON 1720, 1721, 1722, 12609, 14448, 14449

ROTTENBERG, SIMON 5902

ROUCEK, JOSEPH S. 1723

ROUNDTREE, HELEN C. 9810

ROUNDTREE, JOHN G. 19235

ROUNDTREE, LOUISE 490

ROUSE, PARKE JR. 8637

ROUSE-JONES, MARGARET D. 7049

ROUSSEVE, CHARLES B. 12448

ROUT, LESLIE B. 15785

ROUT, LESLIE B., JR. 1724, 2795, 8006, 8007

ROWAN, CHARLES 4256

ROWAN, RICHARD L. 14788

ROWELL, CHARLES H. 491

ROWLAND, ARTHUR R. 492

ROWLAND, DUNBAR 12610, 12611

ROWLAND, REGINALD 18986

ROWLAND, THOMAS B. 9190

ROWLEY, K.M. 7051

ROY, EMILIO 7052

ROY, JOSEPH E.   21075

ROYCE, CHARLES C.   14032

ROZETT, JOHN M.   2797

ROZWENC, EDWIN C.   4257

RUBENSTEIN, HYMIE 16567

RUBIN, JOAN 493

RUBIN, JULIUS   14207, 14451

RUBIN, LOUIS D., JR.   1725, 1726,
    4258

RUBIN, ROGER H.   1727

RUBIN, VERA   4259, 7053, 7054,
    7055

RUBY, BARBARA C.   20602

RUCHAMES, LOUIS   1728, 2798, 2799,
    2800, 2801, 2802, 9812

RUCHKIN, JUDITH P.   9813

RUCKER, ALVIN 14033

RUDD, DANIEL A.   4260

RUDNYANSZKY, LESLIE I.   5904

RUDOLPH, DONNA K.   8010

RUDOLPH, FREDERICK 2803

RUDOLPH, G.A.   8010

RUDOLPH, RICHARD H.   5905

RUDWICK, ELLIOTT   80, 1729, 3993,
    9415, 9416, 19481

RUDWICK, ELLIOTT M.   1730

RUFFIN, EDWARD 20603

RUFFIN, FRANK G.   4261

RUFFIN, GEORGE L.   8640

RUIZ, P.E.   7057

RUKEYSER, M.   20141

RULE', LUCIEN V.   10161

RUMMONDS, F.   8011

RUNCIE, JOHN 2804

RUNES, RICHARD N.   17374

RUPERT, ANTON J.   10074, 10162

RUSCO, ELMER R.   11109

RUSHING, ANDREA B.   494

RUSHTON, RAY 9191

RUSSEL, ROBERT R.   4262, 9192,
    9193, 10851, 14452, 14453,
    14454, 14455, 14456

RUSSELL, HENRY 5906

RUSSELL, JOHN H.   8259, 9815

RUSSELL, MARION J.   495

RUSSELL, MICHELE 2806

RUSSELL, MRS. CHARLES E.B.   5907

RUSSELL, SYLVESTER 17894

RUSSELL-WOOD, A.J.R.   1731, 2807
    8012, 8015, 8016, 8017, 8018,
    8019, 8020, 8021, 16278

RUSSO, PASQUALE 4263

RUTHERFORD, MILDRED L.   2809, 42
    16048

RUTLEDGE, ANNA W.   18680

RUTLEDGE, ARCHIBALD 18317

RUTLEDGE, IAN 6414

RUTLEDGE, IVAN C.   9195, 9196

RUTLEDGE, WILLIAM S.   11781

RUTMAN, ANITA H. 15023, 15786

RUTMAN, DARRETT B. 1733, 8641,
  15023, 15786

RYAN, FRANK 13077

RYAN, LEE W. 4265

RYAN, MARY C. 4266

RYAN, MARY P. 16492

RYAN, SELWYN D. 7058

RYAN, TERRENCE C.I. 5072

RYDER, A.F.C. 5910, 5911, 5912,
  5913

RYDER, CHARLES J. 17895

RYE, STEPHEN H. 9818

RYERSON, PAUL S. 8972

RYLAND, GARNETT 17184

RYLAND, ROBERT 13818

RYMAN, CHERYL 7059

RYWELL, MARTIN 496

S., W.B. 4117

SABIN, JAMES T. 4267, 5914

SABLE, MARTIN H. 497

SADIK, MARVIN S. 4268

SADLER, LYNN B. 12775

SADLER, ROBERT 18987

SAFFORD, FRANK 8022

SAHLI, J.R. 498

SAINSBURY, JOHN A. 10368

SAKLATVALA, BERAM 4269

SALEM, SAM E. 1734

SALERNO, PETER C. 8972

SALISBURY, NANCY L. 4270

SALKEY, ANDREW 7060

SALLEY, ALEXANDER S. 8642, 13078

SALMON, CHARLES S. 7061

SALOUTOS, THEODORE 1735

SALTZMAN, MARTIN 2810

SALVADOR, GEORGE A. 4271

SALWEN, BERT 499, 18525

SAMETH, SIGMUND 14034

SAMPSON, B.K. 9819

SAMPSON, F.A. 500

SAMPSON, R.V. 9197

SAMS, CONWAY W. 5073

SANBORN, FRANKLIN B. 10946

SANCHEZ-ALBORNOZ, NICHOLAS 8023

SANCHEZ-SAAVEDRA, E.M. 9198

SANDAY, PEGGY R. 17473

SANDBO, ANNA L. 4272

SANDERS, CHARLES R. 12776

SANDERS, ISAIAH S. 19404

SANDERS, MARY E. 12450

SANDERS, RONALD 2811

SANDERS, THOMAS G. 8024

SANDERSON, F.E. 501, 5916

SANDERSON, WARREN C. 1737

SANDOVAL, VALERIE 1738

SANDROCK, MARGUERITA J. 12777

SANGSTER, IAN 7062

SANNEH, L.O. 5075

SARASOHN, DAVID 598

SARAYDAR, EDWARD 14458, 14637

SARMIENTO, DOMINGO F. 8025

SASS, HERBERT R. 17474, 17916

SATER, WILLIAM F. 8026

SATTERFIELD, JAMES H. 17185

SATZ, RONALD N. 5917, 5918, 14035

SAUER, CARL O. 7063

SAUL, SUZANNE M. 17186

SAUM, LEWIS O. 4273

SAUNDERS, A.C. DE C.M. 4274

SAUNDERS, D. GAIL 7064

SAUNDERS, EMANUEL 9820, 14459

SAUNDERS, JOHN 8027

SAUNDERS, JOHN V.D. 8028

SAUNDERS, ROBERT M. 9199

SAVADGE, WESLEY R. 5919

SAVAGE, ROSALIND 9821

SAVAGE, W. SHERMAN 4275, 9200,
    11049, 11050, 11051, 11149,
    12778, 19746

SAVAGE, WILLIAM S. 5920

SAVETH, EDWARD N. 502, 1740

SAVITT, TODD L. 13822, 15362,
    15528, 15787, 15789

SAXON, LYLE 12451, 12452, 18318

SAXTON, ALEXANDER 2812, 2813

SAYERS, RAYMOND S. 8029

SAYLOR, W. CROMWELL 14460

SCALLY, MARY A. 17187

SCALLY, SISTER ANTHONY 1741

SCANZONI, JOHN H. 16280

SCARANO, FRANCISCO 7065

SCARANO, FRANCISCO A. 7066

SCARANO, JULITA 8030

SCARBOROUGH, DOROTHY 17896

SCARBOROUGH, RUTH 12165, 12166

SCARBOROUGH, W.S. 14789, 18320,
    19405, 19406

SCARBOROUGH, WILLIAM K. 1742,
    12613, 14461, 14886, 14887,
    15364, 15791

SCARPINO, PHILIP V. 11633, 11634

SCARUPA, HARRIET J. 16282

SCELLE, GEORGES 5921

SCHAEFER, DONALD 14639

SCHAEFER, DONALD F. 14464, 14638

SCHAEFFER, PAUL N. 10755

SCHAEFFER, WENDELL G. 8188

SCHAFER, DANIEL L. 7067

SCHAFER, JOSEPH 9201

SCHAFER, JUDITH K. 12453

SCHAPER, WILLIAM A. 13080

SCHAPSMEIER, EDWARD L. 505

SCHAPSMEIER, FREDERICK H.   505

SCHARF, J. THOMAS   11507

SCHATZ, WALTER   506

SCHEELE, RAYMOND L.   7163

SCHEIBER, H.N.   14143

SCHEIBER, HARRY N.   1743

SCHEIPS, PAUL J.   2814

SCHENCK, WARREN R.   10576

SCHERER, JAMES A.   4276

SCHERER, LESTER B.   8643, 17189

SCHERMAN, KATHARINE   7068

SCHERMERHORN, R.A.   18321

SCHEUB, HAROLD   507

SCHIFFMAN, JOSEPH   2815

SCHIMMEL, JOHANNES C.   17897

SCHLACHTER, GAIL A.   508

SCHLEIN, I.   17898

SCHLENKER, JON A.   13999

SCHLESINGER, ARTHUR M.   1744, 5922

SCHLOBOHM, DIETRICH H.   9202

SCHLOTTERBECK, JOHN   13824

SCHLUTER, HERMAN   4277

SCHMIDT, CYNTHIA E.   17190

SCHMIDT, FREDRIKA T.   2816

SCHMIDT, G.   4278

SCHMIDT, HUBERT G.   10577, 10578, 10579, 10580

SCHMIDT, O.L.   19747

SCHMITZ, M.D.   14639

SCHMITZ, MARK D.   12454, 14463, 14464

SCHNEIDER, FRANK M.   9203

SCHNEIDER, GILBERT D.   19407

SCHNEIDER, MABEL A.   12033

SCHNEIDER, RONALD M.   323

SCHNEIDER, TRACY W.   12780

SCHNELL, KEMPES   9204

SCHNELL, KEMPES Y.   9205

SCHOEN, HAROLD   9823, 9824, 9825

SCHOENBERGER, DALE T.   11052

SCHOENWALD, RICHARD L.   703

SCHOFIELD, M.M.   5923

SCHOMBURG, ARTHUR A.   1745

SCHOR, JOEL   509, 19748

SCHOR, JOEL A.   19749

SCHOULER, JAMES   4279

SCHOUTE, D.   5924

SCHREYER, GEORGE M.   17191

SCHRIVER, EDWARD O.   4280

SCHROEDER, GLENNA R.   4281

SCHUCHTER, ARNOLD   17192

SCHULER, MONICA   1746, 5076, 7072, 7073, 7075, 7076, 8031, 8032, 20147

SCHULMAN, IVAN A.   7077

SCHULTE NORDHOLT, J.W.   4282

SCHULTZ, HAROLD S.   5925

SCHULTZ, THEODORE W. 14465

SCHURZ, WILLIAM L. 8033

SCHUTZ, JOHN A. 7078, 7079

SCHUYLER, GEORGE S. 1747

SCHUYLER, ROBERT L. 7080, 18572

SCHWAAB, EUGENE L. 510

SCHWARTZ, DAVID F. 9206

SCHWARTZ, EUGENIA S. 1391

SCHWARTZ, HAROLD 9207, 19750

SCHWARTZ, JACK 15573

SCHWARTZ, L.P. 9208

SCHWARTZ, PHILIP J. 4283

SCHWARTZ, ROSALIE 19751, 19752

SCHWARTZ, STUART B. 1748, 2817,
7335, 8035, 8038, 8040, 9826,
19753, 20296

SCHWEIKART, LARRY 2818

SCHWENINGER, LOREN 9827, 9828,
9831, 13263, 13264, 15870,
16283, 19755

SCISCO, L.D. 4284, 8260

SCOBIE, EDWARD 2819

SCOFIELD, JOHN 7081

SCOLES, IGNATIUS 8041

SCOMP, H.A. 12167

SCOTT, ANNE F. 4285, 16494, 16495

SCOTT, ARTHUR P. 9209

SCOTT, CLARISSA S. 7082

SCOTT, EDWIN J. 13082

SCOTT, H. HAROLD 5927

SCOTT, HENRY H. 15794

SCOTT, I.B. 4286

SCOTT, JOHN A. 1750, 1751, 4287

SCOTT, JOSEPH W. 2820

SCOTT, KENNETH 5928, 5929, 20149

SCOTT, MARION G. 17899

SCOTT, OSBORNE 19236

SCOTT, PATRICIA B. 511

SCOTT, ROLAND B. 15025

SCOTT, STERLING C. 12456

SCOTT, VIRGINIA 19756

SCOTT, WILLIAM B. 4288

SCOTT, WILLIAM R. 4289

SCRIBNER, ROBERT L. 13827, 1515

SCRUGGS, OTEY 19757

SCRUGGS, OTEY M. 1752, 1753, 17

SCRUGGS, WILLIAM L. 8261

SCUDDER, HAROLD H. 4290

SCULLY, JOHN 18588

SEAGA, EDWARD 7083

SEAGRAVE, CHARLES E. 4291, 1446

SEAL, A.G. 12614

SEAL, ALBERT G. 12615, 12616

SEALE, LEA 18323

SEALE, MARIANNA 18323

SEARCY, J.T. 15795

SEARS, CYRUS 21076

SEAY, DOROTHY 12169

SEBASTIAN, LINDA J.C. 17900

SEBBA, GREGOR 12170

SECRIST, PHILIP 9210

SEDA, ELENA P. 7163

SEEBER, EDWARD D. 4292, 4293

SEEGER, CHARLES 17901

SEFTON, JAMES E. 11943

SEGAL, CHARLES M. 9211

SEHR, TIMOTHY J. 4294

SEIDEN, MELVIN 2822

SEIDLEMAN, MORTCN 19408

SEIP, TERRY L. 9832

SELIGMANN, HERBERT J. 4295

SELJAN, ZORA 18324

SELLERS, CHARLES G. 1839

SELLERS, CHARLES G., JR. 4296, 16050

SELLERS, JAMES B. 9833, 11782

SELLERS, LEILA 13084

SELLIN, J. THORSTEN 4297

SELLIN, J.T. 9212

SELPH, FANNIE E. 4298

SELVA, LANCE H. 2609

SELZER, CATHARINE R. 9834

SENESE, DONALD J. 9213, 9214

SENIOR, CARL H. 7084

SENIOR, W. 5930, 5931

SERAILE, WILLIAM 9836, 20407, 21077, 21078

SERENO, RENZO 17196

SERNETT, MILTON C. 17198, 19237

SETON, IMOGENE H. 5932

SETTLE, E. OPHELIA 18729

SEWARD, RUDY R. 16285

SEWELL, GEORGE A. 12617

SEWELL, RICHARD H. 1755, 11053

SEXSMITH, W.N. 19758

SEXTON, JESSIE E. 4299

SEYMOUR 4300

SHAFER, ROBERT J. 8042

SHAFFER, E.T.H. 1756

SHALER, N.S. 2823, 4302, 4303, 4304, 4305, 11363, 11364, 15797

SHALER, NATHANIEL S. 2824, 4306, 19759

SHALHOPE, ROBERT E. 1757, 2825, 2826

SHALIMAR 5933

SHANKMAN, ARNOLD 1758

SHANNON, A.H. 2827

SHANNON, ALEXANDER H. 2828, 2829, 2830

SHANNON, FRED A. 21079, 21080, 21081

SHAPIRO, EDWARD S. 1759

SHAPIRO, HERBERT 1760, 2831

SHAPIRO, LINN   4307

SHAPIRO, SAMUEL   19760

SHARE, ALLEN J.   1761

SHARMA, MOHAN L.   17902

SHARP, WILLIAM F.   8045, 8046,
    8047, 9837, 14467

SHARPE, ESTHER E.   11054

SHARPLEY, ROBERT H.   15365, 15366

SHARRAR, GEORGE T.   8644

SHARRER, G. TERRY   8645

SHARROW, WALTER G.   4308

SHAW, ELTON R.   13426

SHAW, ERNEST   13829

SHAW, GEORGE C.   9838

SHAW, HELLEN L.   14037

SHAW, JAMES   20408

SHAW, JOANN N.   18681

SHAW, WARREN C.   4309

SHAY, GEORGE H.   4310

SHEA, JOSEPH M.   17200

SHEDD, MARGARET   18471

SHEED, WILFRED   1762

SHEEHAN, ARTHUR   10693

SHEEHAN, ARTHUR T.   10694

SHEEHAN, ELIZABETH   10693

SHEEHAN, ELIZABETH O.   10694

SHEELER, J. REUBEN   8646, 8647

SHEELER, JOHN R.   9215, 9839, 9840,
    13832, 13833

SHEINK, E.W.   2832

SHELDEN, RANDALL G.   13266

SHELDON, A.   19763

SHELDON, GEORGE   10488

SHELDON, JANE M.   19764

SHELDON, MARIANNE B.   9217

SHELE DE VERE, M.R.B.   19765

SHELLEY, B.   4311

SHELLEY, DIAN L.   2833

SHELTON, EDWARD E.   17201

SHELTON, HORACE H.   15155

SHELTON, JANE DE FOREST   10405

SHELTON, JANE T.   12172

SHENKEL, J. RICHARD   12458

SHENTON, JAMES   4312

SHEPARD, ELI   18326

SHEPARD, SARAH M.   4313

SHEPHERD, JAMES F.   5934, 15156

SHEPPARD   18989

SHEPPARD, JILL   7085, 7086

SHEPPARD, R.Z.   1763

SHEPPERD, GLADYS B.   12618

SHEPPERSON, GEORGE   1764, 1765,
    1766, 4314, 4315, 4316, 5077

SHERER, ROBERT G.   19238

SHERER, ROBERT G., JR.   1767, 98

SHERIDAN, RICHARD B.   5935, 5936
    7087, 7089, 7091, 7093, 7094,
    7095, 7096, 7097, 7098, 7099,
    7100, 7101, 7102, 8648, 8649,

14468, 15800

SHERIFF, A.H.M.   5078

SHERLOCK, P.M.   18327

SHERLOCK, PHILIP   7103

SHERLOCK, PHILIP M.   6954

SHERMAN, ALFONSO   4317

SHERMAN, GEORGE R.   21082

SHERMAN, WILLIAM L.   8048, 8049, 8050, 8051

SHERMAN, WILLIAM T.   20409

SHERRARD, OWEN A.   5937

SHERRARD, VIRGINIA B.   16497

SHERRILL, P.M.   12782

SHERWIN, OSCAR   4318, 15157, 15158, 15766

SHERWOOD, FOSTER H.   8932

SHERWOOD, HENRY N.   2834, 4319, 9218, 9843, 9844, 9845, 15574

SHERWOOD, MORGAN B.   1768

SHICK, TOM   2835

SHICK, TOM W.   512, 4320, 4321, 4322

SHIFFRIN, STEVEN H.   19767

SHILLER, SAMUEL   17202

SHILLINGS, DAVID   4323

SHIMKIN, DEMITRI B.   9346, 16286

SHINGLETON, ROYCE   1769

SHINGLETON, ROYCE G.   4324, 5938, 9219, 15451

SHINN, CHARLES H.   16052

SHINODA, YASUKO I.   12783

SHIPMATE JIM   5939

SHIPPEE, LESTER B.   513, 1770

SHIPPEN, EDWARD   5940

SHIVELY, CHARLES   4325

SHOCKLEY, ANN A.   314

SHOCKLEY, GRANT S.   17203

SHOEMAKER, FLOYD C.   11635

SHOFNER, JERRELL H.   9220, 9221, 11946, 11947, 14791

SHORE, JOSEPH   7104

SHORT, K.R.M.   5941, 7105

SHORT, KENNETH R.M.   17205, 17206

SHORTER, CHARLES   11217

SHORTER, EDWARD   15452

SHOWELL, FRANKLIN C.   969

SHOWERS, SUSAN   18328

SHRIDER, J. MORAN   10369

SHRYOCK, RICHARD H.   12174, 15801, 15802, 15803

SHUFELDT, ROBERT W.   2836

SHUGG, ROGER W.   9847, 12459

SHUNK, EDWARD W.   2837

SHURTLEFF, NATHANIEL B.   10490

SHY, JOHN W.   9222

SHYLLON, FOLARIN O.   2838, 2839, 7106

SIBLEY, MARILYN M.   13428

SIDES, SUDIE D.   16053, 16054, 16568

SIEBER, ROY 5079

SIEBERT, WILBUR H. 9348, 11948, 11949, 11950, 19768, 19769, 19770, 19771, 19772, 19773, 19774, 19775, 19776, 19777

SIEG, VERA 514

SIEGEL, BERNARD J. 1771

SIEGEL, FRED 1772, 1773, 1774, 13836

SIGLER, JAY A. 9223

SIGLER, PHIL S. 9849

SIKES, LEWRIGHT 15804

SILBERMAN, CHARLES E. 9224

SILBEY, JOEL H. 2840, 2841

SILCOX, HARRY C. 9850, 9851, 9852

SILIE, RUBEN 947

SILL, DUNKIN H. 10695

SILLEN, SAMUEL 4326

SILVER, JAMES W. 5942, 20607

SILVERA, EDWARD 4327

SILVERMAN, CATHERINE 1775

SILVERMAN, JASON H. 2842, 19778, 19779

SIMBA, MALIK 9225

SIMMEL, GEORG 2843

SIMMONS, DONALD C. 5080

SIMMONS, WILLIAM J. 20152

SIMMS, DAVID MCD 17904

SIMMS, HENRY H. 4328

SIMMS, JAMES M. 17208

SIMMS, L. MOODY JR. 1777, 1778, 1779, 2844

SIMMS, MARION 12460

SIMON, JOHN Y. 21083

SIMON, JULIAN L. 14471

SIMON, KATHLEEN 5081

SIMON, RICHARD S. 4329

SIMONS, A.M. 14472

SIMPKINS, PATRICK L. 12785

SIMPSON, ALBERT F. 4330, 4331

SIMPSON, CRAIG 4332

SIMPSON, DONALD G. 10304

SIMPSON, ELEANOR E. 2845

SIMPSON, GEORGE E. 1780, 7107, 7108, 7110, 7111, 7112, 17210, 17211, 18332

SIMPSON, LESLEY B. 7473, 8054

SIMPSON, MARTHA L. 15453

SIMPSON, ROBERT R. 1781

SIMS, CHARLES F. 17214

SIMS, JANET 160, 515

SIMS, JANET L. 516

SIMS, MICHAEL 517

SINCLAIR, DONALD A. 518

SINCLAIR, WILLIAM A. 4333

SINGAL, DANIEL J. 1782

SINGH, BALJIT 2846

SINGHA, S. 3385

SINGHAM, ARCHIE - 1783

SINGLER, JOHN V.   19409

SINGLETARY, OTIS A.   519, 520

SINGLETON, A.H.   18333

SINGLETON, GEORGE A.   17215, 17216

SINGLETON, THERESA A.   12175, 12176

SINGLETON, WILLIAM H.   12786

SING-NAN, FEN   21084

SINKLER, GEORGE   2847

SINZHEIMER, G.P.G.   14473

SIO, ARNOLD   1784, 7113

SIO, ARNOLD A.   1785, 1786, 1787, 2849, 7114, 9226, 9564

SIOUSSAT, ST. GEORGE L.   1788

SIRES, RONALD V.   7115

SIRMANS, M. EUGENE   8650, 13088

SISAY, HASSAN   8651

SISK, GLENN   12178, 18334

SISK, GLENN N.   11784

SISSON, VIRGIL D.   7116

SISTRUNK, ALBERTHA   10491

SITGREAVES, SAMUEL JR.   521

SITKOFF, HARVARD   522, 1789

SITTERSON, J. CARLYLE   1790, 9856, 12462, 12464, 12465, 12466, 12467, 12468, 14475, 14476

SITTERSON, J.C.   12461

SITTERSON, JOSEPH C.   12469, 12787

SKAGGS, MERRILL M.   1791

SKEMER, DON C.   10696

SKIDMORE, THOMAS E.   1792, 1793, 1794, 2850, 2852, 8056

SKIPPER, OTTIS C.   4334

SKLAIRE, JOAN I.   2853

SKRYGLEY, F.D.   9228

SLATER, MARIAM K.   16289

SLATTERY, J.R.   8652

SLATTERY, JOHN R.   4335, 16502

SLAUGHTER, LINDA W.   21085

SLAUGHTER, SABRA   12969

SLAVENS, GEORGE E.   4341

SLENES, ROBERT W.   8061

SLIBE, MORRELLA J.D.   8062

SLOAN, IRVING J.   528

SLOAN, RUTH C.M.   20162

SLOANE, RUSH R.   19780

SLONAKER, JOHN   529

SLOTKIN, RICHARD   10373

SMALDONE, JOSEPH P.   530

SMALL, EDWIN W.   9858

SMALL, JESSE M.   11637

SMALL, KATHARINE L.   17912

SMALL, MIRIAM R.   9858

SMALL, SANDRA E.   21086, 21087

SMALLEY, EUGENE V.   12471

SMALLPAGE, ERIC   5970

SMALLWOOD, JAMES   10166, 13431

SMALLWOOD, JAMES M. 13432

SMALLWOOD, LAWRENCE L., JR. 7127

SMEDES, SUSAN D. 12619

SMEDLEY, KATHERINE 21088

SMEDLEY, ROBERT C. 11218

SMELSER, MARSHALL 11638

SMETZER, BARBARA 18336

SMILEY, DAVID L. 11365

SMILEY, PORTIA 16537, 18337

SMITH, ABBOT E. 8262

SMITH, ALFRED G. 13091

SMITH, ALFRED G., JR. 13092

SMITH, ALICE R.H. 13093, 13094

SMITH, AMANDA B. 18993

SMITH, ANNA B. 9859

SMITH, ARTHUR F. 7128, 7129, 7130

SMITH, ARTHUR L. 19412

SMITH, BARBARA 1804

SMITH, BURTON M. 1805

SMITH, C. CALVIN 14039

SMITH, C.O. 17223

SMITH, CORTLAND V. 17224

SMITH, DANIEL B. 8666, 11510

SMITH, DANIEL E.H. 13094

SMITH, DAVID 18994

SMITH, DAVID G. 7567

SMITH, DENNIS C. 873, 1806

SMITH, DONALD B. 8063

SMITH, DORIS W. 19782

SMITH, DOUGLAS C. 2860

SMITH, DWIGHT L. 532

SMITH, EARL 1808

SMITH, EDWARD C. 20411

SMITH, EDWIN M. 1809

SMITH, ELBERT B. 4359

SMITH, ELEANOR 16506, 16507

SMITH, ELIZABETH S. 12790

SMITH, ELLEN H. 11511

SMITH, FRANCIS P. 11512

SMITH, FRANK E. 1810

SMITH, G.W. 15271

SMITH, GEORGE W. 21089

SMITH, GREENVILLE 10167

SMITH, H. SHELTON 2861, 17225

SMITH, H.H. 8064

SMITH, HARMON L. 4360

SMITH, HAROLD S. 20414

SMITH, HARRY 18995

SMITH, HELEN W. 11513

SMITH, HELENA M. 2862

SMITH, HENRY L. 19783

SMITH, HERBERT H. 8065

SMITH, HUGH L. 17913

SMITH, JAMES E. 7131, 7132

SMITH, JAMES L. 13844

SMITH, JAMES M. 533

SMITH, JOHN DAVID 535, 536, 1811,
1812, 1813, 1815, 1817, 1818,
1819, 11367, 11368, 13096,
206C8, 21091

SMITH, JORDAN M. ' 9254

SMITH, JOSEPH F. 15534

SMITH, JOSEPH H. 17914, 19784

SMITH, JULIA C. 9255

SMITH, JULIA F. 11951, 11952,
11953, 11954, 11955, 15370,
20163

SMITH, LESLIE S. 11369

SMITH, LUCY H. 17915

SMITH, MARTIN H. 8667, 10407,
10408

SMITH, MICHAEL G. 5971, 7133,
7135, 7136, 7137, 7138, 7139,
7140, 7141

SMITH, MRS. JOHN J. 7142

SMITH, PAGE 13845

SMITH, PATRICIA A. 13433

SMITH, PHILIP R., JR. 21093

SMITH, R.B. 19413

SMITH, RALPH A. 8066, 8067

SMITH, RAYMOND T. 2866, 7143,
8068, 8069, 16296, 16298

SMITH, REED 19414

SMITH, RHEA 11956

SMITH, ROBERT A. 18338

SMITH, ROBERT H., JR. 250

SMITH, ROBERT S. 4658, 5085

SMITH, ROBERT W. 5972, 7144, 7145,
7146, 9258, 14488

SMITH, ROLAND 7147

SMITH, ROLAND M. 537

SMITH, SAM B. 538

SMITH, SAMUEL D. 13270, 13271,
15806

SMITH, SIDONIE 18997

SMITH, SIDONIE A. 18998

SMITH, STEWARD D. 4361

SMITH, T. LYNN 2867, 8071

SMITH, THEODORE C. 1821, 4362

SMITH, THOMAS 4363

SMITH, THOMAS H. 21094

SMITH, THOMAS L. 8073

SMITH, THOMAS V. 4364

SMITH, THOMAS W. 10308

SMITH, TIMOTHY L. 17228

SMITH, VENTURE 18999

SMITH, W. WAYNE 11514

SMITH, WALTER R. 12472

SMITH, WARREN B. 4365, 13098

SMITH, WARREN I. 11785, 11786

SMITH, WILFORD H. 4525

SMITH, WILLIAM B. 2369

SMITH, WILLIAM H. 4366, 9259

SMITH, WILLIAM R. 8668

SMITH, WOODRUFF D. 5196

SMITHER, HARRIET 13436

SMURR, J.W. 11056

SMYLIE, JAMES H. 4367

SMYRL, FRANK H. 13437

SMYTHE, AUGUSTINE T. 17916

SMYTHE, HUGH H. 4368

SMYTHE, MABEL M. 539

SNAVLEY, LARRY M. 20164

SNEED, LEONORA 14843

SNELL, JAMES P. 10586

SNELL, WILLIAM R. 13100

SNIVELY, ETHAN A. 10898

SNOW, LOUDELL F. 18340

SNYDER, CHARLES E. 9260

SNYDER, H. 4369

SNYDER, PERRY A. 12473

SOAPES, THOMAS F. 1822

SOBEL, MECHAL 5086, 17229

SOCOLOW, SUSAN M. 7712, 8074

SOKOLOV, RAYMOND A. 1823

SOLAUN, MAURICIC 2870

SOLIEN, NANCIE L. 7149, 8075

SOLIMAN, ABD E. 4372

SOLOMON, SUSAN 17231

SOLTOW, LEE 14489

SOMMERS, RICHARD J. 21095

SONDLEY, FOSTER A. 12791

SONGY, BENEDICT G. 4373

SONNINO, PAUL 1824

SORRILL, BARBARA 10171

SORSBY, VICTORIA A. 5974

SOSIS, HOWARD J. 17233

SOSNA, MORTON 1825

SOULE, JOSHUA 17234

SOULSBY, HUGH G. 5975, 5976

SOUTH, ELIZABETH G. 4374

SOUTH, S. 12088

SOUTH, STANLEY 18365

SOUTHALL, EUGENE P. 11957, 172.

SOUTHALL, GENEVA H. 17918

SOUTHERN, EILEEN 9862, 17919,
    17920, 17921, 17922

SOUTHERN, EILEEN J. 9863

SOUTHGATE, ROBERT L. 541

SOUTHWOOD, HOWARD D. 1827

SOWELL, THOMAS 4378

SOWLE, PATRICK 12792

SOWLE, PATRICK M. 10172

SPAID, ARTHUR R.M. 10758

SPAIN, DAPHNE 15972

SPALDING, HENRY D. 18342

SPALDING, PHINIZY 12179

SPANGLER, EARL 542, 10968, 109
    10970

SPANGLER, EVE B. 7151

SPEAR, LOIS 1828

SPEARE, SUSAN T. 9261

SPEARS, JAMES E. 15457

SPEARS, JOHN R. 5977, 5978

SPECK, BEATRICE F. 1829

SPECK, F.G. 14040

SPECK, FRANK G. 14041

SPECTOR, ROBERT M. 10494

SPEERS, MARY W.F. 17923

SPEIRAN, KEITH R. 7152

SPELL, SUZANNE 12620

SPELLMAN, PEGGY S. 4380

SPENCER, DAVID E. 1830

SPENCER, JAYME R. 2872

SPENCER, SAMUEL R., JR. 13846

SPENCER, SARA J. 9864

SPENGLER, J.J. 14490

SPENGLER, JOSEPH J. 15029

SPERO, STERLING D. 14796

SPERRY, EARL E. 19787

SPILLER, ROBERT E. 2873

SPINDLER, ADELINE B. 4381

SPINGARN, LAWRENCE P. 7153

SPINNEY, J.D. 5979

SPIVEY, DONALD 2874, 2875

SPOEHR, ALEXANDER 15810

SPRADLING, MARY M. 543, 544

SPRAGGINS, TINSLEY L. 20416, 20611

SPRAGUE, THEODORE W. 7154

SPRATLIN, V.B. 4382

SPRATLIN, VALAUREZ B. 2876

SPRAY, W.A. 10309

SPROAT, JOHN G. 21097

SPRUILL, JULIA C. 16057, 16058

SPURLOCK-EVANS, KARLA J. 545

SPURRELL, MARK 5717

SRYGLEY, FLETCHER D. 11057

ST. CLAIR, LAWRENCE W. 13438

ST. FRANCIS XAVIER UNIVERSITY 10310

STACY, JAMES 17236

STAFFORD, A.O. 18344, 18730

STAFFORD, FRANCES J. 5980

STAHL, ANNIE L.W. 9865, 9866

STAKELY, CHARLES A. 8263

STAMPP, KENNETH 4383

STAMPP, KENNETH M. 1833, 1834, 1835, 1836, 1837, 1838, 1839, 4384, 4385, 4386, 11182, 17237, 17238, 20417, 20612

STANDARD, DIFFEE W. 14797, 14798

STANDIFER, J.A. 546

STANFORD, PETER T. 17239

STANG, ALAN 2878

STANGE, DOUGLAS C. 4387, 9264, 9868, 9869, 17240, 17241

STANLEY, A. KNIGHTON   17242

STANLEY, GERALD   2879, 4388, 11094

STANLEY, HENRY M.   5981

STANLEY, JOHN L.   9870

STANLEY, OMA   19415

STANSBERRY, FREDDYE B.   18345

STANTON, WILLIAM   2880

STAPLER, MAURY   4389

STAPLES, CARLTON A.   10495

STAPLES, KATHERINE E.   2881

STAPLES, ROBERT   16302, 16303,
   16304, 16305, 16503

STAPLES, THOMAS S.   21099

STARIDA, BEVERLY   8506

STARK, ANNE   13439

STARK, BRUCE   10411

STARKE, BARBARA M.   9871

STARKE, CATHERINE J.   2882

STARKEY, MARION L.   4390, 13848,
   14042

STARKEY, OTIS P.   7155

STARKS, GEORGE L., JR.   17925

STARLING, MARION W.   19000, 19001

STARNES, HUGH N.   13101

STAROBIN, ROBERT   2883, 19789

STAROBIN, ROBERT S.   1841, 1842,
   2884, 14491, 14800, 14803,
   19003, 19790, 20167, 20168

STARR, CHESTER G.   14493

STARR, EMMET   14043

STARR, J. BARTON   8669

STARR, RAYMOND   1843, 2885

STAUDENRAUS, P.J.   547, 2886

STAUDENRAUS, PHILIP J.   2887

STAVES, OLIVER W.   4391

STAVISKY, LEONARD   13682

STAVISKY, LEONARD P.   8670, 148
   14806

STEALEY, JOHN E.   9265, 13850,
   14809

STEARNS, A. WARREN   10496

STEARNS, CHARLES   15275

STEARNS, FRANK P.   20418

STEARNS, JEAN   18473

STEARNS, MARSHALL   5087, 18473

STECKEL, RICHARD   14494, 15031,
   15821

STECKEL, RICHARD H.   548, 549,
   14495, 15032, 15035, 16306

STEEL, EDWARD M., JR.   9266, 926

STEELE, ALGERNON O.   17243

STEELY, WILL F.   11370, 17244

STEFFEN, CHARLES G.   11516, 115

STEGMAIER, MARK J.   11518

STEIFFORD, DAVID M.   9874

STEIN, BARBARA H.   8077, 8083

STEIN, HOWARD F.   1844

STEIN, ROBERT   5983, 5984, 5986
   7158

STEIN, ROBERT L.   7160, 7161

STEIN, SHELDON M.   18780

STEIN, STANLEY   8078

STEIN, STANLEY J.   129, 1846, 1847,
   1848, 8079, 8081, 8082, 8083

STEIN, STEPHEN J.   17245

STEINER, BERNARD C.   9268, 10412,
   11519

STEINER, BRUCE E.   13854

STEINER, F.B.   4392

STEINER, H.   4393

STEINER, PAUL E.   21100

STEINER, ROLAND   18346

STEINHAGEN, CAROL T.   4394

STEIRER, WILLIAM F.   4395

STEIRER, WILLIAM F., JR.   1849,
   1850

STENBERG, RICHARD R.   9269, 11058,
   13440

STENSLAND, PER G.   1851

STEPHEN, GEORGE   10173

STEPHENS, H. MORSE   1852

STEPHENS, JEAN B.   11960

STEPHENS, LESTER D.   4396, 12131

STEPHENSON, CLARENCE D.   4397

STEPHENSON, D. GRIER   12182

STEPHENSON, GILBERT T.   2889

STEPHENSON, MARY A.   13855

STEPHENSON, MASON W.   12182

STEPHENSON, N.W.   1853

STEPHENSON, NATHANIEL W.   20613

STEPHENSON, WENDELL H.   1854, 1855,
   1856, 1857, 1858, 1859, 1860,
   1861, 1862, 1863, 1864, 1865,
   1866, 9272, 12475, 12476, 12621,
   15170

STEPTO, R.B.   19004

STEPTO, ROBERT B.   19005

STERKX, H.E.   20614

STERKX, HENRY E.   9875, 9876

STERLING, DOROTHY   13106, 19243,
   19791

STERLING, ELEANORE O.   2890

STERLING, PHILIP   18347, 19792

STERNE, RICHARD S.   16060

STETSON, KENNETH W.   14496

STEVENS, CHARLES E.   19793

STEVENS, HIRAM F.   10971

STEVENS, N.   20171

STEVENS, W. LE CONTE   4398

STEVENS, WILLIAM   4399

STEVENSON, E.B.   2891

STEVENSON, JOHN R.   550

STEVENSON, MARY   13107

STEVENSON, ROBERT   1867, 12477,
   17930

STEVENSON, ROBERT M.   551, 17931

STEWARD, JULIAN H.   4400, 7163

STEWARD, T.B.   7164

STEWARD, THEOPHILUS G. 4401, 4402, 4403, 7165, 8672, 21101

STEWARD, WILLIAM 4403

STEWART, CHARLES 19006

STEWART, CHARLES E. 552

STEWART, FRANK H. 10588

STEWART, HELEN B. 11219

STEWART, JAMES B. 1868, 1869

STEWART, LEROY E. 14044

STEWART, MARJORIE A. 9273

STEWART, SADIE E. 18348

STEWART, T.D. 15809, 15810

STEWART, WILLIAM A. 19416, 19417, 19418, 19419, 19420, 19421, 19422, 19423

STILES, CASSIUS C. 19794

STILL, JAMES 19007

STILL, WILLIAM 19795

STILL, WILLIAM G. 17933

STILLMAN, RACHEL B. 20419

STIRLING, A.P. 3385, 4026

STIRTON, THOMAS 4404

STITT, E.R. 5088

STIVERSON, GREGORY A. 5990, 11520, 14497

STOBER, HORST 5089

STOCKARD, JANICE L. 16511

STOCKBRIDGE, HENRY 15171

STOCKDALE, DAVID C. 14647

STOCKHOLM, RICHARD J. 14812

STOCKING, GEORGE W. 1839

STOCKING, GEORGE W., JR. 2892

STOCKTON, FRANK R. 10589

STODDARD, ALBERT H. 13108

STODDARD, FLORENCE J. 18350

STODDARD, LOTHROP 2893

STODDARD, THEODORE L. 7166, 716

STODDARD, TOM 17934

STOKES, ALLEN H. 14813

STOKES, BEATRICE M. 12478

STOKESBURY, JAMES L. 5992

STONE, ALBERT E. 19008

STONE, ALFRED H. 1870, 1871, 18 2894, 2895, 2896, 4405, 4406, 5090, 9274, 9877, 14498, 1449

STONE, ELIZABETH A. 11248

STONE, HENRY 21102

STONE, JAMES H. 14851

STONE, LUCIE P. 19796

STONE, PAULINE T. 553

STONEQUIST, EVERETT V. 2897

STONEY, SAMUEL G. 13110, 19425

STOREY, JOHN W. 2898

STORING, H.J. 4407

STORING, HERBERT J. 4408

STOUTAMIRE, ALBERT 17935

STOWE, CHARLES E. 17246

STOWE, HARRIET B. 4410

STOWE, STEVEN M. 16061

STRACHE, NEIL E. 554

STRAKER, D. AUGUSTUS 5091

STRATON, JOHN R. 4411

STRAWN, JOHN 1874

STREIFFORD, DAVID M. 2899

STRICK, LISA W. 8673

STRICKER, BARRY A. 17247

STRICKLAND, ARVARH E. 10899, 11639

STRICKLAND, D.A. 5092

STRICKLEN, JEAN B. 4412

STRICKON, ARNOLD 555

STRINE, MARY S. 20175

STRIPLING, PAUL W. 17248

STROBEL, ABNER J. 13441

STROGER, HOWARD 17249

STROMAN, CAROLYN A. 556

STRONG, KATE W. 15812

STROTHER, HORATIO T. 19797, 19798

STROTHER, WILLIAM B. 11372

STROUP, RODGER E. 13111

STROUPE, HENRY S. 557, 4413

STROYER, JACOB 19009

STRUHS, JAMES F. 19800

STRUMOLO, ALBERT 9879

STUART, GEORGE R. 12186

STUART, WILLIAM 9275, 10590, 10591

STUBBS, W.C. 14500

STUBBS, WILLIAM C. 14501

STUCKEY, STERLING 1875, 1876, 1877, 1878, 4414, 4415, 4416, 4417, 5093, 5094, 19801, 20176

STUMP, WILLIAM D. 2900

STURDEVANT, RICK 1824

STURGE, EDMUND 7168

STURM, FRED G. 8084

STYLES, WILLIAM A. 10312

STYRON, WILLIAM 1001, 1879, 1880, 2041

SUAREZ, RALEIGH A., JR. 12479

SUDARKASA, NIARA 16308

SULIVAN, GEORGE L. 5993

SULLIVAN, ALLEN R. 19426

SULLIVAN, HARRY R. 7169

SULLIVAN, LESTER G., JR. 559

SULLIVAN, PHILLIP E. 18353

SULLIVAN, T.P. 18354

SUMMERSELL, CHARLES G. 9278

SUMNERS, BILLY F. 17250

SUNDIATA, I.K. 5995

SUNDIATA, IBRAHIM K. 7170

SUNSERI, ALVIN 1882

SUNSERI, ALVIN R. 11115, 11116, 11117

SUPER, JOHN C. 8085

SUPPIGER, JOSEPH E.   2901

SURET-CANALE, J.   5095

SURET-CANALE, JEAN   5996

SURREY, NANCY M.   12431

SUSSMAN, ROBERT   704, 1883

SUTCH, RICHARD   896, 897, 1884,
    1886, 2902, 14143, 14272, 14435,
    14436, 14503, 14504, 14505,
    14630, 14645, 15112, 15372,
    15374, 16182

SUTHERLAND, DANIEL E.   4419, 4420

SUTHERLAND, G.E.   20420

SUTHERLAND, LOUIS G.   7171

SUTHERN, ORRIN C.   2903

SUTTELL, ELIZABETH L.   5997

SUTTLES, WILLIAM C., JR.   5096,
    17251

SUTTON, BOB   11151

SUTTON, JOEL B.   17937

SWADOS, FELICE   15813

SWALLOW, GEORGE   17252

SWAN, DALE E.   14506, 14507, 14595

SWANEY, CHARLES B.   17253, 17254

SWANSON, WILLIAM J.   1887

SWANTON, JOHN R.   14045

SWART, P.D.   18355

SWARTZLOW, RUBY J.   11640

SWEARINGEN, MACK   12623

SWEAT, EDWARD F.   9880, 9881, 9882,
    9883

SWEENEY, JAMES J.   5097

SWEET, DAVID G.   7172

SWEET, LEONARD I.   4421, 4422

SWEET, WILLIAM W.   17255, 17256
    17257

SWEIG, DONALD   560, 13765

SWEIG, DONALD M.   9885, 15174

SWEM, EARL G.   561

SWIFT, HILDEGARDE H.   20303

SWINNEY, S.H.   10176

SWINT, HENRY L.   21103, 21104,
    21105

SWISHER, CARL B.   9279, 9280

SWISHER, J.A.   9281

SYDER, S.N.   5998

SYDNOR, CHARLES S.   4423, 9283,
    9886, 12624, 12625, 12795,
    13858, 14894, 15039, 19803

SYFERT, DWIGHT N.   5999

SYKES, REVECCA M.   18356

SYMMES, E.   17938

SYNDER, CHARLES E.   4424

SYNNESTVEDT, SIG   20421, 21106

SYNNOTT, ANTHONY   7173

SYNNOTT, ANTHONY J.   7174

SYPHER, WYLIE   4425

SYRETT, JOHN   10177

SZASZ, FERENC M.   4426, 10702

SZASZ, THOMAS S.   2904, 15817,
    20304

SZILAK, DENNIS   5098

SZWED, JOHN   17488

SZWED, JOHN F.   562, 1888, 4427,
    17361, 17362, 17476, 17939,
    17940, 17941, 18357, 18358

TADMAN, MICHAEL   15176, 15177

TAFT, EDNA   7176

TAGGART, HUGH T.   11249

TAKAKI, RONALD   2906, 6000

TAKAKI, RONALD T.   2907, 2908,
    2909

TALBERT, ROY JR.   13859

TALBOTT, FORREST   9284, 9285

TALIB, Y.   6003

TALLANT, ROBERT   12452, 17259

TALLEY, THOMAS W.   18360, 18361

TALLEY, TOMASINA   1890

TALLMADGE, WILLIAM H.   17943

TALLMAN, MARJORIE   18362

TALMADGE, JOHN E.   9286, 12187

TALPALAR, MORRIS   13860

TAMBO, DAVID C.   5099

TAMBS, LEWIS   56

TANDY, JEANNETTE R.   4428

TANG, ANTHONY M.   14503

TANLA-KISHANI, BONGASU   5100

TANNENBAUM, FRANK   1891, 1892,
    7177, 7178, 7180, 8090, 16300

TANNER, EARL C.   11961

TANNER, PAUL   17736

TANSEY, RICHARD   4429

TANSILL, CHARLES C.   2910

TAPP, HAMBLETON   11373, 11374

TARDOLA, M. ELIZABETH   4430

TARLTON, DEWITT T.   14509

TARVER, HAROLD M.   15276

TARVER, JERRY L.   3153

TATE, MERZE   2911, 2912, 2913

TATE, THAD W.   1893, 1894, 8675

TATUM, GEORGIA L.   20182

TAUARES-NERO, JOSE   2914

TAUNAY, AFFONSO D.   6006

TAUSSIG, CHARLES W.   6007

TAUSSIG, MICHAEL   8095, 8096

TAX, SOL   7181

TAXEL, JOEL   1895

TAYLOR, A.A.   13862

TAYLOR, ALRUTHEUS A.   13115, 13273,
    13863, 15178

TAYLOR, BRUCE M.   7182, 7183

TAYLOR, C.H.J.   4431

TAYLOR, CAESAR A.A.   4432

TAYLOR, CELIA B.   18363

TAYLOR, CHARLES E.   7184

TAYLOR, CLARE   4433, 7185, 7186

TAYLOR, CLYDE   19427

TAYLOR, DAVID V.   563

TAYLOR, DOUGLAS M. 7187, 8098, 19428, 19429

TAYLOR, GENEVIEVE 4434

TAYLOR, GEOFFREY 4435

TAYLOR, GEORGE R. 14510

TAYLOR, HUBERT V. 17262, 17263

TAYLOR, J.K. 4436

TAYLOR, JIMMIE 19010

TAYLOR, JOE G. 1896, 6008, 8677, 12483, 12484, 12485, 12487, 20617

TAYLOR, JOHN E. 17944, 17945

TAYLOR, JOHN M. 6009

TAYLOR, JOSEPH H. 21110

TAYLOR, KIT S. 8100, 14511

TAYLOR, MARSHALL W. 16513, 17946

TAYLOR, MORRIS F. 11118

TAYLOR, O.C.W. 19011

TAYLOR, OLIVE A. 17264

TAYLOR, ORVILLE W. 11842, 11844, 11845, 14395, 17265

TAYLOR, PAUL S. 8506, 11095, 14512, 14513, 14514

TAYLOR, QUINTARD JR. 11059

TAYLOR, R.J. 11375

TAYLOR, RICH L. 8101

TAYLOR, RICHARD 20422

TAYLOR, RONALD L. 17477

TAYLOR, ROSSER H. 9288, 9888, 12797, 13116, 14515, 15461

TAYLOR, S.A.G. 7188, 7189

TAYLOR, S.R. 21111

TAYLOR, SALLY 4437

TAYLOR, SUSIE K. 19012

TAYLOR, WILLIAM B. 15377

TAYLOR, WILLIAM M. 4438

TAYLOR, WILLIAM R. 4439

TEAGUE, MICHAEL 6011, 6012

TEAKLE, THOMAS 19808

TEALL, KAY M. 564

TEAMOH, R.T. 21113

TEBEAU, C.W. 16062

TEESDALE, WILLIAM H. 9289

TEGARDEN, J.B.H. 17266

TEILHET, JEHANNE 17478

TELFORD, MARGARET J.A. 13443

TELLER, WALTER 19013

TEMIN, PETER 896, 897, 898, 899 900, 14150, 14151, 14516

TEMPERLY, HOWARD 7190, 7191, 7

TEMPERLY, HOWARD R. 4441

TEMPLE, JOSIAH H. 10497

TENBROEK, JACOBUS 4444

TENHOUTEN, WARREN D. 16310

TENKORANG, S. 6013

TENNEY, JOHN F. 11962

TEPASKE, JOHN J. 19810

TEPER, SHIRLEY 2915

ERBORG—PENN, ROSALYN 565, 16416

ERRELL, LLOYD P. 12139

ERRELL, W.H.H. 21115

ERRILL, TOM E. 1286, 14815

ERRY, GEORGE D. 8678, 9290, 9889,
    13120

ERRY, RODERICK 6014

ETRICK, GWENDOLYN G.P. 17947

EULON, ALAN 7194

HACKER, M. EVA 11096

HANET, OCTAVE 5101, 11847

HELWELL, MIKE 1898, 1899, 1900,
    1976

HEOBALD, STEPHEN L. 17267

HIAM, AMADOU 5102

HIBAULT, CLAUDE 566

HIEME, DARIUS L. 17948

HIGPEN, SAMUEL G. 12628

HIRSK, RICHARD 20305

HOBURN, JOSEPH B. 14046

HOM, WILLIAM T. 9891

HOMAS, ALLEN C. 8679

HOMAS, ASA L. 6016

HOMAS, BENJAMIN P. 4446, 21116

HOMAS, BETTYE 567

HOMAS, COBURN 11788

HOMAS, DAVID H. 18365

HOMAS, DAVID Y. 1901, 4447, 9892,
    11848

THOMAS, EDGAR G. 17269

THOMAS, EMORY M. 13864, 16063,
    16064

THOMAS, HENRY G. 21117

THOMAS, HERBERT A., JR. 15041

THOMAS, HERMAN E. 17270

THOMAS, HUGH 6017, 6018, 7195

THOMAS, J.J. 1902

THOMAS, JOHN I. 5103

THOMAS, KENNETH H., JR. 16311

THOMAS, MARY E. 7198

THOMAS, MRS. Z.V. 15179

THOMAS, PERCIAL M. 13865

THOMAS, ROBERT P. 5208, 5209,
    6020, 8680

THOMAS, TONY 1903

THOMAS, WILLIAM H. 2918, 2919,
    4449, 6021, 14646, 17271, 17272

THOMAS, WILLIAM I. 2920

THOMAS, WILLIAM J. 19430

THOMPSON, ALANA S. 15042

THOMPSON, ALMA M. 570

THOMPSON, ALMOSE A., JR. 5104

THOMPSON, ALVIN O. 2921, 8104

THOMPSON, B.M. 9292

THOMPSON, C. MILDRED 12191

THOMPSON, DANIEL C. 4450, 4451

THOMPSON, DONALD 568

THOMPSON, DONALD P. 7200

THOMPSON, EDGAR   14517

THOMPSON, EDGAR T.   569, 570, 1904,
    2922, 2923, 2924, 2925, 14518,
    14519, 14520, 17273

THOMPSON, ELIZABETH A.J.   17949

THOMPSON, ERA B.   8105, 16312

THOMPSON, ERNEST T.   19244

THOMPSON, HENRY P.   17275

THOMPSON, J. EARL JR.   8681

THOMPSON, LAWRENCE S.   571, 4452

THOMPSON, LEONARD   4753

THOMPSON, LUCILLE S.   572

THOMPSON, MARION M.T.   10592

THOMPSON, MARIVINE K.   17277

THOMPSON, MAURICE   4453

THOMPSON, PATRICK H.   17278

THOMPSON, REBA   17279

THOMPSON, ROBERT F.   5105, 5106,
    5107, 5108, 18474, 18687

THOMPSON, V.B.   7201

THOMPSON, WILLIAM F., JR.   20424

THOMPSON, WINFIELD M.   6024

THOMS, D.W.   6025, 7202, 7203

THORNBROUGH, EMMA L.   1905, 2926,
    9293, 10374, 10921, 21118

THORNBURG, OPAL   12799

THORNE, B.   376

THORNE, IRENE   19813

THORNTON, A.P.   6026, 6027, 7204

THORNTON, ARCHIBALD P.   6028

THORNTON, FLORENCE G.   9295

THORNTON, J. MILLS   11790

THORNTON, JOHN   6029

THORNTON, JONATHAN M.   11791

THORNTON, MARY L.   573

THORP, WILLARD   18366

THORPE, EARL   1906

THORPE, EARL E.   1907, 1908, 1909
    1910, 1911, 1912, 1913, 4454
    11060, 18731, 18783, 18784

THORPE, REED   11119

THORSTENBERG, HERMAN J.   7205

THRIFT, CHARLES T., JR.   17281

THROWER, SARAH S.   17950

THURM, MARCELLA   18691

THURMAN, A. ODELL   11098, 11099

THURMAN, HOWARD   17283, 17951,
    17952

THURMAN, JAN W.   11061

THURMAN, SUE B.   11100

THURSTON, HELEN M.   9296

TICKNOR, CAROLINE   1914, 1915

TIDWELL, J.M.   19431

TIEDEMAN, ARTHUR E.   12489

TIEN, HAN   1916

TIERMAN, STANTON   15180

TIFFANY, NINA M.   19014

TILBY, A. WYATT   7206

TILLER, LESSIE 19432

TILLEY, J.S. 10131

TILLEY, JOHN S. 4455

TILLINGHAST, JOSEPH A. 5109

TILLMAN, KATHERINE D. 16516

TILLY, BETTE B. 13274, 13275

TILTON, EDGAR JR. 10703

TIMBERLAKE, C.L. 11377

TIMMONS, ROBERT 15379

TINDALL, GEORGE B. 13121

TINDALL, P.E.N. 2927

TINKER, HUGH 7207

TINLING, MARION 13866

TINSLEY, VALLIE 17953

TIPTON, F. 15818

TIPTON, FRANK B. 1917

TIRTHA, RANJIT 8106

TISCHLER, NANCY M. 2928, 2929, 2930

TISE, LARRY E. 2931, 2932, 8345, 17284

TITTAMIN, WILLIAM 8682

TITUS, NOEL F. 7208

TOCUS, CLARENCE S. 17954

TODD, ARTHUR 18475, 18476, 18477

TODD, T. WINGATE 15819

TODD, WILLIE G. 17285, 17286

TOKUSHIMA, TATSURO 6031

TOLL, ROBERT C. 2933, 18367

TOLL, WILLIAM 1918, 1919, 1920, 2934, 2936

TOLLE, CHARLES D. 12490

TOLLES, FREDERICK B. 4457

TOLSON, ARTHUR L. 11132

TOMASKE, JOHN A. 14578

TOMICH, DALE 1842, 15279

TOMICH, DALE W. 7209

TOMPKINS, D.A. 4458, 12801

TOOLE, CHRISTINE T. 9895

TOOMER, JEAN 4459

TOOR, FRANCES 18368

TOPLIN, ROBERT B. 1921, 2937, 6032, 7210, 8109, 8113, 8114, 10183, 10186, 19814

TOPPIN, EDGAR A. 574, 8683, 8684

TORCHIA, MARION M. 15820

TORIAN, SARAH 18369

TORODASH, MARTIN 9297

TORSTENSON, JOEL S. 17287

TORTORICI, JOSEPHINE C. 6033

TOUBES, SARAH 19123

TOUCHSTONE, BLAKE 17288

TOUCHSTONE, DONALD B. 17289

TOUSSAINT-SAMSON, ADELE 8115

TOWE, JOSEPH 17955

TOWELL, SHERMAN E. 17290

TOWNE, LAURA M. 13122

TOWNER, LAWRENCE W. 10498, 10499, 10500

TOWNES, A. JANE 10188

TOWNSEND, WILLIAM H. 11378, 11379

TRABUE, CHARLES C. 9298

TRACEY, H. 17956

TRAGLE, HENRY I. 1922, 1923, 13868, 13869, 20188

TRAIL, WILLIAM JR. 10922

TRAUBERT, ANNA E. 13870

TRAYNOR, MARTIN J. 13123

TRECKER, JANICE L. 576

TREDWAY, G.R. 21120

TREE, RONALD L. 7212

TREFOUSSE, HANS L. 10190, 21122

TREGLE, JOSEPH G., JR. 1924, 12491

TRELEASE, ALLEN W. 4461

TREMAIN, MARY 11251, 11252, 11253

TRENCH, CHARLES C. 6036

TRENHOLM, W.L. 4462, 17291

TRENT, WILLIAM P. 4463, 4464

TREPP, JEAN 6037

TRESP, LOTHAR L. 12192

TREUDLEY, MARY 7213

TREVOR-ROPER, HUGH R. 6038

TREXLER, HARRISON A. 11643, 11644, 15280, 15281, 20622

TRICE, KATHERINE 5110

TRIEBER, JACOB 9301

TRIEZENBERG, GEORGE 4465

TRIMBLE, CAIRO A. 9302

TRIMBLE, SARAH R. 13277

TRIMINGHAM, J. SPENCER 5111, 511

TRINDELL, ROGER T. 10593

TRIPATHI, AMALES 1925

TROPER, HAROLD M. 11133

TROSKO, BARBARA R. 8116

TROTTER, JAMES M. 17957

TROUBRIDGE, ST. VINCENT 19433

TROUTMAN, RICHARD L. 10191, 1138 11382, 11383, 11384

TROWBRIDGE, ADA W. 18370

TROWBRIDGE, CHARLES T. 21123

TROWBRIDGE, JOHN T. 4466

TROXLER, GEORGE 4467

TROY, LEON L. 17293

TRUMBULL, JOAN 2938

TRUPIN, JAMES E. 6039

TRUSSELL, JAMES 1064, 15821

TRUTH, SOJOURNER 19016

TRUZZI, MARCELLO 2939

TRYON, WARREN S. 15182

TSCHAN, FRANCIS J. 13871

TUBB, HILDA 18371

TUCKER, DAVID M. 17294

TUCKER, FRANK C. 17295

TUCKER, HELEN A. 14816

TUCKER, LEONARD 7214

TUCKER, ROBERT C. 4468, 13124

TUCKER, ST. GEORGE 13872

TUCKERMAN, C.K. 4469

TUDEN, ARTHUR 4259, 5113, 5114,
5115, 5116

TUELON, ALAN 16519

TULLOCH, HEADLEY 10314

TULLOCH, HUGH 1926, 1927

TULLY, ALAN 8686

TUNNELL, TED 12492, 21124

TUPES, HERSCHEL 11645

TURLEY, DAVID M. 19815

TURNBULL, ROBERT J. 577

TURNER, ARLIN 1928, 4470

TURNER, BLAIR P. 9303, 9304

TURNER, CAROLINE 1929

TURNER, CHARLES W. 13873

TURNER, D.T. 4471

TURNER, DARWIN 1930

TURNER, DARWIN T. 573

TURNER, EDWARD R. 8687, 10760,
10761, 10762, 10764, 10765,
19816

TURNER, EUGENE 2940

TURNER, FREDERICK 6040

TURNER, FREDERICK J. 14527

TURNER, FREDERICK W. 18373

TURNER, HENRY M. 10193

TURNER, IAN B. 11183

TURNER, J. KELLY 12802

TURNER, J. MICHAEL 579

TURNER, JAMES 1931, 1932, 9306

TURNER, JAMES K. 12803

TURNER, JERRY M. 8118

TURNER, JOHN J. 20426

TURNER, LOIS 10973

TURNER, LORENZO D. 580, 4472,
4473, 8119, 13126, 17479, 19017,
19435, 19436, 19437

TURNER, LUCY M. 20193

TURNER, MARY 1933, 19249

TURNER, ROBERT P. 4474

TURNER, SUZANNE L. 12493

TURNER, VICTOR W. 5118

TURNER, WALLACE B. 11385, 11386

TURTON, CECIL M. 19817

TUSHNET, MARK 9307, 9308

TUTTLE, JOSEPH F. 10594, 10595

TUTTLE, W.M., JR. 19818

TUTWILER, JULIA R. 16520

TWE, DIHDWO 4475

TWERSKY, ATARAH S. 2942

TWINING, ALEXANDER C. 10194

TWINING, M.A. 19018

TWINING, MARY 18579

TWINING, MARY A. 5119, 13127,
   13128, 13129, 17483

TWOMBLY, ROBERT C. 8688, 10471,
   10502

TWYMAN, ROBERT W. 486, 15822

TYLDEN, G. 7216

TYLER, ALICE F. 4476

TYLER, LYON G. 16060

TYLER, ROBERT 5120

TYLER, RONNIE 19820

TYLER, RONNIE C. 13445, 13446,
   19821, 20623

TYMS, JAMES D. 17297

TYNER, WAYNE C. 17298

TYSON, GEORGE F., JR. 7217, 7218

U.S. ARMY, BUREAU OF FREE LABOR
   12494

U.S. DEPARTMENT OF COMMERCE,
   CENSUS BUREAU 15046, 15047

U.S. FREEDMEN'S BUREAU 10195

UCHE, KALU O. 4478

UCHENDU, VICTOR 5121

UCHENDU, VICTOR C. 5122

UDAL, J.S. 7219

ULLMAN, DANIEL 21126

ULLMAN, VICTOR 4479, 10315

ULLYAT, A.G. 4480

ULMANN, DORIS 18297

UMOZURIKE, J.D. 9309

UNDERHILL, EDWARD B. 7220

UNDERHILL, LONNIE E. 13989

UNDERWOOD, AGNES N. 10686

UNDERWOOD, JOSEPH H. 4482

UNGAR, HELENE 9899

UNGER, IRWIN 1935, 4483

UNITED STATES, BUREAU OF THE CEN
   15048

UNITED STATES COMMISSION ON CIVI
   RIGHTS 4484, 9310

UNIVERSITY OF PITTSBURGH 584

UNIVERSITY OF TEXAS LIBRARY, AUS
   585

UNTERKOEFLER, ERNEST L. 17299

UNWIN, RAYNER 6043

UPCHURCH, J.T. 4485

URBAN, C. STANLEY 7221, 7222

URBAN, CHESTER S. 7223

URBANSKI, EDMUND S. 7224

USHER, GUY S. 17300

USNER, DANIEL H., JR. 8689

UYA, OKON E. 586, 1936, 1938,
   13132, 13133, 15282, 17485,
   17486, 20196

UZOIGWE, G.N. 6045

UZZELL, W.E. 12804

VACHA, JOHN E. 10196

VACHEENOS, JEAN 16314

VALDES-CRUZ, ROSA 7225, 18375

VALENTI, SUZANNE 4486

VALENTINE, D.T. 10705

VALENTINE, FOY J. 2943

VALLETTE, MARC F. 17301

VALTIERRA, ANGEL 8121

VALUSKA, DAVID L. 21127

VAN ALSTYNE, LAWRENCE 21128

VAN ALSTYNE, RICHARD W. 6047,
9311

VAN ANDEL, M.A. 6048, 6049

VAN BLARCOM, CARCLYN C. 15825

VAN DAM, THEODORE 17360, 17961

VAN DANTZIG, ALBERT 6050

VAN DEBURG, WILLIAM L. 1939, 1940,
1942, 11254, 11521, 14854,
14855, 14856, 19126

VAN DEN BERGHE, PIERRE L. 2944,
2945, 2946, 2947, 2948, 2949,
4487, 8122

VAN DEN BOOGAART, ERNST 6051,
8123

VAN DER ELST, DIRK H. 8124

VAN DEUSEN, JOHN G. 14528

VAN DOREN, CHARLES 8

VAN DYKE, ROGER R. 9900

VAN DYNE, LARRY 1943

VAN EK, JACOB 19824

VAN GUNDY, MORRIS S. 10197

VAN HORNE, JOHN D. 1944, 4488

VAN LIER, R.A.J. 7226, 8125, 8126

VAN METER, BENJAMIN F. 11387

VAN NECK YODER, HILDA 8127

VAN NESS, JAMES S. 15283

VAN PANHUYS, L.C. 8128, 8129

VAN PANHUYS, L.C.R. 8130

VAN PELT, W. WELLS 15978

VAN RENSELARR, H.C. 8143

VAN SERTIMA, IVAN 4489, 19439

VAN VECHTEN, CARL 17962

VAN VELZEN, BONNO T. 8131

VAN VELZEN, H.U.E. 8133

VAN VELZEN, H.U.E. THODEN 7498,
8132

VAN WETERING, W. 8133

VANCE, MAURICE M. 1945

VANCE, ROBERT L.J. 18377

VANCE, RUPERT B. 2950, 14529

VANCE, WILLIAM R. 11388

VANDER VELDE, LEWIS G. 17305

VANDER ZANDEN, JAMES W. 2951

VANDERBILT, KERMIT 2952

VANDERCOOK, JOHN W. 8134

VANDIVER, FRANK 20627

VANDIVER, FRANK E. 11792, 11793,
20630

VANNERSON, JAMES T. 2953

VANRIEL, WESLEY B. 14530

VANSINA, JAN 4753, 4754, 5125,
6053

VARN, SALLIE R. 12196

VASSADY, BELA JR. 7227

VASSAR, RENA 17306

VASSBERG, DAVID E. 8135

VAUGHAN, ALDEN T. 8266

VAUGHN, ROSE E. 9313

VEDDER, RICHARD K. 14531, 14532, 14647, 14819

VEGA-DROUET, HECTOR 5126, 17964

VENABLE, WILLIAM H. 4490, 4491

VENEY, BETHANY 16521

VER STEEG, CLARENCE L. 1946, 8692, 8693

VERGER, PIERRE 6055, 7229, 8136, 8138

VERLINDEN, CHARLES 4492, 14533

VERNON, C.W. 587

VIBERT, FAITH 17307

VICKERY, KENNETH P. 2954

VIGIL, RALPH H. 8139

VILA, ENRIQUETA 6056

VILES, JONAS 11646

VILES, PERRY 6057, 6058

VINCENT, CHARLES 20631

VINCENT, JOHN M. 588

VINIKAS, VINCE 13875

VINOVSKIS, MARIS A. 1947

VIOLETTE, E.M. 9314

VIOLETTE, EUGENE M. 11648

VIRTUE, GEORGE O. 1948

VIVAS SALAS, H. 17308

VLACH, JOHN M. 5127, 13136, 155
15542, 15543, 17309, 18581,
18583, 18586, 18694

VLASEK, DALE R. 1949

VLOCK, LAUREL F. 12805

VOEGELI, JACQUE 20428

VOEGELI, V. JACQUE 20429

VOEGELI, VICTOR J. 20430

VOELZ, PETER M. 7232

VOGT, JOHN 6059, 6060

VOGT, JOHN L. 6061, 6062

VOLK, BETTY 16314

VON HOFE, BARBARA ANNE B. 2958

VON HOLST, HERMAN E. 1950, 4493

VOORHOEVE, JAN 8143, 18378

VOSS, LOUIS 12497

VREDE, A.P. 8144

WACHOLDER, BEN Z. 9315

WACKER, PETER O. 10597

WADDELL, D.A.G. 1951, 6063, 723
8145

WADE, MALVIN 1952

WADE, RICHARD C. 2959, 9904,
13138, 15979, 16316

WADE, RICHARD D. 17311

WADELINGTON, CHARLES W. 2960

WADLEIGH, GEORGE 10516

WADSWORTH, ANNA 18698

WAGANDT, CHARLES L. 10199, 1152
21132, 21134

WAGER, PAUL W. 12739

WAGLEY, C.W. 4494

WAGLEY, CHARLES 1954, 6064, 7234,
   7235, 8147

WAGMAN, MORTON 10706

WAGNER, CLARENCE M. 12198

WAGNER, HENRY R. 8150

WAGNER, KEITH E. 11062

WAGNER, MARIA 2961

WAGNER, MICHAEL J. 8151

WAGSTAFF, H.M. 589

WAGSTAFF, THOMAS 16068

WAGSTAFF, TOM 1955

WAHLE, KATHLEEN O. 1956

WAHLMAN, MAUDE 18587, 18588

WAKELYN, JON 3934

WAKELYN, JON L. 4495, 4496

WALCOTT, RONALD 1957

WALDEN, JEAN E. 17965

WALKER, ALICE 16522

WALKER, ARDA 13278

WALKER, C.E. 590

WALKER, C.T. 1958

WALKER, CAM 21135

WALKER, CLARENCE E. 1917, 16069

WALKER, CORNELIA A. 591

WALKER, DENNIS 8152

WALKER, FRANCIS A. 15051

WALKER, GEORGE 9909, 19826

WALKER, H.J. 4497

WALKER, JACQUELINE B. 12806

WALKER, JAMES 10317

WALKER, JAMES D. 592

WALKER, JAMES W. ST. G. 8697,
   10319, 19827

WALKER, JEAN F. 4498

WALKER, JOHN S. 17313

WALKER, JOSEPH E. 9912, 13279,
   14822, 14823

WALKER, JULIET E.K. 13139

WALKER, MARGARET 4499

WALKER, MARY T. 1960

WALKER, PETER 4500

WALKER, SAUNDERS E. 19440

WALKER, SHEILA S. 17314, 17315

WALKER, THOMAS C. 19022

WALKER, WYATT T. 17966

WALL, BENNETT H. 1961, 1962, 1963,
   12808, 14534, 14535, 15826

WALL, JAMES W. 12810

WALLACE, DAVID D. 13140, 13141,
   14536

WALLACE, HENRY 11389

WALLACE, JAMES O. 13447

WALLACE, ROBERT F. 4501

WALLBRIDGE, EDWIN A. 8153

WALLENSTEIN, PETER 14537

WALLENSTEIN, PETER R.   14538

WALLER, CHARLES   12104

WALLER, CHARLES T.   18228

WALLER, RUBEN   19023

WALLERSTEIN, IMMANUEL   1964, 14539

WALLNER, PETER A.   9319

WALLS, WILLIAM J.   1965

WALSH, L.S.   8698

WALSH, LORENA S.   11526

WALSH, RICHARD   8699, 11527

WALSH, RICHARD C.   17316

WALSH, THEOPH S.   4502

WALTERS, ALEXANDER   11390

WALTERS, BETH   19129

WALTERS, MARY D.   593

WALTERS, RONALD G.   16070

WALTHALL, HOWARD P.   4503

WALTON, DAVID W.   1966

WALTON, FLETCHER   17317

WALTON, GARY M.   5934, 6065

WALTON, GEORGE   14048

WALTON, J.T.   15827

WALTON, JONATHAN W.   10320

WALTON, NORMAN W.   594

WALTON, PERRY   6066

WALVIN, JAMES   141, 1967, 2323,
   2962, 2963, 6352, 9320

WALZ, ROBERT B.   11852

WAMBLE, GASTON H.   11649

WANDER, P.C.   2964

WANDER, PHILIP C.   2965, 2966

WANNAMAKER, RUTH   4504

WANSLEY, JOY   1968

WARD, AILEEN   4506

WARD, HARRY M.   8700

WARD, HAZEL M.   16523

WARD, J.R.   7236

WARD, JOHN W.   1969, 4507

WARD, W.E.F.   5128

WARD, WILLIAM E.F.   6068

WARDELL, MORRIS L.   14049

WARDER, VELMA G.   17967

WARE, CHARLES P.   17499, 17500

WARE, E. RICHMOND   15828

WARGNY, FRANK J.   19251

WARING, JOSEPH I.   13143, 15829,
   15830

WARING, MARY A.   18381, 18382

WARMAN, ARTURO   2967

WARNER, CHARLES D.   4508, 18383

WARNER, LOUIS H.   8154

WARNER, LUCILE S.   4509

WARNER, MARY C.   19829

WARNER, MAUREEN   7237, 7238, 723

WARNER, ROBERT A.   10413

WARREN, DONALD JR.   8155, 8156

WARREN, FRANCIS H.   21136

WARREN, HARRIS G.   12630, 12631,
  12632

WARREN, LOUIS A.   11391

WARREN, ROBERT P.   1001, 2041,
  2968

WARREN, STANLEY JR.   8157

WASHBURN, EMORY   10504

WASHBURN, GEORGIA C.   4512

WASHBURNE, ELIHU B.   10901

WASHINGTON, ALEX   6069

WASHINGTON, AUSTIN D.   10200,
  16317

WASHINGTON, BOOKER T.   4513, 4514,
  4515, 4516, 4517, 4518, 4519,
  4520, 4521, 4522, 4523, 4524,
  4525, 9913, 13878, 13879, 14540,
  14541, 14542, 15383, 17968,
  19025, 19252

WASHINGTON, JOSEPH R., JR.   17320,
  17321, 17322

WASHINGTON, L. BARNWELL   17323

WASHINGTON, MARGARET J.M.   17971

WASHINGTON, NATHANIEL J.   11134

WASHINGTON, SARAH M.   595

WASSING, RENE S.   5130

WASTELL, R.E.P.   7240

WATERMAN, HAZEL   4526

WATERMAN, RICHARD A.   1970, 7241,
  17972, 18384

WATERS, JENNIFER N.   2969

WATERS, JOSEPH G.   4527

WATERS, PHILO W.   4528

WATERS, WILLIAM A.   19331

WATKINS, C.T.H.   17324

WATKINS, FLOYD C.   1971

WATKINS, JAMES L.   4529

WATKINS, MEL   16525

WATKINS, PATRICIA D.   1972

WATKINS, RICHARD H.   4530

WATKINS, SYLVESTRE C.   9914

WATRISS, WENDY   19832

WATSON, A.P.   17325

WATSON, ALAN D.   8702, 8703, 12312,
  16318, 20311

WATSON, ANDREW P.   17326

WATSON, CHARLES S.   4531

WATSON, HARRY L.   1973

WATSON, I.Q.   4532

WATSON, J.H.   10815

WATSON, JACK M.   17976

WATSON, JAMES L.   4533

WATSON, JOHN H.   10816

WATSON, KARL   7242

WATSON, LARRY D.   13144

WATSON, LAURA S.   18335

WATSON, R.L.   5131

WATSON, TOM V.   13448

WATTERS, FANNY C.   12816

WATTERSON, HENRY   4534

WATTS, A. FAULKNER   16526

WATTS, RALPH M.   19833

WAX, DAROLD D.   1975, 2970, 5132,
    6070, 6071, 6072, 6077, 6078,
    8705, 8706, 8707, 10768, 10770,
    10771, 10774, 10775, 13880,
    15187, 15188, 20205

WAXMAN, PERCY   20206

WAY, R.B.   9322

WAYLAND, FRANCIS F.   4535

WAYLAND, JOHN W.   13881

WAYNE, JAMES M.   6079

WAYNE, MICHAEL S.   12633

WEARN, CORNELLA   8708

WEATHERBY, WILLIAM J.   10682

WEATHERFORD, W.D.   4536, 4537

WEATHERFORD, WILLIS D.   2971, 2972,
    4538, 15547, 17327

WEAVER, ESTELLA H.   10202

WEAVER, HERBERT   12634

WEAVER, JOHN C.   6984

WEAVER, ROBERT   4539

WEBB, BERT T.   4540

WEBB, JULIE Y.   15831

WEBB, ROSS A.   11392

WEBB, WILLIAM   19028

WEBBER, ALBERT R.F.   8158

WEBBER, KIKANZA N.   16527

WEBBER, THOMAS L.   16319, 19254

WEBSTER, LAURA J.   21137

WEEDEN, HENRY C.   11393

WEEDEN, HOWARD   17978

WEEDEN, WILLIAM B.   6080, 10807,
    10808

WEEKS, LOUIS   4541, 9915

WEEKS, STEPHEN B.   4542, 4543,
    9916, 9917, 17329, 17330, 202

WEGELIN, OSCAR   16529, 18733

WEGENER, WERNER A.   15982

WEIDMAN, BETTE   4544

WEIGHT, GLENN S.   4545

WEIK, JESSE W.   9323

WEIL, DOROTHY   18386

WEINBAUM, PAUL   9918

WEINBERG, SYDNEY J.   11964

WEINBERGER, ANDREW D.   9324

WEINSTEIN, ALLEN   596, 597, 598

WEINSTEIN, BRIAN   7243

WEINSTEIN, JACOB J.   2973

WEINTRAUB, ANDREW   20431

WEINTRAUB, IRWIN   599

WEISBORD, ROBERT   6031

WEISBORD, ROBERT G.   4546, 4547,
    4548

WEISS, DANIEL   18387

WEISS, NANCY J.   378

WEISS, RICHARD   2672

WEISS, THOMAS   14658

WEISS, THOMAS J.   14659, 14660

WEISSMAN, MICHAELE 16424

WEIXLMANN, JOE   21138

WELBORN, MAX JR.   2974

WELCH, DAVID   17979

WELCH, ELOISE T.   21139

WELCH, G. MURLIN   10948

WELCH, GALBRAITH   5133

WELD, RALPH F.   10414

WELDON, FRED O.   18388, 18389

WELDON, M.C.   20432

WELLARD, JAMES   6082

WELLING, JAMES C.   4549, 10204, 10853, 10854

WELLMAN, MANLY W.   12318

WELLS, ANNA M.   1976, 21140

WELLS, DANIEL W.   10505

WELLS, IDA B.   19029

WELLS, ILA A.   4550

WELLS, JAMES W.   8159

WELLS, ROBERT V.   8709, 15053

WELLS, TOM H.   6083, 6084, 6085, 6086, 12499, 20635

WELSCH, ERWIN K.   600

WENDEL, HUGO C.M.   17331

WENDEL, RUBY L.   4551

WENDT, HERBERT   7244

WENGI, RICHARD A.   11065

WENZEL, CAROL N.   21141

WERNER, JOHN M.   2975

WERNER, RANDOLPH   19834

WERNICK, ROBERT   12202

WERTENBAKER, THOMAS J.   8710, 8711, 13882, 13883

WERTHEIMER, BARBARA M.   8712

WESLAGER, C.A.   15549

WESLEY, CHARLES H.   1977, 1978, 1979, 1980, 1981, 1982, 2976, 2977, 4552, 4553, 4554, 4555, 4556, 4557, 4558, 7245, 7246, 9920, 9921, 9922, 9923, 10207, 10208, 15190, 17980, 19835, 20434, 20636, 20637, 20638, 21142

WESSMAN, JAMES W.   7247

WEST, ANSON   17332

WEST, DENNIS   7248

WEST, DON   4559

WEST, EARLE H.   601, 602

WEST, FRANCIS D.   11965

WEST, GERALD M.   8713

WEST, LANDON   13885

WEST, ROBERT C.   8161, 8162, 8163, 8164

WEST, ROBERT CRAIG   10209

WESTBROOK, ROBERT B.   1983

WESTERGAARD, WALDEMAR   7249, 7250

WESTERGAARD, WALDEMAR C.   7251, 7252

WESTERMANN, WILLIAM L.   9326

WESTERN, JOHN R.   9327

WESTIN, RICHARD B.   21143

WESTMORELAND, GUY T., JR.   603

WETHERELL, CHARLES   15023

WEYL, NATHANIEL   2978, 4560, 4561, 5134

WHALEN, MARY M.F.   9328

WHALEY, H.   20435

WHALEY, MARCELLUS S.   18390

WHALLEY, W.   7253

WHARTENBY, FRANKLEE   14543

WHARTON, LINDA F.   18478

WHARTON, VERNON L.   12635, 21144

WHATLEY, GEORGE C.   11794

WHEATLEY, VERA   4564

WHEELER, JAMES O.   9924

WHEELER, JOSEPH   4565

WHEELER, KENNETH W.   13449

WHEELER, WILLIAM H.   16320

WHEELWRIGHT, DALE G.   15285

WHETTEN, NATHAN L.   8165

WHINNOM, KEITH   19441

WHIPPLE, CHARLES K.   11135

WHIPPLE, EMORY C.   17982, 18479

WHIPPLE, PHILA M.   4567

WHISTLER, OLIVE   10598

WHITE, ALICE P.   12500

WHITE, ARTHUR O.   9926, 9927, 9928, 9929

WHITE, DANA F.   1984

WHITE, DAVID O.   8715, 9930, 993

WHITE, DEBORAH G.   16531

WHITE, DOROTHY W.   11220

WHITE, ELAIN   7254

WHITE, EUGENE E.   17333

WHITE, FRANK B.   13450

WHITE, HENRY A.   13145

WHITE, HENRY C.   14544

WHITE, HOWARD A.   21145, 21146, 21147

WHITE, J.   1985

WHITE, JOHN   1986, 1987, 1988, 4568

WHITE, LAURA A.   4569, 20210

WHITE, LELAND R.   8167

WHITE, LILLIAN O.   17983

WHITE, LONNIE J.   11853

WHITE, MELVIN J.   7255

WHITE, NANCY A.   4571

WHITE, NEWMAN I.   17984, 17985, 17986

WHITE, NIREUS O.   4572

WHITE, RAYMOND E.   13451

WHITE, WILLIAM W.   13452, 13453

WHITELOCK, OTTO V. ST.   7256

WHITELY, WILLIAM G.   11528

WHITEMAN, MAXWELL   604

WHITFIELD, THEODORE M.   13886, 13887, 17334

WHITING, BARTLETT J.   9932

WHITING, HELEN A.   19837

WHITLOW, ROGER   4573

WHITMAN, DANIEL   4574

WHITMAN, KAREN   19838

WHITMAN, LOWELL A.   8717

WHITNEY, ANNIE W.   19442

WHITNEY, EDSON L.   8718, 13147

WHITON, LOUIS C.   8168

WHITRIDGE, ARNOLD   6087

WHITSON, THOMAS   19839

WHITTAKER, CYNTHIA   4575

WHITTEMORE, CHARLES P.   1989

WHITTEN, DAVID O.   12502, 12506,
    13148, 13149, 13150, 14649,
    15191

WHITTEN, NORMAN   17488

WHITTEN, NORMAN E.   8169, 8170

WHITTEN, NORMAN E., JR.   8171,
    8172, 18392

WHITTINGTON, G.P.   12507

WHITTINGTON, JAMES A., JR.   8173

WHYTE, JAMES H.   21148

WICKENDEN, HOMER E.   9933

WIECEK, WILLIAM M.   2979, 9330,
    9331, 9332

WIENER, JONATHAN M.   11795, 11796,
    11797, 11798

WIENER, LEO   4577

WIESENFELD, STEPHEN L.   2980

WIGDERSON, SETH M.   1990

WIGGINS, DAVID K.   15874, 15375,
    15876, 15877, 18481

WIGGINS, WILLIAM H.   18394

WIGGINS, WILLIAM H., JR.   1991,
    18395, 19840

WIGHT, WILLARD E.   9334, 17337

WIGINTON, DOLLIE   11799

WIKRAMANAYAKE, IVY M.   9934

WIKRAMANAYAKE, MARINA   9935

WILBUR, HENRY W.   20436

WILBUR, WALTER   4578

WILCOX, D. RAY   19841

WILCOX, PRESTON   605

WILDER, BURT G.   21149

WILDER, DANIEL W.   10949

WILDY, CLARISSA H.   13454

WILEY, BELL I.   606, 4579, 4580,
    10210, 13280, 14545, 15385,
    15836, 16533, 19842, 20439,
    20643, 20645, 20646, 21150,
    21154

WILFING, CHARLES E.   4581

WILGUS, A. CURTIS   1992

WILGUS, D.K.   17988

WILHELM, BARBARA R.   2816

WILHELM, SIDNEY M.   2982

WILKES, LAURA E.   4582, 4583

WILKIE, JANE R.   15983

WILKINS, JOE B., JR.   7257

WILKINS, MARY V. 15837

WILKINSON, CHARLES B. 2983

WILKINSON, DORIS Y. 607, 1993

WILKINSON, HENRY C. 7258, 7259, 7260

WILKINSON, LUPTON A. 19443

WILKS, IVOR 5135

WILKS, OSCAR C. 13152

WILLCOX, RICHARD R. 6088

WILLCOX, W.F. 1994

WILLEFORD, MARY J. 18396

WILLEFORD, MARY JO 7261

WILLEMS, EMILIO 4587, 8174, 8175

WILLET, N.L. 13153

WILLETT, RALPH 1995, 4568

WILLETTS, GILSON 4588

WILLEY, NATHAN 12508

WILLIAMS, ALFRED M. 18397

WILLIAMS, BEN A. 20648

WILLIAMS, CHANCELLOR 4589

WILLIAMS, CLANTON 11300

WILLIAMS, CLANTON W. 11801

WILLIAMS, CORTEZ H. 4590

WILLIAMS, DANIEL T. 609

WILLIAMS, DARNELL 19445

WILLIAMS, DAVID M. 1996, 6089

WILLIAMS, E. RUSS JR. 9337

WILLIAMS, E.E. 7263

WILLIAMS, E.K. 11222, 15286

WILLIAMS, EDNA G. 13888

WILLIAMS, EDWARD W. 13154

WILLIAMS, EDWIN L., JR. 11967, 11968

WILLIAMS, ELIZABETH J. 12819

WILLIAMS, EMMA I. 13281

WILLIAMS, ERIC 1997, 1998, 2984, 2985, 2986, 6091, 6093, 6094, 7264, 7265, 7268, 7269, 7270, 7271, 7272, 8177

WILLIAMS, ERIC E. 2987, 7273, 7274, 7276, 7277, 8267

WILLIAMS, ERNEST P. 1999

WILLIAMS, ETHEL L. 610, 17341

WILLIAMS, EVAN J. 17342

WILLIAMS, GEORGE H. 11152

WILLIAMS, GEORGE W. 4591, 4592, 19446, 21155

WILLIAMS, GLYNDWR 4593

WILLIAMS, GOMER 6095

WILLIAMS, HELEN 19843

WILLIAMS, HESSIE S. 10213

WILLIAMS, IRENE E. 9338

WILLIAMS, ISSAC D. 19030

WILLIAMS, JACK K. 2000, 6096, 9339, 9340

WILLIAMS, JAMES 19031

WILLIAMS, JANE 19132

WILLIAMS, JERRY T. 612

WILLIAMS, JOHN A. 2001, 2002

WILLIAMS, JOHN G.   13157

WILLIAMS, JOHN H.   8178, 8179, 8180, 8181

WILLIAMS, JOHN J.   7278

WILLIAMS, JOSEPH J.   7279, 7280, 18398

WILLIAMS, JOSEPH S.   13282

WILLIAMS, JUDITH B.   6097

WILLIAMS, KENNY J.   4594

WILLIAMS, LORETTA J.   9938

WILLIAMS, MARIE B.   17989

WILLIAMS, MARY W.   4595, 8182, 8183

WILLIAMS, MELVIN R.   9939, 11255, 11257

WILLIAMS, MICHAEL P.   9941

WILLIAMS, ORA G.   12510

WILLIAMS, OSCAR R.   8720, 10708

WILLIAMS, PAUL V.A.   8184

WILLIAMS, R.K.   11395

WILLIAMS, ROBERT   12820, 17990

WILLIAMS, ROBIN M.   4037

WILLIAMS, ROGER M.   11396

WILLIAMS, SAMUEL C.   14051

WILLIAMS, T. HARRY   20440, 20441, 21158

WILLIAMS, TALCOTT   4596, 4597

WILLIAMS, THELMA A.   17991

WILLIAMS, THOMAS L.   17345

WILLIAMS, WALTER L.   4598, 4599, 12204, 14052

WILLIAMS, WILSON E.   6098, 6099

WILLIAMS-JONES, PEARL   17992

WILLIAMSON, FRANCIS T.   4600

WILLIAMSON, HUGH P.   9342, 9343, 9344, 9345, 11653

WILLIAMSON, JAMES A.   7281, 8185

WILLIAMSON, JOEL   2003, 13158, 15058

WILLIAMSON, JOEL R.   13159, 18788

WILLIAMSON, JOSEPH   10419

WILLIAMSON, ROBERT C.   16326

WILLIAMSON, SAMUEL H.   15156, 15419

WILLIGAN, J. DENNIS   19845

WILLINGHAM, N. LOUISE   613

WILLIS, JEAN L.   8186

WILLIS, JOHN R.   6100

WILLIS, WILLIAM S.   13160

WILLIS, WILLIAM S., JR.   8721, 14054

WILLS, GARY   2989

WILLS, RIDLEY   13283

WILMETH, J. RICHARD   17346

WILMETH, MARLYN W.   17346

WILMORE, GAYRAUD S.   17347, 17348

WILMOTH, ANN G.   9942

WILMS, DOUGLAS C.   12205, 14055

WILSON, ADELAIDE   12206

WILSON, BENJAMIN C.   19846

WILSON, BENJAMIN C., JR.   9943

WILSON, CALVIN D.   4601, 4602

WILSON, CHARLES J.   9944, 9945

WILSON, CHARLES K.   2990

WILSON, EDMUND   2004, 2005, 4603

WILSON, ELLEN G.   4604, 8722

WILSON, EUGENE   15550

WILSON, EUGENE M.   15551

WILSON, F.J.   15608

WILSON, G.R.   17349

WILSON, GEORGE JR.   10934

WILSON, GEORGE R.   10923, 10924

WILSON, GOLD R.   17350

WILSON, HAROLD   4605

WILSON, HAROLD S.   14728

WILSON, HENRY   4606

WILSON, HOWARD H.   6101, 6102

WILSON, JAMES D.   2006

WILSON, JOSEPH T.   4607, 4608,
   10214, 21159

WILSON, L.W.   14056

WILSON, MAJOR L.   4609, 11066,
   11067

WILSON, MARY T.   5136

WILSON, MIRIAM B.   13161

WILSON, MONA   7283

WILSON, NAN   9347

WILSON, OLLY W.   5137

WILSON, PETER J.   7284

WILSON, PRINCE E.   4610

WILSON, RALEIGH A.   14057

WILSON, RICHARD O.   11397

WILSON, ROBERT   13162

WILSON, RUTH D.   2991, 10321

WILSON, SAMUEL JR.   12511

WILSON, THEODORE B.   9348, 9349

WILSON, WARREN W.   14162

WILSON, WILLIAM E.   2992

WILSON, WILLIAM J.   2007, 2993,
   16074

WILSON, WOODROW   2008, 2009, 1534

WILSTACH, PAUL   13889

WILTSHIRE, SUSAN F.   4611

WIMMER, LARRY T.   1064

WINDERS, GERTRUDE H.   19847

WINDLEY, LATHAN A.   614, 19848,
   19849

WINETROUB, HEDDA G.   18789

WINFIELD, ARTHUR A., JR.   15879

WINFREY, DORMAN H.   13455

WINGFIELD, C.L.   12638

WINGFIELD, MARSHALL   13284

WINIUS, GEORGE D.   7509

WINKELMAN, WINNIFRED V.   7285

WINKLER, ALLAN M.   2011

WINKLER, ELIZABETH B.   10215

WINKLER, KAREN J. 2012

WINKS, ROBIN W. 4612, 4613, 10322,
    10323, 10324, 10325, 10326,
    19032, 19033

WINNINGHAM, MRS. DAVID W. 13456

WINSELL, KEITH A. 4614

WINSLOW, DAVID J. 15880

WINSLOW, EUGENE 8723

WINSLOW, HENRY F. 2013

WINSTON, GEORGE T. 2994, 2995

WINSTON, JAMES E. 9946

WINSTON, MICHAEL R. 31, 615, 2014,
    15025

WINSTON, SANFORD 4615

WINTER, HAUSER 11654

WINTERS, CLYDE 5138

WINTERS, JOHN D. 20649

WINTERS, ROBERT E. 12694

WINTHER, OSCAR O. 616, 617

WIPPLER, MIGENE G. 18401

WISCONSIN STATE HISTORICAL SOCIETY
    618

WISE, JENNINGS C. 17995

WISE, JOHN S. 4616

WISE, K.S. 7286

WISEMAN, H.V. 7287

WISER, VIVIAN 11529

WISH, HARVEY 619, 2016, 2017,
    2996, 2997, 4617, 4618, 4619,
    6103, 20213, 20214, 20317

WISNER, ELIZABETH 15838

WITHROW, W.H. 19850

WITTKE, CARL 2998

WOESSNER, HERMAN C. 12513

WOLF, ERIC 4621

WOLF, ERIC R. 7163

WOLF, HAZEL C. 10216

WOLF, JANYCE 330

WOLFE, BERNARD 18402

WOLFF, GERALD 4622

WOLFF, RICHARD D. 6104

WOLFRAM, WALT 19328

WONA 18403

WOOD, BETTY 8222, 12207

WOOD, BETTY C. 12208, 12209

WOOD, CLARENCE A. 10709

WOOD, DONALD 7288

WOOD, ERNIE 9947

WOOD, FORREST G. 21160, 21161

WOOD, GEORGE L. 16075

WOOD, HENRY C. 17996

WOOD, J. TAYLOR 6105

WOOD, JEROME H., JR. 8724, 10778

WOOD, MADELINE J. 6106

WOOD, MINTER 9948, 15985

WOOD, NORMAN B. 4623

WOOD, PETER H. 2018, 2019, 2020,
    2021, 2022, 5140, 6107, 8726,
    8727, 8728, 8729, 14826, 15839,

15840, 17353

WOOD, S.M. 18956

WOOD, STEPHEN W. 17354

WOOD, WALTER K. 13891

WOOD, WILLIAM 13457

WOOD, WILLIAM J. 8269

WOODBRIDGE, H.C. 3003

WOODBURY, NAOMI F. 3004

WOODFORD, JOHN 18590

WOODMAN, HAROLD D. 620, 2023,
    2024, 2025, 2026, 2027, 14550,
    14551, 14552, 14553

WOODRUFF, JAMES F. 11802, 11803

WOODRUFF, MARGUERITE E. 17997

WOODS, DANIEL G. 621

WOODS, FRANCES J. 12516

WOODS, WILLIAM L. 12639

WOODSON, C.G. 19257

WOODSON, CARTER G. 622, 2029,
    3005, 4624, 4625, 4626, 4627,
    4628, 5141, 5142, 9949, 9950,
    9952, 10377, 10378, 10506,
    10710, 11398, 13894, 13895,
    16328, 17355, 19258, 20216

WOODSON, JUNE B. 9953

WOODSON, LEROY H. 4629, 4630

WOODSON, WILLIAM H. 11655

WOODWARD, ADNA 8730

WOODWARD, C. VANN 623, 1001, 2030,
    2031, 2032, 2033, 2035, 2036,
    2037, 2038, 2039, 2040, 2041,
    3006, 3007, 3008, 3009, 4631,
    10217, 10218, 14554, 19851

WOODWARD, DONALD 6108

WOODWARD, GRACE S. 14058

WOODWARD, JAMES E. 9353

WOODWARD, JOSEPH H. 20652

WOODWARD, KENNETH L. 2042, 2043

WOODWARD, MARY V. 4632

WOODWARD, MICHAEL V. 624, 2044,
    2045

WOODWORTH, J.B. 14828

WOOFTER, JAMES J., JR. 13171

WOOLFOLK, GEORGE R. 625, 626,
    9954, 9955, 9956, 9957, 13458
    14555, 14556

WOOLRIDGE, NANCY B. 17356

WOOLSEY, C.M. 10711

WOOLSEY, RONALD C. 11068

WOOSTER, RALPH A. 13462, 13463,
    14557, 15064, 15065

WORCESTER, DONALD E. 8188

WORK, JOHN W. 17998, 17999, 180
    18001, 18002

WORK, M.N. 9958, 18404

WORK, MONROE N. 627, 5143, 5144
    5145, 5146, 5147, 5148, 5149,
    10219, 17489, 17490

WORLEY, TED R. 11854, 11855

WORNER, WILLIAM F. 3011

WORTHAM, SUE C. 13464

WRESZIN, MICHAEL 1789

WRIGHT, ALBERT H. 11969

WRIGHT, BENJAMIN F., JR. 4633

1844

WRIGHT, DAVID 141

WRIGHT, DONALD R. 5150

WRIGHT, G. FREDERICK 12640

WRIGHT, GAVIN 628, 896, 897, 2048, 2049, 2050, 14402, 14558, 14559, 14560, 14561, 14564, 14565, 14652, 14829

WRIGHT, IONE S. 8189

WRIGHT, IRENE A. 6110, 7290, 7291, 9959

WRIGHT, J. LEITCH 8731

WRIGHT, J. LEITCH JR. 8732, 11971, 11972, 11973, 14059

WRIGHT, JAMES M. 7292, 7293, 9960

WRIGHT, JOHN K. 6984

WRIGHT, L.B. 6111

WRIGHT, LOUIS B. 6112, 13896, 13897, 13898

WRIGHT, MARCIA 5151

WRIGHT, MARION M.T. 9354, 9355, 9961, 10600, 10603

WRIGHT, MRS. D. GIRAND 20654

WRIGHT, MRS. FLORENCE B. 19852

WRIGHT, MURIEL H. 14046, 14060

WRIGHT, NATHAN J. 18003

WRIGHT, PHILIP 7294, 7295

WRIGHT, R.R. 4634, 11120

WRIGHT, RICHARD 18405

WRIGHT, RICHARD R. 10779

WRIGHT, RICHARD R., JR. 8190

WRIGHT, ROBERT L. 2072

WRIGHT, W.E.C. 4635

WRIGHT, WILLIAM C. 11530

WRIGHT, WINTHROP R. 3012

WRIGLEY, CHRISTOPHER C. 2051

WRITERS' PROGRAM, GEORGIA 12210

WRITERS' PROGRAM, NEW YORK 629, 10713

WRITERS' PROGRAM, SOUTH CAROLINA 18406

WRITERS' PROGRAM, VIRGINIA 13899

WRITERS PROJECT, GEORGIA 12211

WRITERS PROJECT, NEW YORK (CITY) 6114

WUST, KLAUS 13900

WYATT, EMMA O. 18408

WYATT-BROWN, BERTRAM 2052, 2053, 2054, 4636, 4637, 4638, 17357

WYETH, OLA M. 630

WYLIE, FLOYD M. 4639, 16331

WYLIE, MARGERY B. 631

WYLLY, CHARLES S. 8733

WYNDHAM, HUGH A. 4640, 10220

WYNES, CHARLES E. 4641, 9962

WYNTER, SYLVIA 3013

WYSONG, JACK P. 3014

X.Y. 10507

YANCEY, WILLIAM L. 2758

YANCY, PRESTON M. 4642

YANKOVIC, DONALD J. 11805

YANUCK, JULIUS 9356, 9357, 9358

YARBROUGH, WILLIAM H. 14566, 14567

YASUBA, YASUKICHI 14568

YATES, E.A. 15841

YATES, ELIZABETH 10379

YATES, ELLA G. 632

YATES, IRENE 18409

YATES, JOSEPHINE S. 10221

YATES, NORRIS W. 18004

YEARNS, WILFRED B. 20655

YEARWOOD, SEALE 7296

YEIGH, FRANK 19854

YELLIN, JEAN F. 3015, 4643, 4644

YEO, C.A. 14569

YETMAN, NORMAN R. 2055, 2056, 18790, 18791, 19035, 19138, 19855

YOKLEY, RAYTHA L. 17071

YONKER, THOMAS W. 17358

YOSHPE, HARRY B. 10714, 10715

YOUNG, ALFRED 2057

YOUNG, AURELIA 18005

YOUNG, CARLENE 4645

YOUNG, HENRY J. 17359

YOUNG, HUGH P. 11806

YOUNG, MARY E. 14061

YOUNG, NATHAN B. 4646

YOUNG, PAULINE A. 11224

YOUNG, STARK 2058

YOUNG, TOMMY R. 12517

YOUNG, WILFRED C. 2059

YOUNGER, RICHARD D. 9359

ZABRISKIE, GEORGE A. 18699

ZACHARIAS, DIANNA 633

ZAGOREN, RUBY 10417

ZANGER, JULES 3016

ZANGRANDO, ROBERT L. 3128

ZAVALA, SILVIO A. 8191

ZEICHNER, OSCAR 4647, 9360

ZEITLIN, MAURICE 2060

ZELINSKY, WILBUR 7297, 9963, 15552

ZELNIK, MELVIN 15068

ZEMP, FRANCIS L. 19037

ZEPP, THOMAS M. 14570

ZEUGNER, JOHN 20217

ZILVERSMIT, ARTHUR 2061, 3018, 9964, 10380, 10509, 10510, 10606, 10607

ZIMMERMAN, MATHILDE 6116

ZIRKER, PRISCILLA A. 3019

ZOCHERT, DONALD 4648

ZOELLNER, ROBERT H. 20444

ZOOK, GEORGE F. 6117, 6118, 611

ZOPHY, JON 20992

ZORN, ROMAN J. 9362, 10225, 198

ZORNOW, DAVID M. 8735

ZORNOW, WILLIAM F.   3021, 11258
ZUCKERMAN, MICHAEL   13901
ZUILL, WILLIAM   7298
ZUKE, DOROTHY M.   8736
ZURLO, JOHN A.   4649, 19857